HOLT
SOCIAL
STUDIES

World History

Stanley M. Burstein
Richard Shek

HOLT, RINEHART AND WINSTON

A Harcourt Education Company

Orlando • Austin • New York • San Diego • Toronto • London

Authors

Dr. Stanley M. Burstein

Dr. Stanley M. Burstein is Professor Emeritus of Ancient History and former Chair of the Department of History at California State University, Los Angeles. Dr. Burstein received his B.A., M.A., and Ph.D. degrees from the University of California at Los Angeles. The author of more than 100 books, articles, and chapters on ancient history, Dr. Burstein co-authored *The Ancient World: Readings in Social and Cultural History* (Englewood Cliffs, 2002). His specialties include ancient Greek history, Greek and Roman Egypt, and Kush. Dr. Burstein has served as president of the Association of Ancient Historians and was a member of the Educational Testing Service Task Force for Development of the AP World History Course.

Dr. Richard Shek

Dr. Richard Shek is Professor of Humanities and Religious Studies at California State University, Sacramento. A native of China, Dr. Shek received his B.A. in Tokyo, Japan, and he received his M.A. and a Ph.D. in history from the University of California at Berkeley. His specialties are East Asian cultural and religious history. The author of numerous publications on Confucianism, Daoism, Buddhism, and popular religion in China and Japan, Dr. Shek co-edited *Heterodoxy in Late Imperial China: Essays in Inquiry* (University of California Press, 2004). Dr. Shek was inducted into the International Educators' Hall of Fame in 1999.

ISBN-13: 978-0-03-093664-7

ISBN-10: 0-03-093664-0

7 8 9   032   14 13 12 11 10 09 08

Program Consultants

Contributing Author

Kylene Beers
Senior Reading Researcher
School Development Program
Yale University
New Haven, Connecticut

A former middle school teacher, Dr. Beers has turned her commitment to helping struggling readers into the major focus of her research, writing, speaking, and teaching. She is the current editor of the National Council of Teachers of English literacy journal *Voices from the Middle* and the author of *When Kids Can't Read: What Teachers Can Do* (Heinemann, 2002).

General Editor

Frances Marie Gipson
Secondary Literacy
Los Angeles Unified School District
Los Angeles, California

In her current position, Frances Gipson guides reform work for secondary instruction and supports its implementation. She has designed curriculum at the district, state, and national levels. Her leadership of a coaching collaborative with UCLA's Subject Matter Projects evolved from her commitment to rigorous instruction and to meeting the needs of diverse learners.

Senior Literature and Writing Specialist

Carol Jago
English Department Chairperson
Santa Monica High School
Santa Monica, California

An English teacher at the middle and high school levels for 26 years, Carol Jago also directs the reading and literature project at UCLA and writes a weekly education column for the *Los Angeles Times*. She has been published in numerous professional journals and has authored several books, including *Cohesive Writing: Why Concept is Not Enough* (Boynton/Cook, 2002).

Consultants

John Ferguson, M.T.S., J.D.
Senior Religion Consultant
Assistant Professor
Political Science/Criminal Justice
Howard Payne University
Brownwood, Texas

Rabbi Gary M. Bretton-Granatoor
Religion Consultant
Director of Interfaith Affairs
Anti-Defamation League
New York, New York

J. Frank Malaret
Senior Consultant
Dean, Downtown and West Sacramento Outreach Centers
Sacramento City College
Sacramento, California

Kimberly A. Plummer, M.A.
Senior Consultant
History-Social Science Educator/Advisor
Holt, Rinehart and Winston

Andrés Reséndez, Ph.D.
Senior Consultant
Assistant Professor
Department of History
University of California at Davis
Davis, California

Reviewers

Academic Reviewers

Jonathan Beecher, Ph.D.
Department of History
University of California, Santa
Cruz

Jerry H. Bentley, Ph.D.
Department of History
University of Hawaii

Elizabeth Brumfiel, Ph.D.
Department of Anthropology
Northwestern University
Evanston, Illinois

Eugene Cruz-Uribe, Ph.D.
Department of History
Northern Arizona University

Toyin Falola, Ph.D.
Department of History
University of Texas

Sandy Freitag, Ph.D.
Director, Monterey Bay History
and Cultures Project
Division of Social Sciences
University of California, Santa
Cruz

Yasuhide Kawashima, Ph.D.
Department of History
University of Texas at El Paso

Robert J. Meier, Ph.D.
Department of Anthropology
Indiana University

Marc Van De Mieroop, Ph.D.
Department of History
Columbia University
New York, New York

M. Gwyn Morgan, Ph.D.
Department of History
University of Texas

Robert Schoch, Ph.D.
CGS Division of Natural Science
Boston University

David Shoenbrun, Ph.D.
Department of History
Northwestern University
Evanston, Illinois

Educational Reviewers

Henry John Assetto
Twin Valley High School
Elverson, Pennsylvania

Julie Barker
Pittsford Middle School
Pittsford, New York

Michael Bloom
Ross School
Ross, California

Anthony Braxton
Herbert H. Cruickshank Middle
School
Merced, California

Robert Crane
Taylorsville High School
Salt Lake City, Utah

Katherine A. DeForge
Marcellus High School
Marcellus, New York

Mary Demetrion
Patrick Henry Middle School
Los Angeles, California

Charlyn Earp
Mesa Verde Middle School
San Diego, California

Yolanda Espinoza
Walter Stiern Middle School
Bakersfield, California

Tina Nelson
Deer Park Middle School
Randallstown, Maryland

Don Polston
Lebanon Middle School
Lebanon, Indiana

Robert Valdez
Pioneer Middle School
Tustin, California

UNIT 1 Early Humans and Societies

UNIT 3 Civilization in India and China

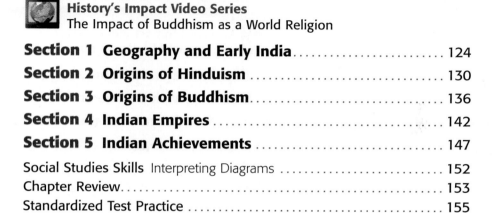

UNIT Foundations of Western Ideas

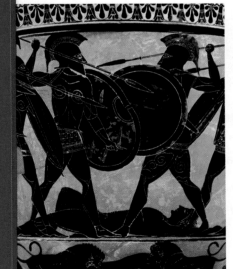

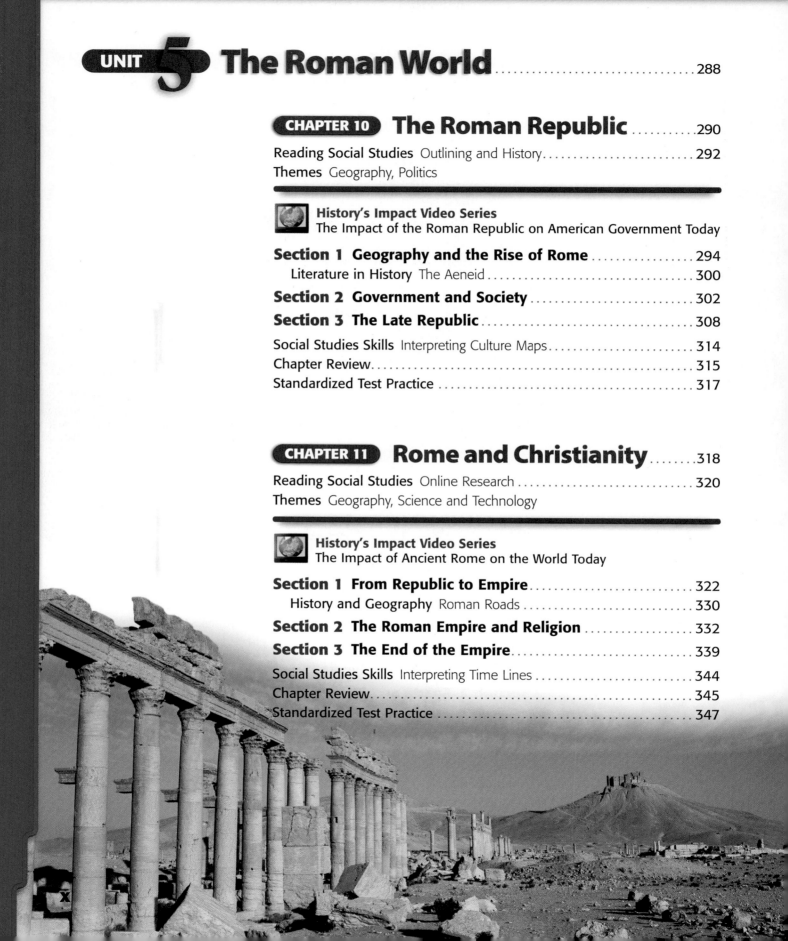

Justinian and Theodora

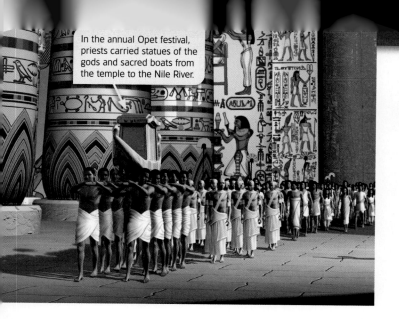

In the annual Opet festival, priests carried statues of the gods and sacred boats from the temple to the Nile River.

Charts, Graphics, and Time Lines

Analyze information presented visually to learn more about history.

Examine key facts and concepts quickly and easily with graphics.

Points of View

See how different people have interpreted historical issues in different ways.

FOCUS ON SPEAKING

Use speaking skills to study and reflect on the events and people who made history.

FOCUS ON WRITING

Use writing to study and reflect on the events and people who made history.

Historic Documents

Examine key documents that have shaped world history.

Reading Social Studies

Learn and practice skills that will help you read your social studies lessons.

History Close-up

See how people lived and how places looked in the past by taking a close-up view of history.

Social Studies Skills

Learn, practice, and apply the skills you need to study and analyze history.

LINKING TO TODAY

Link people and cultures from the past to the world around you today.

Relive history through eyewitness accounts, literature, and documents.

Interpret maps to see where important events happened and analyze how geography has influenced history.

✴ Interactive Maps

Go online to extend your learning with interactive maps.

Reading
like a Historian

Historians use paintings, like the detail of a Japanese folding screen from the 1700s on the next page, to help understand the past. As you study world history, you too will learn how to use different historical sources to **Read like a Historian.**

To find out more about reading like a historian and the historical sources that follow, visit

go.hrw.com
More Online
KEYWORD: HISTORIAN

By Frances Marie Gipson
Secondary Literacy Coordinator
Los Angeles Unified School District, Los Angeles, California

What Does It Mean to Read like a Historian?

In your history class you will be doing a lot of reading, thinking, and problem-solving. Much of your reading and thinking will center on different types of texts or materials. Since you are in a history class reading all sorts of things, a question to consider is, "What does it mean to think, read, and solve problems like a historian?"

Historians work with different types of sources to understand and learn from history. Two categories of sources are **primary** and **secondary** sources.

Primary Sources are historical documents, written accounts by a firsthand witness, or objects that have survived from the past. A study of primary sources might include letters, government documents, diaries, photographs, art objects, stamps, coins, and even clothing.

Secondary Sources are accounts of past events created by people some time after the events happened. This textbook and other books written about historical events are examples of secondary sources.

As you learn more about your work as a historian, you will begin to ask questions and analyze historical materials. You will be working as a detective, digging into history to create a richer understanding of the mysteries of the past.

How to Analyze Written Sources

Primary Sources

Magna Carta

"[17] Ordinary lawsuits shall not follow the royal court around, but shall be held in a fixed place . . .

[20] For a trivial offense, a free man shall be fined only in proportion to the degree of his offense, and for a serious offense correspondingly, but not so heavily as to deprive him of his livelihood.

[28] No constable or other royal official shall take corn or other movable goods from any man without immediate payment, unless the seller voluntarily offers postponement of this . . . "

– Magna Carta, 1215

Asking questions can help you determine the relevance and importance of primary sources such as Magna Carta, a document signed by King John of England in 1215 that limited the king's power. As you read the primary source above and the primary and secondary sources included in this textbook, ask yourself questions like the ones below.

- Who created the source and why?
- Did the writer have firsthand knowledge of the event, or report what others saw or heard?
- Was the writer a neutral party, or did the author have opinions or interests that might have influenced what was recorded?
- Did the writer wish to inform or persuade others?
- Was the information recorded during the event, immediately after the event, or after some lapse of time?

Timbuktu

"Well placed for the caravan trade, it was badly situated to defend itself from the Tuareg raiders of the Sahara. These restless nomads were repeatedly hammering at the gates of Timbuktu, and often enough, they burst them open with disastrous results for the inhabitants. Life here was never quite safe enough to recommend it as the centre [center] of a big state."

–Basil Davidson, from *A History of West Africa*

When reading secondary sources, such as the description of Timbuktu above, historians ask additional questions to seek understanding. They try to source the text, build evidence, and interpret the message that is being conveyed. For historians, reading is a quest to find evidence to answer or challenge a historical problem. As you study secondary sources, ask questions like the ones below.

- Who is the author? What do I know about this author?
- Did the author have firsthand information? What is the author's relationship to the event?
- What might be the author's motivation in writing this piece?
- What type of evidence did the author look at?
- Are any assumptions or bias present?
- How does this document fit into the larger context of the events I am studying?
- What kind of source is it?
- Is the source an original?
- Is the content probable or reasonable?
- What does the date tell me about the event?
- What do I already know about this topic that will help me understand more of what I am reading?

How to Analyze an Artifact

Artifacts, such as this mask of an Aztec god, take many forms. They might be coins, stone tools, pieces of clothing, or even items found in your backpack. As you study artifacts in this textbook, ask yourself questions like the ones below.

- Why was this object created?
- When and where would it have been used?
- Who used the artifact?
- What does the artifact tell me about the technology available at the time it was created?
- What can it tell me about the life and times of the people who used it?
- How does the artifact help to make sense of the time period?

How to Analyze a Historical Map

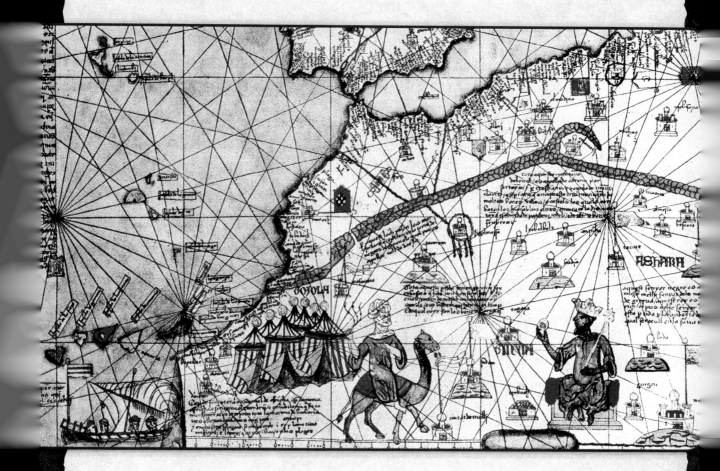

Maps are symbolic representations of places shown in relation to one another. The map above was created around 1375 in Spain and shows part of North Africa. All maps necessarily include some details and leave out others. As you study maps in this textbook, ask questions like the ones below.

- When and where was the map produced?
- What details has the mapmaker chosen to include (or exclude) on this map?
- Why was the map drawn?
- How can I determine if the map is accurate?
- How are maps used to analyze the past, present, and future?

How to
Analyze Art

Art, like the tapestry above, which was created in the 1500s in France, is another important source for historians. One way to study a piece of art is to write down everything that you think is important about it. Then divide the image into four sections and describe the important elements from each section. As you study art in this textbook, ask questions like the ones below.

- What is the setting for the art?
- When and where in the past was the art created?
- What is the subject of the art?
- What other details can I observe?
- What does the art reveal about its subject?
- How can I describe the artist's point of view?

How to Analyze an Infographic

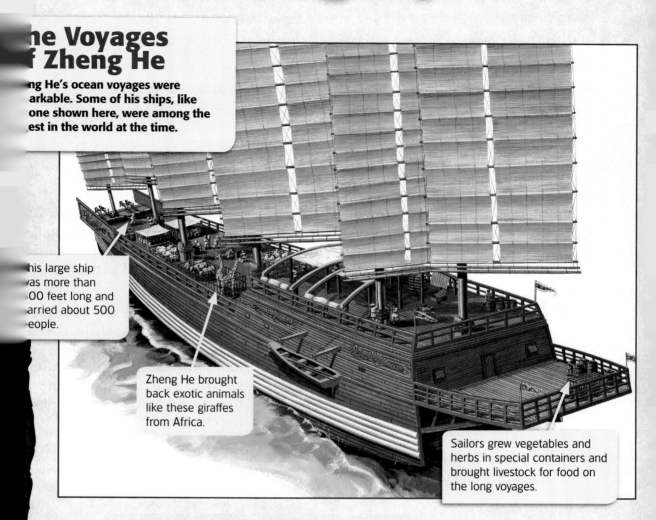

The Voyages of Zheng He

[Zhe]ng He's ocean voyages were [rem]arkable. Some of his ships, like [the] one shown here, were among the [larg]est in the world at the time.

[T]his large ship [w]as more than [5]00 feet long and [c]arried about 500 [p]eople.

Zheng He brought back exotic animals like these giraffes from Africa.

Sailors grew vegetables and herbs in special containers and brought livestock for food on the long voyages.

Infographics give you information in a visual format, using captions and call-out boxes to help explain the intent of the drawing. As you study infographics in this textbook, use the helpful tips and questions below.

- List the parts of the drawing and the importance of each part.
- Describe the focus or significance of the drawing.
- Do the captions and call-out boxes clarify the drawing's purpose?
- Does the drawing help me understand the information that I am studying in my textbook better?

Become an Active Reader

by Dr. Kylene Beers

Did you ever think you would begin reading your social studies book by reading about reading? Actually, it makes better sense than you might think. You would probably make sure you learned some soccer skills and strategies before playing in a game. Similarly, you need to learn some reading skills and strategies before reading your social studies book. In other words, you need to make sure you know whatever you need to know in order to read this book successfully..

Tip #1
Use the Reading Social Studies Pages

Take advantage of the two pages on reading at the beginning of every chapter. Those pages introduce the chapter themes; explain a reading skill or strategy; and identify key terms, people, and academic vocabulary.

Themes

Why are themes important? They help our minds organize facts and information. For example, when we talk about baseball, we may talk about types of pitches. When we talk about movies, we may discuss animation.

Historians are no different. When they discuss history or social studies, they tend to think about some common themes: Economics, Geography, Religion, Politics, Society and Culture, and Science and Technology.

Reading Skill or Strategy

Good readers use a number of skills and strategies to make sure they understand what they are reading. These lessons will give you the tools you need to read and understand social studies.

Key Terms, People, and Academic Vocabulary

Before you read the chapter, review these words and think about them. Have you heard the word before? What do you already know about the people? Then watch for these words and their meanings as you read the chapter.

Tells which theme or themes are important in the chapter

Explains a skill or strategy good readers use

Gives you practice in the reading skill or strategy.

Identifies the important words in the chapter.

Tip #2
Read like a Skilled Reader

You will never get better at reading your social studies book—or any book for that matter—unless you spend some time thinking about how to be a better reader.

Skilled readers do the following:

- They preview what they are supposed to read before they actually begin reading. They look for vocabulary words, titles of sections, information in the margin, or maps or charts they should study.

- They divide their notebook paper into two columns. They title one column "Notes from the Chapter" and the other column "Questions or Comments I Have."

- They take notes in both columns as they read.

- They read like **active readers**. The Active Reading list below shows you what that means.

- They use clues in the text to help them figure out where the text is going. The best clues are called signal words.

  Chronological Order Signal Words:
  first, second, third, before, after, later, next, following that, earlier, finally

  Cause and Effect Signal Words:
  because of, due to, as a result of, the reason for, therefore, consequently

  Comparison/Contrast Signal Words:
  likewise, also, as well as, similarly, on the other hand

Active Reading

Successful readers are **active readers**. These readers know that it is up to them to figure out what the text means. Here are some steps you can take to become an active, and successful, reader.

Predict what will happen next based on what has already happened. When your predictions don't match what happens in the text, re-read the confusing parts.

Question what is happening as you read. Constantly ask yourself why things have happened, what things mean, and what caused certain events.

Summarize what you are reading frequently. Do not try to summarize the entire chapter! Read a bit and then summarize it. Then read on.

Connect what is happening in the part you're reading to what you have already read.

Clarify your understanding. Stop occasionally to ask yourself whether you are confused by anything. You may need to re-read to clarify, or you may need to read further and collect more information before you can understand.

Visualize what is happening in the text. Try to see the events or places in your mind by drawing maps, making charts, or jotting down notes about what you are reading.

Tip #3
Pay Attention to Vocabulary

It is no fun to read something when you don't know what the words mean, but you can't learn new words if you only use or read the words you already know. In this book, we know we have probably used some words you don't know. But, we have followed a pattern as we have used more difficult words.

Key Terms and People
At the beginning of each section you will find a list of key terms or people that you will need to know. Be on the lookout for those words as you read through the section.

The Enlightenment's Roots
The main ideas of the Enlightenment had their roots in other eras. Enlightenment thinkers looked back to the Greeks, Romans, and the history of Christianity. The Renaissance, Reformation, and Scientific Revolution provided ideas also.

Greek and Roman Philosophers
Enlightenment thinkers used ideas from the ancient Greeks and Romans. Greek philosophers had observed an order and regularity in the natural world. Aristotle, for example, taught that people could use logic to discover new truths. Building on Greek ideas, Roman thinkers developed the concept of natural law, the idea that a law governed how the world operated.

With Greek and Roman beliefs as guidelines, Enlightenment thinkers began studying the world in a new way. They applied these beliefs not just to the natural world but also to the human world of society and government.

Christianity
The history of Christianity in Europe provides other clues about ideas that emerged in the Enlightenment. One theologian, Thomas Aquinas, had taught in the Middle Ages that faith paired with reason could explain the world. In spite of Aquinas's use of reason, the Enlightenment was mostly reason, the Enlightenment movement. a secular, or non-religious, mo with the enlightenment thinkers disag and its intolerance toward non-Christian beliefs.

The Renaissance and Reformation
Other reactions to the Christian Church in Europe also influenced the ideas of the Enlightenment. For example, some Renaissance thinkers used Greek and Roman ideas to raise questions about established religious beliefs. These Renaissance thinkers were known as humanists.

Although most humanists were religious, they focused on human value and achievement rather than the glory of God.

The use of reason advanced science and technology, which in turn influenced the Enlightenment. Here, the Italian scientist Alessandro Volta explains a new invention, the battery.

475

reason, the Enlightenmen a **secular**, or non-religious, n Enlightenment thinkers disag

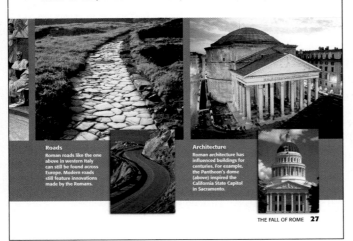

The skill of ancient Roman engineers inspired many later people to copy their techniques. For example, some builders still design stadiums in much the same way Roman engineers did. In fact, many techniques engineers and architects use today were directly inspired by the Roman engineers of 2,000 years ago.

Architecture
Architecture, the art of designing buildings, is closely related to engineering. Roman architects and engineers used many of the same ideas. They constantly sought ways to make larger, stronger buildings.

In addition to being large and strong, however, Roman architects wanted their buildings to be beautiful. Because they admired the beauty of ancient Greek structures, they borrowed Greek ideas. For example, like the Greeks, the Romans used columns and open spaces to make their buildings look elegant and majestic. But the Romans added an **innovation** of their own. They used their engineering skills to make buildings larger and grander than anything the Greeks had built.

Later civilizations greatly admired the Roman architectural style, copying many elements of Roman design in their own buildings. Elements of Roman design are seen in many public buildings even today.

Art
Architecture was not the only field in which the Romans were inspired by the Greeks. Roman works of art also borrowed heavily from earlier Greek examples.

ACADEMIC VOCABULARY
innovation
(i-nuh-VAY-shuhn) a new idea or way of doing something

Roads
Roman roads like the one above in western Italy can still be found across Europe. Modern roads still feature innovations made by the Romans.

Architecture
Roman architecture has influenced buildings for centuries. For example, the Pantheon's dome (above) inspired the California State Capitol in Sacramento.

THE FALL OF ROME **27**

ACADEMIC VOCABULARY

innovation
(i-nuh-VAY-shuhn) a new idea or way of doing something

Academic Vocabulary
When we use a word that is important in all classes, not just social studies, we define it in the margin under the heading Academic Vocabulary. You will run into these academic words in other textbooks, so you should learn what they mean while reading this book.

Words to Know

As you read this social studies textbook, you will be more successful if you know or learn the meanings of the words on this page. There are two types of words listed here. The first list contains academic words, the words we pointed out at the bottom of the previous page. These words are important in all classes, not just social studies. The second list contains words that are special to this particular topic of social studies, world history.

Academic Words

acquire	to get
affect	to change or influence
agreement	a decision reached by two or more people in a group
aspect	part
authority	power or influence; right to rule
classical	referring to the cultures of ancient Greece and Rome
competition	a contest between two rivals
conflict	an open clash between two opposing groups
consequences	effects of a particular event or events
contracts	binding legal agreements
defend	to keep secure from danger
development	creation; the process of growing or improving
distribute	to divide among a group of people
efficient	productive and not wasteful
establish	to set up or create
features	characteristics
function	work or perform
ideals	ideas or goals that people try to live up to
influence	change, or have an effect on
innovation	a new idea, method, or device
logical	reasoned, or well thought out
method	a way of doing something
motive	reason for doing something
neutral	not engaged in either side
opposition	the act of opposing or resisting
policy	rule, course of action
primary	main, most important
principles	basic beliefs, rules, or laws
procedure	the way a task is accomplished
process	a series of steps by which a task is accomplished
purpose	the reason something is done
rebel	to fight against authority
role	a part or function; assigned behavior
strategy	a plan for fighting a battle or war
structure	the way something is set up or organized
values	ideas that people hold dear and try to live by
vary	to be different

Social Studies Words

AD	also CE, refers to dates after Jesus's birth
BC	also BCE, refers to dates before the birth of Jesus of Nazareth
BCE	refers to "Before Common Era," dates before the birth of Jesus of Nazareth
CE	refers to "Common Era," dates after Jesus's birth
century	a period of 100 years
civilization	the culture characteristic of a particular time or place
climate	the weather conditions in a certain area over a long period of time
culture	the knowledge, beliefs, customs, and values of a group of people
custom	a repeated practice; tradition
economy	the system in which people make and exchange goods and services
era	a period of time
geography	the study of the earth's physical and cultural features
physical features	the features on the land's surface, such as mountains and rivers
politics	government
region	an area with one or more features that make it different from surrounding areas
resources	materials found on the earth that people need and value
society	a group of people who share common traditions
trade	the exchange of goods or services

Mapping the Earth

A **globe** is a scale model of the earth. It is useful for showing the entire earth or studying large areas of the earth's surface.

A pattern of lines circles the globe in east-west and north-south directions. It is called a **grid**. The intersection of these imaginary lines helps us find places on the earth.

The east-west lines in the grid are lines of **latitude**. Lines of latitude are called **parallels** because they are always parallel to each other. These imaginary lines measure distance north and south of the **equator**. The equator is an imaginary line that circles the globe halfway between the North and South Poles. Parallels measure distance from the equator in **degrees**. The symbol for degrees is °. Degrees are further divided into **minutes**. The symbol for minutes is ´. There are 60 minutes in a degree. Parallels north of the equator are labeled with an N. Those south of the equator are labeled with an S.

The north-south lines are lines of **longitude**. Lines of longitude are called **meridians**. These imaginary lines pass through the Poles. They measure distance east and west of the **prime meridian**. The prime meridian is an imaginary line that runs through Greenwich, England. It represents 0° longitude.

Lines of latitude range from 0°, for locations on the equator, to 90°N or 90°S, for locations at the Poles. Lines of longitude range from 0° on the prime meridian to 180° on a meridian in the mid-Pacific Ocean. Meridians west of the prime meridian to 180° are labeled with a W. Those east of the prime meridian to 180° are labeled with an E.

Lines of Latitude

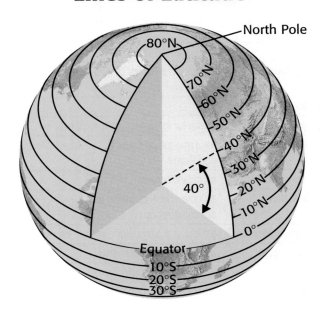

Lines of Longitude

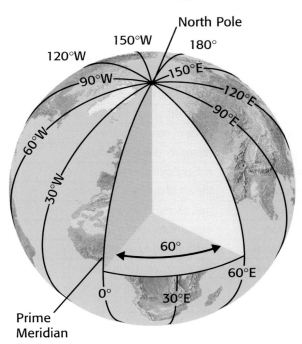

The equator divides the globe into two halves, called **hemispheres**. The half north of the equator is the Northern Hemisphere. The southern half is the Southern Hemisphere. The prime meridian and the 180° meridian divide the world into the Eastern Hemisphere and the Western Hemisphere. However, the prime meridian runs right through Europe and Africa. To avoid dividing these continents between two hemispheres, some mapmakers divide the Eastern and Western hemispheres at 20°W. This places all of Europe and Africa in the Eastern Hemisphere.

Our planet's land surface is divided into seven large landmasses, called **continents**. They are identified in the maps on this page. Landmasses smaller than continents and completely surrounded by water are called **islands**.

Geographers also organize Earth's water surface into parts. The largest is the world ocean. Geographers divide the world ocean into the Pacific Ocean, the Atlantic Ocean, the Indian Ocean, and the Arctic Ocean. Lakes and seas are smaller bodies of water.

Northern Hemisphere

Southern Hemisphere

Western Hemisphere

Eastern Hemisphere

Mapmaking

A **map** is a flat diagram of all or part of the earth's surface. Mapmakers have created different ways of showing our round planet on flat maps. These different ways are called **map projections**. Because the earth is round, there is no way to show it accurately in a flat map. All flat maps are distorted in some way. Mapmakers must choose the type of map projection that is best for their purposes. Many map projections are one of three kinds: cylindrical, conic, or flat-plane.

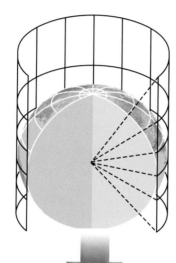

Paper cylinder

Cylindrical Projections

Cylindrical projections are based on a cylinder wrapped around the globe. The cylinder touches the globe only at the equator. The meridians are pulled apart and are parallel to each other instead of meeting at the Poles. This causes landmasses near the Poles to appear larger than they really are. The map below is a Mercator projection, one type of cylindrical projection. The Mercator projection is useful for navigators because it shows true direction and shape. However, it distorts the size of land areas near the Poles.

Mercator projection

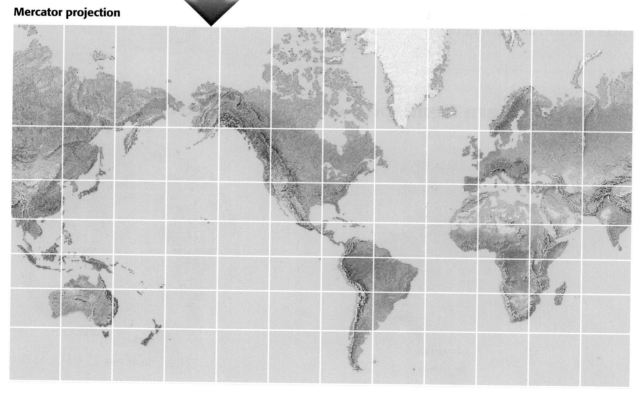

Conic Projections

Conic projections are based on a cone placed over the globe. A conic projection is most accurate along the lines of latitude where it touches the globe. It retains almost true shape and size. Conic projections are most useful for showing areas that have long east-west dimensions, such as the United States.

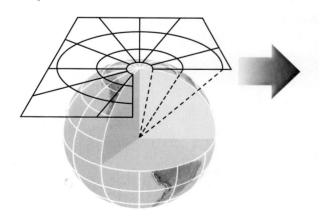

Paper cone

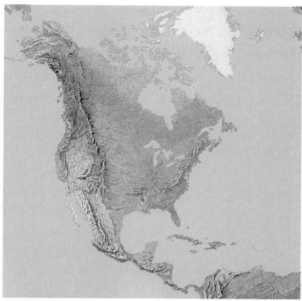

Conic projection

Flat-plane Projections

Flat-plane projections are based on a plane touching the globe at one point, such as at the North Pole or South Pole. A flat-plane projection is useful for showing true direction for airplane pilots and ship navigators. It also shows true area. However, it distorts the true shapes of landmasses.

Flat plane

Flat-plane projection

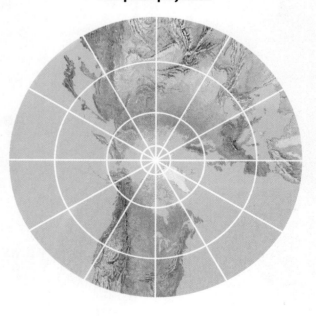

Map Essentials

Maps are like messages sent out in code. Mapmakers provide certain elements that help us translate these codes. These elements help us understand the message they are presenting about a particular part of the world. Of these elements, almost all maps have titles, directional indicators, scales, and legends. The map below has all four of these elements, plus a fifth—a locator map.

❶ Title

A map's **title** shows what the subject of the map is. The map title is usually the first thing you should look at when studying a map, because it tells you what the map is trying to show.

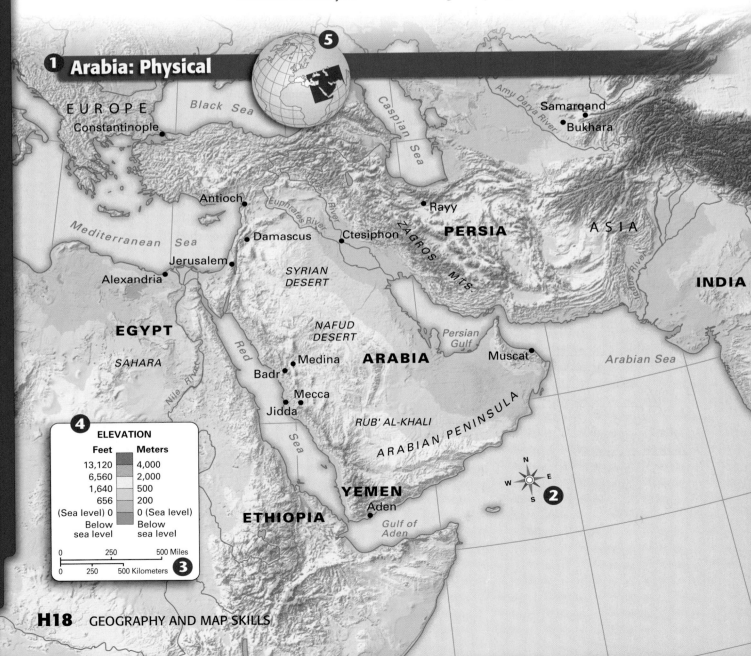

❶ Arabia: Physical

EUROPE
Black Sea
Constantinople

Caspian Sea

Amu Darya River
Samarqand
Bukhara

Antioch
Euphrates River
Rayy
ASIA
PERSIA
Mediterranean Sea
Damascus
Ctesiphon
ZAGROS
Jerusalem
Alexandria
SYRIAN DESERT
MTS.
Indus River
INDIA

EGYPT
NAFUD DESERT
Persian Gulf
SAHARA
Red Sea
Medina
ARABIA
Muscat
Arabian Sea
Badr
Mecca
Jidda
RUB' AL-KHALI
ARABIAN PENINSULA

N
W E
S
❷

YEMEN
Aden
Gulf of Aden
ETHIOPIA

❹ ELEVATION

Feet	Meters
13,120	4,000
6,560	2,000
1,640	500
656	200
(Sea level) 0	0 (Sea level)
Below sea level	Below sea level

0   250   500 Miles
0   250   500 Kilometers **❸**

❷ Compass Rose

A directional indicator shows which way north, south, east, and west lie on the map. Some mapmakers use a "north arrow," which points toward the North Pole. Remember, "north" is not always at the top of a map. The way a map is drawn and the location of directions on that map depend on the perspective of the mapmaker. Most maps in this textbook indicate direction by using a compass rose. A **compass rose** has arrows that point to all four principal directions, as shown.

❸ Scale

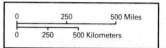

Mapmakers use scales to represent the distances between points on a map. Scales may appear on maps in several different forms. The maps in this textbook provide a bar **scale**. Scales give distances in miles and kilometers.

To find the distance between two points on the map, place a piece of paper so that the edge connects the two points. Mark the location of each point on the paper with a line or dot. Then, compare the distance between the two dots with the map's bar scale. The number on the top of the scale gives the distance in miles. The number on the bottom gives the distance in kilometers. Because the distances are given in large intervals, you may have to approximate the actual distance on the scale.

❹ Legend

The **legend**, or key, explains what the symbols on the map represent. Point symbols are used to specify the location of things, such as cities, that do not take up much space on the map. Some legends, such as the one shown here, show colors that represent certain elevations. Other maps might have legends with symbols or colors that represent things such as roads. Legends can also show economic resources, land use, population density, and climate.

❺ Locator Map

A locator map shows where in the world the area on the map is located. The area shown on the main map is shown in red on the locator map. The locator map also shows surrounding areas so the map reader can see how the information on the map relates to neighboring lands.

Working with Maps

The Atlas at the back of this textbook includes both physical and political maps. Physical maps, like the one you just saw, show the major physical features in a region. These features include things like mountain ranges, rivers, oceans, islands, deserts, and plains. Political maps show the major political features of a region, such as countries and their borders, capitals, and other important cities.

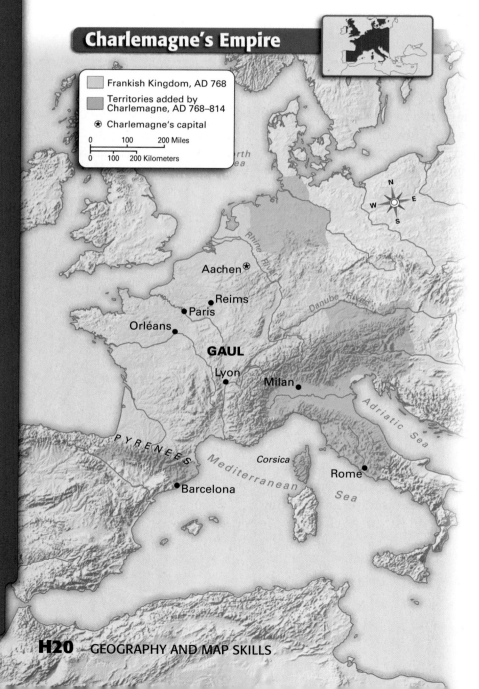

Charlemagne's Empire

Frankish Kingdom, AD 768

Territories added by Charlemagne, AD 768–814

⊛ Charlemagne's capital

0   100   200 Miles

0   100   200 Kilometers

North Sea

Rhine River

Danube River

Aachen ⊛

Reims

Paris

Orléans

GAUL

Lyon

Milan

Adriatic Sea

PYRENEES

Mediterranean Sea

Corsica

Rome

Barcelona

Historical Map

In this textbook, most of the maps you will study are historical maps. Historical maps, such as this one, are maps that show information about the past. This information might be which lands an empire controlled, where a certain group of people lived, what large cities were located in a region, or how a place changed over time. Often colors are used to indicate the different things on the map. Be sure to look at the map title and map legend first to see what the map is showing. What does this map show?

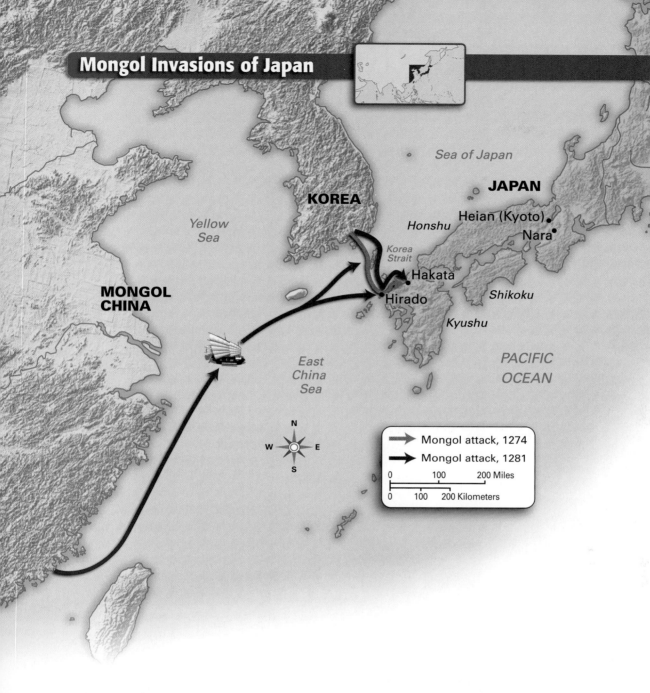

Mongol Invasions of Japan

KOREA

JAPAN

Sea of Japan

Yellow
Sea

Heian (Kyoto)

Honshu

Nara

Korea
Strait

MONGOL
CHINA

Hakata

Hirado

Shikoku

Kyushu

East
China
Sea

PACIFIC
OCEAN

N
W E
S

Mongol attack, 1274
Mongol attack, 1281

0   100   200 Miles

0   100   200 Kilometers

Route Map

One special type of historical map is called a route map. A route map, like the one above, shows the route, or path, that someone or something followed. Route maps can show things like trade routes, invasion routes, or the journeys and travels of people. The routes on the map are usually shown with an arrow. If more than one route is shown, several arrows of different colors may be used. What does this route map show?

The maps in this textbook will help you study and understand history. By working with these maps, you will see where important events happened, where empires rose and fell, and where people moved. In studying these maps, you will learn how geography has influenced history.

Geographic Dictionary

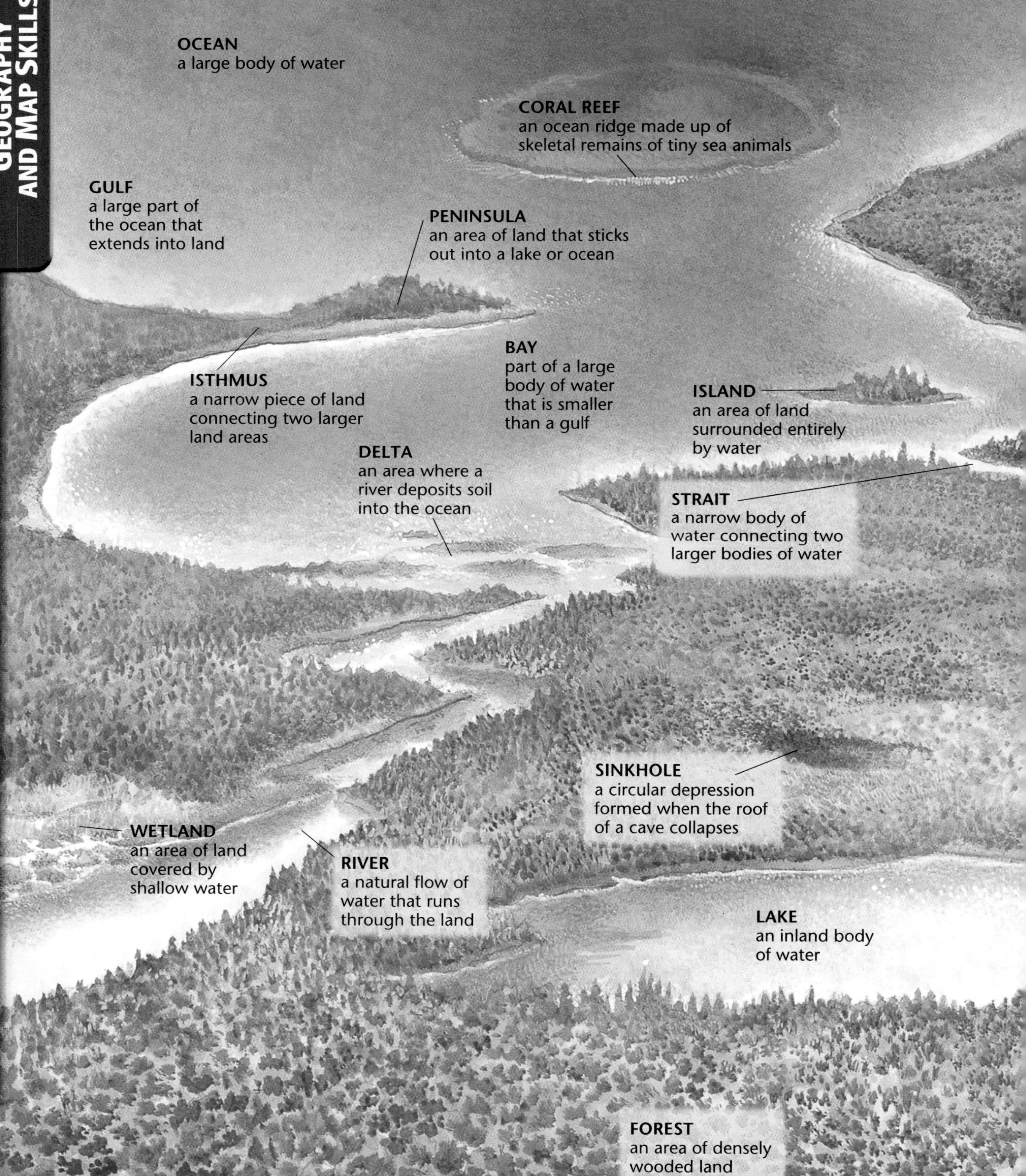

OCEAN
a large body of water

CORAL REEF
an ocean ridge made up of
skeletal remains of tiny sea animals

GULF
a large part of
the ocean that
extends into land

PENINSULA
an area of land that sticks
out into a lake or ocean

ISTHMUS
a narrow piece of land
connecting two larger
land areas

BAY
part of a large
body of water
that is smaller
than a gulf

ISLAND
an area of land
surrounded entirely
by water

DELTA
an area where a
river deposits soil
into the ocean

STRAIT
a narrow body of
water connecting two
larger bodies of water

SINKHOLE
a circular depression
formed when the roof
of a cave collapses

WETLAND
an area of land
covered by
shallow water

RIVER
a natural flow of
water that runs
through the land

LAKE
an inland body
of water

FOREST
an area of densely
wooded land

COAST
an area of land
near the ocean

MOUNTAIN
an area of rugged
land that generally
rises higher than
2,000 feet

VALLEY
an area of low
land between
hills or mountains

GLACIER
a large area of
slow-moving ice

VOLCANO
an opening in Earth's crust
where lava, ash, and gases erupt

CANYON
a deep, narrow valley
with steep walls

HILL
a rounded, elevated
area of land smaller
than a mountain

PLAIN
a nearly
flat area

DUNE
a hill of sand
shaped by wind

OASIS
an area in the
desert with a
water source

DESERT
an extremely dry area with
little water and few plants

PLATEAU
a large, flat,
elevated
area of land

The Five Themes of Geography

Geography is the study of the world's people and places. As you can imagine, studying the entire world is a big job. To make the job easier, geographers have created the Five Themes of Geography. They are: **Location, Place, Human-Environment Interaction, Movement,** and **Region**. You can think of the Five Themes as five windows you can look through to study a place. If you looked at the same place through five different windows, you would have five different perspectives, or viewpoints, of the place. Using the Five Themes in this way will help you better understand the world's people and places.

❶ Location The first thing to study about a place is its location. Where is it? Every place has an absolute location—its exact location on Earth. A place also has a relative location—its location in relation to other places. Use the theme of location to ask questions like, "Where is this place located, and how has its location affected it?"

❷ Place Every place in the world is unique and has its own personality and character. Some things that can make a place unique include its weather, plants and animals, history, and the people that live there. Use the theme of place to ask questions like, "What are the unique features of this place, and how are they important?"

❸ Human-Environment Interaction People interact with their environment in many ways. They use land to grow food and local materials to build houses. At the same time, a place's environment influences how people live. For example, if the weather is cold, people wear warm clothes. Use the theme of human-environment interaction to ask questions like, "What is this place's environment like, and how does it affect the people who live there?"

❹ Movement The world is constantly changing, and places are affected by the movement of people, goods, ideas, and physical forces. For example, people come and go, new businesses begin, and rivers change their course. Use the theme of movement to ask questions like, "How is this place changing, and why?"

❺ Region A region is an area that has one or more features that make it different from surrounding areas. A desert, a country, and a coastal area are all regions. Geographers use regions to break the world into smaller pieces that are easier to study. Use the theme of region to ask questions like "What common features does this area share, and how is it different from other areas?"

Canada

1

LOCATION
Most of the United States is located in the Western Hemisphere, north of Mexico and south of Canada. This location has good farmland, many resources, and many different natural environments.

4

5

United States

3

1

2

Mexico

2

PLACE
New York City is one of the most powerful cities in the world. The people of New York also make the city one of the most ethnically diverse places in the world.

3

HUMAN-ENVIRONMENT INTERACTION
People near Las Vegas, Nevada, transform the desert landscape by building new neighborhoods. Americans modify their environment in many other ways—by controlling rivers, building roads, and creating farmland.

5

REGION
The United States is a political region with one government. At the same time, smaller regions can be found inside the country, such as the Badlands in South Dakota.

4

MOVEMENT
People, goods, and ideas are constantly moving to and from places such as Seattle, Washington. As some places grow, others get smaller, but every place is always changing.

How to Make This Book Work for You

Studying history will be easy for you using this textbook. Take a few minutes to become familiar with the easy-to-use structure and special features of this history book. See how this textbook will make history come alive for you!

Unit

Each chapter of this textbook is part of a Unit of study focusing on a particular time period. Each unit opener provides an illustration, usually showing a young person of the period, and gives you an overview of the exciting topics that you will study in the unit.

Chapter

Each Chapter includes a chapter-opener introduction with a time line of important events, a Social Studies Skills activity, Chapter Review pages, and a Standardized Test Practice page.

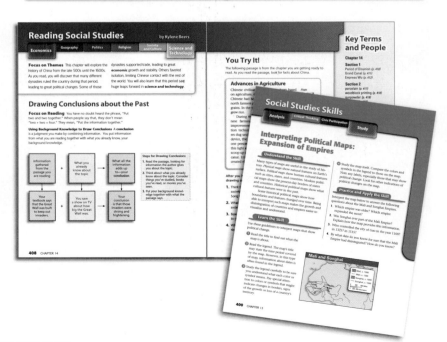

Reading Social Studies These chapter level reading lessons give you skills and practice that you can use to help you read the textbook. Within each chapter there is a Focus on Reading note in the margin on the page where the reading skill is covered. There are also questions in the Chapter Review activity to make sure that you understand the reading skill.

Social Studies Skills The Social Studies Skills lessons give you an opportunity to learn and use a skill that you will most likely use again. You will also be given a chance to make sure that you understand each skill by answering related questions in the Chapter Review activity.

Section

The Section opener pages include Main Idea statements, an overarching big idea statement, and Key Terms and People. In addition, each section includes the following special features.

If You Were There . . . introductions begin each section with a situation for you to respond to, placing you in the time period and in a situation related to the content that you will be studying in the section.

Building Background sections connect what will be covered in this section with what you studied in the previous section.

Short sections of content organize the information in each section into small chunks of text that you shouldn't find too overwhelming.

Taking Notes suggestions and graphic organizers help you read and take notes on the important ideas in the section.

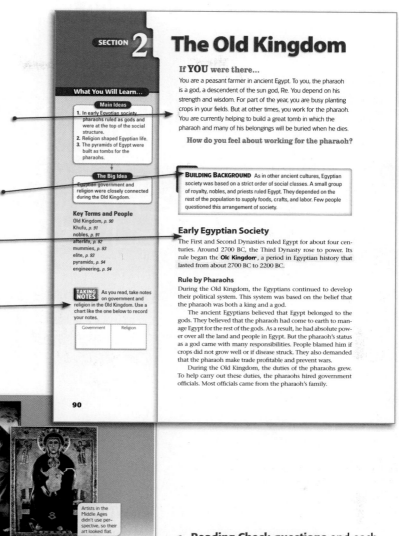

SECTION **2**

The Old Kingdom

What You Will Learn...

Main Ideas
1. In early Egyptian society, pharaohs ruled as gods and were at the top of the social structure.
2. Religion shaped Egyptian life.
3. The pyramids of Egypt were built as tombs for the pharaohs.

The Big Idea
Egyptian government and religion were closely connected during the Old Kingdom.

Key Terms and People
Old Kingdom, *p. 90*
Khufu, *p. 91*
nobles, *p. 91*
afterlife, *p. 92*
mummies, *p. 93*
elite, *p. 93*
pyramids, *p. 94*
engineering, *p. 94*

TAKING NOTES As you read, take notes on government and religion in the Old Kingdom. Use a chart like the one below to record your notes.

Government	Religion

If YOU were there...
You are a peasant farmer in ancient Egypt. To you, the pharaoh is a god, a descendant of the sun god, Re. You depend on his strength and wisdom. For part of the year, you are busy planting crops in your fields. But at other times, you work for the pharaoh. You are currently helping to build a great tomb in which the pharaoh and many of his belongings will be buried when he dies.

How do you feel about working for the pharaoh?

BUILDING BACKGROUND As in other ancient cultures, Egyptian society was based on a strict order of social classes. A small group of royalty, nobles, and priests ruled Egypt. They depended on the rest of the population to supply foods, crafts, and labor. Few people questioned this arrangement of society.

Early Egyptian Society
The First and Second Dynasties ruled Egypt for about four centuries. Around 2700 BC, the Third Dynasty rose to power. Its rule began the **Old Kingdom**, a period in Egyptian history that lasted from about 2700 BC to 2200 BC.

Rule by Pharaohs
During the Old Kingdom, the Egyptians continued to develop their political system. This system was based on the belief that the pharaoh was both a king and a god.

The ancient Egyptians believed that Egypt belonged to the gods. They believed that the pharaoh had come to earth to manage Egypt for the rest of the gods. As a result, he had absolute power over all the land and people in Egypt. But the pharaoh's status as a god came with many responsibilities. People blamed him if crops did not grow well or if disease struck. They also demanded that the pharaoh make trade profitable and prevent wars.

During the Old Kingdom, the duties of the pharaohs grew. To help carry out these duties, the pharaohs hired government officials. Most officials came from the pharaoh's family.

90

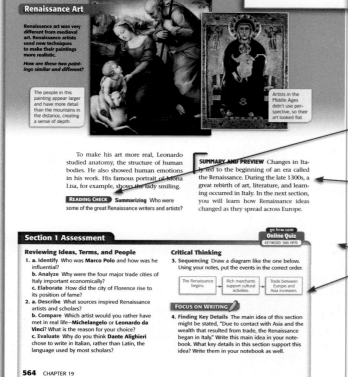

Renaissance Art

Renaissance art was very different from medieval art. Renaissance artists used new techniques to make their paintings more realistic.

How are these two paintings similar and different?

The people in this painting appear larger and have more detail than the mountains in the distance, creating a sense of depth.

Artists in the Middle Ages didn't use perspective, so their art looked flat.

To make his art more real, Leonardo studied anatomy, the structure of human bodies. He also showed human emotions in his work. His famous portrait of Mona Lisa, for example, shows the lady smiling.

READING CHECK Summarizing Who were some of the great Renaissance writers and artists?

SUMMARY AND PREVIEW Changes in Italy led to the beginning of an era called the Renaissance. During the late 1300s, a great rebirth of art, literature, and learning occurred in Italy. In the next section, you will learn how Renaissance ideas changed as they spread across Europe.

Section 1 Assessment

go.hrw.com
Online Quiz
KEYWORD: SN6 HP19

Reviewing Ideas, Terms, and People
1. a. **Identify** Who was **Marco Polo** and how was he influential?
   b. **Analyze** Why were the four major trade cities of Italy important economically?
   c. **Elaborate** How did the city of Florence rise to its position of fame?
2. a. **Describe** What sources inspired Renaissance artists and scholars?
   b. **Compare** Which artist would you rather have met in real life—**Michelangelo** or **Leonardo da Vinci**? What is the reason for your choice?
   c. **Evaluate** Why do you think **Dante Alighieri** chose to write in Italian, rather than Latin, the language used by most scholars?

Critical Thinking
3. **Sequencing** Draw a diagram like the one below. Using your notes, put the events in the correct order.

The Renaissance begins. → Rich merchants support cultural activities. → Trade between Europe and Asia increases.

FOCUS ON WRITING
4. **Finding Key Details** The main idea of this section might be stated, "Due to contact with Asia and the wealth that resulted from trade, the Renaissance began in Italy." Write this main idea in your notebook. What key details in this section support this idea? Write them in your notebook as well.

564 CHAPTER 19

Reading Check questions end each section of content so that you can test whether or not you understand what you have just studied.

Summary and Preview To connect what you have just studied in the section to what you will study in the next section, we include the Summary and Preview.

Section Assessments The section assessment boxes provide an opportunity for you to make sure that you understand the main ideas of the section. We also provide assessment practice online!

Early Humans and Societies

History is the study of the past, and people who study history are called historians. Historians try to learn what life was like for people long ago in places around the world. To understand the people and places of the past, historians study clues and evidence.

Some historians study the earliest humans. Early people hunted animals, gathered plants, and learned how to make stone tools. Eventually, people learned to grow food and raise animals for themselves.

In the next two chapters, you will learn about the subject of history and about the world's earliest peoples.

Explore the Art

In this scene, young Maria de Sautuola discovers prehistoric cave paintings in Altamira, Spain, in 1879. What do these paintings say about the life of early people?

Uncovering the Past

FOCUS ON WRITING

A Job Description What is the job of a historian? an archaeologist? a geographer? In this chapter you will read about the work of people who study the past—its events, its people, and its places. Then you will write a job description to include in a career-planning guide.

History's Impact

▶ **video series**
Watch the video to understand the impact of archaeology on what we have learned about the past.

What You Will Learn…

In this chapter you will learn how historians and geographers study the past. This photo shows clay warriors that were found in China. Finds like these teach us a lot about the history of ancient places.

Reading Social Studies

by Kylene Beers

Focus on Themes This chapter sets the stage for reading the rest of the book. In it you will learn the definitions of many important terms. You will learn how studying history helps you understand the past and the present. You will also read about the study of geography and learn how the world's physical features affected when and where civilization began. Finally, you will begin to think about how **society and culture** and **science and technology** have interacted throughout time.

Specialized Vocabulary of History

Focus on Reading Have you ever done a plié at the barre or sacked the quarterback? You probably haven't if you've never studied ballet or played football. In fact, you may not even have known what those words meant.

Specialized Vocabulary Plié, barre, sack, and quarterback are **specialized vocabulary**, words that are used in only one field. History has its own specialized vocabulary. The charts below list some terms often used in the study of history.

Terms that identify periods of time	
Decade	a period of 10 years
Century	a period of 100 years
Age	a long period of time marked by a single cultural feature
Era	a long period of time marked by great events, developments, or figures
Ancient	very old, or from a long time ago

Terms used with dates	
circa or c.	a word used to show that historians are not sure of an exact date; it means "about"
BC	a term used to identify dates that occurred long ago, before the birth of Jesus Christ, the founder of Christianity; it means "before Christ." As you can see on the time line below, BC dates get smaller as time passes, so the larger the number the earlier the date.
AD	a term used to identify dates that occurred after Jesus's birth; it comes from a Latin phrase that means "in the year of our Lord." Unlike BC dates, AD dates get larger as time passes, so the larger the number the later the date.
BCE	another way to refer to BC dates; it stands for "before the common era"
CE	another way to refer to AD dates; it stands for "common era"

| 300 BC | 200 BC | 100 BC | BC 1 AD | AD 100 | AD 200 | AD 300 |
| 300 BCE | 200 BCE | 100 BCE | BCE 1 CE | 100 CE | 200 CE | 300 CE |

You Try It!

As you read this textbook, you will find many examples of specialized vocabulary terms that historians use. Many of these terms will be highlighted in the text and defined for you as key terms. Others may not be highlighted, but they will still be defined. For some examples, read the passage below. Learning these words as you come across them will help you understand what you read later in the book. For your own reference, you may wish to keep a list of important terms in your notebook.

Vocabulary in Context

We must rely on a variety of sources to learn history. For information on the very first humans, we have fossil remains. A **fossil** is a part or imprint of something that was once alive. Bones and footprints preserved in rock are examples of fossils.

From Chapter 1, page 10

As human beings learned to make things, by accident they also created more sources of information for us. They made what we call **artifacts**, objects created by and used by humans. Artifacts include coins, arrowheads, tools, toys, and pottery.

Answer the following questions about the specialized vocabulary of history.

1. What is a fossil? What is an artifact? How can you tell?

2. Were you born in a BC year or an AD year?

3. Put the following dates in order: AD 2000, 3100 BC, 15 BCE, AD 476, AD 3, CE 1215

4. If you saw that an event happened c. AD 1000, what would that mean?

Academic Vocabulary

Success in school is related to knowing academic vocabulary—the words that are frequently used in school assignments and discussions. In this chapter, you will learn the following academic words:

As you read **Chapter 1,** keep a list in your notebook of specialized vocabulary words that you learn.

Studying History

If YOU were there...

You are a student helping scholars uncover the remains of an ancient city. One exciting day you find a jar filled with bits of clay on which strange symbols have been carved. You recognize the marks as letters because for years you have studied the language of the city's people. This is your chance to put your skills to use!

What might you learn from the ancient writings?

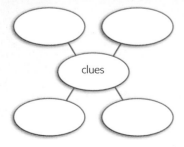

clues

BUILDING BACKGROUND Last year you learned about our country's past. Now you begin a study of world history, which started many centuries before the history of the United States. You will find that we learn about world history in many ways.

The Study of the Past

The people of the ancient world didn't build skyscrapers, invent the automobile, or send spaceships to Mars. But they did remarkable things. Among their amazing feats were building huge temples, inventing writing, and discovering planets. Every step we take—in technology, science, education, literature, and all other fields—builds on what people did long ago. We are who we are because of what people did in the past.

What Is History?

History is the study of the past. A battle that happened 5,000 years ago and an election that happened yesterday are both parts of history.

Historians are people who study history. Their main concern is human activity in the past. They want to know how people lived and why they did the things they did. They try to learn about the problems people faced and how they found solutions.

Historians are interested in how people lived their daily lives. How and where did they work, fight, trade, farm, and worship? What did they do in their free time? What games did they play? In other words, historians study the past to understand people's **culture**—the knowledge, beliefs, customs, and values of a group of people.

What Is Archaeology?

An important field that contributes much information about the past is **archaeology** (ahr-kee-AH-luh-jee). It is the study of the past based on what people left behind.

Archaeologists, or people who practice archaeology, explore places where people once lived, worked, or fought. The things that people left in these places may include jewelry, dishes, or weapons. They range from stone tools to computers.

Archaeologists examine the objects they find to learn what they can tell about the past. In many cases, the objects that people left behind are the only clues we have to how they lived.

READING CHECK **Comparing** How are the fields of history and archaeology similar?

THE IMPACT TODAY

Computers have become an essential tool in modern times.

Studying the Past
Historians and archaeologists study the people and places of the past. For example, by studying the remains of an ancient Egyptian temple (right), they can learn about the lives of the ancient Egyptians (left).

Understanding through History

There are many reasons why people study history. Understanding the past helps us to understand the world today. History can also provide us with a guide to making better decisions in the future.

ACADEMIC VOCABULARY
values ideas that people hold dear and try to live by

Knowing Yourself

History can teach you about yourself. What if you did not know your own past? You would not know which subjects you liked in school or which sports you enjoyed. You would not know what makes you proud or what mistakes not to repeat. Without your own personal history, you would not have an identity.

History is just as important for groups as it is for individuals. What would happen if countries had no record of their past? People would know nothing about how their governments came into being. They would not remember their nation's great triumphs or tragedies. History teaches us about the experiences we have been through as a people. It shapes our identity and teaches us the **values** that we share.

Knowing Others

Like today, the world in the past included many cultures. History teaches about the cultures that were unlike your own. You learn about other peoples, where they lived, and what was important to them. History teaches you how cultures were similar and how they were different.

History also helps you understand why other people think the way they do. You learn about the struggles people have faced. You also learn how these struggles have affected the way people view themselves and others.

Understanding the World

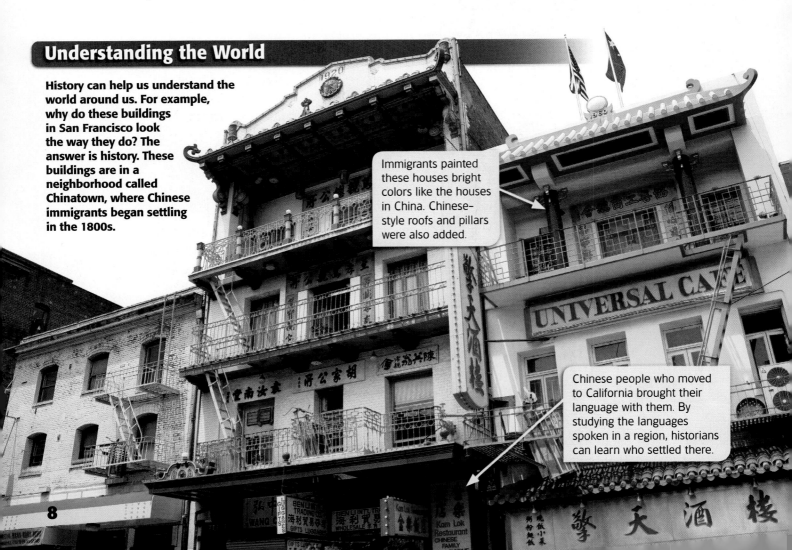

History can help us understand the world around us. For example, why do these buildings in San Francisco look the way they do? The answer is history. These buildings are in a neighborhood called Chinatown, where Chinese immigrants began settling in the 1800s.

Immigrants painted these houses bright colors like the houses in China. Chinese-style roofs and pillars were also added.

Chinese people who moved to California brought their language with them. By studying the languages spoken in a region, historians can learn who settled there.

For example, Native Americans, European settlers, enslaved Africans, and Asian immigrants all played vital roles in our country's history. But the descendants of each group have a different story to tell about their ancestors' contributions.

Learning these stories and others like them that make up history can help you see the viewpoints of other peoples. It can help teach you to respect and understand different opinions. This knowledge helps promote tolerance. History can also help you relate more easily to people of different backgrounds. In other words, knowing about the past can help build social harmony throughout the world today.

Knowing Your World

History can provide you with a better understanding of where you live. You are part of a culture that interacts with the outside world. Even events that happen in other parts of the world affect your culture. History helps you to understand how today's events are shaped by the events of the past. So knowing the past helps you figure out what is happening now.

History is concerned with the entire range of human activities. It is the record of humanity's combined efforts. So while you are studying history, you can also learn more about math, science, religion, government, and many other topics.

Studying the past will also help you develop mental skills. History encourages you to ask important questions. It forces you to analyze the facts you learn. Such analysis teaches you how to recognize which information is important and which is extra. This skill helps you to find the main facts when studying any topic.

History also promotes good decision-making skills. A famous, often repeated saying warns us that those who forget their past are doomed to repeat it. This means

that people who ignore the results of past decisions often make the same mistakes over and over again.

Individuals and countries both benefit from the wisdom that history can teach. Your own history may have taught you that studying for a test results in better grades. In a similar way, world history has taught that providing young people with education makes them more productive when they become adults.

Historians have been talking about the value of history for centuries. More than 2,000 years ago a great Greek historian named Polybius wrote:

FOCUS ON READING
What does the word *century* mean?

*"*The purpose of history is not the reader's enjoyment at the moment of perusal [reading it], but the reformation [improvement] of the reader's soul, to save him from stumbling at the same stumbling block many times over.*"*
–Polybius, from *The Histories, Book XXXVIII*

READING CHECK **Summarizing** What are some benefits of studying history?

Clues from the Past

This archaeologist is examining ancient pottery in Italy to learn about the past.

Using Clues

We must rely on a variety of sources to learn history. For information on the very first humans, we have fossil remains. A **fossil** is a part or imprint of something that was once alive. Bones and footprints preserved in rock are examples of fossils.

As human beings learned to make things, by accident they also created more sources of information for us. They made what we call **artifacts**, objects created by and used by humans. Artifacts include coins, arrowheads, tools, toys, and pottery. Archaeologists examine artifacts and the places where the artifacts were found to learn about the past.

Sources of Information

About 5,000 years ago, people invented writing. They wrote laws, poems, speeches, battle plans, letters, contracts, and many other things. In these written sources, historians have found countless clues about how people lived. In addition, people have recorded their messages in many ways over the centuries. Historians have studied writing carved into stone pillars, stamped onto clay tablets, scribbled on turtle shells, typed with typewriters, and sent by computer.

Historical sources are of two types. A **primary source** is an account of an event created by someone who took part in or witnessed the event. Treaties, letters, diaries, laws, court documents, and royal commands are all primary sources. An audio or video recording of an event is also a primary source.

A **secondary source** is information gathered by someone who did not take part in or witness an event. Examples include history textbooks, journal articles, and encyclopedias. The textbook you are reading right now is a secondary source. The historians who wrote it did not take part in the events described. Instead, they gathered information about these events from different sources.

Written records, like this writing from a tomb in Egypt, are valuable sources of information about the past.

Sometimes, archaeologists must carefully reconstruct artifacts from hundreds of broken pieces, like they did with this statue of an Aztec bat god from Mexico.

Sources of Change

Writers of secondary sources don't always agree about the past. Historians form different opinions about the primary sources they study. As a result, historians may not interpret past events in the same way.

For example, one writer may say that a king was a brilliant military leader. Another may say that the king's armies only won their battles because they had better weapons than their enemies did. Sometimes new evidence leads to new conclusions. As historians review and reanalyze information, their interpretations can and do change.

READING CHECK **Contrasting** How are primary and secondary sources different?

SUMMARY AND PREVIEW We benefit from studying the past. Scholars use many clues to help them understand past events. In the next section you will learn how geography connects to history.

go.hrw.com
Online Quiz
KEYWORD: SN6 HP1

Section 1 Assessment

Reviewing Ideas, Terms, and People

1. **a. Identify** What is **history**?
   b. Explain What kinds of things do historians try to discover about people who lived in the past?
   c. Predict What kinds of evidence will historians of the future study to learn about your **culture**?
2. **a. Describe** How does knowing its own history provide a group with a sense of unity?
   b. Elaborate Explain the meaning of the phrase, "Those who forget their past are doomed to repeat it."
3. **a. Identify** What is a **primary source**?
   b. Explain How did the invention of writing affect the sources on which historians rely?
   c. Elaborate Could a photograph be considered a primary source? Why or why not?

Critical Thinking

4. **Categorizing** Using your notes, identify four types of clues to the past and give at least two examples of each.

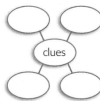
clues

FOCUS ON WRITING

5. **Understanding What Historians Do** What is the difference between a historian and an archaeologist? Take notes about the work these people do.

Studying Geography

What You Will Learn...

Main Ideas

1. Geography is the study of places and people.
2. Studying location is important to both physical and human geography.
3. Geography and history are closely connected.

The Big Idea

Physical geography and human geography contribute to the study of history.

Key Terms

geography, *p. 12*
landforms, *p. 12*
climate, *p. 12*
environment, *p. 13*
region, *p. 15*
resources, *p. 16*

TAKING NOTES As you read, take notes on physical geography and human geography. Use a chart like the one below to record your notes.

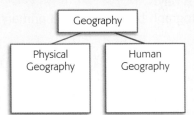

If YOU were there...

Your parents are historians researching a city that disappeared long ago. You go with them to a library to help search for clues to the city's location and fate. While thumbing through a dusty old book, you find an ancient map stuck between two pages. Marked on the map are rivers, forests, mountains, and straight lines that look like roads. It is a map that shows the way to the lost city!

How can this map help you find the city?

BUILDING BACKGROUND You have read how historians and archaeologists help us learn about the past. Another group of scholars—geographers—also contribute to our study of history.

Studying Places and People

When you hear about an event on the news, the first questions you ask may be, "Where did it happen?" and "Who was there?" Historians ask the same questions about events that happened in the past. That is why they need to study geography. **Geography** is the study of the earth's physical and cultural features. These features include mountains, rivers, people, cities, and countries.

Physical Geography

Physical geography is the study of the earth's land and features. People who work in this field are called physical geographers. They study **landforms**, the natural features of the land's surface. Mountains, valleys, plains, and other such places are landforms.

Physical geographers also study **climate**, the pattern of weather conditions in a certain area over a long period of time. Climate is not the same as weather. Weather is the conditions at a specific time and place. If you say that your city has cold winters, you are talking about climate. If you say it is below freezing and snowing today, you are talking about the weather.

Physical Geography

The study of the earth's physical features and processes, such as mountains, rivers, oceans, rainfall, and climate, including this section of California's coast

Human Geography

The study of the earth's people, including their way of life, homes and cities, beliefs, and travels, such as these members of the Dogon people in the country of Mali

Geography

The study of the earth's physical and cultural features

Climate affects many features of a region. For example, it affects plant life. Tropical rain forests require warm air and heavy rain, while a dry climate can create deserts. Climate also affects landforms. For example, constant wind can wear down mountains into flat plains.

Although climate affects landforms, landforms can also affect climate. For example, the Coast Ranges in northern California are mountains parallel to the Pacific coast. As air presses up against these mountains, it rises and cools. Any moisture that the air was carrying falls as rain. Meanwhile, on the opposite side of the range, the Central Valley stays dry. In this way, a mountain range creates two very different climates.

Landforms and climate are part of a place's environment. The **environment** includes all the living and nonliving things that affect life in an area. This includes the area's climate, land, water, plants, soil, animals, and other features.

Human Geography

The other branch of geography is human geography—the study of people and the places where they live. Specialists in human geography study many different things about people and their cultures. What kind of work do people do? How do they get their food? What are their homes like? What religions do they practice?

Human geography also deals with how the environment affects people. For example, how do people who live near rivers protect themselves from floods? How do people who live in deserts survive? Do different environments affect the size of families? Do people in certain environments live longer? Why do some diseases spread easily in some environments but not in others? As you can see, human geographers study many interesting questions about people and this planet.

READING CHECK **Summarizing** What are the two main branches of geography?

Studying Location

Both physical and human geographers study location. Location is the exact description of where something is. Every place on Earth has a specific location.

No two places in the world are exactly alike. Even small differences between places can lead to major differences in how people live. That is why geographers try to understand the effects that different locations have on human populations, or groups of people.

By comparing locations, geographers learn more about the factors that affected each of them. For example, they may study why a town grew in one location while a town nearby got smaller.

Learning from Maps

To study various locations, geographers use maps. A map is a drawing of an area. Some maps show physical **features**. Others show cities and the boundaries of states or countries. Most maps have symbols to show different things. For example, large dots often stand for cities. Blue lines show where rivers flow. Most maps also include a guide to show direction.

People have been making maps for more than 4,000 years. Maps help with many activities. Planning battles, looking for new lands, and designing new city parks all require good maps. On the first day of class, you may have used a map of your school to find your classrooms.

Studying Maps

By studying and comparing maps, you can see how a place's physical and human features are related.

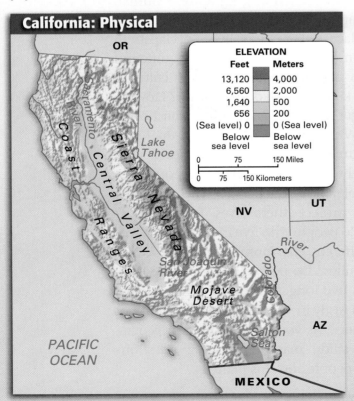

California: Physical

1 What are some of California's main physical features? Where are the state's highest mountains?

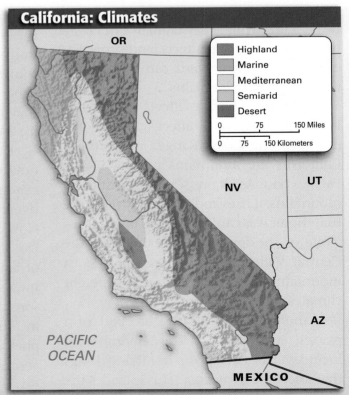

California: Climates

2 What climates are found in California? How are the climate regions related to California's physical features?

Learning about Regions

Learning about regions is another key part of studying geography. A **region** is an area with one or more features that make it different from surrounding areas. These features may be physical, such as forests or grasslands. There may also be differences in climate. For example, a desert area is a type of region. Physical barriers such as mountains and rivers often form a region's boundaries.

Human features can also define regions. An area with many cities is one type of region. An area with only farms is another type. Some regions are identified by the language that people there speak. Other regions are identified by the religion their people practice.

READING CHECK **Categorizing** What are some types of features that can identify a region?

Primary Source

BOOK
What Geography Means

Some people think of geography as the ability to read maps or name state capitals. But as geographer Kenneth C. Davis explains, geography is much more. It is related to almost every branch of human knowledge.

❝Geography doesn't simply begin and end with maps showing the location of all the countries of the world. In fact, such maps don't necessarily tell us much. No—geography poses fascinating questions about who we are and how we got to be that way, and then provides clues to the answers. It is impossible to understand history, international politics, the world economy, religions, philosophy, or 'patterns of culture' without taking geography into account.❞

–Kenneth C. Davis, from *Don't Know Much About Geography*

ANALYSIS SKILL **ANALYZING PRIMARY SOURCES**

Why does the writer think that geography is important?

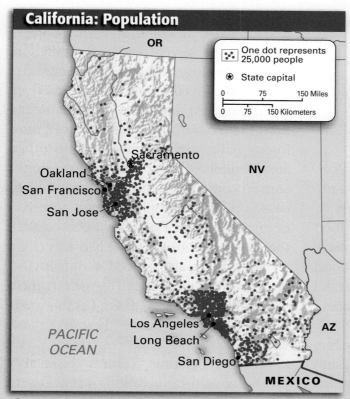

3 Where are California's two main population centers? What kind of climate is found in these areas?

4 How are California's roads related to its physical features? How are they related to its population centers?

One way you can see how geography has shaped history is by studying the locations of cities. Certain locations have strategic advantages over others, and as a result, people choose to create cities there. For example, the city of Rio de Janeiro, Brazil, has easy access to the ocean and breathtaking scenery.

Geography and History

Geography gives us important clues about the people and places that came before us. Like detectives, we can piece together a great deal of information about ancient cultures by knowing where people lived and what the area was like.

Geography Affects Resources

An area's geography was critical to early settlements. People could survive only in areas where they could get enough food and water. Early people settled in places that were rich in **resources**, materials found in the earth that people need and value. All through history, people have used a variety of resources to meet their basic needs.

In early times, essential resources included water, animals, fertile land, and stones for tools. Over time, people learned to use other resources, including metals such as copper, gold, and iron.

Geography Shapes Cultures

Geography also influenced the early development of cultures. Early peoples, for example, developed vastly different cultures because of their environments. People who lived along rivers learned to make fishhooks and boats, while those far from rivers did not. People who lived near forests built homes from wood. In other areas, builders had to use mud or stone. Some people developed religious beliefs based on the geography of their area. For example, ancient Egyptians believed that the god Hapi controlled the Nile River.

Geography also played a role in the growth of civilizations. The world's first societies formed along rivers. Crops grown on the fertile land along these rivers fed large populations.

Some geographic features could also protect areas from invasion. A region surrounded by mountains or deserts, for example, was hard for attackers to reach.

environments in positive and negative ways. People have planted millions of trees. They have created new lakes in the middle of deserts. But people have also created wastelands where forests once grew and built dams that flooded ancient cities. This interaction between humans and their environment has been a major factor in history. It continues today.

READING CHECK **Summarizing** In what ways has geography shaped human history?

SUMMARY AND PREVIEW The field of geography includes physical geography and human geography. Geography has had a major influence on history. In the next chapter you will learn how geography affected the first people.

Geography Influences History

Geography has helped shape history and has affected the growth of societies. People in areas with many natural resources could use their resources to get rich. They could build glorious cities and powerful armies. Features such as rivers also made trade easier. Many societies became rich by trading goods with other peoples.

On the other hand, geography has also caused problems. Floods, for example, have killed millions of people. Lack of rainfall has brought deadly food shortages. Storms have wrecked ships, and with them, the hopes of conquerors. In the 1200s, for example, a people known as the Mongols tried to invade Japan. However, most of the Mongol ships were destroyed by a powerful storm. Japanese history may have been very different if the storm had not occurred.

The relationship between geography and people has not been one-sided. For centuries, people have influenced their

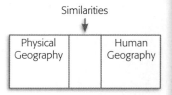

Section 2 Assessment

Reviewing Ideas, Terms, and People

1. **a. Define** What is **geography**?
   b. Summarize What are some of the topics included in human geography?
2. **a. Describe** Identify a **region** near where you live, and explain what sets it apart as a region.
   b. Predict How might a map of a city's **landforms** help an official who is planning a new city park?
3. **a. Recall** Where did early peoples tend to settle?
   b. Compare and Contrast How could a river be both a valuable **resource** and a problem for a region?

Critical Thinking

4. **Comparing and Contrasting** Using your note-taking chart, compare and contrast physical and human geography.

Similarities

Physical Geography		Human Geography

FOCUS ON WRITING

5. **Understanding What Geographers Do** In this section you learned how geographers contribute to the study of history. What is the difference between a physical geographer and a human geographer?

Mapping the Past

Maps are useful tools for historians. By creating a map of how a place used to be, historians can learn where things were located and what the place was like. In other words, by studying a place's geography, we can also learn something about its history.

This map shows the ancient city of Teotihuacán (tay-oh-tee-wah-KAHN) in central Mexico. Teotihuacán reached its height around AD 500. Study this map. What can it tell you about the history of the city?

Pyramid of the Moon

Teotihuacán, c. AD 500

- Pyramid of the Moon
- Pyramid of the Sun
- Houses
- San Juan River
- Street of the Dead
- Citadel
- San Lorenzo River

0	.25	.50 Mile
0	.25	.50 Kilometer

Size and Importance As the map shows, Teotihuacán was a large city. It had many buildings and a large population. From this, you might conclude that the city was important, just as big cities are important today.

Religion The giant buildings that dominate the heart of the city, such as the Pyramid of the Sun, are religious temples. From this, you can conclude that religion was very important to the people of Teotihuacán.

Pyramid of the Sun

Citadel

Street of the Dead

San Juan River

Technology The map shows that this river turns at right angles, just like the city's streets. The people of Teotihuacán must have changed the course of this river. That tells you that they had advanced engineering skills and technology.

GEOGRAPHY SKILLS **INTERPRETING MAPS**

1. **Place** How does the map indicate that Teotihuacán was an important place?
2. **Location** What can you conclude from the fact that large religious buildings are located in the heart of the city?

19

Social Studies Skills

Analysis | Critical Thinking | Economics | Study

Recognizing Bias

Understand the Skill

Everybody has convictions, or things that they strongly believe. However, if we form opinions about people or events based only on our beliefs, we may be showing bias. Bias is an idea about someone or something based solely on opinions, not facts.

There are many types of bias. Sometimes people form opinions about others based on the group to which that person belongs. For example, some people might believe that all teenagers are selfish or that all politicians are dishonest. These are examples of a type of bias called *stereotyping*. Holding negative opinions of people based on their race, religion, age, gender, or similar characteristics is known as *prejudice*.

We should always be on guard for the presence of personal biases. Such biases can slant how we view, judge, and provide information. Honest and accurate communication requires people to be as free of bias as possible.

Learn the Skill

As you read or write, watch out for biases. One way to identify a bias is to look for facts that support a statement. If a belief seems unreasonable when compared to the facts, it may be a sign of bias.

Another sign of bias is a person's unwillingness to question his or her belief if it is challenged by evidence. People sometimes cling to views that evidence proves are wrong. This is why bias is defined as a "fixed" idea about something. It also points out a good reason why we should try to avoid being biased. Our biases can keep us from considering new ideas and learning new things.

You will meet many peoples from the past as you study world history. Their beliefs, behaviors, and ways of life may seem different or strange to you. It is important to remain unbiased and to keep an open mind. Recognize that "different" does not mean "not as good."

Understand that early peoples did not have the technology or the accumulation of past knowledge that we have today. Be careful to not look down on them just because they were less advanced or might seem "simpler" than we are today. Remember that their struggles, learning, and achievements helped make us what we are today.

The following guidelines can help you to recognize and reduce your own biases. Keep them in mind as you study world history.

❶ When discussing a topic, try to think of beliefs and experiences in your own background that might affect how you feel about the topic.

❷ Try to not mix statements of fact with statements of opinion. Clearly separate and indicate what you *know* to be true from what you *believe* to be true.

❸ Avoid using emotional, positive, or negative words when communicating factual information.

Practice and Apply the Skill

Professional historians try to be objective about the history they study and report. Being *objective* means not being influenced by personal feelings or opinions. Write a paragraph explaining why you think being objective is important in the study of history.

Chapter Review

Visual Summary

Use the visual summary below to help you review the main ideas of the chapter.

QUICK FACTS

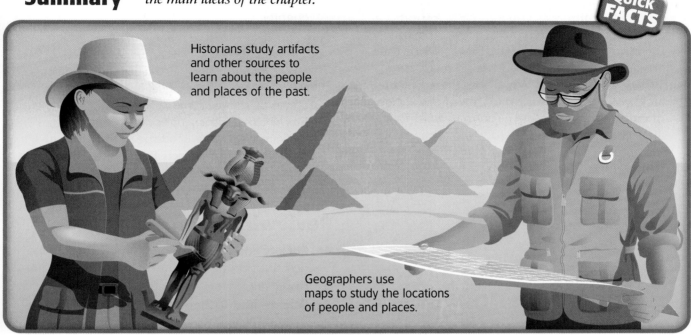

Historians study artifacts and other sources to learn about the people and places of the past.

Geographers use maps to study the locations of people and places.

Reviewing Vocabulary, Terms, and People

*For each statement below, write **T** if it is true or **F** if it is false. If the statement is false, write the correct term that would make the sentence a true statement.*

1. <u>History</u> is the study of the past based on what people left behind.

2. Knowledge, beliefs, customs, and values of a group of people are part of their <u>environment</u>.

3. A handwritten letter from a soldier to his family would be considered a <u>primary source</u>.

4. <u>Geography</u> is the study of the past, whether recent or long ago.

5. Your state probably has many different <u>landforms</u>, such as mountains, plains, and valleys.

6. Weather changes from day to day, but a location's <u>climate</u> does not change as often.

7. <u>Values</u> are ideas that people hold dear and try to live by.

Comprehension and Critical Thinking

SECTION 1 *(Pages 6–11)*

8. **a. Describe** What is history? What is archaeology? How do the two fields work together?

   b. Make Inferences Why may a historian who is still alive disagree with conclusions drawn by a historian who lived a hundred years ago?

   c. Evaluate Do you think primary sources or secondary sources are more valuable to modern historians? Why?

SECTION 2 *(Pages 12–17)*

9. **a. Identify** What are the two main branches of geography, and how does each contribute to our understanding of history?

   b. Analyze If you were asked to divide your state into regions, what features would you use to define those regions? Why?

   c. Predict How might a long period of severe heat or cold affect the history of a city or region?

Using the Internet

go.hrw.com
KEYWORD: SN6 WH1

10. **Activity: Describing Artifacts** Archaeologists study the past based on what people have left behind. Enter the activity keyword and explore recent archaeological discoveries. Select one artifact that interests you and write a short article about it. Write your article as if it will be printed in a school magazine. Describe the artifact in detail: What is it? Who made it? Where was it found? What does the artifact tell archaeologists and historians about the society or culture that created it? You may want to create a chart like the one below to organize your information. If possible, include illustrations with your article.

Artifact	
What is it?	
Who made it?	
Where was it found?	
What does it tell us?	

Social Studies Skills

Recognizing Bias Answer the following questions about personal convictions and bias.

11. What is bias?

12. What is the difference between a personal conviction and a bias?

13. Why do historians try to avoid bias in their writing? What methods might they use to do so?

14. Do you think it is possible for a historian to remove all traces of bias from his or her writing? Why or why not?

Reading Skills

15. **Specialized Vocabulary of History** Read the following passage in which several words have been left blank. Fill in each of the blanks with the appropriate word that you learned in this chapter.

> " Although _____ is defined as the study of the past, it is much more. It is a key to understanding our _____, the ideas, languages, religions, and other traits that make us who we are. In the _____ left behind by ancient peoples we can see reflections of our own material goods: plates and dishes, toys, jewelry, and work objects. These objects show us that human _____ has not changed that much.

Reviewing Themes

16. **Society and Culture** How may a historian's description of a battle reveal information about his or her own society or culture?

17. **Science and Technology** If hundreds of years from now archaeologists study the things we leave behind, what may they conclude about the role of technology in American society? Explain your answer.

FOCUS ON WRITING

18. **Writing Your Job Description** Review your notes on the work of historians, archaeologists, and physical and human geographers. Choose one of these jobs and write a description of it. You should begin your description by explaining why the job is important. Then identify the job's tasks and responsibilities. Finally, tell what kind of person would do well in this job. For example, a historian may enjoy reading and an archaeologist may enjoy working outdoors. When you have finished your description, you may be able to add it to a class or school guide for career planning.

Standardized Test Practice

DIRECTIONS: Read each question, and write the letter of the best response.

1

The object with ancient writing that is shown in this photo is a

A primary source and a resource.

B primary source and an artifact.

C secondary source and a resource.

D secondary source and an artifact.

2 Which of the following is the *best* reason for studying history?

A We can learn the dates of important events.

B We can learn interesting facts about famous people.

C We can learn about ourselves and other people.

D We can hear stories about strange things.

3 The study of people and the places where they live is called

A archaeology.

B environmental science.

C human geography.

D history.

4 Which of the following subjects would interest a physical geographer the *least*?

A a place's climate

B a mountain range

C a river system

D a country's highways

5 The type of evidence that an archaeologist would find most useful is a(n)

A artifact.

B primary source.

C secondary source.

D landform.

6 Which statement *best* describes the relationship between people and natural environments?

A Natural environments do not affect how people live.

B People cannot change the environments in which they live.

C Environments influence how people live, and people change their environments.

D People do not live in natural environments.

7 Each of the following is a primary source *except*

A a photograph.

B a diary.

C a treaty.

D an encyclopedia.

CHAPTER 2

5 MILLION YEARS AGO–
5,000 YEARS AGO

The Stone Ages and Early Cultures

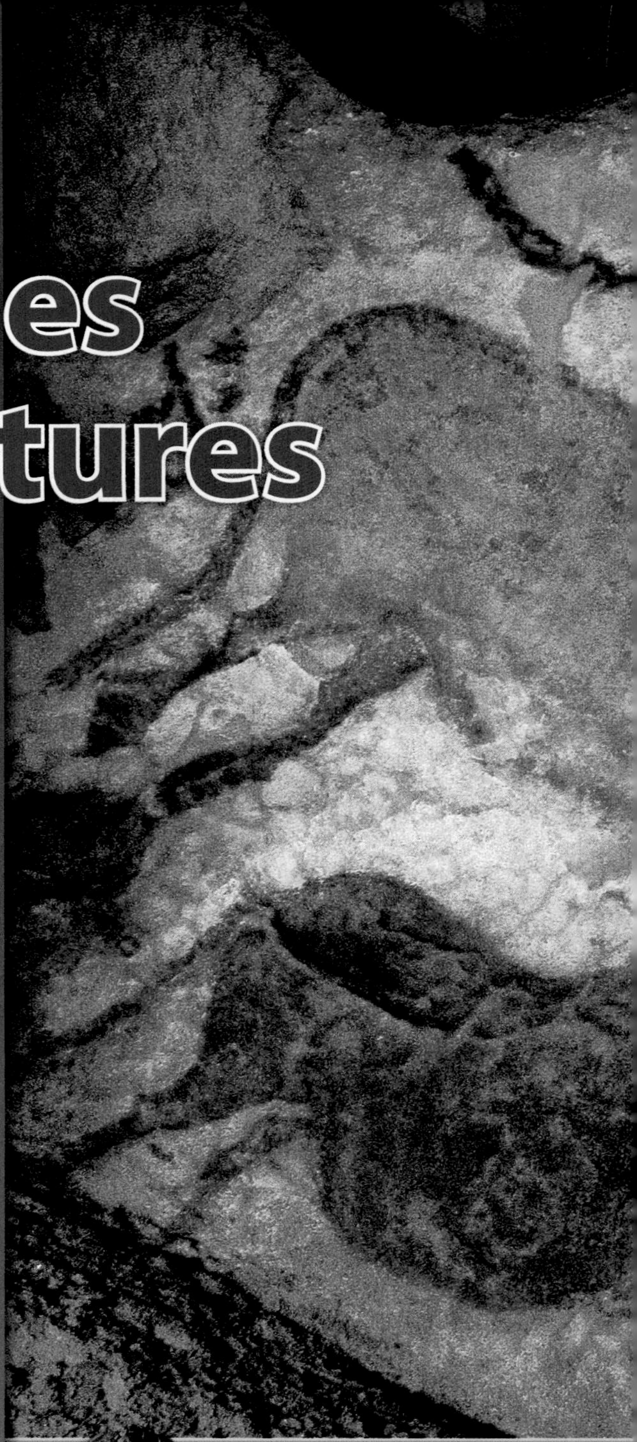

Focus on Writing

A Storyboard Prehistoric humans did not write. However, they did carve and paint images on cave walls. In the spirit of these images, you will create a storyboard that uses images to tell the story of prehistoric humans. Remember that a storyboard tells a story with simple sketches and short captions.

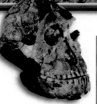

4–5 million
Early humanlike creatures called Australopithecus develop in Africa.

5 MILLION YEARS AGO

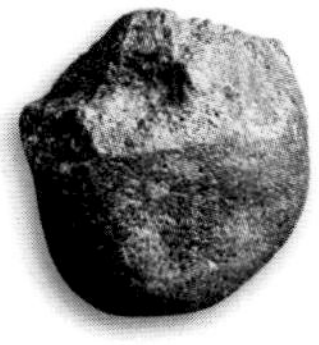

2.6 million
Hominids make the first stone tools.

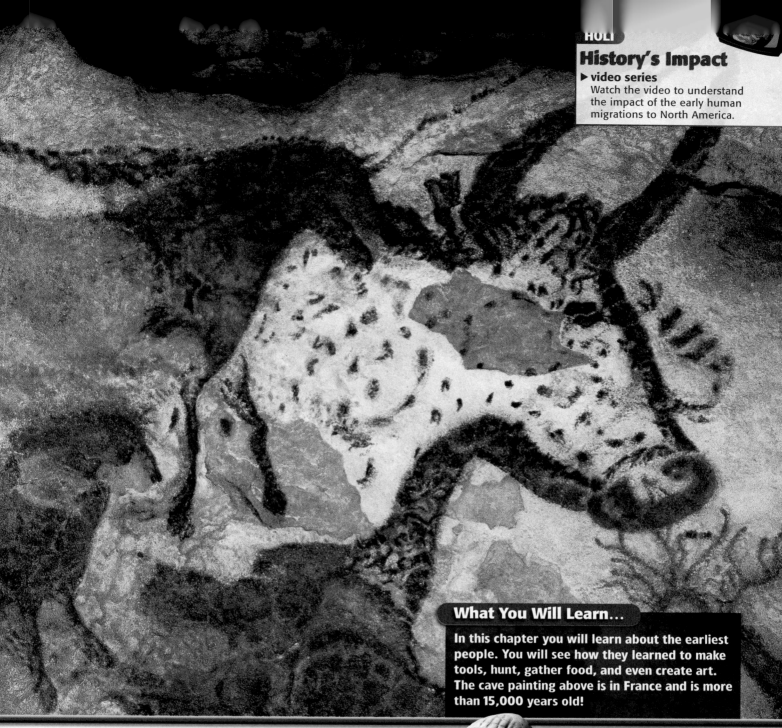

HOLT
History's Impact
▶ video series
Watch the video to understand the impact of the early human migrations to North America.

What You Will Learn...

In this chapter you will learn about the earliest people. You will see how they learned to make tools, hunt, gather food, and even create art. The cave painting above is in France and is more than 15,000 years old!

500,000
By this time, hominids live all across Europe.

500,000 YEARS AGO

200,000
The first modern humans appear in Africa.

11,000
Humans occupy all of the continents except Antarctica.

11,000 YEARS AGO

10,000
Ice ages end. People begin to develop agriculture.

8,500
More than 5,000 people live in Çatal Hüyük, Turkey.

5,000 YEARS AGO

25

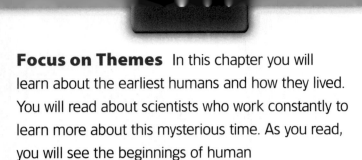

Focus on Themes In this chapter you will learn about the earliest humans and how they lived. You will read about scientists who work constantly to learn more about this mysterious time. As you read, you will see the beginnings of human society and culture—the making of tools, the use of fire, and the creation of language. You will also read about the **geography** of the world and how it shaped where and how early people lived.

Chronological Order

Focus on Reading History, just our like our lives, can be seen as a series of events in time. To understand history and events, we often need to see how they are related in time.

Understanding Chronological Order The word **chronological** means "related to time." Events discussed in this history book are discussed in **sequence**, in the order in which they happened. To understand history better, you can use a sequence chain to take notes about events in the order they happened.

Sequence Chain

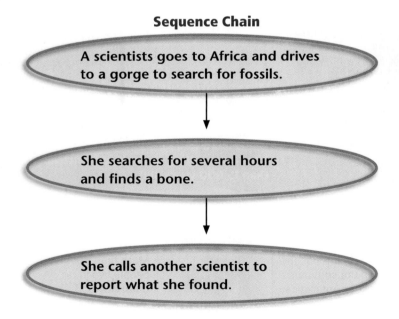

- A scientists goes to Africa and drives to a gorge to search for fossils.
- She searches for several hours and finds a bone.
- She calls another scientist to report what she found.

> Writers sometimes signal chronological order, or sequence, by using words or phrases like these:
>
> *first, before, then, later, soon, after, before long, next, eventually, finally*

You Try It!

The following passage is from the chapter you are about to read. Read the sentences carefully and think about order of events.

Scientists Study Remains

One archaeologist who made important discoveries about prehistory was Mary Leakey. In 1959 she found bones in East Africa that were more than 1.5 million years old. She and her husband, Louis Leakey, believed that the bones belonged to a hominid, an early ancestor of humans . . .

In 1974 anthropologist Donald Johanson found the bones of another early ancestor . . . Johanson named his find Lucy. Tests showed that she lived more than 3 million years ago . . .

In 1994 anthropologist Tim White found even older remains. He believes that the hominid he found may have lived as long as 4.4 million years ago.

From Chapter 2, pages 28–29

After you read the sentences, answer the following questions.

1. Complete the time line below with information about scientists from the passage you just read?

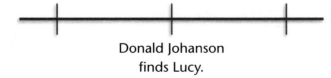

Donald Johanson
finds Lucy.

2. Each of the scientists discussed in the passage found the bones of people who lived at different times. Make another time line that shows the order in which these people lived. What do you notice about this order compared to the order in which the bones were found?

As you read **Chapter 2,** look for words that indicate the order in which events occurred.

The First People

What You Will Learn...

Main Ideas

1. Scientists study the remains of early humans to learn about prehistory.
2. Hominids and early humans first appeared in East Africa millions of years ago.
3. Stone Age tools grew more complex as time passed.
4. Hunter-gatherer societies developed language, art, and religion.

The Big Idea

Prehistoric people learned to adapt to their environment, to make simple tools, to use fire, and to use language.

Key Terms

prehistory, *p. 28*
hominid, *p. 28*
ancestor, *p. 28*
tool, *p. 30*
Paleolithic Era, *p. 31*
society, *p. 33*
hunter-gatherers, *p. 33*

TAKING NOTES As you read, take notes on the advances made by prehistoric humans. Use a chart like this one to record your notes.

Advances

If YOU were there...

You live 200,000 years ago, in a time known as the Stone Age. A local toolmaker has offered to teach you his skill. You watch carefully as he strikes two black rocks together. A small piece flakes off. You try to copy him, but the rocks just break. Finally you learn to strike the rock just right. You have made a sharp stone knife!

How will you use your new skill?

BUILDING BACKGROUND Over millions of years early people learned many new things. Making stone tools was one of the earliest and most valuable skills that they developed. Scientists who study early humans learn a lot about them from the tools and other objects that they made.

Scientists Study Remains

Although humans have lived on the earth for more than a million years, writing was not invented until about 5,000 years ago. Historians call the time before there was writing **prehistory**. To study prehistory, historians rely on the work of archaeologists and anthropologists.

One archaeologist who made important discoveries about prehistory was Mary Leakey. In 1959 she found bones in East Africa that were more than 1.5 million years old. She and her husband, Louis Leakey, believed that the bones belonged to a **hominid** (HAH-muh-nuhd), an early ancestor of humans. An **ancestor** is a relative who lived in the past.

In fact, the bones belonged to an Australopithecus (aw-stray-loh-PI-thuh-kuhs), one of the earliest ancestors of humans. In 1974 anthropologist Donald Johanson (joh-HAN-suhn) found bones from another early ancestor. He described his discovery:

> "We reluctantly headed back toward camp ... I glanced over my right shoulder. Light glinted off a bone. I knelt down for a closer look ... Everywhere we looked on the slope around us we saw more bones lying on the surface."
>
> –Donald Johanson, from *Ancestors: In Search of Human Origins*

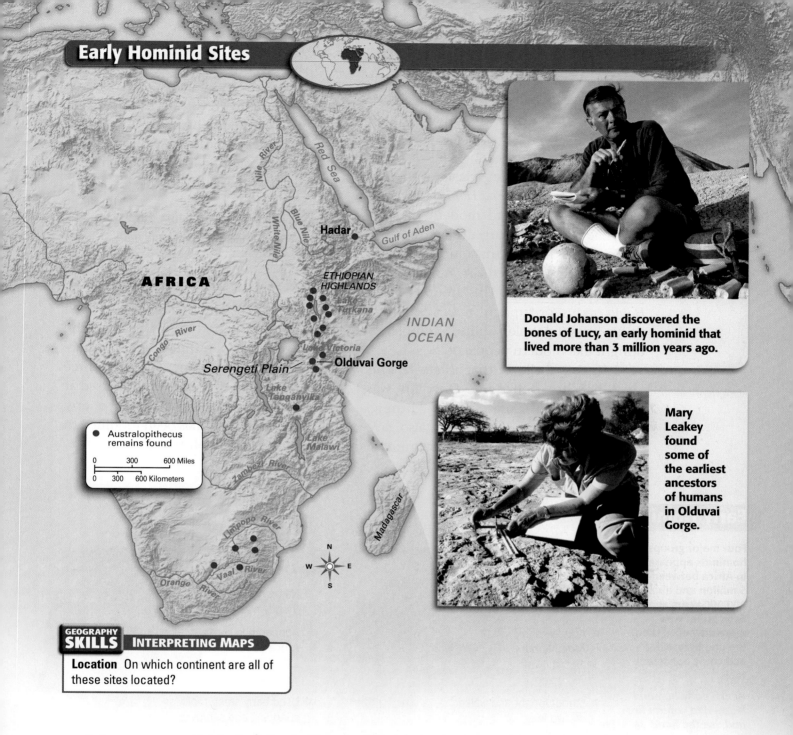

Early Hominid Sites

AFRICA

Nile River
Red Sea
White Nile
Blue Nile
Hadar
Gulf of Aden
ETHIOPIAN HIGHLANDS
Lake Turkana
Congo River
INDIAN OCEAN
Lake Victoria
Serengeti Plain — Olduvai Gorge
Lake Tanganyika
Lake Malawi
Zambezi River
Madagascar
Limpopo River
Vaal River
Orange River

● Australopithecus remains found

0   300   600 Miles
0   300   600 Kilometers

N W E S

Donald Johanson discovered the bones of Lucy, an early hominid that lived more than 3 million years ago.

Mary Leakey found some of the earliest ancestors of humans in Olduvai Gorge.

GEOGRAPHY SKILLS | **INTERPRETING MAPS**

Location On which continent are all of these sites located?

Johanson named his find Lucy. Tests showed that she lived more than 3 million years ago. Johanson could tell from her bones that she was small and had walked on two legs. The ability to walk on two legs was a key step in human development.

In 1994 anthropologist Tim White found even older remains. He believes that the hominid he found may have lived as long as 4.4 million years ago. But some scientists disagree with White's time estimate. Discoveries of ancient bones give us information about early humans and their ancestors, but not all scientists agree on the meaning of these discoveries.

READING CHECK **Drawing Inferences** What can ancient bones tell us about human ancestors?

Hominids and Early Humans

Later groups of hominids appeared about 3 million years ago. As time passed they became more like modern humans.

In the early 1960s Louis Leakey found hominid remains that he called *Homo habilis*, or "handy man." Leakey and his son Richard believed that *Homo habilis* was more closely related to modern humans than Lucy and had a larger brain.

Scientists believe that another group of hominids appeared in Africa about 1.5 million years ago. This group is called *Homo erectus*, or "upright man." Scientists think these people walked completely upright like modern people do.

Scientists believe that *Homo erectus* knew how to control fire. Once fire was started by natural causes, such as lightning, people used it to cook food. Fire also gave them heat and protection against animals.

FOCUS ON READING
Dates in a text can help you keep events in order in your mind.

Eventually hominids developed characteristics of modern humans. Scientists are not sure exactly when or where the first modern humans lived. Many think that they first appeared in Africa about 200,000 years ago. Scientists call these people *Homo sapiens*, or "wise man." Every person alive today belongs to this group.

READING CHECK **Contrasting** How was *Homo erectus* different from *Homo habilis*?

Stone Age Tools

The first humans and their ancestors lived during a long period of time called the Stone Age. To help in their studies, archaeologists divide the Stone Age into three periods based on the kinds of tools used at the time. To archaeologists, a **tool** is any handheld object that has been modified to help a person accomplish a task.

Early Hominids QUICK FACTS

Four major groups of hominids appeared in Africa between 5 million and about 200,000 years ago. Each group was more advanced than the one before it and could use better tools.

Which early hominid learned to control fire and use the hand ax?

Australopithecus

- Name means "southern ape"
- Appeared in Africa about 4–5 million years ago
- Stood upright and walked on two legs
- Brain was about one-third the size of modern humans

Homo habilis

- Name means "handy man"
- Appeared in Africa about 2.4 million years ago
- Used early stone tools for chopping and scraping
- Brain was about half the size of modern humans

An early Stone Age chopper

The first part of the Stone Age is called the **Paleolithic** (pay-lee-uh-LI-thik) **Era**, or Old Stone Age. It lasted until about 10,000 years ago. During this time people used stone tools.

The First Tools

Scientists have found the oldest tools in Tanzania, a country in East Africa. These sharpened stones, about the size of an adult's fist, are about 2.6 million years old. Each stone had been struck with another rock to create a sharp, jagged edge along one side. This process left one unsharpened side that could be used as a handle.

Scientists think that these first tools were mostly used to process food. The sharp edge could be used to cut, chop, or scrape roots, bones, or meat. Tools like these, called choppers, were used for about 2 million years.

Later Tools

Over time people learned to make better tools. For example, they developed the hand ax. They often made this tool out of a mineral called flint. Flint is easy to shape, and tools made from it can be very sharp. People used hand axes to break tree limbs, to dig, and to cut animal hides.

People also learned to attach wooden handles to tools. By attaching a wooden shaft to a stone point, for example, they invented the spear. Because a spear could be thrown, hunters no longer had to stand close to animals they were hunting. As a result, people could hunt larger animals. Among the animals hunted by Stone Age people were deer, horses, bison, and elephantlike creatures called mammoths.

READING CHECK **Summarizing** How did tools improve during the Old Stone Age?

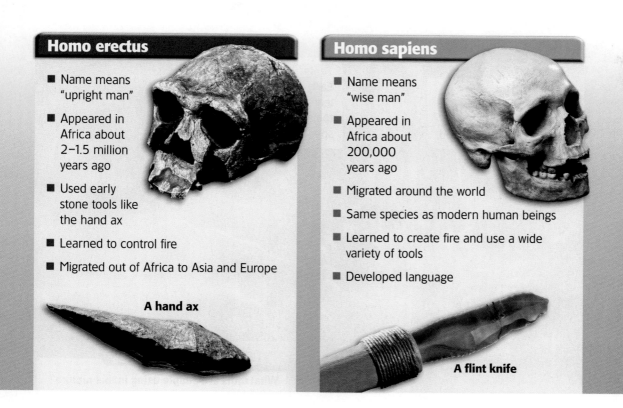

Homo erectus

- Name means "upright man"
- Appeared in Africa about 2–1.5 million years ago
- Used early stone tools like the hand ax
- Learned to control fire
- Migrated out of Africa to Asia and Europe

A hand ax

Homo sapiens

- Name means "wise man"
- Appeared in Africa about 200,000 years ago
- Migrated around the world
- Same species as modern human beings
- Learned to create fire and use a wide variety of tools
- Developed language

A flint knife

Hunter-Gatherers

Early people were hunter-gatherers. They hunted animals and gathered wild plants to survive. Life for these hunter-gatherers was difficult and dangerous. Still, people learned how to make tools, use fire, and even create art.

Hunting
Most hunting was done by men. They worked together to bring down large animals.

Art
People painted herds of animals on cave walls.

Gathering
Most gathering was done by women. They gathered food like wild plants, seeds, fruits, and nuts.

Fire
People learned to use fire to cook their food.

Tools
Early people learned to make tools such as this spear for hunting.

ANALYSIS SKILL **ANALYZING VISUALS**

What tools are people using in this picture?

Hunter-gatherer Societies

As early humans developed tools and new hunting techniques, they formed societies. A **society** is a community of people who share a common culture. These societies developed cultures with languages, religions, and art.

Society

Anthropologists believe that early humans lived in small groups. In bad weather they might have taken shelter in a cave if there was one nearby. When food or water became hard to find, groups of people would have to move to new areas.

The early humans of the Stone Age were **hunter-gatherers**—people who hunt animals and gather wild plants, seeds, fruits, and nuts to survive. Anthropologists believe that most Stone Age hunters were men. They hunted in groups, sometimes chasing entire herds of animals over cliffs. This method was both more productive and safer than hunting alone.

Women in hunter-gatherer societies probably took responsibility for collecting plants to eat. They likely stayed near camps and took care of children.

Language, Art, and Religion

The most important development of early Stone Age culture was language. Scientists have many theories about why language first developed. Some think it was to make hunting in groups easier. Others think it developed as a way for people to form relationships. Still others think language made it easier for people to resolve issues like how to **distribute** food.

Language wasn't the only way early people expressed themselves. They also created art. People carved figures out of stone, ivory, and bone. They painted and carved images of people and animals on cave walls. Scientists still aren't sure why people made art. Perhaps the cave paintings were used to teach people how to hunt, or maybe they had religious meanings.

ACADEMIC VOCABULARY
distribute
to divide among a group of people

LINKING TO TODAY

Stone Tools

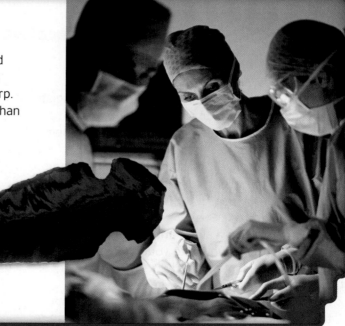

Did you know that Stone Age people's tools weren't as primitive as we might think? They made knife blades and arrowheads—like the one shown below—out of volcanic glass called obsidian. The obsidian blades were very sharp. In fact, they could be 100 times sharper and smoother than the steel blades used for surgery in modern hospitals.

Today some doctors are going back to using these Stone Age materials. They have found that blades made from obsidian are more precise than modern scalpels. Some doctors use obsidian blades for delicate surgery on the face because the stone tools leave "nicer-looking" scars.

 ANALYSIS SKILL **ANALYZING INFORMATION**

How do you think modern obsidian blades are different from Stone Age ones?

Cave Paintings

Thousands of years ago, early people decorated cave walls with paintings like this one. No one knows for sure why people created cave paintings, but many historians think they were related to hunting.

Why do you think this cave painting may be connected to hunting?

Scholars know little about the religious beliefs of early people. Archaeologists have found graves that included food and artifacts. Many scientists think these discoveries are proof that the first human religions developed during the Stone Age.

READING CHECK **Analyzing** What was one possible reason for the development of language?

SUMMARY AND PREVIEW Scientists have discovered and studied the remains of hominids and early humans who lived in East Africa millions of years ago. These Stone Age people were hunter-gatherers who used fire, stone tools, and language. In the next section you will learn how early humans moved out of Africa and populated the world.

Section 1 Assessment

go.hrw.com
Online Quiz
KEYWORD: SN6 HP2

Reviewing Ideas, Terms, and People

1. **a. Identify** Who found the bones of Lucy?
   b. Explain Why do historians need archaeologists and anthropologists to study **prehistory**?
2. **a. Recall** What is the scientific name for modern humans?
   b. Make Inferences What might have been one advantage of walking completely upright?
3. **a. Recall** What kind of **tools** did people use during the **Paleolithic Era**?
   b. Design Design a stone and wood tool you could use to help you with your chores. Describe your tool in a sentence or two.
4. **a. Define** What is a **hunter-gatherer**?
   b. Rank In your opinion, what was the most important change brought by the development of language?

Critical Thinking

5. **Evaluate** Review the notes in your chart on the advances made by prehistoric humans. Using a graphic organizer like the one here, rank the three advances you think are most important. Next to your organizer, write a sentence explaining why you ranked the advances in that order.

   | 1. | 2. | 3. |

FOCUS ON WRITING

6. **Listing Stone Age Achievements** Look back through this section and make a list of important Stone Age achievements. Which of these will you include on your storyboard? How will you illustrate them?

The Iceman

Why was a Stone Age traveler in Europe's highest mountains?

The Iceman's dagger and the scabbard, or case, he carried it in

When did he live? about 5,300 years ago

Where did he live? The frozen body of the Iceman was discovered in the snowy Ötztal Alps of Italy in 1991. Scientists nicknamed him Ötzi after this location.

What did he do? That question has been debated ever since Ötzi's body was found. Apparently, he was traveling. At first scientists thought he had frozen to death in a storm. But an arrowhead found in his shoulder suggests that his death was not so peaceful. After he died, his body was covered by glaciers and preserved for thousands of years.

Why is he important? Ötzi is the oldest mummified human ever found in such good condition. His body, clothing, and tools were extremely well preserved, telling us a lot about life during the Stone Ages. His outfit was made of three types of animal skin stitched together. He wore leather shoes padded with grass, a grass cape, a fur hat, and a sort of backpack. He carried an ax with a copper blade as well as a bow and arrows.

Drawing Conclusions Why do you think the Iceman was in the Alps?

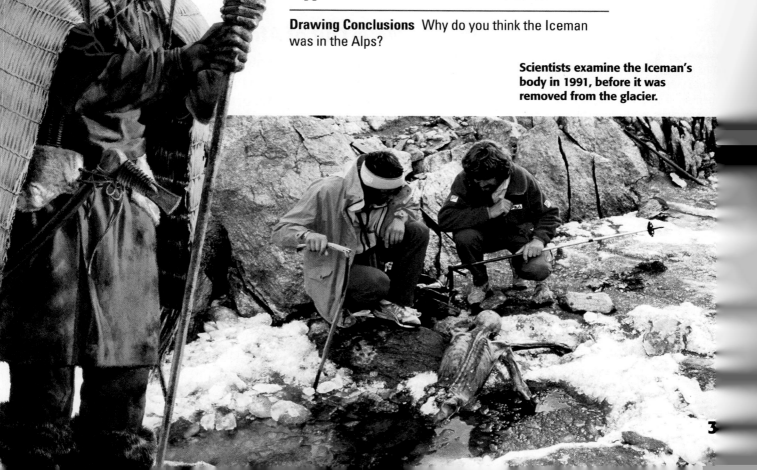

Scientists examine the Iceman's body in 1991, before it was removed from the glacier.

Early Human Migration

What You Will Learn...

Main Ideas

1. People moved out of Africa as the earth's climates changed.
2. People adapted to new environments by making clothing and new types of tools.

The Big Idea

As people migrated around the world they learned to adapt to new environments.

Key Terms

migrate, *p. 36*
ice ages, *p. 36*
land bridge, *p. 36*
Mesolithic Era, *p. 38*

TAKING NOTES As you read, take notes on the sequence and paths of migration of early humans. Record your notes in a graphic organizer like the one below. Add as many ovals as you need to record each stage of migration.

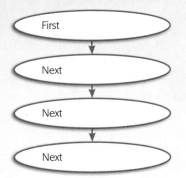

If YOU were there...

Your tribe of hunter-gatherers has lived in this place for as long as anyone can remember. But now there are not enough animals to hunt. Whenever you find berries and roots, you have to share them with people from other tribes. Your leaders think it's time to find a new home in the lands far beyond the mountains. But no one has ever traveled there, and many people are afraid.

How do you feel about moving to a new home?

BUILDING BACKGROUND From their beginnings in East Africa, early humans moved in many directions. Eventually, they lived on almost every continent in the world. People probably had many reasons for moving. One reason was a change in the climate.

People Move Out of Africa

During the Old Stone Age, climate patterns around the world changed, transforming the earth's geography. In response to these changes, people began to **migrate**, or move, to new places.

The Ice Ages

Most scientists believe that about 1.6 million years ago, many places around the world began to experience long periods of freezing weather. These freezing times are called the **ice ages**. The ice ages ended about 10,000 years ago.

During the ice ages huge sheets of ice covered much of the earth's land. These ice sheets were formed from ocean water, leaving ocean levels lower than they are now. Many areas that are now underwater were dry land then. For example, a narrow body of water now separates Asia and North America. But scientists think that during the ice ages, the ocean level dropped and exposed a **land bridge**, a strip of land connecting two continents. Land bridges allowed Stone Age peoples to migrate around the world.

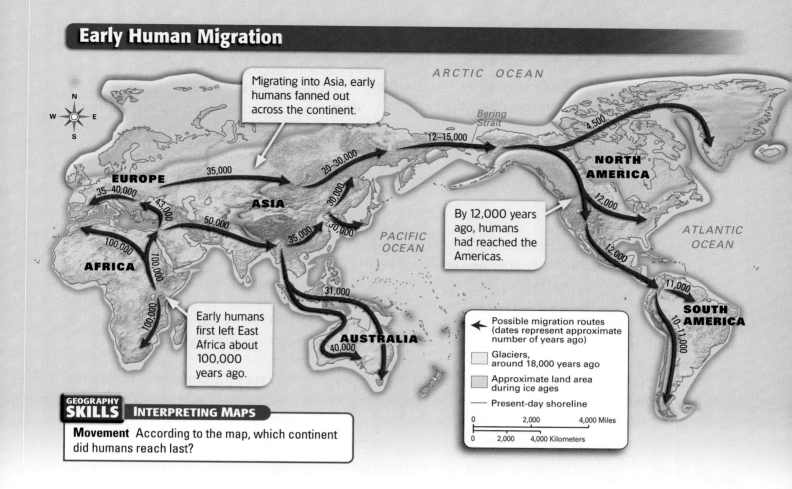

Early Human Migration

Migrating into Asia, early humans fanned out across the continent.

By 12,000 years ago, humans had reached the Americas.

Early humans first left East Africa about 100,000 years ago.

ARCTIC OCEAN

Bering Strait

EUROPE   35,000
35–40,000
43,000
50,000
ASIA
100,000
100,000
100,000
AFRICA
20–30,000
30,000
30,000
35,000
30,000
12–15,000
4,500
NORTH AMERICA
12,000
12,000
11,000
10–11,000
SOUTH AMERICA
PACIFIC OCEAN
ATLANTIC OCEAN
31,000
AUSTRALIA
40,000

Possible migration routes (dates represent approximate number of years ago)

Glaciers, around 18,000 years ago

Approximate land area during ice ages

Present-day shoreline

0   2,000   4,000 Miles
0   2,000   4,000 Kilometers

GEOGRAPHY SKILLS INTERPRETING MAPS

Movement According to the map, which continent did humans reach last?

Settling New Lands

Scientists agree that migration around the world took hundreds of thousands of years. Early hominids, the ancestors of modern humans, migrated from Africa to Asia as early as 2 million years ago. From there, they spread to Southeast Asia and Europe.

Later, humans also began to migrate around the world, and earlier hominids died out. Look at the map to see the dates and routes of early human migration.

Humans began to migrate from East Africa to southern Africa and southwestern Asia around 100,000 years ago. From there, people moved east across southern Asia. They could then migrate to Australia. Scientists are not sure exactly how the first people reached Australia. Even though ocean levels were lower then, there was always open sea between Asia and Australia.

From southwestern Asia, humans also migrated north into Europe. Geographic features such as high mountains and cold temperatures delayed migration northward into northern Asia. Eventually, however, people from both Europe and southern Asia moved into that region.

From northern Asia, people moved into North America. Scientists disagree on when and how the first people arrived in North America. Most scholars think people must have crossed a land bridge from Asia to North America. Once in North America, these people moved south, following herds of animals and settling South America. By 9000 BC, humans lived on all continents of the world except Antarctica.

READING CHECK **Analyzing** How did the ice ages influence human migration?

People Adapt to New Environments

As early people moved to new lands, they found environments that differed greatly from those in East Africa. Many places were much colder and had strange plants and animals. Early people had to learn to adapt to their new environments.

Clothing and Shelter

Although fire helped keep people warm in very cold areas, people needed more protection. To keep warm, they learned to sew animal skins together to make clothing.

In addition to clothing, people needed shelter to survive. At first they took shelter in caves. When they moved to areas with no caves, they built their own shelters. The first human-made shelters were called pit houses. They were pits in the ground with roofs of branches and leaves.

Later, people began to build homes above the ground. Some lived in tents made of animal skins. Others built more permanent structures of wood, stone, clay, or other materials. Even bones from large animals such as mammoths were used in building shelters.

New Tools and Technologies

People also adapted to new environments with new types of tools. These tools were smaller and more complex than tools from the Old Stone Age. They defined the **Mesolithic** (me-zuh-LI-thik) **Era**, or the Middle Stone Age. This period began more than 10,000 years ago and lasted to about 5,000 years ago in some places.

During the Middle Stone Age, people found new uses for bone and stone tools. People who lived near water invented hooks and fishing spears. Other groups invented the bow and arrow.

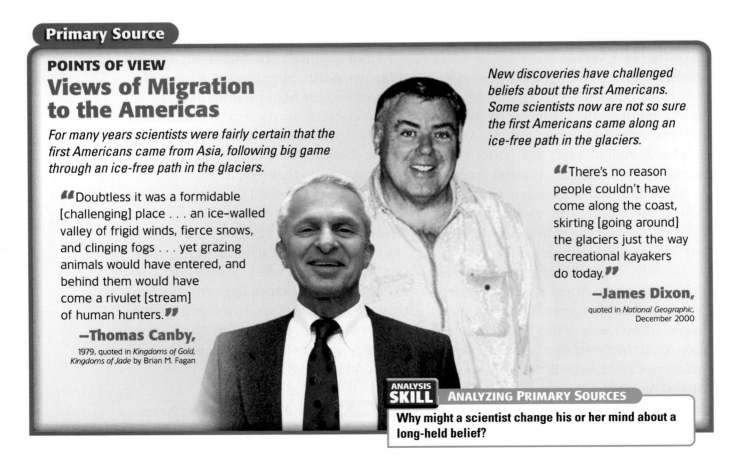

Primary Source

POINTS OF VIEW

Views of Migration to the Americas

For many years scientists were fairly certain that the first Americans came from Asia, following big game through an ice-free path in the glaciers.

❝Doubtless it was a formidable [challenging] place . . . an ice-walled valley of frigid winds, fierce snows, and clinging fogs . . . yet grazing animals would have entered, and behind them would have come a rivulet [stream] of human hunters.❞

—Thomas Canby,
1979, quoted in *Kingdoms of Gold, Kingdoms of Jade* by Brian M. Fagan

New discoveries have challenged beliefs about the first Americans. Some scientists now are not so sure the first Americans came along an ice-free path in the glaciers.

❝There's no reason people couldn't have come along the coast, skirting [going around] the glaciers just the way recreational kayakers do today.❞

—James Dixon,
quoted in *National Geographic,*
December 2000

ANALYSIS SKILL **ANALYZING PRIMARY SOURCES**

Why might a scientist change his or her mind about a long-held belief?

A Mammoth House

Early people used whatever was available to make shelters. In Central Asia, where wood was scarce, some early people made their homes from mammoth bones.

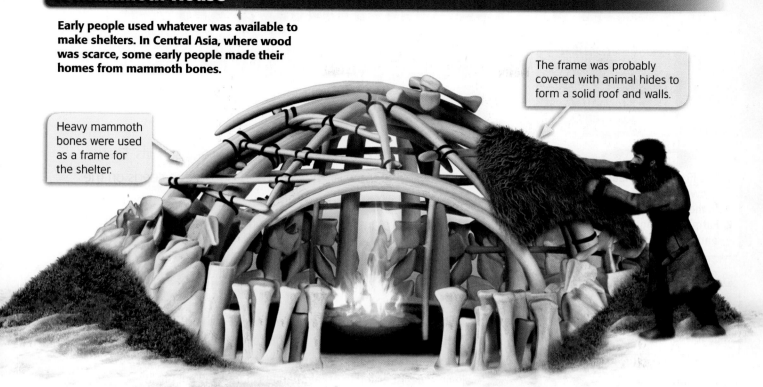

Heavy mammoth bones were used as a frame for the shelter.

The frame was probably covered with animal hides to form a solid roof and walls.

In addition to tools, people developed new technologies to improve their lives. For example, some learned to make canoes by hollowing out logs. They used the canoes to travel on rivers and lakes. They also began to make pottery. The first pets may also have appeared at this time. People kept dogs to help them hunt and for protection. Developments like these, in addition to clothing and shelter, allowed people to adapt to new environments.

READING CHECK Finding Main Ideas
What were two ways people adapted to new environments?

SUMMARY AND PREVIEW Early people adapted to new environments with new kinds of clothing, shelter, and tools. In Section 3 you will read about how Stone Age peoples developed farming.

go.hrw.com
Online Quiz
KEYWORD: SN6 HP2

Section 2 Assessment

Reviewing Ideas, Terms, and People

1. **a. Define** What is a **land bridge**?
   b. Analyze Why did it take so long for early people to reach South America?
2. **a. Recall** What did people use to make tools in the **Mesolithic Era**?
   b. Summarize Why did people have to learn to make clothes and build shelters?

Critical Thinking

3. **Sequencing** Draw the organizer below. Use your notes and sequence chain to show the path of migration around the world.

FOCUS ON WRITING

4. **Illustrating** How will you illustrate early migration on your storyboard? Draw some sketches. How does this information relate to your ideas from Section 1?

Beginnings of Agriculture

What You Will Learn...

Main Ideas

1. The first farmers learned to grow plants and raise animals in the New Stone Age.
2. Farming changed societies and the way people lived.

The Big Idea

The development of agriculture brought great changes to human society.

Key Terms

Neolithic Era, *p. 41*
domestication, *p. 41*
agriculture, *p. 42*
megaliths, *p. 42*

TAKING NOTES As you read, take notes on the different changes related to the development of agriculture. Use a diagram like the one below to help organize your information.

Change in	Details
Climate	
Use of plants	
Use of animals	
Daily life	

If **YOU** were there...

As a gatherer, you know where to find the sweetest fruits. Every summer, you eat many of these fruits, dropping the seeds on the ground. One day you return to find new plants everywhere. You realize that the plants have grown from your dropped seeds.

How could this discovery change your way of life?

BUILDING BACKGROUND The discovery that plants grew from seeds was one of the major advances of the late Stone Age. Other similar advances led to great changes in the way people lived.

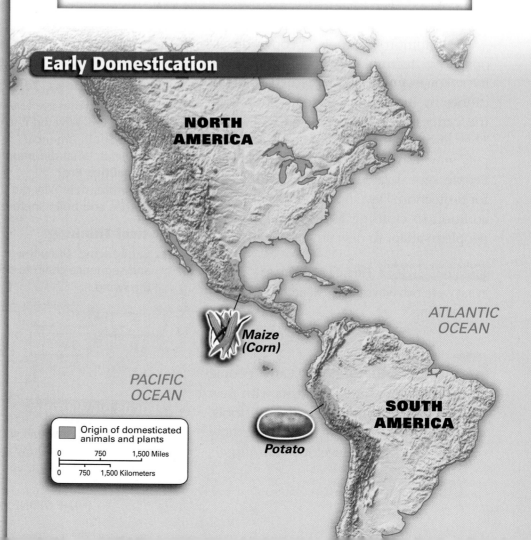

Early Domestication

NORTH AMERICA

ATLANTIC OCEAN

PACIFIC OCEAN

Maize (Corn)

Potato

SOUTH AMERICA

Origin of domesticated animals and plants

0   750   1,500 Miles
0   750   1,500 Kilometers

The First Farmers

After the Middle Stone Age came a period of time that scientists call the **Neolithic** (nee-uh-LI-thik) **Era**, or New Stone Age. It began as early as 10,000 years ago in Southwest Asia. In other places, this era began much later and lasted much longer than it did there.

During the New Stone Age people learned to polish stones to make tools like saws and drills. People also learned how to make fire. Before, they could only use fire that had been started by natural causes such as lightning.

The New Stone Age ended in Egypt and Southwest Asia about 5,000 years ago, when toolmakers began to make tools out of metal. But tools weren't the only major change that occurred during the Neolithic Era. In fact, the biggest changes came in how people produced food.

Plants

After a warming trend brought an end to the ice ages, new plants began to grow in some areas. For example, wild barley and wheat plants started to spread throughout Southwest Asia. Over time, people came to depend on these wild plants for food. They began to settle where grains grew.

People soon learned that they could plant seeds themselves to grow their own crops. Historians call the shift from food gathering to food producing the Neolithic Revolution. Most experts believe that this revolution, or change, first occurred in the societies of Southwest Asia.

Eventually, people learned to change plants to make them more useful. They planted only the largest grains or the sweetest fruits. The process of changing plants or animals to make them more useful to humans is called **domestication**.

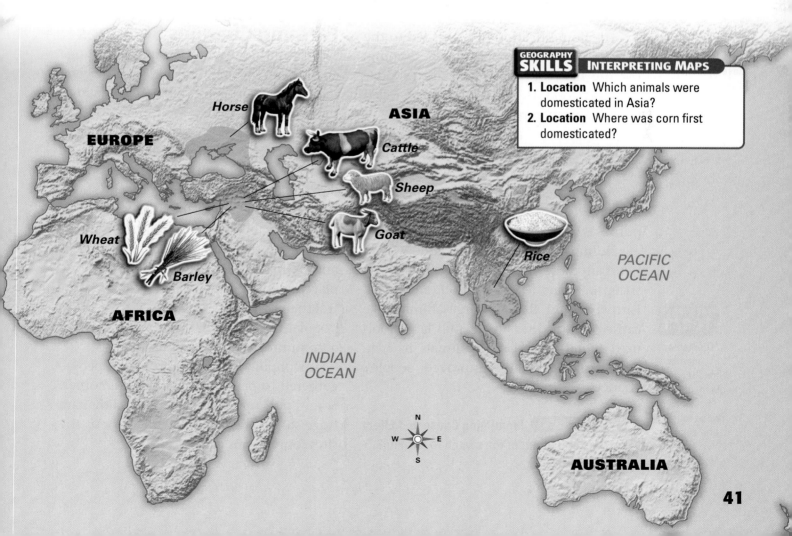

GEOGRAPHY SKILLS INTERPRETING MAPS

1. **Location** Which animals were domesticated in Asia?
2. **Location** Where was corn first domesticated?

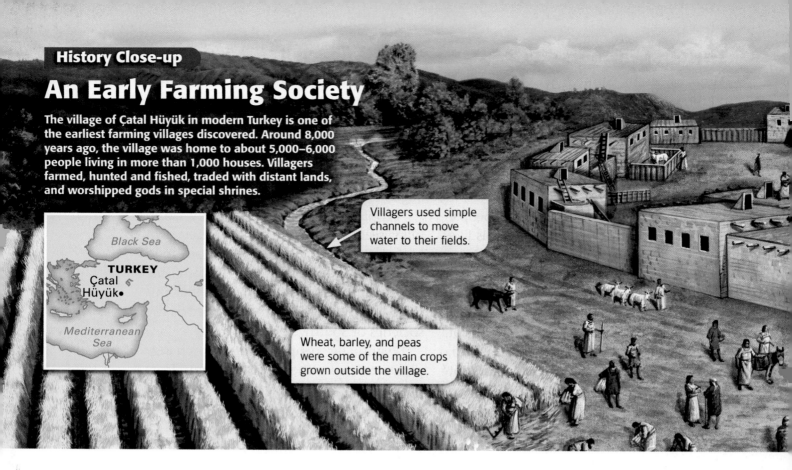

An Early Farming Society

The village of Çatal Hüyük in modern Turkey is one of the earliest farming villages discovered. Around 8,000 years ago, the village was home to about 5,000–6,000 people living in more than 1,000 houses. Villagers farmed, hunted and fished, traded with distant lands, and worshipped gods in special shrines.

Black Sea

TURKEY
Çatal
Hüyük•

Mediterranean
Sea

Villagers used simple channels to move water to their fields.

Wheat, barley, and peas were some of the main crops grown outside the village.

ACADEMIC VOCABULARY
development
creation

The domestication of plants led to the **development** of **agriculture**, or farming. For the first time, people could produce their own food. This development changed human society forever.

Animals

Learning to produce food was a major accomplishment for early people. But learning how to use animals for their own purposes was almost equally important.

Hunters didn't have to follow wild herds anymore. Instead, farmers could keep sheep or goats for milk, food, and wool. Farmers could also use large animals like cattle to carry loads or to pull large tools used in farming. Using animals to help with farming greatly improved people's chances of surviving.

THE IMPACT TODAY

One famous megalith, Stonehenge in England, attracts millions of curious tourists and scholars each year.

READING CHECK Identifying Cause and Effect What was one effect of the switch to farming?

Farming Changes Societies

The Neolithic Revolution brought huge changes to people's lives. With survival more certain, people could focus on activities other than finding food.

Domestication of plants and animals enabled people to use plant fibers to make cloth. The domestication of animals made it possible to use wool from goats and sheep and skins from horses for clothes.

People also began to build permanent settlements. As they started raising crops and animals, they needed to stay in one place. Then, once people were able to control their own food production, the world's population grew. In some areas farming communities developed into towns.

As populations grew, groups of people gathered to perform religious ceremonies. Some put up megaliths. **Megaliths** are huge stones used as monuments or as the sites for religious gatherings.

Houses were made of wood covered with mud. Since they didn't have doors, people entered on ladders through rooftop openings.

Inside their houses, villagers made the earliest known wooden bowls and cups, pottery, and mirrors.

Some houses were built as shrines and had small statues of goddesses and large sculpted bulls' heads.

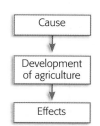

ANALYSIS SKILL **ANALYZING VISUALS**

How did farmers get water to their fields?

Early people probably believed in gods and goddesses associated with the four elements—air, water, fire, and earth—or with animals. For example, one European group honored a thunder god, while another group worshipped bulls. Some scholars also believe that prehistoric peoples also prayed to their ancestors. People in some societies today still hold many of these same beliefs.

READING CHECK Analyzing How did farming contribute to the growth of towns?

SUMMARY AND PREVIEW Stone Age peoples adapted to new environments by domesticating plants and animals. These changes led to the development of religion and the growth of towns. In the next chapter you will learn more about early towns.

go.hrw.com
Online Quiz
KEYWORD: SN6 HP2

Section 3 Assessment

Reviewing Ideas, Terms, and People
1. **a. Define** What is **domestication** of a plant or animal?
   b. Make Generalizations How did early people use domesticated animals?
2. **a. Describe** What were gods and goddesses probably associated with in prehistoric religion?
   b. Explain How did domestication of plants and animals lead to the development of towns?

Critical Thinking
3. **Identifying Cause and Effect** Copy the graphic organizer at right. Use it to show one cause and three effects of the development of agriculture.

Cause
↓
Development of agriculture
↓
Effects

FOCUS ON WRITING
4. **Beginnings of Agriculture** Now that you've read about the birth of agriculture, you're ready to plan your storyboard. Look back through your notes from previous sections and the text of this one. Make a list of the events and ideas you will include on your storyboard. Then plan how you will arrange these items.

Social Studies Skills

Analysis | Critical Thinking | Economics | Study

Identifying Central Issues

Understand the Skill

Central issues are the main problems or topics that are related to an event. The issues behind a historical event can be varied and complicated. Central issues in world history usually involve political, social, economic, territorial, moral, or technological matters. The ability to identify the central issue in an event allows you to focus on information that is most important to understanding the event.

Learn the Skill

In this chapter you learned about prehistory. Some of the events you read about may not seem very important. It is hard for people in the computer age to appreciate the accomplishments of the Stone Age. For example, adding wooden handles to stone tools may seem like a simple thing to us. But it was a life-changing advance for people of that time.

This example points out something to remember when looking for central issues. Try not to use only modern-day values and standards to decide what is important about the past. Always think about the times in which people lived. Ask yourself what would have been important to people living then.

The following guidelines will help you to identify central issues. Use them to gain a better understanding of historical events.

❶ Identify the subject of the information. What is the information about?

❷ Determine the source of the information. Is it a primary source or a secondary source?

❸ Determine the purpose of what you are reading. Why has the information been provided?

❹ Find the strongest or most forceful statements in the information. These are often clues to issues or ideas the writer thinks are the most central or important.

❺ Think about values, concerns, ways of life, and events that would have been important to the people of the times. Determine how the information might be connected to those larger issues.

Practice and Apply the Skill

Apply the guidelines to identify the central issue in the following passage. Then answer the questions.

"What distinguished the Neolithic Era from earlier ages was people's ability to shape stone tools by polishing and grinding. This allowed people to make more specialized tools. Even more important changes took place also. The development of agriculture changed the basic way people lived. Earlier people had been wanderers, who moved from place to place in search of food. Some people began settling in permanent villages. Exactly how they learned that seeds could be planted and made to grow year after year remains a mystery. However, the shift from food gathering to food producing was possibly the most important change ever in history."

1. What is the general subject of this passage?

2. What changes distinguished the Neolithic Era from earlier periods?

3. According to this writer, what is the central issue to understand about the Neolithic Era?

4. What statements in the passage help you to determine the central issue?

Chapter Review

Visual Summary

Use the visual summary below to help you review the main ideas of the chapter.

QUICK FACTS

Hominids developed in Africa and learned how to use tools.

Early humans lived as hunter–gatherers.

Humans migrated around the world, adapting to new environments.

Eventually, people learned how to farm and raise animals.

Reviewing Vocabulary, Terms, and People

For each group of terms below, write a sentence that shows how all the terms in the group are related.

1. prehistory
   ancestor
   hominid
2. domestication
   Neolithic Era
   agriculture
3. Paleolithic Era
   tool
   hunter-gatherers
   develop
4. land bridge
   ice ages
   migrate
5. society
   megaliths
   Neolithic Era

Comprehension and Critical Thinking

SECTION 1 *(Pages 28–34)*

6. **a. Recall** What does *Homo sapiens* mean? When may *Homo sapiens* have first appeared in Africa?

   b. Draw Conclusions If you were an archaeologist and found bead jewelry and stone chopping tools in an ancient woman's grave, what may you conclude?

   c. Elaborate How did stone tools change over time? Why do you think these changes took place so slowly?

SECTION 2 *(Pages 36–39)*

7. **a. Describe** What new skills did people develop to help them survive?

   b. Analyze How did global climate change affect the migration of early people?

   c. Evaluate About 15,000 years ago, where do you think life would have been more difficult—in eastern Africa or northern Europe? Why?

SECTION 3 *(Pages 40–43)*

8. **a. Define** What was the Neolithic Revolution?

 b. Make Inferences How did domestication of plants and animals change early societies?

 c. Predict Why do you think people of the Neolithic Era put up megaliths instead of some other kind of monuments?

Reviewing Themes

9. **Geography** What were three ways in which the environment affected Stone Age peoples?

10. **Society and Culture** How did the development of language change hunter-gatherer society?

Using the Internet   go.hrw.com   KEYWORD: SN6 WH2

11. **Activity: Creating a Skit** In the beginning of the Paleolithic Era, or the Old Stone Age, early humans used modified stones as tools. As the Stone Age progressed, plants and animals became materials for tools too. Enter the activity keyword and research the development of tools and the use of fire. Then create a skit that tells about an early human society discovering fire, creating a new tool, or developing a new way of doing a task.

Reading Skills

Understanding Chronological Order *Below are several lists of events. Arrange the events in each list in chronological order.*

12. Mesolithic Era begins.
  Paleolithic Era begins.
  Neolithic Era begins.

13. *Homo sapiens* appears.
  Homo habilis appears.
  Homo erectus appears.

14. People make stone tools.
  People make metal tools.
  People attach wooden handles to tools.

Social Studies Skills

Identifying Central Issues *Read the primary source passage below and then answer the questions that follow.*

> " Almonds provide a striking example of bitter seeds and their change under domestication. Most wild almond seeds contain an intensely bitter chemical called amygdalin, which (as was already mentioned) breaks down to yield the poison cyanide. A snack of wild almonds can kill a person foolish enough to ignore the warning of the bitter taste. Since the first stage in unconscious domestication involves gathering seeds to eat, how on earth did domestication of wild almonds ever reach that first stage? "
>
> —Jared Diamond, from *Guns, Germs, and Steel*

15. What is the main point of this passage?

16. What does the author suggest is the major issue he will address in the text?

FOCUS ON WRITING

17. **Creating Your Storyboard** Use the notes you have taken to plan your storyboard. What images will you include in each frame of the storyboard? How many frames will you need to tell the story of prehistoric people? How will you represent your ideas visually?

 After you have sketched an outline for your storyboard, begin drawing it. Be sure to include all significant adaptations and developments made by prehistoric people, and don't worry if you can't draw that well. If you like, you might want to draw your storyboard in the simple style of prehistoric cave paintings. As the last frame in your storyboard, write a detailed summary to conclude your story.

Standardized Test Practice

DIRECTIONS: Read each question, and write the letter of the best response.

1 Use the map to answer the following question.

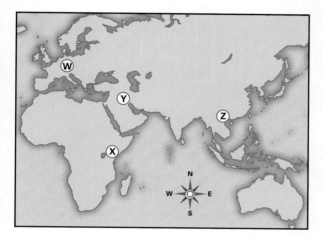

The region in which the first humans lived is shown on the map by the letter

A W.

B X.

C Y.

D Z.

2 The earliest humans lived

A by hunting and gathering their food.

B as herders of sheep and other livestock.

C alone or in pairs.

D in farming villages along rivers and streams.

3 The development of farming brought all of the following changes to the lives of early humans *except*

A the first human-made shelters.

B a larger supply of food.

C the construction of permanent settlements.

D new types of clothing.

4 The region of the world that was likely occupied *last* by early humans was

A northern Asia.

B southern Asia.

C North America.

D South America.

5 Hunter-gatherer societies in the Old Stone Age possessed all of the following *except*

A fire.

B art.

C bone tools.

D religious beliefs.

Connecting with Past Learnings

6 You know that history is the study of people and events from the past. To learn about prehistory, historians would likely study all of the following *except*

A graves.

B journals.

C bones.

D art.

7 A skull from a human who lived during the Neolithic Era would be considered a(n)

A tool.

B artifact.

C fossil.

D secondary source.

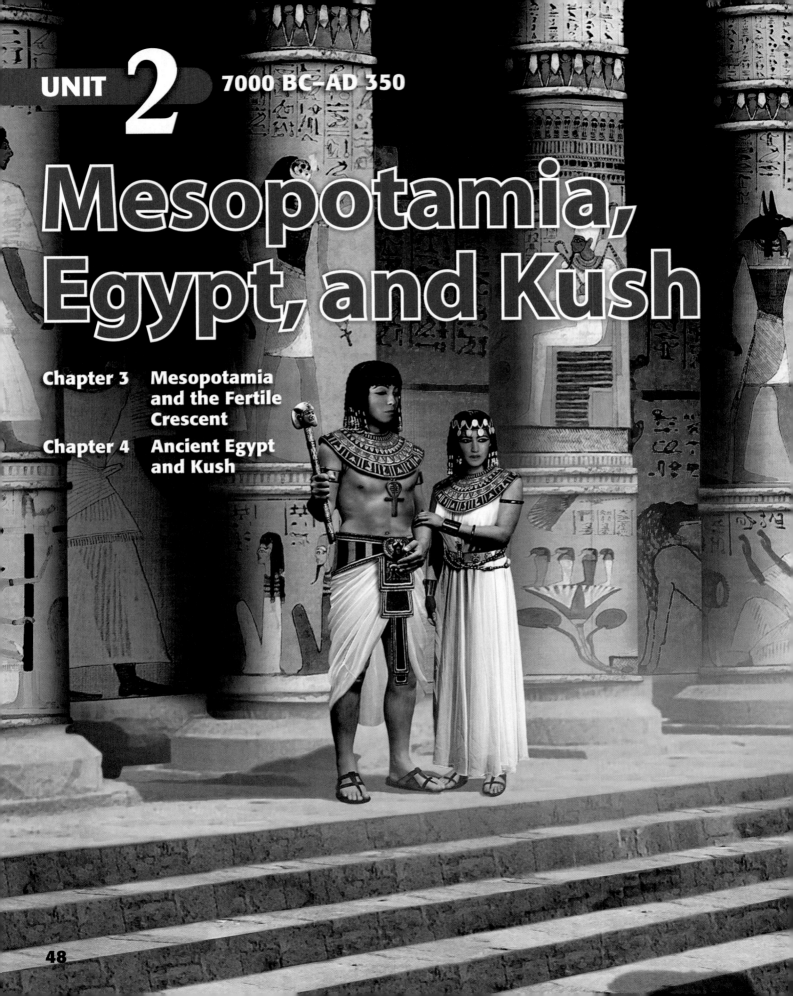

Mesopotamia, Egypt, and Kush

What You Will Learn...

The world's first civilizations developed in Asia and Africa after people learned how to farm. These civilizations began in river valleys, which were perfect places for people to grow crops.

With the development of farming, people no longer had to travel in search of food. Instead, they could settle down in one place. Eventually, people built the first towns and cities and invented government, writing, and the wheel. They also created huge buildings and temples and produced incredible works of art.

In the next two chapters, you will learn about the early civilizations of Mesopotamia, Egypt, and Kush.

Explore the Art

In this scene, the young King Tutankhamen of Egypt stands with his wife at the entrance to a temple. How does this scene show some of the features of Egyptian civilization?

CHAPTER 3 7000–500 BC

Mesopotamia and the Fertile Crescent

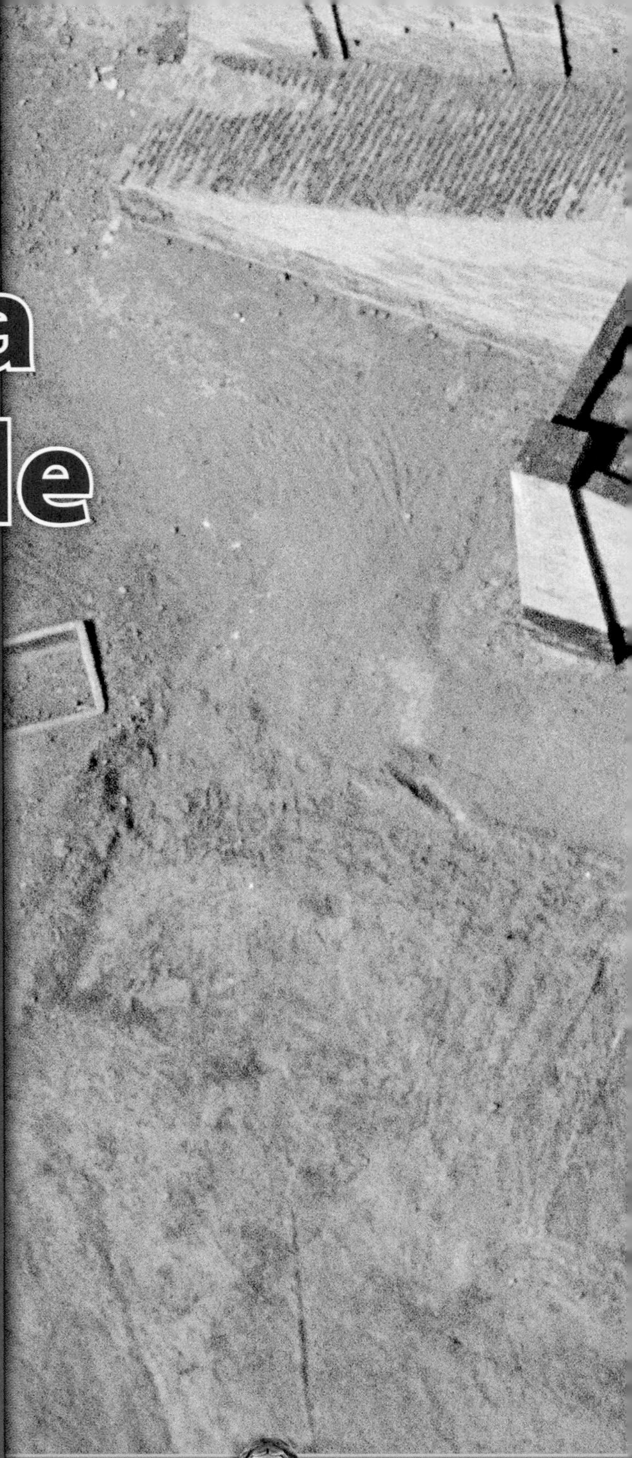

FOCUS ON WRITING

A Letter Most elementary students have not read or heard much about ancient Mesopotamia. As you read this chapter, you can gather information about that land. Then you can write a letter to share some of what you have learned with a young child.

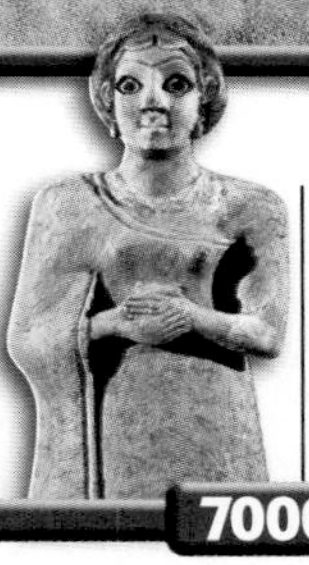

CHAPTER EVENTS

c. 7000 BC
Agriculture first develops in Mesopotamia.

7000 BC

WORLD EVENTS

c. 3100 BC
Menes becomes the first pharaoh of Egypt.

HOLT

History's Impact
▶ **video series**
Watch the video to understand
the impact of a system of laws.

What You Will Learn...

In this chapter you will learn about the early
civilizations of Mesopotamia and the Fertile
Crescent. This photo shows the partially
reconstructed remains of an ancient temple
in Mesopotamia.

c. 2350–2330 BC
Sargon of Akkad
conquers Mesopotamia
and forms the world's
first empire.

c. 1770 BC
Hammurabi
of Babylon
issues a
written code
of laws.

c. 1000 BC
Phoenicians
trade all
around the
Mediterranean.

| 2750 BC | | 2000 BC | | 1250 BC | | 500 BC |

c. 2300 BC
The Harappan
civilization rises
in the Indus Valley.

c. 1500 BC
The Shang
dynasty is
established
in China.

c. 965 BC
Solomon
becomes
king of
Israel.

51

Focus on Themes Chapter three introduces you to a region in Southwest Asia called Mesopotamia, the home of the world's first civilization. You will read about what made this area one where civilizations could begin and grow. You will learn about one group of people—the Sumerians—and their great **technological** inventions. You will also read about other people who invaded Mesopotamia and brought their own rules of governing and **politics** to the area.

Main Ideas in Social Studies

Focus on Reading Have you ever set up a tent? If you have, you know that one pole provides structure and support for the whole tent. A paragraph has a similar structure. One idea—the **main idea**—provides support and structure for the whole paragraph.

Identifying Main Ideas Most paragraphs written about history include a main idea that is stated clearly in a sentence. At other times, the main idea is suggested, not stated. However, that idea still shapes the paragraph's content and the meaning of all of the facts and details in it.

Identifying Main Ideas

1. Read the paragraph. Ask yourself, "What is this paragraph mostly about?"

2. List the important facts and details that relate to that topic.

3. Ask yourself, "What seems to be the most important point the writer is making about the topic?" Or ask, "If the writer could say only one thing about this paragraph, what would it be?" **This is the main idea of the paragraph.**

Having people available to work on different jobs meant that society could accomplish more. Large projects, such as constructing buildings and digging irrigation systems, required specialized workers, managers, and organization. To complete these projects, the Mesopotamians needed structure and rules. Structure and rules could be provided by laws and government.

Topic: The paragraph talks about people, jobs, and structure.

+

Facts and Details:

• People working on different jobs needed structure.

• Laws and government provided this structure.

=

Main Idea: Having people in a society work on many different jobs led to the creation of laws and government.

You Try It!

The passage below is from the chapter you are about to read. Read it and then answer the questions below.

Technical Advances

One of the Sumerians' most important developments was the wheel. They were the first people to build wheeled vehicles, including carts and wagons. Using the wheel, Sumerians invented a device that spins clay as a craftsperson shapes it into bowls. This device is called a potter's wheel.

The plow was another important Sumerian invention. Pulled by oxen, plows broke through the hard soil of Sumer to prepare it for planting. This technique greatly increased farm production. The Sumerians also invented a clock that used falling water to measure time.

Sumerian advances improved daily life in many ways. Sumerians built sewers under city streets. They learned to use bronze to make stronger tools and weapons. They even produced makeup and glass jewelry.

Answer the following questions about finding main ideas.

1. Reread the first paragraph. What is its main idea?

2. What is the main idea of the third paragraph? Reread the second paragraph. Is there a sentence that expresses the main idea of the paragraph? What is that main idea? Write a sentence to express it.

3. Which of the following best expresses the main idea of the entire passage?

  a. The wheel was an important invention.
  b. The Sumerians invented many helpful devices.

As you read Chapter 3, find the main ideas of the paragraphs you are studying.

Academic Vocabulary

Success in school is related to knowing academic vocabulary— the words that are frequently used in school assignments and discussions. In this chapter, you will learn the following academic words:

role *(p. 62)*
impact *(p. 63)*

Geography of the Fertile Crescent

What You Will Learn...

Main Ideas

1. The rivers of Southwest Asia supported the growth of civilization.
2. New farming techniques led to the growth of cities.

The Big Idea

The valleys of the Tigris and Euphrates rivers were the site of the world's first civilizations.

Key Terms

Fertile Crescent, *p. 55*
silt, *p. 55*
irrigation, *p. 56*
canals, *p. 56*
surplus, *p. 56*
division of labor, *p. 56*

TAKING NOTES As you read, take notes on the cause-and-effect relationship between each river valley and the civilization that developed around it. Use a graphic organizer like this one to list causes and effects.

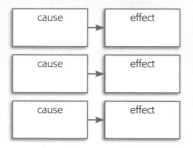

cause	→	effect
cause	→	effect
cause	→	effect

If YOU were there...

You are a farmer in Southwest Asia about 6,000 years ago. You live near a slow-moving river, with many shallow lakes and marshes. The river makes the land in the valley rich and fertile, so you can grow wheat and dates. But in the spring, raging floods spill over the riverbanks, destroying your fields. In the hot summers, you are often short of water.

How can you control the waters of the river?

BUILDING BACKGROUND In several parts of the world, bands of hunter-gatherers began to settle down in farming settlements. They domesticated plants and animals. Gradually their cultures became more complex. Most early civilizations grew up along rivers, where people learned to work together to control floods.

Rivers Support the Growth of Civilization

Early peoples settled where crops would grow. Crops usually grew well near rivers, where water was available and regular floods made the soil rich. One region in Southwest Asia was especially well suited for farming. It lay between two rivers.

The Land Between the Rivers

The Tigris and Euphrates rivers are the most important physical features of the region sometimes known as Mesopotamia (mes-uh-puh-TAY-mee-uh). Mesopotamia means "between the rivers" in Greek.

As you can see on the map, the region called Mesopotamia lies between Asia Minor and the Persian Gulf. The region is part of a larger area called the **Fertile Crescent**, a large arc of rich, or fertile, farmland. The Fertile Crescent extends from the Persian Gulf to the Mediterranean Sea.

In ancient times, Mesopotamia was actually made of two parts. Northern Mesopotamia was a plateau bordered on the north and the east by mountains. Southern Mesopotamia was a flat plain. The Tigris and Euphrates rivers flowed down from the hills into this low-lying plain.

The Rise of Civilization

Hunter-gatherer groups first settled in Mesopotamia more than 12,000 years ago. Over time, these people learned how to plant crops to grow their own food. Every year, floods on the Tigris and Euphrates rivers brought **silt**, a mixture of rich soil and tiny rocks, to the land. The fertile silt made the land ideal for farming.

The first farm settlements formed in Mesopotamia as early as 7000 BC. Farmers grew wheat, barley, and other types of grain. Livestock, birds, and fish were also good sources of food. Plentiful food led to population growth, and villages formed. Eventually, these early villages developed into the world's first civilization.

READING CHECK **Summarizing** What made civilization possible in Mesopotamia?

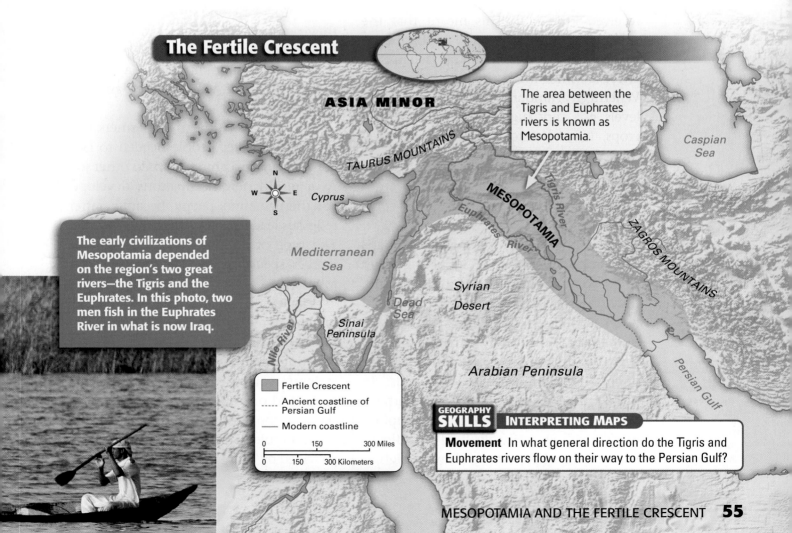

The Fertile Crescent

ASIA MINOR

The area between the Tigris and Euphrates rivers is known as Mesopotamia.

Caspian Sea

TAURUS MOUNTAINS

Cyprus

MESOPOTAMIA

Tigris River

ZAGROS MOUNTAINS

Euphrates River

Mediterranean Sea

The early civilizations of Mesopotamia depended on the region's two great rivers—the Tigris and the Euphrates. In this photo, two men fish in the Euphrates River in what is now Iraq.

Nile River

Dead Sea

Sinai Peninsula

Syrian Desert

Arabian Peninsula

Persian Gulf

Fertile Crescent
Ancient coastline of Persian Gulf
Modern coastline

0   150   300 Miles
0   150   300 Kilometers

GEOGRAPHY SKILLS **INTERPRETING MAPS**

Movement In what general direction do the Tigris and Euphrates rivers flow on their way to the Persian Gulf?

Irrigation and Civilization

Early farmers faced the challenge of learning how to control the flow of river water to their fields in both rainy and dry seasons.

❶ Early settlements in Mesopotamia were located near rivers. Water was not controlled, and flooding was a major problem.

❷ Later, people built canals to protect houses from flooding and move water to their fields.

Farming and Cities

Although Mesopotamia had fertile soil, farming wasn't easy there. The region received little rain. This meant that the water levels in the Tigris and Euphrates rivers depended on how much rain fell in eastern Asia Minor where the two rivers began. When a great amount of rain fell there, water levels got very high. Flooding destroyed crops, killed livestock, and washed away homes. When water levels were too low, crops dried up. Farmers knew they needed a way to control the rivers' flow.

Controlling Water

To solve their problems, Mesopotamians used **irrigation**, a way of supplying water to an area of land. To irrigate their land, they dug out large storage basins to hold water supplies. Then they dug **canals**, human-made waterways, that connected these basins to a network of ditches. These ditches brought water to the fields. To protect their fields from flooding, farmers built up the banks of the Tigris and Euphrates. These built-up banks held back floodwaters even when river levels were high.

THE IMPACT TODAY

People still build dikes, or earthen walls along rivers or shorelines, to hold back water.

Food Surpluses

Irrigation increased the amount of food farmers were able to grow. In fact, farmers could produce a food **surplus**, or more than they needed. Farmers also used irrigation to water grazing areas for cattle and sheep. As a result, Mesopotamians ate a variety of foods. Fish, meat, wheat, barley, and dates were plentiful.

Because irrigation made farmers more productive, fewer people needed to farm. Some people became free to do other jobs. As a result, new occupations developed. For the first time, people became crafters, religious leaders, and government workers. The type of arrangement in which each worker specializes in a particular task or job is called a **division of labor**.

Having people available to work on different jobs meant that society could accomplish more. Large projects, such as constructing buildings and digging irrigation systems, required specialized workers, managers, and organization. To complete these projects, the Mesopotamians needed structure and rules. Structure and rules could be provided by laws and government.

56 CHAPTER 3

3 With irrigation, the people of Mesopotamia were able to grow more food.

4 Food surpluses allowed some people to stop farming and concentrate on other jobs, like making clay pots or tools.

The Appearance of Cities

Over time, Mesopotamian settlements grew in size and complexity. They gradually developed into cities between 4000 and 3000 BC.

Despite the growth of cities, society in Mesopotamia was still based on agriculture. Most people still worked in farming jobs. However, cities were becoming important places. People traded goods there, and cities provided leaders with power bases.

They were the political, religious, cultural, and economic centers of civilization.

READING CHECK **Analyzing** Why did the Mesopotamians create irrigation systems?

SUMMARY AND PREVIEW Mesopotamia's rich, fertile lands supported productive farming, which led to the development of cities. In Section 2 you will learn about some of the first city builders.

go.hrw.com
Online Quiz
KEYWORD: SN6 HP3

Section 1 Assessment

Reviewing Ideas, Terms, and People

1. **a. Identify** Where was Mesopotamia?
   b. Explain How did the **Fertile Crescent** get its name?
   c. Evaluate What was the most important factor in making Mesopotamia's farmland fertile?
2. **a. Describe** Why did farmers need to develop a system to control their water supply?
   b. Explain In what ways did a **division of labor** contribute to the growth of Mesopotamian civilization?
   c. Elaborate How might running large projects prepare people for running a government?

Critical Thinking

3. **Identifying Cause and Effect** Farmers who used the rivers for irrigation were part of a cause-effect chain. Use a chart like this one to show that chain.

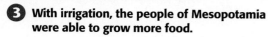

| Water levels in rivers get too low. | → | | → | Mesopotamians enjoy many foods. |

FOCUS ON WRITING

4. **Understanding Geography** Make a list of the words you might use to help young students imagine the land and rivers. Then start to sketch out a picture or map you could use on your poster.

River Valley Civilizations

All of the world's earliest civilizations had something in common—they all arose in river valleys that were perfect locations for farming. Three key factors made river valleys good for farming. First, the fields that bordered the rivers were flat, which made it easier for farmers to plant crops. Second, the soils were nourished by flood deposits and silt, which made them very fertile. Finally, the river provided the water farmers needed for irrigation.

Natural Highways River travel allowed early civilizations to trade goods and ideas. These people are traveling on the Euphrates River, one of the two main rivers of ancient Mesopotamia.

Caspian Sea

M E S O P O T A M I A

Tigris River

Euphrates River

Ur

Mediterranean Sea

Memphis

A F R I C A

EGYPT

Red Sea

Nile River

A R A B I A N
P E N I N S U L A

From Village to City With the development of agriculture, people settled into farming villages. Over time, some of these villages grew into large cities. These ancient ruins are near Memphis, Egypt.

Gift of the River River water was key to farming in early civilizations. This farmer is using water from the Huang He (Yellow River) in China to water her crops.

ASIA

New Activities Food surpluses allowed people to pursue other activities, like crafts, art, and writing. This tile designer lives in the Indus Valley.

CHINA

Huang He
(Yellow River)

• Harappa

HIMALAYAS

Indus River

Ganges River

Chang Jiang
(Yangzi River)

Mohenjo Daro •

INDUS VALLEY

INDIA

Arabian Sea

Bay of Bengal

| 0 | 500 | 1,000 Miles |
| 0 | 500 | 1,000 Kilometers |

GEOGRAPHY **SKILLS** **INTERPRETING MAPS**

1. **Human-Environment Interaction** Why did the first civilizations all develop in river valleys?
2. **Location** Where were the four earliest river valley civilizations located?

INDIAN OCEAN

The Rise of Sumer

What You Will Learn...

Main Ideas

1. The Sumerians created the world's first advanced society.
2. Religion played a major role in Sumerian society.

The Big Idea

The Sumerians developed the first civilization in Mesopotamia.

Key Terms and People

rural, *p. 60*
urban, *p. 60*
city-state, *p. 60*
Gilgamesh, *p. 61*
Sargon, *p. 61*
empire, *p. 61*
polytheism, *p. 62*
priests, *p. 63*
social hierarchy, *p. 63*

TAKING NOTES As you read, use a chart like the one below to take notes on the Sumerian civilization.

Characteristics	Notes
Cities	
Government	
Religion	
Society	

If YOU were there...

You are a crafter living in one of the cities of Sumer. Thick walls surround and protect your city, so you feel safe from the armies of other city-states. But you and your neighbors are fearful of other beings—the many gods and spirits that you believe are every-where. They can bring illness or sandstorms or bad luck.

How might you protect yourself from gods and spirits?

BUILDING BACKGROUND As civilizations developed along rivers, their societies and governments became more advanced. Religion became a main characteristic of these ancient cultures. Kings claimed to rule with the approval of the gods, and ordinary people wore charms and performed rituals to avoid bad luck.

An Advanced Society

In southern Mesopotamia, a people known as the Sumerians (soo-MER-ee-unz) developed the world's first civilization. No one knows where they came from or when they moved into the region. However, by 3000 BC, several hundred thousand Sumerians had settled in Mesopotamia, in a land they called Sumer (soo-muhr). There they created an advanced society.

The City-States of Sumer

Most people in Sumer were farmers. They lived mainly in **rural**, or countryside, areas. The centers of Sumerian society, however, were the **urban**, or city, areas. The first cities in Sumer had about 10,000 residents. Over time, the cities grew. Historians think that by 2000 BC, some of Sumer's cities had more than 100,000 residents.

As a result, the basic political unit of Sumer combined the two parts. This unit was called a city-state. A **city-state** consisted of a city and all the countryside around it. The amount of countryside controlled by each city-state depended on its military strength. Stronger city-states controlled larger areas.

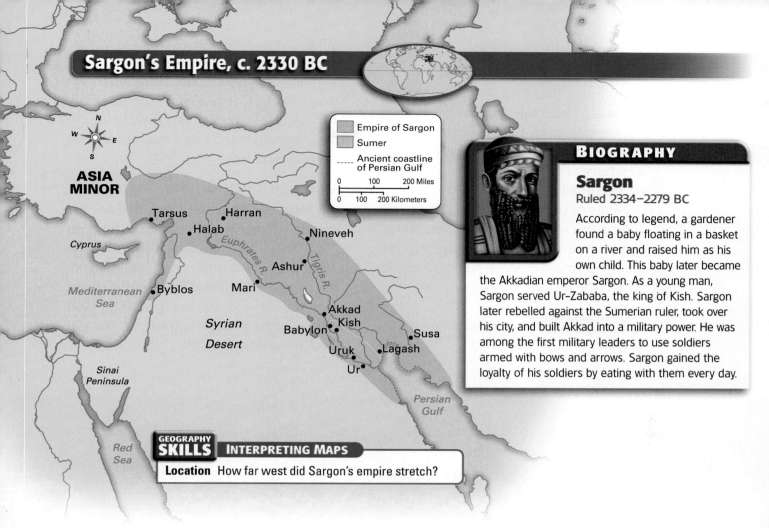

Sargon's Empire, c. 2330 BC

Empire of Sargon
Sumer
- - - - Ancient coastline of Persian Gulf

0   100   200 Miles
0   100   200 Kilometers

ASIA MINOR

N W E S

Tarsus
Halab   Harran
Cyprus   Nineveh
          Ashur
Euphrates R.   Tigris R.
Mediterranean   Byblos   Mari
Sea
          Syrian   Akkad
          Desert   Babylon   Kish
                    Uruk   Lagash   Susa
Sinai   Ur
Peninsula
                    Persian
                    Gulf
Red
Sea

GEOGRAPHY SKILLS INTERPRETING MAPS

Location How far west did Sargon's empire stretch?

BIOGRAPHY

Sargon
Ruled 2334–2279 BC

According to legend, a gardener found a baby floating in a basket on a river and raised him as his own child. This baby later became the Akkadian emperor Sargon. As a young man, Sargon served Ur–Zababa, the king of Kish. Sargon later rebelled against the Sumerian ruler, took over his city, and built Akkad into a military power. He was among the first military leaders to use soldiers armed with bows and arrows. Sargon gained the loyalty of his soldiers by eating with them every day.

City-states in Sumer fought each other to gain more farmland. As a result of these conflicts, the city-states built up strong armies. Sumerians also built strong, thick walls around their cities for protection.

Individual city-states gained and lost power over time. By 3500 BC, a city-state known as Kish had become quite powerful. Over the next 1,000 years, the city-states of Uruk and Ur fought for dominance. One of Uruk's kings, known as **Gilgamesh**, became a legendary figure in Sumerian literature.

Rise of the Akkadian Empire

In time, another society developed along the Tigris and Euphrates. It was created by the Akkadians (uh-KAY-dee-uhns). They lived just north of Sumer, but they were not Sumerians. They even spoke a different language than the Sumerians. In spite of their differences, however, the Akkadians and the Sumerians lived in peace for many years.

That peace was broken in the 2300s BC when **Sargon** sought to extend Akkadian territory. He built a new capital, Akkad (A-kad), on the Euphrates River, near what is now the city of Baghdad. Sargon was the first ruler to have a permanent army. He used that army to launch a series of wars against neighboring kingdoms.

Sargon's soldiers defeated all the city-states of Sumer. They also conquered northern Mesopotamia, finally bringing the entire region under his rule. With these conquests, Sargon established the world's first **empire**, or land with different territories and peoples under a single rule. The Akkadian Empire stretched from the Persian Gulf to the Mediterranean Sea.

Sargon was emperor, or ruler of his empire, for more than 50 years. However, the empire lasted only a century after his death. Later rulers could not keep the empire safe from invaders. Hostile tribes from the east raided and captured Akkad. A century of chaos followed.

Eventually, however, the Sumerian city-state of Ur rebuilt its strength and conquered the rest of Mesopotamia. Political stability was restored. The Sumerians once again became the most powerful civilization in the region.

READING CHECK **Summarizing** How did Sargon build an empire?

Religion Shapes Society

Religion was very important in Sumerian society. In fact, it played a **role** in nearly every aspect of public and private life. In many ways, religion was the basis for all of Sumerian society.

Sumerian Religion

The Sumerians practiced **polytheism**, the worship of many gods. Among the gods they worshipped were Enlil, the lord of the air; Enki, god of wisdom; and Inanna, goddess of love and war. The sun and moon were represented by the gods Utu and Nanna. Each city-state considered one god to be its special protector.

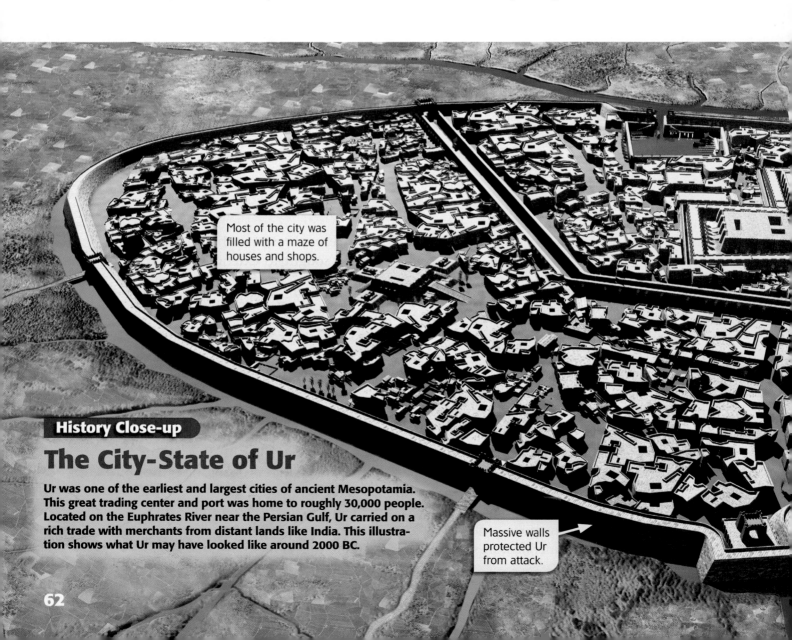

Most of the city was filled with a maze of houses and shops.

History Close-up

The City-State of Ur

Ur was one of the earliest and largest cities of ancient Mesopotamia. This great trading center and port was home to roughly 30,000 people. Located on the Euphrates River near the Persian Gulf, Ur carried on a rich trade with merchants from distant lands like India. This illustration shows what Ur may have looked like around 2000 BC.

Massive walls protected Ur from attack.

The Sumerians believed that their gods had enormous powers. Gods could bring a good harvest or a disastrous flood. They could bring illness, or they could bring good health and wealth. The Sumerians believed that success in every area of life depended on pleasing the gods. Every Sumerian had a duty to serve and to worship the gods.

Priests, people who performed religious ceremonies, had great status in Sumer. People relied on them to help gain the gods' favor. Priests interpreted the wishes of the gods and made offerings to them. These offerings were made in temples, special buildings where priests performed their religious ceremonies.

Sumerian Social Order

Because of their status, priests occupied a high level in Sumer's **social hierarchy**, the division of society by rank or class. In fact, priests were just below kings. The kings of Sumer claimed that they had been chosen by the gods to rule.

Below the priests were Sumer's skilled craftspeople, merchants, and traders. Trade had a great **impact** on Sumerian society. Traders traveled to faraway places and exchanged grain for gold, silver, copper, lumber, and precious stones.

Below traders, farmers and laborers made up the large working class. Slaves were at the bottom of the social order.

ACADEMIC VOCABULARY

impact effect, result

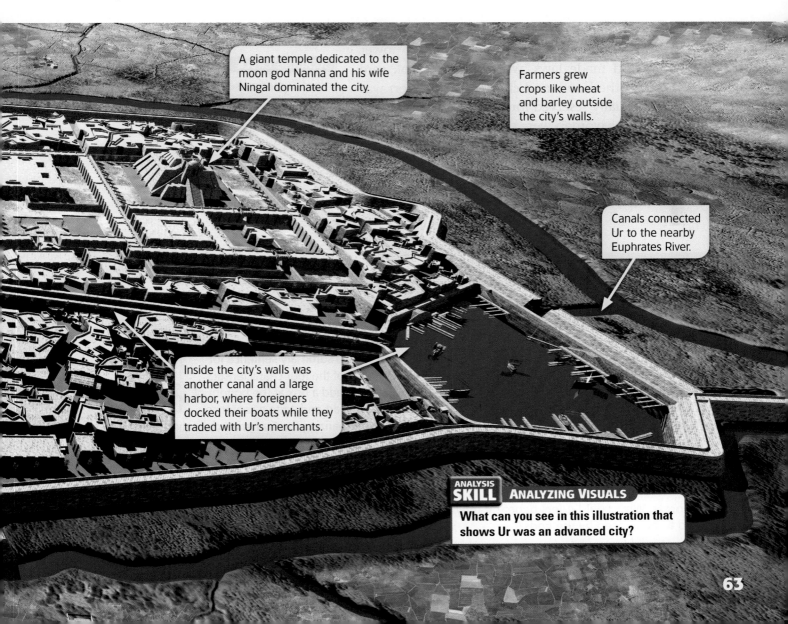

A giant temple dedicated to the moon god Nanna and his wife Ningal dominated the city.

Farmers grew crops like wheat and barley outside the city's walls.

Canals connected Ur to the nearby Euphrates River.

Inside the city's walls was another canal and a large harbor, where foreigners docked their boats while they traded with Ur's merchants.

ANALYSIS SKILL ANALYZING VISUALS

What can you see in this illustration that shows Ur was an advanced city?

Sumerian society was divided into different groups. This ancient artifact shows Sumerian leaders celebrating a military victory while a musician plays his instrument.

Men and Women in Sumer

Sumerian men and women had different roles. In general, men held political power and made laws, while women took care of the home and children. Education was usually reserved for men, but some upper-class women were educated as well.

Some educated women were priestesses in Sumer's temples. Some priestesses helped shape Sumerian culture. One, Enheduanna, the daughter of Sargon, wrote hymns to the goddess Inanna. She is the first known female writer in history.

READING CHECK **Analyzing** How did trade affect Sumerian society?

SUMMARY AND PREVIEW In this section you learned about Sumerian city-states, religion, and society. In Section 3, you will read about the Sumerians' achievements.

Section 2 Assessment

go.hrw.com
Online Quiz
KEYWORD: SN6 HP3

Reviewing Ideas, Terms, and People

1. **a. Recall** What was the basic political unit of Sumer?
   b. Explain What steps did **city-states** take to protect themselves from their rivals?
   c. Elaborate How do you think Sargon's creation of an **empire** changed the history of Mesopotamia? Defend your answer.
2. **a. Identify** What is **polytheism**?
   b. Draw Conclusions Why do you think **priests** were so influential in ancient Sumerian society?
   c. Elaborate Why would rulers benefit if they claimed to be chosen by the gods?

Critical Thinking

3. **Summarizing** In the right column of your note-taking chart, write a summary sentence for each of the four characteristics. Then add a box at the bottom of the chart and write a sentence summarizing the Sumerian civilization.

Characteristics	Notes
Cities	
Government	
Religion	
Society	

Summary Sentence:

FOCUS ON WRITING

4. **Gathering Information about Sumer** What aspects of Sumerian society will you include on your poster? What important people, religious beliefs, or social developments do you think the students should learn?

Sumerian Achievements

If YOU were there...

You are a student at a school for scribes in Sumer. Learning all the symbols for writing is very hard. Your teacher assigns you lessons to write on your clay tablet, but you can't help making mistakes. Then you have to smooth out the surface and try again. Still, being a scribe can lead to important jobs for the king. You could make your family proud.

Why would you want to be a scribe?

BUILDING BACKGROUND Sumerian society was advanced in terms of religion and government organization. The Sumerians were responsible for many other achievements, which were passed down to later civilizations.

The Invention of Writing

The Sumerians made one of the greatest cultural advances in history. They developed **cuneiform** (kyoo-NEE-uh-fohrm), the world's first system of writing. But Sumerians did not have pencils, pens, or paper. Instead, they used sharp tools called styluses to make wedge-shaped symbols on clay tablets.

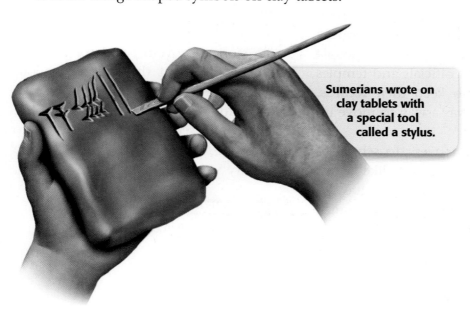

Sumerians wrote on clay tablets with a special tool called a stylus.

What You Will Learn...

Main Ideas

1. The Sumerians invented the world's first writing system.
2. Advances and inventions changed Sumerian lives.
3. Many types of art developed in Sumer.

The Big Idea

The Sumerians made many advances that helped their society develop.

Key Terms

cuneiform, *p. 65*
pictographs, *p. 66*
scribe, *p. 66*
epics, *p. 66*
architecture, *p. 68*
ziggurat, *p. 68*

TAKING NOTES Create a chart like the one below. As you read, list the achievements and advances made by the Sumerian civilization.

Sumerian Advances and Achievements

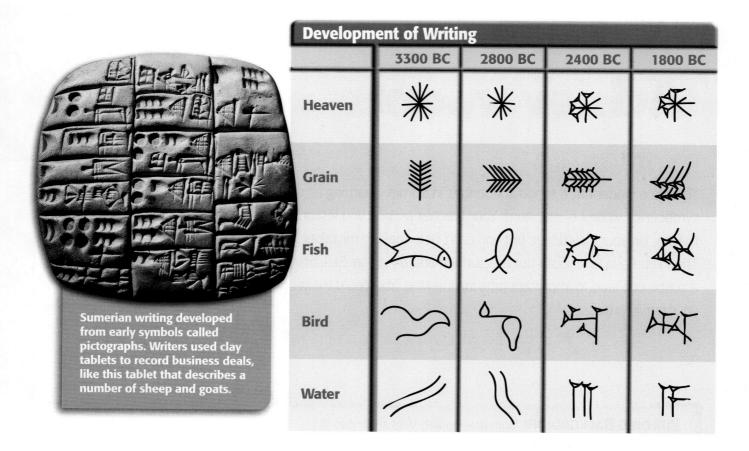

Development of Writing

	3300 BC	2800 BC	2400 BC	1800 BC
Heaven				
Grain				
Fish				
Bird				
Water				

Sumerian writing developed from early symbols called pictographs. Writers used clay tablets to record business deals, like this tablet that describes a number of sheep and goats.

Earlier written communication had used **pictographs**, or picture symbols. Each pictograph represented an object, such as a tree or an animal. But in cuneiform, symbols could also represent syllables, or basic parts of words. As a result, Sumerian writers could combine symbols to express more complex ideas such as "joy" or "powerful."

Sumerians first used cuneiform to keep business records. A **scribe**, or writer, would be hired to keep track of the items people traded. Government officials and temples also hired scribes to keep their records. Becoming a scribe was a way to move up in social class.

Sumerian students went to school to learn to read and write. But, like today, some students did not want to study. A Sumerian story tells of a father who urged his son to do his schoolwork:

" Go to school, stand before your 'school-father,' recite your assignment, open your schoolbag, write your tablet . . . After you have finished your assignment and reported to your monitor [teacher], come to me, and do not wander about in the street. "

–Sumerian essay quoted in *History Begins at Sumer*, by Samuel Noah Kramer

In time, Sumerians put their writing skills to new uses. They wrote works on history, law, grammar, and math. They also created works of literature. Sumerians wrote stories, proverbs, and songs. They wrote poems about the gods and about military victories. Some of these were **epics**, long poems that tell the stories of heroes. Later, people used some of these poems to create *The Epic of Gilgamesh*, the story of a legendary Sumerian king.

READING CHECK **Generalizing** How was cuneiform first used in Sumer?

Advances and Inventions

Writing was not the only great Sumerian invention. These early people made many other advances and discoveries.

Technical Advances

One of the Sumerians' most important developments was the wheel. They were the first people to build wheeled vehicles, including carts and wagons. Using the wheel, Sumerians invented a device that spins clay as a craftsperson shapes it into bowls. This device is called a potter's wheel.

The plow was another important Sumerian invention. Pulled by oxen, plows broke through the hard clay soil of Sumer to prepare it for planting. This technique greatly increased farm production. The Sumerians also invented a clock that used falling water to measure time.

Sumerian advances improved daily life in many ways. Sumerians built sewers under city streets. They learned to use bronze to make stronger tools and weapons. They even produced makeup and glass jewelry.

Math and Sciences

Another area in which Sumerians excelled was math. In fact, they developed a math system based on the number 60. Based on this system, they divided a circle into 360 degrees. Dividing a year into 12 months—a factor of 60—was another Sumerian idea. Sumerians also calculated the areas of rectangles and triangles.

Sumerian scholars studied science, too. They wrote long lists to record their study of the natural world. These tablets included the names of thousands of animals, plants, and minerals.

The Sumerians also made advances in medicine. They used ingredients from animals, plants, and minerals to produce healing drugs. Items used in these medicines included milk, turtle shells, figs, and salt. The Sumerians even catalogued their medical knowledge, listing treatments according to symptoms and body parts.

READING CHECK **Categorizing** What areas of life were improved by Sumerian inventions?

THE IMPACT TODAY

Like the Sumerians we use a base-60 system when we talk about 60 seconds in a minute and 60 minutes in an hour.

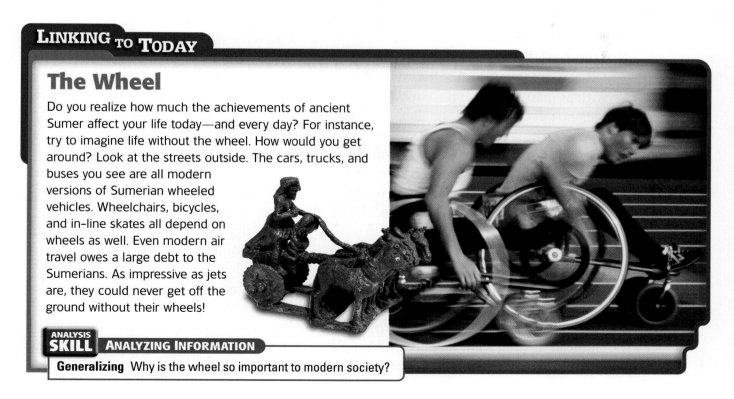

LINKING TO TODAY

The Wheel

Do you realize how much the achievements of ancient Sumer affect your life today—and every day? For instance, try to imagine life without the wheel. How would you get around? Look at the streets outside. The cars, trucks, and buses you see are all modern versions of Sumerian wheeled vehicles. Wheelchairs, bicycles, and in-line skates all depend on wheels as well. Even modern air travel owes a large debt to the Sumerians. As impressive as jets are, they could never get off the ground without their wheels!

ANALYSIS SKILL **ANALYZING INFORMATION**

Generalizing Why is the wheel so important to modern society?

The Sumerians' artistic achievements included beautiful works of gold, wood, and stone.

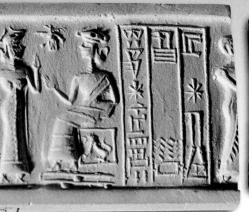

Cylinder seals like this one were carved into round stones and then rolled over clay to leave their mark.

This stringed musical instrument is called a lyre. It features a cow's head and is made of silver decorated with shell and stone.

The Arts of Sumer

The Sumerians' skills in the fields of art, metalwork, and **architecture**—the science of building—are well known to us. The ruins of great buildings and fine works of art have provided us with wonderful examples of the Sumerians' creativity.

Architecture

Most Sumerian rulers lived in large palaces. Other rich Sumerians had two-story homes with as many as a dozen rooms. Most people, however, lived in smaller, one-story houses. These homes had six or seven rooms arranged around a small courtyard. Large and small houses stood side by side along the narrow, unpaved streets of the city. Bricks made of mud were the houses' main building blocks.

City centers were dominated by their temples, the largest and most impressive buildings in Sumer. A **ziggurat**, a pyramid-shaped temple tower, rose above each city. Outdoor staircases led to a platform and a shrine at the top. Some architects added columns to make the temples more attractive.

The Arts

Sumerian sculptors produced many fine works. Among them are the statues of gods created for temples. Sumerian artists also sculpted small objects out of ivory and rare woods. Sumerian pottery is known more for its quantity than quality. Potters turned out many items, but few were works of beauty.

Jewelry was a popular item in Sumer. The jewelers of the region made many beautiful works out of imported gold, silver, and gems. Earrings and other items found in the region show that Sumerian jewelers knew advanced methods for putting gold pieces together.

Cylinder seals are perhaps Sumer's most famous works of art. These small objects were stone cylinders engraved with designs. When rolled over clay, the designs would leave behind their imprint. Each seal left its own distinct imprint. As a result, a person could show ownership of a container by rolling a cylinder over the container's wet clay surface. People could also use cylinder seals to "sign" documents or to decorate other clay objects.

The Sumerians were the first people in Mesopotamia to build large temples called ziggurats.

This gold dagger was found in a royal tomb. The bull's head is made of gold and silver.

ANALYSIS SKILL **ANALYZING VISUALS**
What animal is shown in two of these works?

Some seals showed battle scenes. Others displayed worship rituals. Some were highly decorative, with hundreds of carefully cut gems. They required great skill to make.

The Sumerians also enjoyed music. Kings and temples hired musicians to play on special occasions. Sumerian musicians played reed pipes, drums, tambourines, and stringed instruments called lyres. Children learned songs in school. People sang hymns to gods and kings. Music and dance provided entertainment in marketplaces and homes.

READING CHECK **Drawing Inferences** What might historians learn from cylinder seals?

SUMMARY AND PREVIEW The Sumerians greatly enriched their society. Next you will learn about the later peoples who lived in Mesopotamia.

Section 3 Assessment

go.hrw.com
Online Quiz
KEYWORD: SN6 HP3

Reviewing Ideas, Terms, and People

1. **a. Identify** What is **cuneiform**?
   b. Analyze Why do you think writing is one of history's most important cultural advances?
   c. Elaborate What current leader would you choose to write an **epic** about, and why?
2. **a. Recall** What were two early uses of the wheel?
   b. Explain Why do you think the invention of the plow was so important to the Sumerians?
3. **a. Describe** What was the basic Sumerian building material?
   b. Make Inferences Why do you think cylinder seals developed into works of art?

Critical Thinking

4. **Identifying Effects** In a chart like this one, identify the effect of each Sumerian advance or achievement you listed in your notes.

Advance/ Achievement	Effect

WRITING JOURNAL

5. **Evaluating Information** Review the Sumerian achievements you just read about. Then create a list of Sumerian achievements for your letter. Would this list replace some of the information you collected in Section 2?

MESOPOTAMIA AND THE FERTILE CRESCENT **69**

from The Epic of Gilgamesh

translated by N. K. Sandars

About the Reading The Epic of Gilgamesh *is the world's oldest epic, first recorded—carved on stone tablets—in about 2000 BC. The actual Gilgamesh, ruler of the city of Uruk, had lived about 700 years earlier. Over time, stories about this legendary king had grown and changed. In this story, Gilgamesh and his friend Enkidu seek to slay the monster Humbaba, keeper of a distant forest. In addition to his tremendous size and terrible appearance, Humbaba possesses seven splendors, or powers, one of which is fire. Gilgamesh hopes to claim these powers for himself.*

AS YOU READ Notice both the human qualities and the godly qualities of Gilgamesh.

Humbaba came from his strong house of cedar. He nodded his head and shook it, menacing Gilgamesh; and on him he fastened his eye, the eye of death. Then Gilgamesh called to Shamash and his tears were flowing, "O glorious Shamash, I have followed the road you commanded but now if you send no succor how shall I escape?" ❶ Glorious Shamash heard his prayer and he summoned the great wind, the north wind, the whirlwind, the storm and the icy wind, the tempest and the scorching wind; they came like dragons, like a scorching fire, like a serpent that freezes the heart, a destroying flood and the lightning's fork. The eight winds rose up against Humbaba, they beat against his eyes; he was gripped, unable to go forward or back. ❷ Gilgamesh shouted, "By the life of Ninsun my mother and divine Lugulbanda my father . . . my weak arms and my small weapons I have brought to this Land against you, and now I will enter your house." ❸

So he felled the first cedar and they cut the branches and laid them at the foot of the mountain. At the first stroke Humbaba blazed out, but still they advanced. They felled seven cedars and cut and bound the branches and laid them at the foot of the mountain, and seven times Humbaba loosed his glory on them. As the seventh blaze died out they reached his lair. He slapped his thigh in scorn. He approached like a noble wild bull roped on the mountain, a warrior whose elbows were bound together. The tears started to his eyes and he was pale, "Gilgamesh, let me speak. I have never known a mother, no, nor a father who reared me. I was born of the mountain, he reared me, and Enlil made me the keeper of this forest. Let me go free, Gilgamesh, and I will be your servant, you shall be my lord; all the trees of the forest that I tended on the mountain shall be yours. I will cut them down and build you a palace." . . . ❹

Enkidu said, "Do not listen, Gilgamesh: this Humbaba must die. Kill Humbaba first and his servants after." But Gilgamesh said, "If we touch him the blaze and the glory of light will be put out in confusion, the glory and glamour will vanish, its rays will be quenched." Enkidu said to Gilgamesh, "Not so, my friend. First entrap the bird, and where shall the chicks run then? Afterwards we can search out the glory and the glamour, when the chicks run distracted through the grass."

Gilgamesh listened to the word of his companion, he took the ax in his hand, he drew the sword from his belt, and he struck Humbaba with a thrust of the sword to the neck, and Enkidu his comrade struck the second blow. At the third blow Humbaba fell. Then there followed confusion for this was the guardian of the forest whom they had felled to the ground . . .

When he saw the head of Humbaba, Enlil raged at them. "Why did you do this thing? From henceforth may the fire be on your faces, may it eat the bread that you eat, may it drink where you drink." Then Enlil took again the blaze and the seven splendors that had been Humbaba's: he gave the first to the river, and he gave to the lion, to the stone of execration, to the mountain . . . ❺

O Gilgamesh, king and conqueror of the dreadful blaze; wild bull who plunders the mountain, who crosses the sea, glory to him.

GUIDED READING

WORD HELP

execration a cursing
plunders takes by force

❹ *What effect does Humbaba hope his words will have on Gilgamesh?*

❺ The angry air-god Enlil curses the heroes for slaying Humbaba. He takes back the monster's powers and gives them to other creatures and elements of nature.

In your opinion, is Gilgamesh more or less heroic for slaying Humbaba and angering Enlil?

Archaeologists think this statue from the 700s BC represents Gilgamesh.

CONNECTING LITERATURE TO HISTORY

1. **Analyzing** In Sumerian culture, the gods' powers were thought to be enormous. According to this story, what roles do gods play in people's lives?

2. **Making Inferences** Violence was common in Sumerian society. How does the character of Gilgamesh suggest that Sumerian society could be violent?

Later Peoples of the Fertile Crescent

If YOU were there...

You are a noble in ancient Babylon, an advisor to the great king Hammurabi. One of your duties is to collect all the laws of the kingdom. They will be carved on a tall block of black stone and placed in the temple. The king asks your opinion about the punishments for certain crimes. For instance, should common people be punished more harshly than nobles?

How will you advise the king?

BUILDING BACKGROUND Many peoples invaded Mesopotamia. A series of kings conquered the lands between the rivers. Each new culture inherited the earlier achievements of the Sumerians. Some of the later invasions of the region also introduced skills and ideas that still influence civilization today, such as a written law code.

The Babylonians Conquer Mesopotamia

Although Ur rose to glory after the death of Sargon, repeated foreign attacks drained its strength. By 2000 BC, Ur lay in ruins. With Ur's power gone, several waves of invaders battled to gain control of Mesopotamia.

The Rise of Babylon

Babylon was home to one such group. That city was located on the Euphrates River near what is today Baghdad, Iraq. Babylon had once been a Sumerian town. By 1800 BC, however, it was home to a powerful government of its own. In 1792 BC, Hammurabi (ham-uh-RAHB-ee) became Babylon's king. He would become the city's greatest **monarch** (MAH-nark), a ruler of a kingdom or empire.

Hammurabi's Code

Hammurabi was a brilliant war leader. His armies fought many battles to expand his power. Eventually, he brought all of Mesopotamia into his empire, called the Babylonian Empire, after his capital.

Hammurabi's skills were not limited to the battlefield, though. He was also an able ruler who could govern a huge empire. He oversaw many building and irrigation projects and improved Babylon's tax collection system to help pay for them. He also brought much prosperity through increased trade. Hammurabi, however, is most famous for his code of laws.

Hammurabi's Code was a set of 282 laws that dealt with almost every part of daily life. There were laws on everything from trade, loans, and theft to marriage, injury, and murder. It contained some ideas that are still found in laws today. Specific crimes brought specific penalties. However, social class did matter. For instance, injuring a rich man brought a greater penalty than injuring a poor man.

Hammurabi's Code was important not only for how thorough it was, but also because it was written down for all to see. People all over the empire could read exactly what was against the law.

Hammurabi ruled for 42 years. During his reign, Babylon became the most important city in Mesopotamia. However, after his death, Babylonian power declined. The kings that followed faced invasions from people Hammurabi had conquered. Before long, the Babylonian Empire came to an end.

READING CHECK **Analyzing** What was Hammurabi's most important accomplishment?

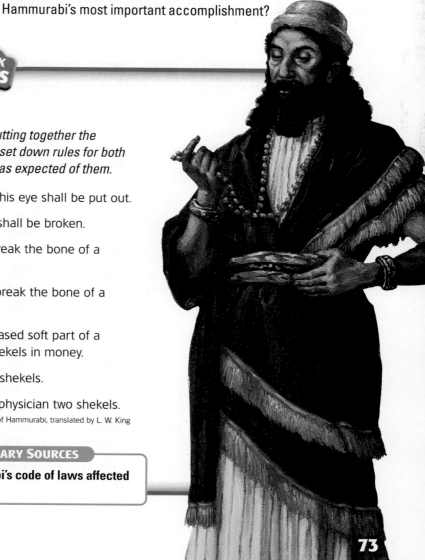

Primary Source

QUICK FACTS

HISTORIC DOCUMENT
Hammurabi's Code

The Babylonian ruler Hammurabi is credited with putting together the earliest known written collection of laws. The code set down rules for both criminal and civil law, and informed citizens what was expected of them.

196. If a man put out the eye of another man, his eye shall be put out.

197. If he break another man's bone, his bone shall be broken.

198. If he put out the eye of a freed man, or break the bone of a freed man, he shall pay one gold mina.

199. If he put out the eye of a man's slave, or break the bone of a man's slave, he shall pay one-half of its value.

221. If a physican heal the broken bone or diseased soft part of a man, the patient shall pay the physician five shekels in money.

222. If he were a freed man he shall pay three shekels.

223. If he were a slave his owner shall pay the physician two shekels.

–Hammurabi, from the Code of Hammurabi, translated by L. W. King

ANALYSIS SKILL **ANALYZING PRIMARY SOURCES**

How do you think Hammurabi's code of laws affected citizens of that time?

Invasions of Mesopotamia

Several other civilizations also developed in and around the Fertile Crescent. As their armies battled each other for fertile land, control of the region passed from one empire to another.

The Hittites and Kassites

FOCUS ON READING
What is the topic of this paragraph? Is the main idea stated in a single sentence?

A people known as the Hittites built a strong kingdom in Asia Minor, in what is today Turkey. Their success came, in part, from two key military advantages they had over rivals. First, the Hittites were among the first people to master ironworking. This meant that they could make the strongest weapons of the time. Second, the Hittites skillfully used the **chariot**, a wheeled, horse-drawn cart used in battle. The chariots allowed Hittite soldiers to move quickly around a battlefield and fire arrows at their enemy. Using these advantages, Hittite forces captured Babylon around 1595 BC.

Hittite rule did not last long, however. Soon after taking Babylon, the Hittite king was killed by an assassin. The kingdom plunged into chaos. The Kassites, a people who lived north of Babylon, captured the city and ruled for almost 400 years.

The Assyrians

Later, in the 1200s BC, the Assyrians (uh-SIR-ee-unz) from northern Mesopotamia briefly gained control of Babylon. However, their empire was soon overrun by invaders. After this defeat, the Assyrians took about 300 years to recover their strength. Then, starting about 900 BC, they began to conquer all of the Fertile Crescent. They even took over parts of Asia Minor and Egypt.

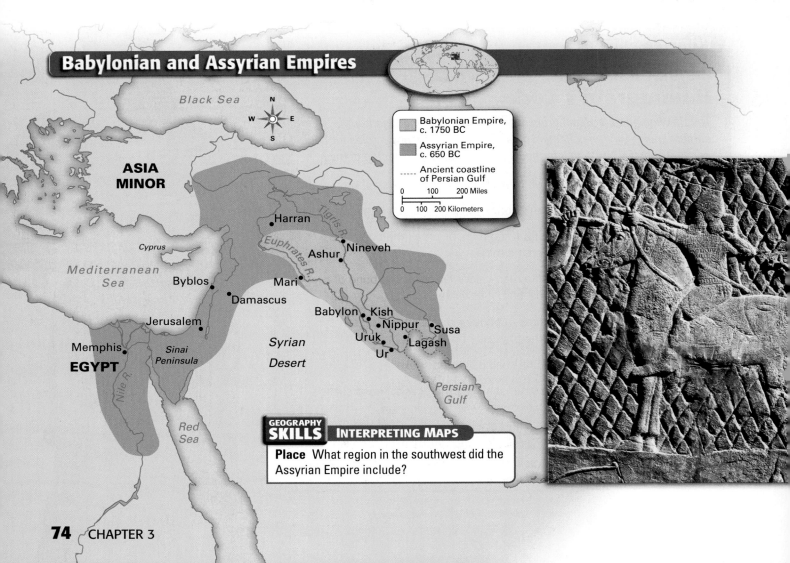

Babylonian and Assyrian Empires

Black Sea

ASIA MINOR

Cyprus

Mediterranean Sea

Harran

Euphrates R.

Tigris R.

Ashur   Nineveh

Byblos   Mari

Damascus

Jerusalem

Babylon   Kish
Nippur   Susa
Uruk   Lagash
Ur

Memphis   Sinai Peninsula   Syrian Desert

EGYPT   Nile R.

Red Sea

Persian Gulf

Babylonian Empire, c. 1750 BC

Assyrian Empire, c. 650 BC

Ancient coastline of Persian Gulf

0   100   200 Miles
0   100   200 Kilometers

GEOGRAPHY SKILLS | **INTERPRETING MAPS**
Place What region in the southwest did the Assyrian Empire include?

The key to the Assyrians' success was their strong army. Like the Hittites, the Assyrians used iron weapons and chariots. The army was very well organized, and every soldier knew his role.

The Assyrians were fierce in battle. Before attacking, they spread terror by looting villages and burning crops. Anyone who still dared to resist them was killed.

After conquering the Fertile Crescent, the Assyrians ruled from Nineveh (NI-nuh-vuh). They demanded heavy taxes from across the empire. Areas that resisted these demands were harshly punished.

Assyrian kings ruled their large empire through local leaders. Each governed a small area, collected taxes, enforced laws, and raised troops for the army. Roads were built to link distant parts of the empire. Messengers on horseback were sent to deliver orders to faraway officials.

The Chaldeans

In 652 BC a series of wars broke out in the Assyrian Empire over who should rule. These wars greatly weakened the empire.

Sensing this weakness, the Chaldeans (kal-DEE-unz), a group from the Syrian Desert, led other peoples in an attack on the Assyrians. In 612 BC, they destroyed Nineveh and the Assyrian Empire.

In its place, the Chaldeans set up a new empire of their own. **Nebuchadnezzar** (neb-uh-kuhd-NEZ-uhr), the most famous Chaldean king, rebuilt Babylon into a beautiful city. According to legend, his grand palace featured the famous Hanging Gardens. Trees and flowers grew on its terraces and roofs. From the ground the gardens seemed to hang in the air.

The Chaldeans admired Sumerian culture. They studied the Sumerian language and built temples to Sumerian gods.

At the same time, Babylon became a center for astronomy. Chaldeans charted the positions of the stars and kept track of economic, political, and weather events. They also created a calendar and solved complex problems of geometry.

READING CHECK **Sequencing** List in order the peoples who ruled Mesopotamia.

The Assyrian Army
The Assyrian army was the most powerful fighting force the world had ever seen. It was large and well organized, and it featured iron weapons, war chariots, and giant war machines used to knock down city walls.

What kinds of weapons can you see in this carving?

Phoenicia, c. 800 BC

The Phoenicians sailed throughout the Mediterranean, building trade networks and founding new cities.

ATLANTIC OCEAN

SPAIN

Strait of Gibraltar

ATLAS MOUNTAINS

The Phoenicians

At the western end of the Fertile Crescent, along the Mediterranean Sea, was a land known as Phoenicia (fi-NI-shuh). It was not home to a great military power and was often ruled by foreign governments. Nevertheless, the Phoenicians created a wealthy trading society.

The Geography of Phoenicia

Today the nation of Lebanon occupies most of what was once Phoenicia. Mountains border the region to the north and east. The western border is the Mediterranean.

Phoenicia had few resources. One thing it did have, however, was cedar. Cedar trees were prized for their timber, a valuable trade item. But Phoenicia's overland trade routes were blocked by mountains and hostile neighbors. Phoenicians had to look to the sea for a way to trade.

THE IMPACT TODAY

Because so many cedar trees have been cut down in Lebanon's forests over the years, very few trees remain.

The Expansion of Trade

Motivated by a desire for trade, the people of Phoenicia became expert sailors. They built one of the world's finest harbors at the city of Tyre. Fleets of fast Phoenician trading ships sailed to ports all around the Mediterranean Sea. Traders traveled to Egypt, Greece, Italy, Sicily, and Spain. They even passed through the Strait of Gibraltar to reach the Atlantic Ocean.

The Phoenicians founded several new colonies along their trade routes. Carthage (KAHR-thij), located on the northern coast of Africa, was the most famous of these. It later became one of the most powerful cities on the Mediterranean.

Phoenicia grew wealthy from its trade. Besides lumber, the Phoenicians traded silverwork, ivory carvings, and slaves. Beautiful glass objects also became valuable trade items after crafters invented glass-blowing—the art of heating and shaping glass. In addition, the Phoenicians made purple dye from a type of shellfish. They then traded cloth dyed with this purple color. Phoenician purple fabric was very popular with rich people.

The Phoenicians' most important achievement, however, wasn't a trade good. To record their activities, Phoenician

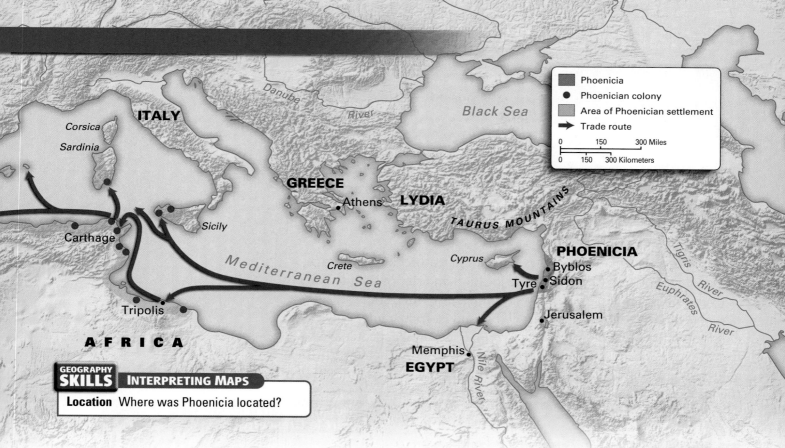

Location Where was Phoenicia located?

traders developed one of the world's first alphabets. An **alphabet** is a set of letters that can be combined to form words. This development made writing much easier. It had a major impact on the ancient world and on our own. In fact, the alphabet we use for the English language is based on the Phoenicians', as modified by later civilizations. Later civilizations, including our own, benefited from the innovations passed along by Phoenician traders.

READING CHECK **Finding Main Ideas** What were the main achievements of the Phoenicians?

SUMMARY AND PREVIEW Many different peoples ruled in the Fertile Crescent after the Sumerians. Some made important contributions that are still valued today. In the next chapter you will learn about two remarkable civilizations that developed along the Nile River.

Section 4 Assessment

go.hrw.com
Online Quiz
KEYWORD: SN6 HP3

Reviewing Ideas, Terms, and People

1. **a. Identify** Where was Babylon located?
   b. Analyze What does **Hammurabi's Code** reveal about Babylonian society?
2. **a. Describe** What two advantages did Hittite soldiers have over their opponents?
   b. Rank Which empire discussed in this section do you feel contributed the most to modern-day society? Why?
3. **a. Identify** For what trade goods were the Phoenicians known? For what else were they known?
   b. Analyze How did Phoenicia grow wealthy?

Critical Thinking

4. **Categorizing** Use your note-taking diagram with the names of the empires. List at least one advance or achievement made by each empire.

FOCUS ON WRITING

5. **Gathering Information about Later Peoples** Several different peoples contributed to civilization in the Fertile Crescent after the Sumerians. Which ones, if any, will you mention in your letter? What will you say?

Social Studies Skills

Interpreting Physical Maps

Understand the Skill

A *physical map* is a map that shows the natural features and landscape, or *topography*, of an area. It shows the location and size of such features as rivers and mountain ranges. Physical maps also often show an area's *elevation*, or how high above sea level the land is. Topography and elevation often influence human activities. For example, people will live where they can find water and defend themselves. Therefore, being able to interpret a physical map can help you better understand how the history of an area unfolded.

Learn the Skill

Follow these steps to interpret a physical map.

1 Read the map's title, distance scale, and legend. These will provide basic information about the map's contents.

2 Note the colors used to show elevation. Use the legend to connect colors on the map to elevations of specific places.

3 Note the shapes of the features, such as how high a mountain range is, how far it stretches, and how long a river is. Note where each feature is in relation to others.

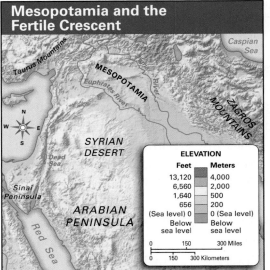

Mesopotamia and the Fertile Crescent

4 Use information from the map to draw conclusions about the effect of the region's topography on settlement and economic activities.

Practice and Apply the Skill

Use the guidelines to answer these questions about the map above.

1. What is the elevation of the western half of the Arabian Peninsula?

2. Describe the topography of Mesopotamia. Why would settlement have occurred here before other places on the map?

3. What feature might have stopped invasions of Mesopotamia?

Chapter Review

Visual Summary

Use the visual summary below to help you review the main ideas of the chapter.

QUICK FACTS

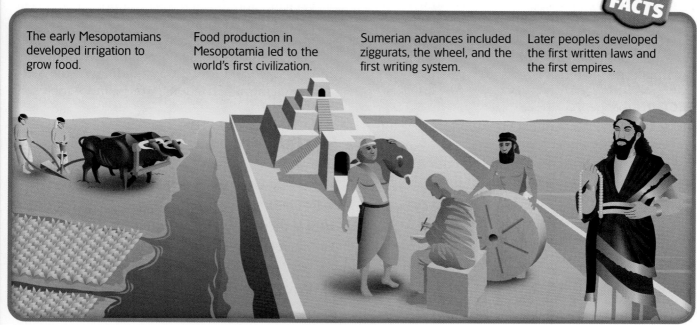

The early Mesopotamians developed irrigation to grow food.

Food production in Mesopotamia led to the world's first civilization.

Sumerian advances included ziggurats, the wheel, and the first writing system.

Later peoples developed the first written laws and the first empires.

Reviewing Vocabulary, Terms, and People

Using your own paper, complete the sentences below by providing the correct term for each blank.

1. Mesopotamian farmers built _____ to irrigate their fields.

2. While city dwellers were urban, farmers lived in _____ areas.

3. The people of Sumer practiced _____, the worship of many gods.

4. Instead of using pictographs, Sumerians developed a type of writing called _____.

5. Horse-drawn _____ gave the Hittites an advantage during battle.

6. The Babylonian king _____ is famous for his code of laws.

7. Another word for effect is _____.

8. Sumerian society was organized in _____, which consisted of a city and the surrounding lands.

Comprehension and Critical Thinking

SECTION 1 *(Pages 54–57)*

9. **a. Describe** Where was Mesopotamia, and what does the name mean?

b. Analyze How did Mesopotamian irrigation systems allow civilization to develop?

c. Elaborate Do you think a division of labor is necessary for civilization to develop? Why or why not?

SECTION 2 *(Pages 60–64)*

10. **a. Identify** Who built the world's first empire, and what did that empire include?

b. Analyze Politically, how was early Sumerian society organized? How did that organization affect society?

c. Elaborate Why did the Sumerians consider it everyone's responsibility to keep the gods happy?

SECTION 3 (Pages 65–69)

11. a. Identify What was the Sumerian writing system called, and why is it so significant?

b. Compare and Contrast What were two ways in which Sumerian society was similar to our society today? What were two ways in which it was different?

c. Evaluate Other than writing and the wheel, which Sumerian invention do you think is most important? Why?

SECTION 4 (Pages 72–77)

12. a. Describe What were two important developments of the Phoenicians?

b. Draw Conclusions Why do you think several peoples banded together to fight the Assyrians?

c. Evaluate Do you think Hammurabi was more effective as a ruler or as a military leader? Why?

Reviewing Themes

13. Science and Technology Which of the ancient Sumerians' technological achievements do you think has been most influential in history? Why?

14. Politics Why do you think Hammurabi is so honored for his code of laws?

Reading Skills

Identifying Main Ideas *For each passage, choose the letter that corresponds to the main idea sentence.*

15. (A) Sumerians believed that their gods had enormous powers. (B) Gods could bring a good harvest or a disastrous flood. (C) They could bring illness or they could bring good health and wealth.

16. (A) The wheel was not the Sumerians' only great development. (B) They developed cuneiform, the world's first system of writing. (C) But Sumerians did not have pencils, pens, or paper. (D) Instead, they used sharp reeds to make wedge-shaped symbols on clay tablets.

Using the Internet

go.hrw.com
KEYWORD: SN6 WH3

17. Activity: Looking at Writing The Sumerians made one of the greatest cultural advances in history by developing cuneiform. This was the world's first system of writing. Enter the activity keyword and research the evolution of language and its written forms. Look at one of the newest methods of writing: text messaging. Then write a paragraph explaining how and why writing was developed and why it was important using text-messaging abbreviations, words, and symbols.

Social Studies Skills

Interpreting Physical Maps *Could you use a physical map to answer the questions below? For each question, answer yes or no.*

18. Are there mountains or hills in a certain region?

19. What languages do people speak in that region?

20. How many people live in the region?

21. What kinds of water features such as rivers or lakes would you find there?

FOCUS ON WRITING

22. Writing Your Letter Use the notes you have taken to create a plan for your letter. You might want to start with a rough outline of two or three main points. For example, one of your main points might be about the land of Mesopotamia. Another might be about the achievements of the Sumerians.

After you have a good plan in mind, you can start to write your letter. As you write, think about the young student who will be reading the letter. What words will he or she understand? How can you capture the student's interest and keep it? If you think it would help the student to see a map or a drawing, create one and attach it to your letter.

DIRECTIONS: Read each question, and write the letter of the best response.

1 Use the map to answer the following question.

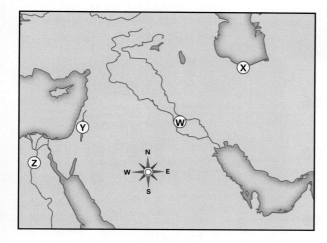

The region known as Mesopotamia is indicated on the map by the letter

A W.

B X.

C Y.

D Z.

2 All of the following ancient civilizations developed in Mesopotamia *except* the

A Akkadians.

B Babylonians.

C Egyptians.

D Sumerians.

3 Which of the following is *not* true of the first writing system?

A It was developed by the Babylonians.

B It began with the use of pictures to represent syllables and objects.

C It was recorded on tablets made of clay.

D It was first used to keep business records.

4 In Sumerian society, people's social class or rank depended on their wealth and their

A appearance.

B religion.

C location.

D occupation.

5 Hammurabi's Code is important in world history because it was an early

A form of writing that could be used to record important events.

B written list of laws that controlled people's daily life and behavior.

C record-keeping system that enabled the Phoenicians to become great traders.

D set of symbols that allowed the Sumerians to communicate with other peoples.

6 What was the most important contribution of the Phoenicians to our civilization?

A purple dye

B their alphabet

C founding of Carthage

D sailing ships

Connecting with Past Learnings

7 In this chapter, you learned about agriculture in Mesopotamia. During what period of prehistory was agriculture first practiced?

A Megalithic Era

B Mesolithic Era

C Paleolithic Era

D Neolithic Era

CHAPTER 4   **4500 BC–AD 400**

Ancient Egypt and Kush

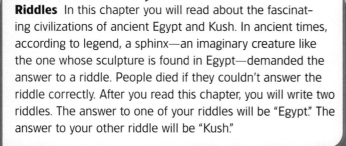

FOCUS ON WRITING

Riddles In this chapter you will read about the fascinating civilizations of ancient Egypt and Kush. In ancient times, according to legend, a sphinx—an imaginary creature like the one whose sculpture is found in Egypt—demanded the answer to a riddle. People died if they couldn't answer the riddle correctly. After you read this chapter, you will write two riddles. The answer to one of your riddles will be "Egypt." The answer to your other riddle will be "Kush."

CHAPTER EVENTS

WORLD EVENTS

c. 4500 BC
Agricultural communities develop in Egypt.

4000 BC

What You Will Learn...

In this chapter you will learn about two great civilizations that developed along the Nile River—Egypt and Kush. This photo shows an ancient temple of Ramses II, one of Egypt's most powerful rulers.

c. 3100 BC
Menes unites Upper and Lower Egypt, establishing the First Dynasty.

c. 2300 BC
The kingdom of Kush sets up its capital at Kerma.

c. 1237 BC
Ramses the Great dies.

c. 730–700 BC
Kush conquers Egypt and establishes the 25th Dynasty.

c. AD 350
Aksum destroys Meroë.

3000 BC   **2000 BC**   **1000 BC**   **400 AD**

c. 3500 BC
The Sumerians create the world's first writing system.

c. 1200 BC
The Olmec form the first urban civilization in the Americas.

c. 1027 BC
The Chou Dynasty begins in China.

c. 500 BC
Buddhism begins to develop in India.

AD 330
Constantinople becomes the capital of the Roman Empire.

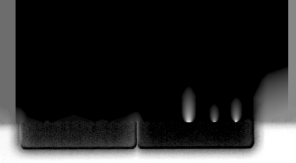

Focus on Themes As you read this chapter, you will learn about the ancient kingdoms of Egypt and Kush. You will see that the **geography** of the areas helped these kingdoms to develop. You will also learn how Egypt conquered and ruled Kush and then how Kush conquered and ruled Egypt. You will learn how the **economies** of these kingdoms, based on trade, grew strong. Finally you will learn about the importance of **religion** to the people of both of these ancient societies.

Causes and Effects in History

Focus on Reading Have you heard the saying, "We have to understand the past to avoid repeating it"? That is one reason we look for causes and effects in history.

Identifying Causes and Effects A **cause** is something that makes another thing happen. An **effect** is the result of something else that has happened. Most historical events have a number of causes as well as a number of effects. You can understand history better if you look for causes and effects of events.

1. *Because the Egyptians had captured and destroyed the city of Kerma, the kings of Kush ruled from the city of Napata.* (p. 109)

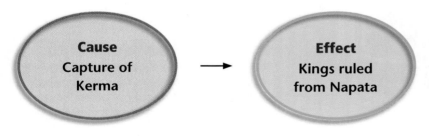

Sometimes writers use words that signal a cause or an effect. Here are some:
Cause—*reason, basis, because, motivated, as*
Effect—*therefore, as a result, for that reason, so*

2. *Piankhi fought the Egyptians because he believed that the gods wanted him to rule all of Egypt.* (p. 110)

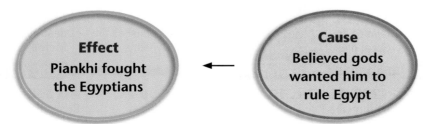

You Try It!

The following selections are from the chapter you are about to read. As you read each, identify which phrase or sentence describes a cause and which describes an effect.

Finding Causes and Effects

1. "During the mid-1000s BC the New Kingdom in Egypt was ending. As the power of Egypt's pharaohs declined, Kushite leaders regained control of Kush. Kush once again became independent." (p. 109)
2. "A series of inept pharaohs left Egypt open to attack." (p. 109)
3. "The Assyrians' iron weapons were better than the Kushites' bronze weapons. Although the Kushites were skilled archers, they could not stop the invaders (p. 111)
4. "Iron ore and wood for furnaces were easily available, so the iron industry grew quickly." (p. 111)

After you read the sentences, answer the following questions.

1. In selection 1, is "Kush once again became independent" the cause of the Egyptians growing weaker or the effect?

2. In selection 2, what left Egypt open to attack? Is that the cause of why Egypt was easily attacked or the effect?

3. In selection 3, who is using the iron weapons, the Assyrians or the Kushites? What was the effect of using the weapons?

4. In selection 4, does the word *so* signal a cause or an effect?

As you read Chapter 4, look for words that signal causes or effects. Make a chart to keep track of these causes and effects.

Key Terms and People

Geography and Ancient Egypt

What You Will Learn...

Main Ideas

1. Egypt was called the gift of the Nile because the Nile River gave life to the desert.
2. Civilization developed along the Nile after people began farming in this region.
3. Strong kings unified all of Egypt.

The Big Idea

The water, fertile soils, and protected setting of the Nile Valley allowed a great civilization to arise in Egypt around 3200 BC.

Key Terms and People

cataracts, *p. 87*
delta, *p. 87*
Menes, *p. 89*
pharaoh, *p. 89*
dynasty, *p. 89*

TAKING NOTES As you read, take notes on characteristics of the Nile River and the way it affected Egypt. Write your notes in a circle like this one.

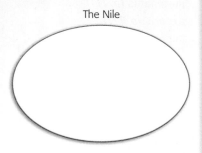

The Nile

If YOU were there...

Your family are farmers in the Nile Valley. Each year when the river's floodwaters spread rich soil on the land, you help your father plant barley. When you are not in the fields, you spin fine linen thread from flax you have grown. Sometimes you and your friends hunt birds in the tall grasses along the riverbanks.

Why do you like living in the Nile Valley?

BUILDING BACKGROUND Mesopotamia was not the only place where an advanced civilization grew up along a great river. The narrow valley of the Nile River in Egypt also provided fertile land that drew people to live there. The culture that developed in Egypt was more stable and long-lasting than those in Mesopotamia.

The Gift of the Nile

Geography played a key role in the development of Egyptian civilization. The Nile River brought life to Egypt. The river was so important to people in this region that the Greek historian Herodotus (hi-RAHD-du-tus) called Egypt the gift of the Nile.

Location and Physical Features

The Nile is the longest river in the world. It begins in central Africa and runs 4,000 miles north to the Mediterranean Sea. Egyptian civilization developed along a 750-mile stretch of the Nile in northern Africa.

Ancient Egypt included two regions, a southern region and a northern region. The southern region was called Upper Egypt. It was so named because it was located upriver in relation to the Nile's flow. Lower Egypt, the northern region, was located downriver. The Nile sliced through the desert of Upper Egypt. There, it created a fertile river valley about 13 miles wide. On either side of the Nile lay hundreds of miles of bleak desert.

As you can see on the map to the right, the Nile rushed through rocky, hilly land south of Egypt. At several points, this terrain caused **cataracts**, or strong rapids, to form. The first cataract, 720 miles south of the Mediterranean, marked the southern border of Upper Egypt. Five more cataracts lay farther south. These rapids made sailing that portion of the Nile very difficult.

In Lower Egypt, the Nile divided into several branches that fanned out and flowed into the Mediterranean Sea. These branches formed a **delta**, a triangle-shaped area of land made of soil deposited by a river. In ancient times, swamps and marshes covered much of the Nile Delta. Some two thirds of Egypt's fertile farmland was located in the Nile Delta.

The Floods of the Nile

Because it received so little rain, most of Egypt was desert. Each year, however, rainfall far to the south of Egypt in the highlands of east Africa caused the Nile to flood. The Nile floods were easier to predict than those of the Tigris and Euphrates rivers in Mesopotamia. Almost every year, the Nile flooded Upper Egypt in midsummer and Lower Egypt in the fall, coating the land around the river with a rich silt.

The silt from the Nile made the soil ideal for farming. The silt also made the land a dark color. That is why the Egyptians called their country the black land. They called the dry, lifeless desert beyond the river valley the red land.

Each year, Egyptians eagerly awaited the flooding of the Nile. For them the river's floods were a life-giving miracle. Without the floods, people never could have settled in Egypt.

READING CHECK **Summarizing** Why was Egypt called the gift of the Nile?

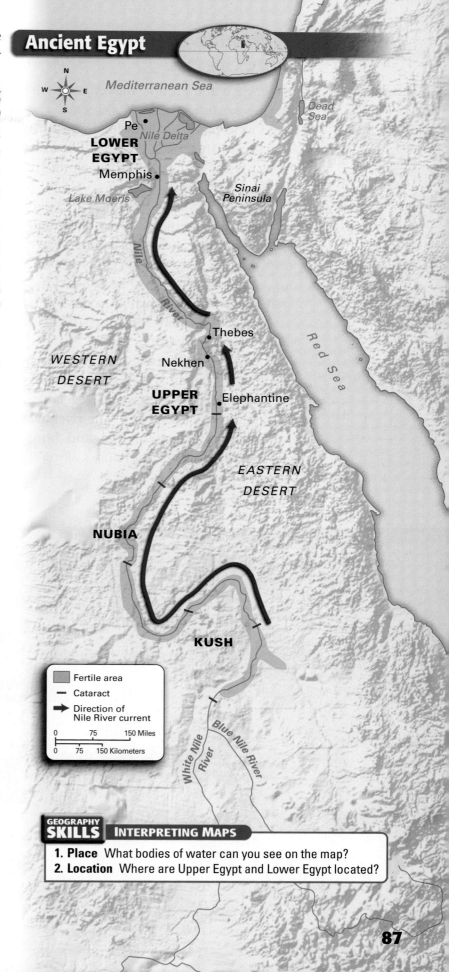

Ancient Egypt

GEOGRAPHY **SKILLS** | **INTERPRETING MAPS**

1. **Place** What bodies of water can you see on the map?
2. **Location** Where are Upper Egypt and Lower Egypt located?

Civilization Develops Along the Nile

Hunter-gatherer groups moved into the Nile Valley more than 12,000 years ago. They found plants, wild animals, and fish there to eat. In time these people learned how to farm, and they settled along the Nile in small villages.

As in Mesopotamia, farmers in Egypt developed an irrigation system. They built basins to collect water during the yearly floods and to store this precious resource long afterward. They also built a series of canals that could be used in the dry months to direct water from the basins to the fields where it was needed.

The Nile provided early Egyptian farmers with an abundance of food. The farmers grew wheat, barley, fruits, and vegetables, and raised cattle and sheep. The river also provided many types of fish, and hunters trapped wild geese and ducks along its banks. Like the Mesopotamians, Egyptians enjoyed a varied diet.

In addition to a stable food supply, the Nile Valley offered another valuable advantage. It had natural barriers that made Egypt hard to invade. The desert to the west was too big and harsh to cross. To the north, the Mediterranean Sea kept many enemies away. The Red Sea provided protection against invasion as well. Cataracts in the Nile made it difficult for outsiders to sail in from the south.

Protected from invaders, the villages of Egypt grew. Wealthy farmers emerged as village leaders, and strong leaders gained control over several villages. By 3200 BC, the villages had banded together and developed into two kingdoms. One was called Lower Egypt and the other was called Upper Egypt.

READING CHECK **Summarizing** What attracted early settlers to the Nile Valley?

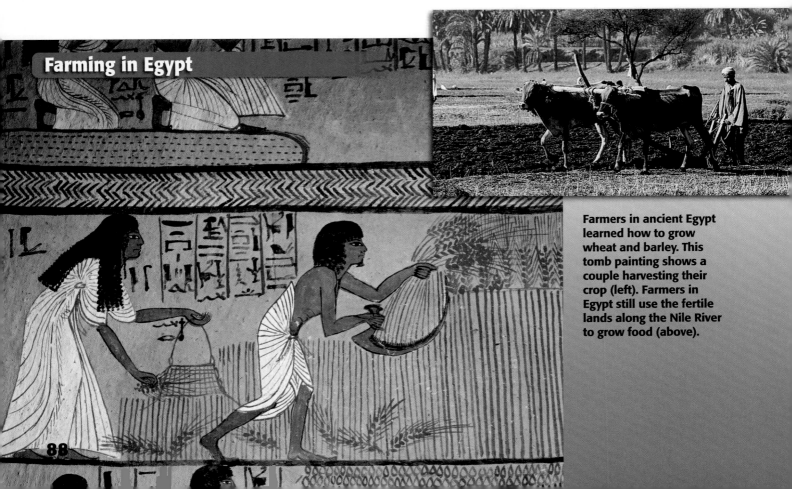

Farming in Egypt

Farmers in ancient Egypt learned how to grow wheat and barley. This tomb painting shows a couple harvesting their crop (left). Farmers in Egypt still use the fertile lands along the Nile River to grow food (above).

Kings Unify Egypt

The king of Lower Egypt ruled from a town called Pe. He wore a red crown to symbolize his authority. Nekhen was the capital city of Upper Egypt. In this kingdom, the king wore a cone-shaped white crown.

Around 3100 BC a leader named **Menes** (MEE-neez) rose to power in Upper Egypt. He sought to finish what an earlier king, called Scorpion, had started. He wanted to unify Upper and Lower Egypt.

The armies of Menes invaded and took control of Lower Egypt. Menes then united the two kingdoms. He married a princess from Lower Egypt to strengthen his control over the unified country. As Egypt's ruler, Menes wore both the white crown of Upper Egypt and the red crown of Lower Egypt. This symbolized his leadership over the two kingdoms. Later, he combined the two crowns into a double crown.

Historians consider Menes to be Egypt's first **pharaoh** (FEHR-oh), the title used by the rulers of Egypt. The title *pharaoh* means "great house." Menes also founded Egypt's first dynasty. A **dynasty** is a series of rulers from the same family.

Menes built a new capital city at the southern tip of the Nile Delta. The city was later named Memphis. For centuries, Memphis was the political and cultural center of Egypt. Many government offices were located there, and the city bustled with artistic activity.

The First Dynasty lasted for about 200 years. Pharaohs who came after Menes also wore the double crown to symbolize their rule over Upper and Lower Egypt. They extended Egyptian territory southward along the Nile and into southwest Asia. Eventually, however, rivals appeared to challenge the First Dynasty for power. These challengers took over Egypt and established the Second Dynasty.

READING CHECK Drawing Inferences
Why do you think Menes wanted to rule over both kingdoms of Egypt?

SUMMARY AND PREVIEW Civilization in ancient Egypt began in the fertile, protected Nile River Valley. People there formed two kingdoms that were later united under one ruler. In the next section, you will learn how Egypt grew and changed under later rulers in a period known as the Old Kingdom.

Section 1 Assessment

go.hrw.com
Online Quiz
KEYWORD: SN6 HP4

Reviewing Ideas, Terms, and People

1. **a. Recall** What were the two regions that made up ancient Egypt?
   b. Make Inferences Why was the Nile Delta well suited for settlement?
   c. Predict How might the Nile's **cataracts** have both helped and hurt Egypt?
2. **a. Describe** What foods did the Egyptians eat?
   b. Analyze What role did the Nile play in supplying Egyptians with these foods?
   c. Elaborate How did the desert on both sides of the Nile help ancient Egypt?
3. **a. Identify** Who was the first **pharaoh** of Egypt?
   b. Draw Conclusions Why did the pharaohs of the First Dynasty wear a double crown?

Critical Thinking

4. **Comparing and Contrasting** Use your notes on the Nile River to complete a Venn diagram like the one shown. List the differences and similarities between the Nile River in Egypt and the Tigris and Euphrates rivers in Mesopotamia.

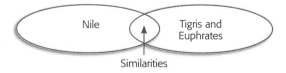

Nile — Similarities — Tigris and Euphrates

FOCUS ON WRITING

5. **Thinking about Geography and Early History** In this section, you read about Egypt's geography and early history. What could you put into your riddle about geography and historical events that would be a clue to the answer?

The Old Kingdom

What You Will Learn...

Main Ideas

1. In early Egyptian society, pharaohs ruled as gods and were at the top of the social structure.
2. Religion shaped Egyptian life.
3. The pyramids of Egypt were built as tombs for the pharaohs.

The Big Idea

Egyptian government and religion were closely connected during the Old Kingdom.

Key Terms and People

Old Kingdom, *p. 90*
Khufu, *p. 91*
nobles, *p. 91*
afterlife, *p. 92*
mummies, *p. 93*
elite, *p. 93*
pyramids, *p. 94*
engineering, *p. 94*

TAKING NOTES As you read, take notes on government and religion in the Old Kingdom. Use a chart like the one below to record your notes.

Government	Religion

If YOU were there...

You are a peasant farmer in ancient Egypt. To you, the pharaoh is a god, a descendent of the sun god, Re. You depend on his strength and wisdom. For part of the year, you are busy planting crops in your fields. But at other times, you work for the pharaoh. You are currently helping to build a great tomb in which the pharaoh and many of his belongings will be buried when he dies.

How do you feel about working for the pharaoh?

BUILDING BACKGROUND As in other ancient cultures, Egyptian society was based on a strict order of social classes. A small group of royalty, nobles, and priests ruled Egypt. They depended on the rest of the population to supply foods, crafts, and labor. Few people questioned this arrangement of society.

Early Egyptian Society

The First and Second Dynasties ruled Egypt for about four centuries. Around 2700 BC, the Third Dynasty rose to power. Its rule began the **Old Kingdom**, a period in Egyptian history that lasted from about 2700 BC to 2200 BC.

Rule by Pharaohs

During the Old Kingdom, the Egyptians continued to develop their political system. This system was based on the belief that the pharaoh was both a king and a god.

The ancient Egyptians believed that Egypt belonged to the gods. They believed that the pharaoh had come to earth to manage Egypt for the rest of the gods. As a result, he had absolute power over all the land and people in Egypt. But the pharaoh's status as a god came with many responsibilities. People blamed him if crops did not grow well or if disease struck. They also demanded that the pharaoh make trade profitable and prevent wars.

During the Old Kingdom, the duties of the pharaohs grew. To help carry out these duties, the pharaohs hired government officials. Most officials came from the pharaoh's family.

The most famous pharaoh of the Old Kingdom was **Khufu** (KOO-foo), who ruled in the 2500s BC. Egyptian legend says that he was cruel, but historical records tell us that the people who worked for him were well fed. Khufu is best known for the monuments that were built to him.

The Social Structure

By 2200 BC, Egypt had about 2 million people. At the top of Egyptian society was the pharaoh. Just below him were the upper classes, which included priests and key government officials. Many of these priests and officials were **nobles**, or people from rich and powerful families.

Below the nobles was a middle class of lesser government officials, scribes, craftspeople, and merchants. Egypt's lower class, about 80 percent of the population, was made up mostly of farmers. During flood season, when they could not work the fields, farmers worked on the pharaoh's building projects. Below farmers in the social order were slaves and servants.

Egypt and Its Neighbors

Although well-protected by its geography, Egypt was not isolated. Other cultures had influenced it for centuries. For example, Sumerian designs are found in Egyptian art. Egyptian pottery also reflects styles from Nubia, a region south of Egypt.

During the Old Kingdom, Egypt began trading with its neighbors. Traders returned from Nubia with gold, ivory, slaves, and stone. Traders traveled to Punt, an area on the Red Sea, to **acquire** incense and myrrh (MUHR). These two items were used to make perfume and medicine. Trade with Syria provided Egypt with wood.

ACADEMIC VOCABULARY
acquire (uh-KWYR) to get

READING CHECK **Generalizing** How was society structured in the Old Kingdom?

Egyptian Society

Pharaoh
The pharaoh ruled Egypt as a god.

Nobles
Officials and priests helped run the government and temples.

Scribes and Craftspeople
Scribes wrote and craftspeople produced goods.

Farmers, Servants, and Slaves
Most Egyptians were farmers. Below them were servants and slaves.

ANALYSIS SKILL **ANALYZING VISUALS**
Which group helped run the government and temples?

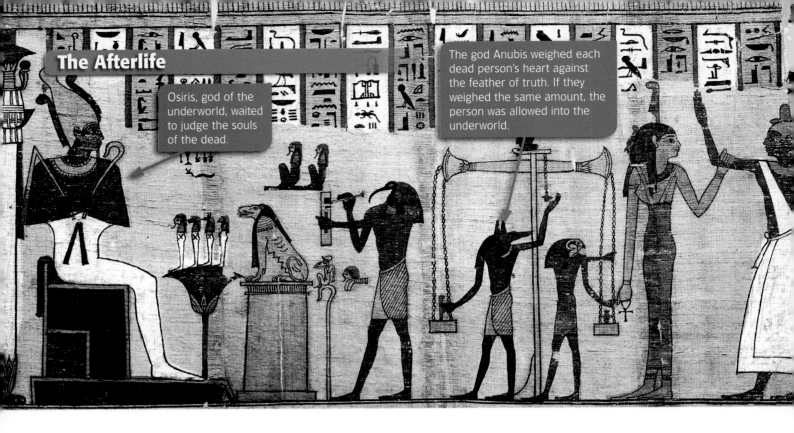

Osiris, god of the underworld, waited to judge the souls of the dead.

The god Anubis weighed each dead person's heart against the feather of truth. If they weighed the same amount, the person was allowed into the underworld.

Religion and Egyptian Life

The ancient Egyptians had strong religious beliefs. Worshipping the gods was a part of their everyday lives. Many Egyptian religious customs focused on what happened after people died.

The Gods of Egypt

Like Mesopotamians, Egyptians practiced polytheism. Before the First Dynasty, each village worshipped its own gods. During the Old Kingdom, however, Egyptian officials tried to give some sort of structure to religious beliefs. Everyone was expected to worship the same gods, though how they worshipped the gods might differ from one region of Egypt to another.

The Egyptians built temples to the gods all over the kingdom. The temples collected payments from both the government and worshippers. These payments allowed the temples to grow more influential.

Over time, certain cities became centers for the worship of certain gods. In Memphis, for example, people prayed to Ptah, the creator of the world.

The Egyptians had gods for nearly everything, including the sun, the sky, and the earth. Many gods mixed human and animal forms. For example, Anubis, the god of the dead, had a human body but a jackal's head. Other major gods included

- Re, or Amon-Re, the sun god
- Osiris, the god of the underworld
- Isis, the goddess of magic, and
- Horus, a sky god, god of the pharaohs

Emphasis on the Afterlife

Much of Egyptian religion focused on the **afterlife**, or life after death. The Egyptians believed that the afterlife was a happy place. Paintings from Egyptian tombs show the afterlife as an ideal world where all the people are young and healthy.

The Egyptian belief in the afterlife stemmed from their idea of *ka* (KAH), or a person's life force. When a person died, his or her *ka* left the body and became a spirit. The *ka*, however, remained linked to the

The body's organs were preserved in special jars and kept next to the mummy.

The body was preserved as a mummy and kept in a case called a sarcophagus.

ANALYSIS SKILL **ANALYZING VISUALS**

According to Egyptian beliefs, how did gods participate in the afterlife?

body and could not leave its burial site. The *ka* had all the same needs that the person had when he or she was living.

To fulfill the *ka's* needs, people filled tombs with objects for the afterlife. These objects included furniture, clothing, tools, jewelry, and weapons. Relatives of the dead were expected to bring food and beverages to their loved ones' tombs so the *ka* would not be hungry or thirsty.

Burial Practices

Egyptian ideas about the afterlife shaped their burial practices. Egyptians believed that a body had to be prepared for the afterlife before it could be buried. This meant the body had to be preserved. If the body decayed, its spirit could not recognize it. That would break the link between the body and spirit. The *ka* would then be unable to receive the food and drink it needed to have a good afterlife.

To keep the *ka* from suffering, the Egyptians developed a <u>method</u> called embalming. Embalming allowed bodies to be preserved for many, many years as **mummies**, specially treated bodies wrapped in cloth. A body that was not embalmed would decay quickly.

Embalming was a complex process that took several weeks. When finished, embalmers wrapped the body with linen cloths and bandages. The mummy was then placed in a coffin. Relatives often wrote magic spells inside the coffin to help the mummy receive food and drink.

Only royalty and other members of Egypt's **elite** (AY-leet), or people of wealth and power, could afford to have mummies made. Peasant families buried their dead in shallow graves at the edge of the desert. The hot dry sand and lack of moisture preserved the bodies naturally.

READING CHECK **Analyzing** How did religious beliefs affect Egyptian burial practices?

ACADEMIC VOCABULARY
method
a way of doing something

The Pyramids

FOCUS ON
READING

What group of words in this paragraph signals an effect?

Egyptians believed that burial sites, especially royal tombs, were very important. As a result, they built spectacular monuments in which to bury their rulers. The most spectacular of all were the **pyramids**, huge stone tombs with four triangle-shaped walls that met in a point on top.

The Egyptians began to build pyramids during the Old Kingdom. Some of the largest pyramids ever constructed were built during this time. Many of these huge structures are still standing. The largest is the Great Pyramid of Khufu near the town of Giza. It covers more than 13 acres at its base and stands 481 feet high. This single pyramid took more than 2 million limestone blocks to build. Historians are still not sure exactly how Egyptians built the pyramids. They are, however, amazing feats of **engineering**, the application of scientific knowledge for practical purposes.

Burial in a pyramid demonstrated a pharaoh's importance. The size was a symbol

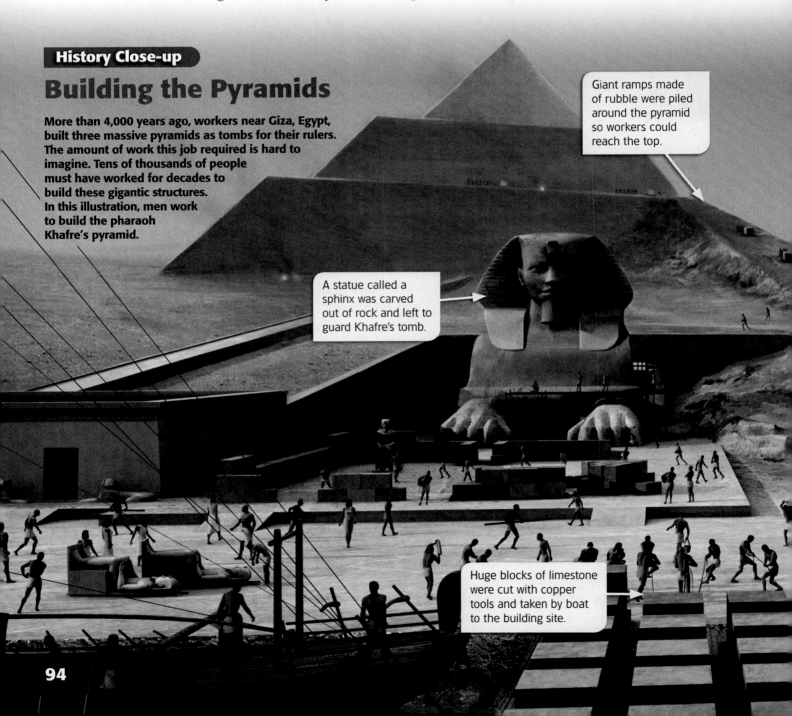

History Close-up

Building the Pyramids

More than 4,000 years ago, workers near Giza, Egypt, built three massive pyramids as tombs for their rulers. The amount of work this job required is hard to imagine. Tens of thousands of people must have worked for decades to build these gigantic structures. In this illustration, men work to build the pharaoh Khafre's pyramid.

Giant ramps made of rubble were piled around the pyramid so workers could reach the top.

A statue called a sphinx was carved out of rock and left to guard Khafre's tomb.

Huge blocks of limestone were cut with copper tools and taken by boat to the building site.

of the pharaoh's greatness. The pyramid's shape, pointing to the skies, symbolized the pharaoh's journey to the afterlife. The Egyptians wanted the pyramids to be spectacular because they believed that the pharaoh, as their link to the gods, controlled everyone's afterlife. Making the pharaoh's spirit happy was a way of ensuring a happy afterlife for every Egyptian.

READING CHECK **Identifying Points of View** Why were pyramids so important to the people of ancient Egypt?

SUMMARY AND PREVIEW During the Old Kingdom, new political and social orders were created in Egypt, and many of the pyramids were built. In Section 3, you will learn about life in later periods, the Middle and New Kingdoms.

Teams of workers dragged the stones on wooden sleds to the pyramid.

ANALYSIS SKILL **ANALYZING VISUALS**

How did workers get their stone blocks to the pyramids?

Section 2 Assessment

Reviewing Ideas, Terms, and People

1. **a. Recall** To what does the term **Old Kingdom** refer?
   b. Analyze Why was the pharaoh's authority never questioned?
   c. Elaborate How did trade benefit the Egyptians?
2. **a. Describe** What did Egyptians mean by the **afterlife**?
   b. Analyze Why was embalming important to the Egyptians?
3. **a. Identify** What is **engineering**?
   b. Elaborate What does the building of the **pyramids** tell us about Egyptian society?

Critical Thinking

4. **Generalizing** Using your notes, complete this graphic organizer with three statements about the relationship between government and religion in the Old Kingdom.

Government and Religion
1.
2.
3.

FOCUS ON WRITING

5. **Noting Characteristics of the Old Kingdom** The Old Kingdom developed special characteristics related to religion and social structure. Write down any of those characteristics you might want to include in your riddle.

ANCIENT EGYPT AND KUSH **95**

The Middle and New Kingdoms

If YOU were there...

You are an official serving Queen Hatshepsut of Egypt. You admire her, but some people think that a woman should not rule. She calls herself king, and she dresses like a pharaoh—even wearing a fake beard. That was your idea! You wish you could help more.

What could Hatshepsut do to show her authority?

BUILDING BACKGROUND The power of the pharaohs expanded during the Old Kingdom. Society was orderly, based on great differences between social classes. But rulers and dynasties changed, and Egypt changed with them. In time, these changes led to new eras in Egyptian history, eras called the Middle and New Kingdoms.

The Middle Kingdom

At the end of the Old Kingdom, the wealth and power of the pharaohs declined. Building and maintaining pyramids cost a lot of money. Pharaohs could not collect enough taxes to keep up with the expenses. At the same time, ambitious nobles used their government positions to take power from the pharaohs.

In time, nobles gained enough power to challenge the pharaohs. By about 2200 BC, the Old Kingdom had fallen. For the next 160 years, local nobles battled each other for power in Egypt. The kingdom had no central ruler. Chaos within Egypt disrupted trade with foreign lands and caused farming to decline. The people faced economic hardship and famine.

Finally, around 2050 BC, a powerful pharaoh named Mentuhotep II defeated his rivals. Once again all of Egypt was united. Mentuhotep's rule began the **Middle Kingdom**, a period of order and stability that lasted until about 1750 BC.

Toward the end of the Middle Kingdom, however, Egypt again experienced internal disorder. Its pharaohs could not hold the kingdom together. There were other problems in Egypt as well. In the mid-1700s BC, a group from Southwest Asia called the Hyksos (HIK-sohs) invaded. They used horses, chariots, and advanced weapons to conquer Lower Egypt, which they ruled for 200 years.

The Egyptians did not like being occupied by the Hyksos. The people of Egypt resented having to pay taxes to foreign rulers. Eventually, the Egyptians fought back. In the mid-1500s BC, Ahmose (AHM-ohs) of Thebes drove the Hyksos out of Egypt. Once the Hyksos were gone, Ahmose declared himself king of all Egypt.

READING CHECK **Summarizing** What problems caused the end of the Middle Kingdom?

The New Kingdom

Ahmose's rise to power marked the beginning of Egypt's 18th Dynasty. More importantly, it was the beginning of the **New Kingdom**, the period during which Egypt reached the height of its power and glory. During the New Kingdom, which lasted from about 1550 BC to 1050 BC, conquest and trade brought tremendous wealth to the pharaohs.

Building an Empire

After battling the Hyksos, Egyptian leaders feared future invasions. To prevent such invasions from occurring, they decided to take control of all possible invasion routes into the kingdom. In the process, these leaders turned Egypt into an empire.

Egypt's first target was the homeland of the Hyksos. After taking over that area, the army continued north and conquered Syria. As you can see from the map on the next page, Egypt had taken over the entire eastern shore of the Mediterranean. It had also defeated the kingdom of Kush, south of Egypt. By the 1400s BC, Egypt was the leading military power in the region. Its empire extended from the Euphrates River to southern Nubia.

Military conquests made Egypt rich. The kingdoms it conquered regularly sent treasures to their Egyptian conquerors. For example, the kingdom of Kush in Nubia sent annual payments of gold, leopard skins, and precious stones to the pharaohs. Assyrian, Babylonian, and Hittite kings also sent expensive gifts to Egypt in an effort to maintain good relations.

Growth and its Effects on Trade

Conquest also brought Egyptian traders into contact with more distant lands. Egypt's trade expanded along with its empire. Profitable **trade routes**, or paths followed by traders, developed. Many of the lands that Egypt took over also had valuable resources for trade. The Sinai Peninsula, for example, had large supplies of turquoise and copper.

BIOGRAPHY

Queen Hatshepsut
Ruled c. 1472–1458 BC

Hatshepsut was married to the pharaoh Thutmose II, her half-brother. He died young, leaving the throne to Thutmose III, his son by another woman. Since Thutmose III was still very young, Hatshepsut took over power. Many people did not think women should rule, but Hatshepsut dressed as a man and called herself king. After Hatshepsut died, her stepson took back power and destroyed all of the monuments Hatshepsut had built during her rule.

Analyze Why do you think some Egyptians objected to the idea of being ruled by a woman?

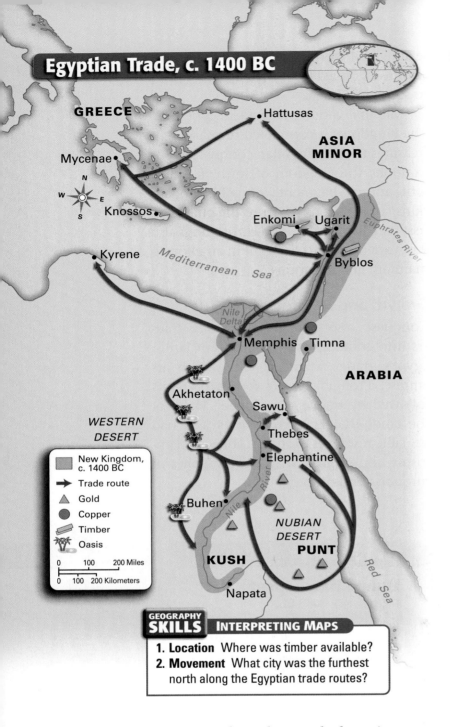

Egyptian Trade, c. 1400 BC

GREECE

Hattusas

ASIA MINOR

Mycenae

Knossos

Enkomi   Ugarit

Euphrates River

Kyrene

Mediterranean Sea

Byblos

Nile Delta

Memphis   Timna

ARABIA

Akhetaton

Sawu

WESTERN DESERT

Thebes

Elephantine

Legend:
- New Kingdom, c. 1400 BC
- → Trade route
- △ Gold
- ● Copper
- ▱ Timber
- 🌴 Oasis

0   100   200 Miles
0   100   200 Kilometers

Buhen

Nile River

NUBIAN DESERT

PUNT

KUSH

Red Sea

Napata

GEOGRAPHY SKILLS   INTERPRETING MAPS

1. **Location** Where was timber available?
2. **Movement** What city was the furthest north along the Egyptian trade routes?

impressive monuments and temples built during her reign. The best known of these structures was a magnificent temple built for her near the city of Thebes (THEEBZ).

Invasions of Egypt

Despite its great successes, Egypt's military might did not go unchallenged. In the 1200s BC the pharaoh Ramses (RAM-seez) II, or **Ramses the Great**, came to power. Ramses, whose reign was one of the longest in Egyptian history, fought the Hittites, a group from Asia Minor. The two powers fought fiercely for years, but neither could defeat the other. Ramses and the Hittite leader eventually signed a peace treaty. Afterwards, the Egyptians and the Hittites became allies.

Egypt faced threats in other parts of its empire as well. To the west, a people known as the Tehenu invaded the Nile Delta. Ramses fought them off and built a series of forts to strengthen the western frontier. This proved to be a wise decision because the Tehenu invaded again a century later. Faced with Egypt's strengthened defenses, however, the Tehenu were defeated once more.

Soon after Ramses the Great died, invaders called the Sea Peoples sailed into southwest Asia. Little is known about these people. Historians are not even sure who they were. All we know is that they were strong warriors who had crushed the Hittites and destroyed cities in southwest Asia. Only after 50 years of fighting were the Egyptians able to turn them back.

Egypt survived, but its empire in Asia was gone. Shortly after the invasions of the Hittites and the Sea Peoples, the New Kingdom came to an end. Egypt once again fell into a period of violence and disorder. Egypt would never again regain its power.

READING CHECK   Identifying Cause and Effect What caused the growth of trade in the New Kingdom?

One ruler who worked to increase Egyptian trade was **Queen Hatshepsut**. She sent Egyptian traders south to trade with the kingdom of Punt on the Red Sea and north to trade with the people of Asia Minor and Greece.

Hatshepsut and later pharaohs used the wealth that they earned from trade to support the arts and architecture. Hatshepsut especially is remembered for the many

Work and Daily Life

Although Egyptian dynasties rose and fell, daily life for Egyptians did not change very much. But as the population grew, society became more complex. A complex society requires people to take on different jobs.

Scribes

Other than priests and government officials, no one in Egypt was more honored than scribes. They worked for the government and for temples. Scribes kept records and accounts for the state. They also wrote and copied religious and literary texts. Scribes did not pay taxes, and many became wealthy.

Artisans, Artists, and Architects

Below scribes on the social scale were artisans whose jobs required advanced skills. Among the artisans who worked in Egypt were sculptors, builders, carpenters, jewelers, metal workers, and leather workers. Most of Egypt's artisans worked for the government or for temples. They made statues, furniture, jewelry, pottery, footwear, and other items.

Architects and artists were also admired in Egypt. Architects designed the temples and royal tombs for which Egypt is famous. Talented architects could rise to become high government officials. Artists, often employed by the state or the temples, produced many different works. Artists often worked in the pharaohs' tombs painting detailed pictures.

Soldiers

After the Middle Kingdom, Egypt created a professional army. The military offered a chance to rise in status. Soldiers received land as payment and could keep treasure they captured in war. Those who excelled could be promoted to officer positions.

Daily Life in Egypt

Servants worked for Egypt's rulers and nobles and did many jobs, like preparing food.

Most Egyptians spent their days in the fields, plowing or otherwise working their crops.

This jar probably held perfume, a valuable trade item.

ANALYSIS SKILL ANALYZING VISUALS

How did most Egyptians spend their days?

Farmers and Other Peasants

Egypt's farmers and other peasants were toward the bottom of the social scale. They made up the vast majority of Egypt's population. Peasant farmers used wooden hoes or cow-drawn plows to prepare the land before the Nile flooded. After the floodwaters had drained away, they planted seeds. Farmers worked together to gather the harvest.

Farmers had to give crops to the pharaoh as taxes. All peasants, including farmers, were subject to special duty. The pharaoh could demand at any time that people work on projects such as building pyramids, mining gold, or fighting in wars.

ACADEMIC VOCABULARY

contracts
binding legal agreements

Slaves

The few slaves in Egypt were considered lower than farmers. They worked on farms, on building projects, and in households. Slaves had some legal rights and in some cases could earn their freedom.

Family Life in Egypt

Most Egyptian families lived in their own homes. Men were expected to marry young so that they could start having children. Most Egyptian women were devoted to their homes and their families. Some, however, had jobs outside the home. A few served as priestesses, and some worked as administrators and artisans. Unlike most women in the ancient world, Egyptian women had certain legal rights. These included the right to own property, make **contracts**, and divorce their husbands.

Children played with toys, took part in ballgames, and hunted. Most boys and girls received an education. At school they learned morals, writing, math, and sports. At age 14, most boys left school to enter their father's profession.

READING CHECK **Categorizing** What types of jobs did people perform in ancient Egypt?

SUMMARY AND PREVIEW Egypt's power and wealth peaked during the New Kingdom. As society became more complex, people in different classes worked at different jobs. Next, you will learn about Egyptian achievements.

Section 3 Assessment

go.hrw.com
Online Quiz
KEYWORD: SN6 HP4

Reviewing Ideas, Terms, and People

1. **a. Recall** What was the **Middle Kingdom**?
   b. Analyze How did Ahmose manage to become king of all Egypt?
2. **a. Identify** Which group of invaders did **Ramses the Great** defeat?
   b. Describe What did **Queen Hatshepsut** do as pharaoh of Egypt?
   c. Predict What do you think is a more reliable source of wealth—trade or payments from conquered kingdoms? Why?
3. **a. Identify** What job employed the most people in ancient Egypt?
   b. Analyze What rights did Egyptian women have?
   c. Evaluate Why do you think scribes were so honored in Egyptian society?

Critical Thinking

4. **Categorizing** Using your notes, fill in the pyramids below with information about political and military factors that led to the rise and fall of the Middle and New Kingdoms.

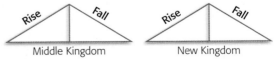

Rise Fall Rise Fall
Middle Kingdom   New Kingdom

FOCUS ON WRITING

5. **Developing Key Ideas from the Middle and New Kingdoms** Your riddle should contain some information about the later pharaohs and daily life in Egypt. Decide which key ideas you should include in your riddle and add them to your list.

Ramses the Great

How Could a Ruler Achieve Fame That Would Last 3,000 Years?

When did he live? the late 1300s and early 1200s BC

Where did he live? As pharaoh, Ramses lived in a city he built on the Nile Delta. The city's name, Pi-Ramesse, means the "house of Ramses."

What did he do? From a young age, Ramses was trained as a ruler and a fighter. Made an army captain at age 10, he began military campaigns even before he became pharaoh. During his reign, Ramses greatly increased the size of his kingdom.

Why is he so important? Many people consider Ramses the last great Egyptian pharaoh. He accomplished great things, but the pharaohs who followed could not maintain them. Both a great warrior and a great builder, he is known largely for the massive monuments he built. The temples at Karnak, Luxor, and Abu Simbel stand as 3,000-year-old symbols of the great pharaoh's power.

Drawing Conclusions Why do you think Ramses built great monuments all over Egypt?

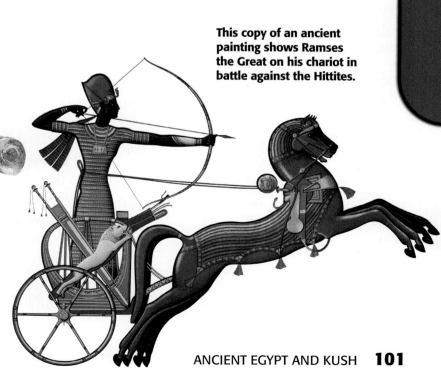

KEY IDEAS

Ramses had a poem praising him carved into the walls of five temples, including Karnak. One verse of the poem praises Ramses as a great warrior and the defender of Egypt.

Gracious lord and bravest king, savior–guard
Of Egypt in the battle, be our ward;
Behold we stand alone, in the hostile Hittite ring,
Save for us the breath of life,
Give deliverance from the strife,
Oh! protect us Ramses Miamun!
Oh! save us, mighty king!

—Pen-ta-ur, from *The Victory of Ramses over the Khita*, in *The World's Story*, edited by Eva March Tappan

This copy of an ancient painting shows Ramses the Great on his chariot in battle against the Hittites.

Egyptian Achievements

Main Ideas

1. The Egyptians developed a writing system using hieroglyphics.
2. The Egyptians created magnificent temples, tombs, and works of art.

The Big Idea

The Egyptians made lasting achievements in writing, architecture, and art.

Key Terms and People

hieroglyphics, *p. 102*
papyrus, *p. 102*
Rosetta Stone, *p. 103*
sphinxes, *p. 104*
obelisk, *p. 104*
King Tutankhamen, *p. 106*

TAKING NOTES As you read, take notes on the many achievements of the ancient Egyptians. In each column of this chart, identify Egyptian advances in the appropriate field.

Writing	Achitecture	Art

If YOU were there...

You are an artist in ancient Egypt. A noble has hired you to decorate the walls of his family tomb. You are standing inside the new tomb, studying the bare walls that you will decorate. No light reaches this chamber, but your servant holds a lantern high. You've met the noble only briefly but think that he is someone who loves his family, the gods, and Egypt.

What will you include in your painting?

BUILDING BACKGROUND The Egyptians had a rich and varied history, but most people today remember them for their cultural achievements, such as their unique writing system. In addition, Egyptian art, including the tomb paintings mentioned above, is admired by millions of tourists in museums around the world.

Egyptian Writing

If you were reading a book and saw pictures of folded cloth, a leg, a star, a bird, and a man holding a stick, would you know what it meant? You would if you were an ancient Egyptian. In the Egyptian writing system, or **hieroglyphics** (hy-ruh-GLIH-fiks), those five symbols together meant "to teach." Egyptian hieroglyphics were one of the world's first writing systems.

Writing in Ancient Egypt

The earliest known examples of Egyptian writing are from around 3300 BC. These early Egyptian writings were carved in stone or on other hard material. Later, the Egyptians learned how to make **papyrus** (puh-PY-ruhs), a long-lasting, paper-like material made from reeds. The Egyptians made papyrus by pressing layers of reeds together and pounding them into sheets. These sheets were tough and durable, yet easy to roll into scrolls. Scribes wrote on papyrus using brushes and ink.

Egyptian Writing

Egyptian hieroglyphics used picture symbols to represent sounds.

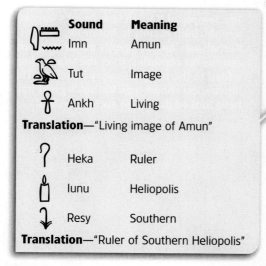

	Sound	Meaning
	Imn	Amun
	Tut	Image
	Ankh	Living

Translation—"Living image of Amun"

	Sound	Meaning
	Heka	Ruler
	Iunu	Heliopolis
	Resy	Southern

Translation—"Ruler of Southern Heliopolis"

ANALYSIS SKILL | **ANALYZING VISUALS**

What does the symbol for ruler look like?

The hieroglyphic writing system used more than 600 symbols, mostly pictures of objects. Each symbol represented one or more sounds in the Egyptian language. For example, a picture of an owl represented the same sound as our letter *M*.

Hieroglyphics could be written either horizontally or vertically. They could be written from right to left or from left to right. These options made hieroglyphics flexible to write but difficult to read. The only way to tell which way a text is written is to look at individual symbols.

The Rosetta Stone

Historians and archaeologists have known about hieroglyphics for centuries, but for a long time they didn't know how to read them. In fact, it was not until 1799 when a lucky discovery by a French soldier gave historians the key they needed to read ancient Egyptian writing.

That key was the **Rosetta Stone**, a stone slab inscribed with hieroglyphics. In addition to hieroglyphics, the Rosetta Stone had text in Greek and a later form of Egyptian. Because the text in all three languages was the same, scholars who knew Greek figured out what the hieroglyphics said.

Egyptian Texts

Because papyrus did not decay in Egypt's dry climate, many Egyptian texts survive. Historians today can read Egyptian government and historical records, science texts, and medical manuals. Literary works have also survived. We can read stories, poems, and mythological tales. Some texts, such as *The Book of the Dead,* tell about the afterlife. Others include love poems and stories about gods and kings.

READING CHECK **Comparing** How is our writing system similar to hieroglyphics?

THE IMPACT TODAY

An object that helps solve a difficult mystery is sometimes called a Rosetta Stone.

Temples, Tombs, and Art

The Egyptians are famous for their architecture and art. The walls of Egypt's magnificent temples and tombs are covered with impressive paintings and carvings.

Egypt's Great Temples

You have already read about the Egyptians' most famous structures, the pyramids. But the Egyptians also built massive temples. Those that survive are among the most spectacular sites in Egypt today.

The Egyptians believed that temples were the homes of the gods. People visited the temples to worship, offer the gods gifts, and ask for favors.

Many Egyptian temples shared similar features. Rows of stone **sphinxes**—imaginary creatures with the bodies of lions and the heads of other animals or humans—lined the path leading to the entrance. The entrance itself was a huge, thick gate. On either side of the gate might stand an **obelisk** (AH-buh-lisk), a tall, four-sided pillar that is pointed on top.

Inside, temples were lavishly decorated, as you can see in the drawing of the Temple of Karnak. Huge columns supported the temple's roof. In many cases, these columns were covered with paintings and hieroglyphics, as were the temple walls. Statues of gods and pharaohs often stood along the walls as well. The sanctuary, the most sacred part of the building, was at the far end of the temple.

The Temple of Karnak is only one of Egypt's great temples. Others were built by Ramses the Great at Abu Simbel and Luxor. Part of what makes the temple at Abu Simbel so impressive is that it is carved out of sandstone cliffs. At the temple's entrance, four 66-foot-tall statues show Ramses as pharaoh. Nearby are some smaller statues of his family.

THE IMPACT TODAY

The Washington Monument, in Washington, DC, was built in the shape of an obelisk.

The Temple of Karnak

The Temple of Karnak was Egypt's largest temple. Built mainly to honor Re, the sun god, Karnak was one of Egypt's major religious centers for centuries. Over the years, pharaohs added to the temple's many buildings. This illustration shows how Karnak's great hall may have looked during an ancient festival.

Karnak's interior columns and walls were painted brilliant colors.

ANALYSIS SKILL ANALYZING VISUALS

What features of Egyptian architecture can you see in this illustration?

Massive columns, some more than 80 feet high, supported the temple's high roof.

High windows let light and air into the temple.

In the annual Opet festival, priests carried statues of the gods and sacred boats from the temple to the Nile River.

Only the pharaoh and priests were allowed inside the temple, which was considered the home of the gods.

Egyptian Art

The ancient Egyptians were masterful artists. Egyptians painted lively, colorful scenes on canvas, papyrus, pottery, plaster, and wood. Detailed works also covered the walls of temples and tombs. The temple art was created to honor the gods, while the tomb art was intended for the enjoyment of the dead in the afterlife.

The subjects of Egyptian paintings vary widely. Some paintings show important historical events, such as the crowning of kings and the founding of temples. Others illustrate major religious rituals. Still other paintings show scenes from everyday life, such as farming or hunting.

Egyptian painting has a distinctive style. People's heads and legs are always seen from the side, but their upper bodies and shoulders are shown straight on. In addition, people do not always appear the same size. Important figures such as pharaohs appear huge in comparison to others. In contrast, Egyptian animals were usually drawn realistically.

Painting was not the only art form in which Egyptians excelled. For example, the Egyptians were skilled stoneworkers. Many tombs included huge statues and detailed carvings on the walls.

The Egyptians also made beautiful objects out of gold and precious stones. They made jewelry for both women and men. This included necklaces, collars, and bracelets. The Egyptians also used gold to make burial items for their pharaohs.

Over the years, treasure hunters emptied many pharaohs' tombs. At least one tomb, however, was not disturbed. In 1922 archaeologists found the tomb of **King Tutankhamen** (too-tang-KAHM-uhn), or King Tut. This tomb was filled with treasures, including jewelry, robes, a burial mask, and ivory statues. King Tut's treasures have taught us much about Egyptian burial practices and beliefs.

READING CHECK **Summarizing** What types of artwork were contained in Egyptian tombs?

SUMMARY AND PREVIEW Ancient Egyptians developed one of the best known cultures in the ancient world. Next, you will learn about a culture that developed in the shadow of Egypt—Kush.

Section 4 Assessment

go.hrw.com
Online Quiz
KEYWORD: SN6 HP4

Reviewing Ideas, Terms, and People

1. **a. Identify** What are **hieroglyphics**?
   b. Contrast How was hieroglyphic writing different from our writing today? from cuneiform used by the Mesopotamians?
   c. Evaluate Why was finding the **Rosetta Stone** so important to scholars?
2. **a. Describe** What were two ways the Egyptians decorated their temples?
   b. Analyze Why were tombs filled with art, jewelry, and other treasures?
   c. Draw Conclusions Why do you think pharaohs like Ramses the Great built huge temples?

Critical Thinking

3. **Summarizing** Draw a chart like the one below. Under each heading, write a statement that summarizes Egyptian achievements in that field.

Writing	Architecture	Art

FOCUS ON WRITING

4. **Adding Up What You Know about Egypt** Look at the notes you have taken at the end of each section. Think about what clues you might include when you write your riddle about Egypt.

Ancient Kush

If **YOU** were there...

You live along the Nile River, where it moves quickly through swift rapids. A few years ago, armies from the powerful kingdom of Egypt took over your country. Some Egyptians have moved here. They bring new customs, and many people are imitating them. Now your sister has a new baby and wants to give it an Egyptian name! This upsets many people in your family.

How do you feel about following Egyptian customs?

BUILDING BACKGROUND Egypt dominated the lands along the Nile, but it was not the only ancient culture to develop along the river. Another kingdom called Kush arose to the south of Egypt. Through trade, conquest, and political dealings, the histories of Egypt and Kush became closely tied together.

The Geography of Early Nubia

South of Egypt, a group of people settled in the region we now call Nubia. These Africans established the first great kingdom in the interior of Africa. We know this kingdom by the name the Egyptians gave it—Kush. The development of Kushite society was greatly influenced by the geography of Nubia, especially the role played by the Nile River.

The ruins of ancient Kushite pyramids stand behind those reconstructed to look the way they did when originally built.

What You Will Learn...

Main Ideas

1. The geography of early Nubia helped civilization develop there.
2. Kush and Egypt traded, but they also fought.
3. Later Kush became a trading power with a unique culture.
4. Both internal and external factors led to the decline of Kush.

The Big Idea

The kingdom of Kush, which arose south of Egypt in a land called Nubia, developed an advanced civilization with a large trading network.

Key Terms and People

Piankhi, *p. 110*
trade network, *p. 111*
merchants, *p. 111*
exports, *p. 111*
imports, *p. 111*
Queen Shanakhdakheto, *p. 113*
King Ezana, *p. 113*

TAKING NOTES As you read, look for information on the rise and fall of Kush. Take notes about your findings in a diagram like the one shown.

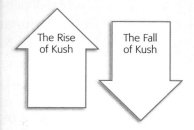

The Rise of Kush   The Fall of Kush

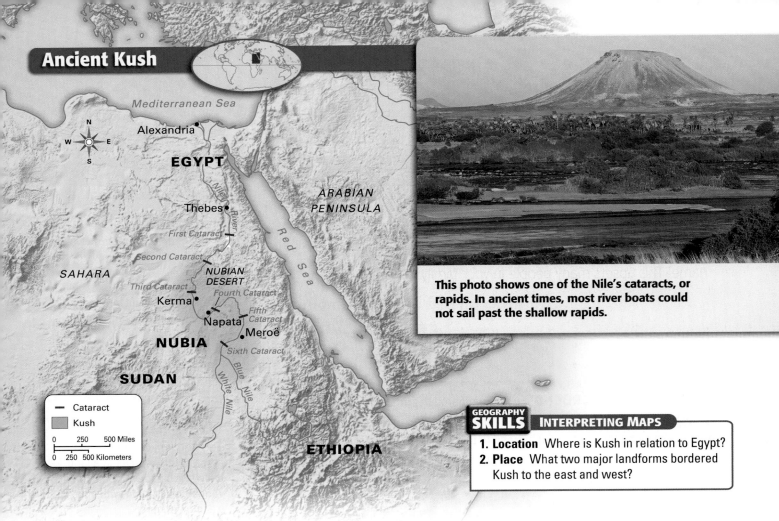

Ancient Kush

Mediterranean Sea

Alexandria

EGYPT

Thebes

First Cataract

Second Cataract

SAHARA

Third Cataract

NUBIAN DESERT

Kerma

Fourth Cataract

Napata

Fifth Cataract

Meroë

NUBIA

Sixth Cataract

SUDAN

White Nile

Blue Nile

ETHIOPIA

ARABIAN PENINSULA

Red Sea

Nile River

N
W E
S

- Cataract
▭ Kush

0   250   500 Miles

0   250 500 Kilometers

This photo shows one of the Nile's cataracts, or rapids. In ancient times, most river boats could not sail past the shallow rapids.

GEOGRAPHY SKILLS INTERPRETING MAPS

1. **Location** Where is Kush in relation to Egypt?
2. **Place** What two major landforms bordered Kush to the east and west?

The Land of Nubia

Today desert covers much of Nubia, but in ancient times the region was more fertile than it is now. Rain flooded the Nile every year, providing a rich layer of silt to nearby lands. The kingdom of Kush developed in this fertile area.

Ancient Nubia was rich in minerals such as gold, copper, and stone. These resources played a major role in the area's history and contributed to its wealth.

Early Civilization in Nubia

Like all early civilizations, the people of Nubia depended on agriculture for their food. Fortunately for them, the Nile's floods allowed the Nubians to plant both summer and winter crops. Among the crops they grew were wheat, barley, and other grains.

Besides farmland, the banks of the Nile also provided grazing land for livestock. As a result, farming villages thrived all along the Nile by 3500 BC.

Over time some farmers grew richer than others. These farmers became village leaders. Sometime around 2000 BC, one of these leaders took control of other villages and made himself king of the region. His new kingdom was called Kush.

The kings of Kush ruled from their capital at Kerma (KAR-muh). This city was located on the Nile just south of the third cataract. Because the Nile's cataracts made parts of the river hard to pass through, they were natural barriers against invaders. For many years the cataracts kept Kush safe from the more powerful Egyptian kingdom to the north.

As time passed, Kushite society grew more complex. Besides farmers and herders, some Kushites became priests and artisans. Early Kush was influenced by cultures to the south. Later, Egypt played a greater role in Kush's history.

READING CHECK Finding Main Ideas How did geography help civilization grow in Nubia?

Kush and Egypt

Kush and Egypt were neighbors. Sometimes the neighbors lived in peace with each other and helped each other prosper. For example, Kush became a major supplier of both slaves and raw materials to Egypt. The Kushites sent materials such as gold, copper, and stone to Egypt. The Kushites also sent the Egyptians ebony, a type of dark, heavy wood, and ivory, the hard white material that makes up elephant tusks.

Egypt's Conquest of Kush

Relations between Kush and Egypt were not always peaceful, however. As Kush grew wealthy from trade, its army grew stronger as well. Egypt's rulers soon feared that Kush would grow even more powerful and attack Egypt.

To prevent such an attack from occurring, the pharaoh Thutmose I sent an army to take control of Kush around 1500 BC. The pharaoh's army conquered all of Nubia north of the Fifth Cataract. As a result, Kush became part of Egypt.

After his army's victory, the pharaoh destroyed Kerma, the Kushite capital. Later pharaohs—including Ramses the Great—built huge temples in what had been Kushite territory.

Effects of the Conquest

Kush remained an Egyptian territory for about 450 years. During that time, Egypt's influence over Kush grew tremendously. Many Egyptians settled in Kush. Egyptian became the language of the region. Many Kushites used Egyptian names and wore Egyptian-style clothing. They also adopted Egyptian religious practices.

A Change in Power

During the mid-1000s BC the New Kingdom in Egypt was ending. As the power of Egypt's pharaohs declined, Kushite leaders regained control of Kush. Kush once again became independent.

We know almost nothing about the history of the Kushites from the time they gained independence until 200 years later. Kush is not mentioned in any historical records that describe those centuries.

The Conquest of Egypt

By around 850 BC Kush had regained its strength. It was once again as strong as it had been before it had been conquered by Egypt. Because the Egyptians had captured and destroyed the city of Kerma, the kings of Kush ruled from the city of Napata. Built by the Egyptians, Napata was on the Nile, about 100 miles southeast of Kerma.

As Kush grew stronger, Egypt was further weakened. A series of inept pharaohs

BIOGRAPHY

Piankhi (PYAN-kee)
c. 751–716 BC

Also known as Piye, Piankhi was among Kush's most successful military leaders. A fierce warrior on the battlefield, the king was also deeply religious. Piankhi's belief that he had the support of the gods fueled his passion for war against Egypt. His courage inspired his troops on the battlefield. Piankhi loved his horses and was buried with eight of his best steeds.

Drawing Conclusions How did Piankhi's belief that he was supported by the gods affect his plans for Egypt?

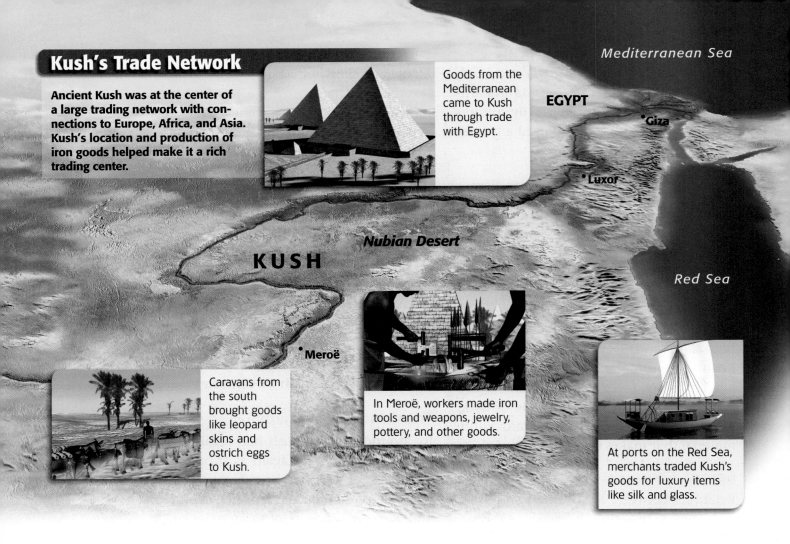

Kush's Trade Network

Ancient Kush was at the center of a large trading network with connections to Europe, Africa, and Asia. Kush's location and production of iron goods helped make it a rich trading center.

Mediterranean Sea

EGYPT

• Giza

• Luxor

Nubian Desert

KUSH

• Meroë

Red Sea

Goods from the Mediterranean came to Kush through trade with Egypt.

Caravans from the south brought goods like leopard skins and ostrich eggs to Kush.

In Meroë, workers made iron tools and weapons, jewelry, pottery, and other goods.

At ports on the Red Sea, merchants traded Kush's goods for luxury items like silk and glass.

left Egypt open to attack. In the 700s BC a Kushite king, Kashta, seized on Egypt's weakness and attacked it. By about 751 BC he had conquered Upper Egypt. He then established relations with Lower Egypt.

After Kashta died, his son **Piankhi** (PYAN-kee) continued to attack Egypt. The armies of Kush captured many cities, including Egypt's ancient capital. Piankhi fought the Egyptians because he believed that the gods wanted him to rule all of Egypt. By the time he died in about 716 BC, Piankhi had accomplished this task. His kingdom extended north from Napata to the Nile Delta.

The Kushite Dynasty

After Piankhi died, his brother Shabaka (SHAB-uh-kuh) took control of the kingdom.

Shabaka then declared himself pharaoh. This declaration began the 25th Dynasty, or Kushite Dynasty, in Egypt.

Shabaka and later rulers of his dynasty believed that they were heirs of the great pharaohs of Egypt's past. They tried to restore old Egyptian cultural practices and renew faded traditions. Some of these practices and traditions had been abandoned during Egypt's period of weakness. For example, Shabaka was buried in a pyramid. The Egyptians had stopped building pyramids for their rulers centuries before.

The Kushite rulers of Egypt built new temples to Egyptian gods and restored old temples. They also worked to preserve Egyptian writings. As a result, Egyptian culture thrived during the 25th Dynasty.

The End of Kushite Rule in Egypt

The Kushite Dynasty remained strong in Egypt for about 40 years. In the 670s BC, however, the powerful army of the Assyrians from Mesopotamia invaded Egypt. The Assyrians' iron weapons were better than the Kushites' bronze weapons. Although the Kushites were skilled archers, they could not stop the invaders. The Kushites were steadily pushed southward. In just 10 years the Assyrians had driven the Kushite forces completely out of Egypt.

READING CHECK **Analyzing** How did internal problems in Egypt benefit Kush?

Later Kush

After they lost control of Egypt, the people of Kush devoted themselves to agriculture and trade, hoping to make their country rich again. Within a few centuries, the kingdom of Kush had indeed become prosperous and powerful once more.

Kush's Iron Industry

The economic center of Kush during this period was at Meroë (MER-oh-wee), the kingdom's new capital. Meroë's location on the east bank of the Nile helped Kush's economy to grow. Large deposits of gold could be found nearby, as could forests of ebony and other wood. More importantly, the area around Meroë was full of rich iron ore deposits.

In this location, the Kushites developed Africa's first iron industry. Iron ore and wood for furnaces were easily available, so the iron industry grew quickly.

The Expansion of Trade

In time, Meroë became the center of a large **trade network**, a system of people in different lands who trade goods. The Kushites sent goods down the Nile to Egypt. From there, Egyptian and Greek **merchants**, or traders, carried goods to ports on the Mediterranean and Red seas and to southern Africa. These goods may have eventually reached India, and perhaps China.

Kush's **exports**—items sent out to other regions—included gold, pottery, iron tools, slaves, and ivory. Kushite merchants also exported leopard skins, ostrich feathers, and elephants. In return, the Kushites received **imports**—goods brought in from other regions—such as fine jewelry and luxury items from Egypt, Asia, and other lands along the Mediterranean Sea.

Kushite Culture

As Kushite trade grew, merchants came into contact with people from other cultures. As a result, the people of Kush combined customs from other cultures with their own unique Kushite culture.

The most obvious influence on Kushite culture was Egypt. Many buildings in Meroë, especially temples, resembled those in Egypt. Many people in Kush worshipped Egyptian gods and wore Egyptian clothing. Kushite rulers used the title *pharaoh* and were buried in pyramids.

Many elements of Kushite culture were not borrowed. Kushite houses and daily life were unique. One Greek geographer noted some Kushite differences.

> "The houses in the cities are formed by interweaving split pieces of palm wood or of bricks. ...They hunt elephants, lions, and panthers. There are also serpents ...and there are many other kinds of wild animals."
> –Strabo, *The Geographies*

In addition to Egyptian gods, the people of Kush worshipped their own gods. They also developed their own written language, Meroitic. Unfortunately, historians are not yet able to understand Meroitic.

THE IMPACT TODAY
More than 50 ancient Kushite pyramids still stand near the ruins of Meroë.

Rulers of Kush

Like the Egyptians, the people of Kush considered their rulers to be gods. Kush's culture was similar to Egypt's, but there were also important differences.

Like the Egyptians, Kush's rulers built pyramids, but they were much smaller and the style was different.

Kush was ruled by a few different powerful queens. Queens seem to have been more important in Kush than in Egypt.

Stone carvings were made to commemorate important buildings and events, just like in Egypt. Kush's writing system was similar to Egyptian hieroglyphics, but scholars have been unable to understand most of it.

ANALYSIS SKILL **ANALYZING VISUALS**

What can you see in the illustration that is similar to Egyptian culture?

Women in Kushite Society

The women of Kush were expected to be active in their society. They worked in the fields, raised children, cooked, and performed other household tasks.

Some Kushite women rose to positions of **authority**. Some served as co-rulers with their husbands or sons. A few women ruled the empire alone. Historians believe that the first woman to rule Kush was **Queen Shanakhdakheto** (shah-nakh-dah-KEE-toh). She ruled from 170 BC to 150 BC.

READING CHECK **Contrasting** How was Kushite culture unlike Egyptian culture?

The Decline of Kush

Kush gradually declined in power. A series of problems within the kingdom weakened its economy. One problem was that Kush's cattle were allowed to overgraze. When cows ate all the grass, wind blew the soil away, causing farmers to produce less food.

In addition, ironmakers used up the forests near Meroë. As wood became scarce, furnaces shut down. Kush produced fewer weapons and trade goods.

Kush was also weakened by a loss of trade. Foreign merchants set up new trade routes that went around Kush. One such trade route bypassed Kush in favor of Aksum (AHK-soom), a kingdom located along the Red Sea in what is today Ethiopia and Eritrea. In the first two centuries AD, Aksum grew wealthy from trade.

By the AD 300s Kush had lost much of its wealth and military might. The king of Aksum took advantage of his former trade rival's weakness. In about AD 350 the Aksumite army of **King Ezana** (AY-zah-nah) destroyed Meroë and took over Kush.

In the late 300s, the rulers of Aksum became Christian. About two hundred years later, the Nubians also converted. The last influences of Kush had disappeared.

READING CHECK **Summarizing** What factors led to the decline of Kush?

SUMMARY AND PREVIEW From their capital at Meroë, the people of Kush controlled a powerful trading network. Next, you will learn about a land that may have traded with Kush—India.

ACADEMIC VOCABULARY

authority power or influence

THE IMPACT TODAY

Much of the population of Ethiopia, which includes what used to be Aksum, is still Christian today.

Section 5 Assessment

go.hrw.com
Online Quiz
KEYWORD: SN6 HP4

Reviewing Ideas, Terms, and People

1. **a. Recall** On which river did Kush develop?
   b. Evaluate How did Nubia's natural resources influence the early history of Kush?
2. **a. Identify** Who was **Piankhi** and why was he important to the history of Kush?
   b. Analyze What were some elements of Egyptian culture that became popular in Kush?
   c. Draw Conclusions Why is the 25th Dynasty significant in the history of both Egypt and Kush?
3. **a. Describe** What advantages did the location of Meroë offer to the Kushites?
   b. Compare How were Kushite and Egyptian cultures similar?
4. **a. Identify** Who conquered Kush in the AD 300s?

b. Evaluate What was the impact of new trading routes on Kush?

Critical Thinking

5. **Identifying Cause and Effect** Create a chart like this one. Using your notes, list an effect for each cause.

Cause	Effect
Thutmose I invades Kush.	
Power of Egyptian pharaohs declines.	
Piankhi attacks Egypt.	

FOCUS ON WRITING

6. **Taking Notes on Kush** Review this section and take notes on those people, places, and events that would make good clues for your riddle about Kush.

Assessing Primary and Secondary Sources

Understand the Skill

Primary sources in history are materials created by people who lived during the times they describe. Examples include letters, diaries, and photographs. *Secondary sources* are accounts written later by someone who was not present. They are designed to teach about or discuss a historical topic. This textbook is an example of a secondary source.

Together, primary and secondary sources can present a good picture of a historical period or event. However, they must be used carefully to make sure that the picture they present is accurate.

Learn the Skill

Here are some questions to ask to help you judge the accuracy of primary and secondary sources.

1 **What is it?** Is it a firsthand account or is it based on information provided by others? In other words, is it primary or secondary?

2 **Who wrote it?** For a primary source, what was the author's connection to what he or she was writing about? For a secondary source, what makes the author an authority on this subject?

3 **Who is the audience?** Was the information meant for the public? Was it meant for a friend or for the writer alone? The intended audience can influence what the writer has to say.

4 **What is the purpose?** Authors of either primary or secondary sources can have reasons to exaggerate—or even lie—to suit their own goals or purposes. Look for evidence of emotion, opinion, or bias in the source. These might influence the accuracy of the account.

5 **Does other evidence support the source?** Look for other information that supports the source's account. Compare different sources whenever possible.

Practice and Apply the Skill

Below are two passages about the military in ancient Egypt. Read them both and use the guidelines to answer the questions that follow.

> "The pharaohs began …leading large armies out of a land that had once known only small police forces and militia. The Egyptians quickly extended their military and commercial influence over an extensive region that included the rich provinces of Syria …and the numbers of Egyptian slaves grew swiftly."
>
> –C. Warren Hollister, from *Roots of the Western Tradition*

> "Let me tell you how the soldier fares …how he goes to Syria, and how he marches over the mountains. His bread and water are borne [carried] upon his shoulders like the load of [a donkey]; they make his neck bent as that of [a donkey], and the joints of his back are bowed [bent]. His drink is stinking water …When he reaches the enemy, he is trapped like a bird, and he has no strength in his limbs."
>
> –from *Wings of the Falcon: Life and Thought of Ancient Egypt*, translated by Joseph Kaster

1. Which quote is a primary source, and which is a secondary source?

2. Is there evidence of opinion, emotion, or bias in the second quote? Explain why or why not.

3. Which information is more likely to be accurate on this subject? Explain your answer.

Chapter Review

Visual Summary

Use the visual summary below to help you review the main ideas of the chapter.

QUICK FACTS

Egypt
Egyptian civilization developed along the Nile River. There, powerful pharaohs ruled a diverse society whose achievements included building impressive pyramids and developing a writing system.

Kush
Kush developed farther south along the Nile. Ruled by their own kings and queens, the Kushites had extensive interaction with the Egyptians and blended Egyptian influences into their own advanced culture.

Reviewing Vocabulary, Terms, and People

For each group of terms below, circle the letter of the term that does not relate to the others. Then write a sentence that explains how the other two terms are related.

1. **a.** cataract
   b. delta
   c. dynasty
2. **a.** afterlife
   b. mummies
   c. engineering
3. **a.** hieroglyphics
   b. Rosetta Stone
   c. obelisk
4. **a.** exports
   b. imports
   c. papyrus

Comprehension and Critical Thinking

SECTION 1 *(pages 86–89)*

5. **a. Describe** Besides crops, what foods did the Nile provide?

   b. Analyze Why did Menes wear a double crown?

   c. Predict What do you think happened in the years when the Nile River did not flood?

SECTION 2 *(pages 90–95)*

6. **a. Identify** In what type of structure were pharaohs buried?

   b. Analyze How were beliefs in the afterlife linked to items placed in tombs?

   c. Elaborate Why did nobles and commoners alike obey the pharaoh?

SECTION 3 *(pages 96–100)*

7 **a. Describe** What factors contributed to Egypt's wealth during the New Kingdom?

b. Analyze How might a young Egyptian rise in social status?

c. Elaborate What caused the New Kingdom to fall?

SECTION 4 *(pages 102–106)*

8. a. Identify What is a sphinx?

b. Describe What was the name of the Egyptian system of writing and how does it differ from our system of writing?

c. Elaborate Why is the temple at Karnak so famous?

SECTION 5 *(pages 107–113)*

9. a. Describe Where did Kushite civilization develop?

b. Draw Conclusions Why did Egypt want to gain control of Kush?

c. Evaluate Why was the 25th Dynasty so important for both Kush and Egypt?

Reviewing Themes

10. Geography Do you think that societies like those in Egypt and Kush could have grown up anywhere besides the Nile River Valley? Why or why not?

11. Religion How did religious beliefs shape both Egyptian and Kushite culture?

12. Economics What led to the creation of Africa's first iron industry in Kush?

Using the Internet

go.hrw.com
KEYWORD: SN6 WH4

13. Activity: Creating Art The Egyptians developed an incredibly artistic civilization. Their architecture included innovative pyramids and temples. Artisans created beautiful paintings, carvings, and jewelry. Enter the activity keyword and research the main features of Egyptian art and architecture. Then imagine you are an Egyptian artisan. Create a piece of art to place inside a pharaoh's tomb. Include hieroglyphics telling the pharaoh about your art.

Reading Skills

Causes and Effects in History Read the following passage and answer the questions.

> Much of Egyptian religion is focused on the afterlife. The Egyptians believed that the afterlife was a happy place. Their belief in the afterlife stemmed from their idea of *ka*, or a person's life force. When a person died, his or her *ka* left the body and became a spirit. The *ka*, however, remained linked to the body and could not leave its burial site. The *ka* had all the same needs that the person had when he or she was living. To fulfill the *ka's* needs, people filled tombs with objects for the afterlife.

14. What is the cause of the Egyptian custom of putting objects in tombs?

15. According to the passage, what is an effect of the Egyptian belief in *ka*?

Social Studies Skills

16. Assessing Primary and Secondary Sources Write three questions you would want to ask about a primary source and three questions you would want to ask about a secondary source that deals with the history of Egypt and Kush.

FOCUS ON WRITING

17. Writing Riddles You have all the information you need for your riddles, but you may have to narrow your list of questions. Choose five details about Egypt and five details about Kush. Then, write a sentence about each detail. Each sentence of your riddle should be a statement ending with "me." For example, if you were writing about the United States, you might say, "In the north, Canada borders me." After writing five sentences for each riddle, end each riddle with "Who am I?"

Standardized Test Practice

DIRECTIONS: Read each question and write the letter of the best response.

1

> Oh great god and ruler, the gift of Re,
>   God of the Sun.
> Oh great protector of Egypt and its people.
> Great one who has saved us from the horrible
>   Tehenu.
> You, who have turned back the Hittites.
> You, who have fortified our western border to
>   forever protect us from our enemies.
> We bless you, oh great one.
> We worship and honor you, oh great pharaoh.

A tribute such as the one above would have been written in honor of which Egyptian ruler?

A Khufu

B Ramses the Great

C King Tutankhamen

D Queen Hatshepsut

2 The Nile helped civilization develop in Egypt and Nubia in all of the following ways *except* by

A providing a source of food and water.

B allowing farming to develop.

C enriching the soil along its banks.

D protecting against invasion from the west.

3 The most fertile soil in Egypt was located in the

A Nile Delta.

B desert.

C cataracts.

D far south.

4 Which of the following statements about the relationship of Egypt and Kush is *NOT* true?

A Egypt ruled Kush for many centuries.

B Kush was an important trading partner of Egypt.

C Egypt sent the first people to colonize Kush.

D Kush ruled Egypt for a period of time.

5 How did Egypt influence Kush?

A Egypt taught Kush how to raise cattle.

B Egypt helped Kush develop its irrigation system.

C Egypt taught Kush to make iron products.

D Kush learned about pyramids from Egypt.

Connecting with Past Learnings

6 In this chapter, you learned about hieroglyphics, one of the world's first writing systems. In Chapter 3, you read about another ancient writing system called

A Sumerian.

B Hammurabi.

C ziggurat.

D cuneiform.

7 In Chapter 3 you read about Sargon I, who first united Mesopotamia under one ruler. Which Egyptian ruler's accomplishments were most similar to Sargon's?

A King Ezana's

B Khufu's

C Menes's

D Hatshepsut's

Civilization in India and China

Two of the earliest civilizations of the ancient world arose in India and in China. In both of these places, river valleys provided the setting for the development of civilization. The Indians and Chinese built large empires and made many advances in science, art, and learning.

These civilizations also gave rise to new spiritual traditions. Two of the world's major religions—Hinduism and Buddhism—began in India. In China, the scholars Confucius and Laozi developed ideas that influenced Chinese thinking and society for more than 2,000 years.

In the next two chapters, you will learn about the advanced civilizations and cultures of India and China.

Explore the Art

In this scene, the Chinese emperor Shi Huangdi oversees the building of a massive wall in 220 BC. Why do you think people might build such a giant barrier?

CHAPTER 5   2300 BC–AD 500

Ancient India

FOCUS ON WRITING

An Illustrated Poster Ancient India was a fascinating place. It was the home of amazing cities, the site of strong empires, and the birthplace of major religions. As you read this chapter, think about how you could illustrate one aspect of Indian culture in a poster. When you finish the chapter, you will design such a poster, which will include captions that explain the illustrations you have drawn.

c. 2300 BC
The Harappan civilization develops.

CHAPTER EVENTS
2300 BC

WORLD EVENTS
2200 BC
The Old Kingdom ends in Egypt.

What You Will Learn...

In this chapter you will learn about the ancient civilization of India, the birthplace of two major world religions—Hinduism and Buddhism. In this photo, crowds of Hindus gather to bathe in the sacred Ganges River.

1500s BC
Aryans begin migrating into India.

c. 1250 BC
Hinduism begins to develop in India.

c. 563 BC
Prince Siddhartha Gautama, or the Buddha, is born in northern India.

c. AD 320
Candra Gupta I founds the Gupta Empire.

1500 BC	1000 BC	500 BC	BC 1 AD	AD 500

c. 1500 BC
The Shang dynasty is established in China.

334 BC
Alexander the Great begins his conquests.

AD 391 All non-Christian religions are banned in the Roman Empire.

ANCIENT INDIA **121**

Reading Social Studies

| Economics | Geography | Politics | Religion | Society and Culture | Science and Technology |

Focus on Themes This chapter outlines and describes the development of India. You will read about India's first civilization, the Harappan civilization, so advanced that the people had indoor bathrooms and their own writing system. You will also learn about the **society and culture** that restricted who Indian people could talk with or marry. Finally, you will read about the **religions** and empires that united India and about the art and literature that Indians created.

Inferences about History

Focus on Reading What's the difference between a good guess and a weak guess? A good guess is an educated guess. In other words, the guess is based on some knowledge or information. That's what an **inference** is, an educated guess.

Making Inferences About What You Read Making inferences is similar to drawing conclusions. You use almost the same process to make an inference: combine information from your reading—what's "inside the text"—with what you already know—what's "outside the text"—and make an educated guess about what it all means. Once you have made several inferences, you may be able to draw a conclusion that ties them all together.

Steps for Making Inferences
1. Ask a question.
2. Note information "inside the Text."
3. Note information "outside the Text."
4. Use both sets of information to make an educated guess, or inference.

Question: Why did Aryan priests have rules for performing sacrifices?	
Inside the Text	**Outside the Text**
Sacred texts tell how to perform sacrifices.	Other religions have duties only priests can perform.
Priests sacrificed animals in fire.	Many ancient societies believed sacrifices helped keep the gods happy.
Sacrifices were offered to the gods.	

Inference: The Aryans believed that performing a sacrifice incorrectly might anger the gods.

You Try It!

The following passage is from the chapter you are about to read. Read the passage and then answer the questions that follow.

Harappan Achievements

Harappan civilization was very advanced. Most houses had bathrooms with indoor plumbing. Artisans made excellent pottery, jewelry, ivory objects, and cotton clothing. They used high-quality tools and developed a system of weights and measures.

From Chapter 5, p. 128

Harappans also developed India's first writing system. However, scholars have not yet learned to read this language, so we know very little about Harappan society. Historians think that the Harappans had kings and strong central governments, but they aren't sure. As in Egypt, the people may have worshipped the king as a god.

Harappan civilization ended by the early 1700s BC, but no one is sure why.

Answer the following questions to make inferences about Harappan society.

1. Do you think the Harappan language was closely related to the languages spoken in India today? Consider the information inside the text and things you have learned outside the text to make an inference about the Harappan language.

4. What have you just learned about Harappan achievements? Think back to other civilizations you have studied that made similar achievements. What allowed those civilizations to make their achievements? From this, what can you infer about earlier Harappan society?

As you read **Chapter 5,** use the information you find in the text to make inferences about Indian society.

Key Terms and People

Chapter 5

Section 1
subcontinent (p. 124)
monsoons (p. 125)
Sanskrit (p. 129)

Section 2
caste system (p. 131)
Hinduism (p. 133)
reincarnation (p. 133)
karma (p. 134)
Jainism (p. 135)
nonviolence (p. 135)

Section 3
fasting (p. 137)
meditation (p.137)
the Buddha (p. 137)
Buddhism (p. 138)
nirvana (p. 138)
missionaries (p.140)

Section 4
Candragupta Maurya (p. 142)
Asoka (p. 143)
Candra Gupta II (p. 144)

Section 5
metallurgy (p. 150)
alloys (p. 150)
Hindu-Arabic numerals (p. 150)
inoculation (p. 150)
astronomy (p. 151)

Academic Vocabulary

Success in school is related to knowing academic vocabulary—the words that are frequently used in school assignments and discussions. In this chapter, you will learn the following academic words:

establish (p. 144)
process (p.150)

Geography and Early India

If YOU were there...

Your people are nomadic herders in southern Asia about 1200 BC. You live in a river valley with plenty of water and grass for your cattle. Besides looking after cattle, you spend time learning songs and myths from the village elders. They say these words hold your people's history. One day, it will be your duty to teach them to your own children.

Why is it important to pass on these words?

BUILDING BACKGROUND Like Mesopotamia and Egypt, India was home to one of the world's first civilizations. Like other early civilizations, the one in India grew up in a river valley. But the society that eventually developed in India was very different from the ones that developed elsewhere.

Geography of India

Look at a map of Asia in the atlas of this book. Do you see the large, roughly triangular landmass that juts out from the center of the southern part of the continent? That is India. It was the location of one of the world's earliest civilizations.

Landforms and Rivers

India is huge. In fact, it is so big that many geographers call it a subcontinent. A **subcontinent** is a large landmass that is smaller than a continent. Subcontinents are usually separated from the rest of their continents by physical features. If you look at the map on the next page, for example, you can see that mountains largely separate India from the rest of Asia.

Among the mountains of northern India are the Himalayas, the highest mountains in the world. To the west are the Hindu Kush. Though these mountains made it hard to enter India, invaders have historically found a few paths through them.

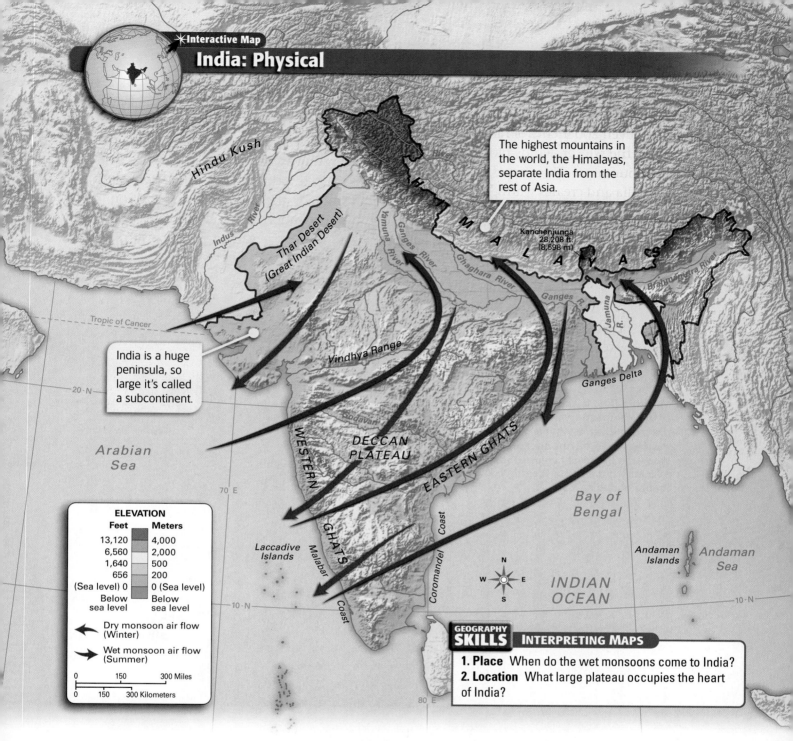

The highest mountains in the world, the Himalayas, separate India from the rest of Asia.

Hindu Kush

Indus River

Thar Desert (Great Indian Desert)

HIMALAYAS

Yamuna River

Ganges River

Ghaghara River

Kanchenjunga 28,208 ft. (8,598 m)

Ganges R.

Jamuna R.

Brahmaputra River

India is a huge peninsula, so large it's called a subcontinent.

Tropic of Cancer

Vindhya Range

Ganges Delta

Godavari

DECCAN PLATEAU

WESTERN GHATS

EASTERN GHATS

Arabian Sea

20°N

70°E

Malabar Coast

Laccadive Islands

Coromandel Coast

Bay of Bengal

Andaman Islands

Andaman Sea

INDIAN OCEAN

N
W   E
S

10°N

10°N

80°E

ELEVATION

Feet	Meters
13,120	4,000
6,560	2,000
1,640	500
656	200
(Sea level) 0	0 (Sea level)
Below sea level	Below sea level

← Dry monsoon air flow (Winter)

→ Wet monsoon air flow (Summer)

0   150   300 Miles
0   150   300 Kilometers

GEOGRAPHY SKILLS INTERPRETING MAPS

1. **Place** When do the wet monsoons come to India?
2. **Location** What large plateau occupies the heart of India?

To the west of the Himalayas is a vast desert. Much of the rest of India is covered by fertile plains and rugged plateaus.

Several major rivers flow out of the Himalayas. The valley of one of them, the Indus, was the location of India's first civilization. The Indus is located in present-day Pakistan, west of India. When heavy snows in the Himalayas melted, the Indus flooded. As in Mesopotamia and Egypt, the flooding left behind a layer of fertile silt. The silt created ideal farmland for early settlers.

Climate

Most of India has a hot and humid climate. This climate is heavily influenced by India's **monsoons**, seasonal wind patterns that cause wet and dry seasons.

In the summer, monsoon winds blow into India from the Indian Ocean, bringing heavy rains that can cause terrible floods. Some parts of India receive as much as 100 or even 200 inches of rain during this time. In the winter, winds blow down from the mountains. This forces moisture out of India and creates warm, dry winters.

READING CHECK **Drawing Conclusions**
How do you think monsoons affected settlement in India?

Harappan Civilization

Historians call the civilization that grew up in the Indus River Valley the Harappan (huh-RA-puhn) civilization. Centered along the Indus, the civilization also controlled large areas on both sides of the river.

Like other ancient societies you have studied, the Harappan civilization grew as irrigation and agriculture improved. As farmers began to produce surpluses of food, towns and cities appeared in India.

History Close-up

Life in Mohenjo Daro

Mohenjo Daro was one of the two major cities of the Harappan civilization. Located next to the Indus River in what is now Pakistan, the city probably covered one square mile. The people who lived in the city enjoyed some of the most advanced comforts of their time, including indoor plumbing.

Harappan merchants used a standard set of weights to measure goods such as precious stones.

India's First Cities

The Harappan civilization was named after the modern city of Harappa (huh-RA-puh), Pakistan. It was near this city that ruins of the civilization were first discovered. From studying these ruins, archaeologists think that the civilization thrived between 2300 and 1700 BC.

The greatest sources of information we have about Harappan civilization are the ruins of two large cities, Harappa and Mohenjo Daro (mo-HEN-joh DAR-oh). The two cities lay on the Indus more than 300 miles apart but were remarkably similar.

Both Harappa and Mohenjo Daro were well planned. Each stood near a towering fortress. From these fortresses, defenders could look down on the cities' brick streets, which crossed at right angles and were lined with storehouses, workshops, market stalls, and houses. In addition, both cities had many public wells.

Next to the city was a huge citadel, or fortress, to guard against invasions.

The houses of Mohenjo Daro had flat roofs. Many had staircases that allowed people to climb to the roof from the street.

The city's streets were paved and well drained. They met at right angles, creating a grid pattern.

Harappan Civilization

HIMALAYAS

Harappa

Mohenjo Daro

Thar Desert

Arabian Sea

Harappan civilization

• Settlement

0 100 200 Miles

0 100 200 Kilometers

ANALYSIS SKILL **ANALYZING VISUALS**

What in this picture suggests that Mohenjo Daro was a well-planned city?

Harappan Achievements

Harappan civilization was very advanced. Most houses had bathrooms with indoor plumbing. Artisans made excellent pottery, jewelry, ivory objects, and cotton clothing. They used high-quality tools and developed a system of weights and measures.

Harappans also developed India's first writing system. However, scholars have not yet learned to read this language, so we know very little about Harappan society. Historians think that the Harappans had kings and strong central governments, but they aren't sure. As in Egypt, the people may have worshipped the king as a god.

Harappan civilization ended by the early 1700s BC, but no one is sure why. Perhaps invaders destroyed the cities or natural disasters, like floods or earthquakes, caused the civilization to collapse.

READING CHECK **Analyzing** Why don't we know much about Harappan civilization?

Harappan Art

Like other ancient peoples, the Harappans made small seals like the one below that were used to stamp goods. They also used clay pots like the one at right decorated with a goat.

Aryan Invasion

Not long after the Harappan civilization crumbled, a new group took power in the Indus Valley. They were called the Aryans (AIR-ee-uhnz), invaders from Central Asia. Some people think they may have helped end the Harappan civilization.

Invaders from the West

The Aryans were skilled warriors. Using chariots and advanced weapons, these invaders took new territory. By 1200 BC Aryan warriors had swept through the Hindu Kush and taken control of the entire Indus Valley. From there they moved east to the Ganges River Valley.

Much of what we know about Aryan society comes from religious writings known as the Vedas (VAY-duhs). These are collections of poems, hymns, myths, and rituals that were written by Aryan priests. Though they are mostly religious, some of the Vedas describe Aryan victories during their invasion of India. You will read more about the Vedas later in this chapter.

Government and Society

As nomads, the Aryans took along their herds of animals as they moved. But over time, they settled in villages and began to farm. Unlike the Harappans, they did not build big cities.

The Aryan political system was also different from the Harappan system. The Aryans lived in small communities, based mostly on family ties. No single ruling authority existed. Instead, each group had its own leader, often a skilled warrior.

Aryan villages were governed by rajas (RAH-juhz). A raja was a leader who ruled a village and the land around it. Villagers farmed some of this land for the raja. They used other sections as pastures for their cows, horses, sheep, and goats.

Although many rajas were related, they didn't always get along. Sometimes rajas joined forces before fighting a common enemy. Other times, however, rajas went to war against each other. In fact, Aryan groups fought each other nearly as often as they fought outsiders.

Language

The first Aryan settlers did not read or write. Because of this, they had to memorize the poems and hymns that were important in their culture, such as the Vedas. If people forgot these poems and hymns, the works would be lost forever.

The language in which these Aryan poems and hymns were composed was **Sanskrit**, the most important language of ancient India. At first, Sanskrit was only a spoken language. Eventually, however, people figured out how to write it down so they could keep records. These Sanskrit records are a major source of information about Aryan society. Sanskrit is no longer spoken today, but it is the root of many modern South Asian languages.

READING CHECK **Identifying** What source provides much of the information we have about the Aryans?

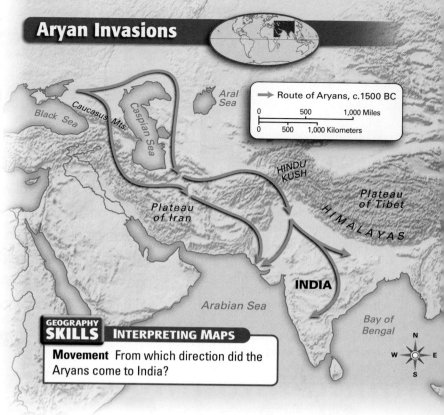

Aryan Invasions

Route of Aryans, c.1500 BC

0   500   1,000 Miles
0 500 1,000 Kilometers

Black Sea
Caucasus Mts.
Caspian Sea
Aral Sea
HINDU KUSH
Plateau of Iran
Plateau of Tibet
HIMALAYAS
INDIA
Arabian Sea
Bay of Bengal

GEOGRAPHY SKILLS **INTERPRETING MAPS**
Movement From which direction did the Aryans come to India?

SUMMARY AND PREVIEW The earliest civilizations in India were centered in the Indus Valley. First the Harappans and then the Aryans lived in this fertile valley. In the next section, you will learn about a new religion that developed in the Indus Valley after the Aryans settled there—Hinduism.

THE IMPACT TODAY
Hindi, the most widely spoken Indian language, is based on Sanskrit.

Section 1 Assessment

go.hrw.com
Online Quiz
KEYWORD: SN6 HP5

Reviewing Ideas, Terms, and People

1. **a. Define** What are **monsoons**?
   b. Contrast How does northern India differ from the rest of the region?
   c. Elaborate Why is India called a **subcontinent**?
2. **a. Recall** Where did Harappan civilization develop?
   b. Analyze What is one reason that scholars do not completely understand some important parts of Harappan society?
3. **a. Identify** Who were the Aryans?
   b. Contrast How was Aryan society different from Harappan society?

Critical Thinking

4. **Drawing Conclusions** Using your notes, draw conclusions about the effect of geography on Indian society. Record your conclusions in a diagram like this one.

Geography of India → Harappan society
Geography of India → Aryan society

FOCUS ON WRITING

5. **Illustrating Geography and Early Civilizations** This section described two possible topics for your poster: geography and early civilizations. Which of them is more interesting to you? Write down some ideas for a poster about your chosen topic.

Origins of Hinduism

Main Ideas

1. Indian society divided into distinct groups under the Aryans.
2. The Aryans practiced a religion known as Brahmanism.
3. Hinduism developed out of Brahmanism and influences from other cultures.
4. The Jains reacted to Hinduism by breaking away to form their own religion.

The Big Idea

Hinduism, the largest religion in India today, developed out of ancient Indian beliefs and practices.

Key Terms

caste system, *p. 131*
Hinduism, *p. 133*
reincarnation, *p. 133*
karma, *p. 134*
Jainism, *p. 135*
nonviolence, *p. 135*

TAKING NOTES As you read this section, take notes on Hinduism using a diagram like the one below. Pay attention to the religion's origins, its teachings, and other religions that developed alongside it.

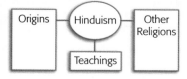

If YOU were there...

Your family are skillful weavers who make beautiful cotton cloth. You belong to the class in Aryan society who are traders, farmers, and craftspeople. Often the raja of your town leads the warriors into battle. You admire their bravery but know you can never be one of them. To be an Aryan warrior, you must be born into that noble class. Instead, you have your own duty to carry out.

How do you feel about remaining a weaver?

BUILDING BACKGROUND As the Aryans moved into India, they developed a strict system of social classes. As the Aryans' influence spread through India, so did their class system. Before long, this class system was a key part of Indian society.

Indian Society Divides

As Aryan society became more complex, their society became divided into groups. For the most part, these groups were organized by people's occupations. Strict rules developed about how people of different groups could interact. As time passed, these rules became stricter and became central to Indian society.

The *Varnas*

According to the Vedas, there were four main *varnas*, or social divisions, in Aryan society. These *varnas* were:

- Brahmins (BRAH-muhns), or priests,
- Kshatriyas (KSHA-tree-uhs), or rulers and warriors,
- Vaisyas (VYSH-yuhs), or farmers, craftspeople, and traders, and
- Sudras (SOO-drahs), or laborers and non-Aryans.

The Brahmins were seen as the highest ranking because they performed rituals for the gods. This gave the Brahmins great influence over the other *varnas*.

The Caste System

As the rules of interaction between *varnas* got stricter, the Aryan social order became more complex. In time, each of the four *varnas* in Aryan society was further divided into many castes, or groups. This **caste system** divided Indian society into groups based on a person's birth, wealth, or occupation. At one time, some 3,000 separate castes existed in India.

The caste to which a person belonged determined his or her place in society. However, this ordering was by no means permanent. Over time, individual castes gained or lost favor in society as caste members gained wealth or power. On rare occasions, people could change caste.

Caste Rules

To keep their classes distinct, the Aryans developed sutras, or guides, which listed all the rules for the caste system. For example, people were not allowed to marry anyone from a different class. It was even forbidden for people from one class to eat with people from another. People who broke the caste rules could be banned from their homes and their castes, which would make them untouchables. Because of these rules, people spent almost all of their time with others in their same class.

READING CHECK **Drawing Inferences** How did a person become a member of a caste?

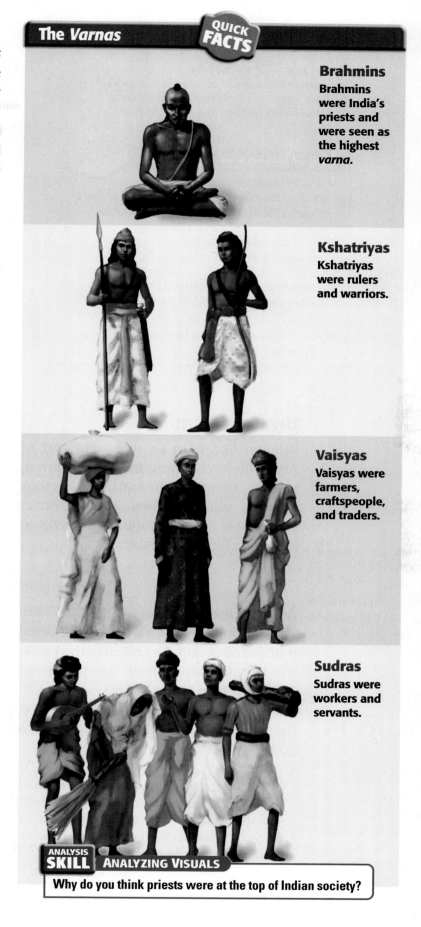

The *Varnas*

QUICK FACTS

Brahmins
Brahmins were India's priests and were seen as the highest *varna*.

Kshatriyas
Kshatriyas were rulers and warriors.

Vaisyas
Vaisyas were farmers, craftspeople, and traders.

Sudras
Sudras were workers and servants.

ANALYSIS SKILL **ANALYZING VISUALS**
Why do you think priests were at the top of Indian society?

Hindu Gods and Beliefs

Hindus believe in many gods, but they believe that all the gods are aspects of a single universal spirit called Brahman. Three aspects of Brahman are particularly important in Hinduism—Brahma, Siva, and Vishnu.

Major Beliefs of Hinduism

- A universal spirit called Brahman created the universe and everything in it. Everything in the world is just a part of Brahman.

- Every person has a soul or *atman* that will eventually join with Brahman.

- People's souls are reincarnated many times before they can join with Brahman.

- A person's karma affects how he or she will be reincarnated.

The god Brahma represents the creator aspect of Brahman. His four faces symbolize the four Vedas.

Brahmanism

Religion had been an important part of Aryan life even before the Aryans moved to India. Eventually, in India, religion took on even more meaning. Because Aryan priests were called Brahmins, their religion is often called Brahmanism.

The Vedas

Aryan religion was based on the Vedas. There are four Vedas, each containing sacred hymns and poems. The oldest of the Vedas, the *Rigveda*, was probably written before 1000 BC. It includes hymns of praise to many gods. This passage, for example, is the opening of a hymn praising Indra, a god of the sky and war.

> *"*The one who is first and possessed of wisdom when born; the god who strove to protect the gods with strength; the one before whose force the two worlds were afraid because of the greatness of his virility [power]: he, O people, is Indra.*"*
>
> –from the *Rigveda*, in *Reading about the World, Volume I*, edited by Paul Brians, et al

Later Vedic Texts

Over the centuries, Aryan Brahmins wrote down their thoughts about the Vedas. In time these thoughts were compiled into collections called Vedic texts.

One collection of Vedic texts describes Aryan religious rituals. For example, it describes how sacrifices should be performed. Priests placed animals, food, or drinks to be sacrificed in a fire. The Aryans believed that the fire would carry these offerings to the gods.

A second collection of Vedic texts describes secret rituals that only certain people could perform. In fact, the rituals were so secret that they had to be done in the forest, far from other people.

The final group of Vedic texts are the Upanishads (oo-PAHN-ee-shads), most of which were written by about 600 BC. These writings are reflections on the Vedas by religious students and teachers.

READING CHECK **Finding Main Ideas** What are the Vedic texts?

Siva, the destroyer aspect of Brahman, is usually shown with four arms and three eyes. Here he is shown dancing on the back of a demon he has defeated.

Vishnu is the preserver aspect of Brahman. In his four arms, he carries a conch shell, a mace, and a discus, symbols of his power and greatness.

Hinduism Develops

The Vedas, the Upanishads, and the other Vedic texts remained the basis of Indian religion for centuries. Eventually, however, the ideas of these sacred texts began to blend with ideas from other cultures. People from Persia and other kingdoms in Central Asia, for example, brought their ideas to India. In time, this blending of ideas created a religion called **Hinduism**, the largest religion in India today.

Hindu Beliefs

The Hindus believe in many gods. Among them are three major gods: Brahma the Creator, Siva the Destroyer, and Vishnu the Preserver. At the same time, however, Hindus believe that each god is part of a single universal spirit called Brahman. They believe that Brahman created the world and preserves it. Gods like Brahma, Siva, and Vishnu represent different aspects of Brahman. In fact, Hindus believe that everything in the world is part of Brahman.

Life and Rebirth

According to Hindu teachings, everyone has a soul, or *atman*, inside them. This soul holds the person's personality, the qualities that make them who they are. Hindus believe that a person's ultimate goal should be to reunite that soul with Brahman, the universal spirit.

Hindus believe that their souls will eventually join Brahman because the world we live in is an illusion. Brahman is the only reality. The Upanishads taught that people must try to see through the illusion of the world. Since it is hard to see through illusions, it can take several lifetimes. That is why Hindus believe that souls are born and reborn many times, each time in a new body. This process of rebirth is called **reincarnation**.

Hinduism and the Caste System

According to the traditional Hindu view of reincarnation, a person who has died is reborn in a new physical form.

More than 800 million people in India practice Hinduism today.

The type of form depends upon his or her **karma**, the effects that good or bad actions have on a person's soul. Evil actions during one's life will build bad karma. A person with bad karma will be born into a lower caste or life form.

In contrast, good actions build good karma. People with good karma are born into a higher caste in their next lives. In time, good karma will bring salvation, or freedom from life's worries and the cycle of rebirth. This salvation is called *moksha*.

Hinduism taught that each person had a duty to accept his or her place in the world without complaint. This is called obeying one's *dharma*. People could build good karma by fulfilling the duties required of their specific caste. Through reincarnation, Hinduism offered rewards to those who lived good lives. Even untouchables could be reborn into a higher caste.

Hinduism was popular at all levels of Hindu society, through all four *varnas*. By teaching people to accept their places in life, Hinduism helped preserve the caste system in India.

Hinduism and Women

Hinduism taught that both men and women could gain salvation. However, Hinduism also taught that women were inferior to men. As a result, Hindu women were not allowed to read the Vedas or other sacred texts.

READING CHECK **Summarizing** What determined how a person would be reborn?

LINKING TO TODAY

Nonviolence

In modern times, nonviolence has been a powerful tool for social protest. Mohandas Gandhi led a long nonviolent struggle against British rule in India. This movement helped India win its independence in 1947. About 10 years later, Martin Luther King Jr. adopted Gandhi's nonviolent methods in his struggle to win civil rights for African Americans. Then, in the 1960s, Cesar Chavez organized a campaign of nonviolence to protest the treatment of farm workers in California. These three leaders proved that people can bring about social change without using violence. As Chavez once explained, "Nonviolence is not inaction. It is not for the timid or the weak. It is hard work. It is the patience to win."

Mohandas Gandhi (top), Martin Luther King Jr. (above), and Cesar Chavez (right)

ANALYSIS SKILL **ANALYZING INFORMATION**

How did these three leaders prove that nonviolence is a powerful tool for social change?

Jains React to Hinduism

Although Hinduism was widely followed in India, not everyone agreed with its beliefs. Some unsatisfied people and groups looked for new religious ideas. One such group was the Jains (JYNZ), believers in a religion called Jainism (JY-ni-zuhm).

Jainism was based on the teachings of a man named Mahavira. Born into the Kshatriya *varna* around 599 BC, he was unhappy with the control of religion by the Brahmins, whom he thought put too much emphasis on rituals. Mahavira gave up his life of luxury, became a monk, and established the principles of Jainism.

The Jains try to live by four principles: injure no life, tell the truth, do not steal, and own no property. In their efforts not to injure anyone or anything, the Jains practice **nonviolence**, or the avoidance of violent actions. The Sanskrit word for this nonviolence is *ahimsa* (uh-HIM-sah). Many Hindus also practice *ahimsa*.

The Jains' emphasis on nonviolence comes from their belief that everything is alive and part of the cycle of rebirth. Jains are very serious about not injuring or killing any creature—humans, animals, insects, or even plants. They do not believe in animal sacrifice, like the ones the ancient Brahmins performed. Because they don't want to hurt living creatures, Jains are vegetarians. They do not eat any food that comes from animals.

READING CHECK Identifying Points of View Why do Jains avoid eating meat?

SUMMARY AND PREVIEW You have learned about two religions that developed in India—Hinduism and Jainism. In Section 3, you will learn about another religion that began there—Buddhism.

These Jain women are wearing masks to make sure they don't accidentally inhale and kill insects.

go.hrw.com
Online Quiz
KEYWORD: SN6 HP5

Section 2 Assessment

Reviewing Ideas, Terms, and People

1. **a. Identify** What is the **caste system**?
   b. Explain Why did strict caste rules develop?
2. **a. Identify** What does the *Rigveda* include?
   b. Analyze What role did sacrifice play in Aryan society?
3. **a. Define** What is **karma**?
   b. Sequence How did Brahmanism develop into **Hinduism**?
   c. Elaborate How does Hinduism reinforce followers' willingness to remain within their castes?
4. **a. Recall** What are the four main teachings of **Jainism**?
   b. Predict How do you think the idea of **nonviolence** affected the daily lives of Jains in ancient India?

Critical Thinking

5. **Analyzing Causes** Draw a graphic organizer like this one. Using your notes, explain how Hinduism developed from Brahmanism, and how Jainism developed from Hinduism.

Brahmanism → Hinduism → Jainism

FOCUS ON WRITING

6. **Illustrating Hinduism** Now you have a new possible topic for your poster. How might you explain a complex religion like Hinduism?

Origins of Buddhism

What You Will Learn...

Main Ideas

1. Siddhartha Gautama searched for wisdom in many ways.
2. The teachings of Buddhism deal with finding peace.
3. Buddhism spread far from where it began in India.

The Big Idea

Buddhism began in India and became a major religion.

Key Terms and People

fasting, *p. 137*
meditation, *p. 137*
the Buddha, *p. 137*
Buddhism, *p. 138*
nirvana, *p. 138*
missionaries, *p. 140*

TAKING NOTES As you read this section, look for information on the basic ideas of Buddhism and on Buddhism's spread. Record what you find in a graphic organizer like this one.

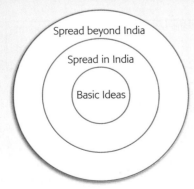

Spread beyond India
Spread in India
Basic Ideas

If YOU were there...

You are a trader traveling in northern India in about 520 BC. As you pass through a town, you see a crowd of people sitting silently in the shade of a huge tree. A man sitting at the foot of the tree begins to speak about how one ought to live. His words are like nothing you have heard from the Hindu priests.

Will you stay to listen? Why or why not?

BUILDING BACKGROUND The Jains were not the only ones to break from Hinduism. In the 500s BC a young Indian prince attracted many people to his teachings about how people should live.

Siddhartha's Search for Wisdom

In the late 500s BC a restless young man, dissatisfied with the teachings of Hinduism, began to ask his own questions about life and religious matters. In time, he found answers. These answers attracted many followers, and the young man's ideas became the foundation of a major new religion in India.

The Quest for Answers

The restless young man was Siddhartha Gautama (si-DAHR-tuh GAU-tuh-muh). Born around 563 BC in northern India, near the Himalayas, Siddhartha was a prince who grew up in luxury. Born a Kshatriya, a member of the warrior class, Siddhartha never had to struggle with the problems that many people of his time faced. However, Siddhartha was not satisfied. He felt that something was missing in his life.

Siddhartha looked around him and saw how hard other people had to work and how much they suffered. He saw people grieving for lost loved ones and wondered why there was so much pain in the world. As a result, Siddhartha began to ask questions about the meaning of human life.

The Great Departure

In this painting, Prince Siddhartha leaves his palace to search for the true meaning of life, an event known as the Great Departure. Special helpers called *ganas* hold his horse's hooves so he won't awaken anyone.

Before Siddhartha reached age 30, he left his home and family to look for answers. His journey took him to many regions in India. Wherever he traveled, he had discussions with priests and people known for their wisdom. Yet no one could give convincing answers to Siddhartha's questions.

The Buddha Finds Enlightenment

Siddhartha did not give up. Instead, he became even more determined to find the answers he was seeking. For several years, he wandered in search of answers.

Siddhartha wanted to free his mind from daily concerns. For a while, he did not even wash himself. He also started **fasting**, or going without food. He devoted much of his time to **meditation**, the focusing of the mind on spiritual ideas.

According to legend, Siddhartha spent six years wandering throughout India. He eventually came to a place near the town of Gaya, close to the Ganges River. There, he sat down under a tree and meditated.

After seven weeks of deep meditation, he suddenly had the answers that he had been looking for. He realized that human suffering comes from three things:

- wanting what we like but do not have,
- wanting to keep what we like and already have, and
- not wanting what we dislike but have.

Siddhartha spent seven more weeks meditating under the tree, which his followers later named the Tree of Wisdom. He then described his new ideas to five of his former companions. His followers later called this talk the First Sermon.

Siddhartha Gautama was about 35 years old when he found enlightenment under the tree. From that point on, he would be called **the Buddha** (BOO-duh), or the "Enlightened One." The Buddha spent the rest of his life traveling across northern India and teaching people his ideas.

THE IMPACT TODAY

Buddhists from all over the world still travel to India to visit the Tree of Wisdom and honor the Buddha.

READING CHECK **Summarizing** What did the Buddha conclude about the cause of suffering?

Teachings of Buddhism

As he traveled, the Buddha gained many followers, especially among India's merchants and artisans. He even taught his views to a few kings. These followers were the first believers in **Buddhism**, a religion based on the teachings of the Buddha.

The Buddha was raised Hindu, and many of his teachings reflected Hindu ideas. Like Hindus, he believed that people should act morally and treat others well. In one of his sermons, he said:

> " Let a man overcome anger by love. Let him overcome the greedy by liberality [giving], the liar by truth. This is called progress in the discipline [training] of the Blessed. "
>
> –The Buddha, quoted in *The History of Nations: India*

Four Noble Truths

At the heart of the Buddha's teachings were four guiding principles. These became known as the Four Noble Truths:

1. Suffering and unhappiness are a part of human life. No one can escape sorrow.

2. Suffering comes from our desires for pleasure and material goods. People cause their own misery because they want things they cannot have.

3. People can overcome desire and ignorance and reach **nirvana** (nir-VAH-nuh), a state of perfect peace. Reaching nirvana frees the soul from suffering and from the need for further reincarnation.

4. People can overcome ignorance and desire by following an eightfold path that leads to wisdom, enlightenment, and salvation.

The chart on the next page shows the steps in the Eightfold Path. The Buddha believed that this path was a middle way between human desires and denying oneself any pleasure. He believed that people should overcome their desire for material goods. They should, however, be reasonable, and not starve their bodies or cause themselves unnecessary pain.

This giant statue of the Buddha is just south of the town of Gaya in Bodh Gaya, India—the place where Buddhists believe Siddhartha reached enlightenment.

The Eightfold Path

1 Right Thought
Believe in the nature of existence as suffering and in the Four Noble Truths.

2 Right Intent
Incline toward goodness and kindness.

3 Right Speech
Avoid lies and gossip.

4 Right Action
Don't steal from or harm others.

5 Right Livelihood
Reject work that hurts others.

6 Right Effort
Prevent evil and do good.

7 Right Mindfulness
Control your feelings and thoughts.

8 Right Concentration
Practice proper meditation.

Challenging Hindu Ideas

Some of the Buddha's teachings challenged traditional Hindu ideas. For example, the Buddha rejected many of the ideas contained in the Vedas, such as animal sacrifice. He told people that they did not have to follow these texts.

The Buddha challenged the authority of the Hindu priests, the Brahmins. He did not believe that they or their rituals were necessary for enlightenment. Instead, he taught that it was the responsibility of each individual to work for his or her own salvation. Priests could not help them. However, the Buddha did not reject the Hindu teaching of reincarnation. He taught that people who failed to reach nirvana would have to be reborn time and time again until they achieved it.

The Buddha was opposed to the caste system. He didn't think that people should be confined to a particular place in society. Everyone who followed the Eightfold Path properly, he said, would achieve nirvana. It didn't matter what *varna* or caste they had belonged to in life as long as they lived the way they should.

The Buddha's opposition to the caste system won him support from the masses. Many of India's herdsmen, farmers, artisans, and untouchables liked hearing that their low social rank would not be a barrier to enlightenment. Unlike Hinduism, Buddhism made them feel that they had the power to change their lives.

The Buddha also gained followers among the higher classes. Many rich and powerful Indians welcomed his ideas about avoiding extreme behavior while seeking salvation. By the time of his death around 483 BC, the Buddha's influence was spreading rapidly throughout India.

READING CHECK **Comparing** How did Buddha's teachings agree with Hinduism?

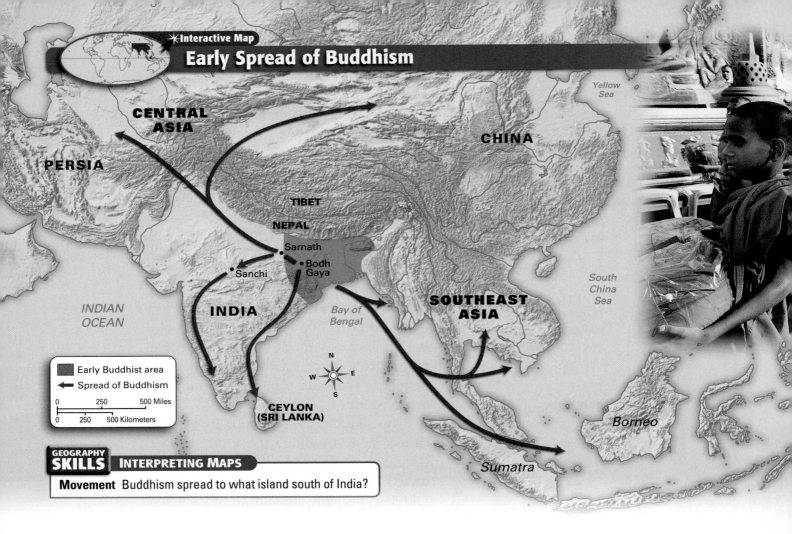

Early Spread of Buddhism

CENTRAL ASIA

PERSIA

CHINA

Yellow Sea

TIBET

NEPAL

Sarnath

Bodh Gaya

Sanchi

INDIAN OCEAN

INDIA

Bay of Bengal

SOUTHEAST ASIA

South China Sea

CEYLON (SRI LANKA)

Borneo

Sumatra

- Early Buddhist area
← Spread of Buddhism

0   250   500 Miles
0 250   500 Kilometers

GEOGRAPHY SKILLS INTERPRETING MAPS

Movement Buddhism spread to what island south of India?

Buddhism Spreads

Buddhism continued to attract followers after the Buddha's death. After spreading through India, the religion began to spread to other areas as well.

Buddhism Spreads in India

According to Buddhist tradition, 500 of the Buddha's followers gathered together shortly after he died. They wanted to make sure that the Buddha's teachings were remembered correctly.

In the years after this council, the Buddha's followers spread his teachings throughout India. The ideas spread very quickly, because Buddhist teachings were popular and easy to understand. Within 200 years of the Buddha's death, his teachings had spread through most of India.

Buddhism Spreads Beyond India

The spread of Buddhism increased after one of the most powerful kings in India, Asoka, became Buddhist in the 200s BC. Once he converted, he built Buddhist temples and schools throughout India. More importantly, though, he worked to spread Buddhism into areas outside of India. You will learn more about Asoka and his accomplishments in the next section.

Asoka sent Buddhist **missionaries**, or people who work to spread their religious beliefs, to other kingdoms in Asia. One group of these missionaries sailed to the island of Sri Lanka around 251 BC. Others followed trade routes east to what is now Myanmar and to other parts of Southeast Asia. Missionaries also went north to areas near the Himalayas.

Young Buddhist students carry gifts in Sri Lanka, one of the many places outside of India where Buddhism spread.

Members of the Theravada branch tried to follow the Buddha's teachings exactly as he had stated them. Mahayana Buddhists, though, believed that other people could interpret the Buddha's teachings to help people reach nirvana. Both branches have millions of believers today, but Mahayana is by far the larger branch.

READING CHECK **Sequencing** How did Buddhism spread from India to other parts of Asia?

SUMMARY AND PREVIEW Buddhism, one of India's major religions, grew more popular once it was adopted by rulers of India's great empires. You will learn more about those empires in the next section.

Missionaries also introduced Buddhism to lands west of India. They founded Buddhist communities in Central Asia and Persia. They even taught about Buddhism as far away as Syria and Egypt.

Buddhism continued to grow over the centuries. Eventually it spread via the Silk Road into China, then Korea and Japan. Through their work, missionaries taught Buddhism to millions of people.

A Split within Buddhism

Even as Buddhism spread through Asia, however, it began to change. Not all Buddhists could agree on their beliefs and practices. Eventually disagreements between Buddhists led to a split within the religion. Two major branches of Buddhism were created—Theravada and Mahayana.

Section 3 Assessment

go.hrw.com
Online Quiz
KEYWORD: SN6 HP5

Reviewing Ideas, Terms, and People

1. **a. Identify** Who was **the Buddha**, and what does the term *Buddha* mean?
   b. Summarize How did Siddhartha Gautama free his mind and clarify his thinking as he searched for wisdom?
2. **a. Identify** What is **nirvana**?
   b. Contrast How are Buddhist teachings different from Hindu teachings?
   c. Elaborate Why do Buddhists believe that following the Eightfold Path leads to a better life?
3. **a. Describe** Into what lands did **Buddhism** spread?
   b. Summarize What role did **missionaries** play in spreading Buddhism?

Critical Thinking

4. **Finding Main Ideas** Draw a diagram like this one. Use it and your notes to identify and describe Buddhism's Four Noble Truths. Write a sentence explaining how these Truths are central to Buddhism.

FOCUS ON WRITING

5. **Considering Indian Religions** Look back over what you've just read and the notes you took about Hinduism earlier. Perhaps you will want to focus your poster on ancient India's two major religions. Think about how you could design a poster around this theme.

ANCIENT INDIA **141**

Indian Empires

What You Will Learn...

Main Ideas

1. The Mauryan Empire unified most of India.
2. Gupta rulers promoted Hinduism in their empire.

The Big Idea

The Mauryas and the Guptas built great empires in India.

Key People

Candragupta Maurya, *p. 142*
Asoka, *p. 143*
Candra Gupta II, *p. 144*

TAKING NOTES As you read, take notes about the rise and fall of ancient India's two greatest empires. Record your notes in a chart like the one shown here.

Mauryan Empire
Gupta Empire

If YOU were there...

You are a merchant in India in about 240 BC. You travel from town to town on your donkey, carrying bolts of colorful cloth. In the heat of summer, you are grateful for the banyan trees along the road. They shelter you from the blazing sun. You stop at wells for cool drinks of water and rest houses for a break in your journey. You know these are all the work of your king, Asoka.

How do you feel about your king?

BUILDING BACKGROUND For centuries after the Aryan invasion, India was divided into small states. Each state had its own ruler and India had no central government. Then, in the 300s BC, a foreign conqueror, Alexander the Great, took over part of northwestern India. His armies soon left, but his influence continued to affect Indian society. Inspired by Alexander's example, a strong leader soon united India for the first time.

Mauryan Empire Unifies India

In the 320s BC a military leader named **Candragupta Maurya** (kuhn-druh-GOOP-tuh MOUR-yuh) seized control of the entire northern part of India. By doing so, he founded the Mauryan Empire. Mauryan rule lasted for about 150 years.

The Mauryan Empire

Candragupta Maurya ruled his empire with the help of a complex government. It included a network of spies and a huge army of some 600,000 soldiers. The army also had thousands of war elephants and thousands of chariots. In return for the army's protection, farmers paid a heavy tax to the government.

In 301 BC Candragupta decided to become a Jainist monk. To do so, he had to give up his throne. He passed the throne to his son, who continued to expand the empire. Before long, the Mauryas ruled all of northern India and much of central India as well.

Asoka

Around 270 BC Candragupta's grandson **Asoka** (uh-SOH-kuh) became king. Asoka was a strong ruler, the strongest of all the Mauryan emperors. He extended Mauryan rule over most of India. In conquering other kingdoms, Asoka made his own empire both stronger and richer.

For many years, Asoka watched his armies fight bloody battles against other peoples. A few years into his rule, however, Asoka converted to Buddhism. When he did, he swore that he would not launch any more wars of conquest.

After converting to Buddhism, Asoka had the time and resources to improve the lives of his people. He had wells dug and roads built throughout the empire. Along these roads, workers planted shade trees and built rest houses for weary travelers. He also encouraged the spread of Buddhism in India and the rest of Asia. As you read in the previous section, he sent missionaries to lands all over Asia.

Asoka died in 233 BC, and the empire began to fall apart soon afterward. His sons fought each other for power, and invaders threatened the empire. In 184 BC the last Mauryan king was killed by one of his own generals. India divided into smaller states once again.

FOCUS ON READING

What can you infer about the religious beliefs of Asoka's sons?

READING CHECK **Finding Main Ideas** How did the Mauryans gain control of most of India?

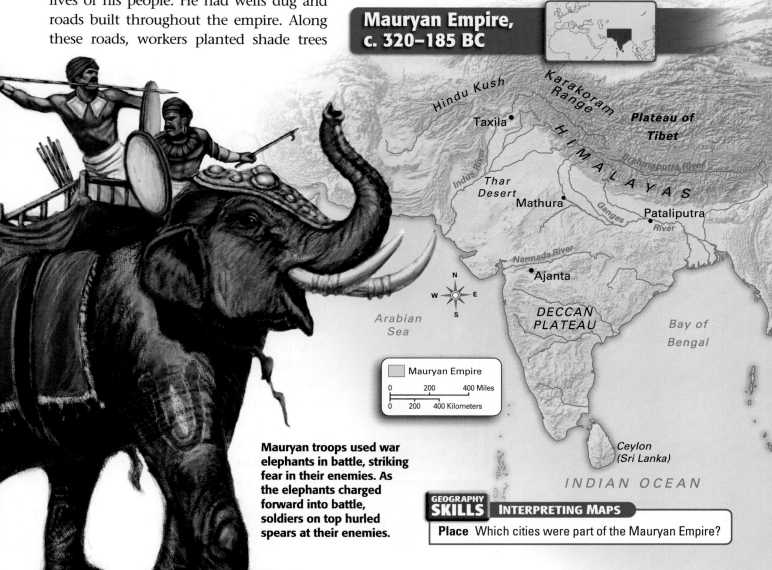

Mauryan troops used war elephants in battle, striking fear in their enemies. As the elephants charged forward into battle, soldiers on top hurled spears at their enemies.

Mauryan Empire, c. 320–185 BC

Hindu Kush · Karakoram Range · Plateau of Tibet · Taxila · HIMALAYAS · Brahmaputra River · Indus River · Thar Desert · Mathura · Ganges River · Pataliputra · Narmada River · Ajanta · Arabian Sea · DECCAN PLATEAU · Bay of Bengal

Mauryan Empire

0   200   400 Miles
0   200   400 Kilometers

Ceylon (Sri Lanka)

INDIAN OCEAN

GEOGRAPHY SKILLS **INTERPRETING MAPS**

Place Which cities were part of the Mauryan Empire?

ANCIENT INDIA   **143**

Gupta Rulers Promote Hinduism

After the collapse of the Mauryan Empire, India remained divided for about 500 years. During that time, Buddhism continued to prosper and spread in India, and so the popularity of Hinduism declined.

A New Hindu Empire

ACADEMIC VOCABULARY

establish to set up or create

Eventually, however, a new dynasty was **established** in India. It was the Gupta (GOOP-tuh) dynasty, which took over India around AD 320. Under the Guptas, India was once again united, and it once again became prosperous.

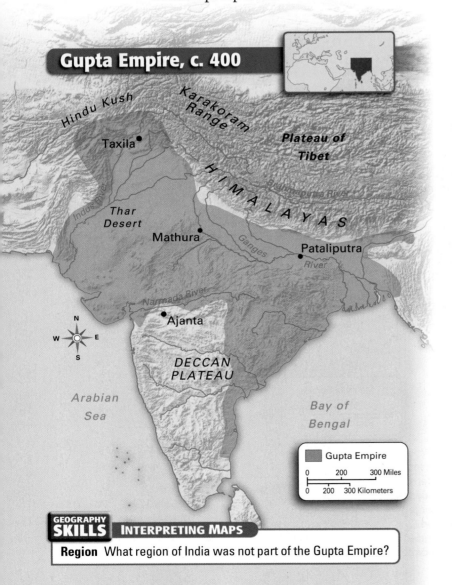

Gupta Empire, c. 400

Hindu Kush

Karakoram Range

Taxila

Plateau of Tibet

HIMALAYAS

Indus River

Thar Desert

Mathura

Ganges River

Pataliputra

Narmada River

Ajanta

DECCAN PLATEAU

Arabian Sea

Bay of Bengal

N W E S

Gupta Empire

0   200   300 Miles
0   200   300 Kilometers

GEOGRAPHY SKILLS | **INTERPRETING MAPS**

Region What region of India was not part of the Gupta Empire?

The first Gupta emperor was Candra Gupta I. Although their names are similar, he was not related to Candragupta Maurya. From his base in northern India, Candra Gupta's armies invaded and conquered neighboring lands. Eventually he brought much of the northern part of India under his control.

Indian civilization flourished under the Gupta rulers. These rulers were Hindu, so Hinduism became India's major religion. The Gupta kings built many Hindu temples, some of which became models for later Indian architecture. They also promoted a revival of Hindu writings and worship practices.

Although they were Hindus, the Gupta rulers also supported the religious beliefs of Buddhism and Jainism. They promoted Buddhist art and built Buddhist temples. They also established a university at Nalanda that became one of Asia's greatest centers for Buddhist studies.

Gupta Society

In 375 Emperor **Candra Gupta II** took the throne in India. Gupta society reached its high point during his rule. Under Candra Gupta II, the empire continued to grow, eventually stretching all the way across northern India. At the same time, the empire's economy strengthened, and people prospered. They created fine works of art and literature. Outsiders admired the empire's wealth and beauty.

Gupta kings believed the social order of the Hindu caste system would strengthen their rule. They also thought it would keep the empire stable. As a result, the Gupta considered the caste system an important part of Indian society.

Gupta rule remained strong in India until the late 400s. At that time the Huns, a group from Central Asia, invaded India from the northwest. Their fierce attacks drained the Gupta Empire of its power and wealth. As the Hun armies marched farther into India, the Guptas lost hope. By the middle of the 500s, Gupta rule had ended, and India had divided into small kingdoms yet again.

SUMMARY AND PREVIEW The Mauryas and Guptas united much of India in their empires. Next you will learn about their many achievements.

READING CHECK **Summarizing** What was the Gupta dynasty's position on religion?

Section 4 Assessment

Reviewing Ideas, Terms, and People

1. **a. Identify** Who created the Mauryan Empire?
   b. Summarize What happened after **Asoka** became a Buddhist?
   c. Elaborate Why do you think many people consider Asoka the greatest of all Mauryan rulers?
2. **a. Recall** What religion did most of the Gupta rulers belong to?
   b. Compare and Contrast How were the rulers **Candragupta Maurya** and Candra Gupta I alike, and how were they different?

Critical Thinking

3. **Categorizing** Draw a chart like this one. Fill it with information about India's rulers.

Ruler	Dynasty	Accomplishments

FOCUS ON WRITING

4. **Comparing Indian Empires** Another possible topic for your poster would be a comparison of the Mauryan and Gupta empires. Make a chart in your notebook that shows such a comparison.

Asoka

How can one decision change a man's entire life?

When did he live? before 230 BC

Where did he live? Asoka's empire included much of northern and central India.

What did he do? After fighting many bloody wars to expand his empire, Asoka gave up violence and converted to Buddhism.

Why is he important? Asoka is one of the most respected rulers in Indian history and one of the most important figures in the history of Buddhism. As a devout Buddhist, Asoka worked to spread the Buddha's teachings. In addition to sending missionaries around Asia, he built huge columns carved with Buddhist teachings all over India. Largely through his efforts, Buddhism became one of Asia's main religions.

Generalizing How did Asoka's life change after he became Buddhist?

KEY EVENTS

c. 270 BC Asoka becomes the Mauryan emperor.

c. 261 BC Asoka's empire reaches its greatest size.

c. 261 BC Asoka becomes a Buddhist.

c. 251 BC Asoka begins to send Buddhist missionaries to other parts of Asia.

This Buddhist shrine, located in Sanchi, India, was built by Asoka.

Indian Achievements

If YOU were there...

You are a traveler in western India in the 300s. You are visiting a cave temple that is carved into a mountain cliff. Inside the cave it is cool and quiet. Huge columns rise all around you. You don't feel you're alone, for the walls and ceilings are covered with paintings. They are filled with lively scenes and figures. In the center is a large statue with calm, peaceful features.

How does this cave make you feel?

BUILDING BACKGROUND The Mauryan and Gupta empires united most of India politically. During these empires, Indian artists, writers, scholars, and scientists made great advances. Some of their works are still studied and admired today.

Religious Art

The Indians of the Mauryan and Gupta periods created great works of art, many of them religious. Many of their paintings and sculptures illustrated either Hindu and Buddhist teachings. Magnificent temples—both Hindu and Buddhist—were built all around India. They remain some of the most beautiful buildings in the world today.

Temples

Early Hindu temples were small stone structures. They had flat roofs and contained only one or two rooms. In the Gupta period, though, temple architecture became more complex. Gupta temples were topped by huge towers and were covered with carvings of the god worshipped inside.

Buddhist temples of the Gupta period are also impressive. Some Buddhists carved entire temples out of mountainsides. The most famous such temple is at Ajanta. Its builders filled the caves with beautiful wall paintings and sculpture.

What You Will Learn...

Main Ideas

1. Indian artists created great works of religious art.
2. Sanskrit literature flourished during the Gupta period.
3. The Indians made scientific advances in metalworking, medicine, and other sciences.

The Big Idea

The people of ancient India made great contributions to the arts and sciences.

Key Terms

metallurgy, *p. 150*
alloys, *p. 150*
Hindu-Arabic numerals, *p. 150*
inoculation, *p. 150*
astronomy, *p. 151*

TAKING NOTES As you read, look for information on achievements of ancient India. Take notes about these achievements in a chart like this one. Enlarge the chart so you have plenty of room to write.

Type of Achievement	Details about Achievements
Religious Art	
Sanskrit Literature	
Scientific Advances	

147

Temple Architecture

This Hindu temple is covered with incredibly detailed carvings and decorations. Many individual sculptures are images of important Hindu gods, like the statue of Vishnu above.

Another type of Buddhist temple was the stupa. Stupas had domed roofs and were built to house sacred items from the life of the Buddha. Many of them were covered with detailed carvings.

Paintings and Sculpture

The Gupta period also saw the creation of great works of art, both paintings and statues. Painting was a greatly respected profession, and India was home to many skilled artists. However, we don't know the names of many artists from this period. Instead, we know the names of many rich and powerful members of Gupta society who paid artists to create works of beauty and significance.

Most Indian paintings from the Gupta period are clear and colorful. Some of them show graceful Indians wearing fine jewelry and stylish clothes. Such paintings offer us a glimpse of the Indians' daily and ceremonial lives.

Artists from both of India's major religions, Hinduism and Buddhism, drew on their beliefs to create their works. As a result, many of the finest paintings of ancient India are found in temples. Hindu painters drew hundreds of gods on temple walls and entrances. Buddhists covered the walls and ceilings of temples with scenes from the life of the Buddha.

Indian sculptors also created great works. Many of their statues were made for Buddhist cave temples. In addition to the temples' intricately carved columns, sculptors carved statues of kings and the Buddha. Some of these statues tower over the cave entrances. Hindu temples also featured impressive statues of their gods. In fact, the walls of some temples, such as the one pictured above, were completely covered with carvings and images.

READING CHECK Summarizing How did religion influence ancient Indian art?

Sanskrit Literature

Sanskrit was the main language of the ancient Aryans. During the Mauryan and Gupta periods, many works of Sanskrit literature were created. These works were later translated into many other languages.

Religious Epics

The greatest of these Sanskrit writings are two religious epics, the *Mahabharata* (muh-HAH-BAH-ruh-tuh) and the *Ramayana* (rah-MAH-yuh-nuh). Still popular in India, the *Mahabharata* is one of the world's longest literary works. It is a story about the struggle between two families for control of a kingdom. Included within the story are many long passages about Hindu beliefs. The most famous is called the *Bhagavad Gita* (BUG-uh-vuhd GEE-tah).

The *Ramayana*, according to Hindu tradition written prior to the *Mahabharata*, tells about a prince named Rama. In truth, the prince was the god Vishnu in human form. He had become human so he could rid the world of demons. He also had to rescue his wife, a princess named Sita. For centuries, the characters of the *Ramayana* have been seen as models for how Indians should behave. For example, Rama is seen as the ideal ruler, and his relationship with Sita as the ideal marriage.

Other Works

Writers in the Gupta period also created plays, poetry, and other types of literature. One famous writer of this time was Kalidasa (kahl-ee-DAHS-uh). His work was so brilliant that Candra Gupta II hired him to write plays for the royal court.

Sometime before 500, Indian writers also produced a book of stories called the *Panchatantra* (PUHN-chuh-TAHN-truh). The stories in this collection were intended to teach lessons. They praise people for cleverness and quick thinking. Each story ends with a message about winning friends, losing property, waging war, or some other idea. For example, the message below warns listeners to think about what they are doing before they act.

> *"*The good and bad of given schemes
> Wise thought must first reveal:
> The stupid heron saw his chicks
> Provide a mongoose meal.*"*
> –from the *Panchatantra*, translated by Arthur William Ryder

Eventually, translations of this collection spread throughout the world. It became popular even as far away as Europe.

READING CHECK **Categorizing** What types of literature did writers of ancient India create?

In this illustration of the *Ramayana*, the monkey king sends the monkey general Hanuman to find Sita. Hanuman helped Rama defeat the demons and win back Sita. Many Indians view him as a model of devotion and loyalty.

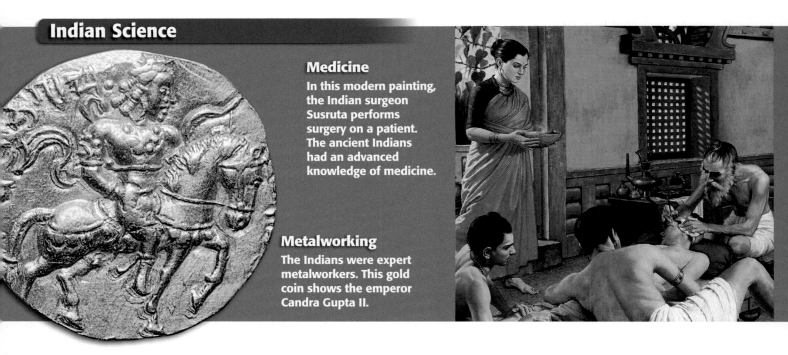

Indian Science

Medicine
In this modern painting, the Indian surgeon Susruta performs surgery on a patient. The ancient Indians had an advanced knowledge of medicine.

Metalworking
The Indians were expert metalworkers. This gold coin shows the emperor Candra Gupta II.

Scientific Advances

Indian achievements were not limited to art, architecture, and literature. Indian scholars also made important advances in metalworking, math, and the sciences.

Metalworking

The ancient Indians were pioneers of **metallurgy** (MET-uhl-uhr-jee), the science of working with metals. Their knowledge allowed them to create high-quality tools and weapons. The Indians also knew **processes** for mixing metals to create **alloys**, mixtures of two or more metals. Alloys are sometimes stronger or easier to work with than pure metals.

Metalworkers made their strongest products out of iron. Indian iron was very hard and pure. These features made the iron a valuable trade item.

During the Gupta dynasty, metalworkers built the famous Iron Pillar near Delhi. Unlike most iron, which rusts easily, this pillar is very resistant to rust. The tall column still attracts crowds of visitors. Scholars study this column even today to learn the Indians' secrets.

ACADEMIC VOCABULARY
process a series of steps by which a task is accomplished

THE IMPACT TODAY
People still get inoculations against many diseases.

Mathematics and Other Sciences

Gupta scholars also made advances in math and science. In fact, they were among the most advanced mathematicians of their day. They developed many elements of our modern math system. The very numbers we use today are called **Hindu-Arabic numerals** because they were created by Indian scholars and brought to Europe by Arabs. The Indians were also the first people to create the zero. Although it may seem like a small thing, modern math wouldn't be possible without the zero.

The ancient Indians were also very skilled in the medical sciences. As early as the AD 100s, doctors were writing their knowledge down in textbooks. Among the skills these books describe is making medicines from plants and minerals.

Besides curing people with medicines, Indian doctors knew how to protect people against disease. The Indians practiced **inoculation** (i-nah-kyuh-LAY-shuhn), or injecting a person with a small dose of a virus to help him or her build up defenses to a disease. By fighting off this small dose, the body learns to protect itself.

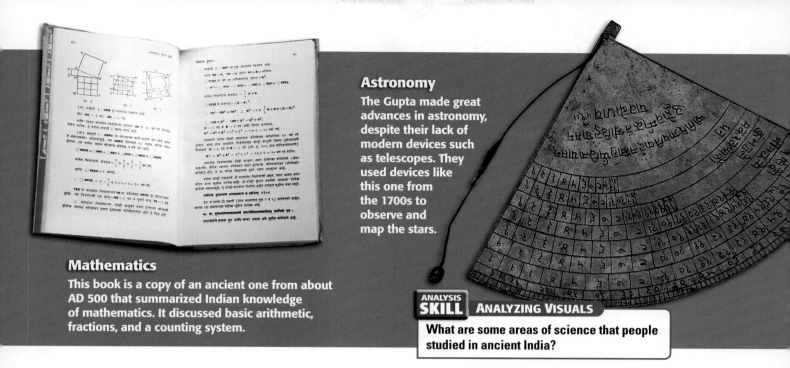

Mathematics
This book is a copy of an ancient one from about AD 500 that summarized Indian knowledge of mathematics. It discussed basic arithmetic, fractions, and a counting system.

Astronomy
The Gupta made great advances in astronomy, despite their lack of modern devices such as telescopes. They used devices like this one from the 1700s to observe and map the stars.

ANALYSIS SKILL ANALYZING VISUALS
What are some areas of science that people studied in ancient India?

For people who were injured, Indian doctors could perform surgery. Surgeons repaired broken bones, treated wounds, removed infected tonsils, reconstructed broken noses, and even reattached torn earlobes! If they could find no other cure for an illness, doctors would cast magic spells to help people recover.

Indian interest in **astronomy**, the study of stars and planets, dates back to early times as well. Indian astronomers knew of seven of the nine planets in our solar system. They knew that the sun was a star and that the planets revolved around it. They also knew that the earth was a sphere and that it rotated on its axis. In addition, they could predict eclipses of the sun and the moon.

READING CHECK Finding Main Ideas What were two Indian achievements in mathematics?

SUMMARY AND PREVIEW From a group of cities on the Indus River, India grew into a major empire whose people made great achievements. In the next chapter, you'll read about another civilization that experienced similar growth—China.

Section 5 Assessment

go.hrw.com
Online Quiz
KEYWORD: SN6 HP5

Reviewing Ideas, Terms, and People

1. **a. Describe** What did Hindu temples of the Gupta period look like?
   b. Analyze How can you tell that Indian artists were well respected?
   c. Evaluate Why do you think Hindu and Buddhist temples contained great works of art?
2. **a. Identify** What is the *Bhagavad Gita*?
   b. Explain Why were the stories of the *Panchatantra* written?
   c. Elaborate Why do you think people are still interested in ancient Sanskrit epics today?
3. **a. Define** What is **metallurgy**?
   b. Explain Why do we call the numbers we use today **Hindu-Arabic numerals**?

Critical Thinking

4. **Categorizing** Draw a chart like this one. Identify the scientific advances that fall into each category below.

Metallurgy	Math	Medicine	Astronomy

FOCUS ON WRITING

5. **Highlighting Indian Achievements** Make a list of Indian achievements that you could include on a poster. Now look back through your notes from this chapter. Which will you choose as the subject of your poster?

Social Studies Skills

Interpreting Diagrams

Understand the Skill

Diagrams are drawings that illustrate or explain objects or ideas. Different types of diagrams have different purposes. The ability to interpret diagrams will help you to better understand historical objects, their functions, and how they worked.

Learn the Skill

Use these guidelines to interpret a diagram:

1 Read the diagram's title or caption to find out what it represents. If a legend is present, study it as well to understand any symbols and colors in the diagram.

2 Most diagrams include labels that identify the object's parts or explain relationships between them. Study these parts and labels carefully.

3 If any written information or explanation accompanies the diagram, compare it to the drawing as you read.

The diagram below is of the Great Stupa at Sanchi in India, which is thought to contain the Buddha's remains. Like most stupas, it was shaped like a dome.

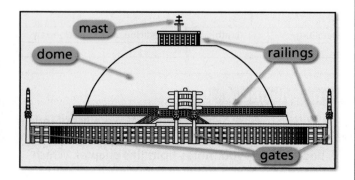

The Sanchi stupa is surrounded by a stone railing with four gates called *torenas*. About halfway up the side of the mound is a second railing next to a walkway. Worshippers move along this walkway in a clockwise direction to honor the Buddha. The stupa is topped by a cube called the *harmika*. Rising from the harmika is a mast or spire. These parts and their shapes all have religious meaning for Buddhists.

Practice and Apply the Skill

Here is another diagram of the Sanchi stupa. Interpret both diagrams on this page to answer the questions that follow.

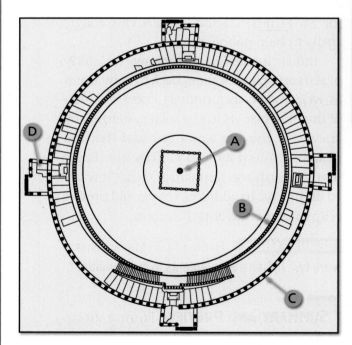

1. Which letter in this diagram labels the *torenas*?

2. What part of the stupa does the letter A label?

3. The walkway and railing are labeled by which letter?

Chapter Review

Visual Summary

Use the visual summary below to help you review the main ideas of the chapter.

QUICK FACTS

The Harappan civilization began in the Indus River Valley.

Hinduism and Buddhism both developed in India.

Indians made great advances in art, literature, science, and other fields.

Reviewing Vocabulary, Terms and People

Fill in the blanks with the correct term or name from this chapter.

1. _____ are winds that bring heavy rainfall.

2. A _____ is a division of people into groups based on birth, wealth, or occupation.

3. Hindus believe in _____, the belief that they will be reborn many times after death.

4. _____ founded the Mauryan Empire.

5. The focusing of the mind on spiritual things is called _____.

6. People who work to spread their religious beliefs are called _____.

7. People who practice _____ use only peaceful ways to achieve change.

8. _____ converted to Buddhism while he was ruler of the Mauryan Empire.

9. A mixture of metals is called an _____.

Comprehension and Critical Thinking

SECTION 1 *(Pages 124–129)*

10. **a. Describe** What caused floods on the Indus River, and what was the result of those floods?

   b. Contrast How was Aryan culture different from Harappan culture?

   c. Elaborate Why is the Harappan culture considered a civilization?

SECTION 2 *(Pages 130–135)*

11. **a. Identify** Who were the Brahmins, and what role did they play in Aryan society?

   b. Analyze How do Hindus believe karma affects reincarnation?

   c. Elaborate Hinduism has been called both a polytheistic religion—one that worships many gods—and a monotheistic religion—one that worships only one god. Why do you think this is so?

SECTION 3 (Pages 136–141)

12. a. Describe What did the Buddha say caused human suffering?

b. Analyze How did Buddhism grow and change after the Buddha died?

c. Elaborate Why did the Buddha's teachings about nirvana appeal to many people of lower castes?

SECTION 4 (Pages 142–145)

13. a. Identify What was Candragupta Maurya's greatest accomplishment?

b. Compare and Contrast What was one similarity between the Mauryas and the Guptas? What was one difference between them?

c. Predict How might Indian history have been different if Asoka had not become a Buddhist?

SECTION 5 (Pages 147–151)

14. a. Describe What kinds of religious art did the ancient Indians create?

b. Make Inferences Why do you think religious discussions are included in the *Mahabharata*?

c. Evaluate Which of the ancient Indians' achievements do you think is most impressive? Why?

Reviewing Themes

15. Religion What is one teaching that Buddhism and Hinduism share? What is one idea about which they differ?

16. Society and Culture How did the caste system affect the lives of most people in India?

Using the Internet

go.hrw.com
KEYWORD: SN6 WH5

17. Activity: Making a Brochure In this chapter, you learned about India's diverse geographical features and the ways in which geography influenced India's history. Enter the activity keyword. Then research the geography and civilizations of India, taking notes as you go. Finally, use the interactive brochure template to present what you have found.

Reading Skills

18. Inferences about History Based on what you learned about the Gupta period, what inference can you draw about religious tolerance in ancient India? Draw a box like the one below to help you organize your thoughts.

Question:	
Inside the Text:	Outside the Text:
Inference:	

Social Studies Skills

19. Understanding Diagrams Look back over the diagram of the Buddhist temple in the skills activity at the end of this chapter. Using this diagram as a guide, draw a simple diagram of your house or school. Be sure to include labels of important features on your diagram. An example has been provided for you below.

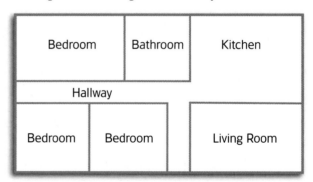

FOCUS ON WRITING ✏

20. Designing Your Poster Now that you have chosen a subject for your poster, it's time to create it. On a large sheet of paper or poster board, write a title that identifies your subject. Then draw pictures, maps, or diagrams that illustrate it.

Next to each picture, write a short caption. Each caption should be two sentences long. The first sentence should identify what the picture, map, or diagram shows. The second sentence should explain why the picture is important to the study of Indian history.

Standardized Test Practice

DIRECTIONS: Read each question, and write the letter of the best response.

1 Use the map to answer the following question.

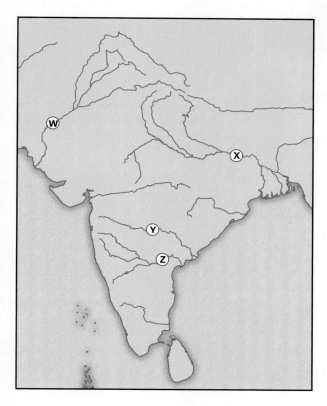

Civilization grew on the Indian subcontinent along the river marked on the map by the letter

A W.

B X.

C Y.

D Z.

2 The people of which *varna* in early India had the hardest lives?

A Brahmins

B Kshatriyas

C Sudras

D Vaisyas

3 What is the *main* goal of people who follow Buddhism as it was taught by the Buddha?

A wealth

B rebirth

C missionary work

D reaching nirvana

4 The Mauryan emperor Asoka is known for all of the following *except*

A expanding the empire across most of India.

B spreading Hinduism.

C working to improve his people's lives.

D practicing nonviolence.

5 Early India's contributions to world civilization included

A developing the world's first calendar.

B creating what is now called algebra.

C inventing the plow and the wheel.

D introducing zero to the number system.

Connecting with Past Learnings

6 In this chapter you learned about two great epics, the *Mahabharata* and the *Ramayana*. Which of the following is also an epic poem that you have studied?

A Hammurabi's Code

B the *Book of the Dead*

C *Gilgamesh*

D the Pyramid Texts

7 As you learned earlier in this course, the ancient Egyptians held elaborate religious rituals. Which of these Indian religions also involved many rituals, including sacrifices?

A Buddhism

B Brahmanism

C Jainism

D Mauryanism

Ancient China

FOCUS ON SPEAKING

Oral Presentation In this chapter you will read about China's fascinating early years. Choose one person or event from that history. You will then tell your classmates why the person or event was important to the history of China.

CHAPTER EVENTS

c. 1500s BC
The Shang dynasty is established in China.

1600 BC

WORLD EVENTS

c. 1480 BC
Queen Hatshepsut rules Egypt.

What You Will Learn...

In this chapter you will learn about the geography, history, and culture of ancient China. China was one of the early centers of civilization. China's two major rivers played key roles in Chinese history and the development of Chinese society.

1100s BC
The Zhou dynasty begins.

551 BC
Confucius is born in China.

221 BC
Shi Huangdi unites China under the Qin dynasty.

206 BC
The Han dynasty begins its rule of China.

1200 BC — **800 BC** — **400 BC** — **BC 1 AD**

c. 965 BC
Solomon becomes king of the Israelites.

c. 500 BC
Buddhism begins to emerge in India.

c. 100 BC
The overland Silk Road connects China and Southwest Asia.

ANCIENT CHINA **157**

Economics	Geography	Politics	Religion	Society and Culture	Science and Technology

Focus on Themes This chapter will describe the early development of China—how Chinese civilization began and took shape under early dynasties. You will see how these dynasties controlled the government and **politics**. You will also see how the Chinese, influenced by the philosopher Confucius, established traditions such as the importance of families. They also encouraged art and learning, helping to shape the **society and culture** that would last for centuries in China.

Summarizing Historical Texts

Focus on Reading When you are reading a history book, how can you be sure that you understand everything? One way is to briefly restate what you've read in a summary.

Writing a Summary A **summary** is a short restatement of the most important ideas in a text. The example below shows three steps used in writing a summary. First underline important details. Then write a short summary of each paragraph. Finally, combine these paragraph summaries into a short summary of the whole passage.

> The first dynasty for which we have clear evidence is the Shang, which was firmly established by the 1500s BC. Strongest in the Huang He Valley, the Shang ruled a broad area of northern China. Shang rulers moved their capital several times, probably to avoid floods or attack by enemies.
>
> The king was at the center of Shang political and religious life. Nobles served the king as advisors and helped him rule. Less important officials were also nobles. They performed specific governmental and religious duties.

Summary of Paragraph 1
China's first dynasty, the Shang, took power in northern China in the 1500s BC.

Summary of Paragraph 2
Shang politics and religion were run by the king and nobles.

Combined Summary
The Shang dynasty, which ruled northern China by the 1500s BC, was governed by a king and nobles.

You Try It!

The following passage is from the chapter you are about to read. As you read it, think about what you would include in a summary.

Early Settlements

Archaeologists have found remains of early Chinese villages. One village near the Huang He had more than 40 houses. Many of them were partly underground and may have had straw-covered roofs. The site also included animal pens, storage pits, and a cemetery.

From Chapter 6 p. 162

Some of the villages along the Huang He grew into large towns. Walls surrounded these towns to defend them against floods and hostile neighbors. In towns like these, the Chinese left many artifacts, such as arrowheads, fishhooks, tools, and pottery. Some village sites even contained pieces of cloth.

After you read the passage, answer the following questions.

1. Read the following summaries and decide which one is the better summary statement. Explain your answer.
   a) Archaeologists have found out interesting things about the early settlements of China. For example, they have discovered that the Chinese had homes with straw-covered roofs, pens for their animals, and even cemeteries. Also, they have found that larger villages were surrounded by walls for defense. Finally, they have found tools like arrowheads and fishhooks.
   b) Archaeologists have found remains of early Chinese villages, some of which grew into large walled settlements. Artifacts found there help us understand Chinese culture.

2. What are three characteristics of a good summary?

Academic Vocabulary

Success in school is related to knowing academic vocabulary—the words that are frequently used in school assignments and discussions. In this chapter, you will learn the following academic words:

vary *(p. 161)*
structure *(p. 168)*
innovation *(p. 182)*
procedure *(p. 187)*

As you read Chapter 6, think about how you would summarize the material you are reading.

Geography and Early China

What You Will Learn...

Main Ideas

1. China's physical geography made farming possible but travel and communication difficult.
2. Civilization began in China along the Huang He and Chang Jiang rivers.
3. China's first dynasties helped Chinese society develop and made many other achievements.

The Big Idea

Chinese civilization began with the Shang dynasty along the Huang He.

Key Terms

jade, *p. 163*
oracle, *p. 164*

TAKING NOTES As you read, take notes on China's geography and its early civilizations. Organize your notes in a table like this one.

Ancient China			
Geography	Earliest Civilization	Xia dynasty	Shang dynasty

If YOU were there...

You live along a broad river in China in about 1400 BC. Your grandfather is a farmer. He tells you wonderful stories about an ancient king. Long ago, this legendary hero tamed the river's raging floods. He even created new rivers. Without him, no one could farm or live in this rich land.

Why is this legend important to your family?

BUILDING BACKGROUND Like other river civilizations, the Chinese people had to learn to control floods and irrigate their fields. China's geographical features divided the country into distinct regions.

China's Physical Geography

Geography played a major role in the development of Chinese civilization. China has many different geographical features. Some features separated groups of people within China. Others separated China from the rest of the world.

A Vast and Varied Land

China covers an area of nearly 4 million square miles, about the same size as the United States. One of the physical barriers that separates China from its neighbors is a harsh desert, the Gobi (GOH-bee). It spreads over much of China's north. East of the Gobi are low-lying plains. These plains, which cover most of eastern China, form one of the world's largest farming regions. The Pacific Ocean forms the country's eastern boundary.

More than 2,000 miles to the west, rugged mountains make up the western frontier. In the southwest the Plateau of Tibet has several mountain peaks that reach more than 26,000 feet. From the plateau, smaller mountain ranges spread eastward. The most important of these ranges is the Qinling Shandi (CHIN-LING shahn-DEE). It separates northern China from southern China.

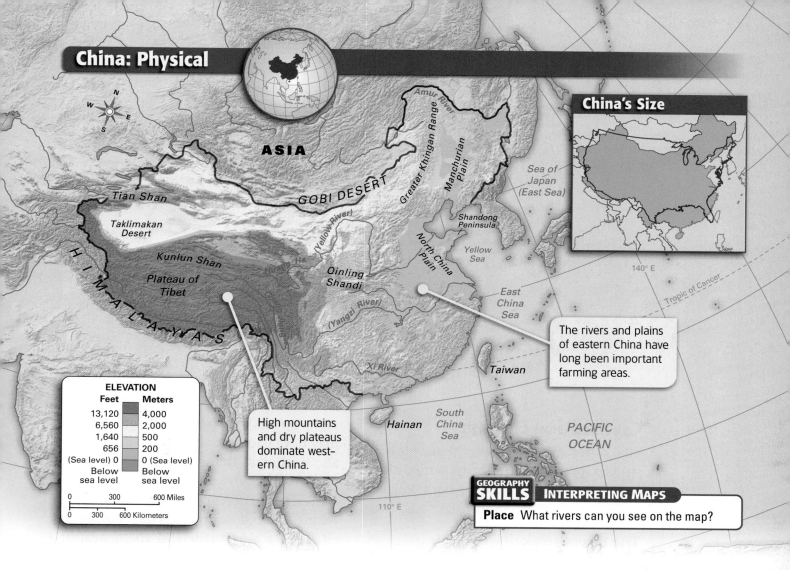

China: Physical

ASIA

Amur River

Greater Khingan Range

Manchurian Plain

GOBI DESERT

Tian Shan

Taklimakan Desert

(Yellow River)

Shandong Peninsula

Kunlun Shan

Huang He

North China Plain

Yellow Sea

Plateau of Tibet

Qinling Shandi

HIMALAYAS

(Yangzi River)

East China Sea

Sea of Japan (East Sea)

China's Size

140° E

Tropic of Cancer

Xi River

Taiwan

ELEVATION

Feet	Meters
13,120	4,000
6,560	2,000
1,640	500
656	200
(Sea level) 0	0 (Sea level)
Below sea level	Below sea level

0   300   600 Miles
0 300 600 Kilometers

Hainan

South China Sea

The rivers and plains of eastern China have long been important farming areas.

PACIFIC OCEAN

High mountains and dry plateaus dominate western China.

110° E

GEOGRAPHY SKILLS **INTERPRETING MAPS**

Place What rivers can you see on the map?

Weather and temperature patterns **vary** widely across China. In the northeast, the climate is cold and dry. Winter temperatures drop well below 0°F. Rivers there are frozen for more than half of the year. In the northwest, the deserts are very dry. But on the eastern plains of China, heavy rains fall. The tropical southeast is the wettest region. Monsoons can bring 250 inches of rain each year. That's enough water to cover a two-story house!

The Rivers of China

Two great rivers flow from west to east in China. The Huang He, or Yellow River, stretches for nearly 3,000 miles across northern China. The river often floods, and the floods leave behind layers of silt on the surrounding countryside. Because these floods can be very destructive, the river is sometimes called China's Sorrow. Over the years, millions of people have died in Huang He floods.

To the south, the Chang Jiang, or Yangzi River, cuts through central China. It flows from the mountains of Tibet to the Pacific Ocean. The Chang Jiang is the longest river in Asia.

In early China, the two rivers helped link people in the eastern part of the country with those in the west. At the same time, the mountains between the rivers limited contact.

ACADEMIC VOCABULARY

vary to be different

READING CHECK **Summarizing** What geographical features limited travel in China?

China is a large country with many different types of environments.

How do these photos show China's diverse geography?

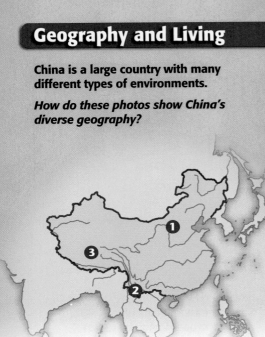

1 In northern China, the Huang He, or Yellow River, has long been the center of civilization. The silt in the river gives it a yellow look.

Civilization Begins

Like other ancient peoples that you have studied, people in China first settled along rivers. There they farmed, built villages, and formed a civilization.

The Development of Farming

Farming in China started along the Huang He and Chang Jiang. The rivers' floods deposited fertile silt. These silt deposits made the land ideal for growing crops.

As early as 7000 BC farmers grew rice in the middle Chang Jiang Valley. North, along the Huang He, the land was better for growing cereals such as millet and wheat.

Along with farming, the early Chinese people increased their diets in other ways. They fished and hunted with bows and arrows. They also domesticated animals such as pigs and sheep. With more sources of food, the population grew.

Early Settlements

Archaeologists have found remains of early Chinese villages. One village site near the Huang He had more than 40 houses. Many of the houses were partly underground and may have had straw-covered roofs. The site also included animal pens, storage pits, and a cemetery.

Some of the villages along the Huang He grew into large towns. Walls surrounded these towns to defend them against floods and hostile neighbors. In towns like these, the Chinese left many artifacts, such as arrowheads, fishhooks, tools, and pottery. Some village sites even contained pieces of cloth.

Separate cultures developed in southern and northeastern China. These included the Sanxingdui (sahn-shing-DWAY) and Hongshan peoples. Little is known about them, however. As the major cultures along the Huang He and Chang Jiang grew, they absorbed other cultures.

Over time, Chinese culture became more advanced. After 3000 BC people used potter's wheels to make more types of pottery. These people also learned to dig water wells. As populations grew, villages spread out over larger areas in both northern and southeastern China.

② Southern China receives more rain than northern China, and farmers can grow several crops of rice a year.

③ Western China's high mountains and wide deserts make travel difficult and isolate China's population centers in the east.

Burial sites have provided information about the culture of this period. Like the Egyptians, the early Chinese filled their tombs with objects. Some tombs included containers of food, suggesting a belief in an afterlife. Some graves contained many more items than others. These differences show that a social order had developed. Often the graves of rich people held beautiful jewelry and other objects made from **jade**, a hard gemstone.

READING CHECK **Generalizing** What were some features of China's earliest settlements?

China's First Dynasties

Societies along the Huang He grew and became more complex. They eventually formed the first Chinese civilization.

The Xia Dynasty

According to ancient stories, a series of kings ruled early China. Around 2200 BC one of them, Yu the Great, is said to have founded the Xia (SHAH) dynasty.

Writers told of terrible floods during Yu's lifetime. According to these accounts, Yu dug channels to drain the water to the ocean. This labor took him more than 10 years and is said to have created the major waterways of north China.

Archaeologists have not yet found evidence that the tales about the Xia are true. However, the stories of Xia rulers were important to the ancient Chinese because they told of kings who helped people solve problems by working together. The stories also explained the geography that had such an impact on people's lives.

The Shang Dynasty

The first dynasty for which we have clear evidence is the Shang, which was firmly established by the 1500s BC. Strongest in the Huang He Valley, the Shang ruled a broad area of northern China. Shang rulers moved their capital several times, probably to avoid floods or attack by enemies.

The king was at the center of Shang political and religious life. Nobles served the king as advisors and helped him rule.

Less important officials were also nobles. They performed specific governmental and religious duties.

The social order became more organized under the Shang. The royal family and the nobles were at the highest level. Nobles owned much land, and they passed on their wealth and power to their sons. Warrior leaders from the far regions of the empire also had high rank in society. Most people in the Shang ruling classes lived in large homes in cities.

Artisans settled outside the city walls. They lived in groups based on what they made for a living. Some artisans made weapons. Other artisans made pottery, tools, or clothing. Artisans were at a middle level of importance in Shang society.

Farmers ranked below artisans in the social order. Farmers worked long hours but had little money. Taxes claimed much of what they earned. Slaves, who filled society's lowest rank, were an important source of labor during the Shang period.

The Shang made many advances, including China's first writing system. This system used more than 2,000 symbols to express words or ideas. Although the system has gone through changes over the years, the Chinese symbols used today are based on those of the Shang period.

Shang writing has been found on thousands of cattle bones and turtle shells. Priests had carved questions about the future on bones or shells, which were then heated, causing them to crack. The priests believed they could "read" these cracks to predict the future. The bones were called oracle bones because an **oracle** is a prediction.

In addition to writing, the Shang also made other achievements. Artisans made beautiful bronze containers for cooking and

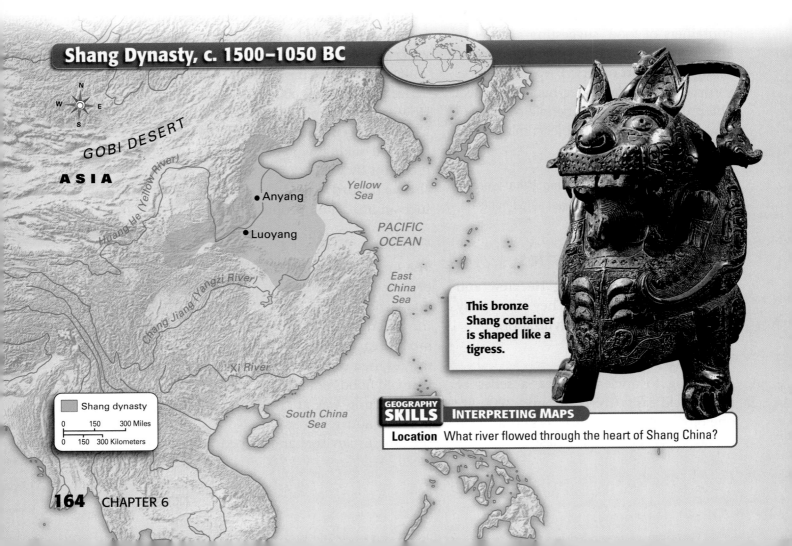

Shang Dynasty, c. 1500–1050 BC

GOBI DESERT

ASIA

Huang He (Yellow River)

• Anyang

• Luoyang

Chang Jiang (Yangzi River)

Xi River

Yellow Sea

PACIFIC OCEAN

East China Sea

South China Sea

Shang dynasty

0   150   300 Miles
0   150   300 Kilometers

This bronze Shang container is shaped like a tigress.

GEOGRAPHY SKILLS   **INTERPRETING MAPS**

Location What river flowed through the heart of Shang China?

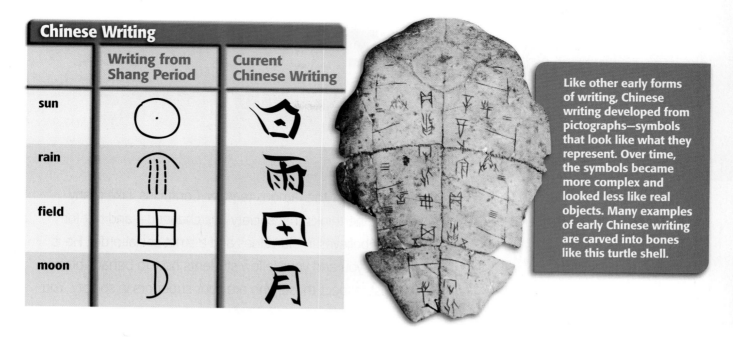

Chinese Writing

	Writing from Shang Period	Current Chinese Writing
sun	⊙	日
rain	☶	雨
field	⊞	田
moon	☽	月

Like other early forms of writing, Chinese writing developed from pictographs—symbols that look like what they represent. Over time, the symbols became more complex and looked less like real objects. Many examples of early Chinese writing are carved into bones like this turtle shell.

religious ceremonies. They also made axes, knives, and ornaments from jade. The military developed war chariots, powerful bows, and bronze body armor. Shang astrologers also made an important contribution. They developed a calendar based on the cycles of the moon.

> **READING CHECK** **Contrasting** What is a major historical difference between the Xia and Shang dynasties?

SUMMARY AND PREVIEW China is a vast land with a diverse geography. Ancient Chinese civilization developed in the fertile valleys of the Huang He and Chang Jiang. Civilization there advanced under Shang rule. People developed a social order, a writing system, and made other achievements. In the next section you will learn about new ideas in China during the rule of the Zhou dynasty.

Section 1 Assessment

go.hrw.com
Online Quiz
KEYWORD: SN6 HP6

Reviewing Ideas, Terms, and People

1. **a. Identify** Name China's two major rivers.
   b. Analyze How did China's geography affect its development?
2. **a. Identify** In which river valley did China's civilization begin?
   b. Explain What made China's river valleys ideal for farming?
   c. Elaborate What do Chinese artifacts reveal about China's early civilization?
3. **a. Describe** How do historians know about the Xia dynasty?
   b. Draw Conclusions What does the use of **oracle** bones tell us about the early Chinese?

Critical Thinking

4. **Comparing and Contrasting** Draw a chart like this one. Use it and your notes to compare and contrast the Xia and Shang dynasties.

Xia dynasty   Shang dynasty

Similarities

> **FOCUS ON SPEAKING**

5. **Thinking about Events** Look back over the section to note the important events of China's earliest times. Think about what it is that makes one event more important than another. Write down your ideas in a notebook.

The Zhou Dynasty and New Ideas

What You Will Learn...

Main Ideas

1. The Zhou dynasty expanded China but then declined.
2. Confucius offered ideas to bring order to Chinese society.
3. Daoism and Legalism also gained followers.

The Big Idea

The Zhou dynasty brought political stability and new ways to deal with political and social changes in ancient China.

Key Terms and People

lords, *p. 167*
peasants, *p. 167*
Confucius, *p. 169*
ethics, *p. 169*
Confucianism, *p. 169*
Daoism, *p. 170*
Laozi, *p. 170*
Legalism, *p. 170*

TAKING NOTES As you read, take notes on changes that occurred during the Zhou dynasty. Use a diagram like the one below to help organize your information.

Politics	Society	Religion and Philosophy

If YOU were there...

You are a student of the famous teacher Confucius. Like many older Chinese, he thinks that society has changed—and not for the better. He believes in old values and a strict social order. He is trying to teach you and your fellow students how to behave properly. You must respect those who are your superiors in society. You must set a good example for others.

How will these teachings affect your life?

BUILDING BACKGROUND The people of the Shang dynasty made many advances, including beautiful metalwork, a writing system, and a calendar. The next dynasty, the Zhou, established other Chinese traditions. Some of these traditions included the importance of family and social order. Later thinkers looked back with admiration to the values of the Zhou period.

The Zhou Dynasty

In the 1100s BC the leaders of a people who came to be known as the Zhou (JOH) ruled over a kingdom in China. They joined with other nearby tribes and attacked and overthrew the Shang dynasty. The Zhou dynasty lasted longer than any other dynasty in Chinese history.

Time Line

The Zhou Dynasty

1100s BC
The Zhou dynasty begins.

551 BC
Confucius is born.

1200 BC — 800 BC — 400 BC

771 BC
Invaders reach the Zhou capital.

481 BC
Civil war spreads across China during the Warring States period.

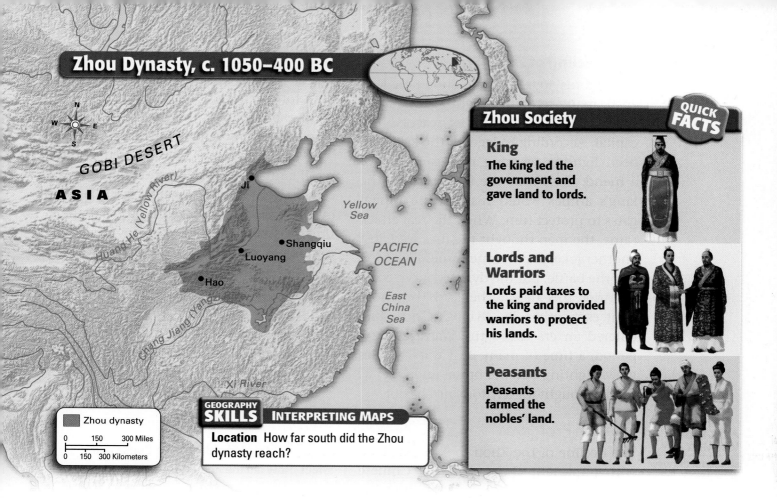

GOBI DESERT

ASIA

Huang He (Yellow River)

Ji

Yellow Sea

Shangqiu
Luoyang

PACIFIC OCEAN

Hao

East China Sea

Chang Jiang (Yangzi)

Xi River

Zhou dynasty

0   150   300 Miles
0   150 300 Kilometers

GEOGRAPHY SKILLS INTERPRETING MAPS

Location How far south did the Zhou dynasty reach?

QUICK FACTS

Zhou Society

King
The king led the government and gave land to lords.

Lords and Warriors
Lords paid taxes to the king and provided warriors to protect his lands.

Peasants
Peasants farmed the nobles' land.

The Zhou Political System

The Zhou kings claimed to possess the mandate of heaven. According to this idea, heaven gave power to the king or leader, and no one ruled without heaven's permission. If a king was found to be bad, heaven would support another leader.

The Zhou came from an area to the west of the Shang kingdom. Early Zhou rulers used the mandate of heaven to justify their rebellion against the Shang. Later Zhou rulers expanded their territory to the northwest and the east. Zhou soldiers then moved south, eventually expanding their rule to the Chang Jiang.

The Zhou established a new political order. They granted land to others in return for loyalty, military support, and other services. The Zhou king was at the highest level. He granted plots of land to **lords**, or people of high rank. Lords paid taxes and provided soldiers to the king as needed. **Peasants**, or farmers with small farms, were at the bottom of the order. Each peasant family received a small plot of land and had to farm additional land for the noble. The system was described in the *Book of Songs*:

" Everywhere under vast Heaven
There is no land that is not the king's
Within the borders of those lands
There are none who are not the king's servants. "
–from the Zhou *Book of Songs*

The Zhou system brought order to China. Ruling through lords helped the Zhou control distant areas and helped ensure loyalty to the king. Over time, however, the political order broke down. Lords passed their power to their sons, who were less loyal to the king. Local rulers gained power. They began to reject the authority of the Zhou kings.

The Decline of Zhou Power

As the lords' loyalty to the Zhou king lessened, many refused to fight against invasions. In 771 BC invaders reached the capital. According to legend, the king had been lighting warning fires to entertain a friend. Each time the fires were lit, the king's armies would rush to the capital gates to protect him. When the real attack came, the men thought the fires were just another joke, and no one came. The Zhou lost the battle, but the dynasty survived.

After this defeat the lords began to fight each other. By 481 BC, China had entered an era called the Warring States period, a time of many civil wars. Armies grew. Fighting became brutal and cruel as soldiers fought for territory, not honor.

ACADEMIC VOCABULARY

structure the way something is set up or organized

Internal Problems

The decline of the Zhou took place along with important changes in the Chinese family **structure**. For many centuries the family had been the foundation of life in China. Large families of several generations formed powerful groups. When these families broke apart, they lost their power. Close relatives became rivals.

Bonds of loyalty even weakened within small families, especially among the upper classes. Sons plotted against each other over inheritances. A wealthy father sometimes tried to maintain peace by dividing his land among his sons. But this created new problems. Each son could build up his wealth and then challenge his brothers. Some sons even killed their own fathers. During the Warring States period, China lacked a strong government to stop the power struggles within the ruling-class families. Chinese society fell into a period of disorder.

READING CHECK **Identifying Cause and Effect** How did the Zhou's decline affect Chinese society?

The Warring States Period

During China's Warring States period, thousands of armies fought each other to gain territory. The armies used new weapons and battle techniques in the civil wars that lasted more than 200 years.

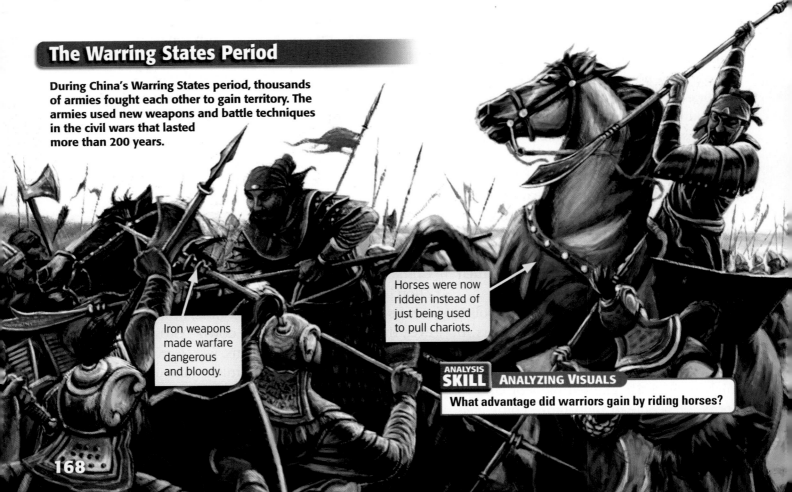

Iron weapons made warfare dangerous and bloody.

Horses were now ridden instead of just being used to pull chariots.

ANALYSIS SKILL **ANALYZING VISUALS**

What advantage did warriors gain by riding horses?

Confucius and Society

During the late Zhou period, thinkers came up with ideas about how to restore order to China. One such person, **Confucius**, became the most influential teacher in Chinese history. Confucius is a Western form of the Chinese title of "Master Kong" or "Kongfuzi."

Confucius felt that China was overrun with rude and dishonest people. Upset by the disorder and people's lack of decency, Confucius said that the Chinese needed to return to **ethics**, or moral values. The ideas of Confucius are known as **Confucianism**.

Confucius wanted China to return to ideas and practices from a time when people knew their proper roles in society. These are basic guidelines that Confucius thought would restore family order and social harmony:

- Fathers should display high moral values to inspire their families.
- Children should respect and obey their parents.
- All family members should be loyal to each other.

Confucius's ideas about government were similar to his ideas about family:

- Moral leadership, not laws, brought order to China.
- A king should lead by example, inspiring good behavior in all of his subjects.
- The lower classes would learn by following the example of their superiors. Confucius expressed this idea when he told kings:

> **"** Lead the people by means of government policies and regulate them through punishments, and they will be evasive and have no sense of shame. Lead them by means of virtue . . . and they will have a sense of shame and moreover have standards. **"**
>
> –Confucius, from *The Analects*

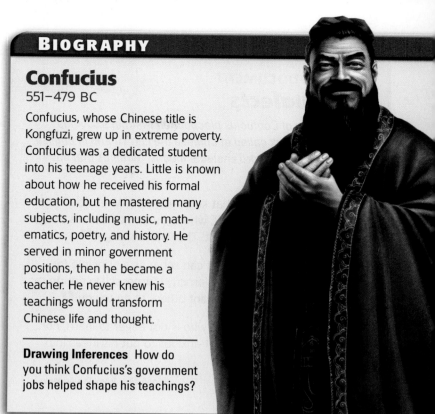

BIOGRAPHY

Confucius
551–479 BC

Confucius, whose Chinese title is Kongfuzi, grew up in extreme poverty. Confucius was a dedicated student into his teenage years. Little is known about how he received his formal education, but he mastered many subjects, including music, mathematics, poetry, and history. He served in minor government positions, then he became a teacher. He never knew his teachings would transform Chinese life and thought.

Drawing Inferences How do you think Confucius's government jobs helped shape his teachings?

As Confucius traveled to many different regions, he earned the reputation of a respected teacher. His ideas were passed down through his students and later compiled into a book called *The Analects*.

Because Confucianism focuses on morality, family, society, and government, people often think of it as a philosophy or way of thinking. But it is much more. Confucianism is a unique teaching that is both philosophical and religious. It has been a guiding force in human behavior and religious understanding in China.

Confucius believed that when people behaved well and acted morally, they were simply carrying out what heaven expected of them. Over the centuries Confucius's ideas about virtue, kindness, and learning became the dominant beliefs in China.

READING CHECK Identifying Points of View
What did Confucius believe about good behavior?

HISTORIC DOCUMENT
The Analects

The followers of Confucius placed their teacher's sayings together in a work called in Chinese the Lun Yü *and in English* The Analects. *The word* analects *means "writings that have been collected."*

❝Yu, shall I teach you what knowledge is? When you know a thing, say that you know it; when you do not know a thing, admit that you do not know it. That is knowledge.❞

❝Is there any one word that can serve as a principle for . . . life? Perhaps the word is reciprocity [fairness]: Do not do to others what you would not want others to do to you.❞

❝I do not enlighten anyone who is not eager to learn, nor encourage anyone who is not anxious to put his ideas into words.❞

—Confucius, from *The Analects*

ANALYSIS SKILL **ANALYZING PRIMARY SOURCES**

What are some of the qualities that Confucius valued?

Daoism and Legalism

Other beliefs besides Confucianism influenced China during the Zhou period. Two in particular attracted many followers.

Daoism

Daoism (DOW-ih-zum) takes its name from *Dao*, meaning "the way." **Daoism** stressed living in harmony with the Dao, the guiding force of all reality. In Daoist teachings, the Dao gave birth to the universe and all things in it. Daoism developed in part as a reaction to Confucianism. Daoists didn't agree with the idea that active, involved leaders brought social harmony. Instead, they wanted the government to stay out of people's lives.

Daoists believed that people should avoid interfering with nature or each other. They should be like water and simply let things flow in a natural way. For Daoists,

Main Ideas of Confucianism **QUICK FACTS**

- People should be respectful and loyal to their family members.
- Leaders should be kind and lead by example.
- Learning is a process that never ends.
- Heaven expects people to behave well and act morally.

the ideal ruler was a wise man who was in harmony with the Dao. He would govern so effortlessly that his people would not even know they were being governed.

Daoists taught that the universe is a balance of opposites: female and male, light and dark, low and high. In each case, opposing forces should be in harmony.

While Confucianism focused its followers' attention on the human world, Daoists paid more attention to the natural world. Daoists regarded humans as just a part of nature, not better than any other thing. In time the Dao, as represented by nature, became so important to the Daoists that they worshipped it.

Laozi (LOWD-zuh) was the most famous Daoist teacher. He taught that people should not try to gain wealth, nor should they seek power. Laozi is credited with writing the basic text of Daoism, *The Way and Its Power*. Later writers created many legends about Laozi's achievements.

Legalism

Legalism, the belief that people were bad by nature and needed to be controlled, contrasted with both Confucianism and Daoism. Unlike the other two beliefs, Legalism was a political philosophy without religious concerns. Instead, it dealt only with government and social control. Followers of Legalism disagreed with the moral preaching of Confucius. Legalists also rejected Daoism because it didn't stress respect for authority.

Legalists felt that society needed strict laws to keep people in line and that punishments should fit crimes. For example, they believed that citizens should be held responsible for each other's conduct. A guilty person's relatives and neighbors should also be punished. This way, everyone would obey the laws.

Unity and efficiency were also important to Legalists. They wanted appointed officials, not nobles, to run China. Legalists wanted the empire to continue to expand. Therefore, they urged the state to always be prepared for war.

Confucianism, Daoism, and Legalism competed for followers. All three beliefs became popular, but the Legalists were the first to put their ideas into practice throughout China.

READING CHECK **Contrasting** How did Daoism and Legalism differ in their theories about government?

BIOGRAPHY

Laozi
c. 500s or 400s BC

Scholars have found little reliable information about Laozi's life. Some believe that his book on Daoism was actually the work of several different authors. Most ancient sources of information about Laozi are myths. For example, one legend states that when Laozi was born, he was already an old man. In Chinese *Laozi* can mean "Old Baby." Over the years, many Daoists have worshipped Laozi as a supernatural being.

Drawing Inferences What do you think it meant to say Laozi was born "old"?

SUMMARY AND PREVIEW When the Zhou dynasty crumbled, political and social chaos erupted. In response, the new teachings of Confucianism, Daoism, and Legalism emerged. In the next section you will learn how the Qin dynasty applied the teachings of Legalism.

Section 2 Assessment

Reviewing Ideas, Terms, and People

1. **a. Identify** What is the mandate of heaven?
   b. Explain Describe the political order used by the Zhou kings to rule distant lands.
   c. Elaborate What happened when nobles began to reject the Zhou king's authority?
2. **a. Identify** Who was **Confucius**?
   b. Analyze Why did many of the teachings of Confucius focus on the family?
3. **a. Identify** Who was the most famous Daoist teacher?
   b. Summarize What were the main ideas of **Daoism**?
   c. Elaborate What might be some disadvantages of **Legalism**?

Critical Thinking

4. **Finding Main Ideas** Draw a chart like the one here. Use it and your notes on the Zhou dynasty to list two main ideas about each set of beliefs.

Confucianism	
Daoism	
Legalism	

FOCUS ON SPEAKING

5. **Exploring the Importance of Historical Figures** Many important people in history are rulers or conquerors. People who think and teach, however, have also played major roles in history. How did thinkers and teachers shape China's history? Write some ideas in your notebook.

The Qin Dynasty

What You Will Learn...

Main Ideas

1. The first Qin emperor created a strong but strict government.
2. A unified China was created through Qin policies and achievements.

The Big Idea

The Qin dynasty unified China with a strong government and a system of standardization.

Key Terms and People

Shi Huangdi, *p. 172*
Great Wall, *p. 175*

TAKING NOTES As you read, take notes on the achievements and policies of Shi Huangdi. Note how he affected life in China. Use a chart like the one below, adding more lines if necessary.

Achievement or Policy	Effect

If YOU were there...

You are a scholar living in China in about 210 BC. You have a large library of Chinese literature, poetry, and philosophy. The new emperor is a harsh ruler with no love for learning. He says you must burn all the books that disagree with his ideas. The idea horrifies you. But if you do not obey, the punishment may be severe.

Will you obey the order to burn your books? Why or why not?

BUILDING BACKGROUND Different dynasties held very different ideas about how to rule. As the Zhou period declined, putting new ideas into effect brought great changes.

The Qin Emperor's Strong Government

The Warring States period marked a time in China when several states battled each other for power. One state, the Qin (CHIN), built a strong army that defeated the armies of the rivaling states. Eventually, the Qin dynasty united the country under one government.

Shi Huangdi Takes the Throne

In 221 BC, the Qin king Ying Zheng succeeded in unifying China. He gave himself the title **Shi Huangdi** (SHEE hwahng-dee), which means "first emperor." Shi Huangdi followed Legalist political beliefs. He created a strong government with strict laws and harsh punishments.

Time Line

The Qin Dynasty

c. 213 BC
Shi Huangdi orders book burnings.

c. 206 BC
The Qin dynasty collapses.

225 BC   215 BC   205 BC

221 BC
Emperor Shi Huangdi unifies China, beginning the Qin dynasty.

210 BC
Shi Huangdi dies.

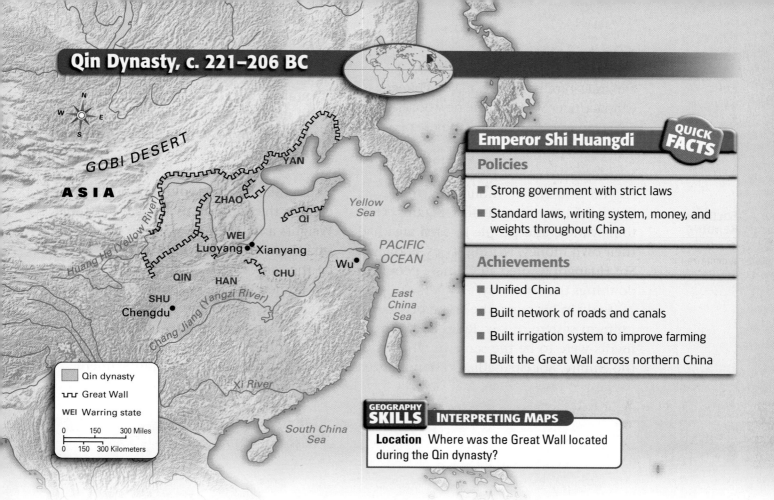

Qin Dynasty, c. 221–206 BC

GOBI DESERT

ASIA

YAN

ZHAO

QI

WEI

Luoyang • • Xianyang

Yellow Sea

QIN   HAN   CHU

Wu •

PACIFIC OCEAN

SHU

Chengdu •

Huang He (Yellow River)

Chang Jiang (Yangzi River)

East China Sea

Xi River

South China Sea

Qin dynasty

⌐⌐⌐ Great Wall

WEI Warring state

0   150   300 Miles
0 150 300 Kilometers

Emperor Shi Huangdi — QUICK FACTS

Policies

- Strong government with strict laws
- Standard laws, writing system, money, and weights throughout China

Achievements

- Unified China
- Built network of roads and canals
- Built irrigation system to improve farming
- Built the Great Wall across northern China

GEOGRAPHY SKILLS | **INTERPRETING MAPS**

Location Where was the Great Wall located during the Qin dynasty?

Shi Huangdi demanded that everyone follow his policies. He ordered the burning of all writings that did not agree with Legalism. The only other books that were saved dealt with farming, medicine, and predicting the future. Many scholars opposed the book burnings. The emperor responded to the opposition by burying 460 scholars alive.

Shi Huangdi also used his armies to expand the empire. First, they occupied the lands around both of China's major rivers. Then his soldiers turned north and advanced almost to the Gobi Desert. To the south, they invaded more lands and advanced as far as the Xi River.

Shi Huangdi ensured that there would not be any future revolts in his new territories. When his soldiers conquered a city, he had them destroy its walls and take all the weapons.

China under the Qin

Shi Huangdi changed China's old political system. He claimed all the power and did not share it with the lords. He even took land away from them and forced thousands of nobles to move with their families to the capital so he could keep an eye on them. He also forced thousands of commoners to work on government building projects. Workers faced years of hardship, danger, and often, death.

To control China, Shi Huangdi divided it into districts, each with its own governor. Districts were subdivided into counties that were governed by appointed officials. This organization helped the emperor enforce his tax system. It also helped the Qin enforce a strict chain of command.

READING CHECK **Summarizing** How did Shi Huangdi strengthen the government?

A Unified China

Qin rule brought other major changes to China. Under Shi Huangdi, new policies and achievements united the Chinese people.

Qin Policies

FOCUS ON READING
How might you summarize the new Qin policies?

As you read earlier, mountains and rivers divided China into distinct regions. Customs varied, and people in each area had their own money, writing styles, and laws. Shi Huangdi wanted all Chinese people to do things the same way.

Early in his reign, the emperor set up a uniform system of law. Rules and punishments were to be the same in all parts of the empire. Shi Huangdi also standardized the written language. People everywhere were required to write using the same set of symbols. People from different regions could now communicate with each other in writing. This gave them a sense of shared culture and a common identity.

Next, the emperor set up a new money system. Standardized gold and copper coins became the currency used in all of China. Weights and measures were also standardized. Even the axle width of carts had to be the same. With all these changes and the unified writing system, trade between different regions became much easier. The Qin government strictly enforced these new standards. Any citizen who disobeyed the laws would face severe punishment.

Guardians of Shi Huangdi's Tomb

In 1974 archaeologists found the tomb of Emperor Shi Huangdi near Xi'an and made an amazing discovery. Buried close to the emperor was an army of more than 6,000 life-size terra-cotta, or clay, soldiers. They were designed to be with Shi Huangdi in the afterlife. In other nearby chambers of the tomb there were another 1,400 clay figures of cavalry and chariots.

MONGOLIA

Huang He (Yellow River)

Xi'an • Shi Huangdi's Tomb

CHINA

Chang Jiang (Yangzi River)

Qin Achievements

New, massive building projects also helped to unify the country. Under Shi Huangdi's rule, the Chinese built a network of roads that connected the capital to every part of the empire. These roads made travel easier for everyone. Each of these new roads was the same width, 50 paces wide. This design helped the army move quickly and easily to put down revolts in distant areas.

China's water system was also improved. Workers built canals to connect the country's rivers. Like the new roads, the canals improved transportation throughout the country. Using the new canals and rivers together made it easier and faster to ship goods from north to south. In addition, the Qin built an irrigation system to make more land good for farming. Parts of that system are still in use today.

Shi Huangdi also wanted to protect the country from invasion. Nomads from the north were fierce warriors, and they were a real threat to China. Hoping to stop them from invading, the emperor built the **Great Wall**, a barrier that linked earlier walls across China's northern frontier. The first section of the wall had been built in the 600s BC to keep invading groups out of China. The Qin connected earlier pieces of the wall to form a long, unbroken structure. Building the wall required years of labor from hundreds of thousands of workers. Many of them died building the wall.

THE IMPACT TODAY

The Great Wall is a major tourist attraction today.

Each terra-cotta soldier was different, with its own facial features, hairstyle, and unique expression. Here, a computer model shows what a soldier might have looked like when it was created.

The Great Wall has been added to and rebuilt many times since Shi Huangdi ruled China.

Rebel forces formed across the country. Each claimed to have received the mandate of heaven to replace the emperor. One of these groups attacked the Qin capital, and the new emperor surrendered. The palace was burned to the ground. Qin authority had disappeared. With no central government, the country fell into civil war.

READING CHECK **Recall** What massive building projects did Shi Huangdi order to unify China?

The Fall of the Qin

Shi Huangdi's policies unified China. However, his policies also stirred resentment. Many peasants, scholars, and nobles hated his harsh ways.

Still, Shi Huangdi was powerful enough to hold the country together. When he died in 210 BC China was unified, but that didn't last. Within a few years, the government began to fall apart.

SUMMARY AND PREVIEW Qin emperor Shi Huangdi's policies and achievements unified China, but his harsh rule led to resentment. After his death, the dynasty fell apart. In the next section you will learn about the Han dynasty that came to power after the end of the Qin.

go.hrw.com
Online Quiz
KEYWORD: SN6 HP6

Section 3 Assessment

Reviewing Ideas, Terms, and People

1. **a. Identify** What does the title **Shi Huangdi** mean?
   b. Explain After unifying China, why did Shi Huangdi divide the country into military districts?
   c. Rate Which of the following acts do you think best showed how powerful Shi Huangdi was—burning books, forcing nobles to move, or forcing commoners to work on government projects? Explain your answer.
2. **a. Recall** Why was the **Great Wall** built?
   b. Summarize What actions did Shi Huangdi take to unify China and standardize things within the empire?
   c. Evaluate In your opinion, was Shi Huangdi a good ruler? Explain your answer.

Critical Thinking

3. **Evaluating** Using your notes and a diagram like this one, rank the effectiveness of the emperor's achievements and policies in unifying China.

Most important		Least important
1.	2.	3.

FOCUS ON SPEAKING

4. **Evaluating Contributions to History** When evaluating a person's contribution to history, it is important to consider both the person's good impact and bad impact. In what ways was Shi Huangdi great? What negative impact did he have on China? Write down your ideas.

Emperor Shi Huangdi

If you were a powerful ruler, how would you protect yourself?

When did he live? c. 259–210 BC

Where did he live? Shi Huangdi built a new capital city at Xianyang, now called Xi'an (SHEE-AHN), in eastern China.

What did he do? Shi Huangdi didn't trust people. Several attempts were made on his life, and the emperor lived in fear of more attacks. He was constantly seeking new ways to protect himself and extend his life. By the time Shi Huangdi died, he didn't even trust his own advisors. Even in death, he surrounded himself with protectors: the famous terra-cotta army.

Why is he important? Shi Huangdi was one of the most powerful rulers in Chinese history. The first ruler to unify all of China, he is also remembered for his building programs. He built roads and canals throughout China and expanded what would become the Great Wall.

Drawing Conclusions Why do you think Shi Huangdi feared for his life?

KEY EVENTS

- **246 BC** Shi Huangdi becomes emperor. Because he is still young, a high official rules in his name.

- **238 BC** He exiles the official, whom he suspects of plotting against him, and rules alone.

- **227 BC** An assassination attempt adds fuel to the emperor's paranoia.

- **221 BC** Shi Huangdi unites all of China under his rule.

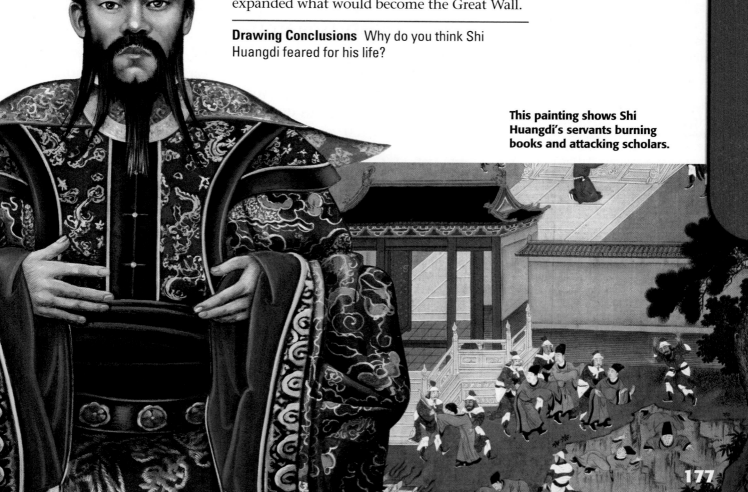

This painting shows Shi Huangdi's servants burning books and attacking scholars.

177

The Han Dynasty

What You Will Learn...

Main Ideas

1. Han dynasty government was based on the ideas of Confucius.
2. Family life was supported and strengthened in Han China.
3. The Han made many achievements in art, literature, and learning.

The Big Idea

The Han dynasty created a new form of government that valued family, art, and learning.

Key Terms

sundial, *p. 182*
seismograph, *p. 182*
acupuncture, *p. 183*

TAKING NOTES As you read, take notes on Han government, family life, and achievements. Use a diagram like the one here to help you organize your notes.

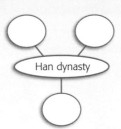

If YOU were there...

You are a young Chinese student from a poor family. Your family has worked hard to give you a good education so that you can get a government job and have a great future. Your friends laugh at you. They say that only boys from wealthy families win the good jobs. They think it is better to join the army.

Will you take the exam or join the army? Why?

BUILDING BACKGROUND Though it was harsh, the rule of the first Qin emperor helped to unify northern China. With the building of the Great Wall, he strengthened defenses on the northern frontier. But his successor could not hold on to power. The Qin gave way to a remarkable new dynasty that would last for 400 years.

Han Dynasty Government

When the Qin dynasty collapsed in 207 BC, several different groups battled for power. After several years of fighting, an army led by Liu Bang (lee-oo bang) won control. Liu Bang became the first emperor of the Han dynasty. This Chinese dynasty lasted for more than 400 years.

The Rise of a New Dynasty

Liu Bang, a peasant, was able to become emperor in large part because of the Chinese belief in the mandate of heaven. He was the first common person to become emperor. He earned people's

Time Line

The Han Dynasty

206 BC
The Han dynasty begins.

200 BC

140 BC
Wudi becomes emperor and tries to strengthen China's government.

BC 1 AD

AD 25
The Han move their capital east to Luoyang.

AD 200

AD 220
The Han dynasty falls.

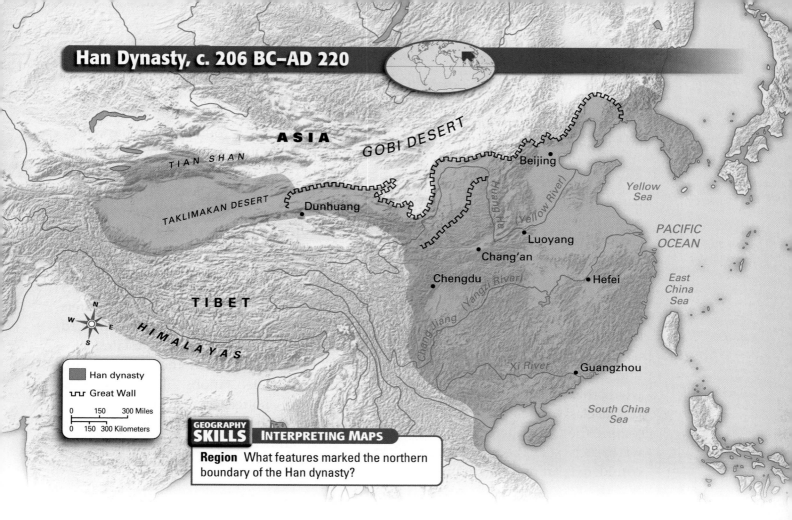

ASIA

TIAN SHAN

GOBI DESERT

TAKLIMAKAN DESERT

Dunhuang

TIBET

HIMALAYAS

Beijing

Huang He

(Yellow River)

Luoyang

Chang'an

Chengdu

Chang Jiang (Yangzi River)

Hefei

Xi River

Guangzhou

Yellow Sea

PACIFIC OCEAN

East China Sea

South China Sea

N
W E
S

Han dynasty

Great Wall

0   150   300 Miles

0 150 300 Kilometers

GEOGRAPHY SKILLS | **INTERPRETING MAPS**

Region What features marked the northern boundary of the Han dynasty?

loyalty and trust. In addition, he was well liked by both soldiers and peasants, which helped him to maintain control.

Liu Bang's rule was different from the strict Legalism of the Qin. He wanted to free people from harsh government policies. He lowered taxes for farmers and made punishments less severe. He gave large blocks of land to his supporters.

In addition to setting new policies, Liu Bang changed the way government worked. He set up a government structure that built on the foundation begun by the Qin. He also relied on educated officials to help him rule.

Wudi Creates a New Government

In 140 BC Emperor Wudi (WOO-dee) took the throne. He wanted to create a stronger central government. To do that, he took land from the lords, raised taxes, and placed the supply of grain under the control of the government.

Under Wudi, Confucianism became China's official government philosophy. Government officials were expected to practice Confucianism. Wudi even began a university to teach Confucian ideas.

If a person passed an exam on Confucian teachings, he could get a good position in the government. However, not just anyone could take the test. The exams were only open to people who had been recommended for government service already. As a result, wealthy or influential families continued to control the government.

READING CHECK **Analyzing** How was the Han government based on the ideas of Confucius?

Family Life

The Han period was a time of great social change in China. Class structure became more rigid. The family once again became important within Chinese society.

Social Classes

Based on the Confucian system, people were divided into four classes. The upper class was made up of the emperor, his court, and scholars who held government positions. The second class, the largest, was made up of the peasants. Next were artisans who produced items for daily life and some luxury goods. Merchants occupied the lowest class because they did not produce anything. They only bought and sold what others made. The military was not an official class in the Confucian system. Still, joining the army offered men a chance to rise in social status because the military was considered part of the government.

This Han artifact is an oil lamp held by a servant.

Lives of Rich and Poor

The classes only divided people into social rank. They did not indicate wealth or power. For instance, even though peasants made up the second highest class, they were poor. On the other hand, some merchants were wealthy and powerful despite being in the lowest class.

People's lifestyles varied according to wealth. The emperor and his court lived in a large palace. Less important officials lived in multilevel houses built around courtyards. Many of these wealthy families owned large estates and employed laborers to work the land. Some families even hired private armies to defend their estates.

The wealthy filled their homes with expensive decorations. These included paintings, pottery, bronze lamps, and jade figures. Rich families hired musicians for entertainment. Even the tombs of dead family members were filled with beautiful, expensive objects.

Most people in the Han dynasty, however, didn't live like the wealthy. Nearly 60 million people lived in China during the Han dynasty, and about 90 percent of them were peasants who lived in the countryside. Peasants put in long, tiring days working the land. Whether it was in the millet fields of the north or in the rice paddies of the south, the work was hard. In the winter, peasants were also forced to work on building projects for the government. Heavy taxes and bad weather forced many farmers to sell their land and work for rich landowners. By the last years of the Han dynasty, only a few farmers were independent.

Chinese peasants lived simple lives. They wore plain clothing made of fiber from a native plant. The main foods they ate were cooked grains like barley. Most peasants lived in small villages. Their small, wood-framed houses had walls made of mud or stamped earth.

The Revival of the Family

Since Confucianism was the official government philosophy during Wudi's reign, Confucian teachings about the family were also honored. Children were taught from birth to respect their elders. Disobeying one's parents was a crime. Even emperors had a duty to respect their parents.

Confucius had taught that the father was the head of the family. Within the family, the father had absolute power. The Han taught that it was a woman's duty to obey her husband, and children had to obey their father.

Han officials believed that if the family was strong and people obeyed the father, then people would obey the emperor, too. Since the Han stressed strong family ties and respect for elders, some men even gained government jobs based on the respect they showed their parents.

Children were encouraged to serve their parents. They were also expected to honor dead parents with ceremonies and offerings. All family members were expected to care for family burial sites.

Chinese parents valued boys more highly than girls. This was because sons carried on the family line and took care of their parents when they were old. On the other hand, daughters became part of their husband's family. According to a Chinese proverb, "Raising daughters is like raising children for another family." Some women, however, still gained power. They could actually influence their sons' families. An older widow could even become the head of the family.

READING CHECK Identifying Cause and Effect
Why did the family take on such importance during the Han dynasty?

During the Han dynasty, the Chinese made many advances in art and learning. Some of these advances are shown here.

Science

This is a model of an ancient Chinese seismograph. When an earthquake struck, a lever inside caused a ball to drop from a dragon's mouth into a toad's mouth, indicating the direction from which the earthquake had come.

Han Achievements

Han rule was a time of great accomplishments. Art and literature thrived, and inventors developed many useful devices.

Art and Literature

The Chinese of the Han period produced many works of art. They became experts at figure painting—a style of painting that includes portraits of people. Portraits often showed religious figures and Confucian scholars. Han artists also painted realistic scenes from everyday life. Their creations covered the walls of palaces and tombs.

In literature, Han China is known for its poetry. Poets developed new styles of verse, including the *fu* style which was the most popular. *Fu* poets combined prose and poetry to create long works of literature. Another style, called *shi*, featured short lines of verse that could be sung. Han rulers hired poets known for the beauty of their verse.

Han writers also produced important works of history. One historian by the name of Sima Qian wrote a complete history of all the dynasties through the early Han. His format and style became the model for later historical writings.

Inventions and Advances

The Han Chinese invented one item that we use every day—paper. They made it by grinding plant fibers, such as mulberry bark and hemp, into a paste. Then they let it dry in sheets. Chinese scholars produced "books" by pasting several pieces of paper together into a long sheet. Then they rolled the sheet into a scroll.

The Han also made other **innovations** in science. These included the sundial and the seismograph. A **sundial** uses the position of shadows cast by the sun to tell the time of day. The sundial was an early type of clock. A **seismograph** is a device that measures the strength of an earthquake. Han emperors were very interested

ACADEMIC VOCABULARY

innovation a new idea, method, or device

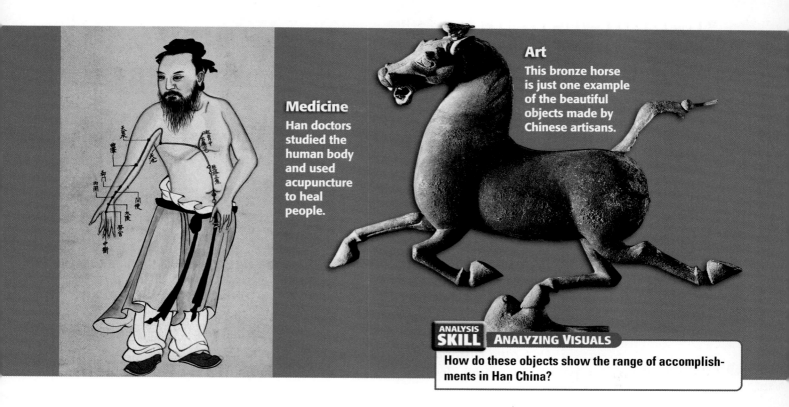

Medicine
Han doctors studied the human body and used acupuncture to heal people.

Art
This bronze horse is just one example of the beautiful objects made by Chinese artisans.

ANALYSIS SKILL **ANALYZING VISUALS**
How do these objects show the range of accomplishments in Han China?

in knowing about the movements of the earth. They believed that earthquakes were signs of future evil events.

Another Han innovation, acupuncture (AK-yoo-punk-cher), improved medicine. **Acupuncture** is the practice of inserting fine needles through the skin at specific points to cure disease or relieve pain. Many Han inventions in science and medicine are still used today.

READING CHECK **Categorizing** What advances did the Chinese make during the Han period?

SUMMARY AND PREVIEW Han rulers moved away from Legalism and based their government on Confucianism. This strengthened family bonds in Han China. In addition, art and learning thrived under Han rule. In the next section you will learn about China's contact beyond its borders.

go.hrw.com
Online Quiz
KEYWORD: SN6 HP6

Section 4 Assessment

Reviewing Ideas, Terms, and People

1. **a. Identify** Whose teachings were the foundation for government during the Han dynasty?
   b. Summarize How did Emperor Wudi create a strong central government?
   c. Evaluate Do you think that an exam system is the best way to make sure that people are fairly chosen for government jobs? Why or why not?
2. **a. Describe** What was the son's role in the family?
   b. Contrast How did living conditions for the wealthy differ from those of the peasants during the Han dynasty?
3. **Identify** What device did the Chinese invent to measure the strength of earthquakes?

Critical Thinking

4. **Analyzing** Use your notes to complete this diagram about how Confucianism influenced Han government and family.

| Government |
| Confucianism |
| Family |

FOCUS ON SPEAKING

5. **Analyzing Impact on History** Sometimes a ruler has the biggest impact on history. Other times, ideas that develop within a society have a greater impact. Which had a greater impact on Han China? Why?

from The Shiji

by Sima Qian

Translated by Burton Watson

About the Reading *The* Shiji, *also called the* Records of the Grand Historian, *is a history that describes more than two thousand years of Chinese culture. The author, Sima Qian (soo-MAH chee-EN), held the title Grand Historian under the Han emperor Wudi. He spent 18 years of his life writing the* Shiji. *His hard work paid off, and his history was well received. In fact, the* Shiji *was so respected that it served as the model for every later official history of China. This passage describes a man named Bu Shi, who attracted the emperor's attention through his generosity and good deeds. Eventually, the emperor invited him to live in the imperial palace.*

AS YOU READ Ask yourself why Sima Qian included Bu Shi in his history.

Bu Shi was a native of Henan, where his family made a living by farming and animal raising. ❶ When his parents died, Bu Shi left home, handing over the house, the lands, and all the family wealth to his younger brother, who by this time was full grown. For his own share, he took only a hundred or so of the sheep they had been raising, which he led off into the mountains to pasture. In the course of ten years or so, Bu Shi's sheep had increased to over a thousand and he had bought his own house and fields. His younger brother in the meantime had failed completely in the management of the farm, but Bu Shi promptly handed over to him a share of his own wealth. This happened several times. Just at that time the Han was sending its generals at frequent intervals to attack the Xiongnu. ❷ Bu Shi journeyed to the capital and submitted a letter to the throne, offering to turn over half of his wealth to the district officials to help in the defense of the border. The emperor dispatched an envoy to ask if Bu Shi wanted a post in the government. ❸

"From the time I was a child," Bu Shi replied, "I have been an animal raiser. I have had no experience in government and would certainly not want such a position" . . .

GUIDED READING

WORD HELP

intervals periods of time
dispatched sent
envoy representative

❶ Henan (HUH-NAHN) is a region of eastern China. It is a productive agricultural region.

❷ The Xiongnu were a tribe of nomads. They lived in the north and often raided towns near China's border.

❸ *Why do you think the emperor invites Bu Shi to work for the government?*

"If that is the case," said the envoy, "then what is your objective in making this offer?"

Bu Shi replied, "The Son of Heaven has sent out to punish the Xiongnu. ❹ In my humble opinion, every worthy man should be willing to fight to the death to defend the borders, and every person with wealth ought to contribute to the expense . . ."

The emperor discussed the matter with the chancellor, but the latter said, "The proposal is simply not in accord with human nature! ❺ Such eccentric people are of no use in guiding the populace, but only throw the laws into confusion. I beg Your Majesty not to accept his offer!"

For this reason the emperor put off answering Bu Shi for a long time, and finally after several years had passed, turned down the offer, whereupon Bu Shi went back to his fields and pastures . . .

The following year a number of poor people were transferred to other regions . . . At this point Bu Shi took two hundred thousand cash of his own and turned the sum over to the governor of Henan to assist the people who were emigrating to other regions . . . At this time the rich families were all scrambling to hide their wealth; only Bu Shi, unlike the others, had offered to contribute to the expenses of the government. ❻ The emperor decided that Bu Shi was really a man of exceptional worth after all . . . Because of his simple, unspoiled ways and his deep loyalty, the emperor finally appointed him grand tutor to his son Liu Hong, the king of Qi.

GUIDED READING

WORD HELP

objective goal
chancellor high official
accord agreement
eccentric someone who acts strangely
populace people
tutor private teacher

❹ The Chinese people believed that their emperor was the "Son of Heaven." They thought he received his power from heavenly ancestors.

❺ The "latter" means the one mentioned last. In this case, the latter is the chancellor.

❻ *What is Bu Shi's attitude toward his wealth? How is it different from the attitude of the rich families?*

In this painting from the 1600s, government officials deliver a letter.

CONNECTING LITERATURE TO HISTORY

1. **Drawing Conclusions** Like many Chinese historians, Sima Qian wanted to use history to teach lessons. What lessons could the story of Bu Shi be used to teach?

2. **Analyzing** The Emperor Wudi based his government on the teachings of Confucius. What elements of Confucianism can you see in this story?

Han Contacts with Other Cultures

What You Will Learn...

Main Ideas

1. Farming and manufacturing grew during the Han dynasty.
2. Trade routes linked China with the Middle East and Rome.
3. Buddhism came to China from India and gained many followers.

The Big Idea

Trade routes led to the exchange of new products and ideas among China, Rome, and other peoples.

Key Terms

silk, *p. 187*
Silk Road, *p. 187*
diffusion, *p. 189*

TAKING NOTES As you read, take notes on Chinese products and trade routes and on the arrival of Buddhism in China. Use a diagram like the one here to help you organize your notes.

Contact with Other Cultures

Products | Trade Routes | Buddhism

If YOU were there...

You are a trader traveling along the Silk Road to China. This is your first journey, but you have heard many stories about the country. You know the trip will be hard, through mountains and deserts and terrible weather. While you expect to make a good profit from silk, you are also curious about China and its people.

What do you expect to find in China?

BUILDING BACKGROUND During the Han dynasty Chinese society returned its focus to Confucian ideas, and new inventions were developed. In addition, increased trade allowed other countries to learn about the rich culture of China.

Farming and Manufacturing

Many advances in manufacturing took place during the Han dynasty. As a result, productivity increased and the empire prospered. These changes paved the way for China to make contact with people of other cultures.

Silk Production

By the Han period, the Chinese had become master ironworkers. They manufactured iron swords and armor that made the army more powerful.

Farmers also gained from advances in iron. The iron plow and the wheelbarrow, a single-wheeled cart, increased farm output. With a wheelbarrow a farmer could haul more than 300 pounds all by himself. With an iron plow, he could till more land and raise more food.

Another item that increased in production during the Han dynasty was **silk**, a soft, light, highly valued fabric. For centuries, Chinese women had known the complicated methods needed to raise silkworms, unwind the silk threads of their cocoons, and then prepare the threads for dyeing and weaving. The Chinese were determined to keep their **procedure** for making silk a secret. Revealing these secrets was punishable by death.

During the Han period, weavers used foot-powered looms to weave silk threads into beautiful fabric. Garments made from this silk were very expensive.

READING CHECK **Finding Main Ideas** How did advances in technology affect farming and silk production?

Trade Routes

Chinese goods, especially silk and fine pottery, were highly valued by people in other lands. During the Han period, the value of these goods to people outside China helped increase trade.

Expansion of Trade

Trade increased partly because Han armies conquered lands deep in Central Asia. Leaders there told the Han generals that people who lived still farther west wanted silk. At the same time, Emperor Wudi wanted strong, sturdy Central Asian horses for his army. China's leaders saw that they could make a profit by bringing silk to Central Asia and trading the cloth for the horses. The Central Asian peoples would then take the silk west and trade it for other products they wanted.

The Silk Road

Traders used a series of overland routes to take Chinese goods to distant buyers. The most famous trade route was known as the **Silk Road**. This 4,000-mile-long network of routes stretched westward from China across Asia's deserts and mountain ranges, through the Middle East, until it reached the Mediterranean Sea.

China still produces about 50 percent of the world's silk.

ACADEMIC VOCABULARY
procedure the way a task is accomplished

PHOTOGRAPH © 2004 MUSEUM OF FINE ARTS, BOSTON

The technique for making silk was a well-kept secret in ancient China, as silk was a valuable trade good in distant lands. Workers made silk from the cocoons of silkworms, just as they do today.

Chinese traders did not travel the entire Silk Road. Upon reaching Central Asia, they sold their goods to local traders who would take them the rest of the way.

Traveling the Silk Road was difficult. Hundreds of men and camels loaded down with valuable goods, including silks and jade, formed groups. They traveled the Silk Road together for protection. Armed guards were hired to protect traders from bandits who stole cargo and water, a precious necessity. Weather presented other dangers. Traders faced icy blizzards, desert heat, and blinding sandstorms.

Named after the most famous item transported along it, the Silk Road was worth its many risks. Silk was so popular in Rome, for example, that China grew wealthy from that trade relationship alone. Traders returned from Rome with silver, gold, precious stones, and horses.

READING CHECK **Summarizing** Why did Chinese trade expand under Han rule?

Buddhism Comes to China

When the Chinese people came into contact with other civilizations, they exchanged ideas along with trade goods. Among these ideas was a new religion. In the first century AD Buddhism spread from India to China along the Silk Road and other trade routes.

Arrival of a New Religion

Over time, the Han government became less stable. People ignored laws, and violence was common. As rebellions flared up, millions of peasants went hungry. Life became violent and uncertain. Many Chinese looked to Daoism or Confucianism to find out why they had to suffer so much, but they didn't find helpful answers.

Buddhism seemed to provide more hope than the traditional Chinese beliefs did. It offered rebirth and relief from suffering. This promise was a major reason the Chinese people embraced Buddhism.

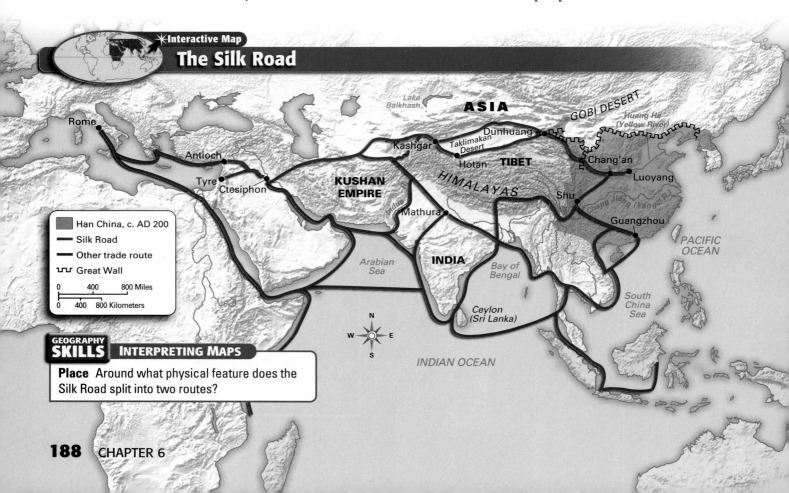

⋇ Interactive Map

The Silk Road

Han China, c. AD 200
Silk Road
Other trade route
Great Wall

0   400   800 Miles
0 400 800 Kilometers

GEOGRAPHY SKILLS **INTERPRETING MAPS**

Place Around what physical feature does the Silk Road split into two routes?

Impact on China

At first, Indian Buddhists had trouble explaining their religion to the Chinese. Then they used ideas found in Daoism to help describe Buddhist beliefs. Many people grew curious about Buddhism.

Before long, Buddhism caught on in China with both the poor and the upper classes. By AD 200, Buddhist altars stood in the emperor's palace.

Buddhism's introduction to China is an example of **diffusion**, the spread of ideas from one culture to another. Elements of Chinese culture changed in response to the new faith. For example, scholars translated Buddhist texts into Chinese. Many Chinese became Buddhist monks and nuns. Artists carved towering statues of Buddha into mountain walls.

READING CHECK **Finding Main Ideas** How did Chinese people learn of Buddhism?

SUMMARY AND PREVIEW Under the Han, trade brought new goods and ideas, including Buddhism, to China. In the next chapter you'll read about the religion of another people—the Jews.

This giant Buddha statue in China is among the largest in the world. It was carved from a hillside and looks down over the meeting place of three rivers.

Section 5 Assessment

go.hrw.com
Online Quiz
KEYWORD: SN6 HP6

Reviewing Ideas, Terms, and People

1. **a. Describe** How did wheelbarrows help farmers?
   b. Summarize How was **silk** made in ancient China?
   c. Elaborate Why did the Chinese keep silk-making methods a secret?

2. **a. Identify** Where did the **Silk Road** begin and end?
   b. Elaborate What information would you use to support the argument that the silk trade must have been very valuable?

3. **a. Identify** What is **diffusion**?
   b. Make Generalizations What Buddhist beliefs appealed to millions of Chinese peasants?

Critical Thinking

4. **Categorizing** Copy the chart here. Use it and your notes on trade to identify goods and ideas that were exchanged along the Silk Road, both into and out of China.

Into China

↑

Trade Along the Silk Road

↓

Out of China

FOCUS ON SPEAKING

5. **Evaluating the Importance of Events** Not all the important events in history are wars or invasions. What peaceful events in this section changed Chinese history? Write down some ideas.

The Silk Road

The Silk Road was a long trade route that stretched across the heart of Asia. Along this route, an active trade developed between China and Southwest Asia by about 100 BC. By AD 100, the Silk Road connected Han China in the east with the Roman Empire in the west.

The main goods traded along the Silk Road were luxury goods—ones that were small, light, and expensive. These included goods like silk, spices, and gold. Because they were small and valuable, merchants could carry these goods long distances and still sell them for a large profit. As a result, people in both the east and the west were able to buy luxury goods that were unavailable at home.

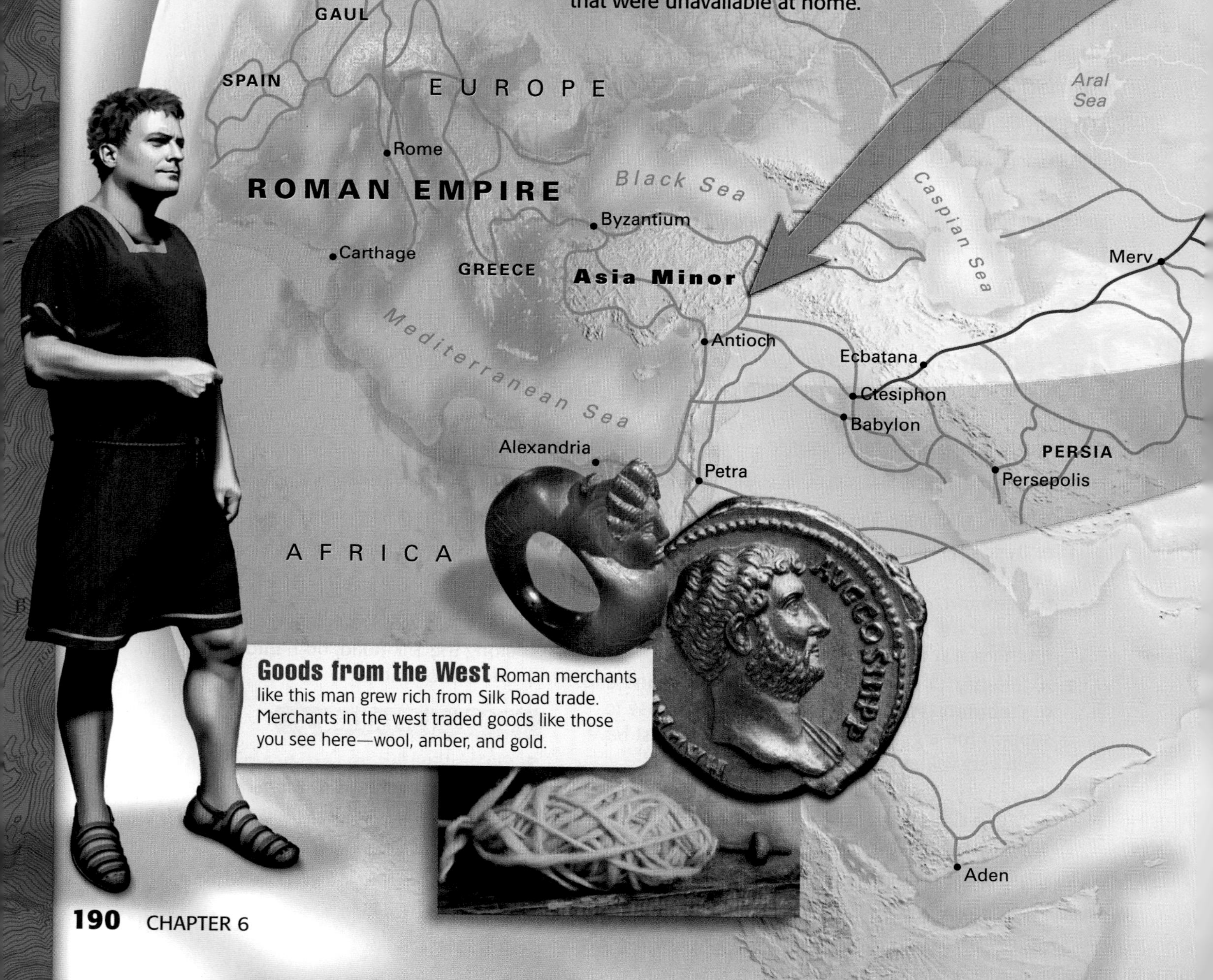

GAUL

SPAIN

EUROPE

Aral Sea

Rome

ROMAN EMPIRE

Black Sea

Caspian Sea

Byzantium

Merv

Carthage

GREECE

Asia Minor

Mediterranean Sea

Antioch

Ecbatana

Ctesiphon

Babylon

PERSIA

Alexandria

Petra

Persepolis

AFRICA

Goods from the West Roman merchants like this man grew rich from Silk Road trade. Merchants in the west traded goods like those you see here—wool, amber, and gold.

Aden

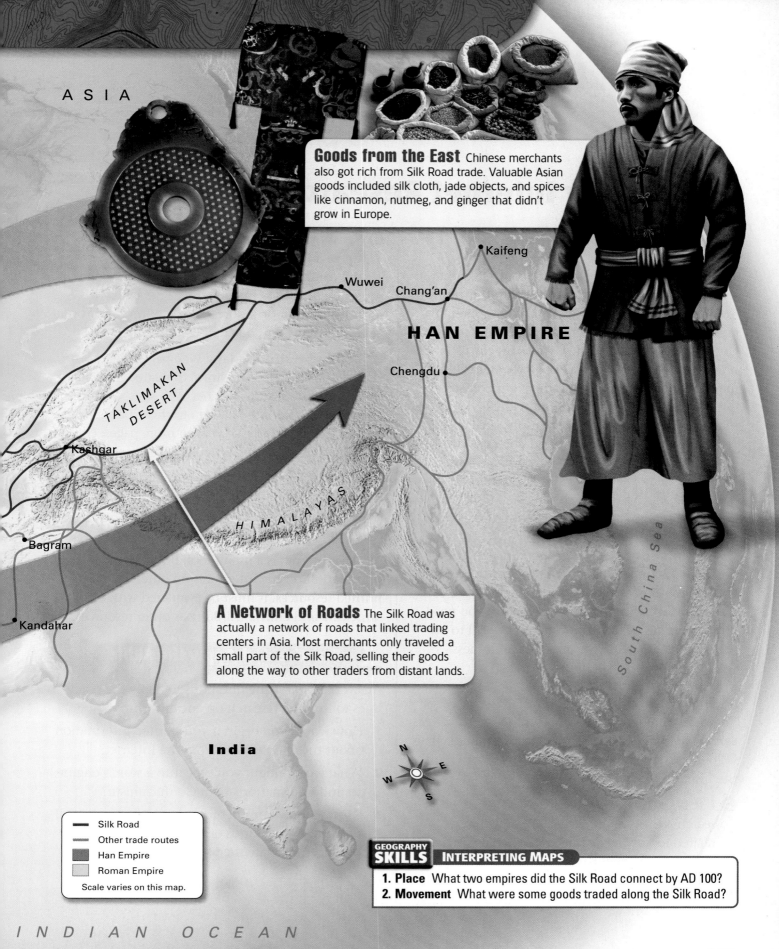

A S I A

Goods from the East Chinese merchants also got rich from Silk Road trade. Valuable Asian goods included silk cloth, jade objects, and spices like cinnamon, nutmeg, and ginger that didn't grow in Europe.

• Kaifeng

Wuwei •   Chang'an •

HAN EMPIRE

Chengdu •

TAKLIMAKAN DESERT

• Kashgar

H I M A L A Y A S

• Bagram

A Network of Roads The Silk Road was actually a network of roads that linked trading centers in Asia. Most merchants only traveled a small part of the Silk Road, selling their goods along the way to other traders from distant lands.

• Kandahar

South China Sea

India

N E S W

Silk Road

Other trade routes

Han Empire

Roman Empire

Scale varies on this map.

I N D I A N   O C E A N

GEOGRAPHY SKILLS ▸ **INTERPRETING MAPS** ▸

1. **Place** What two empires did the Silk Road connect by AD 100?
2. **Movement** What were some goods traded along the Silk Road?

Social Studies Skills

Analysis   Critical Thinking   Economics   Study

Conducting Internet Research

Understand the Skill

The Internet is a huge network of computers that are linked together. You can connect to this network from a personal computer or from a computer at a public library or school. Once connected, you can go to places called Web sites. Web sites consist of one or more Web pages. Each page contains information that you can view on the computer screen.

Governments, businesses, individuals, and many different types of organizations such as universities, news organizations, and libraries have Web sites. Most library Web sites allow users to search their card catalog electronically. Many libraries also have databases on their Web sites. A database is a large collection of related information that is organized by topic.

The Internet can be a very good reference source. It allows you to gather information on almost any topic without ever having to leave your chair. However, finding the information you need can sometimes be difficult. Having the skill to use the Internet efficiently increases its usefulness.

Learn the Skill

There are millions of Web sites on the Internet. This can make it hard to locate specific information. The following steps will help you in doing research on the Internet.

1 **Use a search engine.** This is a Web site that searches other sites. Type a word or phrase related to your topic into the search engine. It will list Web pages that might contain information on your topic. Clicking on an entry in this list will bring that page to your screen.

2 **Study the Web page.** Read the information to see if it is useful. You can print the page on the computer's printer or take notes. If you take notes, be sure to include the page's URL. This is its location or "address" on the Internet. You need this as the source of the information.

3 **Use hyperlinks.** Many Web pages have connections, called hyperlinks, to related information on the site or on other Web sites. Clicking on these links will take you to those pages. You can follow their links to even more pages, collecting information as you go.

4 **Return to your results list.** If the information or hyperlinks on a Web page are not useful, return to the list of pages that your search engine produced and repeat the process.

The Internet is a useful tool. But remember that information on the Internet is no different than printed resources. It must be evaluated with the same care and critical thinking as other resources.

Practice and Apply the Skill

Answer the following questions to apply the guidelines to Internet research on ancient China.

1. How would you begin if you wanted information about the Qin Dynasty from the Internet?

2. What words might you type into a search engine to find information about Confucianism?

3. Use a school computer to research the Great Wall of China. What kinds of pages did your search produce? Evaluate the usefulness of each type.

Chapter Review

Visual Summary

Use the visual summary below to help you review the main ideas of the chapter.

QUICK FACTS

Chinese civilization began along the Huang He (Yellow River).

During the Zhou dynasty, armies fought for power, and the ideas of Confucius spread.

The Qin dynasty unified China with a strong government.

During the Han dynasty, China made advances in learning, and Buddhism spread.

Reviewing Vocabulary, Terms, and People

Match the "I" statement with the person or thing that might have made the statement. Not all of the choices will be used.

a. jade

b. innovation

c. lord

d. oracle

e. peasant

f. Confucius

g. Daoism

h. Shi Huangdi

i. seismograph

j. wheelbarrow

k. Great Wall

l. Legalism

1. "I stressed the importance of living in harmony with nature."

2. "I took a name that means 'first emperor.'"

3. "I stressed that people needed to be controlled with strict laws."

4. "I am a beautiful, hard gemstone that the Chinese made into many objects."

5. "I was built to keep invaders from attacking China."

6. "I can measure the strength of an earthquake."

7. "I am a person of high rank."

8. "I am a new idea, method, or device."

9. "I emphasized the importance of moral values and respect for the family."

10. "I am a farmer who tills a small plot of land."

Comprehension and Critical Thinking

SECTION 1 *(Pages 160–165)*

11. **a. Identify** In what region did the Shang dynasty develop?

    b. Analyze How did China's geography contribute to the country's isolation?

    c. Evaluate Considering the evidence, do you think the Xia dynasty was really China's first dynasty or a myth? Explain your answer.

SECTION 2 *(Pages 166–171)*

12. a. Identify Which Chinese philosophy encouraged strict laws and severe punishments to keep order?

b. Analyze How would Confucianism benefit Chinese emperors?

c. Evaluate Would you be happier under a government influenced by Legalism or by Daoism? In which type of government would there be more order? Explain your answers.

SECTION 3 *(Pages 172–176)*

13. a. Describe What were the main reasons for the fall of the Qin dynasty?

b. Make Inferences Why did Shi Huangdi's armies destroy city walls and take weapons from people they conquered?

c. Evaluate Shi Huangdi was a powerful ruler. Was his rule good or bad for China? Why?

SECTION 4 *(Pages 178–183)*

14. a. Identify During the Han dynasty, who belonged to the first and second social groups?

b. Analyze What was the purpose of the exam system during Wudi's rule?

c. Elaborate What inventions show that the Chinese studied nature?

SECTION 5 *(Pages 186–189)*

15. a. Identify What factors led to the growth of trade during the Han dynasty?

b. Draw Conclusions Who do you think wore silk garments in China?

c. Predict What might have happened if the Chinese had told foreign visitors how to make silk?

Reviewing Themes

16. Politics Why might historians differ in their views of Shi Huangdi's success as a ruler?

17. Society and Culture How did Confucianism affect people's roles in their family, in government, and in society?

Using the Internet

18. Activity: Solving Problems Confucius was one of the most influential teachers in Chinese history. His ideas suggested ways to restore order in Chinese society. Enter the activity keyword and research Confucianism. Take note of the political and cultural problems Confucianism tried to address. Then investigate some of the current political and cultural problems in the United States. Could Confucianism solve problems in the United States? Prepare a persuasive argument to support your answer.

Reading Skills

19. Summarizing Historical Texts From the chapter, choose a subsection under a blue headline. For each paragraph within that subsection, write a sentence that summarizes the paragraph's main idea. Continue with the other subsections under the blue heading to create a study guide.

Social Studies Skills

20. Conducting Internet Research Find a topic in the chapter about which you would like to know more. Use the Internet to explore your topic. Compare the sources you find to determine which seem most complete and reliable. Write a short paragraph about your results.

FOCUS ON SPEAKING

21. Giving Your Oral Presentation You have chosen a person or event and know why your choice was important to Chinese history. Now you must convince your classmates.

First, write a brief description of what the person did or what happened during the event. Then summarize why your person or event is important to Chinese history.

When you give your oral presentation, use vivid language to create pictures in your listeners' minds. Also, use a clear but lively tone of voice.

DIRECTIONS: Read each question, and write the letter of the best response.

1

> The connecting link between serving one's father and serving one's mother is love. The connecting link between serving one's father and serving one's prince is reverence [respect]. Thus the mother [brings forth] love, while the prince brings forth reverence. But to the father belong both—love and reverence . . . Likewise, to serve one's elders reverently paves the way for civic obedience.

The observation and advice in this passage *best* express the teachings of

A Buddhism.
B Confucianism.
C Daoism.
D Legalism.

2 Which feature of China's physical geography did *not* separate its early people from the rest of the world?

A the Gobi
B the Huang-He
C the Pacific Ocean
D the Tibetan Plateau

3 How did the Qin emperor Shi Huangdi unify and control China in the 200s BC?

A He created districts and counties that were governed by appointed officials.
B He gave land to China's nobles so that they would be loyal to him.
C He dissolved the army so that it could not be used against him by his enemies.
D He established the Silk Road to get goods from far away.

4 Which of the following developments in China is an example of diffusion?

A the growth of manufacturing and trade
B the building of the Great Wall
C the spread of Buddhism from India
D the use of inventions to improve farming

5 Which dynasty's rulers created a government based on the ideas of Confucius?

A the Shang dynasty
B the Zhou dynasty
C the Qin dynasty
D the Han dynasty

Connecting with Past Learnings

6 In your studies of ancient India, you learned about the Hindu belief in rebirth. Which belief system that influenced early China also emphasized rebirth?

A Buddhism
B Confucianism
C Daoism
D Legalism

7 What characteristic did early civilization in Mesopotamia share with early civilization in China?

A Both developed paper.
B Both were influenced by Buddhism.
C Both built ziggurats.
D Both first developed in river valleys.

Foundations of Western Ideas

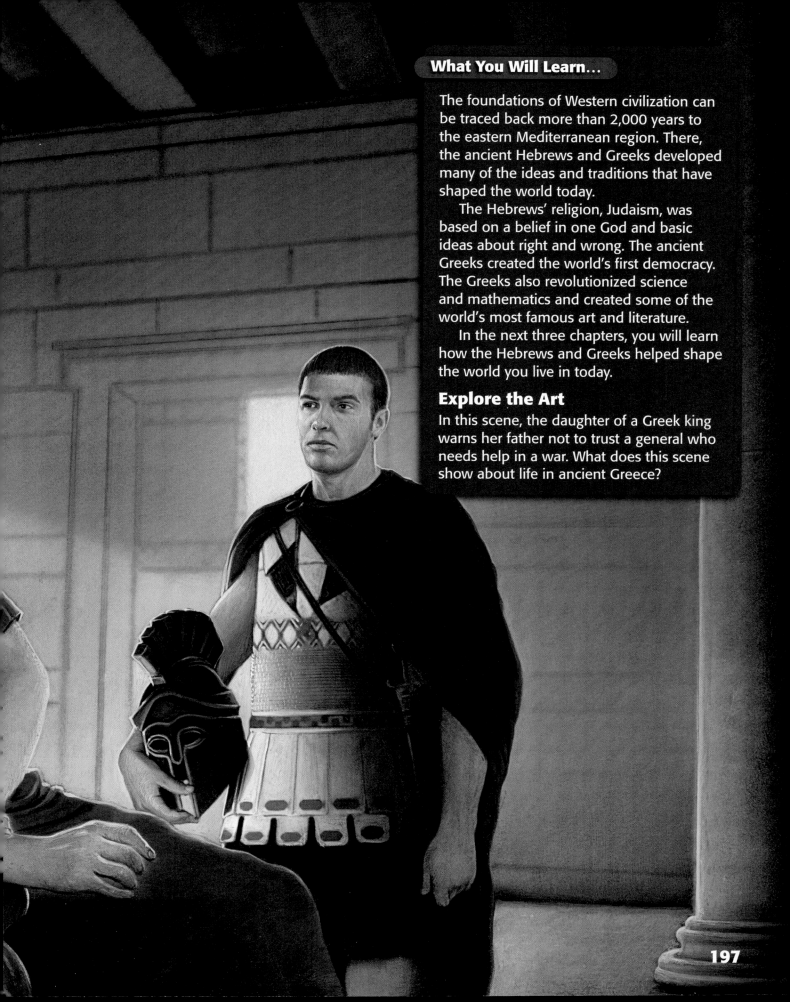

The foundations of Western civilization can be traced back more than 2,000 years to the eastern Mediterranean region. There, the ancient Hebrews and Greeks developed many of the ideas and traditions that have shaped the world today.

The Hebrews' religion, Judaism, was based on a belief in one God and basic ideas about right and wrong. The ancient Greeks created the world's first democracy. The Greeks also revolutionized science and mathematics and created some of the world's most famous art and literature.

In the next three chapters, you will learn how the Hebrews and Greeks helped shape the world you live in today.

Explore the Art

In this scene, the daughter of a Greek king warns her father not to trust a general who needs help in a war. What does this scene show about life in ancient Greece?

CHAPTER 7 2000 BC–AD 70

The Hebrews and Judaism

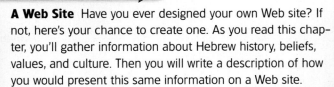

A Web Site Have you ever designed your own Web site? If not, here's your chance to create one. As you read this chapter, you'll gather information about Hebrew history, beliefs, values, and culture. Then you will write a description of how you would present this same information on a Web site.

CHAPTER EVENTS

c. 2000 BC
Abraham leaves Mesopotamia.

2000 BC

WORLD EVENTS

c. 1750 BC
Hammurabi issues his law code.

HOLT

History's Impact
▶ **video series**
Watch the video to under-stand the impact of Judaism throughout the world.

What You Will Learn...

In this chapter you will study the history and culture of the Jewish people. In this photo, hundreds of people pray at the Western Wall, the holiest site in the world of Judaism. The wall is about 2,000 years old.

c. 1200 BC
Moses leads the Hebrews out of Egypt during the Exodus.

586 BC
The Jews are enslaved in Babylon.

AD 70
The Romans destroy the Second Temple in Jerusalem.

1475 BC

950 BC

425 BC

AD 100

c. 1240–1224 BC
Ramses the Great rules Egypt.

c. 563 BC
The Buddha is born in India.

27 BC
Augustus becomes the first Roman emperor.

THE HEBREWS AND JUDAISM **199**

Focus on Themes In this chapter, you will read about the Hebrew people and the religion called Judaism. You will learn about Jewish beliefs, texts such as the Torah and the Dead Sea Scrolls, and leaders such as Abraham and Moses.

As you read, pay close attention to how the Hebrews' beliefs affected where and how they lived. In the process, you will discover that the lives of the early Hebrews revolved around their **religious** beliefs and practices.

Facts and Opinions about the Past

Focus on Reading Why is it important to know the difference between a fact and an opinion? Separating facts from opinions about historical events helps you know what really happened.

Identifying Facts and Opinions Something is a **fact** if there is a way to prove it or disprove it. For example, research can prove or disprove the following statement: "The ancient Jews recorded their laws." But research can't prove the following statement because it is just an **opinion**, or someone's belief: "Everyone should read the records of the ancient Jews."

Use the process below to decide whether a statement is fact or opinion.

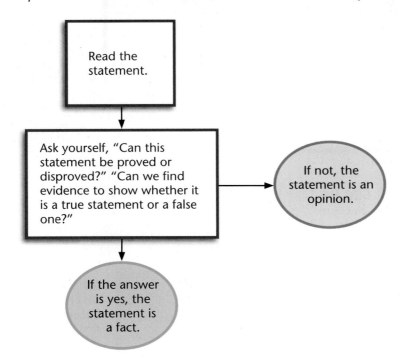

Read the statement.

Ask yourself, "Can this statement be proved or disproved?" "Can we find evidence to show whether it is a true statement or a false one?"

If not, the statement is an opinion.

If the answer is yes, the statement is a fact.

You Try It!

The following passage tells about boys who, years ago, found what came to be called the Dead Sea Scrolls. All the statements in this passage are facts. What makes them facts and not opinions?

Scrolls Reveal Past Beliefs

Until 1947 no one knew about the Dead Sea Scrolls. In that year, young boys looking for a lost goat near the Dead Sea found a small cave. One of the boys went in to explore and found several old jars filled with moldy scrolls.

From Chapter 7, pages 212–213

Scholars were very excited about the boy's find. Eager to find more scrolls, they began to search the desert. Over the next few decades, searchers found several more groups of scrolls.

Careful study revealed that most of the Dead Sea Scrolls were written between 100 BC and AD 50. The scrolls included prayers, commentaries, letters, and passages from the Hebrew Bible. These writings help historians learn about the lives of many Jews during this time.

Identify each of the following as a fact or an opinion and then explain your choice.

1. Boys discovered the Dead Sea Scrolls in 1947.

2. The discovery of the scrolls is one of the most important discoveries ever.

3. All religious leaders should study the Dead Sea Scrolls.

4. The Dead Sea Scrolls were written between 100 BC and AD 50.

Key Terms and People

Chapter 7

Section 1
Judaism *(p. 202)*
Abraham *(p. 202)*
Moses *(p. 203)*
Exodus *(p. 203)*
Ten Commandments *(p. 204)*
David *(p. 205)*
Solomon *(p. 205)*
Diaspora *(p. 206)*

Section 2
monotheism *(p. 208)*
Torah *(p. 210)*
synagogue *(p. 210)*
prophets *(p. 211)*
Talmud *(p. 212)*
Dead Sea Scrolls *(p. 212)*

Section 3
Zealots *(p. 214)*
rabbis *(p. 216)*
Passover *(p. 219)*
High Holy Days *(p. 219)*

Academic Vocabulary

Success in school is related to knowing academic vocabulary—the words that are frequently used in school assignments and discussions. In this chapter, you will learn the following academic word:

principles *(p. 210)*

As you read Chapter 7, look for clues that will help you determine which statements are facts.

The Early Hebrews

What You Will Learn...

Main Ideas

1. Abraham and Moses led the Hebrews to Canaan and to a new religion.
2. Strong kings united the Israelites to fight off invaders.
3. Invaders conquered and ruled the Hebrews after their kingdom broke apart.
4. Some women in Hebrew society made great contributions to their history.

The Big Idea

Originally desert nomads, the Hebrews established a great kingdom called Israel.

Key Terms and People

Judaism, *p. 202*
Abraham, *p. 202*
Moses, *p. 203*
Exodus, *p. 203*
Ten Commandments, *p. 204*
David, *p. 205*
Solomon, *p. 205*
Diaspora, *p. 206*

TAKING NOTES As you read, take notes on the stages of Hebrew and later Jewish history from its beginnings in Canaan to Roman rule. Use a diagram like this one to help you organize your notes.

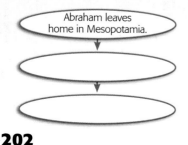

Abraham leaves home in Mesopotamia.

If YOU were there...

You and your family are herders, looking after large flocks of sheep. Your grandfather is the leader of your tribe. One day your grandfather says that your whole family will be moving to a new country where there is more water and food for your flocks. The trip will be long and difficult.

How do you feel about moving to a faraway land?

BUILDING BACKGROUND Like the family described above, the early Hebrews moved to new lands in ancient times. According to Hebrew tradition, their history began when God told an early Hebrew leader to travel west to a new land.

Abraham and Moses Lead the Hebrews

Sometime between 2000 and 1500 BC a new people appeared in Southwest Asia. They were the Hebrews (HEE-brooz). The early Hebrews were simple herders, but they developed a culture that became a major influence on later civilizations.

Most of what is known about early Hebrew history comes from the work of archaeologists and from accounts written by Hebrew scribes. These accounts describe the Hebrews' early history and the laws of **Judaism** (JOO-dee-i-zuhm), the Hebrews' religion. In time these accounts became the Hebrew Bible. The Hebrew Bible is also part of the Christian Bible, which includes the New Testament as well.

The Beginnings in Canaan and Egypt

The Hebrew Bible traces the Hebrews back to a man named **Abraham**. One day, the Hebrew Bible says, God told Abraham to leave his home in Mesopotamia. He was to take his family on a long journey to the west. God promised to lead Abraham to a new land and make his descendants into a mighty nation.

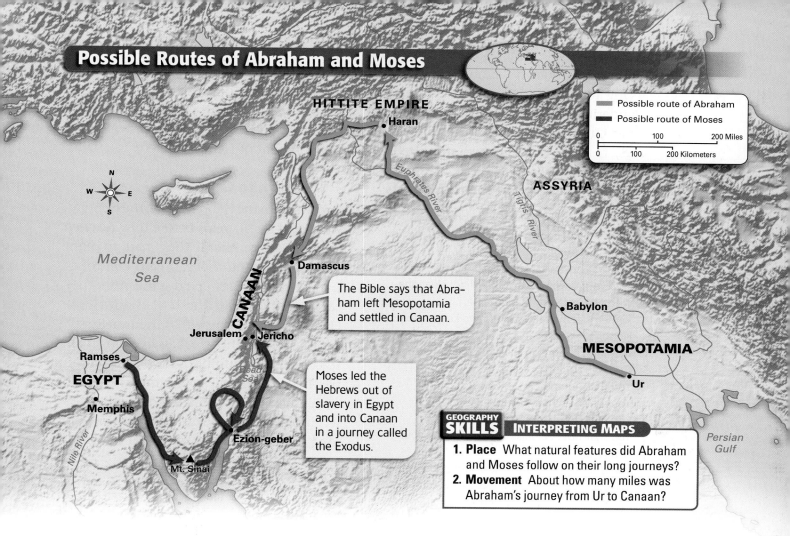

Possible Routes of Abraham and Moses

Legend:
- Possible route of Abraham
- Possible route of Moses

The Bible says that Abraham left Mesopotamia and settled in Canaan.

Moses led the Hebrews out of slavery in Egypt and into Canaan in a journey called the Exodus.

GEOGRAPHY SKILLS — INTERPRETING MAPS

1. **Place** What natural features did Abraham and Moses follow on their long journeys?
2. **Movement** About how many miles was Abraham's journey from Ur to Canaan?

Abraham left Mesopotamia and settled in Canaan (KAY-nuhn), on the Mediterranean Sea. His descendants—the Hebrews—lived in Canaan for many years. Later, however, some Hebrews moved to Egypt, perhaps because of famine in Canaan.

The Hebrews lived well in Egypt, and their population grew. This growth worried Egypt's ruler, the pharaoh. He feared that the Hebrews might soon become too powerful. To stop this from happening, the pharaoh made the Hebrews slaves.

The Exodus

According to the Hebrew Bible, a leader named **Moses** appeared among the Hebrews in Egypt. In the 1200s BC, God told Moses to lead the Hebrews out of Egypt. Moses went to the pharaoh and demanded that the Hebrews be freed. The pharaoh refused. Soon afterward a series of terrible plagues, or disasters, struck Egypt.

The plagues frightened the pharaoh so much that he agreed to free the Hebrews. Overjoyed with the news of their release, Moses led his people out of Egypt in a journey called the **Exodus**. To the Hebrews, the release from slavery proved that God was protecting and watching over them. They believed that they had been set free because God loved them.

The Exodus is a major event in Hebrew history, but other people recognize its significance as well. Throughout history, for example, enslaved people have found hope in the story. Before the Civil War, American slaves sang about Moses to keep their hopes of freedom alive.

For many years after their release, the Hebrews wandered through the desert, trying to return to Canaan. During their wanderings they reached a mountain called Sinai. On that mountain, the Hebrew Bible says, God gave Moses two stone tablets. On the tablets was written a code of moral laws known as the **Ten Commandments**:

> "I the Lord am your God who brought you out of the land of Egypt, the house of bondage: You shall have no other gods besides Me....
> You shall not swear falsely by the name of the Lord your God; for the Lord will not clear one who swears falsely by His name.
> Remember the sabbath day and keep it holy....
> Honor your father and your mother, that you may long endure on the land that the Lord your God is assigning to you.
> You shall not murder.
> You shall not commit adultery.
> You shall not steal.
> You shall not bear false witness against your neighbor.
> You shall not covet your neighbor's house: you shall not covet your neighbor's wife, or his male or female slave, or his ox or his ass, or anything that is your neighbor's."

—Exodus 20:2–14

As you can see, by accepting the Ten Commandments, the Hebrews agreed to worship only God. They also agreed to value human life, self-control, and justice. Over time the commandments shaped the development of Hebrew society.

The Return to Canaan

According to the Hebrew Bible, the Hebrews wandered for 40 years before they reached Canaan. Once there, they had to fight the people living there to gain control of Canaan before they could settle. After they conquered Canaan and settled down, the Hebrews became known as the Israelites.

In Canaan, the Israelites lived in small, scattered communities. These communities had no central government. Instead, each community selected judges as leaders to enforce laws and settle disputes. Before long, though, a threat arose that called for a new kind of leadership.

READING CHECK Identifying Cause and Effect
Why did Abraham leave Mesopotamia?

Time Line

Early Hebrew History

c. 2000 BC
Abraham leaves Mesopotamia and goes to Canaan.

2100 BC

1300 BC

1200s BC
Moses leads the Hebrews on the Exodus out of slavery in Egypt.

1200 BC

Kings Unite the Israelites

The new threat to the Israelites came from the Philistines (FI-li-steenz), who lived along the Mediterranean coast. In the mid-1000s BC the Philistines invaded the Israelites' lands.

Frightened by these powerful invaders, the Israelites banded together under a single ruler who could lead them in battle. That ruler was a man named Saul, who became the first king of Israel. Saul had some success as a military commander, but he wasn't a strong king. He never won the total support of tribal and religious leaders. They often fought against his decisions.

King David

After Saul died, a man once declared an outlaw became king. That king's name was **David**. As a young man, David had been a shepherd. The Hebrew Bible tells how David slew the Philistine giant Goliath, which brought him to the attention of the king. David was admired for his military skills and as a poet; many of the Psalms are attributed to him. For many years, David lived in the desert, gathering support from local people. When Saul died, David used this support to become king.

Unlike Saul, David was well loved by the Israelites. He won the full support of Israel's tribal leaders. David defeated the Philistines and fought and won wars against many other peoples of Canaan. He established the capital of Israel in Jerusalem.

King Solomon

David's son **Solomon** (SAHL-uh-muhn) took the throne in about 965 BC. Like his father, Solomon was a strong king. He expanded the kingdom and made nearby kingdoms, including Egypt and Phoenicia, his allies. Trade with these allies made Israel very rich. With these riches, Solomon built a great temple to God in Jerusalem. This temple became the center of the Israelites' religious life and a symbol of their faith.

READING CHECK **Finding Main Ideas** Why did the Israelites unite under a king?

FOCUS ON READING

Are the sentences in this paragraph facts or opinions? How can you tell?

c. 1000 BC
David becomes king of Israel.

c. 930 BC
Solomon dies. His kingdom is split into the kingdoms of Judah and Israel.

1100 BC   1000 BC   900 BC   800 BC

mid-1000s BC
Saul becomes the first king of Israel.

c. 965 BC
David's son Solomon becomes king of Israel. Solomon builds a great temple in Jerusalem.

ANALYSIS SKILL **READING TIME LINES**

About how many years after Abraham settled in Canaan did Saul become the first king of Israel?

Invaders Conquer and Rule

After Solomon's death in about 930 BC, revolts broke out over who should be king. Within a year, conflict tore Israel apart. Israel split into two kingdoms called Israel and called Judah (JOO-duh). The people of Judah became known as Jews.

The two new kingdoms lasted for a few centuries. In the end, however, both were conquered. The Assyrians defeated Israel around 722 BC. As a result, the kingdom fell apart and most of its people scattered. Judah lasted longer, but before long it was defeated by the Chaldeans.

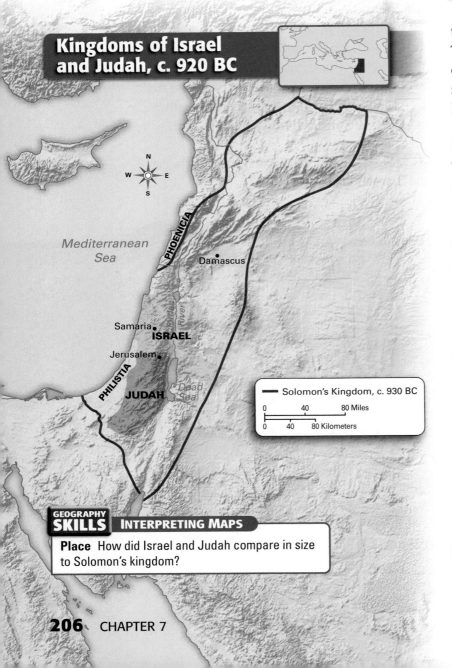

Kingdoms of Israel and Judah, c. 920 BC

Mediterranean Sea

PHOENICIA

Damascus

Samaria

ISRAEL

Jerusalem

PHILISTIA

JUDAH

Dead Sea

— Solomon's Kingdom, c. 930 BC

0   40   80 Miles

0   40   80 Kilometers

N W E S

GEOGRAPHY SKILLS **INTERPRETING MAPS**

Place How did Israel and Judah compare in size to Solomon's kingdom?

The Scattering of the Jews

The Chaldeans captured Jerusalem and destroyed Solomon's Temple in 586 BC. They marched thousands of Jews to their capital, Babylon, to work as slaves. The Jews called this enslavement the Babylonian Captivity. It lasted about 50 years.

In the 530s BC a people called the Persians conquered the Chaldeans and let the Jews return to Jerusalem. But many never took this opportunity to return home. Instead, they moved to other parts of the Persian Empire. Scholars call the scattering of the Jews outside of Israel and Judah the **Diaspora** (dy-AS-pruh).

The rest of the Jews did return home to Jerusalem. There they rebuilt Solomon's Temple, which became known as the Second Temple. The Jews remained under Persian control until the 330s BC, when the Persians were conquered by invaders.

Independence and Conquest

Tired of foreign rule, a Jewish family called the Maccabees (MA-kuh-beez) led a successful revolt in the 160s BC. For about 100 years, the Jews again ruled their own kingdom. Their independence, however, didn't last. In 63 BC the Jews were conquered again, this time by the Romans.

Although Jewish leaders added to the Second Temple under Roman rule, life was difficult. Heavy taxes burdened the people. The Romans were brutal masters who had no respect for the Jewish religion and way of life.

Some rulers tried to force the Jews to worship the Roman Emperor. The Roman rulers even appointed the high priests, the leaders of the Temple. This was more than the Jews could bear. They called on their people to rebel against the Romans.

READING CHECK **Summarizing** How did Roman rule affect Jewish society?

Women in Hebrew Society

Hebrew government and society were dominated by men, as were most ancient societies. Women had few rights. They had to obey their fathers and their husbands. A woman couldn't even choose her own husband. Instead, her husband was chosen by her father. A woman couldn't inherit property either, unless she had no brothers. If she did have a brother, all property went to him.

Some Hebrew women, however, made great contributions to their society. The Hebrew Bible describes them. Some were political and military leaders, such as Queen Esther and the judge Deborah. According to the Hebrew Bible, these women saved the Hebrew people from their enemies. Other women, such as Miriam, the sister of Moses, were spiritual leaders.

Some women in the Hebrew Bible were seen as examples of how Hebrew women should behave. For example, Ruth, who left her people to care for her mother-in-law, was seen as a model of devotion to one's family. The Hebrews told Ruth's story as an example of how people should treat their family members.

READING CHECK **Generalizing** What was life like for most Hebrew women?

Ruth and Naomi

The story of Ruth and Naomi comes from the Book of Ruth, one of the books of the Hebrew Bible. According to this account, Ruth was not a Hebrew, though her husband was. After he died, Ruth and her mother-in-law, Naomi, resettled in Israel. Inspired by Naomi's faith in God, Ruth joined Naomi's family and adopted her beliefs. She dedicated her life to supporting Naomi.

Drawing Inferences What lessons might the Hebrews have used the story of Ruth and Naomi to teach?

SUMMARY AND PREVIEW The history of the Hebrews and Judaism began some 3,500 to 4,000 years ago. The instructions that Jews believe God gave to the early Hebrews shaped their religion, Judaism. In the next section, you will learn about the main teachings of Judaism.

Section 1 Assessment

Reviewing Ideas, Terms, and People

1. a. **Identify** Who was **Abraham**?
   b. **Evaluate** Why was the **Exodus** a significant event in Hebrew history?
2. **Summarize** How did **David** and **Solomon** strengthen the kingdom of Israel?
3. **Describe** What happened during the Babylonian Captivity?
4. a. **Describe** Who had more rights in Hebrew society, men or women?
   b. **Make Inferences** How did Ruth and Naomi set an example for other Hebrews?

Critical Thinking

5. **Evaluating** Review your notes on the Hebrews. In a chart like this one, note the contributions of the four most important people.

Key Figure	Contribution

FOCUS ON WRITING

6. **Taking Notes about Early Hebrew History** Make a list of events and people that played key roles in shaping Hebrew history. Look for ways to group your facts into features on your Web page.

Jewish Beliefs and Texts

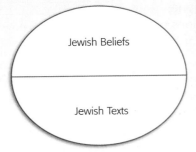
If YOU were there...

You live in a small town in ancient Israel. Some people in your town treat strangers very badly. But you have been taught to be fair and kind to everyone, including strangers. One day, you tell one of your neighbors he should be kinder to strangers. He asks you why you feel that way.

How will you explain your belief in kindness?

BUILDING BACKGROUND The idea that people should be fair and kind to everyone in the community is an important Jewish teaching. Sometimes, their teachings set the Jews apart from other people in society. But at the same time, their shared beliefs tie all Jews together as a religious community.

Jewish Beliefs Anchor Their Society

Religion is the foundation upon which the Jews base their whole society. In fact, much of Jewish culture is based directly on Jewish beliefs. The central beliefs of Judaism are beliefs in God, education, justice, and obedience.

Belief in One God

Most importantly, Jews believe in one God. The Hebrew name for God is YHWH, which is never pronounced by Jews, as it is considered too holy. The belief in only one God is called **monotheism**. Many people believe that Judaism was the world's first monotheistic religion. It is certainly the oldest such religion that is still widely practiced today.

In the ancient world where most people worshipped many gods, the Jews' worship of only God set them apart. This worship also shaped Jewish society. The Jews believed that God had guided their history through his relationships with Abraham, Moses, and other leaders.

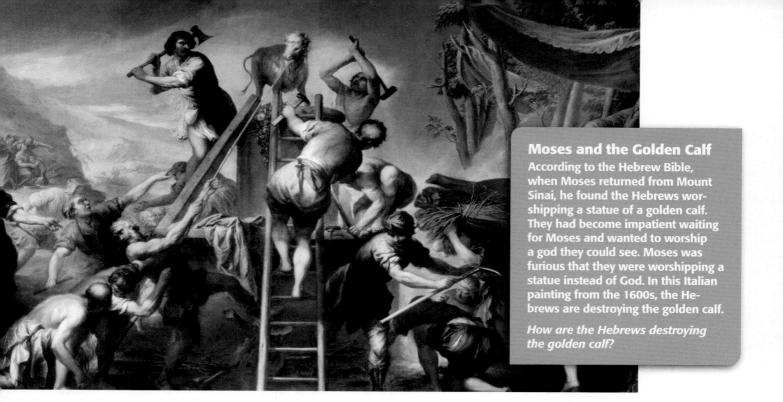

Moses and the Golden Calf
According to the Hebrew Bible, when Moses returned from Mount Sinai, he found the Hebrews worshipping a statue of a golden calf. They had become impatient waiting for Moses and wanted to worship a god they could see. Moses was furious that they were worshipping a statue instead of God. In this Italian painting from the 1600s, the Hebrews are destroying the golden calf.

How are the Hebrews destroying the golden calf?

Belief in Education

Another central element of Judaism is education and study. Teaching children the basics of Judaism has always been important in Jewish society. In ancient Jewish communities, older boys—but not girls—studied with professional teachers to learn their religion. Even today, education and study are central to Jewish life.

Belief in Justice and Righteousness

Also central to the Jews' religion are the ideas of justice and righteousness. To Jews, justice means kindness and fairness in dealing with other people. Everyone deserves justice, even strangers and criminals. Jews are expected to give aid to those who need it, including the poor, the sick, and orphans. Jews are also expected to be fair in business dealings.

Righteousness refers to doing what is proper. Jews are supposed to behave properly, even if others around them do not. For the Jews, righteous behavior is more important than formal ceremonies.

Belief in Obedience and Law

Closely related to the ideas of justice and righteousness is obedience to the law. Moral and religious laws have guided Jews through their history and continue to do so today. Jews believe that God gave them these laws to follow.

The most important Jewish laws are the Ten Commandments. The commandments, however, are only part of Jewish law. Jews believe that Moses recorded a whole system of laws that God had set down for them to obey. Named for Moses, this system is called Mosaic law.

Like the Ten Commandments, Mosaic laws guide many areas of Jews' daily lives. For example, Mosaic law governs how people pray and celebrate holidays. The laws forbid Jews to work on holidays or on the Sabbath, the seventh day of each week. The Sabbath is a day of rest because, in Jewish tradition, God created the world in six days and rested on the seventh. The Jewish Sabbath begins at sundown Friday and ends at nightfall Saturday, the seventh day of the week.

Among the Mosaic laws are rules about the foods that Jews can eat and rules that must be followed in preparing them. For example, the laws state that Jews cannot eat pork or shellfish, which are thought to be unclean. Other laws say that meat has to be killed and prepared in a way that makes it acceptable for Jews to eat. Today foods that have been so prepared are called kosher (KOH-shuhr), or fit.

In many Jewish communities today, people still strictly follow Mosaic law. They are called Orthodox Jews. Other Jews choose not to follow many of the ancient laws. They are known as Reform Jews. A third group, the Conservative Jews, falls between the other two groups. These are the three largest groups of Jews in the world today.

READING CHECK **Generalizing** What are the most important beliefs of Judaism?

Texts List Jewish Beliefs

The laws and **principles** of Judaism are described in several sacred texts, or writings. Among the main texts are the Torah, the Hebrew Bible, and the Commentaries.

The Torah

The ancient Jews recorded most of their laws in five books. Together these books are called the **Torah**, the most sacred text of Judaism. In addition to laws, the Torah includes a history of the Jews until the death of Moses.

Readings from the Torah are central to Jewish religious services today. Nearly every **synagogue** (SI-nuh-gawg), or Jewish house of worship, has at least one Torah. Out of respect for the Torah, readers do not touch it. They use special pointers to mark their places in the text.

Hebrew Texts

The Torah
Using a special pointer called a *yad*, this girl is reading aloud from the Torah. The Torah is the most sacred of Hebrew writings. Jews believe its contents were revealed to Moses by God. The Torah plays a central role in many Jewish ceremonies, like this one.

The Hebrew Bible

The Torah is the first of three parts of a group of writings called the Hebrew Bible, or Tanach (tah-NAHK). The second part is made up of eight books that describe the messages of Hebrew prophets. **Prophets** are people who are said to receive messages from God to be taught to others.

The final part of the Hebrew Bible is 11 books of poetry, songs, stories, lessons, and history. For example, the Book of Daniel tells about a prophet named Daniel, who lived during the Babylonian Captivity. According to the book, Daniel angered the king who held the Jews as slaves. As punishment, the king had Daniel thrown into a den of lions. The story tells that Daniel's faith in God kept the lions from killing him, and he was released. Jews tell this story to show the power of faith.

Also in the final part of the Hebrew Bible are the Proverbs, short expressions of Hebrew wisdom. Many of these sayings are attributed to Hebrew leaders, especially King Solomon. For example, Solomon is supposed to have said, "A good name is to be chosen rather than great riches." In other words, it is better to be seen as a good person than to be rich and not respected.

The third part of the Hebrew Bible also includes the Book of Psalms. Psalms are poems or songs of praise to God. Many of these are attributed to King David. One of the most famous psalms is the Twenty-third Psalm. It includes lines often read today during times of difficulty:

" The Lord is my shepherd; I lack nothing.
    He makes me lie down in green pastures;
        He leads me to water in places of repose;
        He renews my life;
        He guides me in right paths as befits His name. "
—Psalms 23:1–3

The Hebrew Bible
These beautifully decorated pages are from a Hebrew Bible. The Hebrew Bible, sometimes called the Tanach, includes the Torah and other ancient writings.

ANALYSIS SKILL **ANALYZING VISUALS**

How does the Torah look different from the Hebrew Bible and the commentaries?

The Commentaries
The Talmud is a collection of commentaries and discussions about the Torah and the Hebrew Bible. The Talmud is a rich source of information for discussion and debate. Rabbis and religious scholars like these young men study the Talmud to learn about Jewish history and laws.

The Dead Sea Scrolls

The Dead Sea Scrolls were found in this cave, and in similar caves, near Qumran. The hot, dry desert climate preserved the 2,000-year-old scrolls remarkably well.

Why might historians have had trouble reading the Dead Sea Scrolls?

Commentaries

For centuries scholars have studied the Torah and Jewish laws. Because some laws are hard to understand, the scholars write commentaries to explain them.

Many such commentaries are found in the **Talmud** (TAHL-moohd), set of commentaries and lessons for everyday life. The writings of the Talmud were produced between AD 200 and 600. Many Jews consider them second only to the Hebrew Bible in their significance to Judaism.

READING CHECK **Analyzing** What texts do Jews consider sacred?

Scrolls Reveal Past Beliefs

Besides the Torah, the Hebrew Bible, and the Commentaries, many other documents also explain ancient Jewish beliefs. Among the most important are the **Dead Sea Scrolls**, writings by Jews who lived about 2,000 years ago.

Until 1947 no one knew about the Dead Sea Scrolls. In that year, young boys looking for a lost goat near the Dead Sea found a small cave. One of the boys went in to explore and found several old jars filled with moldy scrolls.

Scholars were very excited about the boy's find. Eager to find more scrolls, they began to search the desert. Over the next few decades, searchers found several more groups of scrolls.

Careful study revealed that most of the Dead Sea Scrolls were written between 100 BC and AD 50. The scrolls included prayers, commentaries, letters, and passages from the Hebrew Bible. These writings help historians learn about the lives of many Jews during this time.

READING CHECK **Finding Main Ideas** What did the Dead Sea Scrolls contain?

Judaism and Later Cultures

For centuries, Jewish ideas have greatly influenced other cultures, especially those in Europe and the Americas. Historians call European and American cultures the Western world to distinguish them from the Asian cultures to the east of Europe.

Because Jews lived all over the Western world, people of many cultures learned of Jewish ideas. In addition, these ideas helped shape the largest religion of Western society today, Christianity. Jesus, whose teachings are the basis of Christianity, was Jewish, and many of his teachings reflected Jewish ideas. These ideas were carried forward into Western civilization by both Jews and Christians. Judaism also influenced the development of another major religion, Islam. The first people to adopt Islam believed that they, like the Hebrews, were descendants of Abraham.

How are Jewish ideas reflected in our society? Many people still look to the Ten Commandments as a guide to how they should live. For example, people are expected to honor their parents, families, and neighbors and not to lie or cheat. Although these ideas were not unique to Judaism, it was through the Jews that they entered Western culture.

Not all of the ideas adopted from Jewish teachings come from the Ten Commandments. Other Jewish ideas can also be seen in how people live today. For example, many people do not work on weekends in honor of the Sabbath. In addition, people give money or items to charities to help the poor and needy. This concept of charity is based largely on Jewish teachings.

READING CHECK **Summarizing** How have Jewish ideas helped shape modern laws?

SUMMARY AND PREVIEW Judaism is based on the belief in and obedience to God as described in the Torah and other sacred texts. In the next section you will learn how religion helped unify Jews even when they were forced out of Jerusalem.

go.hrw.com
Online Quiz
KEYWORD: SN6 HP7

Section 2 Assessment

Reviewing Ideas, Terms, and People

1. **a. Define** What is **monotheism**?
   b. Explain What is the Jewish view of justice and righteousness?
2. **a. Identify** What are the main sacred texts of Judaism?
   b. Predict Why do you think the commentaries are so significant to many Jews?
3. **Recall** Why do historians study the Dead Sea Scrolls?
4. **Describe** How are Hebrew teachings reflected in Western society today?

Critical Thinking

5. **Finding Main Ideas** Using the information in your notes, identify four basic beliefs of Judaism and explain them in a diagram like the one shown here.

Jewish Beliefs

FOCUS ON WRITING

6. **Thinking about Basic Values and Teachings** While the information in Section 1 was mostly historical, this section has different kinds of topics. As you write down this information for your Web site, what links do you see between these topics and items already on the list you started in Section 1?

Judaism over the Centuries

What You Will Learn...

Main Ideas

1. Revolt, defeat, and migration led to great changes in Jewish culture.
2. Because Jews settled in different parts of the world, two cultural traditions formed.
3. Jewish traditions and holy days celebrate their history and religion.

The Big Idea

Although many Jews were forced out of Israel by the Romans, shared beliefs and customs helped Jews maintain their religion.

Key Terms

Zealots, *p. 214*
rabbis, *p. 216*
Passover, *p. 219*
High Holy Days, *p. 219*

TAKING NOTES As you read, take notes on events that threatened the survival of Jewish society, and notes on beliefs and customs that helped strengthen it. Use a graphic organizer like this one.

Threatening Events

Helpful Beliefs and Customs

If YOU were there...

Foreign soldiers have taken over your homeland and are forcing you to obey their laws. So, some people are urging you to stand up and fight for freedom. But your conquerors come from a huge, powerful empire. If your people revolt, you have little chance of winning.

Will you join the rebellion? Why or why not?

BUILDING BACKGROUND By about AD 60, many Jews in Jerusalem had to decide whether they would join a rebellion against their foreign conquerors. For a little over a century, Jerusalem had been ruled by Rome. The Romans had a strong army, but their disrespect for Jewish traditions angered many Jews.

Revolt, Defeat, and Migration

The teachings of Judaism helped unite the ancient Jews. After the conquest of Israel by the Romans, many events threatened to tear Jewish society apart.

One threat to Jewish society was foreign rule. By the beginning of the first century AD, many Jews in Jerusalem had grown tired of foreign rule. If they could regain their independence, these Jews thought they could re-create the kingdom of Israel.

Revolt against Rome

The most rebellious of these Jews were a group called the **Zealots** (ZE-luhts). This group didn't think that Jews should answer to anyone but God. As a result, they refused to obey Roman officials. The Zealots urged their fellow Jews to rise up against the Romans. Tensions between Jews and Romans increased. Finally, in AD 66, the Jews revolted. Led by the Zealots, they fought fiercely.

In the end, the Jews' revolt against the Romans was not successful. The revolt lasted four years and caused terrible damage. By the time the fighting ended, Jerusalem lay in ruins. The war had wrecked buildings and cost many lives. Even more devastating to the Jews was the fact that the Romans burned the Second Temple during the last days of fighting in AD 70:

" As the flames went upward, the Jews made a great clamor [shout], such as so mighty an affliction [ordeal] required, and ran together to prevent it; and now they spared not their lives any longer, nor suffered any thing to restrain their force, since that holy house was perishing. "

–Flavius Josephus, *The Wars of the Jews*

After the Temple was destroyed, most Jews lost their will to fight and surrendered. But a few refused to give up their fight. That small group of about 1,000 Zealots locked themselves in a mountain fortress called Masada (muh-SAH-duh).

Intent on smashing the revolt, the Romans sent 15,000 soldiers to capture these Zealots. However, Masada was hard to reach. The Romans had to build a huge ramp of earth and stones to get to it. For two years, the Zealots refused to surrender, as the ramp grew. Finally, as the Romans broke through Masada's walls, the Zealots took their own lives. They refused to become Roman slaves.

THE IMPACT TODAY

The western retaining wall of the Second Temple survived the fire and still stands. Thousands of Jews each year visit the wall.

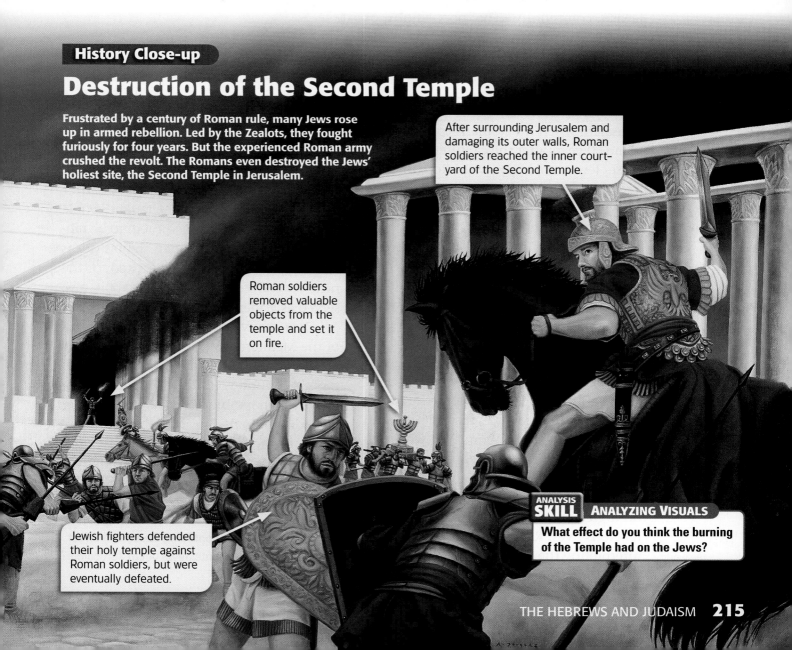

History Close-up

Destruction of the Second Temple

Frustrated by a century of Roman rule, many Jews rose up in armed rebellion. Led by the Zealots, they fought furiously for four years. But the experienced Roman army crushed the revolt. The Romans even destroyed the Jews' holiest site, the Second Temple in Jerusalem.

After surrounding Jerusalem and damaging its outer walls, Roman soldiers reached the inner courtyard of the Second Temple.

Roman soldiers removed valuable objects from the temple and set it on fire.

Jewish fighters defended their holy temple against Roman soldiers, but were eventually defeated.

ANALYSIS SKILL **ANALYZING VISUALS**

What effect do you think the burning of the Temple had on the Jews?

THE HEBREWS AND JUDAISM **215**

Results of the Revolt

With the capture of Masada in AD 73, the Jewish revolt was over. As punishment for the Jews' rebellion, the Romans killed much of Jerusalem's population. They took many of the surviving Jews to Rome as slaves. The Romans dissolved the Jewish power structure and took over the city.

Besides those taken as slaves, thousands of Jews left Jerusalem after the destruction of the Second Temple. With the Temple destroyed, they didn't want to live in Jerusalem anymore. Many moved to Jewish communities in other parts of the Roman Empire. One common destination was Alexandria in Egypt, which had a large Jewish community. The populations of these Jewish communities grew after the Romans destroyed Jerusalem.

A Second Revolt

Some Jews, however, chose not to leave Jerusalem when the Romans conquered it. Some 60 years after the capture of Masada, these Jews, unhappy with Roman rule, began another revolt. Once again, however, the Roman army defeated the Jews. After this rebellion in the 130s the Romans banned all Jews from the city of Jerusalem. Roman officials declared that any Jew caught in or near the city would be killed. As a result, Jewish migration throughout the Mediterranean region increased.

Migration and Discrimination

For Jews not living in Jerusalem, the nature of Judaism changed. Because the Jews no longer had a single temple at which to worship, local synagogues became more important. At the same time, leaders called **rabbis** (RAB-yz), or religious teachers, took on a greater role in guiding Jews in their religious lives. Rabbis were responsible for interpreting the Torah and teaching.

The United States today has a larger Jewish population than any other country in the world.

The Sephardim are descended from Jews who migrated to Spain and Portugal during the Diaspora, or scattering, of the Jews. This Sephardic rabbi is working on part of a Torah scroll.

This change was largely due to the actions of Yohanan ben Zaccai, a rabbi who founded a school at Yavneh, near Jerusalem. In this school, he taught people about Judaism and trained them to be rabbis. Influenced by Yohanan, rabbis' ideas shaped how Judaism was practiced for the next several centuries. Many rabbis also served as leaders of Jewish communities.

Over many centuries, Jews moved out of the Mediterranean region to other parts of the world. In many cases this movement was not voluntary. The Jews were forced to move by other religious groups who discriminated against them or were unfair to them. Jews were forced to leave their cities and find new places to live. As a result, some Jews settled in Asia, Russia, and much later, the United States.

READING CHECK Identifying Cause and Effect
Why did the Romans force Jews out of Jerusalem?

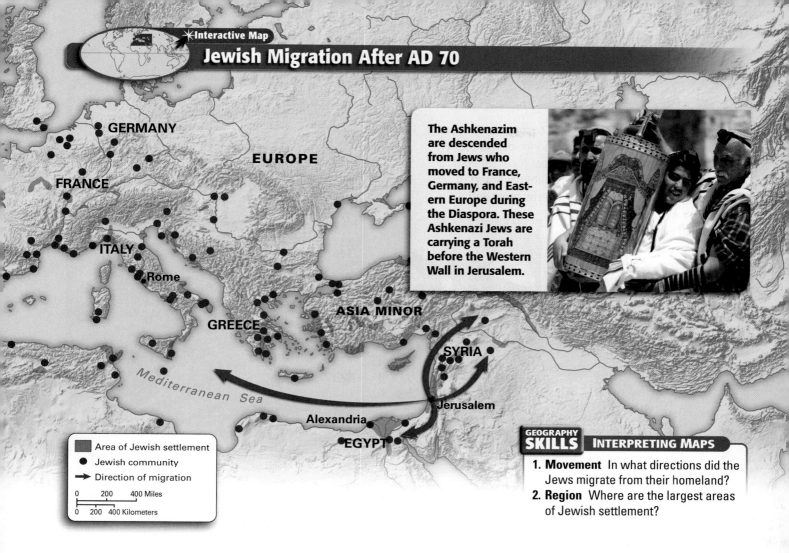

Jewish Migration After AD 70

The Ashkenazim are descended from Jews who moved to France, Germany, and Eastern Europe during the Diaspora. These Ashkenazi Jews are carrying a Torah before the Western Wall in Jerusalem.

GERMANY

EUROPE

FRANCE

ITALY

Rome

GREECE

ASIA MINOR

SYRIA

Jerusalem

Mediterranean Sea

Alexandria

EGYPT

■ Area of Jewish settlement
● Jewish community
→ Direction of migration

0   200   400 Miles
0   200   400 Kilometers

GEOGRAPHY SKILLS | INTERPRETING MAPS

1. **Movement** In what directions did the Jews migrate from their homeland?
2. **Region** Where are the largest areas of Jewish settlement?

Two Cultural Traditions

As you read earlier, the scattering of Jews around the world is called the Diaspora. It began after the Babylonian Captivity in the 500s BC. After that time, Jewish communities developed all around the world.

Jews everywhere shared the basic beliefs of Judaism. For example, all Jews still believed in God and tried to obey his laws as set forth in the sacred texts. But communities in various parts of the world had different customs. As a result, the Jewish communities in different parts of the world began to develop their own languages, rituals, and cultures. These differences led to the creation of two main cultural traditions, both of which still exist today.

The Jews in Eastern Europe

One of the two traditions, the Ashkenazim (ahsh-kuh-NAH-zuhm), is made up of descendants of Jews who moved to France, Germany, and eastern Europe during the Diaspora. For the most part, these Jews had communities separate from their non-Jewish neighbors. Therefore, they developed their own customs that were unlike those of their neighbors. As an example, they developed their own language, Yiddish. Yiddish is similar to German but is written in the Hebrew alphabet.

The Jews in Spain and Portugal

Another Jewish cultural tradition developed during the Diaspora in what are now Spain and Portugal in Western Europe.

THE IMPACT TODAY

Some Yiddish words have entered the English language. For example, *schlep* means "to carry."

A Passover Meal

Passover honors the Exodus, one of the most important events in Hebrew history. In honor of this event from their past, Jews share a special meal called a seder. Each item in the seder symbolizes a part of the Exodus. For example, bitter herbs represent the Hebrews' bitter years of slavery in Egypt. Before eating the meal, everyone reads prayers from a book called the Haggadah (huh–GAH–duh). It tells the story of the Exodus and reminds everyone present of the Jews' history. The small picture shows a seder in a copy of a Haggadah from the 1300s.

ANALYSIS SKILL | **ANALYZING INFORMATION**

How does the Passover seder reflect the importance of the Exodus in Hebrew history?

The descendants of the Jews there are called the Sephardim (suh-FAHR-duhm). They also have a language of their own—Ladino. It is a mix of Spanish, Hebrew, and Arabic. Unlike the Ashkenazim, the Sephardim mixed with the region's non-Jewish residents. As a result, Sephardic religious and cultural practices borrowed elements from other cultures. Known for their writings and their philosophies, the Sephardim produced a golden age of Jewish culture in the AD 1000s and 1100s. During this period, for example, Jewish poets wrote beautiful works in Hebrew and other languages. Jewish scholars also made great advances in mathematics, astronomy, medicine, and philosophy.

READING CHECK Summarizing What were the two main Jewish cultural traditions?

Traditions and Holy Days

Jewish culture is one of the oldest in the world. Because their roots go back so far, many Jews feel a strong connection with the past. They also feel that understanding their history will help them better follow Jewish teachings. Their traditions and holy days help them understand and celebrate their history.

Hanukkah

One Jewish tradition is celebrated by Hanukkah, which falls in December. It honors the rededication of the Second Temple during the revolt of the Maccabees.

The Maccabees wanted to celebrate a great victory that had convinced their non-Jewish rulers to let them keep their religion. According to legend, though, the Maccabees didn't have enough lamp oil to perform the rededication ceremony. Miraculously, the oil they had—enough to burn for only one day—burned for eight full days.

Today Jews celebrate this event by lighting candles in a special candleholder called a menorah (muh-NOHR-uh). Its eight branches represent the eight days through which the oil burned. Many Jews also exchange gifts on each of the eight nights.

Passover

More important than Hanukkah to Jews, Passover is celebrated in March or April. **Passover** is a time for Jews to remember the Exodus, the journey of the Hebrews out of slavery in Egypt.

According to Jewish tradition, the Hebrews left Egypt so quickly that bakers didn't have time to let their bread rise. Therefore, during Passover Jews eat only matzo, a flat, unrisen bread. They also celebrate the holy day with ceremonies and a ritual meal called a seder (SAY-duhr). During the seder, participants recall and reflect upon the events of the Exodus.

High Holy Days

Ceremonies and rituals are also part of the **High Holy Days**, the two most sacred of all Jewish holy days. They take place each year in September or October. The first two days of the celebration, Rosh Hashanah (rahsh uh-SHAH-nuh), celebrate the beginning of a new year in the Jewish calendar.

On Yom Kippur (yohm ki-POOHR), which falls soon afterward, Jews ask God to forgive their sins. Jews consider Yom Kippur to be the holiest day of the entire year. Because it is so holy, Jews don't eat or drink anything for the entire day. Many of the ceremonies they perform for Yom Kippur date back to the days of the Second

Temple. These ceremonies help many Jews feel more connected to their long past, to the days of Abraham and Moses.

READING CHECK **Finding Main Ideas** What name is given to the two most important Jewish holy days?

SUMMARY AND PREVIEW The Jewish culture is one of the oldest in the world. Over the course of their long history, the Jews' religion and customs have helped them maintain a sense of identity and community. This sense has helped the Jewish people endure many hardships. In the next chapter you will learn about another people who made major contributions to Western culture. These were the Greeks.

go.hrw.com
Online Quiz
KEYWORD: SN6 HP7

Section 3 Assessment

Reviewing Ideas, Terms, and People
1. **a. Recall** Who won the battle at Masada?
   b. Evaluate How did the defeat by the Romans affect Jewish history?
2. **a. Identify** What language developed in the Jewish communities of eastern Europe?
   b. Contrast How did communities of Ashkenazim differ from communities of Sephardim?
3. **Identify** What event does **Passover** celebrate?

Critical Thinking
4. **Evaluating** Review your notes. Then use a graphic organizer like the one shown to describe the belief or custom that you think may have had the biggest role in strengthening Jewish society.

Major Belief or Custom

FOCUS ON WRITING

5. **Organizing Your Information** Add notes about what you've just read to the notes you have already collected. Now that you have all your information, organize it into categories that will be windows, links, and other features on your Web page.

Social Studies Skills

Analysis   Critical Thinking   Economics   Study

Identifying Short- and Long-Term Effects

Understand the Skill

Many events of the past are the result of other events that took place earlier. When something occurs as the result of things that happened earlier, it is an effect of those things.

Some events take place soon after the things that cause them. These events are short-term effects. Long-term effects can occur decades or even hundreds of years after the events that caused them. Recognizing cause-and-effect relationships will help you to better understand the connections between historical events.

Learn the Skill

As you learned in Chapter 5, "clue words" can reveal cause-and-effect connections between events. Often, however, no such words are present. Therefore, you should always be looking for what happened as a result of an action or event.

Short-term effects are usually fairly easy to identify. They are often closely linked to the event that caused them. Take this sentence, for example:

" After Solomon's death around 930 BC, revolts broke out over who should be king. **"**

It is clear from this information that a short-term effect of Solomon's death was political unrest.

Now, consider this other passage:

" Some Hebrews . . . moved to Egypt . . . The Hebrews lived well in Egypt and their population grew. But this growing population worried Egypt's ruler, the pharaoh. He feared that the Hebrews would soon take over Egypt. To prevent this from happening, the pharaoh made the Hebrews slaves. **"**

Look carefully at the information in the passage. No clue words exist. However, it shows that one effect of the Hebrews' move to Egypt was the growth of their population. It takes time for a population to increase, so this was a long-term effect of the Hebrews' move.

Recognizing long-term effects is not always easy, however, because they often occur well after the event that caused them. Therefore, the long-term effects of those events may not be discussed at the time. This is why you should always ask yourself why an event might have happened as you study it.

For example, many of our modern laws are a result of the Ten Commandments of the ancient Hebrews. Religion is a major force in history that makes things happen. Other such forces include economics, science and technology, geography, and the meeting of peoples with different cultures. Ask yourself if one of these forces is a part of the event you are studying. If so, the event may have long-term effects.

Practice and Apply the Skill

Review the information in Chapter 7 and answer the following questions.

1. What were the short-term effects of King Solomon's rule of the Hebrews? What long-term benefit resulted from his rule?

2. What was the short-term effect of the destruction of the temple at Jerusalem in AD 70? What effect has that event had on the world today?

Visual Summary

Use the visual summary below to help you review the main ideas of the chapter.

QUICK FACTS

The early Hebrews settled in Canaan.

In Canaan the Hebrews formed the kingdom of Israel and built a great temple to God.

The Romans destroyed the Second Temple in Jerusalem and forced the Jews to leave.

Jewish religion and traditions have united the Jews over the centuries.

Reviewing Vocabulary, Terms, and People

For each group of terms below, write a sentence that shows how the terms in the group are related.

1. Abraham
Judaism

2. Moses
Exodus

3. David
Solomon

4. Torah
Talmud

5. Passover
High Holy Days

6. Moses
Ten Commandments

7. Passover
Exodus

8. monotheism
Judaism

9. synagogues
rabbis

10. principles
Torah

Comprehension and Critical Thinking

SECTION 1 *(Pages 202–207)*

11. a. Describe How did Abraham and Moses shape the history of the Hebrew people?

b. Compare and Contrast What did Saul, David, and Solomon have in common? How did they differ?

c. Evaluate Of Esther, Deborah, Miriam, and Ruth, which do you think provided the best example of how people should treat their families? Explain your answer.

SECTION 2 *(Pages 208–213)*

12. a. Identify What are the basic beliefs of Judaism?

b. Analyze What do the various sacred Jewish texts contribute to Judaism?

c. Elaborate How are Jewish ideas reflected in modern Western society?

SECTION 3 (Pages 214–219)

13. a. Describe What happened as a result of tensions between the Romans and the Jews?

b. Analyze What led to the creation of the two main Jewish cultural traditions?

c. Predict In the future, what role do you think holy days and other traditions will play in Judaism? Explain your answer.

Reading Skills

Identifying Facts and Opinions *Identify each of the following statements as a fact or an opinion.*

14. Much of what we know about Hebrew history comes from the work of archaeologists.

15. Archaeologists should spend more time studying Hebrew history.

16. The Exodus is one of the most fascinating events in world history.

17. Until 1947, scholars did not know about the Dead Sea Scrolls.

18. Hanukkah is a Jewish holy day that takes place every December.

Social Studies Skills

19. Identifying Short- and Long-Term Effects *Identify both the short-term and long-term effects of each of the following events.*

	Short-Term Effects	Long-Term Effects
the Exodus		
the Babylonian Captivity		
the expulsion of the Jews from Jerusalem		

Using the Internet

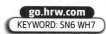
go.hrw.com
KEYWORD: SN6 WH7

20. Activity: Interpreting Maps Migration and conflict were key factors shaping Jewish history and culture. The Exodus, the Babylonian Captivity, and the revolts against Rome forced the Jewish people to adapt their culture and settle in regions outside Israel. Enter the activity keyword. Then create an annotated map showing the birthplace of Judaism and the Jews' movements into other parts of the world. Your map should include a legend as well as labels to identify events and explain their impact on the Jewish people.

Reviewing Themes

21. Religion How did monotheism shape the history of the Hebrews?

22. Religion Do you agree or disagree with this statement: "The history of Judaism is also the history of the Jewish people." Why?

23. Religion How does Mosaic law affect the daily lives of Jewish people?

FOCUS ON WRITING

24. Designing Your Web Site Look back at your notes and how you've organized them. Have you included all important facts and details? Will people be able to find information easily?

What will appear in menus or as hot links, and elsewhere on the page? What images will you include? Draw a rough diagram or sketch of your page. Be sure to label the parts of your page.

Most of the information in your textbook is presented chronologically, by the year or era. How did you present the information?

DIRECTIONS: Read each question, and write the letter of the best response.

1 Use the map to answer the following question.

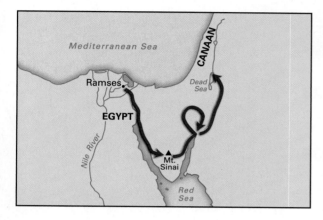

The map above illustrates

A the Babylonian Captivity.

B the Exodus.

C Abraham's migration to Canaan.

D the capture of Jerusalem by the Romans.

2 The Jews believe that the Ten Commandments were given by God to

A Moses.

B Abraham.

C King David.

D King Solomon.

3 The ancient Jews probably were the first people to

A conduct religious ceremonies.

B have a code of laws.

C practice monotheism.

D hold religious beliefs.

4 The basic teachings and laws that guide the Jewish people are found in the

A Talmud.

B Torah.

C Book of the Dead.

D Dead Sea Scrolls.

5 Which group was *most* responsible for the migration of Jews out of Jerusalem to other parts of the Mediterranean region?

A the Israelites

B the Philistines

C the Egyptians

D the Romans

Connecting with Past Learnings

6 Moses issued a set of laws for the Hebrew people to follow. What other ancient leader is famous for issuing a code of laws?

A Gilgamesh

B Tutankhamen

C Asoka

D Hammurabi

7 Jewish teachings required people to honor and respect their parents. This was an idea also common in China. In his writings, who else encouraged people to respect their parents?

A Chandragupta Maurya

B Shi Huangdi

C Confucius

D Abraham

Ancient Greece

FOCUS ON WRITING

A Myth Like most people, the Greeks enjoyed good stories. But they also took their stories seriously. They used stories called myths to explain everything from the creation of the world to details of everyday life. Reading this chapter will provide you with ideas you can use to create your own myth.

CHAPTER EVENTS

c. 2000 BC
The Minoan civilization prospers in Crete.

2000 BC

WORLD EVENTS

c. 2000 BC
The main part of Stonehenge is built in England.

What You Will Learn...

In this chapter you will study Greece—home to one of the great ancient civilizations. In this photo you see the ruins of the temple at Delphi. It was one of the most sacred places in ancient Greece.

c. 1200 BC
The Greeks and Trojans fight the Trojan War.

c. 750 BC
The Greeks begin to build city-states.

c. 500 BC
Athens becomes the world's first democracy.

1700 BC	1400 BC	1100 BC	800 BC	500 BC

c. 1200 BC
The Olmec civilization develops in the Americas.

c. 900 BC
The Phoenicians dominate trade in the Mediterranean.

753 BC
According to legend, Rome is founded.

ANCIENT GREECE   **225**

Focus on Themes In this chapter, you will read about the civilizations of ancient Greece. Whether reading about the Minoans and Mycenaeans or the Spartans and Athenians, you will see that where the people lived affected how they lived.

You will also read how the government of these ancient people changed over the years. By the end of this chapter, you will have learned a great deal about the **geography** and the **politics** of the ancient Greeks.

Greek Word Origins

Focus on Reading Sometimes when you read an unusual word, you can figure out what it means by using the other words around it. Other times you might need to consult a dictionary. But sometimes, if you know what the word's root parts mean, you can figure out its meaning. The chart below shows you several English words that have Greek roots.

In this chapter you'll find...	which means...	and comes from the Greek root
1. geography, *p. 228* (jee-AH-gruh-fee)	the study of the earth's surface	*ge-,* which means "earth" *-graphy,* which means "writing about"
2. acropolis, *p. 232* (uh-KRAH-puh-luhs)	fortress of a Greek city up on a high hill	*acr-,* which means "top" *polis,* which means "city"
3. democracy, *p. 236* (di-MAH-kruh-see)	a form of government in which people hold power	*dem-,* which means "people" *-cracy,* which means "power"
4. tyrant, *p. 237* (TY-ruhnt)	a ruler [in modern times, a harsh ruler]	*tyrannos,* which means "master"
5. oligarchy, *p. 237* (AH-luh-gahr-kee)	rule by a few people	*olig-,* which means "few" *-archy,* which means "rule"
6. mythology, *p. 243* (mi-THAH-luh-jee)	a body of stories about gods and heroes	*mythos,* which means "stories about gods or heroes" *-ology,* which means "study of"

You Try It!

Study each of the words below. Use the chart on the opposite page to find a Greek root or roots for each of them. How do the words' roots relate to their definitions?

Word	Definition
1. geology	a science that deals with the study of the makeup of the earth
2. police	the people who keep order in a city
3. Tyrannosaurus	one of the largest and fiercest dinosaurs
4. architect	the person in charge of designing buildings
5. acrophobia	the fear of heights
6. monarchy	rule by a single person
7. politics	the art or science of governing a city, state, or nation
8. demographer	a scientist who studies the growth of populations

Think about it.

1. How can studying Greek origins help you understand English?

2. Use the chart of roots on the previous page to answer this question. Where do you think a demagogue gets his or her power: the support of the people or a written constitution? Justify your answer.

3. Do you know words in other languages that help you understand English?

Chapter 8

Section 1
polis *(p. 232)*
classical *(p. 232)*
acropolis *(p. 232)*

Section 2
democracy *(p. 236)*
aristocrats *(p. 237)*
oligarchy *(p. 237)*
citizens *(p. 237)*
tyrant *(p. 237)*
Pericles *(p. 240)*

Section 3
mythology *(p. 243)*
Homer *(p. 246)*
Sappho *(p. 247)*
Aesop *(p. 247)*
fables *(p. 247)*

Academic Vocabulary

Success in school is related to knowing academic vocabulary—the words that are frequently used in school assignments and discussions. In this chapter, you will learn the following academic word:

influence *(p. 230)*

As you read Chapter 8, pay close attention to the highlighted words. Many of those words are Greek or come from Greek roots. Refer to the chart on the opposite page to help you understand what those words mean.

Geography and the Early Greeks

If YOU were there...

You live on the rocky coast of a bright blue sea. Across the water you can see dozens of islands and points of land jutting out into the sea. Rugged mountains rise steeply behind your village. It is hard to travel across the mountains in order to visit other villages or towns. Near your home on the coast is a sheltered cove where it's easy to anchor a boat.

What could you do to make a living here?

BUILDING BACKGROUND The paragraph you just read could be describing many parts of Greece, a peninsula in southern Europe. Greece's mountain ranges run right up to the coast in many places, making travel and farming difficult. Although it does not seem like the easiest place in the world to live, Greece was home to some of the ancient world's greatest civilizations.

Greece is a land of rugged mountains, rocky coastlines, and beautiful islands. The trees you see are olive trees. Olives were grown by the early Greeks for food and oil.

Geography Shapes Greek Civilization

The Greeks lived on rocky, mountainous lands surrounded by water. The mainland of Greece is a peninsula, an area of land that is surrounded on three sides by water. But the Greek peninsula is very irregular. It's one big peninsula made up of a series of smaller peninsulas. The land and sea intertwine like your hand and fingers in a bowl of water. In addition, there are many islands. Look at the map of Greece and notice the rugged coastline.

In your mind, picture those peninsulas and islands dominated by mountains that run almost to the sea. Just a few small valleys and coastal plains provide flat land for farming and villages. Now you have an image of Greece, a land where one of the world's greatest civilizations developed.

Mountains and Settlements

Because mountains cover much of Greece, there are few flat areas for farmland. People settled in those flat areas along the coast and in river valleys. They lived in villages and towns separated by mountains and seas.

Travel across the mountains and seas was difficult, so communities were isolated from one another. As a result, the people created their own governments and ways of life. Even though they spoke the same language, Greek communities saw themselves as separate countries.

Seas and Ships

Since travel inland across the rugged mountains was so difficult, the early Greeks turned to the seas. On the south was the huge Mediterranean Sea, to the west was the Ionian (eye-OH-nee-uhn) Sea, and to the east was the Aegean (ee-JEE-uhn) Sea.

Greece: Physical

Black Sea

PINDOS MOUNTAINS

Ionian Sea

GREECE

Gulf of Corinth

Peloponnesus

Mediterranean Sea

Aegean Sea

ASIA MINOR

Rhodes

Crete

ELEVATION

Feet		Meters
6,560		2,000
1,640		500
656		200
(Sea level) 0		0 (Sea level)

0   50   100 Miles
0   50   100 Kilometers

40° N
20° E
25° E
30° E
35° N

GEOGRAPHY SKILLS | **INTERPRETING MAPS**

Location What bodies of water surround Greece?

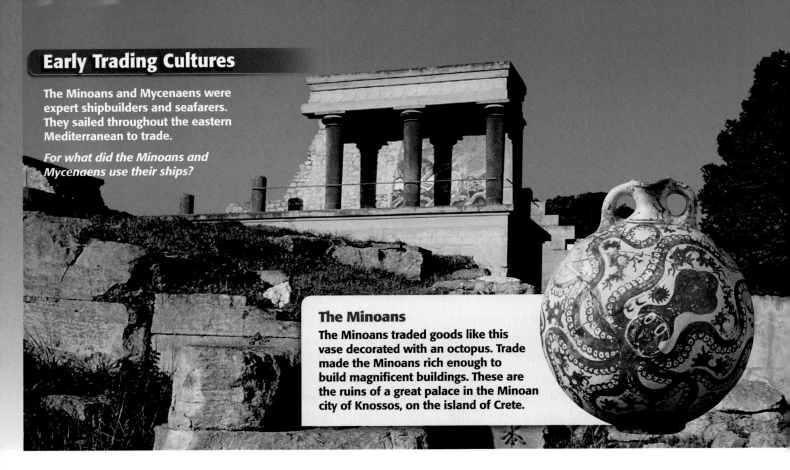

Early Trading Cultures

The Minoans and Mycenaens were expert shipbuilders and seafarers. They sailed throughout the eastern Mediterranean to trade.

For what did the Minoans and Mycenaens use their ships?

The Minoans

The Minoans traded goods like this vase decorated with an octopus. Trade made the Minoans rich enough to build magnificent buildings. These are the ruins of a great palace in the Minoan city of Knossos, on the island of Crete.

It's not surprising that the early Greeks used the sea as a source for food and as a way of trading with other communities.

The Greeks became skilled shipbuilders and sailors. Their ships sailed to Asia Minor (present-day Turkey), to Egypt, and to the islands of the Mediterranean and Aegean seas. As they traveled around these seas, they found sources of food and other products they needed. They also exchanged ideas with other cultures.

READING CHECK Drawing Conclusions

How did mountains affect the location of Greek settlements?

Trading Cultures Develop

Many cultures settled and developed in Greece. Two of the earliest were the Minoans (muh-NOH-uhnz) and the Mycenaens (my-suh-NEE-uhns). By 2000 BC the

Minoans had built an advanced society on the island of Crete. Crete lay south of the Aegean in the eastern Mediterranean. Later, the Mycenaeans built towns on the Greek mainland. These two civilizations **influenced** the entire Aegean region and helped shape later cultures in Greece.

The Minoans

Because they lived on an island, the Minoans spent much of their time at sea. They were among the best shipbuilders of their time. Minoan ships carried goods such as wood, olive oil, and pottery all around the eastern Mediterranean. They traded these goods for copper, gold, silver, and jewels.

Although Crete's location was excellent for Minoan traders, its geography had its dangers. Sometime in the 1600s BC a huge volcano erupted just north of Crete. This eruption created a giant wave that flooded much of Crete. In addition, the eruption

ACADEMIC VOCABULARY

influence change, or have an effect on

230 CHAPTER 8

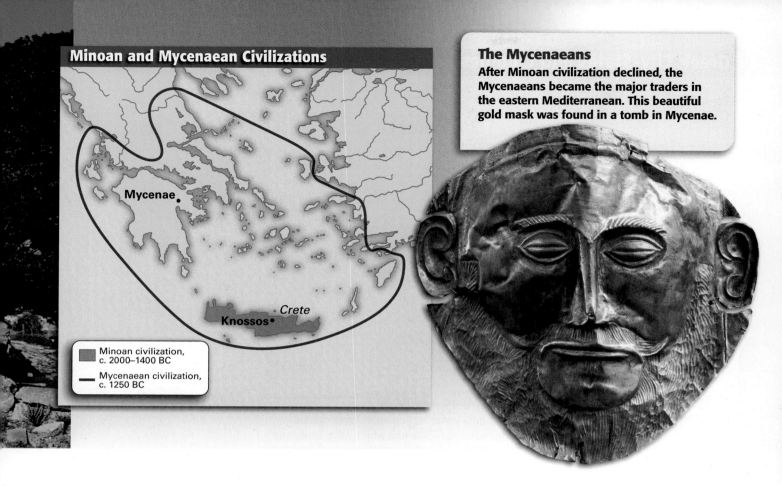

Minoan and Mycenaean Civilizations

Mycenae .

Crete
Knossos•

☐ Minoan civilization,
c. 2000–1400 BC

— Mycenaean civilization,
c. 1250 BC

The Mycenaeans
After Minoan civilization declined, the Mycenaeans became the major traders in the eastern Mediterranean. This beautiful gold mask was found in a tomb in Mycenae.

threw up huge clouds of ash, ruining crops and burying cities. This eruption may have led to the end of Minoan civilization.

The Mycenaeans

Although they lived in what is now Greece and influenced Greek society, historians don't consider the Minoans to be Greek. This is because the Minoans didn't speak the Greek language. The first people to speak Greek, and therefore the first to be considered Greek, were the Mycenaeans.

While the Minoans were sailing the Mediterranean, the Mycenaeans were building fortresses all over the Greek mainland. The largest and most powerful fortress was Mycenae (my-SEE-nee), after which the Mycenaeans were named.

By the mid-1400s, Minoan society had declined. That decline allowed the Mycenaeans to take over Crete and become the major traders in the eastern Mediterranean.

They set up colonies in northern Greece and Italy from which they shipped goods to markets around the Mediterranean and Black seas.

The Mycenaeans didn't think trade had to be conducted peacefully. They often attacked other kingdoms. Some historians think the Mycenaeans attacked the city of Troy, possibly starting the legendary Trojan War, which is featured in many works of literature.

Mycenaean society began to fall apart in the 1200s BC when invaders from Europe swept into Greece. At the same time, earthquakes destroyed many cities. As Mycenaean civilization crumbled, Greece slid into a period of warfare and disorder, a period called the Dark Age.

READING CHECK **Finding Main Ideas**
To what regions did Minoan and Mycenaean traders travel?

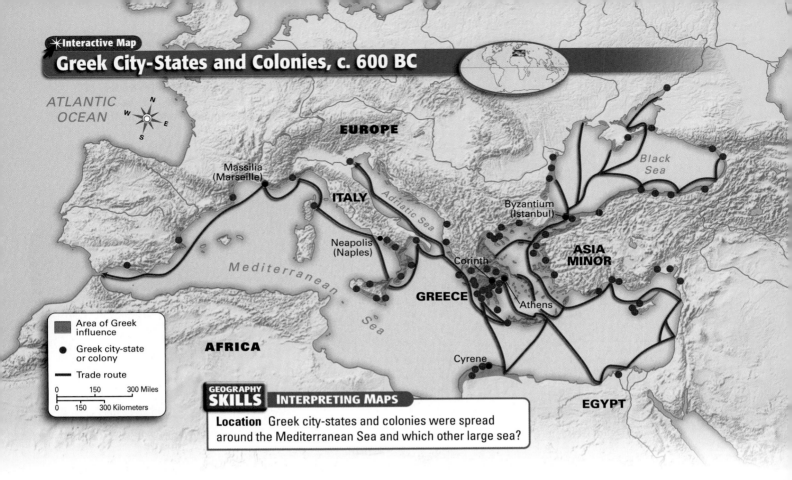

Greek City-States and Colonies, c. 600 BC

ATLANTIC
OCEAN

EUROPE

Massilia
(Marseille)

ITALY

Adriatic Sea

Byzantium
(Istanbul)

*Black
Sea*

Neapolis
(Naples)

Corinth

ASIA
MINOR

Mediterranean

GREECE

Athens

Sea

AFRICA

Cyrene

EGYPT

**Area of Greek
influence**

● Greek city-state
or colony

— Trade route

0   150   300 Miles

0   150   300 Kilometers

**GEOGRAPHY
SKILLS** **INTERPRETING MAPS**

Location Greek city-states and colonies were spread
around the Mediterranean Sea and which other large sea?

Greeks Create City-States

The Greeks of the Dark Age left no written records. All that we know about the period comes from archaeological findings.

About 300 years after the Mycenaean civilization crumbled, the Greeks started to join together in small groups for protection and stability. Over time, these groups set up independent city-states. The Greek word for a city-state is **polis** (PAH-luhs). The creation of city-states marks the beginning of what is known as Greece's classical age. A **classical** age is one that is marked by great achievements.

Life in a City-State

A Greek city was usually built around a strong fortress. This fortress often stood on top of a high hill called the **acropolis** (uh-KRAH-puh-luhs). The town around the acropolis was surrounded by walls for added protection.

**FOCUS ON
READING**

How do Greek roots give you clues to the meaning of *acropolis*?

Not everyone who lived in the city-state actually lived inside the city walls. Farmers, for example, usually lived near their fields outside the walls. In times of war, however, women, children, and elderly people all gathered inside the city walls for protection. As a result, they remained safe while the men of the polis formed an army to fight off its enemies.

Life in the city often focused on the marketplace, or agora (A-guh-ruh) in Greek. Farmers brought their crops to the market to trade for goods made by craftsmen in the town. Because it was a large open space, the market also served as a meeting place. People held both political and religious assemblies in the market. It often contained shops as well.

The city-state became the foundation of Greek civilization. Besides providing security for its people, the city gave them an identity. People thought of themselves as residents of a city, not as Greeks. Because the city-state was so central to their lives, the Greeks expected people to participate in its affairs, especially in its economy and its government.

City-States and Colonization

Life in Greece eventually became more settled. People no longer had to fear raiders swooping down on their cities. As a result, they were free to think about things other than defense. Some Greeks began to dream of becoming rich through trade. Others became curious about neighboring lands around the Mediterranean Sea. Some also worried about how to deal with Greece's growing population. Despite their different reasons, all these people eventually reached the same idea: the Greeks should establish colonies.

Before long, groups from city-states around Greece began to set up colonies in distant lands. After they were set up, Greek colonies became independent. In other words, each colony became a new polis. In fact, some cities that began as colonies began to create colonies of their own. Eventually Greek colonies spread all around the Mediterranean and Black seas. Many big cities around the Mediterranean today began as Greek colonies. Among them are Istanbul (is-tahn-BOOL) in Turkey, Marseille (mahr-SAY) in France, and Naples in Italy.

Patterns of Trade

Although the colonies were independent, they often traded with city-states on the mainland. The colonies sent metals such as copper and iron back to mainland Greece. In return, the Greek city-states sent wine, olive oil, and other products.

Trade made the city-states much richer. Because of their locations, some city-states became great trading centers. By 550 BC the Greeks had become the greatest traders in the whole Aegean region. Greek ships sailed to Egypt and cities around the Black Sea.

READING CHECK **Analyzing** Why did the Greeks develop city-states?

SUMMARY AND PREVIEW In this section you learned about the creation of city-states and how they affected Greek society. In the next section you will read about how the government of one city-state changed as people became more interested in how they were ruled.

go.hrw.com
Online Quiz
KEYWORD: SN6 HP8

Section 1 Assessment

Reviewing Ideas, Terms, and People
1. a. **Identify** What kinds of landforms are found in Greece?
   b. **Interpret** How did the sea help shape early Greek society?
   c. **Predict** How might the difficulty of mountain travel have been a benefit to the Greeks?
2. a. **Recall** What was the first major civilization to develop in Greece?
   b. **Compare** How were the Minoans and Mycenaeans similar?
3. a. **Define** What is a **polis**?
   b. **Elaborate** Why do you think the Greeks built their cities around a high **acropolis**?

Critical Thinking
4. **Summarizing** Using your notes, write one descriptive sentence about Greece's geography and one about city-states. Then write a sentence summarizing the influence of geography on city-states.

| Geography | → | City-States | → | Summary |

FOCUS ON WRITING

5. **Thinking About Geographical Features as Characters** Have you ever thought about physical features as having personalities? For example, you might describe a strong, blustery wind as angry. Think about the physical features of Greece you read about in this section. What kinds of personalities might they have? Write your ideas down in your notebook.

Natural Disaster!

Nature is a powerful force. Throughout history, great natural disasters have affected civilizations. One natural disaster was so devastating that it may have contributed to the destruction of the entire Minoan civilization.

In the 1600s BC a volcano on the Greek island of Thera erupted. The colossal explosion was one of the largest in history. It was so powerful that people could see and hear it from hundreds of miles away. In a moment of nature's fury, the history of the Mediterranean world was changed forever.

BLACK SEA

Troy

ANATOLIA

Mycenae

PELOPONNESUS

Knossos

CRETE

For centuries, the Minoans had thrived on the island of Crete. The Minoans were great sea traders who often sailed to the island of Thera, just 70 miles away.

The eruption of Thera produced fast-moving waves called tsunami (soo-NAH-mee) in the Mediterranean Sea. Scientists today estimate that the waves may have traveled at about 200 miles an hour.

MEDITERRANEAN SEA

N
W E
S

LIBYA

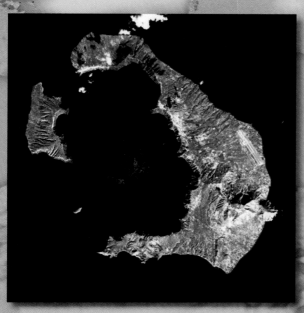

The ancient island of Thera is known as Santorini today. The huge gap on the island's western side and the water in the middle are evidence of the explosion more than 3,500 years ago.

CYPRUS

Aleppo

Jericho

The explosion produced a massive cloud of ash that smothered crops, cities, and people. For years afterward, the ash dimmed the sunlight, making it difficult for farmers to grow their crops.

Three Stages of Disaster

Stage 1

Warning Signs Following a series of earthquakes, the volcano begins to shoot ash into the sky. People flee the island in fear.

Stage 2

Explosion Ash and rock are flung into the air and sweep down the volcano's sides, destroying everything in their path. Cracks through the island rock begin to form from the powerful explosions.

Stage 3

Collapse The volcano collapses and falls into the sea, creating massive waves. The powerful waves slam into Crete, flooding coastal areas.

GEOGRAPHY SKILLS **INTERPRETING MAPS**

1. **Location** What direction did the ash cloud travel after the island's eruption?
2. **Human-Environment Interaction** How might the effects of the ash cloud have influenced Minoan civilization?

E G Y P T

Government in Athens

Main Ideas

1. Aristocrats and tyrants ruled early Athens.
2. Athens created the world's first democracy.
3. Ancient democracy was different than modern democracy.

The Big Idea

The people of Athens tried many different forms of government before creating a democracy.

Key Terms and People

democracy, *p. 236*
aristocrats, *p. 237*
oligarchy, *p. 237*
citizens, *p. 237*
tyrant, *p. 237*
Pericles, *p. 240*

TAKING NOTES As you read, look for information on the various types of government the people of Athens tried. Take notes on a graphic organizer like this one.

Oligarchy	Tyranny	Democracy

If YOU were there...

For many years, your city has been ruled by a small group of rich men. They have generally been good leaders. They have built new buildings and protected the city from enemies. But now a new leader wants to let all free men help run the government. It won't matter whether they are rich or poor. Some people, however, worry about giving power to ordinary people.

What do you think of this new government?

BUILDING BACKGROUND The decision to change a city's government was not unusual in Greece. Many cities tried several forms of government before people were satisfied. To see how these changes came about, we can look at one city whose government changed many times—Athens.

Aristocrats and Tyrants Rule

Greece is the birthplace of **democracy**, a type of government in which people rule themselves. The word democracy comes from Greek words meaning "rule of the people." But Greek city-states didn't start as democracies, and not all became democratic.

Government in Athens QUICK FACTS

Oligarchy

Early Athens was governed by a small group of powerful aristocrats. This type of government is called an oligarchy. Oligarchy means "rule by a few."

Rule by a Few People

Even Athens, the city where democracy was born, began with a different kind of government. In early Athens, kings ruled the city-state. Later, a group of rich landowners, or **aristocrats** (uh-RIS-tuh-krats), took power. A government in which only a few people have power is called an **oligarchy** (AH-luh-gar-kee).

The aristocrats dominated Athenian society. As the richest men in town, they ran the city's economy. They also served as its generals and judges. Common people had little say in the government.

In the 600s BC a group of rebels tried to overthrow the aristocrats. They failed. Possibly as a result of their attempt, however, a man named Draco (DRAY-koh) created a new set of laws for Athens. These laws were very harsh. For example, Draco's laws made minor crimes such as loitering punishable by death.

The people of Athens thought Draco's laws were too strict. In the 590s BC a man named Solon (SOH-luhn) created a set of laws that were much less harsh and gave more rights to nonaristocrats. Under Solon's laws, all free men living in Athens became **citizens**, people who had the right to participate in government. But his efforts were not enough for the Athenians. They were ready to end the rule of the aristocracy.

The Rise of the Tyrants

Because the Athenians weren't pleased with the rule of the aristocrats, they wanted a new government. In 546 BC a noble named Peisistratus (py-SIS-truht-uhs) overthrew the oligarchy. He became the ruler of Athens. Peisistratus was called a **tyrant**, which meant a leader who held power through the use of force.

Today the word *tyrant* means a ruler who is harsh, but the word had a different meaning in ancient Greece. Athenian tyrants were usually good leaders. Tyrants were able to stay in power because they had strong armies and because the people supported them.

Peisistratus brought peace and prosperity to the city. He began new policies meant to unify the city. He created new festivals and built temples and monuments. During his rule, many improvements were made in Athens.

After Peisistratus died, his son took over as tyrant. Many aristocrats, however, were unhappy because their power was gone. Some of these aristocrats convinced a rival city-state to attack Athens. As a result of this invasion, the tyrants lost power and, for a short time, aristocrats returned to power in Athens.

READING CHECK **Finding Main Ideas** What was a tyrant in ancient Greece?

FOCUS ON READING
How do Greek roots give you clues to the meaning of *oligarchy*?

THE IMPACT TODAY

Today very harsh laws or rules are called "draconian" after Draco.

Tyranny
Peisistratus overthrew the oligarchy in 546 BC, and Athens became a tyranny. Tyranny means "rule by a tyrant"—a strong leader who has power.

Democracy
Around 500 BC Athens became a democracy. Democracy means "rule by the people." For the first time in history, a government was based on the votes of its free citizens.

Democracy in Action

Ancient Athens was the birthplace of democracy—the system of government in which the people rule themselves. Democracy was perhaps the greatest achievement of ancient Athens. In time, it became the Greeks' greatest gift to the world.

Only free male citizens of Athens were members of the assembly with the right to vote. Women, slaves, and foreigners could not participate.

In Athenian democracy, people debated issues in the open air, and these debates were noisy affairs.

Voting was usually done by a show of hands, but sometimes assembly members wrote their votes on broken pieces of pottery. Then officials collected these pottery pieces and counted the votes.

Athens Creates Democracy

Around 500 BC a new leader named Cleisthenes (KLYS-thuh-neez) gained power in Athens. Although he was a member of one of the most powerful families in Athens, Cleisthenes didn't want aristocrats to run the government. He thought they already had too much influence. By calling on the support of the people, Cleisthenes was able to overthrow the aristocracy once and for all. In its place, he established a completely new form of government.

Under Cleisthenes' leadership, Athens developed the world's first democracy. For this reason, he is sometimes called the father of democracy.

Democracy under Cleisthenes

Under Cleisthenes, all citizens in Athens had the right to participate in the assembly, or gathering of citizens, that created the city's laws. The assembly met outdoors on a hillside so that everyone could attend the meetings. During meetings, people stood before the crowd and gave speeches on political issues. Every citizen had the right to speak his opinion. In fact, the Athenians encouraged people to speak. They loved to hear speeches and debates. After the speeches were over, the assembly voted. Voting was usually done by a show of hands, but sometimes the Athenians used secret ballots.

The Athenian assembly met on a hill called the Pnyx (pah-NIKS). Sometimes, more than 6,000 men crowded onto the small hill.

Men spoke before the assembly to support or argue against different issues. Persuasive speakers often convinced others to pass laws they supported.

Men in the crowd often argued with speakers.

ANALYSIS SKILL ANALYZING VISUALS

How did people vote in ancient Athens?

The number of people who voted in the assembly changed from day to day. For major decisions, however, the assembly needed about 6,000 people to vote. But it wasn't always easy to gather that many people together in one place.

According to one Greek writer, the government sent slaves to the market to round up more citizens if necessary. In one of the writer's plays, slaves walked through the market holding a long rope between them. The rope was covered in red dye and would mark the clothing of anyone it touched. Any citizen with red dye on his clothing had to go to the assembly meeting or pay a large fine.

Because the assembly was so large, it was sometimes difficult to make decisions. The Athenians therefore selected citizens to be city officials and to serve on a smaller council. These officials decided which laws the assembly should discuss. This helped the government run more smoothly.

Changes in Athenian Democracy

As time passed, citizens gained more powers. For example, they served on juries to decide court cases. Juries had anywhere from 200 to 6,000 people, although juries of about 500 people were much more common. Most juries had an odd number of members to prevent ties.

THE IMPACT TODAY

Like the ancient Greeks, we use juries to decide court cases. But our modern juries have only 12 people.

SPEECH
Pericles' Funeral Oration

In 430 BC Pericles addressed the people of Athens at a funeral for soldiers who had died in battle. In his speech, Pericles tried to comfort the Athenians by reminding them of the greatness of their government.

> Pericles is praising the Athenians for creating a democracy.

"Our form of government does not enter into rivalry with the institutions of others. We do not copy our neighbors, but are an example to them. It is true that we are called a democracy, for the administration is in the hands of the many and not of the few . . . There is no exclusiveness [snobbery] in our public life, and . . . we are not suspicious of one another. . . . "

–Pericles, quoted in Thucydides, *The History of the Peloponnesian War*

> Athenian government was open to all free men, not just a few.

ANALYSIS SKILL **ANALYZING PRIMARY SOURCES**

How do you think Pericles felt Athenian government compared to other cities' governments?

Athens remained a democracy for about 170 years. It reached its height under a brilliant elected leader named **Pericles** (PER-uh-kleez). He led the government from about 460 BC until his death in 429 BC.

Pericles encouraged the Athenians to take pride in their city. He believed that participating in government was just as important as defending Athens in war. To encourage people to participate in government, Pericles began to pay people who served in public offices or on juries. Pericles also encouraged the people of Athens to introduce democracy into other parts of Greece.

End of Democracy in Athens

Eventually, the great age of Athenian democracy came to an end. In the mid-330s BC Athens was conquered by the Macedonians from north of Greece. After the conquest, Athens fell under strong Macedonian influence.

Even after being conquered by Macedonia, Athens kept its democratic government. But it was a democracy with very limited powers. The Macedonian king ruled his country like a dictator, a ruler who held all the power. No one could make any decisions without his approval.

In Athens, the assembly still met to make laws, but it had to be careful not to upset the king. The Athenians didn't dare make any drastic changes to their laws without the king's consent. They weren't happy with this situation, but they feared the king's powerful army. Before long, though, the Athenians lost even this limited democracy. In the 320s BC a new king took over Greece and ended Athenian democracy forever.

READING CHECK **Summarizing** How were citizens involved in the government of Athens?

Ancient Democracy Differs from Modern Democracy

Like ancient Athens, the United States has a democratic government in which the people hold power. But our modern democracy is very different from the ancient Athenians' democracy.

Direct Democracy

All citizens in Athens could participate directly in the government. We call this form of government a direct democracy. It is called direct democracy because each person's decision directly affects the outcome of a vote. In Athens, citizens gathered together to discuss issues and vote on them. Each person's vote counted, and the majority ruled.

The United States is too large for direct democracy to work for the whole country. For example, it would be impossible for all citizens to gather in one place for a debate. Instead, the founders of the United States set up another kind of democracy.

Representative Democracy

The democracy created by the founders of the United States is a representative democracy, or republic. In this system, the citizens elect officials to represent them in the government. These elected officials then meet to make the country's laws and to enforce them. For example, Americans elect senators and representatives to Congress, the body that makes the country's laws. Americans don't vote on each law that Congress passes but trust their chosen representatives to vote for them.

READING CHECK **Contrasting** How are direct democracy and representative democracy different?

Democracy Then and Now — QUICK FACTS

In Athenian Direct Democracy…	In American Representative Democracy…
■ All citizens met as a group to debate and vote directly on every issue.	■ Citizens elect representatives to debate and vote on issues for them.
■ There was no separation of powers. Citizens created laws, enforced laws, and acted as judges.	■ There is a separation of powers. Citizens elect some people to create laws, others to enforce laws, and others to be judges.
■ Only free male citizens could vote. Women and slaves could not vote.	■ Men and women who are citizens have the right to vote.

SUMMARY AND PREVIEW In this section, you learned about the development and decline of democracy in Athens. You also learned how Athenian democracy influenced the government of the United States. In the next section, you will learn about the beliefs and culture of the ancient Greeks and how they affect our culture and literature today.

go.hrw.com
Online Quiz
KEYWORD: SN6 HP8

Section 2 Assessment

Reviewing Ideas, Terms, and People

1. **a. Define** What are **aristocrats**?
   b. Contrast How were **oligarchy** and **tyranny** different?
2. **a. Describe** Describe the **democracy** created by Cleisthenes.
   b. Analyze How did **Pericles** change Athenian democracy?
3. **a. Identify** What type of democracy did Athens have?
   b. Develop In what situations would a representative democracy work better than a direct democracy?

Critical Thinking

4. **Finding Main Ideas** Draw a chart like the one shown. Using your notes, identify who held power in each type of government. Then write a sentence explaining what role common people had in each government.

Oligarchy	Tyranny	Democracy

FOCUS ON WRITING

5. **Connecting Personalities and Governments** Think back to the personalities you assigned to natural features in Section 1. What if people with these same personalities were working to create a government? What kind would they create? Would they rule as tyrants or build a democracy? Write your thoughts in your notebook.

Greek Mythology and Literature

What You Will Learn...

Main Ideas

1. The Greeks created myths to explain the world.
2. Ancient Greek literature provides some of the world's greatest poems and stories.
3. Greek literature lives on and influences our world even today.

The Big Idea

The ancient Greeks created great myths and works of literature that influence the way we speak and write today.

Key Terms and People

mythology, *p. 243*
Homer, *p. 246*
Sappho, *p. 247*
Aesop, *p. 247*
fables, *p. 247*

TAKING NOTES As you read, look for characteristics of Greek myths and literature. Record what you find in a graphic organizer like the one shown.

Greek Myths	Greek Literature

If YOU were there...

As a farmer in ancient Greece, your way of life depends on events in nature. The crops you grow need sunshine and rain, though thunder and lightning scare you. When you look up at the night sky, you wonder about the twinkling lights you see there. You know that at certain times of the year, the weather will turn cold and gray and plants will die. Then, a few months later, green plants will grow again.

How might you explain these natural events?

BUILDING BACKGROUND The Greeks lived in a time long before the development of science. To them, natural events like thunderstorms and changing seasons were mysterious. Today we can explain what causes these events. But to the Greeks, they seemed like the work of powerful gods.

Hephaestus

Hestia

Demeter

Poseidon

Dionysus

Myths Explain the World

The ancient Greeks believed in many gods. These gods were at the center of Greek **mythology**—a body of stories about gods and heroes that try to explain how the world works. Each story, or myth, explained natural or historical events.

Greek Gods

People today have scientific explanations for events like thunder, earthquakes, and volcanic eruptions. The ancient Greeks did not. They believed their gods caused these events to happen, and they created myths to explain the gods' actions.

Among the most important Greek gods were the ones in the picture below:

- Zeus, king of the gods
- Hera, queen of the gods
- Poseidon, god of the sea
- Hades, god of the underworld
- Demeter, goddess of agriculture
- Hestia, goddess of the hearth
- Athena, goddess of wisdom
- Apollo, god of the sun
- Artemis, goddess of the moon
- Ares, god of war
- Aphrodite, goddess of love
- Hephaestus, god of metalworking
- Dionysus, god of celebration
- Hermes, the messenger god

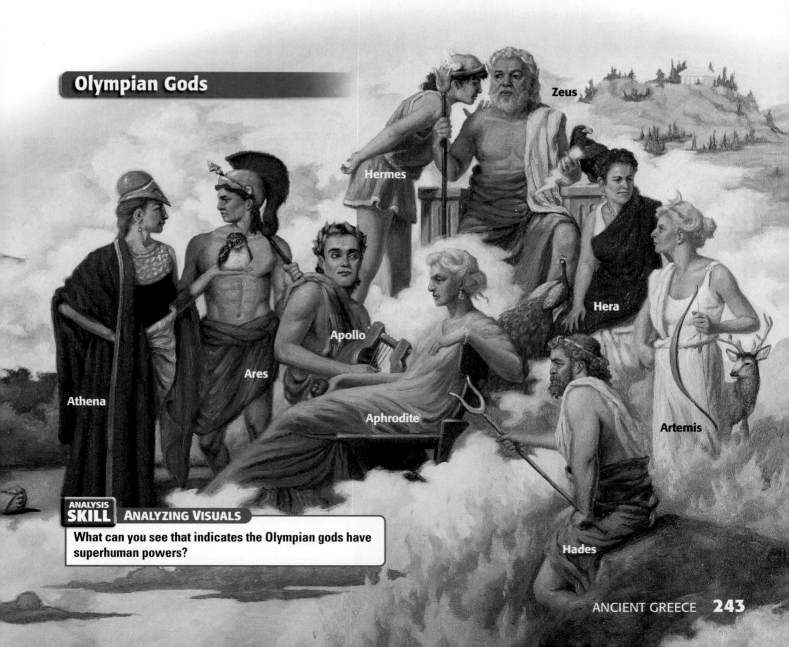

Olympian Gods

Zeus

Hermes

Hera

Apollo

Ares

Athena

Aphrodite

Artemis

Hades

ANALYSIS SKILL ANALYZING VISUALS

What can you see that indicates the Olympian gods have superhuman powers?

Gods and Mythology

The Greeks saw the work of the gods in events all around them. For example, the Greeks lived in an area where volcanic eruptions were common. To explain these eruptions, they told stories about the god Hephaestus (hi-FES-tuhs), who lived underground. The fire and lava that poured out of volcanoes, the Greeks said, came from the huge fires of the god's forge. At this forge he created weapons and armor for the other gods.

The Greeks did not think the gods spent all their time creating disasters, though. They also believed the gods caused daily events. For example, they believed the goddess of agriculture, Demeter (di-MEE-tuhr), created the seasons. According to Greek myth, Demeter had a daughter who was kidnapped by another god. The desperate goddess begged the god to let her daugh-

ter go, and eventually he agreed to let her return to her mother for six months every year. During the winter, Demeter is separated from her daughter and misses her. In her grief, she doesn't let plants grow. When her daughter comes home, the goddess is happy, and summer comes to Greece. To the Greeks, this story explained why winter came every year.

To keep the gods happy, the Greeks built great temples to honor them all around Greece. In return, however, they expected the gods to give them help when they needed it. For example, many Greeks in need of advice traveled to Delphi, a city in central Greece. There they spoke to the oracle, a female priest of Apollo to whom they thought the god gave answers. The oracle at Delphi was so respected that Greek leaders sometimes asked her for advice about how to rule their cities.

Theseus the Hero
According to legend, Athens had to send 14 people to Crete every year to be eaten by the Minotaur, a terrible monster. But Theseus, a hero from Athens, traveled to Crete and killed the Minotaur, freeing the people of Athens from this burden.

LINKING TO TODAY

Let the Games Begin!

One way the ancient Greeks honored their gods was by holding sporting contests like the one shown on the vase. The largest took place every four years at Olympia, a city in southern Greece. Held in honor of Zeus, this event was called the Olympic Games. Athletes competed in footraces, chariot races, boxing, wrestling, and throwing events. Only men could compete. The Greeks held these games every four years for more than 1,000 years, until the AD 320s.

In modern times, people began to hold the Olympics again. The first modern Olympics took place in Athens in 1896. Since then, athletes from many nations have assembled in cities around the world to compete. Today the Olympics include 28 sports, and both men and women participate. They are still held every four years. In 2004 the Olympic Games once again returned to their birthplace, Greece.

ANALYSIS SKILL | **ANALYZING INFORMATION**

How do you think the modern Olympics are similar to the ancient Games? How do you think they are different?

Heroes and Mythology

Not all Greek myths were about gods. Many told about the adventures of great heroes. Some of these heroes were real people, while others were not. The Greeks loved to tell the stories of heroes who had special abilities and faced terrible monsters. The people of each city had their favorite hero, usually someone from there.

The people of Athens, for example, told stories about the hero Theseus. According to legend, he traveled to Crete and killed the Minotaur, a terrible monster that was half human and half bull. People from northern Greece told myths about Jason and how he sailed across the seas in search of a great treasure, fighting enemies the whole way.

Perhaps the most famous of all Greek heroes was a man called Hercules. The myths explain how Hercules fought many monsters and performed nearly impossible tasks. For example, he fought and killed the hydra, a huge snake with nine heads and poisonous fangs. Every time Hercules cut off one of the monster's heads, two more heads grew in its place. In the end, Hercules had to burn the hydra's neck each time he cut off a head to keep a new head from growing. People from all parts of Greece enjoyed stories about Hercules and his great deeds.

READING CHECK **Finding Main Ideas** How did the Greeks use myths to explain the world around them?

Ancient Greek Literature

Because the Greeks loved myths and stories, it is no surprise that they created great works of literature. Early Greek writers produced long epic poems, romantic poetry, and some of the world's most famous stories.

Homer and Epic Poetry

Among the earliest Greek writings are two great epic poems, the *Iliad* and the *Odyssey*, by a poet named **Homer**. Like most epics, both poems describe the deeds of great heroes. The heroes in Homer's poems fought in the Trojan War. In this war, the Mycenaean Greeks fought the Trojans, people of the city called Troy.

The *Iliad* tells the story of the last years of the Trojan War. It focuses on the deeds of the Greeks, especially Achilles (uh-KIL-eez), the greatest of all Greek warriors. It describes in great detail the battles between the Greeks and their Trojan enemies.

The *Odyssey* describes the challenges that the Greek hero Odysseus (oh-DI-see-uhs) faced on his way home from the war. For 10 years after the war ends, Odysseus tries to get home, but many obstacles stand in his way. He has to fight his way past terrible monsters, powerful magicians, and even angry gods.

Both the *Iliad* and the *Odyssey* are great tales of adventure. But to the Greeks Homer's poems were much more than just entertainment. They were central to the ancient Greek education system. People memorized long passages of the poems as part of their lessons. They admired Homer's poems and the heroes described in them as symbols of Greece's great history.

Homer's poems influenced later writers. They copied his writing styles and borrowed some of the stories and ideas he wrote about in his works. Homer's poems are considered some of the greatest literary works ever produced.

In Homer's *Odyssey*, the half woman and half bird Sirens sang sweet songs that made passing sailors forget everything and crash their ships. To get past the Sirens, Odysseus plugged his crew's ears with wax and had himself tied to his ship's mast.

Lyric Poetry

Other poets wrote poems that were often set to music. During a performance, the poet played a stringed instrument called a lyre while reading a poem. These poets were called lyric poets after their instrument, the lyre. Today, the words of songs are called lyrics after these ancient Greek poets.

Most poets in Greece were men, but the most famous lyric poet was a woman named **Sappho** (SAF-oh). Her poems were beautiful and emotional. Most of her poems were about love and relationships with her friends and family.

Fables

Other Greeks told stories to teach people important lessons. **Aesop** (EE-sahp), for example, is famous for his fables. **Fables** are short stories that teach the reader lessons about life or give advice on how to live.

In most of Aesop's fables, animals are the main characters. The animals talk and act like humans. One of Aesop's most famous stories is the tale of the ants and the grasshopper:

BIOGRAPHY

Aesop
before 400 BC

Historians don't know for sure if a man named Aesop ever really lived, but many ancient legends are told about him. According to one story, Aesop was a slave in the 500s BC. Another story says he was an adviser to a king. Some historians think that the fables credited to Aesop were actually written by many different people and collected together under a single name.

Drawing Inferences Why might the Greeks have wanted to list a single author for the fables?

" The ants were spending a fine winter's day drying grain collected in the summertime. A Grasshopper, perishing [dying] with famine [hunger], passed by and earnestly [eagerly] begged for a little food. The Ants inquired [asked] of him, "Why did you not treasure up food during the summer?" He replied, "I had not leisure enough. I passed the days in singing." They then said in derision: "If you were foolish enough to sing all the summer, you must dance supperless to bed in the winter. "

–Aesop, from "The Ants and the Grasshopper"

The lesson in this fable is that people shouldn't waste time instead of working. Those who do, Aesop says, will be sorry.

Another popular fable by Aesop, "The Tortoise and the Hare," teaches that it is better to work slowly and carefully than to hurry and make mistakes. "The Boy Who Cried Wolf" warns readers not to play pranks on others. Since we still read these fables, you may be familiar with them.

READING CHECK **Summarizing** Why did the Greeks tell fables?

Greek Literature Lives

The works of ancient Greek writers such as Homer, Sappho, and Aesop are still alive and popular today. In fact, Greek literature has influenced modern language, literature, and art. Did you know that some of the words you use and some of the stories you hear come from ancient Greece?

Language

Probably the most obvious way we see the influence of the Greeks is in our language. Many English words and expressions come from Greek mythology. For example, we call a long journey an "odyssey" after Odysseus, the wandering hero of Homer's poem. Something very large and powerful is called "titanic." This word comes from the Titans, a group of large and powerful gods in Greek myth.

Many places around the world today are also named after figures from Greek myths. For example, Athens is named for Athena, the goddess of wisdom. Africa's Atlas Mountains were named after a giant from Greek mythology who held up the sky. The name of the Aegean Sea comes from Aegeus, a legendary Greek king. Europe itself was named after a figure from Greek myth, the princess Europa. Even places in space bear names from mythology. For example, Jupiter's moon Io was named after a goddess's daughter.

Literature and the Arts

Greek myths have inspired artists for centuries. Great painters and sculptors have used gods and heroes as the subjects of their works. Writers have retold ancient stories, sometimes set in modern times. Moviemakers have also borrowed stories from ancient myths. Hercules, for example, has been the subject of dozens of films. These films range from early classics to a Walt Disney cartoon.

Mythological references are also common in today's popular culture. Many sports teams have adopted the names of powerful figures from myths, like Titans or

Greek Influence on Language

In Greek Literature and Mythology…	Today…
■ Achilles was a great warrior who was killed when an arrow struck his heel.	■ An "Achilles heel" is a person's weak spot.
■ Hercules was the strongest man on earth who completed 12 almost impossible tasks.	■ When a person has a really hard job to do it is called a "Herculean" task.
■ A fox wanted to eat some grapes but he couldn't reach the branch they were on, so he said, "Those grapes are probably sour anyway."	■ When people pretend they don't want something after they find out they can't have it, they are said to have "sour grapes."
■ King Midas was granted one wish by the god Dionysus, so he wished that everything he touched turned to gold.	■ A person who seems to get rich easily is said to have a "Midas touch."
■ Tantalus was punished for offending the gods. He had to stand up to his chin in water and he was always thirsty, but if he tried to drink the water it went away.	■ Something is "tantalizing" if you want it but it's just out of your reach.

Greek Names Today

The influence of Greek stories and culture can still be seen in names. Astronomers named one of Jupiter's moons Io (EYE-oh) after a woman from Greek mythology. Sports teams also use Greek names. This college mascot is dressed like a Trojan warrior.

Trojans. Businesses frequently use images or symbols from mythology in their advertising. Although people no longer believe in the Greek gods, mythological ideas can still be seen all around us.

READING CHECK Finding Main Ideas
How did Greek myths influence later language and art?

SUMMARY AND PREVIEW The myths, stories, and poems of ancient Greece have shaped how people today speak, read, and write. Like democracy, these myths, stories, and poems are part of ancient Greece's gift to the world. In the next chapter you will learn more about life and culture in ancient Greece.

Section 3 Assessment

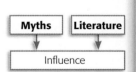
go.hrw.com
Online Quiz
KEYWORD: SN6 HP8

Reviewing Ideas, Terms, and People

1. **a. Define** What is **mythology**?
   b. Summarize Why did the ancient Greeks create myths?
2. **a. Identify** What are **Homer**'s most famous works?
   b. Contrast How are **fables** different from myths?
3. **a. Recall** In what areas have Greek myths influenced our culture?
   b. Analyze Why do you think mythological references are popular with sports teams and businesses today?
   c. Evaluate Why do you think Greek literature has been so influential throughout history?

Critical Thinking

4. **Analyzing** Using your notes and a chart like this, explain the influence of myths and literature on the world today.

Myths	Literature

Influence

FOCUS ON WRITING

5. **Putting Your Ideas Together** Look at your notes from the previous sections. Think about the personalities you gave physical features and government leaders. Now imagine that those personalities belonged to gods. What stories might be told about these gods? Write down some ideas.

ANCIENT GREECE **249**

The Epic Poetry of **Homer**

from the *Iliad*

as translated by Robert Fitzgerald

GUIDED READING

WORD HELP

main strength
resolute determined
imploring begging

❶ *To what is Achilles being compared?*

❷ Priam, Hector's father, knows that the gods have protected and strengthened Achilles.

❸ Achilles' armor was made by the god of metalworking.

Why might the very sight of this armor make Priam afraid?

About the Reading *The* Iliad *describes one part of a ten-year war between the Greeks and the city of Troy. As the poem opens, the Greek hero Achilles (uh-KIL-eez) has left the battle to wait for help from the gods. When he learns that his best friend Patroclus is dead, however, Achilles springs back into action. In this passage, the angry Achilles sprints across the plain toward Troy—and Hector, the Trojan warrior who has killed his friend.*

AS YOU READ Look for words and actions that tell you Achilles is a hero.

Then toward the town with might and main
he ran magnificent, like a racing chariot horse
that holds its form at full stretch on the plain. ❶
So light-footed Achilles held the pace.
And aging Priam was the first to see him
sparkling on the plain, bright as that star
in autumn rising, whose unclouded rays
shine out amid a throng of stars at dusk—
the one they call Orion's dog, most brilliant… ❷
So pure and bright
the bronze gear blazed upon him as he ran.
The old man gave a cry. ❸ With both his hands
thrown up on high he struck his head, then
shouted, groaning, appealing to his dear son.
Unmoved, Lord Hector stood in the gateway,
resolute to fight Achilles.

               Stretching out his hands,
old Priam said, imploring him:

                 "No, Hector!
… don't try to hold your ground against this man,
or soon you'll meet the shock of doom…"

The painting on this vase shows people fighting in the Trojan War.

from the *Odyssey*

About the Reading *The* Odyssey *takes place after the Trojan War has ended. It describes the adventures of another hero, Odysseus (oh-DIS-ee-uhs), as he makes his way home to his kingdom of Ithaca. His voyage is full of obstacles—including the two sea monsters described in this passage. The idea for these monsters probably came from an actual strait in the Mediterranean Sea, where a jagged cliff rose on one side and dangerous whirlpools churned on the other.*

AS YOU READ Try to picture the action in your mind.

GUIDED READING

WORD HELP

travail pain
dire gorge terrible throat
spume foam or froth
maelstrom whirlpool
blanched grew pale
anguish great suffering

❶ Odysseus is the speaker. He is referring to himself and his crew.

Why might the crew be sobbing?

❷ Three times a day, the monster Charybdis (cuh-RIB-duhs) takes in water and then spits it out.

❸ Like many Greek monsters, Scylla (SIL-uh) is part human and part animal. She has the body of a woman, six heads with snake-like necks, and twelve feet.

And all this time,
in travail, sobbing, gaining on the current,
we rowed into the strait—Scylla to port
and on our starboard beam Charybdis, dire
gorge of the salt sea tide. ❶ By heaven! when she
vomited, all the sea was like a cauldron
seething over intense fire, when the mixture
suddenly heaves and rises.
                                    The shot spume
soared to the landside heights, and fell like rain.
But when she swallowed the sea water down
we saw the funnel of the maelstrom, heard
the rock bellowing all around, and dark
sand raged on the bottom far below. ❷
My men all blanched against the gloom, our eyes
were fixed upon that yawning mouth in fear
of being devoured.
                            Then Scylla made her strike,
whisking six of my best men from the ship.
I happened to glance aft at ship and oarsmen
and caught sight of their arms and legs, dangling
high overhead. Voices came down to me
in anguish, calling my name for the last time . . . ❸
                                    We rowed on.

The Rocks were now behind; Charybdis, too,
and Scylla dropped astern.

CONNECTING LITERATURE TO HISTORY

1. **Comparing** Many Greek myths were about heroes who had special abilities. What heroic abilities or traits do Achilles, Hector, and Odysseus share?

2. **Analyzing** The Greeks used myths to explain the natural world. How does the *Odyssey* passage illustrate this?

Social Studies Skills

Analyzing Costs and Benefits

Understand the Skill

Everything you do has both costs and benefits connected to it. *Benefits* are what you gain from something. *Costs* are what you give up to obtain benefits. For example, if you buy a video game, the benefits of your action include the game itself and the enjoyment of playing it. The most obvious cost is what you pay for the game. However, there are also costs that do not involve money. One of these costs is the time you spend playing the game. This is a cost because you give up something else, such as doing your homework or watching a TV show, when you choose to play the game.

The ability to analyze costs and benefits is a valuable life skill as well as a useful tool in the study of history. Weighing an action's benefits against its costs can help you decide whether or not to take it.

Learn the Skill

Analyzing the costs and benefits of historical events will help you to better understand and evaluate them. Follow these guidelines to do a cost-benefit analysis of an action or decision in history.

1 First determine what the action or decision was trying to accomplish. This step is needed in order to determine which of its effects were benefits and which were costs.

2 Then look for the positive or successful results of the action or decision. These are its benefits.

3 Consider the negative or unsuccessful effects of the action or decision. Also think about what positive things would have happened if it had *not* occurred. All these things are its costs.

4 Making a chart of the costs and benefits can be useful. By comparing the list of benefits to the list of costs you can better understand the action or decision and evaluate it.

For example, you learned in Chapter 8 that because of Greece's geography, the early Greeks settled near the sea. A cost-benefit analysis of their dependence on the sea might produce a chart like this one.

Benefits	Costs
Sea was a source of some food.	Would have paid more attention to agriculture than they did.
Didn't have to depend on Greece's poor soil for food.	Had to rely on trade with other peoples for some food and other necessities.
Became great shipbuilders and sailors	
Became great traders and grew rich from trade	
Settled colonies throughout the region	

Based on this chart, one might conclude that the Greeks' choice of where to settle was a good one.

Practice and Apply the Skill

In 546 BC a noble named Peisistratus overthrew the oligarchy and ruled Athens as a tyrant. Use information from the chapter and the guidelines above to do a cost-benefit analysis of this action. Then write a paragraph explaining whether or not it was good for the people of Athens.

Visual Summary

Use the visual summary below to help you review the main ideas of the chapter.

QUICK FACTS

The early Greeks developed trading cultures and independent city-states.

Athens had the world's first direct democracy.

The stories of Greek literature and mythology have influenced language and culture today.

Reviewing Vocabulary, Terms, and People

Unscramble each group of letters below to spell a term that matches the given definition.

1. **olpsi**—a Greek city-state
2. **iciznets**—people who have the right to participate in government
3. **ntaryt**—a person who rules alone, usually through military force
4. **comdeyacr**—rule by the people
5. **bleafs**—stories that teach lessons
6. **tsrarciotas**—rich landowners
7. **coiglhary**—rule by a few people
8. **siclalacs**—referring to a period of great achievements

Comprehension and Critical Thinking

SECTION 1 *(Pages 228–233)*

9. **a. Describe** How did geography affect the development of the Greek city-states?

   b. Compare and Contrast What did the Minoans and Mycenaeans have in common? How were the two civilizations different?

   c. Elaborate How did the concept of the polis affect the growth of Greek colonies?

SECTION 2 *(Pages 236–241)*

10. **a. Identify** What roles did Draco, Solon, and Peisistratus play in the history of Greek government?

   b. Contrast The Greeks tried many forms of government before they created a democracy. How did these various forms of government differ?

   c. Evaluate Do you agree or disagree with this statement: "Representative democracy works better than direct democracy in large countries." Defend your answer.

11. a. Recall Who were some of the main gods of Greek mythology? Who were some of the main heroes?

b. Analyze What are some of the topics that appear in ancient Greek literature, such as the *Iliad* and the *Odyssey*?

c. Predict Do you think the language and literature of ancient Greece will play roles in Western civilization in years to come? Why or why not?

Reading Skills

Greek Word Origins *Look at the list of Greek words and their meanings below. Then answer the questions that follow.*

archos (ruler)	*monos* (single)
bios (life)	*oligos* (few)
geo (earth)	*pente* (five)
micros (small)	*treis* (three)

12. Which of the following words means rule by a single person?

a. oligarchy   **c.** pentarchy

b. monarchy   **d.** triarchy

13. Which of the following words means the study of life?

a. biology   **c.** archaeology

b. geology   **d.** pentology

14. Is something that is *microscopic* very small or very large?

Using the Internet

KEYWORD: SN6 WH8

15. Activity: Comparing Greek Governments Greek government had many forms: tyranny, oligarchy, direct democracy, and monarchy. Create a three-dimensional model, a drawing, or a diagram to illustrate what a person's life under each type of government might have looked like. Include information about the type of government you are representing.

Social Studies Skills

16. Analyzing Costs and Benefits Under Cleisthenes' leadership, Athens developed the world's first democracy. Create a chart comparing costs and benefits of this event. Then write a sentence explaining whether or not it was good for the people of Athens.

Cleisthenes' Leadership

Costs	Benefits

Reviewing Themes

17. Geography How do you think Greek society would have been different if Greece were a land-locked country?

18. Geography How did Crete's physical geography both help and hurt the development of Minoan civilization?

19. Politics Why was citizenship so important in Athens?

FOCUS ON WRITING

20. Writing Your Myth First, decide if your main character is going to be a god or if it will be a human who interacts with the gods. Think about the situations and decisions that your character will face, and how he or she will react to them.

Now it's time to write your myth down. Write a paragraph of seven to eight sentences about your character. You may want to include terrible monsters or heroes with great powers. Don't forget that a myth is supposed to explain something about the world.

Standardized Test Practice

DIRECTIONS: Read each question, and write the letter of the best response.

1

> . . . that multitude of gleaming helms and bossed shields issued from the ships, with plated cuirasses [armor] and ashwood spears. Reflected glintings flashed to heaven, as the plain in all directions shone with glare of bronze and shook with trampling feet of men. Among them Prince Achilles armed. One heard his teeth grind hard together, and his eyes blazed out like licking fire, for unbearable pain had fixed upon his heart. Raging at Trojans, he buckled on the arms Hephaestus forged.

The content of this passage suggests that it was written by

A Homer.

B Zeus.

C Apollo.

D Cleisthenes.

2 **What type of ancient Greek literature would *most* likely describe the deeds of a great hero?**

A fable

B epic poem

C lyric poem

D oration

3 **Which was the main cause for the independence of city-states in ancient Greece?**

A the Greeks' location on the sea

B the threat of warlike neighbors to the north

C the geography of mountainous peninsulas

D the spread of Minoan culture

4 **Athens was ruled by a single person under the type of government known as**

A direct democracy.

B representative democracy.

C oligarchy.

D tyranny.

5 **The citizens' assembly in ancient Athens was an example of**

A trial by jury.

B rule by aristocrats.

C direct democracy.

D representative democracy.

Connecting with Past Learnings

6 **Recently you learned about Hebrew history and beliefs. The ancient Hebrew and Greek civilizations shared all of the following characteristics *except***

A great written works.

B democratic governments.

C strong political leaders.

D influence on later civilizations.

7 **You know that early towns in India were controlled by small groups of priests. Like ancient Greek government, this early Indian government was an example of**

A oligarchy.

B tyranny.

C monarchy.

D democracy.

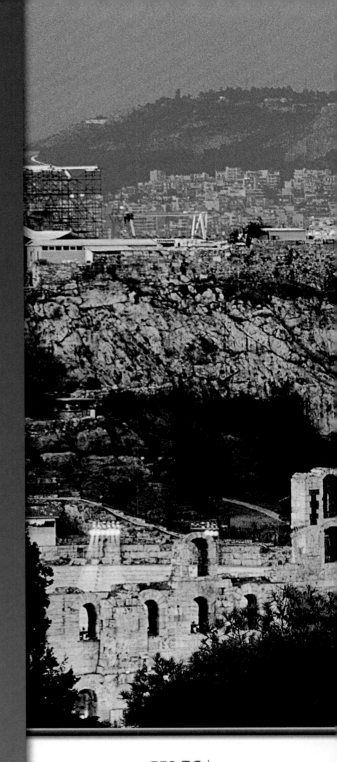

CHAPTER 9 550–30 BC

The Greek World

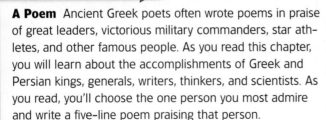

FOCUS ON WRITING

A Poem Ancient Greek poets often wrote poems in praise of great leaders, victorious military commanders, star athletes, and other famous people. As you read this chapter, you will learn about the accomplishments of Greek and Persian kings, generals, writers, thinkers, and scientists. As you read, you'll choose the one person you most admire and write a five-line poem praising that person.

CHAPTER EVENTS

c. 550 BC
Cyrus the Great founds the Persian Empire.

550 BC

WORLD EVENTS

c. 551 BC
Confucius is born in China.

What You Will Learn...

In this chapter you will learn that the ancient Greeks were both fierce fighters and great builders. The ruins shown in this photo are from the Parthenon, a beautiful temple built to celebrate a Greek victory in war.

431 BC
The Peloponnesian War begins.

334–323 BC
Alexander the Great builds his empire.

30 BC
Rome conquers Egypt, ending the Hellenistic Age.

450 BC	350 BC	250 BC	150 BC	50 BC

343 BC
The last Egyptian ruler of Egypt is overthrown.

c. 325 BC
The Mauryan Empire is founded in India.

c. 160 BC
The Maccabees regain Jewish independence.

THE GREEK WORLD **257**

Focus on Themes In this chapter, you will learn about Persia's attempt to take over Greece. You will also read about two great Greek cities, Sparta and Athens, and how they both worked to protect Greece from this invader. Finally, you will discover how, even though another invader conquered Greece, Greek influence continued to spread. Without a doubt, you need to understand the **politics** of the time in order to understand the Greek world and its **society and culture**.

Comparing and Contrasting Historical Facts

Focus on Reading Comparing and contrasting are good ways to learn. That's one reason historians use comparison and contrast to explain people and events in history.

Understanding Comparison and Contrast To **compare** is to look for likenesses, or similarities. To **contrast** is to look for differences. Sometimes writers point out similarities and differences. Other times you have to look for them yourself. You can use a diagram like this one to keep track of similarities and differences as you read.

Greek Cities

Athens

Differences

- Democratic government
- Emphasis on many subjects in education
- Known as the home of artists, writers, and philosophers

Similarities

- Greek language and religion
- More rights for men than for women

Sparta

Differences

- Ruled by kings and officials
- Emphasis only on physical education
- Known for its powerful and disciplined army

Clues for Comparison-Contrast

Writers sometimes signal comparisons or contrasts with words like these:

Comparison—*similarly, like, in the same way, too*

Contrast—*however, unlike, but, while, although, in contrast*

You Try It!

The following passage is from the chapter you are getting ready to read. As you read the passage, look for word clues about similarities and differences.

Boys and Men in Athens

From a young age, Athenian boys from rich families worked to improve both their bodies and their minds. Like Spartan boys, Athenian boys had to learn to run, jump, and fight. But this training was not as harsh or as long as the training in Sparta.

Unlike Spartan men, Athenian men didn't have to devote their whole lives to the army. All men in Athens joined the army, but only for two years. They helped defend the city between the ages of 18 and 20. Older men only had to serve in the army in times of war.

After you read the passage, answer the following questions.

1. What does the word *like* (line 3 of the passage) compare or contrast?

2. Which boys had harsher training, Athenian boys or Spartan boys? What comparison or contrast signal word helped you answer this question?

3. What other comparison or contrast words do you find in the passage? How do these words or phrases help you understand the passage?

4. How are the similarities and differences organized in the passage—alternating back and forth between topics (ABAB) or first one topic and then the next (AABB)?

Academic Vocabulary

Success in school is related to knowing academic vocabulary—the words that are frequently used in school assignments and discussions. In this chapter, you will learn the following academic word:

strategy (p. 262)

As you read Chapter 9, think about the organization of the ideas. Look for comparison and contrast signal words.

Greece and Persia

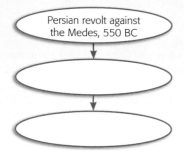

If YOU were there...

You're a great military leader and the ruler of a great empire. You control everything in the nations you've conquered. One of your advisers urges you to force conquered people to give up their customs. He thinks they should adopt your way of life. But another adviser disagrees. Let them keep their own ways, she says, and you'll earn their loyalty.

Whose advice do you take? Why?

BUILDING BACKGROUND Among the rulers who faced decisions like the one described above were the rulers of the Persian Empire. Created in 550 BC, the empire grew quickly. Within about 30 years, the Persians had conquered many peoples, and Persian rulers had to decide how these people would be treated.

Persia Becomes an Empire

While the Athenians were taking the first steps toward creating a democracy, a new power was rising in the East. This power, the Persian Empire, would one day attack Greece. But early in their history, the Persians were an unorganized nomadic people. It took the skills of leaders like Cyrus the Great and Darius I to change that situation. Under these leaders, the Persians created a huge empire, one of the mightiest of the ancient world.

Cyrus the Great

Early in their history, the Persians often fought other peoples of Southwest Asia. Sometimes they lost. In fact, they lost a fight to a people called the Medes (MEEDZ) and were ruled by them for about 150 years. In 550 BC, however, Cyrus II (SY-ruhs) led a Persian revolt against the Medes. His revolt was successful. Cyrus won independence for Persia and conquered the Medes. His victory marked the beginning of the Persian Empire.

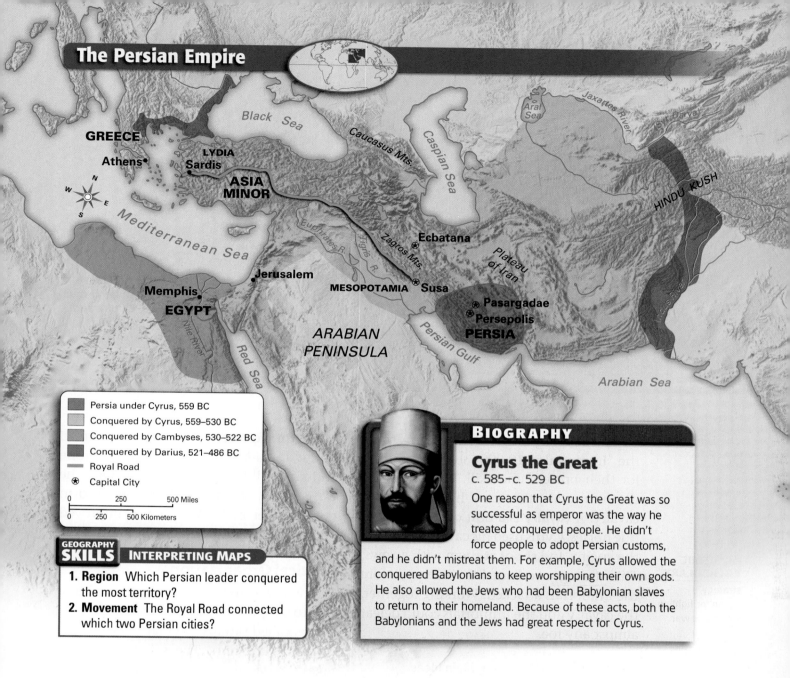

The Persian Empire

GREECE
Athens
LYDIA
Sardis
ASIA MINOR
Mediterranean Sea
Black Sea
Caucasus Mts.
Aral Sea
Jaxartes River
Syr Darya
Caspian Sea
HINDU KUSH
Euphrates R.
Tigris R.
Zagros Mts.
Ecbatana
Plateau of Iran
Susa
MESOPOTAMIA
Jerusalem
Memphis
EGYPT
Nile River
Red Sea
ARABIAN PENINSULA
Persian Gulf
Pasargadae
Persepolis
PERSIA
Arabian Sea

Persia under Cyrus, 559 BC
Conquered by Cyrus, 559–530 BC
Conquered by Cambyses, 530–522 BC
Conquered by Darius, 521–486 BC
Royal Road
⊛ Capital City

0   250   500 Miles
0 250 500 Kilometers

GEOGRAPHY SKILLS   INTERPRETING MAPS

1. **Region** Which Persian leader conquered the most territory?
2. **Movement** The Royal Road connected which two Persian cities?

BIOGRAPHY

Cyrus the Great
c. 585–c. 529 BC

One reason that Cyrus the Great was so successful as emperor was the way he treated conquered people. He didn't force people to adopt Persian customs, and he didn't mistreat them. For example, Cyrus allowed the conquered Babylonians to keep worshipping their own gods. He also allowed the Jews who had been Babylonian slaves to return to their homeland. Because of these acts, both the Babylonians and the Jews had great respect for Cyrus.

As you can see on the map, Cyrus conquered much of Southwest Asia, including nearly all of Asia Minor, during his rule. Included in this region were several Greek cities that Cyrus took over. He then marched south to conquer Mesopotamia.

Cyrus also added land to the east. He led his army into central Asia to the Jaxartes River, which we now call the Syr Darya. When he died around 529 BC, Cyrus ruled the largest empire the world had ever seen.

Cyrus let the people he conquered keep their own customs. He hoped this would make them less likely to rebel. He was right. Few people rebelled against Cyrus, and his empire remained strong. Because of his great successes, historians call him **Cyrus the Great**.

The Persian Army

Cyrus was successful in his conquests because his army was strong. It was strong because it was well organized and loyal.

Persia Under Darius

Sitting on a throne, the emperor Darius meets with an officer of his empire. Darius restored order to the Persian Empire and then expanded it. His army included royal guards like the two shown here.

Why do you think Darius appears larger than the official he is meeting with?

ACADEMIC
VOCABULARY
strategy
a plan for fighting
a battle or war

At the heart of the Persian army were the Immortals, 10,000 soldiers chosen for their bravery and skill. In addition to the Immortals, the army had a powerful cavalry. A **cavalry** is a unit of soldiers who ride horses. Cyrus used his cavalry to charge the enemy and shoot at them with arrows. This <u>strategy</u> weakened the enemy before the Immortals attacked. Working together, the cavalry and the Immortals could defeat almost any foe.

READING CHECK Finding Main Ideas
Who created the Persian Empire?

The Persian Empire Grows Stronger

Cyrus's son Cambyses continued to expand the Persian Empire after Cyrus died. For example, he conquered Egypt and added it to the empire. Soon afterward, though, a rebellion broke out in Persia. During this rebellion, Cambyses died. His death left Persia without a clear leader.

Within four years a young prince named **Darius I** (da-RY-uhs) claimed the throne and killed all his rivals for power. Once he was securely in control, Darius worked to restore order in Persia. He also improved Persian society and expanded the empire.

Political Organization

Darius organized the empire by dividing it into 20 provinces. Then he chose governors called satraps (SAY-traps) to rule the provinces for him. The satraps collected taxes for Darius, served as judges, and put down rebellions within their territories. Satraps had great power within their provinces, but Darius remained the empire's real ruler. His officials visited each province to make sure the satraps were loyal to Darius. He called himself king of kings to remind other rulers of his power.

Persian Society

After Darius restored order to the empire, he made many improvements to Persian society. For example, he built many roads.

Darius had roads built to connect various parts of the empire. Messengers used these roads to travel quickly throughout Persia. One road, called the Royal Road, was more than 1,700 miles long. Even Persia's enemies admired these roads and the Persian messenger system. For example, one Greek historian wrote:

> "Nothing mortal travels so fast as these Persian messengers . . . these men will not be hindered from accomplishing at their best speed the distance which they have to go, either by snow, or rain, or heat, or by the darkness of night."
>
> –Herodotus, from *History of the Persian Wars*

Darius also built a new capital for the empire. It was called Persepolis. Darius wanted his capital to reflect the glory of his empire, so he filled the city with beautiful works of art. For example, 3,000 carvings like the ones on the previous page line the city's walls. Statues throughout the city glittered with gold, silver, and precious jewels.

During Darius's rule a new religion arose in the Persian Empire as well. This religion, which was called Zoroastrianism (zawr-uh-WAS-tree-uh-nih-zuhm), taught that there were two forces fighting for control of the universe. One force was good, and the other was evil. Its priests urged people to help the side of good in its struggle. This religion remained popular in Persia for many centuries.

Persian Expansion

Like Cyrus, Darius wanted the Persian Empire to grow. In the east, he conquered the entire Indus Valley. He also tried to expand the empire westward into Europe. However, before Darius could move very far into Europe, he had to deal with a revolt in the empire.

READING CHECK **Summarizing** How did Darius I change Persia's political organization?

The Persians Fight Greece

In 499 BC several Greek cities in Asia Minor rebelled against Persian rule. To help their fellow Greeks, a few city-states in mainland Greece sent soldiers to join the fight against the Persians.

The Persians put down the revolt, but Darius was still angry with the Greeks. Although the cities that had rebelled were in Asia, Darius was enraged that other Greeks had given them aid. He swore to get revenge on the Greeks.

The Battle of Marathon

Nine years after the Greek cities rebelled, Darius invaded Greece. He and his army sailed to the plains of Marathon near Athens. This invasion began a series of wars between Persia and Greece that historians call the **Persian Wars**.

The Athenian army had only about 11,000 soldiers, while the Persians had about 15,000. However, the Greeks won the battle because they had better weapons and clever leaders.

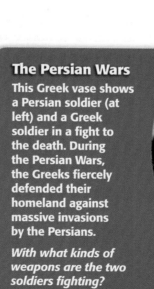

The Persian Wars

This Greek vase shows a Persian soldier (at left) and a Greek soldier in a fight to the death. During the Persian Wars, the Greeks fiercely defended their homeland against massive invasions by the Persians.

With what kinds of weapons are the two soldiers fighting?

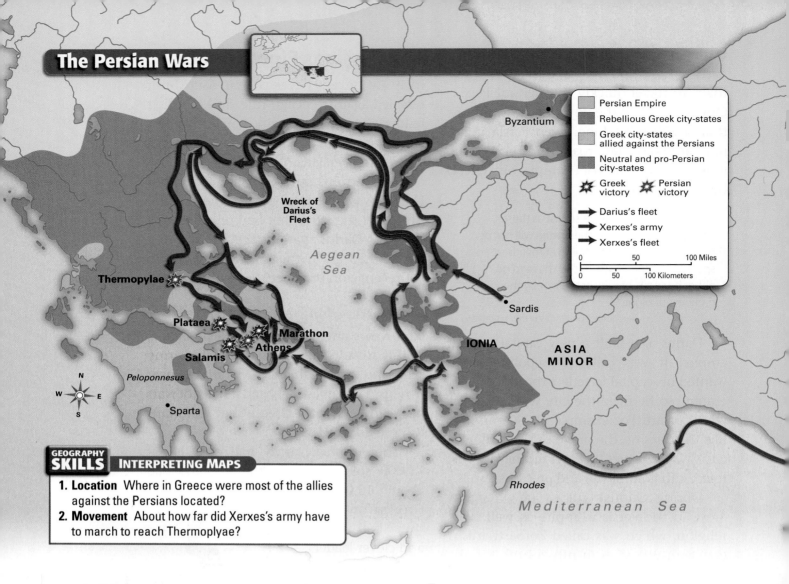

The Persian Wars

Legend:
- Persian Empire
- Rebellious Greek city-states
- Greek city-states allied against the Persians
- Neutral and pro-Persian city-states
- ✦ Greek victory
- ✦ Persian victory
- → Darius's fleet
- → Xerxes's army
- → Xerxes's fleet

0   50   100 Miles
0   50   100 Kilometers

Byzantium
Wreck of Darius's Fleet
Aegean Sea
Thermopylae
Plataea
Marathon
Salamis
Athens
Peloponnesus
Sparta
Sardis
IONIA
ASIA MINOR
Rhodes
Mediterranean Sea

GEOGRAPHY SKILLS · INTERPRETING MAPS

1. **Location** Where in Greece were most of the allies against the Persians located?
2. **Movement** About how far did Xerxes's army have to march to reach Thermoplyae?

THE IMPACT TODAY

Athletes today re-create the Greek messenger's run in 26-mile races called marathons.

According to legend, a messenger ran from Marathon to Athens—a distance of just over 26 miles—to bring news of the great victory. After crying out "Rejoice! We conquer!" the exhausted runner fell to the ground and died.

The Second Invasion of Greece

Ten years after the Battle of Marathon, Darius's son **Xerxes I** (ZUHRK-seez) tried to conquer Greece again. In 480 BC the Persian army set out for Greece. This time they were joined by the Persian navy.

The Greeks prepared to defend their homeland. This time Sparta, a powerful city-state in southern Greece, joined with Athens. The Spartans had the strongest army in Greece, so they went to fight the Persian army. Meanwhile, the Athenians sent their powerful navy to attack the Persian navy.

To slow the Persian army, the Spartans sent about 1,400 soldiers to Thermopylae (thuhr-MAH-puh-lee), a narrow mountain pass. The Persians had to cross through this pass to attack Greek cities. For three days, the small Greek force held off the Persian army. Then the Persians asked a traitorous Greek soldier to lead them through another pass. A large Persian force attacked the Spartans from behind. Surrounded, the brave Spartans and their allies fought to their deaths. After winning the battle, the Persians swept into Athens, attacking and burning the city.

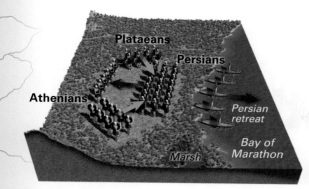

Marathon

At Marathon, the Greeks defeated a larger Persian force by luring the Persians into the middle of their forces. The Athenians then surrounded and defeated the Persians.

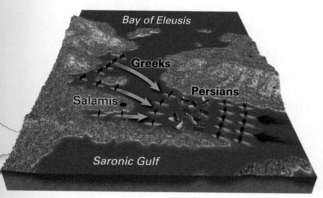

Salamis

At Salamis, the Greeks destroyed the Persian navy by attacking in a narrow strait where the Persian ships could not maneuver well.

Although the Persians won the battle in the pass, the Greeks quickly regained the upper hand. A few days after Athens was burned, the Athenians defeated the Persian navy through a clever plan. They led the larger Persian navy into the narrow straits of Salamis (SAH-luh-muhs). The Persians had so many ships that they couldn't steer well in the narrow strait. As a result, the smaller Athenian boats easily sank many Persian ships. Those ships that were not destroyed soon returned home.

Soon after the Battle of Salamis, an army of soldiers from all over Greece beat the Persians at Plataea (pluh-TEE-uh). This battle ended the Persian Wars. Defeated, the Persians left Greece.

For the Persians, this defeat was humiliating, but it was not a major blow. Their empire remained strong for more than a century after the war. For the Greeks, though, the defeat of the Persians was a triumph. They had saved their homeland.

READING CHECK **Analyzing** Why did Darius and Xerxes want to conquer Greece?

SUMMARY AND PREVIEW Athens and Sparta fought together against Persia. Their friendship didn't last long, though. In the next section, you will learn what happened when they became enemies.

Section 1 Assessment

go.hrw.com
Online Quiz
KEYWORD: SN6 HP9

Reviewing Ideas, Terms, and People

1. **a. Describe** Describe the empire of **Cyrus the Great**.
   b. Make Generalizations Why did peoples conquered by Cyrus the Great seldom rebel?
2. **a. Identify** How did **Darius I** change Persia's political organization?
   b. Make Generalizations How did Persia's roads help improve the empire's organization?
3. **a. Explain** Why did Persia want to invade Greece?
   b. Predict How might the **Persian Wars** have ended if the Spartans had not slowed the Persians at Thermopylae?

Critical Thinking

4. **Categorizing** Review your notes on major events. Using a chart like the one below, list the battles you have identified in the first column. In the other columns identify who fought, who won, and what happened as a result of each battle.

Battle	Armies	Winner	Result

FOCUS ON WRITING

5. **Taking Notes on Persian Leaders** Draw a table with three columns. In the first column, write the names of each leader mentioned in this section. In the second column, list each person's military accomplishments. In the third column, list any other accomplishments.

Sparta and Athens

What You Will Learn...

Main Ideas

1. The Spartans built a military society to provide security and protection.
2. The Athenians admired the mind and the arts in addition to physical abilities.
3. Sparta and Athens fought over who should have power and influence in Greece.

The Big Idea

The two most powerful city-states in Greece, Sparta and Athens, had very different cultures and became bitter enemies in the 400s BC.

Key Terms

alliance, *p. 270*
Peloponnesian War, *p. 271*

TAKING NOTES   As you read, use a chart like the one below to take notes on Athens and Sparta.

	Athens	Sparta
Military		
Education		
Women		

If YOU were there...

Your father, a wandering trader, has decided it is time to settle down. He offers the family a choice between two cities. In one city, everyone wants to be athletic, tough, and strong. They're good at enduring hardships and following orders. The other city is different. There, you'd be admired if you could think deeply and speak persuasively, if you knew a lot about astronomy or history, or if you sang and played beautiful music.

Which city do you choose? Why?

BUILDING BACKGROUND   Two of the greatest city-states in Greece were Sparta and Athens. Sparta, like the first city mentioned above, had a culture that valued physical strength and military might. The Athenian culture placed more value on the mind. However, both city-states had military strength, and they both played important roles in the defense of ancient Greece.

Spartans Build a Military Society

Spartan society was dominated by the military. According to Spartan tradition, their social system was created between 900 and 600 BC by a man named Lycurgus (ly-KUHR-guhs) after a slave revolt. To keep such a revolt from happening again, he increased the military's role in society. The Spartans believed that military power was the way to provide security and protection for their city. Daily life in Sparta reflected this belief.

Boys and Men in Sparta

Daily life in Sparta was dominated by the army. Even the lives of children reflected this domination. When a boy was born, government officials came to look at him. If he was not healthy, the baby was taken outside of the city and left to die. Healthy boys were trained from an early age to be soldiers.

As part of their training, boys ran, jumped, swam, and threw javelins to increase their strength. They also learned to endure the hardships they would face as soldiers. For example, boys weren't given shoes or heavy clothes, even in winter. They also weren't given much food. Boys were allowed to steal food if they could, but if they were caught, they were whipped. At least one boy chose to die rather than admit to his theft:

" One youth, having stolen a fox and hidden it under his coat, allowed it to tear out his very bowels [organs] with its claws and teeth and died rather than betray his theft. "
–Plutarch, from *Life of Lycurgus*

To this boy—and to most Spartan soldiers—courage and strength were more important than one's own safety.

Soldiers between the ages of 20 and 30 lived in army barracks and only occasionally visited their families. Spartan men stayed in the army until they turned 60.

The Spartans believed that the most important qualities of good soldiers were self-discipline and obedience. To reinforce self-discipline they required soldiers to live tough lives free from comforts. For example, the Spartans didn't have luxuries like soft furniture and expensive food. They thought such comforts made people weak. Even the Spartans' enemies admired their discipline and obedience.

Girls and Women in Sparta

Because Spartan men were often away at war, Spartan women had more rights than other Greek women. Some women owned land in Sparta and ran their households when their husbands were gone. Unlike women in other Greek cities, Spartan women didn't spend time spinning cloth or weaving. They thought of those tasks as the jobs of slaves, unsuitable for the wives and mothers of soldiers.

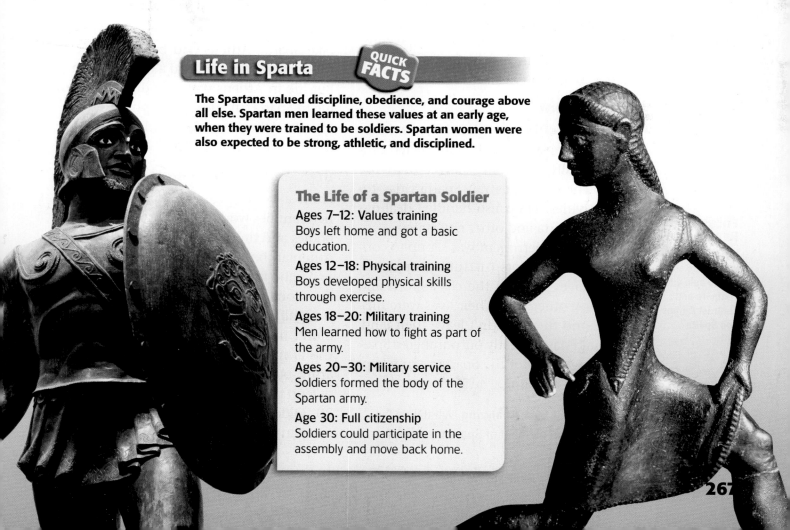

Life in Sparta — QUICK FACTS

The Spartans valued discipline, obedience, and courage above all else. Spartan men learned these values at an early age, when they were trained to be soldiers. Spartan women were also expected to be strong, athletic, and disciplined.

The Life of a Spartan Soldier

Ages 7–12: Values training
Boys left home and got a basic education.

Ages 12–18: Physical training
Boys developed physical skills through exercise.

Ages 18–20: Military training
Men learned how to fight as part of the army.

Ages 20–30: Military service
Soldiers formed the body of the Spartan army.

Age 30: Full citizenship
Soldiers could participate in the assembly and move back home.

POINTS OF VIEW
Views of Education

Plato, an Athenian, thought that education for young boys should train both the mind and the body. He wanted students to be prepared for all aspects of life as adults.

❝And what shall be their education? Can we find a better division than the traditional sort?—and this has two divisions, gymnastics for the body, and music for the soul.❞

—Plato
from The Republic

Lycurgus, a Spartan lawgiver, thought education for boys should teach them how to fight. The historian Plutarch described how education was handled in Sparta under Lycurgus:

❝Reading and writing they gave them, just enough to serve their turn; their chief care was to make them good subjects, and to teach them to endure pain and conquer in battle.❞

—Plutarch
from Life of Lycurgus

ANALYSIS SKILL ANALYZING POINTS OF VIEW

How do Plato's and Lycurgus's viewpoints reflect the ideals of Athens and Sparta?

Spartan women also received physical training. Like the men, they learned how to run, jump, wrestle, and throw javelins. The Spartans believed this training would help women bear healthy children.

Government

Sparta was officially ruled by two kings who jointly led the army. But elected officials actually had more power than the kings. These officials ran Sparta's day-to-day activities. They also handled dealings between Sparta and other city-states.

Sparta's government was set up to control the city's helots (HEL-uhts), or slaves. These slaves grew all the city's crops and did many other jobs. Their lives were miserable, and they couldn't leave their land. Although slaves greatly outnumbered Spartan citizens, fear of the Spartan army kept them from rebelling.

FOCUS ON READING

How can the words *like* and *unlike* help you compare and contrast Athens and Sparta?

READING CHECK **Analyzing** What was the most important element of Spartan society?

Athenians Admire the Mind

Sparta's main rival in Greece was Athens. Like Sparta, Athens had been a leader in the Persian Wars and had a powerful army. But life in Athens was very different from life in Sparta. In addition to physical training, the Athenians valued education, clear thinking, and the arts.

Boys and Men in Athens

From a young age, Athenian boys from rich families worked to improve both their bodies and their minds. Like Spartan boys, Athenian boys had to learn to run, jump, and fight. But this training was not as harsh or as long as the training in Sparta.

Unlike Spartan men, Athenian men didn't have to devote their whole lives to the army. All men in Athens joined the army, but for only two years. They helped defend the city between the ages of 18 and 20. Older men only had to serve in the army in times of war.

In addition to their physical training, Athenian students, unlike the Spartans, also learned other skills. They learned to read, write, and count as well as sing and play musical instruments. Boys also learned about Greek history and legend. For example, they studied the *Iliad*, the *Odyssey*, and other works of Greek literature.

Boys from very rich families often continued their education with private tutors. These tutors taught their students about philosophy, geometry, astronomy, and other subjects. They also taught the boys how to be good public speakers. This training prepared boys for participation in the Athenian assembly.

Very few boys had the opportunity to receive this much education, however. Boys from poor families usually didn't get any education, although most of them could read and write at least a little. Most of the boys from poor families became farmers and grew food for the city's richer citizens. A few went to work with craftspeople to learn other trades.

Girls and Women in Athens

While many boys in Athens received good educations, girls didn't. In fact, girls received almost no education. Athenian men didn't think girls needed to be educated. A few girls were taught how to read and write at home by private tutors. However, most girls only learned household tasks like weaving and sewing.

Despite Athens's reputation for freedom and democracy, women there had fewer rights than women in many other city-states. Athenian women could not

- serve in any part of the city's government, including the assembly and juries,
- leave their homes, except on special occasions,
- buy anything or own property, or
- disobey their husbands or fathers.

In fact, women in Athens had almost no rights at all.

READING CHECK **Identifying Cause and Effect** Why did girls in Athens receive little education?

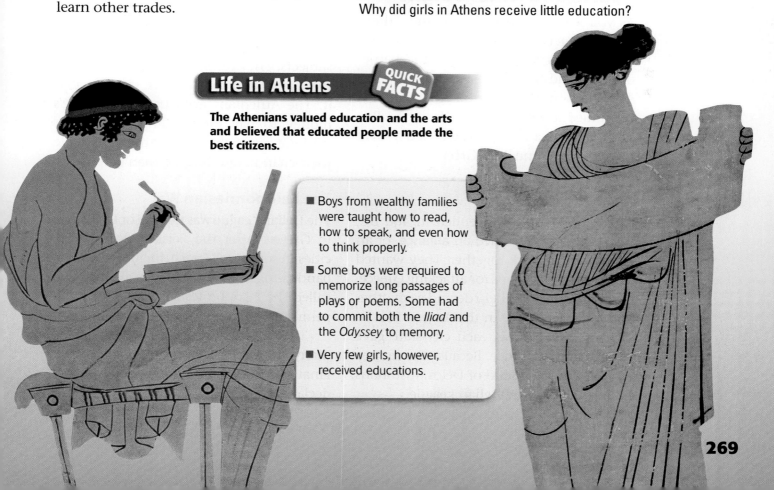

Life in Athens QUICK FACTS

The Athenians valued education and the arts and believed that educated people made the best citizens.

- Boys from wealthy families were taught how to read, how to speak, and even how to think properly.
- Some boys were required to memorize long passages of plays or poems. Some had to commit both the *Iliad* and the *Odyssey* to memory.
- Very few girls, however, received educations.

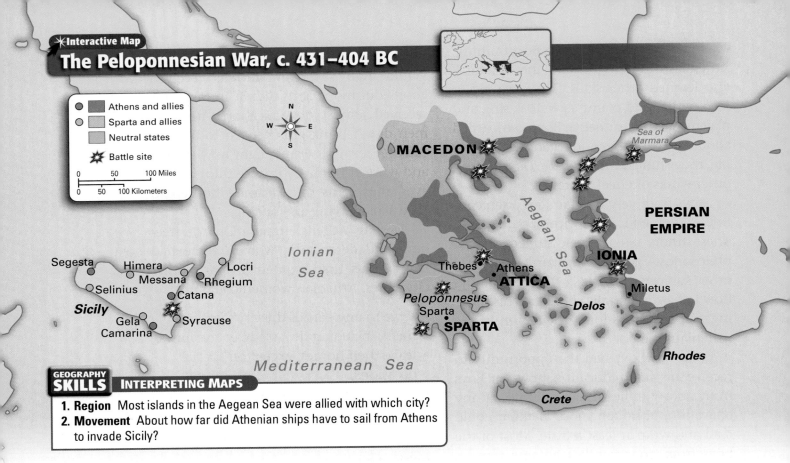

Athens and allies
Sparta and allies
Neutral states
★ **Battle site**

0   50   100 Miles
0   50   100 Kilometers

MACEDON

Sea of Marmara

Aegean Sea

PERSIAN EMPIRE

Ionian Sea

Segesta
Himera
Messana
Selinius
Locri
Rhegium
Catana
Sicily
Gela
Camarina
Syracuse

Thebes
Athens
ATTICA
Peloponnesus
Sparta
SPARTA

IONIA
Miletus
Delos

Rhodes

Mediterranean Sea

Crete

GEOGRAPHY SKILLS | **INTERPRETING MAPS**

1. **Region** Most islands in the Aegean Sea were allied with which city?
2. **Movement** About how far did Athenian ships have to sail from Athens to invade Sicily?

Sparta and Athens Fight

As you learned earlier, Sparta and Athens worked together to win the Persian Wars. The Spartans fought most of the battles on land, and the Athenians fought at sea. After the war, the powerful Athenian fleet continued to protect Greece from the Persian navy. As a result, Athens had a great influence over much of Greece.

Athenian Power

After the Persian Wars ended in 480 BC, many city-states formed an **alliance**, or an agreement to work together. They wanted to punish the Persians for attacking Greece. They also agreed to help defend each other and to protect trade in the Aegean Sea. To pay for this defense, each city-state gave money to the alliance. Because the money was kept on the island of Delos, historians call the alliance the Delian League.

With its navy protecting the islands, Athens was the strongest member of the league. As a result, the Athenians began to treat other league members as their subjects. They refused to let members quit the league and forced more cities to join it. The Athenians even used the league's money to pay for buildings in Athens. Without even fighting, the Athenians made the Delian League an Athenian empire.

The Peloponnesian War

The Delian League was not the only alliance in Greece. After the Persian Wars, many cities in southern Greece, including Sparta, banded together as well. This alliance was called the Peloponnesian League after the peninsula on which the cities were located.

The growth of Athenian power worried many cities in the Peloponnesian League. Finally, to stop Athens's growth, Sparta declared war.

This declaration of war began the **Peloponnesian War**, a war between Athens and Sparta that threatened to tear all of Greece apart. In 431 BC the Spartan army marched north to Athens. They surrounded the city, waiting for the Athenians to come out and fight. But the Athenians stayed in the city, hoping that the Spartans would leave. Instead, the Spartans began to burn the crops in the fields around Athens. They hoped that Athens would run out of food and be forced to surrender.

The Spartans were in for a surprise. The Athenian navy escorted merchant ships to Athens, bringing plenty of food to the city. The navy also attacked Sparta's allies, forcing the Spartans to send troops to defend other Greek cities. At the same time, though, disease swept through Athens, killing thousands. For 10 years neither side could gain an advantage over the other. Eventually, they agreed to a truce. Athens kept its empire, and the Spartans went home.

A few years later, in 415 BC, Athens tried again to expand its empire. It sent its army and navy to conquer the island of Sicily. This effort failed. The entire Athenian army was defeated by Sicilian allies of Sparta and taken prisoner. Even worse, these Sicilians also destroyed most of the Athenian navy.

Taking advantage of Athens's weakness, Sparta attacked Athens, and the war started up once more. Although the Athenians fought bravely, the Spartans won. They cut off the supply of food to Athens completely. In 404 BC, the people of Athens, starving and surrounded, surrendered. The Peloponnesian War was over, and Sparta was in control.

Fighting Among the City-States

With the defeat of Athens, Sparta became the most powerful city-state in Greece. For about 30 years, the Spartans controlled nearly all of Greece, until other city-states started to resent them. This resentment led to a period of war. Control of Greece shifted from city-state to city-state. The fighting went on for many years, which weakened Greece and left it open to attack from outside.

READING CHECK **Identifying Cause and Effect** What happened to Greece after the Peloponnesian War?

SUMMARY AND PREVIEW In this section you read about conflicts among city-states for control of Greece. In the next section, you will learn what happened when all of Greece was conquered by a foreign power.

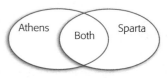

Section 2 Assessment

go.hrw.com
Online Quiz
KEYWORD: SN6 HP9

Reviewing Ideas, Terms, and People

1. **a. Recall** How long did Spartan men stay in the army?
   b. Summarize How did the army affect life in Sparta?
2. **a. Identify** What skills did rich Athenian boys learn in school?
   b. Elaborate How might the government of Athens have influenced the growth of its educational system?
3. **a. Identify** Which city-state won the Peloponnesian War?
   b. Explain Why did many city-states form an **alliance** against Athens?

Critical Thinking

4. **Comparing and Contrasting** Look through your notes on Athens and Sparta to find similarities and differences between the two city-states. Use a graphic organizer like the one on the right to organize the information.

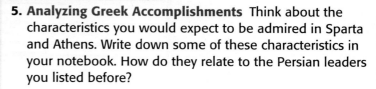

FOCUS ON WRITING

5. **Analyzing Greek Accomplishments** Think about the characteristics you would expect to be admired in Sparta and Athens. Write down some of these characteristics in your notebook. How do they relate to the Persian leaders you listed before?

Alexander the Great

What You Will Learn...

Main Ideas

1. Macedonia conquered Greece in the 300s BC.
2. Alexander the Great built an empire that united much of Europe, Asia, and Egypt.
3. The Hellenistic kingdoms formed from Alexander's empire blended Greek and other cultures.

The Big Idea

Alexander the Great built a huge empire and helped spread Greek culture into Egypt and Asia.

Key Terms and People

Philip II, *p. 272*
phalanx, *p. 273*
Alexander the Great, *p. 274*
Hellenistic, *p. 275*

TAKING NOTES As you read, take notes in a chart like the one below. Record information that tells how Alexander built his empire and how he helped spread Greek culture.

Alexander the Great

Building an Empire	Spreading Greek Culture

If YOU were there...

You are a soldier in the most powerful army in the world. In just eight years, you and your fellow soldiers have conquered an enormous empire. Now your general wants to push farther into unknown lands in search of greater glory. But you're thousands of miles from home, and you haven't seen your family in years.

Do you agree to go on fighting? Why or why not?

BUILDING BACKGROUND The world's most powerful army in the 300s BC was from Macedonia, a kingdom just north of Greece. The Greeks had long dismissed the Macedonians as unimportant. They thought of the Macedonians as barbarians because they lived in small villages and spoke a strange form of the Greek language. But the Greeks underestimated the Macedonians, barbarians or not.

Macedonia Conquers Greece

In 359 BC **Philip II** became king of Macedonia. Philip spent the first year of his rule fighting off invaders who wanted to take over his kingdom. Once he defeated the invaders, he was ready to launch invasions of his own.

Philip's main target was Greece. The leaders of Athens, knowing they were the target of Philip's powerful army, called for all Greeks to join together. Few people responded.

As a result, the armies of Athens and its chief ally Thebes were easily defeated by the Macedonians. Having witnessed this defeat, the rest of the Greeks agreed to make Philip their leader.

Philip's Military Strength

Philip defeated the Greeks because he was a brilliant military leader. He borrowed and improved many of the strategies Greek armies used in battle. For example, Philip's soldiers, like the Greeks, fought as a phalanx (FAY-langks). A **phalanx** was a group of warriors who stood close together in a square. Each soldier held a spear pointed outward to fight off enemies. As soldiers in the front lines were killed, others stepped up from behind to fill their spots.

Philip improved upon the Greeks' idea. He gave his soldiers spears that were much longer than those of his opponents. This allowed his army to attack effectively in any battle. Philip also sent cavalry and archers into battle to support the phalanx.

After conquering Greece, Philip turned his attention to Persia. He planned to march east and conquer the Persian Empire, but he never made it. He was murdered in 336 BC while celebrating his daughter's wedding. When Philip died, his throne—and his plans—passed to his son, Alexander.

READING CHECK **Summarizing** How was Philip II able to conquer Greece?

Alexander Builds an Empire

When Philip died, the people in the Greek city of Thebes rebelled. They thought that the Macedonians would not have a leader strong enough to keep the kingdom together. They were wrong.

Controlling the Greeks

Although he was only 20 years old, Philip's son Alexander was as strong a leader as his father had been. He immediately went south to end the revolt in Thebes.

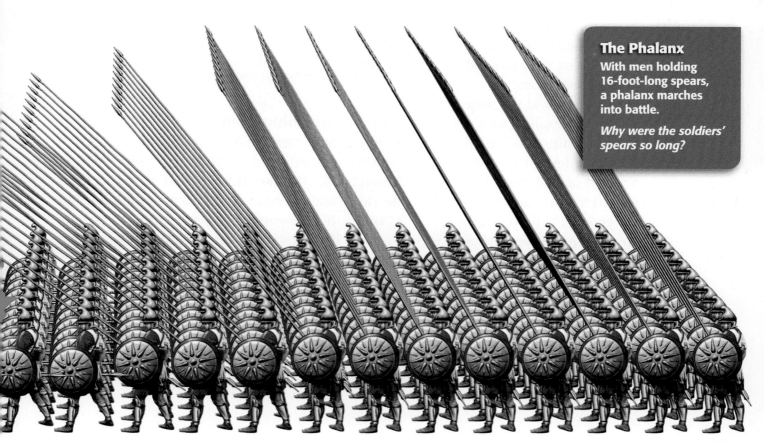

The Phalanx
With men holding 16-foot-long spears, a phalanx marches into battle.

Why were the soldiers' spears so long?

Within a year, Alexander had destroyed Thebes and enslaved the Theban people. He used Thebes as an example to other Greeks of what would happen if they turned against him. Then, confident that the Greeks would not rebel again, he set out to build an empire.

Alexander's efforts to build an empire made him one of the greatest conquerors in history. These efforts earned him the name **Alexander the Great**.

Building a New Empire

Like his father, Alexander was a brilliant commander. In 334 BC he attacked the Persians, whose army was much larger than his own. But Alexander's troops were well trained and ready for battle. They defeated the Persians time after time.

According to legend, Alexander visited a town called Gordium in Asia Minor while he was fighting the Persians. There he heard an ancient tale about a knot tied by an ancient king. The tale said that whoever untied the knot would rule all of Asia. According to the legend, Alexander pulled out his sword and cut right through the knot. Taking this as a good sign, he and his army set out again.

We still use the phrase "cutting the Gordian knot" to mean solving a difficult problem easily.

If you look at the map, you can follow the route Alexander took on his conquests. After defeating the Persians near the town of Issus, Alexander went to Egypt, which was part of the Persian Empire. The Persian governor had heard of his skill in battle. He surrendered without a fight in 332 BC and crowned Alexander pharaoh.

After a short stay in Egypt, Alexander set out again. Near the town of Gaugamela (gaw-guh-MEE-luh), he defeated the Persian army for the last time. After the battle, the Persian king fled. The king soon died, killed by one of his nobles. With the king's death, Alexander became the ruler of what had been the Persian Empire.

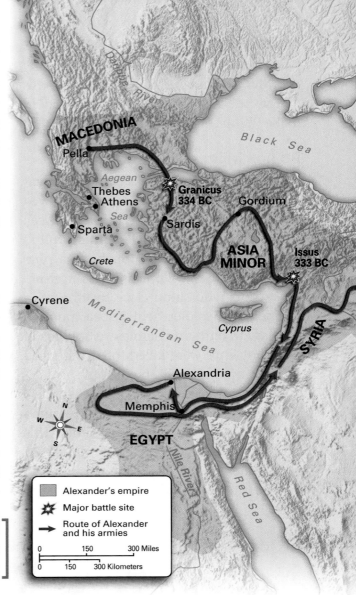

Marching Home

Still intent on building his empire, Alexander led his army through Central Asia. In 327 BC Alexander crossed the Indus River and wanted to push deeper into India. But his exhausted soldiers refused to go any farther. Disappointed, Alexander began the long march home.

Alexander left India in 325 BC, but he never made it back to Greece. In 323 BC, on his way back, Alexander visited the city of Babylon and got sick. He died a few days later at age 33. After he died, Alexander's body was taken to Egypt and buried in a golden coffin.

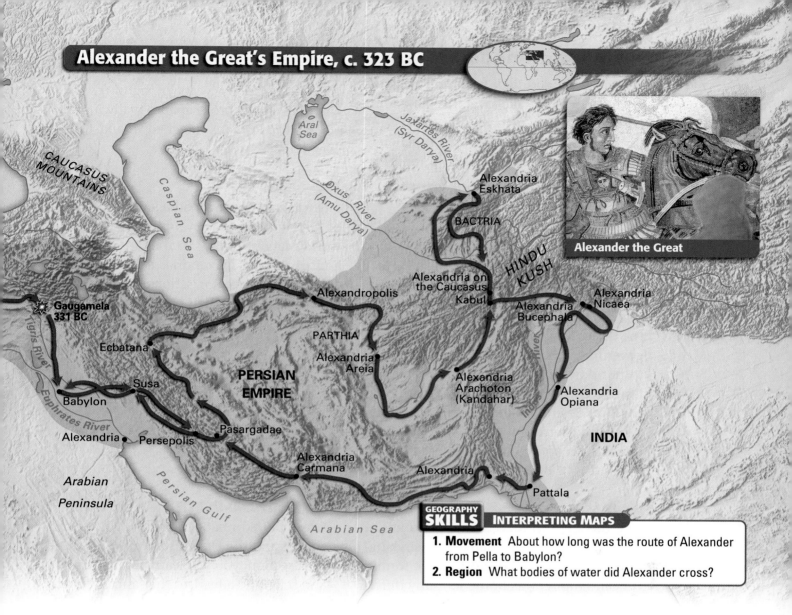

Alexander the Great's Empire, c. 323 BC

Aral Sea

Jaxartes River (Syr Darya)

Caspian Sea

CAUCASUS MOUNTAINS

Oxus River (Amu Darya)

Alexandria Eskhata

BACTRIA

HINDU KUSH

Alexandria on the Caucasus

Alexandropolis

Kabul

Alexandria Nicaea

Alexandria Bucephala

Gaugamela 331 BC

PARTHIA

Alexandria Areia

Ecbatana

PERSIAN EMPIRE

Alexandria Arachoton (Kandahar)

Alexandria Opiana

Susa

Tigris River

Babylon

Euphrates River

Pasargadae

INDIA

Alexandria

Persepolis

Alexandria Carmana

Alexandria

Arabian Peninsula

Persian Gulf

Pattala

Arabian Sea

Alexander the Great

GEOGRAPHY SKILLS — INTERPRETING MAPS

1. **Movement** About how long was the route of Alexander from Pella to Babylon?
2. **Region** What bodies of water did Alexander cross?

Spreading Greek Culture

Alexander's empire was the largest the world had ever seen. An admirer of Greek culture, he worked to spread Greek influence throughout his empire by founding cities in the lands he conquered.

Alexander modeled his new cities after the cities of Greece. He named many of them Alexandria, after himself. He built temples and theaters like those in Greece. He then encouraged Greek settlers to move to the new cities. These settlers spoke Greek, which became common throughout the empire. In time, Greek art, literature, and science spread into surrounding lands.

Even as he supported the spread of Greek culture, however, Alexander encouraged conquered people to keep their own customs and traditions. As a result, a new blended culture developed in Alexander's empire. It combined elements of Persian, Egyptian, Syrian, and other cultures with Greek ideas. Because this new culture was not completely Greek, or Hellenic, historians call it **Hellenistic**, or Greek-like. It wasn't purely Greek, but it was heavily influenced by Greek ideas.

READING CHECK **Sequencing** What steps did Alexander take to create his empire?

Hellenistic Kingdoms

When Alexander died, he didn't have an obvious heir to take over his kingdom, and no one knew who was in power. With no clear direction, Alexander's generals fought for power. In the end, three powerful generals divided the empire among themselves. One became king of Macedonia and Greece, one ruled Syria, and the third claimed Egypt.

Hellenistic Macedonia

As you might expect, the kingdom of Macedonia and Greece was the most Greek of the three. However, it also had the weakest government. The Macedonian kings had to put down many revolts by the Greeks. Damaged by the revolts, Macedonia couldn't defend itself. Armies from Rome, a rising power from the Italian Peninsula, marched in and conquered Macedonia in the mid-100s BC.

Hellenistic Syria

Like the kings of Macedonia, the rulers of Syria faced many challenges. Their kingdom, which included most of the former Persian Empire, was home to many different peoples with many different customs.

Unhappy with Hellenistic rule, many of these people rebelled against their leaders. Weakened by years of fighting, the kingdom slowly broke apart. Finally in the 60s BC the Romans marched in and took over Syria.

Hellenistic Egypt

The rulers of Egypt encouraged the growth of Greek culture. They built the ancient world's largest library in the city of Alexandria. Also in Alexandria, they built the Museum, a place for scholars and artists to meet. Through their efforts, Alexandria became a great center of culture and learning. In the end, the Egyptian kingdom lasted longer than the other Hellenistic kingdoms. However, in 30 BC it too was conquered by Rome.

READING CHECK **Analyzing** Why were three kingdoms created from Alexander's empire?

SUMMARY AND PREVIEW Alexander the Great caused major political changes in Greece and the Hellenistic world. In the next section, you will learn about artistic and scientific advances that affected the lives of people in the same areas.

Section 3 Assessment

Reviewing Ideas, Terms, and People

1. **Identify** What king conquered Greece in the 300s BC?
2. **a. Describe** What territories did **Alexander the Great** conquer?
   b. Interpret Why did Alexander destroy Thebes?
   c. Elaborate Why do you think Alexander named so many cities after himself?
3. **a. Recall** What three kingdoms were created out of Alexander's empire after his death?
   b. Explain Why were these kingdoms called **Hellenistic**?

Critical Thinking

4. **Generalizing** Review your notes on Alexander. Then, write one sentence explaining why he is an important historical figure.

Building an Empire → Why Alexander was important ← Spreading Culture

FOCUS ON WRITING

5. **Evaluating Alexander** Add Alexander the Great to the table you created earlier. Remember that although Alexander was a military man, not all of his accomplishments were in battle.

Greek Achievements

If YOU were there...

Everyone in Athens has been talking about a philosopher and teacher named Socrates, so you decide to go and see him for yourself. You find him sitting under a tree, surrounded by his students. "Teach me about life," you say. But instead of answering, he asks you, "What is life?" You struggle to reply. He asks another question, and another. If he's such a great teacher, you wonder, shouldn't he have all the answers? Instead, all he seems to have are questions.

What do you think of Socrates?

BUILDING BACKGROUND Socrates was only one of the brilliant philosophers who lived in Athens in the 400s BC. The city was also home to some of the world's greatest artists and writers. In fact, all over Greece men and women made great advances in the arts and sciences. Their work inspired people for centuries.

The Arts

Among the most notable achievements of the ancient Greeks were those they made in the arts. These arts included sculpture, painting, architecture, and writings.

Statues and Paintings

The ancient Greeks were master artists. Their paintings and statues have been admired for hundreds of years. Examples of these works are still displayed in museums around the world.

Greek sculpture is admired for its realism, natural look, and details.

Greek statues are so admired because the sculptors who made them tried to make them look perfect. They wanted their statues to show how beautiful people could be. To improve their art, these sculptors carefully studied the human body, especially how it looked when it was moving. Then, using what they had learned, they carved stone and marble statues. As a result, many Greek statues look as though they could come to life at any moment.

Greek painting is also admired for its realism and detail. For example, Greek artists painted detailed scenes on vases, pots, and other vessels. These vessels often show scenes from myths or athletic competitions. Many of the scenes were created using only two colors, black and red. Sometimes artists used black glaze to paint scenes on red vases. Other artists covered whole vases with glaze and then scraped parts away to let the red background show through.

Greek Architecture

If you went to Greece today, you would see the ruins of many ancient buildings. Old columns still hold up parts of broken roofs, and ancient carvings decorate fallen walls. These remains give us an idea of the beauty of ancient Greek buildings.

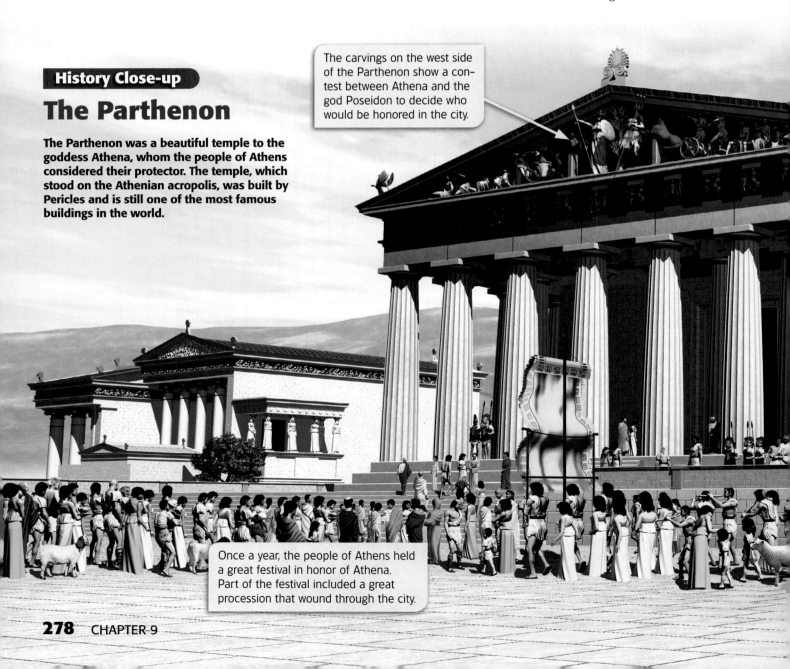

History Close-up

The Parthenon

The Parthenon was a beautiful temple to the goddess Athena, whom the people of Athens considered their protector. The temple, which stood on the Athenian acropolis, was built by Pericles and is still one of the most famous buildings in the world.

The carvings on the west side of the Parthenon show a contest between Athena and the god Poseidon to decide who would be honored in the city.

Once a year, the people of Athens held a great festival in honor of Athena. Part of the festival included a great procession that wound through the city.

The Greeks took great care in designing their buildings, especially their temples. Rows of tall columns surrounded the temples, making the temples look stately and inspiring. Greek designers were very careful when they measured these columns. They knew that columns standing in a long row often looked as though they curved in the middle. To prevent this optical illusion, they made their columns bulge slightly in the middle. As a result, Greek columns look perfectly straight.

Ancient Greek designers took such care because they wanted their buildings to reflect the greatness of their cities. The most impressive of all ancient Greek buildings was the Parthenon (PAHR-thuh-nahn) in Athens, pictured below. This temple to Athena was built in the 400s BC on the Athenian acropolis. It was designed to be magnificent not only outside, but inside as well. As you can see, the interior was decorated with carvings and columns.

New Forms of Writing

Sculpture, painting, and architecture were not the only Greek art forms. The Greeks also excelled at writing. In fact, Greek writers created many new writing forms, including drama and history.

Inside the Parthenon was a magnificent statue of Athena by the sculptor Phidias, whom many people considered the greatest sculptor in all of Greece.

The Parthenon's 46 columns are a type called Doric columns. These simple columns have no decoration at the top.

ANALYSIS SKILL **ANALYZING VISUALS**

Why do you think people are bringing animals and goods with them to the temple?

The Greeks created drama, or plays, as part of their religious ceremonies. Actors and singers performed scenes in honor of the gods and heroes. These plays became a popular form of entertainment, especially in Athens.

In the 400s BC Athenian writers created many of the greatest plays of the ancient world. Some writers produced tragedies, which described the hardships faced by Greek heroes. Among the best tragedy writers were Aeschylus (ES-kuh-luhs) and Sophocles (SAHF-uh-kleez). For example, Sophocles wrote about a Greek hero who mistakenly killed his own father. Other Greek dramatists focused on comedies, which made fun of people and ideas. One famous comedy writer was Aristophanes (ar-uh-STAHF-uh-neez). He used his comedy to make serious points about war, courts of law, and famous people.

The Greeks were also among the first people to write about history. They were interested in the lessons history could teach. One of the greatest of the Greek

historians was Thucydides (thoo-SID-uh-deez). His history of the Peloponnesian War was based in part on his experiences as an Athenian soldier. Even though he was from Athens, Thucydides tried to be **neutral** in his writing. He studied the war and tried to figure out what had caused it. He may have hoped the Greeks could learn from their mistakes and avoid similar wars in the future. Many later historians modeled their works after his.

READING CHECK **Summarizing** What were some forms of art found in ancient Greece?

Philosophy

The ancient Greeks worshipped gods and goddesses whose actions explained many of the mysteries of the world. But by around 500 BC a few people had begun to think about other explanations. We call these people philosophers. They believed in the power of the human mind to think, explain, and understand life.

ACADEMIC VOCABULARY

neutral unbiased, not favoring either side in a conflict

Primary Source

BOOK
The Death of Socrates

In 399 BC Socrates was arrested and charged with corrupting the young people of Athens and ignoring religious traditions. He was sentenced to die by drinking poison. Socrates spent his last hours surrounded by his students. One of them, Plato, later described the event in detail.

Socrates himself does not protest against his sentence but willingly drinks the poison.

The students and friends who have visited Socrates, including the narrator, are much less calm than he is.

"Then raising the cup to his lips, quite readily and cheerfully he drank off the poison. And hitherto most of us had been able to control our sorrow; but now when we saw him drinking . . . my own tears were flowing fast; so that I covered my face and wept . . . Socrates alone retained his calmness: What is this strange outcry? he said . . . I have been told that a man should die in peace. Be quiet then, and have patience."

–Plato, from *Phaedo*

ANALYSIS SKILL **ANALYZING PRIMARY SOURCES**

How does Socrates tell his students to act when they see him drink the poison?

Socrates

Among the greatest of these thinkers was a man named **Socrates** (SAHK-ruh-teez). He believed that people must never stop looking for knowledge.

Socrates was a teacher as well as a thinker. Today we call his type of teaching the Socratic method. Socrates taught by asking questions. His questions were about human qualities such as love and courage. He would ask, "What is courage?" When people answered, he challenged their answers with more questions.

Socrates wanted to make people think and question their own beliefs. But he made people angry, even frightened. They accused him of questioning the authority of the gods. For these reasons, he was arrested and condemned to death. His friends and students watched him calmly accept his death. He took the poison he was given, drank it, and died.

Plato

Plato (PLAYT-oh) was a student of Socrates. Like Socrates, he was a teacher as well as a philosopher. Plato created a school, the Academy, to which students, philosophers, and scientists could come to discuss ideas.

Although Plato spent much of his time running the Academy, he also wrote many works. The most famous of these works was called *The Republic*. It describes Plato's idea of an ideal society. This society would be based on justice and fairness to everyone. To ensure this fairness, Plato argued, society should be run by philosophers. He thought that only they could understand what was best for everyone.

Aristotle

Perhaps the greatest Greek thinker was **Aristotle** (ar-uh-STAH-tuhl), Plato's student. He taught that people should live lives of moderation, or balance. For example,

BIOGRAPHY

Euclid
c. 300 BC

Euclid is considered one of the world's greatest mathematicians. He lived and taught in Alexandria, Egypt, a great center of learning. Euclid wrote about the relationship between mathematics and other fields, including astronomy and music. But it is for geometry that he is best known. In fact, his works were so influential that the branch of geometry we study in school—the study of flat shapes and lines—is called Euclidean geometry.

Drawing Conclusions Why do you think a branch of geometry is named after Euclid?

people should not be greedy, but neither should they give away everything they own. Instead, people should find a balance between these two extremes.

Aristotle believed that moderation was based on **reason**, or clear and ordered thinking. He thought that people should use reason to govern their lives. In other words, people should think about their actions and how they will affect others.

Aristotle also made great advances in the field of logic, the process of making inferences. He argued that you could use facts you knew to figure out new facts. For example, if you know that Socrates lives in Athens and that Athens is in Greece, you can conclude that Socrates lives in Greece. Aristotle's ideas about logic helped inspire many later Greek scientists.

READING CHECK **Generalizing** What did ancient Greek philosophers like Socrates, Plato, and Aristotle want to find out?

Science

THE IMPACT TODAY

Many doctors recite the Hippocratic Oath, a pledge to behave ethically, when they finish medical school.

Aristotle's works inspired many Greek scientists. They began to look closely at the world to see how it worked.

Mathematics

Some Greeks spent their lives studying mathematics. One of these people was **Euclid** (YOO-kluhd). He was interested in geometry, the study of lines, angles, and shapes. In fact, many of the geometry rules we learn in school today come straight from Euclid's writings.

Other Greek mathematicians included a geographer who used mathematics to accurately calculate the size of the earth. Years later, in the AD 300s and 400s, a woman named Hypatia (hy-PAY-shuh) taught about mathematics and astronomy.

Medicine and Engineering

Not all Greek scientists studied numbers. Some studied other areas of science, such as medicine and engineering.

Greek doctors studied the human body to understand how it worked. In trying to cure diseases and keep people healthy, Greek doctors made many discoveries.

The greatest Greek doctor was **Hippocrates** (hip-AHK-ruh-teez). He wanted to figure out what caused diseases so he could better treat them. Hippocrates is better known today, though, for his ideas about how doctors should behave.

Greek engineers also made great discoveries. Some devices they invented are still used today. For example, farmers in many countries still use water screws to bring water to their fields. This device, which brings water from a lower level to a higher one, was invented by a Greek scientist named Archimedes (ahr-kuh-MEED-eez) in the 200s BC. Greek inventors could be playful as well as serious. For example, one inventor created mechanical toys like birds, puppets, and coin-operated machines.

READING CHECK **Summarizing** What advances did Greek scientists make in medicine?

SUMMARY AND PREVIEW Through their art, philosophy, and science, the Greeks have greatly influenced Western civilization. In the next chapter, you will learn about another group that has helped shape the Western world—the Romans.

Section 4 Assessment

go.hrw.com
Online Quiz
KEYWORD: SN6 HP9

Reviewing Ideas, Terms, and People

1. **a. Identify** What two types of drama did the Greeks invent?
   b. Explain Why did Greek columns bulge in the middle?
   c. Elaborate How did studying the human body help Greek artists make their statues look real?
2. **Describe** How did **Socrates** teach? What is this method of teaching called?
3. **a. Identify** In what fields did **Hippocrates** and **Euclid** make their greatest achievements?
   b. Make Inferences Why do some people call Greece the birthplace of the Western world?

Critical Thinking

4. **Summarizing** Add a box to the bottom of your note-taking chart. Use it to summarize Greek contributions in the arts, philosophy, and science.

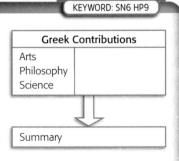

Greek Contributions		
Arts Philosophy Science		
Summary		

FOCUS ON WRITING

5. **Taking Notes about Artists and Thinkers** Add the artists and thinkers from this section to your chart. Because these people were not military leaders, all of your notes will go in the third column of your chart.

Greek Philosophers—
Socrates, Plato, and Aristotle

What would the world be like if no one believed in the importance of knowledge and truth?

When did they live? the 400s and 300s BC

Where did they live? Athens

What did they do? They thought. Socrates, Plato, and Aristotle thought about the world and searched for knowledge, wisdom, and truth. Between them they created the Socratic method of learning, the first political science book, and a method of scientific reasoning.

Why are they important? In most of the ancient world, strong fighters won all the glory. But in Athens, great thinkers and wise men were honored. People listened to them and followed their advice. Even today, people admire the ideas of Socrates, Plato, and Aristotle. Their teachings are at the root of modern philosophy and science.

Making Inferences Do you think these philosophers would have been as influential if they had lived in a different city? Why or why not?

This drawing shows how one artist imagined Plato (left), Aristotle (center), and Socrates (right) to look.

283

Social Studies Skills

Analysis | Critical Thinking | Economics | **Study**

Interpreting Charts and Tables

Understand the Skill

Charts present information visually to make it easier to understand. Different kinds of charts have different purposes. *Organizational charts* can show relationships among the parts of something. *Flowcharts* show steps in a process or cause-and-effect relationships. *Classification charts* group information so it can be easily compared. *Tables* are a type of classification chart that organize information into rows and columns for easy comparison. The ability to interpret charts helps you to analyze information and understand relationships.

Learn the Skill

Use these basic steps to interpret a chart:

1. Identify the type of chart and read its title in order to understand its purpose and subject.
2. Note the parts of the chart. Read the headings of rows and columns to determine the categories and types of information. Note any other labels that accompany the information presented in the chart. Look for any lines that connect its parts. What do they tell you?
3. Study the chart's details. Look for relationships in the information it presents. If it is a classification chart, analyze and compare all content in the rows and columns. In flowcharts and organizational charts, read all labels and other information. Follow and analyze directional arrows or lines.

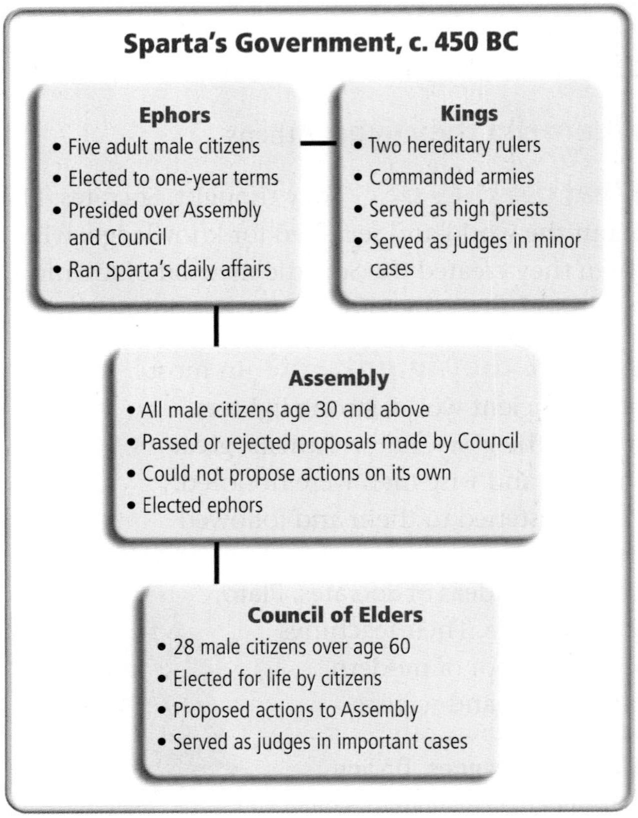

Sparta's Government, c. 450 BC
Ephors
• Five adult male citizens
• Elected to one-year terms
• Presided over Assembly and Council
• Ran Sparta's daily affairs
Kings
• Two hereditary rulers
• Commanded armies
• Served as high priests
• Served as judges in minor cases
Assembly
• All male citizens age 30 and above
• Passed or rejected proposals made by Council
• Could not propose actions on its own
• Elected ephors
Council of Elders
• 28 male citizens over age 60
• Elected for life by citizens
• Proposed actions to Assembly
• Served as judges in important cases

Practice and Apply the Skill

Apply the strategies given to interpret the chart above and answer the following questions.

1. What type of chart is this and what is its purpose?
2. In what ways were the ephors and the Assembly connected?
3. How did the roles of the Assembly and the Council of Elders differ?
4. What position in Spartan government had no direct relationship with the Assembly?

Chapter Review

Visual Summary

Use the visual summary below to help you review the main ideas of the chapter.

QUICK FACTS

Sparta and Athens fought together to defeat Persia in the Persian Wars.

Spartan culture centered on the military, while Athenian culture emphasized government and the arts.

Alexander the Great built a huge empire and spread Greek culture.

The ancient Greeks made lasting contributions to architecture, philosophy, science, and many other fields.

Reviewing Vocabulary, Terms, and People

Choose one word from each word pair to correctly complete each sentence below.

1. A ruler named _____ created the Persian Empire. **(Cyrus the Great/Xerxes I)**

2. A _____ was a group of soldiers that stood in a square to fight. **(cavalry/phalanx)**

3. _____ built the largest empire the world had ever seen. **(Alexander the Great/Aristotle)**

4. The _____ War(s) pitted two city-states against each other. **(Persian/Peloponnesian)**

5. The philosopher _____ taught people by asking them questions. **(Darius/Socrates)**

6. The greatest medical scholar of ancient Greece was _____. **(Philip II/Hippocrates)**

7. Aristotle taught the importance of _____ in his writings. **(reason/alliance)**

8. _____ was a great mathematician. **(Plato/Euclid)**

Comprehension and Critical Thinking

SECTION 1 *(Pages 260–265)*

9. a. **Identify** Who were Cyrus the Great, Darius I, and Xerxes I?

   b. **Analyze** How did the Greeks use strategy to defeat a larger fighting force?

   c. **Elaborate** What were some factors that led to the success of the Persian Empire?

SECTION 2 *(Pages 266–271)*

10. a. **Describe** What was life like for Spartan women? for Athenian women?

    b. **Compare and Contrast** How was the education of Spartan boys different from the education of Athenian boys? What did the education of both groups have in common?

    c. **Evaluate** Do you agree or disagree with this statement: "The Athenians brought the Peloponnesian War on themselves." Defend your argument.

SECTION 3 (Pages 272–276)

11. **a. Describe** How did Philip II improve the phalanx?

b. Analyze How did the cultures that Alexander conquered change after his death?

c. Predict How might history have been different if Alexander had not died so young?

SECTION 4 (Pages 277–282)

12. **a. Identify** What is the Parthenon? For which goddess was it built?

b. Compare What did Socrates, Plato, and Aristotle have in common?

c. Evaluate Why do you think Greek accomplishments in the arts and sciences are still admired today?

Reviewing Themes

13. **Politics** Why did the Persians and the Greeks react differently to the end of the Persian Wars?

14. **Politics** How were the government and the army related in Sparta?

15. **Society and Culture** How were the roles of women different in Athens and Sparta?

Using the Internet

go.hrw.com
KEYWORD: SN6 WH9

16. **Activity: Writing a Dialogue** While rulers such as Alexander and Cyrus fought to gain land, thinkers like Socrates may have questioned their methods. Enter the keyword activity. Write a dialogue between Socrates and a student on whether it was right to invade another country. Socrates should ask at least 10 questions to his student.

Social Studies Skills

17. **Interpreting Charts and Tables** Create a chart in your notebook that identifies key Greek achievements in architecture, art, writing, philosophy, and science. Complete the chart with details from this chapter.

Reading Skills

18. **Comparing and Contrasting Historical Facts** Complete the chart below to compare and contrast two powerful leaders you studied in this chapter, Cyrus the Great and Alexander the Great.

Compare	List two characteristics that Cyrus and Alexander shared.
	a. _____
	b. _____

Contrast	How did Cyrus's and Alexander's backgrounds differ?	
	Cyrus	Alexander
	c. _____	d. _____
	What happened to their empires after they died?	
	Cyrus	Alexander
	e. _____	f. _____

FOCUS ON WRITING

19. **Writing Your Poem** Look back over your notes from this chapter. Ask yourself which of the accomplishments you noted are the most significant. Do you admire people for their ideas? their might? their leadership? their brilliance?

Choose one person whose accomplishments you admire. Look back through the chapter for more details about the person's accomplishments. Then write a poem in praise of your chosen figure. Your poem should be five lines long. The first line should identify the subject of the poem. The next three lines should note his or her accomplishments, and the last line should sum up why he or she is respected.

DIRECTIONS: Read each question and write the letter of the best response.

1

> The freedom which we enjoy in our government extends also to our ordinary life . . . Further, we provide plenty of means for the mind to refresh itself from business. We celebrate games and sacrifices all the year round . . . Where our rivals from their very cradles by a painful discipline seek after manliness . . . we live exactly as we please and yet are just as ready to encounter every legitimate danger.

The information in this passage suggests that the person who wrote it probably lived in

A Athens.

B Persia.

C Sparta.

D Troy.

2 **The Athenians' main rivals were from**

A Sparta.

B Rome.

C Macedonia.

D Persia.

3 **Which people were the chief enemies of the Greeks in the 400s BC?**

A the Romans

B the Persians

C the Egyptians

D the Macedonians

4 **All of the following were Greek philosophers *except***

A Aristotle.

B Plato.

C Socrates.

D Zoroaster.

5 **Hellenistic culture developed as a result of the activities of which person?**

A Darius I

B Philip II

C Cyrus the Great

D Alexander the Great

Connecting with Past Learnings

6 **Cyrus the Great and Alexander the Great both built huge empires. What other leader that you have studied in this course also created an empire?**

A Moses

B Shi Huangdi

C Confucius

D Hatshepsut

7 **In this chapter you have read about many great philosophers and thinkers. Which of the following people you have studied was *not* a philosopher or thinker?**

A Socrates

B Ramses the Great

C Confucius

D Siddhartha Gautama

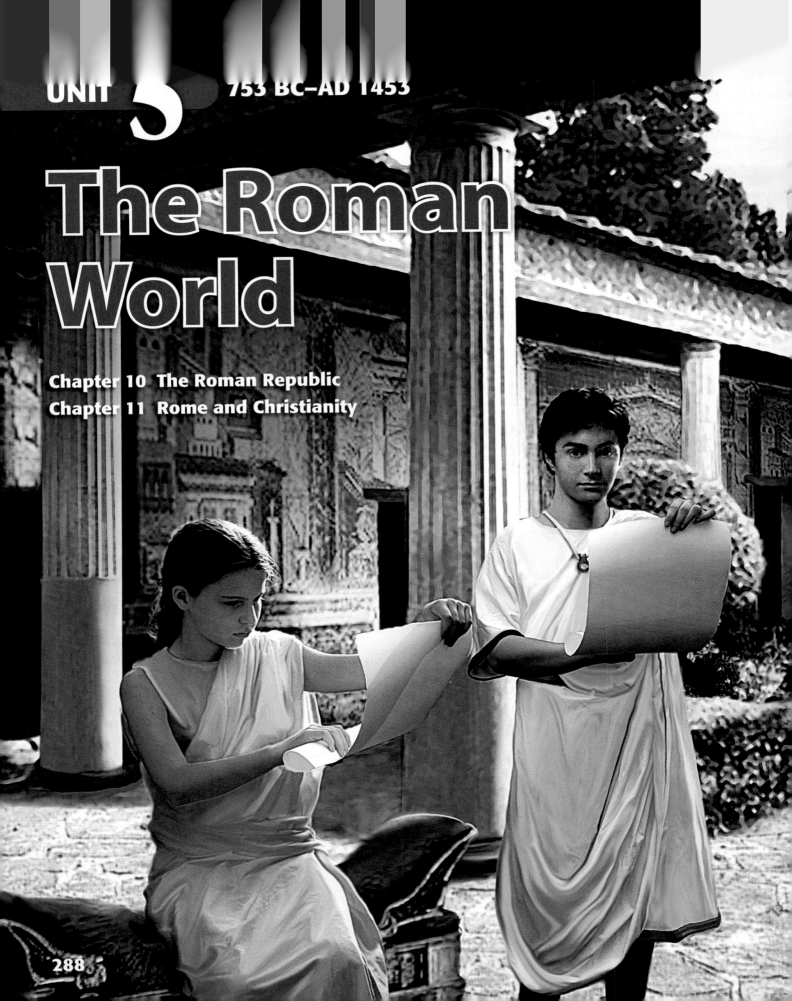

The Roman World

What You Will Learn...

From a small town in Italy, Rome grew to become the center of one of the world's greatest empires. Like the Greeks, whom they admired, the Romans had a lasting influence on world history.

The legacy of Rome was great. The Romans made many huge advances in engineering and architecture, and they developed advanced systems of written laws and government. In the first century AD, a new religion called Christianity appeared and spread throughout the empire.

In the next two chapters, you will learn about the rise of Rome, the growth and spread of Christianity, and the ultimate division and decline of one of the world's greatest empires.

Explore the Art

In this scene, a Roman tutor teaches two young students how to read. What does this scene suggest about life in ancient Rome?

289

The Roman Republic

FOCUS ON SPEAKING

A Legend The ancient Romans created many legends about their early history. They told of heroes and kings who performed great deeds to build and rule their city. As you read this chapter, look for people or events that could be the subjects of legends. When you finish studying this chapter, you will create and present a legend about one of the people or events that you have studied.

CHAPTER EVENTS

753 BC
According to legend, Rome is founded.

800 BC

WORLD EVENTS

c. 700 BC
The Assyrians conquer Israel.

HOLT

History's Impact

▶ video series
Watch the video to understand the impact of Roman government on American government today.

What You Will Learn...

In this chapter you will learn about the history of the Roman Republic. The Roman Forum, the ruins of which are shown above, was a public meeting place at the heart of Rome.

c. 600 BC
The Etruscans take over Rome.

509 BC
The Roman Republic is founded.

264–146 BC
Rome and Carthage fight in the Punic Wars.

27 BC
Augustus becomes Rome's first emperor.

600 BC

400 BC

200 BC

BC 1 AD

490 BC
The Persians invade Greece.

334–323 BC
Alexander the Great builds his empire.

c. 221–206 BC
The Qin dynasty rules China.

Economics	Geography	Politics	Religion	Society and Culture	Science and Technology

Focus on Themes In this chapter, you will read about the Roman Republic, about how Rome's location and **geography** helped it become a major power in the ancient world. You will also read about the city's **politics** and discover how its three-pronged government affected all of society. Finally, you will read about the wars the Roman Republic fought as it expanded its boundaries. You will see how this growth led to problems that were difficult to solve.

Outlining and History

Focus on Reading How can you make sense of all the facts and ideas in a chapter? One way is to take notes in the form of an outline.

Outlining a Chapter Here is an example of a partial outline for Section 1 of this chapter. Compare the outline to the information on pages 294–297. Notice how the writer looked at the heads in the chapter to determine the main and supporting ideas.

> The writer picked up the first heading in the chapter (page 294) as the first main idea. She identified it with Roman numeral I.

Section 1, Geography and the Rise of Rome

I. The Geography of Italy
  A. Physical features—many types of features
    1. Mountain ranges
    2. Hills
    3. Rivers
  B. Climate—warm summers, mild winters
II. Rome's Legendary Origins
  A. Aeneas
    1. Trojan hero
    2. Sailed to Italy and became ruler
  B. Romulus and Remus
    1. Twin brothers
    2. Decided to build city
      a. Romulus killed Remus
      b. City named for Romulus
  C. Rome's Early Kings

> The writer saw two smaller heads under the bigger head on pages 294–295 and listed them as A and B.

> The writer identified two facts that supported II.A (the head on page 296). She listed them as numbers 1 and 2.

> The writer decided it was important to note some individual facts under B.2. That's why she added a and b.

Outlining a Few Paragraphs When you need to outline only a few paragraphs, you can use the same outline form. Just look for the main idea of each paragraph and give each one a Roman numeral. Supporting ideas within the paragraph can be listed with A, B, and so forth. You can use Arabic numbers for specific details and facts.

You Try It!

Read the following passage from this chapter. Then fill in the blanks to complete the outline below.

Growth of Territory

Roman territory grew mainly in response to outside threats. In about 387 BC a people called the Gauls attacked Rome and took over the city. The Romans had to give the Gauls a huge amount of gold to leave the city.

From Chapter 10, page 308

Inspired by the Gauls' victory, many of Rome's neighboring cities also decided to attack. With some difficulty, the Romans fought off these attacks. As Rome's attackers were defeated, the Romans took over their lands. As you can see on the map, the Romans soon controlled all of the Italian Peninsula except far northern Italy.

One reason for the Roman success was the organization of the army. Soldiers were organized in legions . . . This organization allowed the army to be very flexible.

Complete this outline based on the passage you just read.

I. Roman territory grew in response to outside threats.

   A. Gauls attacked Rome in 387 BC.

      1. Took over the city

      2. _____

   B. The Gauls' victory inspired other people to attack Rome.

      1. _____

      2. Romans took lands of defeated foes.

      3. _____

II. _____

   A. Soldiers were organized in legions.

   B. _____

Key Terms and People

Chapter 10

Section 1
Aeneas *(p. 296)*
Romulus and Remus *(p. 297)*
republic *(p. 298)*
dictators *(p. 298)*
Cincinnatus *(p. 298)*
plebeians *(p. 299)*
patricians *(p. 299)*

Section 2
magistrates *(p. 303)*
consuls *(p. 303)*
Roman Senate *(p. 303)*
veto *(p. 304)*
Latin *(p. 304)*
checks and balances *(p. 305)*
Forum *(p. 305)*

Section 3
legions *(p. 309)*
Punic Wars *(p. 309)*
Hannibal *(p. 310)*
Gaius Marius *(p. 312)*
Lucius Cornelius Sulla *(p. 313)*
Spartacus *(p. 313)*

Academic Vocabulary

Success in school is related to knowing academic vocabulary—the words that are frequently used in school assignments and discussions. In this chapter, you will learn the following academic words:

primary *(p. 303)*
purpose *(p. 312)*

As you read Chapter 10, identify the main ideas you would use in an outline of this chapter.

Geography and the Rise of Rome

What You Will Learn...

Main Ideas

1. The geography of Italy made land travel difficult but helped the Romans prosper.
2. Ancient historians were very interested in Rome's legendary history.
3. Once a monarchy, the Romans created a republic.

The Big Idea

Rome's location and government helped it become a major power in the ancient world.

Key Terms and People

Aeneas, p. 296
Romulus and Remus, p. 297
republic, p. 298
dictators, p. 298
Cincinnatus, p. 298
plebeians, p. 299
patricians, p. 299

TAKING NOTES
As you read, take notes in a diagram like the one below. In the first box, describe how Italy's geography set the scene for Rome's rise. Then take notes on the steps in the rise of Rome. Draw as many boxes as you need.

Geography → 1st Step → 2nd Step → 3rd Step

If YOU were there...

You are the ruler of a group of people looking for a site to build a new city. After talking with your advisors, you have narrowed your choice to two possible sites. Both locations have plenty of water and good soil for farming, but they are otherwise very different. One is on top of a tall rocky hill overlooking a shallow river. The other is on a wide open field right next to the sea.

Which site will you choose for your city? Why?

BUILDING BACKGROUND From a small town on the Tiber River, Rome grew into a mighty power. Rome's geography—its central location and good climate—were important factors in its success and growth. The city's rise as a military power began when the Romans went to war and conquered neighboring Italian tribes.

The Geography of Italy

Rome eventually became the center of one of the greatest civilizations of the ancient world. In fact, the people of Rome conquered many of the territories you have studied in this book, including Greece, Egypt, and Asia Minor.

Italy, where Rome was built, is a peninsula in southern Europe. If you look at the map, you can see that Italy looks like a high-heeled boot sticking out into the Mediterranean Sea.

Physical Features

Look at the map again to find Italy's two major mountain ranges. In the north are the Alps, Europe's highest mountains. Another range, the Apennines (A-puh-nynz), runs the length of the Italian Peninsula. This rugged land made it hard for ancient people to cross from one side of the peninsula to the other. In addition, some of Italy's mountains, such as Mount Vesuvius, are volcanic. Their eruptions could devastate Roman towns.

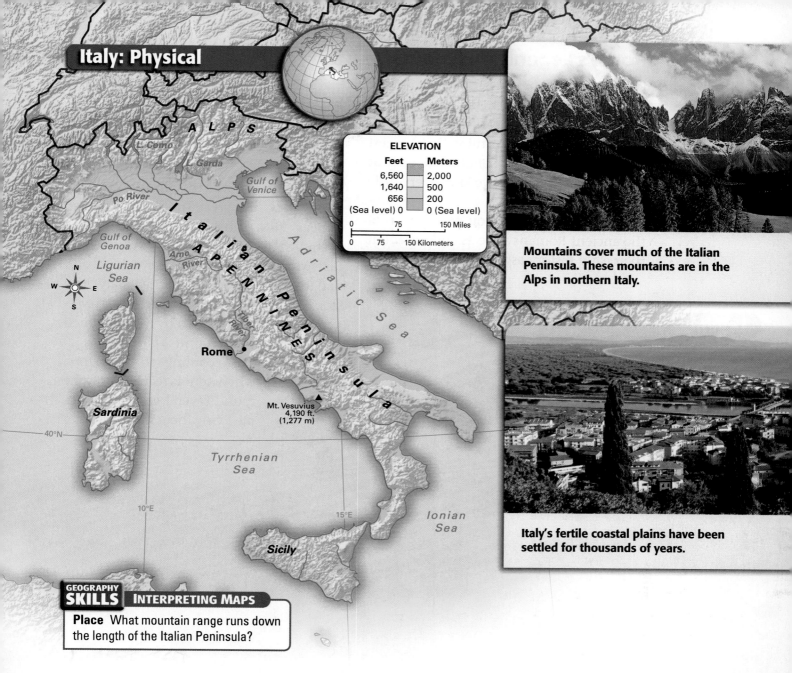

Italy: Physical

ELEVATION

Feet		Meters
6,560		2,000
1,640		500
656		200
(Sea level) 0		0 (Sea level)

0   75   150 Miles

0   75   150 Kilometers

ALPS

L. Como

Garda

Gulf of Venice

Po River

Gulf of Genoa

Italian APENNINES Peninsula

Arno River

Ligurian Sea

Tiber

Adriatic Sea

Rome

Mt. Vesuvius
4,190 ft.
(1,277 m)

Sardinia

40°N

Tyrrhenian Sea

10°E

15°E

Ionian Sea

Sicily

Mountains cover much of the Italian Peninsula. These mountains are in the Alps in northern Italy.

Italy's fertile coastal plains have been settled for thousands of years.

GEOGRAPHY SKILLS **INTERPRETING MAPS**

Place What mountain range runs down the length of the Italian Peninsula?

Not much of Italy is flat. Most of the land that isn't mountainous is covered with hills. Throughout history, people have built cities on these hills for defense. As a result, many of the ancient cities of Italy—including Rome—sat atop hills. Rome was built on seven hills.

Several rivers flow out of Italy's mountains. Because these rivers were a source of fresh water, people also built their cities near them. For example, Rome lies on the Tiber (TY-buhr) River.

Climate

Most of Italy, including the area around Rome, has warm, dry summers and mild, rainy winters. This climate is similar to that of southern California. Italy's mild climate allows people to grow a wide variety of crops. Grains, citrus fruits, grapes, and olives all grow well there. A plentiful food supply was one key factor in Rome's early growth.

READING CHECK Drawing Conclusions
How did Rome's location affect its early history?

Rome's Legendary Origins

Rome's early history is wrapped in mystery. No written records exist, and we have little evidence of the city's earliest days. All we have found are ancient ruins that suggest people lived in the area of Rome as early as the 800s BC. However, we know very little about how they lived.

Would it surprise you to think that the ancient Romans were as curious about their early history as we are today? Rome's leaders wanted their city to have a glorious past that would make the Roman people proud. Imagining that glorious past, they told legends, or stories, about great heroes and kings who built the city.

Aeneas

The Romans believed their history could be traced back to a great Trojan hero named **Aeneas** (i-NEE-uhs). When the Greeks destroyed Troy in the Trojan War, Aeneas fled with his followers. After a long and dangerous journey, he reached Italy. The story of this trip is told in the *Aeneid* (i-NEE-id), an epic poem written by a poet named Virgil (VUHR-juhl) around 20 BC.

According to the story, when Aeneas reached Italy, he found several groups of people living there. He formed an

Legendary Founding of Rome   QUICK FACTS

Roman historians traced their city's history back to legendary figures such as Aeneas, Romulus, and Remus.

Aeneas
According to the *Aeneid*, Aeneas carried his father from the burning city of Troy and then searched for a new home for the Trojans. After traveling around the Mediterranean, Aeneas finally settled in Italy.

alliance with one of these groups, a people called the Latins. Together they fought the other people of Italy. After defeating these opponents, Aeneas married the daughter of the Latin king. Aeneas, his son, and their descendants became prominent rulers in Italy.

Romulus and Remus

Among the descendants of Aeneas were the founders of Rome. According to Roman legends, these founders were twin brothers named **Romulus** (RAHM-yuh-luhs) and **Remus** (REE-muhs). In the story, these boys led exciting lives. When they were babies, they were put in a basket and thrown into the Tiber River. They didn't drown, though, because a wolf rescued them. The wolf cared for the boys for many years. Eventually, a shepherd found the boys and adopted them.

After they grew up, Romulus and Remus decided to build a city to mark the spot where the wolf had rescued them. While they were planning the city, Remus mocked one of his brother's ideas. In a fit of anger, Romulus killed Remus. He then built the city and named it Rome after himself.

Rome's Early Kings

According to ancient historians, Romulus was the first king of Rome, taking the throne in 753 BC. Modern historians believe that Rome could have been founded within 50 years before or after that date.

Roman records list seven kings who ruled the city. Not all of them were Roman. Rome's last three kings were Etruscans (i-TRUHS-kuhnz), members of a people who lived north of Rome. The Etruscans, who had been influenced by Greek colonies in Italy, lived in Italy before Rome was founded.

The Etruscan kings made great contributions to Roman society. They built huge temples and Rome's first sewer. Many historians think that the Romans learned their alphabet and numbers from the Etruscans.

The last Roman king was said to have been a cruel man who had many people killed, including his own advisors. Finally, a group of nobles rose up against him. According to tradition, he was overthrown in 509 BC. The nobles, who no longer wanted kings, created a new government.

READING CHECK **Drawing Conclusions** Why did early Romans want to get rid of the monarchy?

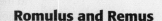

Romulus and Remus
The Romans believed that the twins Romulus and Remus were descendants of Aeneas. In Roman legend, Romulus and Remus were rescued and raised by a wolf. Romulus later killed Remus and built the city of Rome.

The Early Republic

THE IMPACT TODAY

The government of the United States today is a republic.

The government the Romans created in 509 BC was a republic. In a **republic**, people elect leaders to govern them. Each year the Romans elected officials to rule the city. These officials had many powers but only stayed in power for one year. This system was supposed to keep any one person from becoming too powerful in the government.

But Rome was not a democracy. The city's elected officials nearly all came from a small group of wealthy and powerful men. These wealthy and powerful Romans held all the power, and other people had little to no say in how the republic was run.

Challenges from Outside

Shortly after the Romans created the republic, they found themselves at war. For about 50 years the Romans were at war with other peoples of the region. For the most part the Romans won these wars. But they lost several battles, and the wars destroyed many lives and much property.

During particularly difficult wars, the Romans chose **dictators**—rulers with almost absolute power—to lead the city. To keep them from abusing their power, dictators could only stay in power for six months. When that time was over, the dictator gave up his power.

One of Rome's famous dictators was **Cincinnatus** (sin-suh-NAT-uhs), who gained power in 458 BC. Although he was a farmer, the Romans chose him to defend the city against a powerful enemy that had defeated a large Roman army.

Cincinnatus quickly defeated the city's enemies. Immediately, he resigned as dictator and returned to his farm, long before his six-month term had run out.

The victory by Cincinnatus did not end Rome's troubles. Rome continued to fight its neighbors on and off for many years.

Italy, 500 BC

- Romans
- Etruscans
- Greeks
- Carthaginians

0   30   60 Miles
0   30   60 Kilometers

Ligurian Sea

Adriatic Sea

Rome

Tyrrhenian Sea

Ionian Sea

Mediterranean Sea

Carthage

GEOGRAPHY SKILLS | **INTERPRETING MAPS**

Location What group lived mostly north of Rome?

BIOGRAPHY

Cincinnatus
c. 519 BC–?

Cincinnatus is the most famous dictator from the early Roman Republic. Because he wasn't eager to hold on to his power, the Romans considered Cincinnatus an ideal leader. They admired his abilities and his loyalty to the republic. The early citizens of the United States admired the same qualities in their leaders. In fact, some people called George Washington the "American Cincinnatus" when he refused to run for a third term as president. The people of the state of Ohio also honored Cincinnatus by naming one of their major cities, Cincinnati, after him.

Challenges within Rome

Enemy armies weren't the only challenge facing Rome. Within the city, Roman society was divided into two groups. Many of Rome's **plebeians** (pli-BEE-uhnz), or common people, were calling for changes in the government. They wanted more of a say in how the city was run.

Rome was run by powerful nobles called **patricians** (puh-TRI-shuhnz). Only patricians could be elected to office, so they held all political power.

The plebeians were peasants, craftspeople, traders, and other workers. Some of these plebeians, especially traders, were as rich as patricians. Even though the plebeians outnumbered the patricians, they couldn't take part in the government.

In 494 BC the plebeians formed a council and elected their own officials, an act that frightened many patricians. They feared that Rome would fall apart if the two groups couldn't cooperate. The patricians decided that it was time to change the government.

READING CHECK **Contrasting** How were patricians and plebeians different?

Roman Society QUICK FACTS	
Patricians	**Plebeians**
■ Wealthy, powerful citizens	■ Common people
■ Nobles	■ Peasants, craftspeople, traders, other workers
■ Small minority of the population	■ Majority of the population
■ Once controlled all aspects of government	■ Gained right to participate in government
■ After 218 BC, not allowed to participate in trade or commerce	■ Only Romans who could be traders, so many became wealthy

SUMMARY AND PREVIEW In this section you read about the location and founding of Rome, its early rule by kings, and the creation of the city's republican government. In the next section you'll learn more about that government, its strengths and weaknesses, how it worked, and how it changed over time.

Section 1 Assessment

go.hrw.com
Online Quiz
KEYWORD: SN6 HP10

Reviewing Ideas, Terms, and People

1. **a. Describe** Where is Italy located?
   b. Explain How did mountains affect life in Italy?
   c. Predict How do you think Rome's location on the Mediterranean affected its history as it began to grow into a world power?
2. **a. Identify** What brothers supposedly founded the city of Rome?
   b. Summarize What role did **Aeneas** play in the founding of Rome?
3. **a. Describe** What type of government did the Romans create in 509 BC?
   b. Contrast How were **patricians** and **plebeians** different?

Critical Thinking

4. **Categorizing** As you review your notes, separate the legends from the historical events in Rome's founding and growth. Then use a diagram like the one below to list the key legendary events.

   [ ] → [ ] → [ ] → [ ]

FOCUS ON SPEAKING

5. **Gathering Background Ideas** In this section you read about several legends the Romans told about their own history. Look back at the text to get some ideas about what you might include in your own legend. Write some ideas in your notebook.

from the Aeneid

by Virgil

Translated by Robert Fitzgerald

About the Reading *Virgil wrote the* Aeneid *to record the glorious story of Rome's founding and to celebrate the Rome of his day. At the center of the poem stands the hero Aeneas, survivor of the Trojan War and son of the goddess Venus. After wandering for seven years, Aeneas finally reaches southern Italy—then known as Ausonia. Here, Aeneas's friend Ilioneus leads a group of representatives to visit a nearby Latin settlement.*

AS YOU READ Try to identify each group's goals and desires.

GUIDED READING

WORD HELP

tranquilly calmly
astray off course
broached crossed
moored anchored
constraint force
gale storm

❶ Both "Teucrians" and "sons of Dardanus" are ways of referring to Trojans.

❷ Ilioneus says that the Trojans are not lost. A sea-mark is similar to a landmark, a feature sailors use to find their way.

How does Ilioneus address the king? Why do you think he does so?

      Latinus
Called the Teucrians before him, saying
Tranquilly as they entered:
       "Sons of Dardanus—
You see, we know your city and your nation,
As all had heard you laid a westward course—
Tell me your purpose. ❶ What design or need
Has brought you through the dark blue sea so far
To our Ausonian coast? Either astray
Or driven by rough weather, such as sailors
Often endure at sea, you've broached the river,
Moored ship there. Now do not turn away
From hospitality here. Know that our Latins
Come of Saturn's race, that we are just—
Not by constraint or laws, but by our choice
And habit of our ancient god . . ."
Latinus then fell silent, and in turn
Ilioneus began:
       "Your majesty,
Most noble son of Faunus, no rough seas
Or black gale swept us to your coast, no star
Or clouded seamark put us off our course. ❷

Aeneas, from an Italian painting of the 1700s

We journey to your city by design
And general consent, driven as we are
From realms in other days greatest by far
The Sun looked down on, passing on his way
From heaven's far eastern height. ❸ Our line's from Jove,
In his paternity the sons of Dardanus
Exult, and highest progeny of Jove
Include our king himself—Trojan Aeneas,
Who sent us to your threshold . . . ❹
So long on the vast waters, now we ask
A modest settlement of the gods of home,
A strip of coast that will bring harm to no one,
Air and water, open and free to all . . .
Our quest was for your country. Dardanus
Had birth here, and Apollo calls us back,
Directing us by solemn oracles
To Tuscan Tiber . . . ❺ Here besides
Aeneus gives you from his richer years
These modest gifts, relics caught up and saved
From burning Troy . . ."
        Latinus heard
Ilioneus out, his countenance averted,
Sitting immobile, all attention, eyes
Downcast but turning here and there. The embroidered
Purple and the scepter of King Priam
Moved him less in his own kingliness
Than long thoughts on the marriage of his daughter,
As he turned over in his inmost mind
Old Faunus' prophecy.
        "This is the man,"
he thought, "foretold as coming from abroad
To be my son-in-law, by fate appointed,
Called to reign here with equal authority—
The man whose heirs will be brilliant in valor
And win the mastery of the world." ❻

GUIDED READING

WORD HELP

progeny offspring
threshold door
oracle person who gives advice
averted turned away
immobile unmoving

❸ Ilioneus explains that the Trojans have come to Italy "by design"—both on purpose and with help from the gods.

❹ Aeneas and Dardanus, the founder of Troy, were both believed to be descendants of Jove, the king of the gods.

❺ The Romans believed that Troy's founder Dardanus was born in Italy.

What does Ilioneus ask the king to give the Trojans?

❻ Virgil included this vision of Rome's great future to point out the city's greatness to his readers.

CONNECTING LITERATURE TO HISTORY

1. **Analyzing** Rome's leaders wanted their city to have a glorious past that would make the Roman people proud. What details in this passage would make Roman readers proud of their past?

2. **Drawing Conclusions** When Aeneas reached Italy, he formed an alliance with the Latins. Think about how Virgil portrays the Latins in this passage. What words or phrases would you use to describe them? Why might such people make good allies?

Government and Society

What You Will Learn...

Main Ideas

1. Roman government was made up of three parts that worked together to run the city.
2. Written laws helped keep order in Rome.
3. The Roman Forum was the heart of Roman society.

The Big Idea

Rome's tripartite government and written laws helped create a stable society.

Key Terms

magistrates, *p. 303*
consuls, *p. 303*
Roman Senate, *p. 303*
veto, *p. 304*
Latin, *p. 304*
checks and balances, *p. 305*
Forum, *p. 305*

TAKING NOTES As you read, look for information on how government, written laws, and the Forum contributed to the development of Roman society. Record your notes in a chart like the one below.

Roman Government	Written Laws	Roman Forum

If YOU were there...

You have just been elected as a government official in Rome. Your duty is to represent the plebeians, the common people. You hold office for only one year, but you have one important power—you can stop laws from being passed. Now city leaders are proposing a law that will hurt the plebeians. If you stop the new law, it will hurt your future in politics. If you let it pass, it will hurt the people you are supposed to protect.

Will you let the new law pass? Why or why not?

BUILDING BACKGROUND Government in Rome was often a balancing act. Like the politician above, leaders had to make compromises and risk the anger of other officials to keep the people happy. To keep anyone from gaining too much power, the Roman government divided power among many different officials.

Roman Government

When the plebeians complained about Rome's government in the 400s BC, the city's leaders knew they had to do something. If the people stayed unhappy, they might rise up and overthrow the whole government.

To calm the angry plebeians, the patricians made some changes to Rome's government. For example, they created new offices that could only be held by plebeians. The people who held these offices protected the plebeians' rights and interests. Gradually, the distinctions between patricians and plebeians began to disappear, but that took a very long time.

As a result of the changes the patricians made, Rome developed a tripartite (try-PAHR-tyt) government, or a government with three parts. Each part had its own responsibilities and duties. To fulfill its duties, each part of the government had its own powers, rights, and privileges.

Magistrates

The first part of Rome's government was made up of elected officials, or **magistrates** (MA-juh-strayts). The two most powerful magistrates in Rome were called **consuls** (KAHN-suhlz). The consuls were elected each year to run the city and lead the army. There were two consuls so that no one person would be too powerful.

Below the consuls were other magistrates. Rome had many different types of magistrates. Each was elected for one year and had his own duties and powers. Some were judges. Others managed Rome's finances or organized games and festivals.

Senate

The second part of Rome's government was the Senate. The **Roman Senate** was a council of wealthy and powerful Romans that advised the city's leaders. It was originally created to advise Rome's kings. After the kings were gone, the Senate continued to meet to advise consuls.

Unlike magistrates, senators—members of the Senate—held office for life. By the time the republic was created, the Senate had 300 members. At first most senators were patricians, but as time passed many wealthy plebeians became senators as well. Because magistrates became senators after completing their terms in office, most didn't want to anger the Senate and risk their future jobs.

As time passed the Senate became more powerful. It gained influence over magistrates and took control of the city's finances. By 200 BC the Senate had great influence in Rome's government.

Assemblies and Tribunes

The third part of Rome's government, the part that protected the common people, had two branches. The first branch was made up of assemblies. Both patricians and plebeians took part in these assemblies. Their **primary** job was to elect the magistrates who ran the city of Rome.

FOCUS ON READING

If you were outlining the discussion on this page, what headings would you use?

ACADEMIC VOCABULARY

primary main, most important

Government of the Roman Republic

QUICK FACTS

Magistrates	Senate	Assemblies and Tribunes
■ Consuls led the government and army, judged court cases ■ Served for one year ■ Had power over all citizens, including other officials	■ Advised the consuls ■ Served for life ■ Gained control of financial affairs	■ Represented the common people, approved or rejected laws, declared war, elected magistrates ■ Roman citizens could take part in assemblies all their adult lives, tribunes served for one year ■ Could veto the decisions of consuls and other magistrates

Do as the Romans Do

The government of the Roman Republic was one of its greatest strengths. When the founders of the United States sat down to plan our government, they copied many elements of the Roman system. Like the Romans, we elect our leaders. Our government also has three branches—the president, Congress, and the federal court system. The powers of these branches are set forth in our Constitution, just like the Roman officials' powers were. Our government also has a system of checks and balances to prevent any one branch from becoming too strong. For example, Congress can refuse to give the president money to pay for programs. Like the Romans, Americans have a civic duty to participate in the government to help keep it as strong as it can be.

ANALYSIS SKILL **ANALYZING INFORMATION**

Why do you think the founders of the United States borrowed ideas from Roman government?

THE IMPACT TODAY

Like tribunes, the president of the United States has the power to veto actions by other government officials.

The second branch was made up of a group of elected officials called tribunes. Elected by the plebeians, tribunes had the ability to **veto** (VEE-toh), or prohibit, actions by other officials. Veto means "I forbid" in **Latin**, the Romans' language. This veto power made tribunes very powerful in Rome's government. To keep them from abusing their power, each tribune remained in office only one year.

Civic Duty

Rome's government would not have worked without the participation of the people. People participated in the government because they felt it was their civic duty, or their duty to the city. That civic duty included doing what they could to make sure the city prospered. For example,

they were expected to attend assembly meetings and to vote in elections. Voting in Rome was a complicated process, and not everyone was allowed to do it. Those who could, however, were expected to take part in all elections.

Wealthy and powerful citizens also felt it was their duty to hold public office to help run the city. In return for their time and commitment, these citizens were respected and admired by other Romans.

Checks and Balances

In addition to limiting terms of office, the Romans put other restrictions on their leaders' power. They did this by giving government officials the ability to restrict the powers of other officials. For example, one consul could block the actions of the other.

Laws proposed by the Senate had to be approved by magistrates and ratified by assemblies. We call these methods to balance power **checks and balances**. Checks and balances keep any one part of a government from becoming stronger or more influential than the others.

Checks and balances made Rome's government very complicated. Sometimes quarrels arose when officials had different ideas or opinions. When officials worked together, however, Rome's government was strong and efficient, as one Roman historian noted:

> " In unison [together] they are a match for any and all emergencies, the result being that it is impossible to find a constitution that is better constructed. For whenever some common external danger should come upon them and should compel [force] them to band together in counsel [thought] and in action, the power of their state becomes so great that nothing that is required is neglected [ignored]. "
>
> –Polybius, from The Constitution of the Roman Republic

READING CHECK **Finding Main Ideas** What were the three parts of the Roman government?

Written Laws Keep Order

Rome's officials were responsible for making the city's laws and making sure that people followed them. At first these laws weren't written down. The only people who knew all the laws were the patricians who had made them.

Many people were unhappy with this situation. They did not want to be punished for breaking laws they didn't even know existed. As a result, they began to call for Rome's laws to be written down and made accessible to everybody.

Rome's first written law code was produced in 450 BC on 12 bronze tables, or tablets. These tables were displayed in the **Forum**, Rome's public meeting place. Because of how it was displayed, this code was called the Law of the Twelve Tables.

Over time, Rome's leaders passed many new laws. Throughout their history, though the Romans looked to the Law of the Twelve Tables as a symbol of Roman law and of their rights as Roman citizens.

READING CHECK **Drawing Inferences** Why did many people want a written law code?

Primary Source

HISTORIC DOCUMENT
Law of the Twelve Tables

The Law of the Twelve Tables governed many parts of Roman life. Some laws were written to protect the rights of all Romans. Others only protected the patricians. The laws listed here should give you an idea of the kinds of laws the tables included.

A Roman who did not appear before a government official when called or did not pay his debts could be arrested.

[from Table I] If anyone summons a man before the magistrate, he must go. If the man summoned does not go, let the one summoning him call the bystanders to witness and then take him by force.

[from Table III] One who has confessed a debt, or against whom judgment has been pronounced, shall have thirty days to pay it. After that forcible seizure of his person is allowed . . . unless he pays the amount of the judgment.

Women—even as adults— were legally considered to be children.

[from Table V] Females should remain in guardianship even when they have attained their majority.

No one in Rome could be executed without a trial.

[from Table IX] Putting to death of any man, whosoever he might be, unconvicted is forbidden.

–Law of the Twelve Tables, translated in *The Library of Original Sources* edited by Oliver J. Thatcher

ANALYSIS SKILL **ANALYZING PRIMARY SOURCES**

How are these laws similar to and different from our laws today?

The Roman Forum

The Forum was the center of life in ancient Rome. The city's most important temples and government buildings were located there, and Romans met there to talk about the issues of the day. The word *forum* means "public place."

The Roman Forum

The Roman Forum, the place where the Law of the Twelve Tables was kept, was the heart of the city of Rome. It was the site of important government buildings and temples. Government and religion were only part of what made the Forum so important, though. It was also a popular meeting place for Roman citizens. People met there to shop, chat, and gossip.

The Temple of Jupiter stood atop the Capitoline Hill, overlooking the Forum.

Important government records were stored in the Tabularium.

Roman citizens often wore togas, loose-fitting garments wrapped around the body. Togas were symbols of Roman citizenship.

Public officials often addressed people from this platform.

ANALYSIS SKILL **ANALYZING VISUALS**

What can you see in this illustration that indicates the Forum was an important place?

The Forum lay in the center of Rome, between two major hills. On one side was the Palatine (PA-luh-tyn) Hill, where Rome's richest people lived. Across the forum was the Capitoline (KA-pet-uhl-yn) Hill, where Rome's grandest temples stood. Because of this location, city leaders could often be found in or near the forum, mingling with the common people. These leaders used the Forum as a speaking area, delivering speeches to the crowds.

But the Forum also had attractions for people not interested in speeches. Various shops lined the open square, and fights between gladiators were sometimes held there. Public ceremonies were commonly held in the Forum as well. As a result, the forum was usually packed with people.

READING CHECK **Generalizing** How was the Forum the heart of Roman society?

SUMMARY AND PREVIEW In this section you read about the basic structure of Roman government. In the next section you'll see how that government changed as Rome's territory grew and its influence expanded.

The Senate met here in the curia, or Senate House.

Section 2 Assessment

Reviewing Ideas, Terms, and People

1. **a. Identify** Who were the **consuls**?
   b. Explain Why did the Romans create a system of **checks and balances**?
   c. Elaborate How do you think the **Roman Senate** gained power?
2. **a. Recall** What was Rome's first written law code called?
   b. Draw Conclusions Why did Romans want their laws written down?
3. **a. Describe** What kinds of activities took place in the Roman **Forum**?

Critical Thinking

4. **Analyzing** Review your notes on Roman government. Use this diagram to note information about the powers of the parts of Rome's government.

Magistrates

Senate

Assemblies and Tribunes

FOCUS ON SPEAKING

5. **Choosing a Topic** You've just read about Roman laws and government. Would anything related to these topics make good subjects for your legend? Write some ideas in your notebook.

The Late Republic

If YOU were there...

You are a farmer in Italy during the Roman Republic. You are proud to be a Roman citizen, but times are hard. Rich landowners are buying farmland, and many farmers like you have lost their jobs. Some are moving to the city, but you've heard that there are not many jobs there, either. You've also heard that a famous general is raising an army to fight in Asia. That seems very far away, but it would mean good pay.

What might convince you to join the army?

What You Will Learn...

Main Ideas
1. The late republic period saw the growth of territory and trade.
2. Through wars, Rome grew beyond Italy.
3. Several crises struck the republic in its later years.

The Big Idea
The later period of the Roman Republic was marked by wars of expansion and political crises.

Key Terms and People
legions, *p. 309*
Punic Wars, *p. 309*
Hannibal, *p. 310*
Gaius Marius, *p. 312*
Lucius Cornelius Sulla, *p. 313*
Spartacus, *p. 313*

TAKING NOTES As you read, look for information on how Rome expanded beyond Italy and how crises affected the later years of the Roman Republic. Use a diagram like the one below to help you organize your notes.

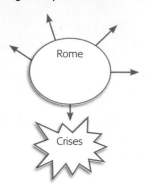

BUILDING BACKGROUND The Roman army played a vital part in the expansion of the republic. Roman soldiers were well trained and defeated many of the city's enemies. As they did so, the Romans took over new lands. As the army conquered these new lands, traders moved in, seeking new products and markets that could make them rich.

Growth of Territory and Trade

After about 400 BC the Roman Republic grew quickly, both geographically and economically. Within 200 years the Roman army had conquered nearly all of Italy. Meanwhile Roman traders had begun to ship goods back and forth around the Mediterranean in search of new products and wealth.

Growth of Territory

Roman territory grew mainly in response to outside threats. In about 387 BC a people called the Gauls attacked Rome and took over the city. The Romans had to give the Gauls a huge amount of gold to leave the city.

Inspired by the Gauls' victory, many of Rome's neighboring cities also decided to attack. With some difficulty, the Romans fought off these attacks. As Rome's attackers were defeated, the Romans took over their lands. As you can see on the map, the Romans soon controlled all of the Italian Peninsula except far northern Italy.

One reason for the Roman success was the organization of the army. Soldiers were organized in **legions** (LEE-juhnz), or groups of up to 6,000 soldiers. Each legion was divided into centuries, or groups of 100 soldiers. This organization allowed the army to be very flexible. It could fight as a large group or as several small ones. This flexibility allowed the Romans to defeat most enemies.

Farming and Trade

Before Rome conquered Italy, most Romans were farmers. As the republic grew, many people left their farms for Rome. In place of these small farms, wealthy Romans built large farms in the countryside. These farms were worked by slaves who grew one or two crops. The owners of the farms didn't usually live on them. Instead, they stayed in Rome or other cities and let others run the farms for them.

Roman trade also expanded as the republic grew. Rome's farmers couldn't grow enough food to support the city's increasing population, so merchants brought food from other parts of the Mediterranean. These merchants also brought metal goods and slaves to Rome. To pay for these goods, the Romans made coins out of copper, silver, and other metals. Roman coins began to appear in markets all around the Mediterranean.

READING CHECK **Identifying Cause and Effect** Why did the Romans conquer their neighbors?

Rome Grows Beyond Italy

As Rome's power grew other countries came to see the Romans as a threat to their own power and declared war on them. In the end the Romans defeated their opponents, and Rome gained territory throughout the Mediterranean.

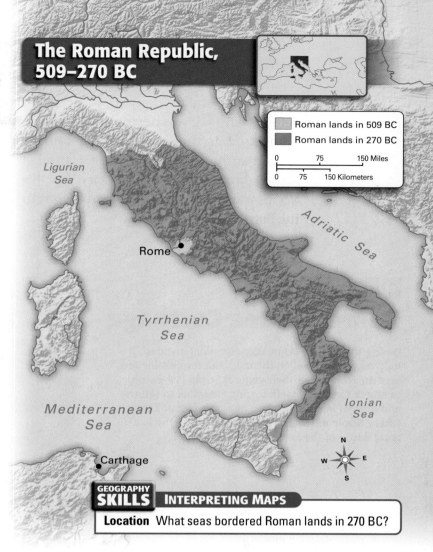

The Roman Republic, 509–270 BC

Roman lands in 509 BC
Roman lands in 270 BC

Ligurian Sea

Rome

Adriatic Sea

Tyrrhenian Sea

Mediterranean Sea

Ionian Sea

Carthage

GEOGRAPHY SKILLS **INTERPRETING MAPS**

Location What seas bordered Roman lands in 270 BC?

The Punic Wars

The fiercest of the wars Rome fought were the **Punic** (PYOO-nik) **Wars**, a series of wars against Carthage, a city in northern Africa. The word *Punic* means "Phoenician" in Latin. As you learned earlier in this book, the Phoenicians were an ancient civilization that had built the city of Carthage.

Rome and Carthage went to war three times between 264 and 146 BC. The wars began when Carthage sent its armies to Sicily, an island just southwest of Italy. In response, the Romans also sent an army to the island. Before long, war broke out between them. After almost 20 years of fighting, the Romans forced their enemies out and took control of Sicily.

In 218 BC Carthage tried to attack Rome itself. An army led by the brilliant general **Hannibal** set out for Rome. Although he forced the Romans right to the edge of defeat, Hannibal was never able to capture Rome itself. In the meantime, the Romans sent an army to attack Carthage. Hannibal rushed home to defend his city, but his troops were defeated at Zama (ZAY-muh) in the battle illustrated below.

By the 140s BC many senators had grown alarmed that Carthage was growing powerful again. They convinced Rome's consuls to declare war on Carthage, and once again the Romans sent an army to Africa and destroyed Carthage. After this victory, the Romans burned the city, killed most of its people, and sold the rest of the people into slavery. They also took control of northern Africa.

Rome Battles Carthage

During the Second Punic War, Hannibal invaded Italy, as you can see on the map. But Rome's leaders sent an army under their general Scipio (SIP-ee-oh) to attack Carthage itself, forcing Hannibal to return and defend his city. The two generals met at Zama, where Scipio defeated Hannibal's army in the last great battle of the Second Punic War.

Rome

Carthage

◼ Carthage	✦ Battle of Zama, 202 BC
◼ Roman Republic	→ Hannibal's route
0 150 300 Miles	→ Scipio's route
0 150 300 Kilometers	

The Romans had the advantage in cavalry, which helped them win the battle.

Some Roman soldiers blew trumpets and yelled to distract the war elephants.

Later Expansion

During the Punic Wars, Rome took control of Sicily, Corsica, Spain, and North Africa. As a result, Rome controlled most of the western Mediterranean region.

In the years that followed, Roman legions marched north and east as well. In the 120s Rome conquered the southern part of Gaul. By that time, Rome had also conquered Greece and parts of Asia.

Although the Romans took over Greece, they were greatly changed by the experience. We would normally expect the victor to change the conquered country. Instead, the Romans adopted ideas about literature, art, philosophy, religion, and education from the Greeks.

READING CHECK **Summarizing** How did the Romans gain territory?

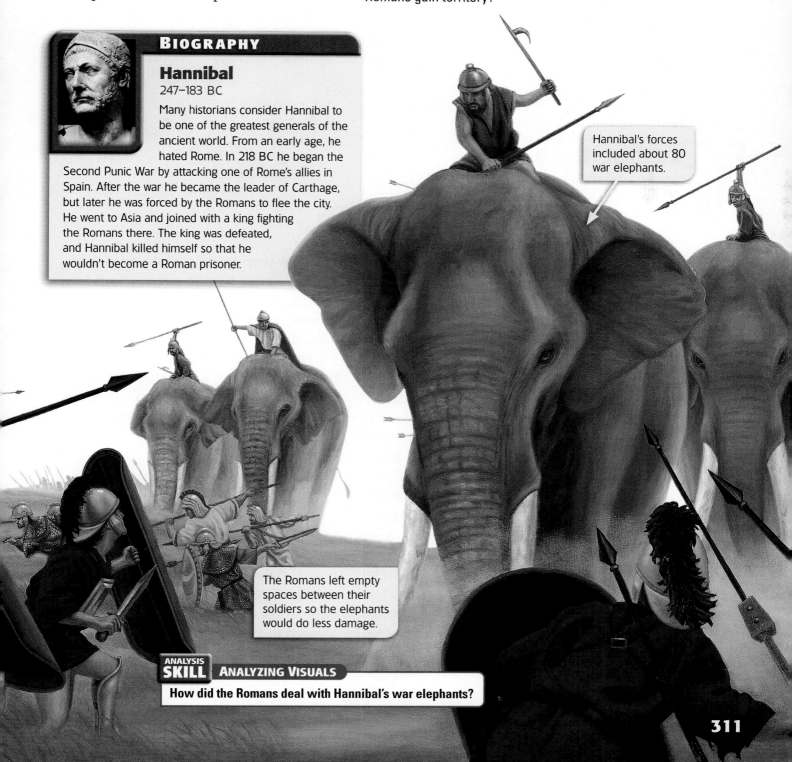

BIOGRAPHY

Hannibal
247–183 BC

Many historians consider Hannibal to be one of the greatest generals of the ancient world. From an early age, he hated Rome. In 218 BC he began the Second Punic War by attacking one of Rome's allies in Spain. After the war he became the leader of Carthage, but later he was forced by the Romans to flee the city. He went to Asia and joined with a king fighting the Romans there. The king was defeated, and Hannibal killed himself so that he wouldn't become a Roman prisoner.

Hannibal's forces included about 80 war elephants.

The Romans left empty spaces between their soldiers so the elephants would do less damage.

ANALYSIS SKILL **ANALYZING VISUALS**

How did the Romans deal with Hannibal's war elephants?

311

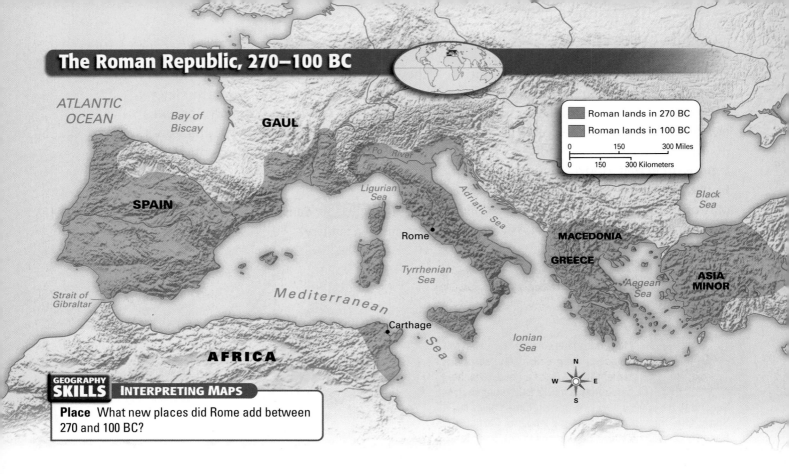

The Roman Republic, 270–100 BC

ATLANTIC OCEAN

Bay of Biscay

GAUL

SPAIN

Strait of Gibraltar

AFRICA

Po River

Ligurian Sea

Rome

Tyrrhenian Sea

Mediterranean

Carthage

Sea

Adriatic Sea

MACEDONIA

GREECE

Ionian Sea

Aegean Sea

Black Sea

ASIA MINOR

Roman lands in 270 BC
Roman lands in 100 BC

0   150   300 Miles
0   150   300 Kilometers

GEOGRAPHY SKILLS INTERPRETING MAPS

Place What new places did Rome add between 270 and 100 BC?

Crises Strike the Republic

As the Romans' territory grew, problems arose in the republic. Rich citizens were getting richer, and many leaders feared that violence would erupt between rich and poor.

Tiberius and Gaius Gracchus

Among the first leaders to address Rome's problems were brothers named Tiberius (ty-BIR-ee-uhs) and Gaius Gracchus (GY-uhs GRAK-uhs). Both served as tribunes.

Tiberius, who took office in 133 BC, wanted to create farms for poor Romans. The **purpose** of these farms was to keep the poor citizens happy and prevent rebellions. Tiberius wanted to create his farms on public land that wealthy citizens had illegally taken over. The public supported this idea, but the wealthy citizens opposed it. Conflict over the idea led to riots in the city, during which Tiberius was killed.

ACADEMIC VOCABULARY

purpose the reason something is done

A few years later Gaius also tried to create new farms. He also began to sell food cheaply to Rome's poor citizens. Like his brother, Gaius angered many powerful Romans and was killed for his ideas.

The violent deaths of the Gracchus brothers changed Roman politics. From that time on people saw violence as a political weapon. They often attacked leaders with whom they disagreed.

Marius and Sulla

In the late 100s BC another social change nearly led to the end of the republic. In 107 BC the Roman army desperately needed more troops. In response, a consul named **Gaius Marius** (MER-ee-uhs) encouraged poor people to join the army. Before, only people who owned property had been allowed to join. As a result of this change, thousands of poor and unemployed citizens joined Rome's army.

Because Marius was a good general, his troops were more loyal to him than they were to Rome. The army's support gave Marius great political power. Following his example, other ambitious politicians also sought their armies' support.

One such politician, **Lucius Cornelius Sulla** (LOO-shuhs kawr-NEEL-yuhs SUHL-uh), became consul in 88 BC. Sulla soon came into conflict with Marius, a conflict that led to a civil war in Rome. A civil war is a war between citizens of the same country. In the end Sulla defeated Marius. He later named himself dictator and used his power to punish his enemies.

Spartacus

Not long after Sulla died, another crisis arose to challenge Rome's leaders. Thousands of slaves led by a former gladiator, **Spartacus** (SPAHR-tuh-kuhs), rose up and demanded freedom.

Spartacus and his followers defeated an army sent to stop them and took over much of southern Italy. Eventually, though, Spartacus was killed in battle. Without his leadership, the revolt fell apart. Victorious, the Romans executed 6,000 rebellious

Lucius Cornelius Sulla
138–78 BC

Although the two eventually became enemies, Sulla learned much of what he knew about military affairs from Gaius Marius. He had been an assistant to Marius before he became consul. Sulla changed Rome's government forever when he became dictator, but he actually had many traditional ideas. For example, he believed the Senate should be the main ruling group in Rome, and he increased its power during his rule.

Analyzing Information Do you think Sulla was a traditional Roman leader? Why or why not?

slaves as an example to others who thought about rebelling. The rebellion was over, but the republic's problems were not.

READING CHECK **Predicting** How do you think Marius and Sulla influenced later leaders?

SUMMARY AND PREVIEW You have read about crises that arose in the late Roman Republic. These crises eventually led to changes in Roman society, as you will see in the next chapter.

go.hrw.com
Online Quiz
KEYWORD: SN6 HP10

Section 3 Assessment

Reviewing Ideas, Terms, and People
1. **a. Define** What was a Roman **legion**?
   b. Explain Why did the Romans decide to conquer all of Italy?
   c. Elaborate How did the growth of territory help increase Roman trade?
2. **a. Recall** Who fought in the **Punic Wars**?
   b. Summarize What led to the beginning of the Punic Wars?
   c. Elaborate Why do you think the Romans borrowed many ideas from Greek culture?
3. **a. Identify** Who was **Spartacus**?
   b. Explain How did the deaths of the Gracchus brothers change Roman politics?

Critical Thinking
4. **Summarizing** Draw a diagram like the one here. Use your notes on crises Rome faced to list three crises during the later period of the republic. Then list two facts about each crisis.

Crises

FOCUS ON SPEAKING

5. **Selecting Characters** In this section you learned about many major figures in Roman history. Choose one of them to be the subject of your legend. Now look back at your notes. How will you make the subject of your legend interesting for your listeners?

Social Studies Skills

Interpreting Culture Maps

Understand the Skill

A culture map is a special type of political map. As you know, physical maps show natural features, such as mountains and rivers. Political maps show the human features of an area, such as boundaries, cities, and roads. The human features shown on a culture map are cultural ones, such as the languages spoken or religions practiced in an area. Historians often use culture maps in their work. Therefore, being able to interpret them is important for understanding history.

Learn the Skill

Follow these guidelines to interpret a culture map.

❶ Use map basics. Read the title to identify the subject. Note the labels, legend, and scale. Pay extra attention to special symbols for cultural features. Be sure you understand what these symbols represent.

❷ Study the map as a whole. Note the location of the cultural symbols and features. Ask yourself how they relate to the rest of the map.

❸ Connect the information on the map to any written information about the subject in the text.

Languages of Italy, 400s BC

Legend:
- Latin
- Umbrian
- Greek
- Etruscan
- Other languages

0   50   100 Miles
0   50   100 Kilometers

Labels: Corsica, Rome, Tyrrhenian Sea, Sardinia, Adriatic Sea, Mediterranean Sea, Sicily

Practice and Apply the Skill

Apply the guidelines to the map on this page and answer the following questions.

1. What makes this map a culture map?

2. What language was most widely spoken on the Italian Peninsula? What other language was widely spoken?

3. Where was Greek spoken? Why did the people there talk in Greek?

4. What language did the Romans speak?

Chapter Review

QUICK FACTS

Visual Summary

Use the visual summary below to help you review the main ideas of the chapter.

The Romans created many legends about their city's glorious history.

The early Romans set up a type of government called a republic.

The Roman Republic conquered lands in Italy and around the Mediterranean.

Reviewing Vocabulary, Terms, and People

Match each numbered definition with the correct lettered vocabulary term.

a. republic
b. plebeians
c. Spartacus
d. legions
e. Aeneas
f. consuls

g. Forum
h. dictator
i. veto
j. Roman Senate
k. patricians
l. primary

1. Rome's public meeting place
2. groups of about 6,000 soldiers
3. the legendary Trojan founder of Rome
4. main, most important
5. a government in which people elect leaders
6. a council that advised Rome's leaders
7. a leader with absolute power for six months
8. the common people of Rome
9. the two most powerful officials in Rome
10. leader of a slave rebellion
11. prohibit
12. noble, powerful Romans

Comprehension and Critical Thinking

SECTION 1 *(Pages 294–299)*

13. **a. Describe** What are two legends that describe Rome's founding? How are the two legends connected?

    b. Compare and Contrast What roles did the plebeians and the patricians take in the early Roman government? In what other ways were the two groups different?

    c. Predict How do you think Italy's geography and Rome's location would affect the spread of Rome's influence?

SECTION 2 (Pages 302–307)

14. a. Describe What were the three parts of Rome's government?

b. Analyze How do checks and balances protect the rights of the people? How do written laws do the same thing?

c. Elaborate What are some places in modern society that serve purposes similar to those of the Roman Forum?

SECTION 3 (Pages 308–313)

15. a. Identify What difficulties did Hannibal, Lucius Cornelius Sulla, and Spartacus cause for Rome?

b. Analyze How did Roman occupations, economics, and society change during the Late Republic?

c. Evaluate Some historians say that Rome and Carthage were destined to fight each other. Why do you think they say this?

Reviewing Themes

16. Politics Why did Roman magistrates only hold office for one year?

17. Geography How do you think Rome's location helped the Romans in their quest to conquer the entire Mediterranean region?

Using the Internet

go.hrw.com
KEYWORD: SN6 WH10

18. Activity: Explaining Roman Society A key reason the Roman Republic fell was because the Roman people gave up on it. The army, once Rome's protector, let itself be turned against the Roman people. The Senate gave up on debate and compromise when it turned to political violence. Enter the keyword. Research the fall of the Roman Republic and create an exhibit for a local history museum. Make sure your exhibit contains information about key figures in the Roman military and government. Use words and pictures to explain the political, religious, and social structures that made Rome an empire and what caused its eventual downfall.

Reading Skills

19. Outlining and History Look back at the discussion "Crises Strike the Republic" in the last section of this chapter. Prepare an outline that will help clarify the people, events, and ideas of this discussion. Before you prepare your outline, decide what your major headings will be. Then choose the details that will appear below each heading. Remember that most outlines follow this basic format:

> I. Main Idea
>   A. Supporting Idea
>   B. Supporting Idea
>   1. Detail
>   2. Detail
> II. Main Idea
>   A. Supporting Idea

Social Studies Skills

Interpreting Culture Maps *Look at the culture map on page 314. Then answer the following questions.*

20. What was the main language spoken in Italy during the 400s BC?

21. Which language do you think was spoken by the fewest people? Why do you think this?

FOCUS ON SPEAKING

22. Presenting Your Legend Now that you've chosen the subject for your legend, it's time to write and present it. As you write your legend, focus on exciting details that will bring the subject to life in your listeners' minds. Once you've finished writing, share your legend with the class. Try to make your legend exciting as you present it. Remember to alter the tone and volume of your voice to convey the appropriate mood.

DIRECTIONS: Read each question, and write the letter of the best response.

1 Use the map to answer the following question.

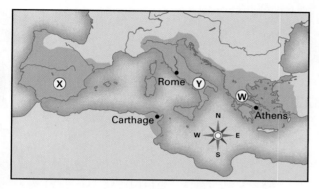

The order in which Rome expanded its control in the Mediterranean region is shown by which of the following sequences of letters?

A Y–W–X

B X–W–Y

C Y–X–W

D W–X–Y

2 Which was the *least* important reason for the growth of Rome's power and influence in the Mediterranean region?

A religion

B trade

C military organization

D wars and conquests

3 According to Roman legend, the city of Rome was founded by

A Latin peoples who moved to Italy from ancient Egypt.

B two men named Romulus and Remus who were raised by a wolf.

C the gods of Greece, who were looking for a new home.

D a Greek warrior named Achilles who had fled from the destruction of Troy.

4 Roman nobles were called

A patricians.

B plebeians.

C tribunes.

D magistrates.

5 Which of the following characteristics did *not* apply to Roman government?

A system of checks and balances

B sense of civic duty

C written code of laws

D equality of all people

Connecting with Past Learnings

6 You learned earlier in this course about other ancient peoples who, like the Romans, founded their civilizations along rivers. These peoples include all of the following *except* the

A Chinese.

B Egyptians.

C Sumerians.

D Hebrews.

7 Virgil's *Aeneid* is similar to what other piece of ancient literature that you've learned about in this course?

A the *Shiji*

B the *Book of the Dead*

C *The Odyssey*

D the *Bhagavad Gita*

Rome and Christianity

FOCUS ON WRITING

Note Cards for a Screenplay Imagine that you are a research assistant for a movie studio that is planning to make a movie about the Roman Empire. Your job is to find out about the important people, places, and events in the history of the empire and to report this information to a group of writers who will create a screenplay. As you read this chapter, look for descriptions of the people, places, and events of the Roman world from the 70s BC to the end of the Eastern Roman Empire.

44 BC
Julius Caesar is assassinated.

CHAPTER EVENTS

27 BC
Augustus becomes Rome's first emperor.

25 BC

WORLD EVENTS

HOLT

History's Impact
▶ video series
Watch the video to understand
the impact of ancient Rome on
the world today.

What You Will Learn...

In this chapter you will learn how Rome became
an empire, how it responded to Christianity,
and how it eventually fell. This photo shows the
Colosseum, an impressive example of ancient
Roman architecture that still influences the
design of stadiums around the world.

c. AD 30
Jesus is
crucified.

AD 312
Emperor Constantine
ends the persecution
of Christians.

AD 476
The last Roman emperor in
the West is overthrown.

AD 1453
The
Byzantine
Empire ends.

BC 1 AD · 250 · 500 · 1450

c. AD 65
Buddhism is
introduced
to China.

AD 250
The Maya
Classic Age
begins in Mexico.

AD 570
Muhammad is born
in Mecca.

ROME AND CHRISTIANITY　**319**

Focus on Themes This chapter describes the development of Rome as it grew from a republic into a strong and vast empire. First, you will learn about the **geographic** expansion of the empire. You will read about powerful leaders such as Julius Caesar, Marc Antony, and Augustus. Finally, you will learn about how the people of the Roman Empire lived and worked. You will read about their many contributions to literature, language, law, and **science and technology**.

Online Research

Focus on Reading Finding information on the World Wide Web can be easy. Just enter a word or two into a search engine and you will instantly find dozens—if not hundreds—of sites full of information.

Evaluating Web Sites However, looking through all those sites can be overwhelming. In addition, not all Web sites have good or accurate information. How do you know which sites are the ones you want? You have to evaluate, or judge, the sites. You can use an evaluation form like the one below to evaluate a Web site.

Evaluating Web-Based Resources

Name of site: _____ Topic of site _____
URL: _____ Date of access: _____

Scroll through the site then answer the questions below.

I. Evaluating the author of the site
   A. Who is the author? What are his or her qualifications?
   B. Is there a way to contact the author?

II. Evaluating the content of the site
   A. Is the site's topic related to the topic you are studying?
   B. Is there enough information at this site to help you?
   C. Is there too much information for you to read or understand?
   D. Does the site include pictures or illustrations to help you understand the information?
   E. Does the site discuss more than one point of view about the topic?
   F. Does the site express the author's opinions rather than facts?
   G. Does the site provide references for any of its information, including quotes?
   H. Are there links to other sites that have valuable information?

III. Evaluating the overall design and quality
   A. Is the site easy to navigate or to find information on?
   B. When was the site last updated?

IV. My overall impression
   A. I think this site has good information that will help me with my research. _____
   B. I think this site either is too hard or too easy or has information I can't verify. _____

You Try It!

The information below is an example of a student's evaluation of a fictional Web site on Julius Caesar. Review the student's answers to the questions on the previous page and then answer the questions at the bottom of the page.

Web Site Evaluation

I. Evaluating the author
    A. Author is listed as Klee O. Patra. She has read many books about Julius Caesar.
    B. No information is listed for contacting the author.

II. Evaluating content of the site
    A. Yes. It is about Julius Caesar.
    B. There appears to be a great deal of information about Julius Caesar.
    C. No, it looks easy to understand.
    D. There are pictures, but most are from movies. There are no maps or historical images.
    E. No.
    F. Yes, it is all about how she loves Caesar.
    G. I can't find any references.
    H. There are two links, but they are both dead.

III. Evaluating overall design and quality
    A. No. It takes a long time to find any specific information. Also, the layout of the page is confusing.
    B. It was last updated in July 1998.

Study the evaluation then answer the following questions.

1. What do you know about the author of this site? Based on the evaluation information, do you think she is qualified to write about Caesar?

2. Does the content of the site seem valuable and reliable? Why?

3. The site has not been updated for many years, but that may not be a major problem for a site about Julius Caesar. Why? When might recent updates be more important?

4. Overall, would you say this site would be helpful? Why or why not?

Key Terms and People

Chapter 11

Section 1
Cicero *(p. 322)*
Julius Caesar *(p. 323)*
Pompey *(p. 323)*
Augustus *(p. 324)*
currency *(p. 326)*
Pax Romana *(p. 326)*
aqueduct *(p. 327)*
Romance languages *(p. 328)*
civil law *(p. 328)*

Section 2
Christianity *(p. 334)*
Jesus of Nazareth *(p. 334)*
Bible *(p. 335)*
crucifixion *(p. 336)*
Resurrection *(p. 336)*
disciples *(p. 336)*
Paul *(p. 337)*
Constantine *(p. 338)*

Section 3
Diocletian *(p. 340)*
Attila *(p. 341)*
corruption *(p. 342)*
Justinian *(p. 342)*
Theodora *(p. 343)*
Byzantine Empire *(p. 343)*

Academic Vocabulary
Success in school is related to knowing academic vocabulary—the words that are frequently used in school assignments and discussions. In this chapter, you will learn the following academic word:

efficient *(p. 342)*

As you read Chapter 11, think about what topics would be interesting to research on the Web. If you do some research on the Web, remember to evaluate the site and its contents.

From Republic to Empire

What You Will Learn...

Main Ideas

1. Disorder in the Roman Republic created an opportunity for Julius Caesar to gain power.
2. The Republic ended when Augustus became Rome's first emperor.
3. The Roman Empire grew to control the entire Mediterranean world.
4. The Romans accomplished great things in science, engineering, architecture, art, literature, and law.

The Big Idea

After changing from a republic to an empire, Rome grew politically and economically, and developed a culture that influenced later civilizations.

Key Terms and People

Cicero, *p. 322*
Julius Caesar, *p. 323*
Pompey, *p. 323*
Marc Antony, *p. 324*
Augustus, *p. 324*
Pax Romana, *p. 326*
aqueduct, *p. 327*
Romance languages, *p. 328*
civil law, *p. 328*

TAKING NOTES As you read, take notes on Rome's change from a republic to an empire and the accomplishments of the empire. Organize your notes in a chart like this one.

Republic to Empire	Accomplishments

If YOU were there...

You are a friend of a famous Roman Senator. Your friend is worried about the growing power of military men in Rome's government. Some other Senators want to take violent action to stop generals from taking over as dictators. Your friend wants your advice: Is violence justified to save the Roman Republic?

What advice will you give your friend?

BUILDING BACKGROUND By the first century BC, the government of the Roman Republic was in trouble. Politicians looked for ways to solve the problems. Philosophers offered ideas, too. In the end, however, the Republic could not survive the great changes that were taking place in Rome.

Disorder in the Republic

Rome in the 70s BC was a dangerous place. Politicians and generals went to war to increase their power even as political order broke down in Rome. There were politically inspired riots to restore the power of the tribunes. All the while, more and more people from throughout the republic flooded into the city, further adding to the confusion.

Calls for Change

Some Romans tried to stop the chaos in Rome's government. One such person was **Cicero** (SIS-uh-roh), a philosopher and gifted orator, or public speaker. In his speeches, Cicero called on upperclass Romans to work together to make Rome a better place. One way to do this, he argued, was to limit the power of generals. Cicero wanted the Romans to give more support to the Senate and to restore checks and balances on government.

But the government did not change. Many Romans didn't agree with Cicero. Others were too busy to listen. Meanwhile, several generals were working to take over the government. The most powerful of these generals was **Julius Caesar** (JOOL-yuhs SEE-zuhr).

Caesar's Rise to Power

Caesar was a great general. Romans admired him for his bravery and skill in battle. His soldiers respected him for treating them well. Between 58 BC and 50 BC Caesar conquered nearly all of Gaul—an area that is today the country of France. He wrote about this conquest in great detail. In this description of one battle, notice how he refers to himself as Caesar:

> " Caesar, having divided his forces … and having hastily [quickly] constructed some bridges, enters their country in three divisions, burns their houses and villages, and gets possession of a large number of cattle and men. "
>
> —Julius Caesar, *The Gallic Wars*

Caesar's military successes made him a key figure in Roman politics. In addition to being a strong leader, Caesar was an excellent speaker. He won many supporters with his speeches in the forum.

Caesar also had powerful friends. Before he went to Gaul, he made an alliance with two of Rome's most influential men, **Pompey** (PAHM-pea) and Crassus (KRAS-uhs). Together the three ruled Rome.

Challenges to Caesar

The partnership lasted about 10 years. But after his conquests in Gaul, Caesar was so popular that even his friends were jealous of him. In 50 BC Pompey's allies in the Senate ordered Caesar to give up command of his armies. They wanted Pompey to control Rome alone.

Caesar refused. Instead he led his troops back toward Rome for a confrontation. Once his men crossed the Rubicon River, the boundary between Gaul and Italy, Caesar knew that there was no turning back.

THE IMPACT TODAY

People now use the phrase "crossing the Rubicon" when they do something that can't be undone.

Julius Caesar conquered Gaul and added it to the empire. This painting from the late 1800s shows a Frankish leader surrendering to Caesar by dropping his weapons at Caesar's feet.

War was certain since Roman law said no general could enter Italy with his army.

Pompey and his allies fled Italy. They didn't think they had enough troops to defeat Caesar. But Caesar's army chased Pompey's forces for a year. They finally defeated Pompey in Greece in 48 BC. Pompey was killed by orders of an Egyptian king.

After Caesar returned to Rome in 45 BC, he made himself dictator for life. Although Caesar worked to improve Roman society, many people resented the way he gained power. They were also concerned that Caesar wanted to become king of Rome.

The Senators were especially angry with Caesar. He had reduced their powers, and they feared his growing strength. On March 15—a date known as the Ides of March—in 44 BC a group of Senators attacked Caesar in the Senate and stabbed him to death.

READING CHECK Sequencing How did Caesar gain power in Rome?

The End of the Republic

After Caesar's assassination, two great leaders emerged to take control of Roman politics. One was Caesar's former assistant, **Marc Antony**. The other was Caesar's adopted son Octavian (ahk-TAY-vee-uhn), later called **Augustus** (aw-GUHS-tuhs).

Antony and Octavian

One priority for Antony and Octavian was punishing the men who killed Caesar. The murderers had thought they would become heroes. Instead they were forced to flee for their lives. Rome was shocked by Caesar's murder. Many people loved Caesar, and riots broke out after his death. In order to end the chaos that followed Caesar's assassination, the Senate had to act quickly to restore order.

At Caesar's funeral, Antony delivered a famous speech that turned even more Romans against the killers. Shortly afterward, he and Octavian set out with an army to try to avenge Caesar's death.

Their army caught up to the killers near Philippi (FI-luh-py) in northern Greece. In 42 BC Antony and Octavian soundly defeated their opponents. After the battle, the last of Caesar's murderers killed themselves.

Octavian Becomes Emperor

After the Battle of Philippi, Octavian returned to Italy. Antony went east to fight Rome's enemies. In 40 BC Antony married Octavian's sister, Octavia. Eight years later, however, he divorced her to marry Cleopatra, the queen of Egypt. Octavian saw this divorce as an insult to his sister and to himself.

Antony's behavior led to civil war in Rome. In 31 BC Octavian sent a fleet to attack Antony. Antony sailed out to meet it, and the two forces met just west of Greece in the Battle of Actium (AK-shee-uhm). Antony's fleet was defeated, but he escaped back to Egypt with Cleopatra. There the two committed suicide so they wouldn't be taken prisoner by Octavian.

Octavian then became Rome's sole ruler. Over the next few years he gained nearly limitless power. He took the title *princeps* (PRIN-seps), or first citizen.

In 27 BC Octavian announced that he was giving up his power to the Senate, but, in reality, he kept all his power. The Senate gave him a new name—Augustus, which means "revered one." Modern historians consider the naming of Augustus to mark the end of the Roman Republic and the beginning of the Roman Empire.

READING CHECK Summarizing How did the Roman Republic become an empire?

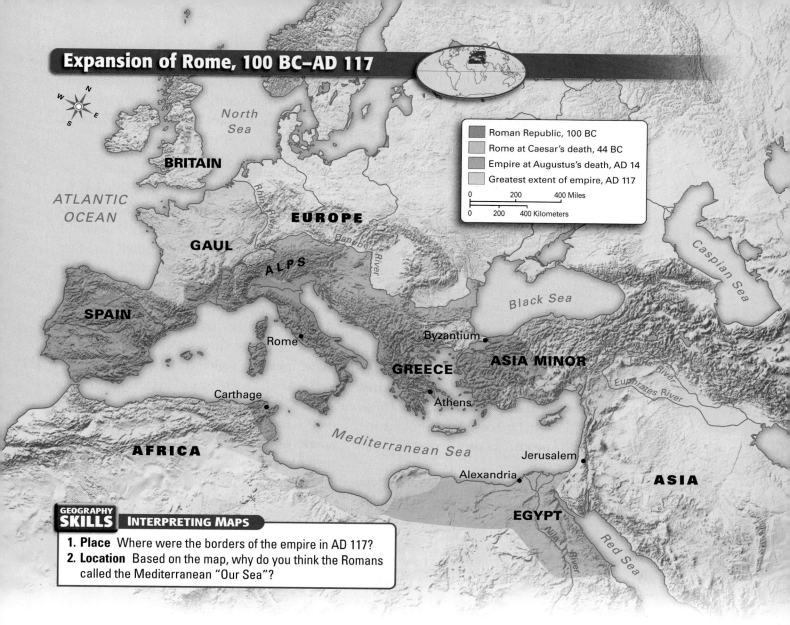

Expansion of Rome, 100 BC–AD 117

Legend:
- Roman Republic, 100 BC
- Rome at Caesar's death, 44 BC
- Empire at Augustus's death, AD 14
- Greatest extent of empire, AD 117

0   200   400 Miles
0   200   400 Kilometers

North Sea

BRITAIN

ATLANTIC OCEAN

EUROPE

GAUL

ALPS

Rhine River

Danube River

SPAIN

Rome

Carthage

GREECE

Athens

Byzantium

ASIA MINOR

Black Sea

Caspian Sea

Euphrates River

Tigris River

AFRICA

Mediterranean Sea

Jerusalem

Alexandria

ASIA

EGYPT

Nile River

Red Sea

GEOGRAPHY SKILLS | **INTERPRETING MAPS**

1. **Place** Where were the borders of the empire in AD 117?
2. **Location** Based on the map, why do you think the Romans called the Mediterranean "Our Sea"?

Rome's Growing Empire

When Rome became an empire, it already controlled most of the Mediterranean world. Augustus and the emperors who followed him further expanded the empire. Some emperors conquered territories to control hostile neighbors. Other Roman leaders wanted to gain control of gold, farmland, and other resources.

By the early AD 100s the Romans had taken over Gaul and much of central Europe. Under the emperor Claudius, the Romans conquered most of the island of Britain. Rome also controlled Asia Minor, Mesopotamia, and the eastern coast of the Mediterranean. All of the north African coast belonged to Rome as well.

The Roman conquests promoted trade. People in Rome needed raw materials that were lacking in Italy. Many of the materials, though, could be found in Rome's provinces, the outlying areas that the Romans controlled. Traders brought metals, cloth, and food from the provinces to the city. They also brought more exotic goods, like spices and silk from Asia and animals from Africa. In return, the Romans sent goods made by artisans to the provinces. These goods included jewelry, glass, and clothing.

To pay for their trade goods, Romans used currency, or money. They traded coins made of gold and silver for the items they wanted. These coins allowed the Romans to trade with people even if they had no items their trade partners wanted. Nearly everyone accepted Roman coins, which helped trade grow even more.

The first 200 years of the Roman Empire was a time of general peace and prosperity. Stable government and a well-run army helped Rome grow wealthy in safety. There were no major wars or rebellions in the empire. We call this peaceful period the **Pax Romana**, or Roman peace. It lasted until the AD 180s.

During the Pax Romana, the empire's population grew. Trade increased, making many Romans wealthy. As a result of these changes, the quality of life improved for people in Rome and its provinces.

READING CHECK Identifying Cause and Effect
How did Rome's territorial expansion affect trade?

Rome's Accomplishments

The Romans made lasting achievements in science, engineering, architecture, and art. In addition, Rome's literary tradition and legal system remain influential today.

Science and Engineering

The Romans took a practical approach to their study of science and engineering. Roman scientists wanted results that could benefit their society. They studied the stars to produce a calendar. They studied plants and animals to learn how to obtain better crops and meat.

To improve health, Roman doctors studied the works of the Greeks. One great doctor in the empire was Galen (GAY-luhn), who lived in the AD 100s. He was a Greek surgeon who studied the body. Galen described the valves of the heart and noted differences between arteries and veins. For centuries doctors based their ideas on Galen's teachings.

The Romans' practical use of science also can be seen in their engineering. The

The Roman Arch

The Romans were the first people to make wide use of the arch. The photograph at right shows a Roman aqueduct supported by hundreds of arches. Below is a drawing showing how Roman engineers built their tall and strong arches.

How did the Romans support arches during their construction?

Romans were great builders. They developed new materials to help their structures last. For example, the Romans made cement by mixing a mineral called lime with volcanic rock and ash. The resulting material dried to be very hard and watertight.

More important than the materials they used, though, were the designs the Romans had for their structures. They built their roads in layers. Each layer was made of a different material. This layered construction made the road highly durable. Many Roman roads have not worn down even after centuries of traffic.

The Romans also created lasting structures by using arches. Because of its rounded shape, an arch can support much more weight than other shapes can. This strength has allowed many arched Roman bridges to last until the present.

The Romans also used arches in their aqueducts (A-kwuh-duhkts). An **aqueduct** is a raised channel used to carry water from mountains into cities. Because they crossed deep valleys, Roman aqueducts needed to be strong. Many still stand today.

Roman builders also learned how to combine arches to create vaults. A vault is a set of arches that supports the roof of a building. The Romans used vaults to create huge, open areas within buildings.

Architecture and Art

The Romans weren't interested only in practicality. They also admired beauty. This appreciation can be seen in the new designs of architecture and art that they created.

Roman architecture also copied some older Greek designs. For example, the Romans used columns to make their public buildings look impressive. The Romans also copied the Greeks by covering many of their buildings with marble.

Their engineering techniques allowed the Romans to make new architectural advances. The vault, for example, let them build huge structures, much larger than anything the Greeks could build. One such structure was the Colosseum in Rome—a huge building constructed for gladiator fights. Many other Roman structures are topped with domes.

Roman artists were known for their beautiful mosaics, paintings, and statues. Mosaics and paintings were used to decorate Roman buildings. Most Roman paintings were frescoes. A fresco is a type of painting done on plaster. Many Roman painters were particularly skilled at creating portraits, or pictures of people. Roman sculptors were also very talented. They studied what the Greeks had done and tried to re-create this brilliance in their own statues.

Literature and Language

Rich in art and architecture, Rome was also home to many of the greatest authors in the ancient world. One such author was Virgil, who wrote a great epic about the founding of Rome, the *Aeneid* (ih-NEE-uhd). Another was Ovid (AHV-uhd), who wrote poems about Roman mythology.

THE IMPACT TODAY

People still build aqueducts today. One of the largest carries water from northern to southern California.

FOCUS ON READING

What key words would you use to search for Web information on a subject discussed in this paragraph?

In addition, Roman writers produced histories, speeches, and dramas that are still studied and enjoyed today.

Virgil, Ovid, and other poets wrote in Latin, the language of government and law. People throughout the Roman world wrote, conducted business, and kept records in Latin. In the eastern half of the empire, Greek was just as important.

Latin later developed into many different languages. These languages are called **Romance languages**. They include Italian, French, Spanish, Portuguese, and Romanian.

Latin also influenced other languages. Many non-Romance languages, including English, contain Latin words. Words like *et cetera, circus,* and *veto* were all originally Latin terms. Latin words are also common in scientific terms and mottoes.

Law

Rome's greatest influence may have been in the field of law. Roman law was enforced across much of Europe. Even after the empire fell, Roman laws continued to exist in the kingdoms that followed.

Over time, Roman law inspired a system called civil law. **Civil law** is a legal system based on a written code of laws, like the one created by the Romans.

Most countries in Europe today have civil law traditions. In the 1500s and 1600s, colonists from some of these countries carried civil law around the world. As a result, many countries in Africa, Asia, and the Americas developed law codes as well.

READING CHECK Finding the Main Idea
How did Roman literature and language influence later societies?

SUMMARY AND PREVIEW Augustus made the Roman Republic into an empire. The empire grew during its first 200 years, and the Romans made many lasting contributions to the world. In the next section, you will learn about an influential development that changed life in Rome—Christianity.

go.hrw.com
Online Quiz
KEYWORD: SN6 HP11

Section 1 Assessment

Reviewing Ideas, Terms, and People

1. **a. Recall** To whom did **Cicero** want to give power?
   b. Making Inferences Why did many Senators consider **Julius Caesar** a threat?
   c. Evaluate What role did the military play in Caesar's rise to power?
2. **a. Identify** Who took over Rome after Caesar's death?
   b. Summarize How did Octavian take power from **Marc Antony**?
   c. Evaluate Why is it significant that Octavian did not take the title of dictator?
3. **a. Identify** What areas of the world did the Romans take over?
   b. Elaborate Why did trade increase during the **Pax Romana**?
4. **a. Recall** What type of law is based on the Roman law code?
   b. Draw Conclusions Latin is no longer spoken. Why do you think people still study it?

Critical Thinking

5. **Analyzing** Review your notes on Rome's accomplishments. Describe how the effects of one Roman accomplishment in each of the fields below is being felt today.

Engineering	
Language	
Law	
Literature	

FOCUS ON WRITING

6. **Taking Notes for a Screenplay** In your notebook, create a three-columned chart labeled "Characters," "Setting," and "Plot." Under the columns, write notes about the people and events from this section that you think would make good material for a movie.

Augustus

What would you do if you had great power?

When did he live? 63 BC–AD 14

Where did he live? Rome

What did he do? As the leader of Rome, Augustus made many improvements in the city. He created a fire department and a police force to protect the city's people. He built new aqueducts and repaired old ones to increase Rome's water supply. Augustus also worked on improving and expanding Rome's road network.

Why is he important? As Rome's first emperor, Augustus is one of the most significant figures in Roman history. Almost singlehandedly, he changed the nature of Roman government forever. But Augustus is also known for the great monuments he had built around Rome. He built a new forum that held statues, monuments, and a great temple to the god Mars. In writing about his life, Augustus declared, "I found Rome a city of brick and left it a city of marble."

Identifying Points of View Why do you think many Romans greatly admired Augustus?

Augustus was responsible for the construction of many impressive buildings in Rome.

KEY EVENTS

45 BC Julius Caesar adopts Octavian as his son and heir.

44 BC Octavian moves to Rome when Caesar dies.

42 BC Octavian and Antony defeat Brutus.

31 BC Octavian defeats Antony.

27 BC Octavian takes the name Augustus and becomes emperor of Rome.

Roman Roads

The Romans are famous for their roads. They built a road network so large and well constructed that parts of it remain today, roughly 2,000 years later. Roads helped the Romans run their empire. Armies, travelers, messengers, and merchants all used the roads to get around. They stretched to every corner of the empire in a network so vast that people even today say that "all roads lead to Rome."

Roman roads stretched as far north as Scotland.

The Romans built about 50,000 miles of roads. That's enough to circle the earth—twice!

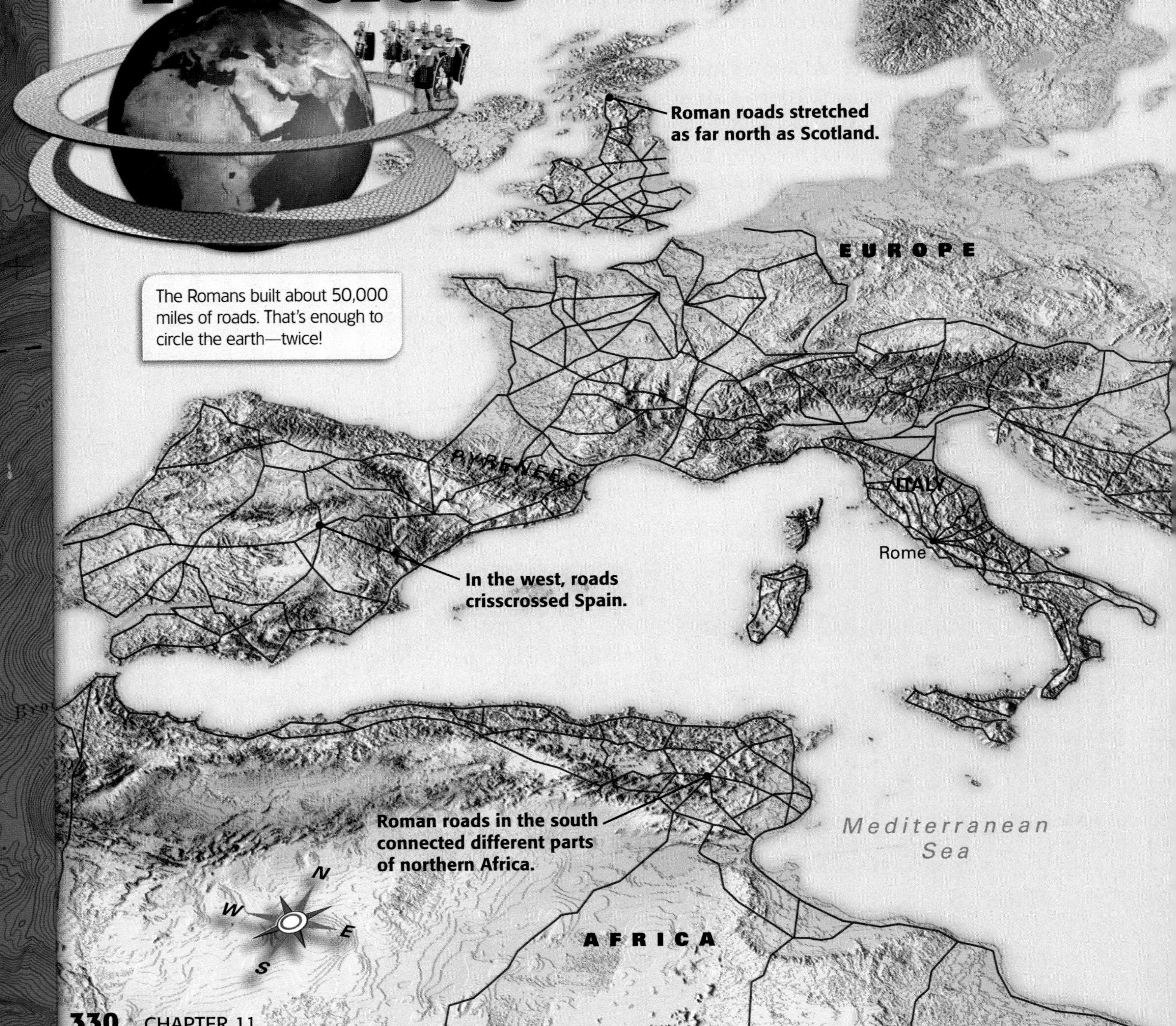

EUROPE

PYRENEES

ITALY

Rome

In the west, roads crisscrossed Spain.

Roman roads in the south connected different parts of northern Africa.

Mediterranean Sea

N

W   E

S

AFRICA

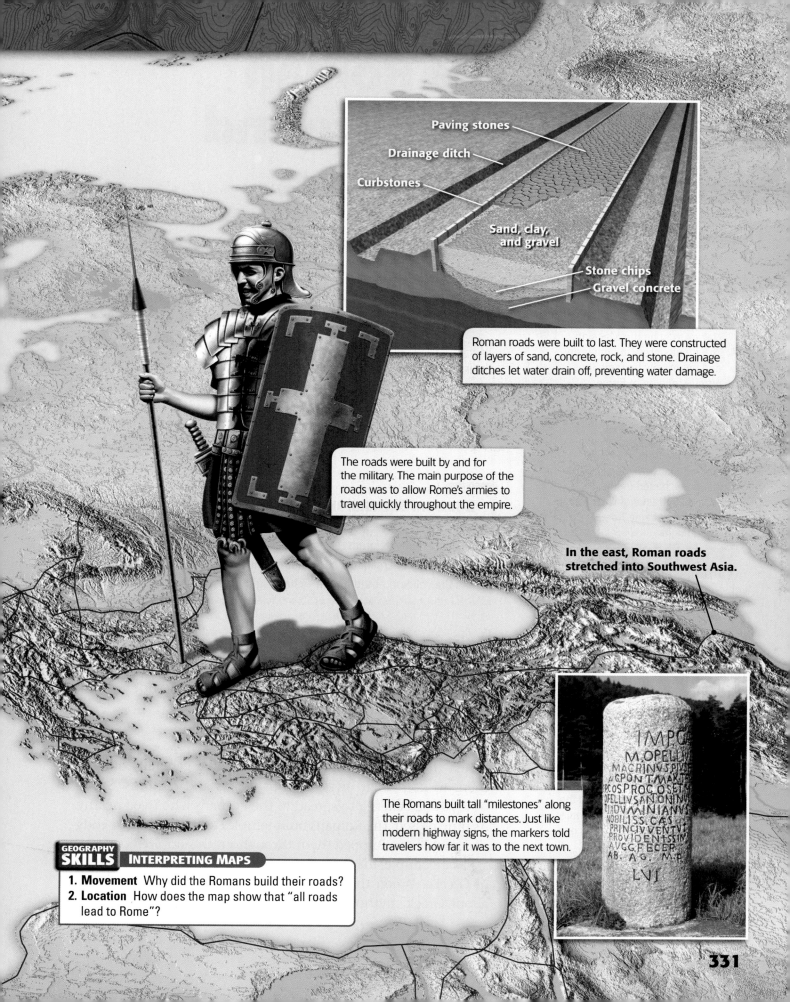

Paving stones

Drainage ditch

Curbstones

Sand, clay, and gravel

Stone chips

Gravel concrete

Roman roads were built to last. They were constructed of layers of sand, concrete, rock, and stone. Drainage ditches let water drain off, preventing water damage.

The roads were built by and for the military. The main purpose of the roads was to allow Rome's armies to travel quickly throughout the empire.

In the east, Roman roads stretched into Southwest Asia.

The Romans built tall "milestones" along their roads to mark distances. Just like modern highway signs, the markers told travelers how far it was to the next town.

IMP.C
M.OPELLI
MACRINVSPIV
AVG.PONT.MAXT
PCOSPROC OSET
OPELLIVSANTONINVS
DIADVMINIANVS
NOBILISS.CÆS
PRINCIVVENTVT
PROVIDENTISSIM
AVGG.FECER
AB. AG. M.P
LVI

GEOGRAPHY SKILLS | **INTERPRETING MAPS**

1. **Movement** Why did the Romans build their roads?
2. **Location** How does the map show that "all roads lead to Rome"?

The Roman Empire and Religion

What You Will Learn...

Main Ideas

1. Despite its general religious tolerance, Rome came into conflict with the Jews.
2. A new religion, Christianity, grew out of Judaism.
3. Many considered Jesus of Nazareth to be the Messiah.
4. Christianity grew in popularity and eventually became the official religion of Rome.

The Big Idea

People in the Roman Empire practiced many religions before Christianity, based on the teachings of Jesus of Nazareth, spread and became Rome's official religion.

Key Terms and People

Christianity, *p. 334*
Jesus of Nazareth, *p. 334*
Messiah, *p. 334*
crucifixion, *p. 336*
Resurrection, *p. 336*
Apostles, *p. 337*
Paul of Tarsus, *p. 337*
Constantine, *p. 338*

TAKING NOTES As you read, take notes on the religious practices in Rome, Jesus's teachings, and the early history of Christianity. Organize your notes in a diagram like this one.

Religion in Rome	Jesus's Teachings	Early Christianity

If YOU were there...

You are a Roman soldier stationed in one of the empire's provinces. You are proud that you've helped bring Roman culture to this place far from the city of Rome. But one group of local people refuses to take part in official Roman holidays and rituals, saying it is against their religious beliefs. Other than that, they seem peaceful. Even so, some soldiers think this group is dangerous.

What will you do about this group?

BUILDING BACKGROUND As the Roman Empire expanded, it came to include many people who spoke many different languages and followed many different religions. While Roman officials were generally tolerant of local religions and cultures, they did not allow anything—like the religion noted above—that might threaten their authority.

Religious Tolerance and Conflict

The Romans were a very religious people. They held many festivals in honor of their gods. However, they did not insist on imposing their beliefs on others.

Freedom of Worship

When the Romans conquered people, they generally allowed them to keep their own religious beliefs and customs. Sometimes these beliefs also spread to the Romans who lived nearby. As time passed, the Romans built temples to these adopted gods, and people worshipped them throughout the empire.

For example, many Romans worshipped the Olympian gods of Greece. When the Romans conquered Greece, they learned about Greek mythology. Before long, the Greek gods became the main gods of Rome as well, although they were known by different names. In the same way, many Romans also adopted gods and beliefs from the Egyptians, Gauls, and Persians.

In their religious lives, the Romans were very practical. They were not sure which gods did or did not exist. To avoid offending any gods, the Romans prayed to a wide variety of gods and goddesses.

The only time the Romans banned a religion was when the rulers of Rome considered it a political problem. In these cases, government officials took steps to prevent problems. Sometimes they placed restrictions on when and where members of a religion could meet. Judaism was one religion that some Roman leaders came to consider a political problem.

Clashes with the Jews

Unlike the Romans, the Jews did not worship many gods. They believed that their God was the only god. Some Romans thought the Jews insulted Rome's gods by not praying to them.

Still, the Romans did not attempt to ban Judaism in the empire. They allowed the Jews to keep their religion and practice it as they pleased. The Jews, however, created political conflict by rebelling against Roman rule. Judea, the territory in which most Jews lived, had been conquered by Rome in 63 BC. Since then, many Jews had resented Roman rule. They did not want to answer to outsiders. As a result, the Jews rebelled against the Romans in AD 66–70. There were other disturbances as well, but each time the Jews were defeated.

The Romans built many temples to honor their many gods. Temples built to honor all the gods were called pantheons, and the most famous of these is the Pantheon in Rome, first built in the 20s BC. Its huge dome awes visitors even today.

The Roman general Titus captured Jerusalem in AD 70. To celebrate this victory, the Romans built this arch that shows Roman soldiers carrying a stolen menorah from Jerusalem's holy Second Temple.

A New Religion

At the beginning of the first century AD, what would become a new religion appeared in Judea. Called **Christianity**, this religion was based on the life and teachings of **Jesus of Nazareth**. Christianity was rooted in the ideas and traditions of Judaism, but it developed as a separate faith.

At the time that Jesus was born, around the end of the first century BC, there were several groups of Jews in Judea. The largest of these groups was very strict in how it practiced Judaism. Members of this group were particularly careful about obeying the laws of Moses, whom you read about in Chapter 7. Jews believe that Moses gave them a set of laws to follow.

As a result of their rigid obedience to the laws, Jews led very structured lives. For example, they performed daily rituals and avoided eating certain foods.

Many Jews followed the laws closely because Jewish prophets had said a new leader would appear among them. Many thought this leader was more likely to appear if they were strict in their religious behavior.

According to the prophecy, the Jews' new leader would be a descendent of King David. When he came, he would restore the greatness of King David's ancient kingdom, Israel. The prophets called this leader the **Messiah** (muh-SY-uh), which means "God's anointed one" in Hebrew. In other words, the Jews believed that God would choose the Messiah that would lead them.

When the Romans took over Judea in 63 BC, many Jews believed that the Messiah would soon appear. Jewish prophets wandered through Judea, announcing that the Messiah was coming. Many Jews anxiously awaited his arrival.

By the early 100s the Romans had become more hostile toward the Jews. Treated harshly and taxed heavily, the Jews grew increasingly bitter. Matters worsened when the emperor Hadrian banned the practice of certain Jewish rituals. He thought this ban would end the Jewish people's desire for independence and cause them to give up Judaism.

Instead Hadrian's actions made the Jews even more upset. Once again they rebelled. This time, Hadrian decided to end the rebellions once and for all.

The Roman army crushed the Jewish revolt, destroyed Jerusalem, and forced the Jews to leave the city. Then the Romans built a new city on the ruins of Jerusalem and brought settlers from other parts of the empire to live there. Jews were forbidden to enter this new city more than once a year. Forced out of their ancient city, many Jews moved into other parts of the Roman world.

READING CHECK Drawing Conclusions
Why did the Romans consider Judaism a threat?

READING CHECK Summarizing Why were Jews waiting for the Messiah to arrive?

Jesus of Nazareth

Jesus of Nazareth, the man many people believe was the Jewish Messiah, lived at the very beginning of the first century AD. Although Jesus was one of the most influential figures in all of world history, we know relatively little about his life. Most of what we know is contained in the Bible, the holy book of the religion of Christianity.

The Christian Bible is made up of two parts. The first part, the Old Testament, is largely the same as the Hebrew Bible. It tells the history and ideas of the Hebrew and Jewish people. The second part, the New Testament, is sacred to Christians. The New Testament is an account of the life and teachings of Jesus and the early history of Christianity. The New Testament also contains letters written by some followers of Jesus.

The Birth of Jesus

According to the Bible, Jesus was born in a town called Bethlehem (BETH-li-hem) at the end of the first century BC. In our dating system, his birth marks the shift from BC to AD. Jesus's mother, Mary, was married to a carpenter named Joseph. But Christians believe God, not Joseph, was Jesus's father.

As a young man, Jesus lived in the town of Nazareth and probably studied with Joseph to become a carpenter. Like most young Jewish men of the time, he also studied the laws and teachings of Judaism. By the time he was about 30, Jesus had begun to travel and teach about religion. Stories of his teachings and actions make up the beginning of the Bible's New Testament. According to the Bible, Jesus created excitement wherever he went.

LINKING TO TODAY

Christian Holidays

For centuries, Christians have honored key events in Jesus's life. Some of these events inspired holidays that Christians celebrate today.

The most sacred holiday for Christians is Easter, which is celebrated each spring. Easter is a celebration of the Resurrection, Jesus's rising from the dead. Christians usually celebrate Easter by attending church services. Many people also celebrate by dyeing eggs because eggs are seen as a symbol of new life.

Another major Christian holiday is Christmas. It honors Jesus's birth and is celebrated every December 25. Although no one knows on what date Jesus was actually born, Christians have placed Christmas in December since the 200s. Today, people celebrate with church services and the exchange of gifts. Some, like people in the picture at right, reenact scenes of Jesus's birth.

ANALYSIS SKILL **ANALYZING INFORMATION**

Why do you think Christians celebrate events in Jesus's life?

Crucifixion and Resurrection

As a teacher, Jesus attracted many followers. As he traveled the Judean countryside, he greatly influenced many who listened to his message. But at the same time, his teachings challenged the authority of political and religious leaders. According to the Bible, Roman leaders arrested Jesus while he was in Jerusalem in or around AD 30.

THE IMPACT TODAY

Because Jesus was crucified, the cross is an important symbol of Christianity today.

Shortly after his arrest, Jesus was executed. He was killed by **crucifixion** (kroo-suh-FIK-shuhn), a type of execution in which a person was nailed to a cross. In fact, the word crucifixion comes from the Latin word for "cross." After Jesus died, his followers buried him.

According to Christian beliefs, Jesus rose from the dead three days after he was crucified. Christians refer to Jesus's rise from the dead as the **Resurrection** (re-suh-REK-shuhn). After the Resurrection, several groups of Jesus's disciples (di-SY-puhls), or followers, claimed to see him again.

Early Christians believe that the Resurrection was a sign that Jesus was the Messiah and the son of God. Some people began to call him Jesus Christ, from the Greek word for Messiah, *Christos*. It is from this word that the words *Christian* and *Christianity* later developed.

The Teachings of Jesus

Jesus had traveled from village to village spreading his message to the Jewish people. Much of Jesus's message was rooted in older Jewish traditions. For example, he emphasized two rules that were also taught in the Torah: love God, and love other people.

Jesus expected his followers to love all people, not just friends or family. He encouraged his followers to be generous to the poor and the sick. He told people that they should even love their enemies. The way people treated others, Jesus said, showed how much they loved God.

Another important theme in Jesus's teachings was salvation, or the rescue of people from sin. Jesus taught that people who were saved from sin would enter the kingdom of God when they died. Many of Jesus's teachings dealt with how people could reach the kingdom. Jesus warned that people who loved money or goods more than they loved God would not be saved.

Over the many centuries since Jesus lived, people have interpreted his teachings in different ways. As a result, many different denominations of Christians have developed. A denomination is a group of people who hold the same religous beliefs. Still, despite their differences, Christians around

The Last Supper

1. Bartholomew
2. James, the Less
3. Andrew
4. Judas
5. Peter
6. John
7. Jesus
8. Thomas
9. James
10. Philip
11. Matthew
12. Thaddeus
13. Simon

This famous painting by Italian artist Leonardo da Vinci shows the Last Supper—the final meal that Jesus and his Apostles shared before Jesus was arrested.

LETTER

Paul's Letter to the Romans

In the late AD 50s Paul traveled to Corinth, a city in Greece. While there, he wrote a letter to the people of Rome. In this letter he told the Romans that he planned to come to their city to deliver God's message. In the meantime, he told them, they should learn to live together peacefully.

"Let love be genuine; hate what is evil, hold fast to what is good; love one another with mutual affection; outdo one another in showing honor. Do not lag in zeal, be ardent [strong] in spirit, serve the Lord. Rejoice in hope, be patient in suffering, persevere in prayer. Contribute to the needs of the saints; extend hospitality to strangers.

Bless those who persecute you; bless and do not curse them. Rejoice with those who rejoice, weep with those who weep. Live in harmony with one another; do not be haughty, but associate with the lowly; do not claim to be wiser than you are. Do not repay anyone evil for evil, but take thought for what is noble in the sight of all. If it is possible, so far as it depends on you, live peaceably with all.**"**

—**Romans 12:9–18 NRSV**

ANALYSIS SKILL **ANALYZING PRIMARY SOURCES**

How did Paul's letter express Jesus's teachings?

---

the world share some basic beliefs about Jesus and his importance.

The Spread of Jesus's Teachings

The **Apostles** (uh-PAHS-uhls) were 12 disciples whom Jesus chose to receive special training. After the Resurrection, the Apostles traveled widely telling about Jesus and his teachings. Some of Jesus's disciples wrote accounts of his life and teachings. These accounts are called the Gospels. Four Gospels are found in the New Testament of the Bible. They were written by men known as Matthew, Mark, Luke, and John. Historians and religious scholars depend on the Gospels for information about Jesus's life.

Probably the most important figure in the spread of Christianity after Jesus's death was named **Paul of Tarsus**. Paul traveled throughout the Roman world spreading Christian teachings. In his letters he wrote about the Resurrection and about salvation. Paul also told Christians that they didn't have to obey all Jewish laws

and rituals. These ideas helped the Christian Church break away from Judaism.

READING CHECK **Summarizing** What do Christians believe happened after Jesus died?

The Growth of Christianity

Early Christians spread Jesus's teachings only among Jews. But Paul and other Christians introduced Christianity to non-Jews as well. As a result, Christianity began to spread rapidly. Within a hundred years after Jesus's death, thousands of Christians lived in the Roman Empire.

However, Christians trying to spread their beliefs faced challenges from local officials. Some officials even arrested and killed Christians who refused to worship Rome's gods. A few Roman emperors feared that Christians would cause unrest, so they banned Christianity. This began a period of persecution (puhr-si-KYOO-shuhn) against Christians. Persecution is the punishment of a group because of its beliefs.

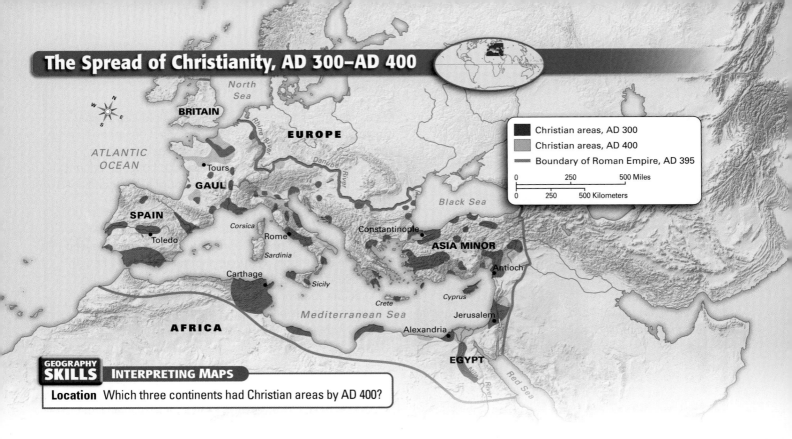

The Spread of Christianity, AD 300–AD 400

North Sea
BRITAIN
EUROPE
ATLANTIC OCEAN
Tours
GAUL
Rhine River
Danube River
SPAIN
Corsica
Rome
Toledo
Sardinia
Carthage
Sicily
AFRICA
Crete
Mediterranean Sea
Alexandria
EGYPT
Nile River
Red Sea
Black Sea
Constantinople
ASIA MINOR
Antioch
Cyprus
Jerusalem

Legend:
- Christian areas, AD 300
- Christian areas, AD 400
- Boundary of Roman Empire, AD 395

0   250   500 Miles
0   250   500 Kilometers

GEOGRAPHY SKILLS **INTERPRETING MAPS**

Location Which three continents had Christian areas by AD 400?

Christians began to meet in secret but continued to spread their faith. In the early 300s, the emperor **Constantine** (KAHN-stuhn-teen) became a Christian. He removed the bans on the religion. A later emperor made Christianity Rome's official religion.

READING CHECK **Identifying Cause and Effect** How did Paul's ideas help to spread Christianity?

SUMMARY AND PREVIEW Although usually tolerant, Roman authorities persecuted Jews and Christians in the empire. However, both Judaism and Christianity survived. In fact, Christianity eventually became the empire's official religion. Next, you will read about the fall of Rome.

Section 2 Assessment

Reviewing Ideas, Terms, and People

1. **a. Recall** Why did Roman leaders ban some religions?
   b. Explain What was one religion that Roman leaders considered a problem? Why?
2. **a. Describe** What traditions were practiced by the Jews of Judea?
   b. Explain Describe Jewish beliefs about the **Messiah**.
3. **a. Identify** From where does most of the information about **Jesus of Nazareth** come?
   b. Analyze How did the teachings of **Paul of Tarsus** change Christianity's relationship to Judaism?
4. **a. Summarize** What challenges did early Christians face in practicing and spreading their religion?
   b. Elaborate How did **Constantine** affect Christianity?

Critical Thinking

5. **Summarizing** Using your notes and a chart like the one below, identify the main teachings of Christianity. Then describe its spread and how Rome's policy toward it changed over time.

Christian Teachings → Spread → Changes in Rome's Policy

FOCUS ON WRITING

6. **Adding Details** Write down some notes and add details to your columns about what life might have been like for Jews and Christians in this period.

The End of the Empire

If YOU were there...

You are a former Roman soldier who has settled on lands in Gaul. In the last few months, groups of foreigners have been raiding local towns and burning farms. The commander of the local army post is an old friend, but he says he is short of loyal soldiers. Many troops have been called back to Rome. You don't know when the next raid will come.

How will you defend your lands?

> **BUILDING BACKGROUND** Though the Roman Empire remained large and powerful, it faced serious threats from both outside and inside. Beyond the borders of the empire, many different groups of people were on the move. They threatened the peace in the provinces—and eventually attacked the heart of the empire itself.

Problems in the Empire

At its height the Roman Empire included all the land around the Mediterranean Sea. In the early AD 100s, the empire stretched from Britain south to Egypt, and from the Atlantic Ocean all the way to the Syrian Desert.

But the empire did not stay that large for long. By the end of the 200s, emperors had given up some of the land the Roman army had conquered. These emperors feared that the empire had become too large to defend or govern efficiently. As later rulers discovered, these emperors were right.

External and Internal Threats

Even as emperors were giving up territory, new threats to the empire were appearing. Tribes of fierce Germanic warriors attacked Rome's northern borders. At the same time, Persian armies invaded in the east. The Romans defended themselves from these invasions for 200 years, but only at great cost.

What You Will Learn...

Main Ideas

1. Many problems threatened the Roman Empire, leading one emperor to divide it in half.
2. Rome declined as a result of invasions and political and economic problems.
3. In the eastern empire, people created a new society and religious traditions that were very different from those in the west.

The Big Idea

Problems from both inside and outside caused the Roman Empire to split into a western half, which collapsed, and an eastern half that prospered for hundreds of years.

Key Terms and People

Diocletian, *p. 340*
Attila, *p. 341*
corruption, *p. 342*
Justinian, *p. 342*
Theodora, *p. 343*
Byzantine Empire, *p. 343*

TAKING NOTES As you read, take notes on the Western Roman Empire and the Eastern Roman Empire. Write your notes in a table like this one.

Western Empire	Eastern Empire

The Romans struggled with problems within the empire as well. The raids against Rome made people near the border nervous. In time, these people abandoned their land. To grow enough food, the Romans invited Germanic farmers to grow crops on Roman lands. These farmers often came from the same tribes that threatened Rome's borders. Over time, whole German communities had moved into the empire. They chose their own leaders and largely ignored the emperors. This caused problems for the Romans.

THE IMPACT TODAY

Constantinople is now called Istanbul, and is a major urban center.

Other internal problems also threatened Rome's survival. Disease swept through the empire, killing many people. The government was also forced to increase taxes to pay for the defense of the empire. Desperate, the Romans looked for a strong emperor. They found one in Diocletian.

Division of the Empire

Diocletian (dy-uh-KLEE-shuhn) became emperor in the late 200s. Convinced that the empire was too big for one person to rule, Diocletian ruled the eastern half and named a co-emperor to rule the west.

Not long after Diocletian left power, the emperor Constantine (KAHN-stuhn-teen) reunited the empire for a short time. He also moved the capital to the east, into what is now Turkey. He built a grand new capital city there. It was called Constantinople (kahn-stant-uhn-OH-puhl), which means "the city of Constantine." Although the empire was still called the Roman Empire, Rome was no longer the real center of power. Power had moved to the east.

READING CHECK **Identifying Cause and Effect** Why did Diocletian divide the Roman Empire?

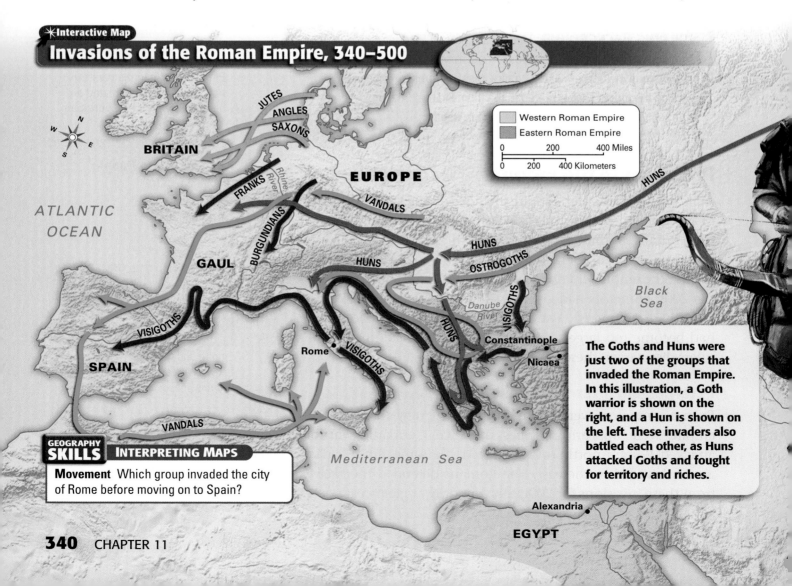

Interactive Map

Invasions of the Roman Empire, 340–500

Western Roman Empire
Eastern Roman Empire

0   200   400 Miles
0   200   400 Kilometers

JUTES
ANGLES
SAXONS
BRITAIN
FRANKS
Rhine River
EUROPE
VANDALS
HUNS
ATLANTIC OCEAN
BURGUNDIANS
GAUL
HUNS
HUNS
OSTROGOTHS
Danube River
VISIGOTHS
Black Sea
VISIGOTHS
Rome
VISIGOTHS
HUNS
Constantinople
Nicaea
SPAIN
VANDALS
Mediterranean Sea
Alexandria
EGYPT

The Goths and Huns were just two of the groups that invaded the Roman Empire. In this illustration, a Goth warrior is shown on the right, and a Hun is shown on the left. These invaders also battled each other, as Huns attacked Goths and fought for territory and riches.

GEOGRAPHY SKILLS **INTERPRETING MAPS**

Movement Which group invaded the city of Rome before moving on to Spain?

The Decline of Rome

As you have read, foreign tribes had settled along the Roman Empire's northern border in the 200s. A century later, these bands of fighters began raiding deep into the heart of the empire.

Early Invasions

The source of these raids was a group of people called the Huns, fierce warriors from Central Asia. The Huns first invaded southeastern Europe and then launched raids on nearby kingdoms. Among the Huns' victims were several groups of people called the Goths, made up of the Visigoths and Ostrogoths. Unable to defeat the Huns, the Goths fled into Roman territory.

Rome's leaders feared that the Goths would destroy Roman land and property. They fought to keep the Goths out of Roman territory. The eastern armies were largely successful. They forced the Goths to move farther west. As a result, however, the western armies were defeated by the Goths. After their victory, large numbers of Goths moved into the Roman Empire.

The Romans fought desperately to keep the Goths from Rome. They even paid the Goths not to attack. In 408, however, the Romans stopped making payments. The Visigoths marched into Rome and sacked, or destroyed, the city in 410. This devastated the Romans. No one had attacked their city in nearly 800 years. Many Romans began to fear for the future of their empire.

The Fall of the Western Empire

The Gothic victory inspired other groups of foreign warriors to invade the western half of the empire. The Vandals, Angles, Saxons, Jutes, and Franks all launched attacks. Meanwhile, the Huns, under a fearsome leader named **Attila** (AT-uhl-uh), raided Roman territory in the east.

Rome needed strong leaders to survive these attacks, but the emperors were weak. Military leaders took power away from the emperors and, by the 450s, ruled Rome.

Conflict among these military leaders gave the invaders an opening. In 476 one of the foreign generals overthrew the last emperor in Rome and named himself king of Italy. Many historians consider this event the end of the Western Roman Empire.

Factors in Rome's Fall

There were several causes of Rome's decline. One was the vast size of the empire. Communication among various parts of the empire was difficult, especially during times of conflict. The Roman world simply became too big to govern effectively.

THE IMPACT TODAY

We still use the word *vandal* today to describe someone who destroys property.

Justinian and Theodora
483–565; c. 500–548

Justinian I was the emperor of the Byzantine Empire from AD 527 to AD 565. As emperor, Justinian reconquered parts of the fallen western empire and simplified Roman laws. He also ordered the building of many beautiful public structures and churches, including the Church of Hagia Sophia.

He married Theodora in about AD 522. Together they worked to restore the power, beauty, and strength of a vast empire. While Justinian was waging military campaigns, Theodora helped create laws to aid women and children and to end government corruption.

Evaluating Which of Justinian and Theodora's accomplishments do you find most impressive? Why?

Political crises also contributed to the decline. By the 400s **corruption**, the decay of people's values, had become widespread in Roman government. Corrupt officials used threats and bribery to achieve their goals, often ignoring the needs of Roman citizens. As a result, Rome's government was no longer **efficient**.

Many wealthy citizens fled to their country estates and created their own armies for protection. Some, however, used these armies to overthrow emperors and take power for themselves. For those people who remained in the cities, life became more difficult. Rome's population decreased, and schools closed. Taxes and prices soared, leaving more Romans poor. By the late 400s Rome was a changed city, and the empire slowly collapsed around it.

ACADEMIC VOCABULARY

efficient (i-FI-shuhnt) productive and not wasteful

READING CHECK Analyzing Information
Why did Rome fall to invaders in the 400s?

A New Eastern Empire

Despite the fall of Rome, the eastern empire grew in wealth and power. Its people created a new society that was different from the society in the west.

Justinian

The eastern emperors dreamed of retaking Rome. For **Justinian** (juh-STIN-ee-uhn), an emperor who ruled from 527 to 565, reuniting the old Roman Empire was a passion. His armies conquered Italy and much land around the Mediterranean.

Justinian's other passions were the law and the church. He ordered officials to remove any out-of-date or unchristian laws. He then organized all the laws into a new legal system called Justinian's Code. By simplifying Roman law, this code helped guarantee fair treatment for all.

Despite his successes, Justinian made many enemies. In 532 an uprising

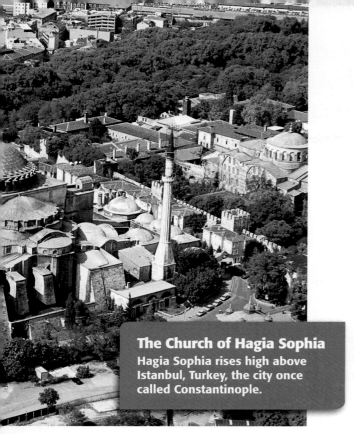

The Church of Hagia Sophia
Hagia Sophia rises high above Istanbul, Turkey, the city once called Constantinople.

threatened to drive him from Constantinople. However, his smart and powerful wife **Theodora** (thee-uh-DOHR-uh) convinced him to stay and fight. Taking her advice, Justinian crushed the riots and ruled effectively for the rest of his reign.

After Justinian's death, the eastern empire began to decline. Invaders took over all the land Justinian had gained. The empire continued to shrink for the next several hundred years. In 1453 the Ottoman Turks captured Constantinople, bringing an end to the Eastern Roman Empire.

Byzantine Society

The society of the eastern empire was distinct from that of the west. Non-Roman influences took hold in the east. People spoke Greek rather than Latin. Historians call the society that developed in the Eastern Roman Empire the **Byzantine** (BI-zuhn-teen) **Empire**, after Byzantium, the Greek town Constantinople had replaced.

The importance of Christianity in the eastern empire is reflected in the Byzantines' beautiful works of art and magnificent churches. As time passed, people began to interpret and practice Christianity differently in the east and the west. Eventually these differences led to a split within the Christian Church. In the 1000s Christians in the east formed the Orthodox Church. As a result, eastern and western Europe were divided by religion.

THE IMPACT TODAY
The Orthodox faith is still the main religion in Russia, Greece, and other parts of eastern Europe.

READING CHECK **Drawing Conclusions**
Why did Justinian reorganize Roman law?

SUMMARY AND PREVIEW After the fall of Rome, Roman power shifted east. The Orthodox Church became a major force in the Byzantine Empire. Next, you will learn about members of another religious group—the Muslims.

go.hrw.com
Online Quiz
KEYWORD: SN6 HP11

Section 3 Assessment

Reviewing Ideas, Terms, and People
1. **a. Recall** To where did Constantine move Rome's capital?
   b. Explain What effect did Roman farmers' fear of raids have on the empire?
2. **a. Identify** Who was **Attila**?
   b. Analyze Why did the Goths move into the Roman Empire?
3. **a. Summarize** What were two of **Justinian's** major accomplishments?
   b. Contrast Name two ways that the **Byzantine Empire** was different from the Western Roman Empire.

Critical Thinking
4. **Drawing Conclusions** Draw a word web like the one shown. In each of the outer circles, list a factor that helped lead to the fall of the Western Roman Empire. You may make more circles if needed.

Fall of the Western Roman Empire

FOCUS ON WRITING

5. **Adding the Final Details** Add the key events, persons, and places that were covered in this section to the list you have been making. Once your list is complete, review it to get an idea of what to include in your screenplay.

Social Studies Skills

Interpreting Time Lines

Understand the Skill

A time line is a visual summary of important events that occurred during a period of history. It displays the events in the order in which they happened. It also shows how long after one event another event took place. In this way time lines allow you to see at a glance what happened and when. You can better see relationships between events and remember important dates when they are displayed on a timeline.

Learn the Skill

Some time lines cover huge spans of time—sometimes even many centuries. Other time lines, such as the one on this page, cover much shorter periods of time.

Time lines can be arranged either vertically or horizontally. This time line is vertical. Its dates are read from top to bottom. Horizontal time lines are read from left to right.

Follow these steps to interpret a time line.

1. Read the time line's title. Note the range of years covered and the intervals of time into which it is divided.

2. Study the order of events on the time line. Note the length of time between events.

3. Note relationships. Ask yourself how an event relates to others on the time line. Look for cause-and-effect relationships and long-term developments.

Practice and Apply the Skill

Interpret the time line to answer the following questions.

1. What is the subject of this time line? What years does it cover?

2. How long did Octavian and Antony rule after dividing Rome?

3. How long after dividing the empire did Antony ally with Cleopatra?

4. What steps did Octavian take to end his alliance with Antony and become emperor? When did he take them? How long did it take?

AUGUSTUS BECOMES EMPEROR

50 BC

45 BC Caesar becomes dictator.

44 BC Caesar is murdered.

43 BC Octavian and Antony decide to rule Rome together.

42 BC Octavian and Antony divide Rome and rule separately.

40 BC

37 BC Antony allies with Cleopatra, queen of Egypt.

31 BC Octavian defeats Antony and Cleopatra in a naval battle near Greece.

30 BC Octavian conquers Egypt. Antony and Cleopatra avoid capture by killing themselves.

30 BC

27 BC Octavian becomes emperor and is renamed Augustus.

23 BC Augustus becomes ruler for life.

Chapter Review

Visual Summary

Use the visual summary below to help you review the main ideas of the chapter.

QUICK FACTS

An architectural wonder, the Colosseum in Rome was the site of many types of public entertainment.

The New Testament of the Bible tells the story of Jesus of Nazareth and his disciples.

The Hagia Sophia, the enormous church built during Justinian's reign, served as the spiritual center of the Byzantine Empire.

Reviewing Vocabulary, Terms, and People

1. The orator and philosopher who called on Romans to work together was

a. Constantine.
c. Augustus.
b. Caesar.
d. Cicero.

2. Latin developed into

a. Byzantium.
c. satire.
b. Romance languages.
d. Latvian.

3. Another word for God's anointed one is

a. disciple.
c. Messiah.
b. Judea.
d. Apostle.

4. The Eastern Roman Empire is also called the

a. Lost Empire.
c. Constantinople Empire.
b. Byzantine Empire.
d. Ottoman Empire.

5. Rome's 200-year period of peace was the

a. Resurrection.
c. crucifixion.
b. Pax Romana.
d. Age of Theodora.

Comprehension and Critical Thinking

SECTION 1 *(pages 322–328)*

6. a. Describe What action did Cicero recommend? How were the goals of Julius Caesar, Pompey, and Crassus different from Cicero's?

b. Analyze What were the most important events in the life of Julius Caesar? What event best qualifies as a turning point in Caesar's life? Defend your choice.

c. Elaborate How did personal relationships—between Marc Antony and Octavian, and between Marc Antony and Cleopatra—affect the history of the Roman Empire?

SECTION 2 *(pages 332–338)*

7. a. Describe How did the Romans' attitude about religion differ from that of the Jews?

b. Compare What were the crucifixion and the Resurrection? What did early Christians believe that the Resurrection showed?

c. Evaluate Why is Paul of Tarsus considered one of the most important people in the history of Christianity?

SECTION 3 *(pages 339–343)*

8. a. Identify Who were the Huns? Who were the Goths? Who were the Visigoths?

b. Compare and Contrast What did Diocletian and Constantine have in common? How did their actions differ?

c. Elaborate Who were Justinian and Theodora, and what did they accomplish?

Reviewing Themes

9. Geography How did the geography of the Roman Empire affect the spread of Christianity?

10. Science and Technology What do you feel was Rome's greatest scientific or technological advance? Why?

Using the Internet

go.hrw.com
KEYWORD: SN6 WH11

11. Activity Enter the keyword. Then create a chart that summarizes the ways in which Justinian's Code influences modern issues such as the rights and responsibilities of individuals.

Reading Skills

12. Online Research Imagine you are evaluating a Web site about ancient Roman architecture. What are some important elements you might look for to determine whether the site will be helpful and accurate? Write three questions you could use to evaluate the site's value.

Social Studies Skills

13. Interpreting Time Lines Look at the time line on page 344. Then, using information you will find in the first section of this chapter, add an entry about Cicero to the time line. Be sure you put it in the correct place.

FOCUS ON WRITING

14. Creating Your Note Cards Now that you've taken notes about the people, places, and events of Rome during this time period, you're ready to prepare note cards. Choose the most interesting details from your chart to include on your cards. On each card write a one-to-two sentence description of a person, place, or event that you think should be featured in this screenplay. Then write another sentence that tells why you think the person, place, or event should be featured. Prepare six cards that you could give to a screenwriter to use to develop the script.

DIRECTIONS: Read each question and write the letter of the best response. Use the time line below to answer question 1.

1

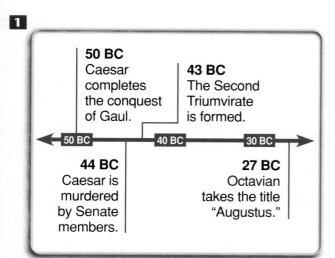

50 BC
Caesar completes the conquest of Gaul.

43 BC
The Second Triumvirate is formed.

50 BC — 40 BC — 30 BC

44 BC
Caesar is murdered by Senate members.

27 BC
Octavian takes the title "Augustus."

Most historians mark the end of the Roman Republic and the beginning of the Roman Empire as taking place in the year

A 50 BC.

B 44 BC.

C 43 BC.

D 27 BC.

2 Which Roman leader seized power from the Senate and became the dictator of the entire Roman Republic?

A Julius Caesar

B Hadrian

C Brutus

D Marc Antony

3 Rome's contributions to the world include all of the following *except*

A techniques used to build strong bridges and other structures.

B the building of pyramids.

C the idea of civil law.

D the use of Latin, which led to the development of the Romance languages.

4 Who was most responsible for spreading the Christian faith immediately after the death of Jesus?

A Octavian

B Diocletian

C Paul of Tarsus

D Theodora of Constantinople

5 In AD 410 the city of Rome was destroyed for the first time in 800 years by the army of a foreign people called the

A Vandals.

B Visigoths.

C Huns.

D Franks.

Connecting with Past Learnings

6 Constantine united the entire Roman Empire and introduced a new religion into the Roman government. Which leader that you learned about in an earlier chapter is known for his similar accomplishments?

A Asoka

B Hammurabi

C Alexander

D Piankhi

7 Earlier in this course, you learned that the Persians threatened Greek civilization for a time. All the following peoples played a similar role in Roman history *except*

A the Byzantines.

B the Goths.

C the Vandals.

D the Huns.

Islamic and African Civilizations

Chapter 12 The Islamic World
Chapter 13 Early African Civilizations

In the 600s a prophet named Muhammad introduced the religion of Islam to the people of Southwest Asia. One hundred years later, Islam had spread throughout the region, across North Africa, and into parts of Europe. Later, Islam spread into West Africa, the home of rich and vibrant trading kingdoms.

In the next two chapters, you will learn about the rise and spread of Islam and the kingdoms of West Africa into which it spread.

Explore the Art

In this scene, a young Muslim traveler named Leo Africanus visits an official of the West African Songhai Empire. What does this scene suggest about the role of Islam in Songhai?

CHAPTER **12** 550–1650

The Islamic World

FOCUS ON WRITING

A Web Site for Children Design a Web site to tell children about the life of the prophet Muhammad, the religion of Islam, and the history and culture of the Muslim people. You'll design five pages: a home page and four links—Who Was Muhammad? What Is Islam? The Islamic Empires, and Islamic Cultural Achievements. As you read, think about what information will be interesting to your audience.

CHAPTER EVENTS

c. 550 Trade routes cross Arabia.

c. 570 Muhammad is born in Mecca.

550

600

WORLD EVENTS

618 The Tang dynasty begins in China.

HOLT

History's Impact
▶ video series
Watch the video to under-
stand the impact of Islamic
traditions on the world today.

What You Will Learn...

In this chapter, you will learn about a religion
called Islam. This photo shows thousands of
people praying in Mecca, the place where
Islam began. Mecca is the most sacred place
in the Islamic world.

622
Muhammad
leaves
Mecca.

632
Muhammad
dies.

762
Baghdad becomes
the capital of the
Islamic Empire.

1453
The Ottomans
capture
Constantinople.

1501
The Safavids
conquer
Persia.

1631
Shah Jahan
begins building
the Taj Mahal.

650

700

1500

1650

657
An Indian
mathematician
introduces
the concept
of zero.

700s
Viking
raids
begin in
northern
Europe.

1215
English nobles force
King John to accept
the Magna Carta.

1521
Cortés
conquers
the Aztec
Empire.

1588
England
defeats the
Spanish
Armada.

Reading Social Studies

by Kylene Beers

Focus on Themes In this chapter, you will learn about the origins and **geographic** spread of one of the world's great **religions**, Islam. You will read about the founder, Muhammad, and how he united much of Arabia under Muslim rule. You will also learn about great conquests and powerful Muslim rulers. Finally, you will read about the outstanding achievements of Islamic scientists, artists, and scholars.

Questioning

Focus on Reading Asking yourself questions is a good way to be sure that you understand what you are reading. You should always ask yourself who the most important people are, when and where they lived, and what they did.

Analytical Questions Questions can also help you make sense of what happened in the past. Asking questions about how and why things happened will help you better understand historical events.

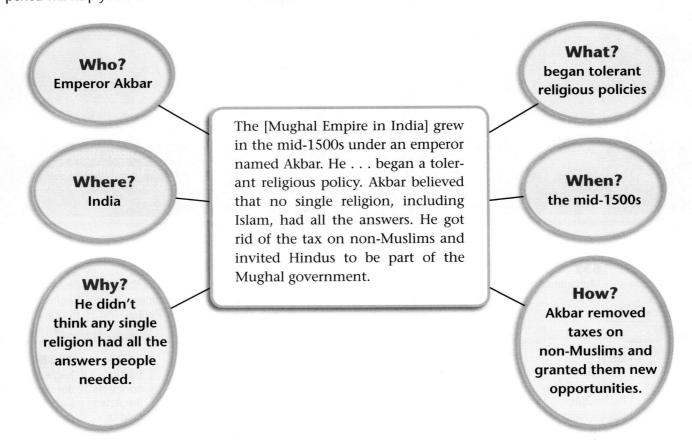

Who?
Emperor Akbar

Where?
India

Why?
He didn't think any single religion had all the answers people needed.

The [Mughal Empire in India] grew in the mid-1500s under an emperor named Akbar. He . . . began a tolerant religious policy. Akbar believed that no single religion, including Islam, had all the answers. He got rid of the tax on non-Muslims and invited Hindus to be part of the Mughal government.

What?
began tolerant religious policies

When?
the mid-1500s

How?
Akbar removed taxes on non-Muslims and granted them new opportunities.

You Try It!

Read the following passage and then answer the questions.

Geography

During the mid-1100s, a Muslim geographer named al-Idrisi collected information from Arab travelers. He was writing a geography book and wanted it to be very accurate. When al-Idrisi had a question about where a mountain, river, or coastline was, he sent trained geographers to figure out its exact location. Using the information the geographers brought back, al-Idrisi made some important discoveries. For example, he proved that land did not go all the way around the Indian Ocean as many people thought.

Answer these questions based on the passage you just read.

1. Who is this passage about?

2. What is he known for doing?

3. When did he live?

4. Why did he do what he did?

5. How did he accomplish his task?

6. How can knowing this information help you understand the past?

As you read **Chapter 12**, ask questions to help you understand what you are reading.

Key Terms and People

Chapter 12

Section 1
oasis *(p. 354)*
caravan *(p. 355)*
Muhammad *(p. 356)*
Islam *(p. 356)*
Muslim *(p. 356)*
Qur'an *(p. 356)*
pilgrimage *(p. 356)*
mosque *(p. 357)*

Section 2
jihad *(p. 359)*
Sunnah *(p. 359)*
Five Pillars of Islam *(p. 360)*

Section 3
Abu Bakr *(p. 362)*
caliph *(p. 362)*
tolerance *(p. 364)*
Janissaries *(p. 364)*
Mehmed II *(p. 364)*
Suleyman I *(p. 364)*
Shia *(p. 365)*
Sunni *(p. 365)*

Section 4
Ibn Battutah *(p. 369)*
Sufism *(p. 369)*
Omar Khayyám *(p. 371)*
patrons *(p. 371)*
minaret *(p. 371)*
calligraphy *(p. 371)*

Academic Vocabulary

Success in school is related to knowing academic vocabulary—the words that are frequently used in school assignments and discussions. In this chapter, you will learn the following academic words:

influence *(p. 356)*
development *(p. 364)*

The Roots of Islam

If YOU were there...

You live in a town in Arabia, in a large merchant family. Your family has grown rich from selling goods brought by traders crossing the desert. Your house is larger than most others in town, and you have servants to wait on you. Although many townspeople are poor, you have always taken such differences for granted. Now you hear that some people are saying the rich should give money to the poor.

How might your family react to this idea?

BUILDING BACKGROUND For thousands of years, traders have crossed the deserts of Arabia to bring goods to market. Scorching temperatures and lack of water have made the journey difficult. But Arabia not only developed into a thriving trade center, it also became the birthplace of a new religion that challenged old ideas.

Life in a Desert Land

The Arabian Peninsula, or Arabia, is located in the southwest corner of Asia. It lies near the intersection of Africa, Europe, and Asia. For thousands of years Arabia's location, physical features, and climate have shaped life in the region.

Physical Features and Climate

Arabia lies in a region with hot and dry air. With a blazing sun and clear skies, summer temperatures in the interior reach 100°F daily. This climate has created a band of deserts across Arabia and northern Africa. Sand dunes, or hills of sand shaped by the wind, can rise to 800 feet high and stretch for hundreds of miles!

Arabia's deserts have a very limited amount of water. What water there is exists mainly in scattered oases. An **oasis** is a wet, fertile area in a desert. Oases have long been key stops along Arabia's overland trade routes.

Two Ways of Life

To live in Arabia's difficult desert environment, people developed two main ways of life. Nomads lived in tents and raised herds of sheep, goats, and camels. The animals provided milk, meat, wool, and leather. The camels also carried heavy loads. Nomads traveled with their herds across the desert in search of food and water for their animals.

Among the nomads, water and grazing land belonged to tribes. Membership in a tribe, a group of related people, offered protection from desert dangers.

While nomads moved around the desert, other Arabs lived a sedentary, or settled, life. These people made their homes in oases where they could farm. These settlements, particularly the ones along trade routes, became towns. Merchants and craftspeople lived there and worked with people in the caravan trade. A **caravan** is a group of traders that travel together.

Towns became centers of trade. Many had a market or bazaar. There, nomads traded animal products and desert herbs for goods such as cooking supplies and clothing. Merchants sold spices, gold, leather, and other goods brought by the caravans.

READING CHECK **Categorizing** What two ways of life were common in Arabia?

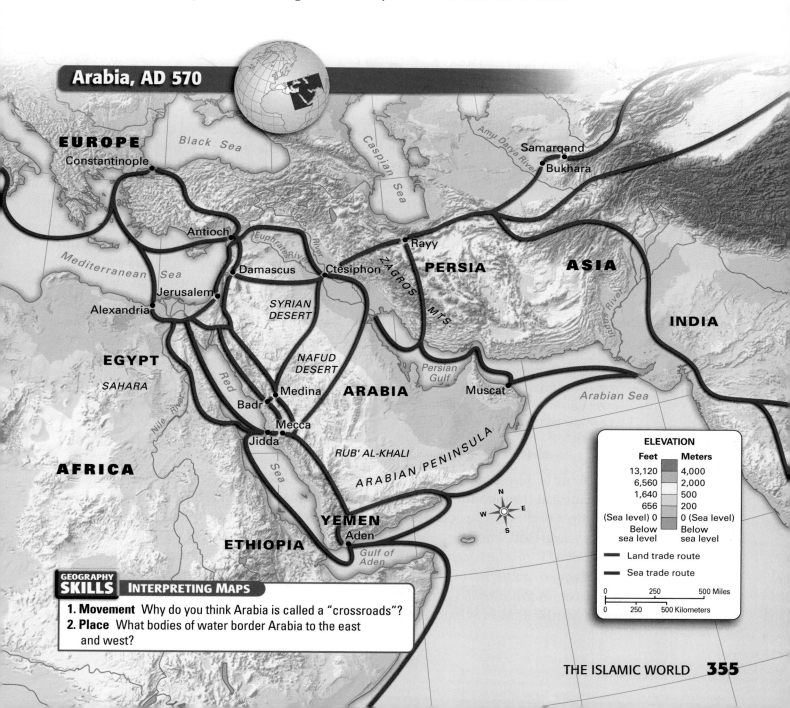

Arabia, AD 570

GEOGRAPHY SKILLS **INTERPRETING MAPS**

1. **Movement** Why do you think Arabia is called a "crossroads"?
2. **Place** What bodies of water border Arabia to the east and west?

A New Religion

In early times, Arabs worshipped many gods. That changed, however, when a man named **Muhammad** brought a new religion to Arabia. Historians know little about Muhammad. What they do know comes from religious writings.

Muhammad Becomes a Prophet

FOCUS ON READING
Write a question you could use to analyze the text in this paragraph. Then answer it.

Muhammad was born into an important family in the city of Mecca around 570. As a child, he traveled with his uncle's caravans. Once he was grown, he managed a caravan business owned by a wealthy woman named Khadijah (ka-DEE-jah). At age 25, Muhammad married Khadijah.

The caravan trade made Mecca a rich city. But most of the wealth belonged to just a few people. Traditionally, wealthy people in Mecca had helped the poor. But as Muhammad was growing up, many rich merchants began to ignore the needy.

Concerned about these changes, Muhammad often went to the hills to pray and meditate. One day, when he was about 40 years old, he went to meditate in a cave. According to religious writings, an angel spoke to Muhammad, telling him to "Recite! Recite!" Muhammad asked what he should recite. The angel answered:

> " Recite in the name of your Lord who created,
> created man from clots of blood!
> Recite! Your Lord is the Most Bountiful One,
> Who by the pen taught man what he did
> not know."
>
> —From *The Koran*, translated by N. J. Dawood

Muslims believe that God had spoken to Muhammad through the angel and had made him a prophet, a person who tells of messages from God. The messages Muhammad received form the basis of the religion called **Islam**. In Arabic, *Islam* means "to submit to God." A follower of Islam is called a **Muslim**. Muslims believe that Muhammad

ACADEMIC VOCABULARY
influence change, or have an effect on

continued receiving messages from God for the rest of his life. These messages were collected in the **Qur'an** (kuh-RAN), the holy book of Islam.

Muhammad's Teachings

In 613 Muhammad began to talk about his messages. He taught that there was only one God, Allah, which means "the God" in Arabic. Islam is monotheistic, a religion based on the belief in one God, like Judaism and Christianity. Although people of all three religions believe in one God, their beliefs about God are not the same.

Muhammad's teachings were new to Arabs, most of whom practiced polytheism. They had many shrines, or special places where they worshipped their gods. A very important shrine, the Kaaba (KAH-bah), was in Mecca. People traveled there every year on a **pilgrimage**, a journey to a sacred place.

Muhammad's teachings upset many Arabs. First, they didn't like being told to stop worshipping their gods. Second, Muhammad's new religion seemed like a threat to people who made money from the yearly pilgrimages to the Kaaba.

Mecca's wealthy merchants didn't like another of Muhammad's teachings: that everyone who believed in Allah would become part of a community in which rich and poor would be equal. Rich merchants also disliked Muhammad's idea that people should give money to help the poor. The merchants wanted to keep all of their money and remain more powerful than the poor.

Islam Spreads in Arabia

At first Muhammad had few followers. Slowly, more people began to listen to his ideas. As Islam began to **influence** people, Mecca's rulers became worried. They threatened Muhammad and even planned to kill him.

A group of people living north of Mecca invited Muhammad to move to their city.

Beginnings of Islam

575   600   625   650

c. 570
Muhammad is born.

c. 610
According to Islamic belief, an angel appears and tells Muhammad to spread the word of God.

613
Muhammad begins to spread his message.

622
Muhammad and his followers leave Mecca for Medina in the hegira. This event marks the beginning of the Islamic calendar.

632
Muhammad dies. Islam begins to spread across Southwest Asia and North Africa.

ANALYSIS SKILL   **READING TIME LINES**

How many years did Muhammad spend spreading his message before he died?

So in 622 Muhammad and many followers went to Medina (muh-DEE-nuh). *Medina* means "the Prophet's city" in Arabic. Muhammad's departure from Mecca is known as the hegira (hi-JY-ruh), or journey.

Muhammad became a spiritual and political leader in Medina. His house became the first **mosque** (mahsk), or building for Muslim prayer.

As the Muslim community in Medina grew stronger, other Arab tribes began to accept Islam. But conflict with the Meccans increased. In 630, after several years of fighting, the people of Mecca gave in. They accepted Islam as their religion.

Soon most of the Arabian tribes accepted Muhammad as their spiritual and political leader and became Muslims. Muhammad died in 632, but the religion he taught would soon spread far beyond Arabia.

READING CHECK   **Summarizing** How did Islam spread in Arabia?

SUMMARY AND PREVIEW The geography of Arabia encouraged trade and influenced the development of nomadic and sedentary lifestyles. In the early 600s Muhammad introduced a new religion to Arabia. Many people in Arabia became Muslims. In the next section, you will learn more about the main Islamic teachings and beliefs.

Section 1 Assessment

go.hrw.com
Online Quiz
KEYWORD: SN6 HP12

Reviewing Ideas, Terms, and People

1. **a. Define** What is an **oasis**?
   b. Make Generalizations Why did towns often develop near oases?
   c. Predict Do you think life would have been better for nomads or townspeople in early Arabia? Explain your answer.
2. **a. Identify** What is a key Islamic belief about God?
   b. Explain According to Islamic belief, how did **Muhammad** get the ideas that started **Islam**?
   c. Evaluate In what ways was Muhammad's time in Medina important to the growth of Islam?

Critical Thinking

3. **Sequencing** Draw a time line like the one below. Using your notes on Muhammad, identify the key dates in his life.

FOCUS ON WRITING

4. **Writing about Muhammad** Review your notes to answer the question, "Who was Muhammad?" It may help to think of Muhammad's life in three parts: "Early Life," "Muhammad Becomes a Prophet," and "Muhammad's Teachings."

Islamic Beliefs and Practices

What You Will Learn...

Main Ideas

1. The Qur'an guides Muslims' lives.
2. The Sunnah tells Muslims of important duties expected of them.
3. Islamic law is based on the Qur'an and the Sunnah.

The Big Idea

Sacred texts called the Qur'an and the Sunnah guide Muslims in their religion, daily life, and laws.

Key Terms

jihad, *p. 359*
Sunnah, *p. 359*
Five Pillars of Islam, *p. 360*

TAKING NOTES As you read, take notes on the most important beliefs and practices of Islam. You can organize your notes in a table like this one.

The Teachings of Islam

If YOU were there...

Your family owns an inn in Mecca. Usually business is pretty calm, but this week your inn is packed. Travelers have come from all over the world to visit your city. One morning you leave the inn and are swept up in a huge crowd of these visitors. They speak many different languages, but everyone is wearing the same white robes. They are headed to the mosque.

What might draw so many people to your city?

BUILDING BACKGROUND One basic Islamic belief is that everyone who can must make a trip to Mecca sometime during his or her lifetime. More Islamic teachings can be found in Islam's holy books—the Qur'an and the Sunnah.

The Qur'an

During Muhammad's life, his followers memorized his messages and his words and deeds. After Muhammad's death, they collected his teachings and wrote them down to form the book known as the Qur'an. Muslims believe the Qur'an to be the exact word of God as it was told to Muhammad.

Beliefs

The central teaching in the Qur'an is that there is only one God—Allah—and that Muhammad is his prophet. The Qur'an says people must obey Allah's commands. Muslims learned of these commands from Muhammad.

Islam teaches that the world had a definite beginning and will end one day. Muhammad said that on the final day God will judge all people. Those who have obeyed his orders will be granted life in paradise. According to the Qur'an, paradise is a beautiful garden full of fine food and drink. People who have not obeyed God, however, will suffer.

Guidelines for Behavior

Like holy books of other religions, the Qur'an describes acts of worship, guidelines for moral behavior, and rules for social life. Muslims look to the Qur'an for guidance in their daily lives. For example, the Qur'an describes how to prepare for worship. Muslims must wash themselves before praying so they will be pure before Allah. The Qur'an also tells Muslims what they should not eat or drink. Muslims are not allowed to eat pork or drink alcohol.

In addition to guidelines for individual behavior, the Qur'an describes relations among people. Many of these ideas changed Arabian society. For example, before Muhammad's time many Arabs owned slaves. Although slavery didn't disappear among Muslims, the Qur'an encourages Muslims to free slaves. Also, women in Arabia had few rights. The Qur'an describes rights of women, including rights to own property, earn money, and get an education. However, most Muslim women still have fewer rights than men.

Another important subject in the Qur'an has to do with **jihad** (ji-HAHD), which means "to make an effort, or to struggle." Jihad refers to the inner struggle people go through in their effort to obey God and behave according to Islamic ways. Jihad can also mean the struggle to defend the Muslim community, or, historically, to convert people to Islam. The word has also been translated as "holy war."

READING CHECK **Analyzing** Why is the Qur'an important to Muslims?

The Sunnah

The Qur'an is not the only source of Islamic teachings. Muslims also study the hadith (huh-DEETH), the written record of Muhammad's words and actions. This record is the basis for the Sunnah. The **Sunnah** (SOOH-nuh) refers to the way Muhammad lived, which provides a model for the duties and the way of life expected of Muslims. The Sunnah guides Muslims' behavior.

The Five Pillars of Islam
QUICK FACTS

Saying "There is no god but God, and Muhammad is his prophet"

Praying five times a day

Giving to the poor and needy

Fasting during the holy month of Ramadan

Traveling to Mecca at least once on a hajj

ANALYSIS SKILL **ANALYZING VISUALS**

Which of the five pillars shows how Muslims are supposed to treat other people?

The Five Pillars of Islam

The first duties of a Muslim are known as the **Five Pillars of Islam**, which are five acts of worship required of all Muslims. The first pillar is a statement of faith. At least once in their lives, Muslims must state their faith by saying, "There is no god but God, and Muhammad is his prophet." Muslims say this when they accept Islam. They also say it in their daily prayers.

The second pillar of Islam is daily prayer. Muslims must pray five times a day: before sunrise, at midday, in late afternoon, right after sunset, and before going to bed. At each of these times, a call goes out from a mosque, inviting Muslims to come pray. Muslims try to pray together at a mosque. They believe prayer is proof that someone has accepted Allah.

The third pillar of Islam is a yearly donation to charity. Muslims must pay part of their wealth to a religious official. This money is used to help the poor, build mosques, or pay debts. Helping and caring for others is important in Islam.

The fourth pillar is fasting—going without food and drink. Muslims fast daily during the holy month of Ramadan (RAH-muh-dahn). The Qur'an says Allah began his revelations to Muhammad in this month. During Ramadan, most Muslims will not eat or drink anything between dawn and sunset. Muslims believe fasting is a way to show that God is more important than one's own body. Fasting also reminds Muslims of people in the world who struggle to get enough food.

The fifth pillar of Islam is the hajj (HAJ), a pilgrimage to Mecca. All Muslims must travel to Mecca at least once in their lives if they can. The Kaaba, in Mecca, is Islam's most sacred place.

The Sunnah and Daily Life

In addition to the five pillars, the Sunnah has other examples of Muhammad's actions and teachings. These form the basis for rules about how to treat others. According to Muhammad's example, people should treat guests with generosity.

In addition to describing personal relations, the Sunnah provides guidelines for relations in business and government. For example, one Sunnah rule says that it is bad to owe someone money. Another rule says that people should obey their leaders.

READING CHECK **Generalizing** What do Muslims learn from the Sunnah?

Islamic Law

The Qur'an and the Sunnah are important guides for how Muslims should live. They also form the basis of Islamic law, or Shariah (shuh-REE-uh). Shariah is a system based on Islamic sources and human reason that judges the rightness of actions an individual or community might take. These actions fall on a scale ranging from required to accepted to disapproved to forbidden. Islamic law makes no distinction between religious beliefs and daily life, so Islam affects all aspects of Muslims' lives.

Sharia sets rewards for good behavior and punishments for crimes. It also describes limits of authority. It was the basis for law in Muslim countries until modern times. Most Muslim countries today blend Islamic law with legal systems like those in the United States or western Europe.

Islamic law is not found in one book. Instead, it is a set of opinions and writings that have changed over the centuries. Different ideas about Islamic law are found in different Muslim regions.

READING CHECK **Finding Main Ideas** What is the purpose of Islamic law?

SUMMARY AND PREVIEW The Qur'an, the Sunnah, and Shariah teach Muslims how to live their lives. In the next chapter, you will learn more about Muslim culture and the spread of Islam from Arabia to other lands.

Sources of Islamic Beliefs

Qur'an	Sunnah	Shariah
Holy book that includes all the messages Muhammad received from God	Muhammad's example for the duties and way of life expected of Muslims	Islamic law, based on interpretations of the Qur'an and Sunnah

Section 2 Assessment

Reviewing Ideas, Terms, and People

1. **a. Recall** What is the central teaching of the Qur'an?
   b. Explain How does the Qur'an help Muslims obey God?
2. **a. Recall** What are the **Five Pillars of Islam**?
   b. Make Generalizations Why do Muslims fast during Ramadan?
3. **a. Identify** What is Islamic law called?
   b. Make Inferences How is Islamic law different from law in the United States?
   c. Elaborate What is a possible reason that opinions and writings about Islamic law have changed over the centuries?

Critical Thinking

4. **Categorizing** Draw a chart like the one to the right. Use it to list three teachings from the Qur'an and three teachings from the Sunnah.

Qur'an	Sunnah

FOCUS ON WRITING

5. **Describing Islam** Answer the following questions to help you write a paragraph describing Islam. What is the central teaching of the Qur'an? How do Muslims honor God? What is the function of the Sunnah?

Islamic Empires

If YOU were there...

You are a farmer living in a village on the coast of India. For centuries, your people have raised cotton and spun its fibers into a soft fabric. One day, a ship arrives in the harbor carrying Muslim traders from far away. They bring interesting goods you have never seen before. They also bring new ideas.

What ideas might you learn from the traders?

BUILDING BACKGROUND You know that for years traders traveled through Arabia to markets far away. Along the way, they picked up new goods and ideas, and they introduced these to the people they met. Some of the new ideas the traders spread were Islamic ideas.

Muslim Armies Conquer Many Lands

After Muhammad's death his followers quickly chose **Abu Bakr** (UH-boo BAK-uhr), one of Muhammad's first converts, to be the next leader of Islam. He was the first **caliph** (KAY-luhf), a title that Muslims use for the highest leader of Islam. In Arabic, the word *caliph* means "successor." As Muhammad's successors, the caliphs had to follow the prophet's example. This meant ruling according to the Qur'an. Unlike Muhammad, however, early caliphs were not religious leaders.

Beginnings of an Empire

Abu Bakr directed a series of battles to unite Arabia. By his death in 634, he had made Arabia into a unified Muslim state. With Arabia united, Muslim leaders turned their attention elsewhere. Their armies, strong after their battles in Arabia, won many stunning victories. They defeated the Persian and Byzantine empires, which were weak from many years of fighting.

When the Muslims conquered lands, they set certain rules for non-Muslims living there. For example, some non-Muslims could not build new places of worship or dress like Muslims. However, Christians and Jews could continue to practice their own religion. They were not forced to convert to Islam.

Growth of the Empire

Many early caliphs came from the Umayyad (oom-EYE-yuhd) family. The Umayyads moved the capital to Damascus, in Muslim-conquered Syria, and continued to expand the empire. They took over lands in Central Asia and in northern India. The Umayyads also gained control of trade in the eastern Mediterranean and conquered parts of North Africa.

The Berbers, the native people of North Africa, resisted Muslim rule at first. After years of fighting, however, many Berbers converted to Islam.

In 711 a combined Arab and Berber army invaded Spain and quickly conquered it. Next the army moved into what is now France, but it was stopped by a Christian army near the city of Tours (TOOR). Despite this defeat, Muslims called Moors ruled parts of Spain for the next 700 years.

A new Islamic dynasty, the Abbasids (uh-BAS-idz), came to power in 749. They reorganized the government to make it easier to rule such a large region.

READING CHECK **Analyzing** What role did armies play in spreading Islam?

Trade Helps Islam Spread

Islam gradually spread through areas the Muslims conquered. Trade also helped spread Islam. Along with their goods, Arab merchants took Islamic beliefs to India, Africa, and Southeast Asia. Though Indian kingdoms remained Hindu, coastal trading cities soon had large Muslim communities. In Africa, societies often had both African and Muslim customs. Many African leaders converted to Islam. Between 1200 and 1600, Muslim traders carried Islam east to what are now Malaysia and Indonesia.

Trade also brought new products to Muslim lands. For example, Arabs learned from the Chinese how to make paper and use gunpowder. New crops such as cotton, rice, and oranges arrived from India, China, and Southeast Asia.

Many Muslim merchants traveled to African market towns too. They wanted African products such as ivory, cloves, and slaves. In return they offered fine white pottery called porcelain from China, cloth goods from India, and iron from Southwest Asia and Europe. Arab traders grew wealthy from trade between regions.

THE IMPACT TODAY

Indonesia now has the largest Muslim population in the world.

The City of Córdoba

By the early 900s, Córdoba, Spain, was one of the wealthiest cities in Europe and a center of Islamic learning. Rich examples of Islamic architecture can still be seen in the city.

A Mix of Cultures

As Islam spread through trade and warfare, Arabs came into contact with people who had different beliefs and lifestyles than they did. Muslims generally practiced religious **tolerance**, or acceptance, with regard to people they conquered. The Muslims did not ban all other religions in their lands. Because they shared some beliefs with Muslims, Christians and Jews in particular kept many of their rights. They did, however, have to pay a special tax. Members of both faiths were also forbidden from converting anyone to their religion.

Many people conquered by the Arabs converted to Islam. These people often adopted other parts of Arabic culture, including the Arabic language. The Arabs, in turn, adopted some customs from the people they conquered. This cultural blending changed Islam from a mostly Arab religion into a religion of many cultures. But the Arabic language and shared religion helped unify the different groups of the Islamic world.

The Growth of Cities

The growing cities of the Muslim world reflected the blending of cultures. Trade had brought people together and created wealth, which supported great cultural **development** in Muslim cities.

Baghdad, in what is now Iraq, became the capital of the Islamic Empire in 762. Trade and farming made Baghdad one of the world's richest cities. Caliphs at Baghdad supported science and the arts. The city was a center of culture and learning.

Córdoba (KAWR-doh-bah), in Spain, became another showplace of Muslim civilization. By the early 900s Córdoba was the largest and most advanced city in Europe.

READING CHECK Finding the Main Idea How did trade affect the spread of Islam?

ACADEMIC VOCABULARY

development the process of growing or improving

Three Muslim Empires

The great era of Arab Muslim expansion lasted until the 1100s. Afterward, three non-Arab Muslim groups built large, powerful empires that took control of much of Europe, Asia, and Africa.

The Ottoman Empire

In the mid-1200s Muslim Turkish warriors known as Ottomans began to take territory from the Christian Byzantine Empire. They eventually ruled land from eastern Europe to North Africa and Arabia.

The key to the empire's expansion was the Ottoman army. The Ottomans trained Christian boys from conquered towns to be soldiers. These slave soldiers, called **Janissaries**, converted to Islam and became fierce warriors. The Ottomans also benefitted from their use of new gunpowder weapons.

In 1453 Ottomans led by **Mehmed II** used huge cannons to conquer Constantinople. With the city's capture, Mehmed defeated the Byzantine Empire. He became known as "the Conqueror." Mehmed made Constantinople, which the Ottomans called Istanbul, his new capital. He also turned the Byzantines' great church, Hagia Sophia, into a mosque.

A later sultan, or Ottoman ruler, continued Mehmed's conquests. He expanded the empire to the east through the rest of Anatolia, another name for Asia Minor. His armies also conquered Syria and Egypt. The holy cities of Mecca and Medina then accepted Ottoman rule.

The Ottoman Empire reached its height under **Suleyman I** (soo-lay-MAHN), "the Magnificent." During his rule from 1520 to 1566, the Ottomans took control of the eastern Mediterranean and pushed farther into Europe, areas they would control until the early 1800s.

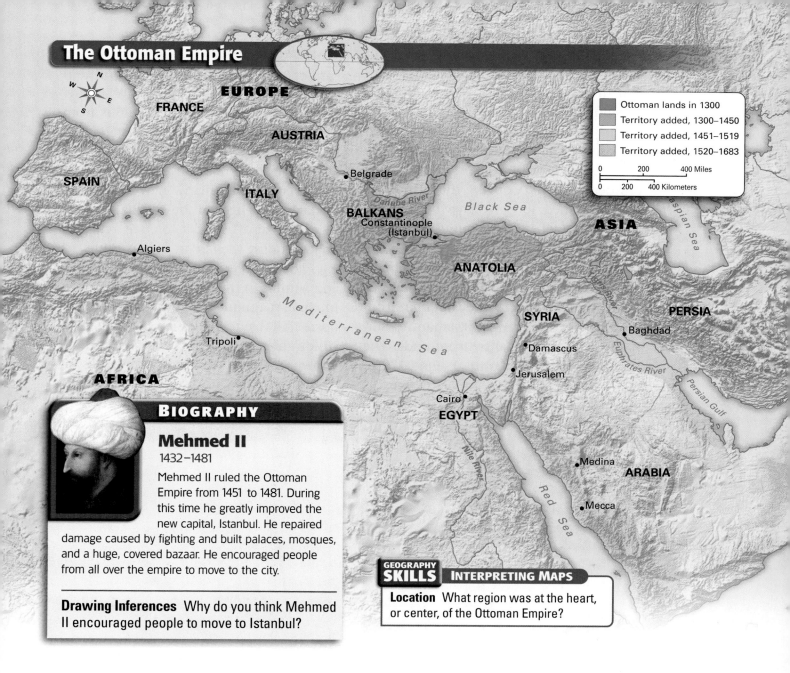

The Ottoman Empire

EUROPE

FRANCE

AUSTRIA

SPAIN

ITALY

•Belgrade

Danube River

Black Sea

BALKANS
Constantinople
(Istanbul)

ASIA

•Algiers

ANATOLIA

Caspian Sea

Mediterranean Sea

SYRIA

PERSIA

•Baghdad

•Damascus

•Tripoli

•Jerusalem

Euphrates River

Persian Gulf

AFRICA

Cairo•

EGYPT

Nile River

•Medina

ARABIA

•Mecca

Red Sea

Ottoman lands in 1300
Territory added, 1300–1450
Territory added, 1451–1519
Territory added, 1520–1683

0   200   400 Miles
0   200   400 Kilometers

BIOGRAPHY

Mehmed II
1432–1481

Mehmed II ruled the Ottoman Empire from 1451 to 1481. During this time he greatly improved the new capital, Istanbul. He repaired damage caused by fighting and built palaces, mosques, and a huge, covered bazaar. He encouraged people from all over the empire to move to the city.

Drawing Inferences Why do you think Mehmed II encouraged people to move to Istanbul?

GEOGRAPHY SKILLS | **INTERPRETING MAPS**

Location What region was at the heart, or center, of the Ottoman Empire?

The Safavid Empire

As the Ottoman Empire reached its height, a group of Persian Muslims known as the Safavids (sah-FAH-vuhds) was gaining power to the east, in the area of present-day Iran. Before long, the Safavids came into conflict with the Ottomans and other Muslims.

The conflict arose from an old disagreement among Muslims about who should be caliph. In the mid-600s, Islam split into two groups. The two groups were the Shia (SHEE-ah) and the Sunni (SOO-nee). The **Shia** were Muslims who thought that only Muhammad's descendants could become caliphs. The **Sunni** didn't think caliphs had to be related to Muhammad. The Ottomans were Sunnis and the Safavid leaders were Shia.

The Safavid Empire began in 1501 when the Safavid leader Esma'il (is-mah-EEL) conquered Persia. He took the ancient Persian title of shah, or king.

Esma'il made Shiism—the beliefs of the Shia—the official religion of the empire. But he wanted to spread Shiism farther.

THE IMPACT TODAY

Most Muslims today belong to the Sunni branch of Islam.

He tried to gain more Muslim lands and convert more Muslims to Shiism. He battled the Uzbek people, but he suffered a crushing defeat by the Ottomans in 1514.

In 1588 the greatest Safavid leader, 'Abbas, became shah. He strengthened the military and gave his soldiers modern gunpowder weapons. Copying the Ottomans, 'Abbas trained foreign slave boys to be soldiers. Under 'Abbas's rule the Safavids defeated the Uzbeks and took back land that had been lost to the Ottomans.

The Safavids blended Persian and Muslim cultural traditions. They built beautiful mosques in their capital, Esfahan (es-fah-HAHN), and grew wealthy from trade. The Safavid Empire lasted until the mid-1700s.

The Mughal Empire

East of the Safavid Empire, in northern India, lay the Mughal (MOO-guhl) Empire. The Mughals were Turkish Muslims from Central Asia. Their empire was established in 1526 by Babur (BAH-boohr).

In the mid-1500s an emperor named Akbar conquered many new lands and worked to strengthen the Mughal government. He also began a tolerant religious policy, ending the tax on non-Muslims.

Akbar's tolerance allowed Muslims and Hindus in the empire to live in peace. In time, a unique Mughal culture developed that blended Persian, Islamic, and Hindu elements. The Mughals became known for their monumental works of

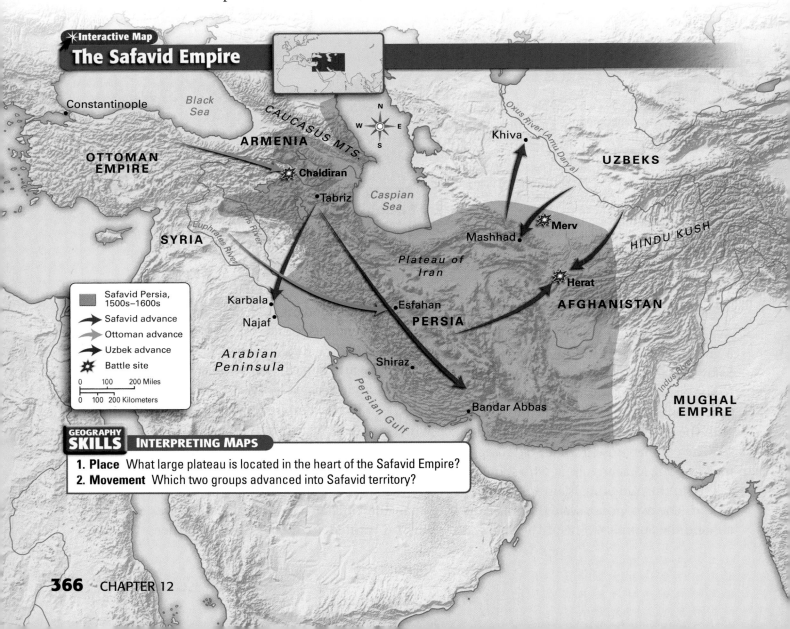

Interactive Map
The Safavid Empire

GEOGRAPHY SKILLS **INTERPRETING MAPS**

1. **Place** What large plateau is located in the heart of the Safavid Empire?
2. **Movement** Which two groups advanced into Safavid territory?

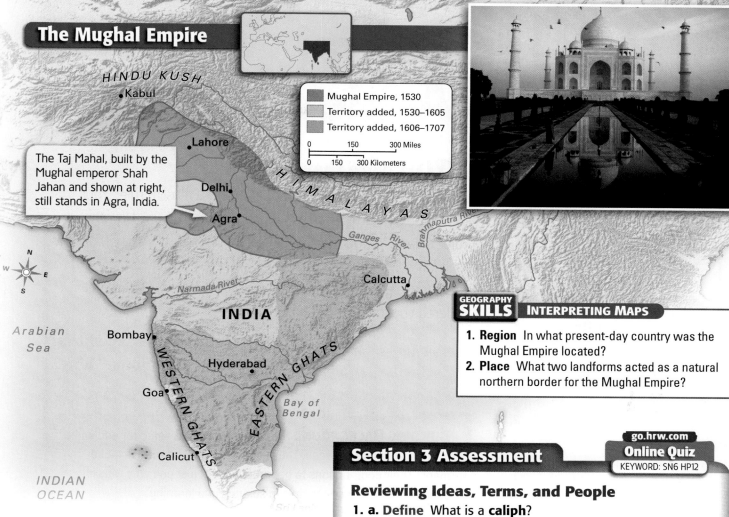

The Mughal Empire

HINDU KUSH
· Kabul

■	Mughal Empire, 1530
▢	Territory added, 1530–1605
▨	Territory added, 1606–1707

0   150   300 Miles
0   150   300 Kilometers

The Taj Mahal, built by the Mughal emperor Shah Jahan and shown at right, still stands in Agra, India.

· Lahore
HIMALAYAS
Delhi ·
Agra ·
Ganges River
Brahmaputra River

· Calcutta

Narmada River

INDIA

Arabian Sea

Bombay ·

Hyderabad ·

Goa ·

WESTERN GHATS
EASTERN GHATS

Bay of Bengal

· Calicut

INDIAN OCEAN

Sri Lanka

GEOGRAPHY SKILLS **INTERPRETING MAPS**

1. **Region** In what present-day country was the Mughal Empire located?
2. **Place** What two landforms acted as a natural northern border for the Mughal Empire?

architecture—particularly the Taj Mahal, a tomb built in the 1600s by emperor Shah Jahan.

In the late 1600s, an emperor reversed Akbar's tolerant policies. He destroyed many Hindu temples, and violent revolts broke out. The Mughal Empire soon fell apart.

READING CHECK **Analyzing** How did the Ottomans gain land for their empire?

SUMMARY AND PREVIEW Islam spread beyond Arabia through warfare and trade. The Ottomans, Safavids, and Mughals built great empires and continued the spread of Islam. In Section 4, you will learn about the cultural achievements of the Islamic world.

Section 3 Assessment

go.hrw.com
Online Quiz
KEYWORD: SN6 HP12

Reviewing Ideas, Terms, and People

1. **a. Define** What is a **caliph**?
   b. Evaluate Do you think the rules that Muslims made for conquered non-Muslims were fair? Why or why not?
2. **a. Identify** Name three places Islam spread to through trade.
   b. Explain How did trade help spread Islam?
3. **a. Recall** Who were the **Janissaries**?
   b. Contrast How did Sunni and Shia beliefs about caliphs differ?

Critical Thinking

4. **Comparing and Contrasting** Draw a chart like the one below. Use your notes to compare and contrast characteristics of the Ottoman, Safavid, and Mughal empires.

	Ottomans	Safavids	Mughals
Leaders			
Location			
Religious policy			

FOCUS ON WRITING

5. **Writing about Islamic Empires** Review this section and write a paragraph about the three powerful Islamic empires that began to form in the 1200s.

Cultural Achievements

What You Will Learn...

Main Ideas

1. Muslim scholars made lasting contributions to the fields of science and philosophy.
2. In literature and the arts, Muslim achievements included beautiful poetry, memorable short stories, and splendid architecture.

The Big Idea

Muslim scholars and artists made important contributions to science, art, and literature.

Key Terms and People

Ibn Battutah, *p. 369*
Sufism, *p. 369*
Omar Khayyám, *p. 371*
patrons, *p. 371*
minaret, *p. 371*
calligraphy, *p. 371*

TAKING NOTES As you read, take notes on the achievements and advances the Muslims made in various fields. In each outer circle of this word web, describe one achievement or advance. You may need to add more circles.

Achievements and Advances

If **YOU** were there...

You are a servant in the court of a powerful Muslim ruler. Your life at court is comfortable, though not one of luxury. Now the ruler is sending your master to explore unknown lands and distant kingdoms. The dangerous journey will take him across seas and deserts. He can take only a few servants with him. He has not ordered you to come but has given you a choice.

Would you join your master's expedition or stay home? Why?

BUILDING BACKGROUND Muslim explorers traveled far and wide to learn about new places. They used what they learned to make maps. Their contributions to geography were just one way Muslim scholars made advancements in science and learning.

Science and Philosophy

The empires of the Islamic world contributed to the achievements of Islamic culture. Muslim scholars made advances in astronomy, geography, math, and science. Scholars at Baghdad and Córdoba translated many ancient writings on these subjects into Arabic. Having a common language helped scholars throughout the

Islamic Achievements

Astronomy

Muslim scientists used astrolabes like this one to figure out their location, direction, and even the time of day. Although the Greeks invented the astrolabe, Muslims scholars greatly improved it.

The use of observatories allowed Muslim scientists to make other significant advances in astronomy too. This observatory was built in the 1700s in Delhi, the capital of Mughal India.

Islamic world share what they learned with each other.

Astronomy

Many Muslim cities had observatories where people could study the sun, moon, and stars. This study of astronomy helped scientists to better understand time and clockmaking. Muslim scientists also improved the astrolabe, which the Greeks had invented to chart the position of the stars. Arab scholars used the astrolabe to figure out their location on Earth.

Geography

Studying astronomy also helped Muslims explore the world. As people learned to use the stars to calculate time and location, merchants and explorers began to travel widely. The explorer **Ibn Battutah** traveled to Africa, India, China, and Spain in the 1320s. To help travelers, Muslim geographers made more accurate maps than were available before, and developed better ways of calculating distances.

Math

Muslim scholars also made advances in mathematics. In the 800s they combined the Indian number system, including the use of zero, with the Greek science of mathematics. A Muslim mathematician used these ideas to write two important books. One laid the foundation for modern algebra. The other explained the new number system. When his works reached Europe, Europeans called the new numbers "Arabic" numerals.

Medicine

Muslims may have made their greatest advances in medicine. They combined Greek and Indian knowledge with discoveries of their own. Muslim doctors started the first pharmacy school to teach people how to make medicine. A doctor in Baghdad discovered how to treat smallpox. Another doctor, known in the West as Avicenna (av-uh-SEN-uh), wrote a medical encyclopedia. It was used throughout Europe until the 1600s and is one of the most famous books in the history of medicine.

Philosophy

Many Muslim doctors and scientists studied the ancient Greek philosophy of rational thought. Others focused on spiritual issues, leading to a movement called **Sufism** (SOO-fi-zuhm). People who practice Sufism are Sufis (SOO-feez). Sufis believe they can find God's love by having a personal relationship with God. Sufism has attracted many followers to Islam.

READING CHECK **Drawing Conclusions**
How did Muslims influence the fields of science and medicine?

THE IMPACT TODAY

We still call the numerals 0, 1, 2, 3, 4, 5, 6, 7, 8, and 9 Arabic or Hindu-Arabic numerals.

Math
Muslim mathematicians combined Indian and Greek ideas with their own to dramatically increase human knowledge of mathematics. The fact that we call our numbers today "Arabic numerals" is a reminder of this contribution.

$$2x + 4$$

Medicine
Muslim doctors made medicines from plants like this mandrake plant, which was used to treat pain and illnesses. Muslim doctors developed better ways to prevent, diagnose, and treat many diseases.

The Blue Mosque

The Blue Mosque in Istanbul was built in the early 1600s for an Ottoman sultan. It upset many people at the time it was built because they thought its six minarets—instead of the usual four—were an attempt to make it as great as the mosque in Mecca.

Domes are a common feature of Islamic architecture. Huge columns support the center of this dome, and more than 250 windows let light into the mosque.

The mosque gets its name from its beautiful blue Iznik tiles.

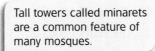

Tall towers called minarets are a common feature of many mosques.

The most sacred part of a mosque is the mihrab, the niche that points the way to Mecca. These men are praying facing the mihrab.

ANALYSIS SKILL **ANALYZING VISUALS**

Why do you think the decoration of the Blue Mosque is so elaborate?

Literature and the Arts

Literature, especially poetry, was popular in the Muslim world. Much poetry was influenced by Sufism. Sufi poets often wrote about their loyalty to God. One of the most famous Sufi poets was **Omar Khayyám** (OH-mahr ky-AHM).

Muslims also enjoyed reading short stories. One famous collection of short stories is *The Thousand and One Nights*. It includes tales about legendary characters such as Sinbad, Aladdin, and Ali Baba.

Architecture was one of the most important Muslim art forms. Rich Muslim rulers became great **patrons**, or sponsors, of architecture. They used their wealth to have beautiful mosques built to honor God and inspire religious followers. The main part of a mosque is a huge hall where people pray. Many mosques also have a large dome and a **minaret**, or narrow tower from where Muslims are called to prayer.

Muslim architects also built palaces, marketplaces, and libraries. Many of these buildings have complicated domes and arches, colored bricks, and decorated tiles.

You may notice, though, that most Muslim art does not show any people or animals. Muslims think only God can create humans and animals or their images. As a result, Muslim art is instead full of complex patterns. Muslim artists also turned to **calligraphy**, or decorative writing. They made sayings from the Qur'an into works of art and used them to decorate mosques and other buildings.

Muslim art and literature combined Islamic influences with the regional traditions of the places Muslims conquered. This mix of Islam with cultures from Asia, Africa, and Europe gave literature and the arts a unique style and character.

READING CHECK **Generalizing** Most mosques include which two architectural elements?

SUMMARY AND PREVIEW Islamic culture produced great achievements in science, philosophy, literature, architecture, and art. In the next chapter, you'll learn about an area that was greatly influenced by Muslim ideas—West Africa.

Section 4 Assessment

go.hrw.com
Online Quiz
KEYWORD: SN6 HP12

Reviewing Ideas, Terms, and People

1. **a. Identify** Who traveled to India, Africa, China, and Spain and contributed his knowledge to the study of geography?
   b. Explain How did Muslim scholars help preserve learning from the ancient world?
   c. Rank In your opinion, what was the most important Muslim scientific achievement? Why?
2. **a. Describe** What function do **minarets** serve in mosques?
   b. Explain How did Muslim artists create art without showing humans or animals?

Critical Thinking

3. **Analyzing** Using your notes, complete a chart like the one at right. For each category in the first column, list one important achievement or advance the Muslims made.

Category	Achievement or Advance
Astronomy	
Geography	
Math	
Medicine	
Philosophy	

FOCUS ON WRITING

4. **Describing Muslim Accomplishments** Review the answers you provided for the graphic organizer above and the information under the Literature and the Arts heading on this page. Then organize what you have learned into a paragraph that describes the cultural achievements of the Muslim world.

Social Studies Skills

Analysis   Critical Thinking   Economics   Study

Understanding Historical Context

Understand the Skill

A *context* is the circumstances under which something happens. *Historical context* includes values, beliefs, conditions, and practices that were common in the past. At times, some of these were quite different than what they are today. To truly understand a historical statement or event, you have to take its context into account. It is not right to judge what people in history did or said based on present-day values alone. To be fair, you must also consider the historical context of the statement or event.

Learn the Skill

To better understand something a historical figure said or wrote, use the following guidelines to understand the context of the statement.

1 Identify the speaker or writer, the date, and the topic and main idea of the statement.

2 Determine the speaker's or writer's attitude and point of view about the topic.

3 Review what you know about beliefs, conditions, or practices related to the topic that were common at the time. Find out more about those times if you need to.

4 Decide how the statement reflects the values, attitudes, and practices of people living at that time. Then determine how the statement reflects values, attitudes, and practices of today.

Applying these guidelines will give you a better understanding of a clash between Muslim and European armies in 1191. The following account of this clash was written by Baha' ad-Din, an advisor to the Muslim leader Saladin. He witnessed the battle.

> " The [king of the] Franks [the Muslim term for all Europeans] …ordered all the Musulman [Muslim] prisoners …to be brought before him. They numbered more than three thousand and were all bound with ropes. The Franks then flung themselves upon them all at once and massacred them with sword and lance in cold blood. "
>
> —Baha' ad-Din, from *The Crusade of Richard I,* by John Gillingham

By modern standards this event seems barbaric. But such massacres were not uncommon in those times. Plus, the description is from one side's point of view. This context should be considered when making judgments about the event.

Practice and Apply the Skill

Baha' ad-Din also described the battle itself. Read the following passage. Then answer the questions.

> " The center of the Muslim ranks was broken, drums and flags fell to the ground …Although there were almost 7,000 …killed that day God gave the Muslims victory over their enemies. He [Saladin] stood firm until …the Muslims were exhausted, and then he agreed to a truce at the enemy's request. "
>
> —Baha' ad-Din, from *Arab Historians of the Crusades,* translated by E. J. Costello

1. What happened to Saladin's army? Why do you think the writer calls the battle a Muslim victory?

2. History records this battle as a European victory. Plus, this account is part of a larger statement written in praise of Saladin. Does this additional context change your understanding and answer to the first question? Explain how or why not.

Visual Summary

Use the visual summary below to help you review the main ideas of the chapter.

QUICK FACTS

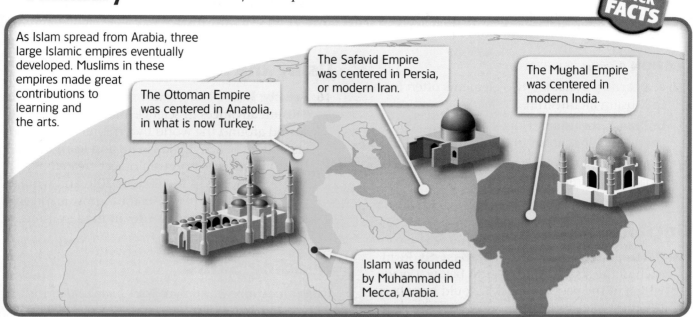

As Islam spread from Arabia, three large Islamic empires eventually developed. Muslims in these empires made great contributions to learning and the arts.

The Ottoman Empire was centered in Anatolia, in what is now Turkey.

The Safavid Empire was centered in Persia, or modern Iran.

The Mughal Empire was centered in modern India.

Islam was founded by Muhammad in Mecca, Arabia.

Reviewing Vocabulary, Terms, and People

For each statement below, write T if it is true and F if it is false. If the statement is false, write the correct term that would make the sentence a true statement.

1. Muslims gather to pray at a **jihad**.

2. Traders often traveled in **caravans** to take their goods to markets.

3. An **Islam** is a person who submits to God and follows the teachings of Muhammad.

4. According to Islamic belief, God's messages to Muhammad during his lifetime make up the **Sunnah**.

5. A **caliph** is a journey to a sacred place.

6. A **minaret** is a tower from where Muslims are called to prayer.

7. **Janissaries** converted to Islam and became fierce warriors in the Ottoman army.

8. The **Sunni** believed that only a descendant of Muhammad could become the highest leader of Islam.

Comprehension and Critical Thinking

SECTION 1 *(pages 354–357)*

9. **a. Recall** What two ways of life developed in Arabia's desert environment?

b. Analyze Why did Muhammad have a hard time getting people in Mecca to accept his teachings?

c. Evaluate What are some possible benefits to a nomadic lifestyle, and what are some possible benefits to a sedentary lifestyle?

SECTION 2 *(pages 358–361)*

10. **a. Define** What is the hajj?

b. Contrast Both the Qur'an and the Sunnah guide Muslims' behavior. Apart from discussing different topics, how do these two differ?

c. Predict Which of the Five Pillars of Islam do you think would be the most difficult to perform? Why?

SECTION 3 (pages 362–367)

11. a. Identify Who was Abu Bakr and why is he important in the history of Islam?

b. Analyze Why did the Safavids come into conflict with the Ottomans?

c. Evaluate In your opinion, was conquest or trade more effective in spreading Islam? Why?

SECTION 4 (pages 368–371)

12. a. Describe What are two elements often found in Muslim architecture?

b. Draw Conclusions How did having a common language help scholars in the Islamic world?

c. Elaborate Why might a ruler want to become a patron of a mosque?

Social Studies Skills

13. Determining the Context of Statements Read each of the statements in List A below. Decide which of the people in List B would have been the most likely writer of each statement.

List A

1. "I have conquered Constantinople."

2. "I want to build a new palace, the finest ever built in India."

3. "I want to conquer more Muslim lands and convert the people within them to Shiism."

4. "I hope my medical encyclopedia helps others to use what I have learned about treating diseases."

5. "I have decided to accept the invitation to move north to Medina."

6. "Being chosen as the first caliph is a high honor for me."

List B

a. Muhammad

b. Mehmed II

c. Avicenna

d. Esma'il

e. Abu Bakr

f. a Mughal emperor

Reviewing Themes

14. Geography How did the geography of the Arabian desert influence the lives of nomads?

15. Religion Take a position, agreeing or disagreeing with this statement: "Muslim leaders were tolerant of those they conquered." Defend your answer.

Using the Internet

go.hrw.com
KEYWORD: SN6 WH12

16. Activity: Researching Muslim Achievements Muslim advances in science, math, and art were spread around the world by explorers and traders. Enter the activity keyword and learn about these advances. Choose an object created by Muslim scholars in the 600s or 700s and write a paragraph that explains its roots, how it spread to other cultures, and its uses in modern times.

Reading Skills

Using Questions to Analyze Text *Imagine that you are a historian who has just finished reading this chapter and you want to learn more about the Islamic world. For each of the topics listed below, write one question for which you could attempt to find an answer in your research. For example, for the topic Islamic law, you might ask, "What Muslim countries today have a legal system that blends Sharia with Western law?*

17. growth of the Ottoman Empire

18. Muslim achievements in math

19. culture and learning in Baghdad

FOCUS ON WRITING

20. Creating Your Web Site Look back over your notes from this chapter. Then, design a home page and the four links titled "Who Was Muhammad?" "What Is Islam?" "The Islamic Empires," and "Islamic Cultural Achievements." Write four or five sentences for each link on your Web site. You may design the pages either online or on a large sheet of paper.

Remember that your audience is children, so you should keep your text simple. Use plenty of vivid language and bright colors to keep your audience interested in your topic.

Standardized Test Practice

DIRECTIONS: Read each question and write the letter of the best response.

> "The office of Imam was set up in order to replace the office of Prophet in the defense of the faith and the government of the world. . . . One group says it derives from reason, since it is the nature of reasonable men to submit to a leader who will prevent them from injuring one another and who will settle quarrels and disputes. . . . Another group says that the obligation derives from Holy Law and not from reason, since the Imam deals with matters of Holy Law. . . ."
>
> —Abu al-Hasan al-Mawardi (972–1058)

1 From the passage, it can be concluded that Imams in early Islam were

A religious leaders.

B government leaders.

C both religious and government leaders.

D neither religious nor government leaders.

2 Which of the following responsibilities of Muslims is not one of the Five Pillars of Islam?

A jihad

B frequent prayer

C hajj

D giving to the poor

3 The teachings of Muhammad are found mainly in the Qur'an and the

A Commentaries.

B Sunnah.

C Analects.

D Torah.

4 Which area of the world was least influenced by Muslim conquest and trade between the AD 600s and 1600s?

A North Africa

B South America

C Southwest Asia

D Southeast Asia

5 Muslim scholars are credited with developing

A geometry.

B algebra.

C calculus.

D physics.

Connecting with Past Learnings

6 Muslims believe that Muhammad revealed Allah's teaching to the world. Which of the following leaders that you learned about earlier did not reveal a religion's teachings to his people?

A Moses

B Hammurabi

C Buddha

D Jesus

7 You have learned that Muslim architects were known for their use of the dome. Which culture that you studied earlier also used many domes?

A the Chinese

B the Egyptians

C the Greeks

D the Romans

Early African Civilizations

FOCUS ON WRITING

A Journal Entry Many people feel that recording their lives in journals helps them to understand their own experiences. Writing a journal entry from someone else's point of view can help you to understand what that person's life is like. In this chapter, you will read about the land, people, and culture of early Africa. Then you will imagine a character and write a journal entry from his or her point of view.

c. 500 BC
West Africans begin using iron and making clay sculptures.

CHAPTER EVENTS

500 BC

WORLD EVENTS

c. 480 BC
Greece defeats Persia in the Persian Wars.

HOLT

History's Impact

▶ video series
Watch the video to understand the impact of early African civilizations on African cultures today.

What You Will Learn...

In this chapter, you will learn about the great empires of West Africa, which grew rich from trade. This photo shows women in front of a mosque in the city of Djenné, in present-day Mali.

c. AD 200
Camels are first used in North Africa, making Saharan trade easier.

1060s
The Empire of Ghana reaches its height.

1324
Mansa Musa leaves Mali on a hajj to Mecca.

1580s
Moroccan invaders begin their conquest of Songhai.

AD 500

1300

1600

1281 The Mongols' attempt to conquer Japan fails.

1337
The Hundred Years' War begins in France.

1521
Spanish explorers conquer the Aztec Empire.

EARLY AFRICAN CIVILIZATIONS **377**

Reading Social Studies

by Kylene Beers

Focus on Themes In this chapter, you will read about West Africa—its physical **geography** and early cultures. You will see West Africa is a land of many resources and varied features. One feature, the Niger River, has been particularly important in the region's history, providing water, food, and transportation for people. In addition, salt and iron deposits can be found in the region. Such resources were the basis for a **technology** that allowed people to create strong tools and weapons.

Organization of Facts and Information

Focus on Reading How are books organized in the library? How are the groceries organized in the store? Clear organization helps us find the product we need, and it also helps us find facts and information.

Understanding Structural Patterns Writers use structural patterns to organize information in sentences or paragraphs. What's a structural pattern? It's simply a way of organizing information. Learning to recognize those patterns will make it easier for you to read and understand social studies texts.

Patterns of Organization		
Pattern	**Clue Words**	**Graphic Organizer**
Cause-effect shows how one thing leads to another	as a result, because, therefore, this led to	Cause → Effect / Effect / Effect
Chronological Order shows the sequence of events or actions.	after, before, first, then, not long after, finally	First → Next → Next → Last
Listing presents information in categories such as size, location, or importance.	also, most important, for example, in fact	Category • Fact • Fact • Fact • Fact

To use text structure to improve your understanding, follow these steps:

1. Look for the main idea of the passage you are reading.

2. Then look for clues that signal a specific pattern.

3. Look for other important ideas and think about how the ideas connect. Is there any obvious pattern?

4. Use a graphic organizer to map the relationships among the facts and details.

You Try It!

The following passages are from the chapter you are about to read. As you read each set of sentences, ask yourself what structural pattern the writer used to organize the information.

Recognizing Structural Patterns

A. "As the people of West Africa became more productive, villages had more than they needed to survive. West Africans began to trade the area's resources with buyers who lived thousands of miles away." (p. 383)

B. "When Sundiata was a boy, a harsh ruler conquered Mali. But as an adult, Sundiata built up an army and won back his country's independence. He then conquered nearby kingdoms, including Ghana, in the 1230s . . . After Sundiata conquered Ghana, he took over the salt and gold trades. He also worked to improve agriculture in Mali." (p. 390)

C. "Four different regions make up the area surrounding the Niger River . . . The northern band is the southern part of the Sahara . . . The next band is the Sahel (sah-HEL), a strip of land with little rainfall that divides the desert from wetter areas . . . Farther south is savannah, or open grassland . . . The fourth band, near the equator, gets heavy rain." (p. 382)

After you read the passages, answer the questions below:

1. What structural pattern did the writer use to organize the information in passage A? How can you tell?

2. What structural pattern did the writer use to organize the information in passage B? How can you tell?

3. What structural pattern did the writer use to organize the information in passage C? How can you tell?

Key Terms and People

Chapter 13

Section 1
rifts *(p. 380)*
sub-Saharan Africa *(p. 380)*
Sahel *(p. 382)*
savannah *(p. 382)*
rain forests *(p. 382)*
extended family *(p. 382)*
animism *(p. 383)*

Section 2
silent barter *(p. 386)*
Tunka Manin *(p. 388)*

Section 3
Sundiata *(p. 390)*
Mansa Musa *(p. 391)*
Sunni Ali *(p. 392)*
Askia the Great *(p. 393)*

Section 4
oral history *(p. 396)*
griots *(p. 396)*
proverbs *(p. 397)*
kente *(p. 399)*

Academic Vocabulary

Success in school is related to knowing academic vocabulary—the words that are frequently used in school assignments and discussions. In this chapter, you will learn the following academic word:

process *(p. 397)*

As you read Chapter 13, think about the organization of the ideas. Look for signal words and ask yourself why the author has arranged the text in this way.

Geography and Early Africa

What You Will Learn...

Main Ideas

1. Landforms, climate, and resources affected the history of West Africa.
2. The way of life of early peoples in West Africa was shaped by family ties, religion, iron technology, and trade.

The Big Idea

Geography, resources, culture, and trade influenced the growth of societies in West Africa.

Key Terms and People

rifts, *p. 380*
sub-Saharan Africa, *p. 380*
Sahel, *p. 382*
savannah, *p. 382*
rain forests, *p. 382*
extended family, *p. 382*
animism, *p. 383*

TAKING NOTES As you read, take notes about the geography and traditional ways of life in Africa. You may wish to use a diagram like the one below to organize your notes.

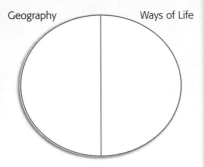

Geography | Ways of Life

If **YOU** were there...

You live in a village near the great bend of the Niger River in Africa in about AD 800. The river is full of life—birds, fish, crocodiles. You use its water to grow crops and raise cattle. Traders use the river to bring wood, gold, and other products from the forests.

Why is this a good place to live?

BUILDING BACKGROUND The continent of Africa is so large that it includes many varied kinds of terrain, from barren deserts to thick rain forests. Each region has a different climate and provides different resources for the people who live there. In West Africa rivers provide water to grow crops in drier areas. The land is also a rich source of minerals, especially gold and iron. These two resources played a large role in the development of West African cultures.

Landforms, Climate, and Resources

Africa is the earth's second largest continent. An immense desert, the Sahara, stretches across most of North Africa. Along the northwestern edge of the Sahara lie the Atlas Mountains. At the opposite edge of the continent, in the southeast, the Drakensberg Mountains rise. In eastern Africa, mountains extend alongside great rifts. These **rifts** are long, deep valleys formed by the movement of the earth's crust. From all these mountains the land dips into plateaus and wide, low plains. The plains of **sub-Saharan Africa**, or Africa south of the Sahara, are crossed by mighty rivers. These rivers include the Congo, the Zambezi, and the Niger.

Regions of West Africa

As a source of water, food, and transportation, the Niger River allowed many people to live in West Africa. Along the Niger's middle section is a low-lying area of lakes and marshes. Many animals find food and shelter there. Fish are also plentiful.

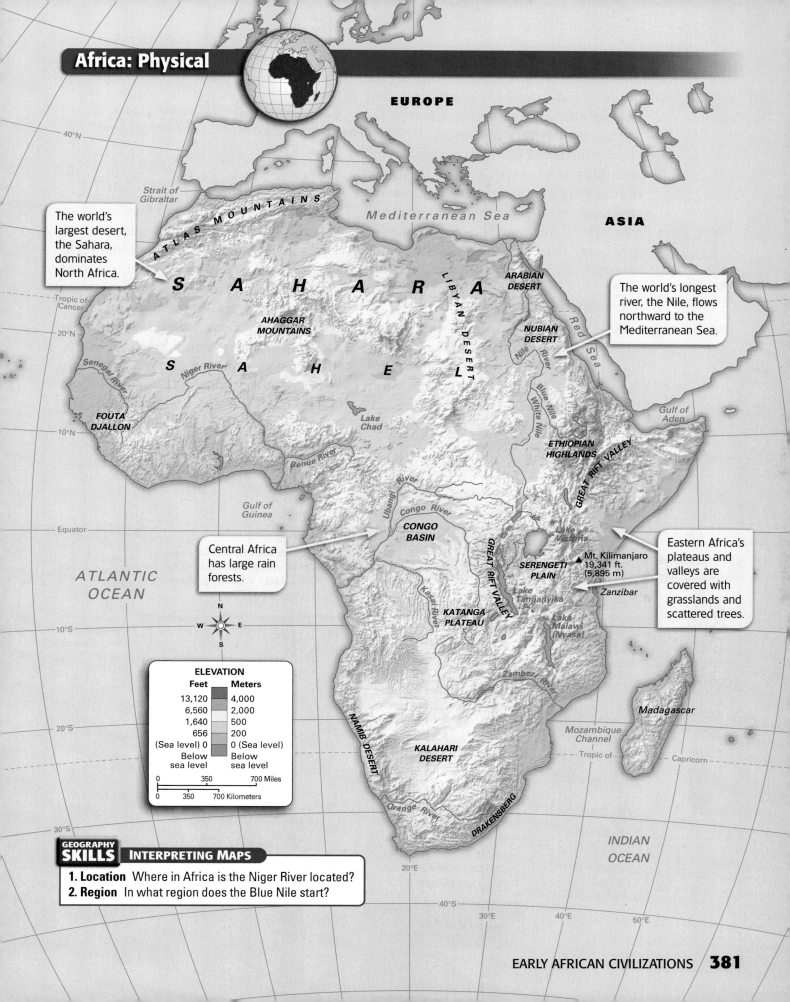

Africa: Physical

EUROPE

ASIA

The world's largest desert, the Sahara, dominates North Africa.

The world's longest river, the Nile, flows northward to the Mediterranean Sea.

Central Africa has large rain forests.

Eastern Africa's plateaus and valleys are covered with grasslands and scattered trees.

Strait of Gibraltar

Mediterranean Sea

ATLAS MOUNTAINS

S A H A R A

LIBYAN DESERT

ARABIAN DESERT

AHAGGAR MOUNTAINS

NUBIAN DESERT

Red Sea

S A H E L

Senegal River

Niger River

Nile River

White Nile

Blue Nile

Gulf of Aden

FOUTA DJALLON

Lake Chad

Benue River

ETHIOPIAN HIGHLANDS

GREAT RIFT VALLEY

Gulf of Guinea

Ubangi River

Congo River

CONGO BASIN

Lake Victoria

Mt. Kilimanjaro 19,341 ft. (5,895 m)

ATLANTIC OCEAN

Kasai River

GREAT RIFT VALLEY

SERENGETI PLAIN

Zanzibar

Lake Tanganyika

KATANGA PLATEAU

Lake Malawi (Nyasa)

Zambezi River

Madagascar

Equator

Tropic of Cancer

40°N

20°N

10°N

10°S

20°S

30°S

Mozambique Channel

Tropic of Capricorn

NAMIB DESERT

KALAHARI DESERT

Orange River

DRAKENSBERG

INDIAN OCEAN

ELEVATION

Feet		Meters
13,120		4,000
6,560		2,000
1,640		500
656		200
(Sea level) 0		0 (Sea level)
Below sea level		Below sea level

| 0 | 350 | 700 Miles |
| 0 | 350 | 700 Kilometers |

GEOGRAPHY SKILLS INTERPRETING MAPS

1. Location Where in Africa is the Niger River located?
2. Region In what region does the Blue Nile start?

20°E   30°E   40°E   50°E

40°S

Four different regions make up the area surrounding the Niger River. The regions run from east to west like broad bands. The northern band is the southern part of the Sahara. Rain is very rare there. The next band is the **Sahel** (sah-HEL), a strip of land with little rainfall that divides the desert from wetter areas. Farther south is the **savannah**, or open grassland with scattered trees. The fourth band, near the equator, gets heavy rain. This band is made of **rain forests**, or moist, densely wooded areas.

THE IMPACT TODAY

Human activities like logging and farming are rapidly destroying Africa's rain forests.

West Africa's Resources

West Africa's land is one of the region's many resources. With its many climates, the land can produce many different crops. Traditional crops grown in West Africa included dates, kola nuts, and grains.

Other resources were minerals. Gold, from the forests, was highly prized. So was salt, which came from the Sahara. Salt kept food from spoiling, and people needed it in their diet to survive Africa's hot climate.

READING CHECK Finding Main Ideas What are some of West Africa's major resources?

Early Peoples' Way of Life

A typical early West African family was an **extended family**. It usually included the father, mother, children, and close relatives in one household. West African society expected each person to be loyal to his or her family. In some areas people also became part of age-sets. In these groups, men born within the same two or three years formed special bonds. Women, too, sometimes formed age-sets.

Loyalty to family and age-sets helped the people of a village to work together. The men hunted, farmed, and raised livestock. Women farmed, collected firewood, ground grain, carried water, and cared for children.

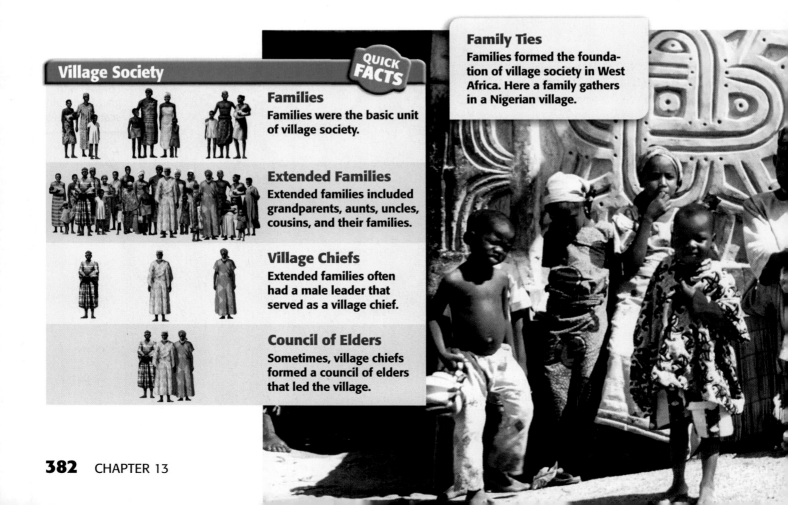

Village Society

QUICK FACTS

Families
Families were the basic unit of village society.

Extended Families
Extended families included grandparents, aunts, uncles, cousins, and their families.

Village Chiefs
Extended families often had a male leader that served as a village chief.

Council of Elders
Sometimes, village chiefs formed a council of elders that led the village.

Family Ties
Families formed the foundation of village society in West Africa. Here a family gathers in a Nigerian village.

Religion was another central feature of village life. Many West Africans believed that their ancestors' spirits stayed nearby. To honor these spirits, families marked places as sacred by putting specially carved statues there. They also offered food to their ancestors. Another common West African belief was **animism**—the belief that bodies of water, animals, trees, and other natural objects have spirits.

As time passed, the people of West Africa developed advanced cultures. Changes in technology helped early communities grow. Around 500 BC West Africans found that they could heat certain kinds of rock to get a hard metal. This was iron. Stronger than other metals, iron was good for making tools and weapons. Iron tools allowed farmers to clear land faster and to grow food more easily than they could with earlier tools.

As the people of West Africa became more productive, villages had more than they needed to survive. West Africans began to trade the area's resources with buyers who lived thousands of miles away.

West Africa's gold and salt mines became a source of great wealth. Traders used camels to cross the Sahara. They took gold, salt, cloth, slaves, and other items to North Africa and the Islamic world.

READING CHECK **Analyzing** How did religion in West Africa reflect the importance of family?

SUMMARY AND PREVIEW Physical geography affected culture and trade in West Africa. When West Africans developed iron technology, communities grew. Trade, especially in gold and salt, expanded. Next, you will read about a West African empire based on this trade—Ghana.

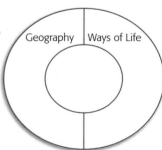
go.hrw.com
Online Quiz
KEYWORD: SN6 HP13

Section 1 Assessment

Reviewing Ideas, Terms, and People

1. **a. Recall** Where in Africa are the **rifts** located?
   b. Explain How were two of West Africa's valuable mineral resources related to local physical geography.
2. **a. Identify** What are two groups to which a person in early West Africa may have owed loyalty?
   b. Analyze How did the use of iron change farming?

Critical Thinking

3. **Drawing Conclusions** Draw a diagram like the one shown. Based on your notes, write a statement in the center circle of the diagram about how Africa's geography has shaped life there.

   Geography | Ways of Life

FOCUS ON WRITING

4. **Reviewing Notes on Early West Africa** Review your notes on the geography and early peoples of West Africa. Consider what your character saw every day. What challenges did the environment present? What role did family, religion, and technology play in your character's way of life?

EARLY AFRICAN CIVILIZATIONS **383**

Crossing the Sahara

Crossing the Sahara has never been easy. Bigger than the entire continent of Australia, the Sahara is one of the hottest, driest, and most barren places on earth. Yet for centuries, people have crossed the Sahara's gravel-covered plains and vast seas of sand. Long ago, West Africans crossed the desert regularly to carry on a rich trade.

Salt, used to preserve and flavor food, was available in the Sahara. Traders from the north took salt south. Camel caravans carried huge slabs of salt weighing hundreds of pounds.

Tindouf

Akjoujt

Taghaza

Walata

Koumbi
Saleh

Timbuktu

Es-Souk

Gao

Takedda

A F R I C A

In exchange for salt, people in West Africa offered other valuable trade goods, especially gold. Gold dust was measured with special spoons and stored in boxes. Ivory, from the tusks of elephants, was carved into jewelry.

Gulf of Guinea

384   CHAPTER 13

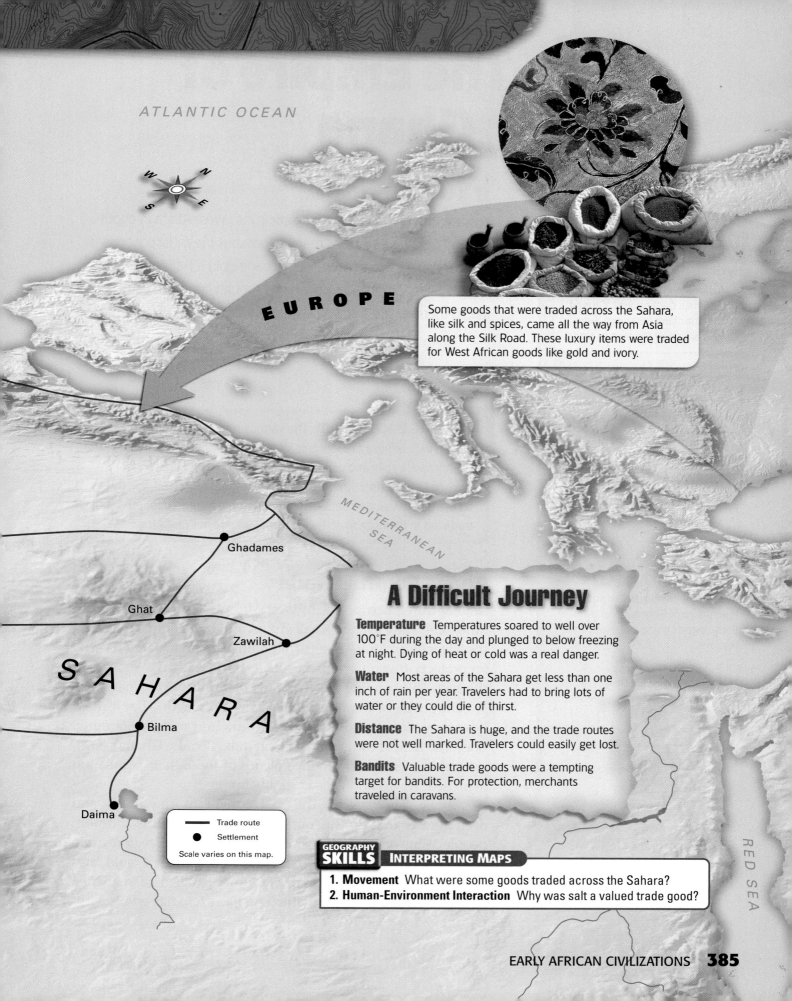

ATLANTIC OCEAN

W N E S

EUROPE

Some goods that were traded across the Sahara, like silk and spices, came all the way from Asia along the Silk Road. These luxury items were traded for West African goods like gold and ivory.

MEDITERRANEAN SEA

● Ghadames

● Ghat

Zawilah ●

S A H A R A

● Bilma

Daima ●

A Difficult Journey

Temperature Temperatures soared to well over 100°F during the day and plunged to below freezing at night. Dying of heat or cold was a real danger.

Water Most areas of the Sahara get less than one inch of rain per year. Travelers had to bring lots of water or they could die of thirst.

Distance The Sahara is huge, and the trade routes were not well marked. Travelers could easily get lost.

Bandits Valuable trade goods were a tempting target for bandits. For protection, merchants traveled in caravans.

——— Trade route
● Settlement
Scale varies on this map.

RED SEA

GEOGRAPHY SKILLS **INTERPRETING MAPS**

1. **Movement** What were some goods traded across the Sahara?
2. **Human-Environment Interaction** Why was salt a valued trade good?

The Empire of Ghana

What You Will Learn...

Main Ideas

1. Ghana controlled trade and became wealthy.
2. Through its control of trade, Ghana built an empire.
3. Ghana's decline was caused by attacking invaders, over-grazing, and the loss of trade.

The Big Idea

The rulers of Ghana built an empire by controlling the salt and gold trade.

Key Terms and People

silent barter, *p. 386*
Tunka Manin, *p. 388*

TAKING NOTES As you read, make a list of important events from the beginning to the end of the empire of Ghana. Keep track of these events using a diagram like this one.

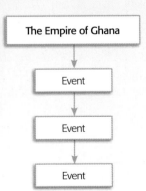

If YOU were there...

You are a trader in a caravan heading into West Africa in about 1000. The caravan carries many goods, but the most precious is salt. Salt is so valuable that people trade gold for it! The gold traders never meet you face to face, though. You wish you could talk to them to find out where they get their gold.

Why do you think the traders are so secretive?

BUILDING BACKGROUND The various regions of Africa provided people with different resources. West Africa, for example, was rich in both fertile soils and minerals, especially gold and iron. Other regions had plentiful supplies of other resources, such as salt. Over time, trade developed between regions with different resources. This trade led to the growth of the first great empire in West Africa.

Ghana Controls Trade

Among the earliest people in West Africa were the Soninke (soh-NING-kee). They lived in small groups and farmed the land along the Niger River. After AD 300, the Soninke began to band together for protection against nomadic herders who wanted to move into the area. This banding together was the beginning of Ghana.

The people of Ghana gradually grew in strength. They learned how to work with iron and how to use iron tools for farming. They also herded cattle for meat and milk. Because Ghana's farmers and herders could produce plenty of food, their population increased. Towns and villages sprang up.

Ghana lay between the vast Sahara to the north and deep forests that spread out to the south. In this location, people were in a good position to trade in the region's two main resources—gold and salt. The exchange of gold and salt sometimes followed a specific process called silent barter. **Silent barter** is a process in which people exchange goods with-

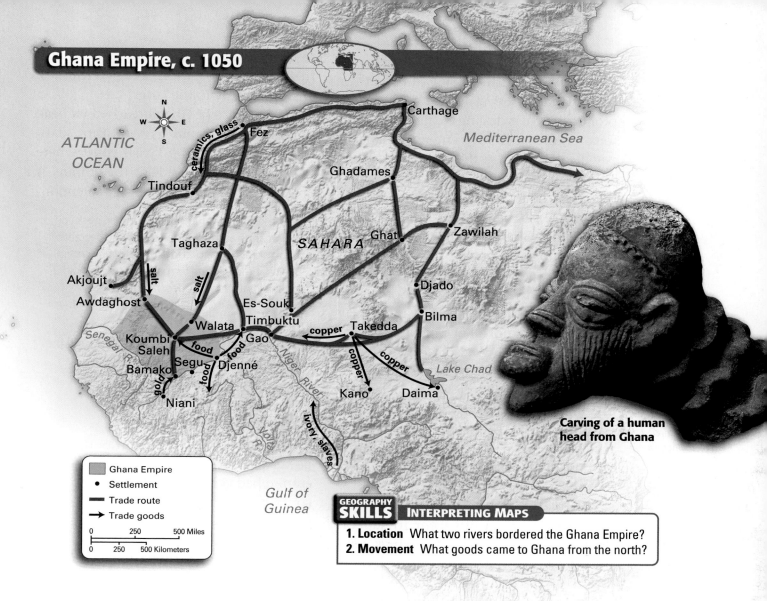

Ghana Empire, c. 1050

ATLANTIC OCEAN

Mediterranean Sea

ceramics, glass

Carthage

Fez

Tindouf

Ghadames

SAHARA

Ghat

Zawilah

Taghaza

Akjoujt

salt

salt

Awdaghost

Djado

Es-Souk

Bilma

Walata

Timbuktu

copper

Takedda

Koumbi Saleh

Gao

food

food

Senegal R.

Bamako

Segu

food

Djenné

copper

copper

gold

Niani

Kano

Daima

Lake Chad

Niger River

Volta R.

ivory, slaves

Gulf of Guinea

Carving of a human head from Ghana

Ghana Empire
Settlement
Trade route
Trade goods

| 0 | 250 | 500 Miles |
| 0 | 250 | 500 Kilometers |

GEOGRAPHY SKILLS — **INTERPRETING MAPS**

1. **Location** What two rivers bordered the Ghana Empire?
2. **Movement** What goods came to Ghana from the north?

out contacting each other directly. In Ghana salt traders left slabs of salt on a riverbank. In exchange, gold miners left what they thought was a fair amount of gold. The method made sure that trade was done peacefully. It also kept the location of the gold mines secret.

As trade in gold and salt increased, Ghana's rulers gained power. They built armies equipped with iron weapons that were superior to the weapons of nearby peoples. Over time, Ghana took over control of trade from the North African merchants. Then, additional goods were added to the mix of items traded. Wheat came from the north. Sheep, cattle, and honey

came from the south. Local products, such as leather and cloth, were also traded. Before long, this extensive trade made Ghana very prosperous indeed.

READING CHECK **Generalizing** How did trade help Ghana develop?

Ghana Builds an Empire

By 800 Ghana was firmly in control of West Africa's trade routes. Nearly all trade between northern and southern Africa passed through Ghana. Ghana's army kept the trade routes safe. Trade increased, and so did Ghana's wealth.

Taxes and Gold

With so many traders passing through their lands, Ghana's rulers looked for ways to profit from their dealings. One way was to force every trader who entered Ghana to pay a special tax on the goods he carried. Then each trader had to pay another tax on the goods he took with him when he left. The people of Ghana also had to pay taxes. In addition, Ghana forced small neighboring tribes to pay tribute.

Ghana's gold mines brought even more income into the royal treasury. Some gold was carried by traders to lands as far away as England. But not all of Ghana's gold was traded. Ghana's kings also kept huge stores of the precious metal for themselves.

FOCUS ON READING
In the section titled "Ghana's Decline," what type of structural pattern is used? How do you know?

The rulers of Ghana banned everyone else in Ghana from owning gold nuggets. Common people could only own gold dust, which they used as money. This ensured that the king was richer than his subjects.

Expansion of the Empire

Part of Ghana's wealth went to support its powerful army. Ghana's kings used this army to conquer many neighboring areas. To keep order in their large empire, Ghana's kings allowed conquered rulers to retain much of their power. These local rulers acted as governors of their territories, answering only to the king.

The empire of Ghana reached its peak under **Tunka Manin** (TOOHN-kah MAH-nin). This king had a lavish court where he displayed the wealth of the empire. A Spanish writer noted the court's splendor.

"The king adorns himself . . . round his neck and his forearms, and he puts on a high cap decorated with gold and wrapped in a turban of fine cotton. Behind the king stand ten pages [servants] holding shields and swords decorated with gold."
–al-Bakri, from *The Book of Routes and Kingdoms*

READING CHECK **Summarizing** How did the rulers of Ghana control trade?

Ghana's Decline

In the mid-1000s, Ghana was rich and powerful, but by the early 1200s, the empire had collapsed. Three major factors contributed to its end.

Invasion

The first factor that hurt Ghana was invasion. A group of North African Muslims called the Almoravids (al-moh-RAH-vidz) attacked Ghana in the 1060s. After 14 years of fighting, the Almoravids defeated the people of Ghana. The Almoravids didn't control Ghana for long, but they weakened the empire. They cut off many trade routes and formed new trading partnerships with Muslim leaders. Without this trade, Ghana could not support its empire.

Overgrazing

A second factor in Ghana's decline also involved the Almoravids. These invaders brought herds of animals with them. These animals ate all the grass in many pastures, leaving the soil exposed to hot desert winds.

BIOGRAPHY

Tunka Manin
Ruled around 1068

All we know about Tunka Manin comes from the writings of a Muslim geographer who wrote about Ghana. From his writings, we know that Tunka Manin was the nephew of the previous king, a man named Basi. Kingship and property in Ghana did not pass from father to son, but from uncle to nephew. Only the king's sister's son could inherit the throne. Once he did become king, Tunka Manin surrounded himself with finery and many luxuries.

Contrasting How was inheritance in Ghana different from inheritance in other societies you have studied?

Overgrazing

Too many animals grazing in one area can lead to problems, such as the loss of farmland that occurred in West Africa.

1 Animals are allowed to graze in areas with lots of grass.

2 With too many animals grazing, however, the grass disappears, leaving the soil below exposed to the wind.

3 The wind blows the soil away, turning what was once grassland into desert.

These winds blew away the soil, leaving it worthless for farming or herding. Many farmers had to leave in search of new homes.

Internal Rebellion

A third factor also helped bring about the decline of Ghana's empire. In about 1200 the people of a country that Ghana had conquered rose up in rebellion. Within a few years these rebels had taken over the entire empire of Ghana.

Once in control, however, the rebels found that they could not keep order.

Weakened, Ghana was attacked and defeated by one of its neighbors. The empire fell apart.

READING CHECK Identifying Cause and Effect Why did Ghana decline in the AD 1000s?

SUMMARY AND PREVIEW The empire of Ghana in West Africa grew rich and powerful through its control of trade routes and its gold production. The empire lasted from about 800 to 1200. In the next section, you will learn about two empires that arose after Ghana—Mali and Songhai.

Section 2 Assessment

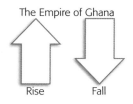

go.hrw.com
Online Quiz
KEYWORD: SN6 HP13

Reviewing Ideas, Terms, and People

1. a. **Identify** What were the two major resources traded in Ghana?
   b. **Explain** How did the **silent barter** system work?
2. a. **Identify** Who was **Tunka Manin**?
   b. **Generalize** What did Ghana's kings do with the money they raised from taxes and gold mining?
   c. **Elaborate** Why did the rulers of Ghana not want everyone to have gold?
3. a. **Recall** What group invaded Ghana in the late 1000s?
   b. **Analyze** How did overgrazing help cause the fall of Ghana?

Critical Thinking

4. **Categorizing** Look through the events you listed in your notes. Decide which contributed to Ghana's rise and which led to its fall. Organize the events in a diagram like this one.

The Empire of Ghana

Rise   Fall

FOCUS ON WRITING

5. **Reviewing Notes on Ghana** Review this section and your notes on the rise and fall of Ghana's trading empire. Keep in mind how your character's life may have been impacted by Ghana's history.

Later Empires

What You Will Learn...

Main Ideas

1. The empire of Mali reached its height under the ruler Mansa Musa, but the empire fell to invaders in the 1400s.
2. The Songhai built a new Islamic empire in West Africa, conquering many of the lands that were once part of Mali.
3. Great Zimbabwe was a powerful state that developed in southern Africa.

The Big Idea

Between 1000 and 1500 three great kingdoms—Mali, Songhai, and Great Zimbabwe—developed in Africa

Key People

Sundiata, *p. 390*
Mansa Musa, *p. 391*
Sunni Ali, *p. 392*
Askia the Great, *p. 393*

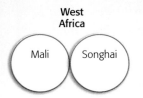

TAKING NOTES As you read, take notes about life in the cultures that developed in West Africa—Mali and Songhai—and the one that developed in southern Africa—Great Zimbabwe.

West Africa | Southern Africa
Mali — Songhai | Great Zimbabwe

If **YOU** were there...

You are a servant of the great Mansa Musa, ruler of Mali. You've been chosen as one of the servants who will travel with him on a pilgrimage to Mecca. The king has given you all fine new clothes of silk for the trip. He will carry much gold with him. You've never left your home before. But now you will see the great city of Cairo, Egypt, and many other new places.

How do you feel about going on this journey?

BUILDING BACKGROUND Mansa Musa was one of Africa's greatest rulers, and his empire, Mali, was one of the largest in African history. Rising from the ruins of Ghana, Mali took over the trade routes of West Africa and grew into a powerful state.

Mali

Like Ghana, Mali (MAH-lee) lay along the upper Niger River. This area's fertile soil helped Mali grow. Mali's location on the Niger also allowed its people to control trade on the river. As a result, the empire grew rich and powerful. According to legend, Mali's rise to power began under a ruler named **Sundiata** (soohn-JAHT-ah).

Sundiata Makes Mali an Empire

When Sundiata was a boy, a harsh ruler conquered Mali. But as an adult, Sundiata built up an army and won back his country's independence. He then conquered nearby kingdoms, including Ghana, in the 1230s.

After Sundiata conquered Ghana, he took over the salt and gold trades. He also worked to improve agriculture in Mali. Sundiata had new farmlands cleared for beans, onions, rice, and other crops. Sundiata even introduced a new crop—cotton. From the cotton fibers people made clothing that was comfortable in the warm climate. They also sold cotton to other people.

To keep order in his prosperous kingdom, Sundiata took power away from local leaders. Each of these local leaders had the title *mansa* (MAHN-sah), a title Sundiata now took

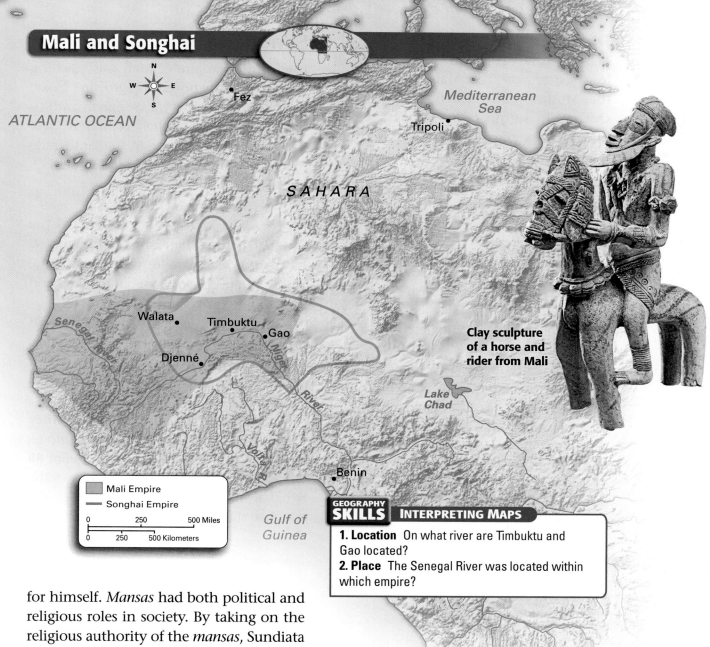

Mali and Songhai

Fez

Tripoli

Mediterranean Sea

ATLANTIC OCEAN

SAHARA

Senegal River

Walata

Timbuktu

Gao

Niger

Djenné

River

Volta River

Lake Chad

Benin

Clay sculpture of a horse and rider from Mali

Mali Empire

Songhai Empire

| 0 | 250 | 500 Miles |

| 0 | 250 | 500 Kilometers |

Gulf of Guinea

GEOGRAPHY SKILLS **INTERPRETING MAPS**

1. Location On what river are Timbuktu and Gao located?

2. Place The Senegal River was located within which empire?

for himself. *Mansas* had both political and religious roles in society. By taking on the religious authority of the *mansas*, Sundiata gained even more power in Mali.

Sundiata died in 1255. Later rulers of Mali took the title of *mansa*. Unlike Sundiata, most of these rulers were Muslims.

Mansa Musa

Mali's most famous ruler was a Muslim named **Mansa Musa** (MAHN-sah moo-SAH). Under his skillful leadership, Mali reached the height of its wealth, power, and fame in the 1300s. Because of Mansa Musa's influence, Islam spread through a large part of West Africa, gaining many new believers.

Mansa Musa ruled Mali for about 25 years, from 1312 to 1337. During that time, Mali added many important trade cities to its empire, including Timbuktu (tim-buhk-TOO).

Religion was very important to Mansa Musa. In 1324 he left Mali on a pilgrimage to Mecca. Through his journey, Mansa Musa introduced his empire to the Islamic world. He spread Mali's fame far and wide.

Mansa Musa also supported education. He sent many scholars to study in Morocco.

These scholars later set up schools in Mali. Mansa Musa stressed the importance of learning to read the Arabic language so that Muslims in his empire could read the Qur'an. To spread Islam in West Africa, Mansa Musa hired Muslim architects to build mosques throughout his empire.

THE IMPACT TODAY

Some of the mosques built by Mansa Musa can still be seen in West Africa today.

The Fall of Mali

When Mansa Musa died, his son Maghan (MAH-gan) took the throne. Maghan was a weak ruler. When raiders from the southeast poured into Mali, he couldn't stop them. The raiders set fire to Timbuktu's great schools and mosques. Mali never fully recovered from this terrible blow. The empire continued to weaken and decline.

In 1431 the Tuareg (TWAH-reg), nomads from the Sahara, seized Timbuktu. The people living at the edges of Mali's empire broke away. By 1500 nearly all of the lands the empire had once ruled were lost. Only a small area of Mali remained.

READING CHECK Sequencing What steps did Sundiata take to turn Mali into an empire?

Songhai

Even as the Empire of Mali was reaching its height, a rival power was growing in the area. That rival was the Songhai (SAHNG-hy) kingdom. From their capital at Gao, the Songhai participated in the same trade that had made Ghana and Mali so rich.

The Building of an Empire

In the 1300s Mansa Musa conquered the Songhai, adding their lands to his empire. But as the Mali Empire weakened in the 1400s, the people of Songhai rebelled and regained their freedom.

The Songhai leaders were Muslims. So too were many of the North African Berbers who traded in West Africa. Because of this shared religion, the Berbers were willing to trade with the Songhai, who grew richer.

As the Songhai gained in wealth, they expanded their territory and built an empire. Songhai's expansion was led by **Sunni Ali** (SOOH-nee ah-LEE), who became ruler of the Songhai in 1464. Before he took over, the Songhai state had been disorganized and

The people of Songhai depended on the Niger River for many things. It was an important transportation route and provided fertile lands and a source of water for farming.

poorly run. As ruler, Sunni Ali worked to unify, strengthen, and enlarge his empire. Much of the land that he added to Songhai had been part of Mali.

As king, Sunni Ali encouraged everyone in his empire to work together. To build religious harmony, he participated in both Muslim and local religions. As a result, he brought stability to Songhai.

Askia the Great

Sunni Ali died in 1492. He was followed as king by his son Sunni Baru, who was not a Muslim. The Songhai people feared that if Sunni Baru didn't support Islam, they would lose their trade with Muslim lands. They rebelled against the king.

The leader of that rebellion was a general named Muhammad Ture (moo-HAH-muhd too-RAY). After overthrowing Sunni Baru, Muhammad Ture chose the title *askia,* a title of high military rank. Eventually, he became known as **Askia the Great**.

Askia supported education and learning. Under his rule, Timbuktu flourished, drawing thousands to its universities, schools, libraries, and mosques. The city was especially known for the University of Sankore (san-KOH-rah). People arrived there from North Africa and other places to study math, science, medicine, grammar, and law. Djenné was another city that became a center of learning.

Most of Songhai's traders were Muslim, and as they gained influence in the empire so did Islam. Askia, himself a devout Muslim, encouraged the growth of Islamic influence. He made many laws similar to those in other Muslim nations.

To help maintain order, Askia set up five provinces within Songhai. He removed local leaders and appointed new governors who were loyal to him. Askia also created a professional army and specialized departments to oversee specific tasks.

BIOGRAPHY

Askia the Great
c. 1443–1538

Askia the Great became the ruler of Songhai when he was nearly 50 years old. He ruled Songhai for about 35 years. During his reign the cities of Songhai gained power over the countryside.

When he was in his 80s, Askia went blind. His son Musa forced him to leave the throne. Askia was sent to live on an island. He lived there for nine years until another of his sons brought him back to the capital, where he died. His tomb is still one of the most honored places in all of West Africa.

Drawing Inferences Why do you think Askia the Great's tomb is still considered an honored place?

Songhai Falls to Morocco

A northern rival of Songhai, Morocco, wanted to gain control of Songhai's salt mines. So the Moroccan army set out for the heart of Songhai in 1591. Moroccan soldiers carried advanced weapons, including the terrible arquebus (AHR-kwih-buhs). The arquebus was an early form of a gun.

The swords, spears, and bows used by Songhai's warriors were no match for the Moroccans' guns and cannons. The invaders destroyed Timbuktu and Gao.

Changes in trade patterns completed Songhai's fall. Overland trade declined as port cities on the Atlantic coast became more important. Africans south of Songhai and European merchants both preferred trading at Atlantic ports to dealing with Muslim traders. Slowly, the period of great West African empires came to an end.

READING CHECK **Evaluating** What do you think was Askia's greatest accomplishment?

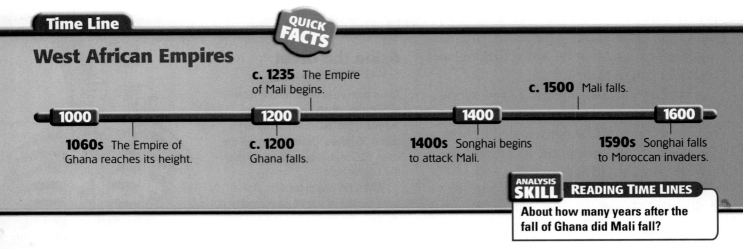

c. **1235** The Empire of Mali begins.

c. **1500** Mali falls.

1000   **1200**   **1400**   **1600**

1060s The Empire of Ghana reaches its height.

c. **1200** Ghana falls.

1400s Songhai begins to attack Mali.

1590s Songhai falls to Moroccan invaders.

ANALYSIS SKILL **READING TIME LINES**

About how many years after the fall of Ghana did Mali fall?

Great Zimbabwe

Strong kingdoms also arose in other parts of Africa. Great Zimbabwe, for example, was a powerful kingdom in southern Africa. Great Zimbabwe was founded in the late 1000s as a small trading and herding center. Gold mining increased in the area in the 1100s. Farming expanded and the kingdom's population grew. In time, Great Zimbabwe became the center of a large trading network.

Trade made Great Zimbabwe's rulers wealthy and powerful. They built a huge stone-walled fortress to protect their capital. In the 1400s the gold trade declined.

THE IMPACT TODAY

The stone fortress remains a major cultural monument in the modern nation of Zimbabwe.

Deprived of its main source of wealth, Great Zimbabwe weakened. By 1500 it was no longer a political and trading center.

READING CHECK **Comparing** How was Great Zimbabwe similar to the empires of West Africa?

SUMMARY AND PREVIEW Sundiata and Mansa Musa helped Mali become a large empire famous for its wealth and centers of learning. Songhai similarly thrived under leaders such as Askia the Great. In the next section, you will read more about the major West African cultures.

Section 3 Assessment

go.hrw.com
Online Quiz
KEYWORD: SN6 HP13

Reviewing Ideas, Terms, and People

1. **a. Identify** Who was **Sundiata**?
   b. Explain What major river was important to the people of Mali? Why?
   c. Elaborate What effects did the rule of **Mansa Musa** have on Mali and West Africa?
2. **a. Identify** Who led the expansion of Songhai in the 1400s?
   b. Explain How did **Askia the Great's** support of education affect Timbuktu?
3. **a. Recall** What made Great Zimbabwe's rulers wealthy and powerful?
   b. Analyze What led to the decline of Great Zimbabwe?

Critical Thinking

4. **Finding Main Ideas** Use your notes to help you list three major accomplishments of Sundiata and Askia.

Sundiata	Askia

FOCUS ON WRITING

5. **Comparing and Contrasting** Review this section and your notes on the empires of Mali and Songhai. Consider how your character's life may have been shaped by the empire in which he or she lived. What were the differences between the empires? How were they the same? How did specific leaders affect the development of the lands they ruled?

Mansa Musa

How could one man's travels become a major historic event?

When did he live? the late 1200s and early 1300s

Where did he live? Mali

What did he do? Mansa Musa, the ruler of Mali, was one of the Muslim kings of West Africa. He became a major figure in African and world history largely because of a pilgrimage he made to the city of Mecca.

Why is he important? Mansa Musa's spectacular journey attracted the attention of the Muslim world and of Europe. For the first time, other people's eyes turned to West Africa. During his travels, Mansa Musa gave out huge amounts of gold. His spending made people eager to find the source of such wealth. Within 200 years, European explorers would arrive on the shores of western Africa.

Identifying Points of View How do you think Mansa Musa changed people's views of West Africa?

This Spanish map from the 1300s shows Mansa Musa sitting on his throne.

KEY FACTS

According to chroniclers of the time, Mansa Musa was accompanied on his journey to Mecca by some 60,000 people. Of those people

- **12,000** were servants to attend to the king.

- **500** were servants to attend to his wife.

- **14,000** more were slaves wearing rich fabrics such as silk.

- **500** carried staffs heavily decorated with gold. Historians have estimated that the gold Mansa Musa gave away on his trip would be worth more than $100 million today.

Historical and Artistic Traditions

What You Will Learn...

Main Ideas

1. West Africans have preserved their history through storytelling and the written accounts of visitors.
2. Through art, music, and dance, West Africans have expressed their creativity and kept alive their cultural traditions.

The Big Idea

Although the people of West Africa did not have a written language, their culture has been passed down through oral history, writings by other people, and the arts.

Key Terms

oral history, *p. 396*
griots, *p. 396*
proverbs, *p. 397*
kente, *p. 399*

 TAKING NOTES As you read, take notes on West African historical and artistic traditions. Write your notes in a diagram like the one below.

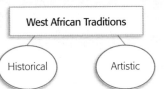

West African Traditions

Historical   Artistic

If **YOU** were there...

You are the youngest and smallest in your family. People often tease you about not being very strong. In the evenings, when work is done, your village gathers to listen to storytellers. One of your favorite stories is about the hero Sundiata. As a boy he was small and weak, but he grew to be a great warrior and hero.

How does the story of Sundiata make you feel?

BUILDING BACKGROUND Although trading empires rose and fell in West Africa, many traditions continued through the centuries. In every town and village, storytellers passed on the people's histories, legends, and wise sayings. These were at the heart of West Africa's arts and cultural traditions.

Preserving History

Writing was never very common in West Africa. In fact, none of the major early civilizations of West Africa developed a written language. Arabic was the only written language they used. The lack of a native written language does not mean that the people of West Africa didn't know their history, though. They passed along information through oral histories. An **oral history** is a spoken record of past events. The task of remembering and telling West Africa's history was entrusted to storytellers.

The Griots

The storytellers of early West Africa were called **griots** (GREE-ohz). They were highly respected in their communities because the people of West Africa were very interested in the deeds of their ancestors. Griots helped keep this history alive for each new generation.

The griots' stories were both entertaining and informative. They told of important past events and of the accomplishments of distant ancestors. For example, some stories explained the rise and fall of the West African empires. Other stories described the actions of powerful kings and warriors. Some griots made their stories more lively by acting out the events like scenes in a play.

In addition to stories, the griots recited **proverbs**, or short sayings of wisdom or truth. They used proverbs to teach lessons to the people. For example, one West African proverb warns, "Talking doesn't fill the basket in the farm." This proverb reminds people that they must work to accomplish things. It is not enough for people just to talk about what they want to do.

In order to tell their stories and proverbs, the griots memorized hundreds of names and events. Through this memorization **process** the griots passed on West African history from generation to generation. However, some griots confused names and

events in their heads. When this happened, the facts of some historical events became distorted. Still, the griots' stories tell us a great deal about life in the West African empires.

West African Epics

Some of the griot poems are epics—long poems about kingdoms and heroes. Many of these epic poems are collected in the *Dausi* (DAW-zee) and the *Sundiata*.

The *Dausi* tells the history of Ghana. Intertwined with historical events, though, are myths and legends. One story is about a seven-headed snake god named Bida. This god promised that Ghana would prosper if the people sacrificed a young woman to him every year. One year a mighty warrior killed Bida. As the god died, he cursed Ghana. The griots say that this curse caused the empire of Ghana to fall.

The *Sundiata* is about Mali's great ruler. According to the epic, when Sundiata was still a boy, a conqueror captured Mali and killed Sundiata's father and 11 brothers.

ACADEMIC
VOCABULARY
process a series
of steps by which
a task is
accomplished

Oral Traditions
West African storytellers called griots had the job of remembering and passing on their people's history. Here, people gather to perform traditional dances and to listen to the stories of a griot.

LINKING TO TODAY

Music from Mali to Memphis

Did you know that the music you listen to today may have begun with the griots? From the 1600s to the 1800s, many people from West Africa were brought to America as slaves. In America, these slaves continued to sing the way they had in Africa. They also continued to play traditional instruments such as the *kora* played by Senegalese musician Soriba Kouyaté (right), the son of a griot. Over time, this music developed into a style called the blues, made popular by such artists as B.B. King (left). In turn, the blues shaped other styles of music, including jazz and rock. So, the next time you hear a Memphis blues track or a cool jazz tune, listen for its ancient African roots!

ANALYSIS SKILL **ANALYZING INFORMATION**

How did West African music affect modern American music?

He didn't kill Sundiata, however, because the boy was sick and didn't seem like a threat. But Sundiata grew up to be an expert warrior. Eventually he overthrew the conqueror and became king.

Visitors' Written Accounts

In addition to the oral histories told about West Africa, visitors wrote about the region. In fact, much of what we know about early West Africa comes from the writings of travelers and scholars from Muslim lands such as Spain and Arabia.

Ibn Battutah was the most famous Muslim visitor to write about West Africa. From 1353 to 1354 he traveled through the region. Ibn Battutah's account of this journey describes the political and cultural lives of West Africans in great detail.

READING CHECK **Drawing Conclusions** Why were oral traditions important in West Africa?

Art, Music, and Dance

Like most peoples, West Africans valued the arts. They expressed themselves creatively through sculpture, mask-making, cloth-making, music, and dance.

Sculpture

Of all the visual art forms, the sculpture of West Africa is probably the best known. West Africans made ornate statues and carvings out of wood, brass, clay, ivory, stone, and other materials.

Most statues from West Africa are of people—often the sculptor's ancestors. Usually these statues were made for religious rituals, to ask for the ancestors' blessings. Sculptors made other statues as gifts for the gods. These sculptures were kept in holy places. They were never meant to be seen by people.

Because their statues were used in religious rituals, many African artists were deeply respected. People thought artists had been blessed by the gods.

Long after the decline of Ghana, Mali, and Songhai, West African art is still admired. Museums around the world display African art. In addition, African sculpture inspired some European artists of the 1900s, including Henri Matisse and Pablo Picasso.

Masks and Clothing

In addition to statues, the artists of West Africa carved elaborate masks. Made of wood, these masks bore the faces of animals such as hyenas, lions, monkeys, and antelopes. Artists often painted the masks after carving them. People wore the masks during rituals as they danced around fires. The way firelight reflected off the masks made them look fierce and lifelike.

Many African societies were famous for the cloth they wove. The most famous of these cloths is called kente (ken-TAY). **Kente** is a hand-woven, brightly colored fabric. The cloth was woven in narrow strips that were then sewn together. Kings and queens in West Africa wore garments made of kente for special occasions.

Music and Dance

In many West African societies, music and dance were as important as the visual arts. Singing, drumming, and dancing were great entertainment, but they also helped people honor their history and mark special occasions. For example, music was played when a ruler entered a room.

Dance has long been a central part of African society. Many West African cultures used dance to celebrate specific events or ceremonies. For example, they may have performed one dance for weddings and another for funerals. In some parts of West Africa, people still perform dances similar to those performed hundreds of years ago.

READING CHECK **Summarizing** Summarize how traditions were preserved in West Africa.

SUMMARY AND PREVIEW The societies of West Africa did not have written languages, but they preserved their histories and cultures through storytelling and the arts. You will next read about another place where traditions are important—China.

Section 4 Assessment

go.hrw.com
Online Quiz
KEYWORD: SN6 HP13

Reviewing Ideas, Terms, and People

1. **a. Define** What is **oral history**?
   b. Make Generalizations Why were **griots** and their stories important in West African society?
   c. Evaluate Why may an oral history provide different information than a written account of the same event?
2. **a. Identify** What were two forms of visual art popular in West Africa?
   b. Make Inferences Why do you think that the sculptures made as gifts for the gods were not meant to be seen by people?
   c. Elaborate What role did music and dance play in West African society?

Critical Thinking

3. **Summarizing** Use a chart like this one and your notes to summarize the importance of each tradition in West Africa.

Tradition	Importance
Storytelling	
Epics	
Sculpture	

FOCUS ON WRITING

4. **Reviewing West African Traditions** Review this section and your notes on the oral and written history of Western Africa and the art, music, and dance of the region. Think about how the griots, visitors from distant lands, or the arts may have affected your character.

Social Studies Skills

Analysis | Critical Thinking | Economics | Study

Interpreting Political Maps

Understand the Skill

Many types of maps are useful in the study of history. *Physical maps* show natural features on Earth's surface. *Political maps* show human cultural features such as cities, states, and countries. Modern political maps show the present-day borders of states and countries. Historical political maps show what cultural features were in the past.

Some historical political maps show how boundaries and features changed over time. Being able to interpret such maps makes the growth and disintegration of countries and empires easier to visualize and understand.

Learn the Skill

Use these guidelines to interpret maps that show political change.

1 Read the title to find out what the map is about.

2 Read the legend. The map's title may state the time period covered by the map. However, in this type of map, information about dates is often found in the legend.

3 Study the legend carefully to be sure you understand what each color or symbol means. Pay special attention to colors or symbols that might indicate changes in borders, signs of the growth or loss of a country's territory.

4 Study the map itself. Compare the colors and symbols in the legend to those on the map. Note any labels, especially those that may show political change. Look for other indications of political changes on the map.

Practice and Apply the Skill

Interpret the map below to answer the following questions about the Mali and Songhai Empires.

1. Which empire was older? Which empire expanded the most?

2. Was Songhai ever part of the Mali Empire? Explain how the map provides this information.

3. Who controlled the city of Gao in the year 1100? in 1325? in 1515?

4. By what date do you know for sure that the Mali Empire had disintegrated? How do you know?

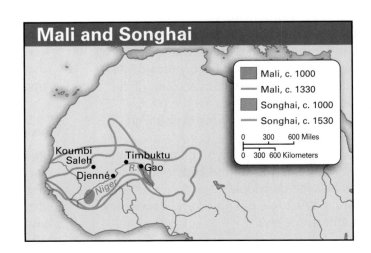

Mali and Songhai

Mali, c. 1000
Mali, c. 1330
Songhai, c. 1000
Songhai, c. 1530

0   300   600 Miles
0   300   600 Kilometers

Koumbi Saleh
Timbuktu
Djenné
R. Gao
Niger

Chapter Review

Visual Summary

Use the visual summary below to help you review the main ideas of the chapter.

QUICK FACTS

The Ghana Empire developed in West Africa and controlled the trade of salt and gold.

Mali's kings built an empire and spread Islam in West Africa.

The Songhai Empire continued to spread Islam.

The history of West Africa has been preserved through story telling, visitors' accounts, art, music, and dance.

Reviewing Vocabulary, Terms, and People

Choose the letter of the answer that best completes each statement below.

1. An area near the equator that has many trees and heavy rainfall may be called a
 a. tropical area.
 b. rain forest.
 c. savannah.
 d. woodland.

2. The belief that natural objects have spirits is called
 a. animism.
 b. vegetism.
 c. animalism.
 d. naturalism.

3. Between the Sahara and the savannah lies the
 a. rain forest.
 b. inland delta.
 c. Zambezi.
 d. Sahel.

4. Mali's rise to power began under a ruler named
 a. Tunka Manin.
 b. Sunni Ali.
 c. Ibn Battutah.
 d. Sundiata.

5. A spoken record of the past is
 a. a Soninke.
 b. an oral history.
 c. a Gao.
 d. an age-set proverb.

6. A West African storyteller is
 a. an Almoravid.
 b. a griot.
 c. an arquebus.
 d. a rift.

7. The Muslim leader of Mali who supported education, spread Islam, and made a famous pilgrimage to Mecca was
 a. Sunni Baru.
 b. Askia the Great.
 c. Mansa Musa.
 d. Muhammad Ture.

8. A brightly colored fabric woven in many African societies is a
 a. kente.
 b. mansa.
 c. Timbuktu.
 d. Tuareg.

Comprehension and Critical Thinking

SECTION 1 *(pages 380–383)*

9. a. Identify Along what river did great civilizations develop in early West Africa?

b. Draw Conclusions Today salt is not nearly as valuable as gold. Why do you think salt was so important in West Africa?

c. Predict How might West Africans have benefited from living in extended families?

SECTION 2 *(pages 386–389)*

10. a. Identify What were the two major trade goods that made Ghana rich? Where did each come from?

b. Make Inferences Why did merchants in Ghana not want other traders to know where their gold came from?

c. Evaluate Who do you think was more responsible for the collapse of Ghana, the people of Ghana or outsiders? Why?

SECTION 3 *(pages 390–394)*

11. a. Describe How did Islam influence society in Mali?

b. Compare and Contrast How were Sundiata and Mansa Musa similar? How were they different?

c. Evaluate Which group do you think played a more important role in Songhai society, warriors or traders?

SECTION 4 *(pages 396–399)*

12. a. Recall What different types of information did griots pass on to their listeners?

b. Analyze Why are the writings of visitors to West Africa so important to our understanding of the region?

c. Evaluate Which of the various arts of West Africa do you think is most important? Why?

Reviewing Themes

13. Geography In which of the four regions were West Africa's two main resources found?

14. Technology How did the development of iron technology affect life in West Africa?

Reading Skills

15. Organization of Facts and Information *Read the paragraph below. What form of organization does the paragraph use? How can you tell?*

> In order to tell their stories and proverbs, the griots memorized hundreds of names and events. Through this memorization process the griots passed on West African history from generation to generation. However, some griots confused names and events in their heads. When this happened, the facts of some historical events became distorted. Still, the griots' stories tell us a great deal about life in the West African empires. *(p. 397)*

Using the Internet

go.hrw.com
KEYWORD: SN6 WH13

16. Activity: Writing a Proverb Does the early bird get the worm? If you go outside at sunrise to check, you missed the fact that this is a proverb that means "The one that gets there first can earn something good." Griots created many proverbs that expressed wisdom or truth. Enter the activity keyword. Then use the Internet resources to write three proverbs that might have been said by griots during the time of the great West African empires. Make sure your proverbs are written from the point of view of a West African person living during those centuries.

Social Studies Skills

Interpreting Maps *Look at the map on page 400. Then answer the following question.*

17. Which empire extended farther eastward?

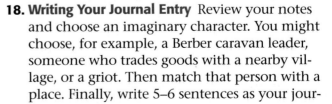

FOCUS ON WRITING

18. Writing Your Journal Entry Review your notes and choose an imaginary character. You might choose, for example, a Berber caravan leader, someone who trades goods with a nearby village, or a griot. Then match that person with a place. Finally, write 5–6 sentences as your journal entry. Include details on what the character sees, feels, and does on a typical day.

Standardized Test Practice

DIRECTIONS: Read each question and write the letter of the best response.

> Well placed for the caravan trade, it was badly situated to defend itself from the Tuareg raiders of the Sahara. These restless nomads were repeatedly hammering at the gates of Timbuktu, and often enough they burst them open with disastrous results for the inhabitants. Life here was never quite safe enough to recommend it as the centre [center] of a big state.
>
> —Basil Davidson, from *A History of West Africa*

1 In this quote, the author is discussing why Timbuktu was

A a good place for universities.

B not a good place for a capital city.

C a good location for trade.

D not a good location for the center of the Tuareg state.

2 In the second sentence of the passage above, what does the phrase *hammering at the gates of Timbuktu* mean?

A driving nails into Timbuktu's gates

B knocking on the door to get into the city

C trying to get into and conquer the city

D making noise to anger the inhabitants

3 The region in Africa of open grasslands and scattered trees is the

A griot.

B Sahara.

C savannah.

D Sahel.

4 How were social groups defined in traditional West African cultures?

A by family and age-set

B by religion and family

C by age-set, family, and religion

D by extended family only

5 The two rulers who were most responsible for spreading Islam in West Africa were

A Sunni Ali and Mansa Musa.

B Sundiata and Sunni Ali.

C Ibn Battutah and Tunka Manin.

D Mansa Musa and Askia the Great.

Connecting with Past Learnings

6 You learned earlier about civilizations that developed along the Tigris and Euphrates rivers in what is now Iraq, and along the Huang He in ancient China. Such developments can be compared to changes along which river in West Africa?

A the Niger

B the Congo

C the Nile

D the Zambezi

7 Like Ghana, which East African kingdom that you learned about earlier grew rich from trade but eventually collapsed due to factors that included overgrazing and invasion?

A Sumer

B Kush

C Babylon

D Mohenjo Daro

Empires of Asia and the Americas

What You Will Learn...

The Asian civilizations of China and Japan were great centers of learning and culture. In China, a series of dynasties ruled a large and unified empire. China made many advances during this time, including the invention of paper money and gunpowder.

To the east, Japan reached a golden age of art and literature during the Heian Period. Later, the country developed a government run by generals called shoguns and warriors known as samurai.

Across the world, people began to build cities and empires in the Americas. Religion and an interest in astronomy guided the lives of these people.

In the next three chapters, you will learn about the history and culture of the people of China, Japan, and the early Americas.

Explore the Art

In this scene, a young Japanese girl is shown writing in her journal. What does the scene suggest about Japanese society?

CHAPTER 14 589–1644

China

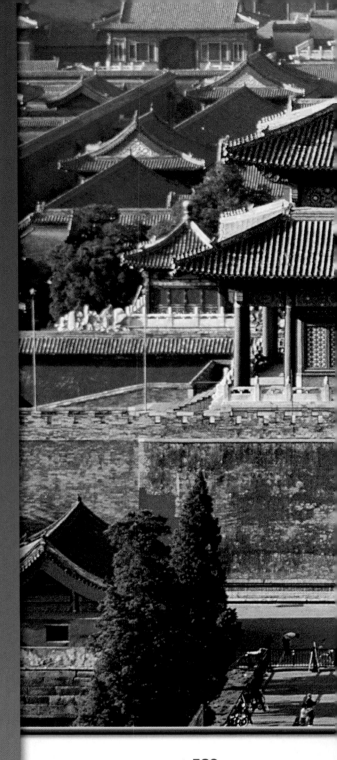

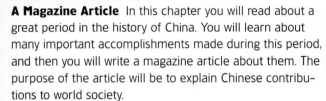

FOCUS ON WRITING

A Magazine Article In this chapter you will read about a great period in the history of China. You will learn about many important accomplishments made during this period, and then you will write a magazine article about them. The purpose of the article will be to explain Chinese contributions to world society.

CHAPTER EVENTS

589
China is reunified under the Sui dynasty.

600

WORLD EVENTS

613
Muhammad begins teaching the basic beliefs of Islam.

HOLT
History's Impact
▶ **video series**
Watch the video to understand the impact of Chinese achievements on world history.

故宫博物院

What You Will Learn...

In this chapter you will learn about Chinese history from the 500s to the 1600s. The magnificent Forbidden City, shown in this photo, was built during this time as a royal palace. Today it is a museum.

730s–760s
Li Bo and Du Fu write some of the greatest poems in Chinese history.

794 The Japanese court is established at Heian.

1279
Mongols found the Yuan dynasty in China.

1060s
The empire of Ghana reaches its height.

1347
The Black Death strikes Europe.

1644
The Ming dynasty ends.

| 800 | 1000 | 1200 | 1400 | 1600 |

Focus on Themes This chapter will explore the history of China from the late 500s until the 1600s. As you read, you will discover that many different dynasties ruled the country during that period, leading to great political changes. Some of those dynasties supported trade, leading to great **economic** growth and stability. Others favored isolation, limiting Chinese contact with the rest of the world. You will also learn that this period saw huge leaps forward in **science and technology**.

Drawing Conclusions about the Past

Focus on Reading You have no doubt heard the phrase, "Put two and two together." When people say that, they don't mean "two + two = four." They mean, "Put the information together."

Using Background Knowledge to Draw Conclusions A **conclusion** is a judgment you make by combining information. You put information from what you are reading together with what you already know, your background knowledge.

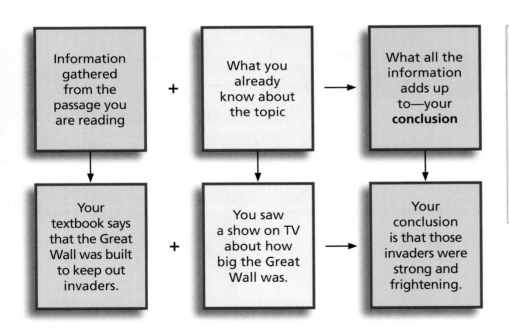

| Information gathered from the passage you are reading | + | What you already know about the topic | → | What all the information adds up to—your **conclusion** |

| Your textbook says that the Great Wall was built to keep out invaders. | + | You saw a show on TV about how big the Great Wall was. | → | Your conclusion is that those invaders were strong and frightening. |

Steps for Drawing Conclusions

1. Read the passage, looking for information the author gives you about the topic.

2. Think about what you already know about the topic. Consider things you've studied, books you've read, or movies you've seen.

3. Put your background knowledge together with what the passage says.

You Try It!

The following passage is from the chapter you are getting ready to read. As you read the passage, look for facts about China.

Advances in Agriculture

From Chapter 14, p. 414

Chinese civilization had always been based on agriculture. Over thousands of years, the Chinese had become expert farmers. In the north farmers grew wheat, barley, and other grains. In the warmer and wetter south they grew rice.

During the Song dynasty, though, Chinese farming reached new heights. The improvement was largely due to new irrigation techniques. For example, some farmers dug underground wells. A new irrigation device, the dragon backbone pump, allowed one person to do the work of several. With this light and portable pump, a farmer could scoop up water and pour it into an irrigation canal. Using these new techniques, farmers created elaborate irrigation systems.

After you have finished the passage, answer the questions below, drawing conclusions about what you have read.

1. Think back on what you've learned about irrigation systems in other societies. What do you think irrigation was like in China before the Song dynasty?

2. What effect do you think this improved irrigation had on Chinese society? Why do you think this?

3. Based on this passage, what kinds of conditions do you think rice needs to grow? How does this compare to the conditions wheat needs?

4. Which crop was most likely grown near the Great Wall—wheat or rice? Why do you think so?

Key Terms and People

Chapter 14

Section 1
Period of Disunion (p. 410)
Grand Canal (p. 411)
Empress Wu (p. 412)

Section 2
porcelain (p. 417)
woodblock printing (p. 418)
gunpowder (p. 418)
compass (p. 418)

Section 3
bureaucracy (p. 422)
civil service (p. 422)
scholar-official (p. 422)

Section 4
Genghis Khan (p. 424)
Kublai Khan (p. 425)
Zheng He (p. 427)
isolationism (p. 430)

Academic Vocabulary

Success in school is related to knowing academic vocabulary—the words that are frequently used in school assignments and discussions. In this chapter, you will learn the following academic words:

function (p. 421)
incentive (p. 422)
consequences (p. 430)

As you read Chapter 14, think about what you already know about China and draw conclusions to fill gaps in what you are reading.

China Reunifies

What You Will Learn...

Main Ideas

1. The Period of Disunion was a time of war and disorder that followed the end of the Han dynasty.
2. China was reunified under the Sui, Tang, and Song dynasties.
3. The Age of Buddhism saw major religious changes in China.

The Big Idea

The Period of Disunion was followed by reunification by rulers of the Sui, Tang, and Song dynasties.

Key Terms and People

Period of Disunion, *p. 410*
Grand Canal, *p. 411*
Empress Wu, *p. 412*

TAKING NOTES As you read, use a chart like this one to keep track of important dates and events in China during the dynasties following the Period of Disunion.

Dynasty	Important Dates	Events and Details

If **YOU** were there...

You are a peasant in China in the year 264. Your grandfather often speaks of a time when all of China was united, but all you have known is warfare among rulers. A man passing through your village speaks of even more conflict in other areas.

Why might you want China to have just one ruler?

BUILDING BACKGROUND Most of China's history is divided into dynasties. The first dynasties ruled China for centuries. But when the Han dynasty collapsed in 220, China plunged into disorder.

The Period of Disunion

When the Han dynasty collapsed, China split into several rival kingdoms, each ruled by military leaders. Historians sometimes call the time of disorder that followed the collapse of the Han the **Period of Disunion**. It lasted from 220 to 589.

Although war was common during the Period of Disunion, peaceful developments also took place at the same time. During this period, nomadic peoples settled in northern China. Some Chinese people adopted the nomads' culture, while the invaders adopted some Chinese practices. For example, one former nomadic ruler ordered his people to adopt Chinese names, speak Chinese, and dress like the Chinese. Thus, the culture of the invaders and traditional Chinese mixed.

A similar cultural blending took place in southern China. Many northern Chinese, unwilling to live under the rule of the nomadic invaders, fled to southern China. There, northern Chinese culture mixed with the more southern cultures.

As a result of this mixing, Chinese culture changed. New types of art and music developed. New foods and clothing styles became popular. The new culture spread over a wider geographic area than ever before, and more people became Chinese.

READING CHECK Finding Main Ideas How did Chinese culture change during the Period of Disunion?

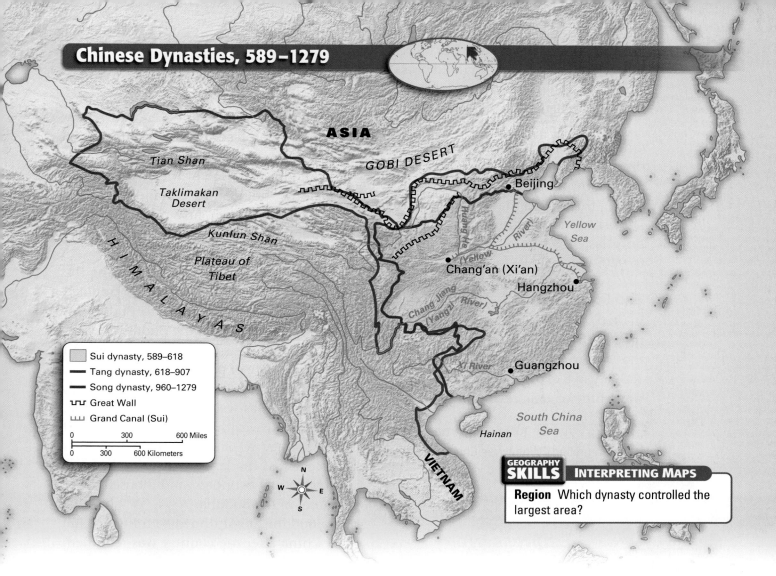

Chinese Dynasties, 589–1279

ASIA

GOBI DESERT

Tian Shan

Taklimakan
Desert

Kunlun Shan

Plateau of
Tibet

HIMALAYAS

Beijing

Huang He
(Yellow
River)

Chang'an (Xi'an)

Hangzhou

Yellow
Sea

Chang Jiang
(Yangzi River)

Xi River

Guangzhou

Hainan

South China
Sea

VIETNAM

Legend:
- Sui dynasty, 589–618
- Tang dynasty, 618–907
- Song dynasty, 960–1279
- ᴸᴸᴸ Great Wall
- ᴸᴸᴸ Grand Canal (Sui)

0   300   600 Miles
0   300   600 Kilometers

N W E S

GEOGRAPHY SKILLS | INTERPRETING MAPS

Region Which dynasty controlled the largest area?

The Sui, Tang, and Song

Finally, after centuries of political confusion and cultural change, China was reunified. For about 700 years, it remained unified under a series of powerful dynasties.

The Sui Dynasty

The man who finally ended the Period of Disunion was a northern ruler named Yang Jian (YANG jee-EN). In 589, he conquered the south, unified China, and created the Sui (SWAY) dynasty.

The Sui dynasty didn't last long, only from 589 to 618. During that time, though, its leaders restored order to China and began the **Grand Canal,** a canal linking northern and southern China.

The Tang Dynasty

A new dynasty arose in China in 618 when a former Sui official overthrew the old government. This dynasty, the Tang, would rule for nearly 300 years. As you can see on the map, China grew under the Tang dynasty to include much of eastern Asia, as well as large parts of Central Asia.

Historians view the Tang dynasty as a golden age of Chinese civilization. One of its greatest rulers was Taizong (TY-tzoong). He conquered many lands, reformed the military, and created law codes. Another brilliant Tang ruler was Xuanzong (SHOO-AN-tzoong). During his reign, culture flourished. Many of China's finest poets wrote while Xuanzong ruled.

The Tang dynasty also included the only woman to rule China—**Empress Wu**. Her methods were sometimes vicious, but she was intelligent and talented.

After the Tang dynasty fell, China entered another brief period of chaos and disorder, with separate kingdoms competing for power. In fact, China was so divided during this period that it is known as Five Dynasties and Ten Kingdoms. The disorder only lasted 53 years, though, from 907 to 960.

The Song Dynasty

In 960, China was again reunified, this time by the Song dynasty. Like the Tang, the Song ruled for about 300 years, until 1279. Also like the Tang, the Song dynasty was a time of great accomplishments.

READING CHECK **Sequencing** When was China reunified? When was China not unified?

BIOGRAPHY

Empress Wu
625–705

Married to a sickly emperor, Empress Wu became the virtual ruler of China in 655. After her husband died, Wu decided her sons were not worthy of ruling. She kept power for herself, and ruled with an iron fist. Those who threatened her power risked death. Unlike many earlier rulers, she chose advisors based on their abilities rather than their ranks. Although she was not well liked, Wu was respected for bringing stability and prosperity to China.

Drawing Conclusions Why do you think Empress Wu was never very popular?

The Age of Buddhism

While China was experiencing changes in its government, another major change was taking place in Chinese culture. A new religion was spreading quickly throughout the vast land.

Buddhism is one of the world's major religions, originating in India around 500 BC. Buddhism first came to China during the Han dynasty. But for some time, there were few Buddhists in China.

Buddhism's status changed during the Period of Disunion. During this troubled time, many people turned to Buddhism. They took comfort in the Buddhist teaching that people can escape suffering and achieve a state of peace.

By the end of the Period of Disunion, Buddhism was well established in China. As a result, wealthy people donated land and money to Buddhist temples, which arose across the land. Some temples were architectural wonders and housed huge statues of the Buddha.

Buddhism continued to influence life in China after the country was reunified. In fact, during the Sui and Tang dynasties, Buddhism continued to grow and spread. Chinese missionaries, people who travel to spread their religion, introduced Buddhism to Japan, Korea, and other Asian lands.

Buddhism influenced many aspects of Chinese culture, including art, literature, and architecture. In fact, so important was Buddhism in China that the period from about 400 to about 845 can be called the Age of Buddhism.

This golden age of Buddhism came to an end when a Tang emperor launched a campaign against the religion. He burned many Buddhist texts, took lands from Buddhist temples, destroyed many temples, and turned others into schools.

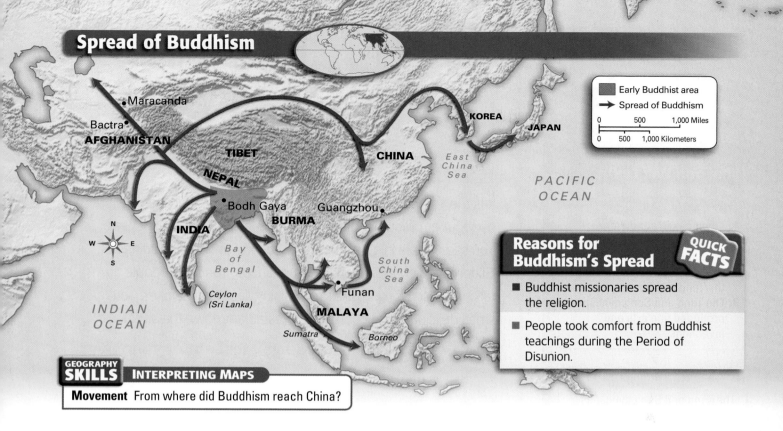

Spread of Buddhism

Maracanda
Bactra
AFGHANISTAN
TIBET
NEPAL
Bodh Gaya
INDIA
BURMA
Guangzhou
KOREA
JAPAN
CHINA
East China Sea
PACIFIC OCEAN
Bay of Bengal
South China Sea
Ceylon (Sri Lanka)
Funan
MALAYA
Sumatra
Borneo
INDIAN OCEAN

Legend:
- Early Buddhist area
- → Spread of Buddhism

0   500   1,000 Miles
0   500   1,000 Kilometers

Reasons for Buddhism's Spread   QUICK FACTS

- Buddhist missionaries spread the religion.
- People took comfort from Buddhist teachings during the Period of Disunion.

GEOGRAPHY SKILLS   INTERPRETING MAPS

Movement From where did Buddhism reach China?

The emperor's actions weakened the influence of Buddhism in China, but they did not destroy it completely. Buddhism continued to play a key role in Chinese society for centuries. As it had during the early Tang period, it continued to shape Chinese art and literature. But even as it influenced life in China, Buddhism changed. People began to blend elements of Buddhism with elements of other philosophies, especially Confucianism and Daoism, to create a new way of thinking.

READING CHECK Identifying Cause and Effect Why did Buddhism spread more easily during the Period of Disunion?

SUMMARY AND PREVIEW From the disorder that followed the fall of the Han dynasty, new dynasties arose to restore order in China. You will read about their many advances in the next section.

Section 1 Assessment

go.hrw.com
Online Quiz
KEYWORD: SN6 HP14

Reviewing Ideas, Terms, and People

1. **a. Define** What was the **Period of Disunion**?
   b. Explain How did Chinese culture change during the Period of Disunion?
2. **a. Identify** Who was **Empress Wu**? What did she do?
   b. Evaluate How do you think the reunification of China affected the common people?
3. **a. Identify** When was the Age of Buddhism in China?
   b. Explain Why did people turn to Buddhism during the Period of Disunion?
   c. Elaborate How did Buddhism influence Chinese culture?

Critical Thinking

4. **Sequencing** Draw a time line like this one. Using your notes on important events, place the main events and their dates on the time line.

200   1300

FOCUS ON WRITING

5. **Getting an Overview** In this section you read an overview of three major dynasties and the contributions of Buddhism. Make a note of any ideas or contributions that you might want to include in your article.

Tang and Song Achievements

What You Will Learn...

Main Ideas

1. Advances in agriculture led to increased trade and population growth.
2. Cities and trade grew during the Tang and Song dynasties.
3. The Tang and Song dynasties produced fine arts and inventions.

The Big Idea

The Tang and Song dynasties were periods of economic, cultural, and technological accomplishments.

Key Terms

porcelain, *p. 417*
woodblock printing, *p. 418*
gunpowder, *p. 418*
compass, *p. 418*

TAKING NOTES As you read, look for information about accomplishments of the Tang and Song dynasties. Keep track of these accomplishments in a chart like this one.

Tang dynasty	Song dynasty

If YOU were there...

It is the year 1270. You are a rich merchant in a Chinese city of about a million people. The city around you fills your senses. You see people in colorful clothes among beautiful buildings. Glittering objects lure you into busy shops. You hear people talking—discussing business, gossiping, laughing at jokes. You smell delicious food cooking at a restaurant down the street.

How do you feel about your city?

BUILDING BACKGROUND The Tang and Song dynasties were periods of great wealth and progress. Changes in farming formed the basis for other advances in Chinese civilization.

Advances in Agriculture

Chinese civilization had always been based on agriculture. Over thousands of years, the Chinese had become expert farmers. In the north farmers grew wheat, barley, and other grains. In the warmer and wetter south they grew rice.

During the Song dynasty, though, Chinese farming reached new heights. The improvement was largely due to new irrigation techniques. For example, some farmers dug underground wells. A new irrigation device, the dragon backbone pump, allowed one person to do the work of several. With this light and portable pump, a farmer could scoop up water and pour it into an irrigation canal. Using these new techniques, farmers created elaborate irrigation systems.

Under the Song, the amount of land under cultivation increased. Lands along the Chang Jiang that had been wild now became farmland. Farms also became more productive, thanks to the discovery of a new type of fast-ripening rice. Because it grew and ripened quickly, this rice enabled farmers to grow two or even three crops in the time it used to take to grow just one.

Chinese farmers also learned to grow new crops, such as cotton, efficiently. Workers processed cotton fiber to make clothes and other goods. The production of tea, which had been grown in China for centuries, also increased.

Agricultural surpluses helped pay taxes to the government. Merchants also traded food crops. As a result, food was abundant not just in the countryside but also in cities. Because food was plentiful, China's population grew quickly. During the Tang dynasty, the population had been about 60 million. During the Song dynasty, the farmers of China fed a country of nearly 100 million people. At the time, China was the largest country in the world.

READING CHECK **Identifying Cause and Effect** How did agricultural advances affect population growth?

THE IMPACT
TODAY
China is still the world's most populous country. More than 1.3 billion people live there today.

Growing Rice

Rice has long been a vital crop in southern China, where the warm, wet climate is perfect for rice growing.

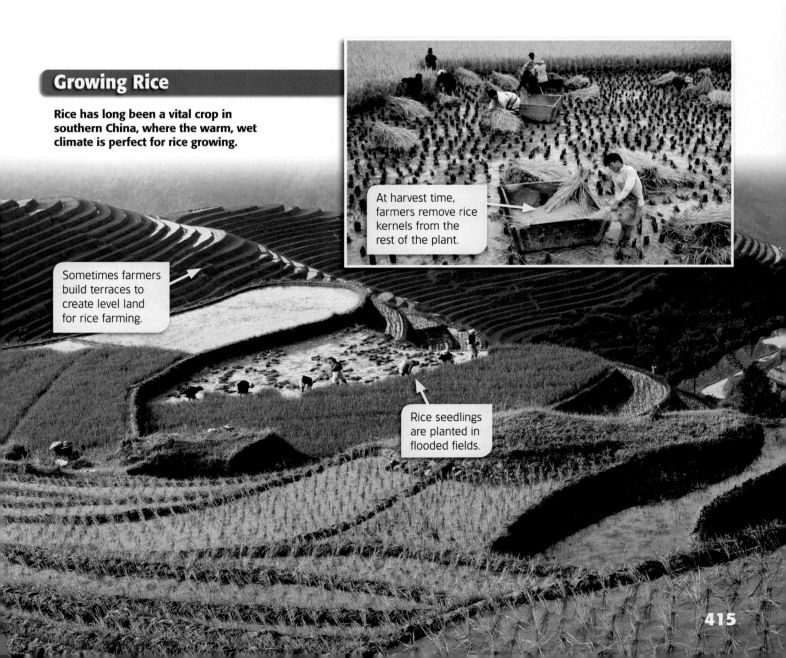

At harvest time, farmers remove rice kernels from the rest of the plant.

Sometimes farmers build terraces to create level land for rice farming.

Rice seedlings are planted in flooded fields.

Cities and Trade

Throughout the Tang and Song dynasties, much of the food grown on China's farms flowed into the growing cities and towns. China's cities were crowded, busy places. Shopkeepers, government officials, doctors, artisans, entertainers, religious leaders, and artists made them lively places as well.

City Life

FOCUS ON READING

What can you conclude about the link between the Grand Canal and the growth of cities?

China's capital and largest city of the Tang dynasty was Chang'an (chahng-AHN), a huge, bustling trade center. With a population of more than a million, it was by far the largest city in the world at the time.

Chang'an, like other trading cities, had a mix of people from many cultures—China, Korea, Persia, Arabia, and Europe. It was also known as a religious and philosophical center, not just for Buddhists and Daoists but for Asian Christians as well.

Cities continued to grow under the Song. Several cities, including the Song capital, Kaifeng (KY-fuhng), had about a million people. A dozen more cities had populations of close to half a million.

Trade in China and Beyond

Trade grew along with Chinese cities. This trade, combined with China's agricultural base, made China richer than ever before.

Much trade took place within China itself. Traders used the country's rivers to ship goods on barges and ships.

The Grand Canal, a series of waterways that linked major cities, carried a huge amount of trade goods, especially farm products. Construction on the canal had begun during the Sui dynasty. During the Tang dynasty, it was improved and expanded. The Grand Canal allowed the Chinese to move goods and crops from distant agricultural areas into cities.

The Grand Canal

Beijing
Huang He (Yellow River)
Yellow Sea
Zhenjiang
Chang'an
Chang Jiang (Yangzi River)
Hangzhou
East China Sea

⊔⊔ Grand Canal (Sui)

The Chinese also carried on trade with other lands and peoples. During the Tang dynasty, most foreign trade was over land routes leading west to India and Southwest Asia, though Chinese traders also went to Korea and Japan in the east. The Chinese exported many goods, including tea, rice, spices, and jade. However, one export was especially important—silk. So valuable was silk that the Chinese tried to keep the method of making it secret. In exchange for their exports, the Chinese imported different foods and plants, wool, glass, gold, and silver.

During the Song dynasty, maritime trade, or sea trade, became more important. China opened its Pacific ports to foreign traders. The sea-trade routes connected China to many other countries. During this time, the Chinese also developed another valuable product—a thin, beautiful type of pottery called **porcelain**.

China's Grand Canal (left) is the world's longest human-made waterway. It was built largely to transport rice and other foods from the south to feed China's cities and armies in the north. Barges like the one above crowd the Grand Canal, which is still an important transportation link in China.

All of this trade helped create a strong economy. As a result, merchants became important members of Chinese society during the Song dynasty. Also as a result of the growth of trade and wealth, the Song invented the world's first system of paper money in the 900s.

READING CHECK Summarizing How far did China's trade routes extend?

Arts and Inventions

While China grew rich economically, its cultural riches also increased. In literature, art, and science, China made huge advances.

Artists and Poets

The artists and writers of the Tang dynasty were some of China's greatest. Wu Daozi (DOW-tzee) painted murals that celebrated Buddhism and nature. Li Bo and Du Fu wrote poems that readers still enjoy for their beauty. This poem by Li Bo expresses the homesickness that one feels late at night:

"Before my bed
there is bright moonlight
So that it seems
like frost on the ground:
Lifting my head
I watch the bright moon,
Lowering my head
I dream that I'm home."
–Li Bo, *Quiet Night Thoughts*

Also noted for its literature, the Song period produced Li Qingzhao (ching-ZHOW), perhaps China's greatest female poet. She once said that the purpose of her poetry was to capture a single moment in time.

Artists of both the Tang and Song dynasties made exquisite objects in clay. Tang figurines of horses clearly show the animals' strength. Song artists made porcelain items covered in a pale green glaze called celadon (SEL-uh-duhn).

THE IMPACT TODAY
Porcelain became so popular in the West that it became known as chinaware, or just china.

Chinese Inventions

Paper
Invented during the Han dynasty around 105, paper was one of the greatest of all Chinese inventions. It gave the Chinese a cheap and easy way of keeping records and made printing possible.

Porcelain
Porcelain was first made during the Tang dynasty, but it wasn't perfected for many centuries. Chinese artists were famous for their work with this fragile material.

Woodblock printing
The Chinese invented printing during the Tang dynasty, centuries before it was known in Europe. Printers could copy drawings or texts quickly, much faster than they could be copied by hand.

Gunpowder
Invented during the late Tang or early Song dynasty, gunpowder was used to make fireworks and signals. The Chinese did not generally use it as a weapon.

Movable type
Inventors of the Song dynasty created movable type, which made printing much faster. Carved letters could be rearranged and reused to print many different messages.

Magnetic compass
Invented no later than the Han period, the compass was greatly improved by the Tang. The new compass allowed sailors and merchants to travel vast distances.

Paper money
The world's first paper money was invented by the Song. Lighter and easier to handle than coins, paper money helped the Chinese manage their growing wealth.

Important Inventions

The Tang and Song dynasties produced some of the most remarkable—and most important—inventions in human history. Some of these inventions influenced events around the world.

According to legend, a man named Cai Lun invented paper in the year 105 during the Han dynasty. A later Tang invention built on Cai Lun's achievement—**woodblock printing**, a form of printing in which an entire page is carved into a block of wood. The printer applies ink to the block and presses paper against the block to create a printed page. The world's first known printed book was printed in this way in China in 868.

Another invention of the Tang dynasty was gunpowder. **Gunpowder** is a mixture of powders used in guns and explosives. It was originally used only in fireworks, but it was later used to make small bombs and rockets. Eventually, gunpowder was used to make explosives, firearms, and cannons. Gunpowder dramatically altered how wars were fought and, in doing so, changed the course of human history.

One of the most useful achievements of Tang China was the perfection of the magnetic **compass**. This instrument, which uses the earth's magnetic field to show direction, revolutionized travel. A compass made it possible to find direction more accurately than ever before. The perfection of the compass had far-reaching effects. Explorers the world over used the compass to travel vast distances. The navigators of trading ships and warships also came to rely on the compass. Thus, the compass has been a key factor in some of the most important sailing voyages in history.

The Song dynasty also produced many important inventions. Under the Song, the Chinese invented movable type. Movable type is a set of letters or characters that are

The Paper Trail

The dollar bill in your pocket may be crisp and new, but paper money has been around a long time. Paper money was printed for the first time in China in the AD 900s and was in use for about 700 years, through the Ming dynasty, when the bill shown here was printed. However, so much money was printed that it lost value. The Chinese stopped using paper money for centuries. Its use caught on in Europe, though, and eventually became common. Most countries now issue paper money.

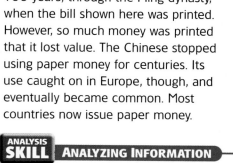

ANALYSIS SKILL **ANALYZING INFORMATION**

What are some advantages of paper money?

used to print books. Unlike the blocks used in block printing, movable type can be rearranged and reused to create new lines of text and different pages.

The Song dynasty also introduced the concept of paper money. People were used to buying goods and services with bulky coins made of metals such as bronze, gold, and silver. Paper money was far lighter and easier to use. As trade increased and many people in China grew rich, paper money became more popular.

READING CHECK Finding Main Ideas What were some important inventions of the Tang and Song dynasties?

SUMMARY AND PREVIEW The Tang and Song dynasties were periods of great advancement. Many great artists and writers lived during these periods. Tang and Song inventions also had dramatic effects on world history. In the next section you will learn about the government of the Song dynasty.

Section 2 Assessment

go.hrw.com
Online Quiz
KEYWORD: SN6 HP14

Reviewing Ideas, Terms, and People

1. **a. Recall** What advances in farming occurred during the Song dynasty?
   b. Explain How did agricultural advancements affect China's population?
2. **a. Describe** What were the capital cities of Tang and Song China like?
   b. Draw Conclusions How did geography affect trade in China?
3. **a. Identify** Who was Li Bo?
   b. Draw Conclusions How may the inventions of paper money and **woodblock printing** have been linked?
   c. Rank Which Tang or Song invention do you think was most important? Defend your answer.

Critical Thinking

4. **Categorizing** Copy the chart at right. Use it to organize your notes on the Tang and Song into categories.

	Tang dynasty	Song dynasty
Agriculture		
Cities		
Trade		
Art		
Inventions		

FOCUS ON WRITING

5. **Identifying Achievements** You have just read about the achievements of the Tang and Song dynasties. Make a list of those you might include in your article.

Confucianism and Government

If **YOU** were there...

You are a student in China in 1184. Night has fallen, but you cannot sleep. Tomorrow you have a test. You know it will be the most important test of your entire life. You have studied for it, not for days or weeks or even months—but for *years*. As you toss and turn, you think about how your entire life will be determined by how well you do on this one test.

How could a single test be so important?

BUILDING BACKGROUND The Song dynasty ruled China from 960 to 1279. This was a time of improvements in agriculture, growing cities, extensive trade, and the development of art and inventions. It was also a time of major changes in Chinese government.

Confucianism

The dominant philosophy in China, Confucianism is based on the teachings of Confucius. He lived more than 1,500 years before the Song dynasty. His ideas, though, had a dramatic effect on the Song system of government.

Confucian Ideas

Confucius's teachings focused on ethics, or proper behavior, for individuals and governments. He said that people should conduct their lives according to two basic principles. These principles were *ren*, or concern for others, and *li*, or appropriate behavior. Confucius argued that society would **function** best if everyone followed *ren* and *li*.

Confucius thought that everyone had a proper role to play in society. Order was maintained when people knew their place and behaved appropriately. For example, Confucius said that young people should obey their elders and that subjects should obey their rulers.

The Influence of Confucianism

After his death, Confucius's ideas were spread by his followers, but they were not widely accepted. In fact, the Qin dynasty officially suppressed Confucian ideas and teachings. By the time of the Han dynasty, Confucianism had again come into favor, and Confucianism became the official state philosophy.

During the Period of Disunion, which followed the Han dynasty, Confucianism was overshadowed by Buddhism as the major tradition in China. As you recall, many Chinese people turned to Buddhism for comfort during these troubled times. In doing so, they largely turned away from Confucian ideas and outlooks.

Later, during the Sui and early Tang dynasties, Buddhism was very influential. Unlike Confucianism, which stressed ethical behavior, Buddhism stressed a more spiritual outlook that promised escape from suffering. As Buddhism became more popular in China, Confucianism lost some of its influence.

ACADEMIC VOCABULARY
function work or perform

In addition to ethics, Confucianism stressed the importance of education. This painting, created during the Song period, shows earlier Confucian scholars during the Period of Disunion sorting scrolls containing classic Confucian texts.

Civil Service Exams

This painting from the 1600s shows civil servants writing essays for China's emperor. Difficult exams were designed to make sure that government officials were chosen by ability—not by wealth or family connections.

Difficult Exams

- Students had to memorize entire Confucian texts.

- To pass the most difficult tests, students might study for more than 20 years!

- Some exams lasted up to 72 hours, and students were locked in private rooms while taking them.

- Some dishonest students cheated by copying Confucius's works on the inside of their clothes, paying bribes to the test graders, or paying someone else to take the test for them.

- To prevent cheating, exam halls were often locked and guarded.

Neo-Confucianism

Late in the Tang dynasty, many Chinese historians and scholars again became interested in the teachings of Confucius. Their interest was sparked by their desire to improve Chinese government and society.

During and after the Song dynasty, a new philosophy called Neo-Confucianism developed. The term *neo* means "new." Based on Confucianism, Neo-Confucianism was similar to the older philosophy in that it taught proper behavior. However, it also emphasized spiritual matters. For example, Neo-Confucian scholars discussed such issues as what made human beings do bad things even if their basic nature was good.

Neo-Confucianism became much more influential under the Song. Later its influence grew even more. In fact, the ideas of Neo-Confucianism became official government teachings after the Song dynasty.

ACADEMIC VOCABULARY
incentive
something that leads people to follow a certain course of action

READING CHECK **Contrasting** How did Neo-Confucianism differ from Confucianism?

Scholar-Officials

The Song dynasty took another major step that affected China for centuries. They improved the system by which people went to work for the government. These workers formed a large **bureaucracy,** or a body of unelected government officials. They joined the bureaucracy by passing civil service examinations. **Civil service** means service as a government official.

To become a civil servant, a person had to pass a series of written examinations. The examinations tested students' grasp of Confucianism and related ideas.

Because the tests were so difficult, students spent years preparing for them. Only a very small fraction of the people who took the tests would reach the top level and be appointed to a position in the government. However, candidates for the civil service examinations had a strong **incentive** for studying hard. Passing the tests meant life as a **scholar-official**—an educated member of the government.

Scholar-Officials

First rising to prominence under the Song, scholar-officials remained important in China for centuries. These scholar-officials, for example, lived during the Qing dynasty, which ruled from the mid-1600s to the early 1900s. Their typical responsibilities might include running government offices; maintaining roads, irrigation systems, and other public works; updating and maintaining official records; or collecting taxes.

Scholar-officials were elite members of society. They performed many important jobs in the government and were widely admired for their knowledge and ethics. Their benefits included considerable respect and reduced penalties for breaking the law. Many also became wealthy from gifts given by people seeking their aid.

The civil service examination system helped ensure that talented, intelligent people became scholar-officials. The civil service system was a major factor in the stability of the Song government.

READING CHECK **Analyzing** How did the Song dynasty change China's government?

SUMMARY AND PREVIEW During the Song period, Confucian ideas helped shape China's government. In the next section, you will read about the two dynasties that followed the Song—the Yuan and the Ming.

go.hrw.com
Online Quiz
KEYWORD: SN6 HP14

Section 3 Assessment

Reviewing Ideas, Terms, and People

1. **a. Identify** What two principles did Confucius believe people should follow?
   b. Explain What was Neo-Confucianism?
   c. Elaborate Why do you think Neo-Confucianism appealed to many people?
2. **a. Define** What was a **scholar-official**?
   b. Explain Why would people want to become scholar-officials?
   c. Evaluate Do you think **civil service** examinations were a good way to choose government officials? Why or why not?

Critical Thinking

3. **Sequencing** Review your notes to see how Confucianism led to Neo-Confucianism and Neo-Confucianism led to government bureaucracy. Use a graphic organizer like the one here.

Confucianism → Neo-Confucianism → Government bureaucracy

FOCUS ON WRITING

4. **Gathering Ideas about Confucianism and Government** In this section you read about Confucianism and new ideas about government. What did you learn that you could add to your list of achievements?

The Yuan and Ming Dynasties

If YOU were there...

You are a farmer in northern China in 1212. As you pull weeds from a wheat field, you hear a sound like thunder. Looking toward the sound, you see hundreds—no, *thousands*—of armed horsemen on the horizon, riding straight toward you. You are frozen with fear. Only one thought fills your mind—the dreaded Mongols are coming.

What can you do to save yourself?

BUILDING BACKGROUND Throughout its history, northern China had been attacked over and over by nomadic peoples. During the Song dynasty these attacks became more frequent and threatening.

The Mongol Empire

Among the nomadic peoples who attacked the Chinese were the Mongols. For centuries, the Mongols had lived as separate tribes in the vast plains north of China. Then in 1206, a powerful leader, or khan, united them. His name was Temüjin. When he became leader, though, he was given a new title: "Universal Ruler," or **Genghis Khan** (JENG-guhs KAHN).

The Mongol Conquest

Genghis Khan organized the Mongols into a powerful army and led them on bloody expeditions of conquest. The brutality of the Mongol attacks terrorized people throughout much of Asia and Eastern Europe. Genghis Khan and his army killed all of the men, women, and children in countless cities and villages. Within 20 years, he ruled a large part of Asia.

Genghis Khan then turned his attention to China. He first led his armies into northern China in 1211. They fought their way south, wrecking whole towns and ruining farmland. By the time of Genghis Khan's death in 1227, all of northern China was under Mongol control.

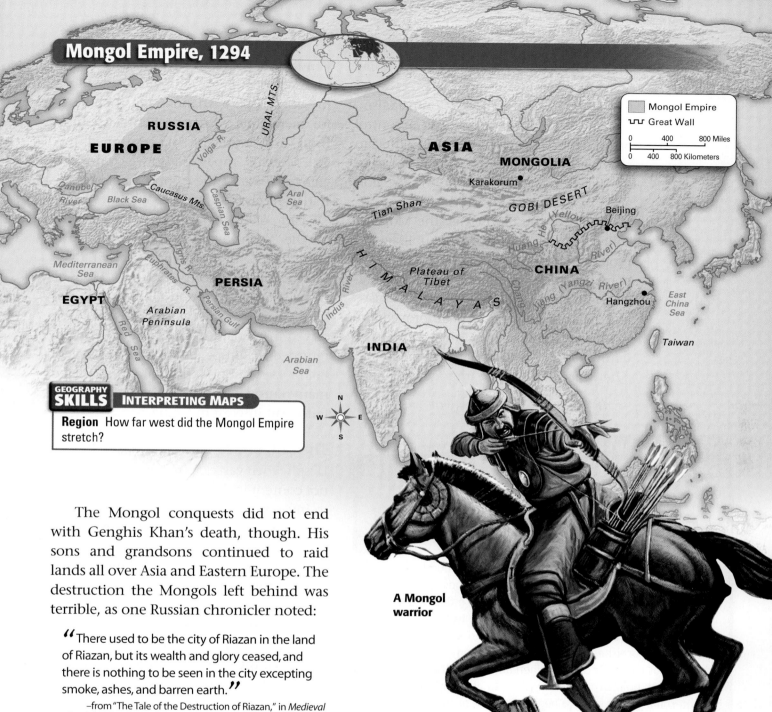

Mongol Empire, 1294

RUSSIA
EUROPE
ASIA
MONGOLIA
URAL MTS.
Danube River
Black Sea
Caucasus Mts.
Volga R.
Caspian Sea
Aral Sea
Tian Shan
Karakorum
GOBI DESERT
Huang He (Yellow River)
Beijing
Mediterranean Sea
Euphrates R.
Tigris R.
PERSIA
HIMALAYAS
Plateau of Tibet
CHINA
Chang Jiang (Yangzi River)
EGYPT
Arabian Peninsula
Persian Gulf
Red Sea
Indus River
Ganges River
INDIA
Arabian Sea
Hangzhou
East China Sea
Taiwan

Mongol Empire
Great Wall
0   400   800 Miles
0   400   800 Kilometers

GEOGRAPHY SKILLS   INTERPRETING MAPS

Region How far west did the Mongol Empire stretch?

N W E S

A Mongol warrior

The Mongol conquests did not end with Genghis Khan's death, though. His sons and grandsons continued to raid lands all over Asia and Eastern Europe. The destruction the Mongols left behind was terrible, as one Russian chronicler noted:

"There used to be the city of Riazan in the land of Riazan, but its wealth and glory ceased, and there is nothing to be seen in the city excepting smoke, ashes, and barren earth."

–from "The Tale of the Destruction of Riazan," in *Medieval Russia's Epics, Chronicles, and Tales*, edited by Serge Zenkovsky

In 1260 Genghis Khan's grandson **Kublai Khan** (KOO-bluh KAHN) became ruler of the Mongol Empire. He completed the conquest of China and in 1279 declared himself emperor of China. This began the Yuan dynasty, a period that some people also call the Mongol Ascendancy. For the first time in its long history, foreigners ruled all of China.

Life in Yuan China

Kublai Khan and the Mongol rulers he led belonged to a different ethnic group than the Chinese did. They spoke a different language, worshipped different gods, wore different clothing, and had different customs. The Chinese resented being ruled by these foreigners, whom they saw as rude and uncivilized.

However, Kublai Khan did not force the Chinese to accept Mongol ways of life. Some Mongols even adopted aspects of the Chinese culture, such as Confucianism. Still, the Mongols made sure to keep control of the Chinese. They prohibited Confucian scholars from gaining too much power in the government, for example. The Mongols also placed heavy taxes on the Chinese.

Much of the tax money the Mongols collected went to pay for vast public-works projects. These projects required the labor of many Chinese people. The Yuan extended the Grand Canal and built new roads and palaces. Workers also improved the roads that were part of China's postal system. In addition, the Yuan emperors built a new capital, Dadu, near modern Beijing.

Primary Source

BOOK
A Chinese City

In this passage Marco Polo describes his visit to Hangzhou (HAHNG-JOH), a city in southeastern China.

"Inside the city there is a Lake . . . and all round it are erected [built] beautiful palaces and mansions, of the richest and most exquisite [finest] structure that you can imagine . . . In the middle of the Lake are two Islands, on each of which stands a rich, beautiful and spacious edifice [building], furnished in such style as to seem fit for the palace of an Emperor. And when any one of the citizens desired to hold a marriage feast, or to give any other entertainment, it used to be done at one of these palaces. And everything would be found there ready to order, such as silver plate, trenchers [platters], and dishes, napkins and table-cloths, and whatever else was needful. The King made this provision for the gratification [enjoyment] of his people, and the place was open to every one who desired to give an entertainment."

–Marco Polo, from *Description of the World*

ANALYSIS SKILL ANALYZING PRIMARY SOURCES

From this description, what impression might Europeans have of Hangzhou?

Mongol soldiers were sent throughout China to keep the peace as well as to keep a close watch on the Chinese. The soldiers' presence kept overland trade routes safe for merchants. Sea trade between China, India, and Southeast Asia continued, too. The Mongol emperors also welcomed foreign traders at Chinese ports. Some of these traders received special privileges.

Part of what we know about life in the Yuan dynasty comes from one such trader, an Italian merchant named Marco Polo. Between 1271 and 1295 he traveled in and around China. Polo was highly respected by the Mongols and even served in Kublai Khan's court. When Polo returned to Europe, he wrote of his travels. Polo's descriptions of China fascinated many Europeans. His book sparked much European interest in China.

The End of the Yuan Dynasty

Despite their vast empire, the Mongols were not content with their lands. They decided to invade Japan. A Mongol army sailed to Japan in 1274 and 1281. The campaigns, however, were disastrous. Violent storms and fierce defenders destroyed most of the Mongol force.

The failed campaigns against Japan weakened the Mongol military. The huge, expensive public-works projects had already weakened the economy. These weaknesses, combined with Chinese resentment, made China ripe for rebellion.

In the 1300s many Chinese groups rebelled against the Yuan dynasty. In 1368 a former monk named Zhu Yuanzhang (JOO yoo-ahn-JAHNG) took charge of a rebel army. He led this army in a final victory over the Mongols. China was once again ruled by the Chinese.

READING CHECK Finding Main Ideas How did the Mongols come to rule China?

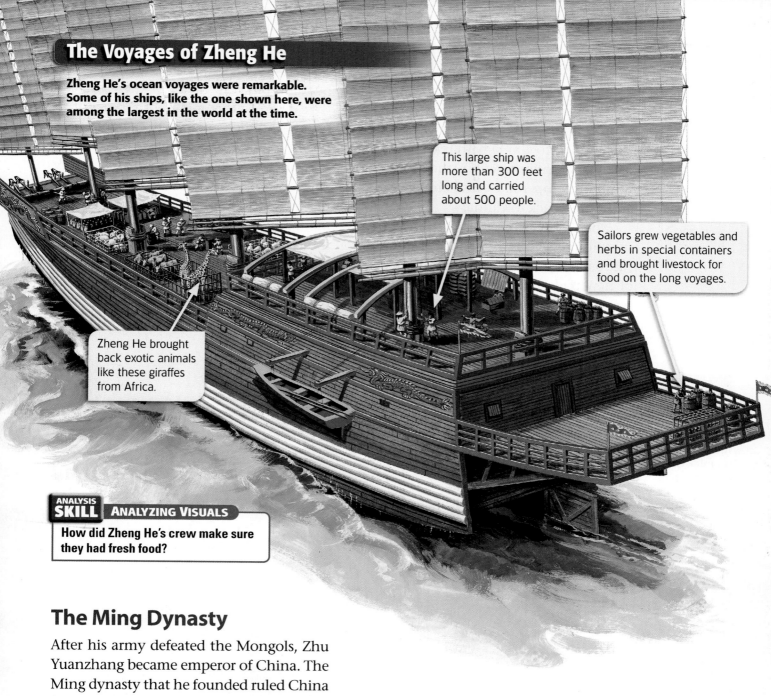

The Voyages of Zheng He

Zheng He's ocean voyages were remarkable. Some of his ships, like the one shown here, were among the largest in the world at the time.

This large ship was more than 300 feet long and carried about 500 people.

Sailors grew vegetables and herbs in special containers and brought livestock for food on the long voyages.

Zheng He brought back exotic animals like these giraffes from Africa.

ANALYSIS SKILL **ANALYZING VISUALS**

How did Zheng He's crew make sure they had fresh food?

The Ming Dynasty

After his army defeated the Mongols, Zhu Yuanzhang became emperor of China. The Ming dynasty that he founded ruled China from 1368 to 1644—nearly 300 years. Ming China proved to be one of the most stable and prosperous times in Chinese history. The Ming expanded China's fame overseas and sponsored incredible building projects across China.

Great Sea Voyages

During the Ming dynasty, the Chinese improved their ships and their sailing skills. The greatest sailor of the period was **Zheng He** (juhng HUH). Between 1405 and 1433, he led seven grand voyages to places around Asia. Zheng He's fleets were huge. One included more than 60 ships and 25,000 sailors. Some of the ships were gigantic too, perhaps more than 300 feet long. That is longer than a football field!

In the course of his voyages Zheng He sailed his fleet throughout the Indian Ocean. He sailed as far west as the Persian Gulf and the easternmost coast of Africa.

Everywhere his ships landed, Zheng He presented leaders with beautiful gifts from China. He boasted about his country and encouraged foreign leaders to send gifts to China's emperor. From one voyage, Zheng He returned to China with representatives of some 30 nations, sent by their leaders to honor the emperor. He also brought goods and stories back to China.

Zheng He's voyages rank among the most impressive in the history of seafaring. Although they did not lead to the creation of new trade routes or the exploration of new lands, they served as a clear sign of China's power.

Great Building Projects

The Ming were also known for their grand building projects. Many of these projects were designed to impress both the Chinese people and their enemies to the north.

In Beijing, for example, Ming emperors built the Forbidden City. This amazing palace complex included hundreds of imperial residences, temples, and other government buildings. Within the buildings were some 9,000 rooms. The name "Forbidden City" came from the fact that the common people were not even allowed to enter the complex. For centuries, this city within a city was a symbol of China's glory.

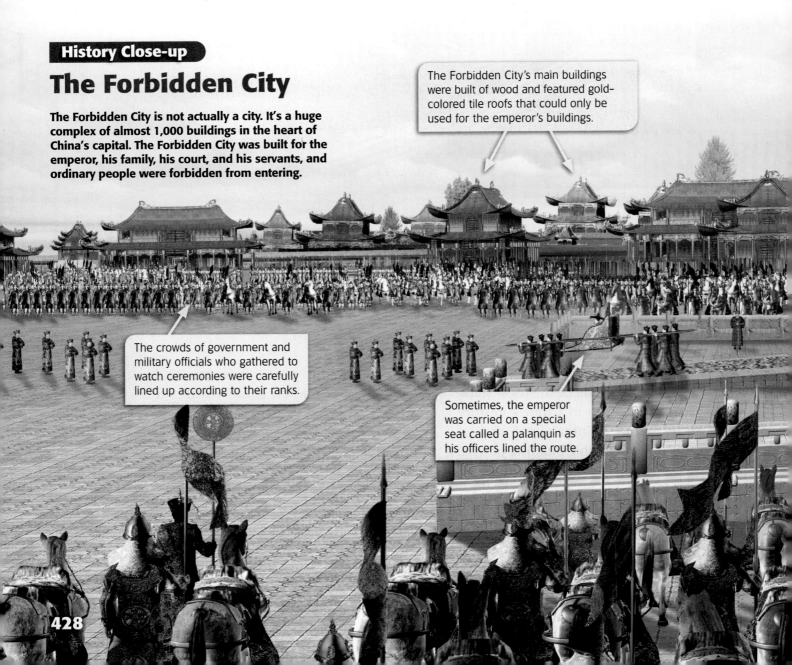

History Close-up

The Forbidden City

The Forbidden City is not actually a city. It's a huge complex of almost 1,000 buildings in the heart of China's capital. The Forbidden City was built for the emperor, his family, his court, and his servants, and ordinary people were forbidden from entering.

The Forbidden City's main buildings were built of wood and featured gold-colored tile roofs that could only be used for the emperor's buildings.

The crowds of government and military officials who gathered to watch ceremonies were carefully lined up according to their ranks.

Sometimes, the emperor was carried on a special seat called a palanquin as his officers lined the route.

Ming rulers also directed the restoration of the famous Great Wall of China. Large numbers of soldiers and peasants worked to rebuild collapsed portions of walls, connect existing walls, and build new ones. The result was a construction feat unmatched in history. The wall was more than 2,000 miles long. It would reach from San Diego to New York! The wall was about 25 feet high and, at the top, 12 feet wide. Protected by the wall—and the soldiers who stood guard along it—the Chinese people felt safe from invasions by the northern tribes.

READING CHECK **Generalizing** In what ways did the Ming dynasty strengthen China?

China Under the Ming

During the Ming dynasty, Chinese society began to change. This change was largely due to the efforts of the Ming emperors. Having expelled the Mongols, the Ming emperors worked to eliminate all foreign influences from Chinese society. As a result, China's government and relations with other countries changed dramatically.

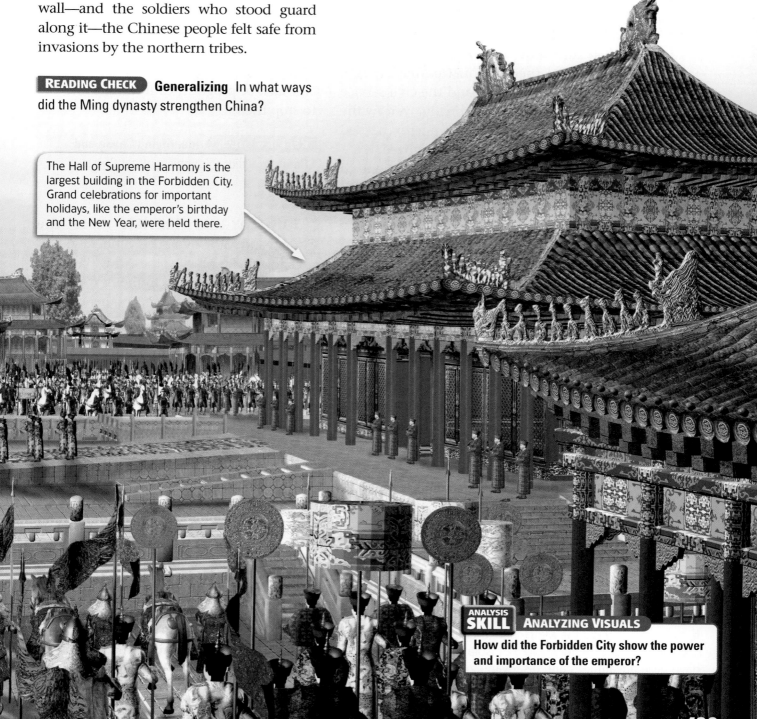

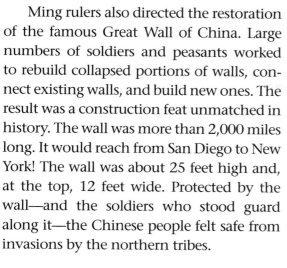

The Hall of Supreme Harmony is the largest building in the Forbidden City. Grand celebrations for important holidays, like the emperor's birthday and the New Year, were held there.

ANALYSIS SKILL **ANALYZING VISUALS**

How did the Forbidden City show the power and importance of the emperor?

429

Government

When the Ming took over China, they adopted many government programs that had been created by the Tang and the Song. However, the Ming emperors were much more powerful than the Tang and Song emperors had been. They abolished the offices of some powerful officials and took a larger role in running the government themselves. These emperors fiercely protected their power, and they punished anyone whom they saw as challenging their authority.

ACADEMIC VOCABULARY
consequences effects of a particular event or events

Despite their personal power, though, the Ming did not disband the civil service system. Because he personally oversaw the entire government, the emperor needed officials to keep his affairs organized.

The Ming also used examinations to appoint censors. These officials were sent throughout China to investigate the behavior of local leaders and to judge the quality of schools and other institutions. Censors had existed for many years in China, but under the Ming emperors their power and influence grew.

Relations with Other Countries

In the 1430s a new Ming emperor made Zheng He return to China and dismantle his fleet. At the same time, he banned foreign trade. China entered a period of isolationism. **Isolationism** is a policy of avoiding contact with other countries.

In the end, this isolationism had great **consequences** for China. In 1644 the Ming dynasty was overthrown. By the late 1800s the Western world had made huge leaps in technological progress. Westerners were then able to gain influence in Chinese affairs. Partly due to its isolation and lack of progress, China was too weak to stop them.

READING CHECK **Identifying Cause and Effect** How did isolationism affect China?

SUMMARY AND PREVIEW Under the Yuan and Ming dynasties, Chinese society changed. Eventually, the Ming began a policy of isolationism. In the next chapter you will read about Japan, another country that was isolated at times.

Section 4 Assessment

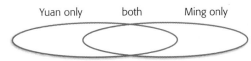

go.hrw.com
Online Quiz
KEYWORD: SN6 HP14

Reviewing Ideas, Terms, and People

1. **a. Identify** Who was **Genghis Khan**?
   b. Explain How did the Mongols gain control of China?
   c. Evaluate Judge this statement: "The Mongols should never have tried to invade Japan."
2. **a. Identify** Who was **Zheng He**, and what did he do?
   b. Analyze What impression do you think the Forbidden City had on the residents of Beijing?
   c. Develop How may the Great Wall have both helped and hurt China?
3. **a. Define** What is **isolationism**?
   b. Explain How did the Ming change China?
   c. Develop How might a policy of isolationism have both advantages and disadvantages?

Critical Thinking

4. **Comparing and Contrasting** Draw a diagram like this one. Use your notes to see how the Yuan and Ming dynasties were alike and different.

   Yuan only   both   Ming only

FOCUS ON WRITING

5. **Identifying Achievements of the Later Dynasties** Make a list of the achievements of the Yuan and Ming dynasties. Then look back over all your notes and rate the achievements or inventions. Which three do you think are the most important?

Kublai Khan

How did a Mongol nomad settle down to rule a vast empire?

When did he live? 1215–1294

Where did he live? Kublai came from Mongolia but spent much of his life in China. His capital, Dadu, was near the modern city of Beijing.

What did he do? Kublai Khan completed the conquest of China that Genghis Khan had begun. He ruled China as the emperor of the Yuan dynasty.

Why is he important? The lands Kublai Khan ruled made up one of the largest empires in world history. It stretched from the Pacific Ocean to Eastern Europe. As China's ruler, Kublai Khan welcomed foreign visitors, including the Italian merchant Marco Polo and the Arab historian Ibn Battutah. The stories these two men told helped create interest in China and its products among Westerners.

Generalizing How did Kublai Khan's actions help change people's views of China?

This painting from the 1200s shows Kublai Khan hunting on horseback.

431

Social Studies Skills

Analysis Critical Thinking Economics Study

Understanding Chance, Error, and Oversight

Define the Skill

History is nothing more than what people thought and did in the past, and the people of the past were just as human as people today. Like us, they occasionally forgot or overlooked things. They made mistakes in their decisions or judgments. Unexpected things happened that they couldn't control. Sometimes, these oversights, errors, and just plain luck shaped history.

Learn the Skill

There are several examples of the role of chance, error, and oversight in Chinese history.

1 Chance Ancient Chinese alchemists were searching for a potion to create everlasting life for the emperor. Although they did not discover the secret of everlasting life, they did discover that mixing certain ingredients together produced an explosion. By chance, they had discovered gunpowder.

2 Oversight As the Mongols were about to attack Western Europe, their khan died. The Mongols had focused so much on their military strength that they had neglected to develop a plan for the continuation of their government. Their law required them to go in person back to their land to elect a new khan. As a result, the Mongols never attacked Western Europe. Instead, they focused on China.

3 Error In the early 1100s, a new empire was gaining strength near Song China. Between the Song and the new empire lay an old enemy of China's. The Song emperor decided to ally himself with the new empire against the old enemy. This proved to be a disastrous decision. The Chinese defeated their old enemy, but China lost its buffer against the new strong empire. The alliance soon fell apart, and the new empire attacked the Song, taking one third of its land.

Practice the Skill

As you read in the chapter, China's silk industry was very successful. But what if chance, error, or oversight had played a role in the silk trade? For each fictional event below, determine whether it would have been a chance, an error, or oversight and describe how it might have affected Chinese history if it had happened.

1. The Chinese taught visitors how to make silk.

2. The Chinese decided that their silk was so valuable that they didn't want to export any of it.

3. The Chinese did not discover how to make silk.

Visual Summary

Use the visual summary below to help you review the main ideas of the chapter.

QUICK FACTS

China was reunified, and Buddhism spread during the Sui and Tang dynasties.

Farming and trade grew under the Tang and Song dynasties.

Confucian thought influenced Chinese government and education.

The powerful Yuan and Ming dynasties strengthened China, and expanded trade, but then China became isolated.

Reviewing Vocabulary, Terms, and People

Match the words or names with their definitions or descriptions.

a. Kublai Khan   **g.** compass

b. movable type   **h.** porcelain

c. scholar-official   **i.** Genghis Khan

d. Empress Wu   **j.** isolationism

e. bureaucracy   **k.** incentive

f. Zheng He   **l.** gunpowder

1. ruthless but effective Tang dynasty ruler

2. a set of letters or characters that can be moved to create different lines of text

3. leader who united the Mongols and began invasion of China

4. body of unelected government officials

5. thin, beautiful pottery

6. a device that indicates direction

7. policy of avoiding contact with other countries

8. founder of the Yuan dynasty

9. a mixture of powders used in explosives

10. commanded huge fleets of ships

11. educated government worker

12. something that leads people to follow a certain course of action

Comprehension and Critical Thinking

SECTION 1 *(Pages 410–413)*

13. a. Identify What period did China enter after the Han dynasty collapsed? What dynasty brought an end to this period?

b. Analyze Why is the Tang dynasty considered a golden age of Chinese civilization?

c. Predict How might Chinese culture have been different in the Tang and Song dynasties if Buddhism had not been introduced to China?

SECTION 2 (Pages 414–419)

14. a. Describe What did Wu Daozi, Li Bo, Du Fu, and Li Qingzhao contribute to Chinese culture?

b. Analyze What led to the growth of cities in China? What were China's cities like during the Tang and Song dynasties?

c. Evaluate Which Chinese invention has had a greater effect on world history—the magnetic compass or gunpowder? Why do you think so?

SECTION 3 (Pages 420–423)

15. a. Define What is Confucianism? How did it change during and after the Song dynasty?

b. Make Inferences Why do you think the civil service examination system was created?

c. Elaborate Why were China's civil service examinations so difficult?

SECTION 4 (Pages 424–430)

16. a. Describe How did the Mongols create their huge empire? What areas were included in it?

b. Draw Conclusions How did Marco Polo and Zheng He help shape ideas about China?

c. Elaborate Why do you think the Ming emperors spent so much time and money rebuilding and enlarging the Great Wall?

Using the Internet

go.hrw.com KEYWORD: SN6 WH14

17. Activity: Creating a Mural The Tang and Song periods saw many agricultural, technological, and commercial developments. New irrigation techniques, movable type, and gunpowder were a few of them. Enter the activity keyword and learn more about such developments. Imagine that a city official has hired you to create a mural showing all of the great things the Chinese developed during the Tang and Song dynasties. Create a large mural that depicts as many advances as possible.

Reviewing Themes

18. Science and Technology How did Chinese inventions alter the course of world history?

19. Economics How did the strong agricultural and trading economy of Tang and Song China affect the country?

Reading Skills

20. Drawing Conclusions about the Past Read the statements about the Ming dynasty below. For each conclusion that follows, decide whether the statements provide suffcent evidence to justify the conclusion.

> The Ming ruled China from 1368 to 1644.
>
> Zhu Yuanzhang was a Ming emperor.
>
> The Great Wall was rebuilt by the Ming.

a. The Great Wall is located in China.

b. Zhu Yuanzhang was a good emperor.

c. Zhu Yuanzhang ruled some time between 1368 and 1644.

d. Zhu Yuanzhang rebuilt the Great Wall.

Social Studies Skills

Chance, Error, and Oversight in History You read in this chapter about how the Mongol rulers of China decided to invade Japan. Three sentences from the text have been revised below. Read each sentence carefully. Then state whether it is an example of oversight, error, or chance.

21. Violent storms destroyed most of the Mongol force.

22. Despite their vast empire, the Mongols were not content with their lands and decided to invade Japan.

FOCUS ON WRITING

23. Writing a Magazine Article Now that you have identified three achievements or inventions you want to write about, begin your article. Open with a sentence that states your main idea. Include three or four sentences about each achievement or invention you have chosen. These sentences should describe the achievement or invention and explain why it was so important. End your article with a sentence or two summarizing China's importance to the world.

DIRECTIONS: Read each question, and write the letter of the best response.

1

This object displays Chinese expertise at working with

A woodblocks.

B gunpowder.

C cotton fibers.

D porcelain.

2 Trade and other contact with peoples far from China stopped under which dynasty?

A Ming

B Yuan

C Song

D Sui

3 Which of the following was *not* a way that Confucianism influenced China?

A emphasis on family and family values

B expansion of manufacturing and trade

C emphasis on service to society

D well-educated government officials

4 What was a major cause for the spread of Buddhism to China and other parts of Asia?

A the teachings of Kublai Khan

B the writings of Confucius

C the travels of Buddhist missionaries

D the support of Empress Wu

5 All of the following flourished during *both* the Tang and the Song dynasties, *except*

A art and culture.

B sea voyages of exploration.

C science and technology.

D trade.

Connecting with Past Learnings

6 Earlier you learned about the deeds of emperor Shi Huangdi. He had laborers work on a structure that Ming rulers improved. What was that structure?

A the Great Wall

B the Great Tomb

C the Forbidden City

D the Temple of Buddha

7 Earlier you learned that the ancient Egyptians increased food production by digging irrigation canals to water their fields. Under which dynasty did the Chinese develop new irrigation techniques to increase their production of food?

A Han

B Ming

C Song

D Sui

Japan

FOCUS ON WRITING

A Travel Brochure You've been hired to create a travel brochure called "Japan's Rich History." Your brochure will describe tourist attractions in Japan that show the country's fascinating past. As you read this chapter, think about how you might encourage people to visit Japan.

CHAPTER EVENTS

c. 550
Buddhism is introduced into Japan from China.

550

WORLD EVENTS

632–651
Arab armies conquer Southwest Asia.

What You Will Learn...

In this chapter, you will learn about the geography and history of early Japan. This photo shows Mount Fuji, a snow-covered volcano that has long been a symbol of Japan.

c. 1000
Lady Murasaki Shikibu writes *The Tale of Genji.*

1192
The first shogun rules Japan.

1603–1868
The Tokugawa shoguns rule Japan.

825

1100

1375

1650

768–814
Charlemagne rules much of western Europe.

1279
The Mongols take over China.

1588
England defeats the Spanish Armada.

Reading Social Studies

by Kylene Beers

Economics Geography **Politics** Religion **Society and Culture** Science and Technology

Focus on Themes As you read this chapter, you will step into the world of early Japan. You will learn about the first Japanese people and their religion, Shinto, and about how the people of China and Korea began to influence the development of Japanese culture. As you read about the history of Japan, you will learn about the **political** systems the Japanese used to govern their nation and their attitudes toward **society and culture**. Finally, you will learn how social elements of medieval Japanese culture continue to affect life in Japan to this day.

Main Ideas and Their Support

Focus on Reading You know that if you take the legs out from under a table it will fall flat on the floor. In just the same way, a main idea will fall flat without details to support it.

Understanding a Writer's Support for Ideas A writer can support main ideas with several kinds of details. These details might be facts, statistics, eyewitness accounts, brief stories, examples, definitions, or comments from experts on the subject.

Notice the types of details the writer uses to support the main idea in the passage below.

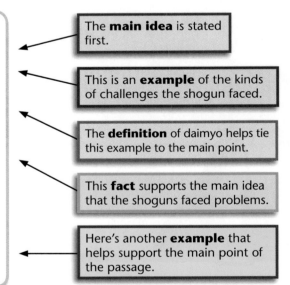

After the Mongol invasion, new problems arose for the shogun. The emperor, tired of having no say in the government, began to fight the shogun for control of the country. At the same time daimyo, the nobles who owned much of Japan's land, fought to break free of the shogun's control. During these struggles for power, small wars broke out all over Japan.

By the 1400s, the shoguns had lost most of their authority. The emperor was still largely powerless, and daimyo ruled much of Japan. Each daimyo controlled his own territory. Within that territory, he made laws and collected taxes. There was no powerful central authority of any sort to impose order in Japan.

- The **main idea** is stated first.
- This is an **example** of the kinds of challenges the shogun faced.
- The **definition** of daimyo helps tie this example to the main point.
- This **fact** supports the main idea that the shoguns faced problems.
- Here's another **example** that helps support the main point of the passage.

You Try It!

The following passage is from the chapter you are about to read. As you read it, look for the writer's main idea and supporting details.

Samurai

The word *samurai* comes from the Japanese word for servant. Every samurai, from the weakest soldier to the most powerful warrior, was supposed to serve his lord. Because all lords in Japan were supposed to serve the emperor, all samurai were required to be loyal to him.

An army of samurai was expensive to support. Few lords could afford to buy armor and weapons for their warriors. As a result, lords paid their samurai with land and food.

From Chapter 15, p. 455

After you read the passage, answer the following questions.

1. Which sentence best states the main idea of the passage?
   a. Samurai, which comes from the word servant, were supposed to serve their lords.
   b. Samurai were paid with land and food.
   c. Few lords could afford to buy armor and weapons for their warriors.

2. Which of the following is not a detail that supports the main idea of the passage?
   a. An army of samurai was expensive to support.
   b. Every samurai was supposed to serve his lord.
   c. In Japan at this time, there were more than 10,000 samurai.

3. Which of the following methods of supporting a main idea does the author use in this passage?
   a. statistics
   b. eyewitness account
   c. facts

Key Terms and People

Chapter 15

Section 1
clans (p. 440)
Shinto (p. 440)
Prince Shotoku (p. 442)
regent (p. 442)

Section 2
court (p. 444)
Lady Murasaki Shikibu (p. 445)
Zen (p. 448)

Section 3
daimyo (p. 454)
samurai (p. 454)
figurehead (p. 455)
shogun (p. 455)

Academic Vocabulary

Success in school is related to knowing academic vocabulary—the words that are frequently used in school assignments and discussions. In this chapter, you will learn the following academic words:

structure (p. 439)
values (p. 457)

As you read Chapter 15, look for the types of details that the writer uses to support the main ideas.

Geography and Early Japan

What You Will Learn...

Main Ideas

1. Geography shaped life in Japan.
2. Early Japanese society was organized in clans, which came to be ruled by an emperor.
3. Japan learned about language, society, and government from China and Korea.

The Big Idea

Japan's early societies were both isolated from and influenced by China and Korea.

Key Terms and People

clans, *p. 442*
Shinto, *p. 442*
Prince Shotoku, *p. 444*
regent, *p. 444*

 TAKING NOTES As you read, take notes on how geography, early peoples, and neighboring countries affected the Japanese people's way of life, government, and religion.

(Way of life) (Government) (Religion)

If **YOU** were there...

You live in a small farming village on one of the islands of Japan. You're very happy with your life. The sea is nearby and food is plentiful. You have a large, extended family to protect and take care of you. Your grandmother says that life in your village has not changed for hundreds of years, and that is good. But now you have heard that some people from across the sea are coming to your village. They are bringing new ideas and new ways of doing things.

How do you feel about these changes?

BUILDING BACKGROUND Japan is a large group of islands located east of the Asian mainland. Life in Japan has always been influenced by many factors. The islands' geography and location shaped how people lived there, and as you read above, visitors from other lands also affected Japanese society.

Geography Shapes Life in Japan

The islands of Japan are really just the tops of undersea mountains and volcanoes, sticking up out of the ocean. Those mountains, as you can see on the map, cover nearly all of Japan. Only about 20 percent of the land is flat. Because it is difficult to live and farm on mountain slopes, most Japanese people have always lived in those flat areas, the coastal plains.

In addition to the mountains and the lack of flat land, the nearness of the sea shaped the lives of Japanese people. Their homes were never far from the sea. Naturally, they turned to the sea for food. They learned to prepare all kinds of seafood, from eel to shark to octopus to seaweed. As a result, seafood has been a key part of the Japanese diet for thousands of years.

The islands' location affected the Japanese people in another way as well. Because they lived on islands, the Japanese were separated from the other people of Asia. This separation allowed

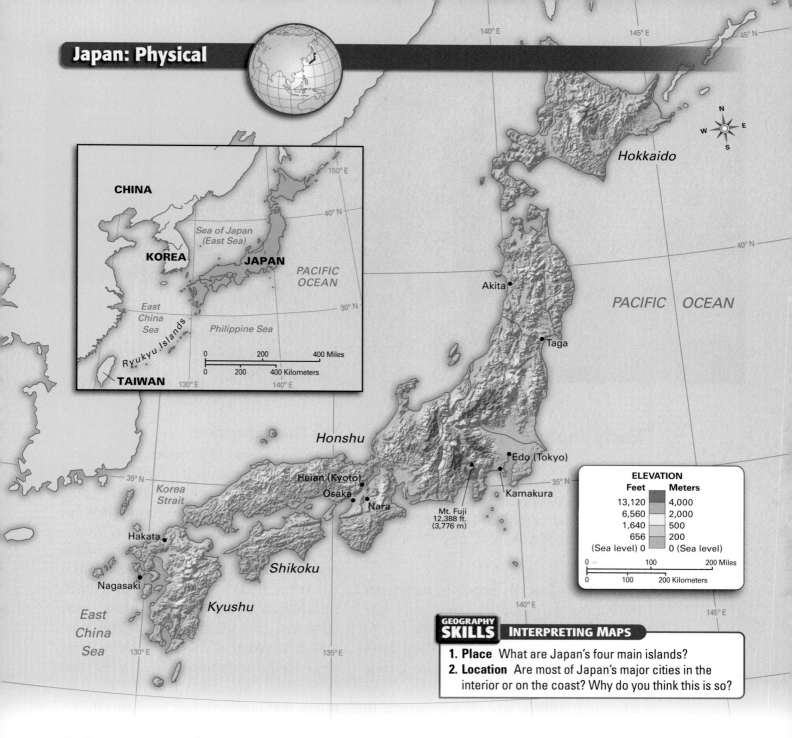

Japan: Physical

CHINA

Sea of Japan
(East Sea)

KOREA   JAPAN   PACIFIC
OCEAN

East
China
Sea

Philippine Sea

Ryukyu Islands

TAIWAN

| 0 | 200 | 400 Miles |
| 0 | 200 | 400 Kilometers |

130° E   140° E

Hokkaido

PACIFIC   OCEAN

Akita

Taga

Honshu

Heian (Kyoto)
Osaka

Nara

Edo (Tokyo)

Kamakura

Mt. Fuji
12,388 ft.
(3,776 m)

Korea
Strait

Hakata

Shikoku

Nagasaki

East
China
Sea

Kyushu

ELEVATION

Feet	Meters
13,120	4,000
6,560	2,000
1,640	500
656	200
(Sea level) 0	0 (Sea level)

| 0 | 100 | 200 Miles |
| 0 | 100 | 200 Kilometers |

GEOGRAPHY SKILLS **INTERPRETING MAPS**

1. **Place** What are Japan's four main islands?
2. **Location** Are most of Japan's major cities in the interior or on the coast? Why do you think this is so?

the Japanese to develop their own culture. For example, they created a religion and a social **structure** very different from those in other parts of Asia. This separation has always been an important part of Japanese society.

Japan isn't totally isolated, however. Look at the inset map above to find Korea and China. As you can see, neither country is very far from the Japanese islands. Korea is only about 100 miles away from Japan. China is about 400 miles away. Those short distances allowed the older Korean and Chinese cultures to influence the new culture of Japan.

READING CHECK **Summarizing** What is Japan's geography like?

ACADEMIC VOCABULARY

structure the way something is set up or organized

A Shinto Shrine
Entering a Shinto shrine, these people walk through a gate called a torii (TOR-ee). The torii marks the boundary of a shrine or other sacred Shinto site. Over time, the torii has become a symbol of Shinto, Japan's ancient religion.

What elements of nature can you see in this painting?

Early Japanese Society

Korea and China did play a major part in shaping Japanese society, but not at first. Early Japan was home to two different cultures, neither of which had any contact with the rest of Asia.

The Ainu

One culture that developed in Japan was the Ainu (EYE-noo). Historians aren't sure exactly when or how the Ainu moved to Japan. Some people think they came from what is now Siberia in eastern Russia. Wherever they came from, the Ainu spoke a language unlike any other language in eastern Asia. They also looked different from the other people of Japan.

Over time, the Ainu began to fight with other people for land. They lost most of these fights, and so they lost their land as well. Eventually the Ainu were driven back onto a single island, Hokkaido. Over time the Ainu culture almost disappeared. Many people gave up the Ainu language and adopted new customs.

THE IMPACT TODAY

Few Ainu remain in Japan today, and most of them live on Hokkaido.

The First Japanese

The people who lived south of the Ainu eventually became the Japanese. They lived mostly in small farming villages. These villages were ruled by powerful **clans**, or extended families. Other people in the village, including farmers and workers, had to obey and respect members of these clans.

At the head of each clan was a chief. In addition to his political power, each chief also had religious duties. The Japanese believed that their clan chiefs were descended from nature spirits called *kami* (KAH-mee). Clan chiefs led their clans in rituals that honored their *kami* ancestors.

Over time, these rituals became a central part of the traditional religion of Japan, **Shinto**. According to Shinto teachings, everything in nature—the sun, the moon, trees, waterfalls, and animals—has *kami*. Shintoists believe that some *kami* help people live and keep them from harm. They build shrines to *kami* and perform ceremonies in which they ask the *kami* to bless them.

The First Emperors

The clans of early Japan weren't all equal. Some clans were larger and more powerful than others. In time a few of these powerful clans built up armies and set out to conquer their neighbors.

One clan that gained power in this way lived in the Yamato region, the western part of Japan's largest island, Honshu. In addition to military might, the Yamato rulers claimed to have a glorious family history. They believed they were descended from the most powerful of all *kami*, the goddess of the sun.

By the 500s the Yamato rulers had extended their control over much of Honshu. Although they didn't control the whole country, the leaders of the Yamato clan began to call themselves the emperors of all Japan.

READING CHECK **Sequencing** How did emperors take power in Japan?

Japan Learns from China and Korea

Early Japanese society received very little influence from cultures on the Asian mainland. Occasionally, officials from China, Korea, or other parts of Asia visited Japan. For the most part, however, these visits didn't have a great impact on the Japanese way of life.

By the mid-500s, though, some Japanese leaders thought that Japan could learn a great deal from other cultures. In particular, they wanted to learn more about the cultures of China and Korea.

To learn what they wanted to know, the rulers of Japan decided to send representatives to China and Korea to gather information about their cultures. They also invited people from China and Korea to move to Japan. The emperors hoped that these people could teach the Japanese new ways of working and thinking.

Influences from China and Korea

QUICK FACTS

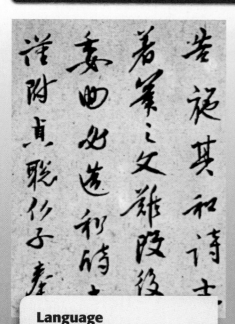

Language
The earliest Japanese writing used Chinese characters.

THE GRANGER COLLECTION, NEW YORK

Philosophy
The ideas of the Chinese philosopher Confucius helped shape Japanese culture and family life.

Religion
Buddhism came to Japan from Korea.

Changes in Language

One of the first things the Japanese learned from China and Korea was language. The early Japanese didn't have a written language. Therefore, many learned to write in Chinese. They continued to speak in Japanese, however, which is very different from Chinese. It wasn't until about 200 years later that people devised a way of writing in Japanese. They used Chinese characters to represent the sounds used in Japanese.

As Japan's contact with China increased, some Japanese people—especially rich and well-educated people—began to write in the Chinese language. Japanese writers used Chinese for their poems and stories. One of the first histories of Japan, written in the 700s, is in Chinese. For many years Chinese was even the official language of Japan's government.

Changes in Religion and Philosophy

One of the people most influential in bringing Chinese ideas to Japan was **Prince Shotoku** (shoh-toh-koo). He served from 593 to 621 as regent (REE-juhnt) for his aunt, the empress. A **regent** is a person who rules a country for someone who is unable to rule alone.

All his life, Prince Shotoku admired Chinese culture. As regent, Shotoku saw a chance for Japan to adopt more Chinese ideas. He sent scholars to China to learn all they could about Chinese society.

The ideas these scholars brought back changed Japanese society. For example, they taught the Japanese about Confucianism.

BIOGRAPHY

Prince Shotoku
573–621

Prince Shotoku was one of Japan's greatest leaders. He helped rule Japan when he was only 20 years old. For many centuries, people have admired him. Legends have developed about his wisdom. According to one early biography, Shotoku was able to talk as soon as he was born and never made a wrong decision.

Prince Shotoku's Japan

Under Prince Shotoku, Buddhism spread across Japan. Shotoku ordered beautiful Buddhist temples to be built, such as the one below in Nara, Japan. The spread of Buddhism changed many areas of Japanese culture during Prince Shotoku's time.

Horyuji Temple in Nara, Japan

Among other things, Confucianism outlined how families should behave. Confucius taught that fathers should rule their families. He believed that wives should obey their husbands, children should obey their parents, and younger brothers should obey older brothers. Families in China lived according to these rules. As Confucian ideas spread through Japan, the Japanese began to live by them as well.

More important than these social changes, though, were the vast religious changes Shotoku made in Japan. He was a Buddhist, and he wanted to spread Buddhism throughout his country. Buddhism wasn't new to Japan. Korean visitors had introduced the religion to Japan about 50 years earlier. But it was not very popular. Most people preferred to keep their traditional religion, Shinto.

Shotoku worked to change people's minds about Buddhism. He built a grand Buddhist temple that still stands today. He also wrote commentaries on Buddhist teachings. Largely because of his efforts, Buddhism became very popular, especially among Japanese nobles.

Changes in Government

Shotoku also wanted to change Japan's government to be more like China's. He especially wanted Japan's emperors to have more power, like China's emperors did.

Afraid that they would lose power to the emperor, many clan leaders opposed Shotoku's government plans. As a result, Japan's emperors gained little power.

READING CHECK **Categorizing** What aspects of Chinese society did Shotoku bring to Japan?

SUMMARY AND PREVIEW In this section, you learned how early Japan grew and developed. Next you'll see how Japan's emperors encouraged nobles to create great works of art and literature.

Statue of the Buddha in Horyuji

go.hrw.com
Online Quiz
KEYWORD: SN6 HP15

Section 1 Assessment

Reviewing Ideas, Terms, and People

1. **a. Recall** What types of landforms cover most of Japan?
   b. Explain How did Japan's location both separate it from and tie it to China and Korea?
2. **a. Define** What is **Shinto**?
   b. Sequence How did the Yamato rulers gain power?
3. **a. Explain** How did **Prince Shotoku** help spread Buddhism in Japan?
   b. Rate What do you think was the most important idea the Japanese borrowed from China or Korea? Why?

Critical Thinking

4. **Categorizing** Draw a diagram like this one. Using your notes on Japan's culture, list ideas that developed within Japan in the circle and ideas that the Japanese borrowed from other people in the arrow.

FOCUS ON WRITING

5. **Taking Notes on Early Japan** Think about the section you have just read. Which details from this section might be appealing to tourists? Write down some thoughts in your notebook. Plan to include them in a section of your travel brochure called "Fun Facts."

Art and Culture in Heian

What You Will Learn...

Main Ideas

1. Japanese nobles created great art in their court at Heian.
2. Buddhism changed in Japan during the Heian period.

The Big Idea

Japanese culture experienced a golden age during the Heian period of the 800s to the 1100s.

Key Terms and People

court, *p. 446*
Lady Murasaki Shikibu, *p. 447*
Zen, *p. 450*

TAKING NOTES As you read, take notes on the changes in Japanese art and religion in the golden age of the Heian period.

	Changes
Art	
Religion	

If YOU were there...

You are a noble, serving the empress of Japan and living in the capital city. While walking in the garden one day, she gives you a small book with blank pages. When you ask her why, she says the book is a diary for you to write in. She tells you that nobles, both men and women, keep diaries to record their lives.

What will you write in your new diary?

BUILDING BACKGROUND In 794 the emperor and empress of Japan moved to Heian (HAY-ahn), a city now called Kyoto. Many nobles, like the one you just read about, followed their rulers to the new city. These nobles loved art and beauty, and they tried to make their new home a beautiful place.

Japanese Nobles Create Great Art

The nobles who followed Japan's emperor to Heian wanted to win his favor by living close to him. In Heian, these nobles created an imperial **court**, a group of nobles who live near and serve or advise a ruler.

Members of the noble court had little to do with the common people of Heian. They lived apart from poorer citizens and seldom left the city. These nobles enjoyed their lives of ease and privilege. In fact, their lives were so easy and so removed from the rest of Japan that many nobles called themselves "dwellers among the clouds."

The nobles of this court loved beauty and elegance. Because of this love, many nobles were great supporters of the arts. As a result, the court at Heian became a great center of culture and learning. In fact, the period between 794 and 1185 was a golden age of the arts in Japan.

Heian (Kyoto)

JOURNAL ENTRY
The Pillow Book

Sei Shonagon (SAY shoh-nah-gohn), author of The Pillow Book, *served Japan's empress from 991 to 1000. The Pillow Book was her journal. In it she wrote poems and thoughts about nature as well as descriptions of daily events. Here she describes the first time she met the empress.*

"When I first entered her Majesty's service I felt indescribably shy, and was indeed constantly on the verge of tears. When I came on duty the first evening, the Empress was sitting with only a three-foot screen in front of her, and so nervous was I that when she passed me some picture or book to look at, I was hardly capable of putting out my hand to take it. While she was talking about what she wanted me to see—telling me what it was or who had made it—I was all the time wondering whether my hair was in order."

−Sei Shonagon, from *The Pillow Book*

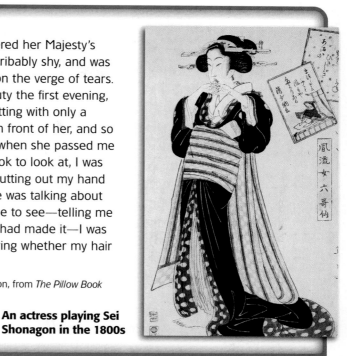

An actress playing Sei Shonagon in the 1800s

ANALYSIS SKILL **ANALYZING PRIMARY SOURCES**

How did Sei Shonagon feel when she met the empress?

Fashion

The nobles' love of beauty began with their own appearances. They had magnificent wardrobes full of silk robes and gold jewelry. Nobles loved elaborate outfits. For example, women wore long gowns made of 12 layers of colored silk cleverly cut and folded to show off many layers at once.

To complete their outfits, nobles often carried delicate decorative fans. These fans were painted with flowers, trees, and birds. Many nobles also attached flowers and long silk cords to their fans.

Literature

In addition to how they looked, Japanese nobles took great care with how they spoke and wrote. Writing was very popular among the nobles, especially among the women. Many women wrote diaries and journals about their lives at court. In their diaries, these women carefully chose their words to make their writing beautiful.

Unlike men, who usually wrote in Chinese, noble women wrote in the Japanese language. As a result, many of the greatest works of early Japanese literature were written by women.

One of the greatest writers in early Japanese history was **Lady Murasaki Shikibu** (moohr-ah-sahk-ee shee-kee-boo). Around 1000, she wrote *The Tale of Genji*. Many historians consider this book to be the world's first full-length novel. Many readers also consider it one of the best.

The Tale of Genji is the story of a prince named Genji and his long quest for love. During his search he meets women from many different social classes.

Many people consider *The Tale of Genji* one of Japan's greatest novels. The characters it describes are very colorful and seem real. In addition, Lady Murasaki's writing is clear and simple but graceful at the same time. She describes court life in Japan with great detail.

Most early Japanese prose was written by women, but both men and women wrote poetry. Nobles loved to read and write poems. Some nobles held parties at which they took turns writing poetry and reading their poems aloud to each other.

Poems from this time usually had only five lines. They followed a specific structure that outlined how many syllables each line could include. Most were about love or nature, but some described everyday events. Here is an example of a nature poem about the end of winter:

"The breezes of spring
Are blowing the ripples astray
Along the water—
Today they will surely melt
The sheet of ice on the pond."

–Kino Tomonori, from the *Gosenshu*

Visual Art

Besides literature, Japan's nobles also loved the visual arts. The most popular art forms of the period were paintings, calligraphy, and architecture.

In their paintings, the nobles of Heian liked bright, bold colors. They also liked paintings that illustrated stories. In fact, many of the greatest paintings from this period illustrate scenes from literature, such as *The Tale of Genji*. Other paintings show scenes from nature or from court life. Many artists painted on doors and furniture rather than on paper.

Another popular form of art in Heian was calligraphy, or decorative writing. Calligraphers spent hours carefully copying poems. They wanted the poems to look as beautiful as they sounded.

The Arts in Heian

Heian was Japan's capital for many centuries. The wealthy nobles who lived there were great supporters of the arts. With their support, literature, painting, calligraphy, and other arts flourished in Heian.

A favorite theme in Japanese painting was *The Tale of Genji*. In this illustration of a scene from the novel, Genji's son is reading a letter as his wife approaches.

Architecture

The nobles of Heian worked to make their city beautiful. They greatly admired Chinese architecture and modeled Heian after the Chinese capital, Chang'an. They copied Chinese building styles, especially in the many temples they built. These styles featured buildings with wooden frames that curved slightly upward at the ends. The wooden frames were often left unpainted to look more natural. Thatched roofs also added to the natural feel.

For other buildings, the nobles liked simple, airy designs. Most buildings were made of wood with tiled roofs and large, open spaces inside. To add to the beauty of these buildings, the nobles surrounded them with elegant gardens and ponds. Similar gardens are still popular in Japan.

Performing Arts

The performing arts were also popular in Japan during the Heian period. The roots of later Japanese drama can be traced back to this time. People often gathered to watch performances by musicians, jugglers, and acrobats. These performances were wild and fun. Especially popular were the plays in which actors skillfully mimicked other people.

In later centuries, these types of performances developed into a more serious form of drama called Noh. Created in the 1300s, Noh plays combine music, speaking, and dance. These plays often tell about great heroes or figures from Japan's past.

THE IMPACT TODAY

Noh plays are still popular in Japan today.

READING CHECK **Categorizing** What forms of art were popular in the Heian period?

The Buddha was a popular subject for statues in the Heian period.

Japanese writing could be an art form in itself. This album made in the shape of a fan is covered in text and pictures.

ANALYSIS SKILL **ANALYZING VISUALS**

How does art from this period reflect the culture of Heian?

Many Zen gardens like this one include raked gravel shaped to look like water and small boulders arranged like mountains.

One new form of Buddhism was very popular with Japan's common people. It was called Pure Land Buddhism and didn't require any special rituals. Instead, Pure Land Buddhists chanted the Buddha's name over and over to achieve an enlightened state.

In the 1100s another popular new form of Buddhism called **Zen** arrived from China. Zen Buddhists believed that neither faith nor good behavior led to wisdom. Instead, people seeking wisdom should practice self-discipline and meditation, or quiet thinking. These ideas appealed to many Japanese, especially warriors. As these warriors gained more influence in Japan, so did Zen Buddhism.

Buddhism Changes

Religion became something of an art form in Heian. The nobles' religion reflected their love of elaborate rituals. Most of the common people in Japan, though equally religious, didn't have the time or money for these ceremonies. As a result, different forms of Buddhism developed in Japan.

READING CHECK Finding Main Ideas How did Buddhism change in Japan?

SUMMARY AND PREVIEW At Heian, Japan's emperors presided over an elegant court. In the next section, you'll learn what happened when emperors and the court lost power and prestige.

go.hrw.com
Online Quiz
KEYWORD: SN6 HP15

Section 2 Assessment

Reviewing Ideas, Terms, and People

1. **a. Recall** Where did Japan's **court** move in the late 700s?
   b. Make Generalizations Why are the 800s to the 1100s considered a golden age for Japanese literature and art?
   c. Evaluate Do you think women in Heian had more rights and freedoms than women in other societies? Why or why not?
2. **a. Identify** What new form of Buddhism developed in Japan?
   b. Compare and Contrast How was religion among Japan's nobles different from religion among the common people?
   c. Elaborate Why do you think Pure Land Buddhism was popular with common people?

Critical Thinking

3. **Categorizing** Draw a Japanese fan like the one shown here. Use your notes about the arts to list two contributions that the Japanese made in each category shown here.

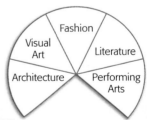

Fashion
Visual Art
Literature
Architecture
Performing Arts

FOCUS ON WRITING

4. **Writing about Japanese Art** Japan's nobles left a legacy of beautiful art that today's visitors can still enjoy. Choose two art forms described in this section and take notes for your brochure. What kinds of pictures could you use to illustrate your text?

Lady Murasaki Shikibu

How would you describe the people you observe in life every day?

When did she live? around 1000

Where did she live? Heian

What did she do? Lady Murasaki was a noble and a servant to the Empress Akiko. While in the empress's service, she wrote lively observations of court life in her diaries. She also wrote the novel *The Tale of Genji*.

Why is she important? *The Tale of Genji* is one of the world's oldest novels, and—some would argue—one of the best. Besides entertaining readers for hundreds of years, *The Tale of Genji* describes the daily lives, customs, and attitudes of Japanese nobles of the time.

Drawing Conclusions What qualified Lady Murasaki to comment on upper-class life in Japan?

This painting from the 1600s is an illustration of court life from *The Tale of Genji*.

from The Tale of Genji

by Lady Murasaki Shikibu
translated by Edward G. Seidensticker

❶ *What kind of modern-day American event might be compared to the emperor's visit?*

❷ *What do Genji's thoughts and actions tell you about his attitude toward his guests?*

About the Reading *The Tale of Genji was written by Lady Murasaki Shikibu at the height of Japan's golden age. This thousand-page novel traces the life and adventures—especially in love—of a noble known as "the shining Genji." Although Genji is the favorite son of the emperor, his mother is only a commoner, so Genji cannot inherit the throne. Instead, it passes first to his half-brother Suzaku (soo-zah-koo) and then to Genji's own son. Here, Genji's son and his half-brother Suzaku visit Genji's mansion in Rokujo (roh-koo-joh), a district of Heian.*

AS YOU READ Look for details that describe the lives of Japanese nobles.

The emperor paid a state visit to Rokujo late in the Tenth Month. ❶ Since the colors were at their best and it promised to be a grand occasion, the Suzaku emperor accepted the invitation of his brother, the present emperor, to join him. It was a most extraordinary event, the talk of the whole court. The preparations, which occupied the full attention of everyone at Rokujo, were unprecedented in their complexity and in the attention to brilliant detail.

Arriving late in the morning, the royal party went first to the equestrian grounds, where the inner guards were mustered for mounted review in the finery usually reserved for the iris festival. There were brocades spread along the galleries and arched bridges and awnings over the open places when, in early afternoon, the party moved to the southeast quarter. The royal cormorants had been turned out with the Rokujo cormorants on the east lake, where there was a handsome take of small fish. Genji hoped that he was not being a fussy and overzealous host, but he did not want a single moment of the royal progress to be dull. ❷ The autumn leaves were splendid, especially in Akikonomu's southwest garden. Walls had been taken down and gates opened, and not so much as an autumn mist was permitted to obstruct the royal view. Genji showed his guests to seats on a higher level than his own. The emperor ordered this mark of inferiority dispensed with, and thought again what a satisfaction it would be to honor Genji as his father.

The lieutenants of the inner guards advanced from the east and knelt to the left and right of the stairs before the royal seats, one presenting the take from the pond and the other a brace of fowl taken by the royal falcons in the northern hills. To no Chujo received the royal command to prepare and serve these delicacies. ❸ An equally interesting repast had been laid out for the princes and high courtiers. The court musicians took their places in late afternoon . . . The concert was quiet and unpretentious and there were court pages to dance for the royal guests. It was as always the excursion to the Suzaku Palace so many years before that people remembered. One of To no Chujo's sons, a boy of ten or so, danced "Our Gracious Monarch" most elegantly. The emperor took off a robe and laid it over his shoulders, and To no Chujo himself descended into the garden for ritual thanks . . .

A painting of Lady Murasaki Shikibu from around 1700

The evening breeze had scattered leaves of various tints to make the ground a brocade as rich and delicate as the brocades along the galleries. The dancers were young boys from the best families, prettily dressed in coronets and the usual grayblues and roses, with crimsons and lavenders showing at their sleeves. They danced very briefly and withdrew under the autumn trees, and the guests regretted the approach of sunset. The formal concert, brief and unassuming, was followed by impromptu music in the halls above, instruments having been brought from the palace collection. As it grew livelier a koto was brought for each of the emperors and a third for Genji. ❹ . . . It was cause for general rejoicing that the two houses should be so close.

GUIDED READING

WORD HELP

brace pair
repast meal
unpretentious simple; modest
coronets small crowns

❸ To no Chujo is Genji's best friend. During the Heian period, food preparation was considered an art, and chefs were highly honored for their skill.

❹ A koto is a stringed instrument sometimes called a Japanese harp.

CONNECTING LITERATURE TO HISTORY

1. **Summarizing** The nobles of the court at Heian loved beauty and elegance. Because of this love, many nobles were great supporters of the arts. Based on this passage, what specific arts did Japanese nobles enjoy?

2. **Generalizing** The nobles enjoyed their lives of ease and privilege. What details suggest that Japanese nobles lived lives of luxury?

3. **Evaluating** After reading this passage, what is your overall impression of Japanese court life?

Growth of a Military Society

What You Will Learn...

Main Ideas

1. Samurai and shoguns took over Japan as emperors lost influence.
2. Samurai warriors lived honorably.
3. Order broke down when the power of the shoguns was challenged by invaders and rebellions.
4. Strong leaders took over and reunified Japan.

The Big Idea

Japan developed a military society led by generals called shoguns.

Key Terms and People

daimyo, *p. 454*
samurai, *p. 454*
figurehead, *p. 455*
shogun, *p. 455*
Bushido, *p. 456*

 TAKING NOTES As you read, use a diagram like the one below to note details about the growth of a military society in Japan.

Rise of Samurai and Shoguns	Life in a Military Society	Challenges to Military Rule

If YOU were there...

You are a Japanese warrior, proud of your fighting skills. For many years you've been honored by most of society, but you face an awful dilemma. When you became a warrior, you swore to protect and fight for both your lord and your emperor. Now your lord has gone to war against the emperor, and both sides have called for you to join them.

How will you decide whom to fight for?

BUILDING BACKGROUND Wars between lords and emperors were not uncommon in Japan after 1100. Closed off from society at Heian, emperors had lost touch with the rest of Japan. As a result, order broke down throughout the islands.

Samurai and Shoguns Take Over Japan

By the late 1100s, Heian was the great center of Japanese art and literature. But in the rest of Japan, life was very different. Powerful nobles fought each other over land. Rebels fought against imperial officials. This fighting destroyed land, which made it difficult for peasants to grow food. Some poor people became bandits or thieves. Meanwhile, Japan's rulers were so focused on courtly life, they didn't notice the many problems growing in their country.

The Rise of the Samurai

With the emperor distracted by life in his court, Japan's large landowners, or **daimyo** (DY-mee-oh), decided that they needed to protect their own lands. They hired **samurai** (SA-muh-ry), or trained professional warriors, to defend them and their property. The samurai wore light armor and fought with swords and bows. Most samurai came from noble families and inherited their positions from their fathers.

The word *samurai* comes from the Japanese word for servant. Every samurai, from the weakest soldier to the most powerful warrior, was supposed to serve his lord. Because all lords in Japan were supposed to serve the emperor, all samurai were required to be loyal to him.

An army of samurai was expensive to support. Few lords could afford to buy armor and weapons for their warriors. As a result, lords paid their samurai with land or food.

Only the most powerful samurai got land for their service. Most of these powerful samurai didn't live on the land they received, but they did profit from it. Every year, the peasant farmers who worked on the land gave the samurai money or food. Samurai who received no land were given food—usually rice—as payment.

Shoguns Rule Japan

Many of the nobles outside Heian were unhappy with the way Japan's government was being run. Frustrated, these nobles wanted a change of leadership. Eventually a few very strong noble clans decided to try to take power for themselves.

Two of these powerful clans went to war with each other in the 1150s. For almost 30 years, the two clans fought. Their fighting was terrible, destroying land and property and tearing families apart.

In the end, the Minamoto clan won. Because he had a very powerful army, and because the emperor was still busy in Heian, the leader of the Minamoto clan was the most powerful man in Japan. He decided to take over ruling the country.

He didn't, however, want to get rid of the emperor. He kept the emperor as a **figurehead**, a person who appears to rule even though real power rests with someone else. As a samurai, the Minamoto leader was supposed to be loyal to the

emperor, but he decided to rule in the emperor's place. In 1192 he took the title **shogun**, a general who ruled Japan in the emperor's name. When he died, he passed his title and power on to one of his children. For about the next 700 years, one shogun would rule in Japan.

READING CHECK **Sequencing** How did the shogun rise to power in Japan?

QUICK FACTS

Samurai Society

Emperor
The emperor was a figurehead for the powerful shogun.

Shogun
A powerful military leader, the shogun ruled in the emperor's name.

Daimyo and Samurai
Daimyo were powerful lords who often led armies of samurai. Samurai warriors served the shogun and daimyo.

Peasants
Most Japanese were poor peasants who had no power.

ANALYSIS SKILL **ANALYZING VISUALS**

Who was the most powerful person in Japan's samurai society?

Samurai Live Honorably

FOCUS ON READING

As you read this section, notice the facts and examples that support the main idea.

Under the shogun, who were military rulers, samurai warriors became more central to Japanese society. As a result, samurai enjoyed many social privileges. Common people had to treat the samurai with respect. Anyone who disrespected a samurai could be killed.

At the same time, tradition placed restrictions on samurai. For example, they couldn't attend certain types of entertainment, such as theater, which were considered beneath them. They also couldn't take part in trade or commerce.

Bushido

More importantly, all samurai had to follow a strict code of rules that taught them how to behave. The samurai code of rules was known as **Bushido** (BOOH-shi-doh). This name means "the way of the warrior." Both men and women from samurai families had to follow Bushido rules.

Bushido required samurai to be brave and honorable fighters. Both men and women of samurai families learned how to fight, though only men went to war. Women learned to fight so they could protect their homes from robbers.

Japan's Samurai

The samurai were bold, highly trained warriors. They followed a strict code of behavior called Bushido, or "the way of the warrior."

What equipment did samurai have to protect themselves?

Samurai wore armor and special helmets. Many carried two swords.

Samurai were often called on to fight, like in the scene above. They were expected to serve with honor and loyalty in battle. The samurai in the scene to the right is writing a poem on a cherry tree. Writing poetry helped train the samurai to concentrate.

Samurai were expected to live simple, disciplined lives. They believed that self-discipline made them better warriors. To improve their discipline, many samurai participated in peaceful rituals that required great concentration. Some created intricate flower arrangements or grew miniature bonsai trees. Others held elaborate tea ceremonies. Many samurai also adopted Zen Buddhism, which stressed self-discipline and meditation.

More than anything else, Bushido required a samurai to be loyal to his lord. Each samurai had to obey his master's orders without hesitation, even if it caused the samurai or his family to suffer. One samurai expressed his duties in this way:

" If one were to say in a word what the condition of being a samurai is, its basis lies first in seriously devoting one's body and soul to his master. "

–Yamamoto Tsunetomo, from *Hagakure*

Obeying his lord was important to the samurai's sense of honor. Honor was the most important thing in a samurai's life. If he did anything to lose honor, a samurai was expected to commit suicide rather than live with his shame. Such shame might be caused by disobeying an order, losing a fight, or failing to protect his lord.

Bushido and Modern Japan

Although it was created as a code for warriors, Bushido influenced much of Japanese society. Even today, many Japanese feel a connection to the samurai. For example, the samurai's dedication and discipline are still greatly admired in Japan. **Values** such as loyalty and honor, the central ideas of the samurai code, remain very important in modern Japan.

ACADEMIC VOCABULARY

values ideas that people hold dear and try to live by

READING CHECK **Finding Main Ideas** What customs did samurai follow?

LINKING TO TODAY

Modern Samurai

Although the samurai class disappeared from Japan at the end of the 1800s, samurai images and values live on. Fierce samurai appear on posters, in advertisements and movies, and in video games, challenging foes with their sharp swords and deadly skills. Many people study the same martial arts, such as sword fighting, that the samurai practiced. In addition, the loyalty that samurai felt toward their lords is still a key part of Japanese society. Many Japanese feel that same loyalty toward other groups—their families, companies, or favorite sports teams. Samurai values such as hard work, honor, and sacrifice have also become deeply rooted in Japanese society.

ANALYSIS SKILL **ANALYZING INFORMATION**

How are Japan's samurai values still alive today?

Mongol Invasions of Japan

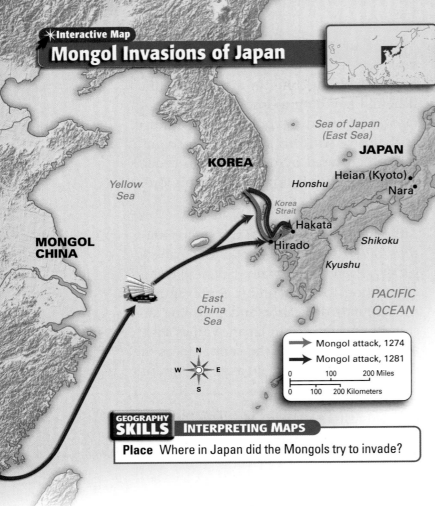

Sea of Japan (East Sea)

JAPAN

KOREA

Heian (Kyoto)

Honshu

Nara

Yellow Sea

Korea Strait

MONGOL CHINA

Hakata

Hirado

Shikoku

Kyushu

East China Sea

PACIFIC OCEAN

→ Mongol attack, 1274
→ Mongol attack, 1281

0   100   200 Miles
0   100   200 Kilometers

N
W   E
S

GEOGRAPHY SKILLS **INTERPRETING MAPS**

Place Where in Japan did the Mongols try to invade?

Order Breaks Down

For about a century, the shoguns kept order in Japan. Supported by the samurai, the shoguns were able to put down challenges to their authority. Eventually, however, more serious challenges arose that brought this order to an end.

Foreign Invasion

One of the greatest challenges to the shoguns was an invasion by the Mongols from China. China's emperor, Kublai Khan, sent an army to conquer the islands in 1274. Faced with invasion, the shogun sent troops to fight the Mongols. In addition, Japan's warring nobles put aside their differences to fight the enemy. The Japanese warriors were aided by a great storm. The storm sank many Mongol ships and forced the Mongols to flee.

In 1281 the Mongols invaded again. This time they sent two huge armies and threatened to overwhelm the Japanese warriors. For weeks, the two armies were locked in deadly combat.

Once again, though, the weather helped the Japanese. A huge storm swept over Japan, sinking most of the Mongol fleet. Many Mongol soldiers drowned, and many more returned to China. The grateful Japanese called the storm that had saved them the kamikaze (kah-mi-KAH-zee), or "divine wind." They believed the gods had sent the storm to save Japan.

But many nobles were left unhappy by the war. They didn't think the shogun gave them enough credit for their part in the fighting. Many came to resent the shogun's power over them.

Internal Rebellion

After the Mongol invasion, new problems arose for the shogun. The emperor, tired of having no say in the government, began to fight the shogun for control of the country. At the same time daimyo, the nobles who owned much of Japan's land, fought to break free of the shogun's control. During these struggles for power, small wars broke out all over Japan.

By the 1400s the shoguns had lost most of their authority. The emperor was still largely powerless, and daimyo ruled much of Japan. Each daimyo controlled his own territory. Within that territory, he made laws and collected taxes. There was no powerful central authority of any sort to impose order in Japan.

READING CHECK **Summarizing** What challenges appeared to the shogun's authority?

Strong Leaders Take Over

Soon new leaders rose to power. They began as local rulers, but these men wanted more power. In the 1500s, each fought to unify all of Japan under his control.

Unification

The first such leader was Oda Nobunaga (ohd-ah noh-booh-nah-gah). Oda gave his soldiers guns that had been brought to Japan by Portuguese traders. This was the first time guns had been used in Japan. With these new weapons, Oda easily defeated his opponents.

After Oda died, other leaders continued his efforts to unify Japan. By 1600, one of them, Tokugawa Ieyasu (toh-koohg-ah-wuh ee-e-yahs-ooh), had conquered his enemies. In 1603 Japan's emperor made Tokugawa shogun. From his capital at Edo (AY-doh)—now Tokyo—Tokugawa ruled all of Japan.

Tokugawa's rise to power began the Tokugawa shogunate (SHOH-guhn-uht), or rule by shoguns of the Tokugawa family. Early in this period, which lasted until 1868, Japan traded with other countries and let Christian missionaries live in Japan.

Isolation

Not all of the shoguns who followed Tokugawa liked this contact with the world, though. Some feared that Japan would become too much like Europe, and the shoguns would lose their power. To prevent such a thing from happening, in the 1630s the ruling shogun closed Japan off from the rest of the world.

Japan's rulers also banned guns. They feared that peasants with guns could defeat their samurai armies. The combination of isolation from the world and limited technology helped extend the samurai period in Japan until the 1800s, far longer than it might have otherwise lasted.

READING CHECK **Drawing Conclusions** How did Japan change in the Tokugawa shogunate?

SUMMARY AND PREVIEW By the 1100s, the growing power of shoguns, daimyo, and samurai had turned Japan into a military society. Next you will read about societies that developed on the other side of the world—in the Americas.

Section 3 Assessment

go.hrw.com
Online Quiz
KEYWORD: SN6 HP15

Reviewing Ideas, Terms, and People

1. **a. Recall** What was the relationship between **samurai** and **daimyo**?
   b. Elaborate Why do you think the first **shogun** wanted to keep the emperor as a **figurehead**?
2. **a. Define** What was **Bushido**?
   b. Explain Why did samurai take up pursuits like flower arranging?
3. **a. Identify** Who invaded Japan in the 1270s and 1280s?
   b. Summarize How did the daimyo help weaken the shoguns?
4. **Identify** What strong leaders worked to unify Japan in the late 1500s?

Critical Thinking

5. **Analyzing** Draw a word web. In the center, write a sentence that describes the samurai. Using your notes about life in a military society, write one of the samurai's jobs, duties, or privileges in each outer circle.

FOCUS ON WRITING

6. **Describing the Samurai** A Japanese history museum will offer a special exhibit on the samurai warrior. Add notes about the samurai to encourage tourists to visit the exhibit. Tell who they were, what they did, and how they lived.

Social Studies Skills

Solving Problems

Understand the Skill

Problem solving is a process for finding good solutions to difficult situations. It involves asking questions, identifying and evaluating information, comparing and contrasting, and making judgments. It is useful in studying history because it helps you better understand problems a person or group faced in the past and how they dealt with those issues.

The ability to understand and evaluate how people solved problems in the past also can help in solving similar problems today. The skill can be applied to many other kinds of difficulties besides historical ones. It is a method for thinking through almost any situation.

Learn the Skill

Using the following steps will help you to better understand and solve problems.

1 **Identify the problem.** Ask questions of yourself and others. This first step helps you to be sure you know exactly what the situation is. It also helps you understand why it is a problem.

2 **Gather information.** Ask other questions and do research to learn more about the problem. For example, what is its history? What caused the problem? What contributes to it?

3 **List options.** Based on the information you have gathered, identify possible options for solving the problem. It will be easier to find a good solution if you have several options.

4 **Evaluate the options.** Weigh each option you are considering. Think of the advantages it has as a solution. Then think of its potential disadvantages. It may help you to compare your options if you make a list of advantages and disadvantages for each possible solution.

5 **Choose and apply a solution.** After comparing the advantages and disadvantages of each possible solution, choose the one that seems best and apply it.

6 **Evaluate the solution.** Once the solution has been tried, evaluate how effective it is in solving the problem. This step will tell you if the solution was a good one, or if you should try another of the options instead. It will also help you know what to do in the future if you happen to face the same problem again.

Practice and Apply the Skill

Read again the "If you were there" in Section 3. Imagine that you are the warrior with this problem. You can apply the steps for solving problems to help you decide what to do. Review the information in the section about the samurai and this time period in Japan's history. Then, in the role of the samurai warrior, answer the questions below.

1. What is the specific problem that you face? Why is it a problem?

2. What events led to your problem? What circumstances and conditions have contributed to it?

3. What options can you think of to solve your problem? List the advantages and disadvantages of each.

4. Which of your options seems to be the best solution for your problem? Explain why. How will you know if it is a good solution?

Chapter Review

Visual Summary

Use the visual summary below to help you review the main ideas of the chapter.

QUICK FACTS

Japan's early culture was influenced by China and Korea.

A golden age of Japanese art and culture occurred during Japan's Heian Period.

After the Heian Period, the Japanese created a military society.

Reviewing Vocabulary, Terms, and People

Unscramble each group of letters below to spell a term that matches the given definition.

1. **etrgne**—a person who rules in someone else's name

2. **misaaru**—a Japanese warrior

3. **aclsn**—large, extended families

4. **elauvs**—ideas that people hold dear

5. **uctro**—a group of nobles who surround a ruler

6. **nguosh**—a great Japanese general who ruled instead of the emperor

7. **enz**—a form of Japanese Buddhism

8. **osnith**—a nature religion that began in Japan

9. **odmiya**—Japanese lords who gave land to samurai

10. **kosouth**—prince who introduced many Chinese ideas to Japan

11. **rctusrteu**—the way something is set up

Comprehension and Critical Thinking

SECTION 1 *(Pages 438–443)*

12. **a. Identify** Who was Prince Shotoku, and what did he do?

    b. Compare and Contrast Why was Japan isolated from China and Korea? How did China and Korea still affect Japan?

    c. Predict How would Japan's physical geography affect the development of Japanese government and society?

SECTION 2 *(Pages 444–448)*

13. **a. Recall** Why is Murasaki Shikibu a major figure in the history of Japanese culture?

    b. Analyze What made the period between the 800s and the 1100s a golden age of the arts in Japan?

    c. Evaluate Would you like to have been a member of the imperial court at Heian? Why or why not?

SECTION 3 *(Pages 454–459)*

14. a. Define What was the Tokugawa shogunate?

   b. Analyze How did Japan develop into a military society? What groups made up that society?

   c. Elaborate What was daily life like for the samurai?

Reviewing Themes

15. Politics How did Prince Shototku try to change the political system in Japan?

16. Science and Technology What new technological advance did Japan's rulers ban, starting in the 1630s? Why?

17. Society and Culture How did Bushido affect modern Japanese culture?

Reading Skills

Main Ideas and Their Support *The passage below is taken from this textbook. Read the passage and then answer the questions that follow.*

> " One of the people most influential in bringing Chinese ideas to Japan was Prince Shotoku. He served from 593 to 621 as regent for his aunt, the empress. A regent is a person who rules a country for someone who is unable to rule alone.
>
> All his life, Prince Shotoku admired Chinese culture. As regent, Shotoku saw a chance for Japan to adopt more Chinese ideas. He sent scholars to China to learn more about Chinese society. "

18. Explain in your own words the main idea of this passage.

19. Which other method might the author have used to make the explanation more informative and interesting? What would this method have contributed to the passage's meaning?

20. What is a definition the author gives in this passage? How does it help support the main idea?

go.hrw.com
KEYWORD: SN6 WH15

Using the Internet

21. Activity: Drawing a Comic Strip A strong military influence affected the governing structure of Japan. Eventually, warriors and generals gained power in Japan as emperors lost some of it. Enter the activity keyword and create a comic strip, similar in style to Japanese anime, about the people who held power. Your characters should include a shogun, a daimyo, a samurai, and an emperor.

Social Studies Skills

22. Solving Problems Imagine that you are a samurai warrior who has been called upon to help fight the Mongol invasion. You are stationed in a small village that is directly in the path of the Mongol army. Some people in the village want to stay and fight the Mongols, but you know they will be killed if they try to fight. The town's leaders want your opinion about what they should do. Write down one or two ideas you might suggest for how to save the people of the village. For each idea, make notes about what consequences your proposed action may have.

FOCUS ON WRITING

23. Creating Your Travel Brochure Look back over your notes from this chapter, and then create a travel brochure that describes Japan's historic attractions. Keep your writing brief—remember that you have to get your audience's attention with just a few words. To help get their attention, draw or find pictures to illustrate your travel brochure.

Standardized Test Practice

DIRECTIONS: Read each question, and write the letter of the best response.

1

I was brought up in a distant province which lies farther than the farthest end of the Eastern Road. I am ashamed to think that inhabitants of the Royal City will think me an uncultured girl.

Somehow I came to know that there are such things as romances in the world and wished to read them. When there was nothing to do by day or at night, one tale or another was told me by my elder sister or stepmother, and I heard several chapters about the shining Prince Genji.

From the content of this passage, it can be concluded that its author was a

A   samurai warrior.

B   noble woman from Heian.

C   farmer from northern Japan.

D   daimyo.

2   **The importance of loyalty, honor, and discipline in Japanese society today are *mainly* the result of what influence in Japan's history?**

A   the code of the samurai

B   the teachings of Shinto

C   the reforms of Prince Shotoku

D   the spread of Chinese Buddhism

3   **Most great works of early Japanese literature were written by**

A   Buddhist scholars.

B   samurai warriors.

C   Shinto priests.

D   noble women.

4   **The influence of China and Korea on Japan's history, culture, and development is found in all of the following *except***

A   Japan's first writing system.

B   the traditional Japanese diet.

C   early rules for family behavior.

D   the practice of Buddhism.

5   **The main function of samurai in Japanese society was to**

A   write poetry.

B   manage farmland.

C   defend lords.

D   conquer China.

Connecting with Past Learnings

6   **Early Japanese society under the clans was not a single unified country but many small states. This type of government *most* resembled that of**

A   the early city-states of ancient Greece.

B   the Roman Empire during the Pax Romana.

C   the Old Kingdom of ancient Egypt.

D   the New Kingdom of ancient Egypt.

7   **The nobles of Heian placed great emphasis on art and learning, just like the people of which ancient Greek city-state that you learned about earlier?**

A   Sparta

B   Athens

C   Macedonia

D   Troy

The Early Americas

FOCUS ON WRITING

A Newspaper Article You are a writer for a European newspaper who is traveling with some explorers to the Americas. Your newspaper wants you to write an article to share what you have seen with readers back home in Europe. As you read this chapter, you will decide what to write about—the land, the people, or the events that occurred after the explorers arrived.

REGION EVENTS

c. AD 200
The Maya begin building large cities in the Americas.

c. 900
The Maya Classic Age ends.

500 BC

WORLD EVENTS

c. 500 BC
Athens develops the world's first democracy.

What You Will Learn...

In this chapter you will learn about the growth and development of the Maya, Aztec, and Inca civilizations in the Americas. The ruins of the Inca city Machu Picchu, shown here, lie high in the Andes Mountains.

c.1325
The Aztecs set up their capital at Tenochtitlán.

c. 1440
Pachacuti begins to expand the Inca Empire.

1519
Cortés arrives in Mexico.

1537
Pizarro conquers the Inca Empire.

1350

1450

1550

1337
The Hundred Years' War between France and England begins.

1433
China's emperor ends ocean exploration of Asia and Africa.

1453
The Ottomans conquer Constantinople.

1517
Martin Luther posts his Ninety-five Theses.

by Kylene Beers

Economics	Geography	Politics	Religion	Society and Culture	Science and Technology

Focus on Themes In this chapter, you will read about the development of civilizations in the Americas—in Mesoamerica, which is in the southern part of North America, and in the Andes, which is in South America. As you read about the Maya in Mesoamerica, the Aztecs in central Mexico, and the Incas in South America, you will see how the **geography** of the areas affected their way of life. You will learn that these ancient civilizations made interesting advancements in **science**.

Analyzing Historical Information

Focus on Reading History books are full of information. As you read, you are confronted with names, dates, places, terms, and descriptions on every page. Because you're faced with so much information, you don't want to have to deal with unimportant or untrue material in a history book.

Identifying Relevant and Essential Information Information in a history book should be relevant, or related to the topic you're studying. It should also be essential, or necessary, to understanding that topic. Anything that is not relevant or essential distracts from the important material you are studying.

The passage below comes from an encyclopedia, but some irrelevant and nonessential information has been added so that you can learn to identify it.

The Maya

The first sentence of the paragraph expresses the main idea. Anything that doesn't support this idea is nonessential.

Who They Were Maya were an American Indian people who developed a magnificent civilization in Mesoamerica, which is the southern part of North America. They built their largest cities between AD 250 and 900. Today, many people travel to Central America to see Maya ruins.

The last sentence does not support the main idea and is nonessential.

This paragraph discusses Maya communication. Any other topics are irrelevant.

Communication The Maya developed an advanced form of writing that used many symbols. Our writing system uses 26 letters. They recorded information on large stone monuments. Some early civilizations drew pictures on cave walls. The Maya also made books of paper made from the fig tree bark. Fig trees need a lot of light.

The needs of fig trees have nothing to do with Maya communication. This sentence is irrelevant.

Portions of this text and the one on the next page were taken from the 2004 World Book Online Reference Center.

You Try It!

The following passage has some sentences that aren't important, necessary, or relevant. Read the passage and identify those sentences.

The Maya Way of Life

Religion The Maya believed in many gods and goddesses. More than 160 gods and goddesses are named in a single Maya manuscript. Among the gods they worshipped were a corn god, a rain god, a sun god, and a moon goddess. The early Greeks also worshipped many gods and goddesses.

Family and Social Structure Whole families of Maya—including parents, children, and grandparents—lived together. Not many houses today could hold all those people. Each family member had tasks to do. Men and boys, for example, worked in the fields. Very few people are farmers today. Women and older girls made clothes and meals for the rest of the family. Now most people buy their clothes.

After you read the passage, answer the following questions.

1. Which sentence in the first paragraph is irrelevant to the topic? How can you tell?

2. Which three sentences in the second paragraph are not essential to learning about the Maya? Do those sentences belong in this passage?

Academic Vocabulary

Success in school is related to knowing academic vocabulary—the words that are frequently used in school assignments and discussions. In this chapter, you will learn the following academic words:

As you read Chapter 16, practice detemining what is relevant information for each section.

The Maya

What You Will Learn...

Main Ideas

1. Geography helped shape the lives of the early Maya in Mesoamerica.
2. During the Classic Age, the Maya built great cities linked by trade.
3. Maya culture was influenced by social structure, religion, and achievements in science and the arts.
4. The decline of Maya civilization began in the 900s, for reasons that are still unclear.

The Big Idea

The Maya developed an advanced civilization that thrived in Mesoamerica from about 250 until the 900s.

Key Terms and People

maize, *p. 468*
Pacal, *p. 469*
observatories, *p. 472*

TAKING NOTES As you read, take notes on different aspects of Maya civilization. Use a chart like this one to help you organize your notes.

Geography	
Cities and trade	
Society and religion	
Achievements	
Decline	

If YOU were there...

You are a Maya farmer, growing corn in fields outside a city. Often you enter the city to join in religious ceremonies. You watch the king and his priests standing at the top of a tall pyramid. They wear capes of brightly colored feathers and gold ornaments that glitter in the sun. Far below them, thousands of worshippers crowd into the plaza with you to honor the gods.

How do these ceremonies make you feel?

BUILDING BACKGROUND Religion was very important to the Maya, one of the early peoples in the Americas. The Maya believed the gods controlled everything in the world around them.

Geography and the Early Maya

The region known as Mesoamerica stretches from the central area of Mexico south to the northern part of Central America. It was in this region that a people called the Maya (MY-uh) developed a remarkable civilization.

Around 1000 BC the Maya began settling in the lowlands of what is now northern Guatemala. Thick tropical forests covered most of the land, but the people cleared areas to farm. They grew a variety of crops, including beans, squash, avocados, and **maize**, or corn. The forests provided valuable resources, too. Forest animals such as deer, rabbits, and monkeys were sources of food. In addition, trees and other plants made good building materials. For example, some Maya used wooden poles and vines, along with mud, to build their houses.

The early Maya lived in small, isolated villages. Eventually, though, these villages started trading with one another and with other groups in Mesoamerica. As trade increased, the villages grew. By about AD 200, the Maya had begun to build large cities in Mesoamerica.

READING CHECK Finding Main Ideas How did the early Maya make use of their physical environment?

The Classic Age

The Maya civilization reached its height between about AD 250 and 900. This time in Maya history is known as the Classic Age. During this time, Maya territory grew to include more than 40 large cities.

Maya cities were really city-states. Each had its own government and its own king. No single ruler ever united the many cities into one empire. However, trade helped hold Maya civilization together. People exchanged goods for products that were not available locally. For example, Maya in the lowlands exported forest goods, cotton, and cacao (kuh-KOW) beans, which are used in making chocolate. In return, they received obsidian (a glasslike volcanic rock), jade, and colorful bird feathers.

Through trade, the Maya got supplies for construction. Maya cities had grand buildings, such as palaces decorated with carvings and paintings. The Maya also built stone pyramids topped with temples. Some temples honored local kings. For example, in the city of Palenque (pah-LENG-kay), the king **Pacal** (puh-KAHL) built a temple to record his achievements.

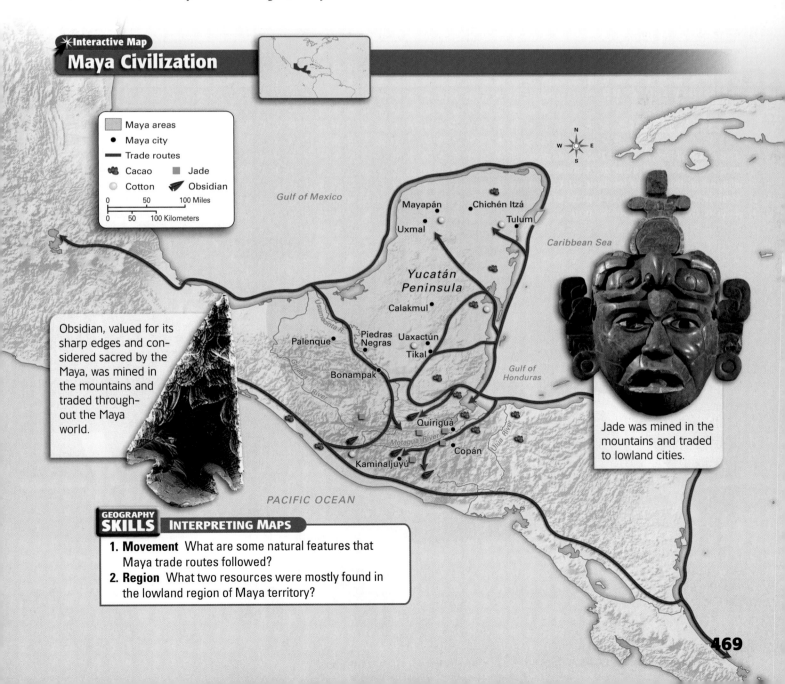

★Interactive Map
Maya Civilization

Maya areas
● Maya city
▬ Trade routes
🌰 Cacao ▪ Jade
○ Cotton ➤ Obsidian

0   50   100 Miles
0   50   100 Kilometers

Gulf of Mexico

Mayapán Chichén Itzá
Uxmal Tulum
Caribbean Sea

Yucatán Peninsula

Calakmul

Usumacinta R.
Palenque Piedras Negras Uaxactún
Grijalva River Tikal
Bonampak
Gulf of Honduras

Quiriguá
Motagua River
Copán
Ulúa River
Kaminaljuyú

PACIFIC OCEAN

Obsidian, valued for its sharp edges and considered sacred by the Maya, was mined in the mountains and traded throughout the Maya world.

Jade was mined in the mountains and traded to lowland cities.

GEOGRAPHY SKILLS   INTERPRETING MAPS

1. **Movement** What are some natural features that Maya trade routes followed?
2. **Region** What two resources were mostly found in the lowland region of Maya territory?

In addition to palaces and temples, the Maya built canals and paved large plazas, or open squares, for public gatherings. Farmers used stone walls to shape hillsides into flat terraces so they could grow crops on them. Almost every Maya city also had a stone court for playing a special ball game. Using only their heads, shoulders, or hips, players tried to bounce a heavy, hard rubber ball through stone rings attached high on the court walls. The winners of these games received jewels and clothing.

READING CHECK **Analyzing** Why is Maya civilization not considered an empire?

Maya Culture

In Maya society, people's everyday lives were heavily influenced by two main forces. One was the social structure, and the other was religion.

Social Structure

The king held the highest position in Maya society. Because he was believed to be related to the gods, the king had religious as well as political authority. Priests, merchants, and noble warriors were also part of the upper class. Together with the king, they held all the power in Maya society.

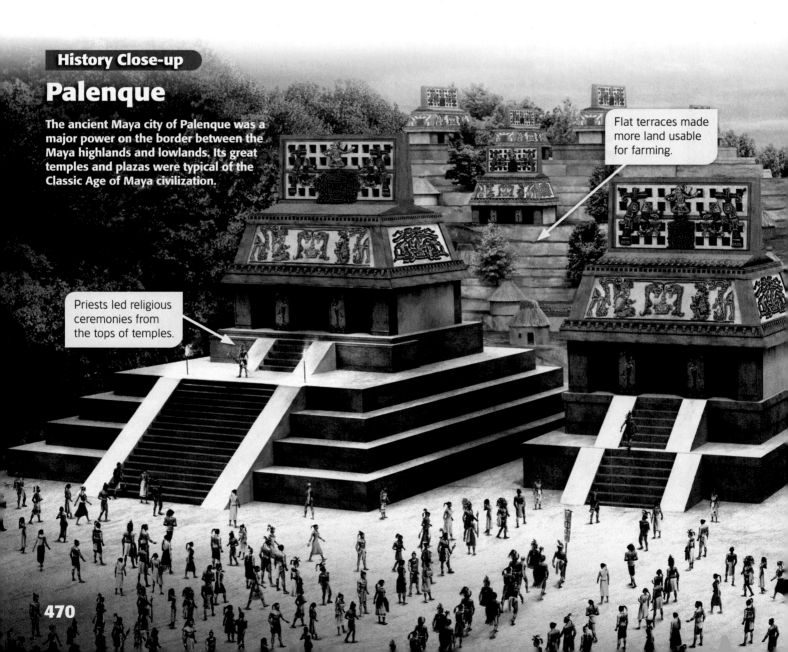

History Close-up

Palenque

The ancient Maya city of Palenque was a major power on the border between the Maya highlands and lowlands. Its great temples and plazas were typical of the Classic Age of Maya civilization.

Flat terraces made more land usable for farming.

Priests led religious ceremonies from the tops of temples.

Most Maya, though, belonged to the lower class. This group was made up of farming families who lived outside the cities. The women cared for the children, cooked, made yarn, and wove cloth. The men farmed, hunted, and crafted tools.

Lower-class Maya had to "pay" their rulers by giving the rulers part of their crops and goods such as cloth and salt. They also had to help construct temples and other public buildings. If their city went to war, Maya men had to serve in the army, and if captured in battle, they usually became slaves. Slaves carried goods along trade routes or worked as servants or farmers for upper-class Maya.

Religion

The Maya worshipped many gods, including a creator, a sun god, a moon goddess, and a maize god. Each god was believed to control a different **aspect** of daily life.

According to Maya beliefs, the gods could be helpful or harmful, so people tried to please the gods to get their help. The Maya believed their gods needed blood to prevent disasters or the end of the world. Every person offered blood to the gods by piercing their tongue or skin. On special occasions, the Maya also made human sacrifices. They usually used prisoners captured in battle, offering their hearts to stone carvings of the gods.

ACADEMIC VOCABULARY

aspect a part of something

Maya temples were shaped like mountains, which the Maya considered sacred because they allowed people to approach the gods.

BIOGRAPHY

Pacal
603–683

Pacal became king of the Maya city of Palenque when he was just 12 years old. As king, Pacal led many important community events, such as religious dances and public meetings. When he died he was buried at the bottom of the Temple of the Inscriptions shown to the near left.

Maya buildings were covered with stucco and painted in bright colors.

ANALYSIS SKILL **ANALYZING VISUALS**

In what ways might Palenque's setting have helped the city? In what ways might it have hurt the city?

Maya Astronomy and Writing

October 28, AD 709

She is letting blood.

Lady Xoc

Lord of Yaxchilán

This photo (left) shows the observatory at the Maya city of Chichén Itzá. The stone carving (above) is an artistic and written record of a religious ceremony.

Achievements

FOCUS ON
READING
Is any information in this paragraph irrelevant?

The Maya's religious beliefs led them to make impressive advances in science. They built **observatories**, or buildings from which people could study the sky, so their priests could watch the stars and plan the best times for religious festivals. With the knowledge they gained about astronomy, the Maya developed two calendars. One, with 365 days, guided planting, harvesting, and other farming activities. This calendar was more accurate than the calendar used in Europe at that time. The Maya also had a separate 260-day calendar that they used for keeping track of religious events.

The Maya could measure time accurately partly because they were skilled mathematicians. They created a number system that helped them make complex calculations, and they were among the first people with a symbol for zero. The Maya used their number system to record key dates in their history.

The Maya also developed a writing system. In a way, it was similar to Egyptian hieroglyphics, because symbols represented both objects and sounds. The Maya carved series of these symbols into large stone tablets to record their history and the achievements of their kings. They also wrote in bark paper books and passed down stories and poems orally.

The Maya created amazing art and architecture as well. Maya jade and gold jewelry was exceptional. Also, their huge temple-pyramids were masterfully built. The Maya had neither metal tools for cutting nor wheeled vehicles for carrying supplies. Instead, workers used obsidian tools to cut limestone into blocks. Then workers rolled the giant blocks over logs and lifted them with ropes. The Maya often decorated their buildings with paintings.

READING CHECK **Categorizing** What groups made up the different classes in Maya society?

Decline of Maya Civilization

Maya civilization began to collapse in the AD 900s. People stopped building temples and other structures. They left the cities and moved back to the countryside. What caused this collapse? Historians aren't sure, but they think a combination of factors was probably responsible.

One factor could have been the burden on the common people. Maya kings forced their subjects to farm for them or work on building projects. Perhaps people didn't want to work for the kings. They might have decided to **rebel** against their rulers' demands and abandon their cities.

Increased warfare between cities could also have caused the decline. Maya cities had always fought for power. But if battles became more widespread or destructive, they would have cost many lives and disrupted trade. People might have fled the cities for their safety.

A related theory is that perhaps the Maya could not produce enough to feed everyone. Growing the same crops year after year could have weakened the soil. In addition, as the population grew, the demand for food would have increased. To meet this demand, cities might have begun competing fiercely for new farmland. But the resulting battles would have ruined more crops, damaged more land, and created even greater food shortages.

Climate change could have played a role, too. Scientists know that Mesoamerica suffered from droughts during the period when the Maya were leaving their cities. Droughts would have made it hard to grow enough food for city dwellers.

Whatever the reasons, the collapse of Maya civilization happened gradually. The Maya scattered after 900, but they did not disappear entirely. In fact, the Maya civilization later revived in the Yucatán Peninsula. But by the time Spanish conquerors reached the Americas in the 1500s, Maya power had faded.

READING CHECK **Summarizing** What factors may have caused the end of Maya civilization?

SUMMARY AND PREVIEW The Maya built a civilization that peaked between about 250 and 900 but later collapsed for reasons still unknown. In Section 2, you will learn about another people of Mesoamerica, the Aztecs.

ACADEMIC VOCABULARY
rebel
to fight against authority

Section 1 Assessment

go.hrw.com
Online Quiz
KEYWORD: SN6 HP16

Reviewing Ideas, Terms, and People

1. **a. Recall** What resources did the Maya get from the forest?
   b. Elaborate How do you think Maya villages grew into large cities?
2. **a. Describe** What features did Maya cities include?
   b. Make Inferences How did trade strengthen the Maya civilization?
3. **a. Identify** Who belonged to the upper class in Maya society?
   b. Explain How did the Maya try to please their gods?
   c. Rank What do you think was the most impressive cultural achievement of the Maya? Why?
4. **a. Describe** What happened to the Maya after 900?
   b. Evaluate What would you consider to be the key factor in the collapse of Maya civilization? Explain.

Critical Thinking

5. **Evaluating** Draw a diagram like the one to the right. Use your notes to rank Maya achievements, with the most important at the top.

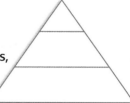

FOCUS ON WRITING

6. **Gathering Information about the Maya** Part of your article would likely be devoted to the Maya. Use the map and pictures in this section to help you decide which places to write about. How would you describe the land and the Maya cities? What would you add about the history and culture of the Maya?

The Aztecs

Main Ideas

1. The Aztecs built a rich and powerful empire in central Mexico.
2. Life in the empire was shaped by social structure, religion, and warfare.
3. Hernán Cortés conquered the Aztec Empire in 1521.

The Big Idea

The strong Aztec Empire, founded in central Mexico in 1325, lasted until the Spanish conquest in 1521.

Key Terms and People

causeways, *p. 474*
conquistadors, *p. 478*
Hernán Cortés, *p. 478*
Moctezuma II, *p. 478*

TAKING NOTES As you read, take notes on the founding of the Aztec Empire, life in the empire at its height, and the fall of the Aztec Empire. Use a diagram like the one here to help you organize your notes.

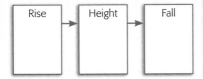

Rise	Height	Fall

If YOU were there...

You live in a village in southeast Mexico that is ruled by the powerful Aztec Empire. Each year your village must send the emperor many baskets of corn. You have to dig gold for him, too. One day some pale, bearded strangers arrive by sea. They want to overthrow the emperor, and they ask for your help.

Should you help the strangers? Why or why not?

BUILDING BACKGROUND The Aztecs ruled a large empire in Mesoamerica. Each village they conquered had to contribute heavily to the Aztec economy. This system helped create a mighty state, but one that did not inspire loyalty.

The Aztecs Build an Empire

The first Aztecs were farmers who migrated from the north to central Mexico. Finding the good farmland already occupied, they settled on a swampy island in the middle of Lake Texcoco (tays-KOH-koh). There, in 1325, they began building their capital and conquering nearby towns.

War was a key factor in the Aztecs' rise to power. The Aztecs fought fiercely and demanded tribute payments from the people they conquered. The cotton, gold, and food that poured in as a result became vital to their economy. The Aztecs also controlled a huge trade network. Merchants carried goods to and from all parts of the empire. Many merchants doubled as spies, keeping the rulers informed about what was happening in their lands.

War, tribute, and trade made the Aztec Empire strong and rich. By the early 1400s the Aztecs ruled the most powerful state in Mesoamerica. Nowhere was the empire's greatness more visible than in its capital, Tenochtitlán (tay-NAWCH-teet-LAHN).

To build this amazing island city, the Aztecs first had to overcome many geographic challenges. One problem was difficulty getting to and from the city. The Aztecs addressed this challenge by building three wide **causeways**—raised roads across water or wet ground—to connect the island to the lake shore.

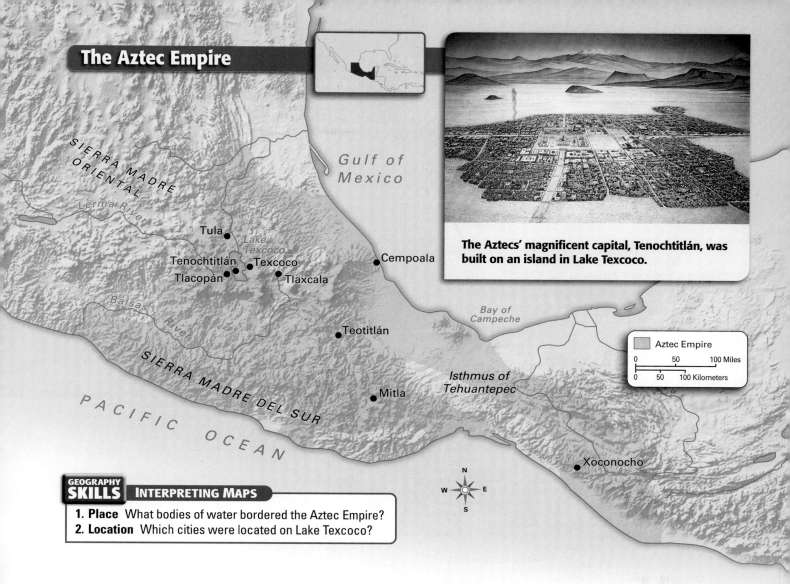

The Aztec Empire

The Aztecs' magnificent capital, Tenochtitlán, was built on an island in Lake Texcoco.

GEOGRAPHY SKILLS **INTERPRETING MAPS**

1. **Place** What bodies of water bordered the Aztec Empire?
2. **Location** Which cities were located on Lake Texcoco?

They also built canals that crisscrossed the city. The causeways and canals made travel and trade much easier.

Tenochtitlán's island location also limited the amount of land available for farming. To solve this problem, the Aztecs created floating gardens called *chinampas* (chee-NAHM-pahs). They piled soil on top of large rafts, which they anchored to trees that stood in the water.

The Aztecs made Tenochtitlán a truly magnificent city. Home to some 200,000 people at its height, it had huge temples, a busy market, and a grand palace.

READING CHECK **Finding Main Ideas** How did the Aztecs rise to power?

Life in the Empire

The Aztecs' way of life was as distinctive as their capital city. They had a complex social structure, a demanding religion, and a rich culture.

Aztec Society

The Aztec emperor, like the Maya king, was the most important person in society. From his great palace, he attended to law, trade, tribute, and warfare. Trusted nobles helped him as tax collectors, judges, and other government officials. Noble positions were passed down from fathers to sons, and young nobles went to school to learn their responsibilities.

THE IMPACT TODAY

Mexico's capital, Mexico City, is located where Tenochtitlán once stood.

Tenochtitlán

The Aztecs turned a swampy, uninhabited island into one of the largest and grandest cities in the world. The first Europeans to visit Tenochtitlán were amazed. At the time, the Aztec capital was about five times bigger than London.

The Great Temple stood at the heart of the city. On top of the temple were two shrines—a blue shrine for the rain god and a red shrine for the sun god.

Gold, silver, cloaks, and precious stones were among the many items sold at the market.

A network of canals linked different parts of the city.

Aztec farmers grew crops on "floating gardens" called *chinampas*.

ANALYSIS SKILL **ANALYZING VISUALS**

What is the most important building in this picture? How can you tell?

Aztec Arts: Ceremonial Jewelry

Aztec artists were very skilled. They created detailed and brightly colored items. This double-headed serpent was probably worn during religious ceremonies. The man on the right is wearing it on his chest.

What are some features of Aztec art that you can see in these pictures?

Just below the emperor and his nobles was a class of warriors and priests. Warriors were highly respected and had many privileges, but priests were more influential. They led religious ceremonies, passed down history, and, as keepers of the calendars, decided when to plant and harvest.

The next level of Aztec society included merchants and artisans. Below them, in the lower class, were farmers and laborers, who made up the majority of the population. Many didn't own their land, and they paid so much in tribute that they often found it tough to survive. Only slaves, at the very bottom of society, struggled more.

Religion and Warfare

Like the Maya, the Aztecs worshipped many gods who were believed to control both nature and human activities. To please the gods, Aztec priests regularly made human sacrifices. Most victims were battle captives or slaves. In ritual ceremonies, priests would slash open their victims' chests to "feed" human hearts and blood to the gods. The Aztec sacrificed as many as 10,000 people a year. To supply enough victims, Aztec warriors waged frequent battles with neighboring peoples.

Cultural Achievements

As warlike as the Aztecs were, they also appreciated art and beauty. Architects and sculptors created fine stone pyramids and statues. Artisans used gold, gems, and bright feathers to make jewelry and masks. Women embroidered colorful designs on the cloth they wove.

The Aztecs valued learning as well. They studied astronomy and devised a calendar much like the Maya one. They took pride in their history and kept detailed written records. They also had a strong oral tradition. Stories about ancestors and the gods were passed from one generation to the next. The Aztecs also enjoyed fine speeches and riddles such as these:

> "What is a little blue-green jar filled with popcorn? Someone is sure to guess our riddle: it is the sky.
>
> What is a mountainside that has a spring of water in it? Our nose."
> –Bernardino de Sahagún, from *Florentine Codex*

Knowing the answers to riddles showed that one had paid attention in school.

READING CHECK **Identifying Cause and Effect** How did their religious practices influence Aztec warfare?

Cortés Conquers the Aztecs

In the late 1400s the Spanish arrived in the Americas, seeking adventure, riches, and converts to Catholicism. One group of **conquistadors** (kahn-kees-tuh-DOHRZ), or Spanish conquerors, reached Mexico in 1519. Led by **Hernán Cortés** (er-NAHN kawr-TAYS), their <u>motives</u> were to find gold, claim land, and convert native peoples.

ACADEMIC
VOCABULARY
motive
reason for doing
something

The Aztec emperor, **Moctezuma II** (MAWK-tay-SOO-mah), cautiously welcomed the strangers. He believed Cortés to be the god Quetzalcoatl (ket-suhl-kuh-WAH-tuhl), whom the Aztecs believed had left Mexico long ago. According to legend, the god had promised to return in 1519.

Moctezuma gave the Spaniards gold and other gifts, but Cortés wanted more. He took the emperor prisoner, enraging the Aztecs, who attacked the Spanish. They managed to drive out the conquistadors, but Moctezuma was killed in the fighting.

Within a year, Cortés and his men came back. This time they had help from other Indians in the region who resented the Aztecs' harsh rule. In addition, the Spanish had better weapons, including armor, cannons, and swords. Furthermore, the Aztecs were terrified of the enemy's big horses—animals they had never seen before. The Spanish had also unknowingly brought deadly diseases such as smallpox to the Americas. These diseases weakened or killed thousands of native people. In 1521 the Aztecs surrendered. Their once mighty empire came to a swift end.

READING CHECK **Summarizing** What factors helped the Spanish defeat the Aztecs?

SUMMARY AND PREVIEW The Aztec Empire, made strong by warfare and tribute, fell to the Spanish in 1521. Next you will learn about another empire in the Americas, that of the Incas.

Section 2 Assessment

go.hrw.com
Online Quiz
KEYWORD: SN6 HP16

Reviewing Ideas, Terms, and People

1. a. Recall Where and when did Aztec civilization develop?
b. Explain How did the Aztecs in Tenochtitlán adapt to their island location?
c. Elaborate How might Tenochtitlán's location have been both a benefit and a hindrance to the Aztecs?
2. a. Recall What did the Aztecs feed their gods?
b. Rate Consider the roles of the emperor, warriors, priests, and others in Aztec society. Who do you think had the hardest role? Explain.
3. a. Identify Who was **Moctezuma II**?
b. Make Generalizations Why did allies help **Cortés** defeat the Aztecs?
c. Predict The Aztecs vastly outnumbered the **conquistadors**. If the Aztecs had first viewed Cortés as a threat rather than a god, how might history have changed?

Critical Thinking

4. Evaluating Draw a diagram like the one shown. Use your notes to identify three factors that contributed to the Aztecs' power. Put the factor you consider most important first, and put the least important last. Explain your choices.

1.	2.	3.

FOCUS ON WRITING

5. Describing the Aztec Empire Tenochtitlán would certainly be described in your article. Make notes about how you would describe Tenochtitlán. Be sure to explain the causeways, *chinampas*, and other features. What activities went on in the city? Your article should also describe the events that occurred when the Spanish discovered the Aztec capital. Make notes on the fall of the Aztec Empire.

The Incas

If YOU were there...

You live in the Andes Mountains, where you raise llamas. You weave their wool into warm cloth. Last year, soldiers from the powerful Inca Empire took over your village. They brought in new leaders, who say you must all learn a new language and send much of your woven cloth to the Inca ruler. They also promise that the government will provide for you in times of trouble.

How do you feel about living in the Inca Empire?

BUILDING BACKGROUND The Incas built their huge empire by taking over village after village in South America. They brought many changes to the people they conquered before they were themselves conquered by the Spanish.

The Incas Create an Empire

While the Aztecs were ruling Mexico, the Inca Empire arose in South America. The Incas began as a small tribe in the Andes. Their capital was Cuzco (KOO-skoh) in what is now Peru.

In the mid-1400s a ruler named **Pachacuti** (pah-chah-KOO-tee) began to expand Inca territory. Later leaders followed his example, and by the early 1500s the Inca Empire was huge. It stretched from modern Ecuador to central Chile and included coastal deserts, snowy mountains, fertile valleys, and thick forests. About 12 million people lived in the empire. To rule effectively, the Incas formed a strong central government.

The Incas lived in a region of high plains and mountains.

What You Will Learn...

Main Ideas

1. The Incas created an empire with a strong central government in South America.
2. Life in the Inca Empire was influenced by social structure, religion, and the Incas' cultural achievements.
3. Francisco Pizarro conquered the Incas and took control of the region in 1537.

The Big Idea

The Incas controlled a huge empire in South America, but it was conquered by the Spanish.

Key Terms and People

Pachacuti, *p. 479*
Quechua, *p. 480*
masonry, *p. 481*
Atahualpa, *p. 482*
Francisco Pizarro, *p. 482*

TAKING NOTES As you read, take notes on the Inca Empire. In each circle of a diagram like the one below, fill in details about geography, government, society, religion, achievements, and conquest by the Spanish.

Inca Empire

Central Rule

Pachacuti did not want the people he conquered to have too much power. He began a policy of removing local leaders and replacing them with new officials he trusted. He also made the children of conquered leaders travel to Cuzco to learn about Inca government and religion. When the children were grown, they were sent back to govern their villages, where they taught people the Inca way of life.

As another means of unifying the empire, the Incas used an official Inca language, **Quechua** (KE-chuh-wuh). Although people spoke many other languages, all official business had to be done in Quechua. Even today, many people in Peru speak Quechua.

A Well-Organized Economy

The Inca government strictly controlled the economy and told each household what work to do. Most Incas had to spend time working for the government as well as themselves. Farmers tended government land in addition to their own. Villagers made cloth and other goods for the army. Some Incas served as soldiers, worked in mines, or built roads and bridges. In this way, the people paid taxes in the form of labor rather than money. This labor tax system was called the *mita* (MEE-tah).

Another feature of the Inca economy was that there were no merchants or markets. Instead, government officials would **distribute** goods collected through the *mita*. Leftover goods were stored in the capital for emergencies. If a natural disaster struck, or if people simply could not care for themselves, the government provided supplies to help them.

ACADEMIC VOCABULARY
distribute
to divide among a group of people

READING CHECK Summarizing How did the Incas control their empire?

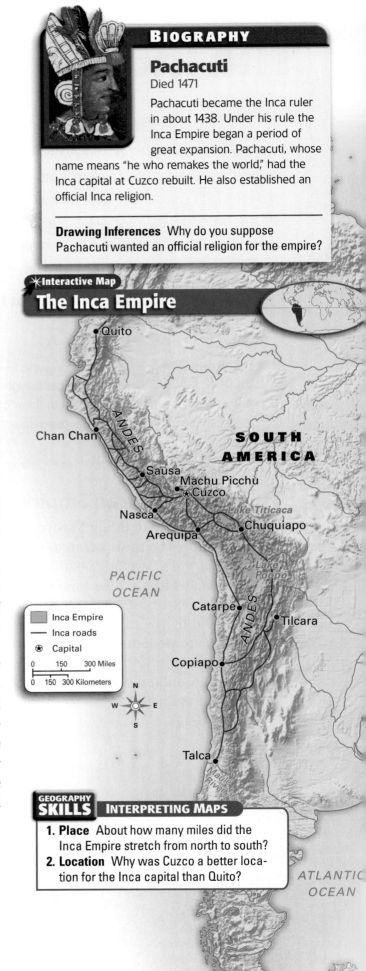

BIOGRAPHY

Pachacuti
Died 1471

Pachacuti became the Inca ruler in about 1438. Under his rule the Inca Empire began a period of great expansion. Pachacuti, whose name means "he who remakes the world," had the Inca capital at Cuzco rebuilt. He also established an official Inca religion.

Drawing Inferences Why do you suppose Pachacuti wanted an official religion for the empire?

★Interactive Map
The Inca Empire

- Quito
- Chan Chan
- ANDES
- SOUTH AMERICA
- Sausa
- Machu Picchu
- Cuzco
- Nasca
- Lake Titicaca
- Chuquiapo
- Arequipa
- PACIFIC OCEAN
- Lake Poopó
- Catarpe
- ANDES
- Tilcara
- Copiapo
- Talca
- Maule River
- ATLANTIC OCEAN

Inca Empire
— Inca roads
⊛ Capital

0   150   300 Miles
0   150   300 Kilometers

N
W   E
S

GEOGRAPHY SKILLS INTERPRETING MAPS
1. **Place** About how many miles did the Inca Empire stretch from north to south?
2. **Location** Why was Cuzco a better location for the Inca capital than Quito?

Most Incas were farmers. The Incas in this drawing from the mid-1500s are harvesting potatoes.

Life in the Inca Empire

Because the rulers controlled Inca society so closely, the common people had little personal freedom. At the same time, the government protected the general welfare of all in the empire. But that did not mean everyone was treated equally.

Social Divisions

Inca society had two main social classes. The emperor, priests, and government officials made up the upper class. Members of this class lived in stone houses in Cuzco and wore the best clothes. They didn't have to pay the labor tax, and they enjoyed many other privileges. Inca rulers, for example, could relax in luxury at Machu Picchu (MAH-choo PEEK-choo). This royal retreat lay nestled high in the Andes. Palaces and gardens could be found behind its gated wall.

The lower class in Inca society included farmers, artisans, and servants. There were no slaves, however, because the Incas did not practice slavery. Most Incas were farmers. In the warmer valleys, they grew crops like maize and peanuts. In the cooler mountains, they carved terraces into the hillsides and grew potatoes. High in the Andes, people raised llamas—South American animals related to camels—for meat and wool.

Lower-class Incas dressed in plain clothes and lived simply. By law, they couldn't own more goods than what they needed to survive. Most of what they produced went to the *mita* and the upper class.

Religion

The Inca social structure was partly related to religion. For example, the Incas thought that their rulers were related to the sun god and never really died. As a result, priests brought mummies of former kings to many ceremonies. People gave these royal mummies food and gifts.

Inca ceremonies often included sacrifices. But unlike the Maya and the Aztecs, the Incas rarely sacrificed humans. Instead they sacrificed llamas, cloth, or food.

In addition to practicing the official religion, people outside Cuzco worshipped other gods at local sacred places. The Incas believed certain mountaintops, rocks, and springs had magical powers. Many Incas performed sacrifices at these places as well as at the temple in Cuzco.

Achievements

Inca temples were grand buildings. The Incas were master builders, known for their expert **masonry**, or stonework. They cut stone blocks so precisely that they didn't need cement to hold them together. The Incas also built a network of roads. Two major highways ran the length of the empire and linked to many other roads.

The Incas produced works of art as well. Artisans made pottery and gold and silver jewelry. They even created a life-sized cornfield of gold and silver, crafting each cob, leaf, and stalk individually. Inca weavers also made some of the finest textiles in the Americas.

The ruins of Machu Picchu draw thousands of tourists to Peru every year.

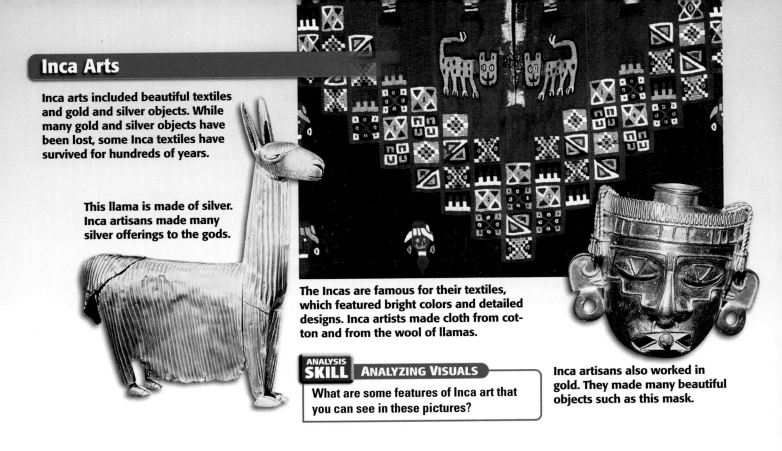

Inca Arts

Inca arts included beautiful textiles and gold and silver objects. While many gold and silver objects have been lost, some Inca textiles have survived for hundreds of years.

This llama is made of silver. Inca artisans made many silver offerings to the gods.

The Incas are famous for their textiles, which featured bright colors and detailed designs. Inca artists made cloth from cotton and from the wool of llamas.

ANALYSIS SKILL **ANALYZING VISUALS**

What are some features of Inca art that you can see in these pictures?

Inca artisans also worked in gold. They made many beautiful objects such as this mask.

While such artifacts tell us much about the Incas, nothing was written about their empire until the Spanish arrived. Indeed, the Incas had no writing system. Instead, they kept records with knotted cords called *quipus* (KEE-pooz). Knots in the cords represented numbers. Different colors stood for information about crops, land, and other important topics.

The Incas also passed down their history orally. People sang songs and told stories about daily life and military victories. Official "memorizers" learned long poems about Inca legends and history. Eventually, after the conquistadors came, records were written in Spanish and Quechua. We know about the Incas from these records and from the stories that survive in the songs, dances, and religious practices of the people in the region today.

READING CHECK **Contrasting** How did daily life differ for upper- and lower-class Incas?

Pizarro Conquers the Incas

The arrival of conquistadors changed more than how the Incas recorded history. In the late 1520s, a civil war began in the Inca Empire after the death of the ruler. Two of the ruler's sons, **Atahualpa** (ah-tah-WAHL-pah) and Huáscar (WAHS-kahr), fought to claim the throne. Atahualpa won the war in 1532, but fierce fighting had weakened the Inca army.

On his way to be crowned as king, Atahualpa got news that a band of about 180 Spanish soldiers had arrived in the Inca Empire. They were conquistadors led by **Francisco Pizarro**. When Atahualpa came to meet the group, the Spanish attacked. They were greatly outnumbered, but they caught the unarmed Incas by surprise. They quickly captured Atahualpa and killed thousands of Inca soldiers.

To win his freedom, Atahualpa asked his people to fill a room with gold and silver for Pizarro. Incas brought jewelry, states, and other valuable items from all parts of the empire. Melted down, the precious metals may have totaled 24 tons. They would have been worth millions of dollars today. Despite this huge payment, the Spaniards killed Atahualpa. They knew that if they let the Inca ruler live, he might rally his people and overpower their forces.

Some Incas fought back after the emperor's death. In 1537, though, Pizarro defeated the last of the Incas. Spain took control over the entire Inca Empire and ruled the region for the next 300 years.

READING CHECK **Identifying Cause and Effect** What events ended the Inca Empire?

SUMMARY AND PREVIEW The Incas built a huge empire with a strong central government, but they could not withstand the Spanish conquest in 1537. In the next chapter, you will turn to Europe in an earlier age—an age before the Spanish even learned of the Americas.

Section 3 Assessment

Reviewing Ideas, Terms, and People

1. **a. Identify** Where was the Inca Empire located? What kinds of terrain did it include?
   b. Explain How did the Incas control their economy?
   c. Evaluate Do you think the *mita* system was a good government policy? Why or why not?
2. **a. Describe** What social classes existed in Inca society?
   b. Make Inferences How might the Inca road system have helped strengthen the empire?
3. **a. Recall** When did the Spanish gain full control over Inca lands?
   b. Analyze Why do you think **Pizarro** was able to defeat the much larger forces of the Incas?
   c. Elaborate What effect do you think the civil war with his brother had on **Atahualpa**'s kingship? How might history have been different if the Spanish had not arrived until a few years later?

Critical Thinking

4. **Analyzing** Draw a diagram like the one below. Using your notes, write a sentence in each box about how that topic influenced the topic its arrow points to.

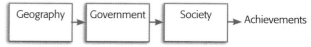

Geography → Government → Society → Achievements

FOCUS ON WRITING

5. **Adding Information about the Inca Empire** Your article would also describe the lands where the Incas lived. How would you highlight the diversity of the geography? What specific sites would you describe? Include some comments about how the Incas' building activities related to their environment. You will also want to include information on what happened when the Spanish arrived.

Inca Roads

Inca roads were more than just roads—they were engineering marvels. The Incas built roads across almost every kind of terrain imaginable: coasts, deserts, forests, grasslands, plains, and mountains. In doing so, they overcame the geography of their rugged empire.

Although the Incas had no wheeled vehicles, they relied on their roads for transportation, communication, and government administration. The roads symbolized the power of the Inca government.

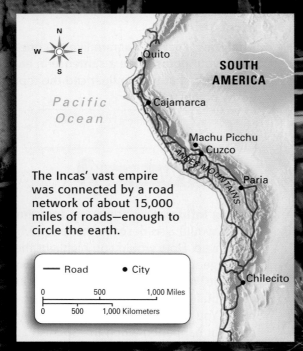

SOUTH AMERICA

Pacific Ocean

Quito
Cajamarca
Machu Picchu
Cuzco
Paria
Chilecito

ANDES MOUNTAINS

The Incas' vast empire was connected by a road network of about 15,000 miles of roads—enough to circle the earth.

— Road   • City

0   500   1,000 Miles
0   500   1,000 Kilometers

Many roads were just three to six feet wide, but that was wide enough for people on foot and for llamas, which the Incas used as pack animals.

Inca engineers built rope bridges to cross the valleys of the Andes Mountains. Rope bridges could stretch more than 200 feet across high gorges.

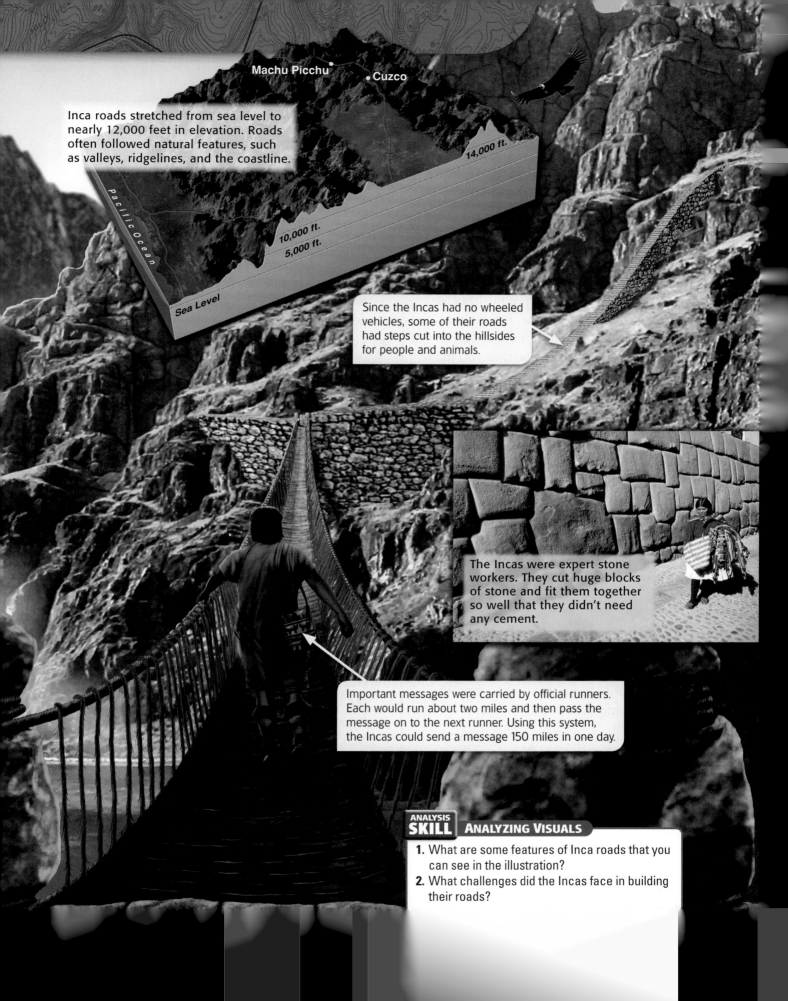

Inca roads stretched from sea level to nearly 12,000 feet in elevation. Roads often followed natural features, such as valleys, ridgelines, and the coastline.

Machu Picchu • Cuzco

Pacific Ocean

14,000 ft.

10,000 ft.

5,000 ft.

Sea Level

Since the Incas had no wheeled vehicles, some of their roads had steps cut into the hillsides for people and animals.

The Incas were expert stone workers. They cut huge blocks of stone and fit them together so well that they didn't need any cement.

Important messages were carried by official runners. Each would run about two miles and then pass the message on to the next runner. Using this system, the Incas could send a message 150 miles in one day.

ANALYSIS SKILL **ANALYZING VISUALS**

1. What are some features of Inca roads that you can see in the illustration?
2. What challenges did the Incas face in building their roads?

Social Studies Skills

Analyzing Economic Effects

Understand the Skill

Most decisions people make or actions they take have several effects. Effects can be political, social, personal, or economic. For example, think about the effects of a decision you might make to get a summer job. A social effect might be that you make new friends at your job. A personal effect might be that you have less time for other activities that you enjoy. An economic effect would be that you have more money to spend.

Throughout history, many decisions have had economic effects—either intended or unintended. Even a decision made for a political, social, or environmental reason can have economic effects. Since economic circumstances have often been a factor in the rise and fall of civilizations, learning to analyze economic effects can be useful in your study of history.

Learn the Skill

Analyzing economic effects can help you to better understand and evaluate historical events. Follow these guidelines to understand economic effects of decisions and actions in history.

1 Determine who made the decision or took the action and decide what the goal was.

2 Consider whether the goal was to improve or change economic circumstances.

3 Sometimes an economic effect is not the main effect of a decision. Think about any unintended consequences of the decision or action. Consider whether any social or political effects are also economic effects.

4 Note that sometimes economic effects can be viewed either positively or negatively depending on whom they affect.

Practice and Apply the Skill

Review the information in the chapter about the Maya. Use that information to help you answer the following questions.

1. What was an economic effect of the Maya in lowland cities exporting forest goods and cotton? Was that effect expected or unexpected?

2. What might have been a positive economic effect of the Maya king's making lower-class Maya farm and work for him? What might have been a negative effect?

3. Do you think the development of the Maya calendar had any economic effects? Why or why not?

4. What economic effects did warfare have on Maya civilization? Were these effects expected or unexpected?

Chapter Review

Visual Summary

Use the visual summary below to help you review the main ideas of the chapter.

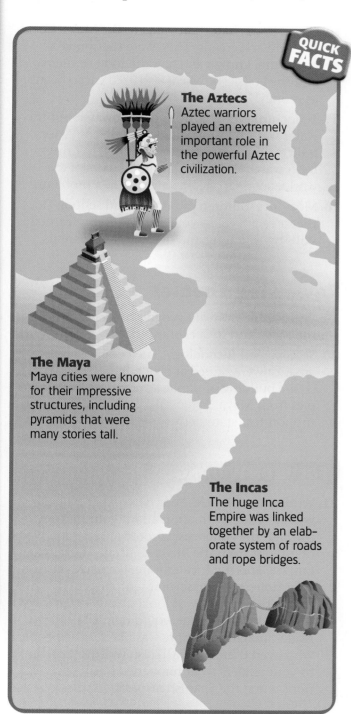

QUICK FACTS

The Aztecs
Aztec warriors played an extremely important role in the powerful Aztec civilization.

The Maya
Maya cities were known for their impressive structures, including pyramids that were many stories tall.

The Incas
The huge Inca Empire was linked together by an elaborate system of roads and rope bridges.

Reviewing Vocabulary, Terms and People

For each statement below, write T if it is true and F if it is false. If the statement is false, replace the underlined term with one that would make the sentence a true statement.

1. The main crops of the Maya included **maize** and beans.

2. The **Quechua** came to the Americas to find land, gold, and converts to Catholicism.

3. The Aztecs mistook **Hernán Cortés** for the god Quetzalcoatl.

4. Maya priests studied the sun, moon, and stars from stone **observatories**.

5. **Francisco Pizarro** led a party of Spanish soldiers to Mexico in 1519.

6. **Atahualpa** tried to buy his freedom by having his people deliver great riches to the Spanish.

7. The official language of the Inca Empire was **Pachacuti**.

8. The Aztecs built raised roads called **masonry** to cross from Tenochtitlán to the mainland.

9. **Moctezuma II** was the Inca leader at the time of the Spanish conquest.

10. Many people in Mesoamerica died at the hands of the **conquistadors**.

Comprehension and Critical Thinking

SECTION 1 *(Pages 468–473)*

11. **a. Recall** Where did the Maya live, and when was their Classic Age?

    b. Analyze What was the connection between Maya religion and astronomy?

    c. Elaborate Why did Maya cities trade with each other? Why did they fight?

SECTION 2 *(Pages 474–478)*

12. a. Describe What was Tenochtitlán like? Where was it located?

b. Make Inferences Why do you think warriors were such respected members of Aztec society?

c. Evaluate What factor do you think played the biggest role in the Aztecs' defeat? Defend your answer.

SECTION 3 *(pages 479–483)*

13. a. Identify Name two Inca leaders and explain their roles in Inca history.

b. Draw Conclusions What geographic and cultural problems did the Incas overcome to rule their empire?

c. Predict Do you think most people in the Inca Empire appreciated or resented the *mita* system? Explain your answer.

Social Studies Skills

14. Analyzing Economic Effects Organize your class into groups. Choose one member of your group to represent the ruler of a Maya city. The rest of the group will be his or her advisers. As a group, decide on some policies for your city. For example, will you go to war, or will you trade? Will you build a new palace, or will you construct terraces for farming? Once you have determined policies for your city, share your ideas with representatives of other cities. As a class, discuss the economic effects of each policy you have chosen.

Using the Internet

go.hrw.com
KEYWORD: SN6 WH16

15. Making Diagrams In this chapter you learned about the rise and fall of Maya civilization and of the Aztec and Inca empires. What you may not know is that the rise and fall of empires is a pattern that occurs again and again throughout history. Enter the activity keyword. Then create a diagram that shows both the factors that cause empires to form and the factors that cause empires to fall apart.

Reading Skills

Analyzing Historical Information *In each numbered passage below, the first sentence expresses the main idea. One of the following sentences is irrelevant or nonessential to the main idea. Identify the irrelevant or nonessential sentence in each passage.*

16. Cacao beans had great value to the Maya. Cacao trees are evergreens. They were the source of chocolate, known as a favorite food of rulers and the gods. The Maya also used cacao beans as money.

17. Tenochtitlán was surrounded by water, but the water was undrinkable. As a result, the Aztecs built a stone aqueduct, or channel, to bring fresh water to the city. In many parts of the world, access to clean water is still a problem.

18. Most Inca children did not attend school. Does that idea appeal to you? Inca children learned skills by watching and helping their parents.

Reviewing Themes

19. Geography How did geography play a role in the Maya and Inca economies?

20. Science and Technology The people of Mesoamerica were skilled at civil engineering—that is, the building of public structures. Give examples from Maya, Aztec, and Inca civilization to support this statement.

FOCUS ON WRITING

21. Writing Your Article Your newspaper article will include information about your journey through the Americas. Choose at least one place of interest from the Maya civilization, the Aztec Empire, and the Inca Empire. For each site, use your notes to write several sentences to describe its location and how it looked at its height. Try to include details that would help a European reader imagine what life was like for the people who lived there. You will also want to explain to your readers what happened to these civilizations when the Spanish arrived.

DIRECTIONS: Read each question, and write the letter of the best response. Use the map below to answer question 1.

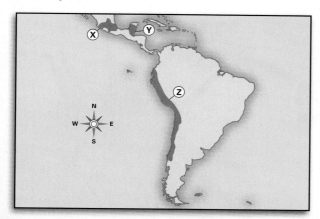

1 The Aztec and Inca empires are indicated on this map by

A X for the Inca and Y for the Aztec.

B Y for the Aztec and Z for the Inca.

C Y for the Inca and Z for the Aztec.

D X for the Aztec and Z for the Inca.

2 Maya, Aztec, and Inca societies were similar in many ways. Which of the following practices were common to all three civilizations?

A producing works of art and keeping written records

B engaging in trade and demanding tribute payments

C offering sacrifices to the gods and building stone temples

D practicing slavery and worshipping many gods

3 Farming was important to the Maya, the Aztecs, and the Incas. Which of the following is *not* a true statement?

A The Maya grew crops on *chinampas.*

B Farmers in all three civilizations grew maize, but only the Incas raised llamas.

C Maya farmers might not have been able to produce enough food for the entire population.

D Maya and Aztec priests decided the best times to plant and harvest.

4 The following factors all helped the Spanish to conquer the Aztecs and the Incas *except*

A European diseases.

B a greater number of soldiers.

C superior weapons.

D existing problems within the empires.

5 Which statement *best* describes the social structure in Maya, Aztec, and Inca civilizations?

A The ruler held the highest position in society, and slaves held the lowest.

B The Aztecs had a simpler class structure than the Maya or the Incas.

C Social divisions were very important to the Maya and the Aztecs, but power and wealth were equally distributed in the Inca Empire.

D Social class helped shape daily life, with the upper class enjoying special privileges made possible by the labor of the common people.

Connecting with Past Learnings

6 In this chapter you read that Maya civilization during the Classic Age included independent city-states. What other civilization that you have studied was organized into city-states?

A ancient Greece

B ancient Persia

C Han China

D the Roman Empire

7 The Maya and the Incas both believed their rulers were related to the gods. Which ancient people believed the same thing?

A Jews

B Indians

C Phoenicians

D Egyptians

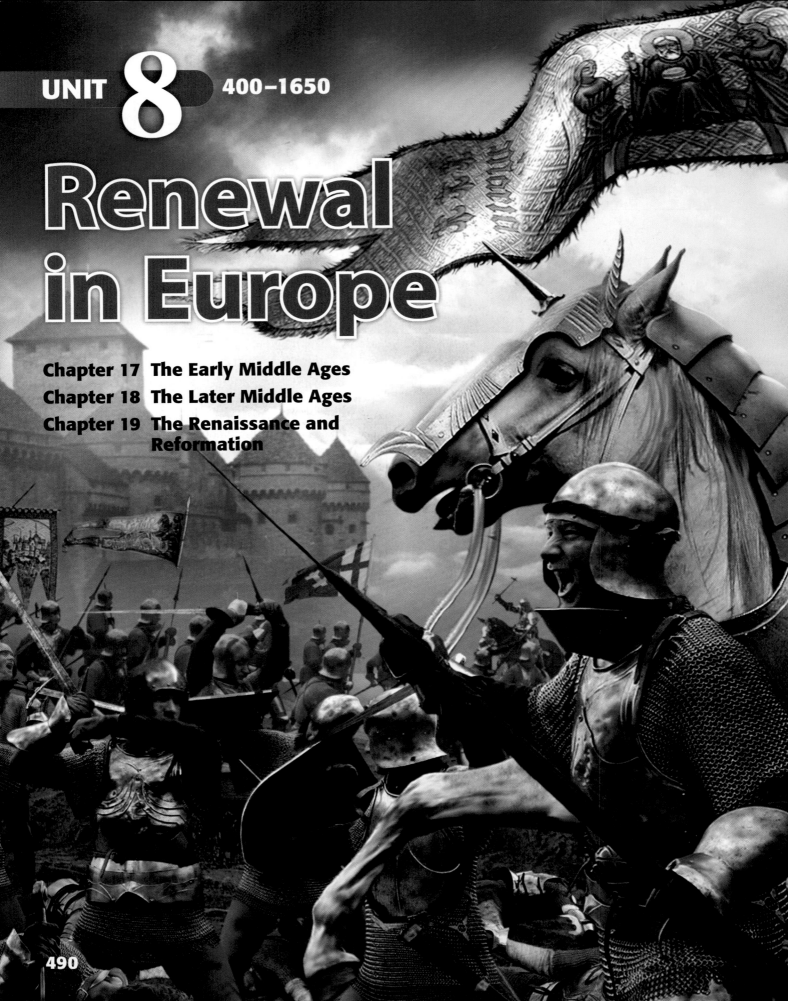

UNIT 8 400–1650

Renewal in Europe

When the Roman Empire collapsed, Europe lost its center of power, and a new period called the Middle Ages began. During the Middle Ages, Europe was divided into small kingdoms. At the same time, though, the strong influence of the Christian church tied most Europeans together.

Later, during the Renaissance and Reformation, people changed the way they looked at the world. They developed new ideas about art, politics, and religion, ideas that changed Europe forever.

In the next three chapters, you will learn about life during the Middle Ages, the Renaissance, and the Reformation.

Explore the Art

In this scene, French teenager Joan of Arc carries a religious flag as she leads an army into battle during the Middle Ages. What does the scene suggest about the struggles of that period?

The Early Middle Ages

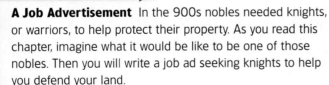

FOCUS ON WRITING

A Job Advertisement In the 900s nobles needed knights, or warriors, to help protect their property. As you read this chapter, imagine what it would be like to be one of those nobles. Then you will write a job ad seeking knights to help you defend your land.

CHAPTER EVENTS

c. 430
Saint Patrick brings Christianity to Ireland.

400

WORLD EVENTS

476
Rome falls.

HOLT

History's Impact
▶ video series
Watch the video to understand the legacy of the feudal system in Europe.

What You Will Learn...

In this chapter you will learn about the social and economic systems in Europe during a time called the Middle Ages. This photo shows Caernarfon Castle in Wales. Built in the late 1200s, the castle showed the king's power and provided defense from invasions.

700s–800s
The Vikings raid Europe.

800
Charlemagne is crowned emperor of much of Europe.

1066
Feudalism is introduced into Britain.

600

800

1000

1200

613
Muhammad begins teaching people about Islam.

794
Heian becomes the capital of Japan.

1000s
The Chinese invent gunpowder.

1076
Ghana falls to Muslim invaders.

THE EARLY MIDDLE AGES **493**

Focus on Themes In this chapter you will read about Europe during the early Middle Ages. You will learn how the geography of the land affected growth and trade and see how the Christian **religion** spread throughout northern Europe during this time. You will learn about the invaders who tried to conquer the land and see how the feudal system developed. As you read, you will understand how this feudal system shaped the entire **society and culture** of the people.

Evaluating Sources

Focus on Reading As you have already learned, historians study both primary and secondary sources to learn about the past. By studying both types, they can get a better picture of what life was like.

Assessing Primary and Secondary Sources However, not all sources are accurate or reliable. You need to be careful when you read historical sources. Checklists like the ones below can help you judge which sources are reliable and worth using in your research.

Checklist for Primary Sources

✔ Who is the author? Does he or she seem trustworthy?

✔ Was the author actually present for the event described in the source?

✔ How soon after the event occurred was the source written?

✔ Can the information in the source be verified in other primary or secondary sources?

Historians in the past were not always careful about what they put in their books. Some included rumors, gossip, or hearsay.

The more time that passed between the event and the writing, the greater the chance of errors or distortion in the description.

Not everyone who writes about history is a good historian. Try to use sources by qualified writers.

Good historians will always tell you where they got their information. If information isn't documented, you can't always trust that it is true or accurate.

Checklist for Secondary Sources

✔ Who is the author? What are his or her credentials, or qualifications for writing?

✔ Where did the author get his or her information?

✔ Is the information in the source properly documented?

✔ Has the author drawn valid conclusions from his or her sources?

You Try It!

The following passage of a primary source can be found in the chapter you are about to read. As you read this passage, ask yourself what you could learn from this source.

The Benedictine Rule

For bedding, a mattress, a blanket, a coverlet and a pillow are enough. The beds should be frequently inspected by the Abbot as a precaution against private possessions. If anyone is found to have anything which was not given him by the Abbot, he is to undergo the severest punishment; and that this vice of personal ownership may be totally eliminated, everything necessary should be given by the Abbot; namely a cowl, a tunic, stockings, shoes, a belt, a knife, a pen, a needle, a handkerchief and writing tablets, so that all excuses about necessity are removed.

From Chapter 17, page 502

After you read the passage, answer the following questions.

1. The passage you have just read is from a code of rules that monks lived by in the early 500s. If a historian wanted to study how monks lived at that time, would this be a good source to use? Why or why not?

2. Where else might a historian look to verify the information found in this source?

3. Would this be a good source to study to learn how monks live today? Why or why not?

Academic Vocabulary

Success in school is related to knowing academic vocabulary—the words that are frequently used in school assignments and discussions. In this chapter, you will learn the following academic words:

role *(p. 510)*
elements *(p. 514)*

As you read Chapter 17, look at the primary sources included in the chapter. Why do you think these sources were chosen to be included?

Geography of Europe

What You Will Learn...

Main Ideas

1. The physical features of Europe vary widely from region to region.
2. Geography has shaped life in Europe, including where and how people live.

The Big Idea

Because Europe has many types of landforms and climates, different ways of life have developed there.

Key Terms

Eurasia, *p. 496*
topography, *p. 496*

TAKING NOTES As you read, use a chart like the one below to take notes on the geography of three regions of Europe.

	Geography
Northern Europe	
Southern Europe	
Scandinavia	

If YOU were there...

Your village is on the banks of a river. The river has created a flat plain where you can grow crops. The river also gives you a way to get to the sea and to trade with villages farther inland. You love your village and think it's the perfect place to live. But your favorite uncle, the one everyone looks up to, says he is very worried. Your village is in a very dangerous place.

Why do you think your uncle is worried?

BUILDING BACKGROUND Many villages in Europe were built on rivers. But rivers were only one of the physical features that affected where and how people lived in Europe. All of Europe's features—its landforms, its waterways, and its climates—played roles in shaping people's lives.

The Physical Features of Europe

Europe is a small continent, but it is very diverse. Many different landforms, water features, and climates can be found there.

Although we call Europe a continent, it is actually part of **Eurasia**, the large landmass that includes both Europe and Asia. Geographers consider the Ural Mountains to be the boundary between the two continents.

Landforms and Waterways

Look at the map of Europe. You can see that different parts of Europe have very different features. In other words, Europe's topography (tuh-PAH-gruh-fee) varies widely from place to place. **Topography** refers to the shape and elevation of land in a region.

Mountain ranges cover much of southern Europe. Some peaks in the Alps reach higher than 15,000 feet. The highest mountains have large snowfields and glaciers.

ARCTIC OCEAN

ASIA

20°W

20°E   30°E   40°E   70°N

Iceland

SCANDINAVIAN PENINSULA

URAL MOUNTAINS

60°N

Norwegian Sea

N. Dvina River

British Isles

PENNINES

North Sea

Gulf of Bothnia

Baltic Sea

N O R T H E R N   E U R O P E A N   P L A I N

Kama River

50°N

ATLANTIC OCEAN

English Channel

Paris

Rhine

Seine River

Elbe River

Oder River

Vistula River

Dniester River

Don River

Volga River

Dnieper River

Bay of Biscay

Mont Blanc
15,781 ft.
(4,810 m)

A L P S

CARPATHIAN MTS.

Mt. Elbrus
18,510 ft.
(5,642 m)

CAUCASUS MTS.

Caspian Sea

PYRENEES

ITALIAN PENINSULA

Corsica

Adriatic Sea

BALKAN PENINSULA

Black Sea

ASIA

IBERIAN PENINSULA

40°N

Sardinia

Balearic Islands

Strait of Gibraltar

Tyrrhenian Sea

Sicily

Aegean Sea

Crete

Mediterranean Sea

ELEVATION

Feet		Meters
13,120		4,000
6,560		2,000
1,640		500
656		200
(Sea level) 0		0 (Sea level)
Below sea level		Below sea level

Ice cap

0   250   500 Miles

0   250   500 Kilometers

GEOGRAPHY SKILLS INTERPRETING MAPS

1. **Region** What four peninsulas do you see labeled?
2. **Movement** How might the Alps have affected the movement of peoples?

North of the Alps, the land is much flatter than in southern Europe. In fact, most of northern Europe is part of the vast Northern European Plain. As you can see on the map, this plain stretches all the way from the Atlantic Ocean in the west to the Ural Mountains in the east. In the past, this huge expanse of land was covered with thick forests. Many types of trees grew well in the plain's rich, fertile soils.

The Northern European Plain is also the location of most of Europe's major rivers. Many of these rivers begin with melting snow in the southern mountains and flow out across the plain on their way northward to the sea.

If you travel even farther north from the Northern European Plain, the land starts to rise again. Far northern Europe has many rugged hills and low mountains.

Geography and Living

Europe's geography has influenced the development of different ways of life. It has influenced, for example, what crops people have grown and where cities have developed.

❸ Norway

❷ Germany

❶ Italy

❶ Farmers have long grown olives and other hardy crops in the drier, warmer areas along the Mediterranean in southern Europe.

You can see these hills and mountains in the northern part of the British Isles and in Scandinavia, Europe's largest peninsula. Scandinavia is only one of Europe's many peninsulas. Smaller peninsulas extend into the sea from many parts of Europe. These peninsulas give Europe a very long, jagged coastline.

Climate and Vegetation

Like its landforms, Europe's climates and vegetation vary widely from region to region. For example, southern Europe is largely warm and sunny. As a result, shrubs and trees that don't need a lot of water are common there.

Most of northwestern Europe, in contrast, has a mild and cooler, wetter climate. Cold winds from the north and northeast can bring freezing weather in winter.

Freezing weather is much more common in Scandinavia, though. That region is very cold throughout the year. Snow falls for much of the year, and few plants can survive the region's cold climates.

READING CHECK Summarizing How do Europe's landforms and climates vary by region?

Geography Shapes Life

As in other parts of the world, geography has affected history in Europe. It influenced where and how people lived.

Southern Europe

In southern Europe, most people lived on coastal plains or in river valleys where the land was flat enough to farm. People grew crops like grapes and olives that could survive the region's dry summers. In the mountains where the land was steep or rocky, people raised sheep and goats.

Because southern Europe has many peninsulas, people there don't live far from the sea. As a result, many became traders and seafarers.

Northern Europe

Most people in northern Europe lived farther from the sea. They still had access to the sea, however, through northern Europe's rivers. Because rivers were an easy method of transportation, towns grew up along them. Rivers also provided protection. The city of Paris, France, for example, was built on an island in a river to make the city hard for raiders to reach.

2 Cities have grown along rivers such as the Rhine in Germany. Rivers have been routes for moving people and goods.

3 Many people in cold, snowy Scandinavia have settled on the coasts, looking to the sea and lands beyond for the resources they need.

In the fields around cities, farmers grew all sorts of crops. These fields were excellent farmlands, but the flat land also made an easy route for invaders to follow. No mountains blocked people's access to northern Europe, and as a result, the region was frequently invaded.

READING CHECK **Contrasting** How did geography influence where people lived in Europe?

SUMMARY AND PREVIEW You have just read about the role Europe's geography played in its history. Because Europe has so many types of landforms and climates, many different ways of life developed there. Also, northern Europe had few natural barriers to prevent invasions. In the next section, you will learn how Europe changed when invasions did occur.

go.hrw.com
Online Quiz
KEYWORD: SN6 HP17

Section 1 Assessment

Reviewing Ideas, Terms, and People

1. **a. Define** What is **topography**?
   b. Compare and Contrast How is southern Europe's climate like or unlike your climate?
2. **a. Describe** Where do most people in southern Europe live?
   b. Draw Conclusions Do you think Europe's major farming regions are in the north or the south? Why?
   c. Elaborate How might the region's climate affect how people live in Scandinavia?

Critical Thinking

3. **Categorizing** Draw a chart like the one to the right. Using your notes, list the landforms, climates, and vegetation of northern Europe, southern Europe, and Scandinavia.

	Landforms	Climates	Vegetation
Northern Europe			
Southern Europe			
Scandinavia			

FOCUS ON WRITING

4. **Thinking about Geography** If you were a noble living in northern Europe, what might your life be like? How would the landforms and climate affect people in your area? Why might you need the protection of knights? Write some ideas down in your notebook.

Europe after the Fall of Rome

Main Ideas

1. Christianity spread to northern Europe through the work of missionaries and monks.
2. The Franks, led by Charlemagne, created a huge Christian empire and brought together scholars from around Europe.
3. Invaders threatened much of Europe in the 700s and 800s.

The Big Idea

Despite the efforts of Christians to maintain order, Europe was a dangerous place after the fall of Rome.

Key Terms and People

Middle Ages, *p. 500*
medieval, *p. 500*
Patrick, *p. 501*
monks, *p. 502*
monasteries, *p. 502*
Benedict, *p. 502*
Charlemagne, *p. 503*

TAKING NOTES As you read, look for information about how events and people in the Middle Ages affected Europe. Record your notes in a chart like this one.

	Effects on Europe
Fall of Roman Empire	
Spread of Christianity	
Charlemagne	
Invaders	

If YOU were there...

You're returning to your village in northern Europe after a hard day working in the fields. But as you reach the top of a hill, you smell smoke. Alarmed, you break into a run. Finally, your village comes into sight, and your fears are realized. Your village is on fire! In the distance, you can see sails moving away on the river.

What do you think has happened to your village?

BUILDING BACKGROUND Europe was a dangerous place after Rome fell. Without the Roman government, Europe had no central authority to keep order. As a result, outlaws and bandits became common. At the same time, new groups of people were moving into Europe. Violence was common. Distressed, people looked for ways to bring order and comfort into their lives.

Christianity Spreads to Northern Europe

As the Roman Empire fell, various groups from the north and east moved into former Roman lands. As they moved in, these groups created their own states. The rulers of these states, usually powerful warlords, began to call themselves kings. These kings often fought among themselves. As a result, by the early 500s Europe was divided into many small kingdoms.

The creation of these kingdoms marked the beginning of the **Middle Ages**, a period that lasted from about 500 to about 1500. We call this time the "middle" ages because it falls between ancient times and modern times. Another name for the Middle Ages is the **medieval** (mee-DEE-vuhl) period, from the Latin words for "middle age."

At the beginning of the Middle Ages, many of the kingdoms of northern Europe were not Christian. Christianity was only common in places that had been part of the Roman Empire, such as Italy and Spain. As time passed, however, Christianity

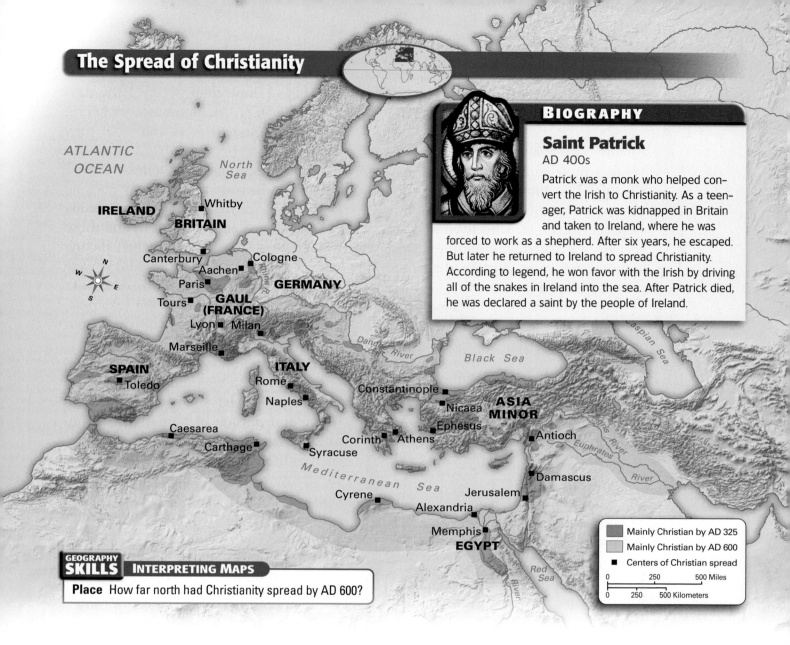

The Spread of Christianity

ATLANTIC OCEAN

North Sea

IRELAND

Whitby

BRITAIN

Canterbury

Cologne

Aachen

Paris

GERMANY

Tours

GAUL
(FRANCE)

Lyon

Milan

Marseille

Danube River

Black Sea

Caspian Sea

SPAIN

ITALY

Toledo

Rome

Constantinople

Naples

Nicaea

ASIA MINOR

Ephesus

Caesarea

Corinth

Athens

Antioch

Carthage

Syracuse

Euphrates River

Tigris River

Mediterranean Sea

Damascus

Cyrene

Jerusalem

Alexandria

Memphis

EGYPT

Red Sea

BIOGRAPHY

Saint Patrick
AD 400s

Patrick was a monk who helped convert the Irish to Christianity. As a teenager, Patrick was kidnapped in Britain and taken to Ireland, where he was forced to work as a shepherd. After six years, he escaped. But later he returned to Ireland to spread Christianity. According to legend, he won favor with the Irish by driving all of the snakes in Ireland into the sea. After Patrick died, he was declared a saint by the people of Ireland.

Legend
- Mainly Christian by AD 325
- Mainly Christian by AD 600
- ■ Centers of Christian spread

0   250   500 Miles
0   250   500 Kilometers

GEOGRAPHY SKILLS | **INTERPRETING MAPS**

Place How far north had Christianity spread by AD 600?

slowly spread farther north. This spread was largely through the efforts of two groups of Christians—missionaries and monks.

Missionaries

Perhaps the most powerful force that helped spread Christianity into northern Europe was the pope. Over the years, many popes sent missionaries to teach people in northern kingdoms about Christianity. Missionaries are people who try to convert others to a particular religion. Some missionaries traveled great distances to spread Christianity to new lands.

One of the first places to which popes sent missionaries was Britain. These missionaries traveled all over the island, and eventually most people in Britain became Christian. From Britain, other missionaries carried Christianity into what are now France and Germany.

Not all missionaries, though, were sent by the pope. In fact, one of the first missionaries to travel to northern Europe was **Patrick**, who took it upon himself to teach people about Christianity. In the mid-400s Patrick traveled from Britain to Ireland to convert the people there.

Unlike most missionaries, Patrick traveled alone. Although he faced resistance to his teachings, he eventually converted the Irish people to Christianity.

Monks

While missionaries traveled to spread Christian teachings, men called monks were equally dedicated to their faith. **Monks** were religious men who lived apart from society in isolated communities. In these communities, monks spent their time in prayer, work, and meditation.

Communities of monks, or **monasteries**, were built all over Europe in the Middle Ages. Life in a monastery was strictly organized. The monks had to follow rules that were intended to help them live as good Christians. These rules outlined the day-to-day affairs of the monastery, including how monks should dress and what they should eat.

Most European monasteries followed a set of rules created in the early 500s by an Italian monk named **Benedict**. His code was called the Benedictine Rule, and those who followed it were called Benedictine monks. But not all monks in Europe were Benedictines. Different groups of monks created their own rules. For example, monks in Ireland were very different from monks in France or Germany.

Even though they lived apart from society, monks had a big influence on Europe. Monks performed many services, both inside and outside of monasteries. Monasteries sometimes provided basic services, such as health care, that were unavailable to many members of their communities. The poor and needy would arrive at a monastery and the monks would give them aid.

In addition to giving aid to people in their communities, monks

- ran schools and copied books for those who couldn't read or write,
- collected and saved ancient writings from Greece and Rome,
- served as scribes and advisors to local rulers.

Monks also helped spread Christian teachings into new areas. Many monasteries were built in remote locations where Christians had never traveled before. People living near the monasteries learned about Christianity from the monks.

READING CHECK Summarizing How did missionaries and monks help spread Christianity into new areas?

HISTORIC DOCUMENT
The Benedictine Rule

The Benedictine Order was the largest group of monks in Europe in the early Middle Ages. In his rule, Benedict listed the guidelines monks had to follow. Here he describes what each monk was allowed to own.

Monks were not allowed to own any property.

An abbot is the head of a monastery.

"For bedding, a mattress, a blanket, a coverlet and a pillow are enough. The beds should be frequently inspected by the Abbot as a precaution against private possessions. If anyone is found to have anything which was not given him by the Abbot, he is to undergo the severest punishment; and that this vice [wickedness] of personal ownership may be totally eliminated, everything necessary should be given by the Abbot; namely, a cowl [hood], a tunic [long shirt], stockings, shoes, a belt, a knife, a pen, a needle, a handkerchief and writing tablets, so that all excuses about necessity are removed.**"**

–from *The Rule of Saint Benedict*, translated by Abbot Parry

ANALYSIS SKILL ANALYZING PRIMARY SOURCES

Why do you think Benedictine monks were only allowed a few simple possessions?

Charlemagne

What would you do if you ruled much of Europe?

When did he live? 742–814

Where did he live? Charlemagne, or Charles the Great, ruled most of what are now France and Germany. He lived mainly in his capital, Aachen, near the modern city of Cologne, Germany.

What did he do? Through his wars of conquest, Charlemagne united many of the tribes of central and western Europe into a single empire.

KEY EVENTS

771 Charlemagne becomes king of the Franks.

773 Charlemagne becomes an ally of the pope after rescuing him from invaders.

794 Charlemagne makes Aachen his capital.

800 Pope Leo III names Charlemagne emperor.

Why is he important? While Europe was still reeling from the collapse of Rome, Charlemagne brought people together. He helped Europeans realize that they shared common bonds, such as Christianity, that linked them. In other words, he helped people see themselves as Europeans, not members of tribes.

Drawing Conclusions How did this change in view affect later European society?

This painting shows Charlemagne being crowned by the pope in AD 800.

Feudalism and Manor Life

What You Will Learn...

Main Ideas

1. Feudalism governed how knights and nobles dealt with each other.
2. Feudalism spread through much of Europe.
3. The manor system dominated Europe's economy.
4. Towns and trade grew and helped end the feudal system.

The Big Idea

A complex web of duties and obligations governed relationships between people in the Middle Ages.

Key Terms and People

knights, *p. 506*
vassal, *p. 507*
feudalism, *p. 507*
William the Conqueror, *p. 508*
manor, *p. 509*
serfs, *p. 509*
Eleanor of Aquitaine, *p. 510*

TAKING NOTES As you read, pay attention to the duties and obligations of different people in the Middle Ages. Record your notes in a chart like this one.

	Duties and Obligations
Lords	
Knights	
Serfs	
Skilled workers	
Merchants	

If YOU were there...

You are a peasant in the Middle Ages, living on the land of a noble. Although you and your family work very hard for many hours of the day, much of the food you grow goes to the noble and his family. Your house is very small, and it has a dirt floor. Your parents are tired and weak, and you wish you could do something to improve their lives.

Is there any way you could change your life?

BUILDING BACKGROUND Hard work was a constant theme in the lives of peasants in the Middle Ages. They worked long hours and had to obey the wishes of nobles. But most nobles weren't free to live as they chose either. They were sworn to obey more powerful nobles, who had to obey the wishes of the king. Life in the Middle Ages was one big web of duties and obligations.

Feudalism Governs Knights and Nobles

When the Vikings, Magyars, and Muslims began their raids in the 800s, the Frankish kings were unable to defend their empire. Their army was too slow to defend against the lightning-fast attacks of their enemies. Because they couldn't depend on protection from their kings, nobles had to defend their own lands. As a result, the power of nobles grew, and kings became less powerful. In fact, some nobles became as powerful as the kings themselves. Although these nobles remained loyal to the king, they ruled their lands as independent territories.

Knights and Land

To defend their lands, nobles needed soldiers. The best soldiers were **knights**, warriors who fought on horseback. However, knights needed weapons, armor, and horses. This equipment was expensive, and few people had money in the early Middle Ages.

As a result, nobles gave knights fiefs (FEEFS), or pieces of land, instead of money for their military service. A noble who gave land to a knight in this way was called a lord.

In return for the land, a knight promised to support the noble in battle or in other matters. A knight who promised to support a lord in exchange for land was called a **vassal**. The vassal swore that he would always remain loyal to his lord. Historians call this system of promises that governed the relationships between lords and vassals **feudalism** (FYOO-duh-lih-zuhm).

A Lord's Duties

The ties between lords and vassals were the heart of feudalism. Each group had certain responsibilities toward the other. A lord had to send help to his vassals if an enemy attacked. In addition, he had to be fair toward his vassals. He couldn't cheat them or punish them for no reason. If a lord failed to do what he was supposed to, his vassals could break all ties with him.

To defend their lands, many lords built castles. A castle is a large building with strong walls that can easily be defended against attacks. Early castles didn't look like the towering structures we see in movies and storybooks. Those great castles were built much later in the Middle Ages. Most early castles were made of wood, not stone. Nevertheless, these castles provided security in times of war.

A Vassal's Duties

When a lord went to war, he called on his vassals to fight with him. But fighting wasn't a vassal's only duty. For example, vassals had to give their lords money on special occasions, such as when a lord's son became a knight or when his daughter got married. A vassal also had to give his lord food and shelter if he came to visit. If a vassal gained enough land, he could

become a lord. In this way a person might be both a lord and a vassal. A knight could also accept fiefs from two different lords and become a vassal to both. Feudal obligations could become confusing.

READING CHECK **Sequencing** What led to the creation of feudalism?

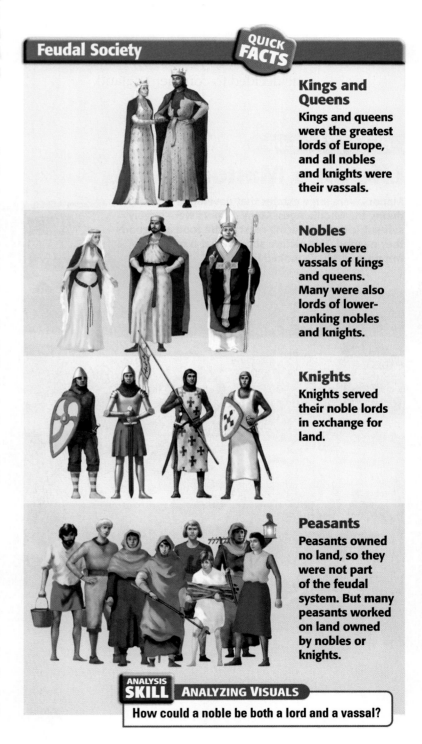

Feudal Society QUICK FACTS

Kings and Queens
Kings and queens were the greatest lords of Europe, and all nobles and knights were their vassals.

Nobles
Nobles were vassals of kings and queens. Many were also lords of lower-ranking nobles and knights.

Knights
Knights served their noble lords in exchange for land.

Peasants
Peasants owned no land, so they were not part of the feudal system. But many peasants worked on land owned by nobles or knights.

ANALYSIS SKILL **ANALYZING VISUALS**
How could a noble be both a lord and a vassal?

THE IMPACT
TODAY

Though many people have tried to invade England since, William's invasion in 1066 was the last time England was conquered.

Feudalism Spreads

Feudalism was first created by the Franks. Before long the system began to spread into other kingdoms. In the 1000s, Frankish knights introduced feudalism into northern Italy, Spain, and Germany. Feudalism then spread into eastern Europe.

Feudalism also reached Britain in the 1000s. It was brought there by a French noble named William, who was the duke of Normandy in northern France. In 1066, he decided to conquer England.

William and his knights sailed into England and defeated the English king in a battle near the town of Hastings. After winning the battle, William declared himself the new king of England. He became known as **William the Conqueror**. To reward his knights for their part in the victory, William gave them large estates of land in his new country. This was the beginning of feudalism in England.

READING CHECK Sequencing How did feudalism spread to England?

History Close-up

Life on a Manor

Manors were large estates that developed in Europe during the Middle Ages. Many manors were largely self-sufficient, producing most of the food and goods they needed. This picture shows what a manor in Britain might have looked like.

The lord of the manor lived in a large stone house called the manor house.

Peasants grew vegetables in small gardens near their houses.

In the fall, peasants worked to harvest crops like wheat.

The Manor System

When a knight received a fief from his lord, he needed a way to farm it. Knights were fighters who didn't have time to work in the fields. At the same time, peasants, or small farmers, needed to grow food to live. Very few peasants, however, owned any land.

As a result, a new economic system developed. Under this system, knights allowed peasants to farm land on their large estates. In return, the peasants had to give the knights food or other payment.

The large estate owned by a knight or lord was called a **manor**. In general, each manor included a large house or castle, pastures, fields, and forests. It also had a village where the peasants who worked on the manor lived.

Peasants, Serfs, and Other Workers

Most medieval lords kept about one-fourth to one-third of their land for their own use. The rest of the land was divided among peasants and **serfs**—workers who were tied to the land on which they lived.

The village church was built on a small piece of land that belonged to the lord.

Sheep grazed on grassy fields, and villagers used sheep's wool to make clothes.

The village black-smith made iron tools for farming.

Harvested wheat was taken to the mill and ground into flour, which was used to make bread.

ANALYSIS SKILL **ANALYZING VISUALS**

What goods can you see being produced on this manor?

509

Although they weren't slaves, serfs weren't allowed to leave their land without the lord's permission. Serfs spent much of their time working in their lords' fields. In return for this work, they got a small piece of land to farm for themselves. They also received their lords' protection against outlaws and raiders.

The lives of serfs and peasants weren't easy. Farm labor was hard, and they often worked in the fields late into the night. Men did most of the farming. Women made clothing, cooked, grew vegetables, and gathered firewood. Even children worked, tending sheep and chickens.

In addition to peasants and serfs, most manors had several skilled workers. These workers traded their goods and services to the peasants in exchange for food. Lords wanted the people who lived on the manor to produce everything they needed, including food and clothing.

ACADEMIC VOCABULARY
role assigned behavior

Manor Lords

The lord of a manor controlled everything that happened on his lands. His word was law. The lord resolved any disputes that arose on the manor and punished people who misbehaved. He also collected taxes from the people who lived on his manor.

As you would expect, manor lords and ladies lived more comfortably than other people on the manor. They had servants and large houses. Still, their lives weren't easy. Lords who survived diseases faced the possibility of being killed in war.

Women in the Middle Ages

Regardless of their social class, women in the Middle Ages had fewer rights than men. Women generally had to obey the wishes of their fathers or husbands. But women still had important **roles** in society. As you have read, peasant women worked to support their families. Noblewomen also had duties. They ran manor households and supervised servants. Women governed manors when their husbands went to war. Some noblewomen, like the French woman **Eleanor of Aquitaine**, had great political power. Other women who wanted power and influence joined the most powerful of institutions, the Christian Church.

READING CHECK Contrasting How were the lives of nobles and peasants different?

BIOGRAPHY

Eleanor of Aquitaine
c. 1122–1204

Eleanor of Aquitaine was one of the most powerful people of the Middle Ages. She ruled Aquitaine, a region in southwestern France, as the king's vassal. In 1137 Eleanor became queen of France when she married King Louis VII. Later, she divorced Louis and became queen of England by marrying King Henry II of England. Even while she was queen of England, she spent much of her time ruling her own territory. Eleanor had many children, and two of her sons later became kings of England.

Drawing Conclusions
Why do you think Eleanor had more power than other women in the Middle Ages?

Towns and Trade Grow

In the Middle Ages, most people lived on manors or on small farms, not in towns. As a result, most towns were small. After about 1000, however, this situation began to change. Some towns became big cities. At the same time, new towns appeared.

What led to the growth of medieval towns? For one thing, Europe's population increased, partly because more food was available. New technology helped farmers produce larger harvests than ever before. Among these improvements was a heavier plow. With this plow farmers could dig deeper into the soil, helping their plants grow better. Another new device, the horse collar, allowed farmers to plow fields using horses. In times past, farmers had used oxen, which were strong but slow. With horses, farmers could tend larger fields, grow more food, and feed more people.

Towns also grew because trade increased. As Europe's population grew, so did trade. Trade routes spread all across Europe. Merchants also brought goods from Asia and Africa to sell in markets in Europe. The chance to make money in trade led many people to leave their farms and move to cities, causing cities to grow even larger.

In time, the growth of trade led to the decline of feudalism. Knights began to demand money for their services instead of land. At the same time, serfs and peasants left their manors for towns, slowly weakening the manor system.

READING CHECK Identifying Cause and Effect
Why did towns and trade grow in the Middle Ages?

Medieval Market
In the Middle Ages, some towns held large trade fairs each year. This illustration shows a bishop blessing a trade fair in France.

SUMMARY AND PREVIEW In this section, you learned about European feudalism and the social and economic relationships it created among people. In the next section, you'll read about how this system compares to one that developed halfway around the world in Japan.

Section 3 Assessment

go.hrw.com
Online Quiz
KEYWORD: SN6 HP17

Reviewing Ideas, Terms, and People

1. **a. Define** What was a **knight**?
   b. Explain Why did **vassals** have to serve lords?
   c. Elaborate Do you think knights or lords benefited more from **feudalism**? Why?
2. **Explain** How did **William the Conqueror** help spread feudalism?
3. **a. Describe** What was a typical **manor** like?
   b. Elaborate How do you think most **serfs** felt about the manor system?
4. **a. Recall** What led to the growth of Europe's population in the Middle Ages?
   b. Draw Conclusions Why do you think many peasants left their farms for cities?

Critical Thinking

5. **Analyzing** Draw a flow chart like the one below. Review your notes and then, in each box, list the duties and obligations that each group had toward the other.

   Lords → ← Knights → ← Serfs

FOCUS ON WRITING

6. **Writing about Knights** Take notes on the knights described in this section and how what you've learned will affect your search for knights. What kinds of people will you hire? How will you pay them? Write your answers in your notebook.

Feudal Societies

If YOU were there...

You want to be a squire, a young person who trains to be a knight. Your best friend thinks you are foolish. He says that you'll have to swear a vow of loyalty to your lord, and you'll have to fight in battles for him. Your sister told you that you will have to follow a strict code of honor. But you still want to be a knight.

Why do you want to be a knight?

BUILDING BACKGROUND Knights were an important part of feudal society. People who wanted to be knights did have to swear vows of loyalty, fight in battles, and follow a code of honor. But European knights were not the only people who had to live by these rules. Half a world away, Japanese samurai lived under similar obligations. In fact, if you look at these two societies, you will see that many striking similarities existed between them.

Feudal Societies Share Common Elements

Feudalism was not unique to Europe. As you have already read, the Japanese developed a very similar system halfway around the world from Europe at about the same time. But how similar were the two societies?

Lords and Vassals

In Europe, the basis for the feudal system was land. Kings and lords gave land to knights. In return, the knights promised to serve their lords and fight for them when necessary. Many knights owned large manors. Peasants and serfs worked on the manors and paid the lords in food.

A very similar system existed in Japan. There, the emperor gave land to great lords who were later called daimyo. In turn, these lords employed warriors called samurai. Like European knights, the samurai promised to serve and fight for their lords. In exchange, the samurai received rice and grain. Lords got the grain from peasants who farmed their land. Peasants had to pay their lords in grain.

What You Will Learn...

Main Ideas

1. Feudal societies shared common elements in Europe and Japan.
2. Europe and Japan differed in their cultural elements such as religion and art.

The Big Idea

Although the feudal systems of Europe and Japan were similar, their cultures were very different.

Key Terms

chivalry, *p. 513*
haiku, *p. 514*

TAKING NOTES As you read, take notes on the feudal systems and cultures of Europe and Japan in the Middle Ages.

	Europe	Japan
Fuedal system		
Warriors		
Religion		
Arts		

Samurai and Knights

Although Japanese samurai and European knights never actually met, they had much in common. Both were the elite warriors of their time and place.

ANALYSIS SKILL **ANALYZING VISUALS**

How are the samurai and knight similar? How are they different?

Knights and Samurai

The lives of knights and samurai were, in many ways, very similar. Both had to swear vows of loyalty to their lords. These lords expected them to fight well and to be fearless in battle. The lords also expected their knights or samurai to live disciplined and honorable lives.

Both European knights and Japanese samurai had to follow strict codes of honor that governed how they behaved. You have already learned about Bushido, the Japanese code of the samurai. Europeans called their code of honorable behavior for knights **chivalry** (SHIV-uhl-ree). Like Bushido, chivalry required knights to be brave and loyal but humble and modest at the same time. It also required them to be kind and generous when dealing with people, especially women.

Because of their loyalty and dedication, both knights and samurai were greatly admired by other members of their societies. This admiration can often be seen in literary descriptions of the men, such as this description of the French knight Roland and his comrades who are greatly outnumbered by their enemies:

"The battle is fearful and full of grief.
Oliver and Roland strike like good men,
the Archbishop, more than a thousand blows,
and the Twelve Peers do not hang back, they strike!
the French fight side by side, all as one man.
The pagans die by hundreds, by thousands:
whoever does not flee finds no refuge from death,
like it or not, there he ends his days."

–from *The Song of Roland*, translated by Frederick Goldin

Even though Roland and the others were almost certain that they would die, they continued to fight. They became heroes, admired for their courage and bravery.

FOCUS ON READING

Why do you think a primary source is included here?

The Japanese also admired their warriors for their courage. A passage from a Japanese text shows a similar admiration for warriors fighting impossible odds:

"Where Naozane galloped, Sueshige followed; where Sueshige galloped, Naozane followed. Neither willing to be outdone, they dashed in by turns, whipping their horses and attacking until the sparks flew… Naozane pulled out the arrows that were lodged in his own armor, tossed them aside, faced the stronghold with a scowl, and shouted in a mighty voice, 'I am Naozane, the man who left Kamakura last winter determined to give his life for Lord Yoritomo… Confront me! Confront me!'"

–from *The Tale of the Heike*, translated by Helen Craig McCullough

READING CHECK **Comparing** How were European knights and Japanese samurai similar?

Europe and Japan Differ

Although European and Japanese societies were the same in some ways, in most ways they were not. Their two cultures were also very different.

Perhaps the main difference between medieval Europeans and Japanese was religion. Nearly all Europeans were Christian, while the Japanese blended **elements** of Buddhism, Shinto, and Confucianism. European and Japanese religions taught very different ways of looking at the world. People in those places, therefore, did not act the same way.

The differences between Europe and Japan can also be seen in the artistic forms popular in each place. European art in the Middle Ages dealt mostly with religious themes. Paintings showed scenes from the Bible, and writers tried to inspire people with stories about great Christians.

In Japan, on the other hand, most art dealt with natural themes. Paintings of nature were common, and people built many gardens. Buildings blended with nature, rather than standing out. Japanese literature also celebrated nature. For example, Japanese poets in the 1600s created **haiku** (HY-koo), short, three-line poems of 17 syllables that describe nature scenes.

Art in Europe and Japan

The medieval arts of Europe and Japan were very different. European art often emphasized religion, while Japanese art often emphasized nature.

In what ways are these two paintings different?

Comparing and Contrasting Europe and Japan

Feudal Europe
- Christianity
- Religious themes in art and literature

- Feudal government
- Royalty (kings and queens, emperor)
- Nobles (lords, daimyo)
- Warriors (knights, samurai)
- Warrior codes of honor (chivalry, Bushido)
- Peasants worked land

Feudal Japan
- Buddhism, Shinto, Confucianism
- Nature themes in art and literature

Here is one example of haiku:

Very soon they die—
but of that there is no sign
in the locust-cry.
–Matsuo Basho, from *Anthology of Japanese Literature*,
edited by Donald Keene

Although European and Japanese feudal systems seemed similar, the cultures that lay behind them were different. Still, it is remarkable to think that feudal systems so similar could exist so far apart.

READING CHECK **Contrasting** How were feudal European and Japanese cultures different?

SUMMARY AND PREVIEW In this section you learned how to compare feudalism in Europe and Japan. Although both Europe and Japan had feudal societies, there were many differences in the two societies. Feudalism lasted much longer in Japan than it did in Europe, not disappearing until the 1800s. In the next chapter you will learn about how European society changed after feudalism disappeared in the later Middle Ages. One major change was the growing importance of religion.

go.hrw.com
Online Quiz
KEYWORD: SN6 HP17

Section 4 Assessment

Reviewing Ideas, Terms, and People

1. **a. Define** What was **chivalry**?
   b. Compare What were three characteristics knights and samurai shared?
   c. Develop Why do you think feudal systems developed in both Europe and Japan?

2. **a. Identify** What was the religion of most people in medieval Europe? What religions influenced most people in Japan?
   b. Contrast How were the subjects of **haiku** different from medieval European poems?
   c. Evaluate In your opinion, were European and Japanese societies more similar to or different from each other? Explain your answer.

Critical Thinking

3. **Comparing and Contrasting** Draw a chart like the one below. Using your notes, list two similarities and one key difference between knights and samurai.

Similarities	Difference
1.	1.
2.	

FOCUS ON WRITING

4. **Describing Chivalry** Think about what you've just learned about chivalry. What kinds of rules will you expect your knights to follow? How will you explain these rules to them?

Social Studies Skills

Interpreting Diagrams

Understand the Skill

Diagrams are drawings that use lines and labels to explain or illustrate something. Different types of diagrams have different purposes. *Pictorial diagrams* show an object in simple form, much like it would look if you were viewing it. *Cutaway diagrams* show the "insides" of an object. *Component diagrams* show how an object is organized by separating it into parts. Such diagrams are sometimes also called *schematic drawings*. The ability to interpret diagrams will help you to better understand a historical object, its function, and how it worked.

Learn the Skill

Use these basic steps to interpret a diagram:

1. Determine what type of diagram it is.

2. Read the diagram's title or caption to find out what it represents.

3. Look for any labels and read them carefully. Most diagrams include text that identifies the object's parts or explains relationships between the parts.

4. If a legend is present, study it to identify and understand any symbols and colors that are used in the diagram.

5. Look for numbers or letters that might indicate a sequence of steps. Also look for any arrows that might show direction or movement.

An Early Castle

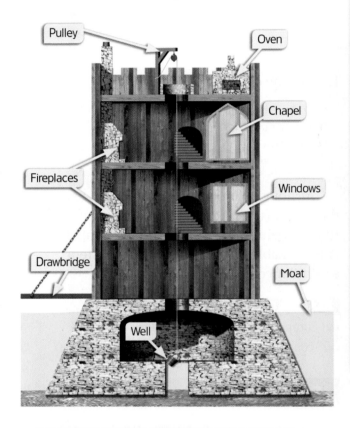

Pulley · Oven · Chapel · Fireplaces · Windows · Drawbridge · Moat · Well

Practice and Apply the Skill

Interpret the diagram above, of an early castle, and answer the following questions.

1. What type of diagram is this?
2. What labels in diagram suggest how the castle was heated?
3. What was the purpose of the pulley?
4. Of what materials was the castle made?
5. What features of the castle helped make it secure against attack?

Chapter Review

Visual Summary

Use the visual summary below to help you review the main ideas of the chapter.

QUICK FACTS

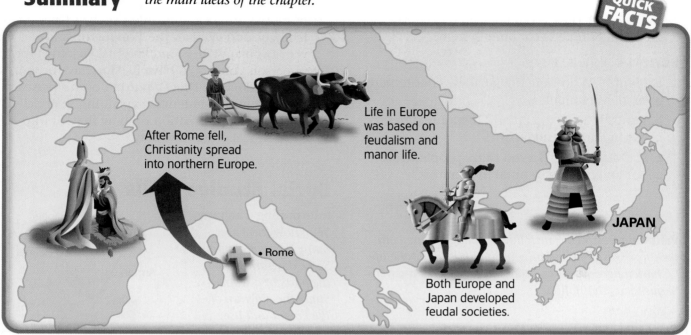

After Rome fell, Christianity spread into northern Europe.

• Rome

Life in Europe was based on feudalism and manor life.

Both Europe and Japan developed feudal societies.

JAPAN

Reviewing Vocabulary, Terms, and People

Write each word defined below, circling each letter that is marked by a star. Then write the word these letters spell.

1. *_ _ _ _ _—religious men who lived in isolated communities

2. *_ _ _ _ _ _ _ of Aquitaine—one of the most powerful women of the Middle Ages

3. _ _ _ _ *_ _ _ _ _ _—a political system in which land is given for military service

4. _ _ *_ _ _ _ _ _—a code of behavior that knights had to follow

5. _ *_ _ _ _—farm workers who were tied to the land they worked

6. *_ _ _ _ _ _—someone who received land in exchange for military service

7. _ *_ _ _ _—a large estate

8. _ _ _ _ _ *_ _ _ _ _ _ _—Frankish king who created a huge empire

Comprehension and Critical Thinking

SECTION 1 *(Pages 496–499)*

9. a. Identify What region of Europe has the best land for farming?

b. Analyze How have rivers and seas influenced life in Europe?

c. Evaluate Based on its geography, in which part of Europe would you want to live? Why would you want to live there?

SECTION 2 *(Pages 500–504)*

10. a. Identify What two groups of people were largely responsible for the northern spread of Christianity?

b. Compare In what way was the empire of the Franks under Charlemagne like the Roman Empire?

c. Elaborate How do you think the building of new monasteries helped spread Christianity?

SECTION 3 *(Pages 506–511)*

11. **a. Describe** What were women's lives like during the Middle Ages?

    b. Analyze How did knights and lords try to make their manors self-sufficient?

    c. Elaborate How was feudalism related to medieval Europe's economic system?

SECTION 4 *(Pages 512–515)*

12. **a. Identify** Who were the Japanese counterparts of medieval knights?

    b. Contrast How did art and literature differ between Europe and Japan?

    c. Elaborate Why do you think people wrote about knights and samurai in literature?

Reading Skills

Evaluating Sources *The following passages are both taken from historians writing in the 800s about the life of Charlemagne. Read both passages and then answer the questions that follow.*

> " I consider that it would be foolish for me to write about Charlemagne's birth and childhood …for nothing is set down in writing about this and nobody can be found still alive who claims to have any personal knowledge of these matters. I have therefore decided to leave out what is not really known …"
>
> –Einhard, from *Two Lives of Charlemagne*, translated by Lewis Thorpe

> " When I was a child, he was already a very old man. He brought me up and used to tell me about these events. I was a poor pupil, and I often ran away, but in the end he forced me to listen."
>
> –Notker, from *Two Lives of Charlemagne*, translated by Lewis Thorpe

13. Are these passages primary or secondary sources?

14. Which historian do you think would be the most credible, or believable?

Reviewing Themes

15. **Religion** Do you think religion helped to unify or divide Europeans in the Middle Ages? Why?

16. **Society and Culture** Do you think religion or government had more influence on medieval societies? Why?

Using the Internet
go.hrw.com KEYWORD: SN6 WH17

17. **Activity: Researching Daily Life** Feudalism created a web of relationships and duties between different people in medieval Europe. Enter the activity keyword and research the lives of monks and peasants, rulers such as Charlemagne and William the Conqueror, and warriors like Vikings and knights. Pick the type of person you would have liked to have been in the Middle Ages. Draw a portrait of this person. Then write 5–6 sentences explaining their daily life. Include information on how they fit into the political order of society.

Social Studies Skills

Interpreting Diagrams
You know there are many types of diagrams. Some diagrams show the parts of a whole. Study the diagram of the knight and use it to answer the questions that follow.

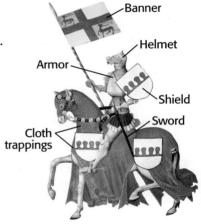

Banner, Helmet, Armor, Shield, Sword, Cloth trappings

18. Which parts of a knight's outfit were used for protection? Which might help him be recognized in battle?

19. What did a knight use as a weapon?

20. Why might a knight carry a banner?

FOCUS ON WRITING

21. **Writing a Job Ad** "Wanted: Brave and Loyal Knights." Use your notes from this chapter to write a job ad. Start your ad by explaining why you need knights to help you. Then write a description of the type of people who will be suitable for the job and how they will be expected to behave. Be sure to mention in your ad what knights will receive in exchange for their service.

DIRECTIONS: Read each question, and write the letter of the best response.

1

PERSON A

Obligations to Person B
- Provide Protection
- Provide Land

PERSON B

Obligations to Person A
- Provide Loyalty
- Provide Military Service

In this diagram, Person B is probably a

A lord.

B vassal.

C serf.

D peasant.

2 **One thing that continued to grow and spread across Europe after the fall of the Roman Empire was**

A Christianity.

B Roman culture.

C Bushido.

D republican government.

3 **Why would feudalism have taken hold more strongly in northern Europe than in southern Europe?**

A Fewer geographic barriers protected northern Europeans from invasion by enemies.

B Southern Europeans were more interested in fishing than in farming.

C A larger number of towns grew up along the rivers of northern Europe.

D Most people in southern Europe lived along the region's long coastlines.

4 **Which of these descriptions does *not* apply to feudalism as it developed in Europe?**

A growing power of kings

B powerful nobles

C clearly defined roles in society

D duties and obligations

5 **One way in which society developed *differently* in Europe and Japan was in**

A the relationship between lords and vassals.

B the duties and obligations in each system.

C the themes of their art and literature.

D the behavior of knights and samurai.

Connecting with Past Learnings

6 **Charlemagne was a brilliant warrior and a strong king. The achievements of which ancient figure have the *least* in common with those of Charlemagne?**

A Julius Caesar

B Alexander the Great

C Aristotle

D Shi Huangdi

7 **Serfs were tied to the land on which they worked. A serf in medieval Europe held a place in society that was *most* like**

A a Brahman in ancient India.

B a peasant in ancient China.

C a Christian in ancient Rome.

D a trader in ancient Egypt.

CHAPTER **18** 1000–1500

The Later Middle Ages

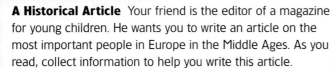

FOCUS ON WRITING

A Historical Article Your friend is the editor of a magazine for young children. He wants you to write an article on the most important people in Europe in the Middle Ages. As you read, collect information to help you write this article.

CHAPTER EVENTS

1066 Feudalism is introduced into Britain.

1000

WORLD EVENTS

1055 The Seljuk Turks take control of Baghdad.

What You Will Learn...

In this chapter, you will learn about life in Europe during the later Middle Ages. Christianity was a major influence on people's lives during these years. This photo shows the monastery at Mont St. Michel in France.

1096–1291
Crusaders battle for control of the Holy Land.

1347–1351
The Black Death kills about 25 million people in Europe.

1492
The Spanish drive the Jews out of Spain.

1100 | 1200 | 1300 | 1400 | 1500

1192 The first shogun takes power in Japan.

1405–1433
Admiral Zheng He leads Chinese sea expeditions of Asia and Africa.

1492
Christopher Columbus lands in the Americas.

THE LATER MIDDLE AGES **521**

| Economics | Geography | Politics | Religion | Society and Culture | Science and Technology |

Focus on Themes In this chapter, you will learn about Europe in the late Middle Ages, a period of important change and new developments. You will see how the Christian **religion** was a major influence on people's lives. You will also read about the conflict between religious and political leaders and how this conflict shaped **society and culture**. Finally, you will learn about important events that changed medieval society and opened up the way towards the development of modern life.

Stereotypes and Bias in History

Focus on Reading Historians today try to be impartial in their writing. They don't let their personal feelings affect what they write. Writers in the past, however, didn't always feel the need to be impartial. Their writings were sometimes colored by their attitudes about other people, places, and ideas.

Identifying Stereotypes and Bias Two ways in which writing can be colored by the author's ideas are stereotypes and bias. A **stereotype** is a generalization about whole groups of people. **Bias** is an attitude that one group is superior to another. The examples below can help you identify stereotypes and bias in the things you read.

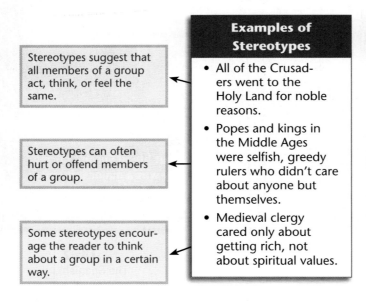

Stereotypes suggest that all members of a group act, think, or feel the same.

Stereotypes can often hurt or offend members of a group.

Some stereotypes encourage the reader to think about a group in a certain way.

Examples of Stereotypes

- All of the Crusaders went to the Holy Land for noble reasons.
- Popes and kings in the Middle Ages were selfish, greedy rulers who didn't care about anyone but themselves.
- Medieval clergy cared only about getting rich, not about spiritual values.

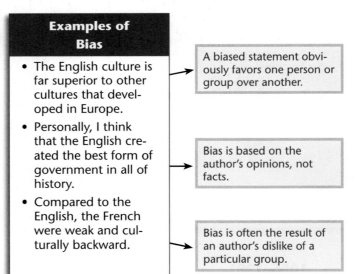

Examples of Bias

- The English culture is far superior to other cultures that developed in Europe.
- Personally, I think that the English created the best form of government in all of history.
- Compared to the English, the French were weak and culturally backward.

A biased statement obviously favors one person or group over another.

Bias is based on the author's opinions, not facts.

Bias is often the result of an author's dislike of a particular group.

You Try It!

The following passage was written by a French poet and knight named Rutebeuf. Rutebeuf, who lived from about 1245 to 1285, explains his reasons for not wanting to join the Crusades. As you read the passage, look for examples of stereotypes and bias in his writing.

A Knight Speaks

Am I to leave my wife and children, all my goods and inheritance, to go and conquer a foreign land which will give me nothing in return? I can worship God just as well in Paris as in Jerusalem . . . . Those rich lords and prelates [priests] who have grabbed for themselves all the treasure on earth may well need to go on Crusade. But I live at peace with my neighbors. I am not bored with them yet and so I have no desire to go looking for a war at the other end of the world. If you like heroic deeds, you can go along and cover yourself with glory: tell the Sultan from me that if he feels like attacking me I know very well how to defend myself. But so long as he leaves me alone, I shall not bother my head about him. All you people, great and small, who go on pilgrimage to the Promised Land, ought to become very holy there: so how does it happen that the ones who come back are mostly bandits?

–Rutebeuf, from *The Medieval World* by Freidrich Heer, translated by Janet Sondheimer

Review the graphic organizer on the previous page. Then answer the following questions about the passage you just read.

1. Does the author show a bias against any groups in medieval society?

2. What is the author's opinion about rich lords and prelates? Do you think his opinion is justified? Why or why not?

3. What stereotype about Crusaders does the writer include in the passage?

4. How do you think a Crusader would feel about this passage? Why?

As you read Chapter 18, notice how the authors of this book have avoided making stereotypes and expressing bias about European society and culture.

Key Terms and People

Academic Vocabulary

Success in school is related to knowing academic vocabulary— the words that are frequently used in school assignments and discussions. In this chapter, you will learn the following academic words:

authority (p. 526)
policy (p. 548)

Popes and Kings

If YOU were there...

You are 13 years old, the youngest child of the king of France. One day your father announces that he wants to make an alliance with a powerful noble family. To seal the alliance, he has arranged for you to marry one of his new ally's children. Your father wants you to be happy and asks what you think of the idea. You know the alliance will make your father's rule more secure, but it means leaving home to marry a stranger.

What will you say to your father?

BUILDING BACKGROUND In the Middle Ages, kings were some of the most powerful men in Europe. Many kings, like the one described above, looked for ways to increase their power. But in their search for power, these kings had to deal with other powerful leaders, including popes. These other leaders had their own plans and goals.

Popes and Kings Rule Europe

In the early Middle Ages, great nobles and their knights held a great deal of power. As time passed, though, this power began to shift. More and more, power came into the hands of two types of leaders, popes and kings. Popes had great spiritual power, and kings had political power. Together, popes and kings controlled most of European society.

The Power of the Popes

In the Middle Ages, the pope was the head of the Christian Church in Western Europe. Since nearly everyone in the Middle Ages belonged to this church, the pope had great power. People saw the pope as God's representative on Earth. They looked to him for guidance about how to live and pray.

Because the pope was seen as God's representative, it was his duty to decide what the church would teach. From time to time, a pope would write a letter called a bull to explain a religious teaching or outline a church policy. In addition, the pope decided when someone was acting against the church.

If the pope felt someone was working against the church, he could punish the person in many ways. For serious offenses, the pope or other bishops could choose to **excommunicate**, or cast out from the church, the offender. This punishment was deeply feared because Christians believed that a person who died while excommunicated would not get into heaven.

In addition to spiritual power, many popes had great political power. After the Roman Empire collapsed, many people in Italy looked to the pope as their leader. As a result, some popes began to live like royalty. They became rich and built huge palaces. At the same time, they came into conflict with Europe's other political leaders, kings.

The Power of Kings

As you can see on the map below, Europe in 1000 was divided into many small states. Most of these states were ruled by kings, some of whom had little real power. In a few places, though, kings had begun to take firm control of their countries. Look at the map to find England, France, and the Holy Roman Empire. At this time, Europe's most powerful kings ruled those three countries.

In England and France, kings inherited their thrones from their fathers. At times, nobles rebelled against the kings, but the kings usually reestablished order fairly quickly. They maintained this order through alliances as well as warfare.

THE IMPACT TODAY

Hundreds of millions of people around the world consider the pope their spiritual leader.

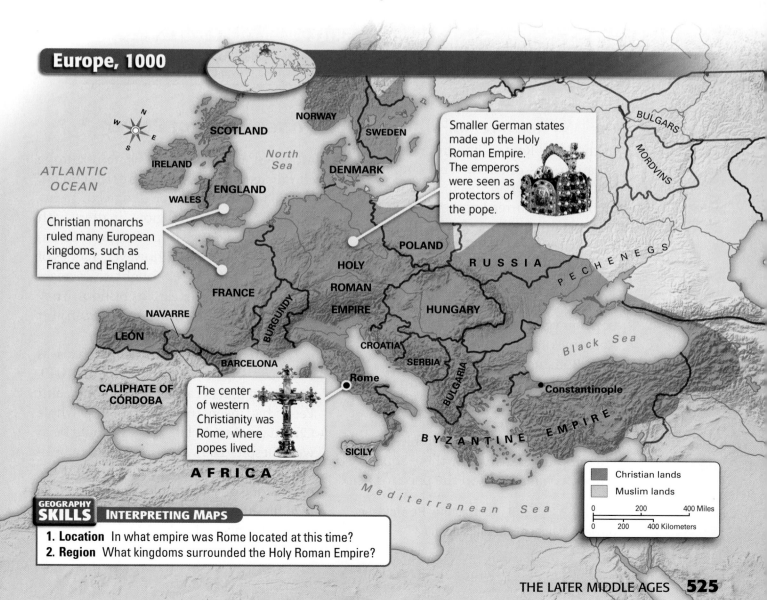

Europe, 1000

Christian monarchs ruled many European kingdoms, such as France and England.

Smaller German states made up the Holy Roman Empire. The emperors were seen as protectors of the pope.

The center of western Christianity was Rome, where popes lived.

NORWAY

SCOTLAND

SWEDEN

BULGARS

MORDVINS

IRELAND

North Sea

ATLANTIC OCEAN

DENMARK

ENGLAND

WALES

POLAND

HOLY

RUSSIA

PECHENEGS

FRANCE

ROMAN

EMPIRE

HUNGARY

NAVARRE

BURGUNDY

LEÓN

Black Sea

BARCELONA

CROATIA

CALIPHATE OF CÓRDOBA

Rome

SERBIA

BULGARIA

Constantinople

BYZANTINE EMPIRE

SICILY

AFRICA

Mediterranean Sea

Christian lands

Muslim lands

0   200   400 Miles

0   200   400 Kilometers

GEOGRAPHY SKILLS **INTERPRETING MAPS**

1. **Location** In what empire was Rome located at this time?
2. **Region** What kingdoms surrounded the Holy Roman Empire?

POINTS OF VIEW
Views of Power

Pope Gregory VII thought popes should have the power to choose bishops. He believed popes—not kings—got their power from God.

❝Who does not know that kings and princes derive their origin from men ignorant of God who raised themselves above their fellows by . . . every kind of crime? . . . Does anyone doubt that the priests of Christ are to be considered as fathers and masters of kings and princes and of all believers?❞

—**Pope Gregory VII,**
from a letter to the Bishop of Metz, 1081, in *Readings in Medieval History*, ed. by Patrick Geary

Emperor Henry IV thought popes had too much power. He argued that kings should choose bishops because God had chosen the king.

❝Our Lord, Jesus Christ, has called us to kingship, but has not called you to the priesthood . . . You who have not been called by God have taught that our bishops who have been called by God are to be [rejected] . . .❞

—**Emperor Henry IV,**
from a letter to Pope Gregory VII, 1076, in *Readings in Medieval History*, ed. by Patrick Geary

ANALYSIS SKILL **IDENTIFYING POINTS OF VIEW**

What words indicate Pope Gregory's view that the church has more power than monarchs do?

The Holy Roman Empire

In the Holy Roman Empire, however, the situation was different. This empire grew out of what had been Charlemagne's empire. As you read earlier, Charlemagne built his empire in the 700s with the pope's approval.

In the mid-900s, another emperor took the throne with the approval of the pope. Because the empire was approved by the pope and people saw it as a rebirth of the Roman Empire, it became known as the Holy Roman Empire.

Holy Roman emperors didn't inherit their crowns. Instead, they were elected by the empire's nobles. Sometimes, these elections led to fights between nobles and the emperor. In the worst of these squabbles, emperors had to call on the pope for help.

READING CHECK **Contrasting** How did the powers of popes and kings differ?

ACADEMIC VOCABULARY

authority power, right to rule

Popes Fight for Power

Although the people of western Europe considered the pope the head of the church, people in eastern Europe disagreed. There, bishops controlled religious matters with little or no guidance from the pope. Beginning in the mid-1000s, however, a series of clever and able popes sought to increase their **authority** over eastern bishops. They believed all religious officials should answer to the pope.

Among those who believed this was Pope Leo IX, who became pope in 1049. He argued that because the first pope, Saint Peter, had been the leader of the whole Christian Church, later popes should be as well. Despite Leo's arguments, many bishops in eastern Europe, most notably the bishop of Constantinople, wouldn't recognize his authority. In 1054, Leo decided to excommunicate that bishop.

Leo's decision created a permanent split within the church. Christians who agreed with the bishop of Constantinople formed the Orthodox Church. Those who supported Leo's authority became known as Roman Catholics. With their support, the pope became head of the Roman Catholic Church and one of the most powerful figures in western Europe.

READING CHECK **Generalizing** How did Leo IX try to increase popes' authority?

Kings and Popes Clash

As popes worked to increase their power, they often came into conflict with kings. For example, kings thought they should be able to select bishops in their countries. Popes, on the other hand, argued that only they could choose religious officials.

In 1073 a new pope came to power in Rome. His name was **Pope Gregory VII**. Trouble arose when Gregory disapproved of a bishop chosen by the Holy Roman **Emperor Henry IV**. Angry because the pope questioned his authority, Henry convinced Germany's bishops that they should remove Gregory as pope. In response, the pope excommunicated Henry. He called on the empire's nobles to overthrow Henry.

Desperate to stay in power, Henry went to Italy to ask the pope for forgiveness. Gregory refused to see him. For three days Henry stood barefoot in the snow outside the castle where Pope Gregory was staying. Eventually, Gregory accepted Henry's apology and allowed the emperor back into the church. Gregory had proven himself more powerful than the emperor, at least for that moment.

The fight over the right to choose bishops continued even after Henry and Gregory died. In 1122 a new pope and emperor reached a compromise. They decided that church officials would choose all bishops and abbots. The bishops and abbots, however, would still have to obey the emperor.

This compromise did not end all conflict. Kings and popes continued to fight for power throughout the Middle Ages, changing lives all over Europe.

READING CHECK **Identifying Causes and Effects** What caused Gregory and Henry's power struggle?

SUMMARY AND PREVIEW In this section you read about the powers of popes and kings. In many cases, these powers led to conflict between the two. In the next section, though, you will read about popes and kings working together against a common enemy.

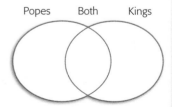

Section 1 Assessment

go.hrw.com
Online Quiz
KEYWORD: SN6 HP18

Reviewing Ideas, Terms, and People
1. **a. Describe** What was the pope's role in the Roman Catholic Church?
   b. Draw Conclusions How did cooperation with the pope help kings like Charlemagne and the early Holy Roman Emperors?
2. **Explain** Why did Pope Leo IX **excommunicate** the bishop of Constantinople?
3. **a. Identify** With whom did **Pope Gregory VII** clash?
   b. Elaborate Why do you think the pope made **Emperor Henry IV** wait for three days before forgiving him?

Critical Thinking
4. **Comparing** Draw a diagram like the one shown here. Use it and your notes to compare the power of popes to the power of kings.

Popes   Both   Kings

FOCUS ON WRITING

5. **Taking Notes on the Popes and Kings** Who were the popes and kings you read about in this section? Why were they important? Start a list of important people.

The Crusades

What You Will Learn...

Main Ideas

1. The pope called on Crusaders to invade the Holy Land.
2. Despite some initial success, the later Crusades failed.
3. The Crusades changed Europe forever.

The Big Idea

The Christian and Muslim cultures fought over holy sites during a series of medieval wars.

Key Terms and People

Crusades, *p. 528*
Holy Land, *p. 528*
Pope Urban II, *p. 528*
King Richard I, *p. 530*
Saladin, *p. 530*

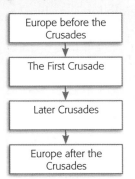

TAKING NOTES As you read, take notes on what happened in Europe before, during, and after the Crusades. Use a diagram like the one here to help you organize your notes.

Europe before the Crusades
↓
The First Crusade
↓
Later Crusades
↓
Europe after the Crusades

If YOU were there...

You belong to a noble family that has produced many great knights. One day your uncle, the head of the family, tells you that the pope has called on warriors to defend holy places in a faraway land. Your uncle is too old to fight, so it falls on you to answer the pope's call to war. The journey will be long and dangerous. Still, you will see new places and possibly win glory for your family.

How do you feel about joining this war?

BUILDING BACKGROUND In the early Middle Ages few people traveled far from home. They spent most of their lives in a single village or farm. As time passed, however, Europeans learned of other people and places. Their contacts with some of these people were peaceful. With others, though, the contact was not peaceful. Wars broke out. The most famous of these wars were the Crusades.

Crusaders Invade the Holy Land

The **Crusades** were a long series of wars between Christians and Muslims in Southwest Asia. They were fought over control of Palestine, a region of Southwest Asia. Europeans called Palestine the **Holy Land** because it was the region where Jesus had lived, preached, and died.

Causes of the Crusades

For many years, Palestine had been in the hands of Muslims. In general, the Muslims did not bother Christians who visited the region. In the late 1000s, though, a group of Turkish Muslims entered the area and captured the city of Jerusalem. Pilgrims returning to Europe said that these Turks had attacked them in the Holy Land, which was no longer safe for Christians.

Before long, the Turks began to raid the Byzantine Empire. The Byzantine emperor, fearing an attack on Constantinople, asked **Pope Urban II** of the Roman Catholic Church for help. Although the Byzantines were Orthodox Christians and not Catholic, the pope agreed to the request.

Crusader Battlefield

The Holy Land was the scene of many bloody battles during the Crusades, like the one near the city of Antioch shown in this medieval painting. The men at right show what Crusaders may have worn.

What was the goal of the Crusaders?

The Call to Arms

Pope Urban called on Christians from all over Europe to retake the Holy Land from the Muslim Turks. He challenged Europe's kings and nobles to quit fighting among themselves and fight together against the Turks. In response, people joined the pope's army by the thousands.

Crusaders from all over Europe flocked to France to prepare for their long journey. They sewed crosses onto their clothing to show that they were fighting for God. In fact, the word *crusade* comes from the Latin for "marked with a cross." As they marched off to war, the Crusaders yelled their rallying cry, "God wills it!"

Why would people leave home to fight in a distant land? Some just hoped to save their souls or to do what they thought God wanted. They thought that God would look favorably on them for fighting his enemies, as one French abbot noted:

"What a glory to return in victory from such a battle! . . . if they are blessed who die in the Lord, how much more are they who die for the Lord!"

—Saint Bernard of Clairvaux, from *In Praise of the New Knighthood*

Other Crusaders wanted land and treasure. Still others were looking for something to do. Adventure called to them.

The First Crusade

About 5,000 Crusaders left Europe for the Holy Land in 1096. Some of the first ones to set out were peasants, not soldiers. On their way to the Holy Land, these peasant Crusaders attacked Jews in Germany. They blamed the Jews for Jesus's death.

Before they even reached the Holy Land, Turkish troops killed most of these untrained, poorly equipped peasants.

The nobles and knights fared better. When they reached Jerusalem in 1099, they found the Muslim army disorganized and unready to fight. After about a month of fighting, the Crusaders took Jerusalem.

After the Europeans took Jerusalem, they set up four small kingdoms in the Holy Land. The rulers of these kingdoms created lord and vassal systems like they had known at home. They also began to trade with people back in Europe.

READING CHECK **Summarizing** What did the First Crusade accomplish?

Later Crusades Fail

The kingdoms the Christians created in the Holy Land didn't last, though. Within 50 years the Muslims had started taking land back from the Christians. In response, the Europeans launched more Crusades.

The Second and Third Crusades

French and German kings set off in 1147 to retake land from the Muslims. This Second Crusade was a terrible failure. Poor planning and heavy losses on the journey to the Holy Land led to the Christians' total defeat. Ashamed, the Crusaders returned to Europe in less than a year.

The Third Crusade began after the Muslims retook Jerusalem in 1189. The rulers of England, France, and the Holy Roman Empire led their armies to the Holy Land to fight for Jerusalem, but problems soon arose. The German king died, and the French king left. Only **King Richard I** of England stayed in the Holy Land.

King Richard's main opponent in the Third Crusade was **Saladin**, the leader of the Muslim forces. Saladin was a brilliant

BIOGRAPHY

Richard I
1157–1199

Called "Lion Heart" for his courage, Richard I was a skilled soldier and a great general. He did not succeed in taking Jerusalem during the Third Crusade, but he earned the respect of Muslims and Christians alike. Since his death, he has become the hero of countless stories and legends.

ATLANTIC OCEAN

leader. Even Crusaders respected his kindness toward fallen enemies. In turn, the Muslims admired Richard's bravery.

For months, Richard and Saladin fought and negotiated. Richard captured a few towns and won protection for Christian pilgrims. In the end, however, he returned home with Jerusalem still in Muslim hands.

The Fourth Crusade

In 1201 French knights arrived in Venice ready to sail to the Holy Land to begin a Fourth Crusade. However, the knights didn't have money to pay for the voyage. For payment the Venetians asked the knights to conquer Zara, a rival trade city. The knights agreed. Later they also attacked Constantinople and carried off many treasures. The city that had been threatened by Muslims before the Crusades had been sacked by Christians!

The End of the Crusades

Other Crusades followed, but none was successful. By 1291 the Muslim armies had taken back all of the Holy Land, and the

The Major Crusades, 1096–1204

★ Interactive Map

N W E S

North Sea

ENGLAND

Dover

HOLY ROMAN EMPIRE

Paris

Vézelay

Regensburg

Vienna

Lyon

Clermont

Trieste

Venice

Genoa

Marseille

Zadar

Corsica

Rome

Sardinia

Mediterranean Sea

Black Sea

Constantinople

SELJUK TURKS

BYZANTINE EMPIRE

Sicily

Crete

Edessa

Antioch

Tripoli

HOLY LAND

Acre

Jerusalem

BIOGRAPHY

Saladin
1137–1193

Saladin is often called one of the greatest generals of the Middle Ages. The Muslim leader successfully held Jerusalem against Richard I in the Third Crusade. Saladin's people considered their leader a wise ruler. Crusaders respected his sometimes kind treatment of fallen enemies. Many Christians saw him as a model of knightly chivalry.

Legend:
- Western Christian lands, 1095
- Eastern Christian lands, 1095
- Islamic lands, 1095
- First Crusade, 1096–1099
- Second Crusade, 1147–1149
- Third Crusade, 1189–1192
- Fourth Crusade, 1201–1204

0   100   200 Miles
0   100   200 Kilometers

GEOGRAPHY SKILLS INTERPRETING MAPS

1. **Place** From which countries did the first three Crusades start out?
2. **Movement** About how far was the journey from Paris to Jerusalem?

Crusades had ended. Why did the Crusades fail? There were many reasons.

- The Crusaders had to travel huge distances just to reach the war. Many died along the way.
- Crusaders weren't prepared to fight in Palestine's desert climate.
- The Christians were outnumbered by their well-led and organized Muslim foes.

- Christian leaders fought among themselves and planned poorly.

Whatever the reasons for their failure, the Crusades ended just as they had begun so many years before, with the Holy Land under Muslim control.

READING CHECK Analyzing How did geography limit the success of the Crusades?

Crusades Change Europe

FOCUS ON READING

How might stereotype and bias have affected Christian and Muslim relationships?

Although the Crusades failed, they changed Europe forever. Trade between Europe and Asia grew. Europeans who went to the Holy Land learned about products such as apricots, rice, and cotton cloth. Crusaders also brought ideas of Muslim thinkers to Europe.

Politics in Europe also changed. Some kings increased their power because many nobles and knights had died in the Holy Land. These kings seized lands that were left without clear owners. During the later Crusades, kings also gained influence at the popes' expense. The popes had wanted the church to be in charge of all the Crusades. Instead, rulers and nobles took control.

The Crusades had lasting effects on relations among peoples as well. Because some Crusaders had attacked Jews, many Jews distrusted Christians. In addition, tension between the Byzantines and western Christians increased, especially after Crusaders attacked Constantinople.

The greatest changes occurred with Christian and Muslim relationships. Each group learned about the other's religion and culture. Sometimes this led to mutual respect. In general, though, the Crusaders saw Muslims as unbelievers who threatened innocent Christians. Most Muslims viewed the Crusaders as vicious invaders. Some historians think that the distrust that began during the Crusades still affects Christian and Muslim relationships today.

READING CHECK **Finding Main Ideas** What were some results of the Crusades?

SUMMARY AND PREVIEW In this section you learned how religious beliefs led to a series of wars. In the next section you will learn about the role of religion in most people's daily lives in the Middle Ages.

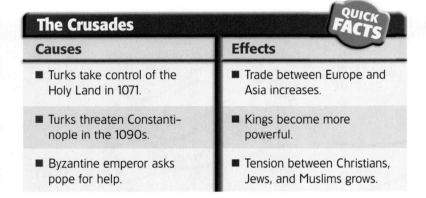

The Crusades QUICK FACTS

Causes	Effects
■ Turks take control of the Holy Land in 1071.	■ Trade between Europe and Asia increases.
■ Turks threaten Constantinople in the 1090s.	■ Kings become more powerful.
■ Byzantine emperor asks pope for help.	■ Tension between Christians, Jews, and Muslims grows.

Section 2 Assessment

Reviewing Ideas, Terms, and People

1. a. Recall What did **Pope Urban II** ask Christians to do?
   b. Elaborate Why do you think so many people were willing to go on a Crusade?
2. a. Identify In which Crusade did **Saladin** and **King Richard I** fight?
   b. Rank Which Crusade do you think was the least successful? Why?
3. a. Identify What new products were introduced to Europe after the Crusades?
   b. Draw Conclusions Why did the Crusades change relationships between Christians and other groups?

Critical Thinking

4. Comparing and Contrasting Draw a diagram like the one here. Use it and your notes to compare and contrast Europe before and after the Crusades.

Europe Before		Europe After
1. 2. 3.	The Crusades	1. 2. 3.

go.hrw.com
Online Quiz
KEYWORD: SN6 HP18

FOCUS ON WRITING

5. Thinking about the Crusades Look back through what you've just read and make a list of people who were important in the Crusades. What made them important?

Christianity and Medieval Society

If YOU were there...

You are a stone carver, apprenticed to a master builder. The bishop has hired your master to design a huge new church. He wants the church to inspire and impress worshippers with the glory of God. Your master has entrusted you with the decoration of the outside of the church. You are excited by the challenge.

What kind of art will you create for the church?

BUILDING BACKGROUND Thousands of churches were built across Europe in the Middle Ages. People took great pride in their churches because religion was very important to them. In fact, Christianity was a key factor in shaping medieval society.

The Church Shapes Society and Politics

Nearly everyone who lived in Europe during the Middle Ages was Christian. In fact, Christianity was central to every part of life. Church officials, called **clergy**, and their teachings were very influential in European culture and politics.

The towers of old Christian churches still rise above many European towns and cities. Christianity became a strong influence on European life in the Middle Ages.

What You Will Learn...

Main Ideas

1. The Christian Church shaped both society and politics in medieval Europe.
2. Orders of monks and friars did not like the church's political nature.
3. Church leaders helped build the first universities in Europe.
4. The church influenced the arts in medieval Europe.

The Big Idea

The Christian Church was central to life in the Middle Ages.

Key Terms and People

clergy, *p. 533*
religious order, *p. 536*
Francis of Assisi, *p. 536*
friars, *p. 536*
Thomas Aquinas, *p. 537*
natural law, *p. 538*

TAKING NOTES As you read, take notes on the many roles the Catholic Church played in Europe in the Middle Ages. Organize your notes in a chart like this one.

The Church in the Middle Ages

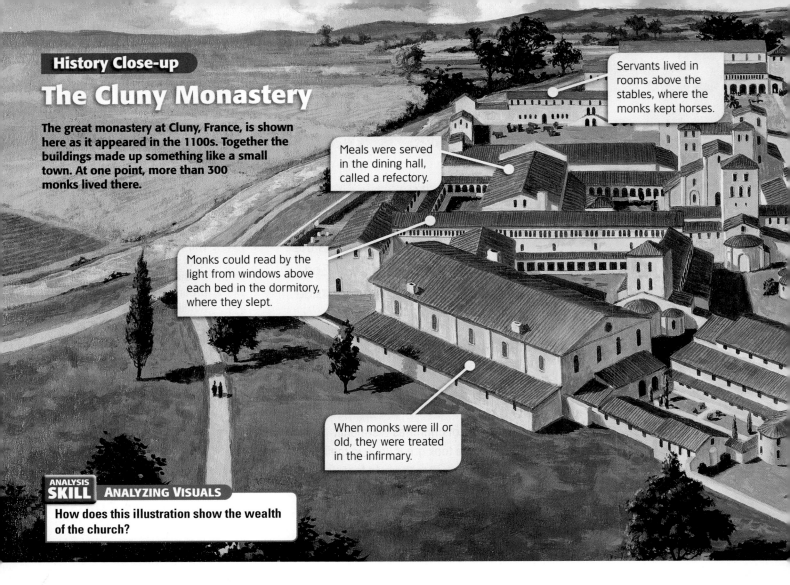

The Cluny Monastery

The great monastery at Cluny, France, is shown here as it appeared in the 1100s. Together the buildings made up something like a small town. At one point, more than 300 monks lived there.

Servants lived in rooms above the stables, where the monks kept horses.

Meals were served in the dining hall, called a refectory.

Monks could read by the light from windows above each bed in the dormitory, where they slept.

When monks were ill or old, they were treated in the infirmary.

ANALYSIS SKILL ANALYZING VISUALS

How does this illustration show the wealth of the church?

The Church and Society

In the Middle Ages, life revolved around the local church. Markets, festivals, and religious ceremonies all took place there.

For some people, however, the local church was not enough. They wanted to see important religious sites—the places where Jesus lived, where holy men and women died, and where miracles happened. The church encouraged these people to go on pilgrimages, journeys to religious locations. Among the most popular destinations were Jerusalem, Rome, and Compostela, in northwestern Spain. Each of these cities had churches that Christians wanted to visit.

Another popular pilgrimage destination was Canterbury, near London in England. Hundreds of visitors went to the cathedral in Canterbury each year. One such visit is the basis for one of the greatest books of the Middle Ages, *The Canterbury Tales* by Geoffrey Chaucer (CHAW-suhr). Chaucer's book tells of a group of pilgrims who feel drawn, like many people, to Canterbury:

"When in April the sweet showers fall
And pierce the drought of March to the root . . .
Then people long to go on pilgrimages
And palmers long to seek the stranger strands
Of far-off saints, hallowed in sundry lands
And specially, from every shire's end
Of England, down to Canterbury they wend."
—Geoffrey Chaucer, from *The Canterbury Tales*

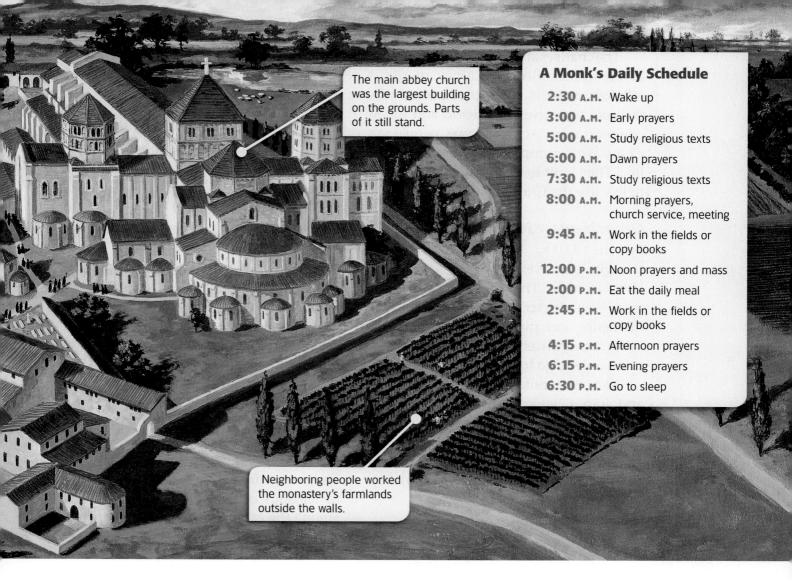

The main abbey church was the largest building on the grounds. Parts of it still stand.

A Monk's Daily Schedule

2:30 A.M.	Wake up
3:00 A.M.	Early prayers
5:00 A.M.	Study religious texts
6:00 A.M.	Dawn prayers
7:30 A.M.	Study religious texts
8:00 A.M.	Morning prayers, church service, meeting
9:45 A.M.	Work in the fields or copy books
12:00 P.M.	Noon prayers and mass
2:00 P.M.	Eat the daily meal
2:45 P.M.	Work in the fields or copy books
4:15 P.M.	Afternoon prayers
6:15 P.M.	Evening prayers
6:30 P.M.	Go to sleep

Neighboring people worked the monastery's farmlands outside the walls.

The Church and Politics

The church also gained political power during the Middle Ages. Many people left land to the church when they died. In fact, the church was one of the largest landholders in Europe. Eventually, the church divided this land into fiefs. In this way, it became a feudal lord.

Of all the clergy, bishops and abbots were most involved in political matters. They often advised local rulers. Some clergy got so involved with politics that they spent little time dealing with religious affairs.

READING CHECK **Analyzing** In what ways were clergy members important political figures?

Monks and Friars

Some people were unhappy with the political nature of the church. They thought the clergy should focus only on spiritual matters. These people feared that the church had become obsessed with wealth and power.

The Monks of Cluny

Among those unhappy with the church were a group of French monks. In the early 900s they started a monastery in the town of Cluny (KLOO-nee). The monks of Cluny followed a strict schedule of prayers and religious services. They paid little attention to the world, concerning themselves only with religious matters.

The changes at Cluny led to the creation of a religious order, the Cluniac monks. A **religious order** is a group of people who dedicate their lives to religion and follow common rules. Across Europe, people saw Cluny as an example of how monks should live. They built new monasteries and tried to live like the Cluniacs.

Other New Orders

By the 1100s, though, some monks thought that even Cluny's rules weren't strict enough. They created new orders with even stricter rules. Some took vows of silence and stopped speaking to each other. Others lived in tiny rooms and left them only to go to church services.

Men were not the only ones to create and join religious orders. Women were allowed to join these kinds of orders as well. Communities of nuns called convents appeared across Europe. Like monks, these nuns lived according to a strict set of rules. The nuns of each convent prayed and worked together under the watchful eyes of an abbess, the convent's leader.

Although monks and nuns lived apart from other people, they did a great deal for society. For example, they collected and stored texts that explained Christian teachings. Monks spent hours copying these documents, and they sent copies to monasteries across Europe.

The Friars

Not everyone who joined a religious order wanted to live apart from society. Some wanted to live in cities and spread Christian teachings. As a result, two new religious orders were begun in the early 1200s.

These orders were the Dominicans and the Franciscans, named for their founders, Dominic de Guzmán and **Francis of Assisi**. Because they didn't live in monasteries, members of these orders were not monks. They were **friars**, people who belonged to religious orders but lived and worked among the general public.

Friars lived simply, wearing plain robes and no shoes. Like monks, they owned no property. They roamed about, preaching and begging for food. For that reason, friars were also called mendicants, from a Latin word for beggars.

The main goal of the friars was to teach people how to live good Christian lives. They taught people about generosity and kindness. A prayer credited to Francis illustrates what the friars hoped to do:

"Lord, make me an instrument of your peace. Where there is hatred, let me sow love; where there is injury, pardon; where there is doubt, faith; where there is despair, hope; where there is darkness, light; and where there is sadness, joy."

–Francis of Assisi, from *The Prayer of Saint Francis*

READING CHECK Summarizing Why did people create new religious orders?

BIOGRAPHY

Saint Francis of Assisi
c. 1182–1226

Born in Assisi, Italy, Francis was the son of a wealthy merchant. As a young man, however, Francis gave all his money and possessions away and left his father's house. He lived a simple life, preaching and tending to people who were poor or ill. Francis considered everyone his brother or sister, including animals. He encouraged people to take care of animals just as they would take care of other people. Within a few years other people had begun to copy his lifestyle. In 1210 they became the first members of the Franciscan Order.

Making Generalizations How do you think Francis's generosity and compassion might inspire Christians to follow the church's teachings?

School Days

Did you know that many customs that schools and universities follow today began in the Middle Ages? For example, medieval teachers taught groups of students instead of individuals. Classes ran according to a fixed schedule, and students had to take tests. At night, students went to their rooms to study and complete assignments. Many students participated in sports such as races and ball games after classes. At graduation, students dressed up in caps and gowns. All of these customs are still common today.

Medieval universities were not exactly the same as universities are now, however. Medieval students entered the university at age 14, and only boys could attend.

ANALYSIS SKILL | **ANALYZING INFORMATION**

Why do you think some customs followed by universities in the Middle Ages have lasted until today?

Universities Are Built

While some people were drawing away from the world in monasteries and convents, others were looking for ways to learn more about it. In time, their search for knowledge led to the creation of Europe's first universities.

Some of the earliest universities were created by the church. The church's goal was to teach people about religion. Other universities were created by groups of students who went searching for teachers who could tell them about the world.

Most teachers in these universities were members of the clergy. Besides religion, schools taught law, medicine, astronomy, and other courses. All classes were taught in Latin. Although relatively few people in Europe spoke Latin, it was the language of scholars and the church.

As people began to study new subjects, some of them developed new ideas about the world. In particular, they wondered how human reason and Christian faith were related. In the past, people had believed that some things could be proven with reason, but other things had to be taken on faith. Some people in universities, though, began to wonder if the two ideas could work together.

One such person was the Dominican philosopher **Thomas Aquinas** (uh-KWY-nuhs). Thomas was a teacher at the University of Paris. He argued that rational thought could be used to support Christian beliefs. For example, he wrote an argument to prove the existence of God.

Thomas also believed that God had created a law that governed how the world operated. He called it **natural law**. If people could study and learn more about this law, he argued, they could learn to live the way God wanted.

READING CHECK **Generalizing** How did universities help create new ideas?

The Church and the Arts

In addition to politics and education, the church was also a strong influence on art and architecture. Throughout the Middle Ages, religious feeling inspired artists and architects to create beautiful works of art.

Religious Architecture

Many of Europe's churches were incredible works of art. The grandest of these churches were cathedrals, large churches in which bishops led religious services. Beginning in the 1100s Europeans built their cathedrals using a dramatic new style called Gothic architecture.

Gothic cathedrals were not only places to pray, but also symbols of people's faith.

Gothic Architecture

One of the most beautiful of all Gothic cathedrals is in Chartres (SHAHRT), near Paris, France. At 112 feet high it is about as tall as a 10-story building.

As a result, they were towering works of great majesty and glory.

What made these Gothic churches so unusual? For one thing, they were much taller than older churches. The walls often rose up hundreds of feet, and the ceilings seemed to reach to heaven. Huge windows of stained glass let sunlight pour in, filling the churches with dazzling colors. Many of these amazing churches still exist. People continue to worship in them and admire their beauty.

Religious Art

Medieval churches were also filled with beautiful objects created to show respect for God. Ornate paintings and tapestries covered the walls and ceilings. Even the clothing priests wore during religious services was attractive. Their robes were often highly decorated, sometimes with threads made out of gold.

Many of the books used during religious ceremonies were beautiful objects. Monks had copied these books carefully.

BIOGRAPHY

Saint Thomas Aquinas
1225–1274

Though he was born in Italy, Thomas Aquinas lived most of his life in France. As a student and then a teacher at the University of Paris, Thomas spent most of his time in study.

He wrote a book called the *Summa Theologica*, in which he argued that science and religion were related.

Although some people did not like Thomas's ideas, most considered him the greatest thinker of the Middle Ages. Later teachers modeled their lessons after his ideas.

Making Generalizations Why might people believe someone is a great thinker even if they disagree with his or her ideas?

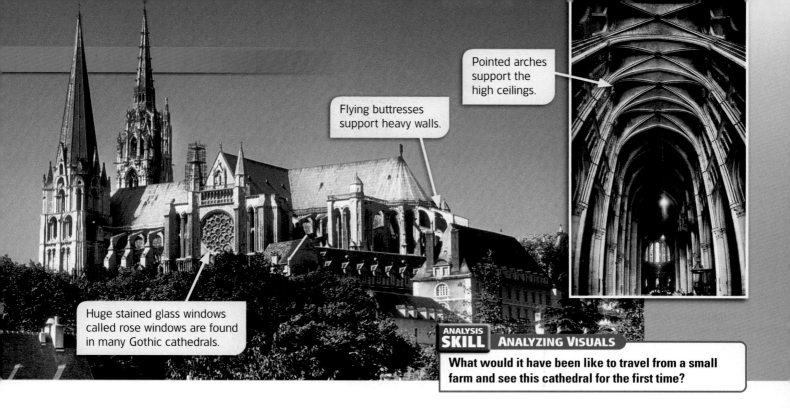

Pointed arches support the high ceilings.

Flying buttresses support heavy walls.

Huge stained glass windows called rose windows are found in many Gothic cathedrals.

ANALYSIS SKILL **ANALYZING VISUALS**

What would it have been like to travel from a small farm and see this cathedral for the first time?

They also decorated them using bright colors to adorn the first letters and the borders of each page. Some monks added thin sheets of silver and gold to the pages. Because the pages seem to glow, we use the word *illuminated* to describe them.

READING CHECK **Generalizing** How were medieval art and religion related?

SUMMARY AND PREVIEW Besides its religious role, the church played important roles in politics, education, and the arts. The church changed as time passed. In the next section, you will learn about other changes that took place in Europe at the same time. These changes created new political systems around the continent.

Section 3 Assessment

go.hrw.com
Online Quiz
KEYWORD: SN6 HP18

Reviewing Ideas, Terms, and People

1. **a. Recall** What are church officials called?
   b. Explain Why did people go on pilgrimages?
2. **a. Identify** What new monastery founded in France in the 900s served as an example to people around Europe?
   b. Contrast How were **friars** different from monks?
3. **Analyze** How did **Thomas Aquinas** think reason and faith could work together?
4. **a. Identify** What new style of religious architecture developed in Europe in the 1100s?
   b. Elaborate Why do you think so much of the art created in the Middle Ages was religious?

Critical Thinking

5. **Categorizing** Draw a chart like the one below. Using your notes, decide which of the church's roles were political,

The Church in the Middle Ages		
Political	Intellectual	Artistic

   which were intellectual, and which were artistic. List each role in the appropriate column of your chart.

FOCUS ON WRITING

6. **Taking Notes on Church Leaders** In this section, you've read about at least two people who became saints. Add them to your list and note why they're important.

Political and Social Change

What You Will Learn...

Main Ideas

1. Magna Carta caused changes in England's government and legal system.
2. The Hundred Years' War led to political changes in England and France.
3. The Black Death, which swept through Europe in the Middle Ages, led to social changes.

The Big Idea

Europe's political and social systems underwent great changes in the late Middle Ages.

Key Terms and People

Magna Carta, *p. 540*
Parliament, *p. 541*
Hundred Years' War, *p. 542*
Joan of Arc, *p. 542*
Black Death, *p. 543*

TAKING NOTES As you read, take notes on the major events of the later Middle Ages and the political and social changes surrounding them. Use a diagram like this one to help you organize your notes.

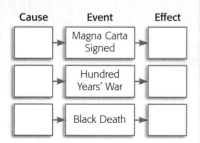

Cause	Event	Effect
	Magna Carta Signed	
	Hundred Years' War	
	Black Death	

If YOU were there...

You are a baron, one of England's great nobles, living in northern Britain. Winter is approaching, and it looks like it will be very cold soon. To prepare for the winter, you send some of your servants to a forest on your land to gather firewood. When they return, though, they don't have much wood. The king has chopped down many of the trees in your forest to build a new castle. Dismayed, you send a messenger to ask the king to pay a fair price for the wood, but he refuses.

How can you get the king to respect your rights?

BUILDING BACKGROUND Beginning with William the Conqueror, the kings of England fought to increase their power. By the 1200s, the kings felt that they could do as they pleased, whether their nobles agreed with them or not. The kings' attitudes upset many nobles, especially when kings began to create new taxes or take the nobles' property. Some nobles began to look for ways to limit kings' powers and protect their own rights.

Magna Carta Causes Change in England

In 1215 a group of nobles decided to force the king to respect their rights. In the middle of a field called Runnymede near London, they made King John approve a document they had written. This document listing rights that the king could not ignore was called **Magna Carta**. Its name is a Latin phrase meaning "Great Charter."

William the Conqueror

HISTORIC DOCUMENT
Magna Carta

Magna Carta was one of the first documents to protect the rights of the people. Magna Carta was so influential that the British still consider it part of their constitution. Some of its ideas are also in the U.S. Constitution. Included in Magna Carta were 63 demands that English nobles made King John agree to follow. A few of these demands are listed here.

Demand 31 defended people's right to own any property, not just wood.

Magna Carta guaranteed that everyone had the right to a fair trial.

To all free men of our kingdom we have also granted, for us and our heirs for ever, all the liberties written out below, to have and to keep for them and their heirs, of us and our heirs.

(16) No man shall be forced to perform more service for a knight's 'fee', or other free holding of land, than is due from it.

(31) Neither we nor any royal official will take wood for our castle, or for any other purpose, without the consent [permission] of the owner.

(38) In future no official shall place a man on trial upon his own unsupported statement, without producing credible [believable] witnesses to the truth of it.

—Magna Carta, from a translation by the British Library

ANALYSIS SKILL **ANALYZING PRIMARY SOURCES**

In what ways do you think the ideas listed above influenced modern democracy?

The Effects of Magna Carta

Magna Carta required the king to honor certain rights. Among these rights was habeas corpus (HAY-bee-uhs KOHR-puhs), a Latin phrase meaning "you have the body." The right of habeas corpus meant that people could not be kept in jail without a reason. They had to be charged with a crime and convicted at a jury trial before they could be sent to prison. Before, kings could arrest people for no reason at all.

More importantly, Magna Carta required that everyone—even the king—had to obey the law. The idea that everyone must follow the law became one of the basic principles of English government.

Changes after Magna Carta

Magna Carta inspired the English to find more ways to limit the king's power. A council of nobles was created to advise the king. In time, the council developed into **Parliament** (PAHR-luh-muhnt), the law-making body that governs England today. Over the years, membership in Parliament was opened to knights and town leaders. By the late Middle Ages, kings could do little without Parliament's support.

The English continued to work to secure and protect their rights. To ensure that everyone was treated fairly, people demanded that judges be free of royal control. Many people believed judges chosen by the king would always side with him. Eventually, in the late 1600s, the king agreed to free the courts of his control. This creation of an independent judicial system was a key step in bringing democracy to England.

READING CHECK **Summarizing** How did Magna Carta and Parliament limit the king's power?

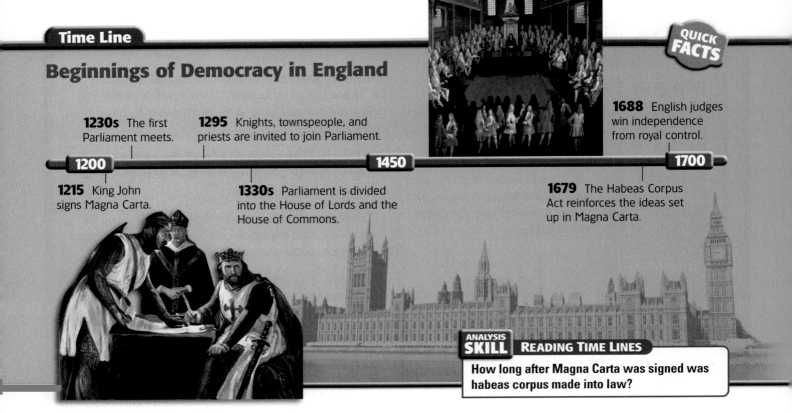

Beginnings of Democracy in England

1230s The first Parliament meets.

1295 Knights, townspeople, and priests are invited to join Parliament.

1688 English judges win independence from royal control.

1200

1450

1700

1215 King John signs Magna Carta.

1330s Parliament is divided into the House of Lords and the House of Commons.

1679 The Habeas Corpus Act reinforces the ideas set up in Magna Carta.

ANALYSIS SKILL **READING TIME LINES**

How long after Magna Carta was signed was habeas corpus made into law?

THE IMPACT TODAY

Joan of Arc is still a national hero in France.

The Hundred Years' War

Although Magna Carta changed England's government, it had no effect outside of that country. Kings in other parts of Europe continued to rule as they always had. Eventually, however, these kings also had to face great political changes.

The Course of the War

One of the countries in which political change occurred was France. In 1328 the king of France died with no sons, and two men claimed his throne. One was French. The other was the king of England. In the end, the French man became king.

This did not sit well with the English king, and a few years later he invaded France. This invasion began a long conflict between England and France that came to be called the **Hundred Years' War**.

At first the English armies did well, winning most of the battles. After nearly 100 years of fighting, however, a teenage peasant girl, **Joan of Arc**, rallied the French troops. Although the English eventually captured and killed Joan, it was too late. The French drove the English from their country in 1453.

Results of the War

The Hundred Years' War changed the governments of both England and France. In England, Parliament's power grew because the king needed Parliament's approval to raise money to pay for the costly war. As Parliament gained more influence, the king lost power.

In France, on the other hand, the king's power grew. During the war, the king had become popular with his nobles. Fighting the English had created a bond between them. As a result, the nobles supported the king after the war as well.

READING CHECK **Contrasting** How did the governments of England and France change after the war?

The Black Death

While the English and French fought the Hundred Years' War, an even greater crisis arose. This crisis was the **Black Death**, a deadly plague that swept through Europe between 1347 and 1351.

The plague originally came from central and eastern Asia. Unknowingly, traders brought rats carrying the disease to Mediterranean ports in 1347. From there it quickly swept throughout much of Europe. Fleas that feasted on the blood of infected rats passed on the plague to people.

The Black Death was not caused by one disease but by several different forms of plague. One form called bubonic plague (byoo-BAH-nik PLAYG) could be identified by swellings called buboes that appeared on victims' bodies. Another even deadlier form could spread through the air and kill people in less than a day.

The Black Death killed so many people that many were buried quickly without priests or ceremonies. In some villages nearly everyone died or fled as neighbors fell ill. In England alone, about 1,000 villages were abandoned.

The plague killed millions of people in Europe and millions more around the world. Some historians think Europe lost about a third of its population—perhaps 25 million people. This huge drop in population caused sweeping changes in Europe.

In most places, the manor system fell apart completely. There weren't enough people left to work in the fields. Those peasants and serfs who had survived the plague found their skills in high demand. Suddenly, they could demand wages for their labor. Once they had money, many fled their manors completely, moving instead to Europe's growing cities.

READING CHECK **Identifying Cause and Effect** What effects did bubonic plague have in Europe?

SUMMARY AND PREVIEW Magna Carta, the Hundred Years' War, and the Black Death changed European society. In the next section, you will learn about other changes in society, changes brought about by religious differences.

Section 4 Assessment

Reviewing Ideas, Terms, and People

1. **a. Identify** What document did English nobles hope would limit the king's power?
   b. Explain How was the creation of **Parliament** a step toward the creation of democracy in England?
2. **a. Identify** Who rallied the French troops during the **Hundred Years' War**?
   b. Elaborate The Hundred Years' War caused much more damage in France than in England. Why do you think this was the case?
3. **a. Describe** What was the **Black Death**?
   b. Explain How did the Black Death contribute to the decline of the manor system?
   c. Elaborate Why do you think the Black Death was able to spread so quickly through Europe?

Critical Thinking

4. **Evaluating** Copy the diagram below. Use it to rank the significance of the effects of Magna Carta, the Hundred Years' War, and the Black Death. Next to the diagram, write a sentence to explain your choices.

   Most Significant
   1.
   2.
   3.
   Least Significant

FOCUS ON WRITING

5. **Rating Importance** After reading this section, you'll probably want to add King John to your list. You should also start to think about which people were the most important. Rank the people on your list from most to least important.

The Black Death

"And they died by the hundreds," wrote one man who saw the horror, "both day and night." The Black Death had arrived. The Black Death was a series of deadly plagues that hit Europe between 1347 and 1351, killing millions. People didn't know what caused the plague. They also didn't know that geography played a key role in its spread—as people traveled to trade, they unwittingly carried the disease with them to new places.

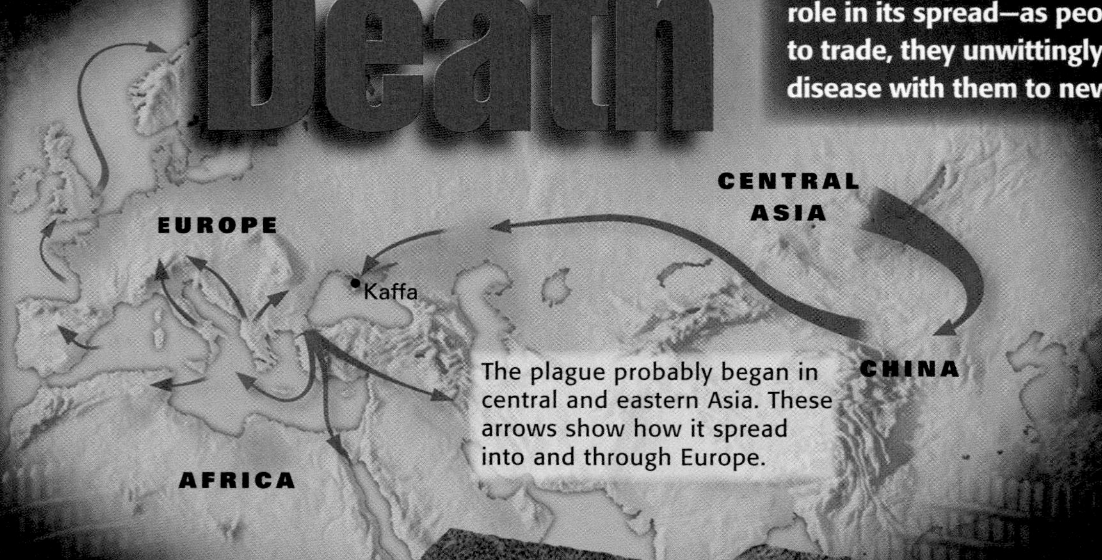

EUROPE

CENTRAL ASIA

CHINA

•Kaffa

AFRICA

The plague probably began in central and eastern Asia. These arrows show how it spread into and through Europe.

This ship has just arrived in Europe from the east with trade goods—and rats with fleas.

The fleas carry the plague and jump onto a man unloading the ship. Soon, he will get sick and die.

The plague is so terrifying that many people think it's the end of the world. They leave town for the country, spreading the Black Death even farther.

People dig mass graves to bury the dead. But often, so many victims are infected that there is no one left to bury them.

The garbage and dirty conditions in the town provide food and a home for the rats, allowing the disease to spread even more.

So many people die so quickly that special carts are sent through the streets to gather the bodies.

GEOGRAPHY SKILLS **INTERPRETING MAPS**

1. How did the Black Death reach Europe from Asia?
2. What helped spread the plague within Europe?

Challenges to Church Authority

Main Ideas

1. The church reacted to challengers by punishing people who opposed its teachings.
2. Christians fought Moors in Spain and Portugal in an effort to drive all Muslims out of Europe.
3. Jews faced discrimination across Europe in the Middle Ages.

The Big Idea

In the Middle Ages, the Christian Church dealt harshly with people who did not respect its authority.

Key Terms and People

heresy, *p. 546*
Reconquista, *p. 547*
King Ferdinand, *p. 548*
Queen Isabella, *p. 548*
Spanish Inquisition, *p. 548*

TAKING NOTES As you read, look for information about groups of people who challenged the authority of the Catholic Church or were seen as the church's enemies. Use a diagram like the one below to help you organize your notes.

Challengers

If YOU were there...

You are a student at a university in Córdoba, Spain. Your fellow students include Christians, Muslims, and Jews. But a new king and queen want all Muslims and Jews to leave Spain.

How will the rulers' decision affect your friends?

BUILDING BACKGROUND As you have read, most Europeans in the Middle Ages belonged to the Catholic Church. As Christianity spread in Europe, many Jews and Muslims were pressured to become Christian or leave their homes. At the same time, others openly challenged the church's authority.

The Church Reacts to Challengers

By around 1100, some Christians had begun to question church teachings. They felt that the clergy focused more on money and land than on God. Others didn't agree with the church's ideas. They began to preach their own ideas about religion.

Religious ideas that oppose accepted church teachings are called **heresy** (HER-uh-see). People who hold such ideas are called heretics. Church officials sent priests and friars throughout Europe to find possible heretics. Most of these priests and friars tried to be fair. A few tortured people until they confessed to heresy, even if they were innocent. Most people found guilty in these trials were fined or put in prison. Others were killed.

In the early 1200s, Pope Innocent III decided that heresy was too great a threat to ignore. He called a crusade against heretics in southern France. With this call, the pope encouraged the king of France and his knights to rid their country of heretics. The result was a bloody war that lasted about 20 years. The war destroyed towns and cost thousands of people their lives.

READING CHECK **Finding Main Ideas** How did church leaders try to fight heresy?

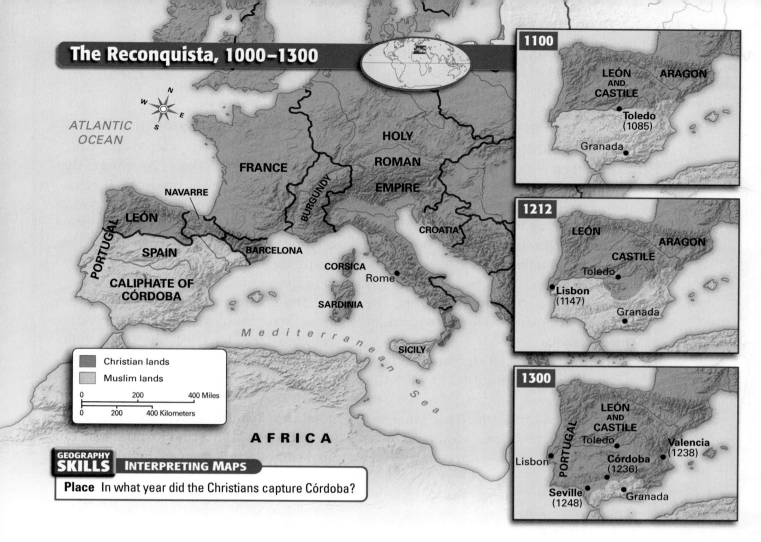

The Reconquista, 1000–1300

ATLANTIC OCEAN

FRANCE

HOLY ROMAN EMPIRE

NAVARRE

LEÓN

PORTUGAL

SPAIN

BARCELONA

CALIPHATE OF CÓRDOBA

CROATIA

CORSICA

Rome

SARDINIA

Mediterranean Sea

SICILY

AFRICA

Christian lands
Muslim lands

0   200   400 Miles
0   200   400 Kilometers

1100
LEÓN AND CASTILE
ARAGON
Toledo (1085)
Granada

1212
LEÓN
ARAGON
CASTILE
Toledo
Lisbon (1147)
Granada

1300
LEÓN AND CASTILE
PORTUGAL
Toledo
Valencia (1238)
Lisbon
Córdoba (1236)
Seville (1248)
Granada

GEOGRAPHY SKILLS **INTERPRETING MAPS**

Place In what year did the Christians capture Córdoba?

Christians Fight the Moors

France was not the only place where Christians fought people they saw as the church's enemies. In Spain and Portugal, armed Christian warriors fought to drive the Muslim Moors out of their lands.

The Weakening of Muslim Control

By the late 900s the once powerful Muslim government of Spain had begun to weaken. Political and religious leaders fought each other for power. Various ethnic groups also fought each other.

In 1002 the Muslim government fell apart completely. Caught up in fighting among themselves, Muslim leaders were too busy to guard against the Christian kingdoms of northern Spain.

The Fight against the Moors

For centuries, the kingdoms of northern Spain had been small and weak. But as the Moors' power declined, these little Christian kingdoms seized the opportunity to attack. Slowly, they took land away from the Moors. They called their efforts to retake Spain from the Moors the **Reconquista** (reh-kahn-KEES-tuh), or reconquest.

In 1085 Castile (ka-STEEL), the largest of the Spanish kingdoms, won a great victory against the Moors. The Castilian victory inspired other Christian kingdoms to fight the Moors. The kingdoms of Aragon and Portugal soon joined the fight.

The Christian armies won victory after victory. By the 1250s, the victorious Christian armies had nearly pushed the Moors completely out of Europe.

THE IMPACT TODAY

Although the Moors were driven out, many places in Spain and Portugal still bear names that came from Arabic, the language the Moors spoke.

ACADEMIC
VOCABULARY

policy rule,
course of action

The only territory still under Muslim control was a small kingdom called Granada (grah-NAH-dah).

The Rise of Portugal and Spain

As a result of their victories, both Portugal and Spain grew more powerful than before. Portugal, once a part of Castile, broke free and declared its independence. Meanwhile, Castile and Aragon decided to unite.

In 1469 Ferdinand, the prince of Aragon, married Isabella, a Castilian princess. Ten years later, they became king and queen of their countries. Together, they ruled all of Spain as **King Ferdinand** and **Queen Isabella**.

Ferdinand and Isabella finally brought an end to the Reconquista. In 1492 their army conquered Granada, the last Muslim stronghold in Spain. That same year, they required all Spanish Jews to convert to Christianity or leave the country. A few years later, they banned the practice of Islam as well. Through this **policy**, all of Spain became Christian.

The Spanish Inquisition

Ferdinand and Isabella wanted only Christians in their kingdom. To ensure that Christianity alone was practiced, they created the **Spanish Inquisition**, an organization of priests that looked for and punished anyone in Spain suspected of secretly practicing their old religion. Later, the Inquisition spread to Portugal as well.

The Spanish and Portuguese Inquisitions were ruthless in seeking heretics, Muslims, and Jews. People found guilty of heresy were sentenced in public ceremonies. Many of those found guilty were killed. They were often burned to death. In total, the Spanish sentenced about 2,000 people to die. Almost 1,400 more were put to death by the Portuguese Inquisition.

READING CHECK **Summarizing** What was the purpose of the Spanish Inquisition?

Jews Face Discrimination

Heretics and Muslims were not the only groups punished for their beliefs in the Middle Ages. European Jews also suffered. This suffering was caused by Christians who believed that the Jews had been responsible for the death of Jesus. These Christians thought Jews should be punished.

You have already read about how Jews were killed during the Crusades. You have also read that Jews were forced to leave their homes in Spain. Similar things happened all over Europe. Rulers, supported by the church, forced Jews to leave their countries. For example, in 1290, the king of England arrested all English Jews and forced them to leave the country. The same thing happened in France in 1306 and again in 1394.

BIOGRAPHY

Queen Isabella
1451–1504

Although she is considered one of the greatest monarchs in Spanish history, Isabella was never actually the queen of Spain. She was the queen of Castile, but she had no official power in her husband's kingdom, Aragon. In practice, however, the two ruled both kingdoms together.

In addition to her role in the Reconquista, Isabella made great contributions to Spanish society. She encouraged religion and education and supported many artists. She also helped pay for the transatlantic voyages of Christopher Columbus, during which he discovered America.

Analyzing How did Isabella help promote Spanish culture?

The Spanish Inquisition

The painting shows accused heretics, in the pointed hats, before the Spanish Inquisition. The Spanish artist Francisco Goya painted it in the early 1800s.

How did the artist show what the accused heretics are feeling?

In the Holy Roman Empire, frightened people blamed Jews for the arrival of the Black Death. Many Jews had to flee their homes to escape angry mobs. Because the Jews were not Christian, many Europeans didn't want them in their towns.

READING CHECK **Summarizing** How were Jews discriminated against in the Middle Ages?

SUMMARY AND PREVIEW During the Middle Ages, religion shaped how people thought, what they did, and where they lived. In some places religion led to wars and punishment for those who didn't agree with the Catholic Church. In the next chapter, you will learn about the era that followed the Middle Ages.

Section 5 Assessment

go.hrw.com
Online Quiz
KEYWORD: SN6 HP18

Reviewing Ideas, Terms, and People

1. **a. Define** What is **heresy**?
   b. Explain Why did the church send priests and friars to find heretics?
2. **a. Identify** Who did Spanish Christians try to drive out of their lands?
   b. Explain What was the purpose of the **Spanish Inquisition**?
   c. Predict How might Spanish history have been different if the Spanish had not defeated the Moors?
3. **Summarize** How did kings and other rulers punish Jews in the Middle Ages?

Critical Thinking

4. **Categorizing** Draw a chart like the one here. Use your notes to help you fill in each box with a description of Christians' reactions to that group.

Heretics	Moors	Jews

FOCUS ON WRITING

5. **Choosing Important People** There are two more people in this section to add to your list. How do you rank them on the list of most-to-least important? Who do you feel is most important?

Social Studies Skills

Analysis   Critical Thinking   Economics   Study

Understanding Transportation Maps

Define the Skill

Transportation maps show routes of travel and trade. These maps help you understand about the movement of people, products, and ideas between places in the world.

Learn the Skill

Follow these steps to interpret a transportation map.

1. Read the map's title. This will tell you what general information is shown on the map. Study the legend. Look for any symbols that relate to routes or methods of transportation.

2. Note any lines or arrows on the map. These lines and arrows often indicate routes of movement. Study these carefully. Note their starting and ending points and where they pass in between.

3. Study the whole map. Read all the labels. Transportation maps can tell you about the history of an area. For example, they can show how geography influenced the area's development.

Practice the Skill

Use the map below to answer the questions.

1. Which Crusade passed through Rome?

2. Which city did three Crusades travel through?

3. How did the later Crusades differ from the earlier ones in type of transportation used?

4. Why do you think all four Crusades passed through territory of the Byzantine Empire?

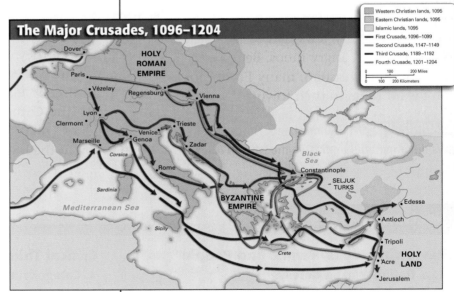

The Major Crusades, 1096–1204

Chapter Review

Visual Summary

Use the visual summary below to help you review the main ideas of the chapter.

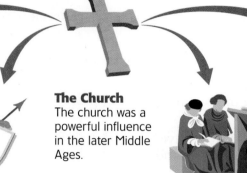

Government
The church and monarchy often worked together but sometimes were rivals.

Crusades
The pope called for Christians to retake the Holy Land.

The Church
The church was a powerful influence in the later Middle Ages.

Education and Society
The church helped guide learning and reacted to challenges to its authority.

Art and Architecture
Christianity inspired great forms of art and architecture.

Reviewing Vocabulary, Terms, and People

Match the words with their definitions.

1. excommunicate
2. religious order
3. Crusades
4. clergy
5. heresy
6. Thomas Aquinas
7. Magna Carta
8. Spanish Inquisition

a. church officials
b. punished non-Christians in Spain
c. religious ideas that oppose church teachings
d. an English document limiting the king's powers
e. cast out from the church
f. thought faith and reason could be used together
g. a group of people who dedicate their lives to religion, live together, and follow the same rules
h. wars fought to regain the Holy Land

Comprehension and Critical Thinking

SECTION 1 *(Pages 524–527)*

9. **a. Describe** What was the relationship between Charlemagne and the pope like?

   b. Contrast How did the opinions of popes like Gregory VII about power differ from those of kings like Henry IV?

   c. Evaluate Do you think conflict with kings strengthened or weakened medieval popes? Why?

SECTION 2 *(Pages 528–532)*

10. **a. Identify** What was the main goal of the Crusades?

    b. Draw Conclusions Why do you think the Crusades changed the relationships between Christians and other groups?

    c. Evaluate Which Crusade do you think was most successful? Which was least successful? Why?

SECTION 3 *(Pages 533–539)*

11. a. Describe How did Christianity shape art and education in the Middle Ages?

b. Analyze Why was Christianity so influential in so many areas of medieval life?

c. Elaborate How were the changes that took place in the medieval church related to its growing power and wealth?

SECTION 4 *(Pages 540–543)*

12. a. Describe What was the Black Death, and how did it affect Europe?

b. Make Inferences Why do some people consider Magna Carta to represent the beginning of democracy in England?

c. Predict How might Europe's history have been different if England had won the Hundred Years' War?

SECTION 5 *(Pages 546–549)*

13. a. Identify What were the results of the Reconquista?

b. Draw Conclusions Why were the Spanish and Portuguese Inquisitions so feared?

c. Elaborate Why do you think some Christians considered heresy such a threat?

Reviewing Themes

14. Religion In what ways did the Crusades demonstrate the power of the church in Europe?

15. Society and Culture How did the church affect the lives of ordinary people?

Using the Internet
go.hrw.com
KEYWORD: SN6 WH18

16. Activity: Evaluating Sources A challenge for anyone trying to understand the Middle Ages is evaluating the primary and secondary sources. Enter the activity keyword, and then rate the listed sources. Explain whether the source is a primary or secondary source, whether you think it is believable, and your reasoning.

Reading Skills

Stereotypes and Bias in History *The passage below is taken from a collection of stories called the* Decameron *by the Italian writer Boccaccio. In it, he describes the arrival of the Black Death in his home city of Florence. Read the passage and then answer the questions that follow.*

> " I say, then, that it was the year of the bountiful Incarnation of the Son of God, 1348. The mortal pestilence then arrived in the excellent city of Florence, which surpasses every other Italian city in nobility. Whether through the operations of the heavenly bodies, or sent upon us mortals through our wicked deeds by the just wrath of God for our correction, the plague had begun some years before in Eastern countries. It carried off uncounted numbers of inhabitants, and kept moving without cease from place to place. It spread in piteous fashion towards the West. "

17. Do you think Boccaccio expresses any bias about the city of Florence in this passage?

18. Do any words or phrases in the passage indicate stereotypes or bias about the people of Florence?

Social Studies Skills

19. Understanding Transportation Maps Look at the map on page 550. Then describe the route taken by members of the First Crusade. Include information on directions traveled and method of transportation.

FOCUS ON WRITING

20. Writing Your Article Review your notes. Be sure you've identified the three people you think are the most important and why they're important. Now write an article explaining why these people were so important to Europe in the Middle Ages. Keep your article short: one or two sentences to introduce your topic, a sentence or two about each important person, and a one- or two-sentence conclusion.

DIRECTIONS: *Read each question, and write the letter of the best response.*

1

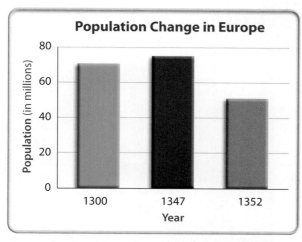

Population Change in Europe

Population (in millions)

80
60
40
20
0

1300   1347   1352
Year

What historical event was responsible for the population trend shown in the graph?

A the Crusades

B the Black Death

C the Hundred Years' War

D the Spanish Inquisition

2 Which of the following had the *greatest* influence on the lives of most Europeans during the Middle Ages?

A towns and trade

B the king

C religion and the church

D universities

3 One reason the Crusades failed to conquer the Holy Land permanently was because

A the fighting was a long distance from Europe.

B Crusader armies had better weapons than the Muslims did.

C religion was not important to most Europeans.

D the power of the popes declined.

4 Which statement *best* describes the relationship between popes and kings during Europe's Middle Ages?

A Popes became more powerful than kings.

B Many popes became kings, and many kings became popes.

C Popes and kings often disagreed with each other.

D Kings had more power than popes did.

5 Before the Reconquista, most of the Iberian Peninsula was controlled by

A Spaniards.

B Portuguese.

C Crusaders.

D Muslims.

Connecting with Past Learnings

6 Muslim culture spread all the way to Spain through conquest and trade. Which culture spread across much of the ancient world in the same way?

A Japanese

B Harappan

C Roman

D Sumerian

7 Magna Carta helped introduce democratic ideas to England. The first democracy in the ancient world arose in

A Greece.

B China.

C India.

D Rome.

CHAPTER 19 · 1270–1650

The Renaissance and Reformation

FOCUS ON WRITING

A Book Jacket You work at a publishing company, and you've been asked to design a book jacket for a book about the Renaissance and Reformation. As you read this chapter, consider which main ideas and important details you should include in the description on the back page, which image you might pick for the front, and what you should call the book.

CHAPTER EVENTS

1200

WORLD EVENTS

1271
Marco Polo travels to China.

1201
The Fourth Crusade begins.

History's Impact
▶ video series
Watch the video to understand the impact of the Renaissance and the Reformation.

What You Will Learn...

In this chapter, you will learn how the Renaissance changed thinking in Europe and led to the Reformation. The Renaissance began in Italy's great trading cities, like Venice, shown here. Venice is an island city crisscrossed with canals, so its "streets" are actually waterways.

c. 1450
Gutenberg develops his printing press.

1517
Martin Luther announces his 95 Theses criticizing the Catholic Church.

1648
The Thirty Years' War ends.

1350

1500

1650

1368
The Ming dynasty begins in China.

1453
The Ottomans conquer Constantinople.

1537
Spanish conquistadors conquer the Inca Empire.

1603
The Tokugawa shoguns come to power in Japan.

Reading Social Studies

by Kylene Beers

Focus on Themes This chapter takes you into Italy in the 1300s to 1600s. At that time scholars, artists, and scientists built on classical Greek and Roman roots to make new advances in **society and culture** and the arts. You will read how Italy's **geographical** location, along with the invention of the printing press and the reopening of routes between China and Europe made the Renaissance a worldwide event with effects far beyond Italy.

Greek and Latin Word Roots

Focus on Reading During the Renaissance, scientists and scholars became interested in the history and languages of ancient Greece and Rome. Many of the words we use every day are based on words spoken by people in these ancient civilizations.

Common roots The charts below list some Greek and Latin roots found in many English words. As you read the charts, try to think of words that include each root. Then think about how the words' meanings are related to their roots.

Common Latin Roots		
Root	**Meaning**	**Sample words**
-aud-	hear	audience, audible
liter-	writing	literature, literary
re-	again	repeat, redo
-script-	write	script, manuscript
sub-	below	submarine, substandard
trans-	across	transport, translate

Common Greek Roots		
Root	**Meaning**	**Sample words**
anti-	against	antifreeze, antiwar
astr-	star	asteroid, astronaut
-chron-	time	chronicle, chronology
dia-	across, between	diagonal, diameter
micr-	small	microfilm, microscope
-phono-	sound	telephone, symphony

You Try It!

Each of the following sentences is taken from the chapter you are about to read. After you've read the sentences, answer the questions at the bottom of the page.

Getting to the Root of the Word

1. Many Italian writers contributed great works of <u>literature</u> to the Renaissance. (*p. 562*)
2. As Protestantism spread in the later 1500s and 1600s, Catholic leaders <u>responded</u>. (*p. 572*)
3. They studied <u>astronomy</u> to learn about the sun, stars, and planets. (*p. 566*)
4. In 1456 Gutenberg printed the Bible in Latin. It was later <u>translated</u> and printed in other languages. (*p. 566*)
5. Also, parallel lines, such as on floor tiles, are drawn <u>diagonally</u>. (*p. 563*)

Answer the following questions about the underlined words. Use the Common Roots charts on the opposite page for help.

1. Which of the underlined words has a root word that means "writing?" How does knowing the root word help you figure out what the word means?

2. What does the root word *astr-* mean? How does that help you figure out the meaning of *astronomy?*

3. In the second sentence, what do you think *responded* means? How could this be related to the root *re-?*

4. What's the root word in *translated?* What does *translated* mean? How is that definition related to the meaning of the root word?

5. What does the word *diagonally* mean? How is that meaning related to the meaning of *dia-?*

6. How many more words can you think of that use the roots in the charts on the opposite page? Make a list and share it with your classmates.

Academic Vocabulary

Success in school is related to knowing academic vocabulary—the words that are frequently used in school assignments and discussions. In this chapter, you will learn the following academic words:

classical *(p. 562)*
affect *(p. 566)*
agreement *(p. 575)*

As you read Chapter 19, be on the lookout for words with Greek and Latin root words like those listed in the chart on the opposite page. Use the chart to help you figure out what the words mean.

The Italian Renaissance

What You Will Learn...

Main Ideas

1. Increased trade with Asia brought wealth to Italian trade cities, leading to the Renaissance.
2. Italian writers and artists contributed great works during the Renaissance.

The Big Idea

The growth of wealthy trading cities in Italy led to a rebirth of the arts and learning called the Renaissance.

Key Terms and People

Marco Polo, *p. 559*
Renaissance, *p. 561*
humanism, *p. 561*
Dante Alighieri, *p. 562*
Niccolo Machiavelli, *p. 562*
Michelangelo, *p. 563*
Leonardo da Vinci, *p. 563*

TAKING NOTES As you read, look for information about the growth of trade and cities. Note how this growth influenced writers and artists. Use a diagram like the one below to record your notes.

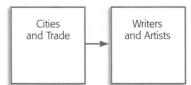

Cities and Trade → Writers and Artists

If YOU were there...

You are a historian living in Florence, Italy, in the late 1300s. In your writing you describe the wonders of your city today. But the place was very different only about 50 years ago. At that time, the Black Death was sweeping through the city. In fact, your own grandfather was killed by the terrible disease. Some 50,000 of the city's other citizens also died from the plague. Now, though, Florence is known for its beauty, art, and learning.

How did your city change so quickly?

BUILDING BACKGROUND By the late 1300s the Black Death's horrors had passed. Europeans could worry less about dying and concentrate more on living. They wanted to enjoy some of life's pleasures—art, literature, and learning. Increased trade with faraway lands would help spark new interest in these activities.

Trade with Asia

It seems strange that the Black Death had any positive results, but that is what happened. Though the death toll was terrible, the disease didn't damage farmland, buildings, ships, machines, or gold. People who survived used these things to raise more food and make new products. Wages rose as workers, now in short supply, demanded higher pay. Europe's economy began to grow again.

As more goods became available, prices went down. Trade increased, and new products appeared in the markets. Some of these goods came from thousands of miles away. To learn how these items ended up in Europe, we need to go back in time.

The Silk Road Reopens

The Chinese and Romans did business together from about AD 1 to 200. Products moved between East and West along the Silk Road. This was a caravan route that started in China and ended at the

Mediterranean Sea. When the Roman Empire and the Han dynasty fell, soldiers no longer protected travelers. As a result, use of the Silk Road declined. Then in the 1200s the Mongols took over China. They once again made the roads safer for travelers and traders. Among these traders were a remarkable man from Venice named **Marco Polo** and his family.

The Polos traveled from Europe to China, where they saw many amazing things, such as paper money, and coal used for fuel. In China they also met with the Mongol emperor Kublai Khan. He invited them to stay in his court and made Marco Polo a government official. The Polos spent 20 years in Asia before returning to Venice. There, a writer helped Polo record his journey. Polo's descriptions made many Europeans curious about Asia. People began to desire Asian goods, and trade between Asia and Europe grew. Italian merchants organized much of this trade.

Trade Cities in Italy

By the 1300s four northern Italian cities had become trading centers—Florence, Genoa (JEN-uh-wuh), Milan (muh-LAHN), and Venice. These cities bustled with activ-ity. Shoppers there could buy beautiful things from Asia. Residents could meet strangers from faraway places and hear many languages on the streets.

Italian cities played two important roles in trade. One role was as ports on the Mediterranean Sea. Venice and Genoa were the main port cities. Merchant ships brought spices and other luxuries from Asia into the cities' harbors. Merchants then shipped the goods all across Europe.

Florence was a banking and trade center. The city's wealthy leaders used their money to beautify the city with impressive buildings and art.

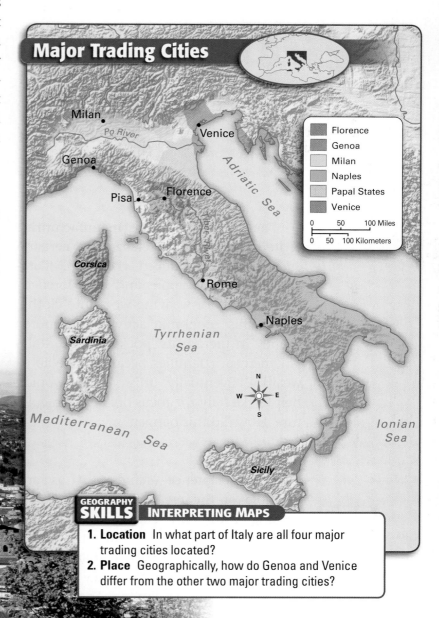

Major Trading Cities

Florence
Genoa
Milan
Naples
Papal States
Venice

0   50   100 Miles
0   50   100 Kilometers

Milan
Po River
Venice
Genoa
Adriatic Sea
Pisa
Florence
Tiber River
Corsica
Rome
Sardinia
Tyrrhenian Sea
Naples
Mediterranean Sea
Sicily
Ionian Sea

GEOGRAPHY SKILLS | **INTERPRETING MAPS**

1. **Location** In what part of Italy are all four major trading cities located?
2. **Place** Geographically, how do Genoa and Venice differ from the other two major trading cities?

History Close-up

Florence

A market in Florence buzzes with activity in this scene showing what Florence may have looked like in the 1400s.

Merchants traded goods from Europe and Asia in the city's markets.

Cloth was a major trade good in Florence.

Bankers kept detailed records of their investments.

The other role was as manufacturing centers. Each city specialized in certain crafts. Venice produced glass. In Milan workers made weapons and silk. Florence was a center for weaving wool into cloth. All of this economic activity put more money in merchants' pockets. Some Italian merchant families became incredibly wealthy. Eventually, this wealth would help make Italy the focus of European culture. How did this happen?

Florence

One city—Florence—stands out as an example of the great trade and wealth coming into Italy during the 1300s. Florence's wealth began with the wool trade, but banking increased that wealth. Bankers in Florence kept money for merchants from all over Europe. The bankers also earned money by making loans and charging interest. Interest is a fee that lenders charge people who borrow money from them. This fee is usually a certain percentage of the loan.

The greatest of the Florence bankers were the Medici (MED-i-chee) family. In the early 1400s they were the richest family in the city. Their fortune gave the Medicis political power too. You see, in most big Italian cities, a single rich family controlled the government. The head of the family ruled the city. By 1434 Cosimo de' Medici (KOH-zee-moh day MED-i-chee) ruled Florence.

Cosimo de' Medici wanted Florence to be the most beautiful city in the world. He hired artists to decorate his palace. He also paid architects to redesign many of Florence's buildings.

Cosimo de' Medici also valued education. After all, his banks needed workers who could read, write, and understand math.

THE IMPACT TODAY

Bankers in Florence during this time developed a bookkeeping system that is still used today.

City leaders hired architects and artists to create beautiful buildings like this famous church called the Duomo.

Visitors to Florence helped spread Renaissance ideas throughout Europe.

ANALYSIS SKILL **ANALYZING VISUALS**
What can you see in this illustration that shows the wealth of Florence?

To improve education, he built libraries and collected books. Under the Medicis, Florence became the center of Italian art, literature, and culture. In other Italian cities, rich families tried to outdo each other in their support of the arts and learning.

Beginning of the Renaissance

This love of art and education was a key feature of a time we call the Renaissance (re-nuh-SAHNS). The word **Renaissance** means "rebirth" and refers to the period that followed Europe's Middle Ages.

What was being "reborn"? Interest in art and literature revived, especially in ancient Greek and Roman works. Appreciation also developed for the importance of people as individuals. These ideas were very different from those of the Middle Ages.

READING CHECK **Summarizing** How did trade lead to the Renaissance in Italy?

Italian Writers and Artists

New ways of thinking emerged during the Renaissance. At the same time, the period brought a renewed emphasis on the past. These trends inspired Italian writers and artists to produce many brilliant works.

Sources of Inspiration

During the Middle Ages, most thinkers in Europe had devoted themselves to religious study. By the 1300s, however, scholars had begun to broaden their interests. They studied poetry, history, art, and the Greek and Latin languages. Together, these subjects are known as the humanities because they explore human activities rather than the physical world or the nature of God. The study of the humanities led to a movement called **humanism**, a way of thinking and learning that stresses the importance of human abilities and actions.

FOCUS ON READING
What word in this paragraph, besides *Renaissance*, uses a Latin root that means "again"? How does the meaning of the word reflect the meaning of the Latin root?

BOOK
The Prince

In The Prince, *Machiavelli offers advice for rulers on how to stay in power. In this famous passage, he explains why in his view it is better for rulers to be feared than to be loved.*

❝A controversy has arisen about this: whether it is better to be loved than feared, or vice versa. My view is that it is desirable to be both loved and feared; but it is difficult to achieve both and, if one of them has to be lacking, it is much safer to be feared than loved . . . For love is sustained by a bond of gratitude which, because men are excessively self-interested, is broken whenever they see a chance to benefit themselves. But fear is sustained by a dread of punishment that is always effective.❞

ANALYSIS SKILL   ANALYZING PRIMARY SOURCES

Do you think that Machiavelli gave good advice in this passage? Why or why not?

This interest in the humanities was linked to the rediscovery of ancient writings. In the 1300s Turks conquered much of the Byzantine Empire. Scholars seeking to escape the Turks fled to Italy. With them they carried rare works of literature.

Many of the works they brought to Italy were ancient **classical** writings, such as works by Greek thinkers. Scholars were excited by the return of these writings and went looking for ancient Latin texts too. They found many in monasteries, where monks had preserved works by Roman writers. As scholars rediscovered the glories of Greece and Rome, they longed for a renewal of classical culture.

Renaissance artists and architects were also drawn to the past. Classical statues and ruins of Roman buildings still stood in Italy. These ancient ruins and statues inspired painters and sculptors.

ACADEMIC VOCABULARY

classical referring to the cultures of ancient Greece or Rome

Italian Writers

Many Italian writers contributed great works of literature to the Renaissance. The earliest was the politician and poet **Dante Alighieri** (DAHN-tay ahl-eeg-YEH-ree). Before Dante, most medieval authors had written in Latin, the language of the church. Dante wrote in Italian, which was the common language of the people. This showed that he considered Italian, the people's language, to be as good as Latin.

A later Italian writer, **Niccolo Machiavelli** (neek-koh-LOH mahk-yah-VEL-lee), was also a politician. In 1513 he wrote a short book called *The Prince*. It gave leaders advice on how they should rule.

Machiavelli didn't care about theories or what *should* work. He was only interested in what really happened in war and peace. He argued that to be successful, rulers had to focus on the "here and now," not on theories. Machiavelli thought that rulers sometimes had to be ruthless to keep order. In this way, Machiavelli serves as a good example of Renaissance interest in human behavior and society.

Two Masters

Michelangelo
1475–1564
Michelangelo produced some the most famous works of art in world history. Like many of his masterpieces, his powerful statue of the Hebrew king David and his remarkable painting for the Sistine Chapel (both at right) were created for the Roman Catholic Church.

Italian Art and Artists

During the Renaissance, Italian artists created some of the most beautiful paintings and sculptures in the world. Ideas about the value of human life affected the art of the time. Artists showed people in a more realistic way than medieval artists had done. Renaissance artists studied the human body and drew what they saw. However, because artists often used classical statues as their guides, many of the human beings they drew were as perfect as Greek gods.

Artists also used a new technique called perspective—a way of showing depth and distance on a flat surface. Perspective is created by various means. For example, people in the background of a painting are shown smaller than people in the front. Sharper colors are used for objects seen up close, while distant images are made to look hazier. Also, parallel lines, such as on floor tiles, are drawn diagonally. This is another way to give the illusion of distance between the people or objects shown.

Two Masters

There were several great Italian Renaissance artists. But two stand out above the rest. Each is an example of what we call a Renaissance person—someone who can do practically anything well.

One of these great Italian masters was **Michelangelo** (mee-kay-LAHN-jay-loh). He had many talents. Michelangelo designed buildings, wrote poetry, carved sculptures, and painted magnificent pictures. Perhaps his most famous work is a painting that covers the ceiling of the Sistine Chapel in the Vatican. The muscular human figures in this immense painting remind the viewer of Greek or Roman statues.

The true genius of the Renaissance was **Leonardo da Vinci**. In addition to being an expert painter, Leonardo was a sculptor, architect, inventor, engineer, town planner, and mapmaker. Both nature and technology fascinated Leonardo. Detailed drawings of plants, animals, and machines fill the sketchbooks that he left behind.

Leonardo da Vinci
1452–1519

Leonardo showed artistic talent at a young age, but no one could have known that he would become one of the great geniuses of history. His Mona Lisa (far right) is one of the most famous paintings in the world. Leonardo also left behind notebooks that were filled with examples of his other interests. His self-portrait (above right) and anatomical sketches (right) reveal his attention to detail and study of the human body. His ideas for a human-powered flying machine are reflected in the model above.

Renaissance Art

Renaissance art was very different from medieval art. Renaissance artists used new techniques to make their paintings more realistic.

How are these two paintings similar and different?

The people in this painting appear larger and have more detail than the mountains in the distance, creating a sense of depth.

Artists in the Middle Ages didn't use perspective, so their art looked flat.

To make his art more real, Leonardo studied anatomy, the structure of human bodies. He also showed human emotions in his work. His famous portrait of Mona Lisa, for example, shows the lady smiling.

READING CHECK Summarizing Who were some of the great Renaissance writers and artists?

SUMMARY AND PREVIEW Changes in Italy led to the beginning of an era called the Renaissance. During the late 1300s, a great rebirth of art, literature, and learning occurred in Italy. In the next section, you will learn how Renaissance ideas changed as they spread across Europe.

Section 1 Assessment

Reviewing Ideas, Terms, and People

1. **a. Identify** Who was **Marco Polo** and how was he influential?
   b. Analyze Why were the four major trade cities of Italy important economically?
   c. Elaborate How did the city of Florence rise to its position of fame?
2. **a. Describe** What sources inspired Renaissance artists and scholars?
   b. Compare Which artist would you rather have met in real life—**Michelangelo** or **Leonardo da Vinci**? What is the reason for your choice?
   c. Evaluate Why do you think **Dante Alighieri** chose to write in Italian, rather than Latin, the language used by most scholars?

Critical Thinking

3. **Sequencing** Draw a diagram like the one below. Using your notes, put the events in the correct order.

| The Renaissance begins. | → | Rich merchants support cultural activities. | → | Trade between Europe and Asia increases. |

FOCUS ON WRITING

4. **Finding Key Details** The main idea of this section might be stated, "Due to contact with Asia and the wealth that resulted from trade, the Renaissance began in Italy." Write this main idea in your notebook. What key details in this section support this idea? Write them in your notebook as well.

The Renaissance beyond Italy

If YOU were there...

You are a student from Holland, studying law at the university in Bologna, Italy. Life in Renaissance Italy is so exciting! You've met artists and writers and learned so much about art and literature. You can hardly wait to tell people at home about everything you've learned. But now a lawyer in Bologna has offered you a chance to stay and work in Italy.

Will you stay in Italy or return to Holland?

> **BUILDING BACKGROUND** By the late 1400s the Renaissance spirit was spreading from Italy to other parts of Europe. Artists, writers, and scholars came to Italy to study. Then they taught others what they had learned and brought paintings and sculptures from Italy back home. They also picked up new ideas. Soon, printing and books made these new ideas available to even more people.

Advances in Science and Education

Many of the texts rediscovered in the 1300s dealt with science. Europeans could once again read works by ancient scientists in the original Greek. After learning from these works, Renaissance scholars went on to make their own scientific advances.

Mathematics and the Sciences

Some Renaissance scientists thought mathematics could help them understand the universe. They studied ancient math texts and built on the ideas in them. In the process, they created many of the symbols we use in math today. These include the symbols for the square root ($\sqrt{}$) and for positive (+) and negative (-) numbers.

Advances in mathematics led to advances in other fields of science. Engineers and architects, for example, used new mathematical formulas to design ways to strengthen buildings.

What You Will Learn...

Main Ideas

1. During the Renaissance, advances in science and education were made.
2. New ideas from the Renaissance spread across Europe through the development of paper, printing, and new universities.

The Big Idea

The Renaissance spread far beyond Italy, and as it spread, it changed.

Key Terms and People

Petrarch, *p. 566*
Johann Gutenberg, *p. 566*
Christian humanism, *p. 567*
Desiderius Erasmus, *p. 567*
Albrecht Dürer, *p. 568*
Miguel de Cervantes, *p. 568*
William Shakespeare, *p. 568*

TAKING NOTES As you read, draw a graphic organizer like the one below. In the outer circles, describe the ideas, art, and literature of the Renaissance outside of Italy. Add new circles as necessary.

Renaissance beyond Italy

Other Renaissance scientists wanted to know more about the sky and what was in it. They studied astronomy to learn about the sun, stars, and planets. Through their efforts, Renaissance scientists learned that the earth moves around the sun.

Changes in Education

During the Renaissance, students continued to study religious subjects, but they learned about the humanities as well. History became especially important. The Renaissance scholar **Petrarch** (PE-trahrk) warned against ignoring history:

> "O inglorious age! that scorns antiquity, its mother, to whom it owes every noble art … What can be said in defense of men of education who ought not to be ignorant of antiquity [ancient times] and yet are plunged in … darkness and delusion?"
>
> —Francesco Petrarch, from a 1366 letter to Boccaccio

ACADEMIC VOCABULARY

affect
to change or influence

Petrarch's ideas would **affect** education for many years. Education and new ways of spreading information would take the Renaissance far beyond Italy.

READING CHECK **Summarizing** What fields of study advanced during the Renaissance?

The Spread of New Ideas

Travelers and artists helped spread Renaissance ideas throughout Europe. But the development of printing played a giant role. It allowed thousands of people to read books for the first time ever.

Paper and Printing

Papermaking spread from China to the Middle East, and then to Europe. Several European factories were making paper by the 1300s. Cheaper and easier to prepare, paper soon replaced the processed animal skins on which people had written before.

In the mid-1400s a German named **Johann Gutenberg** (GOOT-uhn-berk) developed a printing press that used movable type. That is, each letter was on a separate piece of metal. A worker fitted letters into a frame, spread ink on the letters, and then pressed a sheet of paper against the letters. An entire page was printed at once. The worker could then rearrange the letters in the frame to create a new page.

In 1456 Gutenberg printed the Bible in Latin. It was later translated and printed

Time Line

Printing in Europe

1000 Printing has not developed in Europe yet. Books are copied by hand, usually by monks.

c. 1455 Johann Gutenberg develops the printing press. It uses movable type, which makes the mass production of books possible and allows ideas to spread more quickly.

1000

1300

1300s Factories in Europe begin making paper using techniques introduced from Asia.

in other languages. As the Bible became increasingly available, more people learned to read. They then wanted more education.

New Universities

Students from around Europe traveled to Italy to study. At Italian universities, they picked up humanist ideas, which they took back to their own countries.

Over time, new universities opened in France, Germany, and the Netherlands. Because they were set up by humanists, Renaissance ideas about the value of individuals spread throughout Europe.

Although only men could attend universities, many noble families in Italy educated their daughters at home. Some of these women married nobles from other parts of Europe and became influential. They used their positions to encourage the spread of Renaissance ideas in the lands that their husbands ruled.

The Northern Renaissance

As humanism spread into northern Europe, it took on a more religious form. Scholars there focused on the history of Christianity, not Greece or Rome. This **Christian humanism** was a blend of humanist and religious ideas.

Many northern scholars came to feel that the church was corrupt and did not follow Jesus's teachings. A Dutch priest named **Desiderius Erasmus** (des-i-DEER-ee-uhs i-RAZ-mus) was the most important voice for reform. Erasmus criticized corrupt clergy and wanted to get rid of some church rituals that he considered meaningless. Instead of rituals, he emphasized devotion to God and the teachings of Jesus.

Northern Europeans also brought key changes to Renaissance art. For example, they used a more realistic style than Italian artists did. People in northern paintings don't look like Greek gods. Instead, they are more lifelike, with physical flaws. Northern artists also worked on a broader range of subjects. Many painted scenes of daily life, rather than the biblical scenes and classical myths favored by Italian artists.

One of the most famous artists of the northern Renaissance was a gifted German.

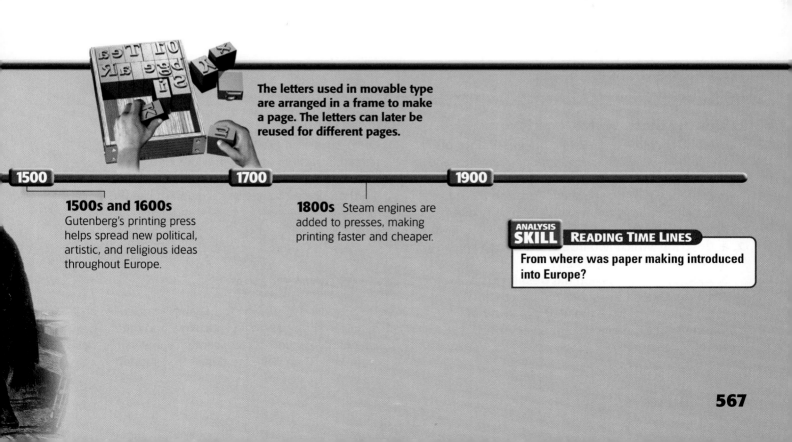

The letters used in movable type are arranged in a frame to make a page. The letters can later be reused for different pages.

1500 — 1700 — 1900

1500s and 1600s Gutenberg's printing press helps spread new political, artistic, and religious ideas throughout Europe.

1800s Steam engines are added to presses, making printing faster and cheaper.

ANALYSIS SKILL **READING TIME LINES**

From where was paper making introduced into Europe?

William Shakespeare

1564–1616

Many people consider William Shakespeare the greatest playwright of all time. His plays are still hugely popular around the world. Shakespeare was such an important writer that he even influenced the English language. He invented common phrases such as *fair play* and common words such as *lonely*. In fact, Shakespeare is probably responsible for more than 2,000 English words.

Drawing Inferences How do you think Shakespeare invented new words and phrases?

His name was **Albrecht Dürer** (AWL-brekt DYUR-uhr). Dürer studied anatomy so that he could paint people more realistically. He showed objects in great detail. Dürer is most famous for his prints. A print is a work of art that is reproduced from an original.

Literature beyond Italy

Writers in other countries besides Italy also included Renaissance ideas in their works. Like Dante, they wrote in the languages of their home countries. In Spain **Miguel de**

Cervantes (mee-GEL day ser-VAHN-tays) wrote *Don Quixote* (kee-HOH-tay). In this book Cervantes poked fun at the romantic tales of the Middle Ages. Like many writers of his day, Cervantes thought that his own time was much better than the Middle Ages.

Many readers consider **William Shakespeare** the greatest writer in the English language. Although he also wrote poems, Shakespeare is most famous for his plays. He wrote more than 30 comedies, tragedies, and histories. London audiences of the late 1500s and early 1600s packed the theatre to see his works performed. Ever since then, people have enjoyed Shakespeare's language and his understanding of humanity.

READING CHECK **Analyzing** How did travel and marriage spread Renaissance ideas?

SUMMARY AND PREVIEW The development of paper, the printing press, and new universities helped spread the Renaissance beyond Italy. Northern artists and writers altered Renaissance ideas. Next, you will learn about new religious ideas that swept through Europe at about the same time.

Section 2 Assessment

Reviewing Ideas, Terms, and People

1. **a. Identify** Name and explain the importance of one Renaissance achievement in mathematics and one achievement in astronomy.
   b. Evaluate Why do you think **Petrarch** placed so much emphasis on the study of history during the Renaissance?
2. **a. Describe** Which two inventions helped spread the Renaissance beyond Italy?
   b. Analyze What position did **Desiderius Erasmus** take on the subject of church rituals?
   c. Evaluate Why have the works of **William Shakespeare** remained so popular around the world for centuries?

Critical Thinking

3. **Comparing and Contrasting** Using your notes from this section and the previous one, compare and contrast the Italian Renaissance and the Northern Renaissance. Use a diagram like this one.

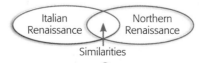

Italian Renaissance

Northern Renaissance

Similarities

FOCUS ON WRITING

4. **Finding the Main Idea** You already wrote a list of details to support a main idea. Now find the main idea of this section. Write a sentence that states that main idea. Then write the details that support it.

The Reformation of Christianity

If YOU were there...

You live in a small town in Germany in the 1500s. The Catholic Church has a lot of influence here. Often, church officials clash with local nobles over who has the final say in certain political issues. The church also demands that the nobles pay high taxes. Lately, however, a local priest has been openly criticizing church leaders. He wants to make some changes.

How do you think the nobles will respond to him?

BUILDING BACKGROUND By the early 1500s Renaissance ideas had caused many Europeans to view their lives with a more critical eye. They thought their lives could be changed for the better. One area that some people thought needed improvement was religion.

Reformers Call for Change

By the late Renaissance some people had begun to complain about problems in the Catholic Church. They called on its leaders to end corruption and focus on religion. Their calls led to the **Reformation**, a reform movement against the Roman Catholic Church.

Unpopular Church Practices

Those who wanted to reform the church had many complaints. Some thought that priests and bishops weren't religious anymore. Others felt that the pope was too involved in politics, neglecting his religious duties. Many thought the church had grown too rich. The Roman Catholic Church had become one of the richest institutions in Europe because it didn't have to pay taxes.

Many people objected to the ways the church earned its money. One common method was the sale of indulgences. An indulgence was a document given by the pope that excused a person from penalties for the sins that he or she had committed.

What You Will Learn...

Main Ideas

1. Reformers called for change in the Catholic Church, but some broke away to form new churches.
2. The Catholic Reformation was an attempt to reform the church from within.
3. The political impact of the Reformation included religious wars and social change.

The Big Idea

Efforts to reform the Roman Catholic Church led to changes in society and the creation of new churches.

Key Terms and People

Reformation, *p. 569*
Martin Luther, *p. 570*
Protestants, *p. 570*
John Calvin, *p. 571*
Catholic Reformation, *p. 572*
Jesuits, *p. 572*
federalism, *p. 575*

TAKING NOTES As you read, take notes on efforts to reform the Catholic Church, both by Protestants—people who broke away from the church—and by Catholics.

Protestants	Catholics

According to the church, an indulgence reduced the time that a person would serve in purgatory. In Catholic teachings, purgatory was a place where souls went to make up for their sins before they went to heaven. Many Christians thought that by selling indulgences, the church was letting people buy their way into heaven.

Martin Luther

By the early 1500s scholars in northern Europe were calling for church reforms. On October 31, 1517, a priest named **Martin Luther** added his voice to the call for reform. He nailed a list of complaints about the church to the door of a church in Wittenberg (VIT-uhn-berk) in the German state of Saxony. Luther's list is called the Ninety-Five Theses (THEE-seez). Thanks to the newly invented printing press, copies of this list spread to neighboring states.

Luther's complaints angered many Catholics. Pope Leo X called Luther a heretic and excommunicated him. Germany's ruler, the Holy Roman Emperor, ordered Luther to appear before a diet, or council of nobles and church officials, in the German city of Worms (VOHRMS). The emperor called Luther an outlaw and ordered him to leave the empire. But one noble secretly supported Luther and helped him to hide from the emperor.

Luther's ideas eventually led to a split in the church. Those who protested against the Roman Catholic church became known as **Protestants** (PRAH-tuhs-tuhnts). Those Protestants who followed Luther's teachings were specifically known as Lutherans.

Luther taught that anyone could have a direct relationship with God. They didn't need priests to talk to God for them. This idea is called the priesthood of all believers.

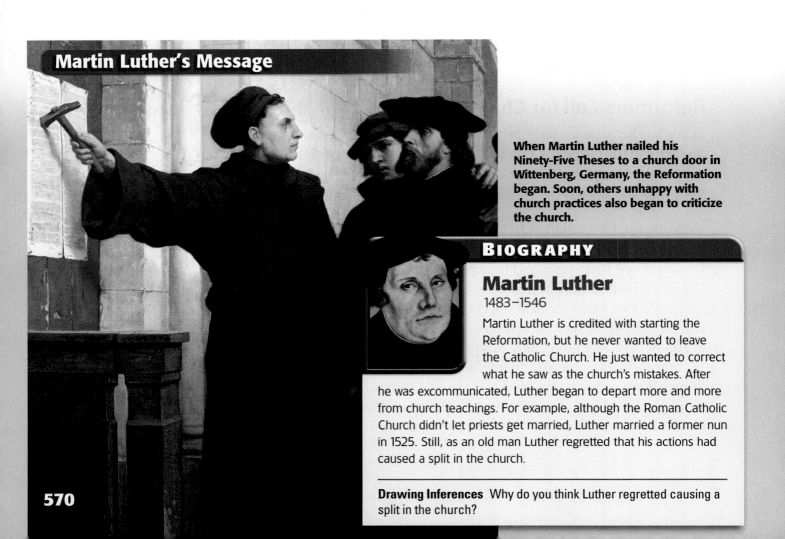

Martin Luther's Message

When Martin Luther nailed his Ninety-Five Theses to a church door in Wittenberg, Germany, the Reformation began. Soon, others unhappy with church practices also began to criticize the church.

BIOGRAPHY

Martin Luther
1483–1546

Martin Luther is credited with starting the Reformation, but he never wanted to leave the Catholic Church. He just wanted to correct what he saw as the church's mistakes. After he was excommunicated, Luther began to depart more and more from church teachings. For example, although the Roman Catholic Church didn't let priests get married, Luther married a former nun in 1525. Still, as an old man Luther regretted that his actions had caused a split in the church.

Drawing Inferences Why do you think Luther regretted causing a split in the church?

It challenged the traditional structure and power of the church. But Luther encouraged people to live as the Bible, not priests or the pope, said.

To help people understand how God wanted them to live, Luther translated the Bible's New Testament into German, his native language. For the first time many Europeans who didn't know Greek or Latin could read the Bible for themselves. In addition to translating the Bible, Luther wrote pamphlets, essays, and songs about his ideas, many of them in German.

Many German nobles liked Luther's ideas. They particularly supported Luther's position that the clergy should not interfere with politics. Because these nobles allowed the people who lived on their lands to become Lutheran, the Lutheran Church soon became the dominant church in most of northern Germany.

Other Reformers

Even before Luther died in 1546, other reformers across Europe had begun to follow his example. William Tyndale (TIN-duhl), an English professor, thought that everyone should be able to read and interpret the Bible. This belief went against the teachings of the Catholic Church, which held that only the clergy could interpret the Bible. When Tyndale translated the Bible into English, Catholic authorities had him executed.

A more influential reformer than Tyndale was **John Calvin**. One of Calvin's main teachings was predestination, the idea that God knew who would be saved even before they were born. Nothing people did during their lives would change God's plan. However, Calvin also thought that it was important to live a good life and obey God's laws.

THE IMPACT TODAY

Many of the songs Luther wrote are still sung in Protestant churches around the world.

Primary Source

HISTORIC DOCUMENT
Luther's Ninety-Five Theses

In Wittenberg, nailing documents to the church door was a common way of sharing ideas with the community. The Ninety-Five Theses Martin Luther posted, however, created far more debate than other such documents. The items listed here, selected from Luther's list, argued against the sale of indulgences.

Luther thought that only God—not the pope—could grant forgiveness.

Luther thought buying indulgences was useless.

(5) The pope will not, and cannot, remit [forgive] other punishments than those which he has imposed by his own decree [ruling] or according to the canons [laws].

(21) Therefore, those preachers of indulgences err [make a mistake] who say that, by the pope's indulgence, a man may be exempt from all punishments, and be saved.

(30) Nobody is sure of having repented [been sorry] sincerely enough; much less can he be sure of having received perfect remission of sins.

(43) Christians should be taught that he who gives to the poor, or lends to a needy man, does better than buying indulgences.

(52) It is a vain and false thing to hope to be saved through indulgences, though the commissary [seller]—nay, the pope himself—was to pledge his own soul therefore.

—Martin Luther, *Ninety-Five Theses*

 ANALYSIS SKILL ANALYZING PRIMARY SOURCES

Why did Martin Luther argue against the sale of indulgences?

BIOGRAPHY

John Calvin
1509–1564

Calvin was probably the most influential figure of the Reformation after Luther. Through his writings and preaching, Calvin spread basic Reformation ideas such as the right of the common people to make church policy. Unlike many other religious leaders, Calvin didn't think that the pursuit of profits would keep businesspeople from being saved. This idea would eventually help lead to the growth of capitalism.

Making Inferences Why might Calvin's economic ideas have been popular with the people of Geneva?

In 1541 the people of Geneva, Switzerland, made Calvin their religious and political leader. He and his followers, called Calvinists, passed laws to make people live according to Calvin's teachings. Calvin hoped to make Geneva an example of a good Christian city.

In England the major figure of the Reformation was King Henry VIII. Henry asked the pope to officially end his marriage, but the pope refused. Furious, Henry decided that he was not going to obey the pope anymore. In 1534 he declared himself the head of a new church, called the Church of England, or Anglican Church.

Henry broke from the Catholic Church for personal reasons, not religious ones. As a result, he didn't change many church practices. The rituals and beliefs of the Anglican Church stayed very much like those of the Catholic Church. But Henry's actions opened the door for other Protestant beliefs to take hold in England.

THE IMPACT TODAY

The Jesuit Order runs Catholic schools and universities all around the world.

READING CHECK **Summarizing** What were Martin Luther's main religious teachings?

The Catholic Reformation

As Protestantism spread in the later 1500s and 1600s, Catholic leaders responded. Their effort to stop the spread of Protestantism and to reform the Catholic Church from within was known as the **Catholic Reformation**, or the Counter-Reformation.

Catholic Culture in Spain

Even before the Catholic Reformation, Spain's rulers had been battling to drive non-Catholics from their lands. In 1492 the king and queen defeated the last Muslim forces in Spain. They then forced all Muslims and Jews remaining in the country to convert to Catholicism.

The Spanish monarchs also ordered the Spanish Inquisition to find and punish any Muslims or Jews who had converted to Catholicism but still secretly kept their old beliefs.

The Inquisition was ruthless in carrying out this duty. It later sought out Protestants. Once the Inquisition had punished all Muslim, Jewish, and Protestant believers, Spain's Catholic Church had no opposition.

Catholic Reforms

In other parts of Europe, Catholic leaders were responding to the criticisms of Protestants. Catholic reformers created new religious orders, or communities, in southern Europe. These orders wanted to win people back to the Catholic Church.

The first of the new orders was founded in 1534 by a Spanish noble, Saint Ignatius (ig-NAY-shuhs) of Loyola. This new order was the Society of Jesus, or the Jesuits. The **Jesuits** were a religious order created to serve the pope and the church. Ignatius had fought as a knight, and the Jesuits were trained to be as disciplined as soldiers in their religious duties. By teaching people about Catholic ideas, Jesuits hoped to turn people against Protestantism.

The Council of Trent

Many Catholic leaders felt more change was needed. They called together the Council of Trent, a meeting of church leaders in Trent, Italy. Clergy from across Europe came to discuss, debate, and eventually reform Catholic teachings.

The council restated the importance of the clergy in interpreting the Bible, but it created new rules that clergy had to follow. One rule ordered bishops to live in the areas they oversaw. The council also officially rejected the ideas of the Protestant leaders.

Some Catholic Reformation leaders wanted to punish Protestants as heretics. To lead this campaign, the pope created religious courts to punish any Protestants found in Italy. He also issued a list of books considered dangerous for people to read, including many by Protestant leaders. People reading books on this list could be excommunicated from the Catholic Church.

Catholic Missionaries

Many Catholics dedicated their lives to helping the church grow. They became missionaries, traveling to foreign countries to spread their faith. As this missionary activity greatly increased during the Catholic Reformation, Catholic teachings spread around the world.

Many of the new missionaries were Jesuits. Jesuit priests went to Africa, Asia, and America. Probably the most important missionary of the period was the Jesuit priest Saint Francis Xavier (ZAYV-yuhr). He brought Catholicism to parts of India and Japan in the mid-1500s.

Around the world Catholic missionaries baptized millions of people. Through their efforts the Catholic Reformation reached far beyond Europe.

READING CHECK **Finding Main Ideas** What were the goals of Catholic Reformation leaders?

The Council of Trent

Results of the Council of Trent QUICK FACTS

- The selling of indulgences is banned

- Bishops must live in the areas they oversee

- The ideas of Luther, Calvin, and other Reformation leaders are rejected

The Council of Trent met between 1545 and 1563 to clarify church teachings that had been criticized by Protestants. The council played a key role in revitalizing the Catholic Church in Europe.

Protestant Self-Government

This painting from the 1600s shows a Protestant church in France. Members of a congregation like this one would elect leaders and make their own rules. The rise of self-government was one result of the Reformation.

Some Results of the Reformation

QUICK FACTS

- Religious conflicts spread across Europe

- Church leaders reform the Catholic Church

- Missionaries spread Catholicism around the world

- Northern Europe becomes largely Protestant

- Local Protestant churches practice self-government

The Political Impact

The Reformation created division within Europe. In Spain most people were Catholic. In the northern countries most people were Protestant. The Holy Roman Empire was a patchwork of small kingdoms, some Catholic and some Protestant. These divisions often led to political conflicts.

Religious Wars

Although most people in France were Catholic, some became Protestants. French Protestants were called Huguenots (HYOO-guh-nahts). Tensions increased between the two religious groups after the French king, who was Catholic, banned all Protestant religions. In 1562 violence broke out.

The war between French Catholics and Huguenots continued off and on for decades. The conflict finally ended in 1598. In that year King Henry IV issued the Edict of Nantes (NAHNT), a law granting religious freedom in most of France. Protestants could worship anywhere except in Paris and a few other cities.

Religious wars caused even more destruction in the Holy Roman Empire. There, the king of Bohemia sparked a conflict when he forced everyone in his kingdom to become Catholic. In 1618 Protestants rose up in revolt. The rebellion spread through the Holy Roman Empire, starting what is known as the Thirty Years' War.

The Holy Roman Emperor sought help from other Catholic countries. The Protestants also sought allies. The Catholic king of France agreed to help them because he didn't like the Holy Roman Emperor.

After 30 years of fighting, Europe's rulers worked out a peace agreement in 1648. This **agreement**, the Treaty of Westphalia, allowed rulers to determine whether their countries would be Catholic or Protestant. The treaty also made the states of Germany independent of the Holy Roman Empire.

Social Changes

The Reformation led not only to political changes but to social changes too. Before the Reformation, most Europeans had no voice in governing the Catholic Church. They simply followed the teachings of their priests and bishops. However, many Protestant churches didn't have priests, bishops, or other clergy. Instead each congregation, or community of worshippers, made its own rules and elected its own leaders. People began to think that their own ideas, not just the clergy's, were important.

Once people began to govern their own churches, they also wanted political power. In some places congregations ruled their towns, not just their churches. In the American colonies of New England, for instance, congregations met to decide how their towns would be run. These town meetings were an early form of self-government, in which people rule themselves.

As time passed, some congregations gained even more power. Their decisions came to affect more aspects of people's lives or to control events in larger areas. The power of these congregations didn't replace national governments, but national rulers began to share some power with local governments. The sharing of power between local governments and a strong central government is called **federalism**.

Once people began to think that their ideas were important, they began to raise questions. They wanted to know more about the world around them. In addition, many people refused to accept information based on someone else's authority. They didn't care if the person was an ancient writer or a religious leader. The desire to investigate led people to turn to science.

READING CHECK **Analyzing** How did Europe change after the Thirty Years' War?

ACADEMIC VOCABULARY

agreement a decision reached by two or more people or groups

SUMMARY AND PREVIEW In the 1500s Protestants challenged the Catholic Church. Catholic leaders adopted religious reforms to preserve the church's influence. The religious changes of the Reformation led to conflict and social changes. In the next chapter, you'll learn about the growth of science and the Scientific Revolution.

Section 3 Assessment

go.hrw.com
Online Quiz
KEYWORD: SN6 HP19

Reviewing Ideas, Terms, and People

1. **a. Recall** What were three complaints people had about the Catholic Church in the early 1500s?
   b. Contrast How did **Martin Luther's** ideas about interpreting the Bible differ from Catholics' ideas?
2. **a. Define** What was the **Catholic Reformation**?
   b. Analyze What was the goal of the Spanish Inquisition?
3. **a. Identify** Where did the Thirty Years' War begin?
   b. Sequence How did the **Reformation** lead to the growth of **federalism**?

Critical Thinking

4. **Analyzing** Using your notes on the reformers and a diagram like the one below, explain how tensions between Protestants and Catholics led to conflict and violence in Europe.

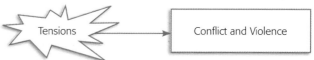

Tensions → Conflict and Violence

FOCUS ON WRITING

5. **Choosing Important Details** Write the main idea and supporting details of the section in your notebook. Then go over your notes to choose the most important or intriguing details to include on your book jacket. Put a check mark next to the details you think you'll include.

from Romeo and Juliet

by William Shakespeare

About the Reading *Shakespeare's plays spotlight an enormous range of human experiences—including love, loss, and everything in between. Even though* Romeo and Juliet *ends in disaster, its message is a hopeful one. Its main characters, two teenaged members of warring families, meet at a party and fall instantly in love. In this scene, which takes place later that evening, a troubled Romeo sees Juliet on her balcony.*

AS YOU READ Notice the words Romeo uses to describe Juliet's beauty.

Rom. But soft, what light through yonder window breaks?
It is the east, and Juliet is the sun. ❶
Arise, fair sun, and kill the envious moon,
Who is already sick and pale with grief
That thou, her maid, art far more fair than she . . .
Two of the fairest stars in all the heaven,
Having some business, do entreat her eyes
To twinkle in their spheres till they return.
What if her eyes were there, they in her head?
The brightness of her cheek would shame those stars,
As daylight doth a lamp; her eyes in heaven
Would through the airy region stream so bright
That birds would sing and think it were not night.
See how she leans her cheek upon her hand!
O that I were a glove upon that hand,
That I might touch that cheek!
Jul. Ay me!
Rom. She speaks!
O, speak again, bright angel, for thou art
As glorious to this night, being o'er my head,
As is a winged messenger of heaven
Unto the white-upturned wond'ring eyes
Of mortals that fall back to gaze on him,

❶ Romeo compares Juliet to the sun and claims that even the moon will be jealous of her beauty.

To what else does he compare her in this speech?

When he bestrides the lazy puffing clouds,
And sails upon the bosom of the air.
Jul. O Romeo, Romeo, wherefore art thou Romeo? **❷**
Deny thy father and refuse thy name;
Or, if thou wilt not, be but sworn my love,
And I'll no longer be a Capulet.
Rom. [Aside.] Shall I hear more, or shall I speak at this?
Jul. 'Tis but thy name that is my enemy;
Thou art thyself, though not a Montague.
What's Montague? It is nor hand nor foot,
Nor arm nor face, nor any other part
Belonging to a man. O, be some other name!
What's in a name? That which we call a rose
By any other word would smell as sweet;
So Romeo would, were he not Romeo call'd,
Retain that dear perfection which he owes
Without that title. Romeo, doff thy name,
And for thy name, which is no part of thee,
Take all myself. **❸**
Rom. I take thee at thy word.
Call me but love, and I'll be new baptized;
Henceforth I never will be Romeo.
Jul. What man art thou that thus bescreen'd in night
So stumblest on my counsel?
Rom. By a name
I know not how to tell thee who I am.
My name, dear saint, is hateful to myself,
Because it is an enemy to thee;
Had I it written, I would tear the word.
Jul. My ears have not yet drunk a hundred words
Of thy tongue's uttering, yet I know the sound.
Art thou not Romeo, and a Montague?
Rom. Neither, fair maid, if either thee dislike.

WORD HELP

bestrides mounts
wherefore why
doff remove
counsel secret thoughts

❷ Juliet is not asking where Romeo is. She is asking why he is Romeo, her family's enemy.

❸ Juliet says that she could be with Romeo if he were from a different family.

What does she ask him to do?

A painting of Romeo and Juliet from the 1800s

CONNECTING LITERATURE TO HISTORY

1. **Evaluating** Renaissance humanists explored human activities and focused on human actions. Why do you think the actions of Romeo and Juliet are still important to audiences today?

2. **Analyzing** Medieval writings often focused on religious topics. But the Renaissance humanists believed that people could write about many subjects other than religion. Based on this passage, what new topic did some humanist writers explore?

Social Studies Skills

Analysis   Critical Thinking   Economics   Study

Understanding Graphs

Understand the Skill

Graphs are drawings that display information in a clear, visual form. There are three main types of graphs. *Line graphs* show changes in something over time. *Bar graphs* compare quantities within a category. Some bar graphs may illustrate changes over time as well. *Circle graphs*, also called *pie graphs*, represent the parts that make up a whole of something. Each piece of the circle, or "pie," shows what proportion that part is of the whole.

Graphs let you see relationships more quickly and easily than tables or written explanations do. The ability to read and interpret graphs will help you to better understand and use statistical information in history.

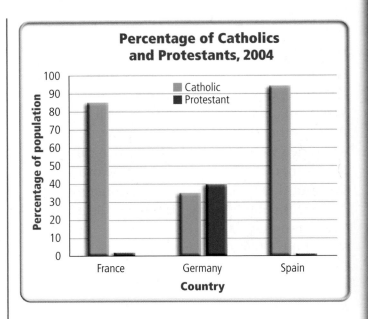

Percentage of Catholics and Protestants, 2004

Learn the Skill

Use the following guidelines to understand and interpret data presented in a graph.

1. Read the graph's title to identify the subject. Note the type of graph. This will give you clues about its purpose.

2. Study the graph's parts and read its labels. Note the subjects or categories that are graphed. Also note the units of measure. If the graph uses different colors, determine what each means.

3. Analyze the data. Note any increases or decreases in quantities. Look for trends or changes over time. Determine any other relationships in the data that is graphed.

Practice and Apply the Skill

The Reformation brought changes to Christianity in Europe. The effects of these changes can still be seen there today. Use the graph to answer the following questions.

1. What kind of graph is this?

2. What is the purpose of the graph?

3. What percentage of the population in France is Catholic?

4. In what country are there more Protestants than Catholics?

Visual Summary

Use the visual summary below to help you review the main ideas of the chapter.

QUICK FACTS

Italian trade wealth supported a rebirth of the arts and learning, inspiring great works of Renaissance genius.

The printing press played a key role in spreading the ideas of the Renaissance beyond Italy.

Reformers criticized practices of the Catholic Church and eventually broke away to form Protestant churches.

Reviewing Vocabulary, Terms, and People

Copy each sentence onto your own paper and fill in the blank with the word or name in the word pair that best completes the sentence.

1. The trader from Venice who traveled to China and met with Kublai Khan was _____ _____ (Cosimo de Medici/Marco Polo).

2. A way of thinking and learning that stresses the importance of human abilities and actions is called _____ (humanism/the Renaissance).

3. _____ (Leonardo da Vinci/ Michelangelo) was a painter, sculptor, inventor, engineer, and mapmaker.

4. _____ (Albrecht Dürer/Johann Gutenberg) developed a printing press that used movable type.

5. Poet _____ (Miguel de Cervantes/ William Shakespeare) also wrote more than 30 plays.

6. The _____ (Spanish Inquisition/ Reformation) was a movement to reform the Catholic Church during the late Renaissance.

7. The priest who posted a list of 95 complaints about the church was _____ (Pope Leo X/Martin Luther).

8. _____ (John Calvin/Dante Alighieri) believed in predestination, as well as in the importance of living a good life and obeying God's laws.

9. The _____ (congregation/Council of Trent) was a meeting held to discuss and reform practices of the Catholic Church.

10. Sharing power between local governments and a strong central government is called _____ (federalism/indulgences).

Comprehension and Critical Thinking

SECTION 1 *(Pages 558–564)*

11. a. Identify What were the four main trade cities of Italy during the 1300s?

b. Analyze In what sense was the Renaissance a rebirth?

SECTION 2 *(Pages 565–568)*

12. a. Recall How did new ideas about education spread beyond Italy?

b. Contrast How was Northern European art different from Italian art?

c. Elaborate The printing press significantly changed the history of the world. In your opinion, what other inventions have had a major impact on world history?

SECTION 3 *(Pages 569–575)*

13. a. Recall Where did more Protestants live, in northern or southern Europe?

b. Draw Conclusions How did Protestant religions come into being?

Reviewing Themes

14. Geography How did their location help Italy's major port cities develop trade networks?

15. Society and Culture Give three non-religious effects of the Renaissance and Reformation.

Using the Internet

go.hrw.com
KEYWORD: SN6 WH19

16. Activity: Supporting a Point of View The Renaissance was a time of great advances in literature, the arts, science, and math. Individuals such as Marco Polo, William Shakespeare, Leonardo da Vinci, and Johann Gutenberg helped change people's view of the world. Enter the activity keyword and learn about the important people and events of the Renaissance. Then create a political cartoon about an event or person in the chapter. Pick the point of view of a supporter or critic and use your cartoon to explain how he or she would have viewed your topic.

Reading Skills

Greek and Latin Word Roots *Answer the following questions about the Greek and Latin roots of words from this chapter.*

17. Based on the definition of *perspective,* what do you think the Latin root *spec-* means. *Hint*: Think about other words that use this root, such as *spectator* and *spectacles.*

a. to feel

b. to see

c. to hear

d. to understand

18. The prefix *per-* in perspective means "through." Based on this meaning, what do you think the word *permeate* means?

a. to spread through

b. to dissolve in

c. to disappear from

d. to climb over

Social Studies Skills

19. Understanding Graphs What kind of graph (line, bar, or circle) would you create to show how the number of Protestants in the Netherlands rose and fell during the 1600s? Explain your answer.

FOCUS ON WRITING

20. A Book Jacket Now that you have all the main ideas and supporting details, it is time to create your book jacket. Remember to put the title on the front cover. Illustrate the front page with a picture that you feel best illustrates the Renaissance and Reformation. On the back cover, list the main ideas and supporting details that you have already identified. What do you think will attract people to your book?

DIRECTIONS: Read each question, and write the letter of the best response. Use the primary source below to answer question 1.

> "I realize that women have accomplished many good things and that even if evil women have done evil, ... the benefits accrued [gained] ... because of good women—particularly the wise and literary ones ... outweigh the evil. Therefore, I am amazed by the opinion of some men who claim they do not want their daughters, wives, or kinswomen [female relatives] to be educated because their mores [morals] will be ruined as a result."
>
> —Christine de Pizan, from the *Book of the City of Ladies*, 1405

1 The content of this passage suggests that the person who wrote it was

A a rich Italian merchant.

B Niccolo Machiavelli.

C a supporter of humanism.

D Marco Polo.

2 Which person's contribution was *most* important in spreading the ideas of the Renaissance beyond Italy?

A Cosimo de' Medici

B Johann Gutenberg

C Leonardo da Vinci

D Dante Alighieri

3 In general, the artists and architects of the Renaissance were financially supported by

A rich families and church leaders.

B large European universities.

C the most powerful nations in Europe.

D the printing industry.

4 Reformers found fault with all the following practices of the Catholic Church *except*

A its sale of indulgences.

B its support of monotheism.

C the clergy's involvement in corruption.

D the church owning vast wealth.

5 Which person is generally credited with starting the Reformation?

A Desiderius Erasmus

B Martin Luther

C John Calvin

D King Henry VIII

Connecting with Past Learning

6 Italy in the Renaissance was not a unified country, but several small independent states. Which of the following cultures had a similar structure?

A ancient Greece during the Golden Age

B the Fertile Crescent during the Stone Age

C the New Kingdom of ancient Egypt

D Rome during the Pax Romana

7 In many places in Europe in the 1500s, Protestants were persecuted for their beliefs. Other people that you have studied who were persecuted for what they believed were

A Egyptians under Alexander the Great.

B Hindus in India.

C Christians in the early Roman Empire.

D Buddhists in China.

UNIT 9

The Early Modern World

The world changed dramatically with the Scientific Revolution and the Age of Exploration. New inventions allowed European explorers to sail around the globe. They found new continents and began to see what the shape of the world was really like. Contacts between distant peoples and lands changed societies and economies around the world.

At the same time, European thinkers developed new ideas about government during a period known as the Enlightenment. These ideas led people to take up arms in revolutions and fight for their freedom.

In the next two chapters, you will learn how both European exploration and the Enlightenment helped shape the world.

Explore the Art

In this scene, young sailor Diego Bermúdez tends a sail on Columbus's first voyage to the Americas. Why might a young boy like Diego have joined Columbus on such a dangerous voyage?

CHAPTER **20** 1400–1700

Science and Exploration

FOCUS ON SPEAKING

An Informative Report A teacher at an elementary school has asked you to create an informative oral report for fifth graders about changes in Europe, Africa, Asia, and the Americas during the Scientific Revolution and the Age of Exploration. As you read this chapter, look for the important people and events that you will discuss. After you have finished the chapter, you will prepare a short speech and create a simple visual aid to refer to during your presentation.

CHAPTER EVENTS

1416
Henry the Navigator sets up his school of navigation.

1492
Columbus arrives in the Americas.

1400

WORLD EVENTS

1431
Joan of Arc is burned at the stake.

What You Will Learn...

In this chapter you will learn about the discoveries and inventions of the Scientific Revolution and the changes brought about by the European Age of Exploration. This photo shows a powerful telescope that astronomers use to study the skies.

1519
Magellan sails around the tip of South America.

1530s
Copernicus develops his theory of the sun-centered solar system.

1609
Galileo uses his telescope to study planets.

1687
Sir Isaac Newton publishes *Principia Mathematica*.

1600

1700

c. 1500
Askia the Great rules Songhai.

1649
Shah Jahan finishes building the Taj Mahal.

1690
John Locke argues that people have certain natural rights.

Focus on Themes In this chapter you will read about how a new way of looking at science was developed, as well as how the Scientific Revolution led to profound changes in **society and culture**. You will also learn about the European explorers who sailed to the Americas and the routes they followed to get there. You will also learn how their explorations led to the creation of a new **economic** system called capitalism.

Vocabulary Clues

Focus on Reading When you are reading your history textbook, you may often come across a word you do not know. If that word isn't listed as a key term, how do you find out what it means?

Using Context Clues Context means surroundings. Authors often include clues to the meaning of a difficult word in its context. You just have to know how and where to look.

Clue	How It Works	Example	Explanation
Direct Definition	Includes a definition in the same or a nearby sentence	European countries practiced mercantilism, in which a government controls all economic activity in a country and its colonies to make the government stronger and richer.	The phrase *"in which a government controls all economic activity in a country and its colonies to make the government stronger and richer"* defines *mercantilism*.
Restatement	Uses different words to say the same thing	Observation of the real world had disproved, or shown to be false, the teachings of an ancient authority.	The word *disproved* is another way to say *shown to be false*.
Comparisons or Contrasts	Compares or contrasts the unfamiliar word with a familiar one	Kepler discovered that the planets moved in elliptical, rather than in circular, orbits.	The word *rather* indicates that *elliptical* means something different from *circular*.

You Try It!

The following sentences are from this chapter. Each uses a definition or restatement clue to explain unfamiliar words. See if you can use the context to figure out the meaning of the words in italics.

Vocabulary Clues

1. These thinkers were *rationalists*, people who looked at the world in a rational, or reasonable and logical, way. (p. 589)
2. Its author was Polish astronomer Nicolaus Copernicus. The book was called *On the Revolution of the* Celestial Spheres. (p. 590)
3. Although Magellan was killed before he could complete the voyage, his crew became the first to *circumnavigate*, or go all the way around, the globe. (p. 595)
4. Capitalism is an economic system in which individuals and private businesses run most industries. (p. 601)

After you read the sentences, answer the following questions.

1. In example 1, what does the word *rationalists* means? What hints did you find in the sentence to figure that out?

2. In example 2, what is the meaning of *Celestial Spheres*? What hint helps you understand what this phrase means?

3. What is the definition of *circumnavigate* in example 3? What kind of context clues did you find in that sentence?

4. In example 4, what does *capitalism* mean? How do you know?

Key Terms and People

Chapter 20

Section 1
Scientific Revolution *(p. 588)*
theories *(p. 588)*
Ptolemy *(p. 589)*
Nicolaus Copernicus *(p. 590)*
Johannes Kepler *(p. 590)*
Galileo Galilei *(p. 591)*
Sir Isaac Newton *(p. 591)*
scientific method *(p. 592)*

Section 2
Henry the Navigator *(p. 595)*
Vasco da Gama *(p. 595)*
Christopher Columbus *(p. 595)*
Ferdinand Magellan *(p. 595)*
circumnavigate *(p. 595)*
Sir Francis Drake *(p. 596)*
Spanish Armada *(p. 596)*

Section 3
plantations *(p. 598)*
mercantilism *(p. 599)*
capitalism *(p. 601)*
market economy *(p. 601)*

Academic Vocabulary

Success in school is related to knowing academic vocabulary—the words that are frequently used in school assignments and discussions. In this chapter, you will learn the following academic words:

logical *(p. 589)*
principles *(p. 592)*

As you read Chapter 20, look for phrases between commas or dashes. Those phrases might be the definition or restatement of an unfamiliar word or term.

The Scientific Revolution

If **YOU** were there...

You are a student in Germany in the early 1500s. You love to watch the changing phases of the moon and draw the star patterns at different times of the year. You've asked your teachers many questions. Why does the moon hang in the sky? Why do the stars move? But their answers don't seem convincing to you.

How can you find the answers to your questions?

BUILDING BACKGROUND In the 1500s, Europe was undergoing dramatic changes. The Renaissance was well under way. During the Renaissance, educated people began to focus more on the world they lived in. It was a time of great advancements in art, writing, and education. The stage was set for another revolution in thinking.

The Birth of Modern Science

The series of events that led to the birth of modern science is called the **Scientific Revolution**. It occurred in Europe between about 1540 and 1700. Before the Scientific Revolution, most educated people who studied the world relied on explanations from authorities like ancient Greek writers or Catholic Church officials. After the Scientific Revolution, educated people felt freer to question old beliefs. They gained knowledge by studying the world around them and using logic to explain what they saw.

Understanding Science

The word *science* comes from a Latin word meaning "knowledge" or "understanding." So it is not surprising that science involves a particular way of gaining knowledge about the world. Science starts with observation. Scientists observe, or look at, the world. By observing the world they can identify facts about it. But scientists do more than identify facts. They use logic to explain what they have observed. The explanations scientists develop to explain observed facts are called **theories**.

Scientists design experiments to test whether their theories are correct. If the experiments show that the theory makes sense, the theory is accepted. If the experiments do not support the theory, scientists develop a new theory.

As you can see, scientific knowledge is based on observations, facts, and **logical** ideas, or theories, about them. Before the Scientific Revolution, this method of gaining knowledge was uncommon.

Roots of the Revolution

Many scientific ideas had been expressed in ancient times. Greek thinkers, such as Aristotle and **Ptolemy** (TAHL-uh-mee), wrote about astronomy, geography, and logic. These thinkers were rationalists, people who looked at the world in a rational, or reasonable and logical, way.

Muslim scholars translated the works of Greek thinkers into Arabic. They also added their own ideas about how the world worked. Arabic writings were later translated into Latin, allowing Europeans to study past rational thought. As the Europeans learned from these writings, their own view of the world became more rational.

Developments in Europe also helped bring about the Scientific Revolution. One such development was the growth of humanism during the Renaissance. Humanist artists and writers encouraged study of the natural world. Another development was the popularity of alchemy (AL-kuh-mee). A forerunner of chemistry, alchemy involved experiments whose aim was to turn common metals into gold.

READING CHECK **Finding Main Ideas** What was the Scientific Revolution?

ACADEMIC VOCABULARY

logical reasoned, well thought out

Greek Thinkers
The ancient Greeks developed theories about how the world worked that influenced later scientific thinkers. This famous painting from the early 1500s by the Italian artist Raphael shows some influential Greek thinkers.

Philosophers like Plato and Aristotle used reason and logic to understand the world.

Pythagoras studied numbers and believed that things could be predicted and measured.

Euclid discovered basic mathematical laws that helped explain the natural world.

589

Discoveries and Inventions

During the Renaissance, European scholars eagerly studied the works of Greek rationalists. Then an event took place that caused Europeans to doubt the Greeks. In 1492 Christopher Columbus sailed west across the Atlantic Ocean in hopes of reaching Asia. To navigate, he relied in part on a map of the world that Ptolemy had created.

Columbus never reached Asia. He ran into North America instead, a land mass Ptolemy knew nothing about. Europeans were stunned that observation of the real world had disproved the teachings of an ancient authority. Soon scholars began to question the accuracy of other authorities. They also began to make important discoveries of their own.

Advances in Astronomy

In 1543 an astronomer published a book that contradicted Ptolemy on another matter. Many historians think the publication of this book marks the beginning of the Scientific Revolution. The book was called *On the Revolution of the Celestial Spheres.*

Its author was Polish astronomer **Nicolaus Copernicus** (kuh-PUHR-ni-kuhs).

Nearly 1,400 years before Copernicus, Ptolemy had written that the sun and planets orbited, or circled around, the earth. As Copernicus studied the movements of the planets, however, he learned that Ptolemy's theory made little sense.

So Copernicus came up with a different explanation for what he observed. His theory was that the planets moved around the sun in circular orbits. Though he never proved this theory, Copernicus inspired fresh thinking about science.

Another leading astronomer, Tycho Brahe (TEE-koh BRAH-huh), worked in Denmark. In the late 1500s, he charted the positions of more than 750 stars. In his work, Brahe set an example by emphasizing careful observation and detailed, accurate records. Careful recording of information is necessary so that other scientists can use what has previously been learned.

Brahe was assisted by German astronomer **Johannes Kepler**. Later, Kepler tried to map the orbits of the planets. But Kepler

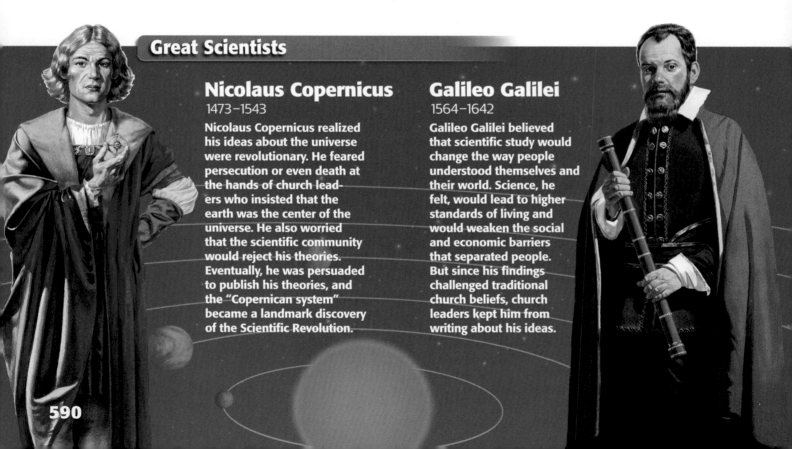

Great Scientists

Nicolaus Copernicus
1473–1543

Nicolaus Copernicus realized his ideas about the universe were revolutionary. He feared persecution or even death at the hands of church leaders who insisted that the earth was the center of the universe. He also worried that the scientific community would reject his theories. Eventually, he was persuaded to publish his theories, and the "Copernican system" became a landmark discovery of the Scientific Revolution.

Galileo Galilei
1564–1642

Galileo Galilei believed that scientific study would change the way people understood themselves and their world. Science, he felt, would lead to higher standards of living and would weaken the social and economic barriers that separated people. But since his findings challenged traditional church beliefs, church leaders kept him from writing about his ideas.

ran into a problem. He discovered that the planets did not move in circular orbits as Copernicus had thought. The planets instead move in elliptical, or oval, orbits around the sun. Kepler's basic ideas about the planets' movements are still accepted by scientists today.

Italian scientist **Galileo Galilei** (gal-uh-LEE-oh gal-uh-LAY) was the first person to study the sky with a telescope. Galileo saw craters and mountains on the moon and discovered that moons orbit Jupiter.

Galileo was also interested in how falling objects behave. Today, we use the term *mechanics* for the study of objects and motion. Galileo's biggest contribution to science was the way he learned about mechanics. Instead of just observing things in nature, he set up experiments. In fact, Galileo was the first scientist to routinely use experiments to test his theories.

Sir Isaac Newton

The high point of the Scientific Revolution came with the publication of *Principia Mathematica*. The author of this book,

published in 1687, was the English scientist **Sir Isaac Newton**. Newton was one of the greatest scientists who ever lived. Some of his theories have been proven so many times that they are now called laws.

One of Newton's laws is called the law of gravity. You may know that gravity is the force that attracts objects to each other. It's the force that makes a dropped apple fall to the ground and that keeps the planets in orbit around the sun.

Newton's other three laws are called the laws of motion. They describe how objects move in space. Newton went on to explain how much of the physical world worked. His laws became the foundation of nearly all scientific study until the 1900s.

New Inventions

During the Scientific Revolution, scientists made dramatic advances in technology. Around 1590 a Dutch lens maker invented a simple microscope. By the mid-1600s, a microscope was used to observe tiny plants and animals living in drops of pond water.

In 1593 Galileo invented the thermometer to measure temperature. In 1609 he built a much-improved telescope that he used to make his important observations and discoveries.

In 1643, an Italian scientist invented the barometer, a device that measures air pressure. Used to help forecast the weather, the barometer, like other inventions of the time, gave scientists new ways to learn about their world.

THE IMPACT TODAY
Astronomers still study Kepler's ideas, which they call his laws of planetary motion.

FOCUS ON READING
Which sentence in this paragraph contains a direct definition of an unfamiliar word?

READING CHECK
Summarizing What were two major achievements in astronomy during this era?

Sir Isaac Newton
1642–1727

Sir Isaac Newton was interested in learning about the nature of light, so he conducted a series of experiments. In Newton's time, most people assumed that light was white. Newton proved, however, that light is actually made up of all of the colors of the rainbow. His research on light became the basis for his invention of the reflecting telescope—the type of telescope that is found in most large observatories today.

Effects on Society

The Scientific Revolution changed the way we learn about the world. People started to pursue science in a systematic fashion. Two men in particular, Francis Bacon and Rene Descartes (ruh-NAY day-CART), encouraged the use of orderly experiments and clear reasoning. Their ideas helped shape the **scientific method**, a step-by-step process for performing experiments and other scientific research. The basics of this method—observation and experimentation—are the main **principles** of modern science.

ACADEMIC
VOCABULARY
principles
basic beliefs,
rules, or laws

The Scientific Revolution affected other areas of life too. Philosophers thought observation and logic could explain problems like poverty and war. By using reason, they hoped to find ways to improve society.

As scientists discovered laws that governed nature, some thinkers began to believe that certain laws governed human behavior as well. If all people were governed by the same laws, then it stood to reason that all people must be equal. This idea of equality was important in the development of democratic ideas in Europe.

Science also created conflict as some scientific discoveries raised questions about church teachings. Church officials feared that science might lead people to doubt key elements of their faith, undermining the church's influence.

Catholic leaders tried to force scientists to reject any findings that contradicted church teachings. For example, they threatened Galileo with torture unless he accepted the church's belief that the earth did not move. Despite such conflicts, science continued to develop rapidly.

READING CHECK **Analyzing** Why was the church troubled by the Scientific Revolution?

SUMMARY AND PREVIEW The Scientific Revolution was the birth of modern science. Scientists developed new methods and inventions to make key discoveries. Next, you will learn about the age of European exploration.

Section 1 Assessment

Reviewing Ideas, Terms, and People

1. **a. Recall** When did the **Scientific Revolution** take place?
   b. Analyze Why was the Scientific Revolution important in world history?
   c. Predict What might cause scientists to reject a popular **theory**?
2. **a. Recall** What event caused Europeans to doubt the ideas of ancient Greek authorities?
   b. Analyze What was the most important contribution **Galileo Galilei** made to modern science?
   c. Evaluate Why do you think **Sir Isaac Newton** is considered to be one of the greatest scientists of all time?
3. **a. Describe** What is the **scientific method**?
   b. Contrast How did the views of science and the church differ?
   c. Elaborate What effect did the Scientific Revolution have on some philosophers?

Critical Thinking

4. **Identifying Effects** Based on your notes, list four major thinkers of the Scientific Revolution and their greatest achievements. Then write a statement that summarizes their effects on society.

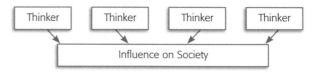

FOCUS ON SPEAKING

5. **Organizing Information** To prepare for your presentation, create a two-column chart. Label one column "Scientific Revolution," and the other "Exploration." From your notes, select the key people and events that you will discuss in your report. Put these in your first column.

Great Voyages of Discovery

If YOU were there...

Your uncle is a Portuguese ship captain who has just come back from a long sea voyage. He shows you a map of the new lands he has seen. He tells wonderful stories about strange plants and animals. You are studying to become a carpenter, but you wonder if you might like to be an explorer like your uncle instead.

How would you decide which career to choose?

BUILDING BACKGROUND A spirit of adventure swept across Europe in the 1400s. Improved maps showed new lands. Travelers' tales encouraged people to dream of finding riches and adventure.

Desire and Opportunity to Explore

Why did people seek to explore the world in the 1400s? First, they wanted Asian spices. Italy and Egypt controlled the trade routes to Asia, charging very high prices for spices. As a result, many countries wanted to find a direct sea route that led to Asia.

What You Will Learn...

Main Ideas

1. Europeans had a desire and opportunity to explore in the 1400s and 1500s.
2. Portuguese and Spanish explorers discovered new trade routes, lands, and people.
3. The English and French claimed land in North America.

The Big Idea

European explorers brought knowledge, wealth, and influence to their countries.

Key Terms and People

Henry the Navigator, *p. 595*
Vasco da Gama, *p. 595*
Christopher Columbus, *p. 595*
Ferdinand Magellan, *p. 595*
circumnavigate, *p. 595*
Sir Francis Drake, *p. 596*
Spanish Armada, *p. 596*

TAKING NOTES As you read, make a list of the major explorers of the Age of Exploration and their discoveries. You can use a chart like the one below, adding rows as needed.

Explorer	Discovery

This photo shows replicas of the three ships that Christopher Columbus used to sail to the Americas in 1492.

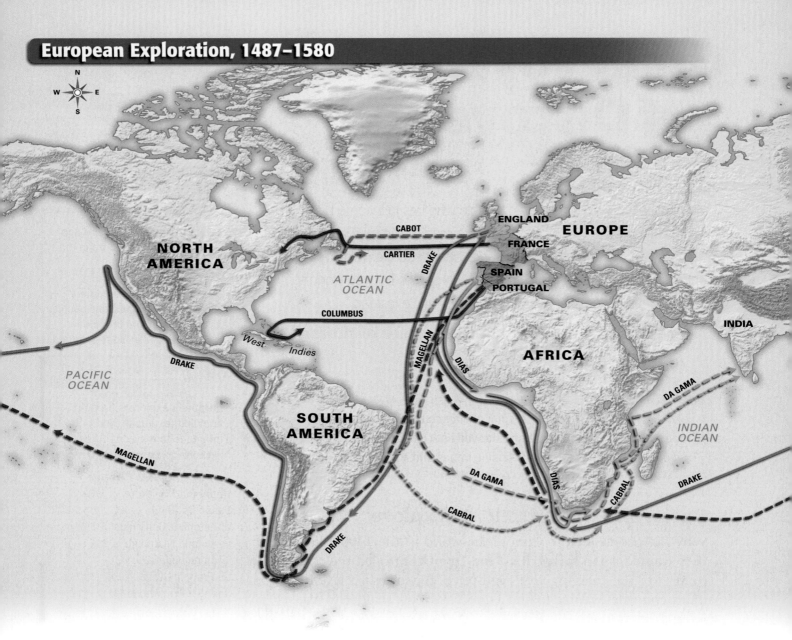

This way they could get spices without having to buy from Italian or Egyptian traders.

Religion gave explorers another reason to set sail. European Christians wanted to convert more people to their religion to counteract the spread of Islam in Europe, Africa, and Asia.

Advances in technology made exploration possible. Sailors used the astrolabe and the compass to find routes to faraway places. More accurate maps allowed sailors to sail from port to port without having to stay right along the coast the entire way.

Other advances came in shipbuilding. The Portuguese began building ships called caravels (KER-uh-velz). Caravels used triangular sails that, unlike traditional square sails, allowed ships to sail against the wind. By replacing oars on the ship's sides with rudders at the back of the ship, the Portuguese also greatly improved steering. The new caravels helped Portugal take the lead in the European Age of Exploration.

READING CHECK **Finding Main Ideas** What advances in technology aided exploration?

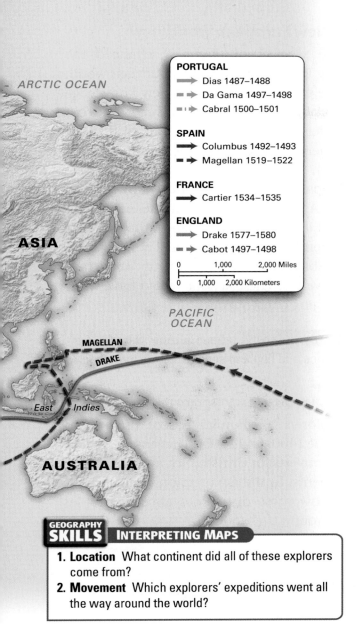

PORTUGAL
→ Dias 1487–1488
→ Da Gama 1497–1498
→ Cabral 1500–1501

SPAIN
→ Columbus 1492–1493
→ Magellan 1519–1522

FRANCE
→ Cartier 1534–1535

ENGLAND
→ Drake 1577–1580
→ Cabot 1497–1498

0   1,000   2,000 Miles
0   1,000   2,000 Kilometers

ARCTIC OCEAN

ASIA

PACIFIC OCEAN

MAGELLAN

DRAKE

East Indies

AUSTRALIA

GEOGRAPHY SKILLS | INTERPRETING MAPS

1. **Location** What continent did all of these explorers come from?
2. **Movement** Which explorers' expeditions went all the way around the world?

Portuguese and Spanish Explorations

Prince **Henry the Navigator** was responsible for much of Portugal's success on the seas. He built an observatory and a navigation school to teach sailors how to find their way on long ocean voyages. Some Portuguese sailors sailed south along the coast of Africa. In 1498 **Vasco da Gama** sailed around Africa and landed on the west coast of India. A sea route to Asia had been found.

Reaching the Americas

An Italian sailor, **Christopher Columbus**, thought he had already figured out a shorter way to Asia—sailing west across the Atlantic. He told the Spanish monarchs Ferdinand and Isabella his plan and promised them riches, new territory, and Catholic converts if they funded his journey. Isabella agreed.

In August 1492 Columbus set sail with 88 men and three small ships. On October 12, he and his crew landed on an island in the Bahamas. Columbus believed he had reached Asia. He didn't realize the continent of North America lay in front of him.

A Portuguese explorer later discovered South America by accident while trying to sail around Africa. Then, in 1519, **Ferdinand Magellan** (muh-JEHL-uhn) led a voyage around South America's southern tip. He continued sailing into the Pacific even though his ships were low on food and water. Although Magellan was killed before he could complete the voyage, his crew became the first to **circumnavigate**, or go all the way around, the globe.

Conquest of the "New World"

Spanish explorers called the Americas the "New World." When they arrived in these lands in the early 1500s, the Aztec Empire in Mexico and the Inca Empire in Peru were at the height of their powers. The Spanish saw these empires as good sources of gold and silver. They also wanted to convert the native peoples to Christianity.

Having better weapons, the Spanish quickly conquered the Aztecs and Incas. The Spanish also brought new diseases that over time killed possibly three-quarters of the native peoples. Soon, Spain ruled large parts of North and South America.

READING CHECK **Identifying Points of View** Why do you think European explorers called the Americas the "New World"?

The English and French in America

England and France also wanted to find a new route to Asia. After Spain and Portugal gained control of the southern routes, the English and French sent explorers to look for a waterway through North America. Though these explorers did not find such a passage, they claimed land in North America for England and France.

Competing for Land and Wealth

Besides looking for a route to Asia, England hoped to find riches in the New World. But Spain controlled the gold and silver of the former Aztec and Inca empires. When English sailors, such as **Sir Francis Drake**, began stealing treasure from Spanish transport ships, Spain became furious.

In 1588 Spain sent 130 ships to attack England. This fleet, called the **Spanish Armada**, was part of Spain's large navy. But the English had faster ships and better guns. They defeated the Armada and saved England from invasion. Spain now had a rival for rule of the seas.

A New European Worldview

The voyages of discovery changed the way Europeans thought about their world. The explorations brought new knowledge about geography and proved some old beliefs wrong. Europeans learned that the Americas were a separate landmass from Asia. Geographers made more accurate maps that reflected this new knowledge.

As Europeans studied the new maps and laid claim to new lands, they saw the potential for great wealth. They began to establish colonies and set up new trade networks. These actions would have wide-ranging consequences.

READING CHECK Generalizing Why did France and England send explorers to America?

SUMMARY AND PREVIEW European explorers sailed on voyages of discovery in the 1400s and 1500s. They found wealth, converts for Christianity, and new continents. In the next section, you will read how these discoveries affected peoples around the world.

Section 2 Assessment

go.hrw.com
Online Quiz
KEYWORD: SN6 HP20

Reviewing Ideas, Terms, and People

1. **a. Describe** What were caravels? How were they better than what they replaced?
   b. Explain What motivated Europeans to explore the world in the 1400s and 1500s?
2. **a. Identify** Who led the first voyage to **circumnavigate** the globe?
   b. Analyze How did the Spanish conquer the Aztec and Inca empires?
3. **a. Recall** Where did the English and French look for a route to Asia?
   b. Draw Conclusions How did power shift in Europe after the defeat of the **Spanish Armada**?
   c. Evaluate When claiming land in the New World for themselves, Europeans ignored the ownership rights of native peoples. What is your opinion of this?

Critical Thinking

4. **Drawing Conclusions** Add another column to the chart you created. In this last column, write a statement drawing a conclusion about the significance of each discovery.

Explorer	Discovery	Significance

FOCUS ON SPEAKING

5. **Collecting Information** Review your notes and this section. Select what you consider to be the three most important events of the European Age of Exploration. Describe these in the second column of your chart.

New Systems of Trade

If YOU were there...

You live in a coastal town in Spain in the 1500s. This week, several ships have returned from the Americas, bringing silver for the royal court. But that's not all. The crew has also brought back some strange foods. One sailor offers you a round, red fruit. Natives in the Americas call it a "tomatl," he tells you. He dares you to taste it, but you are afraid it might be poison.

Will you taste the tomato? Why or why not?

BUILDING BACKGROUND New fruits and vegetables such as tomatoes and potatoes looked very strange to Europeans in the 1500s. But new foods were only one part of a much larger exchange of products and ideas that resulted from the voyages of discovery.

Exchanging Plants, Animals, and Ideas

The exchange of plants, animals, and ideas between the New World (the Americas) and the Old World (Europe) is known as the **Columbian Exchange**. It changed lives around the world.

What You Will Learn...

Main Ideas

1. Europe, Asia, Africa, and the Americas exchanged plants, animals, and ideas.
2. In the 1600s and 1700s, new trade patterns developed and power shifted in Europe.
3. Market economies changed business in Europe.

The Big Idea

Exchanges between the Old World and the New World influenced the development of new economic systems: mercantilism and capitalism.

Key Terms
plantations, *p. 598*
mercantilism, *p. 599*
capitalism, *p. 601*
market economy, *p. 601*

TAKING NOTES Copy the diagram below. As you read, fill it in with information about the changes in Europe during the 1500s and 1600s.

New Products	New Trade Patterns	New Economic Systems

European manufactured goods, like this mirror, were new to the Americas.

Europeans brought new ideas and technologies when they settled new lands. This illustration shows a scene in what is now New Mexico.

Missions and settlements helped spread Christianity and European languages.

Europeans brought animals like oxen to pull carts.

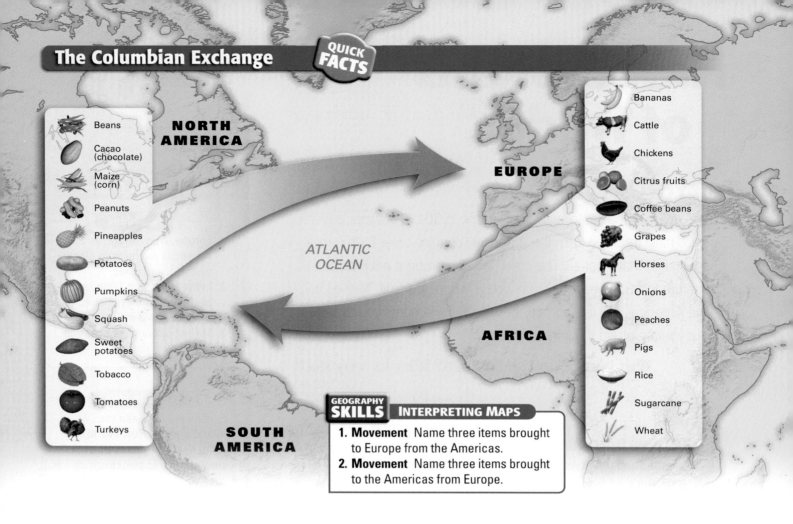

QUICK FACTS

NORTH AMERICA

Beans
Cacao (chocolate)
Maize (corn)
Peanuts
Pineapples
Potatoes
Pumpkins
Squash
Sweet potatoes
Tobacco
Tomatoes
Turkeys

EUROPE

ATLANTIC OCEAN

AFRICA

SOUTH AMERICA

Bananas
Cattle
Chickens
Citrus fruits
Coffee beans
Grapes
Horses
Onions
Peaches
Pigs
Rice
Sugarcane
Wheat

GEOGRAPHY SKILLS | INTERPRETING MAPS

1. **Movement** Name three items brought to Europe from the Americas.
2. **Movement** Name three items brought to the Americas from Europe.

Europeans introduced many new plants to the Americas, including bananas, sugarcane, oranges, onions, and lettuce. Europeans also brought new animals such as cows, goats, sheep, pigs, horses, and chickens to the New World.

In the Americas, Europeans found plants and animals they had never seen. They took some back to Europe, as well as to Africa and Asia. This exchange of plants changed the eating habits of people around the world. Some of the foods new to Europeans were tomatoes, potatoes, beans, squash, and chocolate.

In addition, Europeans introduced their culture to the places they explored. Missionaries went to Asia, Africa, and the Americas to convert the peoples there to Christianity. Missionaries taught European languages to native peoples as well.

Europeans also brought technologies such as guns and steel to the New World. The introduction of sheep and sugarcane created new industries. Artisans made new kinds of textiles from the wool that the sheep provided. Colonists also began to grow sugarcane on **plantations**, or large farms.

Plantations and mines in the Americas made money for Portugal and Spain. However, many American Indians who were forced to work on the land died from harsh treatment and European diseases. Europeans then started using enslaved Africans as workers. Soon, thousands of Africans were being shipped to the Americas as slave labor. The use of slave labor continued in parts of the Americas until the late 1800s.

READING CHECK Identifying Cause and Effect
What caused the Columbian Exchange?

Trade and Economic Power

The exchange of products between European countries and their colonies changed economic relations around the world. European countries saw their colonies as a way to get rich.

This view of the colonies was part of an economic system called **mercantilism**—a system in which a government controls all economic activity in a country and its colonies to make the government stronger and richer. Mercantilism was the main economic policy in Europe between 1500 and 1800.

Under mercantilism, governments did everything they could to get more gold and silver, which were considered to be the measure of a country's strength. Countries also tried to export more goods than they imported. In this way, they could keep a favorable balance of trade—the relationship between the value of imports and exports.

New Trading Patterns

Mercantilism created new patterns of global trade. One involved the exchange of raw materials from colonies in the Americas, manufactured products from Europe, and slaves from Africa. This three-pronged network was known as the triangular trade.

The Atlantic slave trade was a major part of the triangular trade. European traders crammed enslaved Africans on ships for the long voyage to the Americas. Chained together without enough food and water, many slaves got sick and died. Between the late 1500s and early 1800s Europeans shipped millions of enslaved Africans to colonies in the New World.

Power Shifts in Europe

In the 1500s Portugal and Spain, the early leaders in exploration, were also the leading economic powers. That changed as the Dutch and English became stronger.

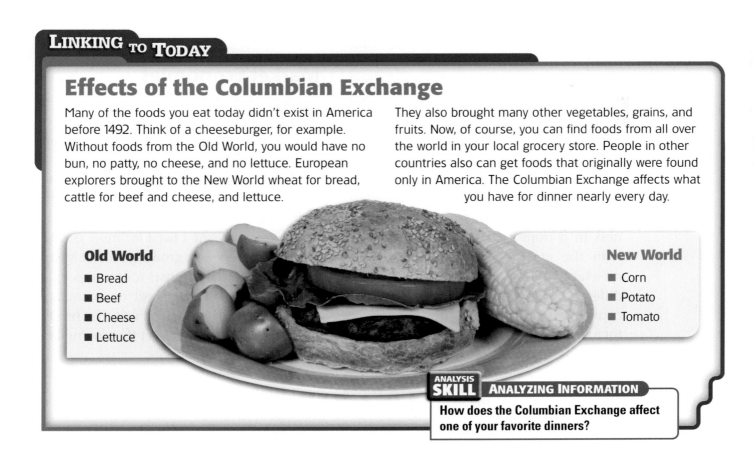

LINKING TO TODAY

Effects of the Columbian Exchange

Many of the foods you eat today didn't exist in America before 1492. Think of a cheeseburger, for example. Without foods from the Old World, you would have no bun, no patty, no cheese, and no lettuce. European explorers brought to the New World wheat for bread, cattle for beef and cheese, and lettuce.

They also brought many other vegetables, grains, and fruits. Now, of course, you can find foods from all over the world in your local grocery store. People in other countries also can get foods that originally were found only in America. The Columbian Exchange affects what you have for dinner nearly every day.

Old World
- Bread
- Beef
- Cheese
- Lettuce

New World
- Corn
- Potato
- Tomato

ANALYSIS SKILL ANALYZING INFORMATION

How does the Columbian Exchange affect one of your favorite dinners?

Supply and Demand QUICK FACTS

Market economies are based on the idea of supply and demand. This idea states that people will produce goods that other people want. In Europe, market economies developed as populations grew and the world economy developed.

1 Population grew in Europe. With more people, there was a greater demand for goods.

2 Since people wanted more goods, companies worked to make, or supply, more goods.

The Netherlands became a great trading power in the 1600s as the Dutch used their shipbuilding, sailing, and business skills to boost their overseas commerce. Dutch merchants formed a company to trade directly with Asia. The Dutch soon controlled many islands in Southeast Asia and trading posts in India, Japan, and southern Africa.

England also benefited greatly from increased trade. New trading posts in India and China, along with its colonies in North America, gave England access to huge markets and many resources.

Banking

Increased trade created a need for banks. Realizing this, the Dutch and the English each set up banks. Banking improved business in a number of ways. For example, with the growth of international trade, merchants had to deal with money from different countries. At banks, merchants could exchange money from one country for money from another and be certain that they were getting the proper value. Banks also loaned money to people who wanted to start new businesses. In doing so, banks contributed to economic growth.

Banking and new trade routes, along with increased manufacturing, brought wealth to England and the Netherlands. The economic power in Europe shifted.

READING CHECK Identifying Cause and Effect
Why did power shift from Spain and Portugal to England and the Netherlands in the 1600s?

Market Economies

Economic growth and new wealth changed business in Europe. Because more people had wealth, they started buying more manufactured goods.

There were several reasons for the increased demand for manufactured goods. First, Europe's population was growing. More people meant a need for more goods. Second, farmers were growing food at lower costs. With lower expenses for food, people had more money to spend on manufactured goods. A third reason was that newly founded colonies had to get their manufactured goods from Europe.

As the demand rose, businesspeople realized they could make more money by finding better ways to make manufactured

3 Finally, the supply of goods met the demand for goods.

goods. They wanted to increase the supply of goods offered to meet the demand. This new way of doing business can be considered the beginning of capitalism. **Capitalism** is an economic system in which individuals and private businesses run most industries. Competition among these businesses affects how much goods cost.

Competition among different businesses is most successful in a market economy.

In a **market economy**, individuals decide what goods and services they will buy and sell. The government does not make these decisions for people. A market economy works on a balance between supply and demand. If there is a great demand for a product, a seller will increase the supply in order to make more money.

The ability of individuals to control how they make and spend money is a benefit of a market economy and capitalism. In the 1800s capitalism would become the basis for most economic systems in western Europe and the Americas.

READING CHECK **Summarizing** What is a market economy?

SUMMARY AND PREVIEW The Columbian Exchange brought new plants, animals, and technology, as well as social and cultural changes, to Europe, Africa, Asia, and the Americas. New economic systems were developed too—mercantilism and, later, capitalism. Next, you'll learn about political changes in Europe.

go.hrw.com
Online Quiz
KEYWORD: SN6 HP20

Section 3 Assessment

Reviewing Ideas, Terms, and People

1. **a. Identify** Name some plants and animals that were part of the Columbian Exchange.
   b. Evaluate Who do you think benefitted more from the Columbian Exchange—Europeans or people in the Americas?
2. **a. Describe** What was the triangular trade?
   b. Analyze How did economic power shift in Europe in the 1600s?
   c. Elaborate How were colonies important to a country that was following the economic policy of **mercantilism**?
3. **a. Recall** In what kind of an economic system do individuals and private businesses run most of the industries?
   b. Explain How do supply and demand work in a market economy?

Critical Thinking

4. **Analyzing** Using your notes, explain how the availability of new products led to new trade patterns and new economic systems in Europe. Write your explanations in the arrows of a diagram like the one below.

| New Products | | New Trade Patterns | | New Economic Systems |

FOCUS ON SPEAKING

5. **Understanding Economics** From your notes and reading, select the three most important effects of the interaction between the Old and New Worlds. Describe these in your chart.

from Girl with a Pearl Earring

by Tracy Chevalier (1964–   )

About the Reading *The 1999 novel* Girl with a Pearl Earring *is a work of historical fiction. It is set in the bustling city of Delft, the Netherlands, during the 1660s. At this time, the Netherlands was one of the wealthiest, most powerful nations in the world. Nevertheless, many Dutch commoners struggled to pay high taxes. The main character of this novel is the teenaged daughter of one such commoner. To help support her family, Griet works as a maid to the family of a middle-class artist. The artist, Johannes Vermeer, was one of the greatest Dutch painters of his time.*

AS YOU READ Picture the city of Delft in your mind.

I had walked along that street all my life, but had never been so aware that my back was to my home. When I reached the end and turned out of sight of my family, though, it became a little easier to walk steadily and look around me. The morning was still cool, the sky a flat grey-white pulled close over Delft like a sheet, the summer sun not yet high enough to burn it away. The canal I walked along was a mirror of white light tinged with green. As the sun grew brighter the canal would darken to the color of moss.

Frans, Agnes, and I used to sit along that canal ❶ and throw things in—pebbles, sticks, once a broken tile—and imagine what they might touch on the bottom—not fish, but creatures from our imagination, with many eyes, scales, hands and fins. Frans thought up the most interesting monsters. Agnes was the most frightened. I always stopped the game, too inclined to see things as they were ❷ to be able to think up things that were not.

❸ There were a few boats on the canal, moving towards Market Square. It was not market day, however, when the canal was so full you couldn't see the water. One boat was carrying river fish for the stalls at Jeronymous Bridge. Another sat low on the water, loaded with bricks. The man poling the boat called out a greeting to me. I merely nodded and lowered my head so that the edge of my cap hid my face.

GUIDED READING

WORD HELP

inclined likely

❶ A major canal connected Delft to the cities of Rotterdam and The Hague.

What tells you that the canal was a central part of Griet's life?

❷ Griet claims that she is a realist—that she saw things "as they were."

What does this tell you about the description of the city that follows?

❸ *What details in this paragraph and the next suggest that Delft had a thriving economy?*

I crossed a bridge over the canal and turned into the open space of Market Square, even then busy with people criss-crossing it on their way to some task—buying meat at the Meat Hall, or bread at the baker's, taking wood to be weighed at the Weigh House. Children ran errands for their parents, apprentices for their masters, maids for their households. Horses and carts clattered across the stones. To my right was the Town Hall, with its gilded front and white marble faces gazing down from the keystones above the windows. To my left was the New Church, where I had been baptized sixteen years before. Its tall, narrow tower made me think of a stone birdcage. Father had taken us up it once. I would never forget the sight of Delft spread below us, each narrow brick house and steep red roof and green waterway and city gate marked forever in my mind, tiny and yet distinct. I asked my father then if every Dutch city looked like that, but he did not know. He had never visited any other city, not even The Hague, two hours away on foot.

I walked to the center of the square. There the stones had been laid to form an eight-pointed star set inside a circle. Each point aimed towards a different part of Delft. I thought of it as the very center of the town, and as the center of my life. Frans and Agnes and I had played in that star since we were old enough to run in the market. In our favorite game, one of us chose a point and one of us named a thing—a stork, a church, a wheelbarrow, a flower—and we ran in that direction looking for that thing. We had explored most of Delft that way.

One point, however, we had never followed. I had never gone to Papists' Corner, where the Catholics lived. The house where I was to work was just ten minutes from home, the time it took a pot of water to boil, but I had never passed by it.

❹ I knew no Catholics. There were not so many in Delft, and none in our street or in the shops we used. It was not that we avoided them, but they kept to themselves.

Girl with a Pearl Earring (1665), by Johannes Vermeer

WORD HELP

apprentices people who work for or train under a master craftsman

gilded overlaid with a thin layer of gold

keystones the top center stones in an arch

❹ Most people in the Netherlands were Protestant.

How does Griet's description of Delft reflect what you learned about the Reformation?

CONNECTING LITERATURE TO HISTORY

1. **Analyzing** New trade routes and banking, along with increased manufacturing, brought wealth to the Netherlands. What details in this excerpt point to the economic success of the Dutch?

2. **Drawing Inferences** The Netherlands became a great trading power. What geographical feature of Delft—and, more broadly, the Netherlands—helped its merchants to succeed in trade?

Social Studies Skills

Analyzing Tables

Understand the Skill

Like graphs, tables present numerical data. The figures are usually listed side by side for easy reference and comparison. A table is especially useful for organizing several categories of data. Since the figures in each row or column are related, you can easily compare numbers, and see relationships.

Learn the Skill

Follow these guidelines to read and analyze a table.

1 Read the table's title to determine its subject. All the data presented in the table will be related in some way to this subject.

2 Identify the data. Note the headings and labels of the table's columns and rows. This will tell you how the figures are organized. A table may also contain notes in parentheses. These explain the units in which the data should be read.

3 Study the information. Note the numbers in each row and column. Read across rows and down columns.

4 Use critical thinking skills to compare and contrast numbers, identify cause-and-effect relationships, note patterns of information, and draw conclusions.

Practice and Apply the Skill

The table below provides information on the planets in the solar system. Interpret the table to answer the following questions.

1. Which planets were unknown to Kepler, Galileo, and other scientists of the 1500s and 1600s?

2. What relationship does the table show between the length of a planet's year and its distance from the sun?

Planets of the Solar System					
Planet	When discovered	Diameter (in miles)	Minimum distance from Earth (in millions of miles)	Distance from Sun (in millions of miles)	Length of year (in Earth years)
Mercury	ancient times	3,024	57	36	0.24
Venus	ancient times	7,504	26	67	0.62
Earth	——————	7,909	——————	93	1.00
Mars	ancient times	4,212	49	141	1.88
Jupiter	ancient times	88,534	390	482	11.86
Saturn	prehistoric times	74,400	792	885	29.46
Uranus	1781	32,488	1,687	1,780	84.01
Neptune	1846	31,279	2,695	2,788	164.80

Visual Summary

Use the visual summary below to help you review the main ideas of the chapter.

QUICK FACTS

During the Scientific Revolution, scientists used observation, experimentation, and new inventions to greatly increase their knowledge of the world. This knowledge was also expanded by the European exploration of distant lands, made possible by technical advances in shipbuilding.

Reviewing Vocabulary, Terms, and People

For each statement below, write T if it is true and F if it is false. If the statement is false, write the correct term that would make the sentence a true statement.

1. **Galileo Galilei** was the first person to study the sky with a telescope.

2. An explanation that a scientist develops to explain observed facts is called a **scientific method**.

3. **Sir Isaac Newton** developed the theory that the planets orbit around the sun.

4. **Christopher Columbus** led the first voyage to **circumnavigate** the globe.

5. In 1588 an English navy was sent to destroy a fleet of ships called the **Spanish Armada**.

6. **Henry the Navigator** was responsible for much of Portugal's success on the seas.

7. The Spanish created large farms called **plantations** in the Americas.

Comprehension and Critical Thinking

SECTION 1 *(Pages 588–592)*

8. **a. Recall** When did the Scientific Revolution occur?

 b. Compare and Contrast How were Copernicus's and Kepler's theories about the movement of the planets similar? How were they different?

 c. Elaborate Choose one new invention from the period of the Scientific Revolution and explain how it affects your life.

SECTION 2 *(pages 593–596)*

9. **a. Recall** What did these people achieve: Vasco da Gama, Christopher Columbus, and Ferdinand Magellan?

 b. Draw Conclusions How did new navigation tools, caravels, and better maps affect travel by sea?

 c. Predict If the Spanish Armada had defeated the English, how might history have changed?

10. **a. Identify** Name three plants and three animals that Europeans brought to the Americas.

    b. Compare and Contrast What were some positive and negative results of the Columbian Exchange?

    c. Evaluate How did the founding of colonies affect manufacturing?

Social Studies Skills

Analyzing Tables *An invention from the Scientific Revolution—the barometer—is used to record air pressure during a hurricane. Scientists measure the strength of a hurricane on a scale from 1–5, with 5 being the strongest. Study the data in the table below about Hurricane Frances in 2004. Use the table to answer the questions that follow.*

Date and time	Wind speed (mph)	Air pressure (mb)	Category
9/1 12:00 noon	120	937	4
9/2 12:00 noon	125	939	4
9/3 12:00 noon	110	957	3
9/4 12:00 noon	90	960	2
9/5 11:00 am	80	963	1

11. What happened to the air pressure as the hurricane got weaker?

12. On what days did the air pressure of the hurricane measure 950 mb or greater?

Using the Internet

go.hrw.com
KEYWORD: SN6 WH20

13. **Activity: Researching Scientists and Their Discoveries** Amazing discoveries were made during the Scientific Revolution. Enter the activity keyword. Then create a chart of important scientists of that time, their key discoveries or inventions, the way the discoveries influenced society, and how information about the discoveries has evolved over time.

Reading Skills

Vocabulary Clues *Read the sentence, then answer the questions.*

> Catholic Church leaders tried strongly to impel scientists to reject any findings that contradicted church teachings.

14. What is the meaning of the word *impel*? What clues tell you its meaning?

15. What does the word *contradict* mean? How can you tell from the sentence? How could you restate the meaning by using words you know?

Reviewing Themes

16. **Society and Culture** How did the birth of science lead to the growth of democratic ideas?

17. **Economics** What led to the shift from mercantilism to capitalism?

18. **Economics** To make wise buying decisions in a market economy, individuals must know how to analyze advertisements, determine if they can afford a particular item, and judge whether their money might be better spent in other ways. Think of an item that you might like to buy. Describe the steps you would take in deciding whether to make the purchase.

FOCUS ON SPEAKING

19. **Giving Your Report** Look over the notes you made in your chart. Decide on an organized way to present your information. Then write your speech. Remember that your audience is young, so keep your content simple. Support your key points with interesting details. Use plenty of expressive language to keep your audience interested. Create a colorful, easy-to-follow visual to refer to as you speak.

DIRECTIONS: Read each question, and write the letter of the best response.

1 Use the diagram to answer the following question.

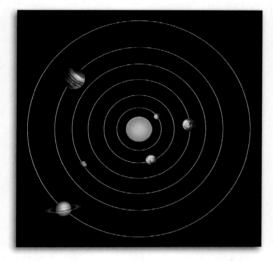

The pioneering work of which early scientist produced this understanding of the solar system?

A Francis Bacon

B Nicolaus Copernicus

C Ptolemy

D Isaac Newton

2 The fundamental principles of the modern scientific method are

A logic and mathematical theories.

B common beliefs of science and religion.

C very detailed record keeping.

D observation and experimentation.

3 Who was the first person to lead a voyage that went all the way around the world?

A Pedro Cabral

B Ferdinand Magellan

C Vasco da Gama

D Francis Drake

4 The Columbian Exchange is responsible for all of the following *except*

A the spread of disease from Europe to America.

B the introduction of the horse to Europe.

C the spread of American crops to Africa and Asia.

D the introduction of firearms to America.

5 According to the policy of mercantilism, what was the main purpose of colonies?

A to be a source of slaves to work in the ruling country

B to provide a place where the ruling country could send undesirable people

C to help the ruling country have a favorable balance of trade

D to serve as bases from which the ruling country could launch attacks on enemies

Connecting with Past Learnings

6 The event you learned about earlier in this course that was *most* responsible for the Scientific Revolution was

A the Renaissance.

B the fall of Rome.

C the development of feudalism.

D the invention of the printing press.

7 One result of the Columbian Exchange was the spread of Christianity. What other reason for Christianity's spread have you learned about this year?

A the Crusades

B the Spanish Inquisition

C the Reformation

D the Catholic Reformation

Enlightenment and Revolution

FOCUS ON WRITING

A Persuasive Article Imagine that you are a philosopher writing an article arguing for the ideas of the Enlightenment. How would you persuade people who don't agree with the new ideas? How will you change their minds? You will write a persuasive article in favor of Enlightenment ideas to be published in a pamphlet.

CHAPTER EVENTS

1642
Civil war begins in England.

1650

WORLD EVENTS

1647
Construction on the Taj Mahal is completed.

History's Impact

▶ **video series**
Watch the video to understand the impact of the Declaration of Independence on the development of American government and society.

What You Will Learn...

In this chapter you will learn how ideas of the Enlightenment led to revolutions around the world. This photo shows a reenactment of one of these revolutions—the American Revolution.

1690 John Locke argues that government's power should be limited.

1759 Mary Wollstonecraft is born in London.

1776 The American colonies declare their independence.

1789 The French Revolution begins.

1700

1707 The Mughal Empire ends in India.

1750

1769 Spanish missionaries begin founding missions in California.

1780 Tupac Amaru leads a peasant revolt against Peru's colonial rulers.

1800

Reading Social Studies

by Kylene Beers

Economics | Geography | Politics | Religion | Society and Culture | Science and Technology

Focus on Themes This chapter will introduce you to the Enlightenment, an era of great **political** thinkers, writers, and activists. You will learn about some of these figures, among the most influential people in all of world history. In their ideas, you will see the roots of our modern government, a government brought about by bold statesmen who inspired a revolution. You will also see how similar revolutions changed **society and culture** in countries around the world.

Summarizing Historical Texts

Focus on Reading History is made up of issues, questions about what to do in a particular situation. Throughout history, people have looked at issues from all sides. Each person's view of the issue shaped what he or she thought should be done.

Identifying Points of View The way a person views an issue is called his or her **point of view**, or perspective. Points of view can be shaped by many factors, such as a person's background or political beliefs. When you read a historical document, figuring out the author's point of view can help you understand his or her opinions about an issue.

Thomas Jefferson, from the Declaration of Independence

The history of the present King of Great Britain is a history of repeated injuries and usurpations, all having in direct object the establishment of a direct Tyranny over these States. To prove this, let Facts be submitted to a candid world.

He has refused his Assent to Laws, the most wholesome and necessary to the public good.

He has forbidden his Governors to pass Laws of immediate and pressing importance, unless suspended in their operation till his Assent should be obtained; and when so suspended, he has utterly neglected to attend to them.

→ **Consider the author's background—** Jefferson was a leader in the American colonies.

→ **Look for emotional language—** Words like injuries and usurpations make Jefferson's opinion clear.

→ **Look at the evidence—** Jefferson uses only examples of the king's flaws.

Put it all together to determine the author's point of view— Jefferson was opposed to the policies of the English king and wanted a change in government.

610 CHAPTER 21

You Try It!

Read the following passage from this chapter. Then answer the questions that follow.

Rousseau

French thinker Jean-Jacques Rousseau criticized divine right. He believed in popular sovereignty—the idea that governments should express the will of the people. In *The Social Contract*, published in 1762, Rousseau declared, "Man is born free, but he is everywhere in chains." According to Rousseau, citizens submit to the authority of government to protect their own interests, entering into a "social contract." This contract gives the government the power to make and enforce laws as long as it serves the people. The government should give up that power if it is not serving the people.

From Chapter 21, p. 618

Think about the passage you have just read and then answer the questions below.

1. What do you think was Rousseau's point of view about France's government?

2. What words or phrases in this passage helped you identify his point of view?

3. How did Rousseau's own beliefs and ideas affect his point of view?

4. Do you think Rousseau's point of view was similar to or different from that of the king of France?

5. Who do you think would more likely share Rousseau's point of view: a wealthy French noble or a colonist planning a rebellion? Why do you think so?

Academic Vocabulary

Success in school is related to knowing academic vocabulary—the words that are frequently used in school assignments and discussions. In this chapter, you will learn the following academic words:

contract *(p. 617)*
ideals *(p. 624)*

As you read Chapter 21, try to determine the points of view of the various people you are studying.

Ideas of the Enlightenment

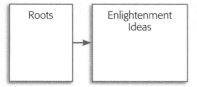

If YOU were there...

You are a student in the early 1700s. It seems your teacher can pass or fail whomever he wants. You think the teacher should make his decisions about grades based on what a student has learned. You come up with a new idea—testing students so they can prove what they know. You think this idea will improve your grades as well as relations in your school.

Will you challenge the teacher's authority?

BUILDING BACKGROUND In the 1600s and 1700s, people like the student mentioned above began to question sources of authority in society—particularly those of religion and government. They thought that using reason and logic would lead to improvements in society. Their ideas spread quickly in Europe.

The Age of Reason

Discoveries made during the Scientific Revolution and on the voyages of discovery led to changes in Europe. A number of scholars were beginning to challenge long-held beliefs about science, religion, and government.

These new scholars relied on reason, or logical thought, instead of religious teachings to explain how the world worked. They believed human reason could be used to achieve three great goals—knowledge, freedom, and happiness—and that achieving these goals would improve society. The use of reason in guiding people's thoughts about philosophy, society, and politics defined a time period called the **Enlightenment**. Because of its emphasis on the use of reason, the Enlightenment was also known as the Age of Reason.

READING CHECK Finding Main Ideas How did the Enlightenment thinkers explain the world?

The Enlightenment's Roots

The main ideas of the Enlightenment had their roots in other eras. Enlightenment thinkers looked back to the Greeks, Romans, and the history of Christianity. The Renaissance, Reformation, and Scientific Revolution provided ideas also.

Greek and Roman Philosophers

Enlightenment thinkers used ideas from the ancient Greeks and Romans. Greek philosophers had observed an order and regularity in the natural world. Aristotle, for example, taught that people could use logic to discover new truths. Building on Greek ideas, Roman thinkers developed the concept of natural law, the idea that a law governed how the world operated.

With Greek and Roman beliefs as guidelines, Enlightenment thinkers began studying the world in a new way. They applied these beliefs not just to the natural world but also to the human world of society and government.

Christianity

The history of Christianity in Europe provides other clues about ideas that emerged in the Enlightenment. One theologian, Thomas Aquinas, had taught in the Middle Ages that faith paired with reason could explain the world. In spite of Aquinas's use of reason, the Enlightenment was mostly a **secular**, or non-religious, movement. Enlightenment thinkers disagreed with the church's claims to authority and its intolerance toward non-Christian beliefs.

The Renaissance and Reformation

Other reactions to the Christian Church in Europe also influenced the ideas of the Enlightenment. For example, some Renaissance thinkers used Greek and Roman ideas to raise questions about established religious beliefs. These Renaissance thinkers were known as humanists.

Although most humanists were religious, they focused on human value and achievement rather than the glory of God.

The use of reason advanced science and technology, which in turn influenced the Enlightenment. Here, the Italian scientist Alessandro Volta explains a new invention, the battery.

Ideas of the Enlightenment

QUICK FACTS

- The ability to reason is what makes humans unique.
- Reason can be used to solve problems and improve people's lives.
- Reason can free people from ignorance, superstition, and unfair government.
- The natural world is governed by laws that can be discovered through reason.
- Like the natural world, human behavior is governed by natural laws.
- Governments should reflect natural laws and encourage education and debate.

Renaissance humanists believed people could improve their world by studying it and changing it. These ideas contributed to the Enlightenment idea of progress—the idea that humans were capable of improving their world.

Some Reformation ideas also reappeared during the Enlightenment. Like Martin Luther and other reformers, Enlightenment scholars questioned church authority. They found that religious beliefs didn't always fit in with what they learned from their logical study of the world.

The Scientific Revolution

The Scientific Revolution also influenced Enlightenment thinkers. Through experiments, scientists like Newton and Galileo had discovered that the world did not work exactly the way the church explained it. Using scientific methods of study, scientists discovered laws that governed the natural world. Enlightenment thinkers took the idea of natural laws one step further. They believed that natural laws must also govern human society and government.

READING CHECK Identifying Main Ideas
What were some movements that influenced the Enlightenment?

New Ideas

Enlightenment thinkers borrowed ideas from history to develop a new worldview. They believed the use of reason could improve society. To achieve this progress, they had to share their ideas with others.

French Philosophers

French philosophers popularized many Enlightenment ideas. One philosopher, **Voltaire** (vohl-TAYR), mocked government and religion in his writings. Instead of trusting God to improve human happiness, Voltaire believed humans could improve their own existence.

Having gotten in trouble for some of his writings, Voltaire also spoke out against censorship—removal of information considered harmful. He argued, "I [may] disapprove of what you say, but I will defend to the death your right to say it." His statement emphasized the Enlightenment goal of freedom of thought.

Enlightenment thinkers made an effort to share their thoughts with the public. Philosopher Denis Diderot (dee-DROH) edited a book called the *Encyclopedia*. This book included articles by more than 100 experts on science, technology, and history. The French king and the pope both banned the *Encyclopedia*.

In spite of censorship, Enlightenment ideas spread. One important place for the exchange of ideas was the **salon**, a social gathering held to discuss ideas. Women often hosted the salons. Most Enlightenment thinkers did not view women as equal to men. However, in hosting salons women could influence opinions.

British Writers

Women and men also began to publish their ideas in books, pamphlets, and newspaper articles. British writer **Mary Wollstonecraft**, for example, argued that women should have the same rights as men.

Enlightenment thinkers even applied their ideas of freedom and progress to economics. British writer Adam Smith believed economics was governed by natural laws. He argued that governments should not try to control the economy and that economic growth came when individuals were free to make their own choices. Like many Enlightenment thinkers, his ideas would have a lasting effect.

READING CHECK **Summarize** How did Enlightenment thinkers spread their ideas?

SUMMARY AND PREVIEW Scholars during the Enlightenment drew on ideas from previous eras. They proposed ideas about the importance of reason and progress. In the next section you will learn how the Enlightenment changed ideas about government.

Section 1 Assessment

Reviewing Ideas, Terms, and People

1. **a. Define** What was the **Enlightenment**?
   b. Explain What was the main goal of most Enlightenment thinkers?
2. **a. Define** What does it mean to say that the Enlightenment was a **secular** movement?
   b. Explain What was the connection between the discoveries of the Scientific Revolution and the Enlightenment?
   c. Elaborate How did the idea of natural law contribute to the Enlightenment?
3. **a. Describe** How did **Voltaire** feel about censorship?
   b. Explain What did Adam Smith contribute to Enlightenment ideas?

Critical Thinking

4. **Summarize** Draw a chart like this one. Using your notes, summarize how each source contributed to Enlightenment ideas.

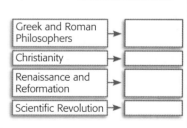

Greek and Roman Philosophers	→	
Christianity	→	
Renaissance and Reformation	→	
Scientific Revolution	→	

FOCUS ON WRITING

5. **Arguing for Enlightenment Ideas** Review the section for new ideas about science, religion, women's rights, and economics. How may these ideas help people? Write down what you could say in favor of Enlightenment ideas on these topics.

New Views on Government

What You Will Learn...

Main Ideas

1. The Enlightenment influenced some monarchies.
2. Enlightenment thinkers helped the growth of democratic ideas.
3. In America, the Enlightenment inspired a struggle for independence.

The Big Idea

Enlightenment ideas influenced the growth of democratic governments in Europe and America.

Key Terms and People

John Locke, *p. 617*
natural rights, *p. 618*
Charles-Louis Montesquieu, *p. 618*
Jean-Jacques Rousseau, *p. 618*
popular sovereignty, *p. 618*
Benjamin Franklin, *p. 619*
Thomas Jefferson, *p. 619*

TAKING NOTES As you read, use a chart like the one below to take notes on how the Enlightenment influenced democratic ideas in Europe and America.

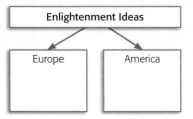

If YOU were there...

You are in a coffee house, discussing everything from politics to religion with friends. It is 1770. Suddenly, someone next to you questions the king's right to rule. Other people begin to agree with that person. As you listen to their logic, you wonder about other ways to run a government.

Would you support a government that didn't include a king or queen? Why or why not?

BUILDING BACKGROUND For centuries, Europe's monarchs had struggled with nobles and with church leaders for power. In England, Parliament limited the monarch's power. In some other countries, however, the kings and queens ruled without limits. The Enlightenment would change governments in Europe and in America.

Enlightenment Influence on Monarchies

In the 1600s and 1700s kings, queens, and emperors ruled Europe. (See the map.) Many of these monarchs believed that they ruled through divine right. That is, they thought that God had given them the right to rule as they chose. They also thought they shouldn't be limited by bodies such as England's parliament. King Louis XIV of France saw himself as the entire government. He declared, *"L'état, c'est moi!"* or "I am the state."

Although monarchs such as Louis XIV held the most power, other groups in society also had privileges. In France, for example, the nobles paid few taxes and held the highest positions in the army. The French clergy paid no taxes at all. However, most of the French people, the commoners, were poor, paid high taxes, and had no role in their government.

Outside of France, some monarchs began to change their ideas about how they ruled. They applied Enlightenment ideas to government. These rulers became known as enlightened despots.

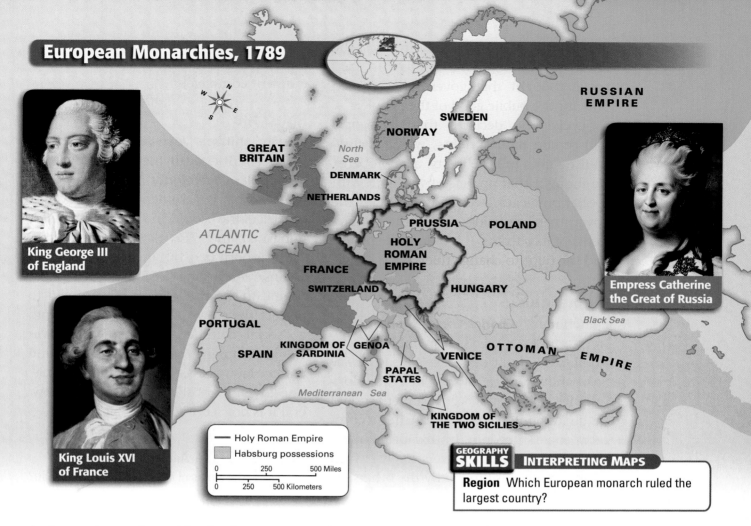

European Monarchies, 1789

King George III of England

King Louis XVI of France

RUSSIAN EMPIRE

SWEDEN

NORWAY

GREAT BRITAIN

North Sea

DENMARK

NETHERLANDS

ATLANTIC OCEAN

PRUSSIA

POLAND

HOLY ROMAN EMPIRE

FRANCE

SWITZERLAND

HUNGARY

Empress Catherine the Great of Russia

Black Sea

PORTUGAL

SPAIN

KINGDOM OF SARDINIA

GENOA

VENICE

OTTOMAN EMPIRE

PAPAL STATES

Mediterranean Sea

KINGDOM OF THE TWO SICILIES

— Holy Roman Empire
▧ Habsburg possessions

0   250   500 Miles
0   250   500 Kilometers

GEOGRAPHY SKILLS **INTERPRETING MAPS**

Region Which European monarch ruled the largest country?

A despot is a ruler with absolute power. The enlightened despots tried to make life better for the commoners. They also thought they could make their countries stronger if the commoners were happier. Frederick II of Prussia was one such ruler. He approved reforms in law and education. Empress Catherine the Great of Russia was another enlightened despot. Her reforms gave the Russian nobility greater rights and powers.

Although the enlightened despots made some improvements in their countries, many Enlightenment thinkers looked for bigger changes. They began to consider the need for democracy.

READING CHECK **Contrasting** How do rule by divine right and rule by an enlightened despot differ?

Democratic Ideas

Some Enlightenment thinkers only challenged the idea of rule by divine right. Others went further. They developed some completely new ideas about how governments should work. Three of these thinkers—Locke, Montesquieu, and Rousseau—tried to identify the best possible form of government. The ideas of these Enlightenment thinkers contributed to the creation of modern democracy.

Locke

The English philosopher **John Locke** had a major influence on Enlightenment political thought. In 1690, he published *Two Treatises on Government*. In this work, Locke argued for government as a **contract** between the ruler and the people.

ACADEMIC VOCABULARY

contract a binding legal agreement

Because a contract bound both sides, the ruler's power would be limited. In fact, Locke thought that government existed only for the public good of the people.

Locke also declared that all people had certain **natural rights**, which included the rights to life, liberty, and property. He thought that no person was born with special privileges. According to Locke, the government should protect the natural rights of its citizens. If it didn't, the people had the right to change rulers.

Montesquieu

Frenchman **Charles-Louis Montesquieu** (mohn-te-SKYOO) was a member of the nobility. He built on Locke's ideas in *The Spirit of the Laws*, published in 1748. Montesquieu claimed that a government should be divided into separate branches to protect people's freedom. In this idea, known as the separation of powers, each branch of government is limited by the others. As a result, the separate branches must share power. None of them can control the government completely.

Rousseau

French thinker **Jean-Jacques Rousseau** (roo-SOH) criticized divine right. He believed in **popular sovereignty** (SAHV-ruhn-tee)— the idea that governments should express the will of the people. In *The Social Contract*, published in 1762, Rousseau declared, "Man is born free, but he is everywhere in chains." According to Rousseau, citizens submit to the authority of government to protect their own interests, entering into a "social contract." This contract gives the government the power to make and enforce laws as long as it serves the people. The government should give up that power if it is not serving the people.

READING CHECK Analyzing What idea appears in the works of both Locke and Rousseau?

Enlightenment Thinkers

The ideas of Locke, Montesquieu, and Rousseau contributed to the creation of modern democracy.

Who believed in separation of government powers?

THE GRANGER COLLECTION, NEW YORK

John Locke
1632–1704
■ Government's power is limited.
■ People have natural rights, such as life, liberty, and property.

Charles-Louis Montesquieu
1689–1755
■ The powers of government should be separated into separate branches.

The Enlightenment in America

The ideas of these three philosophers spread throughout Europe. From Europe, they spread to the British colonists living in North America. Enlightenment ideas would have a big effect on America's history.

The British colonists already knew basic ideas about participation in government. Because they were British citizens, the colonists knew about Parliament and its control over the British monarch. When the British government began to chip away at what the colonists saw as their rights, the colonists fought back.

British Policy in North America

To learn more about this struggle, we must go back to the founding of the colonies. Other countries besides Britain settled and controlled land in North America. One of them was France.

Jean-Jacques Rousseau
1712–1778

- Governments should express the will of the people.
- People enter into a social contract with their government, giving it the right to create and enforce laws.

In North America the French and British had many disagreements. These conflicts led to war. Even though the British eventually defeated the French, years of fighting cost Britain a lot of money.

To raise funds, the British government created new taxes in the colonies. One tax added to the cost of molasses. Another new tax, called the Stamp Act, required colonists to pay more for newspapers, some legal documents, and other printed materials. People in England didn't have to pay these taxes. As a result, the colonists thought the taxes were unfair. The colonists wanted to be treated as British citizens. They wanted the same rights as Europeans.

Colonists' Views

Many colonial leaders were familiar with the ideas of the Enlightenment. Two leaders in particular—**Benjamin Franklin** and **Thomas Jefferson**—would apply those ideas to the colonists' complaints.

In 1766 philosopher and scientist Benjamin Franklin went to London. There he addressed the House of Commons in Parliament. He argued that the British government had no right to tax the colonists because they had no representative in Parliament. His argument against "taxation without representation" inspired riots against the tax in the colonies. The riots persuaded the British government to get rid of the Stamp Act.

Thomas Jefferson was a farmer, scientist, and scholar. He had been influenced by the Scientific Revolution. John Locke was another source of inspiration. In keeping with Locke's ideas, Jefferson believed that Britain had no right to govern or impose taxes on the colonies. He supported the idea of independence for the colonies. Jefferson also supported the separation of religious and political power. In this way, he reflected the Enlightenment's secular attitudes.

FOCUS ON READING

Why did the colonists' point of view on taxes differ from the view of the British government?

The Enlightenment Reaches America

1690 John Locke publishes *Two Treatises on Civil Government.*

1748 Montesquieu publishes *The Spirit of the Laws.*

1762 Rousseau publishes *The Social Contract.*

1690 · 1745 · 1755 · 1765 · 1775

1766 Benjamin Franklin argues against unfair tax policies in the American colonies.

1774 Thomas Jefferson argues that only voluntary loyalty to the king ties the American colonies to Great Britain.

THE GRANGER COLLECTION, NEW YORK

ANALYSIS SKILL **READING TIME LINES**
Who might have been influenced by Rousseau's writings?

Jefferson would later become president of the United States. His philosophies and achievements, based on Enlightenment ideas, helped to establish the democratic government and the rights we enjoy today in the United States.

READING CHECK **Finding Main Ideas** Why did some colonists want to be independent of Britain?

SUMMARY AND PREVIEW In the 1600s and 1700s some European monarchs thought they had a divine right to rule. As Enlightenment thinkers proposed new ways of thinking, people questioned the monarchs' rights. Democratic ideas spread. In the next section you will learn how these ideas changed governments in England, France, and America.

Section 2 Assessment

go.hrw.com
Online Quiz
KEYWORD: SN6 HP21

Reviewing Ideas, Terms, and People

1. **a. Define** What does divine right mean?
   b. Explain What did enlightened despots try to do?
2. **a. Define** What are **natural rights**?
   b. Explain What did Locke believe was the purpose of government?
   c. Elaborate Why would separation of powers protect people's freedoms?
3. **a. Describe** What role did **Benjamin Franklin** play in the American colonists' disagreement with the British government?
   b. Elaborate Why do you think many Americans consider **Thomas Jefferson** a hero?

Critical Thinking

4. **Summarizing** Draw a chart like the one here. Using your notes, list 5 important people. Explain how each person's idea influenced democracy in Europe and America.

Person	Ideas

FOCUS ON WRITING

5. **Organizing Ideas about Government** Note ways Enlightenment ideas might improve government by making it more effective or fair. How would you present your arguments to someone who favors monarchy or rule by divine right?

John Locke

Would you risk arrest for your beliefs in people's rights?

When did he live? 1632–1704

Where did he live? England and the Netherlands

What did he do? Locke worked as a professor, physician, and government official. He wrote about the human mind, science, government, religion, and other topics.

Why is he important? Locke believed in the right of common people to think and worship as they pleased and to own property. He also had great faith in science and people's basic goodness. Not everyone liked his ideas. At one point Locke fled to Holland to avoid arrest by political enemies. Locke's ideas have inspired political reforms in the West for some 300 years.

Drawing Inferences Why do you think some people disliked Locke's ideas?

KEY IDEAS

" Men being, as has been said, by nature, all free, equal, and independent, no one can be . . . subjected to the political power of another, without his own consent. The only way whereby any one divests himself of his natural liberty . . . is by agreeing with other men to join and unite into a community. "

–John Locke, from *Second Treatise of Civil Government*

This book printed in 1740 is a collection of John Locke's writings.

THE

WORKS

OF

JOHN LOCKE, Efq;

In Three Volumes.

The CONTENTS of which follow in the next Leaf.

With Alphabetical Tables.

VOL. I.

The FOURTH EDITION.

LONDON,

Printed for Edmund Parker, at the Bible and Crown, in Lombard-Street; Edward Symon, against the Royal-Exchange, in Cornhill; Charles Hitch, at the Red-Lion, in Paternoster-Row; and John Pemberton, at the Golden-Buck, in Fleetstreet.

M. DCC. XL.

The Age of Revolution

Main Ideas

1. Revolution and reform changed the government of England.
2. Enlightenment ideas led to democracy in America.
3. The French Revolution caused major changes in France's government.

The Big Idea

Revolutions changed the governments of Britain, the American colonies, and France.

Key Terms

English Bill of Rights, *p. 623*
Declaration of
  Independence, *p. 624*
Declaration of the Rights of Man
  and of the Citizen, *p. 627*

TAKING NOTES As you read, keep track of major events that led to changes in government in England, America, and France. Use a diagram like this one to help organize your notes.

Major Events	
England	
America	
France	

If YOU were there...

You live near Boston, Massachusetts. British soldiers have moved in and taken over your house. They say that the law allows them to take whatever they need. But your father doesn't want the soldiers living in your house and eating your food. What can he do to fight the king's laws?

Should your father disobey the king? Why or why not?

BUILDING BACKGROUND British soldiers in the North American colonies were just one sign that trouble was brewing. Ideas about the rights of the people were in conflict with ideas about the rights of monarchs. In England, the North American colonies, and France, this conflict led to violent revolutions.

Revolution and Reform in England

Enlightenment ideas inspired commoners to oppose monarchies that ruled without concern for the people's needs. However, the monarchs wouldn't give up their privileges. In England, Parliament forced the monarchy to change.

Trouble with Parliament

For many years, the English Parliament and the English monarchy had had an uneasy relationship. Parliament demanded that its rights and powers be respected. However, the monarchy stood for rule by divine right. The relationship between English monarchs and Parliament got worse.

The conflict led to a civil war in 1642. Representatives of Parliament led by Oliver Cromwell took over the country. The king, Charles I, was charged with various crimes and beheaded in 1649. Cromwell became a dictator. The years of his rule were troubled and violent.

George Washington led the colonial army to victory over the British in the American Revolution. In this 1851 copy of a famous painting, Washington is shown leading his troops across the Delaware River to attack British forces.

By 1660 many English people were tired of turmoil and wanted to restore the monarchy. They invited the dead king's son to return and rule England as Charles II. They made Charles promise to allow Parliament to keep the powers it had won in the civil war. These powers included the right to approve new taxes. Parliament was able to work with Charles II during most of his rule. However, when Charles died and his brother James became king, the trouble began again.

James II, an unpopular Catholic, tried to promote his religious beliefs in England, a Protestant country. As a result, Parliament invited the Protestant William of Orange, James's son-in-law, to invade England. When William and his wife, Mary, arrived in England in 1688, James and his family fled to France.

New Rights for the English People

Parliament offered the throne to William and Mary on one condition. They had to accept the **English Bill of Rights**, a document that listed rights for Parliament and the English people. This document, approved in 1689, drew on the principles of Magna Carta, which limited a ruler's power and recognized some rights for the people.

Magna Carta had been in place for hundreds of years, but the monarchs had not honored it. William and Mary agreed to honor Magna Carta. They also agreed that Parliament could pass laws and raise taxes. As a result, the monarchs ruled according to laws passed by Parliament. Divine right to rule had ended in England.

READING CHECK Sequencing What events led to the creation of the English Bill of Rights?

Democracy in America

Although the power of the monarchs was limited in England, some people in North America were not satisfied. Colonists there grew increasingly unhappy with both the king and Parliament.

A New Country

Some colonists disliked the laws and taxes that the British government had imposed. In addition, colonists were used to ruling themselves through their own assemblies, or congresses. They also believed that a faraway king and parliament could not understand life in America.

Many colonists protested British laws they thought were unfair. As conflict continued, colonial leaders met to resolve the crisis. At this meeting, called the First Continental Congress, the delegates decided to resist the British. Not all colonists wanted independence, but they did want to have fair laws and to feel safe. They created militias, or groups of armed men, to protect themselves from the British troops stationed in the colonies.

Fighting began in April of 1775 when a militia exchanged fire with British troops. In 1776 the colonial leaders gathered again. At that meeting, Thomas Jefferson wrote the **Declaration of Independence**, a document declaring the colonies' independence from British rule. Like Magna Carta, the Declaration stated people's rights to certain liberties. The Declaration begins with a sentence that also expresses Enlightenment **ideals**:

> *"*We hold these truths to be self-evident, that all men are created equal, that they are endowed by their Creator with certain unalienable Rights, that among these are Life, Liberty and the Pursuit of Happiness.*"*
>
> –from the *Declaration of Independence*

In this passage, the word *unalienable* means "cannot be taken away." This wording shows the influence of John Locke's ideas

ACADEMIC VOCABULARY

ideals ideas or goals that people try to live up to

Documents of Democracy   QUICK FACTS

The growth of modern democracy was greatly influenced by several key documents, which are shown here.

Which two documents contain some of John Locke's ideas?

Magna Carta (1215)
- Limited the power of the monarchy
- Identified people's rights to property
- Established people's right to trial by a jury

The English Bill of Rights (1689)
- Outlawed cruel and unusual punishment
- Guaranteed free speech for members of Parliament

about natural rights. In addition, the Declaration of Independence said that people unhappy with their government had the right to change it. This statement builds on the ideas of Rousseau as well as Locke.

The Declaration of Independence was signed by representatives from all of the colonies. A new nation—the United States of America—was born.

A New Government

The British government finally agreed to end the fighting and recognize the United States. American leaders then met to form a new government. They wrote a set of rules called the Articles of Confederation. Under the Articles, the central government was weak. The Americans were afraid that a strong central government would be too much like a monarchy. However, the weak government didn't serve the needs of the people. A new government plan was needed.

Virginia farmer James Madison was a main author of the new plan—the Constitution. This document reflected the ideas of Montesquieu, who had proposed the separation of powers in 1748. In keeping with Montesquieu's idea, the Constitution divided power among three branches of government:

- The legislative branch, called Congress, would make laws.
- The executive branch, headed by the president, would enforce laws.
- The judicial branch, or court system, would interpret laws.

The Constitution did not address the rights of women or of slaves, and men without land couldn't vote. It did, however, guarantee the rights of most citizens.

READING CHECK **Finding Main Ideas** How were ideas of Enlightenment thinkers reflected in the American Revolution and the new American government?

The United States Declaration of Independence (1776)
- Declared that people have natural rights that governments must protect
- Argued that people have the right to replace their government

The French Declaration of the Rights of Man and of the Citizen (1789)
- Stated that the French government received its power from the people
- Strengthened individual rights and equality

Women's March on Versailles
During the French Revolution, about 6,000 women marched to the palace at Versailles to demand bread from the king.

The French Revolution

As the Americans fought for and created a new nation, the French people paid close attention to events. They were inspired by the Americans to fight for their own rights.

An Unfair Society

The French king ruled over a society split into three groups called estates. The clergy were members of the First Estate and enjoyed many privileges. Nobles made up the Second Estate. They held important positions in the military, the government, and the courts.

Most French people belonged to the Third Estate. Included were peasants, craftworkers, and shopkeepers. The Third Estate paid the highest taxes but had few rights. Many members of the Third Estate were poor and hungry. They felt that the king didn't understand their problems. While the common people starved, King Louis XVI had

THE IMPACT TODAY
July 14, Bastille Day, is France's independence day.

fancy parties. His queen, Marie-Antoinette, spent huge amounts of money on clothes.

Meanwhile, the government was badly in debt. Louis XVI wanted to raise money by taxing the rich. To do so, in 1789 he called together members of the three estates.

The meeting did not go smoothly. Some members of the Third Estate were familiar with Enlightenment ideas. These members demanded a real voice in the meeting's decisions. Eventually, the Third Estate members formed a separate group called the National Assembly. This group demanded that the king accept a constitution limiting his powers.

Louis XVI refused to agree to such demands, angering the common people of Paris. Violence broke out on July 14, 1789. On that day a mob stormed a Paris prison, the Bastille. After forcing the guards to surrender, the mob took guns stored inside the building and freed the prisoners. The French Revolution had begun.

Revolution and Change

After the Bastille fell, the revolution spread to the countryside. Peasants there were afraid that the king and nobles would crush the revolution. In events called the Great Fear, peasants took revenge on their noble landlords for years of poor treatment. In their rage and fear, the peasants burned country houses and monasteries.

Other leaders of the revolution were taking peaceful steps. The National Assembly wrote a constitution. It included some of the same ideas found in the writings of Enlightenment philosophers, the English Bill of Rights, and the Declaration of Independence. Called the **Declaration of the Rights of Man and of the Citizen**, this document guaranteed some freedoms for citizens and distributed the payment of taxes more fairly. Among the rights the Declaration supported were freedom of speech, of the press, and of religion. It also guaranteed that men could take part in the government.

Louis XVI was forced to accept the new laws, but new laws did not satisfy the revolution's leaders. In 1792 they ended the monarchy and created a republic. The next year, the leaders put Louis XVI on trial and executed him.

Facing unrest, in 1793 the new French government began to order trials of anyone who questioned its rule. In the period that followed, called the Reign of Terror, thousands of people were executed with the guillotine. This machine beheaded victims quickly with a heavy blade. The Reign of Terror ended when one of its main leaders, Maximilien Robespierre, was himself executed in July of 1794.

Although the Reign of Terror was a grim chapter in the story of the French Revolution, the revolution wasn't a failure. Eventually, France created a democratic government. Enlightenment ideas about freedom were powerful. Once they took hold, they would not go away. Many Europeans and Americans enjoy freedoms today thanks to Enlightenment ideas.

READING CHECK **Summarizing** What is the Declaration of the Rights of Man and of the Citizen?

SUMMARY AND PREVIEW Questions about divine right led to struggles between the English monarchy and Parliament. Enlightenment ideas inspired the American Revolution and led to democracy in the United States. The French also formed a republic. In the next chapter you will learn about revolutions and independence in countries around the world.

Section 3 Assessment

go.hrw.com
Online Quiz
KEYWORD: SN6 HP21

Reviewing Ideas, Terms, and People

1. **a. Describe** What caused the conflict between the English monarchy and Parliament?
   b. Compare What was the connection between Magna Carta and the **English Bill of Rights**?
2. **a. Identify** What basic rights were listed in the **Declaration of Independence**?
   b. Explain How were Montesquieu's ideas reflected in the U.S. Constitution?
3. **a. Describe** How was French society organized before the French Revolution?
   b. Compare What did the Great Fear and the Reign of Terror have in common?

Critical Thinking

4. **Sequencing** Use a time line like the one below to show the sequence and dates of revolutionary events in Britain, France, and America.

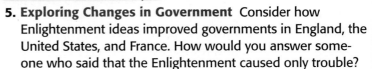

FOCUS ON WRITING

5. **Exploring Changes in Government** Consider how Enlightenment ideas improved governments in England, the United States, and France. How would you answer someone who said that the Enlightenment caused only trouble?

Social Studies Skills

Understanding Continuity and Change

Understand the Skill

A well-known saying claims that "the more things change, the more they stay the same." Nowhere does this observation apply better than to the study of history. Any look back over the past will show many changes—nations expanding or shrinking, empires rising and falling, changes in leadership, and people on the move, to name just a few.

The reasons for change have not varied, however. The same general forces have driven the actions of people and nations across time. These forces are the "threads" that run through history and give it continuity, or connectedness. They are the "sameness" in a world of continuous change.

Learn the Skill

You can find the causes of all events of the past in one or more of these major forces or themes that connect all history.

1. **Cooperation and Conflict:** Throughout time, people and groups have worked together to achieve goals. They have also opposed others who stood in the way of their goals.

2. **Cultural Invention and Interaction:** The values and ideas expressed in peoples' art, literature, customs, and religion have enriched the world. But the spread of cultures and their contact with other cultures have produced conflict also.

3. **Geography and Environment:** Physical environment and natural resources have shaped how people live. Efforts to gain, protect, or make good use of land and resources have been major causes of cooperation and conflict in history.

4. **Science and Technology:** Technology, or the development and use of tools, has helped people make better use of their environment. Science has changed their knowledge of the world, and changed their lives, too.

5. **Economic Opportunity and Development:** From hunting and gathering to herding, farming, manufacturing, and trade, people have tried to make the most of their resources. The desire for a better life has also been a major reason people have moved from one place to another.

6. **The Impact of Individuals:** Political, religious, military, business, and other leaders have been a major influence in history. The actions of many ordinary people have also shaped history.

7. **Nationalism and Imperialism:** Nationalism is the desire of a people to have their own country. Imperialism is the wish to control other peoples. Both have existed through history.

8. **Political and Social Systems:** People have always been part of groups—families, villages, nations, or religious groups, for example. The groups to which people belong affect how they relate to people around them.

Practice and Apply the Skill

Check your understanding of the sources of continuity and change in history by answering the following questions.

1. How does the Enlightenment illustrate cultural invention and interaction in history?

2. What other forces in history were at work during the Enlightenment? Explain your answer.

Chapter Review

Visual Summary

Use the visual summary below to help you review the main ideas of the chapter.

QUICK FACTS

The Enlightenment

Enlightenment ideas helped inspire revolutions in America and Europe.

Enlightenment thinkers developed new ideas about government and society.

New governments created influential documents based on Enlightenment ideas that guaranteed people's rights and freedoms.

Reviewing Vocabulary, Terms, and People

Match the words or names with their definitions or descriptions.

a. Enlightenment

b. English Bill of Rights

c. Voltaire

d. John Locke

e. natural rights

f. popular sovereignty

g. secular

h. Charles-Louis Montesquieu

i. Benjamin Franklin

1. non-religious

2. argued for the colonists' rights before Parliament

3. a period also known as the Age of Reason

4. proposed the separation of powers

5. document that William and Mary had to sign before they could rule

6. spoke out against censorship

7. the idea that governments should express the will of the people

8. included life, liberty, and property in Locke's view

9. argued against divine right in *Two Treatises on Civil Government*

Comprehension and Critical Thinking

SECTION 1 *(Pages 612–615)*

10. a. Identify What three goals did Enlightenment thinkers believe the use of reason could achieve?

b. Compare How was the influence of Greek and Roman ideas similar to the influence of the Scientific Revolution on the Enlightenment?

c. Elaborate Voltaire and others have argued against censorship. Is censorship ever acceptable? Explain your answer.

SECTION 2 *(Pages 616–620)*

11. a. Identify Who were two important leaders in the American colonies?

b. Compare and Contrast What ideas did Locke and Rousseau share? How did these ideas differ from most monarchs' ideas about government?

c. Elaborate Do you think things would have happened the same or differently in the colonies if colonial leaders had not been familiar with Enlightenment ideas? Explain your answer.

SECTION 3 *(Pages 622–627)*

12. a. Identify What event started the French Revolution?

b. Analyze What basic ideas are found in both the English Bill of Rights and Magna Carta?

c. Elaborate The way people interpret the Constitution has changed over the years. What do you think is a reason for this change?

Social Studies Skills

13. Understanding Continuity and Change in History The Enlightenment was a period of great change in Europe and America. However, it was also driven by some of the same forces that have driven the actions of people and nations across time. Choose one of the factors listed below that helped promote change during the Enlightenment. Write a sentence explaining how this factor influenced the Enlightenment. Then, choose one factor that shows historical continuity during the Enlightenment. Write a sentence explaining the influence of that factor on the Enlightenment.

Cooperation and Conflict	Economic Opportunity and Development
Cultural Invention and Interaction	Impact of Individuals
Geography and Environment	Nationalism and Imperialism
Science and Technology	Political and Social Systems

Reviewing Themes

14. Politics How did the English Bill of Rights and the Declaration of the Rights of Man and of the Citizen change the power of monarchs?

15. Society and Culture How would daily life have changed for a peasant after the French Revolution?

Using the Internet

go.hrw.com KEYWORD SN6 WH21

16. Activity: Making a Collage The Age of Enlightenment was a time of religious, political, and economic change. Enlightenment thinkers such as John Locke, Benjamin Franklin, and Charles-Louis Montesquieu created ripples of change in democratic thought and institutions. Enter the activity keyword and learn more about these and other Enlightenment figures. Pick your favorite person and create a collage about his or her life and ideas.

Reading Skills

Understanding Points of View *Read the passage below and answer the questions that follow.*

> " From whatever side we approach our principle, we reach the same conclusion, that the social compact sets up among the citizens an equality of such a kind, that they all bind themselves to observe the same conditions and should therefore all enjoy the same rights. "
>
> –Jean-Jacques Rousseau, from *The Social Contract*

17. What is Rousseau's point of view about rights?

18. Who might disagree with Rousseau?

FOCUS ON WRITING

19. Writing Your Article Use the work you have already done to write your persuasive article. In 3–4 sentences, introduce the ideas of the Enlightenment. In the next paragraph, discuss the benefits of these ideas to society and government. Conclude with a summary of your main points and a call to action—what you want readers of your article to do or think.

DIRECTIONS: Read each question, and write the letter of the best response.

1

> We hold these truths to be self-evident, that all men are created equal, that they are endowed by their Creator with certain unalienable Rights, that among these are Life, Liberty, and the pursuit of Happiness. That to secure these rights, Governments are instituted [organized] among Men, deriving [getting] their just powers from the consent of the governed, That whenever any Form of Government becomes destructive of these ends it is the Right of the People to alter or abolish it, and to institute new Government . . .
>
> —from *The Declaration of Independence*, 1776

This passage is based *mainly* on the ideas of which Enlightenment thinker?

A Voltaire
B John Locke
C Adam Smith
D Charles-Louis Montesquieu

2 The idea that a king's rule is limited is contained in which earlier document in English history?

A Magna Carta
B Ninety-Five Theses
C Proclamation of 1763
D The Declaration of Independence

3 The period of history known as the Enlightenment grew out of all of the following *except*

A the Renaissance.
B the ideas of the ancient Greeks.
C the Scientific Revolution.
D the writings of Confucius.

4 The U.S. Constitution divides the power to govern among the president, the Congress, and the courts. This approach to government is based on the ideas of which Enlightenment thinker?

A John Locke
B Denis Diderot
C Charles-Louis Montesquieu
D Mary Wollstonecraft

5 What view did the political thinkers of the Enlightenment share with the scientists of the Scientific Revolution?

A a belief in reason
B a belief in human rights
C a belief in divine right
D a belief in democracy

Connecting with Past Learnings

6 You already learned about the Greek philosopher Plato, who taught that society should be based on fairness and justice for all. Which European later *best* expressed Plato's idea?

A Oliver Cromwell
B Sir Isaac Newton
C Adam Smith
D Jean-Jacques Rousseau

7 You have learned about various forms of government. The Enlightenment idea that governments should express the will of the people was illustrated in ancient history by

A the Ten Commandments.
B the Roman Republic.
C the city-states of Mesopotamia.
D the teachings of the Buddha.

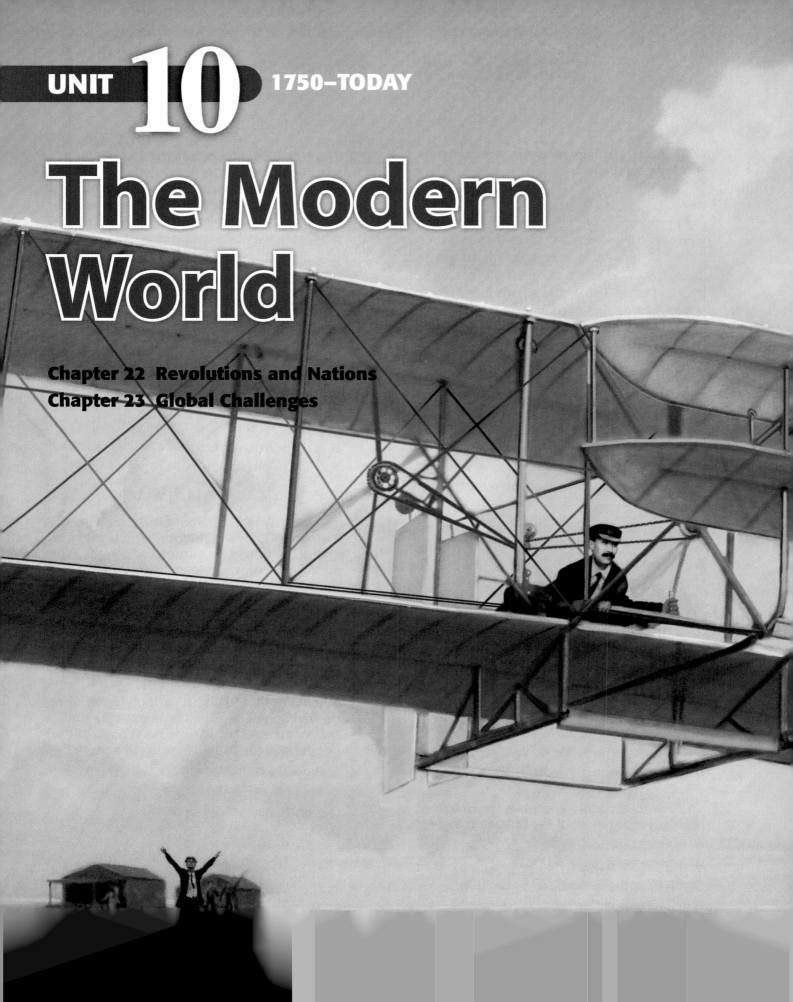

UNIT 10 1750–TODAY

The Modern World

Chapter 22 Revolutions and Nations
Chapter 23 Global Challenges

What You Will Learn...

During the past two centuries, people all over the world have seen tremendous change. Kings and empires have given way to democratic governments and independent states. Products once made by hand in homes are now mass-produced in factories. These changes did not come easily or overnight. In the nineteenth century, many countries were involved in political, economic, and technological revolutions. In the twentieth century, two world wars were fought. Today, technological and scientific advances continue to change our world in ways that were once unimaginable.

Explore the Art

In this scene from Kitty Hawk, North Carolina, the Wright brothers make the first successful human-powered flight. Their achievement was a giant step in making our world a smaller place. What do you think it might have been like to witness this important event?

CHAPTER **22** 1750–1914

Revolutions and Nations

FOCUS ON WRITING

Journal Writing Many people throughout history have written in journals to record their personal experiences. As you read this chapter, you will create a journal page (or pages) based on events and people from the time period of the French and Industrial revolutions. You will write your journal as if you were a citizen of Europe during this interesting time.

CHAPTER EVENTS

1750

1778
The French
Revolution
begins.

HOLT

History's Impact
▶ video series
Watch the video to understand the impact of America's foreign policy on its neighbors.

What You Will Learn...

In this chapter, you will learn about a period of big changes in Europe that affected much of the world. Change came from revolutionary movements, the Industrial Revolution, and new political philosophies. This photo shows the Arc de Triomphe in Paris, which was ordered built by Napoleon Bonaparte.

1804
Napoleon is crowned emperor of France.

1853
Commodore Matthew Perry urges the Japanese to open ports to American trade.

1856
Henry Bessemer develops a way to convert iron into steel.

1879
The electric light bulb is invented.

1800

1850

1900

1815 Napoleon is defeated at the Battle of Waterloo and is ordered out of Europe.

1848 Revolutions break out in Italy, France, Germany, and the Austrian Empire.

1871
The German Empire is proclaimed.

635

Focus on Themes In this chapter you will learn about a period of many changes in Europe and how they affected life in other parts of the world. You will read how **political** changes like revolutionary movements spread from Europe to South America and how colonial policies influenced many of the world's regions. You will also learn about **economic** changes, including the Industrial Revolution, that led to a transformation of the world's economy. As you read about these changes, you will be able to compare the actions of different leaders.

Comparing Historical Texts

Focus on Reading A good way to learn what people in the past thought is to read what they wrote. However, most documents will tell you only one side of the story. By comparing writings by different people, you can learn a great deal about the sides of a historical issue or debate.

Comparing Texts When you compare historical texts, you should consider the following: who wrote the documents, and what the documents were meant to achieve. To do this, you need to find the writer's main point or points.

Nationalism. . . attacks democracy,. . . fights socialism and undermines pacifism, humanitarianism and internationalism. . . It declares the program of liberalism finished.

> –Alfredo Rocco, *What Is Nationalism and What Do the Nationalists Want?*, 1914 (quoted in Eric Hobsbawm, *The Age of Empire 1875–1914*. New York: Pantheon, 1987, p. 142)

The State, therefore, is not only a high moral good in itself, but is also the assurance for the people's endurance. Only through it can their moral development be perfected, for the living sense of citizenship inspires the community in the same way as a sense of duty inspires the individual. . . . The grandeur of war lies in the utter annihilation of puny man in the great conception of the State, and it brings out the full magnificence of the sacrifice of fellow-countrymen for one another. In war the chaff is winnowed from the wheat.

> –Heinrich von Treitschke, quoted in *Introduction to Contemporary Civilization in the West,* New York: Columbia University Press, 1954. pp. 550–566) [found at http://www2.ctc.edu/~ttaylor//treit.htm]

Document 1	Document 2
Rocco	von Treitschke
Nationalism is opposed to liberalism, international cooperation, peace, and democracy.	Nationalism encourages moral development, a sense of duty, and, through war, brings out the best in people and separates the strong from the weak.

Both Sides of the Issue
To some, nationalism was bad because it created unhealthy competition and led to war. Others felt it was good because it created a stronger state and better citizens.

You Try It!

Read the following passages, both of which express a contemporary opinion about Napoleon. As you read, look for the main point each writer makes.

> If Bonaparte was a conqueror, he conquered the grand conspiracy of kings against the abstract right of the human race to be free. . . If he was ambitious his greatness was not founded on the . . . surrender of the rights of human nature.
>
> —William Hazlitt, *Political Essays, with Sketches of Public Characters,* 1819

> There are only two alternatives: to take the chains of slavery or to fight for freedom. Bonaparte tyrannizes our independence by the most violent means: fire and death. . . . Are we going to allow Napoleon's eagles to come and seize our homes, outrage our families, despoil our GOD of his holy vessels, as they have just done in Portugal?
>
> —Proclamation at La Coruña, 1808

After you read the passages, answer the following questions

1. What is the main point Hazlitt makes in his passage?

2. What is the main point made in the Spanish proclamation?

3. How can a comparison of these two passages help you understand the issues that shaped people's attitudes toward the French emperor?

> **As you read Chapter 22,** think about the kinds of historical documents the author had to compare in order to write the chapter.

Academic Vocabulary

Success in school is related to knowing academic vocabulary—the words that are frequently used in school assignments and discussions. In this chapter, you will learn the following academic words:

opposition *(p. 639)*
conflict *(p. 642)*

The Spread of Revolutionary Ideals

What You Will Learn...

Main Ideas

1. During the Napoleonic Era, Napoleon conquered vast territories in Europe and spread reforms across the continent.
2. At the Congress of Vienna, European leaders tried to restore the old monarchies and ensure peace.
3. Inspired by revolutionary ideals in Europe, Latin American colonies began to win their independence.

The Big Idea

Napoleon's quest to rule Europe was eventually thwarted, but not before the ideals of the French Revolution spread throughout the continent and Latin America.

Key Terms and People

Napoleon Bonaparte, p. 638
coup d'état, p. 638
Klemens von Metternich, p. 640
conservatism, p. 641
liberalism, p. 641
Simon Bolívar, p. 642

TAKING NOTES As you read, note the names of leaders who fought for or against the spread of revolutionary ideals. Use a chart like this one for your notes on these leaders, where they lived, and what their goals were.

Leader	Place	Goal

If YOU were there...

You are living in Paris in 1799. You have complained for years about the weak, corrupt government officials who rule your country. Just days ago, however, a popular general led an overthrow of the government. His supporters say he is strong and patriotic.

Will you support this new leader?

BUILDING BACKGROUND The general who took over the government of France was indeed strong. His rule led to great changes not only in France but throughout Europe.

The Napoleonic Era

After the French Revolution, a young general named **Napoleon Bonaparte** became a hero in France. He defeated rebels at home and foreign armies that threatened the new republic. Before long, Napoleon seized political power and made France into a great empire that dominated Europe.

The Rise of an Emperor

By the late 1790s the French had had enough of violence. They wanted order and strong leaders, not the weak politicians who were running the country. In 1799 Napoleon took part in a **coup d'état** (koo day-tah), the forceful overthrow of a government. Napoleon took the top position in the new government of France. Then in 1804, with his popularity soaring, he crowned himself emperor.

Napoleon was a remarkable military leader. Under his command, the French army won a series of dazzling victories against Austria, Prussia, and Russia. French troops conquered many

Early Victories

Between 1805 and 1808, Napoleon's armies defeated the armies of Austria, Prussia, and Russia. As a result, these countries were forced to become allies of France. This painting shows Napoleon during his victory against the Russian army at the Battle of Friedland in 1807.

BIOGRAPHY

Napoleon Bonaparte
1769–1821

Napoleon was only five feet, two inches tall, but in military matters, he was a towering genius. He learned the value of artillery as a young officer. He grouped his cannons on the battlefield to maximize their effect. Napoleon also stressed mobility. He won many battles by quickly moving his troops into place to surround the enemy. But Napoleon's energy and decision-making skills declined in his later years. By 1814 Napoleon's brilliance had faded. His army could not hold off the forces that had united against him.

Analyzing What two military techniques did Napoleon use to win many of his battles?

countries and forced others to become allies of France. By 1810 Napoleon was the master of Europe. His empire stretched across most of the continent.

Napoleon wanted an efficient government, and he created one. He put in place a system of public education. He made taxes fairer. He also created the Bank of France as a central financial institution. Perhaps most significantly, he issued a set of laws, called the Napoleonic Code, for his empire. The code reflected many of the ideals of the French Revolution. All men were equal before the law. All received the same civil rights, including trial by jury. All could practice religion freely.

With these reforms, Napoleon brought new liberties to the people of the French Empire. Yet his legal code denied rights to women. In addition, Napoleon did not allow fair elections. He restricted freedom of the press. Napoleon also tolerated no **opposition** to his rule, and he harshly punished those hostile to him.

The Defeat of Napoleon

Great Britain was the one enemy Napoleon could not defeat. In 1805 the British navy destroyed the French fleet at the Battle of Trafalgar, off the coast of Spain. In response, Napoleon ordered all nations in Europe to stop trading with Great Britain.

When Russia ignored this order, Napoleon invaded with a force of 600,000 men. The decision was a disaster for the French.

ACADEMIC VOCABULARY

opposition
the act of opposing or resisiting

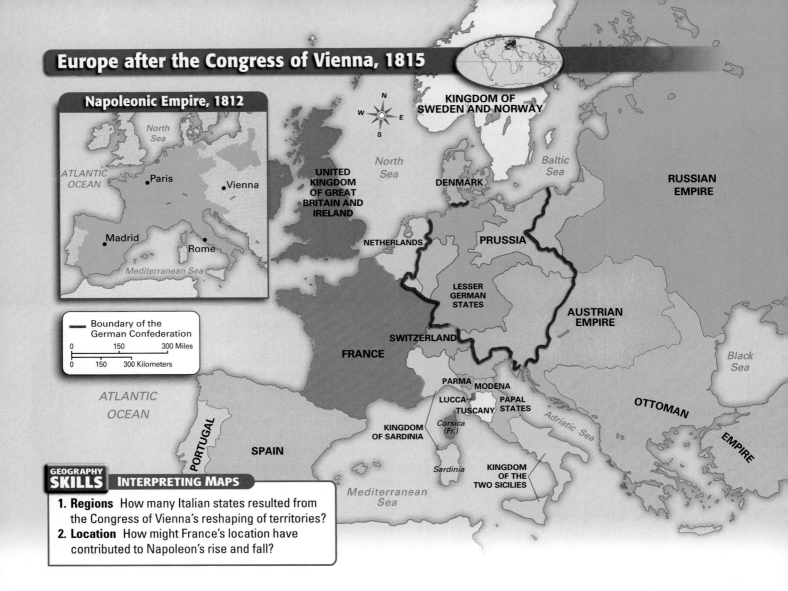

Europe after the Congress of Vienna, 1815

Napoleonic Empire, 1812

North Sea

ATLANTIC OCEAN

Paris

Vienna

Madrid

Rome

Mediterranean Sea

— Boundary of the German Confederation

0   150   300 Miles
0   150   300 Kilometers

KINGDOM OF SWEDEN AND NORWAY

North Sea

DENMARK

Baltic Sea

RUSSIAN EMPIRE

UNITED KINGDOM OF GREAT BRITAIN AND IRELAND

NETHERLANDS

PRUSSIA

LESSER GERMAN STATES

AUSTRIAN EMPIRE

SWITZERLAND

FRANCE

Black Sea

ATLANTIC OCEAN

PARMA MODENA
LUCCA   PAPAL
TUSCANY STATES

Corsica (Fr.)

Adriatic Sea

OTTOMAN

PORTUGAL

SPAIN

KINGDOM OF SARDINIA

Sardinia

KINGDOM OF THE TWO SICILIES

EMPIRE

Mediterranean Sea

GEOGRAPHY SKILLS **INTERPRETING MAPS**

1. **Regions** How many Italian states resulted from the Congress of Vienna's reshaping of territories?
2. **Location** How might France's location have contributed to Napoleon's rise and fall?

Smart Russian tactics and harsh winter weather forced the French into a bloody retreat.

With Napoleon's army weakened, Austria, Great Britain, Prussia, and Russia joined forces to defeat the French. These allies captured Paris in March 1814. In April they forced Napoleon to give up power and leave France. A year later, he returned and raised a new army. The British and Prussians, however, dealt Napoleon his final defeat at the Battle of Waterloo in Belgium in June 1815. The allies then sent Napoleon away to a small island in the Atlantic. He died there six years later.

READING CHECK **Summarizing** What changes did Napoleon bring to Europe?

The Congress of Vienna

After Napoleon's defeat in 1814, European leaders met in Vienna to draw up a peace settlement. They wanted to restore stability to a continent that had been torn apart by two decades of war.

Redrawing the Map

Countries across Europe sent representatives to the Congress of Vienna. But the leaders of powerful Austria, Britain, Prussia, and Russia made all the important decisions. Prince **Klemens von Metternich** (MEH-tuhr-nik) of Austria led the meetings.

At first the congress offered generous peace terms to France. But after Napoleon returned in 1815, the diplomats were not so lenient. After the Battle of Waterloo, they sent an army to take control of France. France had to give back the territory it had conquered. The French also had to pay 700 million francs to rebuild Europe. In addition, diplomats added and subtracted territory to reshape the different kingdoms along France's borders. They did this to try to balance the strength of the different countries in Europe. After Napoleon, the diplomats wanted to make sure that no single European power could ever again threaten the rest of the continent.

Containing the French Revolution

Metternich and the other leaders at the Congress of Vienna opposed the ideals of the French Revolution. They instead promoted **conservatism**, a movement to preserve the old social order and governments. The diplomats at Vienna wanted to return Europe to the way it was before the French Revolution.

The Congress of Vienna restored the old European monarchies. Royal families returned to power in Spain, Portugal, and the Italian states. In France, Louis XVIII took the throne, putting the Bourbon family back in power. The new king, however, did have to accept a constitution that left some of the reforms of the French Revolution in place.

Despite the efforts of Metternich, the ideals of democratic revolution did not die. **Liberalism**, a movement for individual rights and liberties, gained strength in the following decades. In the 1820s liberal uprisings erupted in Spain, Portugal, and a number of Italian states. But conservative forces rallied to preserve the old order. The dreams of liberals would have to wait.

READING CHECK **Identifying Bias** What did the diplomats at the Congress of Vienna fear?

Latin American Independence

The ideals of the French Revolution also inspired uprisings across the Atlantic. European powers had ruled Latin America for 300 years. The people living in these colonies now wanted to control their own affairs. In the 1800s they launched a series of revolts to throw off European rule.

Haiti, a Caribbean island under French rule, was the first colony in Latin America to gain independence. In the 1790s Toussaint-L'Ouverture (TOO-san LOO-ver-toor), himself a freed slave, led a rebellion of the island's African slaves. Although Napoleon sent an army to retake the island, Haitian fighters defeated the French troops. In 1804 Haiti declared its independence.

The movement for freedom quickly spread to the continent of South America.

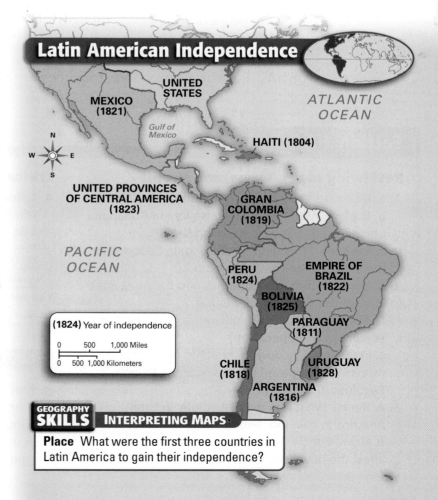

Latin American Independence

UNITED STATES

MEXICO (1821)

ATLANTIC OCEAN

Gulf of Mexico

HAITI (1804)

UNITED PROVINCES OF CENTRAL AMERICA (1823)

GRAN COLOMBIA (1819)

PACIFIC OCEAN

PERU (1824)

EMPIRE OF BRAZIL (1822)

BOLIVIA (1825)

PARAGUAY (1811)

(1824) Year of independence

0   500   1,000 Miles
0 500 1,000 Kilometers

CHILE (1818)

URUGUAY (1828)

ARGENTINA (1816)

GEOGRAPHY SKILLS **INTERPRETING MAPS**

Place What were the first three countries in Latin America to gain their independence?

ACADEMIC
VOCABULARY

conflict
an open clash
between two
opposing groups

FOCUS ON
READING

Who from this
same time period
might have written
an account with a
different opinion
of Spanish rule in
South America?

The revolutionary leaders **Simon Bolívar** (see-MOHN boh-LEE-vahr) and José de San Martín led independence movements across the continent. Bolívar condemned the Spanish rulers in a fiery declaration:

> "They have committed every manner of crime, reducing the Republic of Venezuela to the most frightful desolation [state of ruin]. Justice therefore demands vengeance, and necessity compels us to exact [get] it. Let the monsters who infest Colombian soil, who have drenched it in blood, be cast out forever."
>
> Simon Bolívar, from *Proclamation to the People of Venezuela*

Bolívar's successes inspired other revolutionaries to fight for liberation. Independence movements flared up across Latin America. One by one, the colonies threw off European rule. Neither Spain nor Portugal could hold onto their New World empires. By 1831 a dozen Latin American nations had won their freedom.

Independence, however, brought new challenges to Latin America. Bolívar hoped to establish peaceful constitutional governments. But the new nations fought over borders. There was also **conflict** between conservatives and liberals in the new countries. Conservatives, mostly from the upper classes, wanted the wealthy to control government at any cost. Liberals, mostly from the lower classes, favored the creation of democracies. It was hard for inexperienced new leaders to rule under these conditions. Throughout the region, unstable governments rose and fell.

READING CHECK Finding Main Ideas
Name three key leaders in the movement for Latin American independence.

SUMMARY AND PREVIEW After gaining power in France, Napoleon conquered much of Europe. After his defeat, European leaders met in Vienna to try to restore stability to the continent. In Latin America, revolutionary ideals led to independence movements. In Section 2, you will learn about the changes brought about by a different kind of revolution—the Industrial Revolution.

go.hrw.com
Online Quiz
KEYWORD: SN6 HP22

Section 1 Assessment

Reviewing Ideas, Terms, and People

1. **a. Describe** What is a **coup d'état**?
   b. Explain What events led to **Napoleon Bonaparte** being forced to leave France in 1814?
   c. Evaluate How did the Napoleonic Code reflect the ideals of the French Revolution?
2. **a. Recall** Which four countries had the most influence at the Congress of Vienna?
   b. Contrast What is the difference between **conservatism** and **liberalism**?
   c. Evaluate Why do you think the old European monarchies opposed the ideals of the French Revolution?
3. **a. Recall** What was the first colony in Latin America to gain independence?
   b. Draw Conclusions How did independence affect the new Latin American countries?

Critical Thinking

4. **Categorizing** Using your notes on the spread of revolutionary ideas, identify two achievements and one failure of each leader. Use a chart like this one.

Leader	Achievements	Failure
Napoleon Bonaparte		
Klemens von Metternich		
Simon Bolívar		

FOCUS ON WRITING

5. **Gathering Background** Make a list of the key events that took place during this time. Think about how these events might have affected people living then. Next, make a list of different types of persons who might have been affected.

Simon Bolívar

When did he live? 1783–1830

Where did he live? Simon Bolívar was born in Caracas, Venezuela. As a teenager he moved to Spain to finish his education. Bolívar spent most of his adult life in South America where he lived mostly in Venezuela and Colombia.

What did he do? Simon Bolívar led independence movements in Bolivia, Colombia, Ecuador, and Venezuela. He later worked to build unity among Latin America's new countries.

Why was he important? At the time of Simon Bolívar's birth, European powers governed Latin America. Bolívar helped inspire resistance to colonial rule. He led several military campaigns to drive the Spanish out of Colombia and Venezuela. Bolívar later helped liberate Upper Peru. The people there named their new nation Bolivia, in his honor. Bolívar sought to establish the new nations as constitutional republics. Rebellions and unrest, however, defeated these efforts.

Drawing Inferences How do you think Simon Bolívar's actions promoted independence in other parts of Latin America besides Bolivia, Colombia, Ecuador, and Venezuela?

Simon Bolívar's victories over Spanish forces won independence for many South American countries.

KEY EVENTS

1811
Venezuela declares its independence on July 5.

1813
Bolívar defeats the Spanish at the Battle of Lastaguanes in Venezuela.

1819
Bolívar captures Bogotá, Colombia, after defeating the Spanish at the Battle of Boyacá.

1825
Bolivia declares its independence.

1826
Bolívar hosts a congress in Panama to promote Latin American unity.

The Industrial Revolution

What You Will Learn...

Main Ideas

1. During the Industrial Revolution, new machines and methods dramatically changed the way that goods were produced.
2. Industrialization and the factory system brought a new way of life to Europe and America.

The Big Idea

The Industrial Revolution created an economy based on factory-made goods, bringing sweeping changes to Europe and America.

Key Terms and People

factory system, *p. 645*
laissez-faire, *p. 646*
socialism, *p. 646*
Karl Marx, *p. 646*

TAKING NOTES Create a concept web like the one below. As you read, fill in the outer ovals with facts about the new inventions, factory system, and ways of life created during the Industrial Revolution.

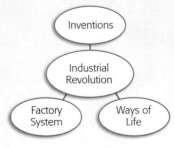

If YOU were there...

For years your father has woven cloth to make a living. But new machines can now weave cloth much faster than people can, and your father has lost his job. Many people you know are moving to the city to work in factories. Everyone has heard, though, that factory work is exhausting, dangerous, and pays poorly.

What do you think your father should do?

BUILDING BACKGROUND The Industrial Revolution began in Great Britain in the late 1700s and spread to western Europe and the United States during the 1800s. As work shifted away from homes into factories, workers saw their way of life change forever.

Key Inventions, 1733–1856

1733
Flying Shuttle
John Kay's invention sped up weaving so much that weavers outpaced their supply of thread.

1764
Spinning Jenny
James Hargreaves's invention made thread fast enough to keep up with the flying shuttle.

New Machines and Methods

In the 1700s and 1800s new inventions completely changed the way people worked. At the same time, scientific discoveries led to key advances in health.

New Inventions

Starting in the early 1700s a series of new inventions completely changed the way goods were made. In this time, called the Industrial Revolution, machines in factories began to perform the work that before had been done by hand at home or in small shops. This period of industrialization began in Great Britain but soon spread.

The textile, or cloth-weaving, industry was the first to change. Inventions like the flying shuttle, spinning jenny, and cotton gin combined to greatly increase cotton production and speed up the weaving process. As a result, Great Britain's textile industry grew rapidly.

In 1769 James Watt developed an efficient steam engine that could power the new factory machines. Since iron was used to make steam-powered machines, demand for iron grew. In 1856 Henry Bessemer developed a way to cheaply convert iron into steel. Because steel was stronger than iron, the steel industry grew as well.

New inventions also improved transportation and communication. Steamships made river travel faster. Steam-powered trains replaced slow animal-drawn carts. In addition, a new device called the telegraph made it possible to quickly send messages over long distances.

The Factory System

Before industrialization, each good had been individually made by hand. You can imagine what a slow process this was. Industrialization shifted production to a factory system. In the **factory system**, machines rapidly produce large quantities of goods at factories.

Advances in transportation improved the efficiency of the factory system. Trains and steamships could bring raw materials to the factories and carry finished goods away. Products could then be shipped quickly to faraway markets.

THE IMPACT TODAY

Today, cell phones and email make communicating over long distances faster and easier than ever.

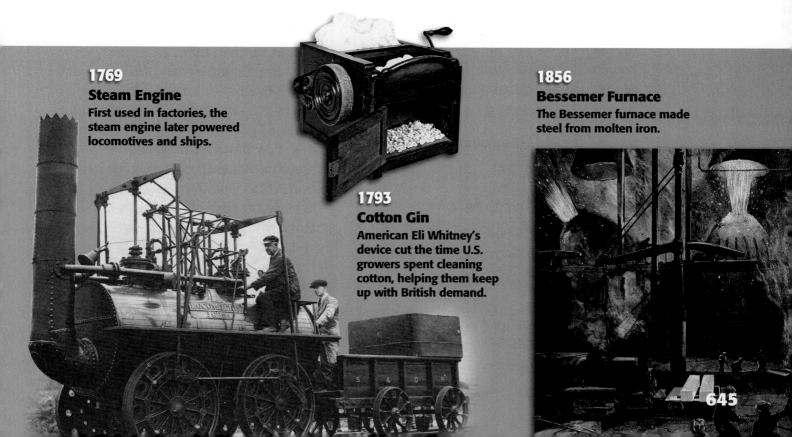

1769
Steam Engine
First used in factories, the steam engine later powered locomotives and ships.

1793
Cotton Gin
American Eli Whitney's device cut the time U.S. growers spent cleaning cotton, helping them keep up with British demand.

1856
Bessemer Furnace
The Bessemer furnace made steel from molten iron.

The new industries that sprang up during this period needed money to operate. Bankers, merchants, and rich landowners provided capital, money to invest in activities that produce more money. Because they, not the government, were funding industrialization, capitalists wanted government to stay out of business matters. They wanted **laissez-faire** (leh-say-FAR), a "let things be" attitude on the part of government toward industry. Governments agreed and placed very few regulations on business.

Industrialization spread to the United States by the early 1800s. By the century's end industrialization had spread to a number of countries in western Europe.

Scientific Advances

The Industrial Age was also a time of increased scientific research. In medicine, Edward Jenner developed a treatment to prevent smallpox—one of the deadliest diseases of the time. Louis Pasteur discovered that germs cause disease, and he developed ways to kill them. These discoveries improved the health of millions and saved many lives.

In chemistry and physics, scientists made important discoveries about the structure of atoms, the small particles that make up everything in the universe. Major breakthroughs were also made in the fields of geology and psychology, the study of the mind.

READING CHECK **Summarizing** How did new inventions promote industrialization?

A New Way of Life

The Industrial Revolution changed the work experience and way of life for millions of people in Europe and America.

The Workers

During the 1800s machines began to do much of the work once done by weavers,

Romanticism and Realism

During the 1800s two major artistic movements emerged: romanticism and realism. Romantic artists rebelled against the changes brought by the Industrial Revolution. They focused on beauty and nature and tried to show life as they thought it should be. Realists, on the other hand, attempted to show life as it actually was. They often dealt with the social and economic effects of the Industrial Revolution.

Describe the subject matter of the images on the right. Identify which work is an example of romanticism and which is an example of realism.

artisans, and farmworkers. As a result, many people had no way to support themselves. Unemployed workers moved from farms to the cities and took jobs in the new factories. As a result, cities quickly grew.

Factory workers faced difficult conditions. Working long days on the machines was tiring and dangerous. Wages were poor. Women and children had to work too, but for lower pay than men.

In addition, industrial cities were harsh places to live in. Factories polluted the air. Housing was crowded and poorly built. Garbage filled the streets. Crime became a part of daily life in many areas.

Because of these problems, some reformers wanted to replace the capitalist system. In its place, they promoted **socialism**, a social system in which businesses are either owned by the workers or controlled by the government. Socialists hoped that ending private ownership of industries would stop the poor treatment of workers. German philosopher **Karl Marx** called for workers to unite in a revolution to bring down the capitalist system.

A Growing Middle Class

Some people benefited more than others from the changes of the 1800s. The middle class grew to include factory managers, merchants, clerks, engineers, doctors, and other well-educated professionals. People in the middle class earned good incomes and could afford comfortable lives.

The middle and upper classes also had time to read, visit museums, and attend plays and concerts. Two major trends in the arts competed for their attention. Romanticism stressed beauty, nature, emotions, and simpler times. Realism tried to show everyday life as it really was.

READING CHECK Finding Main Ideas What changes did industrialization bring about?

REVIEW AND PREVIEW New inventions shifted the production of goods to factories. As a result, work experiences changed, cities grew, and the middle class expanded. Next, you will learn about nationalism and imperialism and their effects around the world.

go.hrw.com
Online Quiz
KEYWORD: SN6 HP22

Section 2 Assessment

Reviewing Ideas, Terms, and People

1. **a. Describe** What were some transportation and communication advances during the Industrial Revolution?
   b. Contrast How did work under the **factory system** differ from work done at home or in small shops?
2. **a. Recall** What led to the rapid growth of cities?
   b. Contrast What is the main difference between capitalism and **socialism**?

Critical Thinking

3. **Identifying Cause and Effect** Using your notes, complete a diagram like the one below. In the boxes, explain how each change in society led to the one that follows.

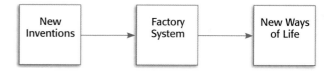

| New Inventions | → | Factory System | → | New Ways of Life |

FOCUS ON WRITING

4. **Character Development** Select a person from your list that would make an interesting character in your journal. As you add events from this section, add one or two details that could help bring your character to life.

Nationalism and Colonial Empires

What You Will Learn...

Main Ideas

1. Nationalism sparked independence movements in Europe and the unification of Italy and Germany.
2. Colonial empires grew in the late 1800s as industrialism led to a new wave of imperialism.

The Big Idea

Nationalism led to the creation of powerful nation-states that competed with each other to build large empires throughout the world.

Key Terms and People

nationalism, *p. 648*
nation-states, *p. 648*
Giuseppe Garibaldi, *p. 649*
Otto von Bismarck, *p. 650*
imperialism, *p. 651*
Matthew Perry, *p. 651*

TAKING NOTES As you read, take notes on nationalism and colonialism. Notice how each of these factors changed life in various places around the world.

Nationalism	Colonialism

If YOU were there...

You and everyone you know are Italian. You are all proud of the language, culture, and history you share. But you live in a part of Italy that is ruled by Austria. Recently you have heard of a movement to unite all Italians into one kingdom to be ruled by Italians.

Will you support such an effort?

BUILDING BACKGROUND During the 1800s industrialization was not the only important change occurring in Europe. Many groups were getting tired of living in empires ruled by faraway leaders who did not speak their language, share their culture, or have their interests in mind. These groups took steps to form their own countries and rule themselves.

Nationalism

Nationalism is devotion and loyalty to one's country. It typically develops among people who share a common language and religion and who believe that they share a common history or culture. Nationalism was a powerful force in the 1800s. It fueled the independence movements in Latin America. It also led a number of groups in Europe to create their own nations. As these new nations emerged, the map of Europe once again changed.

Nationalist Uprisings

In the early 1800s many peoples conquered by Napoleon resented French domination. They wanted to rule themselves, not answer to a foreign power. They also wanted to unite with others who shared their language, beliefs, and customs. Nationalists supported the idea of independent **nation-states**, self-governing countries made up of people with a common cultural background.

After Napoleon's defeat, growing feelings of nationalism led various groups in Europe to rebel against foreign control.

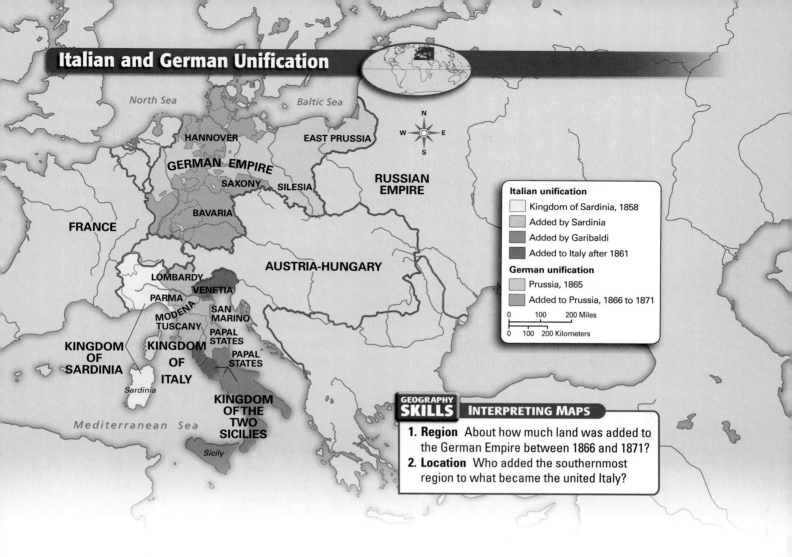

Italian and German Unification

North Sea

Baltic Sea

HANNOVER

EAST PRUSSIA

GERMAN EMPIRE

SAXONY   SILESIA

RUSSIAN EMPIRE

BAVARIA

FRANCE

AUSTRIA-HUNGARY

LOMBARDY

VENETIA

PARMA

MODENA

SAN MARINO

TUSCANY

PAPAL STATES

KINGDOM OF SARDINIA

KINGDOM OF ITALY

PAPAL STATES

Sardinia

KINGDOM OF THE TWO SICILIES

Mediterranean Sea

Sicily

Italian unification
- Kingdom of Sardinia, 1858
- Added by Sardinia
- Added by Garibaldi
- Added to Italy after 1861

German unification
- Prussia, 1865
- Added to Prussia, 1866 to 1871

0   100   200 Miles

0   100   200 Kilometers

GEOGRAPHY SKILLS | INTERPRETING MAPS

1. **Region** About how much land was added to the German Empire between 1866 and 1871?
2. **Location** Who added the southernmost region to what became the united Italy?

While some succeeded, others did not. Greece, for example, won its independence from the Ottoman Empire in 1829. But a wave of revolutions in 1848 all failed. Hungarian and Czech (CHEK) nationalists in the Austrian Empire were defeated. Italians and Germans also failed in their efforts to form their own countries. They would succeed, however, in later years.

The Unification of Italy

In the early 1800s what is now Italy was divided into separate states. An Italian king ruled Sardinia in the north, but Austria ruled other northern states. The Bourbon family ruled Sicily in the south, and the pope controlled the area around Rome.

As nationalism grew, more and more Italians embraced the idea of unifying as one country. Nationalist efforts repeatedly failed, however, until Camillo di Cavour (kuh-VOOR) became prime minister of Sardinia. Cavour modernized Sardinia's army, formed shrewd alliances, and fought a war that drove the Austrians from the north. The other Italian states in the region then united with Sardinia in 1860.

That same year **Giuseppe Garibaldi** gathered more than 1,000 passionate followers and overthrew the government in Sicily. A few months later, Garibaldi and Cavour joined their lands together. In 1861 Italy became a united kingdom. Ten years later Rome became its capital.

German Unification

Like the Italians, German-speaking peoples were divided into many separate states in the mid-1800s. But the spirit of nationalism had been growing among Germans since the days of Napoleon. As Italy unified, German nationalism became even stronger.

Prussia was the largest of the German states. Austria was its closest rival. In the 1860s the Prussian prime minister, **Otto von Bismarck**, devised a plan to create a unified Germany under Prussian domination. Bismarck built a strong army and won wars against Denmark and Austria. Prussia's victories gave it more territory and secured its leadership of the northern German states.

ACADEMIC
VOCABULARY

competition
a contest
between two
rivals

Bismarck's next step was to wage war against France. Moved by nationalism, the southern German states sided with Prussia. They won a quick victory and agreed to unite permanently. Bismarck's plan had worked. The German Empire was proclaimed in January 1871. King Wilhelm of Prussia became emperor, ruling over all the German states except Austria.

Germany then concentrated on building its economic and military strength. It also joined other European powers in the fierce **competition** for colonies.

READING CHECK **Identifying Cause and Effect** How did the French Empire and Napoleon's policies lead to nationalism in Europe?

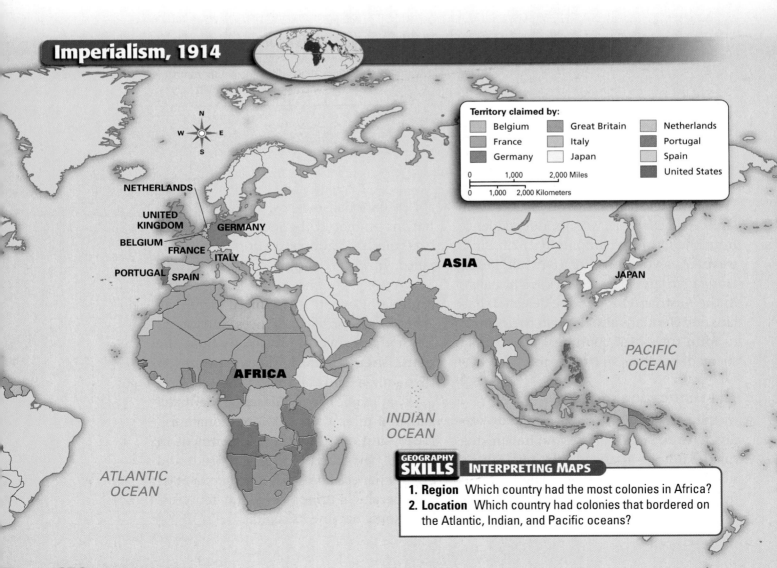

Imperialism, 1914

Territory claimed by:

Belgium	Great Britain	Netherlands
France	Italy	Portugal
Germany	Japan	Spain
		United States

0   1,000   2,000 Miles

0   1,000   2,000 Kilometers

NETHERLANDS

UNITED KINGDOM   GERMANY

BELGIUM   FRANCE

PORTUGAL SPAIN   ITALY

ASIA

JAPAN

AFRICA

PACIFIC OCEAN

INDIAN OCEAN

ATLANTIC OCEAN

GEOGRAPHY SKILLS **INTERPRETING MAPS**

1. **Region** Which country had the most colonies in Africa?
2. **Location** Which country had colonies that bordered on the Atlantic, Indian, and Pacific oceans?

U.S. Commodore Matthew Perry arrived in Japan in 1853 to negotiate with the Japanese about opening their ports.

Colonial Empires

European nations had been building global empires since the 1400s. In the late 1800s, however, the race for colonies grew heated. New, strong nations like Germany and Italy challenged Britain and France for territory. Japan modernized its economy and acquired colonies in East Asia. At the same time, the United States increased its influence in the Caribbean and the Pacific.

Causes of Imperialism

Imperialism is the control of a region or country by another country. A major cause of increased imperialism in the 1800s was industrialization. Industrial nations needed raw materials for their factories. But many of these materials were plentiful only on other continents. As a result, many Europeans wanted to control these faraway places. Industrialists also argued that colonies would provide nations with markets for their finished goods.

Nationalism was also involved. Citizens believed that a large empire increased their nation's power. In addition, many people promoted imperialism for social reasons. For example, missionaries traveled to colonies to spread their religion. Other imperialists felt they had a duty to export their "superior" culture to peoples they viewed as less advanced.

Empire Building in Africa and Asia

Africa became a major target of the imperialist powers. Before 1880 Europeans ruled only a few colonies in Africa. Within 25 years, however, they had swallowed up almost the entire continent. British, French, and other imperialists profited from mining operations and the production of palm oil and other crops. But for many Africans, colonial rule meant forced labor and the disruption of their culture.

European imperialism also extended into Asia. Great Britain ruled over India and Burma (now Myanmar). Russia expanded into Central Asia. France established the large colony of Indochina in Southeast Asia. Britain and France forced China to open itself to trade with terms that greatly favored Europeans. Western powers intruded in Japan, too, but with different results.

Japanese Imperialism

In 1853 the United States sent a powerful naval force to Japan. At the head of this force was Commodore **Matthew Perry**.

Perry's assignment was to negotiate a treaty that would open Japan to American trade. The following year, the Japanese agreed to Perry's terms, but Japan was determined to avoid foreign domination. The country quickly industrialized its economy and built a strong military. Becoming an imperial power itself, Japan took Korea and Taiwan from China in 1895. Ten years later Japan defeated Russia in a war that brought the Japanese even more land.

American Expansion

The United States also expanded its territory in the 1800s. In 1823 President James Monroe issued the Monroe Doctrine. This policy stated that the United States would oppose any European efforts to re-colonize newly independent Latin American republics or to interfere in their affairs. The doctrine allowed the United States to become the dominant power in the region.

In the 1840s the United States conquered nearly half of Mexico's territory. This covered the area from Texas to California. In 1898 the United States gained control of the Philippines and Puerto Rico in a war with Spain. Hawaii became a U.S. territory that same year.

In 1903 the United States took over part of Panama to build a canal linking the Atlantic and Pacific oceans. The canal shortened the sea route from New York to San Francisco by about 8,000 miles. This made the shipment of goods from coast to coast much cheaper and faster than before. Protecting this important new route would keep the United States involved in Latin American affairs for years to come.

READING CHECK **Analyzing** How did the Industrial Revolution affect imperialism?

SUMMARY AND PREVIEW The growth of nationalism led to independence movements and the unification of Italy and Germany. Industrialism helped fuel new imperialism. Industrial powers acquired colonies and built large global empires. Next, you will learn about changes that occurred in the 1900s.

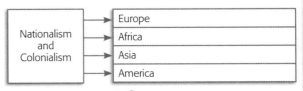

go.hrw.com
Online Quiz
KEYWORD: SN6 HP22

Section 3 Assessment

Reviewing Ideas, Terms, and People

1. **a. Describe** What characteristics and traits do people usually have in common that bring about feelings of **nationalism**?
   b. Explain During the unification of Italy, who led his followers in an overthrow of Sicily's government? To whose lands did he then add Sicily?
   c. Analyze Why did Prussia feel that it needed to defeat Austria?
2. **a. Recall** Which nation became an imperial power in East Asia?
   b. Explain What is the relationship between industrialization and **imperialism**?
   c. Analyze Why do you think that United States President James Monroe issued the Monroe Doctrine?

Critical Thinking

3. **Categorizing** Use your notes to complete the chart below showing the effects of nationalism and colonialism on each place.

Nationalism and Colonialism	Europe
	Africa
	Asia
	America

FOCUS ON WRITING

4. **Refining Your Character** Review this section and your notes on any other specific events your character might have taken part in or been affected by. Use details from this section to form a more complete picture of your character.

WORD HELP

kinsmen relatives

compound group of family homes

kinship feelings between relatives

abominable worthy of hatred

❶ Uchendu, Unachukwu, and Emefo are other elderly relatives of Okwonko.

❷ Families were breaking apart because some members accepted the Christian faith of the colonizers while others held onto the tribe's traditional religious beliefs.

from Things Fall Apart

by Chinua Achebe (1930–)

About the Reading *In* Things Fall Apart, *Nigerian writer Chinua Achebe tells about an African village and how it is forever changed by the arrival of European colonizers. The Europeans bring a new religion and government that threaten the traditional beliefs and way of life of the villagers. Here, the main character, Okwonko, is hosting a feast for his relatives. A family elder makes a speech to thank Okwonko for arranging the gathering. He also expresses his concerns about the arrival of the Europeans.*

AS YOU READ Identify what the speaker feels is most important for young people to realize.

"A man who calls his kinsmen to a feast does not do so to save them from starving. They all have food in their own homes. When we gather together in the moonlit village ground it is not because of the moon. Every man can see it in his own compound. We come together because it is good for kinsmen to do so. You may ask why I am saying all this. I say it because I fear for the younger generation, for you people." He waved his arm where most of the young men sat. "As for me, I have only a short while to live, and so have Uchendu and Unachukwu and Emefo. ❶ But I fear for you young people because you do not understand how strong is the bond of kinship. You do not know what it is to speak with one voice. And what is the result? An abominable religion has settled among you. A man can now leave his father and his brothers. ❷ He can curse the gods of his fathers and his ancestors, like a hunter's dog that suddenly goes mad and turns on his master. I fear for you; I fear for the clan."

CONNECTING LITERATURE TO HISTORY

1. **Analyzing** The family relationship was a very important part of African society before and after the arrival of European colonizers. Why did the speaker think that the new religion brought by the Europeans was a threat to families?

2. **Comparing** The speaker says, "We come together because it is good for kinsmen to do so." Do you think many people have this view today? When do you gather with relatives? How do such get-togethers strengthen the "bonds of kinship"?

Social Studies Skills

Understanding Supply and Demand

Understand the Skill

Making decisions as a group is a complicated and difficult skill to learn. However, it is an important skill at all levels of society—from governing a nation to choosing a movie to see with friends. At every level, success is based on the ability of group members to work together in effective and cooperative ways.

Learn the Skill

Being part of an effective group requires certain behaviors.

1. Be an active member. Take part in setting the group's goals and in making its decisions.

2. Take a position. State your views and work to persuade other members to accept them. However, also be open to negotiating and compromising to settle differences within the group.

3. Be willing to take charge if leadership is needed. But also be willing to follow the leadership of other members.

4. When you disagree with a point someone makes, make it clear that you still respect that person's opinion.

5. Never make another member feel that his or her comments are stupid, unwanted, or not valuable. But let people know if you think they're not respecting your opinions.

Practice and Apply the Skill

Divide into a small group of four or five students. Imagine you are all members of a family living in the American or European countryside in the early 1800s. Your family has farmed the same piece of land for many generations, but your life is hard and you have little money for anything more than food and shelter. Now you have heard that, in a nearby city, workers can earn three times as much as you earn on your family's farm. But getting such a job would require you to move to the city, making it difficult for your family to get together, even for holidays and special occasions. In addition, life in the city would be very different from what you are used to. Together, decide what to do. Make a plan with roles for all family members. After your group has made its plan, answer the following questions.

1. Did your group create a plan to improve the family's life and financial situation? Did you take into account both benefits and disadvantages? What did you contribute toward the plan?

2. How well did your group work together? What role did you play in that?

3. Was your group able to make a decision? If not, why? If so, was compromise involved? Explain why or why not.

Visual Summary

Use the visual summary below to help you review the main ideas of the chapter.

QUICK FACTS

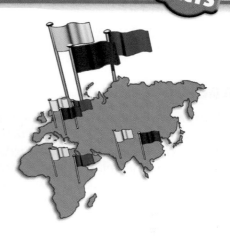

New Nations
Resentment against French domination during Napoleon's rule sparked nationalism across much of Europe.

Industrialism
As production shifted from homes to factories, work changed, cities grew, and the middle class expanded.

Empires
Industrialism, nationalism, and other factors fueled imperialism among European and other powers in the 1800s.

Reviewing Vocabulary, Terms, and People

For each pair of terms below, write a sentence that shows how the terms are related.

1. Napoleon Bonaparte
   coup d'état
2. Klemens von Metternich
   conservatism
3. Karl Marx
   socialism
4. nationalism
   nation-state
5. Otto von Bismarck
   imperialism
6. Simon Bolívar
   liberalism
7. factory system
   laissez-faire

Comprehension and Critical Thinking

SECTION 1 *(pages 638–643)*

8. **a. Identify** List the four countries that controlled all the important decisions made at the Congress of Vienna.

   b. Analyze How were Napoleon's forces weakened and then defeated?

   c. Elaborate Describe the problems that faced South American nations after they threw off colonial rule.

SECTION 2 *(pages 644–647)*

9. **a. Recall** How did production methods change during the Industrial Revolution?

   b. Draw Conclusions Why did capitalists prefer laissez-faire policies toward industry?

   c. Evaluate What was it like to live in an industrial city in the mid-1800s?

SECTION 3 *(pages 648–652)*

10. a. Describe What series of events transformed a number of separate German states into a unified imperialist power?

b. Contrast What arguments were made in favor of imperialism? What arguments could be made against it?

c. Elaborate What was the result of Commodore Matthew Perry's trip to Japan?

Reading Skills

11. Comparing Historical Texts *Read the selections below. Then answer the questions that follow. The first selection was written by an English reformer named Annie Besant in support of striking match factory workers. The second selection is an answer from a match girl at the factory.*

> Born in slums, driven to work while still children, undersized because under-fed, oppressed because helpless, flung aside as soon as worked out, who cares if they die or go on to the streets…? Girls are used to carry boxes on their heads until the hair is rubbed off and the young heads are bald at fifteen years of age. Country clergymen with shares in Bryant & May's draw down on your knee your fifteen year old daughter; pass your hand tenderly over the silky clustering curls, rejoice in the dainty beauty of the thick, shiny tresses. —*The Link* (23rd June, 1888)

> Dear Lady they have been trying to get the poor girls to say that it is all lies that has been printed and trying to make us sign papers that it is all lies; dear Lady nobody knows what it is we have put up with and we will not sign them. We thank you very much for the kindness you have shown to us. My dear Lady we hope you will not get into any trouble on our behalf as what you have spoken is quite true. — July 4, 1888

12. Why do you think Annie Besant addresses her comment to "Country clergymen with shares in Bryant & May's"?

13. Who is "they" that the match girl refers to in her letter? What do "they" want the girls to do?

Reviewing Themes

14. Politics What political goals did the Congress of Vienna try to achieve?

15. Economics What are three changes that the factory system caused?

Using the Internet

16. Activity: Analyzing Art If art is the mirror of society, then what is reflected when new social forces surge across the globe? You have seen the ways in which the spread of revolutionary ideas, the Industrial Revolution, nationalism, and imperialism disrupted and replaced the social customs and power relations that had existed before. Artisans became factory workers, power shifted from kings to the upper and middle classes, nationalism created nation-states, and lands far from Europe became European colonies. Enter the activity keyword. Then research the way in which these forces have been portrayed in art. After viewing the slide show, complete the interactive worksheet.

Social Studies Skills

17. Understanding Supply and Demand Write two to three sentences explaining how the concept of supply and demand applied to some aspect of the Industrial Revolution.

FOCUS ON WRITING

18. Writing Your Journal Entry Review your notes and decide what you will focus on for your journal entry. First, find an appropriate date to write at the top of your page. Next, use your section notes to help you write one or two introductory sentences to give your readers a sense of who you are and what is going on right now in your life. Complete your journal entry by telling what happened, how you were involved, and what other people were part of this experience. Remember, writing in a journal combines facts with feelings.

DIRECTIONS: Read each question, and write the letter of the best response.

1

> We are Prussians, and Prussians we shall remain . . . We do not wish to see the Kingdom of Prussia obliterated in the putrid [rotten] brew of cosy south German sentimentality [emotional sappiness].

The statement above was most likely made by which of the following rulers?

A Napoleon Bonaparte

B Simon Bolívar

C Camillo di Cavour

D Otto von Bismarck

2 Under Napoleon Bonaparte, the French army won victories against all of the following countries *except*

A Austria.

B Prussia.

C Great Britain.

D Russia.

3 After gaining independence, many new Latin American nations experienced internal conflict between which two groups?

A republicans and democrats

B liberals and conservatives

C socialists and capitalists

D nationalists and imperialists

4 Which of these did NOT help the United States to remain involved in Latin American affairs?

A the Monroe Doctrine

B conquering much of Mexico's territory

C building the Panama Canal

D Matthew Perry's visit to Japan

5 The Industrial Revolution began in

A Great Britain.

B Germany.

C France.

D the Austrian Empire.

Connecting with Past Learnings

6 The Panama Canal made trade between Latin America and the United States much easier. Which of the following that you have previously learned about played a key role in the trade between Egypt and Kush?

A the Nile River

B the Silk Road

C gold coin currency

D the Tigris and Euphrates rivers

7 In this chapter you read about the development of science and technology in the Industrial Age. Prior to the 1800s, many improvements in science and engineering were made in all of the following time periods *except*

A the Scientific Revolution.

B the Old Kingdom.

C the Middle Ages.

D the Renaissance.

CHAPTER 23 1900–TODAY

Global Challenges

FOCUS ON WRITING

A Cover Story Think about the different news magazines that you have seen at bookstores, newsstands, or the library. What is featured on the cover? As you read this chapter, look for people or events that could be the subject of a cover story for a magazine from the time period you are studying. When you finish reading this chapter, choose an event or person and write a short article about this subject for your cover story.

CHAPTER EVENTS

1919
The Treaty of Versailles sets peace terms at the end of World War I.

1900

HOLT
History's Impact
▶ video series
Watch the video to understand the impact of World War II.

What You Will Learn...

In this chapter you will learn about the two world wars that took place in the 1900s. You will also learn about the spread of democracy and the challenges facing the world. This photo captures the old and new ways of life in Singapore, a country that has prospered in the global economy.

1933 Adolf Hitler takes over Germany.

1949 Mao Zedong takes power in China.

1961 The Soviets build the Berlin Wall.

1998 The euro becomes the official currency of the European Union.

1940

1960

1980

2000

1945 World War II ends after atomic bombs are dropped on Japan.

1969 U.S. astronauts walk on the moon.

1989 The Berlin Wall falls, and the Cold War ends.

2004 The Olympic games are held in Athens, Greece.

GLOBAL CHALLENGES **659**

Focus on Themes In this chapter you will learn about the two world wars that took place in the first half of the twentieth century. You will also learn about the spread of democracy and the many challenges facing the world today. You will see how throughout the world, **geography** and **politics** were intertwined as they influenced the way people lived during the twentieth century and today.

Public Documents in History

Focus on Reading Historians use many types of documents to learn about the past. These documents can often be divided into two types—private and public. Private documents are those written for a person's own use, such as letters, journals, or notebooks. Public documents, on the other hand, are available for everyone to read and examine. They include such things as laws, tax codes, and treaties.

Studying Public Documents Studying public documents from the past can tell us a great deal about politics and society of a particular time. However, public documents can often be confusing or difficult to understand. When you read such a document, you may want to use a list of questions like the one below to be sure you understand what you're reading.

Question Sheet for Public Documents

1. What is the topic of the document?

2. Do I understand what I'm reading?

3. Is there any vocabulary in the document that I do not understand?

4. What parts of the document should I re-read?

5. What are the main ideas and details of the document?

6. What have I learned from reading this document?

You can often figure out the topic of a public document from the title and introduction.

Public documents often use unfamiliar words or use familiar words in unfamiliar ways. For example, the document on the next page uses the word *commodities*. Do you know what the word means in this context? If not, you should look it up.

Many public documents deal with several issues and will therefore have several main ideas.

You Try It!

The passage below is from a food rationing notice distributed in America during World War II. Read the passage and then answer the questions that follow.

POINT RATIONING

The purpose of point rationing is to guarantee everyone a fair share of scarce but essential goods while at the same time giving everyone a variety of items from which to choose. There are three chief differences between point rationing and the coupon rationing which is now in effect for sugar and coffee.

The first important difference is this: under straight coupon rationing one coupon entitles the consumer to buy a specific amount of a single commodity—such as one sugar coupon entitles you to buy a specified amount of sugar. But in point rationing one set of coupons covers a whole group of commodities. For instance, your week's meat ration coupons would enable you to choose your ration freely among beef, veal, pork, lamb, or mutton . . .

War Ration Book Two will have four pages of blue stamps and four pages of red stamps. The blue stamps will be used for the first group of goods to be rationed by points. The red stamps will be used for the second group of point-rationed items. The number on each stamp tells how many points the stamp is worth. The letter on each stamp tells for what period it is good.

Answer the following questions about the document you just read.

1. What is this document about?

2. What was the main idea or ideas of this document? What supporting details were included?

3. Are there any other words in this passage with which you are unfamiliar? How might not knowing those words hinder your understanding of the passage?

Academic Vocabulary

Success in school is related to knowing academic vocabulary—the words that are frequently used in school assignments and discussions. In this chapter, you will learn the following academic word:

defend (p. 663)

As you read **Chapter 23,** think about public documents the authors might have read in order to write the text.

World War I

If YOU were there...

On a summer day in 1914 you're visiting the capital of your province. Suddenly, you hear angry voices and shouting in the streets. You run toward the noise and are told that a Serbian nationalist has just killed the heir to the Austro-Hungarian throne. You're upset and worried about what this might mean for your future.

How do you think Austro-Hungary will react?

BUILDING BACKGROUND In the early 1900s tensions in Europe were nearing a breaking point. Issues at home and overseas pit European powers against each other. As rulers grew increasingly nervous, they built up their armies and formed new alliances to respond to the growing danger.

The Onset of War

In the summer of 1914 war broke out in Europe. Many nations from around the world soon joined in the fighting. A number of factors led to this global conflict, which became known as World War I.

Underlying Causes

By the 1900s nationalism had created rivalries among the countries of Europe. People were willing to go to war to prove the superiority of their nation. At the same time, some groups that wanted to form their own nation-states were still ruled by others. For example, people in the Balkan Peninsula in southeastern Europe wanted independence from Austria-Hungary. They started nationalist movements that created tensions in the Balkans.

Imperialism added to Europe's problems. As you read in Chapter 22, industrial nations competed fiercely for colonies. Many people believed that if their country had an empire, it was a great power. The race to grab overseas territories led to several crises that nearly resulted in war.

In the early 1900s European nations also began to build large armies. A number of them spent heavily on modern weapons.

What You Will Learn...

Main Ideas

1. The onset of World War I can be traced to nationalism, imperialism, and the buildup of military forces in Europe.
2. The Allies' victory over the Central Powers came soon after the United States entered the war.
3. The Treaty of Versailles changed the map of Europe and created resentment.
4. The Russian Revolution resulted in the world's first Communist state.

The Big Idea

World War I, fought from 1914 to 1918, caused terrible destruction and changed Europe forever.

Key Terms and People

communism, *p. 665*
Vladimir Lenin, *p. 665*

TAKING NOTES As you read, identify the two major alliances that fought in the war. In a chart like the one below, list the countries that belonged to each alliance.

World War I Alliances	
Allies	Central Powers

European Alliances, 1914

NORWAY
SWEDEN
North Sea
GREAT BRITAIN
DENMARK
Baltic Sea
NETHERLANDS
ATLANTIC OCEAN
English Channel
BELGIUM
GERMAN EMPIRE
RUSSIA
LUXEMBOURG
FRANCE
Bay of Biscay
SWITZERLAND
AUSTRIA-HUNGARY
ROMANIA
Black Sea
SERBIA
BULGARIA
ITALY
PORTUGAL
SPAIN
Corsica
MONTENEGRO
ALBANIA
Sardinia
OTTOMAN EMPIRE
Balearic Islands
Mediterranean Sea
Sicily
GREECE

Triple Alliance
Triple Entente
Neutral countries

0   200   400 Miles
0   200   400 Kilometers

The assassination of Archduke Francis Ferdinand and his wife sparked the beginning of World War I.

GEOGRAPHY SKILLS INTERPRETING MAPS

1. Place Which group held the most land, the Triple Entente or the Triple Alliance?
2. Location Which member of the Triple Alliance shared borders with two countries in the Triple Entente?

Countries used their armies both to show strength and to threaten their enemies.

The rising nationalism, tense rivalries, and growing armies caused European nations to fear each other. They began to make new alliances to protect themselves. Members of the same alliance promised to **defend** each other if any were attacked.

The Spark for War

In 1914 Europe was on the brink of war. Tension boiled between Austria-Hungary and Serbia over a part of Austria-Hungary that the Serbs badly wanted. Then, on June 28, a Serbian nationalist killed Archduke Francis Ferdinand, the heir to the Austro-Hungarian throne, and his wife. Seeking revenge, Austria-Hungary declared war on Serbia.

The alliance system split Europe into two warring sides. The Central Powers were led by Austria-Hungary and Germany.

Against them stood the Allies: Great Britain, France, and Russia. In time, other countries from around the globe joined in the fight.

READING CHECK Summarizing What were the main causes of World War I?

The Allies' Victory

Germany struck the first blow. It sent a large army into Belgium and France. But French and British troops stopped the Germans near Paris. Both sides then dug miles of trenches, deep ditches from which the soldiers defended their positions. Generals repeatedly ordered their men to charge enemy lines. But new, deadly machine guns cut down soldiers as they tried to move forward. This trench warfare cost millions of lives. Neither side could advance, resulting in a bloody stalemate that lasted over three years.

ACADEMIC VOCABULARY
defend
to keep secure from danger

Meanwhile, German leaders decided to use another new weapon, the submarine, in the war at sea. To stop the English from receiving food and supplies, German submarines began to sink ships headed for Britain. The United States warned Germany not to attack unarmed ships. When Germany ignored these warnings, the United States joined the Allies in April 1917.

Help from American forces gave the Allies a fresh advantage. Soon afterward, though, the exhausted Russians pulled out of the war. Germany then tried a new attack on France. U.S. and Allied troops stopped the Germans and pushed them out of France. Germany's allies also suffered serious defeats in 1918. By November the Central Powers had collapsed.

READING CHECK **Drawing Conclusions** How did the United States affect the outcome of the war?

The Treaty of Versailles

After the war, leaders of the Allies met at Versailles (ver-SY), near Paris, to discuss peace terms. U.S. president Woodrow Wilson proposed a plan intended to promote democracy and prevent future wars. One of his ideas was to create the League of Nations, an organization where countries would try to solve their problems peacefully.

Wilson also believed that nationalities should rule themselves. Acting on this view, the Allies redrew the map of Europe. They took land from Russia and Germany and broke up Austria-Hungary and the Ottoman Empire. From these lands, seven new countries were created.

The Allies also forced Germany to accept blame for starting the war. Germany had to slash the size of its army, give up its colonies, and pay for war damages.

History Close-up
Trench Warfare

Trenches were dug in a zigzag pattern so that the enemy could not stand at one end and fire down the length of a trench.

German and Allied trenches were separated by lines of barbed wire. Some trenches were lined with concrete so that they could withstand attacks using artillery.

A series of trenches at the back were used to deliver food, ammunition, and mail to soldiers on the front lines.

Some trenches served as first-aid posts where wounded soldiers were cared for until they could be evacuated.

ANALYSIS SKILL **ANALYZING VISUALS**

Identify three different ways that soldiers tried to defend themselves in their trenches.

Many people disliked the Treaty of Versailles. Germans thought it was too harsh. Not all nationalities got their own nation. Some countries resented losing land. So, instead of leading to lasting peace, the treaty set the stage for further conflict.

READING CHECK **Analyzing** Why were many people unhappy with the Treaty of Versailles?

The Russian Revolution

Another result of World War I was revolution in Russia. Problems and anger had been growing there for decades. Peasants and workers struggled in poverty. Wartime food shortages and heavy losses of life further turned people against the government. In March 1917 Czar Nicholas II, Russia's ruler, was forced to give up power.

A new government took over, but it could not keep order. Uprisings swept across Russia. The Bolsheviks, supporters of communism, grew in strength. **Communism** is an economic and political system in which the government owns all businesses and controls the economy. **Vladimir Lenin**, the Bolshevik leader, built support among workers and soldiers. In November 1917 the Bolsheviks overthrew the new government, and Lenin created the world's first Communist state, the Union of Soviet Socialist Republics, or the Soviet Union.

READING CHECK **Summarizing** How did the Bolsheviks gain power in Russia?

SUMMARY AND PREVIEW The Allies won World War I, but peace did not last long. Next you will learn about World War II.

Because military tanks were not damaged by either machine gun or rifle fire, their use marked the beginning of the end for trench warfare.

Troops hurled hand grenades into opposing trenches and at oncoming troops to prevent them from advancing.

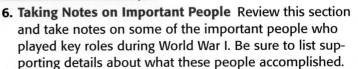

go.hrw.com
Online Quiz
KEYWORD: SN6 HP23

Section 1 Assessment

Reviewing Ideas, Terms, and People

1. **a. Recall** Why did Austria-Hungary declare war on Serbia?
   b. Analyze What conditions made Europe ripe for war in 1914?
2. **a. Describe** What were the effects of trench warfare?
   b. Explain Why did the United States join the Allies?
3. **a. Describe** How was Germany punished for its role in World War I?
   b. Evaluate Was the Treaty of Versailles successful?
4. **a. Identify** Who led the Russian Revolution?
   b. Contrast How did the Soviet Union differ from Russia under Czar Nicholas II?

Critical Thinking

5. **Summarizing** Using your notes, choose one member of each alliance and explain what happened to it after the war.

Member of the Allies	Member of the Central Powers

FOCUS ON WRITING

6. **Taking Notes on Important People** Review this section and take notes on some of the important people who played key roles during World War I. Be sure to list supporting details about what these people accomplished.

World War II

If YOU were there...

In December 1941 you are spending a quiet Sunday listening to the radio. Suddenly the radio broadcast is interrupted by an announcer's voice, and you are shocked by what you hear. Japan has just launched a massive air raid on the U.S. Navy at Pearl Harbor, Hawaii. You are saddened and angered by the attack.

What do you think the U.S. response should be?

What You Will Learn...

Main Ideas

1. Another global conflict, World War II, pitted the Allies against the Axis Powers from 1939 to 1945.
2. The results of World War II included a staggering loss of life and a new power struggle between the United States and the Soviet Union.

The Big Idea

World War II, the most destructive conflict in history, was followed by the Cold War between the United States and the Soviet Union.

Key Terms and People

fascism, *p. 667*
the Allies, *p. 667*
Axis Powers, *p. 667*
Franklin Roosevelt, *p. 667*
Holocaust, *p. 668*
genocide, *p. 668*
Cold War, *p. 669*
Mao Zedong, *p. 669*

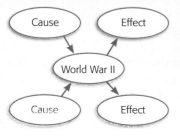

TAKING NOTES As you read, identify events that led to World War II and those that resulted from the war. Use a graphic organizer like this one to keep track of your thoughts.

> **BUILDING BACKGROUND** Many countries faced deep economic and political problems as a result of World War I. Dictators rose to power in a number of countries but did not bring solutions. Instead they attacked their neighbors and plunged the world back into war.

Another Global Conflict

In the 1920s Europe struggled to recover from World War I. The situation grew worse in 1929 and the early 1930s, when the Great Depression, a severe economic slump, swept the globe. By the 1940s the world would once again be at war.

Leaders of War QUICK FACTS

Allies

Winston Churchill
Prime Minister of
Great Britain

Franklin Roosevelt
President of
the United States

Joseph Stalin
Premier of
the Soviet Union

The Rise of Dictators

As troubles grew, people looked to strong leaders. In Japan, the military took over the government. In the Soviet Union, Joseph Stalin took power after Lenin died. A ruthless ruler, Stalin killed or sent to forced labor camps anyone he thought was disloyal.

Brutal dictators also arose in Italy and Germany. They attracted followers by preaching **fascism** (FA-shiz-um), a political philosophy based on nationalism and strong government. In 1922 Benito Mussolini made Italy the first fascist state. Adolf Hitler led the fascist Nazi (NOT-see) movement in Germany. He took over the German government in 1933.

Axis Powers and Aggression

Bitter about the Versailles Treaty, Hitler aimed to take revenge for Germany's loss in World War I by expanding German territory. After invading other nearby countries, he attacked Poland in 1939. In response, Great Britain and France, known as **the Allies**, declared war on Germany. The next year, Hitler countered with an alliance of his own. Germany, Italy, and Japan joined forces to become the **Axis Powers**.

World War II was a new kind of war. Tanks and trucks allowed armies to move quickly. Bombers flew long distances to strike enemy targets. With these tactics, Germany quickly defeated Poland in what the Germans called a blitzkrieg, or "lightning war." Hitler's forces soon overran other European countries too.

When France fell in 1940, British Prime Minister Winston Churchill rallied his people, and the British air force held off the Germans. Hitler's troops then invaded the Soviet Union. Both sides suffered heavy losses before the Soviets were finally able to force the Germans into retreat.

Victory of the Allies

On December 7, 1941, Japan attacked the U.S. Navy at Pearl Harbor, Hawaii. Led by President **Franklin Roosevelt**, the United States joined the Allies. For the next two and a half years battles raged in Europe, North Africa, the Middle East, Asia, and the islands of the South Pacific Ocean. Then in June 1944 U.S. and British troops landed in France and pushed into Germany. Soviet forces advanced from the east. Germany surrendered in May 1945.

FOCUS ON READING
What type of public documents might be helpful in learning more about the U.S. decision to enter World War II?

Axis Powers

Adolf Hitler
Chancellor of Germany

Benito Mussolini
Prime Minister of Italy

Hideki Tojo
Prime Minister of Japan

A PERSONAL ACCOUNT
The Diary of Anne Frank

Anne Frank was a Jewish teenager living in Germany when Hitler came to power. When the Nazis' treatment of German Jews became unbearable, Anne and her family fled to Amsterdam. Soon afterward, however, Nazis began rounding up Jews there, so the Franks were forced into hiding. Anne kept a diary of this time. In the entry from that diary shown above, Anne writes about events shortly after her family went into hiding.

Our many Jewish friends and acquaintances are being taken away in droves [large numbers]. The Gestapo [German secret police] is treating them very roughly and transporting them in cattle cars [train cars used to move livestock] to Westerbork, the big camp in Drenthe to which they're sending all the Jews .... We assume that most of them are being murdered. —October 9, 1942

Anne was right. The Nazis sent millions of Jews to concentration camps—special camps where Jews and others were worked to death or murdered. Yet in the entry below, less than a month before being found by the Nazis and taken to a concentration camp where she later died, Anne refuses to lose hope.

What do you think Anne meant when she said her ideals are absurd?

It's a wonder I haven't abandoned all my ideals, they seem so absurd and impractical. Yet I cling to them because I still believe, in spite of everything, that people are truly good at heart. —July 15, 1944

ANALYSIS SKILL ANALYZING PRIMARY SOURCES

Despite her terrible situation, why do you think Anne believed that "people are truly good at heart"?

U.S. leaders thought a powerful new weapon, the atomic bomb, could end the war with Japan. In August 1945 the United States dropped atomic bombs on the cities of Hiroshima and Nagasaki. Days later Japan surrendered. The war was over.

READING CHECK Evaluating What led to the Allies' victory in World War II?

Results of the War

THE IMPACT TODAY

The United Nations is still an important organization that tries to promote peace in the world.

World War II was the deadliest conflict in human history. More than 34 million soldiers were injured, and 22 million died. Over 30 million civilians also lost their lives. Many were victims of the **Holocaust** (HO-luh-kost), the Nazis' effort to wipe out

the Jewish people. The Nazis rounded up Jews throughout Europe and sent them to special camps where they were killed. Six million Jews died in this **genocide** (JE-nuh-side), the deliberate destruction of a people. Millions of other people, including Slavs, Gypsies, and those with disabilities, were killed too.

Thousands of civilians died in Japan when the atomic bombs were dropped. These nuclear weapons had terrifying implications. People feared that another war could wipe out humanity. Near the end of the war, leaders of the Allies worked together to form the United Nations to help solve world disputes peacefully.

The world, though, was vastly changed. The war had weakened the economies and governments of many nations. The United States and the Soviet Union were left as the world's strongest powers. Allies during the war, the two nations now distrusted each other. This distrust led to the **Cold War**, a period of tense rivalry between the superpowers but no direct fighting.

The Soviets set up Communist states in Eastern Europe. The United States took action by giving economic aid to help the democracies of Western Europe. Germany ended up divided between the two. West Germany became a democracy. East Germany became a Communist nation.

The Cold War also extended into Asia. In 1945 Korea, like Germany, was divided into two parts. Soviet forces occupied the northern half, where a Communist government took power. U.S. troops took control of the southern half, where an anti-Communist government was established. In 1949 **Mao Zedong** (mau zuh-DUNG) formed a Communist government in China.

READING CHECK **Analyzing** What were the two strongest countries after World War II?

Causes and Effects of World War II

Causes
- Germany invades neighboring countries in an effort to build a new German Empire under Nazi rule.
- Japan invades countries in Asia to gain access to raw materials.

Effects
- More than 50 million people are killed.
- The Jewish population in Europe is nearly completely wiped out by the Holocaust.
- The United States and the Soviet Union emerge as the world's strongest powers.

SUMMARY AND PREVIEW Between 1939 and 1945, the world's major powers fought the deadliest, most destructive conflict the world has ever known. Next, you will read about the Cold War and later developments of the post-war period.

go.hrw.com
Online Quiz
KEYWORD: SN6 HP23

Section 2 Assessment

Reviewing Ideas, Terms, and People
1. **a. Recall** What is **fascism**? Why did this philosophy become popular in Europe in the years following World War I?
   b. Explain What role did the British air force play in World War II?
   c. Analyze How did the entry of the United States into the war affect its outcome?
2. **a. Describe** What happened to Europe's Jewish population during World War II?
   b. Explain What is the purpose of the United Nations and when was it formed?
   c. Draw Conclusions Why do you think Germany was divided into two parts after World War II?

Critical Thinking
3. **Analyzing** Using your notes, identify the major effects of World War II. For each effect you note, write a sentence explaining how the war caused it. Use a diagram like the one below.

```
           ┌──────────────────────────┐
         ┌→│ Effect:                  │
┌──────┐ │ └──────────────────────────┘
│World │ │ ┌──────────────────────────┐
│War II│─┼→│ Effect:                  │
└──────┘ │ └──────────────────────────┘
         │ ┌──────────────────────────┐
         └→│ Effect:                  │
           └──────────────────────────┘
```

FOCUS ON WRITING

4. **Taking Notes on Important Events** Make a list of the key events of World War II. For each event, write a sentence about the key people involved.

Land, Air, and Sea

World War II was a truly global conflict that involved countries from nearly every part of the world. During the war, which lasted from September 1939 to September 1945, battles were fought in Europe, the Soviet Union, the Middle East, Africa, Asia, and the islands of the Pacific. A key factor in the fighting was the use of newly developed tanks, planes, and ships. These advanced war machines could cover much more territory than ever before, and they played major roles in the deadly battles waged on land, in the air, and at sea.

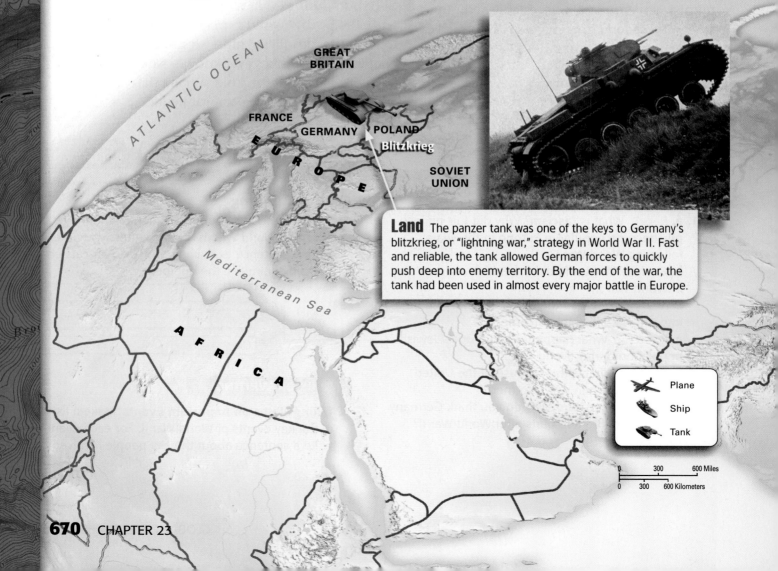

ATLANTIC OCEAN

GREAT BRITAIN

FRANCE

GERMANY

POLAND

EUROPE

Blitzkrieg

SOVIET UNION

Mediterranean Sea

AFRICA

Land The panzer tank was one of the keys to Germany's blitzkrieg, or "lightning war," strategy in World War II. Fast and reliable, the tank allowed German forces to quickly push deep into enemy territory. By the end of the war, the tank had been used in almost every major battle in Europe.

Plane

Ship

Tank

0   300   600 Miles

0   300   600 Kilometers

Air The B29 bomber plane could fly almost 6,000 miles without refueling, which gave it the ability to strike targets far from its base. This is one reason the B29 was used to drop the atomic bombs on the Japanese cities of Hiroshima and Nagasaki.

Sea In June 1942 several of the Japanese ships shown at left took part in the Battle of Midway. In this battle, the U.S. Navy defeated the Japanese attackers and destroyed a number of their key ships, becoming the strongest naval power in the Pacific.

Atomic Bombs

JAPAN

Battle of Midway

A S I A

P A C I F I C   O C E A N

GEOGRAPHY SKILLS INTERPRETING MAPS

1. **Place** Based on Japan's geography, why do you think having a strong navy and air force was particularly important for this country during the war?
2. **Movement** Why was the B29 bomber plane's ability to fly such a long distance without refueling important?

Toward the Present Day

What You Will Learn...

Main Ideas

1. Colonialism ended after World War II as countries in Asia, the Middle East, and Africa gained independence.
2. The Cold War ended with democracy on the rise and communism in retreat.
3. Worldwide terrorism has become a great threat to peace.
4. Global interdependence creates new opportunities and challenges for all of us today.

The Big Idea

Since World War II, countries around the world have gone through dramatic political, economic, and technological changes.

Key Terms and People

Mohandas Gandhi, p. 673
ideologies, p. 674
Korean War, p. 674
Vietnam War, p. 675
Ronald Reagan, p. 675
Mikhail Gorbachev, p. 675
terrorism, p. 676

TAKING NOTES As you read, make a list of major events that happened in various parts of the world. You may want to organize your list in a table like this one.

Asia	Africa	Europe	United States

If YOU were there...

You are a present-day student studying world history. You've learned about everything from ancient times to the modern era. You've noticed that throughout history, people have had to react to important changes and difficult challenges.

What important changes or challenges do you see in today's world?

BUILDING BACKGROUND World War II resulted in major changes around the world. Change is still occurring—in politics, in economics, and in the way we live.

The End of Colonialism

As you have read, World War II weakened the nations of Europe both economically and politically. As a result, they were unable to hold onto their overseas empires.

Independence in Asia and the Middle East

Great Britain viewed India as the "crown jewel" in its empire—its largest and most profitable colony. However, in the 1920s

Time Line

The Spread of Independence, 1947–Today

1957 Ghana gains independence from Great Britain.

1940

1960

1947 India gains independence from Great Britain.

1948 Israel declares statehood.

1963 Kenya is granted independence from Great Britain.

and 1930s **Mohandas Gandhi** led a growing independence movement in India. He inspired thousands to join him in nonviolent protests against British rule. After World War II, Britain agreed to give up control. India, however, was home to two major religious groups—Hindus and Muslims. Neither group wanted to be governed by the other. In 1947 Britain split the colony in two and granted each part independence. The larger part, India, had a Hindu majority. The smaller part, Pakistan, became a Muslim nation.

Meanwhile, in Southeast Asia, the French and Dutch struggled to hold onto their colonies. Indonesia threw off Dutch rule in 1949, but it took a bitter war before the Vietnamese freed themselves from France in 1954.

Several Arab states in the Middle East also gained independence after World War II. Then, in 1947, the United Nations voted to divide the Palestine Mandate, formerly under British control, into Jewish and Arab states. While the Arabs rejected this decision, the Jews accepted it. In 1948 they created the State of Israel. Arab armies then attacked Israel, but Israel defeated them.

New Nations in Africa

The nations of Europe also lost their colonies in Africa as nationalism swept through the continent. Ghana won independence from the British in 1957. The rest of Great Britain's African empire dissolved rapidly in the 1960s.

Movements against French rule in Africa also gained strength. France granted independence to Morocco and Tunisia in 1956. Algeria had to fight a bloody eight-year war to win its freedom. To avoid any more wars, France peacefully granted independence to its other African colonies.

Other European countries, including Italy, Belgium, and Portugal, also lost their colonies in Africa. By 1981 European rule in Africa had ended, but foreign interest in the continent did not lessen.

Alliances in Africa

As the United States and the Soviet Union struggled against each other in the Cold War, they competed for allies. They were both interested in Africa's newly independent nations. As a result, both countries sent economic and military aid to former colonies in an effort to gain their support.

Some African nations sided with the United States. Others sided with the Soviet Union. Many of the new nations, however, chose not to side with either country. They remained **neutral** during the Cold War.

ACADEMIC VOCABULARY
neutral
not choosing either side

READING CHECK **Analyzing** Why did European countries lose their colonies after World War II?

1971
Bangladesh separates from Pakistan.

1980

1980
Zimbabwe (formerly Rhodesia) gains independence.

2002
East Timor is recognized as an independent state.

2000

ANALYSIS SKILL **READING TIME LINES**

How many years passed between the time the first and last countries shown on this time line gained their independence?

The Cold War

The Cold War divided the world into Communist and non-Communist sides. The two sides would struggle against each other for over 40 years. By 1992, however, most Communist governments, including the Soviet Union, would collapse.

Fighting the Cold War

In the 1950s and 1960s an arms race developed between the Soviet Union and the United States. Both superpowers built huge numbers of missiles, bombers, and nuclear weapons. Americans and Soviets realized, however, that if nuclear weapons were ever used, millions of people would be killed. Much of the world would be destroyed. Although they were rivals, both countries knew they could not afford armed conflict.

The Cold War, then, was a battle between **ideologies** (i-dee-AH-luh-jeez), or systems of beliefs. Each side believed its economic and political system was best. The United States believed in capitalism and democracy. The Soviets believed in communism. They saw capitalist nations as greedy and corrupt. Americans, on the other hand, saw themselves as defenders of the free, democratic world.

Berlin, Germany's capital, became a source of tension in Cold War Europe. After World War II the city, like Germany itself, was divided in two. The Soviets controlled the eastern half. The Western Allies (the U.S., Britain, and France) controlled the western half. While conditions in West Germany began to improve, those in East Germany did not. Thousands of East Germans began fleeing to West Berlin. To stop them, the Soviets built a wall along the border in 1961. Topped with barbed wire and patrolled by armed guards, the Berlin Wall became a symbol of the Cold War.

In Asia the Cold War turned violent. In 1950 Communist North Korea invaded non-Communist South Korea, starting the **Korean War**. The United Nations sent troops from the United States and its allies to defend South Korea. China's army helped North Korea. After three years of

The Fall of Communism

The Berlin Wall stood for 28 years as a barrier separating Communist East Germany from democratic West Germany. When East Germany opened its borders in November 1989, Germans from both east and west celebrated by tearing down the wall. The event became a symbol of the end of Communism in Eastern Europe.

fighting, the war ended with no winner. Korea remained divided.

Vietnam was also split in two—a Communist north and a non-Communist south. In 1957 the Communists began the **Vietnam War** to overthrow the south. The United States sent thousands of troops and massive aid to support the south. Still, the Communists prevailed. In 1976 Vietnam was reunited as a Communist country.

Meanwhile, Soviet troops crushed democratic movements in Hungary and Czechoslovakia. Then, in 1979, the Soviets invaded Afghanistan to strengthen its Communist government. Afghan rebels, aided by the U.S., fiercely battled the invaders. In 1989 the Soviets left in defeat.

The Triumph of Democracy

By the 1980s the Soviet economy was in trouble. At the same time, President **Ronald Reagan** was expanding U.S. military forces and weapons. Trying to keep up with the Americans created more problems for the Soviet economy. The Communist nations of Eastern Europe also faced economic hardships. They were heavily in debt, and their people were living in poverty.

The Soviet leader **Mikhail Gorbachev** (GOR-buh-chof) saw the serious problems facing his country and Eastern Europe. He proposed a number of reforms to change the Soviet economy. To win support for these reforms, Gorbachev promoted openness. The government loosened its control over its people. Soviet citizens could discuss ways to change the system and were even allowed to criticize their government.

Gorbachev's new policies inspired reform movements throughout Eastern Europe. In a single year, 1989, Communist regimes in Bulgaria, Czechoslovakia, East Germany, Hungary, Poland, and Romania all toppled. Joyful Germans tore down the Berlin Wall, and East and West Germany reunited as a democracy in 1990. The following year, states within the Soviet Union demanded their independence. In December 1991 the Soviet Union broke into 15 independent countries.

China resisted the push for change. In 1989 when students protested to demand democratic reforms, troops were sent to smash the movement. China, however, wanted Western technology. It began to change its economic policies and adopted some capitalistic practices so that it could trade with capitalist nations. China has remained Communist, but its markets are opening to the West.

Japan, by contrast, embraced democracy and capitalism after World War II. With American help, it became a peaceful, prosperous country. Today it is a stable democracy and an economic giant.

ANALYSIS SKILL **ANALYZING VISUALS**

Why do you think Germans were so happy about the fall of the Berlin Wall?

READING CHECK Identifying Points of View

Why did the United States and the Soviets avoid direct warfare during the Cold War?

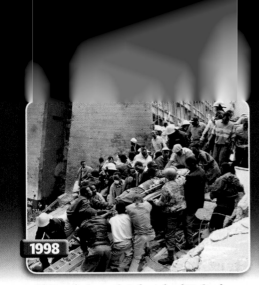

1998

Al Qaeda terrorists bombed United States embassies in two African nations, Kenya and Tanzania. The blasts killed more than 250 people.

2000

An al Qaeda terrorist bombing in Aden, Yemen, targeted a U.S. Navy ship, the *Cole*. The bomb killed 17 sailors and created a huge gash in the ship's side.

2001

On September 11, 2001, al Qaeda terrorists attacked the World Trade Center in New York City and the Pentagon in Washington, D.C. Over 3,000 people died as a result.

Worldwide Terrorism

Terrorism around the world has increased over the past two decades. **Terrorism** is criminal activity involving the use of violence to create fear and to push for political change. Terrorist acts include shootings, bombings, kidnappings, and hijackings.

Modern Terrorism

Although terrorism has been practiced for thousands of years, attacks became more common and deadly in the 1900s. An early example was Northern Ireland. In 1922 the British granted self-rule to part of Ireland but kept control of Northern Ireland. A group named the Irish Republican Army, or IRA, wanted independence for all of Ireland. The IRA began terrorist attacks to try to achieve this goal. Shootings and bombings killed hundreds of British soldiers and others. Then, in 1998, the British agreed to grant self-rule to Northern Ireland. In 2005, the IRA officially disarmed.

Many other groups have since adopted terrorist tactics. Nationalists fighting for Algerian independence bombed French civilians. In Spain terrorists fight for the independence of the Basque (bask) region–a part of Spain with its own culture and language. Other terrorist groups are active in South America, Africa, and Asia.

Terrorism has been a major tactic in the Israeli-Palestinian conflict. After Israel defeated several of its Arab neighbors in the Six-Day War in 1967, a large number of Palestinians came under Israeli rule. The Palestine Liberation Organization (PLO) launched a terrorism campaign against Israel. The PLO's stated goal was to destroy Israel. The PLO gained global attention by hijacking an Israeli jet in 1968. In 1972 Palestinian terrorists murdered Israeli athletes at the Olympic Games. Since that time, Palestinian attacks have killed hundreds of Jews, and Israel has retaliated against these attacks.

Israelis and Palestinians have tried several times to work out a peaceful way to settle their differences. But these attempts have been unsuccessful. A peaceful resolution to their dispute continues to present a difficult challenge to both sides.

2002

More than 200 people died when terrorists bombed two night clubs in Bali, Indonesia, in October 2002. The bombings were the deadliest terrorist attacks in the history of Indonesia.

2004

On March 11, 2004, terrorists bombed a morning commuter train as it pulled into a stop in Madrid, Spain. The bombing killed 190 people and wounded 1,800 more.

2004

People around the world were stunned when terrorists took over a school in Beslan, Russia, and held children hostage. Over 300 people died during this attack.

A New Kind of War

Terrorism against Americans increased in the 1990s. Osama bin Laden, a Muslim extremist based in Afghanistan, ordered many of the attacks. Bin Laden used al Qaeda (al KI-duh), a terrorist group, to wage war on the United States. In 1993 terrorists exploded a bomb under the World Trade Center in New York City. That blast killed 6 and injured 1,000. Five years later, the U.S. embassies in Kenya and Tanzania were bombed. More than 250 people were killed. The following year terrorists bombed the U.S. warship *Cole* in a port in Yemen. This attack killed 17 U.S. sailors and injured dozens more.

The deadliest terrorist attacks in history occurred on September 11, 2001. On that day al Qaeda terrorists hijacked four American planes. The hijackers crashed two jets into the World Trade Center towers in New York and one into the Pentagon in Washington, D.C. After passengers in the fourth jet fought the terrorists, the jet crashed in a Pennsylvania field. More than 3,000 people died in the attacks.

In response, U.S. president George W. Bush declared war on terrorism. He sent forces to Afghanistan where they killed or captured many Al Qaeda members. They also helped a new government take power. Afghans elected a new president in 2004 and a new parliament in 2005.

President Bush believed Iraqi leader Saddam Hussein was another threat to Americans. In 2003 U.S. troops invaded Iraq and removed Saddam from power. After years of war, Iraq is slowly rebuilding. In January 2005 millions of Iraqis voted in their country's first free election in 50 years. Shortly after, Iraqis approved a constitution for their country. In December 2005 Iraqis braved threats of violence to hit the polls once again, this time to elect their first full-term government.

Recent terrorist attacks have also claimed hundreds of lives in Indonesia, Spain, Russia, Israel, and Iraq. But world leaders have begun to work together to combat this problem. The leaders hope that international cooperation will help end this threat to world peace.

READING CHECK **Generalizing** How has terrorism changed since 1990?

Global Interdependence

You've probably heard the saying, "It's a small world." Today this is truer than ever. New forms of communication bring people together. We exchange goods and services widely. We also depend on each other for the well-being of the planet.

The Global Economy

In the global economy, nations around the world are linked in a single economic network. Natural resources, capital, product parts, finished goods, and workers move from country to country in an international process of producing goods and services. Faster trains, planes, and ships make this movement possible. New trade agreements between countries also help to expand the global trade network.

Other technology has furthered the development of the global economy. Businesspeople use mobile phones, email, and video conferences to communicate.

Cable TV networks provide breaking news from around the world. Shoppers in many countries now find an amazing selection of goods at their local stores and on the Internet. People can make a purchase from almost anywhere in the world with just the click of a mouse.

The World of Tomorrow

Outside of the global economy, other developments have created new challenges. The population explosion is just one example. In 1930 there were 2 billion people on our planet. In 1988 there were 5 billion. By 2000 the world's population reached 6 billion. Many scientists fear that our population could soon overwhelm the earth's resources.

Protecting the environment is another challenge. Pollution has destroyed many forests, rivers, and lakes. Timber cutting has reduced the rain forests of Latin America and Africa. Overgrazing has led to the expansion of deserts. In addition, gasses

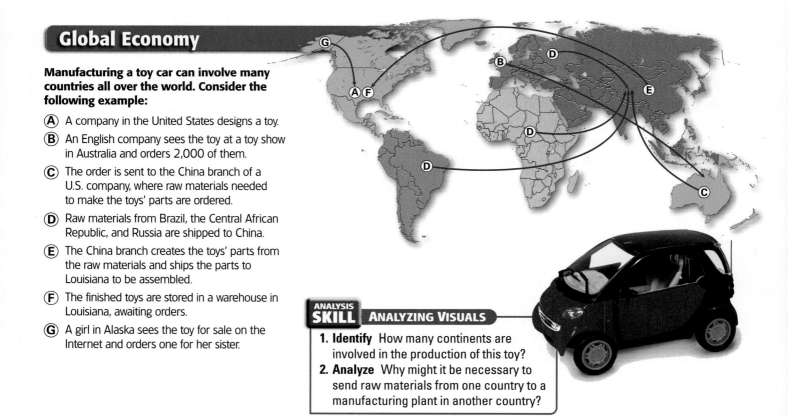

Global Economy

Manufacturing a toy car can involve many countries all over the world. Consider the following example:

(A) A company in the United States designs a toy.

(B) An English company sees the toy at a toy show in Australia and orders 2,000 of them.

(C) The order is sent to the China branch of a U.S. company, where raw materials needed to make the toys' parts are ordered.

(D) Raw materials from Brazil, the Central African Republic, and Russia are shipped to China.

(E) The China branch creates the toys' parts from the raw materials and ships the parts to Louisiana to be assembled.

(F) The finished toys are stored in a warehouse in Louisiana, awaiting orders.

(G) A girl in Alaska sees the toy for sale on the Internet and orders one for her sister.

ANALYSIS SKILL **ANALYZING VISUALS**

1. **Identify** How many continents are involved in the production of this toy?
2. **Analyze** Why might it be necessary to send raw materials from one country to a manufacturing plant in another country?

released into the air have damaged parts of Earth's atmosphere. Some fear that this could lead to a dangerous rise in temperatures around the world.

Individuals and organizations are working to solve these environmental problems. In 2004, for example, Wangari Maathai (wan-GAH-ree mah-DIE-ye) of Kenya received the Nobel Peace Prize for her work in planting more than 30 million trees across the continent of Africa.

In spite of the challenges that we face, our successes in the following areas over the last 100 years give us many reasons to be optimistic:

- **Space** The Soviet Union launched the world's first space satellite, and two American astronauts walked on the moon. Since then, 16 nations have begun working together to build a station in space.
- **Technology** Miniaturization allowed us to develop portable radios and digital watches. It also made it possible to increase the power and speed of computers while shrinking their size.
- **Medicine** The discovery of antibiotics and the structure of DNA enables us to control many diseases and to find cures for others. Laser technology allows us to repair unhealthy tissue.

Accomplishments like these give us reason to believe that we will continue to meet challenges with strength and creativity.

READING CHECK Identifying Cause and Effect What has led to the rise of a global economy?

SUMMARY AND PREVIEW After World War II, most European colonies became independent. The Cold War ended as communism collapsed in Europe. Terrorism has emerged as a threat to global peace, but nations are working together to build a more secure world and a better future for the world's citizens.

BIOGRAPHY

Wangari Maathai
1940–

In 2004 Wangari Maathai became the first African woman to win the Nobel Peace Prize. Maathai was awarded the prize for her work with the Green Belt Movement. This group, which Maathai founded, started as an effort to help reforest Africa. But it has also worked to fight poverty, hunger, and political corruption. The Nobel committee said about their choice, "We believe that Maathai is a strong voice speaking for the best forces in Africa to promote peace and good living conditions on that continent."

Drawing Conclusions Why do you think the Nobel Committee honored the Green Belt Movement?

Section 3 Assessment

go.hrw.com
Online Quiz
KEYWORD: SN6 HP23

Reviewing Ideas, Terms, and People

1. **a. Identify** Who was the leader of the independence movement in India?
   b. Analyze Why was the colony of India divided into two countries?
   c. Make Inferences Why do you think some African countries chose not to side with either the United States or the Soviet Union during the Cold War?
2. **a Recall** Why was the Berlin Wall built?
   b. Elaborate What was the result of **Mikhail Gorbachev's** attempt to improve the Soviet economy?
3. **a. Identify** What is al Qaeda?
   b. Predict Do you think the world will ever be safe from **terrorism**? Why or why not?
4. **a. Describe** What types of items move from country to country in a global economy?
   b. Draw Conclusions Why is international cooperation necessary for solving environmental problems?

Critical Thinking

5. **Sequencing** Using your notes, create a time line that shows major events since World War II in the order they occurred.

1950	1960	1970	1980	1990	2000

FOCUS ON WRITING

6. **Choosing a Topic** You've just read about other important events and people from the most recent period of history. Would one of these events or people make a good cover story for your magazine? Make a list of any topics that you would consider writing about.

Social Studies Skills

Analysis   Critical Thinking   Economics   Study

Understanding Historical Interpretation

Understand the Skill

Historical interpretations are ways of explaining the past. They are based on what is known about the people, ideas, and events that make up history.

Two historians can look at the same set of facts about a historical topic and see things in different ways. Each historian decides which facts are the most important in explaining what happened and why. One person may believe certain facts are important, while someone else may believe other facts are more important. The amount of attention paid to different facts can lead historians to come up with different explanations of what happened in the past and why it happened.

The result of focusing on different facts is different interpretations of history. In addition, new facts that are uncovered about a topic may cause historians to reconsider their ideas, and still more historical interpretations may result. The ability to recognize and evaluate different historical interpretations is a valuable skill in the study of history.

Learn the Skill

Use the following guidelines to better understand and evaluate differing historical interpretations of people and events.

❶ Identify the main idea in how the topic is explained. What conclusions are reached? Conclusions may not be directly stated. They may only be hinted at in the information provided.

❷ Identify the facts on which the writer has relied. Do these facts seem to support his or her explanation and conclusions?

❸ Determine if the writer or speaker has ignored important information about the topic. If so, the interpretation may be inaccurate or deliberately slanted to prove a particular point of view.

Just because interpretations differ, one is not necessarily right and others wrong. As long as a person considers all the evidence, and draws conclusions based on a fair evaluation of that evidence, his or her interpretation is probably acceptable.

Remember, however, that trained historians let the facts *lead* them to conclusions. People who *start* with a conclusion, select only facts that support it, and ignore opposing evidence may produce interpretations that have little value for understanding history.

Practice and Apply the Skill

Reread the text under the heading "The Triumph of Democracy" in Section 3. Suppose that Historian A believes the Cold War ended mostly because of Ronald Reagan's expansion of U.S. military forces, and Historian B believes it ended mostly because of Mikhail Gorbachev's reforms in the Soviet Union. Answer the following questions to evaluate their explanations.

1. What kinds of evidence might support Historian A's interpretation?

2. What kinds of evidence might support Historian B's interpretation?

3. Suppose each historian asks you to write a paper supporting his or her position. Which historian would you support? Explain why.

Chapter Review

Visual Summary

Use the visual summary below to help you review the main ideas of the chapter.

QUICK FACTS

Countries around the globe face a new enemy—terrorism.

Today the world is linked together economically and technologically.

Global Challenges

Protecting the environment is an important world concern.

During the 1900s, two major wars involved much of the globe.

Reviewing Vocabulary, Terms, and People

Match each "I" statement below with the person or thing that could have made the statement. Not all of the choices will be used.

1. I am a system in which the government owns all businesses and controls the economy.
2. I led the independence movement in India.
3. I was the leader of the Bolsheviks in Russia.
4. I created the first fascist state in the world.
5. I led the Nazi movement in Germany.
6. I served as prime minister of Great Britain during World War II.
7. I was president of the United States when Pearl Harbor was attacked.
8. I was president of the United States when the Berlin Wall fell.
9. I was the Soviet leader whose reforms led to the end of communism in Eastern Europe and the Soviet Union.

10. I am criminal activity that involves the use of violence to create fear and to push for political change.

   a. Vladimir Lenin
   b. Franklin Roosevelt
   c. Mohandas Gandhi
   d. Mikhail Gorbachev
   e. Adolf Hitler
   f. terrorism
   g. Benito Mussolini
   h. communism
   i. Joseph Stalin
   j. Winston Churchill
   k. Ronald Reagan
   l. fascism

Comprehension and Critical Thinking

SECTION 1 *(pages 662–665)*

11. a. Describe Why was Austria-Hungary having problems with people who lived in the Balkans?

b. Analyze How did President Woodrow Wilson's ideas affect the Treaty of Versailles?

c. Evaluate Why did the Russian people force Czar Nicholas II out of power?

SECTION 2 *(pages 666–669)*

12. a. Recall Why did the United States decide to drop atomic bombs on Hiroshima and Nagasaki?

b. Elaborate How was Great Britain able to withstand German advances in World War II?

SECTION 3 *(pages 672–679)*

13. a. Identify After what event did France decide to peacefully grant independence to its remaining colonies in Africa?

b. Make Inferences Why do you think the United States and the Soviet Union never directly went to war against each other?

Reviewing Themes

14. Geography How did imperialism contribute to tensions in Europe before the outbreak of World War I?

15. Politics How did the alliances formed after World War II lead to more than 40 years of international conflict?

Using the Internet

go.hrw.com
KEYWORD: SN6 WH23

16. Activity: Conflict in the Modern World Since the end of the Cold War, countries have gone through many changes. Some changes have led to tension, which has given birth to terrorist organizations and a buildup of weapons. Enter the activity keyword. Use the Internet to research terrorist groups, weapons of mass destruction, and their locations. Create a world map to show where weapons of mass destruction and terrorist groups are located. Include a legend to explain your map.

Reading Skills

17. Public Documents in History *Read the list of documents below. Then classify each document listed as either a public or private document.*

a. the letters of Winston Churchill

b. the Treaty of Versailles

c. Vladimir Lenin's diary

d. the U.S. declaration of war against Japan

e. newspaper articles about the September 11, 2001, attacks

Social Studies Skills

Understanding Historical Interpretation *Reread the "If You Were There" scenario in Section 1. Suppose that Historian A believes that rivalries among European countries were caused by people wanting to prove the superiority of their nation. Suppose that Historian B believes that some groups wanted to form their own nation-states and break away from the rule of others. Answer the following questions to evaluate the historians' possible explanations of the killing of the heir to the Austro-Hungarian throne.*

18. Is the fact that the person killed was heir to the throne relevant to either historian's argument? Why or why not?

19. Is the fact that the killing was committed by a Serbian nationalist strong evidence to support either Historian A's or Historian B's interpretation? Explain why or why not?

FOCUS ON WRITING

20. Writing Your Cover Story Review your notes and decide whether you will write about a person or event. Which do you think would make the strongest cover story for your magazine? What are the important facts that you will need to include about your subject? How will you help your reader see why your subject was important enough to be featured on the cover of a magazine? Once you have decided on your topic, write a short article about your chosen subject.

Standardized Test Practice

DIRECTIONS: Read each question and write the letter of the best response.

1

> "World War I has shown that countries should try to solve their problems peacefully."
>
> "I have a plan to prevent future wars and promote democracy."
>
> "Nationalities should rule themselves."

Which person would have been *most* likely to have said these things?

A   Adolf Hitler

B   Winston Churchill

C   Wangari Maathai

D   Woodrow Wilson

2   The political philosophy that is based on nationalism and a strong government is called

A   Nazism

B   fascism

C   blitzkrieg

D   Bolshevism

3   Which was *not* a cause of World War I?

A   nationalism

B   imperialism

C   the assassination of the heir to the Austro-Hungarian throne

D   attacks by the Irish Republican Army

4   Which world leader was *most* involved in the end of the Cold War?

A   Joseph Stalin

B   Franklin Roosevelt

C   Mikhail Gorbachev

D   Mao Zedong

5   Which of the following countries did *not* become Communist following World War II?

A   China

B   North Korea

C   East Germany

D   Japan

Connecting with Past Learnings

6   In an earlier chapter you learned about the Treaty of Westphalia and how it resulted in the states of Germany becoming independent. Which treaty listed below redrew the map of Europe following World War I?

A   The Austria-Hungary Treaty

B   The Treaty of Versailles

C   The Treaty of the Pacific

D   The Roosevelt Doctrine

7   In this chapter you have read about many world leaders. Which of the following people you have studied was *not* a political leader?

A   Petrarch

B   Cosimo de' Medici

C   Napoleon Bonaparte

D   Justinian

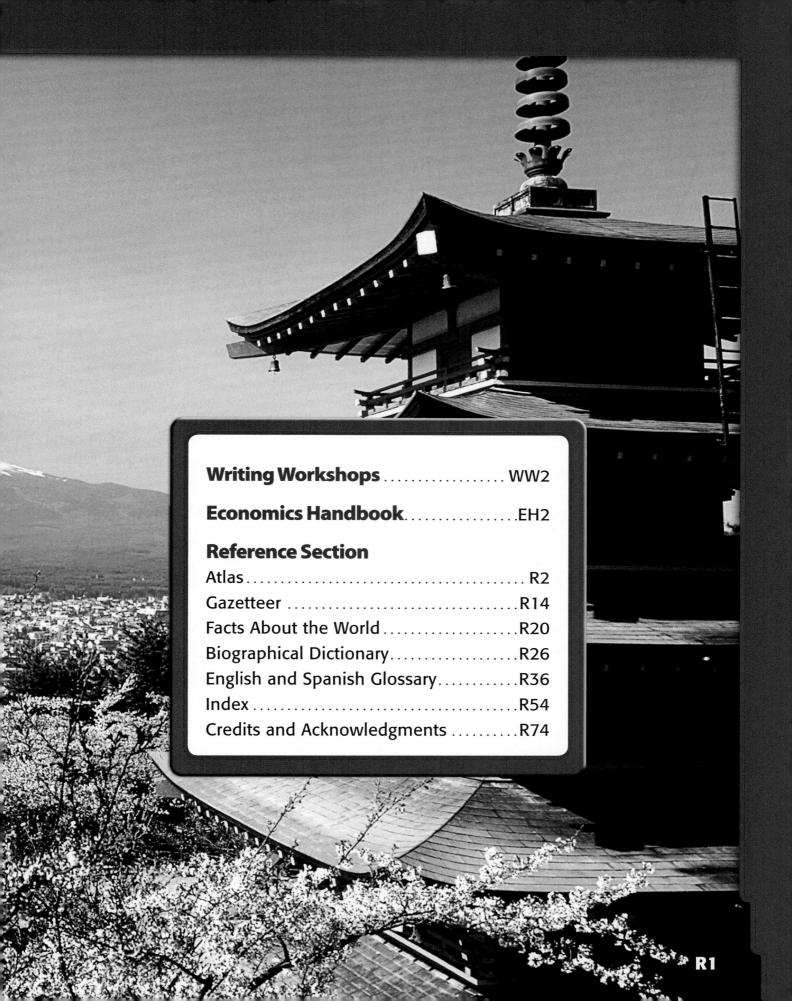

Assignment

Write a paper comparing and contrasting two early human societies.

TIP **Using a Graphic Organizer**

A Venn diagram can help you see ways that the two societies are similar and different.

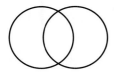

Comparing and Contrasting Societies

Comparing means finding likenesses between or among things. Contrasting means finding differences. You often compare and contrast things to understand them better and see how they are related.

1. Prewrite

Getting Started

Unlike most essays, a compare and contrast paper has two subjects. However, it still has only one big idea, or thesis. For example, your idea may be to show how two societies dealt with the same problem or to show how two human societies changed over time.

Begin by choosing two subjects. Then identify specific points of similarities and differences between the two. Support each point with historical facts, examples, and details.

Organizing Your Information

Choose one of these two ways to organize your points of comparison.

- Present all the points about the first subject and then all the points about the second subject: AAABBB, or block style
- Alternate back and forth between the first subject and the second subject: ABABAB, or point-by-point style

2. Write

This framework will help you use your notes to write a first draft.

A Writer's Framework

Introduction
- Clearly identify your two subjects.
- Give background information readers will need in order to understand your points of comparison between the societies.
- State your big idea, or main purpose in comparing and contrasting these two societies.

Body
- Present your points of comparison in block style or point-by-point style.
- Compare the two societies in at least two ways, and contrast them in at least two ways.
- Use specific historical facts, details, and examples to support each of your points.

Conclusion
- Restate your big idea.
- Summarize the points you have made in your paper.
- Expand on your big idea, perhaps by relating it to your own life, to other societies, or to later historical events.

3. Evaluate and Revise

Evaluating

Use the following questions to discover ways to improve your paper.

Evaluation Questions for a Comparison/Contrast Paper

- Do you introduce both of your subjects in your first paragraph?
- Do you state your big idea, or thesis, at the end of your introduction?
- Do you present two or more similarities and two or more differences between the two societies?

- Do you use either the block style or point-by-point style of organization?
- Do you support your points of comparison with enough historical facts, details, and examples?
- Does your conclusion restate your big idea and summarize your main points?

TIP **Help with Punctuation**
Use the correct punctuation marks before and after clue words within sentences. Usually, a comma comes before *and, but, for, nor, or, so,* and *yet,* with no punctuation after the word. When they are in the middle of a sentence, clue words and phrases such as *however, similarly, in addition, in contrast,* and *on the other hand* usually have a comma before and after them.

Revising

When you are revising your paper, you may need to add comparison-contrast clue words. They will help your readers see the connections between ideas.

Clue Words for Similarities	Clue Words for Differences
also, another, both, in addition, just as, like, similarly, too	although, but, however, in contrast, instead, on the other hand, unlike

4. Proofread and Publish

Proofreading

Before sharing your paper, you will want to polish it by correcting any remaining errors. Look closely for mistakes in grammar, spelling, capitalization, and punctuation. To avoid two common grammar errors, make sure that you have used the correct form of *–er* or *more* and *–est* or *most* with adjectives and adverbs when making comparisons.

Publishing

One good way to share your paper is to exchange it with one or more classmates. After reading each other's papers, you can compare and contrast them. How are your papers similar? How do they differ? If possible, share papers with someone whose big idea is similar to yours.

● Practice and Apply

Use the steps and strategies outlined in this workshop to write your compare and contrast paper.

A Description of a Historical Place

If a picture is worth a thousand words, then a thousand words could add up to a good description. Writers turn to description when they want to explain what a place is like—what you would see if you were there, or what you might hear, smell, or touch.

Assignment

Write a description of a place—a city, village, building, or monument—in ancient Mesopotamia, Egypt, or the Fertile Crescent.

1. Prewrite

Picking a Subject and a Main Idea

Think about the civilizations of ancient Mesopotamia, Egypt, and the Fertile Crescent. Which civilization seems most interesting to you? What villages, cities, or buildings seem interesting? Select one place and use this textbook, the Internet, or sources in your library to find out more about it.

You also need to decide on your point of view about your subject. For example, was this place scary, exciting, or overwhelming?

TIP **Organizing Details**

Organize the details you gather in one of these ways.

- **Spatial Order** Arrange details according to where they are. You can describe things from right to left, top to bottom, or faraway to close up.
- **Chronological Order** Arrange details in the order they occurred or in the order that you experienced them.
- **Order of Importance** Arrange details from the most to least important or vice versa.

Choosing Details

As you conduct your research, look for details to show your readers what it would have been like to actually be in that place.

- **Sensory Details** What color(s) do you associate with your subject? What shape or shapes do you see? What sounds would you hear if you were there? What could you touch—rough walls, dry grass, a smooth, polished stone?
- **Factual Details** How big was this place? Where was it located? When did it exist? If people were there, what were they doing?

When you choose the details to use in your description, think about your point of view on this place. If it was exciting, choose details that will help you show that.

2. Write

This framework will help you use your notes to write a first draft.

A Writer's Framework

Introduction	Body	Conclusion
■ Identify your subject and your point of view on it. ■ Give your readers any background information that they might need.	■ Describe your subject, using sensory and factual details. ■ Follow a consistent and logical order.	■ Briefly summarize the most important details about the place. ■ Reveal your point of view about the place.

3. Evaluate and Revise

Evaluating

Use the following questions to discover ways to improve your paper.

Evaluation Questions for a Description of a Place

- Do you immediately catch the reader's interest?
- Do you use sensory and factual details that work together to create a vivid picture of your subject?
- Do you clearly state your point of view or most important idea?

- Is the information organized clearly?
- Do you end the description by summarizing the most important details?

TIP **Showing Location** When describing the physical appearance of something, make sure you use precise words and phrases to explain where a feature is located. Some useful words and phrases for explaining location are *below, beside, down, on top, over, next to, to the right,* and *to the left.*

Revising

We often help others understand or imagine something by making a comparison. Sometimes we compare two things that are really very much alike. For example, "The city grew like San Diego did. It spread along a protected harbor." At other times we compare two things that are not alike. These comparisons are called figures of speech, and they can help your readers see something in an interesting way.

- Similes compare two unlike things by using words such as *like* or *so.* **EXAMPLE** *The city center curved around the harbor like a crescent moon.*
- Metaphors compare two unlike things by saying one is the other. **EXAMPLE** *The city was the queen of the region.*

When you evaluate and revise your description, look for ways you can make your subject clearer by comparing it to something else.

4. Proofread and Publish

- Make sure you use commas correctly with a list of details. **EXAMPLE** *The temple was 67 feet high, 35 feet wide, and 40 feet deep.*
- Share your paper with students who wrote about a similar place. What details do your descriptions share? How are they different?
- Find or create a picture of the place you have described. Ask a classmate or a family member to read your description and compare it to the picture.

Practice and Apply

Use the steps and strategies outlined in this workshop to write your description of a place in ancient Mesopotamia or Africa.

Why Things Happen

Why do civilizations so often develop in river valleys? Why did early people migrate across continents? You learn about the forces that drive history when you ask why things happened. Then you can share what you learned by writing an expository essay, explaining why events turned out as they did.

Assignment

Write an expository essay explaining one of these topics:

■ Why the Aryans developed the caste system

■ Why Confucius is considered the most influential teacher in Chinese history

---

TIP **Organizing Information**

Essays that explain why should be written in a logical order. Consider using one of these:

■ **Chronological order**, the order in which things happened

■ **Order of importance**, the order of the least important reason to the most important, or vice versa.

---

1. Prewrite

Considering Topic and Audience

Choose one of the two topics in the assignment, and then start to think about your big idea. Your big-idea statement might start out like this:

■ The Aryans developed the caste system to . . .

■ Confucius is considered the most influential teacher in Chinese history because he . . .

Collecting and Organizing Information

You will need to collect information that answers the question *Why*. To begin, review the information in this unit of your textbook. You can find more information on your topic in the library or on the Internet.

You should not stop searching for information until you have at least two or three answers to the question *Why*. These answers will form the points to support your big idea. Then take another look at your big idea. You may need to revise it or add to it to reflect the information you have gathered.

2. Write

Here is a framework that can help you write your first draft.

A Writer's Framework

Introduction	Body	Conclusion
■ Start with an interesting fact or question. ■ Identify your big idea. ■ Include any important background information.	■ Include at least one paragraph for each point supporting your big idea. ■ Include facts and details to explain and illustrate each point. ■ Use chronological order or order of importance.	■ Summarize your main points. ■ Using different words, restate your big idea.

3. Evaluate and Revise

Evaluating

Effective explanations require clear, straightforward language. Use the following questions to discover ways to improve your draft.

Evaluation Questions for an Expository Essay

- Does your essay begin with an interesting fact or question?
- Does the introduction identify your big idea?
- Have you developed at least one paragraph to explain each point?
- Is each point supported with facts and details?

- Have you organized your points clearly and logically?
- Did you explain any unusual words?
- Does the conclusion summarize your main points?
- Does the conclusion restate your big idea in different words?

Revising

Reread your draft. See whether each point is connected logically to the main idea and the other points you are making. If needed, add transitions—words and phrases that show how ideas fit together.

To connect points and information in time, use words like *after*, *before*, *first*, *later*, *soon*, *eventually*, *over time*, *as time passed*, and *then*. To show order of importance, use transitional words and phrases like *first*, *last*, *mainly*, *to begin with*, and *more important*.

4. Proofread and Publish

Proofreading

If you create a bulleted or numbered list, be sure to capitalize and punctuate the list correctly.

- **Capitalization:** It is always acceptable to capitalize the first word of each item in the list.
- **Punctuation:** (1) If the items are sentences, put a period at the end of each. (See the list in the tip above.) (2) If the items are not complete sentences, you usually do not need any end punctuation.

Publishing

Share your explanation with students from another class. After they read it, ask them to summarize your explanation. How well did they understand the points you wanted to make?

● Practice and Apply

Use the steps and strategies in this workshop to write your explanation.

TIP **Using Lists** To make an explanation easier to follow, look for information that can be presented in a list.

Sentence/Paragraph Form Confucius gave the Chinese people guidelines for behavior. He felt that fathers should display high moral values, and he thought it was important that women obey their husbands. Children were to be obedient and respectful.

List Form
Confucius gave the Chinese people guidelines for behavior:

- Fathers should display high moral values.
- Wives should obey their husbands.
- Children should obey and respect their parents.

A Social Studies Report

The purpose of a social studies report is to share information. Often, this information comes from research. You begin your research by asking questions about a subject.

Assignment

Collect information and write an informative report on a topic related to the Hebrews or the ancient Greeks.

 TIP Narrowing a Topic

Broad: Sparta

Less Broad: Women and Girls in Sparta

Focus Question: What was life like for women and girls in Sparta?

1. Prewrite

Choosing a Subject

You could ask many questions about the unit you have just studied.

- Why was Ruth an important person in the history of the Jewish religion?
- What was the role of mythology in the lives of the ancient Greeks?
- What were the most important accomplishments of Alexander the Great?

Jot down some topics that interested you. Then, brainstorm a list of questions about one or more of these topics. Make sure your questions are narrow and focused. Choose the question that seems most interesting.

Finding Historical Information

Use at least three sources besides your textbook to find information on your topic. Good sources include

- books, maps, magazines, newspapers
- television programs, movies, videos
- Internet sites, CD-ROMs, DVDs

Keep track of your sources of information by writing them in a notebook or on cards. Give each source a number as shown below.

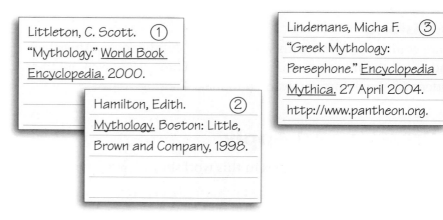

Littleton, C. Scott. ①
"Mythology." World Book Encyclopedia. 2000.

Hamilton, Edith. ②
Mythology. Boston: Little, Brown and Company, 1998.

Lindemans, Micha F. ③
"Greek Mythology: Persephone." Encyclopedia Mythica. 27 April 2004. http://www.pantheon.org.

Taking Notes

Take notes on important facts and details from your sources. Historical writing needs to be accurate. Carefully record all names, dates, and other information from sources. Copy any direct quotation word for word and enclose the words in quotation marks. Along with each note, include the number of its source and its page number.

Stating the Big Idea of Your Report

You can easily turn your original question into the big idea for your report. If your question changes a bit as you do your research, rewrite it before turning it into a statement. The big idea of a report is often, but not always, stated in the first paragraph.

Organizing Your Ideas and Information

Sort your notes into topics and subtopics. Put them in an order that is logical, that will make sense to your reader. We often use one of these ways to organize information:

- placing events and details in the order they happened
- grouping causes with their effects
- grouping information by category, usually in the order of least to most important

Here is a partial outline for a paper on Greek mythology.

Big Idea: The ancient Greeks told myths to explain the world.
I. Purpose of mythology in ancient Greece
  A. Greeks' questions about the world around them
  B. Greeks' use of myths for answers
II. Myths about everyday events in the Greeks' lives
  A. The myth of Hestia, goddess of the home
  B. The myth of Hephaestus, god of crafts and fire
III. Myths about the natural world of the Greeks
  A. The myth of Apollo, god of the sun
  B. The myth of Persephone, goddess of the seasons

TIP **Statement or Question**
Your big idea statement can be a statement of the point you want to make in your paper.

> The ancient Greeks used mythology to explain nature.

It can also be a question, similar to your original research question.

> How did the ancient Greeks use mythology to explain their lives?

TIP **Making the Most of Your Outline** If you write each of your topics and subtopics as a complete sentence, you can use those sentences to create your first draft.

2. Write

It is good to write a first draft fairly quickly, but it's also helpful to organize it as you go. Use the following framework as a guide.

A Writer's Framework

Introduction
- Start with a quotation or interesting historical detail.
- State the big idea of your report.
- Provide any historical background readers need in order to understand your big idea.

Body
- Present your information under at least three main ideas.
- Write at least one paragraph for each of these main ideas.
- Add supporting details, facts, or examples to each paragraph.

Conclusion
- Restate your main idea, using slightly different words.
- Close with a general comment about your topic or tell how the historical information in your report relates to later historical events.

Studying a Model

Here is a model of a social studies report. Study it to see how one student developed a social studies paper. The first and the concluding paragraphs are shown in full. The paragraphs in the body of the paper are summarized.

INTRODUCTORY PARAGRAPH

Attention grabber

Statement of Big Idea

The ancient Greeks faced many mysteries in their lives. How and why did people fall in love? What made rain fall and crops grow? What are the planets and stars, and where did they come from? Through the myths they told about their heroes, gods, and goddesses, the Greeks answered these questions. They used mythology to explain all things, from everyday events to forces of nature to the creation of the universe.

Body Paragraphs

The first body paragraph opens with a statement about how the Greeks used myths to explain their daily lives. Then two examples of those kinds of myths are given. The student summarizes myths about Aphrodite, goddess of love, and Hephaestus, god of crafts and fire.

In the next paragraph, the student shows how the Greeks used myths to explain the natural world. The example of such a story is Persephone and her relationship to the seasons.

The last paragraph in the body contains the student's final point, which is about creation myths. The two examples given for these myths are stories about Helios, god of the sun, and Artemis, goddess of the moon.

CONCLUDING PARAGRAPH

First two sentences restate the thesis

Last three sentences make a general comment about the topic, Greek myths.

The Greeks had a huge number of myths. They needed that many to explain all of the things that they did and saw. Besides explaining things, myths also gave the Greeks a feeling of power. By praying and sacrificing to the gods, they believed they could affect the world around them. All people want to have some control over their lives, and their mythology gave the Greeks that feeling of control.

Notice that each paragraph is organized in the same way as the entire paper. Each paragraph expresses a main idea and includes information to support that main idea. One big difference is that not every paragraph requires a conclusion. Only the last paragraph needs to end with a concluding statement.

3. Evaluate and Revise

It is important to evaluate your first draft before you begin to revise it. Follow the steps below to evaluate and revise your draft.

Evaluating and Revising an Informative Report

1. Does the introduction grab the readers' interest and state the big idea of your report?
2. Does the body of your report have at least three paragraphs that develop your big idea? Is the main idea in each paragraph clearly stated?
3. Have you included enough information to support each of your main ideas? Are all facts, details, and examples accurate? Are all of them clearly related to the main ideas they support?
4. Is the report clearly organized? Does it use chronological order, order of importance, or cause and effect?
5. Does the conclusion restate the big idea of your report? Does it end with a general comment about your topic?
6. Have you included at least three sources in your bibliography? Have you included all the sources you used and not any you did not use?

4. Proofread and Publish

Proofreading

To correct your report before sharing it, check the following:
- the spelling and capitalization of all proper names for specific people, places, things, and events
- punctuation marks around any direct quotation
- punctuation and capitalization in your bibliography

Publishing

Choose one or more of these ideas to share your report.
- Create a map to accompany your report. Use a specific color to highlight places and routes that are important in your report.
- File a copy of your report in your school's library for other students' reference. Include illustrations to go with the report.
- If your school has a Web site, you might post your report there. See if you can link to other sources on your topic.

TIP Bibliography
- Underline the titles of all books, television programs, and Web sites.
- Use quotation marks around titles of articles and stories.

● Practice and Apply

Use the steps and strategies outlined in this workshop to research and write an informative report.

Assignment

Write about a problem the Romans faced and what their solution was or what you think would be a better solution.

Historical Problem and Solution

History is the story of how individuals have solved political, economic, and social problems. Learning to write an effective problem-solution paper will be useful in school and in many other situations.

1. Prewrite

Identifying a Problem

Think of a problem the Romans faced. Look at the problem closely. What caused it? What were its effects? Here is an example.

Problem: The Gauls overran Rome.

Solution A: Pay the Gauls a huge ransom to leave Rome. [caused other cities to attack in the hope of getting similar ransoms]

Solution B: Attack other cities. [caused other cities to stop attacking Rome; let Rome gain power and wealth]

Finding a Solution and Proof

Compare the Roman solution to the problem to one they didn't try. Choose either the Roman solution or your own solution to write about. Your explanation should answer these questions.

- How does the solution address the cause of the problem?
- How does the solution fix the effects of the problem?

Use historical evidence to support what you say about the problem:

- facts, examples, or quotations
- comparisons with similar problems your readers know about

2. Write

This framework can help you clearly explain the problem and its solution.

A Writer's Framework

Introduction
- Tell your reader what problem the Romans faced.
- Explain the causes and effects of the problem.
- State your purpose in presenting this problem and its solution.

Body
- Explain the solution.
- Connect the solution directly to the problem.
- Give supporting historical evidence and details that show how the solution deals with the problem.

Conclusion
- Summarize the problem and the solution.
- Discuss how well the solution deals with the problem.

3. Evaluate and Revise

Evaluating

Now you'll want to evaluate your draft to see where you can improve your paper. Try using the following questions to decide what to revise.

Evaluation Questions for a Historical Problem and Solution

- Does your introduction state the problem clearly and describe it fully?
- Does the introduction give causes and effects of the problem?
- Do you clearly explain how the solution relates to the problem?

- Do you give supporting historical evidence showing how the solution deals with the problem?
- Do you conclude by summarizing the problem and the solution?

Revising

Revise your draft to make what you say clear and convincing. You may need to

- Add historical facts, examples, quotations and other evidence to give your readers all the information they need to understand the problem and solution
- Reorganize paragraphs to present information in a clear, logical order
- Insert words like *thus, therefore,* and *as a result* to show how causes link to effects and how the solution deals with the problem

4. Proofread and Publish

Proofreading

To improve your paper before sharing it, check the following:
- spelling of all names, places, and other historical information, especially Latin words, because they can be tricky
- punctuation around linking words such as *so, thus,* and *in addition* that you use to connect causes with effects and solutions with problems

Publishing

Choose one or more of these ideas to share your report.
- Create a poster that Roman leaders might put up to announce how they will solve the problem.
- Hold a debate between teams of classmates who have chosen similar problems but different solutions. Have the rest of the class vote on whose solutions are best.

● Practice and Apply

Use the steps and strategies outlined in this workshop to write a problem-solution paper.

TIP **Problem-Solution Clue Words.** It's not enough simply to tell your reader what the problem and solution are. You need to show how they are related. Here is a list of words and phrases that will help you do so.

as a result	therefore
consequently	this led to
nevertheless	thus

TIP **Seeing Your Paper as Others See It.** To you, your paper makes perfect sense. To others, it may not. Whenever possible, ask someone else to read your paper. Others can see flaws and errors that you never will see. Listen closely to questions and suggestions. Do your best to see the other person's point before defending what you have written.

A Summary of a History Lesson

Assignment

Write a summary of one section in a chapter you read in Unit 6, "Islamic and African Civilizations."

After you read something, do you have trouble recalling what it was about? Many people do. Writing a summary briefly restating the main ideas and details of something you have read can help you remember it.

1. Prewrite

Reading to Understand

The first thing you need to do is to read the section at least twice.

- **Read** it straight through the first time to see what it is about.
- **Reread** it as many times as necessary to be sure you understand the main topic of the whole section.

Identifying the Main Idea

Next, identify the main idea in each paragraph or for each heading in the chapter. Look back at the facts, examples, quotations, and other information in each of them. Ask yourself, *What is the main idea that they all support, or refer to?* State this idea in your own words.

Noting Details

Note the information that directly and best supports each main idea. Often, several details and examples are given to support a single idea. Choose only those that are most important and provide the strongest support.

2. Write

As you write your summary, refer to the framework below to help you keep on track.

> **TIP** How Long Is a Summary?
>
> Here are some guidelines you can use to plan how much to write in a summary. If you are summarizing
>
> - only a few paragraphs, your summary should be about one third as long as the original.
> - longer selections such as an article or textbook chapter, write one sentence for each paragraph or heading in the original.

A Writer's Framework

Introduction
- Give the section number and title.
- State the main topic of the section.
- Introduce the first main heading in the section and begin your summary by identifying the main idea and supporting information under it.

Body
- Give the main idea, along with its most significant supporting details, for each heading in the section.
- Use words and phrases that show connections between ideas.
- Use your own words as much as you can, and limit quotations in number and length.

Conclusion
- Restate the main idea of the section.
- Comment on maps, charts, other visual content, or other features that were especially important or useful.

3. Evaluate and Revise

Now you need to evaluate your summary to make sure that it is complete and accurate. The following questions can help you decide what to change.

Evaluation Questions for a Summary

- Does your introduction identify the number and title of the section and its main topic?
- Do you identify the main idea of the section?
- Do you include supporting details for each heading or paragraph in the section?
- Do you connect ideas and information by using words that show how they are related?

- Have you written the summary in your own words and limited the number and length of your quotations?
- Does your conclusion state the underlying meaning, or main idea, of the section?

TIP **Finding Main Ideas in a History Chapter** Boldfaced headings in textbooks usually tell what subject is discussed under those headings. The first and last sentences of paragraphs under headings can also be a quick guide to what is said about a subject.

4. Proofread and Publish

Proofreading

Be sure to enclose all quotations in quotation marks and to place other marks of punctuation correctly before or after closing quotation marks.

- **Commas** and **periods** go **inside** closing quotation marks.
- **Semicolons** and **dashes** go **outside** closing quotation marks.
- **Question marks** and **exclamation points** go **inside** closing quotation marks **when they are part of the quotation** and **outside when they are not**.

TIP **Using Special Historical Features** Don't forget to look at maps, charts, timelines, pictures, historical documents, and even study questions and assignments. They often contain important ideas and information.

Publishing

Team up with classmates who have written summaries on different sections of the same chapter you have. Review each other's summaries. Make sure the summaries include all the main ideas and most significant details in each section.

Collect all the summaries to create a chapter study guide for your team. If possible, make copies for everyone on the team. You may also want to make extra copies so that you can trade study guides with teams who worked on other chapters.

● Practice and Apply

Use the steps and strategies outlined in this workshop to write a summary of one section of a chapter in this unit.

Assignment

Write an essay stating your opinion on this topic or another historical topic of your choice: All great empires are likely to end in the same way the Maya and Aztec empires did.

TIP **Fact vs. Opinion** A fact is a statement that can be proved true. Facts include

- measurements
- dates
- locations
- definitions

An opinion is a statement of a personal belief. Opinions often include judgmental words and phrases such as *better, should,* and *think.*

Persuasion and Historical Issues

The study of history raises questions, or issues, that can be argued from both sides. Effective persuasive writing supports a point of view with evidence.

1. Prewrite

Taking a Position

Do you think all great empires will follow the same course as the Maya and Aztecs, or could an empire take a different course? Write a sentence that states your position, or opinion about, this topic or another topic.

Supporting Your Position

To convince your audience to agree with your position, you will need reasons and evidence. **Reasons** tell *why* a writer has a particular point of view. **Evidence** backs up, or helps prove, the reasons. Evidence includes facts, examples, and opinions of experts, like historians. You can find this evidence in this textbook or other books recommended by your teacher.

Organizing Reasons and Evidence

Try to present your reasons and evidence in order of importance, so that you can end with your most convincing points. Use transitions such as *mainly, last,* and *most important* to emphasize ideas.

2. Write

This framework can help you state your position clearly and present convincing reasons and evidence.

A Writer's Framework

Introduction	**Body**	**Conclusion**
■ Introduce the topic by using a surprising fact, quotation, or comparison to get your reader's attention. ■ Identify at least two differing positions on this topic. ■ State your own position on the topic.	■ Present at least two reasons to support your position. ■ Support each reason with evidence (facts, examples, expert opinions). ■ Organize your reasons and evidence in order of importance with your most convincing reason last.	■ Restate your position. ■ Summarize your supporting reasons and evidence. ■ Project your position into history by using it to predict the course of current and future events.

3. Evaluate and Revise

Evaluating

Use the following questions to evaluate your draft and find ways to make your paper more convincing.

Evaluation Questions for a Persuasive Essay

- Does your introduction include an opinion statement that clearly states your position?
- Have you given at least two reasons to support your position?
- Do you provide convincing evidence to back up your reasons?

- Are your reasons and evidence organized by order of importance, ending with the most important?
- Does your conclusion restate your position and summarize your reasons and evidence? Do you apply your opinion to future history?

Revising

Strengthen your argument with loaded words. Loaded words are words with strong positive or negative connotations.
- Positive—leader
- Negative—tyrant, despot
- Neutral—ruler, emperor

Loaded words can add powerful emotional appeals to your reader's feelings and help convince them to agree with your opinion.

4. Proofread and Publish

Proofreading

Keep the following guidelines in mind as you reread your paper.
- Wherever you have added, deleted, or changed anything, make sure your revision fits in smoothly and does not introduce any errors.
- Double-check names, dates, and other factual information.

Publishing

Team up with one of your classmates who has taken the same position you have. Combine your evidence to create the most powerful argument you can. Challenge a team that has taken an opposing view to a debate. Ask the rest of the class for feedback: Which argument was more convincing? What were the strengths and weaknesses of each position?

Practice and Apply

Use the steps and strategies outlined in this workshop to write a persuasive composition.

TIP **Using a Computer to Check Spelling in History Papers** Whenever you can, use a spell-checker program to help you catch careless errors. However, keep in mind that it will not solve all your spelling problems.

- It will not catch misspellings that correctly spell other words, such as *their, they're,* and *there,* or *an* instead of *and.*
- It will highlight but not give the preferred spelling for many proper names.
- It cannot be relied upon for correct capitalization.

A Historical Narrative

Assignment

A narrative is a story that may be true or fictional. Write a fictional historical narrative set in Europe during the Middle Ages.

What was life like in Europe in the Middle Ages? Where did people live? How did they spend their days? You can learn more about history by researching and writing a narrative that is set in a different time and place.

1. Prewrite

Planning Character and Setting

You should write your narrative from the point of view of someone who lived during that time.

- **The Narrator** Is the person telling your story a knight, a peasant, or a priest? A lady or a lady's maid?
- **The Event** What event or incident will your narrator experience? A jousting tournament? A Viking invasion? A religious pilgrimage? A famine or fire in the village?
- **The Setting** How will the time, between 800 and 1200 AD, and place, somewhere in Europe, affect this person? What will he or she want out of life or would fear or admire?

> **TIP** **Adding Details** Help your audience get a feel for the setting by using sensory details. As you think about everyday life in the Middle Ages, make note of details that describe how things might have looked, felt, sounded, smelled, or tasted.

Developing a Plot

Select an event or incident, and then ask yourself these questions.

- How would the event have unfolded? In other words, what would have happened first, second, third, and so on?
- What problem might face your narrator during this event? How could your narrator solve this problem?

2. Write

Have your narrator tell what happened in the first person, using *I, me, we, us,* etc. For example, *I woke up early. We stopped by a stream.* Then use the framework below to help you write your first draft.

A Writer's Framework

Introduction	Body	Conclusion
■ Grab the reader's attention. ■ Offer needed background information about the place and the people involved in the event.	■ Start with the beginning of the incident or event, and present the actions in the order they happen. ■ Build to a suspenseful moment when the outcome is uncertain.	■ Show how the narrator solves his or her problem. ■ Explain how the narrator changes or how his or her life changes.

3. Evaluate and Revise

Evaluating

Read through the first draft of your narrative. Then use the guidelines below to consider its content and organization.

Evaluation Questions for a Fictional Historical Narrative

- Do you grab the reader's attention at the very beginning?
- Do you include background information to explain the time, place, and people involved in the event?
- Do you use first-person pronouns to show that your narrator is the central person in the event?

- Do you tell the actions in the order they happen or happened?
- Do you show how the narrator solves the problem or how it is solved for him or her?
- Do you explain how the narrator changes as a result of the event?

Revising

Before you share your narrative with others, have a classmate read it and retell the narrative to you. Add details at any point where his or her retelling seems uncertain or dull. Add transitions to show how events are connected in time.

4. Proofread and Publish

Proofreading

Weak word choice can drain the life from your narrative. Vague nouns and adjectives do little to spark the interest and imagination of readers. In contrast, precise words make your story come alive. They tell readers exactly what the characters and setting are like.

- **Vague Nouns or Pronouns** Words like *man* and *it* tell your readers little. Replace them with precise words, like *peasant* or *cottage*.
- **Vague adjectives** Would you prefer an experience that is *nice* or *fun*, or one that is *thrilling, exhilarating, or stirring*?

Publishing

You can publish your historical narrative by reading it aloud in class or by posting it on a class authors' wall. You may also publish all the narratives in your class as an Internet page or in a photocopied literary magazine.

● Practice and Apply

Use the steps and strategies outlined in this workshop to write your historical narrative.

TIP **Describing Actions** We communicate not only with our words but also with our actions. By describing specific actions—movements, gestures, and facial expressions—you can make people in your narrative live and breathe.

TIP **Connecting Events** To improve your narrative, use transitions such as *next, later,* and *finally* to show the order in which the events and actions happen or happened.

Cause and Effect in History

Assignment

Write a paper explaining one of the following topics:
(1) The effects of the Columbian exchange
(2) The causes of the French Revolution

TIP **Adding Facts and Details** For each cause or effect you identify, you need supporting facts and examples.

Example

Effect: New plants and animals introduced to Americas

- European seeds
- Bananas, sugarcane, onions
- Domesticated animals
- Cows, goats, sheep

"**W**hy did it happen?" "What happened as a result?" Historians ask questions like these in order to study the causes and effects of historical events. In this way, they learn more about historical events and the links that form the chain between them.

1. Prewrite

Identifying Causes and Effects

A **cause** is an action or event that causes another event or situation to happen. An **effect** is what happens as a result of an event or situation. To understand historical events, we sometimes look at causes, sometimes look at effects, and sometimes look at both. For example, we could look at the causes behind Columbus's discovery of a new land, but we could also limit our discussion to the effects.

Collecting and Organizing Information

After choosing the topic you want to write about, gather information from the chapter in this textbook, an encyclopedia, or another library source. You can use graphic organizers like the ones below to organize your information:

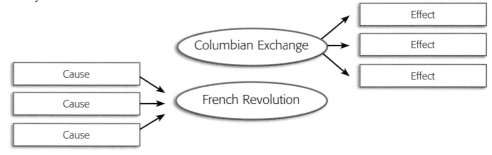

2. Write

You can use this framework to help you write your first draft.

A Writer's Framework

Introduction	Body	Conclusion
■ Briefly identify the event that you will discuss. [Columbian Exchange or French Revolution] ■ Identify at least three causes or effects you will discuss.	■ Explain the causes or effects one at a time, providing supporting facts and examples for each. ■ Present the causes or effects in order of importance, placing the most important point last.	■ Summarize your ideas about the causes or effects of the event.

3. Evaluate and Revise

Evaluating

Use the following questions to discover ways to improve your draft.

Evaluation Questions for an Explanation of Causes or Effects

- Does your introduction identify the event you are going to explain?
- Does your introduction identify the causes or effects you will discuss?
- Do you explain the causes or effects one at a time, using facts and examples to support each one?

- Do you present the causes or effects in order of importance? Do you discuss the most important cause or effect last?
- Does the conclusion summarize causes or effects and their importance?

Revising

Keep a sharp eye out for false cause-and-effect relationships. The fact that one event happened after another does not mean that the first event caused the second.

> **Historical events:** Columbus sailed to America in 1492. John Cabot sailed to Canada in 1497.
>
> **False cause-and-effect relationship:** Because Columbus sailed to America in 1492, John Cabot sailed to Canada in 1497. [Although Columbus's voyage happened before Cabot's discovery, it was not a cause.]

4. Proofread and Publish

Proofreading

As you proofread your paper, check to see whether you have unclear pronoun references. They occur when you have two different nouns or phrases the pronoun might refer to.

> **Unclear** After the explorers conquered the native peoples, many of *them* died. [Does *them* refer to the explorers or the native peoples?]
>
> **Clear** After the explorers conquered the native peoples, many of the native peoples died.

Publishing

With classmates who wrote about the same topic, create a booklet of essays to display in your classroom or in the school library.

● Practice and Apply

Use the steps and strategies outlined in this workshop to write an explanation of causes or effects.

TIP **Saving the Best for the Last** Why would you place the most important cause or effect at the end of your paper, rather than at the beginning? Think about your own experience. When you read something, what part do you remember best—the first or the last? When you hear a speech or your teacher presents a lesson, what sticks in your mind?

Most of the time, we remember what we heard last or read last. That is why it is often a good idea to "save the best for last."

TIP **Signaling Causes and Effects** Signal that you are about to discuss a cause or an effect with words and phrases like these:

- **Words and phrases that signal causes:** *because, due to, given that, since*

- **Words and phrases that signal effects:** *therefore, thus, consequently, so, as a result, for that reason*

A Biographical Narrative

Write a biographical narrative about a significant event in the life of a historical figure discussed in Unit 10, such as Simon Bolívar, Winston Churchill, Anne Frank, or Ronald Reagan.

TIP **Organizing Information**
Think about the historical forces that shaped the experiences and actions of the person you choose. Then, select an important event in that person's life to show how he or she contributed to history. Arrange details about the event from most to least important.

People have shaped the world. How does a single person, working alone or with others, change the course of history? What were the critical events in their lives? How did living in a specific time and place affect those events? These are questions we ask as we try to understand our world.

1. Prewrite

- **Choose** a person who has, in some way, affected the history or the world since 1750.
- **Choose** a specific event or incident in the person's life. For example, you might choose to discuss Simon Bolívar's role in driving the Spanish out of Bolivia.

Collecting and Organizing Information

- **Look** for information about your topic in the library or on the Internet. Book-length biographies about the person you choose are a good source.
- **Identify** the parts of the event. Organize them in chronological, or time, order. Note specific details about the people, actions, and places important to the event.

2. Write

As you write your biographical narrative, refer to the framework below to help you keep on track.

A Writer's Framework

Introduction
- Introduce the person and the event.
- Identify the importance of the event.

Body
- Write at least one paragraph for each major part of the event. Include specific details.
- Use chronological, or time order, to organize the parts of the event.

Conclusion
- Restate the importance of the event.
- Summarize the contributions of the person in the final paragraph.

3. Evaluate and Revise

Now you need to evaluate your biographical narrative and make sure that is complete and accurate. The following questions can help you decide what to change.

Evaluation Questions for a Biographical Narrative

- Does your introduction identify the person and event and describe the importance of each?
- Do you have one paragraph for each major part of the event?
- Do you include specific details about people, actions and places?

- Do you use chronological order, the order in time, to organize the parts of the event?
- Does your conclusion summarize the importance of the person and the event?

4. Proofread and Publish

Proofreading

Keep the following guidelines in mind as you proofread your paper.
- Make sure your transitional phrases—such as then, next, later, or finally, help clarify the order of the actions that took place.
- Make sure you capitalized all proper names

Publishing

Team up with classmates who have written biographical narratives on different people. Review each other's essays. Make sure that each biographical narrative clearly describes the contributions of a historical figure and an event from that person's life.

You can share your biographical narrative by creating a biographical dictionary. Collect all biographical narratives to create a class biographical dictionary for Unit 10. If possible make copies for everyone to use as a study tool.

● Practice and Apply

Use the steps and strategies outlined in this workshop to write a biographical narrative of a person from Unit 10.

Economics Handbook

What Is Economics?

Economics may sound dull, but it touches almost every part of the human experience, past and present. Here are some examples of the kinds of economic choices you may have made yourself:

- Which pair of shoes to buy—the ones on sale or the ones you really like, which cost much more
- Whether to continue saving your money for the DVD player you want or use some of it now to go to a movie
- Whether to give some money to a fundraiser for a new park or to housing for the homeless

As these examples show, we can think of economics as a study of choices. These choices are the ones people make to satisfy their needs or their desires.

Studying economics will help you understand the choices made by other people. Learning from their experiences—and their mistakes—will help you better understand history and the world in which we live. It will also help you make better economic choices.

Glossary of Economic Terms

Here are some of the words we use to talk about economics:

ECONOMIC SYSTEMS

Countries have developed different economic systems to help them make choices, such as what goods and services to produce, how to produce them, and for whom to produce them. The most common economic systems in the world are market economies and mixed economies.

capitalism See market economy.

command economy an economic system in which the central government makes all economic decisions, such as in the countries of Cuba and North Korea

communism a political system in which the government owns all property and runs a command economy

free enterprise a system in which businesses operate with little government involvement, such as in a country with a market economy

market economy an economic system based on private ownership, free trade, and competition; the government has little to say about what, how, or for whom goods and services are produced; examples include Germany and the United States

mixed economy an economy that is a combination of command, market, and traditional economies

traditional economy an economy in which production is based on customs and tradition, and in which people often grow their own food, make their own goods, and use barter to trade

THE ECONOMY AND MONEY

People, businesses, and countries obtain the items they need and want through economic activities such as producing, selling, and buying goods or services. Countries differ in the amount of economic activity that they have and in the strength of their economies.

consumer a person who buys goods or services for personal use

consumer good a finished product sold to consumers for personal or home use

corporation a business in which a group of owners share in the profits and losses

currency paper or coins that a country uses for its money supply

demand the amount of goods and services that consumers are willing and able to buy at a given time

depression a severe drop in overall business activity over a long period of time

developed countries countries with strong economies and a high quality of life; often have high per capita GDPs and high levels of industrialization and technology

developing countries countries with less productive economies and a lower quality of life; often have less industrialization and technology

economic development the level of a country's economic activity, growth, and quality of life

economy the structure of economic life in a country

goods objects or materials that humans can purchase to satisfy their wants and needs

gross domestic product (GDP) total market value of all goods and services produced in a country in a given year; *per capita GDP* is the average value of goods and services produced per person in a country in a given year

industrialization the process of using machinery for all major forms of production

inflation an increase in overall prices

investment the purchase of something with the expectation that it will gain in value; usually property, stocks, etc.

money any item, usually coins or paper currency, that is used in payment for goods or services

producer a person or group that makes goods or provides services to satisfy consumers' wants and needs

productivity the amount of goods or services that a worker or workers can produce within a given amount of time

profit the gain or excess made by selling goods or services over their costs

purchasing power the amount of income that people have available to spend on goods and services

services any activities that are performed for a fee

standard of living how well people are living; determined by the amount of goods and services they can afford

stock a share of ownership in a corporation

supply the amount of goods and services that are available at a given time

INTERNATIONAL TRADE

Countries trade with each other to obtain resources, goods, and services. Growing global trade has helped lead to the development of a global economy.

balance of trade the difference between the value of a country's exports and imports

barter the exchange of one good or service for another

black market the illegal buying and selling of goods, often at high prices

comparative advantage the ability of a company or country to produce something at a lower cost than other companies or countries

competition rivalry between businesses selling similar goods or services; a condition that often leads to lower prices or improved products

e-commerce the electronic trading of goods and services, such as over the Internet

exports goods or services that a country sells and sends to other countries

free trade trade among nations that is not affected by financial or legal barriers; trade without barriers

imports goods or services that a country brings in or purchases from another country

interdependence a relationship between countries in which they rely on one another for resources, goods, or services

market the trade of goods and services

market clearing price the price of a good or service at which supply equals demand

one-crop economy an economy that is dominated by the production of a single product

opportunity cost the value of the next-best alternative that is sacrificed when choosing to consume or produce another good or service

scarcity a condition of limited resources and unlimited wants by people

specialization a focus on only one or two aspects of production in order to produce a product more quickly and cheaply; for example, one worker washes the wheels of the car, another cleans the interior, and another washes the body

trade barriers financial or legal limitations to trade; prevention of free trade

trade-offs the goods or services sacrificed in order to consume or produce another good or service

underground economy illegal economic activities and unreported legal economic activities

PERSONAL ECONOMICS

Individuals make personal choices in how they manage and use their money to satisfy their needs and desires. Individuals have the choice to spend, save, or invest their money.

budget a plan listing the expenses and income of an individual or organization

credit a system that allows consumers to pay for goods and services over time

debt an amount of money that is owed

financial institutions businesses that keep and invest people's money and loan money to people; include banks or credit unions

income a gain of money that comes typically from labor or capital

interest the money that a borrower pays to a lender in return for a loan

loan money given on the condition that it will be paid back, often with interest

savings money or income that is not used to purchase goods or services

tax a required payment to a local, state, or national government; different kinds of taxes include sales taxes, income taxes, and property taxes

wage the payment a worker receives for his or her labor

RESOURCES

People and businesses need resources—such as land, labor, and money—to produce goods and services.

capital generally refers to wealth, in particular wealth that can be used to finance the production of goods or services

human capital sometimes used to refer to human skills and education that affect the production of goods and services in a company or country

labor force all people who are legally old enough to work and are either working or looking for work

natural resource any material in nature that people use and value

nonrenewable resource a resource that cannot be replaced naturally, such as coal or petroleum

raw material a natural resource used to make a product or good

renewable resource a resource that Earth replaces naturally, such as water, soil, and trees

ORGANIZATIONS

Countries have formed many organizations to promote economic cooperation, growth, and trade. These organizations are important in today's global economy.

European Union (EU) an organization that promotes political and economic cooperation in Europe

International Monetary Fund (IMF) a UN agency that promotes cooperation in international trade and that works to maintain stability in the exchange of countries' currencies

Organization of Economic Cooperation and Development (OECD) an organization of countries that promotes democracy and market economies

United Nations (UN) an organization of countries that promotes peace and security around the globe

World Bank a UN agency that provides loans to countries for development and recovery

World Trade Organization (WTO) an international organization dealing with trade between nations

Economic Handbook Review

Reviewing Vocabulary and Terms

On a separate sheet of paper, fill in the blanks in the following sentences:

ECONOMIC SYSTEMS

1. **A.** Businesses are able to operate with little government involvement in a _____ system.
   B. In a _____, a central government makes all economic decisions.
   C. _____ is a political system in which the government owns all property and runs a command economy.
   D. Economies that combine parts of command, market, or traditional economies are called _____.
   E. _____ is another name for a market economy, which is based on private ownership, free trade, and competition.

THE ECONOMY AND MONEY

2. **A.** _____ are objects or materials that people can buy to satisfy their needs and wants.
   B. A _____ is any activity that is performed for a fee.
   C. A person who buys goods or services is a _____, and a person or group that makes goods or provides services is a _____.
   D. The amount of goods and services that consumers are willing and able to buy at any given time is known as _____.
   E. The total value of all the goods and services produced in the United States in one year is its _____.

INTERNATIONAL TRADE

3. A. If we have an unlimited demand for a natural resource, such as oil, and there is only so much oil in the ground, we have a condition called _____.

B. Goods or services that a country sells to other countries are _____.

C. Rivalry between producers that provide the same good or service is called _____.

D. If a country is able to produce a good or service at a lower cost than other countries, it is said to have a _____.

E. Trade among nations that is not limited by legal or economic barriers is called _____.

PERSONAL ECONOMICS

4. A. A _____ is a required payment to a local, state, or national government that is used to support public services such as education, road construction, and government aid.

B. The money we do not spend on goods or services is our _____.

C. You can use _____ to pay for goods and services over time.

D. The payment that a worker receives for his or her labor is called a _____.

E. Individuals and companies use _____ to plan and manage their expenses and income.

Economics and History

1. Work with a partner to investigate trade and interdependence in ancient Asia, Europe, Africa, or the Americas. Choose two ancient societies or civilizations and, for each, focus on the following questions: Where was the civilization located? What resources were available? What goods and resources were exported? With whom did trade take place? What goods and resources were imported? Then, identify two positive or negative effects of trade for each civilization. Write a brief report summarizing your findings and present it to your class.

2. Keep a journal of all the economic choices that you make during your morning routine. What basic needs and wants do you satisfy? What goods, services, and natural resources do you consume before school? Then create a journal from the point of view of a person living in either an ancient civilization, Europe during the Middle Ages, or North America during the Industrial Revolution. Once you have completed your journals, write a paragraph discussing how technology has, over time, changed the way people obtain and use the items they need and want.

3. With three or four partners, create a historical skit that illustrates one of the following basic economic concepts: scarcity and limited resources, supply and demand, or opportunity costs and trade-offs. For example, a skit might explore supply and demand by showing how an increased demand for manufactured goods contributed to the development of market economies in Europe during the 1600s. Write a script for your skit. Then practice the skit and perform it for the class.

RESOURCES

5. A. Diamonds and gold are examples of
_____, which are any materials in nature
that people use and value.

B. The _____ consists of all people who
are legally able to work and are working or
looking for work.

C. Wealth that can be used to finance the
production of goods and services is called
_____.

D. Oil is an example of a _____, which is a
resource that cannot be replaced naturally.

E. Water and trees are examples of _____,
resources that Earth replaces naturally.

ORGANIZATIONS

6. A. Many European countries have joined the
_____ to help promote political and
economic cooperation across Europe.

B. The _____ consists of many agencies
that promote peace and security around
the world.

C. The _____ is a UN agency that provides
loans to countries to help them develop
their economies.

D. The _____ is a UN agency that helps
protect the stability of countries' currencies.

E. Many democratic countries promote market
economies through the _____.

Activities

Economics Today

1. With a group, choose five countries to research. Look up the per capita GDP
and the life expectancy rates for each of these countries in the regional atlas.
Then use your textbook, go to your library, or use the Internet to research
the literacy rate and the number of TVs per 1,000 people for each of these
countries. Organize this information in a five-column chart like the one
shown here. Study the information to see if you can find any patterns. Write
a brief paragraph explaining what you have learned about the five countries.

Region				
Country	Per Capita GDP (U.S. $)	Life Expectancy at Birth	Literacy Rate	TVs per 1,000 People

2. Work with a partner to identify some of the many types of currency used
in either Africa, Europe, or Asia. Then imagine that you are the owners of
a business in the United States. You have created a new product that you
want to sell in the continent you selected, but people there do not use the
same currency as you do. To sell your product, you will need to be able to
exchange one type of currency for another. Search the Internet or look in
a newspaper to find a list of currency exchange rates. For example, if your
product sells for 1,000 dollars, what should the cost be in euros? In British
pounds? In South African rand? In Japanese yen?

3. Conduct research to find the following information for each country in the chart below: main trading partners, exports, imports, industrial products, agricultural products, and resources. Organize the information into a second chart. Then use the information in the two charts to write a one-page report explaining how international trade, specialization, and available resources affects each country's per capita GDP and standard of living.

THE WORLD ALMANAC
Facts about Countries

COUNTRY Capital	FLAG	POPULATION	AREA (sq mi)	PER CAPITA GDP (U.S. $)	LIFE EXPECTANCY AT BIRTH	TVS PER 1,000 PEOPLE
Afghanistan Kabul		29.9 million	250,001	$800	42.9	14
Ethiopia Addis Ababa		73.1 million	435,186	$800	48.8	5
Germany Berlin		82.4 million	137,847	$28,700	78.7	581
Japan Tokyo		127.4 million	145,883	$29,400	81.2	719
Kazakhstan Astana		15.2 million	1,049,155	$7,800	66.6	240
Saudi Arabia Riyadh		26.4 million	756,985	$12,000	75.5	263
United States Washington, D.C.		295.7 million	3,718,710	$40,100	77.7	844

4. With a partner, compare prices in two grocery stores. Create a chart showing the price of five items in the two stores. Also, figure the average price of the items in each store. How do you think the fact that the stores are near each other affects prices? How might prices be different if one store went out of business? How might the prices be different or similar if the United States had a command economy? Present what you have learned about prices and competition to your class.

World: Political

ARCTIC OCEAN

Greenland
(DENMARK)

ALASKA
(U.S.)

ICELAND

60°N

CANADA

Godthåb

Aleutian Islands

Vancouver
Winnipeg

NORTH
AMERICA

Ottawa   Montreal

Chicago

Toronto

New York City

UNITED
STATES

Washington,
D.C.

40°N

ATLANTIC
OCEAN

Rabat
Casablanca

Los Angeles

MOROCCO

Houston

Bermuda
(U.K.)

WESTERN
SAHARA
(Sovereignty
Disputed)

MEXICO

Tropic of Cancer

20°N

Mexico
City

MAURITANIA   MA

Nouakchott

HAWAII
(U.S.)

CAPE VERDE

SENEGAL
Dakar

Bamako   BURKIN
FAS

GAMBIA
GUINEA-BISSAU   GUINEA

GHAN
SIERRA   CÔTE
LEONE   D'IVOIRE
LIBERIA

Caracas

VENEZUELA   GUYANA

KIRIBATI

PACIFIC
OCEAN

Equator   0°

Bogotá

Georgetown
Paramaribo   SURINAME
FRENCH GUIANA
(FRANCE)

COLOMBIA

N

Galápagos
Islands
(ECUADOR)

Quito
ECUADOR

W   E

S

PERU

SOUTH
AMERICA

SAMOA

American
Samoa

Lima

BRAZIL

BOLIVIA
La Paz

Brasília

Sucre

20°S

TONGA

PARAGUAY

Rio de Janeiro

Tropic of Capricorn

São Paulo

CHILE

Asunción

ATLANTIC
OCEAN

URUGUAY

Buenos
Aires

Santiago

Montevideo

ARGENTINA

Boundaries

National capitals

Other cities

0   500   1,000 Miles

0   500 1,000 Kilometers

Projection: Mollweide

40°S

Falkland
Islands
(U.K.)

South
Georgia
(U.K.)

South Sandwich
Islands

60°S

160°W   140°W   120°W   100°W   80°W   60   40°W   20°W

Antarctic Circle

90°W   80°W

FLORIDA
(U.S.)

70°W   Tropic of Cancer

0   200   400 Miles

Nassau

60°W

0   200   400 Kilometers

Projection: Mercator

BAHAMAS

ATLANTIC   OCEAN

Havana

Turks and Caicos Is.
(U.K.)

20°N

GULF OF
MEXICO

CUBA

Virgin Islands
(U.S. and U.K.)

Cayman Is.
(U.K.)

HAITI   DOMINICAN
REPUBLIC

1

MEXICO

BELIZE
Belmopan

Port-au-Prince

Santo
Domingo

Guadeloupe (FRANCE)

2

JAMAICA

Kingston

Puerto Rico
(U.S.)

3

GUATEMALA
HONDURAS

CARIBBEAN   SEA

Martinique (FRANCE)

4   6

Guatemala City
San Salvador

Tegucigalpa
NICARAGUA

Netherlands
Antilles
(NETHERLANDS)

5   7

EL SALVADOR

Managua

Aruba
(NETHERLANDS)

N

Port-of-
Spain   TRINIDAD AND
TOBAGO

W   E

COSTA RICA

Panama
City

10°N

S

San José

PANAMA

VENEZUELA

PACIFIC   OCEAN

COLOMBIA

GUYANA

90°W

COUNTRY	CAPITAL
1 Antigua and Barbuda	St. Johns
2 St. Kitts and Nevis	Basseterre
3 Dominica	Roseau
4 St. Lucia	Castries
5 St. Vincent and the Grenadines	Kingstown
6 Barbados	Bridgetown
7 Grenada	St. George's

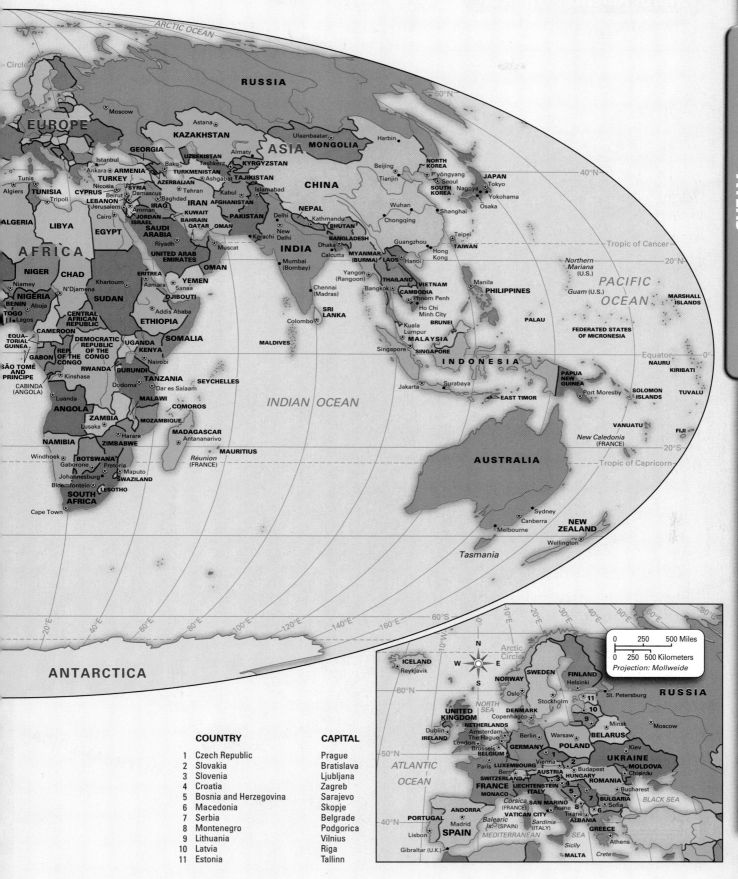

	COUNTRY	CAPITAL
1	Czech Republic	Prague
2	Slovakia	Bratislava
3	Slovenia	Ljubljana
4	Croatia	Zagreb
5	Bosnia and Herzegovina	Sarajevo
6	Macedonia	Skopje
7	Serbia	Belgrade
8	Montenegro	Podgorica
9	Lithuania	Vilnius
10	Latvia	Riga
11	Estonia	Tallinn

North America: Physical

ARCTIC OCEAN

ASIA

EUROPE

North Pole

POLAR ICE PACK

St. Lawrence Island

Bering Sea

Nunivak Island

BROOKS RANGE

Beaufort Sea

Queen Elizabeth Islands

Ellesmere Island

Greenland

Denmark Strait

Mt. McKinley 20,320 ft. (6,194 m)

ALASKA RANGE

Yukon River

Banks Island

Baffin Bay

Cape Farewell

Kodiak Island

Gulf of Alaska

YUKON PLATEAU

Great Bear Lake

Mackenzie River

Victoria Island

Baffin Island

Davis Strait

Alexander Archipelago

R O C K Y

Peace River

Great Slave Lake

Southampton Island

Hudson Strait

Labrador Sea

Queen Charlotte Islands

Athabasca River

Lake Athabasca

C A N A D I A N

Coats Island

Mansel Island

Vancouver Island

PACIFIC OCEAN

Saskatchewan River

Nelson River

Hudson Bay

S H I E L D

Anticosti Island

Newfoundland

Mount Rainier 14,410 ft. (4,392 m)

CASCADE RANGE

Columbia R.

G R E A T

Lake Winnipeg

Prince Edward Island

Gulf of St. Lawrence

Cape Breton Island

Cape Mendocino

COAST RANGES

Missouri River

Superior

St. Lawrence River

SIERRA NEVADA

CENTRAL VALLEY

GREAT BASIN

BLACK HILLS

M O U N T A I N S

P L A I N S

L. Michigan

Huron

Lake Ontario

APPALACHIAN

Cape Cod

Long Island

ATLANTIC OCEAN

DEATH VALLEY

Platte River

INTERIOR PLAINS

Ohio River

Bermuda

Mount Whitney 14,494 ft. (4,418 m)

COLORADO PLATEAU

OZARK PLATEAU

Cumberland R.

MOUNTAINS

PIEDMONT

Cape Hatteras

Guadalupe Island

Arkansas River

Red River

Tennessee River

Mississippi River

ATLANTIC COASTAL PLAIN

BAJA CALIFORNIA

Rio Grande

Brazos River

GULF COASTAL PLAIN

FLORIDA PENINSULA

Cape Canaveral

Gulf of California

SIERRA MADRE OCCIDENTAL

SIERRA MADRE ORIENTAL

Gulf of Mexico

Florida Keys

Bahamas

Straits of Florida

Tropic of Cancer

Popocatépetl 17,887 ft. (5,452 m)

YUCATÁN PENINSULA

Cuba

Greater Antilles

Hispaniola

Puerto Rico

Lesser Antilles

SIERRA MADRE DEL SUR

Jamaica

Caribbean Sea

Trinidad

CENTRAL AMERICA

Lake Nicaragua

ISTHMUS OF PANAMA

SOUTH AMERICA

Equator

ELEVATION

Feet	Meters
13,120	4,000
6,560	2,000
1,640	500
656	200
(Sea level) 0	0 (Sea level)
Below sea level	Below sea level

Ice cap

0   300   600 Miles

0   300   600 Kilometers

Projection: Azimuthal Equal Area

North America: Political

ARCTIC OCEAN

+North Pole

ASIA

EUROPE

Bering Strait

St. Lawrence Island
Nunivak Island

Point Barrow

Beaufort Sea

Banks Island

Queen Elizabeth Islands

Ellesmere Island

Greenland (DENMARK)

ICELAND

Baffin Bay

Denmark Strait

ALASKA (U.S.)

Yukon River

Mackenzie River

Victoria Island

Baffin Island

Davis Strait

Cape Farewell

Anchorage

Kodiak Island

Gulf of Alaska

Great Bear Lake

Southampton Island

Coats Island

Mansel Island

Hudson Strait

Labrador Sea

Juneau

Alexander Archipelago

Peace River

Great Slave Lake

Hudson Bay

PACIFIC OCEAN

Queen Charlotte Islands

Edmonton

CANADA

Anticosti Island

Newfoundland

Vancouver Island

Calgary

Lake Winnipeg

St. Pierre and Miquelon (FRANCE)

Vancouver

Winnipeg

Prince Edward Island

Cape Breton Island

Seattle

Portland

Columbia River

Missouri River

Lake Superior

Quebec

Montreal

Ottawa

Toronto

Lake Huron

Lake Ontario

Lake Erie

Boston

Cape Cod

New York City

Cape Mendocino

Snake River

Minneapolis

Lake Michigan

Milwaukee

Detroit

Cleveland

Philadelphia

Baltimore

ATLANTIC OCEAN

San Francisco

San Jose

Great Salt Lake

Salt Lake City

Platte River

Chicago

Columbus

Washington, D.C.

Denver

UNITED STATES

Indianapolis

St. Louis

Ohio R.

Norfolk

Los Angeles

San Diego

Tijuana

Colorado River

Kansas City

Cape Hatteras

Bermuda (U.K.)

Phoenix

Memphis

Atlanta

Birmingham

Red River

Mississippi River

Dallas

Rio Grande

Austin

San Antonio

Houston

New Orleans

Jacksonville

Cape Canaveral

Gulf of California

Monterrey

Gulf of Mexico

Florida Keys

Miami

THE BAHAMAS

Nassau

Turks and Caicos Islands (U.K.)

Tropic of Cancer

MEXICO

Straits of Florida

DOMINICAN REPUBLIC

Puerto Rico (U.S.)

San Juan

ST. KITTS & NEVIS

ANTIGUA & BARBUDA

Guadeloupe (FRANCE)

Guadalajara

Mexico City

Havana

CUBA

Puebla

Balsas R.

Mérida

Cayman Is. (U.K.)

Kingston

HAITI

Port-au-Prince

Santo Domingo

Virgin Is. (U.S., U.K.)

Martinique (FRANCE)

DOMINICA

BARBADOS

JAMAICA

ST. LUCIA

ST. VINCENT AND THE GRENADINES

GRENADA

Belmopan

BELIZE

Caribbean Sea

Netherlands Antilles (NETHERLANDS)

GUATEMALA

Guatemala City

HONDURAS

Tegucigalpa

Aruba (NETHERLANDS)

TRINIDAD AND TOBAGO

San Salvador

EL SALVADOR

NICARAGUA

Managua

Panama Canal

SOUTH AMERICA

COSTA RICA

San José

PANAMA

Panama City

Legend

- Boundaries
- ⊛ National capitals
- • Other cities

0   300   600 Miles

0   300   600 Kilometers

Projection: Azimuthal Equal Area

0° Equator

South America: Physical

CENTRAL AMERICA

Caribbean Sea

Panama Canal

Gulf of Panama

Malpelo Island

Margarita Island

Tobago

Trinidad

Lake Maracaibo

Orinoco River Delta

LLANOS

Meta River

Orinoco River

Angel Falls

GUIANA HIGHLANDS

Devil's Island
Cape Orange

Amazon River Delta

ATLANTIC OCEAN

Mount Tolima
18,425 ft.
(5,616 m)

Caqueta River

Orinoco River

Río Negro

Japurá River

AMAZON BASIN

Amazon River

Tapajós River

Tocantins River

Equator

Galápagos Islands

Gulf of Guayaquil

Mount Chimborazo
20,561 ft.
(6,267 m)

ANDES

Marañón River

Ucayali River

Amazon River

Juruá River

Purus River

Madeira River

Xingu River

Araguaia River

Paranaíba River

São Francisco River

BRAZILIAN HIGHLANDS

Mount Huascarán
22,205 ft.
(6,768 m)

MATO GROSSO PLATEAU

PACIFIC OCEAN

Ancohuma Peak
20,958 ft.
(6,388 m)

Mamoré River

Guaporé River

BRAZILIAN PLATEAU

ATACAMA DESERT

CHACO

Paraguay River

San Ambrosio Island

San Félix Island

Tropic of Capricorn

ANDES

Salado River

Paraná River

Uruguay River

Mount Aconcagua
22,834 ft.
(6,960 m)

Salado River

Juan Fernández Islands

PAMPAS

Río de la Plata

ATLANTIC OCEAN

Colorado River

Gulf of San Matías

Chiloé Island

Chonos Archipelago

PATAGONIA

Gulf of San Jorge

Cape Tres Puntas

Bahía Grande

Strait of Magellan

Falkland Islands

Tierra del Fuego

Cape Horn

South Georgia Islands

South America: Political

CENTRAL
AMERICA

Caribbean Sea

Barranquilla
Cartagena
Caracas

VENEZUELA

Lake
Maracaibo

Georgetown
Paramaribo
GUYANA
Cayenne
SURINAME
FRENCH
GUIANA
(FRANCE)

Medellín

Bogotá

COLOMBIA

Cali

Orinoco River

ATLANTIC
OCEAN

Malpelo
Island
(COLOMBIA)

Quito

ECUADOR

Guayaquil

Río Negro

Amazon

Amazon River

Belém

Galápagos
Islands
(ECUADOR)

Equator

Equator 0°

PERU

Marañón River

Ucayali River

BRAZIL

Recife

Trujillo

Callao
Lima

São Francisco River

Salvador

PACIFIC
OCEAN

Arequipa

Lake
Titicaca
La Paz
Lake
Poopó

BOLIVIA

Sucre

Brasília

Belo Horizonte

Paraguay River

Campinas
São Paulo

PARAGUAY

Rio de Janeiro

Asunción

Tropic of Capricorn

Tropic of
Capricorn

San Ambrosio
Island
(CHILE)

San Félix Island
(CHILE)

Curitiba

Paraná
River

Pôrto Alegre

Uruguay River

CHILE

Juan Fernández
Islands
(CHILE)

Córdoba

Rosario

URUGUAY

Valparaíso
Santiago

Buenos Aires

Montevideo

ATLANTIC
OCEAN

Río de la Plata

ARGENTINA

Legend

▨	Boundaries
⊛	National capitals
•	Other cities

0   250   500 Miles
0   250   500 Kilometers
Projection: Azimuthal Equal Area

Strait of
Magellan

Falkland
Islands (U.K.)

South Georgia
Island
(U.K.)

Tierra del
Fuego

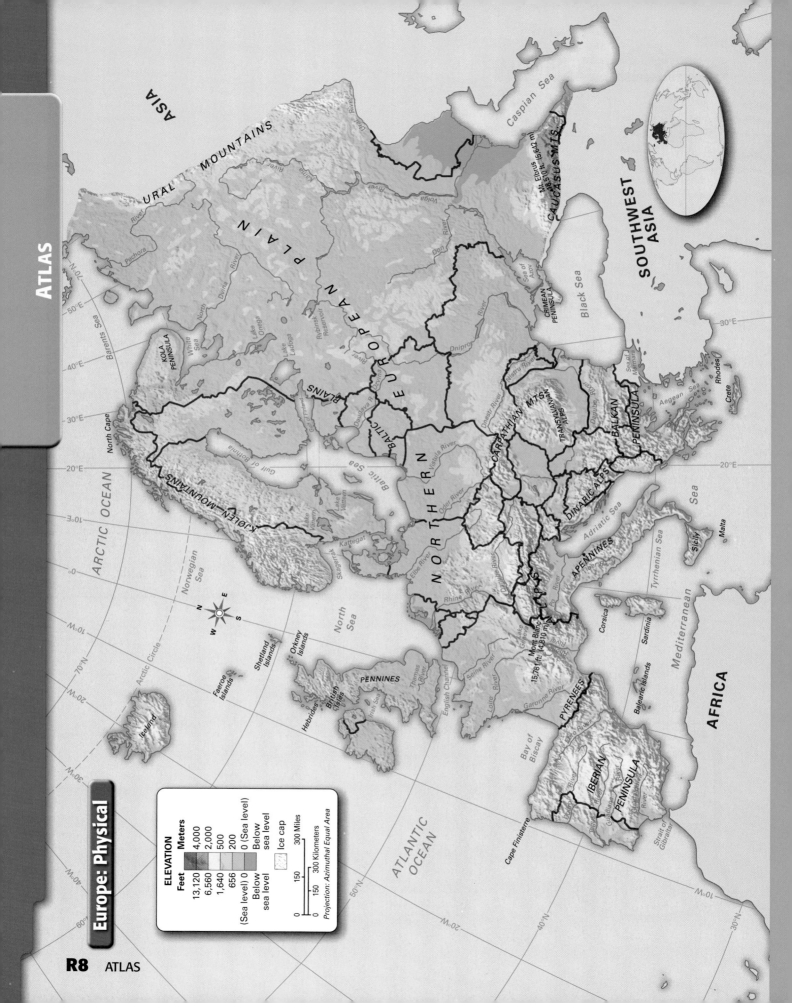

Europe: Physical

ELEVATION

Feet	Meters
13,120	4,000
6,560	2,000
1,640	500
656	200
(Sea level) 0	0 (Sea level)
Below sea level	Below sea level

Ice cap

0   150   300 Miles
0   150   300 Kilometers

Projection: Azimuthal Equal Area

ASIA

URAL MOUNTAINS

NORTHERN EUROPEAN PLAIN

Barents Sea

Caspian Sea

Mt. Elbrus 18,510 ft. (5,642 m)

CAUCASUS MTS.

SOUTHWEST ASIA

Black Sea

CRIMEAN PENINSULA

Sea of Azov

KOLA PENINSULA

White Sea

North Cape

Pechora River

Dvina River

Volga River

Don River

Dnipro River

Ural River

Kama River

Lake Onega

Lake Ladoga

Rybinsk Reservoir

ARCTIC OCEAN

Norwegian Sea

North Cape

KJÖLEN MOUNTAINS

Gulf of Bothnia

Gulf of Finland

Lake Vänern

Lake Vättern

Kattegat

Skagerrak

BALTIC PLAINS

BALTIC SEA

Daugava River

Vistula River

Oder River

Elbe River

Nistru River

Dnestr River

CARPATHIAN MTS.

TRANSYLVANIAN ALPS

BALKAN PENINSULA

DINARIC ALPS

Danube River

Sea of Marmara

Aegean Sea

Rhodes

Crete

Sea

APENNINES

Adriatic Sea

ALPS

Mont Blanc 15,781 ft. (4,810 m)

Lake Geneva

Rhine River

Rhône River

Po River

Tiber River

Tyrrhenian Sea

Sicily

Malta

Corsica

Sardinia

Mediterranean Sea

Iceland

Faeroe Islands

Shetland Islands

Orkney Islands

Hebrides

British Isles

PENNINES

North Sea

Irish Sea

Thames River

English Channel

Seine River

Loire River

Garonne River

Bay of Biscay

PYRENEES

IBERIAN PENINSULA

Ebro River

Duero River

Tagus River

Guadiana River

Guadalquivir River

Cape Finisterre

Strait of Gibraltar

ATLANTIC OCEAN

AFRICA

Arctic Circle

Europe: Political

Boundaries

✦ National capitals

• Other cities

| 0 | 150 | 300 Miles |

| 0 | 150 | 300 Kilometers |

Projection: Azimuthal Equal Area

ASIA

URAL MOUNTAINS

RUSSIA

Ural River

Nizhny Novgorod

Volga River

Moscow

Don River

Caspian Sea

SOUTHWEST ASIA

Barents Sea

White Sea

North Cape

ARCTIC OCEAN

Arctic Circle

Black Sea

St. Petersburg

FINLAND

Helsinki

Gulf of Finland

Tallinn

ESTONIA

LATVIA

Riga

LITHUANIA

Vilnius

RUSSIA

Minsk

BELARUS

Kiev

UKRAINE

MOLDOVA

Chișinău

Dniester River

ROMANIA

Bucharest

Danube River

Sofia

BULGARIA

Skopje

MACEDONIA

Aegean Sea

Rhodes

Crete

Athens

GREECE

ALBANIA

Tiranë

SWEDEN

Gulf of Bothnia

Stockholm

Göteborg

Baltic Sea

Warsaw

POLAND

Kraków

SLOVAKIA

Bratislava

Budapest

HUNGARY

Zagreb

CROATIA

SLOVENIA

BOSNIA AND HERZEGOVINA

Sarajevo

SERBIA

Belgrade

MONTENEGRO

Podgorica

Adriatic Sea

Sea

NORWAY

Oslo

Bergen

DENMARK

Copenhagen

North Sea

Hamburg

Berlin

Dresden

GERMANY

Elbe River

Prague

CZECH REPUBLIC

Vienna

AUSTRIA

Munich

LIECHTENSTEIN

Vaduz

Bern

SWITZERLAND

Milan

San Marino

SAN MARINO

Rome

VATICAN CITY

ITALY

MONACO

Monaco

Naples

Sicily

MALTA

Valletta

Mediterranean

Ljubljana

AFRICA

ICELAND

Reykjavík

Faeroe Islands (DENMARK)

Shetland Islands

SCOTLAND

Edinburgh

NORTHERN IRELAND

Belfast

Liverpool

UNITED KINGDOM

ENGLAND

WALES

London

Dublin

IRELAND

British Isles

Channel Islands (U.K.)

English Channel

THE NETHERLANDS

Amsterdam

The Hague

BELGIUM

Brussels

LUXEMBOURG

Luxembourg

Cologne

Bonn

Paris

FRANCE

Rhine River

Lyon

Marseille

Seine River

Bay of Biscay

PYRENEES

Andorra la Vella

ANDORRA

Barcelona

Balearic Islands (SPAIN)

Corsica (FRANCE)

Sardinia (ITALY)

SPAIN

Madrid

Valencia

Seville

Gibraltar (U.K.)

Strait of Gibraltar

PORTUGAL

Lisbon

Tagus River

ATLANTIC OCEAN

Asia: Physical

ELEVATION

Feet	Meters
13,120	4,000
6,560	2,000
1,640	500
656	200
0 (Sea level)	0 (Sea level)
Below sea level	Below sea level

Ice cap

0 250 500 750 Miles
0 250 500 750 Kilometers

Projection: Azimuthal Equal Area

EUROPE

AFRICA

AUSTRALIA

PACIFIC OCEAN

INDIAN OCEAN

North Pole

Arctic Circle

Tropic of Cancer

Equator

Wrangel Island
New Siberian Islands
Franz Josef Land
Novaya Zemlya
Taymyr Peninsula
North Land
Kamchatka Peninsula
Aleutian Islands
Sakhalin Island
Kuril Islands
Hokkaido
Honshu
Shikoku
Kyushu
Korea Strait
Okinawa
Ryukyu
Taiwan
Hainan
Luzon
Mindanao
Philippines
Borneo
Celebes
Bangka
Sumatra
Java
Mentawai Islands
Nicobar Islands
Andaman Islands
Sri Lanka
Maldives
Lakshadweep Islands
Socotra Island
Cyprus
Sinai Peninsula

Bering Sea
Sea of Okhotsk
Sea of Japan (East Sea)
Yellow Sea
East China Sea
South China Sea
Gulf of Tonkin
Gulf of Thailand
Celebes Sea
Banda Sea
Java Sea
Arafura Sea
Andaman Sea
Bay of Bengal
Arabian Sea
Gulf of Oman
Persian Gulf
Gulf of Aden
Red Sea
Mediterranean Sea
Black Sea
Caspian Sea
Sea of Azov
Bosporus
Barents Sea
Kara Sea
Laptev Sea

CENTRAL RANGE
KOLYMA MTS.
CHERSKY RANGE
VERKHOYANSKIY RANGE
STANOVOY MOUNTAINS
YABLONOVY RANGE
GREATER KHINGAN RANGE
SAYAN MOUNTAINS
ALTAY MOUNTAINS
CENTRAL SIBERIAN PLATEAU
WEST SIBERIAN PLAIN
URAL MOUNTAINS
KAZAKH UPLANDS
TIAN SHAN
TARIM BASIN
TAKLIMAKAN DESERT
KUNLUN MOUNTAINS
PLATEAU OF TIBET
HINDU KUSH
HIMALAYAS
Mount Everest 29,035 ft. (8,850 m)
MONGOLIAN PLATEAU
GOBI
NORTH CHINA PLAIN
QIN LING
BOHAI HILLS
INDOCHINA PENINSULA
MALAY PENINSULA
MADOKE MOUNTAINS
New Guinea

S I B E R I A

USTYURT PLATEAU
TURAN LOWLAND
KYZYL KUM
KARA KUM
GREAT SALT DESERT
ZAGROS MTS.
CAUCASUS MTS.
Mount Ararat 16,945 ft. (5,165 m)
ANATOLIAN PLATEAU
SYRIAN DESERT
AN-NAFUD
RUB' AL-KHALI
THAR DESERT
INDO-GANGETIC PLAIN
DECCAN PLATEAU
WESTERN GHATS
EASTERN GHATS

Amur River
Aldan River
Lena River
Lower Tunguska River
Yenisey River
Angara River
Lake Baikal
Ob River
Irtysh River
Ishim River
Tobol River
Balqash Lake
Syr Darya
Amu Darya
Yellow River (Huang He)
Yangtze River
Mekong River
Chao Phraya River
Salween River
Brahmaputra River
Ganges River
Indus River
Sutlej River
Godavari River
Euphrates River
Tigris River

10°S, 0°, 10°N, 20°N, 30°N, 40°N, 50°N, 60°N, 70°N, 80°N
40°E, 50°E, 60°E, 70°E, 80°E, 90°E, 100°E, 110°E, 120°E, 130°E, 140°E, 150°E, 160°E, 170°E, 180°, 170°W

Asia: Political

Boundaries
⊛ National capitals
• Other cities

| 0 | 250 | 500 | 750 Miles |
| 0 | 250 | 500 | 750 Kilometers |

Projection: Two-Point Equidistant

North Pole

Aleutian Islands

Bering Sea

Sea of Okhotsk

Kuril Islands (RUSSIA)

Sakhalin Island

Vladivostok

Sapporo

JAPAN
Tokyo
Yokohama
Osaka Nagoya
Kyoto
Kobe Hiroshima
Nagasaki

Yakutsk

RUSSIA

URAL MOUNTAINS

Irkutsk

Ulaanbaatar

MONGOLIA

Novosibirsk

Omsk

Yekaterinburg
Chelyabinsk

Astana

Lake Balkhash

KAZAKHSTAN

Almaty

Moscow

Ural River

Caspian Sea

Barents Sea
Kara Sea
Laptev Sea

EUROPE

Arctic Circle

RUSSIA

Black Sea

GEORGIA
T'bilisi
Baku
ARMENIA AZERBAIJAN
Ankara yerevan
Istanbul
Izmir TURKEY
Tabriz
Mosul
Baghdad
Isfahan
Tehran
IRAN
Shiraz
Mashhad
TURKMENISTAN
Ashgabat
UZBEKISTAN
Tashkent
KYRGYZSTAN
Bishkek
TAJIKISTAN
Dushanbe
Kabul
AFGHANISTAN
Kandahar
Islamabad
Lahore
Faisalabad
Peshawar
PAKISTAN
Karachi

Nicosia CYPRUS
Beirut LEBANON
Damascus SYRIA
Aleppo
Tel Aviv ISRAEL
Jerusalem
Amman JORDAN
IRAQ
Basra
KUWAIT
Kuwait City
Manama BAHRAIN
Doha QATAR
Abu Dhabi
Riyadh UNITED ARAB EMIRATES
Mecca
Jidda
SAUDI ARABIA
Masqat (Muscat)
OMAN
Socotra (YEMEN)
Sanaa YEMEN

Mediterranean Sea
Red Sea
Gulf of Aden
Persian Gulf
Arabian Sea

AFRICA

Tigris
Euphrates

Harbin
Changchun
Fushun
Dalian
Great Wall of China
Beijing
NORTH KOREA
P'yongyang
SOUTH KOREA
Seoul
Pusan

Qingdao
Yellow Sea
Nanjing
Shanghai
East China Sea
Ryukyu Islands (JAPAN)
Tropic of Cancer

Xi'an
Wuhan
Chongqing
CHINA
Chengdu

Huang He (Yellow River)
Chang Jiang (Yangtze River)

TAIWAN
Taipei

Guangzhou
Hong Kong
Macao
Hainan (CHINA)

PHILIPPINES
Manila

PACIFIC OCEAN

Nu River
Brahmaputra River
NEPAL
Kathmandu
BHUTAN
Thimphu
BANGLADESH
Dhaka
Chittagong
MYANMAR (BURMA)
Mandalay
Yangon (Rangoon)

Delhi
New Delhi
Jaipur
Ahmadabad
Bhopal
Nagpur
INDIA
Hyderabad
Mumbai (Bombay)
Bangalore
Chennai (Madras)
Kolkata (Calcutta)
Ganges River
Indus River

SRI LANKA
Colombo

MALDIVES
Male

Lakshadweep Islands (INDIA)

Andaman Islands (INDIA)
Nicobar Islands (INDIA)

Bay of Bengal

INDIAN OCEAN

LAOS
Vientiane
THAILAND
Bangkok
CAMBODIA
Phnom Penh
VIETNAM
Hanoi
Ho Chi Minh City
Gulf of Thailand
South China Sea

Bandar Seri Begawan
BRUNEI
MALAYSIA
Kuala Lumpur
SINGAPORE
Singapore
Medan

INDONESIA
Jakarta
Bandung
Semarang
Surabaya
Ujung Pandang
Java Sea
Celebes Sea
Arafura Sea

New Guinea

EAST TIMOR

AUSTRALIA

Equator

ATLAS

EUROPE

SOUTHWEST ASIA

Azores

Madeira Islands

Strait of Gibraltar

ATLAS MOUNTAINS

Mediterranean Sea

Gulf of Sidra

LIBYAN DESERT

QATTARA DEPRESSION

Suez Canal

Persian Gulf

Canary Islands

Tropic of Cancer

Cape Blanc

EL DJOUF

S A H A R A

AHAGGAR MOUNTAINS

AIR MTS.

TIBESTI MOUNTAINS

Lake Nasser

Nile River

NUBIAN DESERT

Red Sea

Cape Verde Islands

Cape Verde

Senegal River

S A H E L

S U D A N

Niger River

Lake Chad

CHAD BASIN

White Nile

Blue Nile

Gulf of Aden

FOUTA DJALLON

White Volta

Black Volta

Lake Volta

Benue River

SUDAN BASIN

ETHIOPIAN HIGHLANDS

HORN OF AFRICA

SOMALI PENINSULA

Cape Palmas

Gulf of Guinea

ADAMAWA MTS.

Ubangi River

Congo River

Lake Albert

Lake Edward

Lake Turkana

RIFT VALLEY

Cape Lopez

CONGO BASIN

Kasai River

MITUMBA MOUNTAINS

WESTERN RIFT VALLEY

EASTERN

Lake Kivu

SERENGETI PLAIN

Mount Kenya 17,058 ft. (5,199 m)

Mount Kilimanjaro 19,340 ft. (5,895 m)

Equator

INDIAN OCEAN

Equator

N W E S

Lake Tanganyika

MASAI STEPPE

Zanzibar

Seychelles

Ascension

ATLANTIC OCEAN

Cunene River

Lake Rukwa

Lake Mweru

Lake Malawi (Nyasa)

Cape Delgado

Comoro Islands

Okavango Delta

Lake Kariba

Victoria Falls

Zambezi River

Mozambique Channel

Madagascar

Mauritius

KALAHARI BASIN

NAMIB DESERT

KALAHARI DESERT

Limpopo River

Réunion

Tropic of Capricorn

Orange River

Vaal River

GREAT KARROO

DRAKENSBERG MOUNTAINS

Cape of Good Hope

ELEVATION

Feet	Meters
13,120	4,000
6,560	2,000
1,640	500
656	200
(Sea level) 0	0 (Sea level)
Below sea level	Below sea level

0   250   500 Miles

0   250   500 Kilometers

Projection: Azimuthal Equal Area

EUROPE

Azores
(PORTUGAL)

40°N

Madeira
(PORTUGAL)

Strait of
Gibraltar

Casablanca ⊛ Rabat

Algiers Tunis

Mediterranean Sea

**SOUTHWEST
ASIA**

TUNISIA

Tripoli ⊛

30°N

Canary Islands
(SPAIN)

MOROCCO

Alexandria

Suez Canal

ALGERIA

LIBYA

Giza ⊛ Cairo

El Aaiún

Nile River

EGYPT

WESTERN
SAHARA
(Claimed by
Morocco)

Tropic of Cancer

Lake
Nasser

20°N

MAURITANIA

Nouakchott ⊛

MALI

NIGER

CHAD

Khartoum ⊛

ERITREA

⊛ Asmara

Red Sea

Gulf of Aden

**CAPE
VERDE**

⊛ Praia

SENEGAL

Dakar ⊛

Niger River

Niamey ⊛

DJIBOUTI

⊛ Djibouti

10°N

GAMBIA

Banjul ⊛

Bamako ⊛

**BURKINA
FASO**

Lake
Chad

N'Djamena ⊛

SUDAN

Blue Nile

10°N

Bissau

**GUINEA-
BISSAU**

GUINEA

Ouagadougou ⊛

BENIN

NIGERIA

ETHIOPIA

⊛ Addis Ababa

Conakry ⊛

TOGO

Abuja ⊛

Freetown ⊛

**CÔTE
D'IVOIRE**

GHANA

SIERRA LEONE

Yamoussoukro ⊛

Lomé ⊛

Lagos

**CENTRAL AFRICAN
REPUBLIC**

Monrovia ⊛

Abidjan

Accra ⊛

Porto-
Novo ⊛

LIBERIA

Gulf of
Guinea

CAMEROON

Bangui ⊛

SOMALIA

Malabo ⊛

EQUATORIAL GUINEA

Yaoundé ⊛

UGANDA

KENYA

⊛ Mogadishu

SÃO TOMÉ AND PRÍNCIPE

São Tomé ⊛

**REPUBLIC
OF THE
CONGO**

Congo River

Kisangani

Kampala ⊛

0° Equator

Libreville ⊛

Nairobi

Equator 0°

GABON

**DEMOCRATIC
REPUBLIC
OF THE CONGO**

RWANDA

⊛ Kigali

**INDIAN
OCEAN**

W ⊕ E

Brazzaville ⊛

Bujumbura ⊛

BURUNDI

Victoria ⊛

Lake
Victoria

Mombasa

SEYCHELLES

CABINDA
(ANGOLA)

Kinshasa ⊛

TANZANIA

Pemba

Dodoma ⊛

Zanzibar

Luanda ⊛

Dar es Salaam

**ATLANTIC
OCEAN**

Lake
Tanganyika

Lake Malawi
(Nyasa)

COMOROS

⊛ Moroni

10°S

St. Helena
(U.K.)

Lubumbashi

MALAWI

10°S

ANGOLA

ZAMBIA

Lilongwe ⊛

Lusaka ⊛

Zambezi River

MOZAMBIQUE

Antananarivo ⊛

MAURITIUS

20°S

Harare ⊛

MADAGASCAR

Port Louis ⊛

Réunion
(FRANCE)

ZIMBABWE

NAMIBIA

Bulawayo

BOTSWANA

Tropic of Capricorn

Windhoek ⊛

┌──────────────────────────────┐
│ ▬▬ Boundaries   │
│ ⊛ National capitals   │
│ • Other cities   │
│ 0   250   500 Miles   │
│ 0 250 500 Kilometers   │
│ *Projection: Azimuthal Equal Area* │
└──────────────────────────────┘

Gaborone ⊛

Pretoria ⊛

Maputo ⊛

Johannesburg

Mbabane ⊛

SWAZILAND

Bloemfontein

Maseru ⊛

LESOTHO

30°S

Orange River

SOUTH AFRICA

30°S

Cape Town

Gazetteer

A

Aachen (AH-kuhn) (51°N, 6°E) a city in Germany; it was the capital of Charlemagne's empire (p. 503)

Aegean Sea (ee-JEE-uhn) a sea east of Greece; the sea provided Greeks with a source of food and a means of trading with other peoples (p. 229)

Africa the second-largest continent (p. 380)

Akkad (AH-kahd) (33°N, 44°E) a city along the Euphrates River near modern Baghdad; started by Akkadian emperor Sargon in 2300s BC (p. 61)

Aksum (AHK-soom) an ancient state in southeast Nubia on the Red Sea, in what are now Ethiopia and Eritea; through trade, Aksum became the most powerful state in the region (p. 113)

Alexandria (31°N, 30°E) a city in Egypt, named after Alexander the Great (p. 276)

Alps a mountain range that extends across south-central Europe (p. 496)

Andes Mountains a mountain range along the west coast of South America (p. 479)

Arabian Peninsula an arid region in southwest Asia; Islam developed there (p. 354)

Asia the world's largest continent, bounded by the Arctic, Pacific, and Indian oceans (p. 124)

Asia Minor a large peninsula in western Asia, between the Black Sea and the Mediterranean Sea, forming modern Turkey (p. 74)

Athens (38°N, 24°E) an ancient city and modern capital of Greece; the world's first democracy developed in Athens around 500 BC (p. 237)

Atlas Mountains a mountain range along the northwest coast of Africa (p. 380)

Australia an island continent between the South Pacific and Indian oceans (p. 37)

Aztec Empire an empire in what is now Mexico; reached its height in the early 1500s (p. 474)

B

Babylon (32°N, 45°E) an ancient city on the lower Euphrates River near what is now Baghdad (p. 72)

Baghdad (BAG-dad) (33°N, 44°E) the capital of Iraq, on the Tigris River; was the center of Islam from the mid-700s to the 800s (p. 364)

Bahamas a group of islands in the Atlantic Ocean off the southeastern coast of Florida; Christopher Columbus landed in the Bahamas on his first voyage to the Americas (p. 595)

Berlin (53°N, 13°E) a city in Germany; it was split in two after World War II and reunited as a democracy in 1990 (p. 675)

Bethlehem (BETH-li-hem) (32°N, 35°E) an ancient town in Judea; traditionally regarded as the birthplace of Jesus (p. 335)

Black Sea a sea between southeast Europe and Asia, north of Asia Minor (p. 233)

Byzantium (buh-ZAN-tee-uhm) an ancient Greek city in what is now Turkey; Constantinople was built on its site (p. 343)

C

Canaan (KAY-nuhn) a region in what is now Israel near the coast of the Mediterranean Sea; according to the Bible, Abraham settled in Canaan and his Hebrew descendants lived there for many years (p. 203)

Canterbury (51°N, 1°E) a city near London, England; it was a popular pilgrimage destination during the Middle Ages and the subject of Chaucer's *The Canterbury Tales* (p. 534)

Carthage (KAHR-thij) (37°N, 10°E) a key trade center built by the Phoenicians on the northern coast of Africa; it became one of the most powerful cities in the Mediterranean (p. 76)

Central America the narrow region between North America and South America; parts of the northern countries of Central America make up the area known as Mesoamerica (p. 468)

Chang Jiang (or Yangzi River) a river that cuts through central China, flowing from the mountains of Tibet to the Pacific Ocean (p. 161)

Chile a country in western South America; the Inca Empire stretched into central Chile (p. 479)

China a country in East Asia; a series of dynasties turned China into a world power (p. 160)

Cluny (KLOO-nee) (46°N, 5°E) a town in France; a group of monks formed a religious order there in the early 900s (p. 535)

Congo River a river that flows through the plains of sub-Saharan Africa (p. 380)

Constantinople (kahn-stant-uhn-OH-puhl) (41°N, 29°E) the capital of the Byzantine Empire, located in modern Turkey between the Black Sea and the Mediterranean Sea (p. 340)

Córdoba (KAWR-doh-bah) (38°N, 5°W) a city in southern Spain; it was the center of Muslim rule in Spain (p. 364)

Crete an island in the eastern Mediterranean Sea, south of the Greek mainland; a civilization formed there around 2000 BC (p. 230)

Cuzco (KOO-skoh) (14°S, 72°W) a city in Peru; it was the capital of the Inca Empire (p. 479)

Damascus (34°N, 36°E) an ancient city and the modern capital of Syria; it was important in the spread of Christianity (p. 363)

Dead Sea a salty lake on the boundary between Israel and Jordan; 2,000-year-old scrolls discovered near there helped scholars learn about the history of the Jews (p. 212)

Delhi (29°N, 77°E) a historic city and capital of modern India; it was ruled by the Gupta dynasty (p. 150)

Delphi an ancient city in central Greece; Greeks traveled here to get advice from an oracle of Apollo (p. 244)

Djenné a city in present-day Mali that was a center of trade and learning during the Songhai Empire (p. 393)

Drakensburg Mountains a mountain range near the coast of southeastern Africa (p. 380)

Edo (AY-doh) (36°N, 140°E) a city that became the capital of Japan in 1603 under the Tokugawa shogunate; it is now called Tokyo (p. 459)

Egypt (EE-juhpt) a country in northeast Africa and location of the mouth of the Nile River; ancient Egypt was famous for temples, pyramids, art, and cultural achievements, such as an early writing system (p. 86)

Esfahan (es-fah-HAHN) (33°N, 52°E) a city in modern Iran; it was capital of the Safavid Empire and was considered one of the world's most magnificent cities during the 1600s (p. 366)

Euphrates River a river that flows mainly through Iraq and empties into the Persian Gulf; silt from the Euphrates helped form the Fertile Crescent in Mesopotamia (p. 55)

Eurasia a large landmass that includes Europe and Asia (p. 496)

Europe a continent of many peninsulas located between Asia and the Atlantic Ocean (p. 496)

Fertile Crescent a large arc of rich farmland between the Persian Gulf and the Mediterranean Sea (p. 55)

Florence (44°N, 11°E) a city in Italy; ruled by the Medici family in the 1400s, it was a major center for culture and trade (p. 559)

GAZETTEER

Gao (GOW) (16°N, 0°W) a major ancient trading city in Africa that was the capital of the Songhai Empire (p. 392)

Gaul an ancient region in western Europe, consisting mainly of parts of modern France and Belgium (p. 323)

Gaya (25°N, 85°E) a town in India; according to legend, Siddhartha Gautama found enlightenment in Gaya (p. 137)

Geneva (46°N, 6°E) a city in Switzerland; John Calvin hoped to make Geneva a model Christian city (p. 572)

Genoa (JEN-uh-wuh) (44°N, 10°E) a port city in Italy (p. 559)

Germany a country in north-central Europe; it was the major aggressor in both world wars (p. 667)

Ghana (GAH-nuh) a West African country located between the Niger and Senegal rivers; it was the site of a powerful empire established around 300 (p. 386)

Gibraltar, Strait of (ji-BRAHL-ter) a strait, or narrow sea passage, between Spain and Morocco, connecting the Mediterranean Sea and the Atlantic Ocean (p. 76)

Giza (30°N, 31°E) an Egyptian city and the site of large pyramids, including the Great Pyramid of Khufu (p. 94)

Gobi (GOH-bee) a desert covering much of northern China; the Gobi helped isolate China from its neighbors (p. 160)

Great Britain a kingdom in Western Europe made up of England, Scotland, and Wales (p. 645)

Greece a country in southern Europe with mountains, rugged coastlines, and scenic islands; the country is called the birthplace of democracy (p. 228)

Haiti a Caribbean country that was one of the first to throw off European colonial rule (p. 641)

Harappa (huh-RA-puh) a city that thrived between 2300 and 1700 BC in the Indus Valley, in what is now Pakistan (p. 127)

Heian (35°N, 136°E) a city in Japan now called Kyoto; it was a cultural center and capital of Japan for many centuries (p. 448)

Himalayas a mountain range on the northern Indian border; it is the highest mountain range in the world (p. 124)

Hiroshima (34°N, 132°E) a city in Japan; the United States dropped the first atomic bomb on this city, hoping it would end World War II (p. 668)

Honshu Japan's largest island (p. 445)

Huang He (Yellow River) a river that stretches nearly 3,000 miles across China; it is sometimes called China's Sorrow (p. 161)

Inca Empire an empire in South America that stretched from what is now northern Ecuador to central Chile; it reached its height in the early 1500s (p. 479)

India a country and subcontinent in south Asia; India was home to one of the world's oldest civilizations (p. 124)

Indus Valley a river valley in modern Pakistan where one of the earliest civilizations began (p. 125)

Ionian Sea (eye-OH-nee-uhn) a sea west of Greece (p. 229)

Israel a country between the Mediterranean Sea and Jordan; it was the homeland of the ancient Hebrews (pp. 206, 673)

Italy a country in southern Europe located on a peninsula in the Mediterranean; it was once the center of the Roman Empire (p. 294)

J

Japan a mountainous island country off the eastern coast of Asia near China and the Koreas (p. 440)

Jerusalem (32°N, 35°E) a city in Israel; as part of the Holy Land, Muslims and Christians fought to control it during the Crusades (p. 205)

Judea territory where most of the ancient Jews lived; it was conquered by Rome in 63 BC (p. 333)

Judah (JOO-duh) one of the two kingdoms created when Israel was divided; the people in Judah came to be called Jews (p. 206)

K

Kaifeng (KY-fuhng) (35°N, 114°E) the capital of China during the Song dynasty (p. 416)

Kerma (KAR-muh) a city on the Nile in the kingdom of Kush; it was captured by Egypt, forcing the Kushites to move their capital to Napata (p. 108)

Kish a city-state in Sumer that became powerful around 3500 BC (p. 61)

Korea a country in eastern Asia near China and Japan that influenced early Japanese culture; it is now divided into two countries—communist North Korea and non-communist South Korea (p. 674)

Kush the first great kingdom in Africa's interior; Kush ruled Egypt and at other times was ruled by Egypt (p. 107)

M

Macedonia a small kingdom located west of the Black Sea and north of the Aegean Sea; Macedonians conquered Greece in the 300s BC (p. 272)

Mali (MAH-lee) a West African country along the upper Niger River; it was the location of an empire that reached its height around 1300 (p. 390)

Mecca (21°N, 40°E) an ancient city in Arabia and birthplace of Muhammad (p. 356)

Medina (muh-DEE-nuh) (24°N, 40°E) a city in Arabia, north of Mecca; people there were among the first to accept Islam (p. 357)

Mediterranean Sea a large sea surrounded by Europe, Africa, and Asia (p. 229)

Memphis (30°N, 31°E) an Egyptian capital city at the southern tip of the Nile Delta; built around 3100 BC, it was the political and cultural center of Egypt for centuries (p. 89)

Meröe (MER-oh-wee) an ancient capital of Kush, located on the east bank of the Nile (p. 111)

Mesoamerica a region that includes the southern part of modern Mexico and part of Central America; the region was home to the Maya civilization (p. 468)

Mesopotamia (mes-uh-puh-TAY-mee-uh) the region in southwest Asia between the Tigris and Euphrates rivers; it was the site of some of the world's earliest civilizations (p. 55)

Milan (muh-LAHN) (45°N, 9°E) a city in Italy; it was a major trading center during the 1300s (p. 559)

Mohenjo Daro (mo-HEN-joh DAR-oh) (27°N, 68°E) an ancient city of the Harappan civilization, located in what is now Pakistan (p. 127)

Mount Sinai according to the Bible, the mountain in Egypt where God gave Moses the stone tablets containing the Ten Commandments (p. 204)

Mycenae (my-SEE-nee) an ancient Greek city; the site of a strong fortress built by the Mycenaeans (p. 231)

Napata a city built by the Egyptians on the Nile River; it was the capital of Kush in the 700s and 600s BC (p. 109)

Niger River a major river in West Africa (p. 380)

Nile the longest river in the world; it flows from central Africa to the Mediterranean and was vital to the development of civilizations in Egypt and Kush (p. 86)

Nineveh (37°N, 43°E) an ancient capital of Assyria, located on the Tigris River (p. 75)

Normandy (49°N, 0°E) a region in northern France; it was home of William the Conqueror, who became king of England in 1066 (p. 508)

North America a large continent in the northern and western hemispheres, bordered on the west by the Pacific Ocean and on the east by the Atlantic Ocean (p. 37)

Northern European Plain a vast, flat land area that stretches from the Atlantic Ocean in the west to the Ural Mountains in the east (p. 497)

Nubia (NOO-bee-ah) a region in northeastern Africa on the Nile, south of Egypt; the kingdom of Kush developed in Nubia (p. 107)

P

Palenque (pah-LENG-kay) (18°N, 92°W) an ancient Maya city in what is now southern Mexico (p. 469)

Panama a country in Central America; the U.S. took control of a part of Panama in 1903 to build a canal connecting the Atlantic and Pacific oceans (p. 652)

Pearl Harbor (21°N, 158°W) a U.S. Navy base in Hawaii; it was attacked by the Japanese in 1941, drawing American forces into World War II (p. 667)

Persia an ancient empire in Southwest Asia in what is now Iran; it was one of the most powerful empires of the ancient world (p. 260)

Phoenicia (fi-NI-shuh) an ancient country that was a strip of land at the western end of the Fertile Crescent, along the Mediterranean Sea; Phoenicians were some of the leading traders of the ancient world (p. 76)

Plateau of Tibet a high plateau in central Asia, mostly in Tibet and China (p. 160)

Q–R

Qinling Shandi (chin-LING SHAHN-dee) a mountain range that extends east from the Plateau of Tibet; it separates northern and southern China (p. 160)

Roman Empire a large and powerful empire that included all land around the Mediterranean Sea; it reached its height around AD 117 (p. 324)

Rome (42°N, 13°E) a city in Italy near the Mediterranean Sea; it was the capital of the Roman Empire (p. 294)

Sahara the world's largest desert, located in northern Africa (p. 380)

Sahel (sah-HEL) a semi-arid strip of land between the Sahara Desert and wetter areas to the south (p. 382)

Scandinavia a large peninsula in northern Europe (p. 498)

Silk Road an ancient trade route from China through Central Asia to the Mediterranean (p. 558)

Songhai (SAHNG-hy) a large and powerful empire in West Africa during the 1400s and 1500s (p. 392)

South America a large continent in the southern and western hemispheres, bordered on the west by the Pacific Ocean and on the east by the Atlantic Ocean (p. 37)

Sparta (37°N, 22°E) an ancient city in Greece; its society was dominated by the military (p. 266)

Sub-Saharan Africa the area of Africa south of the Sahara (p. 380)

Sumer (soo-muhr) the region in southern Mesopotamia where the world's first civilization developed (p. 60)

Tanzania a country in East Africa; fossils from the earliest humans were discovered there (p. 31)

Tenochtitlán (tay-NAWCH-teet-LAHN) (19°N, 99°W) the capital of the Aztec Empire; it is now the site of Mexico City (p. 474)

Thebes (38°N, 23°E) an ancient Greek city destroyed by Alexander (p. 273)

Tiber River a river that flows out of Italy's mountains; Rome was built on the Tiber (p. 295)

Tigris River a river that flows mainly through modern Iraq; silt from the Tigris and Euphrates formed the Fertile Crescent, where the world's first farming civilizations developed (p. 55)

Tikal (tee-KAHL) (17°N, 90°W) a major Maya city in what is now Guatemala (p. 469)

Timbuktu (tim-BUK-too) (17°N, 3°W) a city in West Africa that began as a camp for traders around 1100 and became a major center of culture and learning (p. 391)

Troy (40°N, 26°E) an ancient city in what is now Turkey; according to Greek legend and literature, it was the site of the Trojan War (p. 246)

Turkey (39°N, 32°E) a country occupying Asia Minor and the southeast portion of the Balkan Peninsula; Roman emperor Constantine moved Rome's capital east, building the city of Constantinople, now called Istanbul (p. 340)

U–V

Ur a city in ancient Sumer, located on the Euphrates River near the Persian Gulf; one of the largest cities of ancient Mesopotamia (p. 61)

Ural Mountains a mountain range that forms a natural boundary between Europe and Asia (p. 496)

Uruk a city in ancient Sumer, located on the Euphrates River; Uruk and Ur fought for dominance around 3500–2500 BC (p. 61)

Venice (45°N, 12°E) a city in Italy that was a major trading center during the 1300s (p. 559)

Versailles (49°N, 2°E) a city near Paris, France; Allied leaders met there to draft a peace plan after World War I (p. 664)

Vienna (48°N, 16°E) capital of Austria; European leaders met there to draw up peace terms for France after the defeat of Napoleon (p. 640)

Vietnam (18°N, 107°E) a country in Southeast Asia; it was reunified by the Communists in 1976 after the end of the Vietnam War (p. 675)

W

Waterloo (51°N, 4°E) a town in Belgium; it was the site of a battle at which the British and Prussians defeated Napoleon (p. 640)

Wittenberg (vit-uhn-BERK) (52°N, 13°E) the city in Germany where Martin Luther nailed his Ninety-Five Theses to the door of a church (p. 570)

X–Z

Xi'an (34°N, 109°E) the capital of China during the Tang dynasty (p. 177)

Yucatán Peninsula a peninsula in southeast Mexico; many Maya cities were built there (p. 469)

Zambezi River a river that flows through southeast Africa (p. 380)

Ancient Civilizations

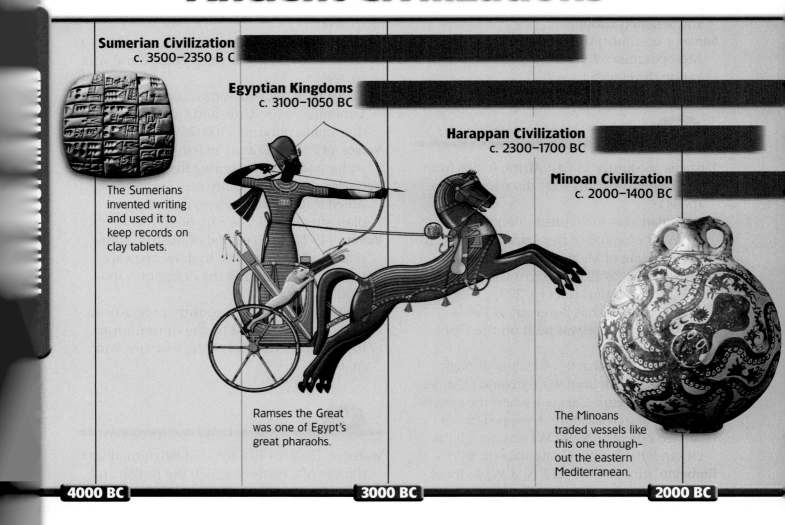

Sumerian Civilization
c. 3500–2350 B C

The Sumerians invented writing and used it to keep records on clay tablets.

Egyptian Kingdoms
c. 3100–1050 BC

Harappan Civilization
c. 2300–1700 BC

Minoan Civilization
c. 2000–1400 BC

Ramses the Great was one of Egypt's great pharaohs.

The Minoans traded vessels like this one through-out the eastern Mediterranean.

4000 BC   3000 BC   2000 BC

Important Dates

c. 4000–3000 BC The first cities are founded in Sumer.

c. 3500 BC The Sumerians invent writing.

c. 3500 BC Maize (corn) is domesticated in Mesoamerica.

c. 3200 BC The Sumerians invent the wheel.

c. 3100 BC Upper Egypt and Lower Egypt are united.

c. 2500 BC The Great Pyramid of Khufu is built in Egypt.

c. 2350 BC The first empire is created in Mesopotamia.

c. 2000 BC Judaism begins to develop.

c. 1750 BC The earliest known set of written laws is issued by Hammurabi.

c. 1250 BC Hinduism begins to develop.

c. 1100 BC The Phoenicians create an alphabet.

c. 1050 BC Saul becomes the first King of Israel.

c. 500 BC Buddhism begins to develop.

c. 500 BC Athens becomes the world's first democracy.

c. 140 BC Confucianism becomes China's official government philosophy.

c. 100 BC The Silk Road connects China and Southwest Asia.

27 BC The Roman Empire begins.

c. AD 30 Christianity begins to develop.

c. AD 200 The Maya build large cities in Mesoamerica.

c. AD 320 The Gupta dynasty begins in India.

AD 476 The western Roman Empire falls.

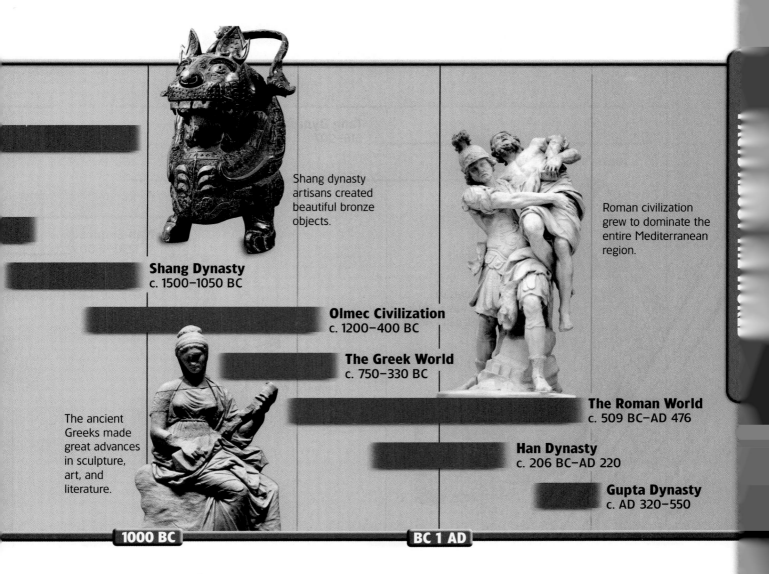

Shang dynasty artisans created beautiful bronze objects.

Shang Dynasty
c. 1500–1050 BC

Roman civilization grew to dominate the entire Mediterranean region.

Olmec Civilization
c. 1200–400 BC

The Greek World
c. 750–330 BC

The ancient Greeks made great advances in sculpture, art, and literature.

The Roman World
c. 509 BC–AD 476

Han Dynasty
c. 206 BC–AD 220

Gupta Dynasty
c. AD 320–550

1000 BC

BC 1 AD

Important People

Sargon (c. 2350 BC) was a king of Akkad, a land north of Sumer. He created a powerful army and used it to build the world's first empire.

Abraham (c. 2000 BC) is the biblical figure to whom the ancient Hebrews traced their ancestry and religion. He is believed to have traveled from his home in Mesopotamia to Canaan around 2000 BC.

Hammurabi (ruled c. 1792–1750 BC) founded the Babylonian Empire and issued the first known written code of laws.

Queen Hatshepsut (ruled c. 1503–1482 BC) was a ruler of Egypt who expanded trade routes.

Siddhartha Gautama (c. 563–483 BC) was an Indian prince who became known as the Buddha. His teachings became the foundation for Buddhism.

Confucius (c. 551–479 BC) was a Chinese philosopher and teacher. His teachings, known as Confucianism, became a major philosophy in China.

Alexander the Great (c. 356–323 BC) built one of the largest empires in the ancient world and spread Greek culture throughout his empire.

Pericles (c. 495–429 BC) was an Athenian orator and politician. During his 30-year rule, Athenian democracy reached its height.

Shi Huangdi (c. 259–210 BC), the first Qin emperor, united China for the first time and built what would become the Great Wall of China.

Augustus (c. 63 BC–AD 14) was Rome's first emperor. During his reign Rome entered the Pax Romana.

Jesus of Nazareth (c. AD 1–30) was one of the most influential people in history. His life and teachings were the basis for Christianity.

Medieval to Early Modern Times

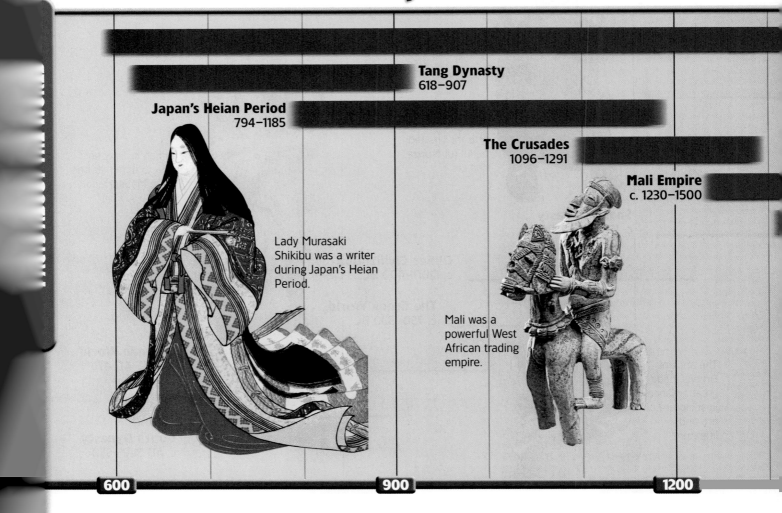

Tang Dynasty
618–907

Japan's Heian Period
794–1185

The Crusades
1096–1291

Mali Empire
c. 1230–1500

Lady Murasaki Shikibu was a writer during Japan's Heian Period.

Mali was a powerful West African trading empire.

600 | 900 | 1200

Important Dates

476 The western Roman Empire falls.

534 The Byzantine emperor Justinian creates a unified code of laws.

581 The Sui dynasty reunites China.

622 Muhammad leaves Mecca for Medina.

711 The Moors invade Spain.

800 Pope Leo III crowns Charlemagne Emperor of the Romans.

1066 William the Conqueror leads the Norman invasion of Britain.

1192 The first shogun takes power in Japan.

1215 A group of nobles forces King John to sign Magna Carta.

1324 Mansa Musa leaves Mali on a hajj to Mecca.

1347–1351 The Black Death strikes Europe.

1453 The Ottoman Turks capture Constantinople.

1478 The Spanish Inquisition begins.

1492 Christopher Columbus sails to the Americas.

1517 Martin Luther posts his Ninety-Five Theses.

1521 Hernán Cortés conquers the Aztec Empire.

1533 Francisco Pizarro conquers the Inca Empire.

1545–1563 The Council of Trent meets to reform Catholic teachings.

1588 England defeats the Spanish Armada.

1633 Galileo is put on trial for promoting ideas that go against the Catholic Church.

1776 The American colonies declare independence from Great Britain.

1789 The French Revolution begins when a mob storms the Bastille in Paris.

Byzantine Empire c. 476–1453

Renaissance artist Leonardo da Vinci painted the famous *Mona Lisa.*

The Taj Mahal was built by the Mughal emperor Shah Jahan.

The Renaissance c. 1300–1600

Aztec Empire c. 1325–1521

Age of Exploration c. 1450–1650

The Reformation 1517–c. 1650

Mughal Empire c. 1530–1800

Compasses like this one helped explorers navigate the seas during the Age of Exploration.

Scientific Revolution c. 1540–1700

Enlightenment c. 1650–1800

1500

1800

Important People

Muhammad (c. 570–632) was the founder of Islam. He spread Islam's teachings to the people of Arabia. His teachings make up the Qur'an.

Charlemagne (742–814) was a Frankish king who ruled most of what is now France and Germany. He helped promote Christianity in western Europe.

Lady Murasaki Shikibu (c. 1000) was a court lady during Japan's Heian Period. She wrote *The Tale of Genji,* considered by some to be the world's first novel.

Kublai Khan (1215–1294) was a Mongol ruler who completed the conquest of China and founded the Yuan dynasty.

Mansa Musa (c. 1300) was the ruler of the Mali Empire at the height of its wealth and power. He helped spread Islam throughout West Africa.

Johann Gutenberg (c. 1390–1468) was a German inventor who invented a method of printing with moveable type.

Christopher Columbus (1451–1506) was an Italian navigator who sailed to the Americas for Spain searching for a route to Asia.

Leonardo da Vinci (1452–1519) painted the *Mona Lisa,* one of the world's most admired paintings.

Sir Isaac Newton (1642–1727) was one of the most influential scientists in history. He proposed a law of gravity to explain the movement of objects.

The Modern World

Napoleon

1804
Politics
Napoleon is crowned emperor of France.

1829
Politics Greece wins independence from the Ottoman Empire.

1850s–1890
Society and Culture
Artists portray ordinary people and events realistically during the Realism movement.

1800

1823
Politics
The Monroe Doctrine makes the United States the dominant power in the Western Hemisphere.

1830s
Science and Technology
The Industrial Revolution transforms life in Great Britain and soon spreads to other countries.

1875

1871
Politics Otto von Bismarck founds the German Empire.

Otto von Bismarck

Events and People

Politics

1790s Toussaint-L'Ouverture successfully leads a rebellion of slaves against French rule in Haiti.

1811 Simon Bolívar helps Venezuela fight for its independence from Spain, influencing independence movements in Bolivia, Colombia, and Ecuador.

1837 Queen Victoria begins her 63-year reign in the United Kingdom.

1868 Tokugawa Keiki resigns as the last shogun of Japan.

1916 Jeanette Rankin becomes the first woman elected to the United States House of Representatives.

1933 Mohandas Gandhi begins a 21-day hunger strike as a non-violent protest against British rule in India.

1949 Mao Zedong transforms China into a Communist nation.

1994 Nelson Mandela is elected the first black president of South Africa after many years of struggling against apartheid.

Science and Technology

1856 Henry Bessemer develops a method for converting iron into steel.

1903 Orville and Wilbur Wright complete the first controlled aircraft flight.

1905 Albert Einstein introduces the theory of relativity.

Israeli flag

1948
Politics
The country
of Israel is
established.

1989
Politics Communist control
collapses in Bulgaria, Czechoslovakia,
East Germany, Hungary, Poland,
and Romania.

1950 ———————————————————— **2025**

1939–1945
Politics World
War II is fought
in Europe, North
Africa, and Asia
between the Axis
powers and Allies.

1957
Science and Technology
The Soviet Union launches
the satellite Sputnik 1, beginning the space race.

1983
**Society and
Culture** The
Internet becomes
available to the
general public.

2001
Politics Terrorists attack the
World Trade Center in New York
City and the Pentagon in Washing-
ton, D.C. on September 11, 2001.

Sputnik 1

1911 Marie Curie wins the Nobel Prize in chemistry
for discovering several radioactive elements.

1925 George Washington Carver publishes a book
on how to find industrial uses for agricultural
products.

1969 Neil Armstrong becomes the first person to
walk on the moon.

1996 Ian Wilmut clones a mammal, Dolly the
sheep.

Society and Culture

1824 Louis Braille introduces a reading system for
the blind.

1848 Karl Marx and Friedrich Engels introduce *The
Communist Manifesto.*

1880 Pyotr Ilyich Tchaikovsky pens the *1812 Over-
ture* to commemorate Russia's victory over
Napoleon in 1812.

1921 Pablo Picasso paints *The Three Musicians,* one
of the most renowned cubist works.

1937 Zora Neale Hurston writes *Their Eyes Were
Watching God.*

1997 J. K. Rowling publishes the first Harry Potter
book.

2004 Lance Armstrong wins a record 6th Tour de
France bicycle race.

(Activity)

Create a three-circle Venn diagram comparing and
contrasting the historical development of Western,
Eastern, and African cultures. Use specific examples
from the time line.

Biographical Dictionary

A

'Abbas (1571–1629) Safavid leader, he took back land that had been lost to the Ottomans. He also made great contributions to the Safavid economy and culture. (p. 366)

Abraham Biblical figure, according to the Bible, God led Abraham to Canaan, and Abraham's descendants became the Jewish people. (p. 202)

Abu Bakr (UH-boo BAK-uhr) (c. 573–634) The first caliph, he ruled the Muslim world after Muhammad's death. (p. 362)

Aeneas (i-NEE-uhs) (c. 2500s BC) Legendary Roman hero, the Romans traced their history back to Aeneas. Aeneas was a Trojan hero who left Troy after the Trojan War, eventually settling in Italy. (p. 296)

Aesop (EE-sahp) (before 400 BC) Ancient Greek storyteller, he was famous for his fables—short stories that teach important lessons about life. (p. 247)

Akbar (1542–1605) Mughal emperor, he conquered new lands and worked to make the Mughal government stronger. He also began a tolerant religious policy that helped unify the empire (p. 366).

Alexander the Great (c. 356–323 BC) Macedonian ruler, he was one of the greatest military commanders in history. The son of Philip II, Alexander conquered large areas of Asia and parts of Europe and Africa and spread Greek culture throughout his empire. (p. 274)

Ali (died 1492) Sunni, or emperor, of Songhai, he conquered Mali and made Songhai into a powerful state. (p. 392)

Antony, Marc (c. 82–30 BC) Roman general, he fought against Octavian after the death of Julius Caesar. Antony was allied with Cleopatra of Egypt, but was defeated by Octavian at the Battle of Actium in 31 BC. (p. 324)

Aquinas, Thomas (uh-KWY-nuhs) (1225–1274) Dominican philosopher, he argued that rational thought could be used to support Christian belief. (p. 538)

Aristotle (ar-uh-STAH-tuhl) (384–322 BC) Greek philosopher, he was a student of Plato. Aristotle taught that people should live lives of moderation and use reason in their lives. (p. 283)

Askia the Great (c. 1443–1538) Songhai ruler, he overthrew Sunni Baru. His reign was the high point of Songhai culture. (p. 393)

Asoka (uh-SOH-kuh) (ruled 270–232 BC) Ruler of the Mauryan Empire, he extended his control over most of India and promoted the spread of Buddhism. (p. 146)

Atahualpa (ah-tah-WAHL-pah) (1502–1533) The last Inca king, he was killed by Francisco Pizarro. (p. 483)

Attila (AT-uhl-uh) (c. 406–453) Leader of the Huns, he led invasions of Constantinople, Greece, Gaul, and northern Italy and was greatly feared by the Romans. (p. 341)

Augustus (aw-GUHS-tuhs) (63 BC–AD 14) First Roman emperor, he was originally named Octavian. He was the great-nephew of Julius Caesar and gained control of Rome after defeating Marc Antony in battle. As emperor, Augustus built many monuments and a new forum. (p. 329)

B

Babur (BAH-boohr) (1483–1530) Indian emperor, he founded the Mughal Empire. (p. 366)

Benedict (c. 480–547) Italian saint and monk, he created a set of rules for monks to follow. (p. 502)

Bismarck, Otto von (1815–1898) Prussian prime minister, he led the unification of Germany and the creation of the German Empire. (p. 650)

Bolívar, Simon (see-MON bo-LEE-var) (1783–1830) Latin American revolutionary leader, he inspired revolutionary movements in Bolivia, Colombia, Ecuador, and Venezuela. (p. 643)

Bonaparte, Napoleon (1769–1821) French general and emperor, he took over France after the French Revolution and conquered much of Europe. (p. 639)

Brahe, Tycho (TYOO-koh BRAH-huh) (1546–1601) Danish astronomer of the Scientific Revolution, he emphasized the importance of careful observation. (p. 590)

Buddha (BOO-duh) (c. 563–483 BC) Founder of Buddhism, he was originally an Indian prince named Siddhartha Gautama. He founded the Buddhist religion after a long spiritual journey through India. (p. 137)

Caesar, Julius (JOOL-yuhs SEE-zuhr) (100–44 BC) Roman general, he was one of the greatest military leaders in history. Caesar conquered most of Gaul and was named dictator for life, but was later murdered by a group of senators. (p. 323)

Calvin, John (1509–1564) Christian reformer, he taught about predestination, living good lives, and obeying God's laws. (p. 572)

Candra Gupta II (kuhn-druh-GOOP-tuh) (300s–400s) Gupta emperor, he ruled India during the height of Gupta power. (p. 144)

Candragupta Maurya (kuhn-druh-GOOP-tuh MOUR-yuh) (late 300s BC) Mauryan ruler, he founded the Mauryan Empire in northern India. (p. 142)

Cervantes, Miguel de (mee-GEL day ser-VAHN-tays) (1547–1616) Spanish writer, he wrote *Don Quixote.* (p. 568)

Charlemagne (SHAHR-luh-mayn) (742–814) King of the Franks, he was a brilliant warrior and strong leader. He was crowned Emperor of the Romans in 800. (p. 505)

Charles I (1600–1649) King of England, his conflict with Parliament caused the English Civil War. He was beheaded in 1649. (p. 622)

Charles II (1630–1685) King of England, he was the son of Charles I. He was asked by Parliament to rule England after the death of Oliver Cromwell. (p. 623)

Chaucer, Geoffrey (CHAW-suhr) (c. 1342–1400) Medieval English poet, he wrote *The Canterbury Tales.* (p. 534)

Churchill, Winston (1874–1965) British prime minister, he rallied the English people during World War II. (p. 667)

Cicero (SIS-uh-roh) (106–43 BC) Roman orator and philosopher, he tried to limit the power of Rome's generals and give control of the government back to the Senate. (p. 322)

Cincinnatus (sin-suh-NAT-uhs) (born c. 519) Roman dictator, he was chosen by the Romans to defend their lands from attack. Later, he willingly gave up power and was considered an ideal leader by the Romans. (p. 298)

Cleisthenes (KLYS-thuh-neez) Athenian statesman, he is considered the father of Athenian democracy. (p. 238)

Charlemagne

BIOGRAPHICAL DICTIONARY

Cleopatra (69–30 BC) Egyptian queen, she became a devoted ally of Julius Caesar and Marc Antony. After Antony was defeated by Octavian, she committed suicide. (p. 324)

Clovis (c. 466–511) King of the Franks, he was a Christian leader who built a huge kingdom in Gaul. (p. 503)

Columbus, Christopher (1451–1506) Italian sailor supported by the rulers of Spain, he reached the Americas in 1492, becoming the first European to do so. (p. 595)

Confucius (551–479 BC) Chinese philosopher, he emphasized ethical behavior for individuals and governments. He was the most influential teacher in Chinese history. (p. 169)

Constantine (KAHN-stuhn-teen) (c. 280–337) Roman emperor, he was the first Roman emperor to become a Christian. Constantine moved the empire's capital from Rome to Constantinople and removed bans on Christianity. (p. 338)

Copernicus, Nicolaus (kih-PUHR-ni-kuhs) (1473–1543) Polish astronomer, his book *On the Revolution of the Celestial Spheres* helped begin the Scientific Revolution. (p. 590)

Cortés, Hernán (er-NAHN kawr-TAYS) (1485–1547) Spanish conquistador, he went to Mexico in search of gold and conquered the Aztec Empire. (p. 477)

Cromwell, Oliver (1599–1658) Leader of Parliament, he overthrew King Charles I in 1642 and became ruler of England. (p. 622)

Cyrus the Great (SY-ruhs) (c. 585–529 BC) Persian emperor, he created the Persian Empire by conquering most of Southwest Asia. (p. 261)

da Gama, Vasco See Gama, Vasco da.

da Vinci, Leonardo See Leonardo da Vinci.

Daniel Biblical figure, according to the Hebrew Bible, he was a prophet who was thrown into a lions' den after angering the king. Daniel survived because of his faith in God. (p. 211)

Dante (DAHN-tay) (1265–1321) Italian Renaissance poet, he wrote *The Divine Comedy* in the Italian language. (p. 562)

Darius I (da-RY-uhs) (550–486 BC) Persian emperor, he restored order to the Persian Empire after a period of rebellion. Darius I built roads and made other improvements to Persian society. (p. 262)

David (c. 1000 BC) King of Israel, he defeated the Philistines and established the capital in Jerusalem as a governmental and religious center. (p. 205)

Diderot, Denis (duh-NEE dee-DROH) (1713–1784) French Enlightenment philosopher, he edited a multi-volume book called the *Encyclopedia*. (p. 614)

Diocletian (dy-uh-KLEE-shuhn) (c. 245–c. 316) Roman emperor, he divided the Roman Empire into eastern and western halves. (p. 340)

Du Fu (712–770) One of China's greatest poets, he lived during the Tang dynasty. (p. 417)

Dürer, Albrecht (AWL-brekt DYUR-uhr) (1471–1528) German Renaissance artist, he is famous for his prints and woodcuts. (p. 568)

Eleanor of Aquitaine (c. 1122–1204) Queen of France and England, she was one of the most powerful women in Europe in the Middle Ages. (p. 510)

Erasmus, Desiderius (des-i-DEER-ee-uhs i-RAZ-mus) (1466–1536) Dutch priest, he published *In Praise of Folly* in which he criticized corrupt clergy. His criticisms helped inspire the Protestant Reformation. (p. 567)

Esma'il (is-mah-EEL) (1487–1524) Ruler of Persia, he founded the Safavid Empire. (p. 365)

Euclid (YOO-kluhd) (c. 300 BC) Greek mathematician, he was one of the greatest mathematicians in history. Euclid is famous for his contributions to the field of geometry. (p. 281)

Ezana (AY-zah-nah) (c. 300s) Aksumite ruler, he destroyed Meroë and took over the kingdom of Kush around AD 350. (p. 113)

Ferdinand (1452–1516) King of Spain, he and his wife Isabella completed the Reconquista. They forced Jews in Spain to become Christian or leave and banned Islam. (p. 548)

Francis of Assisi (c. 1182–1226) Italian saint, he encouraged people to be kind to others and founded the Franciscan Order. (p. 536)

Franklin, Benjamin (1706–1790) American colonial leader, he argued that the British government had no right to tax the colonists because they had no representation in Parliament. (p. 619)

Galen (129–c. 199) Greek surgeon of the Roman Empire, he described heart valves and studied arteries and veins. (p. 326)

Galilei, Galileo (gal-uh-LEE-oh gal-uh-LAY)  (1564–1642) Italian scientist, he was the first scientist to routinely use experiments to test theories. He was placed on trial for supporting theories that contradicted Church teachings. (p. 591)

Gama, Vasco da (c. 1460–1524) Portuguese sailor, he sailed around Africa to reach India. (p. 595)

Gandhi, Mohandas (1869–1948) Hindu nationalist leader, he led nonviolent protests against British rule in India. (p. 673)

Garibaldi, Giuseppe (1807–1882) Italian military and political leader, he led the movement for Italian unification. (p. 649)

Genghis Khan (JENG-guhs KAHN) (c. 1162–1227) Ruler of the Mongols, he led his people in attacks against China and against other parts of Asia. His name means "universal leader." (p. 424)

Gilgamesh (c. 3000 BC) King of Uruk, a city-state in Sumer, he became a legendary figure in Sumerian literature. (p. 61)

Gorbachev, Mikhail (gor-buh-chof) (1931–) Leader of the Soviet Union, he proposed reforms and openness that encouraged changes in government throughout Eastern Europe. (p. 675)

Gregory VII (1020–1085) A powerful medieval pope, he fought with Holy Roman Emperor Henry IV over the power to choose church officials. (p. 527)

Gutenberg, Johann (YOH-hahn GOO-tuhn-berk) (c. 1400–1468) German printer, he developed a printing press that used movable type. (p. 566)

Hadrian (76–138) Roman emperor, he conquered most of Britain and built a huge wall across the northern part of the island to keep barbarian invaders from the north out of Roman territory. (p. 334)

Eleanor of Aquitaine

BIOGRAPHICAL DICTIONARY

Hammurabi (ruled c. 1792–1750 BC) Babylonian ruler, he was a brilliant military leader who brought all of Mesopotamia into the Babylonian Empire. Hammurabi is known for a unified code of 282 laws, the earliest known set of written laws, that was produced during his reign. (p. 72)

Hannibal (247–183 BC) Carthaginian general, he was one of the greatest generals of the ancient world. Hannibal invaded Italy during the Second Punic War but was eventually defeated by Scipio at the Battle of Zama. (p. 311)

Hatshepsut (ruled c. 1503–1482 BC) Egyptian queen, she worked to increase trade with places outside of Egypt and ordered many impressive monuments and temples built during her reign. (p. 97)

Henry IV (1050–1106) Holy Roman Emperor, he fought against Pope Gregory VII over the power to choose church officials. (p. 527)

Henry VIII (1491–1547) King of England, he split with the Catholic Church and declared himself head of the Church of England, or Anglican Church. (p. 572)

Henry the Navigator (1394–1460 Prince of Portugal, he helped promote exploration by Portuguese sailors. (p. 595)

Hippocrates (hip-ahk-ruh-teez) (c. 460–c. 377 BC) Greek doctor, he is regarded as the father of medicine. Hippocrates tried to find out what caused diseases and is known today for his ideas on how doctors should conduct themselves. (p. 282)

Hitler, Adolf (1889–1945) German dictator, his aggression launched World War II. (p. 667)

Homer (800s–700s BC) Greek poet, he wrote the *Iliad* and the *Odyssey,* two famous Greek epic poems. They describe the deeds of heroes during and after the Trojan War. (p. 246)

Hypatia (hy-PAY-shuh) (c. 370–415) Greek mathematician and astronomer, she made important contributions to science. (p. 282)

Ibn Battutah (1304–c. 1368) Muslim traveler and writer, he visited Africa, India, China, and Spain. (p. 398)

Iceman (c. 3300 BC) Stone Age traveler, he was found in the Alps in 1991. Scientists have learned a great deal about Stone Age people from his clothing and tools. (p. 35)

Ieyasu, Tokugawa See Tokugawa Ieyasu.

Ignatius of Loyola (ig-NAY-shuhs) (1491–1556) Spanish noble and saint, he founded the Society of Jesus, or the Jesuits. (p. 572)

Isabella (1451–1504) Queen of Spain, she helped complete the Reconquista. She and her husband banned Islam and forced all Jews in Spain to become Christian or leave. She also paid for the voyages of Christopher Columbus. (p. 548)

James II (1633–1701) King of England, he tried to re-introduce Roman Catholicism to England, a Protestant country. He was replaced as ruler by William and Mary. (p. 623)

Jefferson, Thomas (1743–1826) American colonial leader and author of the Declaration of Independence, he believed that Britain had no right to govern or impose taxes on the colonies. (p. 619)

Jesus (c. AD 1–c. 30) Founder of Christianity, he taught about kindness and love for God. His teachings spread throughout the Roman Empire and the world. (p. 334)

Joan of Arc (c. 1412–1431) French peasant girl, she rallied the French troops during the Hundred Years' War. (p. 542)

Justinian (juh-STIN-ee-uhn) (c. 483–565) Emperor of the eastern Roman Empire, he organized all Roman laws into a legal system called Justinian's Code. He also reconquered much of the Mediterranean and built Hagia Sophia. (p. 342)

Kepler, Johannes (1571–1630) German astronomer, he proved that the planets orbit the sun. (p. 590)

Khadijah (ka-DEE-jah) (600s) Muhammad's wife, she was a successful trader. (p. 356)

Khayyám, Omar See Omar Khayyám.

Khufu (KOO-foo) (ruled 2500s BC) Egyptian pharaoh, he ruled during Egypt's Old Kingdom and is known for the many monuments built to honor him. (p. 91)

Kublai Khan (KOO-bluh KAHN) (1215–1294) Mongol ruler, he completed the conquest of China and founded the Yuan dynasty. (p. 431)

Laozi (LOWD-zuh) (c. 500s or 400s BC) Chinese philospoher, he was the most famous Daoist teacher. Laozi is credited with writing *The Way and Its Power,* Daoism's basic text. (p. 170)

Lenin, Vladimir (1870–1924) Russian revolutionary leader, he led the overthrow of the Russian government in 1917 to create the first Communist state. (p. 665)

Leonardo da Vinci (1452–1519) Genius of the Renaissance, he was a painter, sculptor, inventor, engineer, town planner, and mapmaker. (p. 563)

Li Bo (701–762) One of China's greatest poets, he lived during the Tang dynasty. (p. 417)

Li Qingzhao (ching-ZHOW) (1081–1141) China's greatest female poet, she lived during the Song dynasty. (p. 417)

Liu Bang (lee-oo BANG) Chinese emperor, he founded the Han dynasty. (p. 178)

Locke, John (1632–1704) English philosopher, he thought that government was a contract between the ruler and the people. (p. 621)

Louis XIV (1638–1715) French king, he believed that he ruled by divine right. (p. 616)

Louis XVI (1754–1793) French king at the time of the French Revolution, he refused to sign a constitution limiting his power. He was tried and later executed. (p. 626)

Luther, Martin (1483–1546) German priest credited with starting the Reformation, he nailed a list of complaints about the Catholic Church to a church door in Wittenberg, Germany. (p. 570)

Maathai, Wangari (wan-GAH-ree mah-DY-yee) Nobel Prize winner, she was honored in 2004 for her efforts in planting more than 30 million trees across Africa. She was the first African woman to receive the Nobel Peace Prize. (p. 679)

Machiavelli, Niccolo (mahk-yah-VEL-lee) (1469–1527) Italian writer and politician, he wrote *The Prince* in which he advised leaders on how to rule. (p. 562)

Madison, James (1751–1836) American colonial leader, he was the primary author of the Constitution. (p. 625)

Magellan, Ferdinand (muh-JEHL-uhn) (c. 1480–1521) Portuguese explorer sailing for Spain, his crew was the first to circumnavigate the globe. (p. 595)

Mansa Musa See Musa.

Mao Zedong (mow zuh-doong) Chinese leader, he made China a Communist state in 1949. (p. 669)

Marius, Gaius (GY-uhs MER-ee-uhs) (157–86 BC) Roman consul, he was a popular general who encouraged the unemployed poor to join the Roman army. (p. 312)

Marx, Karl (1818–1883) German philosopher, he called on workers to overthrow capitalism. His ideas helped inspire socialism. (p. 646)

Medici, Cosimo de' (KOH-zee-moh day MED-i-chee) (1389–1464) Italian banker and leader of Florence, he wanted to make Florence the greatest city in the world. His actions helped bring about the Renaissance. (p. 560)

Mehmed II (1432–1481) Ottoman sultan, he defeated the Byzantine Empire in 1453. (p. 365)

Menes (MEE-neez) (c. 3100 BC) Legendary Egyptian ruler, he unified the kingdoms of Upper and Lower Egypt and built the new capital city of Memphis. (p. 89)

Metternich, Klemens von (meh-tuhr-nik) Austrian prince, he led the Congress of Vienna in setting peace terms after the defeat of Napoleon. (p. 640)

Michelangelo (mee-kay-LAHN-jay-loh) (1475–1564) Italian Renaissance artist, he designed buildings, wrote poetry, and created sculptures and paintings. (p. 562)

Moctezuma II (MAWK-tay-soo-mah) (1466–1520) The last Aztec emperor, he was killed in the Spanish conquest led by Cortés. (p. 477)

Montesquieu, Charles-Louis (mohn-te-SKYOO) (1689–1755) French Enlightenment thinker, he believed that government should be divided into separate branches to protect people's freedom. (p. 618)

Moses (c. 1200s BC) Biblical figure, according to the Bible, he led the Hebrew people out of Egypt and back to Canaan in the Exodus. During this journey, Moses received the Ten Commandments from God. (p. 203)

Muhammad (c. 570–632) Founder of Islam, he spread Islam's teachings to the people of Arabia. His teachings make up the Qu'ran. (p. 356)

Murasaki Shikibu (moohr-ah-sahk-ee shee-kee-boo) (c. 978–c. 1026) Japanese noble and writer, she wrote *The Tale of Genji,* the world's first known novel. (p. 451)

Musa (moo-sah) (died c. 1332) Mali's greatest and most famous *mansa,* or ruler, he was a devout Muslim. He made a famous pilgrimage to Mecca that helped spread Mali's fame. (p. 395)

Mussolini, Benito (1883–1945) Italian dictator, he made Italy a fascist state shortly before World War II. (p. 667)

Naomi (nay-OH-mee) Bibilical figure, according to the Bible, she had a strong faith in God. (p. 207)

Nebuchadnezzar (neb-uh-kuhd-NEZ-uhr) (ruled 605–561 BC) Chaldean king, he rebuilt Babylon into a beautiful city, which featured the famed Hanging Gardens. (p. 75)

Newton, Sir Isaac (1642–1727) English scientist, he studied and simplified the work of earlier scientists. He identified four laws that explained how the physical world works. (p. 591)

Oda Nobunaga (ohd-ah noh-booh-nah-gah) (1534–1582) Japanese shogun, he fought to unify all of Japan. (p. 459)

Omar Khayyám (OH-mahr-ky-AHM) (c. 1048–c. 1131) Sufi poet, mathematician, and astonomer, he wrote *The Rubáiyát.* (p. 371)

Ovid (AHV-uhd) (43 BC–AD 17) Roman poet and author, he was one of the greatest authors of the ancient world and wrote poems on Roman mythology. (p. 327)

Murasaki Shikibu

Pacal (puh-KAHL) (603–683) Maya king of Palenque, he had a temple built in the city to record his achievements. (p. 469)

Pachacuti (pah-chah-KOO-tee) (died 1471) Inca ruler, he greatly expanded the Incas' territory. (p. 480)

Patrick (400s) Christian saint, he converted the people of Ireland to Christianity. (p. 501)

Paul (c. AD 10–67) One of the most important figures in the spread of Christianity, he worked to spread Jesus's teachings and wrote letters that explained key ideas of Christianity. (p. 337)

Peisistratus (py-SIS-truht-uhs) (500s BC) Athenian tyrant, he brought peace and prosperity to the city. (p. 237)

Pericles (PER-uh-kleez) (495–429 BC) Athenian leader, he encouraged the spread of democracy and led Athens when the city was at its height. (p. 266)

Perry, Matthew (1794–1858) American naval commander, he negotiated a trade agreement with Japan in 1854. (p. 651)

Petrarch (PEH-trahrk) (1304–1374) Early Italian Renaissance scholar, he wrote about the importance of knowing history. (p. 566)

Philip II (ruled 359–336 BC) Macedonian king, he was a brilliant military leader who defeated the Greeks. Alexander the Great was his son. (p. 272)

Piankhi (PYAHN-kee) (c. 751–716 BC) Ruler of Kush, he was one of Kush's most successful military leaders. His army captured all of Egypt. (p. 109)

Pizarro, Francisco (1475–1541) Spanish conquistador, he conquered the Inca Empire. (p. 483)

Plato (PLAYT-oh) (428–389 BC) Greek philosopher, he was a student of Socrates. Plato started a school in Athens called the Academy and wrote *The Republic,* which describes an ideal society run by philosophers. (p. 283)

Polo, Marco (1254–1324) Italian trader, he traveled to China and later wrote about his trip. During his time in China he served as a government official in Kublai Khan's court. (p. 559)

Pompey (106–48 BC) Roman general, he was an ally of Caesar but later the two went to war and Pompey was defeated in Egypt. (p. 323)

Ptolemy (TAHL-uh-mee) (AD 100s) Ancient Greek astronomer and geographer, he studied the skies and made maps of the Mediterranean region. (p. 589)

Ramses the Great (ram-seez) (late 1300s and early 1200s BC) Egyptian pharaoh, he expanded the kingdom and built lasting temples at Karnak, Luxor, and Abu Simbel. Ramses the Great is often considered one of Egypt's greatest rulers. (p. 101)

Reagan, Ronald (1911–2004) U.S. president, he expanded U.S. military forces to put more pressure on the Soviet Union. (p. 675)

Richard I (1157–1199) King of England, he led Christian soldiers in the Third Crusade. He earned the respect of his enemies as well as Christian soldiers for his bravery and his fairness. (p. 530)

Robespierre, Maximilien (roh-bes-pyer) (1758–1794) A leader of the French Revolution, his execution ended the Reign of Terror. (p. 627)

Romulus and Remus (c. 753 BC) Legendary figures in Roman history, they built a city that eventually became Rome. (p. 297)

Rousseau, Jean-Jacques (roo-soh) (1712–1778) French philosopher, he believed in popular sovereignty and the social contract between citizens and their governments. (p. 207)

Ruth Biblical figure, according to the Bible, she left her family to care for her mother-in-law, Naomi. Ruth is an example of a model of devotion. (p. 207)

Saladin (1137–1193) Muslim general, he led the Muslim forces during the Third Crusade. (p. 531)

Sappho (SAF-oh) (c. 610–580 BC) Greek poet, she was one of the most famous lyric poets of Greece. (p. 247)

Sargon (c. 2300 BC) King of Akkad, a land north of Sumer, he built the world's first empire after defeating Sumer and northern Mesopotamia. (p. 61)

Shah Jahan (1592–1666) Ruler of the Mughal Empire, he built the Taj Mahal to honor his wife. (p. 367)

Shakespeare, William (1564–1616) English Renaissance writer and playwright, he is considered by many to be the greatest English writer of all time. (p. 568)

Shanakhdakheto (shah-nahk-dah-KEE-toh) (ruled 170–150 BC) Ruler of Kush, historians think she was the first woman to rule Kush. Her tomb is one of the largest pyramids in Meroë. (p. 113)

Shi Huangdi (SHEE hwahng-dee) (259–210 BC) Ruler of China, he united China for the first time. He built roads and canals and began the Great Wall of China. Shi Huangdi also imposed a standard system of laws, money, weights, and writing system in China. (p. 177)

Shikibu, Murasaki See Murasaki Shikibu.

Shotoku (shoh-toh-koo) (573–621) Japanese regent, he was one of Japan's greatest leaders. He was influential in bringing Buddhism and Chinese ideas to Japan. (p. 444)

Smith, Adam (1723–1790) British economist, he argued that governments should not interfere in economic matters and that economic growth came when individuals were free to make their own choices. (p. 615)

Socrates (SAHK-ruh-teez) (470–399 BC) Greek philosopher, his teaching style was based on asking questions. He wanted people to question their own beliefs. Socrates was arrested and condemned to death for challenging authority. (p. 283)

Solomon (SAHL-uh-muhn) (ruled c. 965–930 BC) King of Israel, he formed alliances with nearby kingdoms and built a temple to God in Jerusalem. (p. 205)

Spartacus (SPAHR-tuh-kuhs) (c. 73 BC) Former Roman gladiator, he led a slave revolt against Rome. (p. 313)

Stalin, Joseph (1879–1953) Soviet leader, he took over the Soviet government after Lenin died. He killed or sent to labor camps thousands of people he considered disloyal. (p. 667)

Suleyman I (soo-lay-MAHN) (c. 1494–1566) Ottoman ruler, he governed the empire at its height. (p. 364)

Sulla, Lucius Cornelius (LOO-shuhs kawr-NEEL-yuhs SUHL-uh) (138–78 BC) Roman consul, he battled Gaius Marius in a civil war. (p. 313)

Sundiata (soohn-JAHT-ah) (died 1255) Founder of the Empire of Mali, his reign is recorded in legends. (p. 390)

Sunni Ali See Ali.

Taizong (TY-tzong) (600–649) Chinese emperor of the Tang dynasty, he conquered much of Asia, reformed the military, and created codes of law. (p. 411)

Theodora (thee-uh-DOHR-uh) (c. 500–548) Wife of the Byzantine emperor Justinian, she was a smart and powerful woman who helped him rule effectively. (p. 342)

Thucydides (c. 400s BC) Greek historian, he was a former Athenian soldier who wrote a history of the Peloponnesian War based on his experiences. He tried to be impartial and study the causes and effects of war in hopes that future Greeks would not repeat their mistakes. (p. 280)

Tokugawa Ieyasu (toh-koohg-ah-wuh ee-eyahs-ooh) (1543–1616) Japanese shogun, he unified all of Japan and began the Tokugawa shogunate. (p. 459)

Tunka Manin (TOOHN-kah MAH-nin) (ruled c. 1068) King of the Empire of Ghana, his kingdom was visited by Muslim writers. (p. 388)

Tutankhamen (too-tang-KAHM-uhn) (c. 1300 BC) Egyptian pharaoh, he died while still a young king. The discovery of his tomb in 1922 has taught archaeologists much about Egyptian culture. (p. 106)

Tyndale, William (TIN-duhl) (c. 1494–1536) English professor, he translated the Bible into English. He was later executed as a heretic. (p. 571)

Urban II (c. 1035–1099) Medieval pope, he called on Christians to launch the First Crusade. (p. 528)

Voltaire (vohl-TAYR) (1694–1778) French philosopher, he mocked government and religion in his writings. (p. 615)

William and Mary (1650–1702; 1662–1694) Rulers of England, they agreed to the English Bill of Rights, which limited their powers and recognized some rights for English citizens. (p. 623)

William the Conqueror (c. 1028–1087) Powerful French noble who conquered England, he brought feudalism to Britain. (p. 508)

Wollstonecraft, Mary (1759–1797) British writer, she argued that women should have the same rights as men. (p. 615)

Wu (625–705) Empress of China during the Tang dynasty, she ruled ruthlessly and brought prosperity to China. (p. 412)

Xavier, Francis (ZAYV-yuhr) (1506–1552) Jesuit priest and missionary, he introduced Catholicism to parts of India and Japan. (p. 573)

Yang Jian (YANG jee-en) (541–604) Chinese emperor, he reunified China after the Period of Disunion and established the Sui dynasty. (p. 411)

Yohanan ben Zaccai (yoh-HAN-uhn ben ZAK-ay-y) (c. AD 70) Jewish teacher, he built a school near Jerusalem where he trained rabbis to carry on the Jewish religion after the Temple had been destroyed by the Romans. (p. 216)

Zedong, Mao See Mao Zedong.

Zheng He (juhng HUH) (c. 1371–c. 1433) Chinese admiral during the Ming Dynasty, he led great voyages that spread China's fame throughout Asia. (p. 427)

Zhu Yuanzhang (JOO yoo-ahn-JAHNG) (1368–1398) Emperor of China and founder of the Ming dynasty, he led an army that overthrew the Mongols. (p. 426)

Voltaire

BIOGRAPHICAL DICTIONARY

English and Spanish Glossary

MARK	AS IN	RESPELLING	EXAMPLE
a	alphabet	a	*AL-fuh-bet
ā	Asia	ay	AY-zhuh
ä	cart, top	ah	KAHRT, TAHP
e	let, ten	e	LET, TEN
ē	even, leaf	ee	EE-vuhn, LEEF
i	it, tip, British	i	IT, TIP, BRIT-ish
ī	site, buy, Ohio	y	SYT, BY, oh-HY-oh
	iris	eye	EYE-ris
k	card	k	KAHRD
kw	quest	kw	KWEST
ō	over, rainbow	oh	OH-vuhr, RAYN-boh
u̇	book, wood	ooh	BOOHK, WOOHD
ȯ	all, orchid	aw	AWL, AWR-kid
ȯi	foil, coin	oy	FOYL, KOYN
au̇	out	ow	OWT
ə	cup, butter	uh	KUHP, BUHT-uhr
ü	rule, food	oo	ROOL, FOOD
yü	few	yoo	FYOO
zh	vision	zh	VIZH-uhn

*A syllable printed in small capital letters receives heavier emphasis than the other syllable(s) in a word.

Phonetic Respelling and Pronunciation Guide

Many of the key terms in this textbook have been respelled to help you pronounce them. The letter combinations used in the respelling throughout the narrative are explained in the following phonetic respelling and pronunciation guide. The guide is adapted from *Merriam-Webster's Collegiate Dictionary, Eleventh Edition; Merriam-Webster's Biographical Dictionary;* and *Merriam-Webster's Geographical Dictionary.*

A

acropolis (uh-KRAH-puh-luhs) a high hill upon which a Greek fortress was built (p. 232)
acrópolis colina elevada sobre la que se construyó una fortaleza griega (pág. 232)

acupuncture (AK-yoo-punk-cher) the Chinese practice of inserting fine needles through the skin at specific points to cure disease or relieve pain (p. 183)
acupuntura práctica china que consiste en insertar pequeñas agujas en la piel en puntos específicos para curar enfermedades o aliviar el dolor (pág. 183)

afterlife life after death, much of Egyptian religion focused on the afterlife (p. 92)
la otra vida vida después de la muerte (pág. 92)

agriculture farming (p. 42)
agricultura cultivo de la tierra (pág. 42)

alliance an agreement to work together (p. 270)
alianza acuerdo de colaboración (pág. 270)

Allies Great Britain, France, the Soviet Union, and the United States joined together in World War II against Germany, Italy, and Japan (p. 667)
Aliados Unión de Gran Bretaña, Francia, la Unión Soviética y Estados Unidos contra Alemania, Italia y Japón durante la Segunda Guerra Mundial (pág. 667)

alloy a mixture of two or more metals (p. 150)
aleación mezcla de dos o más metales (pág. 150)

alphabet a set of letters that can be combined to form words (p. 77)
alfabeto conjunto de letras que pueden combinarse para formar palabras (pág. 77)

ancestor a relative who lived in the past (p. 28)
antepasado pariente que vivió hace muchos años (pág. 28)

animism the belief that bodies of water, animals, trees, and other natural objects have spirits (p. 383)

animismo creencia de que las masas de agua, los animales, los árboles y otros elementos naturales tienen espíritu (pág. 383)

Apostles (uh-PAHS-uhls) the 12 chosen disciples of Jesus who spread his teachings (p. 337)

apóstoles los 12 discípulos elegidos por Jesucristo que difundieron sus enseñanzas (pág. 337)

aqueduct (A-kwuh-duhkt) a human-made raised channel that carries water from distant places (p. 327)

acueducto canal hecho por el ser humano que transporta agua desde lugares alejados (pág. 327)

archaeology (ar-kee-AH-luh-jee) the study of the past based on what people left behind (p. 7)

arqueología estudio del pasado a través de los objetos que dejaron las personas tras desaparecer (pág. 7)

architecture the science of building (p. 68)

arquitectura ciencia de la construcción (pág. 68)

aristocrat (uh-RIS-tuh-krat) a rich landowner or noble (p. 237)

aristócrata propietario de tierras o noble rico (pág. 237)

artifact an object created and used by humans (p. 10)

artefacto objeto creado y usado por los humanos (pág. 10)

astronomy the study of stars and planets (p. 151)

astronomía estudio de las estrellas y los planetas (pág. 151)

Axis Powers The name for the alliance formed by Germany, Italy, and Japan alliance during World War II (p. 667)

Potencias del Eje Alianza que formaron Alemania, Italia y Japón durante la Segunda Guerra Mundial (pág. 667)

Black Death a deadly plague that swept through Europe between 1347 and 1351 (p. 543)

Peste Negra plaga mortal que azotó Europa entre 1347 y 1351 (pág. 543)

Buddhism a religion based on the teachings of the Buddha that developed in India in the 500s BC (p. 138)

budismo religión basada en las enseñanzas de Buda, originada en la India en el siglo VI a. C. (pág. 138)

bureaucracy a body of unelected government officials (p. 422)

burocracia cuerpo de empleados no electos del gobierno (pág. 422)

Bushido (BOOH-shi-doh) the code of honor followed by the samurai in Japan (p. 456)

Bushido código de honor por el que se regían los samuráis en Japón (pág. 456)

Byzantine Empire the society that developed in the eastern Roman Empire after the fall of the western Roman Empire (p. 343)

Imperio bizantino sociedad que surgió en el Imperio romano de oriente tras la caída del Imperio rhomano de occidente (pág. 343)

caliph (KAY-luhf) a title that Muslims use for the highest leader of Islam (p. 362)

califa título que los musulmanes le dan al líder supremo del Islam (pág. 362)

calligraphy decorative writing (p. 371)

caligrafía escritura decorativa (pág. 371)

canal a human-made waterway (p. 56)

canal vía de agua hecha por el ser humano (pág. 56)

capitalism an economic system in which individuals and private businesses run most industries (p. 601)

capitalismo sistema económico en el que los individuos y las empresas privadas controlan la mayoría de las industrias (pág. 601)

caravan a group of traders that travel together (p. 355)
caravana grupo de comerciantes que viajan juntos (pág. 355)

caste system the division of Indian society into groups based on rank, wealth, or occupation (p. 131)
sistema de castas división de la sociedad india en grupos basados en la clase social, el nivel económico o la profesión (pág. 131)

cataracts rapids along a river, such as those along the Nile in Egypt (p. 87)
rápidos fuertes corrientes a lo largo de un río, como las del Nilo en Egipto (pág. 87)

Catholic Reformation the effort of the late 1500s and 1600s to reform the Catholic Church from within; also called the Counter-Reformation (p. 572)
Reforma católica iniciativa para reformar la Iglesia católica desde dentro que tuvo lugar a finales del siglo XVI y en el XVII; también conocida como Contrarreforma (pág. 572)

causeway a raised road across water or wet ground (p. 474)
carretera elevada carretera construida sobre agua o terreno pantanoso (pág. 474)

cavalry a unit of soldiers who ride horses (p. 262)
caballería grupo de soldados a caballo (pág. 262)

chariot a wheeled, horse-drawn cart used in battle (p. 74)
cuadriga carro tirado por caballos usado en las batallas (pág. 74)

checks and balances a system that balances the distribution of power in a government (p. 305)
pesos y contrapesos sistema creado para equilibrar la distribución del poder en un gobierno (pág. 305)

chivalry (SHIV-uhl-ree) the code of honorable behavior for medieval knights (p. 513)
caballería código de comportamiento y honor de los caballeros medievales (pág. 513)

Christian humanism the combination of humanist and religious ideas (p. 567)
humanismo cristiano combinación de ideas humanistas y religiosas (pág. 567)

Christianity a religion based on the teachings of Jesus of Nazareth that developed in Judea at the beginning of the first century AD (p. 334)
cristianismo religión basada en las enseñanzas de Jesús de Nazaret que se desarrolló en Judea a comienzos del siglo I d. C. (pág. 334)

circumnavigate to go all the way around (p. 595)
circunnavegar rodear por completo (pág. 595)

citizen a person who has the right to participate in government (p. 237)
ciudadano persona que tiene el derecho de participar en el gobierno (pág. 237)

city-state a political unit consisting of a city and its surrounding countryside (p. 60)
ciudad estado unidad política formada por una ciudad y los campos que la rodean (pág. 60)

civil law a legal system based on a written code of laws (p. 328)
derecho civil sistema jurídico basado en un código de leyes escritas (pág. 328)

civil service service as a government official (p. 422)
administración pública servicio como empleado del gobierno (pág. 422)

clan an extended family (p. 442)
clan familia extensa (pág. 442)

classical an age marked by great achievements (p. 232)
clásica época marcada por grandes logros (pág. 232)

clergy church officials (p. 533)
clero funcionarios de la Iglesia (pág. 533)

climate the average weather conditions in a certain area over a long period of time (p. 12)
clima condiciones del tiempo medias de una zona específica durante un largo período de tiempo (pág. 12)

Cold War a period of distrust between the United States and Soviet Union after World War II, when there was a tense rivalry between the two superpowers but no direct fighting (p. 669)
Guerra fría período de desconfianza entre Estados Unidos y la Unión Soviética que siguió a la Segunda Guerra Mundial; existía una rivalidad tensa entre las dos superpotencias, pero no se llegó a la lucha real (pág. 669)

compass an instrument that uses the earth's magnetic field to indicate direction (p. 418)
brújula instrumento que utiliza el campo magnético de la Tierra para indicar la dirección (pág. 418)

communism an economic and political system in which the government owns all businesses and controls the economy (p. 665)
comunismo sistema económico y político en el que el gobierno es propietario de todos los medios de producción y controla la economía (pág. 665)

Confucianism a philosophy based on the ideas of Confucius that focuses on morality, family order, social harmony, and government (p. 169)
confucianismo filosofía basada en las ideas de Confucio que se basa en la moralidad, el orden familiar, la armonía social y el gobierno (pág. 169)

conquistadors (kahn-kees-tuh-DOHRS) Spanish soldiers (p. 478)
conquistadores soldados españoles (pág. 478)

conservatism a movement that arose to preserve the old social order and governments in an effort to return Europe to the way it was before the French Revolution (p. 641)
conservadurismo movimiento surgido con el fin de preservar los antiguos gobiernos y orden social en un esfuerzo por que Europa volviese a la situación en la que se encontraba antes de la Revolución francesa (pág. 641)

consuls (KAHN-suhlz) the two most powerful officials in Rome (p. 303)
cónsules los dos funcionarios más poderosos en Roma (pág. 303)

corruption the decay of people's values (p. 342)
corrupción decadencia de los valores de las personas (pág. 342)

coup d'état (KOO DAY-tah) the forceful overthrow of a government (p. 638)
golpe de estado derrocamiento forzoso de un gobierno (pág. 638)

court a group of nobles who live near and serve or advise a ruler (p. 448)
corte grupo de nobles que viven cerca de un gobernante y lo sirven o aconsejan (pág. 448)

crucifixion (kroo-suh-FIK-shuhn) a type of execution in which a person was nailed to a cross (p. 336)
crucifixión tipo de ejecución en la que se clavaba a una persona en una cruz (pág. 336)

Crusades a long series of wars between Christians and Muslims in Southwest Asia fought for control of the Holy Land from 1096 to 1291 (p. 528)
cruzadas larga sucesión de guerras entre cristianos y musulmanes en el sudoeste de Asia para conseguir el control de la Tierra Santa; tuvieron lugar entre el año 1096 y el año 1291 (pág. 528)

culture the knowledge, beliefs, customs, and values of a group of people (p. 7)
cultura el conocimiento, las creencias, las costumbres y los valores de un grupo de personas (pág. 7)

cuneiform (kyoo-NEE-uh-fohrm) the world's first system of writing; developed in Sumer (p. 65)
cuneiforme primer sistema de escritura del mundo; desarrollado en Sumeria (pág. 65)

currency money (p. 326)
moneda dinero (pág. 326)

D

daimyo (DY-mee-oh) large landowners of feudal Japan (p. 454)
daimyo grandes propietarios de tierras del Japón feudal (pág. 454)

Daoism (DOW-ih-zum) a philosophy that developed in China and stressed the belief that one should live in harmony with the Dao, the guiding force of all reality (p. 170)
taoism filosofía que se desarrolló en China y que enfatizaba la creencia de que se debe vivir en armonía con el Tao, la fuerza que guía toda la realidad (pág. 170)

Dead Sea Scrolls writings about Jewish beliefs created about 2,000 years ago (p. 212)
manuscritos del mar Muerto escritos sobre las creencias judías, redactados hace unos 2,000 años (pág. 212)

Declaration of Independence a document written in 1776 that declared the American colonies' independence from British rule (p. 624)
Declaración de Independencia documento redactado en 1776 que declaró la independencia de las colonias de Norteamérica del dominio británico (pág. 624)

Declaration of the Rights of Man and of the Citizen a document written in France in 1789 that guaranteed specific freedoms for French citizens (p. 627)
Declaración de los Derechos del Hombre y del Ciudadano documento redactado en Francia en 1789 que garantizaba libertades específicas para los ciudadanos franceses (pág. 627)

delta a triangle-shaped area of land made from soil deposited by a river (p. 87)
delta zona de tierra de forma triangular creada a partir de los sedimentos que deposita un río (pág. 87)

democracy a type of government in which people rule themselves (p. 236)
democracia tipo de gobierno en el que el pueblo se gobierna a sí mismo (pág. 236)

Diaspora (dy-AS-pruh) the scattering of the Jews outside of Judah after the Babylonian Captivity (p. 206)
diáspora la dispersión de los judíos desde Judá tras el cautiverio en Babilonia (pág. 206)

dictator a ruler who has almost absolute power (p. 298)
dictador gobernante que tiene poder casi absoluto (pág. 298)

diffusion the spread of ideas from one culture to another (p. 189)
difusión traspaso de ideas de una cultura a otra (pág. 189)

division of labor an arrangement in which each worker specializes in a particular task or job (p. 56)
división del trabajo organización mediante la que cada trabajador se especializa en un trabajo o tarea en particular (pág. 56)

domestication the process of changing plants or animals to make them more useful to humans (p. 41)
domesticación proceso en el que se modifican los animales o las plantas para que sean más útiles para los humanos (pág. 41)

dynasty a series of rulers from the same family (p. 89)
dinastía serie de gobernantes pertenecientes a la misma familia (pág. 89)

E

elite (AY-leet) people of wealth and power (p. 93)
élite personas ricas y poderosas (pág. 93)

empire land with different territories and peoples under a single rule (p. 61)
imperio zona que reúne varios territorios y pueblos bajo un mismo gobierno (pág. 61)

engineering the application of scientific knowledge for practical purposes (p. 94)
ingeniería aplicación del conocimiento científico para fines prácticos (pág. 94)

English Bill of Rights a document approved in 1689 that listed rights for Parliament and the English people and drew on the principles of Magna Carta (p. 623)
Declaración de Derechos inglesa documento aprobado en 1689 que enumeraba los derechos del Parlamento y del pueblo de Inglaterra, inspirada en los principios de la Carta Magna (pág. 623)

Enlightenment a period during the 1600s and 1700s when reason was used to guide people's thoughts about society, politics, and philosophy (p. 612)
Ilustración período durante los siglos XVII y XVIII en el que la razón guiaba la opinión de las personas acerca de la sociedad, la política y la filosofía (pág. 612)

environment all the living and nonliving things that affect life in an area (p. 13)
medio ambiente todos los seres vivos y elementos inertes que afectan la vida de un área (pág. 13)

epics long poems that tell the stories of heroes (p. 66)
poemas épicos poemas largos que narran hazañas de héroes (pág. 66)

ethics moral values (p. 169)
ética valores morales (pág. 169)

excommunicate to cast out from the church (p. 525)
excomulgar expulsar de la Iglesia (pág. 525)

Exodus the journey of the Hebrews, led by Moses, from Egypt to Canaan after they were freed from slavery (p. 203)
Éxodo viaje de los hebreos, guiados por Moisés, desde Egipto hasta Canaán después de su liberación de la esclavitud (pág. 203)

exports items sent to other regions for trade (p. 111)
exportaciones productos enviados a otras regiones para el intercambio commercial (pág. 111)

extended family a family group that includes the father, mother, children, and close relatives (p. 382)
familia extensa grupo familiar que incluye al padre, la madre, los hijos y los parientes cercanos (pág. 382)

F

fable a short story that teaches a lesson about life or gives advice on how to live (p. 247)
fábula relato breve que presenta una enseñanza u ofrece algún consejo sobre la vida (pág. 247)

factory system a system in which machines rapidly manufacture large quantities of items (p. 645)
sistema de fábrica un sistema en el que se fabrican grandes cantidades de artículos con gran rapidez mediante el uso de máquinas (pág. 645)

fascism (FASH-iz-uhm) a political system based on nationalism and strong government; Adolph Hitler in Germany and Benito Mussolini in Italy were the first fascist leaders (p. 667)
fascismo sistema político basado en el nacionalismo y en un gobierno fuerte; los primeros líderes fascistas fueron Adolph Hitler en Alemania y Benito Mussolini en Italia (pág. 667)

ENGLISH AND SPANISH GLOSSARY

fasting going without food for a period of time (p. 137)

ayunar dejar de comer durante un período de tiempo (pág. 137)

federalism the sharing of power between local governments and a strong central government (p. 575)

federalismo sistema de distribución del poder entre los gobiernos locales y un gobierno central fuerte (pág. 575)

Fertile Crescent an area of rich farmland in Southwest Asia where the first civilizations began (p. 55)

Media Luna de las tierras fértiles zona de ricas tierras de cultivo situada en el sudoeste de Asia, en la que comenzaron las primeras civilizaciones (pág. 55)

feudalism (FYOO-duh-lih-zuhm) the system of obligations that governed the relationships between lords and vassals in medieval Europe (p. 507)

feudalismo sistema de obligaciones que gobernaba las relaciones entre los señores feudales y los vasallos en la Europa medieval (pág. 507)

figurehead a person who appears to rule even though real power rests with someone else (p. 455)

títere persona que aparentemente gobierna aunque el poder real lo ostenta otra persona (pág. 455)

Five Pillars of Islam five acts of worship required of all Muslims (p. 360)

los cinco pilares del Islam cinco prácticas religiosas que los musulmanes tienen que observar (pág. 360)

Forum a Roman public meeting place (p. 305)

foro lugar público de reuniones en Roma (pág. 305)

fossil a part or imprint of something that was once alive (p. 10)

fósil parte o huella de un ser vivo ya desaparecido (pág. 10)

friar a member of a religious order who lived and worked among the public (p. 536)

fraile miembro de una orden religiosa que vivía y trabajaba entre la gente (pág. 536)

G

genocide the deliberate destruction of a people (p. 668)

genicidio la eliminación intencionada de un pueblo (pág. 668)

geography the study of Earth's physical and cultural features (p. 12)

geografía estudio de las características físicas y culturales de la Tierra (pág. 12)

Grand Canal a canal linking northern and southern China (p. 411)

canal grande un canal que conecta el norte con el sur de China (pág. 411)

Great Wall a barrier made of walls across China's northern frontier (p. 175)

Gran Muralla barrera formada por muros situada a lo largo de la frontera norte de China (pág. 175)

griot a West African storyteller (p. 396)

griot narrador de relatos de África occidental (pág. 396)

gunpowder a mixture of powders used in guns and explosives (p. 418)

pólvora mezcla de polvos utilizada en armas de fuego y explosivos (pág. 418)

H

haiku a type of Japanese poem with three lines and 17 syllables that describes nature scenes (p. 514)

haiku tipo de poema japonés de tres líneas y 17 sílabas en el que se describen escenas de la naturaleza (pág. 514)

Hammurabi's Code a set of 282 laws governing daily life in Babylon; the earliest known collection of written laws (p. 73)
Código de Hammurabi conjunto de 282 leyes que regían la vida cotidiana en Babilonia; la primera colección de leyes escritas conocida (pág. 73)

Hellenistic Greek-like; heavily influenced by Greek ideas (p. 275)
helenístico al estilo griego; muy influido por las ideas de la Grecia clásica (pág. 275)

heresy (HER-uh-see) religious ideas that oppose accepted church teachings (p. 546)
herejía ideas religiosas que se oponen a la doctrina oficial de la Iglesia (pág. 546)

hieroglyphics (hy-ruh-GLIH-fiks) the ancient Egyptian writing system that used picture symbols (p. 102)
jeroglíficos sistema de escritura del antiguo Egipto, en el cual se usaban símbolos ilustrados (pág. 102)

High Holy Days the two most sacred of all Jewish holidays—Rosh Hashanah and Yom Kippur (p. 219)
Supremos Días Santos los dos días más sagrados de las festividades judías, Rosh Hashanah y Yom Kippur (pág. 219)

Hindu-Arabic numerals the number system we use today; it was created by Indian scholars during the Gupta dynasty (p. 150)
numerales indoarábigos sistema numérico que usamos hoy en día; fue creado por estudiosos de la India durante la dinastía Gupta (pág. 150)

Hinduism the main religion of India; it teaches that everything is part of a universal spirit called Brahman (p. 133)
hinduismo religión principal de la India; sus enseñanzas dicen que todo forma parte de un espíritu universal llamado Brahman (pág. 133)

history the study of the past (p. 6)
historia el estudio del pasado (pág. 6)

Holocaust the Nazis' effort to wipe out the Jewish people in World War II, when 6 million Jews throughout Europe were killed (p. 668)
Holocausto intento de los Nazis de eliminar al pueblo judío; hecho acaecido durante la Segunda Guerra Mundial en el que se asesinó a 6 millones de judíos en toda Europa (pág. 668)

Holy Land the region on the eastern shore of the Mediterranean Sea where the Jewish religion began and where Jesus lived, preached, and died (p. 528)
Tierra Santa región de la costa este del mar Mediterráneo en donde comenzó la religión judía y en la que Jesús vivió, predicó y murió (pág. 528)

hominid an early ancestor of humans (p. 28)
homínido antepasado primitivo de los humanos (pág. 28)

humanism the study of history, literature, public speaking, and art that led to a new way of thinking in Europe in the late 1300s (p. 561)
humanismo estudio de la historia, la literatura, la oratoria y el arte que produjo una nueva forma de pensar en Europa a finales del siglo XIV (pág. 561)

Hundred Years' War a long conflict between England and France that lasted from 1337 to 1453 (p. 542)
Guerra de los Cien Años largo conflicto entre Inglaterra y Francia que tuvo lugar entre 1337 y 1453 (pág. 542)

hunter-gatherers people who hunt animals and gather wild plants, seeds, fruits, and nuts to survive (p. 33)
cazadores y recolectores personas que cazan animales y recolectan plantas, semillas, frutas y nueces para sobrevivir (pág. 33)

ice ages long periods of freezing weather (p. 36)
eras glaciales largos períodos de clima helado (pág. 36)

ENGLISH AND SPANISH GLOSSARY

ideologies (i-dee-AH-luh-jeez) systems or beliefs (p. 674)
ideologías sistemas de creencias (pág. 672)

imperialism the control of a region or country by another country (p. 651)
imperialismo el control de una región o país por parte de otro país (pág. 651)

imports goods brought in from other regions (p. 111)
importaciones bienes que se introducen en un país procedentes de otras regiones (pág. 111)

inoculation (i-nah-kyuh-LAY-shuhn) injecting a person with a small dose of a virus to help build up defenses to a disease (p. 150)
inoculación acto de inyectar una pequeña dosis de un virus a una persona para ayudarla a crear defensas contra una enfermedad (pág. 150)

irrigation a way of supplying water to an area of land (p. 56)
irrigación método para suministrar agua a un terreno (pág. 56)

Islam a religion based on the messages Muhammad is believed to have received from God (p. 356)
Islam religión basada en los mensajes que se cree que Mahoma recibió de Dios (pág. 356)

isolationism a policy of avoiding contact with other countries (p. 430)
aislacionismo política de evitar el contacto con otros países (pág. 430)

jade a hard gemstone often used in jewelry (p. 163)
jade piedra preciosa de gran dureza que se suele utilizar en joyería (pág. 163)

Jainism an Indian religion based on the teachings of Mahavira that teaches all life is sacred (p. 135)
jainismo religión de la India basada en las enseñanzas de Mahavira, que proclama que toda forma de vida es sagrada (pág. 135)

Janissary an Ottoman slave soldier (p. 364)
jenízaro soldado esclavo otomano (pág. 364)

Jesuits members of a Catholic religious order created to serve the pope and the church (p. 572)
jesuitas miembros de una orden religiosa católica creada para servir al Papa y a la Iglesia (pág. 572)

jihad (ji-HAHD) to make an effort or to struggle; has also been interpreted to mean holy war (p. 359)
yihad esforzarse o luchar; se ha interpretado también con el significado de guerra santa (pág. 359)

Judaism (JOO-dee-i-zuhm) the religion of the Hebrews (practiced by Jews today); it is the world's oldest monotheistic religion (p. 202)
judaísmo religión de los hebreos (practicada por los judíos hoy en día); es la religión monoteísta más antigua del mundo (pág. 202)

karma in Buddhism and Hinduism, the effects that good or bad actions have on a person's soul (p. 134)
karma en el budismo y el hinduismo, los efectos que las buenas o malas acciones producen en el alma de una persona (pág. 134)

kente a hand-woven, brightly colored West African fabric (p. 399)
kente tela muy colorida, tejida a mano, característica de África occidental (pág. 399)

knight a warrior in medieval Europe who fought on horseback (p. 506)
caballero guerrero de la Europa medieval que luchaba a caballo (pág. 506)

Korean War Communist North Korea invaded non-Communist South Korea in 1950; after three years of fighting, Korea remained divided (p. 674)
Guerra de Corea guerra iniciada cuando Corea del Norte, de régimen comunista, invadió Corea del Sur, de régimen no comunista; tras tres años de enfrentamientos, Corea siguió dividida (pág. 672)

L

laissez-faire (leh-say-FAYR) a "let things be" attitude on the part of government toward industry (p. 646)
laissez-faire actitud de los gobiernos de "dejar hacer" a las industrias (pág. 646)

land bridge a strip of land connecting two continents (p. 36)
puente de tierra franja de tierra que conecta dos continentes (pág. 36)

landforms the natural features of the land's surface (p. 12)
accidentes geográficos características naturales de la superficie terrestre (pág. 12)

Latin the language of the Romans (p. 304)
latín idioma de los romanos (pág. 304)

Legalism the Chinese belief that people were bad by nature and needed to be controlled (p. 170)
legalismo creencia china de que las personas eran malas por naturaleza y debían ser controladas (pág. 170)

legion (LEE-juhn) a group of up to 6,000 Roman soldiers (p. 309)
legión grupo que podía incluir hasta 6,000 soldados romanos (pág. 309)

liberalism a movement for individual rights and liberties (p. 641)
liberalismo movimiento a favor de los derechos del individuo y las libertades (pág. 641)

lord a person of high rank who owned land but owed loyalty to his king (p. 167)
señor feudal persona de alto nivel social que poseía tierras y debía lealtad al rey (pág. 167)

M

magistrate (MA-juh-strayt) an elected official in Rome (p. 303)
magistrado funcionario electo en Roma (pág. 303)

Magna Carta a document signed in 1215 by King John of England that required the king to honor certain rights (p. 540)
Carta Magna documento firmado por el rey Juan de Inglaterra en 1215 que exigía que el rey respetara ciertos derechos (pág. 540)

maize (MAYZ) corn (p. 468)
maíz cereal también conocido como elote o choclo (pág. 468)

manor a large estate owned by a knight or lord (p. 509)
señorío gran finca perteneciente a un caballero o señor feudal (pág. 509)

market economy an economic system in which individuals decide what goods and services they will buy (p. 601)
economía de mercado sistema económico en el que los individuos deciden qué tipo de bienes y servicios desean comprar (pág. 601)

masonry stonework (p. 481)
mampostería obra de piedra (pág. 481)

medieval (mee-DEE-vuhl) referring to the Middle Ages (p. 500)
medieval relativo a la Edad Media (pág. 500)

meditation deep, continued thought that focuses the mind on spiritual ideas (p. 137)
meditación reflexión profunda y continua, durante la cual la persona se concentra en ideas espirituales (pág. 137)

megalith a huge stone monument (p. 42)
megalito enorme monumento de piedra (pág. 42)

mercantilism a system in which a government controls all economic activity in a country and its colonies to make the government stronger and richer (p. 599)
mercantilismo sistema en el que el gobierno controla toda la actividad económica de un país y sus colonias con el fin de hacerse más fuerte y más rico (pág. 599)

merchant a trader (p. 111)
mercader comerciante (pág. 111)

ENGLISH AND SPANISH GLOSSARY

Mesolithic Era the middle part of the Stone Age; marked by the creation of smaller and more complex tools (p. 38)
Mesolítico período central de la Edad de Piedra, caracterizado por la creación de herramientas más pequeñas y complejas (pág. 38)

Messiah (muh-sy-uh) in Judaism, a new leader that would appear among the Jews and restore the greatness of ancient Israel (p. 334)
Mesías en el judaísmo, nuevo líder que aparecería entre los judíos y restablecería la grandeza del antiguo Israel (pág. 334)

metallurgy (MET-uhl-uhr-jee) the science of working with metals (p. 150)
metalurgia ciencia de trabajar los metales (pág. 150)

Middle Ages a period that lasted from about 500 to 1500 in Europe (p. 500)
Edad Media nombre con el que se denomina el período que abarca aproximadamente desde el año 500 hasta el 1500 en Europa (pág. 500)

Middle Kingdom the period of Egyptian history from about 2050 to 1750 BC and marked by order and stability (p. 96)
Reino Medio período de la historia de Egipto que abarca aproximadamente del 2050 al 1750 a. C. y que se caracterizó por el orden y la estabilidad (pág. 96)

migrate to move to a new place (p. 36)
migrar desplazarse a otro lugar (pág. 36)

minaret a narrow tower from which Muslims are called to prayer (p. 371)
minarete torre fina desde la que se llama a la oración a los musulmanes (pág. 371)

missionary someone who works to spread religious beliefs (p. 140)
misionero alguien que trabaja para difundir sus creencias religiosas (pág. 140)

monarch (MAH-nark) a ruler of a kingdom or empire (p. 72)
monarca gobernante de un reino o imperio (pág. 72)

monastery a community of monks (p. 502)
monasterio comunidad de monjes (pág. 502)

monk a religious man who lived apart from society in an isolated community (p. 502)
monje religioso que vivía apartado de la sociedad en una comunidad aislada (pág. 502)

monotheism the belief in only one god (p. 208)
monoteísmo creencia en un solo dios (pág. 208)

monsoon a seasonal wind pattern that causes wet and dry seasons (p. 125)
monzón viento estacional cíclico que causa estaciones húmedas y secas (pág. 125)

mosque (MAHSK) a building for Muslim prayer (p. 357)
mezquita edificio musulmán para la oración (pág. 357)

mummy a specially treated body wrapped in cloth for preservation (p. 93)
momia cadáver especialmente tratado y envuelto en tela para su conservación (pág. 93)

Muslim a follower of Islam (p. 356)
musulmán seguidor del Islam (pág. 356)

mythology stories about gods and heroes that try to explain how the world works (p. 243)
mitología relatos sobre dioses y héroes que tratan de explicar cómo funciona el mundo (pág. 243)

N

nationalism a devotion and loyalty to one's country; develops among people with a common language, religion, or history (p. 648)
nacionalismo sentimiento de lealtad a un país; se desarrolla entre personas con un idioma, religión o historia en común (pág. 648)

nation-states self-governing countries made up of people with a common cultural background (p. 648)
naciones-estado países con gobierno independiente formados por personas con un origen cultural común (pág. 648)

natural law a law that people believed God had created to govern how the world operated (p. 538)
  ley natural ley que las personas pensaban que Dios había creado para controlar el funcionamiento del mundo (pág. 538)

natural rights the belief that developed during the Enlightenment that people had certain rights, such as the right to life, liberty, and property (p. 618)
  derechos naturales creencia que se desarrolló durante la Ilustración de que las personas tenían ciertos derechos, como el derecho a la vida, a la libertad y a la propiedad (pág. 618)

Neolithic Era the New Stone Age; when people learned to make fire and tools such as saws and drills (p. 41)
  Neolítico Nueva Edad de Piedra; el ser humano aprendió a producir fuego y a fabricar herramientas como sierras y taladros manuales (pág. 41)

New Kingdom the period from about 1550 to 1050 BC in Egyptian history when Egypt reached the height of its power and glory (p. 97)
  Reino Nuevo período de la historia egipcia que abarca aproximadamente desde el 1550 hasta el 1050 a. C., en el que Egipto alcanzó la cima de su poder y su gloria (pág. 97)

nirvana in Buddhism, a state of perfect peace (p. 138)
  nirvana en el budismo, estado de paz perfecta (pág. 138)

noble a rich and powerful person (p. 91)
  noble persona rica y poderosa (pág. 91)

nonviolence the avoidance of violent actions (p. 135)
  no violencia rechazo de las acciones violentas (pág. 135)

oasis a wet, fertile area within a desert (p. 354)
  oasis zona húmeda y fértil en un desierto (pág. 354)

obelisk (AH-buh-lisk) a tall, pointed, four-sided pillar in ancient Egypt (p. 104)
  obelisco pilar alto, de cuatro caras y acabado en punta, propio del antiguo Egipto (pág. 104)

observatories buildings used to study astronomy; Mayan priests watched the stars from these buildings (p. 472)
  observatorios edificios que sirven para estudiar la astronomía; los sacerdotes mayas observaban las estrellas desde estos edificios (pág. 472)

Old Kingdom the period from about 2700 to 2200 BC in Egyptian history that began shortly after Egypt was unified (p. 90)
  Reino Antiguo período de la historia egipcia que abarca aproximadamente del 2700 hasta el 2200 a. C. y comenzó poco después de la unificación de Egipto (pág. 90)

oligarchy (AH-luh-gar-kee) a government in which only a few people have power (p. 237)
  oligarquía gobierno en el que sólo unas pocas personas tienen el poder (pág. 237)

oracle a prediction by a wise person, or a person who makes a prediction (p. 164)
  oráculo predicción de un sabio o de alguien que hace profecías (pág. 164)

oral history a spoken record of past events (p. 396)
  historia oral registro hablado de hechos ocurridos en el pasado (pág. 396)

Paleolithic Era (pay-lee-uh-LI-thik) the first part of the Stone Age; when people first used stone tools (p. 31)
  Paleolítico primera parte de la Edad de Piedra; cuando el ser humano usó herramientas de piedra por primera vez (pág. 31)

papyrus (puh-PY-ruhs) a long-lasting, paper-like material made from reeds that the ancient Egyptians used to write on (p. 102)
  papiro material duradero hecho de juncos, similar al papel, que los antiguos egipcios utilizaban para escribir (pág. 102)

ENGLISH AND SPANISH GLOSSARY

Parliament (PAHR-luh-muhnt) the lawmaking body that governs England (p. 541)
Parlamento órgano legislador que gobierna Inglaterra (pág. 541)

Passover a holiday in which Jews remember the Exodus (p. 219)
Pascua judía festividad en la que los judíos recuerdan el Éxodo (pág. 219)

patricians (puh-TRI-shunz) the nobility in Roman society (p. 299)
patricios nobles de la sociedad romana (pág. 299)

patron a sponsor (p. 371)
mecenas patrocinador (pág. 371)

Pax Romana Roman Peace; a period of general peace and prosperity in the Roman Empire that lasted from 27 BC to AD 180 (p. 326)
Pax Romana Paz Romana; período de paz y prosperidad generales en el Imperio romano que duró del 27 a. C. al 180 d. C. (pág. 326)

peasant a farmer with a small farm (p. 167)
campesino agricultor dueño de una pequeña granja (pág. 167)

Peloponnesian War a war between Athens and Sparta in the 400s BC (p. 270)
guerra del.Peloponeso guerra entre Atenas y Esparta en el siglo V a. C. (pág. 270)

Period of Disunion the time of disorder following the collapse of the Han Dynasty (p. 410)
período de desunión la época de desorden que siguió el derrumbe de la dinastía Han (pág. 410)

Persian Wars a series of wars between Persia and Greece in the 400s BC (p. 263)
guerras persas serie de guerras entre Persia y Grecia en el siglo V a. C. (pág. 263)

phalanx (FAY-langks) a group of Greek warriors who stood close together in a square formation (p. 273)
falange grupo de guerreros griegos que se mantenían unidos en formación compacta y cuadrada (pág. 273)

pharaoh (FEHR-oh) the title used by the rulers of Egypt (p. 89)
faraón título usado por los gobernantes de Egipto (pág. 89)

pictograph a picture symbol (p. 66)
pictograma símbolo ilustrado (pág. 66)

pilgrimage a journey to a sacred place (p. 356)
peregrinación viaje a un lugar sagrado (pág. 356)

plantation a large farm (p. 598)
plantación hacienda de grandes dimensiones (pág. 598)

plebeians (pli-BEE-uhnz) the common people of ancient Rome (p. 299)
plebeyos gente común de la antigua Roma (pág. 299)

polis (PAH-luhs) the Greek word for a city-state (p. 232)
polis palabra griega para designar una ciudad estado (pág. 232)

polytheism the worship of many gods (p. 62)
politeísmo culto a varios dioses (pág. 62)

popular sovereignty the Enlightenment idea that governments should express the will of the people (p. 618)
soberanía popular idea de la Ilustración que consiste en que los gobiernos deben expresar la voluntad del pueblo (pág. 618)

porcelain a thin, beautiful pottery invented in China (p. 417)
porcelana cerámica bella y delicada creada en China (pág. 417)

prehistory the time before there was writing (p. 28)
prehistoria período anterior a la existencia de la escritura (pág. 28)

priest a person who performs religious ceremonies (p. 63)
sacerdote persona que lleva a cabo ceremonias religiosas (pág. 63)

primary source an account of an event by someone who took part in or witnessed the event (p. 10)
fuente primaria relato de un hecho por parte de alguien que participó o presenció el hecho (pág. 10)

prophet someone who is said to receive messages from God to be taught to others (p. 211)
profeta alguien del que se cree que recibe mensajes de Dios para transmitírselos a los demás (pág. 211)

Protestant a Christian who protested against the Catholic Church (p. 570)
protestante cristiano que protestaba en contra de la Iglesia católica (pág. 570)

proverb a short saying of wisdom or truth (p. 397)
proverbio refrán breve que expresa sabiduría o una verdad (pág. 397)

Punic Wars a series of wars between Rome and Carthage in the 200s and 100s BC (p. 309)
guerras púnicas sucesión de guerras entre Roma y Cartago en los siglos III y II a. C. (pág. 309)

pyramid a huge triangular tomb built by the Egyptians and other peoples (p. 94)
pirámide tumba triangular y gigantesca construida por los egipcios y otros pueblos (pág. 94)

Q

Quechua (KE-chuh-wuh) the language of the Inca (p. 480)
quechua idioma de los incas (pág. 480)

Qur'an (kuh-RAN) the holy book of Islam (p. 356)
Corán libro sagrado del Islam (pág. 356)

R

rabbi (RAB-eye) a Jewish religious leader and teacher (p. 216)
rabino líder y maestro religioso judío (pág. 216)

rain forest a moist, densely wooded area that contains many different plants and animals (p. 382)
selva tropical zona húmeda y con muchos árboles que contiene muchas variedades de plantas y animales (pág. 382)

reason clear and ordered thinking (p. 281)
razón pensamiento claro y ordenado (pág. 281)

Reconquista (re-kahn-KEES-tuh) the effort of Christian kingdoms in northern Spain to retake land from the Moors during the Middle Ages (p. 547)
Reconquista esfuerzo de los reinos cristianos del norte de España por recuperar los territorios en posesión de los moros durante la Edad Media (pág. 547)

Reformation (re-fuhr-MAY-shuhn) a reform movement against the Roman Catholic Church that began in 1517; it resulted in the creation of Protestant churches (p. 569)
Reforma movimiento de reforma contra la Iglesia católica romana que comenzó en 1517; resultó en la creación de las iglesias protestantes (pág. 569)

regent a person who rules a country for someone who is unable to rule alone (p. 444)
regente persona que gobierna un país en lugar de alguien que no puede hacerlo por su cuenta (pág. 444)

region an area with one or more features that make it different from surrounding areas (p. 15)
región zona con una o varias características que la diferencian de las zonas que la rodean (pág. 15)

reincarnation a Hindu and Buddhist belief that souls are born and reborn many times, each time into a new body (p. 133)
reencarnación creencia hindú y budista de que las almas nacen y renacen muchas veces, siempre en un cuerpo nuevo (pág. 133)

religious order a group of people who dedicate their lives to religion and follow common rules (p. 536)
orden religiosa grupo de personas que dedican su vida a la religión y respetan una serie de normas comunes (pág. 536)

Renaissance (re-nuh-SAHNS) the period of "rebirth" and creativity that followed Europe's Middle Ages (p. 561)
Renacimiento período de "volver a nacer" y creatividad posterior a la Edad Media en Europa (pág. 561)

republic a political system in which people elect leaders to govern them (p. 298)
república sistema político en el que el pueblo elige a los líderes que lo gobernarán (pág. 298)

resources the materials found on Earth that people need and value (p. 16)
recursos materiales de la Tierra que las personas necesitan y valoran (pág. 16)

Resurrection in Christianity, Jesus's rise from the dead (p. 336)
Resurrección en el cristianismo, la vuelta a la vida de Jesús (pág. 336)

rift a long, deep valley formed by the movement of the earth's crust (p. 380)
fisura valle largo y profundo formado por el movimiento de la corteza terrestre (pág. 380)

Roman Senate a council of wealthy and powerful citizens who advised Rome's leaders (p. 303)
Senado romano consejo de ciudadanos ricos y poderosos que aconsejaba a los gobernantes de Roma (pág. 303)

Romance languages languages that developed from Latin, such as Italian, French, Spanish, Portuguese, and Romanian (p. 328)
lenguas romances lenguas que surgieron del latín, como el italiano, el francés, el español, el portugués y el rumano (pág. 328)

Rosetta Stone a huge stone slab inscribed with hieroglyphics, Greek, and a later form of Egyptian that allowed historians to understand Egyptian writing (p. 103)
piedra Roseta gran losa de piedra en la que aparecen inscripciones en jeroglíficos, en griego y en una forma tardía del idioma egipcio que permitió a los historiadores descifrar la escritura egipcia (pág. 103)

rural a countryside area (p. 60)
rural zona del campo (pág. 60)

Sahel (sah-HEL) a semiarid region in Africa just south of the Sahara that separates the desert from wetter areas (p. 382)
Sahel región semiárida de África, situada al sur del Sahara, que separa el desierto de otras zonas más húmedas (pág. 382)

salon a social gathering held to discuss ideas during the Enlightenment (p. 615)
tertulia reunión social para debatir ideas; se acostumbraban celebrar durante la Ilustración (pág. 615)

samurai (SA-muh-rye) a trained professional warrior in feudal Japan (p. 454)
samurai guerrero profesional del Japón feudal (pág. 454)

Sanskrit the most important language of ancient India (p. 129)
sánscrito el idioma más importante de la antigua India (pág. 129)

savannah an open grassland with scattered trees (p. 382)
sabana pradera abierta con árboles dispersos (pág. 382)

scholar-official an educated member of the government (p. 422)

    funcionario erudito miembro culto del gobierno (pág. 422)

science a particular way of gaining knowledge about the world (p. 588)

    ciencia manera específica de adquirir conocimientos sobre el mundo (pág. 588)

scientific method a step-by-step method for performing experiments and other scientific research (p. 592)

    método científico método detallado para realizar experimentos y otros tipos de investigaciones científicas (pág. 592)

Scientific Revolution a series of events that led to the birth of modern science; it lasted from about 1540 to 1700 (p. 588)

    Revolución científica serie de acontecimientos que condujeron al nacimiento de la ciencia moderna; se extendió desde alrededor del 1540 hasta el 1700 (pág. 588)

scribe a writer (p. 66)

    escriba escritor (pág. 66)

secondary source information gathered by someone who did not take part in or witness an event (p. 10)

    fuente secundaria información recopilada por alguien que no participó ni presenció un hecho (pág. 10)

secular non-religious (p. 613)

    seglar no religioso, laico (pág. 613)

seismograph a device that measures the strength of an earthquake (p. 182)

    sismógrafo aparato que mide la fuerza de un terremoto (pág. 182)

serf a worker in medieval Europe who was tied to the land on which he or she lived (p. 509)

    siervo trabajador de la Europa medieval que estaba atado al territorio en el que vivía (pág. 509)

Shia (SHEE-ah) a member of the second-largest branch of Islam (p. 365)

    shia miembro de la segunda rama más importante del Islam (pág. 365)

Shinto the traditional religion of Japan (p. 442)

    sintoísmo religión tradicional de Japón (pág. 442)

shogun a general who ruled Japan in the emperor's name (p. 455)

    shogun general que gobernaba Japón en nombre del emperador (pág. 455)

silent barter a process in which people exchange goods without contacting each other directly (p. 386)

    trueque silencioso proceso mediante el que las personas intercambian bienes sin entrar en contacto directo (pág. 386)

silk a soft, light, and highly valued fabric developed in China (p. 187)

    seda tejido suave, ligero y muy apreciado que se originó en China (pág. 187)

Silk Road a network of trade routes that stretched across Asia from China to the Mediterranean Sea (p. 187)

    Ruta de la Seda red de rutas comerciales que se extendían a lo largo de Asia desde China hasta el mar Mediterráneo (pág. 187)

silt a mixture of fertile soil and tiny rocks that can make land ideal for farming (p. 55)

    cieno mezcla de tierra fértil y piedrecitas que pueden crear un terreno ideal para el cultivo (pág. 55)

social hierarchy the division of society by rank or class (p. 63)

    jerarquía social división de la sociedad en clases o niveles (pág. 63)

socialism a political and economic system in which the government owns the means of production (p. 646)

    socialismo sistema social en el que los medios de producción pertenecen a los trabajadores o están controlados por el gobierno (pág. 646)

society a community of people who share a common culture (p. 33)

    sociedad comunidad de personas que comparten la misma cultura (pág. 33)

ENGLISH AND SPANISH GLOSSARY

Spanish Armada a large fleet of Spanish ships that was defeated by England in 1588 (p. 596)

Armada española gran flota de barcos españoles que fue derrotada por Inglaterra en 1588 (pág. 596)

Spanish Inquisition an organization of priests in Spain that looked for and punished anyone suspected of secretly practicing their old religion (p. 548)

Inquisición española organización de sacerdotes que perseguía y castigaba a las personas que no eran cristianas en España (pág. 548)

sphinx (sfinks) an imaginary creature with a human head and the body of a lion that was often shown on Egyptian statues (p. 104)

esfinge criatura imaginaria con cabeza humana y cuerpo de león que aparecía re-presentada a menudo en las estatuas egipcias (pág. 104)

subcontinent a large landmass that is smaller than a continent, such as India (p. 124)

subcontinente gran masa de tierra menor que un continente, como la India (pág. 124)

sub-Saharan Africa Africa south of the Sahara (p. 380)

África subsahariana parte de África que queda al sur del Sahara (pág. 380)

Sufism (soo-fi-zuhm) a movement in Islam that taught people they can find God's love by having a personal relationship with God (p. 369)

sufismo movimiento perteneciente al Islam que enseñaba a las personas que pueden hallar el amor de Dios si establecen una relación personal con Él (pág. 369)

sundial a device that uses the position of shadows cast by the sun to tell the time of day (p. 182)

reloj de sol dispositivo que utiliza la posición de las sombras que proyecta el sol para indicar las horas del día (pág. 182)

Sunnah (sooh-nuh) a collection of writings about the way Muhammad lived that provides a model for Muslims to follow (p. 359)

Sunna conjunto de escritos sobre la vida de Mahoma que proporciona un modelo de comportamiento para los musulmanes (pág. 359)

Sunni a member of the largest branch of Islam (p. 365)

suní miembro de la rama más importante del Islam (pág. 365)

surplus more of something than is needed (p. 56)

excedente cantidad que supera lo que se necesita (pág. 56)

synagogue (si-nuh-gawg) a Jewish house of worship (p. 210)

sinagoga lugar de culto judío (pág. 210)

Talmud (tahl-moohd) a set of commentaries and lessons for everyday life in Judaism (p. 212)

Talmud Conjunto de comentarios y lecciones para la vida diaria en el judaísmo (pág. 212)

Ten Commandments in the Bible, a code of moral laws given to Moses by God (p. 204)

los Diez Mandamientos en la Biblia, código de leyes morales que Dios le entregó a Moisés (pág. 204)

terrorism criminal activity involving the use of violence to create fear and push for political change (p. 676)

terrorismo actividad criminal que implica el uso de la violencia para crear miedo y promover cambios politicos (pág. 676)

theory an explanation a scientist develops based on facts (p. 588)

teoría explicación que desarrolla un científico basándose en hechos (pág. 588)

tolerance acceptance (p. 364)

tolerancia aceptación (pág. 364)

tool an object that has been modified to help a person accomplish a task (p. 30)
herramienta objeto que ha sido modificado para ayudar a una persona a realizar una tarea (pág. 30)

topography the shape and elevation of land in a region (p. 496)
topografía forma y elevación del terreno en una región (pág. 496)

Torah the most sacred text of Judaism (p. 210)
Torá el texto más sagrado del judaísmo (pág. 210)

trade network a system of people in different lands who trade goods back and forth (p. 111)
red comercial sistema de personas en diferentes lugares que comercian productos entre sí (pág. 111)

trade route a path followed by traders (p. 97)
ruta comercial itinerario seguido por los comerciantes (pág. 97)

tyrant an ancient Greek leader who held power through the use of force (p. 237)
tirano gobernante de la antigua Grecia que mantenía el poder mediante el uso de la fuerza (pág. 237)

urban a city area (p. 60)
urbano zona de ciudad (pág. 60)

vassal a knight who promised to support a lord in exchange for land in medieval Europe (p. 507)
vasallo caballero de la Europa medieval que prometía apoyar a un señor feudal a cambio de tierras (pág. 507)

veto (VEE-toh) to reject or prohibit actions and laws of other government officials (p. 304)
vetar rechazar o prohibir acciones y leyes de otros funcionarios del gobierno (pág. 304)

Vietnam War started in 1957 by the Communists in North Vietnam to overthrow the South; Communists prevailed and in 1976 Vietnam was reunited as a Communist country (p. 675)
Guerra de Vietnam guerra iniciada en 1957 por el régimen comunista de Vietnam del Norte para derrocar al gobierno de Vietnam del Sur; los comunistas se impusieron y Vietnam se reunificó en 1976 como un país comunista (pág. 675)

woodblock printing a form of printing in which an entire page is carved into a block of wood, covered with ink, and pressed to a piece of paper to create a printed page (p. 418)
xilografía forma de impresión en la que una página completa se talla en una plancha de madera, se cubre de tinta y se presiona sobre un papel para crear la página impresa (pág. 418)

X, Y, Z

Zealots (ZE-luhts) radical Jews who supported rebellion against the Romans (p. 214)
zelotes judíos radicales que apoyaron la rebelión contra los romanos (pág. 214)

Zen a form of Buddhism that emphasizes meditation (p. 452)
zen forma del budismo que se basa en la meditación (pág. 452)

ziggurat a pyramid-shaped temple in Sumer (p. 68)
zigurat templo sumerio en forma de pirámide (pág. 68)

Index

INDEX

printing: movable type and, 418–419, 418f, 566f; wood-block, 418f

prophets, 211

Protestants, 570; in France, 574; self-government and, 574f; Spanish Inquisition and, 572

proverbs, 397

provinces, 325

Prussia: Congress of Vienna and, 640; Napoleon's victories against, 639; victories against Napoleon by, 640; war against Denmark and Austria and, 650

Psalms 23:1-3, 211

Ptah (Egyptian god), 92

Ptolemy, 589, 590

Puerto Rico, 652

Punic Wars, 309–311

Punt, 91, 98

Pure Land Buddhism, 450

purgatory, 570

pyramids, 94–95, 107p, 110, 111, 112p

Pythagoras, 589

Q

Qin dynasty, 172–176, 173m

Qing dynasty, 423

Qinling Shandi, 160

Quechua, 480, 482

Quetzalcoatl (Aztec god), 478

Quick Facts: Early Hominids, 30; Hammurabi's Code, 73; Major Beliefs of Hinduism, 132; The Eightfold Path, 139; Zhou Society, 167; Main Ideas of Confucianism, 170; Emperor Shi Huangdi, 173; Government in Athens, 237; Democracy Then and Now, 241; Life in Sparta, 267; Life in Athens, 269; Legendary Founding of Rome, 296; Government of the Roman Republic, 303; Roman Accomplishments, 327; The Five Pillars of Islam, 360; Sources of Islamic Beliefs, 361; Village Society, 382; West African Empires, 394; Chapter 13 Visual Summary, 401; Chinese Inventions, 418; Influ-

ences from China and Korea, 443; Samurai Society, 455; Feudal Society, 507; Comparing and Contrasting Europe and Japan, 515; The Crusades, 532; Beginnings of Democracy in England, 542; Results of the Council of Trent, 573; Protestant Self-Government, 574; Columbian Exchange, 598; Supply and Demand, 600; Ideas of the Enlightenment, 614; Documents of Democracy, 624; Chapter 1 Visual Summary, 21; Chapter 2 Visual Summary, 45; Chapter 3 Visual Summary, 79; Chapter 4 Visual Summary, 115; Chapter 5 Visual Summary, 153; Chapter 6 Visual Summary, 193; Chapter 7 Visual Summary, 221; Chapter 8 Visual Summary, 253; Chapter 9 Visual Summary, 285; Chapter 10 Visual Summary, 315; Chapter 11 Visual Summary, 345; Chapter 12 Visual Summary, 373; Chapter 14 Visual Summary, 433; Chapter 15 Visual Summary, 435; Chapter 16 Visual Summary, 487; Chapter 17 Visual Summary, 517; Chapter 18 Visual Summary, 551; Chapter 19 Visual Summary, 579; Chapter 20 Visual Summary, 605; Chapter 21 Visual Summary, 629; Chapter 22 Visual Summary, 655, Chapter 23 Visual Summary, 681

quipus, 482

Qumran, 212

Qur'an, 356, 358–359, 360, 361, 362, 371, 392

R

rabbis, 216

rain forests, 382, 678

raja, 128–129

Ramadan, 360

Ramayana, 149

Ramses II (king of Egypt), 98, 101f, 109; temples and, 83, 104

Re (Egyptian god), 92

Reading Skills: Understanding Specialized Vocabulary, 4; Chronological Order, 26; Main Ideas in Social Studies, 54; Causes and Effects in History, 84; Inferences about History, 122; Summarizing Historical Texts, 158; Facts and Opinions about the Past, 200; Understanding Word Origins, 224; Comparing and Contrasting Historical Facts, 258; Outlining and History, 292; Online Research, 320; Using Questions to Analyze Tests, 352; Organization of Facts and Information, 378; Drawing Conclusions about the Past, 408; Main Ideas and Their Support, 440; Analyzing Historical Information, 466; Evaluating Sources, 484; Stereotypes and Bias in History, 522; Greek and Latin Word Roots, 556; Vocabulary Clues, 586; Points of View in Historical Texts, 610; Comparing Historical Texts, 636; Public Documents, 600

Reagan, Ronald, 675

realism, 646f

reason, 281

Reason, Age of. *See* **Enlightenment**

Reconquista, 547, 547m

Red Sea, 88, 91

Reformation, 569–575; Catholic, 572–575; Enlightenment and, 613–614; political impact of, 574–575; religious wars and, 574–575; social changes and, 575

Reform Jews, 210

regent, 444

Reign of Terror, 627

reincarnation, 133, 139

religion(s): arts and, 538–39; Aztec, 477, 481; Buddhism as. *See* Buddhism; Christianity as. *See* Christianity; Confucianism as. *See* Confucianism; Daoism as, 170, 171, 188, 189, 413; Egyptian life and, 92–93; in Europe, religion in Japan versus, 514; as foundation of Sumerian society, 62–63;

Credits and Acknowledgments

Acknowledgments

For permission to reproduce copyrighted material, grateful acknowledgment is made to the following sources:

Cesar E. Chavez Foundation: Quote from "Core Values of Cesar E. Chavez' from *Cesar E. Chavez Foundation* Web site; accessed September 24, 2004, at http://www.cesar-chavezfoundation.org. Copyright © by Cesar E. Chavez Foundation.

Columbia University Press: From *Records of the Grand Historian of China, Vol. II: The Age of Emperor Wu* by Burton Watson. Copyright © 1961 by Columbia University Press. From "Heinrich Von Treitschke" from *Introduction to Contemporary Civilization in the West* by the staff of Columbia College. Copyright © 1946, 1954, 1960 by Columbia University Press.

Doubleday, a division of Random House, Inc., www.randomhouse.com: From "A Personal Account: The Diary of Anne Frank" from *The Diary of a Young Girl: The Definitive Edition* by Anne Frank, edited by Otto H. Frank & Mirjam Pressler, translated by Susan Massotty. Copyright © 1995 by Doubleday, a division of Random House, Inc.

Benedict Fitzgerald for the Estate of Robert Fitzgerald: From *The Iliad* by Homer, translated by Robert Fitzgerald. Copyright © 1974 by Robert Fitzgerald. From *The Odyssey* by Homer, translated by Robert Fitzgerald. Copyright © 1961, 1963, by Robert Fitzgerald; copyright renewed © 1989 by Benedict R. C. Fitzgerald, on behalf of the Fitzgerald Children.

Penelope Fitzgerald for the Estate of Robert Fitzgerald: From *The Aeneid* by Virgil, translated by Robert Fitzgerald. Translation copyright © 1980, 1982, 1983 by Robert Fitzgerald.

Grove Press, Inc.: From "Poetry from the Six Collections" by Ki no Tomonori from *Anthology of Japanese Literature: From the earliest era to the mid-nineteenth century,* compiled and edited by Donald Keene. Copyright © 1955 by Grove Press.

Harcourt Education: From *Things Fall Apart* by Chinua Achebe. Copyright © 1959 by Chinua Achebe.

The Jewish Publication Society: Exodus 20:2–14 and Psalms 23:1–3 from *Tanakh: A New Translation of the Holy Scriptures According to the Traditional Hebrew Text.* Copyright © 1985 by the Jewish Publication Society.

Kendall/Hunt Publishing Company: From *Kings, Saints, and Parliaments: A Sourcebook for Western Civilization, 1050–1700,* edited by Sears McGee, et al. Copyright © 1994 by Kendall/Hunt Publishing Company.

Alfred A. Knopf, a division of Random House, Inc., www.randomhouse.com: From *The Tale of Genji* by Lady Murasaki Shikibu, translated by Edward G. Seidensticker. Copyright © 1976 by Edward G. Seidensticker.

Caroline Miley: From "Proclamation at La Coruña 1808 before the Napoleonic Invasion of Spain," translated by Caroline Miley, from the *Napoleon Series* Web site, accessed February 2, 2005, at http://www.napoleon-series.org/research/miscellaneous/c_lacoruna.html. Originally printed in Spanish on the Spanish language Web site, *The Royal Green Jackets.* Copyright © by Caroline Miley.

Penguin Books Ltd.: "Quiet Night Thoughts" by Li Po from *Li Po and Tu Fu: Poems,* translated by Arthur Cooper. Copyright © 1973 by Arthur Cooper. From *The Epic of Gilgamesh: an English version with an Introduction by N. K. Sandars.* Copyright © 1960, 1964, 1972 by N. K. Sandars.

Plume, a division of Penguin Group (USA) Inc: From *Girl with a Pearl Earring* by Tracy Chevalier. Copyright © 1999 by Tracy Chevalier. Originally published by Dutton.

John Porter: From *Polybius 6.11–18: The Constitution of the Roman Republic,* translated by John Porter. Copyright © 1995 by John Porter, University of Saskatchewan.

Royal Green Jackets: From "Proclamation at La Coruña 1808 before the Napoleonic Invasion of Spain," translated by Caroline Miley. Originally printed in Spanish on the Spanish language Web site, *The Royal Green Jackets.* Copyright © by Royal Green Jackets.

Simon & Schuster Adult Publishing Group: From *Popol Vuh: The Definitive Edition of the Mayan Book of the Dawn of Life and the Glories of Gods and Kings* by Dennis Tedlock. Copyright © 1985, 1996 by Dennis Tedlock.

The University of Chicago Press: From *The Panchatantra,* translated from the Sanskrit by Arthur William Ryder. Copyright 1925 by the University of Chicago Press.

The Arthur Waley Estate: From *The Pillow Book of Sei Shonagon,* translated by Arthur Waley. Copyright 1928, 1929, 1949, 1957 by The Arthur Waley Estate.

Weidenfeld & Nicolson, Ltd.: Excerpt (Retitled "A Knight Speaks") by Rutebeuf from *The Medieval World: Europe 1100–1350* by Friedrich Heer, translated from the German by Janet Sondheimer. Copyright © 1961 by George Weidenfeld and Nicolson Ltd. English translation copyright © 1962 by George Weidenfeld and Nicolson Ltd.

Sources Cited:

From "Richard the Lionheart Massacres the Saracens, 1191" from the *Eyewitness to History* Web site, accessed November 1, 2004, at www.eyewitnesstohistory.com.

From "Saladin and the Third Crusade" from *Arab Historians of the Crusades—Selected and Translated from the Arabic Sources* by Francesco Gabrieli, translated and edited by E. J. Costello. Published by University of California Press, 1969.

Illustrations and Photo Credits

Cover: Roy Ooms/Masterfile

Front Matter: ii (tl), Seth Joel ; ii (cr), Clay McClachlan; v, Musée des Antiquités St Germain en Laye/Dagli Orti/The Art Archive; vi, Ancient Art & Architecture Collection, Ltd.; vii (br), Musée Cernuschi Paris / Dagli Orti/Art Archive; viii, The Art Archive / National Archaeological Museum Athens / Dagli Orti; ix, Anders Blomqvist/Lonely Planet Images; x, Richard T. Nowitz/National Geographic Image Collection; xi (tr), Private Collection, Credit: Heini Schneebeli/Bridgeman Art Library; xii, Snark/Art Resource, NY; xiii, Angelo Cavalli/SuperStock; xiv, SuperStock; xv, Ray Manley/SuperStock; xvi, SuperStock; xvii, Thomas Kienzle/AP/Wide World Photos.; H2, Roger Viollet/Getty Images; H4, Dept. of the Environment, London, UK,/Bridgeman Art Library; H6, Copyright British Museum, London; H7, The Granger Collection, New York; H8, The Concert at the Fountain, Loire workshop, c. 1570-80 (tapestry), French school, (15th century)/Musee des Gobelins, Paris, France, Lauros/The Bridgeman Art Library; H25 (t), Daily News Pix; H25 (c), Robert Maass/Corbis; H25 (br), Glen Allison/Getty Images; H25 (bl), Randy Wells/Corbis.

Back Matter: R20 (tl), Gianni Dagli Orti/Corbis; R20 (cr), Scala/Art Resource, NY; R21 (tl), Musée Cernuschi Paris / Dagli Orti/Art Archive; R21 (cl), National Archaeological Museum Athens / Dagli Orti/Art Archive; R21 (r) Timothy McCarthy/Art Resource, NY; R22 (cl), The Art Archive; R22 (cr), Private Collection, Credit: Heini Schneebeli/Bridgeman Art Library; R23 (cr), Hilarie Kavanagh/Stone/Getty Images; R23 (cl), Liu Liqun/Corbis; R23 (tc), Gianni Dagli Orti/Corbis; R24 (cr), SuperStock; R24 (cl), Hulto-Deutsch Collection/Corbis; R24 (tr), Snark/Art Resource, NY; R25 (tr), Robert Maas/Corbis; R25 (cr), Beth A. Keiser/AP/Wide World Photos.

Unit 1, Chapter One: 2-3 (all), O. Louis Mazzatenta/National Geographic Image Collection; 7, Rohan/Stone/Getty Images; 8 (b), Garry Gay/Alamy Images; 10 (t), Eric Vandeville/Gamma Press, Inc.; 11 (tl), Instituto Nacional de Antropología y Historia, Mexico (Detail); 11 (tr), Bojan Brecelj/Corbis/SABA; 11 (tc), Instituto Nacional de Antropología y Historia, Mexico (Detail); 13 (tr), Gamma Press, Inc.; 13 (tl), Anne Rippy/Image Bank/Getty Images; 16 (t), Gavin Hellier/Robert Harding World Imagery/Getty Images; 19 (tr), Kevin Schafer/Corbis; 23, Egyptian National Museum, Cairo, Egypt/ET Archive, London/SuperStock; **Chapter Two:** 24-25 (all), Pierre Vauthey/Sygma/Corbis; 24 (bc), Kenneth Garrett/National Geographic

L. Stanfield/National Geographic Image Collection; 334, INDEX/Bridgeman Art Library; 335 (cr), Scrovegni Chapel Padua / Dagli Orti (A)/Art Archive; 335 (br), Howie McCormick, The Ironton Tribune/AP/Wide World Photos; 336, Alinari/Art Resource, NY; 337, Johnny van Haeften Gallery, London, UK/Bridgeman Art Library; 342-343 (all), Danny Lehman/Corbis.

Unit 6, Chapter Twelve: 350-351 (all), Ali Kazuyoshi Nomachi/Pacific Press Service; 350 (cl), Scala/Art Resource, NY; 350 (br), Réunion des Musées Nationaux/Art Resource, NY; 351 (br), Army Museum Madrid/Dagli Orti/Art Archive; 359, Ali Kazuyoshi Nomachi/Pacific Press Service; 363 (bl), Ian Dagnall/Alamy Images; 363 (br), Vanni Archive/Corbis; 365, The Granger Collection, New York; 367, Hilarie Kavanagh/Stone/Getty Images; 368 (bl), Bibliotheque Nationale de Cartes et Plans, Paris, France/Bridgeman Art Library; 368 (br), R & S Michaud/Woodfin Camp & Associates; 369 (br), R & S Michaud/Woodfin Camp & Associates; 370 (tl), Helene Rogers/Art Directors & TRIP Photo Library; 370 (cl), Robert Frerck/Odyssey/Chicago; 370 (tr), Art Directors & TRIP Photo Library; **Chapter Thirteen:** 376-377 (all), PhotoDisc; 376 (br), Werner Forman/Art Resource, NY; 377 (bc), The Art Archive; 377 (br), Trustees of the British Museum, London; 377 (bl), G K & Vikki Hart/Image Bank/Getty Images; 377 (cr), Erich Lessing/Art Resource, NY; 377 (cl), Werner Forman/Art Resource, NY; 382 (r), Robert Frerck/Odyssey/Chicago; 384 (cl), Dagli Orti (A)/The Art Archive; 384 (br), Dagli Orti (A)/The Art Archive; 384 (bl), Aldo Tutino/Art Resource, NY; 384 (tr), Nik Wheeler/Corbis; 385 (cr), Reza/Webistan/Corbis; 385 (tr), HIP/Scala/Art Resource, NY; 387 (cr), Dr. Roderick McIntosh; 389, Steve McCurry/Magnum Photos; 391 (tr), Private Collection, Credit: Heini Schneebeli/Bridgeman Art Library; 392, Sandro Vannini/Corbis; 395 (br), The Granger Collection, New York; 397, Pascal Meunier / Cosmos/Aurora Photos; 398 (tr), AFP/Getty Images; 398 (c), Reuters/Corbis.

Unit 7, Chapter Fourteen: 406-407 (all), Dallas and John Heaton/Corbis; 406 (br), Art Directors & TRIP Photo Library; 407 (cr), Freelance Consulting Services Pty Ltd/Corbis; 407 (bl), Sekai Bunka Photo/Ancient Art & Architecture Collection, Ltd.; 407 (br), G K & Vikki Hart/PhotoDisc; 415 (b), Keren Su/China Span; 415 (cr), Keren Su/Corbis; 416 (b), Carl & Ann Purcell/Corbis; 417, Ric Ergenbright/Corbis; 418 (b), Liu Liqun/Corbis; 418 (c), China Photo/Reuters/Corbis; 418 (t), Paul Freeman/Private Collection/Bridgeman Art Library; 419 (tr), Tom Stewart/Corbis; 419 (tc), Private Collection/Bridgeman Art Library; 420, Traditionally attributed to: Yan Liben, Chinese, died in 673. Northern Qi Scholar's Collating Classic Texts (detail). Chinese, Northern Song dynasty, 11th century. Object place: China. Ink and color on silk. 27.6 x 114 cm (10 7/8 x 44 7/8 in.). Museum of Fine Arts, Boston. Denman Waldo Ross Collection. 31.123/Museum of Fine Arts, Boston; 422 (tc), Snark/Art Resource, NY; 431 (br), National Palace Museum, Taipei, Taiwan/Bridgeman Art Library; 432-433 (all), Keren Su/Corbis; **Chapter Fifteen:** 436-

437 (all), Spectrum Colour Library; 436 (br), Royalty Free/Corbis; 437 (cl), The Art Archive; 437 (cr), National Museum, Tokyo/A.K.G., Berlin/SuperStock; 437 (bc), (Detail) Bibliotheque Nationale, Paris, France/Bridgeman Art Library; 437 (br), Erich Lessing/Art Resource, NY; 442, Rijksmuseum voor Volkenkunde Leiden (Leyden) / Dagli Orti/Art Archive; 443 (bl), Ronald Sheridan/Ancient Art & Architecture Collection, Ltd.; 443 (bc), The Granger Collection, New York; 443 (br), Royalty Free/Corbis; 444 (b), Kenneth Hamm/Photo Japan; 444 (cr), Bettmann/Corbis; 445, Art Directors & TRIP Photo Library; 447, (Detail) Musee des Beaux-Arts, Angers, France/Giraudon/Bridgeman Art Library; 448, Archivo Iconografico, S.A./Corbis; 449 (cr), Burstein Collection/Corbis; 449 (bl), Sakamoto Photo Research Laboratory/Corbis; 450, Catherine Karnow/Corbis; 451 (br), Sekai Bunka Photo/Ancient Art & Architecture Collection, Ltd.; 456 (cl), Roger Viollet/Getty Images; 456 (bc), Fitzwilliam Museum, University of Cambridge, UK/Bridgeman Art Library; 457 (tr), Gunshots/Art Archive; 457 (bc), Kenneth Hamm/Photo Japan; **Chapter Sixteen:** 464-465 (all), Angelo Cavalli/SuperStock; 464 (br), Gianni Dagli Orti/Corbis; 465 (cl), The Trustees Of The British Museum; 465 (c), Werner Forman/Art Resource, NY; 465 (cr), Fundacion Miguel Mujica Gallo, Museo do Oro del Peru; 465 (bl), British Library/Art Archive; 465 (br), Freer Gallery of Art, Smithsonian Institution, Washington D.C., Purchase F1932.28/Freer Gallery of Art and the Arthur M Sackler Gallery of Art/Smithsonian; 469 (bl), Justin Kerr, K4809/Kerr Associates; 469 (cr), Erich Lessing/Art Resource, NY; 471 (cr), Scala/Art Resource, NY; 472 (tl), Robert Frerck/Odyssey Productions, Chicago; 472 (tr), The Trustees Of/The British Museum (Detail); 475 (tr), Mexican National Museum, Mexico City 9-2256/D.Donne Bryant/DDB Stock Photography; 477 (tc), Trustees of the British Museum, London; 479, Robert Frerck/Odyssey/Chicago; 481 (tc), The Granger Collection, New York; 482 (tl), American Museum of Natural History, New York, USA/Bridgeman Art Library; 482 (tr), Stuart Franklin/Magnum Photos; 482 (cr), Museo del Banco Central del Ecuador - Quito. 0-19224/D. Donne Bryant/DDB Stock Photography; 485 (cr), Kevin Schafer/Corbis.

Unit 8, Chapter Seventeen: 492-493 (all), Robert Harding Picture Library; 492 (br), The Crosiers/Gene Plaisted, OSC; 493 (c), SuperStock; 493 (bl), The Granger Collection, New York; 493 (bc), Art Archive; 498, Vittoriano Rastelli/Corbis; 499 (tl), Stephen Studd/Stone/Getty Images; 499 (tr), Stefano Scata/Getty Images; 501, The Crosiers/Gene Plaisted, OSC; 504 (tr), North Wind Picture Archives; 505 (br), Scala/Art Resource, NY; 511, Bibliotheque Nationale, Paris, France/Bridgeman Art Library; 513 (tl), Sakamoto Photo Research Library/Corbis; 513 (tr), Alinari/Art Resource, NY; 514 (br), Freer Gallery of Art, Smithsonian Institution, Washington D.C. Purchase, F1963.5/Freer Gallery of Art and the Arthur M Sackler Gallery of Art/Smithsonian; 514 (bl), Archivo Iconografico, S.A./Corbis; **Chapter Eighteen:** 520-521 (all), Archivo Iconografico, S.A./Corbis; 520 (br), The

British Museum/HIP/Topham/The Image Works, Inc.; 521 (cl), The British Library/Topham-HIP/The Image Works, Inc.; 521 (cr), G K & Vikki Hart/PhotoDisc; 521 (bc), ChinaStock; 525 (bl), Elio Ciol/Corbis; 525 (cr), Erich Lessing/Art Resource, NY; 526 (tr), Hulton Archive/Getty Images; 526 (tl), Hulton Archive/Getty Images; 529 (t), Archivo Iconografico, S.A./Corbis; 530, Mary Evans Picture Library; 531 (tr), Galleria degli Uffizi Florence / Dagli Orti/Art Archive; 533, Ben Mangor/SuperStock; 537 (tr), Archivo Iconografico, S.A./Corbis; 537 (c), Jim Cummins/Corbis; 538 (tr), Erich Lessing/Art Resource, NY; 539 (tl), Vanni/Art Resource, NY; 539 (tr), Gjon Mili//Time Life Pictures/Getty Images Editorial; 540, Ancient Art & Architecture Collection, Ltd.; 541 (t), Dept. of the Environment, London, UK/Bridgeman Art Library; 542 (tr), The Granger Collection, New York; 542 (c), Wolfgang Kaehler/Corbis; 542 (cl), Bettmann/Corbis; 549, Scala / Art Resource, NY; **Chapter Nineteen:** 554-555 (all), Ray Manley/SuperStock; 554 (br), Giraudon/Art Resource, NY; 555 (cr), AKG-Images; 555 (bl), Réunion des Musées Nationaux/Art Resource, NY; 555 (br), Dorling Kindersley Ltd. Picture Library; 559, Bo Brännhage/Panoramic Images; 562 (t), Erich Lessing/Art Resource, NY; 562 (br), Rabatti - Domingie/AKG-images; 563 (bl), SuperStock; 563 (cr), The Granger Collection, New York; 563 (c), Scala/Art Resource, NY; 563 (br), Gianni Dagli Orti/Corbis; 563 (cl), Bettmann/Corbis; 564 (tr), Scala/Art Resource, NY; 564 (tl), Scala/Art Resource, NY; 566 (bl), The Bodleian Library, Oxford/Art Archive; 566 (br), The Granger Collection, New York; 568, National Portrait Gallery, London/SuperStock; 570 (br), Scala/Art Resource, NY; 570 (bl), AKG-Images; 573, Archivo Iconografico, S.A./Corbis; 574, Erich Lessing/Art Resource, NY; 577, AKG-Images.

Unit 9, Chapter Twenty: 584-585 (all), Bill Ross/Corbis; 585 (cl), Royal Society, London, UK/Bridgeman Art Library; 585 (cr), Galleria degli Uffizi Florence / Dagli Orti (A)/Art Archive; 585 (bc), Hilarie Kavanagh/Stone/Getty Images; 589, Erich Lessing/Art Resource, NY; 593, Image courtesy of NASA/Kennedy Space Center; 597, Giovanna Paponetti; 599, Victoria Smith/HRW; 603, Scala/Art Resource, NY; **Chapter Twenty One:** 608-609 (all), Phil Degginger/Alamy Images; 609 (cl), Philip Mould, Historical Portraits Ltd, London, UK/Bridgeman Art Library; 609 (c), Tate Gallery, London/Art Resource, NY; 609 (cr), Explorer, Paris/SuperStock; 609 (bl), Burstein Collection/Corbis; 609 (bc), David Muench/Corbis; 613, Scala/Art Resource, NY; 617 (tl), National Portrait Gallery, London/SuperStock; 617 (cl), Alexander Burkatovski/Corbis; 617 (tr), Erich Lessing/Art Resource, NY; 618 (l), The Granger Collection, New York; 618 (r), Stefano Bianchetti/Corbis; 619, Réunion des Musées Nationaux/Art Resource, NY; 620, The Granger Collection, New York; 621 (bc), Archivo Iconografico, S.A./Corbis; 623, Metropolitan Museum of Art, New York, USA/Bridgeman Art Library; 624 (cl), Bettmann/Corbis; 624 (bl), Dept. of the Environment, London, UK/Bridgeman Art Library; 624 (cr), The Granger Collection, New York; 624 (br), Custody of the House

Staff Credits

The people who contributed to *Holt Social Studies: World History* are listed below. They represent editorial, design, intellectual property resources, production, emedia, and permissions.

Lissa B. Anderson, Melanie Baccus, Charles Becker, Jessica Bega, Ed Blake, Gillian Brody, Shirley Cantrell, Erin Cornett, Rose Degollado, Chase Edmond, Mescal Evler, Rhonda Fariss, Marsh Flournoy, Leanna Ford, Bob Fullilove, Matthew Gierhart, Janet Harrington, Rhonda Haynes, Rob Hrechko, Wilonda Ieans, Cathy Jenevein, Kadonna Knape, Cathy Kuhles, Debbie Lofland, Bob McClellan, Joe Melomo, Richard Metzger, Andrew Miles, Cynthia Munoz, Karl Pallmeyer, Chanda Pearmon, Jarred Prejean, Shelly Ramos, Désirée Reid, Curtis Riker, Marleis Roberts, Diana Rodriguez, Gene Rumann, Annette Saunders, Jenny Schaeffer, Kay Selke, Ken Shepardson, Michele Shukers, Chris Smith, Christine Stanford, Elaine Tate, Jeannie Taylor, Joni Wackwitz, Ken Whiteside